PHILIP'S

G000292764

STREET ATLAS

Derbyshire

Buxton, Chesterfield, Derby, Matlock, Swadlincote

www.philips-maps.co.uk

First published in 1995 by

Philip's, a division of
Octopus Publishing Group Ltd
www.octopusbooks.co.uk
2-4 Heron Quays, London E14 4JP
An Hachette Livre UK Company

Third colour edition 2006
Second impression with revisions 2008
DBYCB

ISBN-10   0-540-08844-7 (spiral)
ISBN-13   978-0-540-08844-7 (spiral)

© Philip's 2008

Ordnance Survey®

This product includes mapping data licensed
from Ordnance Survey® with the permission of
the Controller of Her Majesty's Stationery Office.
© Crown copyright 2008. All rights reserved.
Licence number 100011710.

Printed by Toppan, China

Contents

III   **Key to map symbols**

IV   **Key to map pages**

VI   **Route planning**

X   **Administrative and Postcode boundaries**

1   **Street maps** at 3½ inches to 1 mile

266   **Street maps of centres of Chesterfield and Derby** at 7 inches to 1 mile

268   **Index** of towns and villages

271   **Index** of streets, hospitals, industrial estates, railway stations, schools, shopping centres, universities and places of interest

Digital Data

The exceptionally high-quality mapping found in this atlas is available as digital data in TIFF format, which is easily convertible to other bitmapped (raster) image formats.

The index is also available in digital form as a standard database table. It contains all the details found in the printed index together with the National Grid reference for the map square in which each entry is named.

For further information and to discuss your requirements, please contact james.mann@philips-maps.co.uk

Motorway with junction number	
Primary route – dual/single carriageway	
A road – dual/single carriageway	
B road – dual/single carriageway	
Minor road – dual/single carriageway	
Other minor road – dual/single carriageway	
Road under construction	
Tunnel, covered road	
Rural track, private road or narrow road in urban area	
Gate or obstruction to traffic (restrictions may not apply at all times or to all vehicles)	
Path, bridleway, byway open to all traffic, road used as a public path	
Pedestrianised area	
DY7 **Postcode boundaries**	
County and unitary authority boundaries	
Railway, tunnel, railway under construction	
Tramway, tramway under construction	
Miniature railway	
Walsall **Railway station**	
Private railway station	
South Shields **Metro station**	
Tram stop, tram stop under construction	
Bus, coach station	

◆ **Ambulance station**	
◆ **Coastguard station**	
◆ **Fire station**	
◆ **Police station**	
✚ **Accident and Emergency entrance to hospital**	
Ⓗ **Hospital**	
✛ **Place of worship**	
🅸 **Information Centre** (open all year)	
🛒 **Shopping Centre**	
P P&R **Parking, Park and Ride**	
PO **Post Office**	
△ 🚐 **Camping site, caravan site**	
⚑ ✕ **Golf course, picnic site**	
Prim Sch **Important buildings, schools, colleges, universities and hospitals**	
Built up area	
Woods	
River Medway **Water name**	
River, weir, stream	
Canal, lock, tunnel	
Water	
Tidal water	
Church **Non-Roman antiquity**	
ROMAN FORT **Roman antiquity**	
87 **Adjoining page indicators and overlap bands** The colour of the arrow and the band indicates the scale of the adjoining or overlapping page (see scales below)	
237	

Acad	**Academy**	Inst	**Institute**	Recn Gd	**Recreation Ground**
Allot Gdns	**Allotments**	Ct	**Law Court**		
Cemy	**Cemetery**	L Ctr	**Leisure Centre**	Resr	**Reservoir**
C Ctr	**Civic Centre**	LC	**Level Crossing**	Ret Pk	**Retail Park**
CH	**Club House**	Liby	**Library**	Sch	**School**
Coll	**College**	Mkt	**Market**	Sh Ctr	**Shopping Centre**
Crem	**Crematorium**	Meml	**Memorial**	TH	**Town Hall/House**
Ent	**Enterprise**	Mon	**Monument**	Trad Est	**Trading Estate**
Ex H	**Exhibition Hall**	Mus	**Museum**	Univ	**University**
Ind Est	**Industrial Estate**	Obsy	**Observatory**	W Twr	**Water Tower**
IRB Sta	**Inshore Rescue Boat Station**	Pal	**Royal Palace**	Wks	**Works**
		PH	**Public House**	YH	**Youth Hostel**

■ The small numbers around the edges of the maps identify the 1 kilometre National Grid lines
■ The dark grey border on the inside edge of some pages indicates that the mapping does not continue onto the adjacent page

The scale of the maps on the pages numbered in blue is 5.52 cm to 1 km • 3½ inches to 1 mile • 1: 18103	0 ¼ ½ ¾ 1 mile
	0 250m 500m 750m 1 kilometre

The scale of the maps on pages numbered in red is 11.04 cm to 1 km • 7 inches to 1 mile • 1: 9051	0 220 yards 440 yards 660 yards ½ mile
	0 125m 250m 375m ½ kilometre

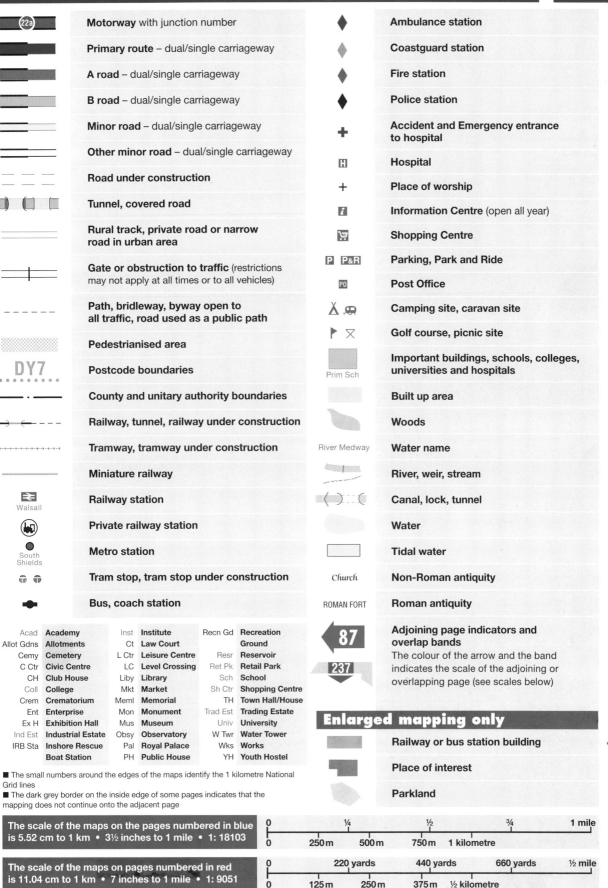

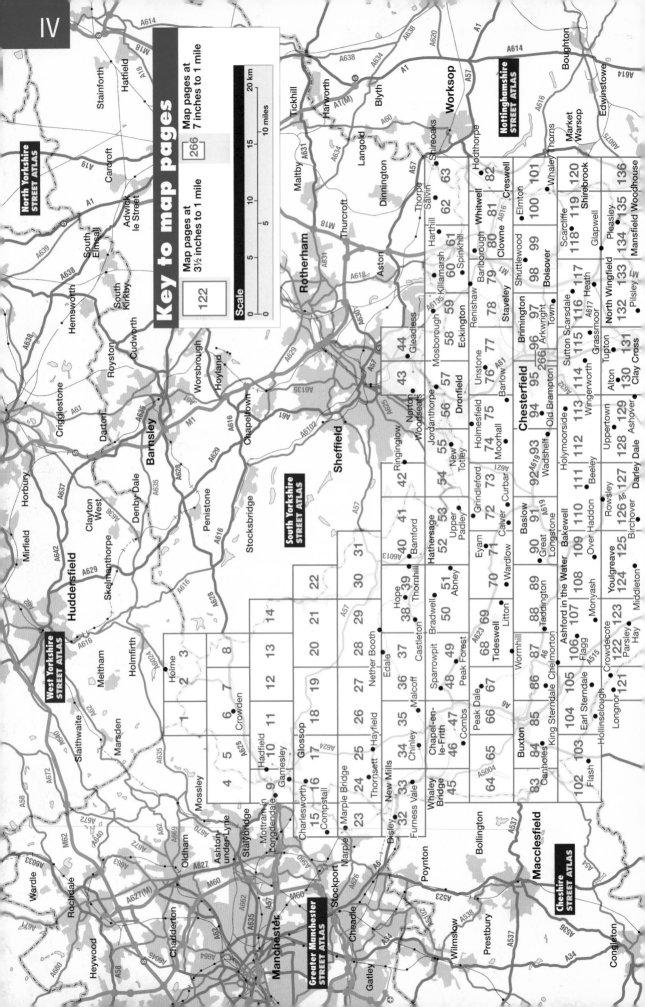

IV

Key to map pages

Map pages at
3½ inches to 1 mile
122

Map pages at
7 inches to 1 mile
266

Scale
0
0
5
5
10
10 miles
15
20 km

North Yorkshire
STREET ATLAS

West Yorkshire
STREET ATLAS

South Yorkshire
STREET ATLAS

Nottinghamshire
STREET ATLAS

Greater Manchester
STREET ATLAS

Cheshire
STREET ATLAS

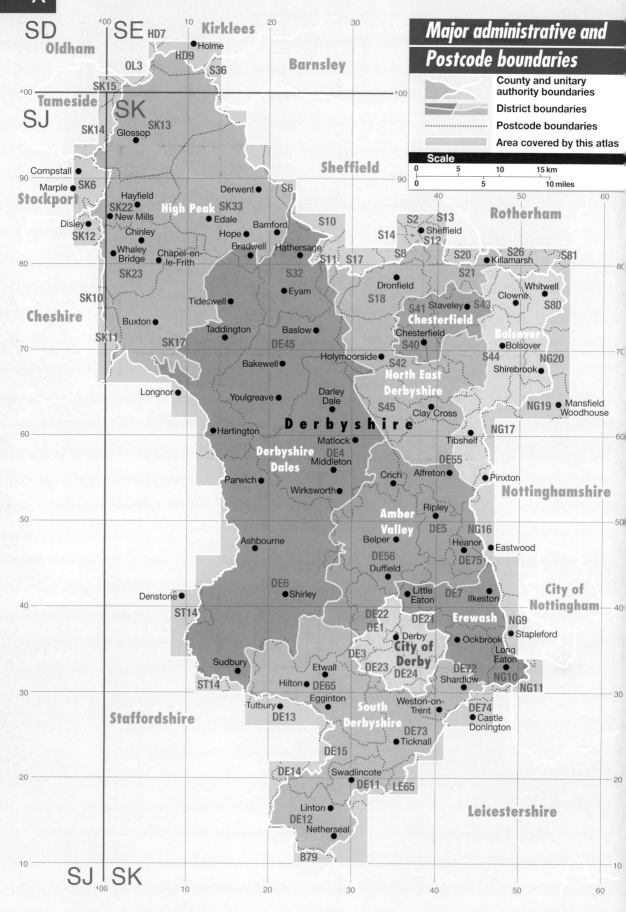

Major administrative and Postcode boundaries

County and unitary authority boundaries
District boundaries
Postcode boundaries
Area covered by this atlas

Scale
0   5   10   15 km
0   5   10 miles

SD   SE   HD7   Kirklees
Oldham
OL3   HD9   Holme
SK15   S36   Barnsley

Tameside
SJ   SK
SK14   SK13   Glossop   Sheffield
Compstall
Marple   SK6   Derwent   S6
Stockport   Hayfield   SK33   Rotherham
SK22   New Mills   S2   S13
High Peak   Edale   S14   Sheffield   S12
Disley   Hope   Bamford   S10
SK12   Chinley   Bradwell   Hathersage   S8   S20   S26   S81
Whaley   Chapel-en-   S11   S17   Killamarsh
Bridge   le-Frith   S32   S21
SK23   S18   S41   Staveley   S43   Clowne   Whitwell
SK10   Tideswell   Eyam   Dronfield   Chesterfield   S80
Cheshire   S18   Chesterfield   Bolsover
Buxton   Taddington   Baslow   S40   Bolsover
SK11   SK17   DE45   S42   S44   Shirebrook   NG20
Bakewell   Holymoorside   North East   Shirebrook
Longnor   Derbyshire   NG19   Mansfield
Youlgreave   Darley   S45   Woodhouse
Dale   Clay Cross
Hartington   Derbyshire   Matlock   Tibshelf   NG17
DE4   Middleton   DE55
Derbyshire   Crich   Alfreton   Pinxton
Dales   Wirksworth   Nottinghamshire
Parwich   Ripley
Amber   NG16
Ashbourne   Valley   DE5   Heanor   Eastwood
Belper   DE75
DE56   Duffield   Ilkeston   City of
Denstone   DE6   Little   DE7   Nottingham
Shirley   Eaton   Erewash   NG9
ST14   DE22   DE21   Stapleford
DE1   Derby   Ockbrook   Long
DE3   City of   Eaton
Sudbury   DE23   Derby   DE72   NG10
Etwall   DE24   Shardlow   NG11
Hilton   DE65   Weston-on-   DE74   Castle
Tutbury   Egginton   Trent   Donington
DE13   South   DE73   Ticknall
Staffordshire   Derbyshire   DE15   Leicestershire
DE14   Swadlincote
DE11   LE65
Linton
DE12   Netherseal
B79

SJ   SK

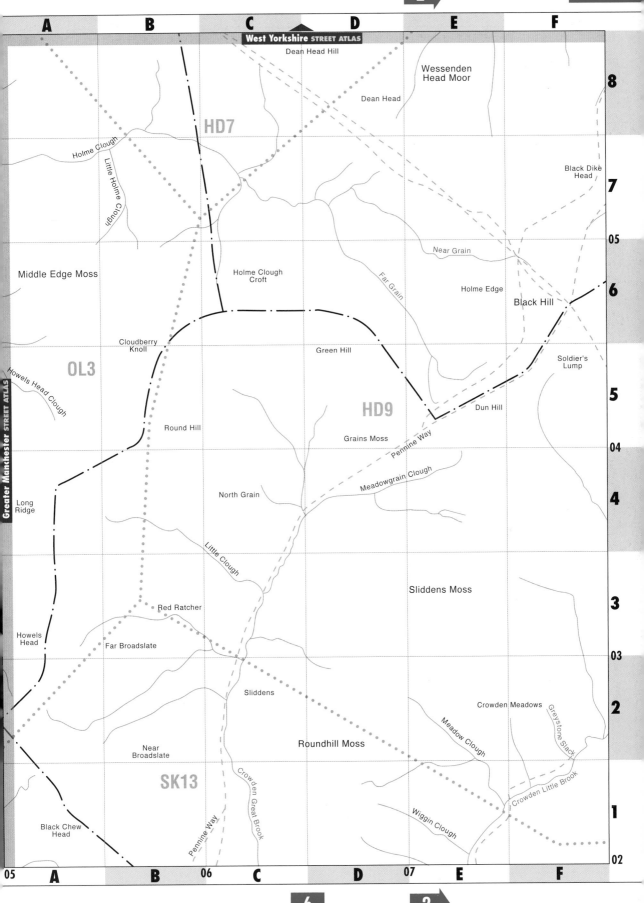

West Yorkshire STREET ATLAS

Greater Manchester STREET ATLAS

A   B   C   D   E   F

8

7

05

6

05

5

04

4

03

3

03

2

1

02

Dean Head Hill

Wessenden
Head Moor

HD7

Dean Head

Holme Clough

Little Holme Clough

Black Dike
Head

Near Grain

Middle Edge Moss

Holme Clough
Croft

Far Grain

Holme Edge

Black Hill

Howels Head Clough

OL3

Cloudberry
Knoll

Green Hill

Soldier's
Lump

Round Hill

HD9

Dun Hill

Grains Moss

Pennine Way

04

Long
Ridge

North Grain

Meadowgrain Clough

Little Clough

Sliddens Moss

Red Ratcher

Howels
Head

Far Broadslate

Sliddens

Crowden Meadows

Greystone Stack

Near
Broadslate

Roundhill Moss

Meadow Clough

Crowden Little Brook

SK13

Crowden Great Brook

Black Chew
Head

Pennine Way

Wiggin Clough

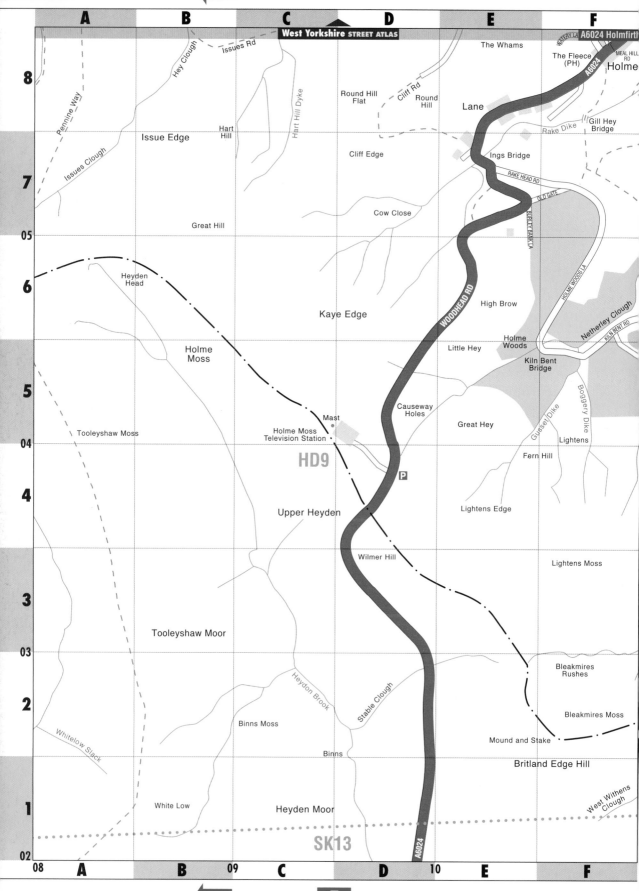

A   B   C   D   E   F

8

Pennine Way

Issues Rd

Hey Clough

Hart Hill Dyke

Issue Edge

Hart Hill

Cliff Rd

Round Hill Flat

Round Hill

The Whams

The Fleece (PH)

A6024

MEAL HILL RD

Holme

A6024 Holmfirth

WATERY LA

Lane

Gill Hey Bridge

Rake Dike

7

Issues Clough

Cliff Edge

Ings Bridge

RAKE HEAD RD

OLD GATE

05

Great Hill

Cow Close

BURLEY BANK LA

HOLME WOODS LA

6

Heyden Head

Kaye Edge

High Brow

Netherley Clough

KILN BENT RD

Holme Moss

Little Hey

Holme Woods

Kiln Bent Bridge

5

Tooleyshaw Moss

Mast

Causeway Holes

Great Hey

Gusset Dike

Boggery Dike

Lightens

04

Holme Moss Television Station

HD9

P

Fern Hill

4

Upper Heyden

Lightens Edge

Wilmer Hill

Lightens Moss

3

Tooleyshaw Moor

Heydon Brook

Stable Clough

Bleakmires Rushes

03

Binns Moss

2

Whitelow Slack

Binns

Mound and Stake

Bleakmires Moss

Britland Edge Hill

1

White Low

Heyden Moor

West Withens Clough

SK13

A6024

02

08   A   B   09   C   D   10   E   F

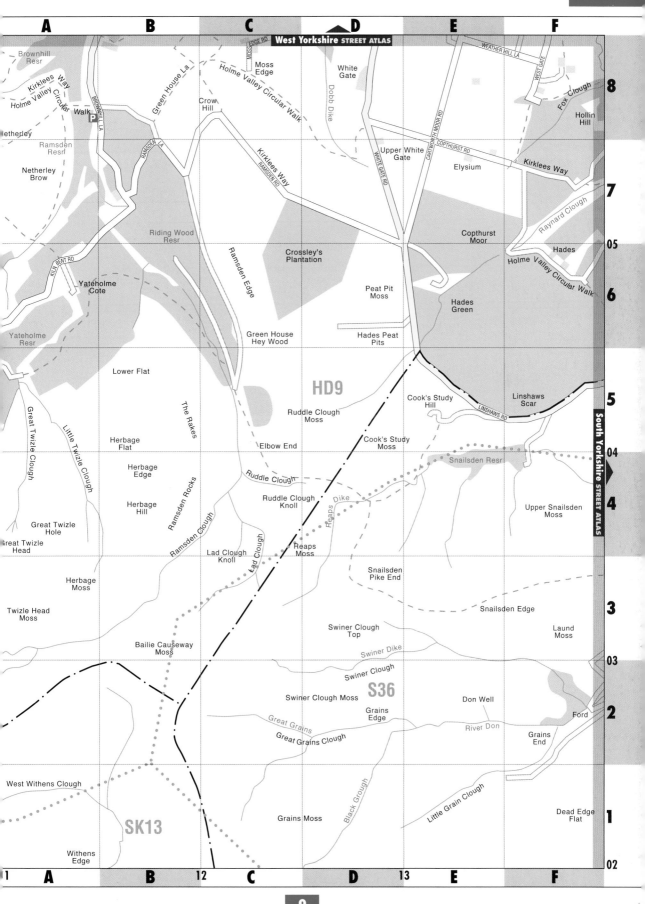

A   B   C   D   E   F

8

7

05

6

5

04

4

3

03

2

1

02

Brownhill
Resr

Kirklees Valley Way
Holme Valley Circular Walk

Netherley

Ramsden
Resr

Netherley
Brow

Yateholme
Cote

Yateholme
Resr

Great Twizle Clough

Little Twizle Clough

Great Twizle
Hole

Great Twizle
Head

Herbage
Moss

Twizle Head
Moss

West Withens Clough

SK13

Withens
Edge

Green House La

Crow
Hill

Riding Wood
Resr

Lower Flat

The Rakes

Herbage
Flat

Herbage
Edge

Herbage
Hill

Ramsden Rocks

Ramsden Clough

Bailie Causeway
Moss

BROWNHILL LA

RAMSDEN LA

KILN BENT RD

Kirklees Way

RAMSDEN RD

Ramsden Edge

Green House
Hey Wood

HD9

Ruddle Clough
Moss

Elbow End

Ruddle Clough

Ruddle Clough
Knoll

Lad Clough
Knoll

Lad Clough

Reaps
Moss

Swiner Clough
Moss

Great Grains

Great Grains Clough

Grains Moss

Grains
Moss

Moss
Edge

MOSS EDGE RD

Holme Valley Circular Walk

White
Gate

Dobb Dike

WHITE GATE RD

Upper White
Gate

Crossley's
Plantation

Peat Pit
Moss

Hades Peat
Pits

Cook's Study
Moss

Reaps Dike

Snailsden
Pike End

Swiner Clough
Top

Swiner Dike

Swiner Clough

S36

Grains
Edge

Black Grough

WEATHER HILL LA

CARTWORTH MOOR RD

COPTHURST RD

Elysium

Copthurst
Moor

Hades
Green

Cook's Study
Hill

LINSHAWS RD

Snailsden Resr

Snailsden Edge

Don Well

River Don

Little Grain Clough

WEST GATE

Fox Clough

Hollin
Hill

Kirklees Way

Raynard Clough

Hades

Holme Valley Circular Walk

Linshaws
Scar

Upper Snailsden
Moss

Laund
Moss

Ford

Grains
End

Dead Edge
Flat

P   Walk

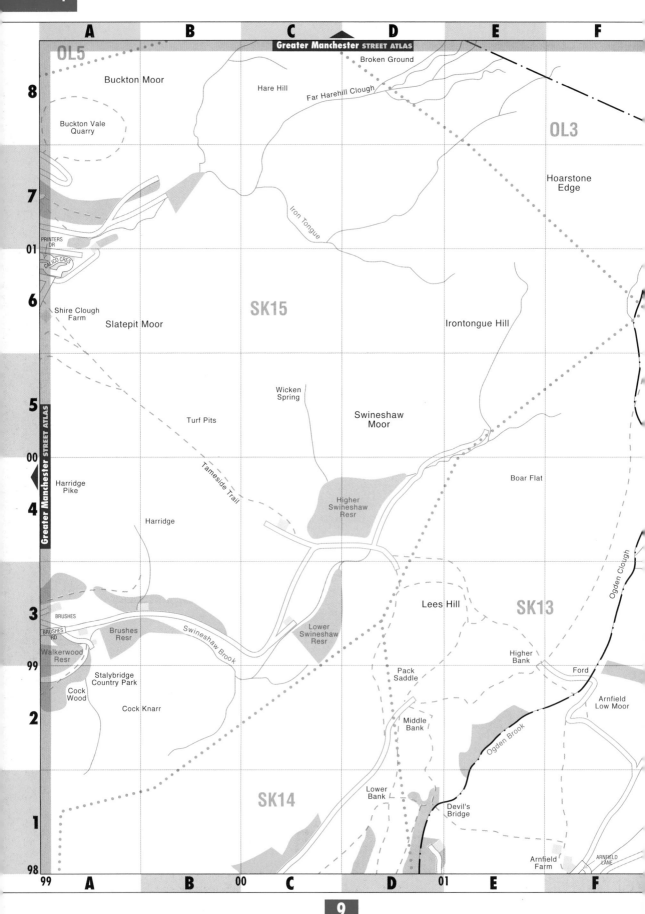

OL5

Buckton Moor

Buckton Vale
Quarry

Hare Hill

Broken Ground

Far Harehill Clough

OL3

Hoarstone
Edge

PRINTERS
DR

CALICO CRES

Iron Tongue

SK15

Shire Clough
Farm

Slatepit Moor

Irontongue Hill

Wicken
Spring

Turf Pits

Swineshaw
Moor

Tameside Trail

Boar Flat

Harridge
Pike

Higher
Swineshaw
Resr

Harridge

BRUSHES

Lees Hill

SK13

Ogden Clough

BRUSHES
RD

Brushes
Resr

Swineshaw Brook

Lower
Swineshaw
Resr

Higher
Bank

Ford

Walkerwood
Resr

Pack
Saddle

Arnfield
Low Moor

Cock
Wood

Stalybridge
Country Park

Cock Knarr

Middle
Bank

Ogden Brook

SK14

Lower
Bank

Devil's
Bridge

Arnfield
Farm

ARNFIELD
LANE

Greater Manchester STREET ATLAS

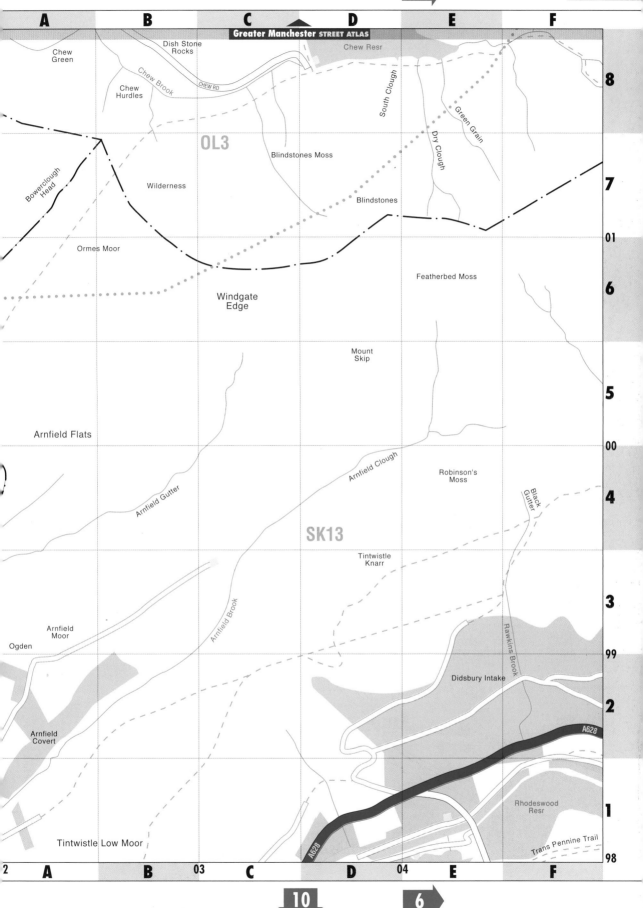

A   B   C   D   E   F

Greater Manchester STREET ATLAS

Chew Green

Dish Stone
Rocks

Chew Resr

8

Chew Brook

CHEW RD

Chew
Hurdles

South Clough

OL3

Blindstones Moss

Dry Clough

Green Grain

Bowerclough
Head

Wilderness

Blindstones

7

01

Ormes Moor

Featherbed Moss

6

Windgate
Edge

Mount
Skip

5

00

Arnfield Flats

Arnfield Clough

Robinson's
Moss

Black Gutter

4

Arnfield Gutter

SK13

Tintwistle
Knarr

3

Arnfield Brook

Arnfield
Moor

Rawkins Brook

Ogden

99

Didsbury Intake

2

Arnfield
Covert

A628

1

Rhodeswood
Resr

Tintwistle Low Moor

Trans Pennine Trail

98

2   A   03   B   C   04   D   E   F

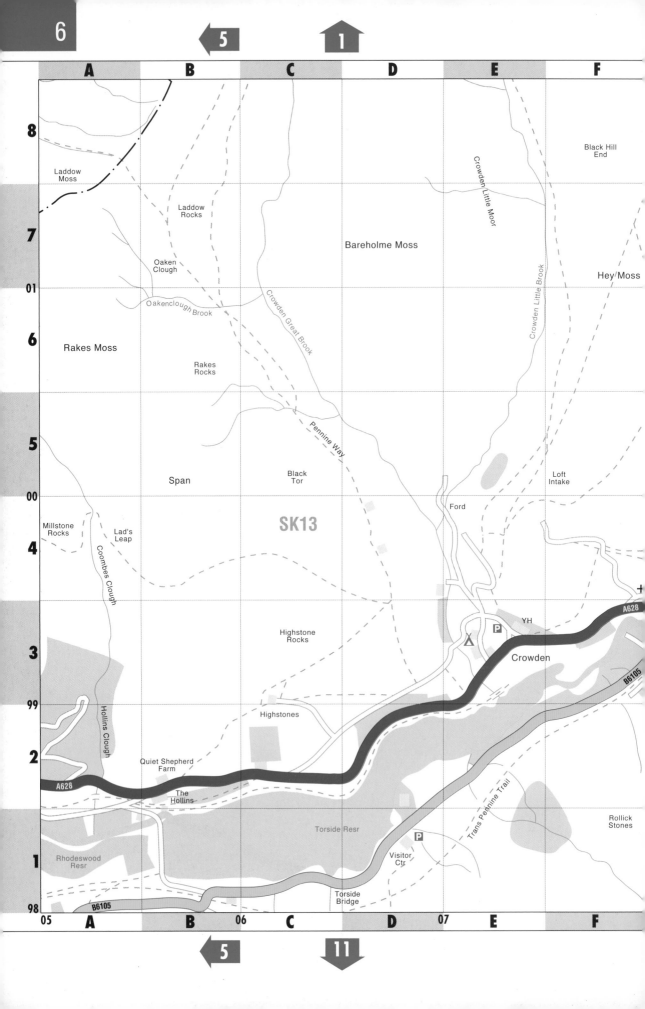

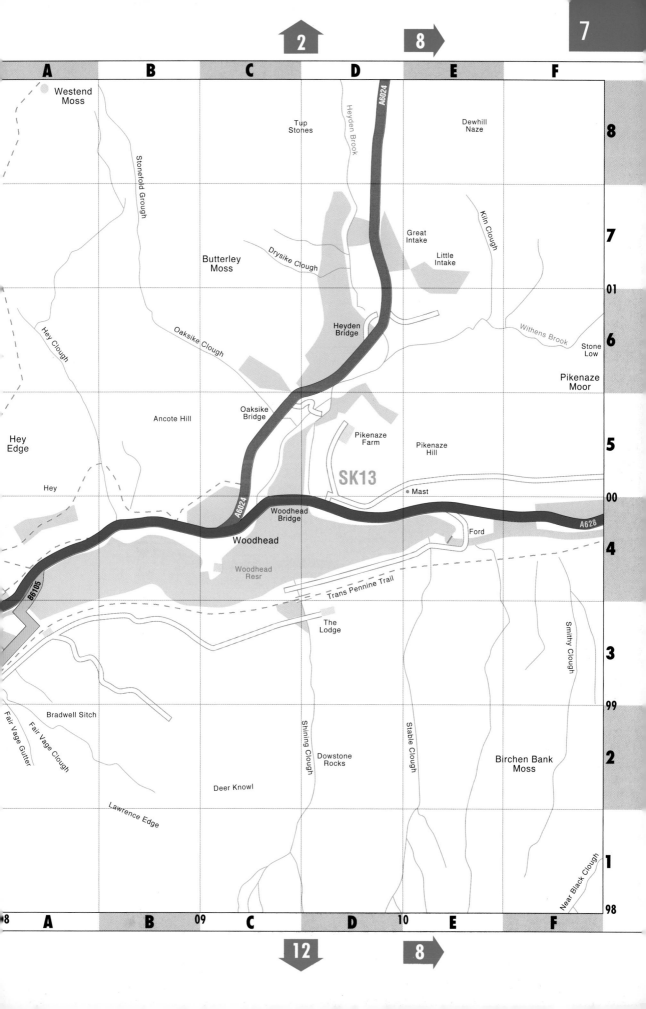

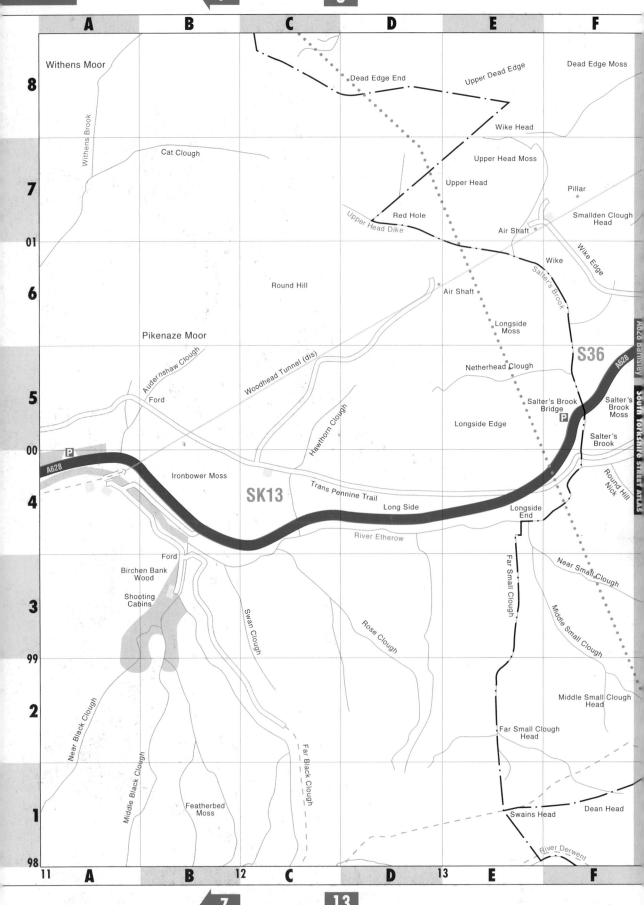

A   B   C   D   E   F

Withens Moor

8

Withens Brook

Cat Clough

7

01

Round Hill

6

Pikenaze Moor

Audernshaw Clough

Woodhead Tunnel (dis)

Hawthorn Clough

5

Ford

00

A628

4

Ironbower Moss

SK13

Trans Pennine Trail

Long Side

Long Side

River Etherow

Ford

Birchen Bank
Wood

Shooting
Cabins

3

Swan Clough

Rose Clough

Near Black Clough

Middle Black Clough

99

Featherbed
Moss

Far Black Clough

2

1

98

Dead Edge End

Upper Dead Edge

Dead Edge Moss

Wike Head

Upper Head Moss

Upper Head

Pillar

Red Hole

Smallden Clough
Head

Upper Head Dike

Air Shaft

Air Shaft

Wike

Wike Edge

Salter's Brook

Longside
Moss

S36

Netherhead Clough

Salter's Brook
Bridge

Longside Edge

Salter's
Brook
Moss

P

Salter's
Brook

A628

Longside
End

Round Hill
Nick

Far Small Clough

Near Small Clough

Middle Small Clough

Middle Small Clough
Head

Far Small Clough
Head

Swains Head

Dean Head

River Derwent

A628 Barnsley   South Yorkshire STREET ATLAS

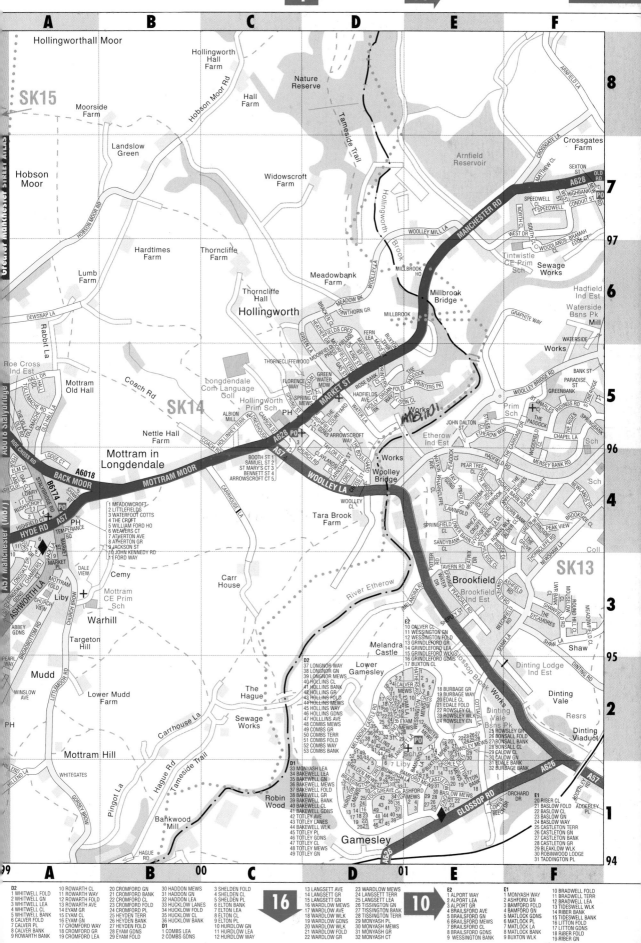

D2
1 WHITWELL FOLD
2 WHITWELL GN
3 WHITWELL LEA
4 WHITWELL CL
5 WHITWELL BANK
6 CALVER FOLD
7 CALVER PL
8 CALVER BANK
9 ROWARTH BANK
10 ROWARTH CL
11 ROWARTH WAY
12 ROWARTH FOLD
13 ROWARTH AVE
14 EYAM GR
15 EYAM CL
16 EYAM GN
17 CROMFORD WAY
18 CROMFORD GR
19 CROMFORD LEA
20 CROMFORD GN
21 CROMFORD BANK
22 CROMFORD CL
23 CROMFORD FOLD
24 CROMFORD PL
25 HEYDEN TERR
26 HEYDEN BANK
27 HEYDEN FOLD
28 EYAM GDNS
29 EYAM FOLD

30 HADDON MEWS
31 HADDON GN
32 HADDON LEA
33 HUCKLOW LANES
34 HUCKLOW FOLD
35 HUCKLOW CL
36 HUCKLOW BANK

D1
1 COMBS LEA
2 COMBS GDNS

3 SHELDEN FOLD
4 SHELDEN CL
5 SHELDEN PL
6 ELTON LEA
7 ELTON CL
8 ELTON PL
9 HURDLOW GN
10 HURDLOW CL
11 HURDLOW LEA
12 HURDLOW WAY

13 LANGSETT AVE
14 LANGSETT GR
15 LANGSETT TERR
16 LANGSETT LEA
17 WARDLOW MEWS
18 WARDLOW WLK
19 WARDLOW AVE
20 WARDLOW WLK
21 WARDLOW GR
22 WARDLOW LEA

23 WARDLOW MEWS
24 LANGSETT GN
25 LANGSETT TERR
26 TISSINGTON GN
27 TISSINGTON TERR
28 TISSINGTON WLK
29 MONYASH WAY
30 MONYASH MEWS
31 MONYASH GR
32 MONYASH CT

E2
1 ALPORT WAY
2 ALPORT LEA
3 ALPORT GR
4 BRAILSFORD AVE
5 BRAILSFORD GN
6 BRAILSFORD CL
7 BRAILSFORD GDNS
8 BRAILSFORD BANK
9 WESSINGTON BANK

E1
1 MONYASH WAY
2 ASHFORD GN
3 BAMFORD FOLD
4 BAMFORD GN
5 MATLOCK GDNS
6 MATLOCK CL
7 MATLOCK LA
8 MATLOCK PL
9 BUXTON WLK

10 BRADWELL FOLD
11 BRADWELL TERR
12 BRADWELL LEA
13 TIDESWELL WLK
14 RIBER BANK
15 TIDESWELL BANK
16 LITTON FOLD
17 LITTON GDNS
18 RIBER FOLD
19 RIBER GN

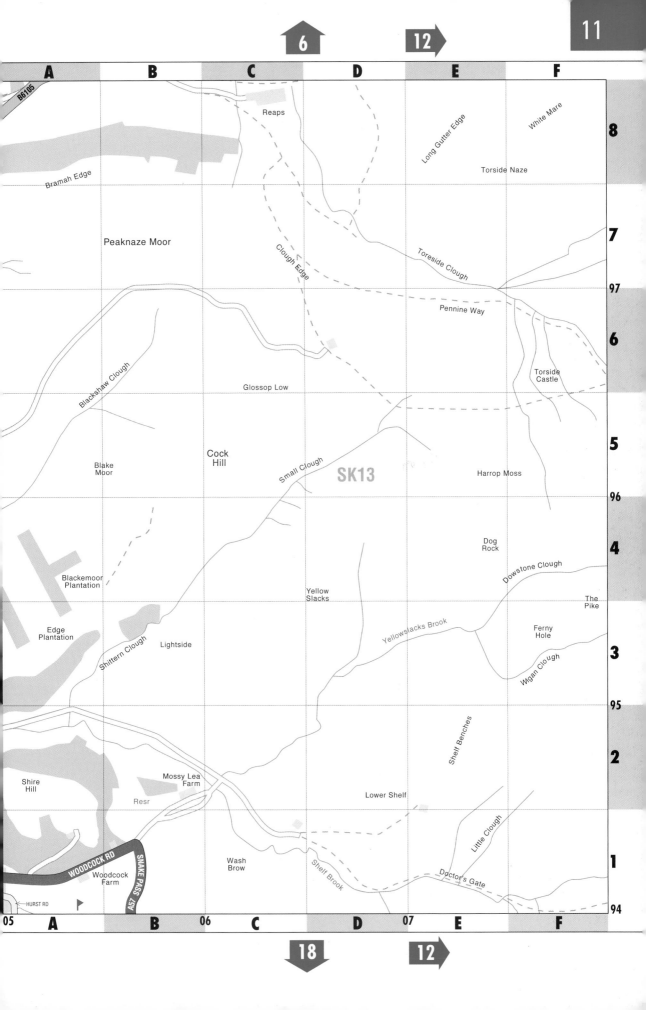

11
7

| | A | B | C | D | E | F |

Wildboar Clough

Round Hill

8

Shining Clough Moss

Near Black Clough

Bleaklow Meadows

7

Sykes Moor

97

Near Bleaklow Stones

6

Wildboar Grain

Far Moss

Bleaklow

SK13

Bleaklow Hill

5

Joseph Patch

Bleaklow Head

Alport Head

Wain Stones

96

Pennine Way

4

Dowstone Clough

Shelf Moss

Far Fork Grain

Near Fork Grain

Hern Stones

3

95

The Swamp

Shelf Moor

Hern Clough

Grains in the Water

2

Lower Shelf Stones

Higher Shelf Stones

Alport Low

Crooked Clough

S33

Ashton Clough

1

White Clough

Devil's Dike

Gathering Hill

94

| 08 | A | B | 09 | C | D | 10 | E | F |

11
19

A B C D E F

Black
Moss

Middle Black Clough

Featherbed
Moss

8

White
Stones

Swains
Greave

7

97

Barrow
Stones

Barrow Clough

6

SK13

Bleaklow
Stones

Grinah
Stones

Round
Hill

5

96

Westend
Head

Grinah Grain

Deep Grain

4

The Ridge

Ridgewalk Moor

3

95

S33

River Westend

2

Ravens Clough

1

Over Wood
Moss

94

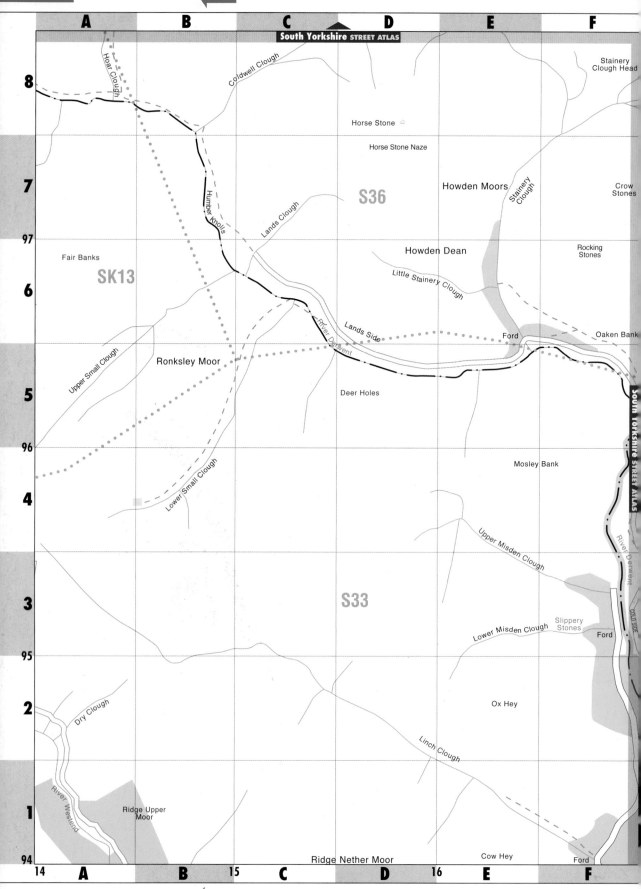

South Yorkshire STREET ATLAS

Hoar Clough
Coldwell Clough
Stainery Clough Head
Horse Stone
Horse Stone Naze
S36
Howden Moors
Stainery Clough
Crow Stones
Humber Knolls
Lands Clough
97
Howden Dean
Rocking Stones
Fair Banks
SK13
Little Stainery Clough
River Derwent
Lands Side
Ford
Oaken Bank
Upper Small Clough
Ronksley Moor
Deer Holes
Mosley Bank
Lower Small Clough
Upper Misden Clough
S33
Lower Misden Clough
Slippery Stones
Ford
Dry Clough
Ox Hey
River Westend
Linch Clough
Cow Hey
Ford
Ridge Upper Moor
Ridge Nether Moor

South Yorkshire STREET ATLAS
River Derwent
COLD SIDE

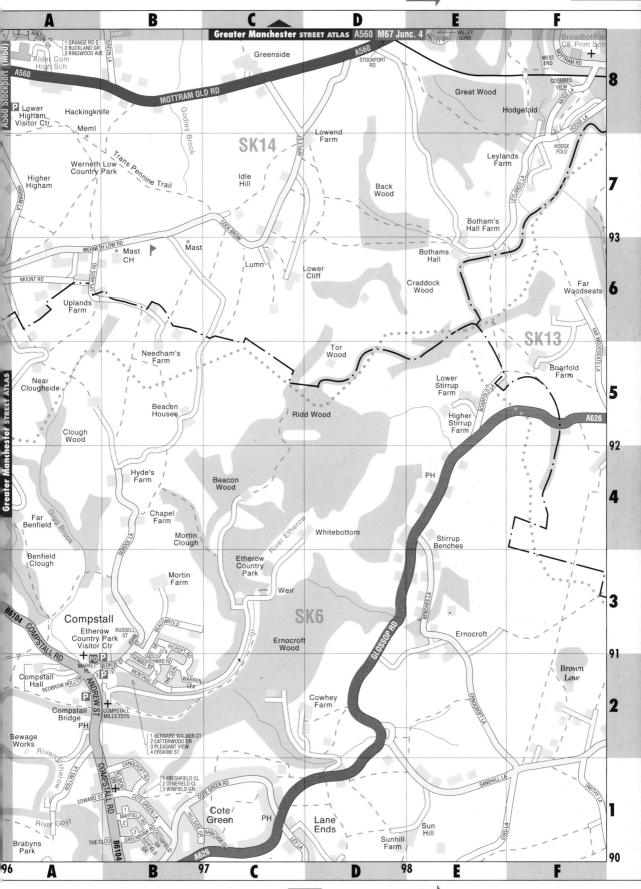

Greater Manchester STREET ATLAS | A560 | M67 Junc. 4

A B C D E F

A Abou Stockport (WBU)

A560

1 GRANGE RD S
2 BUCKLAND GR
3 RINGWOOD AVE

Alder Com
High Sch

Broadbottom
CE Prim Sch

WEST
END

MOTTRAM RD

COOMBES
VIEW

8

Greenside

Stockport
RD

Great Wood

Hodgefold

Lower
Higham
Visitor Ctr

Hackingknife

Meml

MOTTRAM OLD RD

HINTON GR

GREEN LA

Godley Brook

APPLE ST

Lowend
Farm

Leylands
Farm

MOSS LA

HODGE LA

HODGE
FOLD

7

SK14

Higher
Higham

Werneth Low
Country Park

Trans Pennine Trail

Idle
Hill

Back
Wood

Botham's
Hall Farm

LEYLANDS LA

93

HIGHAM LA

WERNETH LOW RD

UPLANDS RD

COCK BROW

Mast

Mast
CH

Lumn

Lower
Cliff

Lower
Cliff

Bothams
Hall

Craddock
Wood

Far
Woodseats

6

MOUNT RD

Uplands
Farm

SK13

FAR WOODSEATS LA

92

Near
Cloughside

Needham's
Farm

Tor
Wood

Lower
Stirrup
Farm

Boarfold
Farm

BOARFOLD LA

5

Clough
Wood

Beacon
Houses

Ridd Wood

Higher
Stirrup
Farm

A626

92

Hyde's
Farm

Beacon
Wood

PH

4

Far
Benfield

Gigg Brook

Chapel
Farm

Mortin
Clough

SCHOOL LA

River Etherow

Whitebottom

Stirrup
Benches

Benfield
Clough

Mortin
Farm

Etherow
Country
Park

Weir

BENCHES LA

3

B6104

COMPSTALL RD

Compstall

Etherow
Country Park
Visitor Ctr

RUSSELL
ST

BEACONFOLD

JOHN ST

RICROFT RD

Ernocroft
Wood

SK6

GLOSSOP RD

Ernocroft

ERNOCROFT LA

91

Compstall
Hall

REDBROW HOLLOW

P P

MARKET
PL

THOMAS ST

ORCHARD RD

MONTAGU ST

THE CEA

GEORGE ST

WARREN
LEA

Brown
Low

2

Compstall
Bridge

ANDREW ST

P

PH

Compstall
Mills Ests

1 BERNARD WALKER CT
2 CATTERWOOD DR
3 PLEASANT VIEW
4 ERSKINE ST

Cowhey
Farm

SANDHILL LA

Sewage
Works

River Etherow

ROLLINS LA

ERNOCROFT RD

BELMONT DR

COMPSTALL RD

EDWARD ST

COTE GREEN LA

1 FRESHFIELD CL
2 DENEFIELD CL
3 WINFIELD GR

HILLSIDE GR

CROSSFIELD GR

COTE GREEN RD

Lane
Ends

Sun
Hill

GIBB LA

SMITHY LA

1

River Goyt

Brabyns
Park

THE CLOSE

B6104

MAYFIELD RD

GREENBANK GR

ASHFIELD GR

BANKSIDE CT

Cote
Green

PH

LEYLA

A626

Sunhill
Farm

90

96 A B 97 C D 98 E F

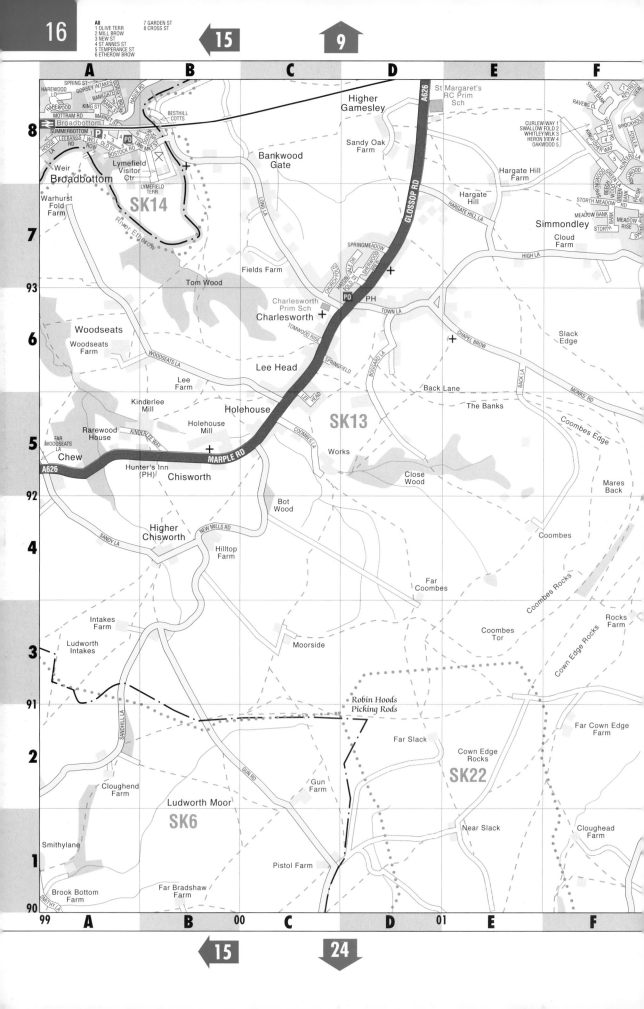

16

A8
1 OLIVE TERR
2 MILL BROW
3 NEW ST
4 ST ANNES ST
5 TEMPERANCE ST
6 ETHEROW BROW
7 GARDEN ST
8 CROSS ST

15 9

A   B   C   D   E   F

Spring St
Harewood Lo
Harewood
Mottram Rd
Gorsey Intakes
Bank Gate
King St
Market
Hague Rd
Besthill Cotts

Higher Gamesley
St Margaret's RC Prim Sch

Swift Bank
Ravens Cl
Valley Rd
Brockholes
Kingster Way
Hunters Cl

Broadbottom
Summerbottom
Leebangs Rd
Well La
Old St
Bostock Rd
Lymefield Visitor Ctr
Lymefield Terr

SK14

Bankwood Gate

Sandy Oak Farm

Hargate Hill Farm

Hargate Hill

Simmondley

Curlew Way 1
Swallow Fold 2
Whitley Wlk 3
Heron View 4
Oakwood 5

Springwood
Beech
Green
Springmeadow
Storth Meadow
Meadow Bank
Storth
Meadow Rise

8

Weir
Broadbottom

River Etherow

Warhurst Fold Farm

Fields Farm

Tom Wood

Glossop Rd

A626

Hargate Hill La

High La

Cloud Farm

7

93

Woodseats

Woodseats Farm

Woodseats La

Springmeadow
Maynard's Dale Dr
Sherwood Fern
Church Fold

Charlesworth Prim Sch
Charlesworth
PO PH

Town La

Chapel Brow

Slack Edge

Monks Rd

6

Lee Head

Lee Farm

Tomwood Rise

Springfield

Boggard La

Back Lane

The Banks

Back La

Coombes Edge

5

Kinderlee Mill

Rarewood House

Kinderlee Way

Holehouse
Holehouse Mill

Marple Rd

Coombes La

Lee Head

Works

Close Wood

SK13

Mares Back

92

Chew
A626
Hunter's Inn (PH)
Chisworth

Higher Chisworth

Sandy La

New Mills Rd

Hilltop Farm

Bot Wood

Coombes

4

Coombes Rocks

Intakes Farm

Ludworth Intakes

Moorside

Far Coombes

Coombes Tor

Rocks Farm

Cown Edge Rocks

3

91

Robin Hoods Picking Rods

Far Slack

Far Cown Edge Farm

2

Cloughend Farm

Ludworth Moor

SK6

Gun Rd

Gun Farm

Cown Edge Rocks

SK22

Cloughead Farm

Sandhill La

1

Smithylane

Brook Bottom Farm

Far Bradshaw Farm

Smithy La

Pistol Farm

Near Slack

90

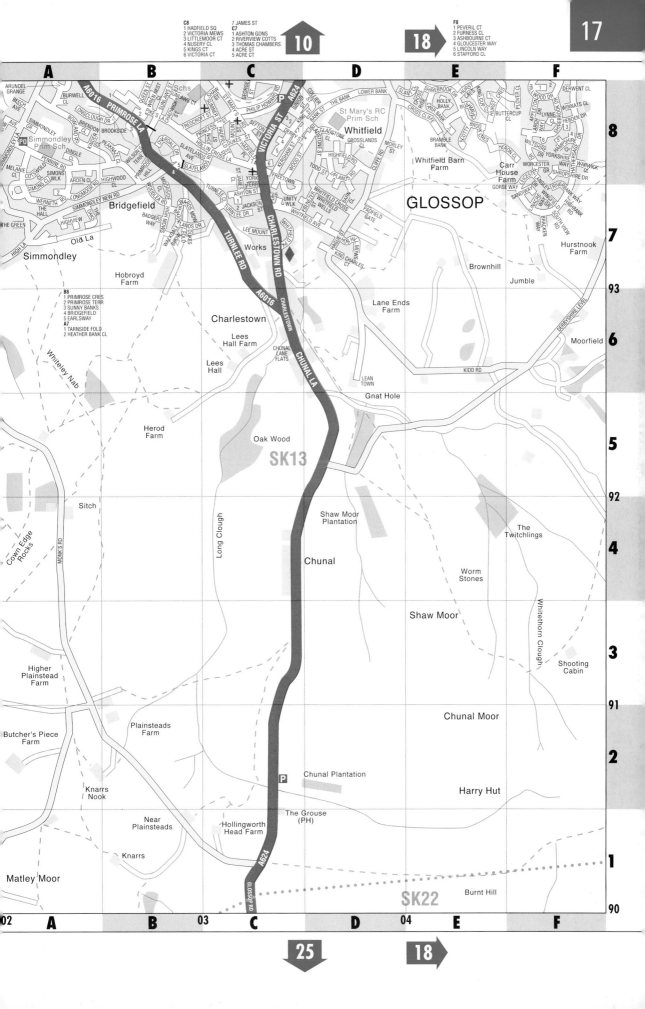

A B C D E F

CH

Hill End Farm

Hurst Resr

A57

Lordship Hill

Hey Clough

Old Dike

Birchen Orchard Clough

Lower Ridge

8

DERBYSHIRE LEVEL

Hurst Brook

SNAKE RD

Ramsley Clough

Cabin Clough

Coldharbour Moor

7

93

Ramsley Moor

Higher Ridge

Span Moor

Span Clough

Holden Clough

A57

6

Hurst Moor

5

SK13

Wood's Cabin

Bostock Plantation

Highmoor Pits

92

Black Moor

Bray Clough

Fairvage Clough

Moss Castle

Glead Hill

Pennine Way

4

Bakestone Delph Clough

3

Within Clough

S33

91

2

Snake Path

River Ashop

Mill Hill

Ashop Head

SK22

Pennine Way

1

90

05 A 06 B C 07 D E F

A B C D E F

8

Rose Clough

Crooked Clough

Devil's Dike

Pennine Way

Doctor's Gate

Urchin Clough

SK13

Old Woman

7

93

Snake Pass

Doctor's Gate Culvert

SNAKE RD

Nether North Grain

Upper North Grain

6

Thomason's Hollow

Featherbed Moss

Lady Clough Moor

5

Featherbed Top

Salvin Ridge

92

S33

Lady Clough

4

Within Clough

Upper Gate Clough

Snake Woodland Forest Walk

91

Red Clough

Nether Gate Clough

Snake Plantations

P

3

Ashop Clough

Saukin Ridge

A57

2

Urchin Clough

Rough Bank

Snake Path

River Ashop

Black Ashop Moor

1

SK22

90

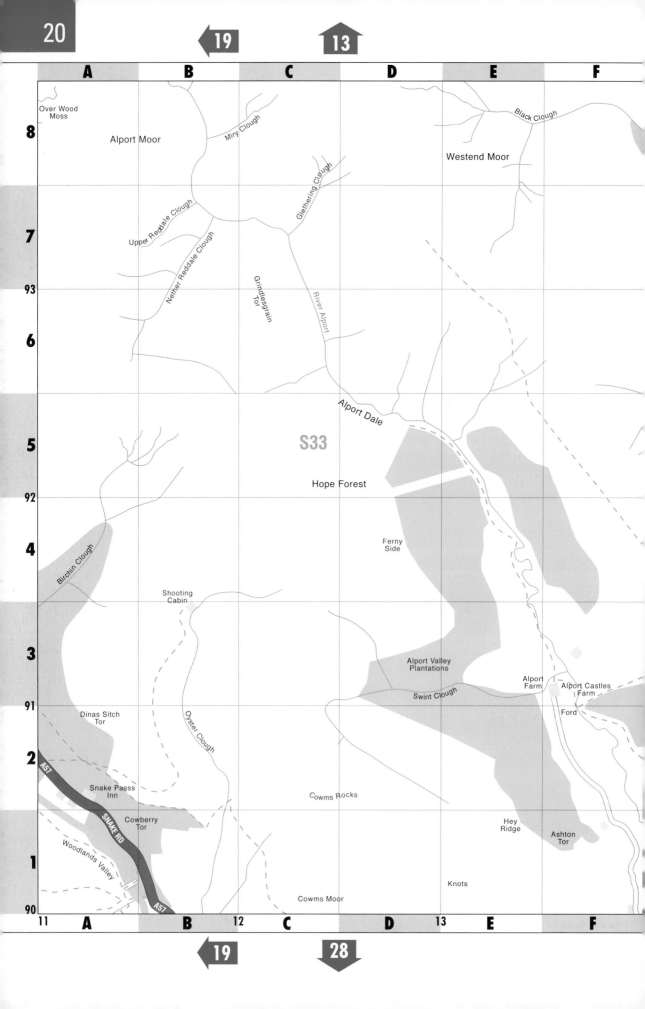

19
13

A   B   C   D   E   F

Over Wood
Moss

8   Alport Moor   Miry Clough   Black Clough

                                                    Westend Moor

                        Glethering Clough

7   Upper Reddale Clough

93   Nether Reddale Clough

     Grindlesgrain
     Tor

6   River Alport

                          Alport Dale

5   S33

92   Hope Forest

                          Ferny
                          Side

4   Birchin Clough

     Shooting
     Cabin   Alport Valley
                                   Plantations

3   Swint Clough   Alport   Alport Castles
                                                               Farm   Farm

91   Dinas Sitch   Oyster Clough   Ford
     Tor

2   A57
     Snake Passs
     Inn   Cowms Rocks

     Cowberry   Hey   Ashton
     Tor   Ridge   Tor
     SNAKE RD

1   Woodlands Valley

                                   Knots

90   A57   Cowms Moor

11   A   B   12   C   D   13   E   F

19
28

14

22

A	B	C	D	E	F

Upper Wood

Banktop Hey

Ronksley South Plantation

8

Ford

Ridge Clough

Nether Wood Plantation

River Westend

Ridge Wood

7

Banktop Plantation

Ford

Howden Resr

93

Fagney Plantation

Hern Side

6

Fagney Clough

Fox's Piece

West Cable Tip Plantation

Howden Dam

Ditch Clough Plantation

Morebottom Cottage

Ditch Clough

Green Clough

5

Island Plantation

92

Bank Clough

S33

Chapel Plantation

Birchinlee East Plantation

4

Birchin Hat

Birchinlee

Derwent Resr

Calfhey Wood

Alport Castles

The Towe

Birchinlee Pasture

Little Moor

3

Cote Clough

91

Castles Wood

Ouzelden Clough
Ouzelden Brook

Gores Farm

Hucklow Lees Barn

Birchinlee New Piece

2

Whitefield Pits

Gores Plantation

Allport Grain

Gores Heights

River Alport

Rowlee Pasture

1

Nabs Wood

90

A	B	C	D	E	F

14

15

16

29

22

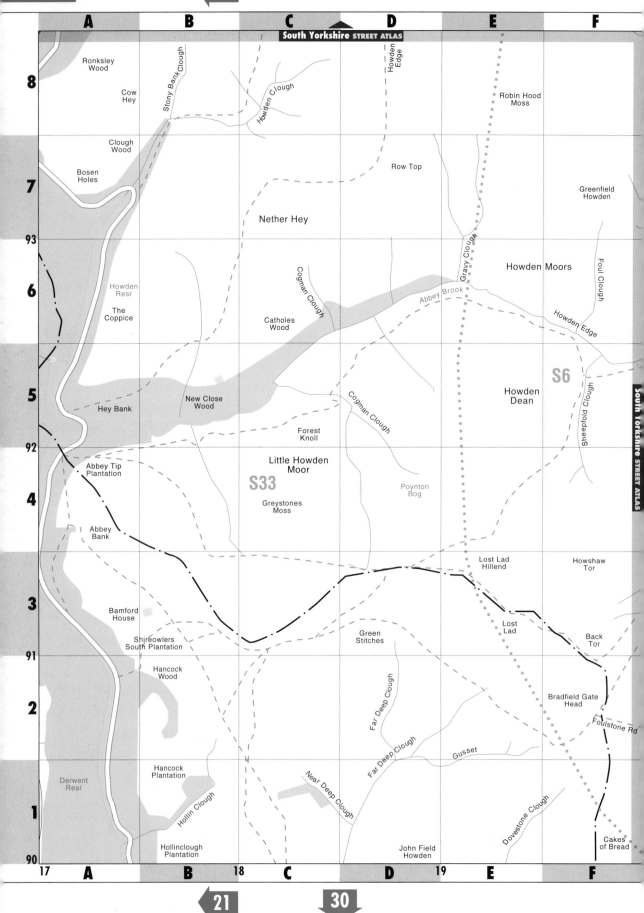

A **B** **C** **D** **E** **F**

8

Ronksley
Wood

Cow
Hey

Stony Bank Clough

Howden Clough

Howden
Edge

Robin Hood
Moss

7

Clough
Wood

Bosen
Holes

Row Top

Greenfield
Howden

93

Nether Hey

Gravy Clough

Howden Moors

Foul Clough

6

Howden
Resr

The
Coppice

Cogman Clough

Catholes
Wood

Abbey Brook

Howden Edge

S6

5

Hey Bank

New Close
Wood

Cogman Clough

Howden
Dean

Sheepfold Clough

92

Forest
Knoll

Little Howden
Moor

Poynton
Bog

Abbey Tip
Plantation

S33

4

Greystones
Moss

Abbey
Bank

Lost Lad
Hillend

Howshaw
Tor

3

Bamford
House

Lost
Lad

Back
Tor

Shireowlers
South Plantation

Green
Stitches

91

Hancock
Wood

Bradfield Gate
Head

2

Far Deep Clough

Foulstone Rd

Hancock
Plantation

Far Deep Clough

Gusset

1

Derwent
Resr

Near Deep Clough

Dovestone Clough

Hollin Clough

Hollinclough
Plantation

John Field
Howden

Cakes
of Bread

90

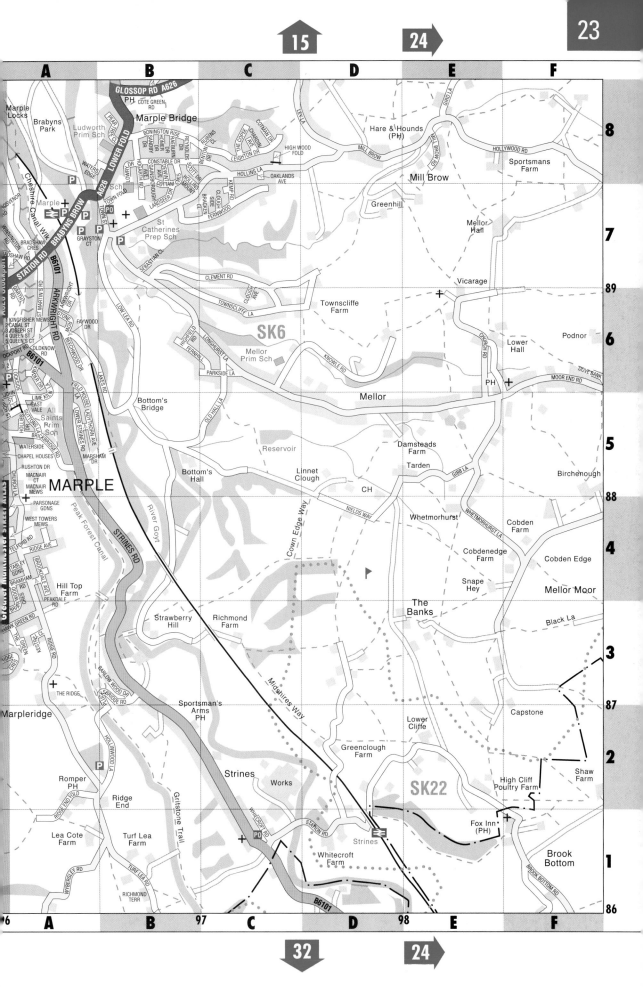

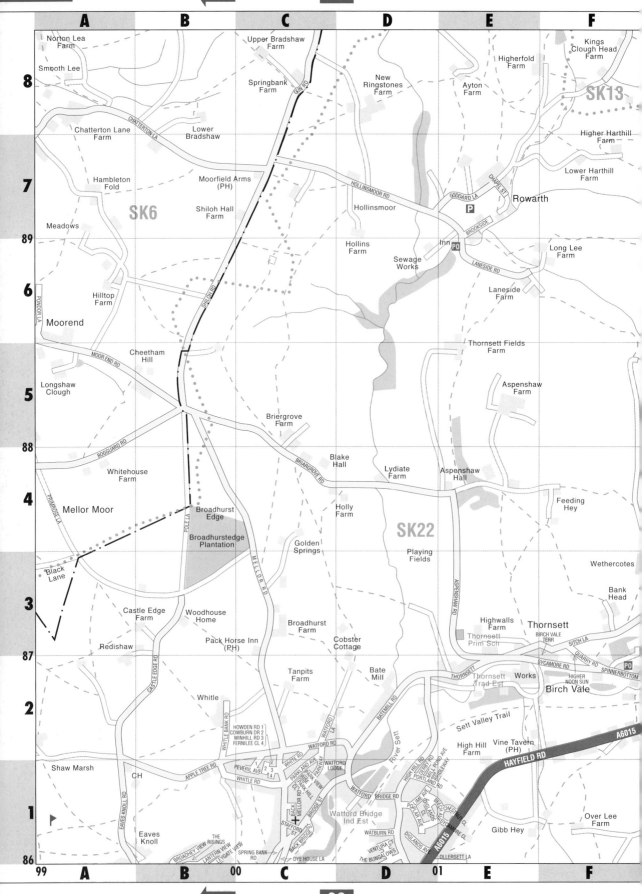

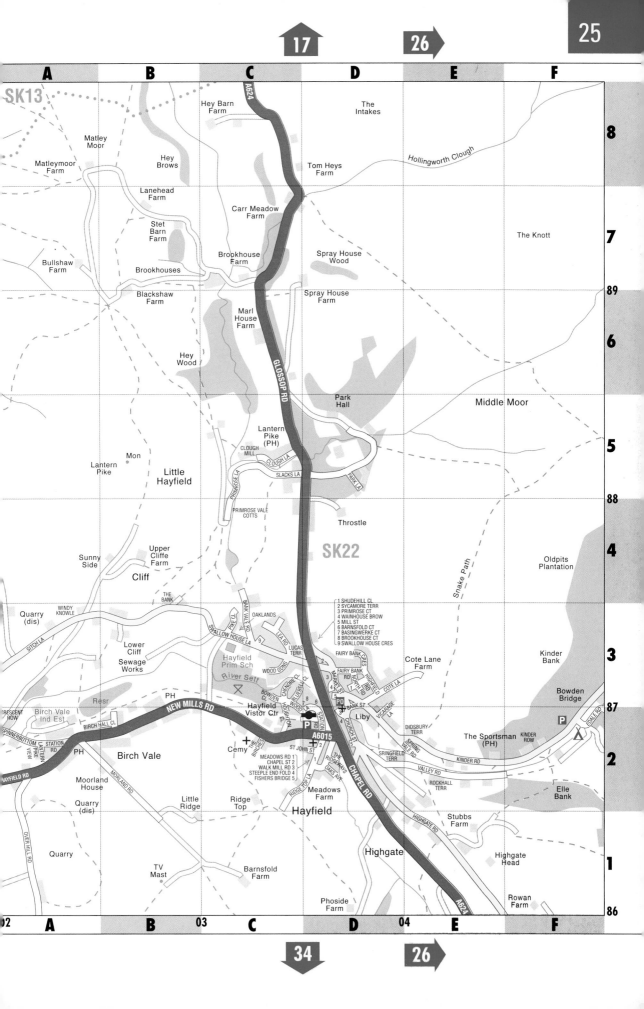

SK13

A B C D E F

8
7
89
6
5
88
4
3
87
2
1
86

Matley Moor

Matleymoor Farm

Hey Brows

Hey Barn Farm

The Intakes

Hollingworth Clough

Lanehead Farm

Carr Meadow Farm

Tom Heys Farm

The Knott

Stet Barn Farm

Brookhouse Farm

Spray House Wood

Bullshaw Farm

Brookhouses

Blackshaw Farm

Spray House Farm

Marl House Farm

Hey Wood

Park Hall

Middle Moor

Lantern Pike (PH)

GLOSSOP RD

A624

CLOUGH MILL

CLOUGH LA

SLACKS LA

PARK LA

Lantern Pike

Mon

Little Hayfield

PRIMROSE LA

PRIMROSE VALE COTTS

Throstle

SK22

Snake Path

Oldpits Plantation

Upper Cliffe Farm

Sunny Side

Cliff

THE BANK

BANK VALE RD

OAKLANDS

PIKE CL

1 SHUDEHILL CL
2 SYCAMORE TERR
3 PRIMROSE CT
4 WAINHOUSE BROW
5 MILL ST
6 BARNSFOLD CT
7 BASINGWERKE CT
8 BROOKHOUSE CT
9 SWALLOW HOUSE CRES

Kinder Bank

Quarry (dis)

WINDY KNOWLE

SWALLOW HOUSE LA

LEA RD

9

LUCAS TERR

FAIRY BANK CRES

MARKET ST

SWALLOW HOUSE CRES

Cote Lane Farm

Bowden Bridge

SITCH LA

Lower Cliff

Sewage Works

Hayfield Prim Sch

WOOD GDNS

CHEDDLE CL

FAIRY BANK RD NORTH

FAIRY BANK RD

COTE LA

KINDER RD

EDALE RD

P

△

Resr

River Sett

BOWDEN CL

HOLLINGHILL RD

WOOD ST

BANK ST

VICARAGE LA

Kinder Row

The Sportsman (PH)

CRESCENT ROW

Birch Vale Ind Est

PH

BIRCH HALL CL

NEW MILLS RD

PH

Hayfield Vistor Ctr

P

STATION RD

PO

Liby

Didsbury Terr

Springfield Terr

SPRING VALE RD

SPINNERBOTTOM RD

LANTERN PIKE VIEW

STATION RD

Birch Vale

Cemy

THE BIRCHES

ST JOHN ST

A6015

CHURCH ST

VALLEY RD

Valley Rd

ROCKHALL TERR

Elle Bank

HAYFIELD RD

Moorland House

MORLAND RD

Quarry (dis)

Little Ridge

Ridge Top

RIDGE TOP LA

MEADOWS RD 1
CHAPEL ST 2
WALK MILL RD 3
STEEPLE END FOLD 4
FISHERS BRIDGE 5

OAKS AVE

THE RIDGEWAYS

Meadows Farm

Hayfield

CHAPEL RD

HIGHGATE RD

Stubbs Farm

OVER HILL RD

Quarry

TV Mast

Barnsfold Farm

Highgate

Highgate Head

Phoside Farm

A624

Rowan Farm

A B C D E F

8

Leygatehead
Moor

7

William Clough

Pennine Way

Sandy
Heys

89

6

Nab
Brow

Hollin
Head

Mermaid's
Pool

White Brow

River Kinder

5

Kinder
Reservoir

Red Brook

SK22 Blackshaws

Kinder
Head

88

Upper Moor

Marepiece
Wood

4

Upper
House

Farlands

River Kinder

Booth

Cluther
Rocks

Kinder Rd

The
Cote

3

Broad
Clough

Kinder
Low

Hill
Houses

The Three
Knolls

Pennine Way

87

Edale Rd

2

Tunstead Clough
Farm

River Sett

Tunstead
House

Stones
House

Kinderlow
End

Oaken Clough

Swine's
Back

The
Ashes

S33

1

Harry Moor

Edale
Cross

86

05 A B 06 C D 07 E F

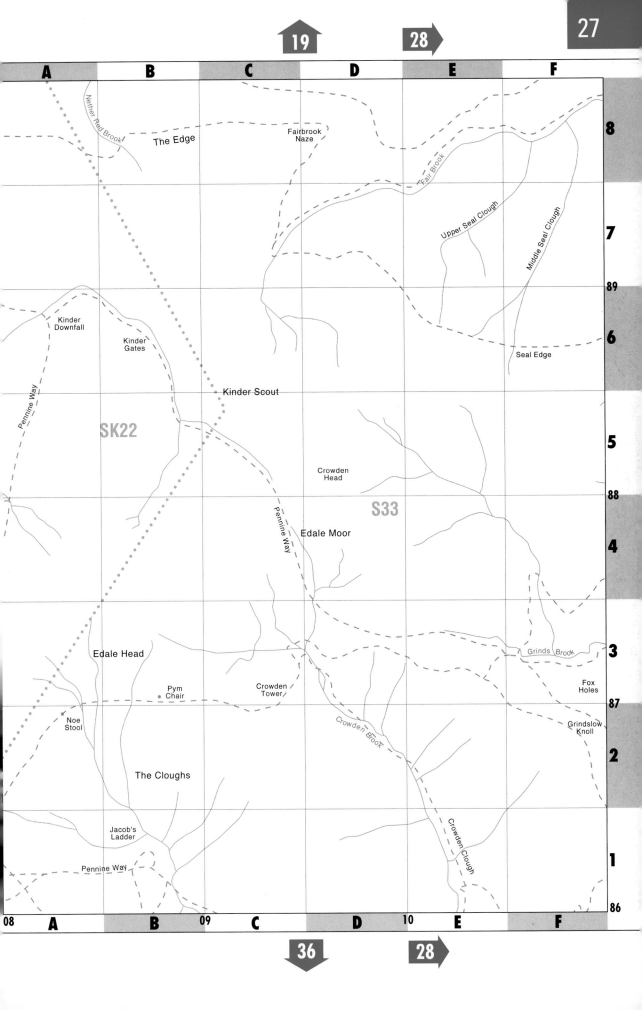

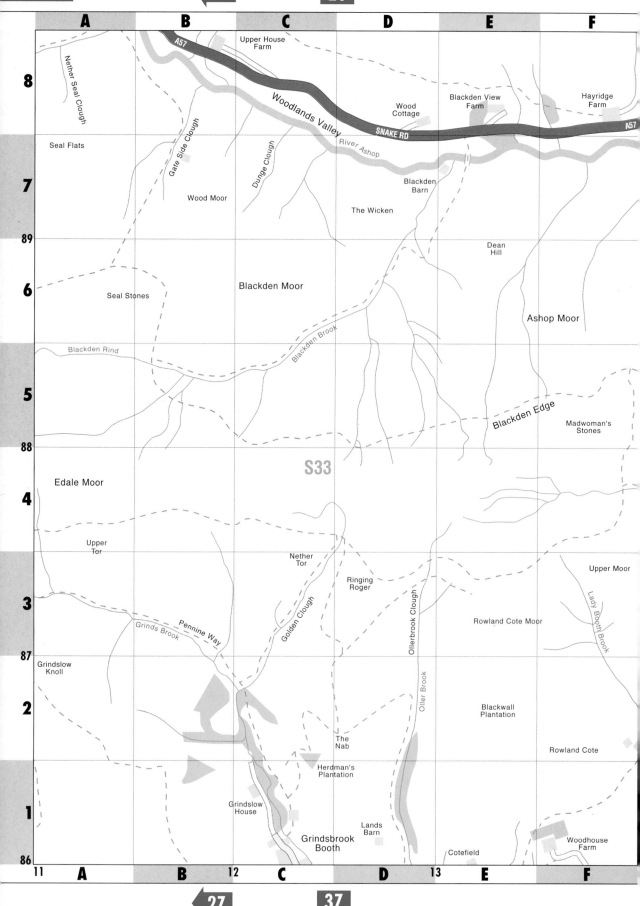

A57

Upper House
Farm

Nether Seal Clough

Woodlands Valley

Wood
Cottage

Blackden View
Farm

Hayridge
Farm

8

Seal Flats

Gate Side Clough

SNAKE RD

A57

River Ashop

7

Wood Moor

Dunge Clough

Blackden
Barn

The Wicken

89

Dean
Hill

6

Seal Stones

Blackden Moor

Blackden Brook

Ashop Moor

Blackden Rind

5

Blackden Edge

Madwoman's
Stones

88

S33

Edale Moor

4

Upper
Tor

Nether
Tor

Ringing
Roger

Ollerbrook Clough

Upper Moor

3

Grinds Brook

Pennine Way

Golden Clough

Rowland Cote Moor

Lady Booth Brook

87

Grindslow
Knoll

Oller Brook

2

Blackwall
Plantation

Rowland Cote

1

Grindslow
House

The
Nab

Herdman's
Plantation

Lands
Barn

Woodhouse
Farm

Grindsbrook
Booth

Cotefield

86

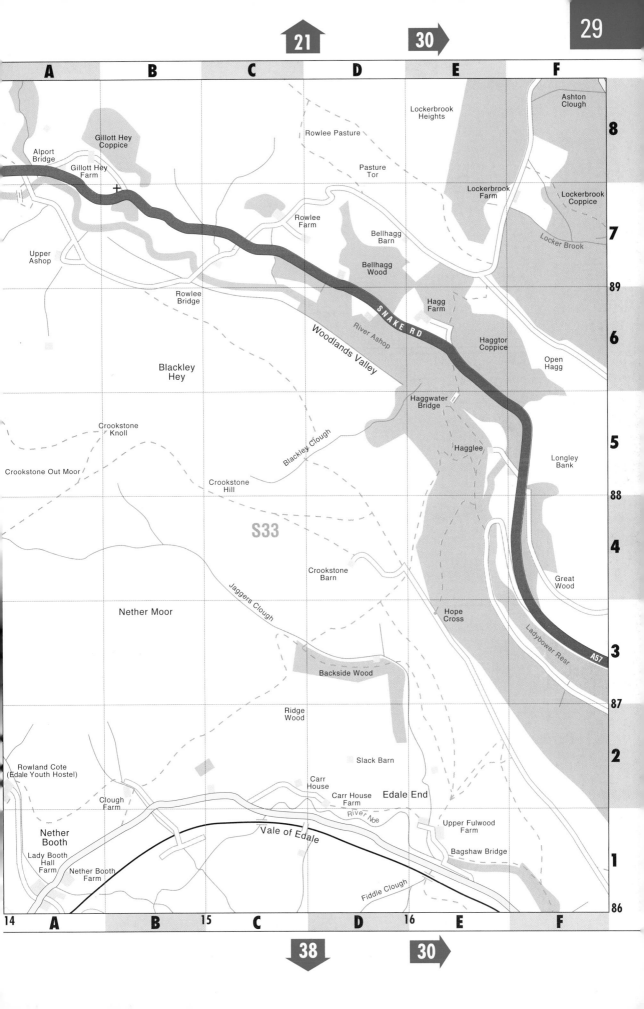

29
22

A **B** **C** **D** **E** **F**

8

Derwent Resr

Pike Low

Dovestone Tor

Briery Side

Dovestone Clough

Mill Brook

7

Jubilee Cottages

Trail

Lanehead

Derwent Edge

Salt Cellar

Old House

Warren Plantation

DERWENT LA

89

Derwent Aqueduct

Derwent

Wellhead Barn

White Tor

6

Ridges Coppice

Wellhead

Ashes Farm

High House

Hagg Side

Grindle Clough

5

Ladybower Resr

Grainfoot Clough

S33

88

Bridge-end Pasture

Lee Wood

4

Hursthead Cote

Hurst Clough

Lodge Cote

Whinstone Lee Tor

Two Thorne Fields Farm

3

A57

Fearfall Wood

Lead Hill

87

Grimbocar Wood

SNAKE RD

Crook Hill

Crookhill Farm

2

Nabs

Toadhole Cote

Saw Mill

Ashopton

Rough Wood

Wooler Knoll

Ashopton Viaduct

A57

1

Ladybower Resr

86

17 **A** **B** 18 **C** **D** 19 **E** **F**

29
39

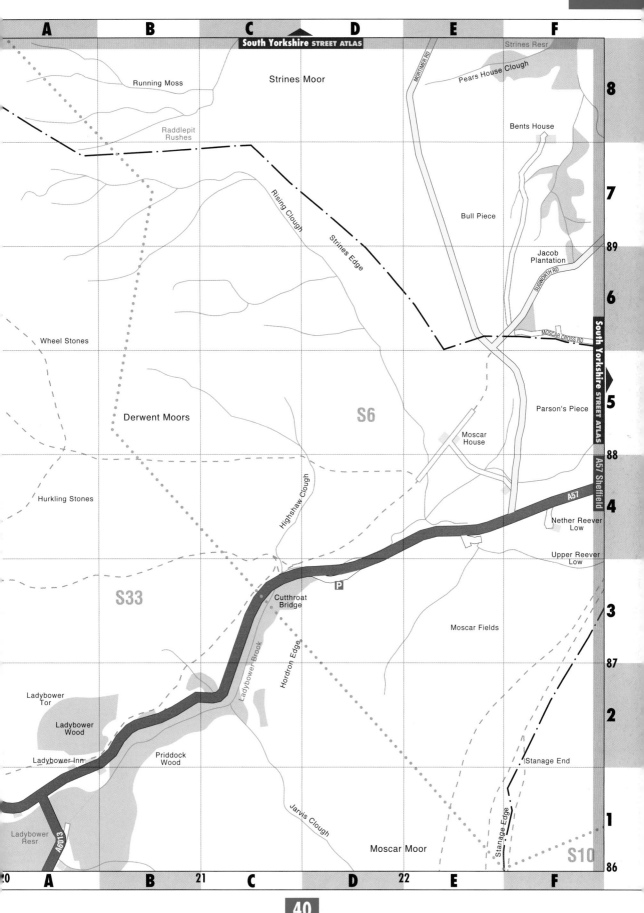

South Yorkshire STREET ATLAS

South Yorkshire STREET ATLAS

Running Moss

Strines Moor

Strines Resr

Pears House Clough

Bents House

Raddlepit
Rushes

Bull Piece

Rising Clough

Strines Edge

Jacob
Plantation

Wheel Stones

MOSCAR CROSS RD

Derwent Moors

S6

Parson's Piece

Moscar
House

A57 Sheffield

Hurkling Stones

Highshaw Clough

A57

Nether Reever
Low

Upper Reever
Low

S33

Cutthroat
Bridge

Moscar Fields

Ladybower Brook

Hordron Edge

Ladybower
Tor

Ladybower
Wood

Priddock
Wood

Stanage End

Ladybower Inn

Jarvis Clough

Moscar Moor

Stanage Edge

Ladybower
Resr

S10

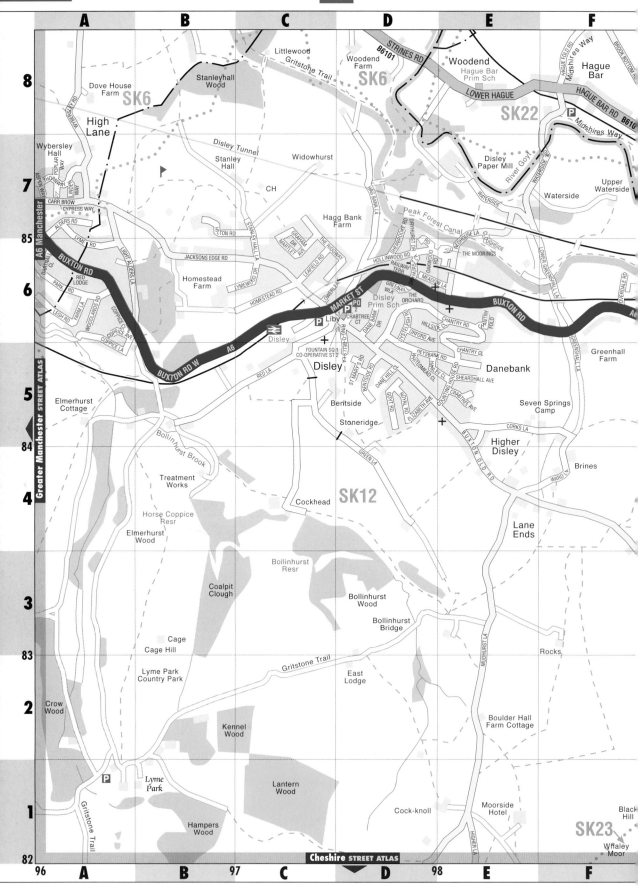

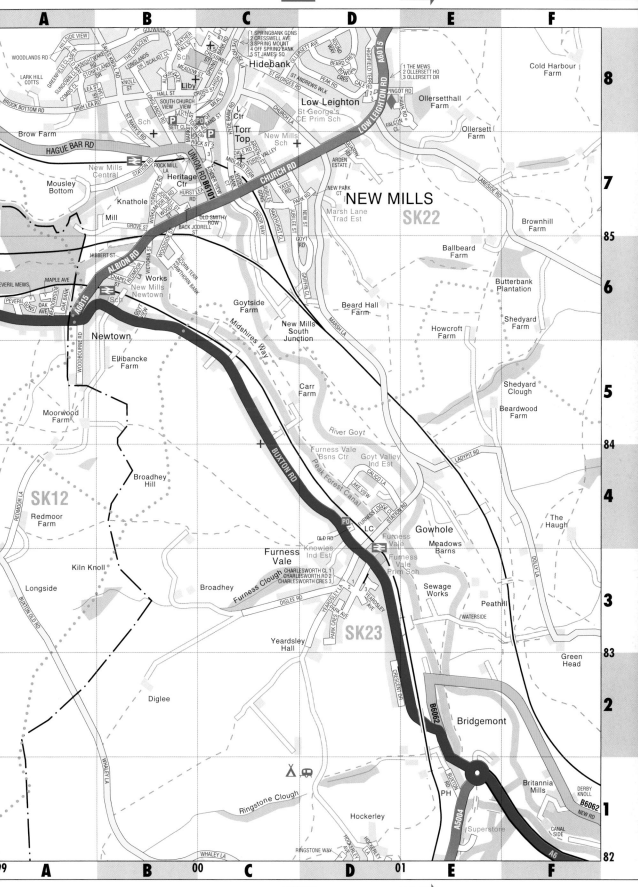

C7
1 FOUNDRY CT
2 LOWER ROCK ST
3 BACK UNION RD
4 LEES MILL

24

34

1 SPRINGBANK GDNS
2 CRESSWELL AVE
3 SPRING MOUNT
4 OFF SPRING BANK
5 ST JAMES' SQ

WOODLANDS RD
HILLSIDE VIEW
LARK HILL COTTS
BROOK BOTTOM RD
Hidebank
Low Leighton
St George's CE Prim Sch
1 THE MEWS
2 OLLERSETT HO
3 OLLERSETT DR
Cold Harbour Farm
Ollersetthall Farm
8

Brow Farm
HAGUE BAR RD
New Mills Central
Torr Top
New Mills Sch
CHURCH RD
Ollersett Farm
7

Mousley Bottom
Knathole
Mill
Heritage Ctr
Arden Estate
New Park Ct
NEW MILLS
Marsh Lane Trad Est
SK22
Brownhill Farm
85

HIBBERT ST
ALBION RD
Works
New Mills Newtown Sch
Goytside Farm
Beard Hall Farm
Ballbeard Farm
Butterbank Plantation
6

EVERIL MEWS
MAPLE AVE
PEVERIL GDNS
Newtown
Ellibancke Farm
Midshires Way
New Mills South Junction
Howcroft Farm
Shedyard Farm
Shedyard Clough
5

Moorwood Farm
Carr Farm
River Goyt
Beardwood Farm
84

SK12
Broadhey Hill
BUXTON RD
Peak Forest Canal
Furness Vale Bsns Ctr
Goyt Valley Ind Est
CALICO LA
LAKE VIEW
LADYPIT RD
4

REDMOOR LA
Redmoor Farm
OLD RD
Knowles Ind Est
Furness Vale
LC
Furness Vale
Gowhole
Meadows Barns
The Haugh
DOLLY LA

Kiln Knoll
Furness Vale
Broadhey
Furness Clough
CHARLESWORTH CL 1
CHARLESWORTH RD 2
CHARLESWORTH CRES 3
Furness Vale Prim Sch
Sewage Works
Peathill
3

Longside
BUXTON OLD RD
DIGLEE RD
YEARDSLEY AVE
PARK CRES PARK AVE
SK23
WATERSIDE
83

Yeardsley Hall
CRESCENT DR
Green Head

Diglee
B6062
Bridgemont
2

WHALEY LA
Ringstone Clough
PH
BUXTON RD
Britannia Mills
DERBY KNOLL
B6062
NEW RD
1

WHALEY LA
Ringstone Way
Hockerley
A5004
Superstore
CANAL SIDE
A6
82

45

34

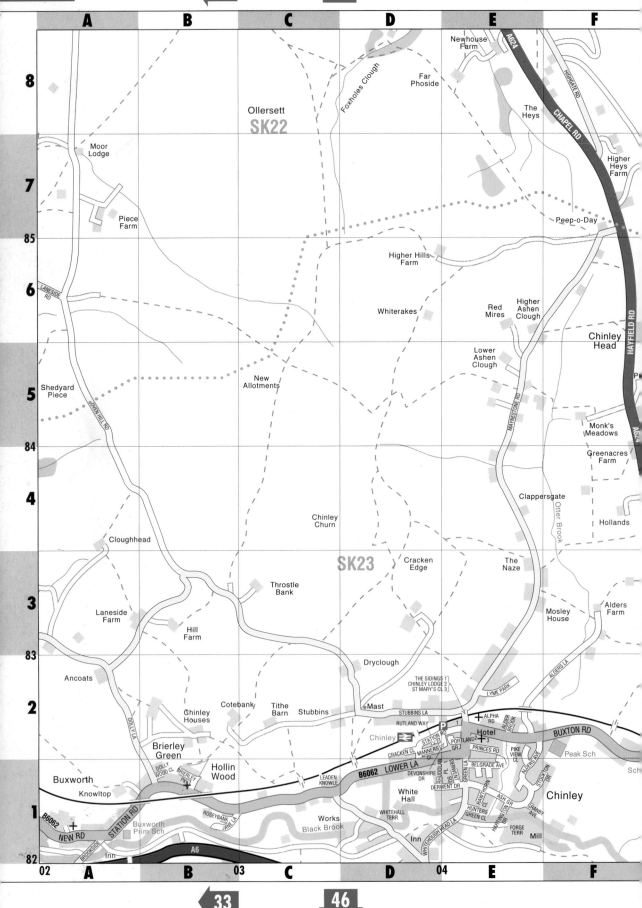

A   B   C   D   E   F

8

7

85

6

5

84

4

3

83

2

1

82

Ollersett
SK22

Foxholes Clough

Newhouse
Farm

Far
Phoside

The Heys

Higher Heys
Farm

Moor
Lodge

Peep-o-Day

Piece
Farm

Higher Hills
Farm

Chinley
Head

Whiterakes

Red
Mires

Higher
Ashen
Clough

Laneside
RD

Lower
Ashen
Clough

Shedyard
Piece

New
Allotments

Monk's
Meadows

Greenacres
Farm

Chinley
Churn

Clappersgate

Hollands

SK23

Cracken
Edge

The
Naze

Cloughhead

Otter Brook

Mosley
House

Alders
Farm

Throstle
Bank

Laneside
Farm

Hill
Farm

Dryclough

Alders LA

Ancoats

THE SIDINGS 1
CHINLEY LODGE 2
ST MARY'S CL 3

LYME PARK

Cotebank

Tithe
Barn

Stubbins

Mast

STUBBINS LA

Alpha
RD

ALDER
BROOK

BUXTON RD

Chinley
Houses

RUTLAND WAY

P   1

Hotel
3

Peak Sch

Brierley
Green

Chinley

STATION
RD

PORTLAND
PL

Princes RD

PIKE
VIEW
CL

Buxworth

Hollin
Wood

DOLLY
WOOD CL

BRIERLEY
PK

MANNERS RD

BELGRADE AVE

Knowltop

LEADEN
KNOWLE

B6062 LOWER LA

DEVONSHIRE
DR

White
Hall

HAWTHORN
CL

Chinley

B6062

NEW RD

STATION RD

BROOKSIDE

Buxworth
Prim Sch

ROSEYBANK

JANE LA

Black Brook

Works

WHITEHALL
TERR

DERWENT DR

HUNTERS
GREEN CL

HARPINGTON DR

FORGE
TERR

Mill

Inn

A6

Inn

CHAPEL RD

HIGHGATED

A624

HAYFIELD RD

MAYNESTONE RD

DOLLY LA

OVEN HILL RD

WHITEHOUGH HEAD LA

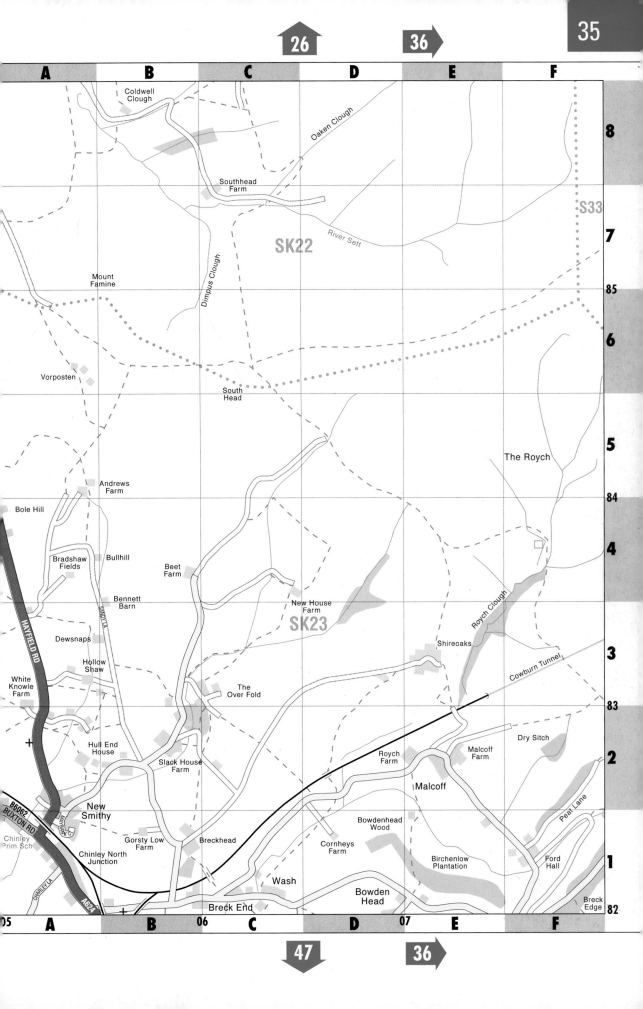

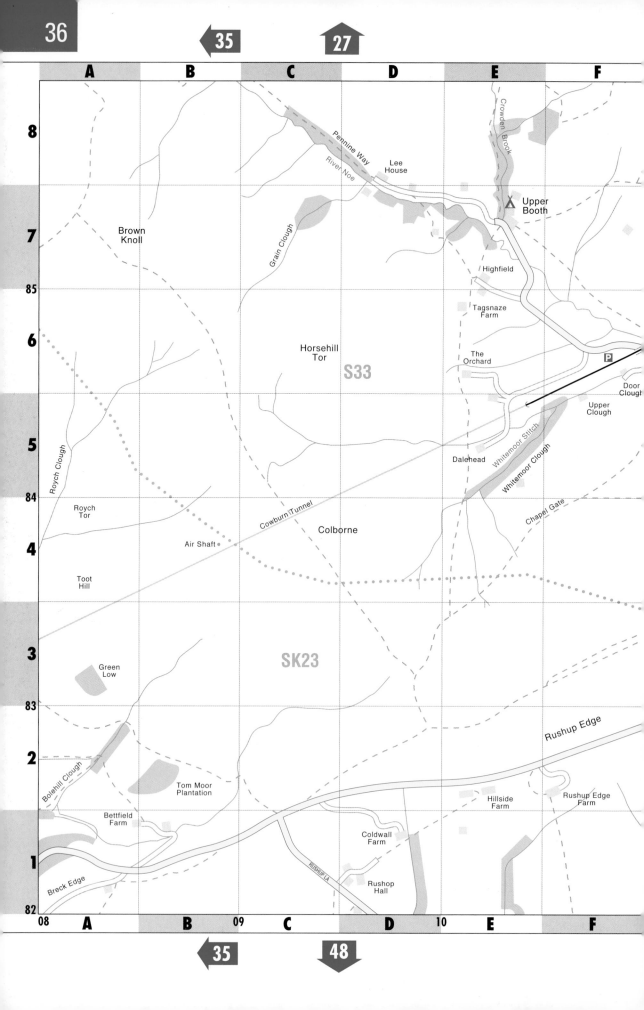

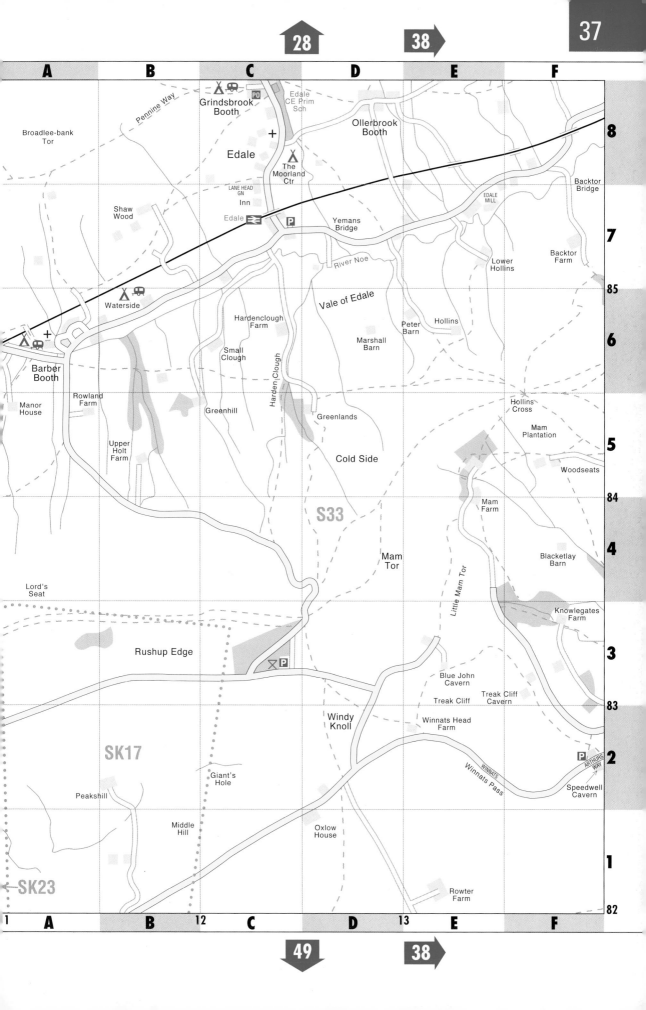

A B C D E F

8

7

85

6

5

84

4

83

3

2

1

82

Broadlee-bank Tor

Grindsbrook Booth

Edale CE Prim Sch

Ollerbrook Booth

Edale

The Moorland Ctr

Backtor Bridge

LANE HEAD GN Inn

EDALE MILL

Shaw Wood

Edale

Yemans Bridge

Lower Hollins

Backtor Farm

Pennine Way

River Noe

Vale of Edale

Waterside

Hardenclough Farm

Peter Barn

Hollins

Small Clough

Marshall Barn

Hollins Cross

Barber Booth

Manor House

Rowland Farm

Greenhill

Harden Clough

Greenlands

Mam Plantation

Woodseats

Upper Holt Farm

Cold Side

Mam Farm

S33

Mam Tor

Blacketlay Barn

Lord's Seat

Little Mam Tor

Knowlegates Farm

Rushup Edge

Blue John Cavern

Treak Cliff Cavern

Treak Cliff

SK17

Windy Knoll

Winnats Head Farm

Giant's Hole

Winnats Pass

ARTHURS WAY

Speedwell Cavern

Peakshill

Middle Hill

Oxlow House

SK23

Rowter Farm

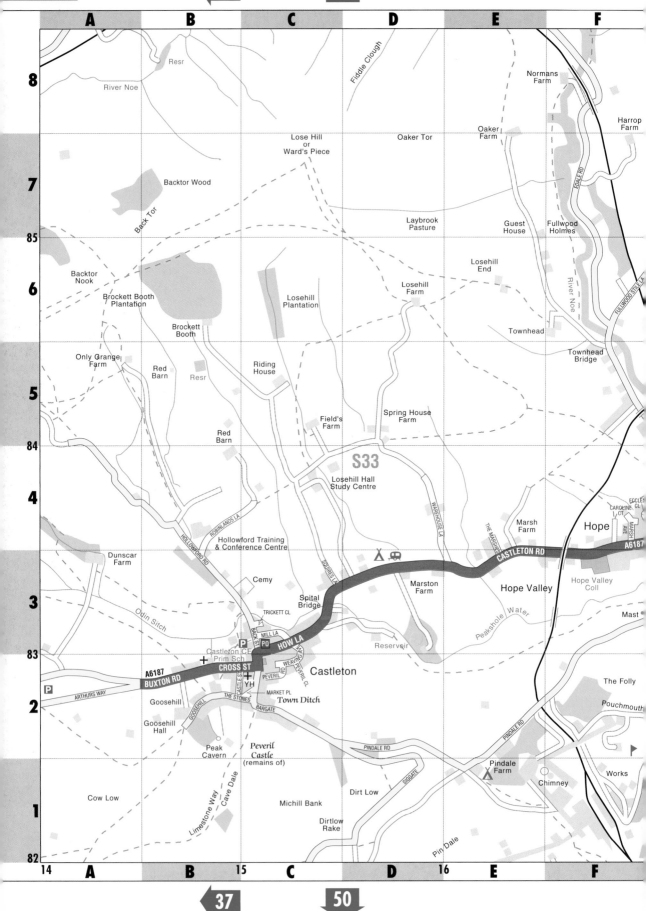

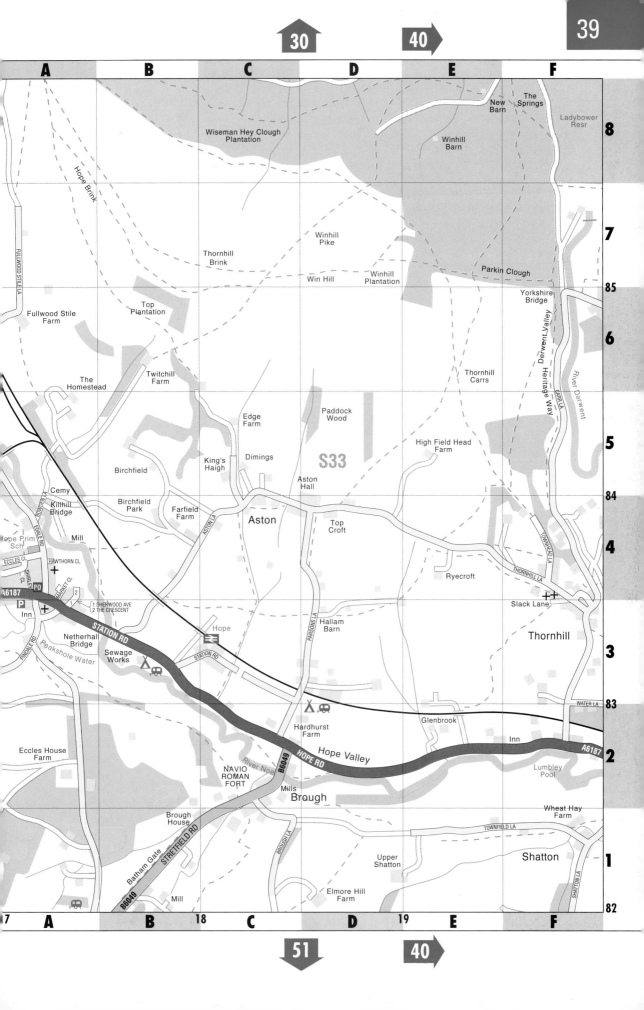

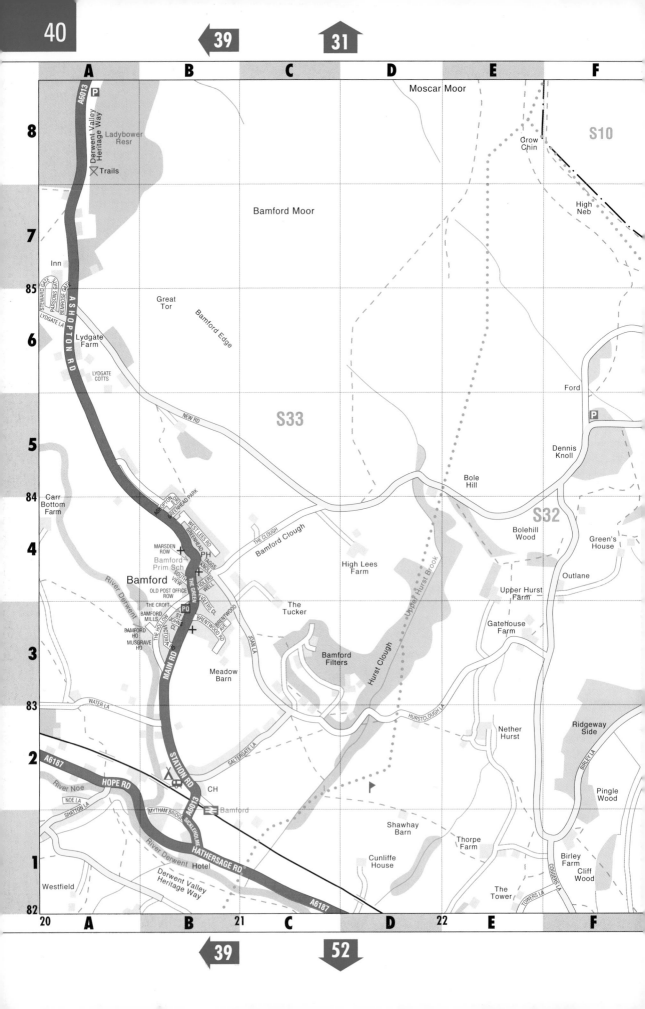

South Yorkshire STREET ATLAS

A · B · C · D · E · F

High Lad Ridge

Rape Piece

Hallam Moors

8

Broadshaw
Plantation

Redmires
Resrs

REDMIRES RD

7

Gin Piece

Broadshaw

Fairthorn
Lodge

85

Stanedge
Lodge

S10

Spring
Piece

6

Buck
Stone

Stanage Edge

Fair-thorn Clough

LONG CSWY

Stanedge
Pole

5

Sheepwash
Bank

84

Stanage
Plantation

White Path Moss

Friar's Ridge

4

Robin Hood's
Cave

North
Lees

Hook's Car

Cowper
Stone

RINGINGLOW RD

3

Hood Brook

Bronte
Cottage

Cattis Side

Cattis-side Moor

Hookcar
Sitch

S32

83

Cowclose

Carhead
Rocks

Overstones
Farm

CAR HEIGHT

2

Brookfield Manor
(Training Ctr)

Birchin
Wood

Fiddler's Elbow

Leveret Croft

Kimber Court
Farm

BAULK LA

Moorseats

Callow
Bank

1

Moorseats
Wood

Carr Head

Higger Tor

Toothill Farm

82

23 · A · B · 24 · C · D · 25 · E · F

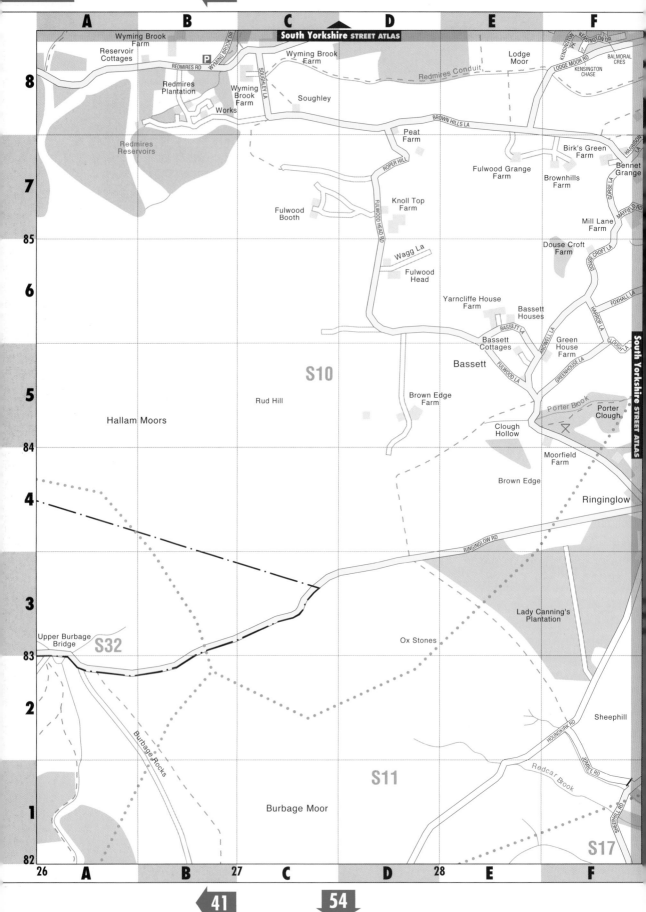

A B C D E F

8

Wyming Brook Farm
Reservoir Cottages
REDMIRES RD
P
WYMING BROOK DR
Wyming Brook Farm
Lodge Moor
KENSINGTON PK
KENSINGTON DR
LODGE MOOR RD
BALMORAL CRES
Redmires Plantation
Works
Wyming Brook Farm
SOUGHLEY LA
Soughley
Redmires Conduit
KENSINGTON CHASE
HARRISON LA

Redmires Reservoirs

7

Peat Farm
BROWN HILLS LA
ROPER HILL
Birk's Green Farm
Fulwood Grange Farm
Brownhills Farm
Bennet Grange
GORSE LA
MAYFIELD RD

Fulwood Booth
FULWOOD HEAD RD
Knoll Top Farm
Mill Lane Farm

85

Wagg La
Douse Croft Farm
DOUSE CROFT LA

6

Fulwood Head
Yarncliffe House Farm
Bassett Houses
FOXHALL LA

HOWELL LA
HARROP LA
CLOUGH LA

Bassett Cottages
Bassett
Green House Farm

S10

Bassett
FULWOOD LA
GREENHOUSE LA

5

Rud Hill
Brown Edge Farm
Porter Brook
Porter Clough

Hallam Moors
Clough Hollow

84

Moorfield Farm
Brown Edge

4

Ringinglow

3

Lady Canning's Plantation
RINGINGLOW RD
Ox Stones

Upper Burbage Bridge
S32

83

2

BURBAGE ROCKS
HOUNDKIRK RD
Sheephill
JUMBLE RD

S11
Redcar Brook

1

Burbage Moor
SHEEPHILL RD
S17

82

26 A B 27 C D 28 E F

South Yorkshire STREET ATLAS

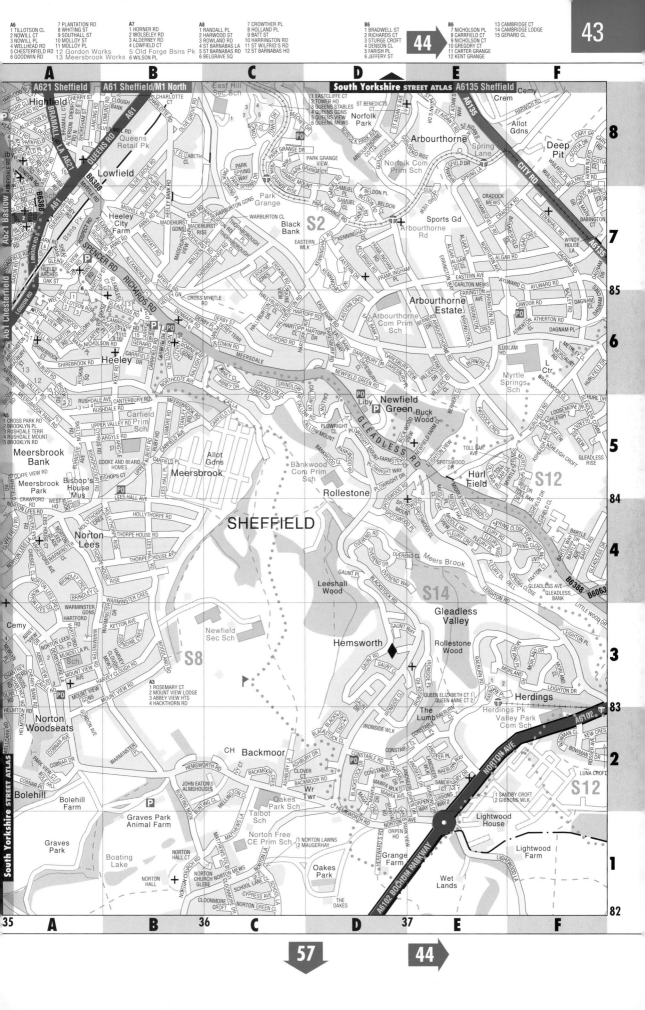

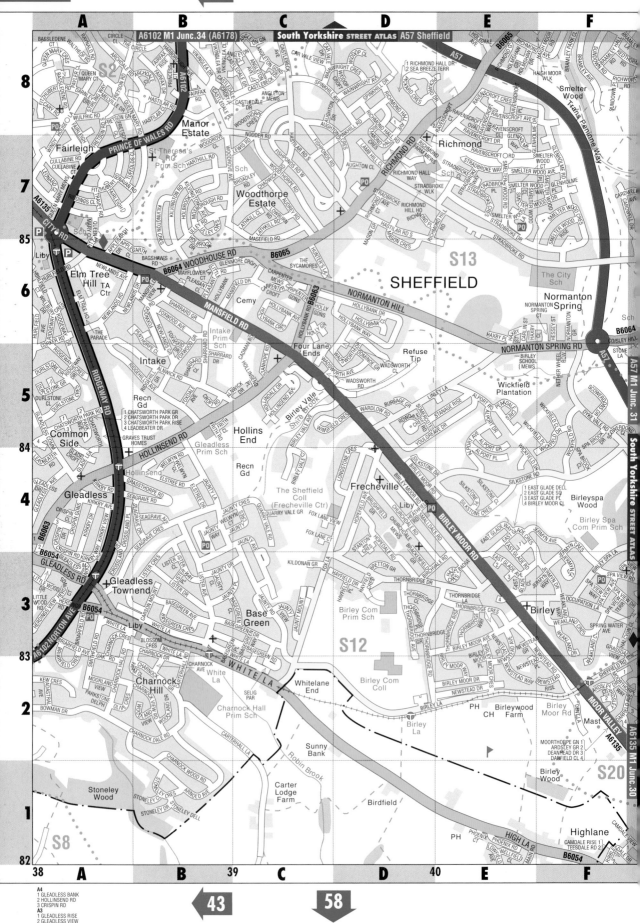

South Yorkshire STREET ATLAS A57 Sheffield

A4
1 GLEADLESS BANK
2 HOLLINSEND RD
3 CRISPIN RD
A3
1 GLEADLESS RISE
2 GLEADLESS VIEW

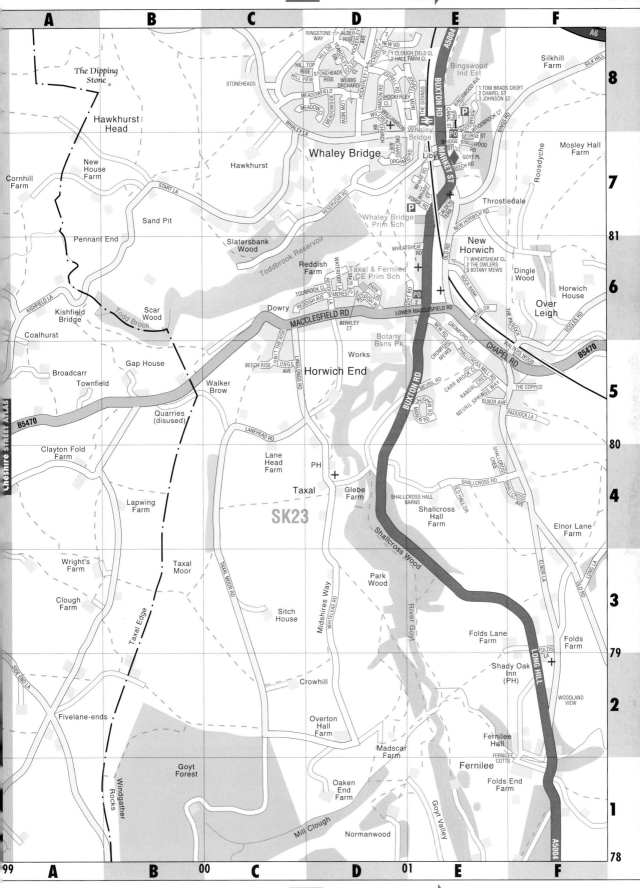

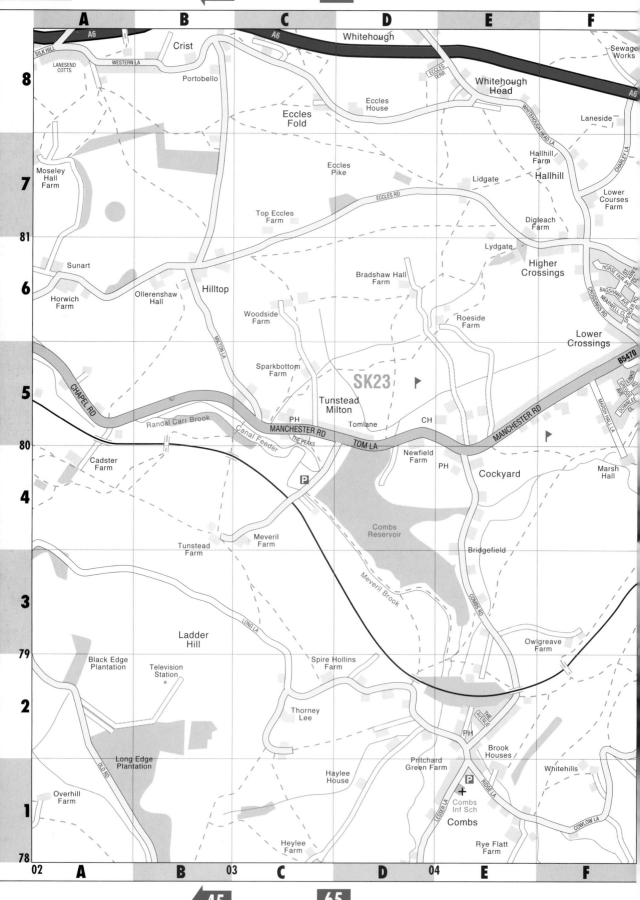

A B C D E F

Bridgeholm Green
A624
CHARLEY LA
Mill
BRIDGEHOLM MILL
Chapel Milton
1 CROSS KEYS ROW
2 HILLSIDE
HAYFIELD RD
Chestnut Centre Conservatory Pk
Slackhall Farm
Slackhall
Mag Low
8

Higher Courses Farm
BOWDEN LA
STODHART FLATS
Bowden Hey Farm
BROOK FOLD
Bowden Hey Rd
Black Brook
SHEFFIELD RD
Slacke Hall
Maglow Farm
7

Works
WHEATFIELDS 1
FROOD CL 2
POPLAR TERR 3
CARRIERS MDW 4
COARSES VIEW 5
VALLEY DR 6
SAGE MEWS 7
THE GREEN
CRANSIDE AVE
HAYFIELD RD
A624
Townend
FRITH KNOLL RD
Wks
7 SMITHBROOK CL
8 BARLOW RD
Bagshaw Hall Farm
Bagshaw
81

CHURCH BR 1
TERRACE RD 2
CROSS ST 3
HARDCASTLE MEWS 4
THE COTTAGES 5
ALDER GROVE 6
CHERRY TREE CT 7
BURRFIELDS RD
DANESWAY
HEAD DR
Burrfields
MARKET ST
PO
WESLEY CT
QUENTIN RD
BUXTON RD
B5470
Laneside
81

WOODBINE TERR
ECCLES RD
HORSE FAIR AVE
MIDLAND RD
CHURCH LA
MARKET ST
Liby
TH
PARK VIEW DR
Sch
HEYWORTH ST
BERESFORD RD
ELDON ST
LONGSON RD
ANCHOR AVE
NETHERFIELD RD
BROOKLANDS
9 JAVELIN
BROOKLANDS
Blackbrook
BLACKBROOK LA
Blackbrook
Peaslows Farm
6

SPENCER AVE
MELLOR LA
CROSSINGS AVE
CROSSINGS RD
MIDLAND RD
SEATON RD
ROEBUCK MEWS
MARKET ST
PO
HIGH ST
Sch
Chapel-en-le-Frith
WEST HORDERNS
GRANGE PARK RD
THORNBROOK RD
PARK CRES
EASTBROOK
WARNBROOK AVE
THORNEY
MOSS VIEW RD
WILLSHAW RD
BERESFORD AVE
ANCHOR FOLD
HOMESTEAD WAY
JOHNSON WAY
9 ASHFIELD RD
10 BURDEKIN CL
Smithfield
High Leigh
Blackbrook Farm
BUXTON RD
5

FRITH VIEW RD
ELMFIELD
FINKS RD
MANCHESTER RD
HORDERNS RD
LANESIDE CL
HORDERNS LA
KNOWLE AVE
HOLLIN DR
CROMWELL AVE
ROWTON GRANGE RD
GRANGE AVE
BROOKSIDE RD
GRANGE PARK AVE
WILLOW DR
WARM BROOK
1 WATERS EDGE LA
2 OAK CL
3 LOWER EAVES VIEW
4 THORNBROOK CL
5 EAVES AVE
6 GREEN PARK AVE
Lower Eaves
5

Marshgreen Farm
ALSTON RD
JUBILEE RD
SYCAMORE RD
LONGMEADE DR
SCHOFIELD RD
LONG LA
WOODLANDS RD
ASHBOURNE LA
Eaves Hall
Eaves Tunnel
Lower Plumpton
80

Down Lee Farm
LC
Chapel-en-le-Frith
Ridge Lodge
1 BRIDGEWAY
2 THE HAWTHORNS
3 GISBOURNE DR
Windy Wall Farm
Paradise Farm
Bolt Edge
Higher Plumpton
Barmoor Clough
A6
A623
4

Top Lodge
Ridge Reservoirs
Ridge Farm
Hollinknoll
Martinside
Sittinglow
Platting Farm
Tunnel
HIGHER HALLSTEADS
SK17
3

Bank Hall
Ridge Hall
COWLOW LA
Cow Low
Dove Holes Tunnel
MEADOW LA
Hallsteads Farm
79

Castle Naze
Combs Edge
Short Edge
Cowlow
Lady Low
Meadows Farm
HIGHFIELD AVE
MEADOW CL
Dove Holes
HALLSTEADS CL
HALLSTEADS
BEELOW CL
WAINS CL
WALKER BROW
THE MEADOWS
BEAUMONT DR
2

Bull Ring Henge
Dove Holes CE Prim Sch
ALEXANDER RD
HORSESHOE AVE
STATION RD
A6
Dove Holes
1

SK23

78

47
36

	A	B	C	D	E	F

8 Stonyford

SK23

7 Bella Vista

81 Peaslows

Goldpiece Farm

6 Peaslows Farm

Sparrowpit

BAGSHAW LA

The Wanted Inn (PH)

Rushup Farm

Gautries Side

RUSHUP LA

Whitelee

Pot Holes

Bull Pit

Perryfoot

Coalpit Hole

Perry Dale

Gautries Hill

Rake Vein

5 Mast

Bennett Edge Farm

Higher Barmoor Farm

Haddock Low

Harratt Grange

Nether Barn

80 Boltedge Farm

Bennettston Hall Hotel

Ebbing and Flowing Well

Middle Barmoor Farm

Pedlicote Farm

4 Barmoor Farm

Barmoor

SK17

Chamberkno

A623

Chamber Farm

3 Lower Barmoor Farm

Bee Low Quarry

Lower Bee Low

79 Lodesbarn

Freshfields Farm Donkey Sanctuary

Ivy House

2 Ridgeclose Farm

Backlane Farm

Greenknoll Farm

1 Lodes Marsh

BATHAM GATE

Kemp's Hill

78 Dove Holes Quarry

Laughman Tor

08	A	B	09	C	D	10	E	F

47
67

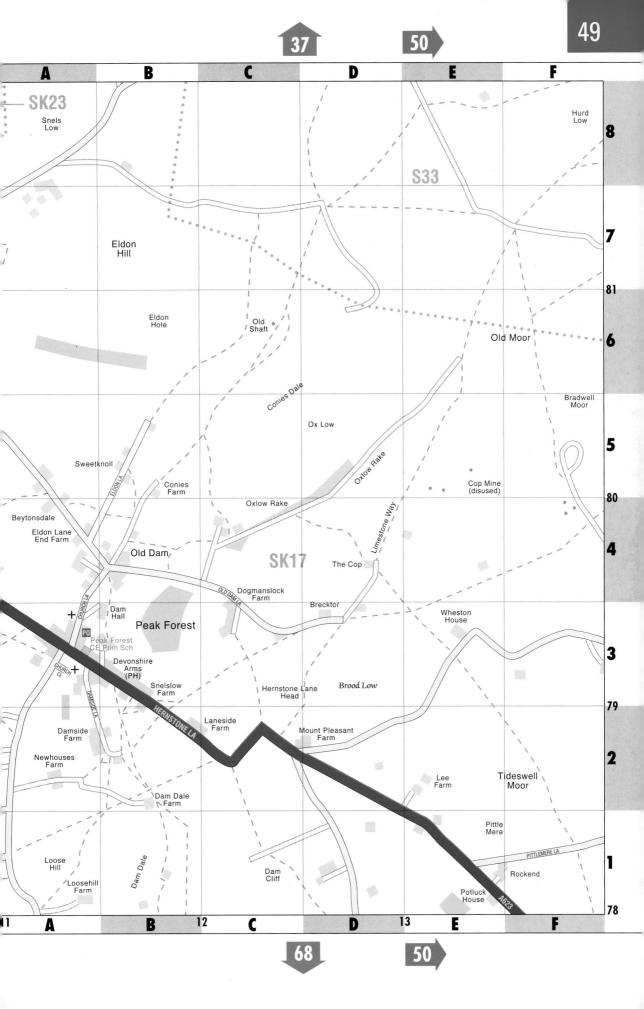

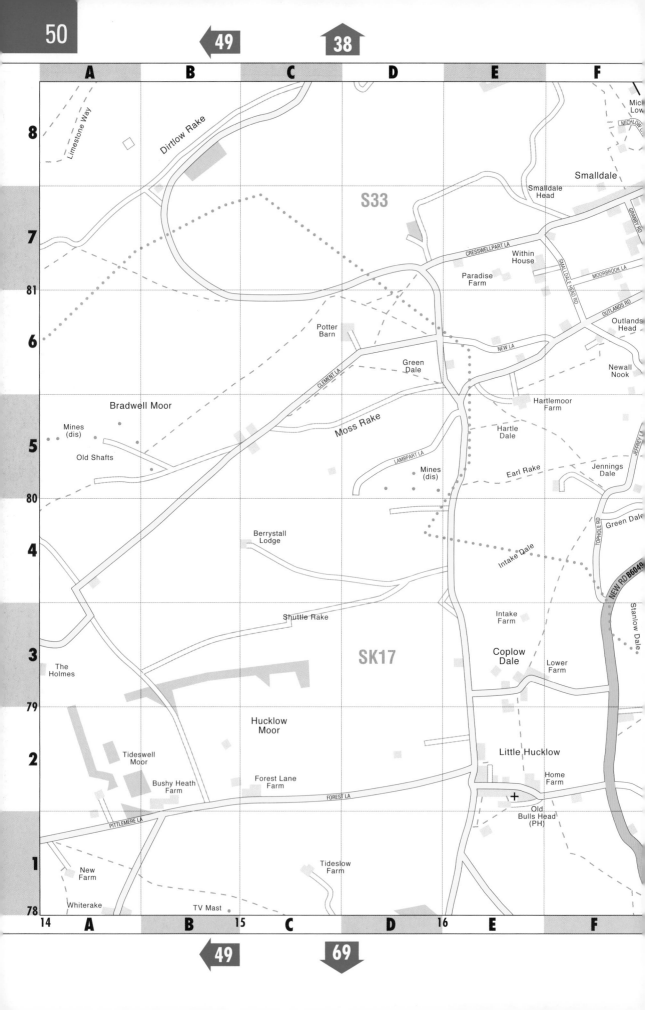

A   B   C   D   E   F

Limestone Way

Dirtlow Rake

8

Mich
Low
MICHLOW LA

Smalldale

S33

Smalldale
Head

7

CRESSWELLPART LA   Within
House

GRANBY RD

81

Paradise
Farm

SMALLDALE HEAD RD

MOORBROOK LA

OUTLANDS RD

Outlands
Head

6

Potter
Barn

NEW LA

Newall
Nook

CLEMENT LA

Green
Dale

Bradwell Moor

Mines
(dis)

Moss Rake

Hartlemoor
Farm

Hartle
Dale

5

Old Shafts

LAMBPART LA

Mines
(dis)

Earl Rake

Jennings
Dale

JEFFREY LA

80

TOPHOLE RD

Green Dale

Berrystall
Lodge

Intake Dale

NEW RD B6049

4

Stanlow Dale

Shuttle Rake

Intake
Farm

3

The
Holmes

SK17

Coplow
Dale

Lower
Farm

79

Hucklow
Moor

Little Hucklow

2

Tideswell
Moor

Home
Farm

Bushy Heath
Farm

Forest Lane
Farm

FOREST LA

✚

Old
Bulls Head
(PH)

PITTLEMERE LA

1

New
Farm

Tideslow
Farm

78

Whiterake

TV Mast

14   A   B   15   C   D   16   E   F

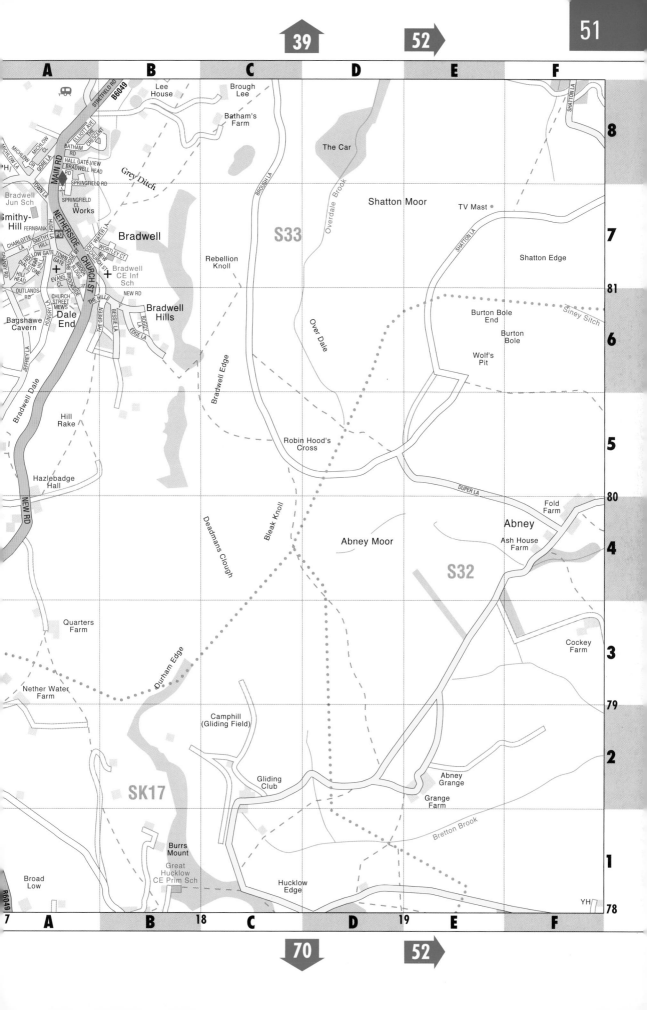

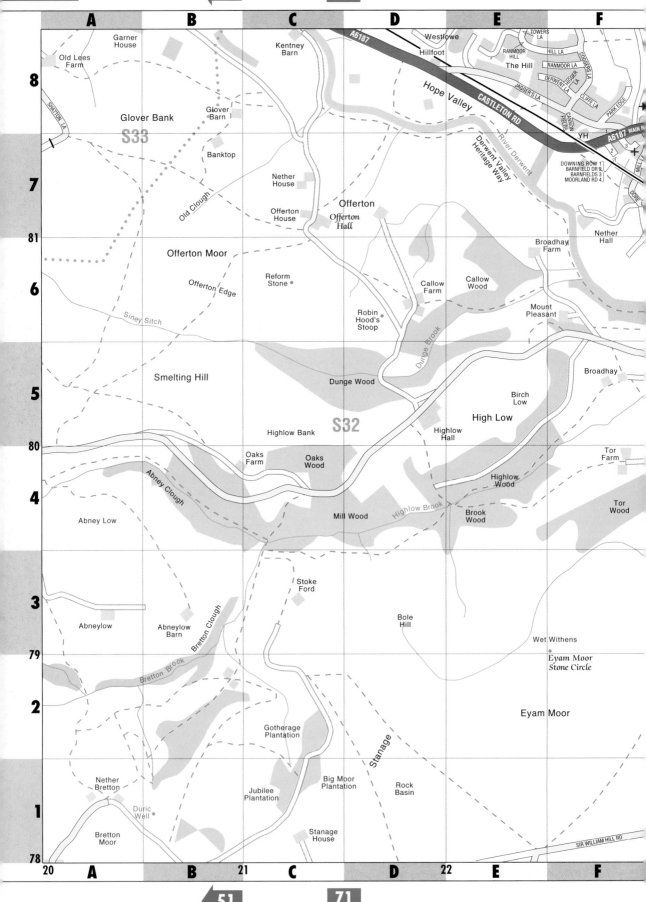

A   B   C   D   E   F

8

Old Lees Farm
Garner House
Kentney Barn
Westlowe
Hillfoot
TOWERS LA
RANMOOR HILL
The Hill
RANMOOR LA
HILL LA
COGGERS LA

Hope Valley

Glover Bank
Glover Barn
S33

DERWENT LA
TRIGGER LA
JAGGER'S LA
CASTLETON RD
CLIFFE LA
PARK EDGE

7

Banktop
Nether House

River Derwent
YH
A6187 MAIN R
2
3
DORE L

Offerton House
Offerton
Offerton Hall

Derwent Valley Heritage Way

DOWNING ROW 1
BARNFIELD DR 2
BARNFIELDS 3
MOORLAND RD 4.

81

Offerton Moor
Broadhay Farm
Nether Hall

6

Offerton Edge
Reform Stone
Callow Farm
Callow Wood
Mount Pleasant

Siney Sitch
Robin Hood's Stoop

Dunge Brook

Broadhay

5

Smelting Hill
Dunge Wood
Birch Low
High Low

Highlow Bank
S32
Highlow Hall

80

Oaks Farm
Oaks Wood
Highlow Wood
Tor Farm

4

Abney Clough
Abney Low
Mill Wood
Highlow Brook
Brook Wood
Tor Wood

3

Abneylow
Abneylow Barn
Bretton Clough
Stoke Ford
Bole Hill
Wet Withens

79

Bretton Brook
Eyam Moor Stone Circle

2

Gotherage Plantation
Stanage
Eyam Moor

Nether Bretton
Duric Well
Big Moor Plantation
Rock Basin

1

Jubilee Plantation
Bretton Moor
Stanage House
SIR WILLIAM HILL RD

78

20   A   B   21   C   D   22   E   F

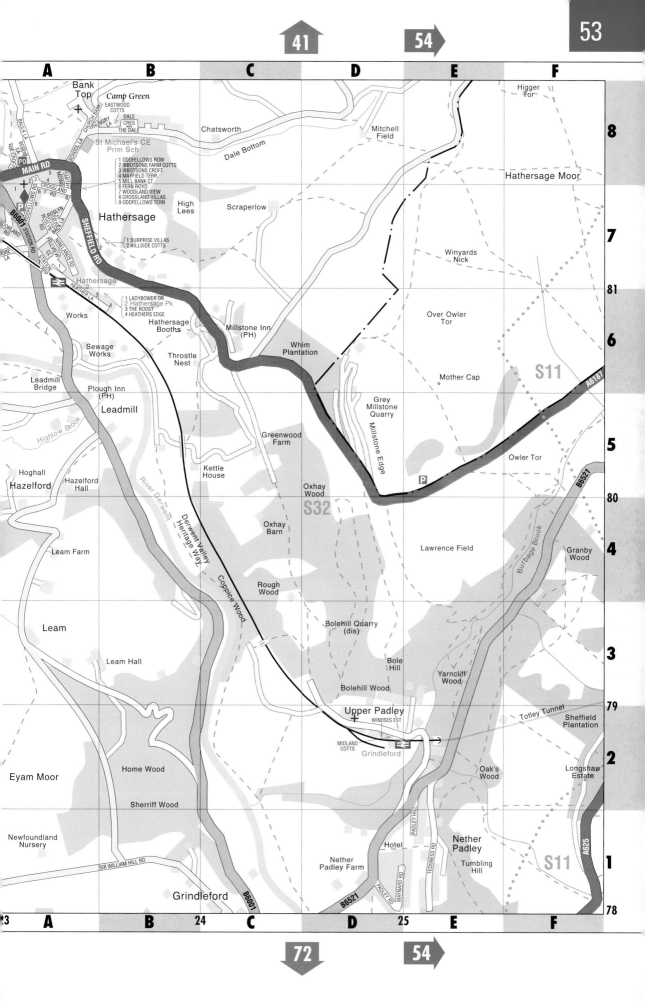

53
42

A   B   C   D   E   F

8

S32

Houndkirk Moor

SHEEPHILL RD

A625

Houndkirk Hill

WHITELOW LA

Carl Wark

Burbage Brook

7

HOUNDKIRK RD

81

Parson House Farm
(Outdoor Pursuits Ctr)

Blacka Moor

Blacka Plantation

6

Burbage Bridge

A6187

A6187 HATHERSAGE RD

A625

Blacka Dike

Lenny Hill

Fox House Inn

Stony Ridge

S11

Cowsick

Blacka Hill

5

B6521

STONY RIDGE RD

OWLER BAR RD

S17

Lodge P

Nell Croft

80

Longshaw Estate Visitor Centre

LONGSHAW LODGE

Robin Hood's Well

Wimble Holme Hill

Longshaw Estate Trail

A6187

4

Little John's Well

Totley Moor

Sheffield Country Wlk

Totley Tunnel

Moss Rd

Brown Edge

3

Longshaw Estate

Totley Moss

79

P

B6054

S32

2

A625

Bar Brook

White Edge Lodge

Salter Sitch

Flask Edge

1

Lady's Cross

Barbrook Bridge

White Edge Moor

B6054

78

26   A   B   27   C   D   28   E   F

53
73

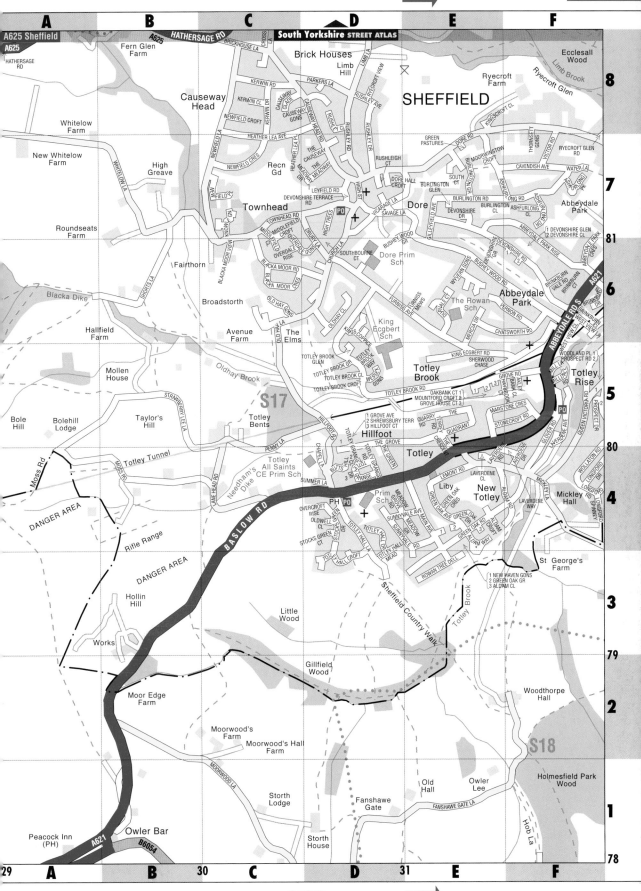

A5
1 QUEEN VICTORIA RD
2 WOODLAND PL
3 EVERARD GLADE
4 LADYBOWER CT
5 DERWENT CT

B5
1 PROSPECT CT
2 MOORVIEW CT

◄ **55**

E6
1 ATLANTIC CRES
2 GERVASE WLK
E8
1 ABBEY BROOK CT

F8
1 CHANCET WOOD RD
2 ROXTON AVE
3 CHARLES ASHMORE RD
4 LITTLE NORTON LA

A621 Sheffield   South Yorkshire STREET ATLAS   A61 Sheffield

Abbeydale Industrial Mus

Beauchief Abbey LA

Beauchief Abbey (rems of)

Parkbank Wood

Ecclesall Wood

Mill Pond

S7

Limb Bridge

Ladies' Spring Wood

Beauchief Hall

Cockshutt Farm

Beauchief

Gulleys Wood

SHEFFIELD

S8

Abbeydale Park

Dore

1 LADIES SPRING DR
2 LADIES SPRING CT
3 LADIES SPRING GR
4 TWENTYWELL CT
5 DORE CT
6 ABBEYDALE CT
7 WOODBANK CT
8 RIVER CT

CH

Beauchief Park

Greenhill

Greenhill Prim Sch

Liby

Old Park Wood

Poynton Wood

S17

Castlerow View

Lower Bradway

GREENHILL PARKWAY

Greenhill Park

Bradway Bank

Twentywell

Sir Harold Jackson Prim Sch

Mast

BRADWAY RD

Bradway Tunnel

Lowedges Prim Sch

Upper Bradway

CONALAN AVE

Bradway

CH

Border View Farm

Bowshaw Farm

Bowshaw

Mickley Farm

Upper Birchitt

ROD MOOR RD

Works

MICKLEY LA

Sheffield Country Walk

Bowshaw

Rod Moor

Mickley

S18

Barnes Farm

Stubley Hollow Riding Ctr

STUBLEY HOLLOW

NORTHERN COMM

Dronfield Woodhouse

PH

Green Lea

STUBLEY LA

Summerwood Top

Birchin Lee Farm

William Levick Prim Sch

DRONFIELD

Hall Farm

CARR LA

B6056

Gosforth Valley

Gosforth Brigg Prim Sch

Holmesfield Park Wood

St Andrew's CE Prim Sch

HOLMESFIELD RD

B6054 MAIN RD

East Hollow

Sports Ctr

C1
1 THORNTON PL
2 OXCLOSE DR
3 ROSTON CL
4 IVAN BROOK CL
5 HAZELWOOD CL
6 WINGFIELD CL

D1
1 LYNWOOD CL
2 SHERWOOD PL
3 ROSTON CL
4 RADBOURNE COMM
D2
1 MILLSTONE CL
2 BUCKINGHAM CL

E1
1 CASTLERIGG WAY
2 PATTERDALE CL
3 CONSTABLE CL
4 LANDSEER CL
E8
1 ABBEY BROOK CL

F1
1 HOGARTH RISE
2 HEATHFIELD CL
3 GOSFORTH CRES
4 MANOR BGLWS

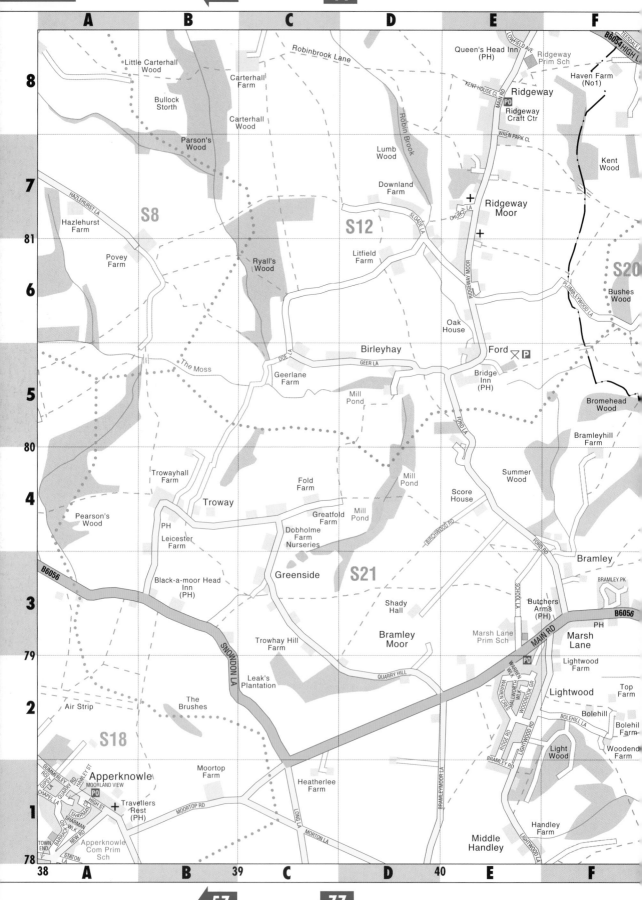

A B C D E F

8

Little Carterhall Wood

Carterhall Farm

Bullock Storth

Carterhall Wood

Parson's Wood

Robinbrook Lane

Queen's Head Inn (PH)

Ridgeway Prim Sch

Ridgeway

Haven Farm (No1)

Robin Brook

Lumb Wood

Kent Wood

7

HAZLEHURST LA

Hazlehurst Farm

S8

Downland Farm

Ridgeway Moor

Kent Wood

81

Povey Farm

Ryall's Wood

S12

Litfield Farm

Oak House

S20

6

Bushes Wood

SLOADE LA

RIDGEWAY MOOR

PLUMBLEYWOOD LA

The Moss

DOE LA

Geerlane Farm

Birleyhay

GEER LA

Mill Pond

Ford

Bridge Inn (PH)

Bromehead Wood

5

Bramleyhill Farm

80

Trowayhall Farm

Fold Farm

Mill Pond

Summer Wood

FORD LA

4

Pearson's Wood

Troway

PH

Leicester Farm

Greatfold Farm

Dobholme Farm Nurseries

Mill Pond

Score House

BIRCHWOOD RD

Bramley

BRAMLEY PK

FORD RD

B6056

Black-a-moor Head Inn (PH)

Greenside

S21

Shady Hall

Bramley Moor

Butchers Arms (PH)

Marsh Lane Prim Sch

Marsh Lane

B6056

PH

3

SNONDON LA

Trowhay Hill Farm

QUARRY HILL

SCHOOL LA

MAIN RD

Lightwood Farm

79

Leak's Plantation

Lightwood

2

Air Strip

The Brushes

RIDGE RD

WARREN WLK

BRAMLEY RD

Light Wood

BOLEHILL LA

Bolehill

Top Farm

Bolehil Farm

Woodend Farm

S18

Moortop Farm

Heatherlee Farm

BRAMLEYMOOR LA

1

Apperknowle

MOORLAND VIEW

Travellers Rest (PH)

MOORTOP RD

LONG LA

MORTON LA

Handley Farm

Apperknowle Com Prim Sch

TOWN END

STATON LA

Middle Handley

LIGHTWOOD LA

78

38 A B 39 C 40 D E F

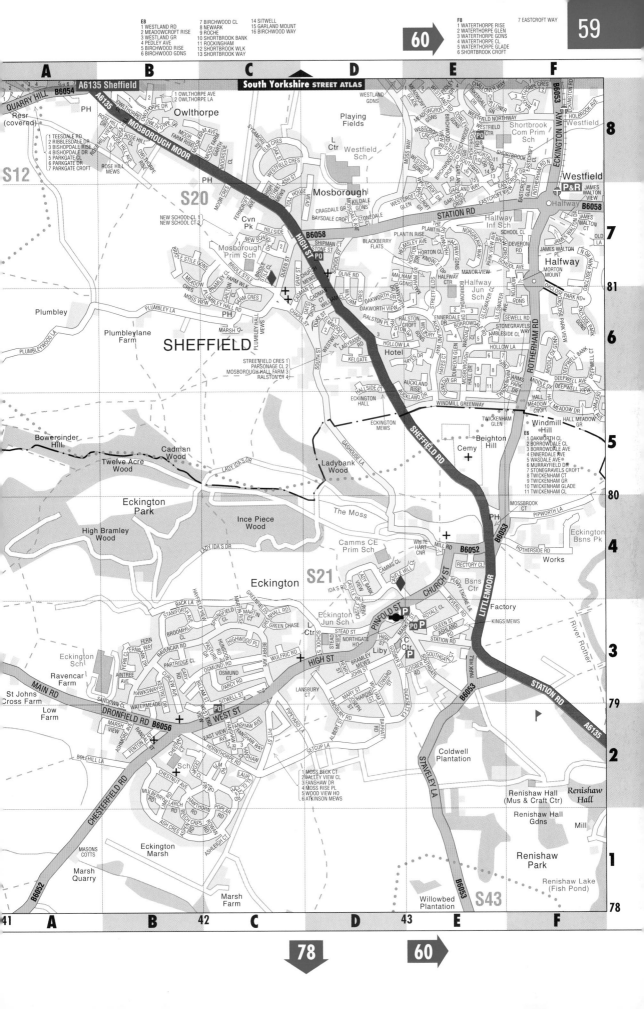

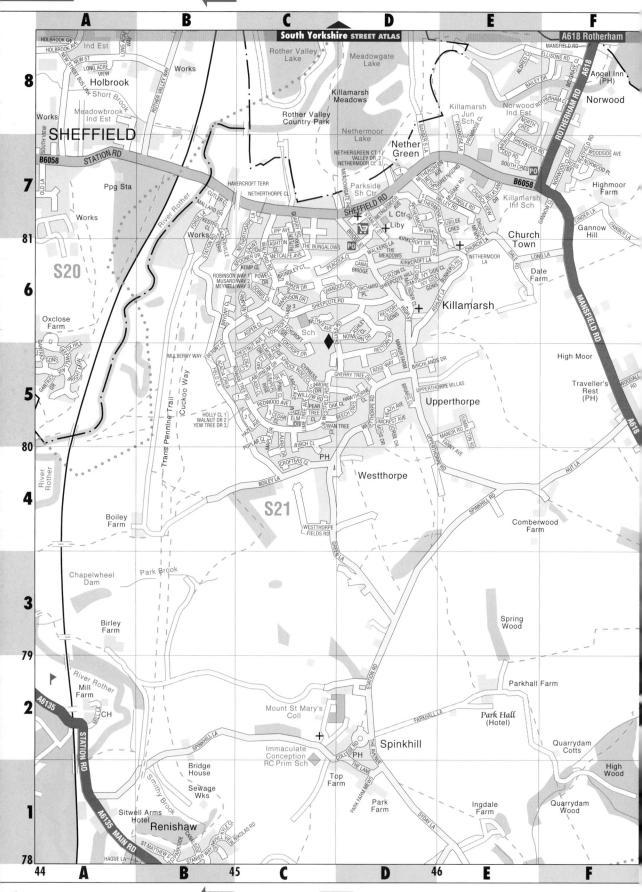

South Yorkshire STREET ATLAS

A618 Rotherham

A B C D E F

South Yorkshire STREET ATLAS

M1 Leeds

8

Nor
Wood

Spoil
Heap

Hard
Field

Broad Bridge Dike

Baugy
Hill

WALSKER LA

Top
Farm

Poplar
Farm

North
Farm

NORTH FARM CL

HUDSON
CL

NORTHLANDS

CASSON DR

GLEBE AVE

HARD LA

MANOR RD

THORPE RD

7

81

CARVER LA

Killamarsh
Pond

Woodall
Pond

Woodall

Beehive
Farm

CHAPEL YD

GLEBE FARM CL

RECTORY GDNS

STREET FARM CL

6

KILLAMARSH LA

Low
Plantation

Sewage
Wks

WOODALL LA

Broad
Bridge

PL Ctr PH

JACKYS LA

UNION RD

ORCHARD LEE

KYE LA

Harthill

S21

WOODALL
RD

Woodall
Bottoms

WOODHALL
HOUSE
FARM

Stone
Hill

S26

Harthill
Resr

GREYSTONES CT

DARLEY CL

CARVER
WAY

CARVER CR

DE SUTTON PL

DISHWELL LA

SOUTH FARM AVE

DOCTOR LA

SERLBY LA

OSBORNE CROFT

DR WARREN PL

THE DOWNINGS

SERLBY DR

COMMON RD

HARTHILL FIELD RD

5

80

WOODALL
RD

Motel

PEREGRINE WAY

PRYOR MEDE

PRIORY
CT

CRESCENT

WINNEY HILL

THE HOFINGE

4

MANSFIELD
RD

DOWCAR LA

HEWITT PL

FIRVALE

Fir
Hill

Woodall
Common

Woodall
Common

Birkenhead
Wood

Carr Farm
Cottage

WINNEY LA

Carr
Farm

3

79

The
Pebley
(PH)

Pebleygrove
Farm

Pebley
Resr

Harthill
Field

Pebley Oaks

ROTHERHAM RD

S43

Crabtree
Wood

Car
Plantation

HARTHILL LA

S80

2

WARD LA

Hawke
Wood

Garden
Plantation

Nitticarhill
Wood

Nitticarhill Rd

Butcherlawn
Pond

Nitticarhill

Longrybank
Wood

Barlborough
Hall Sch

A6(18)

1

78

47 A 48 C D 49 E F

M1

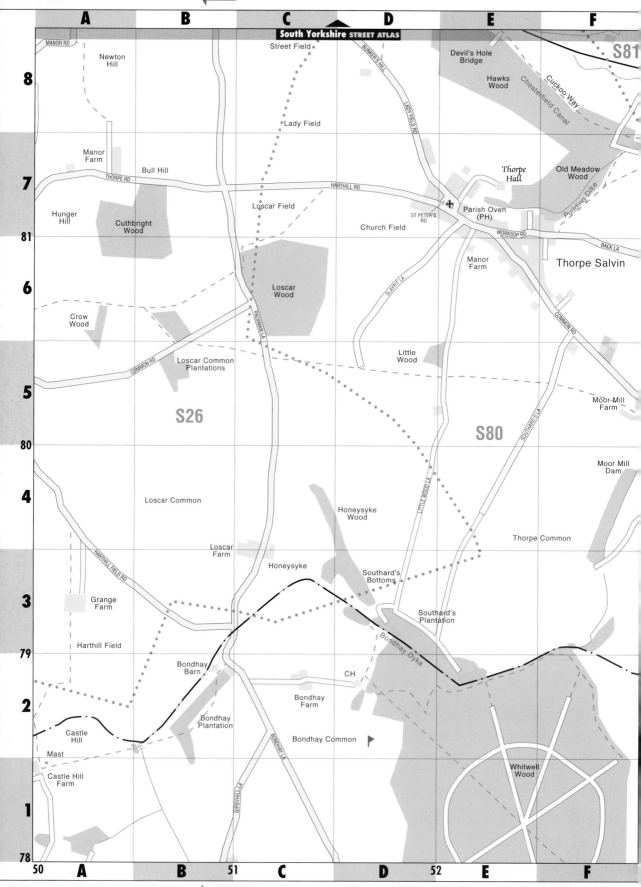

South Yorkshire STREET ATLAS

S81

8

Newton Hill

Street Field

Devil's Hole Bridge

Hawks Wood

Cuckoo Way

Chesterfield Canal

Lady Field

Manor Farm

Bull Hill

THORPE RD

7

Thorpe Hall

Old Meadow Wood

Pudding Dike

HARTHILL RD

Loscar Field

ST PETER'S RD

Parish Oven (PH)

Hunger Hill

Cuthbright Wood

Church Field

81

WORKSOP RD

BACK LA

Thorpe Salvin

6

Loscar Wood

SLAYPIT LA

Manor Farm

Crow Wood

PACKMAN LA

COMMON RD

Little Wood

Loscar Common Plantations

COMMON RD

5

S26

Moor-Mill Farm

SOUTHARD'S LA

80

S80

Moor Mill Dam

4

Loscar Common

Honeysyke Wood

LITTLE WOOD LA

Thorpe Common

HARTHILL FIELD RD

Loscar Farm

Honeysyke

Southard's Bottoms

Southard's Plantation

3

Grange Farm

Bondhay Dyke

Harthill Field

79

Bondhay Barn

CH

2

Bondhay Plantation

Bondhay Farm

Bondhay Common

Whitwell Wood

Castle Hill

Mast

GIPSYHILL LA

BONDHAY LA

Castle Hill Farm

1

78

50   51   52

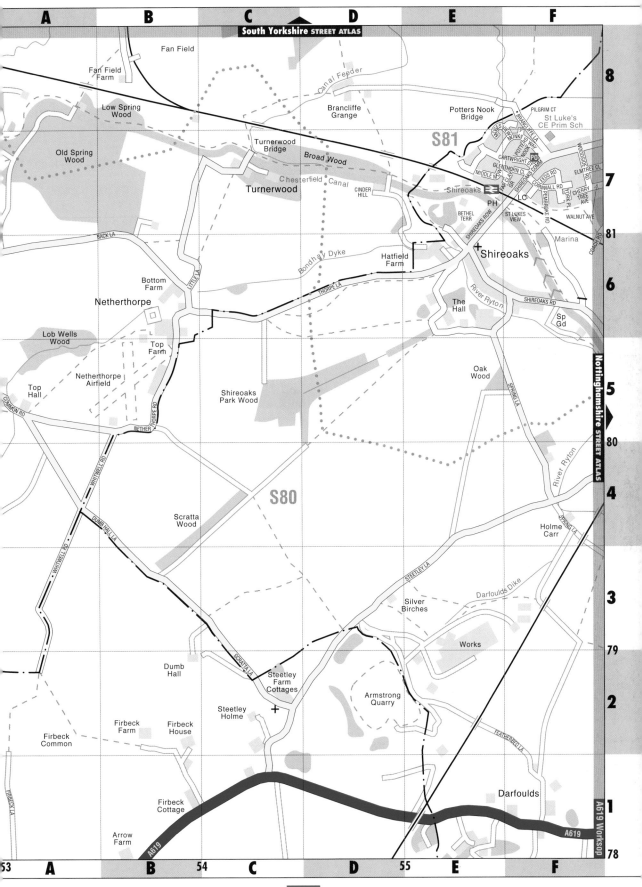

South Yorkshire STREET ATLAS

A B C D E F

8

Fan Field

Fan Field
Farm

Canal Feeder

Low Spring
Wood

Brancliffe
Grange

Potters Nook
Bridge

Pilgrim Ct

St Luke's
CE Prim Sch

Old Spring
Wood

Turnerwood
Bridge

Broad Wood

S81

7

Chesterfield Canal

Turnerwood

CINDER
HILL

Shireoaks

PH

LC

Bethel
Terr

St Lukes
View

Walnut Ave

Marina

81

BACK LA

Bottom
Farm

LITTLE LA

Bondhay Dyke

THORPE LA

Hatfield
Farm

Shireoaks

River Ryton

Shireoaks Rd

6

Netherthorpe

The
Hall

Sp
Gd

Lob Wells
Wood

Top
Farm

Oak
Wood

SPRING LA

5

Top
Hall

Netherthorpe
Airfield

Shireoaks
Park Wood

80

COMMON RD

THORPE RD

NETHER

River Ryton

WHITTWELL RD

S80

4

DUMB HALL LA

Scratta
Wood

Holme
Carr

SPRING LA

WHITTWELL RD

STEETLEY LA

Darfoulds Dike

3

Silver
Birches

SCRATTA LA

Works

79

Dumb
Hall

Steetley
Farm
Cottages

Armstrong
Quarry

2

Steetley
Holme

Firbeck
Farm

Firbeck
House

FEATHERBED LA

Firbeck
Common

Darfoulds

A619 Worksop

1

FIRBECK LA

Firbeck
Cottage

A619

Arrow
Farm

A619

78

53 A B 54 C D 55 E F

Nottinghamshire STREET ATLAS

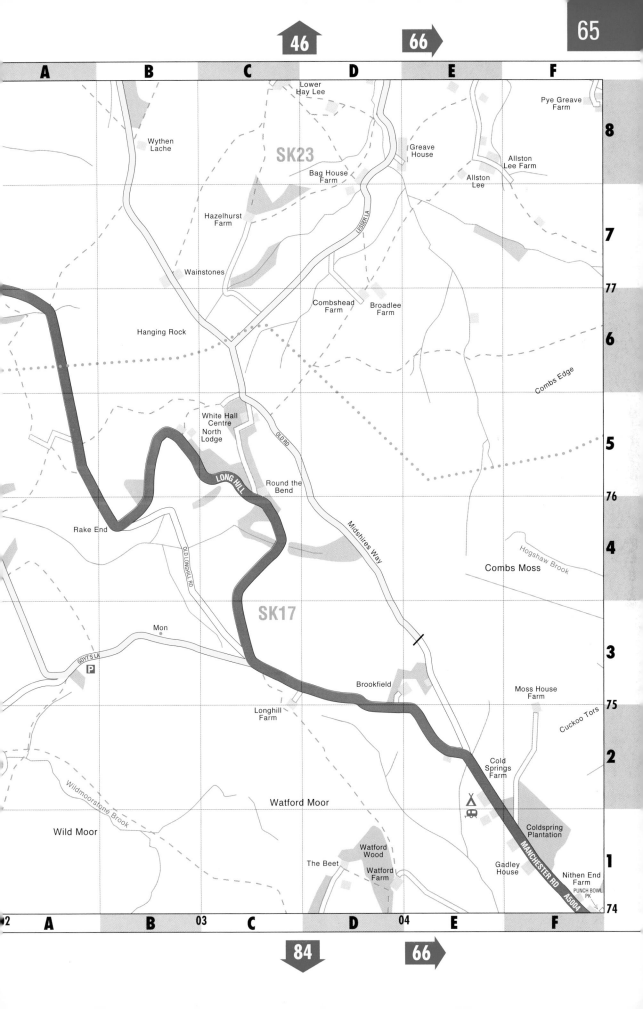

A   B   C   D   E   F

8
Pyegreave Brook
Hob Tor
Resrs
PO · 1 · 2 · PH   DALE RD
BEECH LA
A6
BUXTON RD
1 STATION RD
1,2 HALLSTEADS
+
Ashpiece Farm
LONGRIDGE LA

7
SK23
P
Bibbington

77

6
Combs Moss
Black Edge
Blackedge Resr
Field Farm
BATHAM GATE

5
Blackedge Farm
Tom Thorn Farm
Batham Gate

76
SK17
Thorn Head Farm
WATERSWALLOWS LA
Tomthorn

4
Hogshaw Brook
High Peak Nurseries

3
Television Station
Mast
Resr
Turner Lodge
Brook House
Breezemount Farm
Brownedge Plantation
Waterswallows Green
Light Wood
Lightwood Resr
Frome Lodge
Brookhouse Farm

75

2
Works
Hogshaw Brook
NURSERY DR
BROWN EDGE RD
The Barms Farm
DAISYMERE LA
LADYCROFT
BUXTON
Fairfield Common
WATERSWALLOWS RD
Nunsfield Farm

1
Corbar Hill
WYE HO
CORBAR RD
LIGHTWOOD RD
SYCAMORE WAY
SHERATON CL
ASPEN CL
BIRCH CL
CHESTNUT CL
WILLIAMSON AV
LANSDOWNE RD
St Anne's RC Prim Sch
BARMS WAY
NUNSFIELD RD
GLENWOOD RD
ST PETER'S RD
LINKS VIEW
DAKIN ST
NORTH RD
A6
CROSS ST
GOLF TERR
MONTPELIER PL
CHERRY TREE DR
ASHWOOD RD
WATERSWALLOWS MEWS
DAKIN CT
TOWN END
CH
LESSER LA
Townend Farm
Corbar Woods
CORBAR WOODS LA
LASCELLES RD
FAIRFIELD RD A6

74
05   A   B   06   C   D   07   E   F

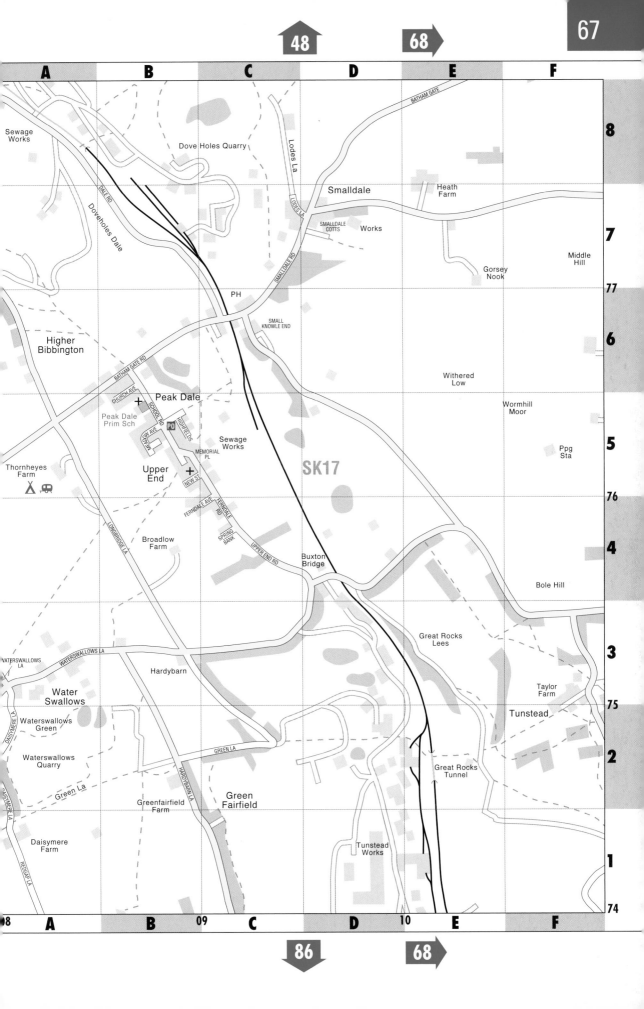

A B C D E F

8

Sewage
Works

Dove Holes Quarry

Lodes La

BATHAM GATE

Smalldale

Heath
Farm

7

SMALLDALE
COTTS

Works

SMALLDALE RD

LODES LA

Middle
Hill

Gorsey
Nook

77

PH

6

SMALL
KNOWLE END

Higher
Bibbington

Withered
Low

Wormhill
Moor

BATHAM GATE RD

CHURCH AVE

SCHOOL RD

Peak Dale

Ppg
Sta

5

Peak Dale
Prim Sch

MEADOW AVE

HIGHFIELDS

PO

SK17

Sewage
Works

MEMORIAL
PL

Thornheyes
Farm

Upper
End

NEW ST

76

FERNDALE AVE

FERNDALE RD

SPRING BANK

Broadlow
Farm

UPPER END RD

Buxton
Bridge

Bole Hill

4

LONGBRIDGE LA

Great Rocks
Lees

3

WATERSWALLOWS LA

Hardybarn

Taylor
Farm

WATERSWALLOWS
LA

Water
Swallows

Tunstead

75

DAISYMERE LA

Waterswallows
Green

GREEN LA

Great Rocks
Tunnel

2

Waterswallows
Quarry

HARDYBARN LA

Green La

Green
Fairfield

REDGAP LA

DAISYMERE LA

Greenfairfield
Farm

Daisymere
Farm

Tunstead
Works

1

74

08 A B 09 C D 10 E F

67
49

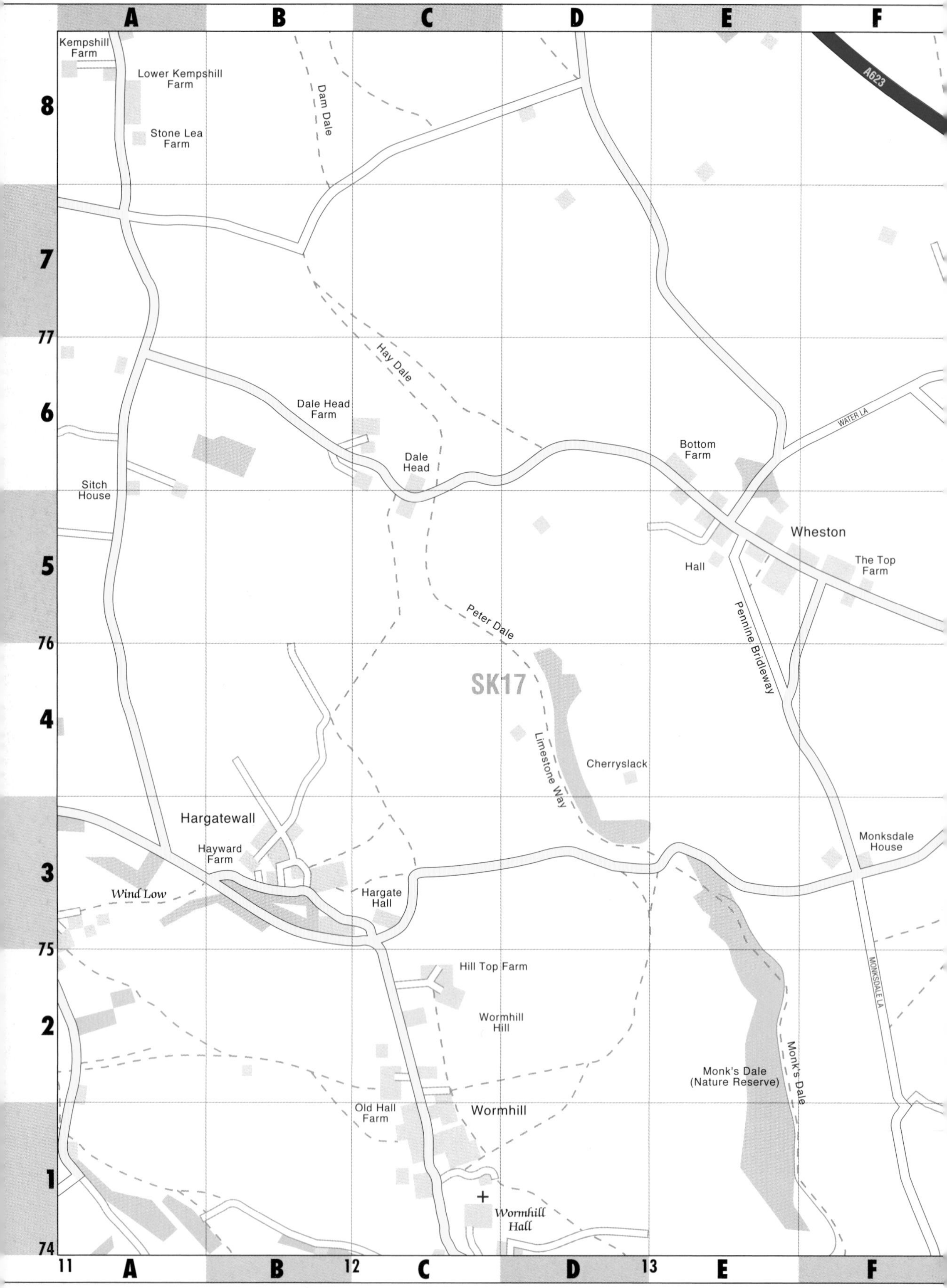

A B C D E F

A623

Kempshill Farm

Lower Kempshill Farm

8

Stone Lea Farm

Dam Dale

7

77

Hay Dale

Dale Head Farm

6

Dale Head

Bottom Farm

Water La

Sitch House

Wheston

5

Hall

The Top Farm

Peter Dale

76

SK17

Pennine Bridleway

4

Limestone Way

Cherryslack

Monksdale House

Hargatewall

Hayward Farm

3

Wind Low

Hargate Hall

Monksdale La

75

Hill Top Farm

2

Wormhill Hill

Monk's Dale

Monk's Dale (Nature Reserve)

Old Hall Farm

Wormhill

1

+ Wormhill Hall

74

11 A B 12 C D 13 E F

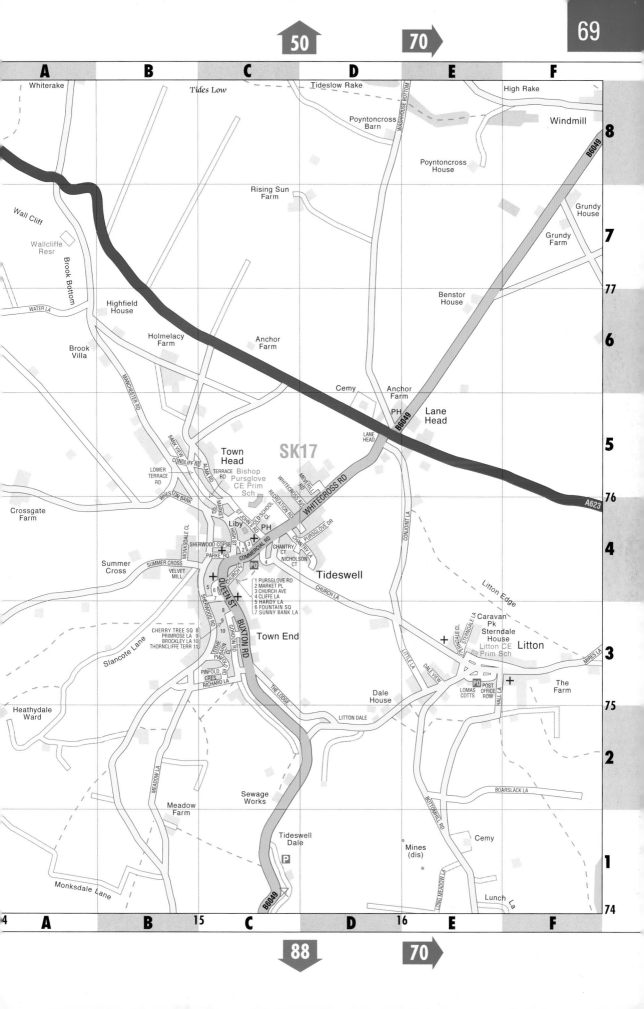

69 51

	A	B	C	D	E	F

B6049

Artis Farm

Great Hucklow

PH

Rose Farm

Grindlow

Hall Farm

Roods Farm

Bretton Mount

Shepherd's Park

BRADSHAW LA

8

7

77

Stanleymoor Farm

Stanley Moor

Silly Dale

Little Moor

Manor Farm

Foolow

Inn

Old Hall Farm

Waterfall Farm

Linen Dale

6

TROT LA

Stanley Lodge

Stanley House

Brosterfield Farm

BROSTERFIELD CVN SITE

Opencast Workings

Tideswell Lane

5

76

A623

SK17

Littonfields

PH

Somerset House Farm

Wardlow Mires

B6465

Watergrove

A623

Housley

Housley House

S32

Castlegate Stud Farm

4

MIRES LA

Peter's Stone

THUNDERPIT LA

3

Meadow Farm

Manor Farm

White House Farm

Gregory Farm

Wardlow

PH

White Rake

Mines (dis)

75

2

Tansley Dale

Cressbrook Dale

Hall Farm

Wardlow Hay Farm

B6465

Longstone Moor

1

74

17	A	B	18	C	D	19	E	F

69 89

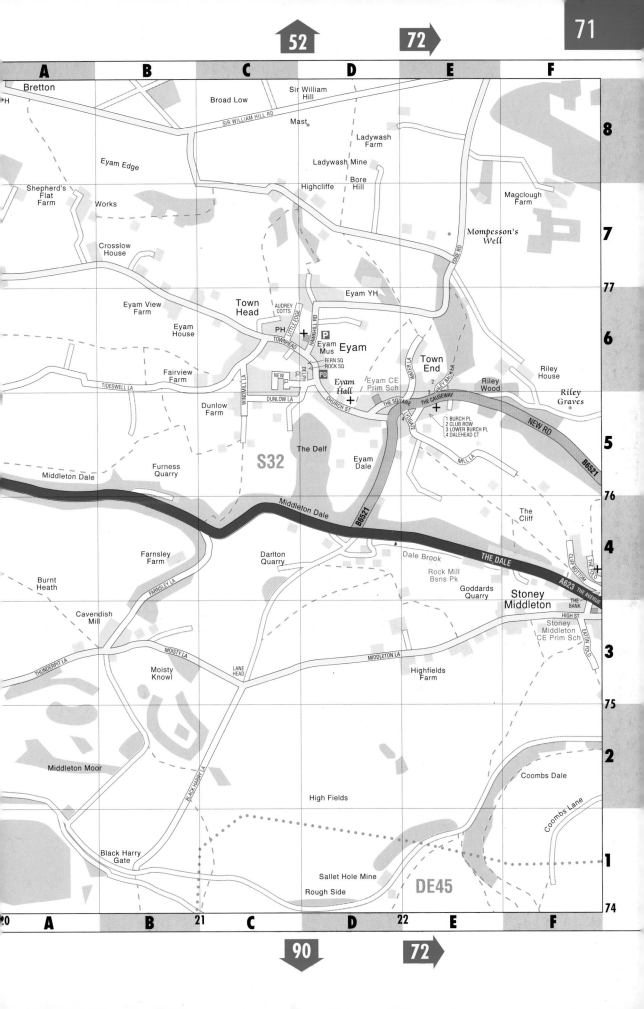

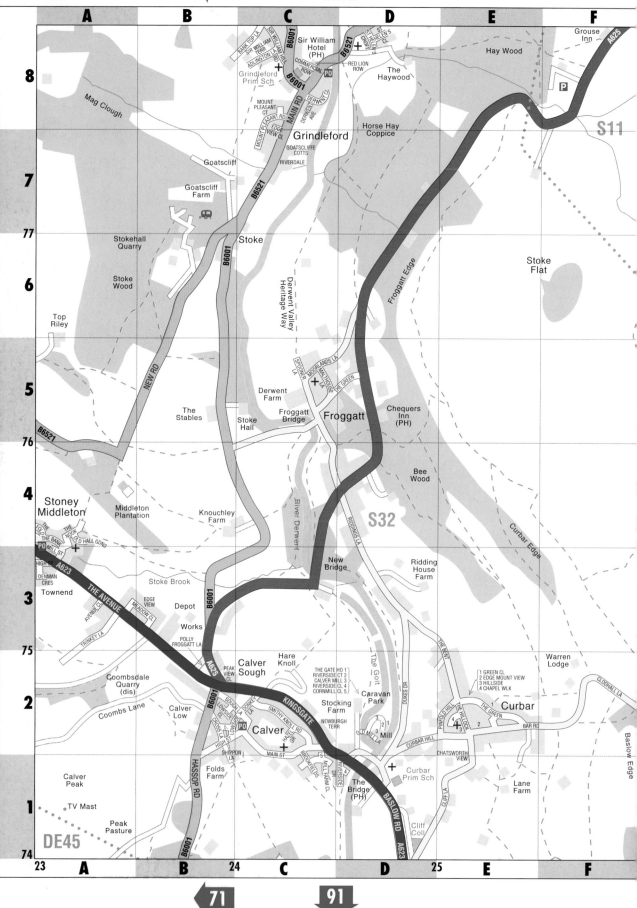

A **B** **C** **D** **E** **F**

B6054

B6054

Saltersitch
Bridge

8

Bar Brook

Bucka
Hill

A621

S11

7

White Edge Moor

Hurkling
Stone

Barbrook
Reservoir

77

Greaves's
Piece

Works

CAR RD

6

White Edge

Car
Top

S17

5

Big Moor

76

4

S32

Bar Brook

Ramsley
Moor

S18

3

Ramsley
Lodge

75

Swine
Sty

2

P

Ramsley
Reservoir

Sandyford Brook

DE45

1

Leash Fen

Eaglestone
Flat

S42

A621

Blake Brook

74

26 **A** **B** 27 **C** **D** 28 **E** **F**

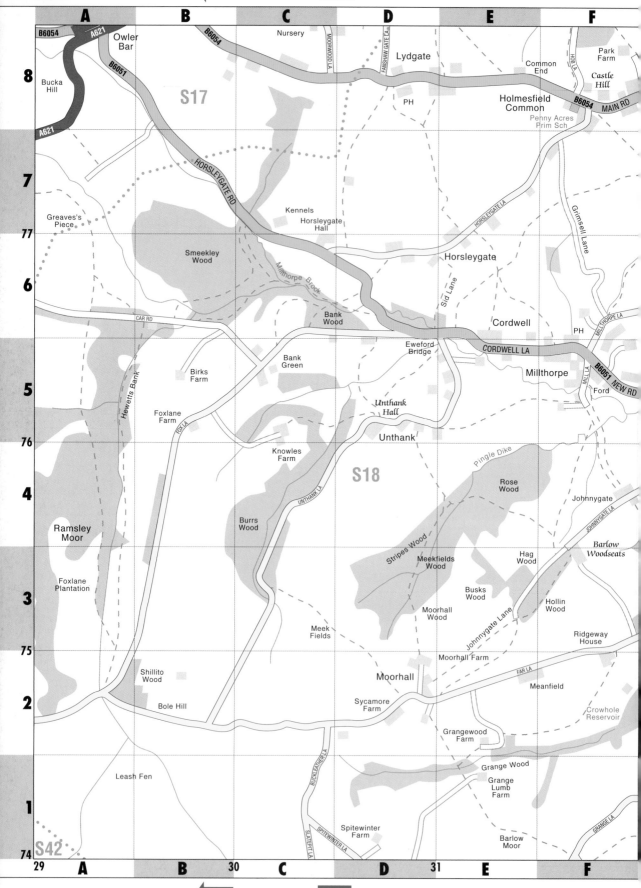

A B C D E F

8

B6054 A621
Owler Bar
B6051
Bucka Hill
A621

S17

Nursery
MOORWOOD LA
FANSHAW GATE LA
Lydgate
Common End
HOB LA
Park Farm
Castle Hill
PH
Holmesfield Common
B6054 MAIN RD
Penny Acres Prim Sch

7

HORSLEYGATE RD
Greaves's Piece
Kennels
Horsleygate Hall
HORSLEYGATE LA
Horsleygate
Grimsell Lane

77

Smeekley Wood
Millthorpe Brook
Sid Lane

6

CAR RD
Bank Wood
Cordwell
MILLTHORPE LA
PH
Eweford Bridge
CORDWELL LA
Bank Green
Birks Farm
Millthorpe
B6051 NEW RD

5

Hewetts Bank
Foxlane Farm
FOX LA
Unthank Hall
MILL LA
Ford

76

Knowles Farm
Unthank
Pingle Dike
Rose Wood
Johnnygate

4

S18
UNTHANK LA
JOHNNYGATE LA
Barlow Woodseats
Ramsley Moor
Burrs Wood
Stripes Wood
Hag Wood
Meekfields Wood
Hollin Wood
Busks Wood

3

Foxlane Plantation
Moorhall Wood
Johnnygate Lane
Ridgeway House
Meek Fields
Moorhall Farm
FAR LA

75

Shillito Wood
Meanfield
Moorhall
Crowhole Reservoir

2

Bole Hill
Sycamore Farm
Grangewood Farm
Grange Wood

Leash Fen
BUCKLEATHER LA
Grange Lumb Farm

1

SLATEPIT LA
SPITEWINTER LA
Spitewinter Farm
Barlow Moor
GRANGE LA

74

S42

29 A B 30 C D 31 E F

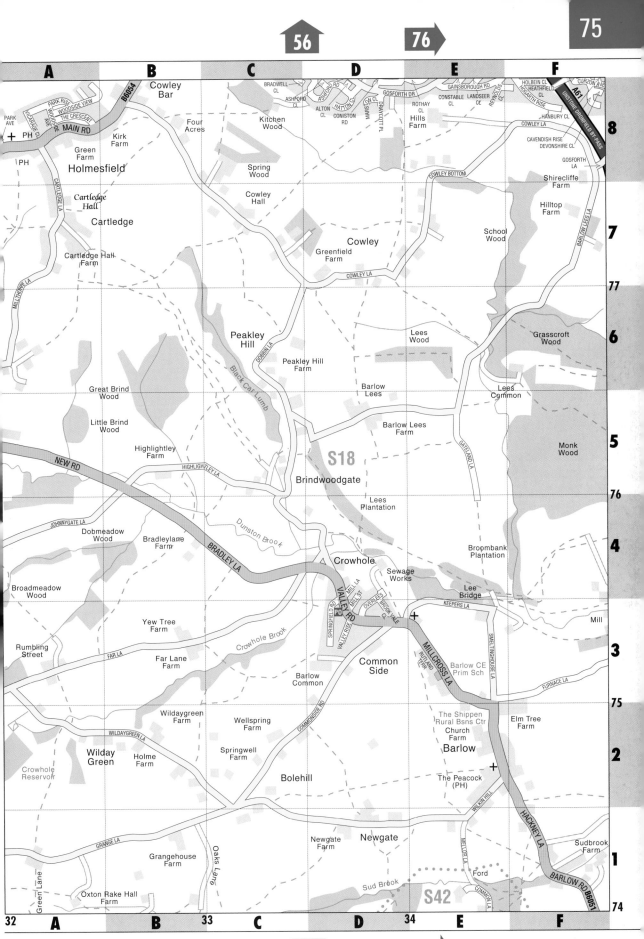

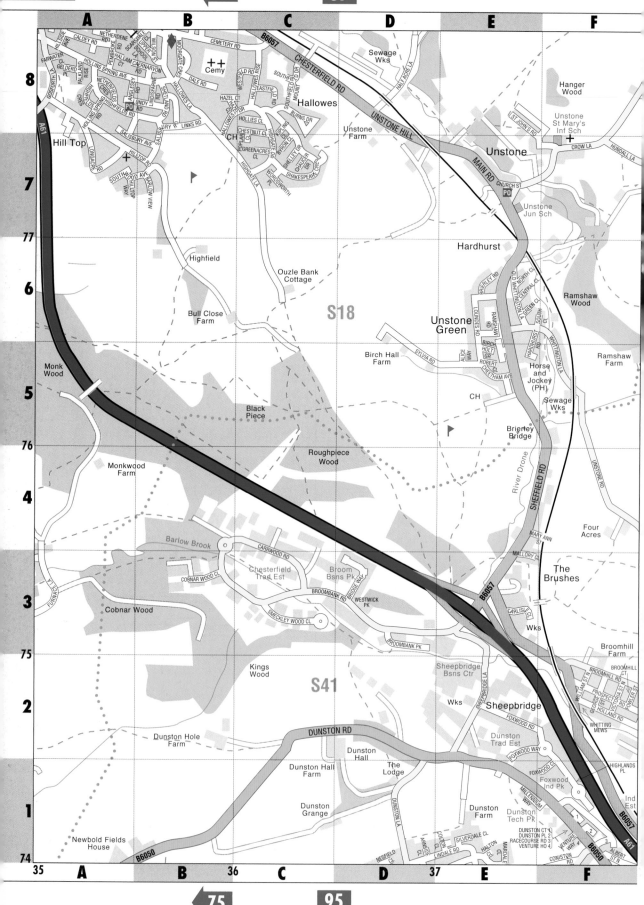

A   B   C   D   E   F

8

HILLSIDE
CALDEY RD
GOSFORTH
NETHERDENE
HALLAM
SCARSDALE
WILSON CL
MOORGATE CRES
CEMETERY RD
B6057
CHESTERFIELD RD
Sewage Wks
HALT ACRE LA
Hanger Wood

FARWATER
CL
GELDERD
FALKLAND
RISE
HOLLINS SPRING AVE
CAERNARVON
HALLOWES LA
DALE RD
WESTFIELD RD
HALLOWES RISE
SOUTHFIELD
OLD MOUNT RD
UNSTONE HILL
St JOHN'S RD
Unstone St Mary's Inf Sch
A61
ANGLESEY
NETHERFIELD CL
SHETLAND RD
LINDISFARNE
HAZEL CT
HALLOWESTOR
HAZEL RD
Hallowes
Unstone Farm
Unstone
CROW LA
HUNDALL LA

Hill Top
PO
HIGHFIELDS
LUNDY RD
SALISBURY AVE
LINKS RD
HOLLIES CL
CHESTNUT CL
GREENACRES CL
SAPLING
HEDGATE
WYNDON CL
BURNS DR
CH
MAIN RD
CHURCH ST
PO

7

LONGACRE RD
SOUTH AVE
HILLTOP RD
OLD AVE
HILLTOP
BARLOW VIEW
HILLTOP WAY
SHELLEY DR
SPACER DR
WIDEWORTH
SHAKESPEARE CRES
Unstone Jun Sch

77

Highfield
Ouzle Bank Cottage
Hardhurst

6

Bull Close Farm
S18
Unstone Green
BRIERLEY RD
OLD WHITTINGTON LA
NORTH CL
CENTRAL CL
GREEN CL
SOUTH
Ramshaw Wood

Monk Wood
Birch Hall Farm
SYLVA RD
ALICE WAY
ROBERT CL
CHEETHAM AVE
LOUNDES RD
RAMSHAW RD
BIRCH HOLT GR
HARDHURST RD
WHITTINGTON LA
Horse and Jockey (PH)
Ramshaw Farm

5

Black Piece
CH
Brierley Bridge
Sewage Wks

76

Monkwood Farm
Roughpiece Wood
River Drone
SHEFFIELD RD
UNSTONE RD

4

Four Acres
MARY ANN ST
MALLORY CL
The Brushes

3

FURNACE LA
Barlow Brook
CARRWOOD RD
COBNAR WOOD CL
Chesterfield Trad Est
Broom Bsns Pk
BRIDGE WAY
WESTWICK PK
BROOMBANK RD
B6057
CARLISLE CL
Wks
Broomhill Farm
BROOMHILL RD

Cobnar Wood
SMECKLEY WOOD CL
BROOMBANK PK
WILLIAM ST
GEORGE ST
PROSPECT RD
FOWLER ST
HOLLAND RD

75

Kings Wood
S41
Sheepbridge Bsns Ctr
SHEEPBRIDGE LA
Wks
Sheepbridge
FOXWOOD RD
WHITTING MEWS
HIGHLANDS PL

2

Dunston Hole Farm
DUNSTON RD
Dunston Hall
Dunston Hall Farm
The Lodge
DUNSTON LA
FOXWOOD WAY
FOXWOOD CL
Dunston Trad Est
Foxwood Ind Pk
Ind Est

1

Newbold Fields House
B6050
Dunston Grange
Dunston Farm
Dunston Tech Pk
MILLENNIUM WAY
DUNSTON CT 1
DUNSTON PL 2
RACECOURSE RD 3
VENTURE HO 4
VENTURE WAY
ALBERT ST N
B6050
A61
B6057

NESFIELD CT
POTON CL
LINDALE RD
ARNGATE CL
SILVERDALE CL
HALTON
MARDALE
CONISTON RD

74

35   A   B   36   C   D   37   E   F

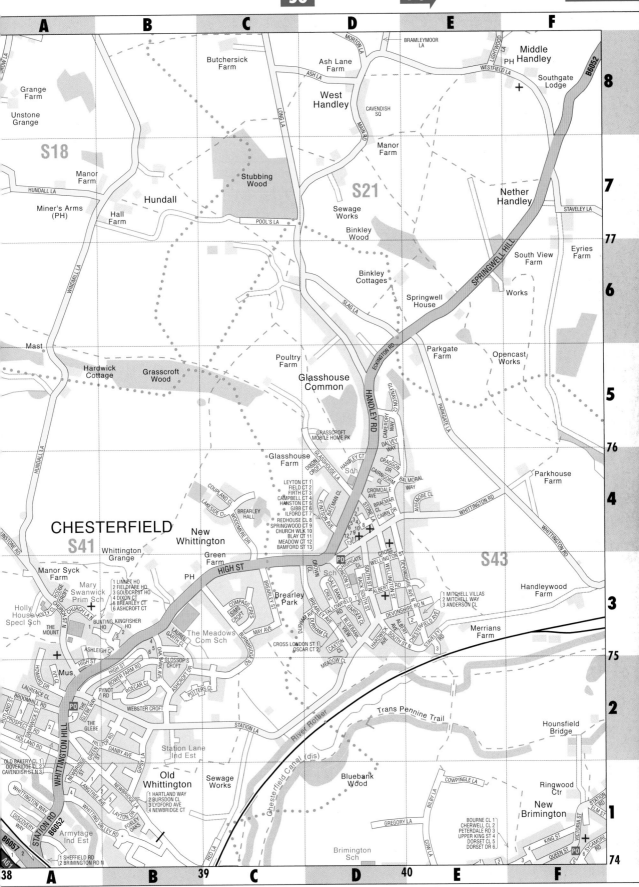

B3
1 ACTON CT
2 CHIGWELL WAY
3 KINGSTON CT
4 ROMFORD WAY
5 RICHMOND CT
6 CHELMSFORD WAY
7 CRICKLEWOOD CT
8 EALING CT
9 DUEWELL CT

10 CAMBERWELL CT
11 DULWICH CT
12 GREENWICH CT
13 CHISWICK CT

E2
1 BARNFIELD CL
2 DEVONSHIRE CL
3 DEVONSHIRE ST
4 KEDLESTON CT
5 HARDWICK CT
6 ARUNDEL CT
7 WELBECK CT
8 MELBOURNE CT
9 PORTER HO

F2
1 WATERINGBURY GR
2 TUDOR ST
3 NETHERTHORPE RD
4 WHITEHEAD ST
5 LEANDER CT
6 MALLARD CT

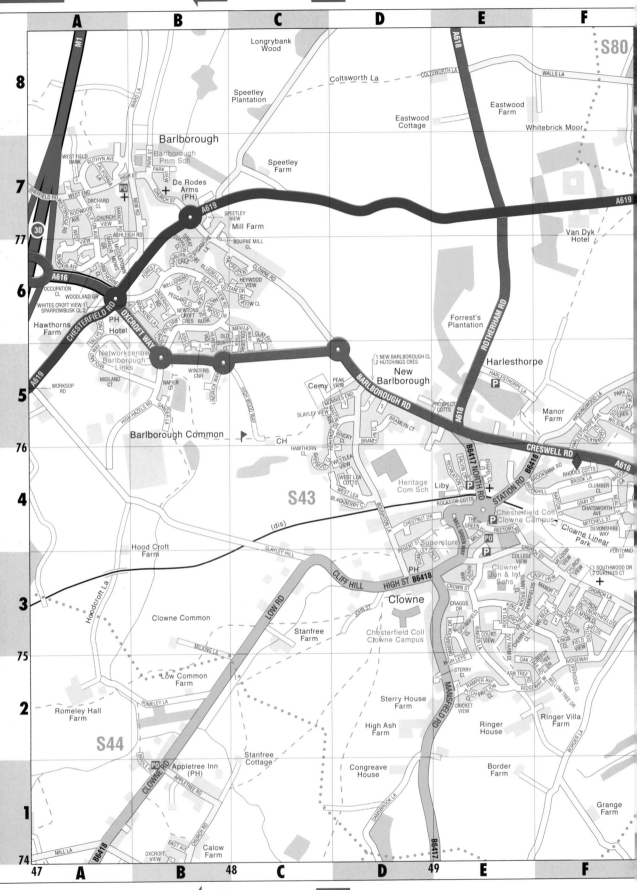

S80

A B C D E F

8

Longrybank
Wood

Coltsworth La

COLTSWORTH LA

WALLS LA

Speetley
Plantation

Eastwood
Cottage

Eastwood
Farm

Whitebrick Moor

Barlborough

Speetley
Farm

7

WEST FIELD
BANK

Barlborough
Prim Sch

De Rodes
Arms
(PH)

A619

Speetley
View

Mill Farm

A619

Van Dyk
Hotel

77

30

BOURNE MILL
CL

HEYWOOD
VIEW

CLOWNE RD

A616

OCCUPATION
CL

WOODLAND GR

WHITES CROFT VIEW 1
SPARROWBUSK CL 2

Forrest's
Plantation

Harlesthorpe

6

Hawthorns
Farm

PH
Hotel

OLD
QUARRY

CLAY PIT

1 NEW BARLBOROUGH CL
2 HUTCHINGS CRES

ROTHERHAM RD

HARLESTHORPE LA

Manor
Farm

A619

WORKSOP
RD

MIDLAND
CT

NAPIER
CT

WINDERS
CNR

Cemy

PEAK
VIEW

New
Barlborough

BARLBOROUGH RD

PROSPECT
COTTS

P

CRESWELL RD

A616

5

Barlborough Common

CH

SLAYLEY VIEW

MONNIES END

HAWTHORN
CL

BRICKY
CL

BRAMLYN CT

BRAM

A618

HICKINWOOD LA

PARK VIEW

SOUTHGATE
CRES

WILSON AVE

76

WEST LEA
COTTS

WEST LEA

BLACKBERRY C

Heritage
Com Sch

Liby

B6417 NORTH RD

STATION RD

B6418

CRESWELL RD

RHODES COTTS

CLUMBER
CL

GRAY ST

CHATSWORTH
AVE

4

S43

(dis)

Hood Croft
Farm

CHESTNUT DR

P

P

Superstore

RECTORY
RD

P

Chesterfield Coll
Clowne Campus

THE
GREEN

MILL ST

PO

Clowne Linear
Park

DEVONSHIRE
WAY

PORTLAND
CL

1 SOUTHWOOD DR
2 DUKERIES CT

SLAYLEY HILL

LOW RD

CLIFF HILL

HIGH ST

B6418

JOHN ST

REGENT ST

PH

CHURCH
ST

Clowne
Jun & Inf
Schs

MANOR
CL

CHURCH LA

3

Clowne Common

Stanfree
Farm

Clowne

Chesterfield Coll
Clowne Campus

CRAGGS
DR

CROWN ST

RINGER
WY

SPRINGFIELD

COURT
VIEW

RIDGEWAY

75

MILKING LA

High LEYS

STERRY
CL

PITCH PAVILION

ASH TREE CL

OAK TREE CL

WILLOW TREE DR

2

Low Common
Farm

ROMELEY LA

Sterry House
Farm

RAMPER AVE

CRICKET
VIEW

Ringer
House

Ringer Villa
Farm

Romeley Hall
Farm

MANSFIELD RD

BORDER LA

S44

Stanfree
Cottage

High Ash
Farm

Congreave
House

Border
Farm

Grange
Farm

1

PO

Appletree Inn
(PH)

CLOWNE RD

APPLETREE RD

CHURCH RD

DAMSBROOK LA

B6417

MILL LA

B6418

OXCROFT
VIEW

EAST AVE

CHURCH LA

Calow
Farm

74

47   A   48   B   C   48   D   49   E   F

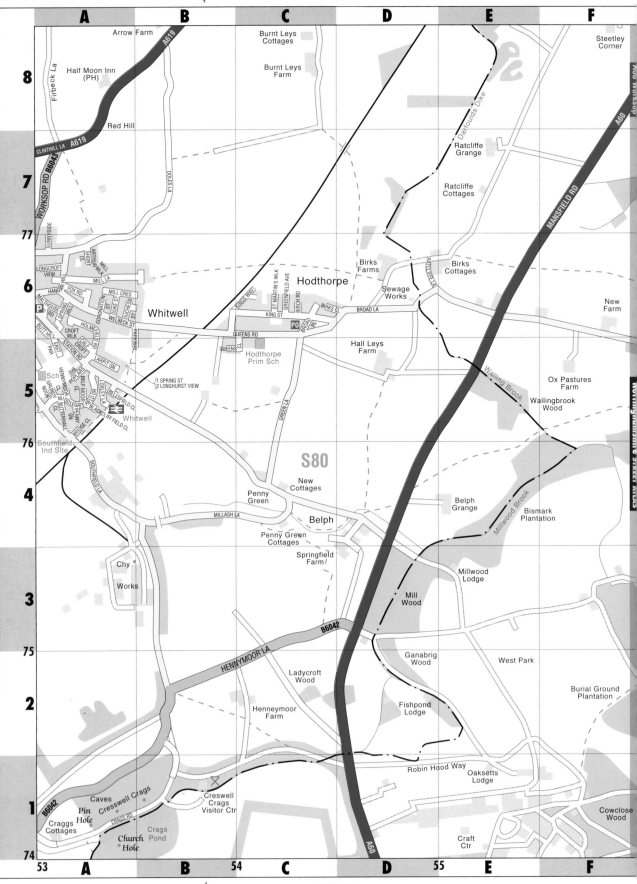

| | A | B | C | D | E | F |

8

Firbeck La

Half Moon Inn (PH)

Arrow Farm

A619

Burnt Leys Cottages

Burnt Leys Farm

Steetley Corner

A60 Worksop

Red Hill

7

WORKSOP RD B6043

CLINTHILL LA   A619

DOLES LA

Daffoulds Dike

Ratcliffe Grange

Ratcliffe Cottages

MANSFIELD RD

A60

77

SUNNYSIDE

Birks Farms

Birks Cottages

New Farm

6

LONGCROFT VIEW

ARTHUR WLK

SHORT CL

MILL

CALF

MILL LA

HANG

FOX RD

MILL CRES

DUKE ST

CRESCENT

WELBECK ST

DUKES ST

Whitwell

KINGS WAY

ST MARTIN'S WLK

GREENFIELD AVE

BIRCH RD

KING ST

BIRKS CL

BIRKS CL

Hodthorpe

Sewage Works

BROAD LA

MALTHOUSE

RD

SPRING

BUTT HILL

HOLMEFIELD RD

CROFT WLK

CROFT

STATION RD

PARKWAY

QUEENS RD

QUEENS CL

PO

BROAD PL

Hall Leys Farm

Walling Brook

New Farm

5

EAST

PAR

SchL

THE POPLARS

HENNYMOOR

BELF MOOR RD

DOLEGATE

PENNY

BLACKCLIFF FIELD CL

BELSFIELD CL

LOXLEY LA

LARPIT GN

1 SPRING ST
2 LONGHURST VIEW

Whitwell

Hodthorpe Prim Sch

GREEN LA

Ox Pastures Farm

Wallingbrook Wood

76

Southfield Ind Site

GRUBBY NOOK

BUTTERHALL

BRIDGE CL

SOUTHFIELD LA

S80

Millwood Brook

Bismark Plantation

4

MILLASH LA

New Cottages

Penny Green

Belph

Penny Green Cottages

Belph Grange

3

Chy

Works

Springfield Farm

Mill Wood

Millwood Lodge

75

HENNYMOOR LA

B6042

Ganabrig Wood

West Park

2

Ladycroft Wood

Henneymoor Farm

Fishpond Lodge

Burial Ground Plantation

1

B6042

Pin Hole

Caves Cresswell Crags

CRAGS RD

Craggs Cottages

Church Hole

Crags Pond

Creswell Crags Visitor Ctr

Robin Hood Way

Oaksetts Lodge

A60

Craft Ctr

Cowclose Wood

74

| | A | B | C | D | E | F |

53   54   55

Nottinghamshire Street Atlas

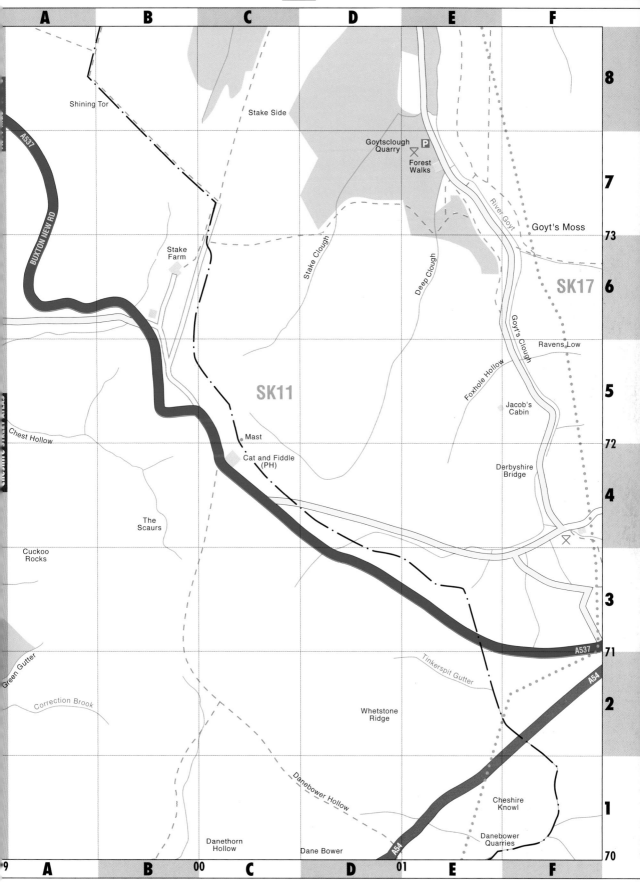

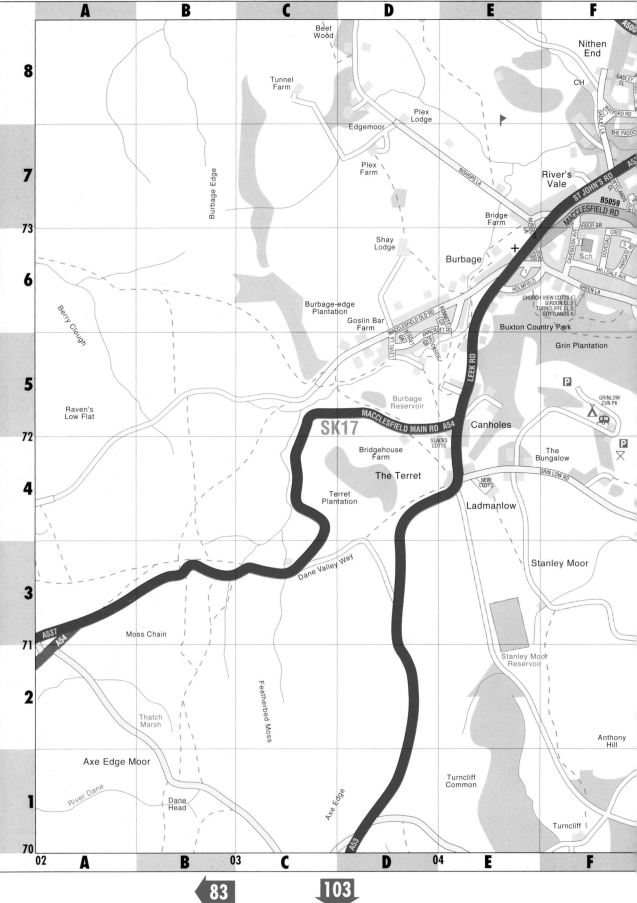

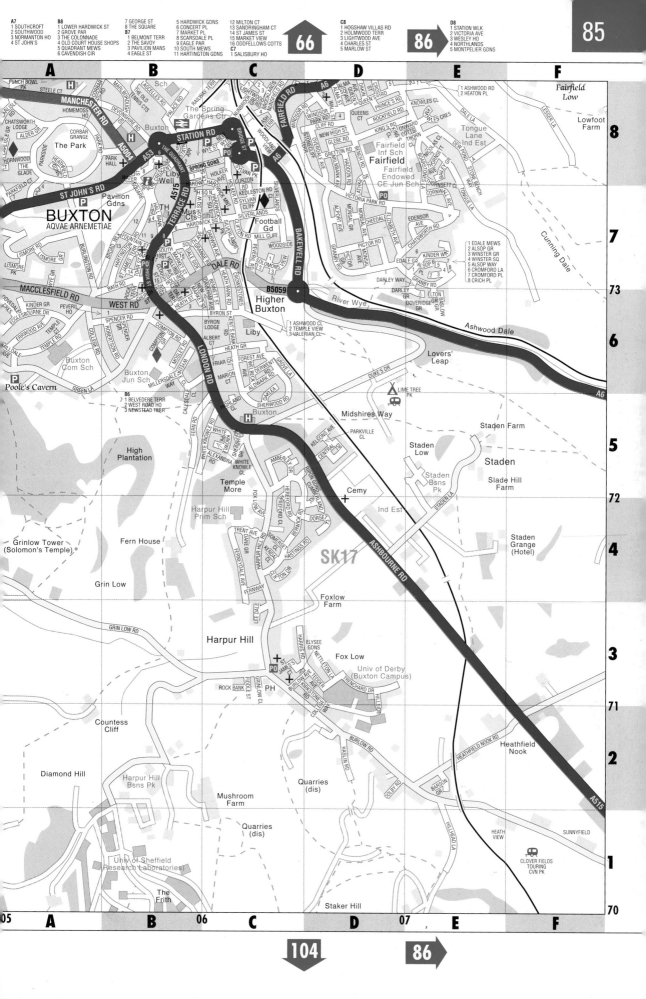

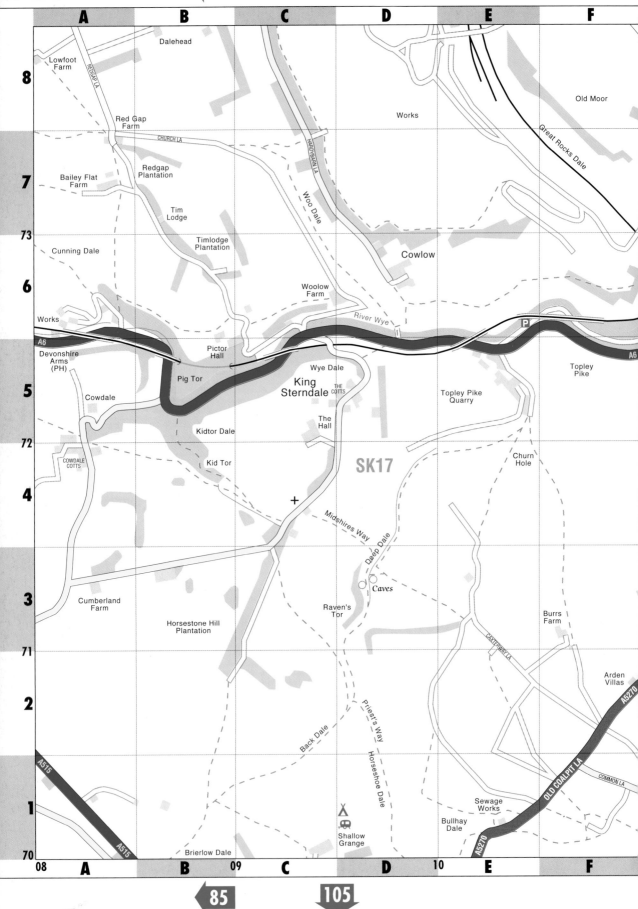

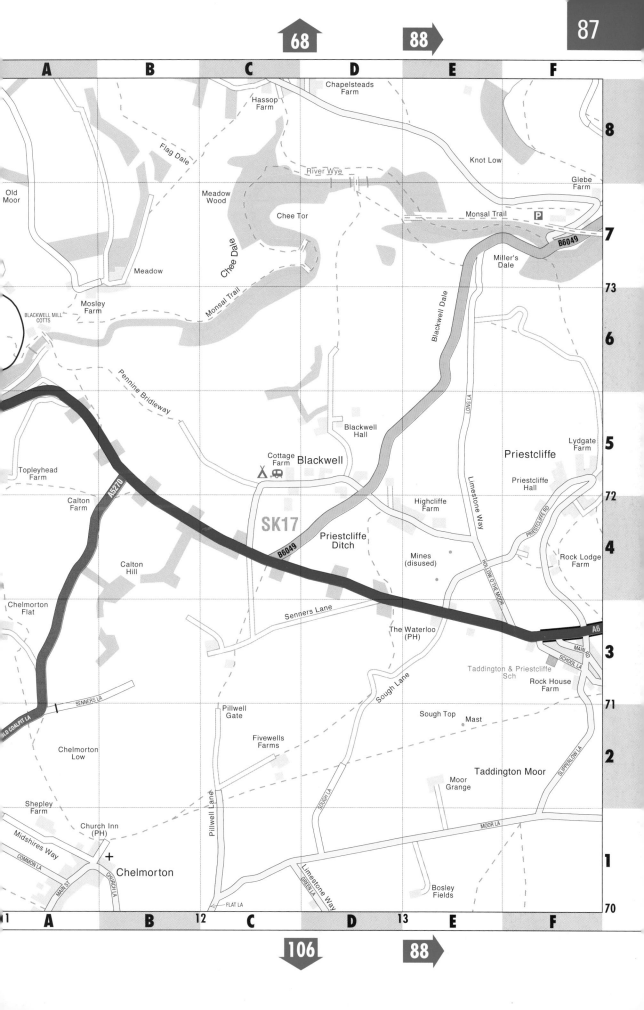

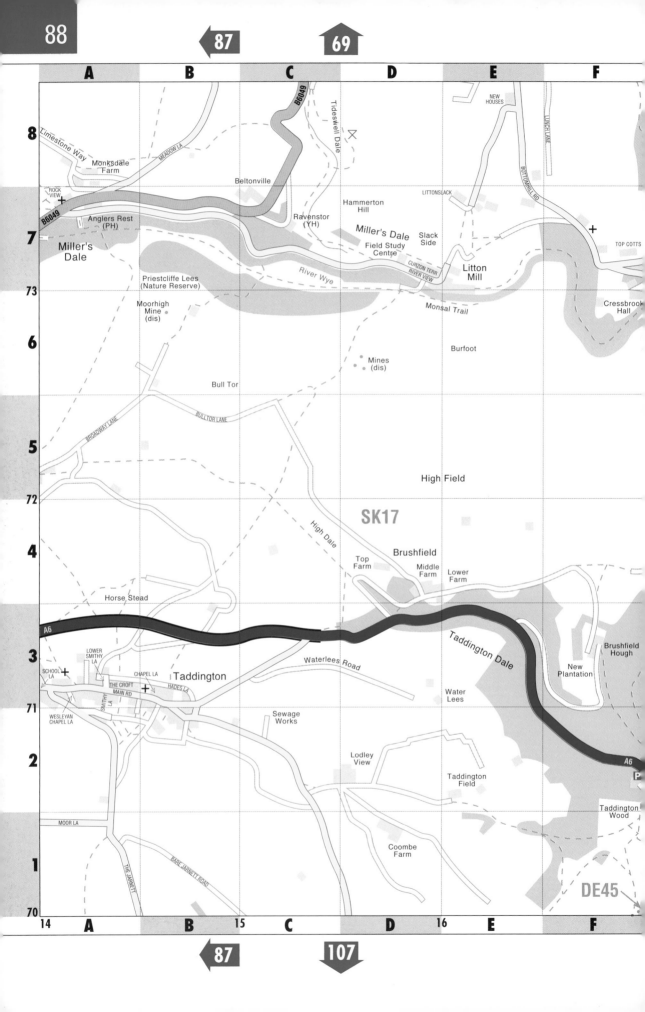

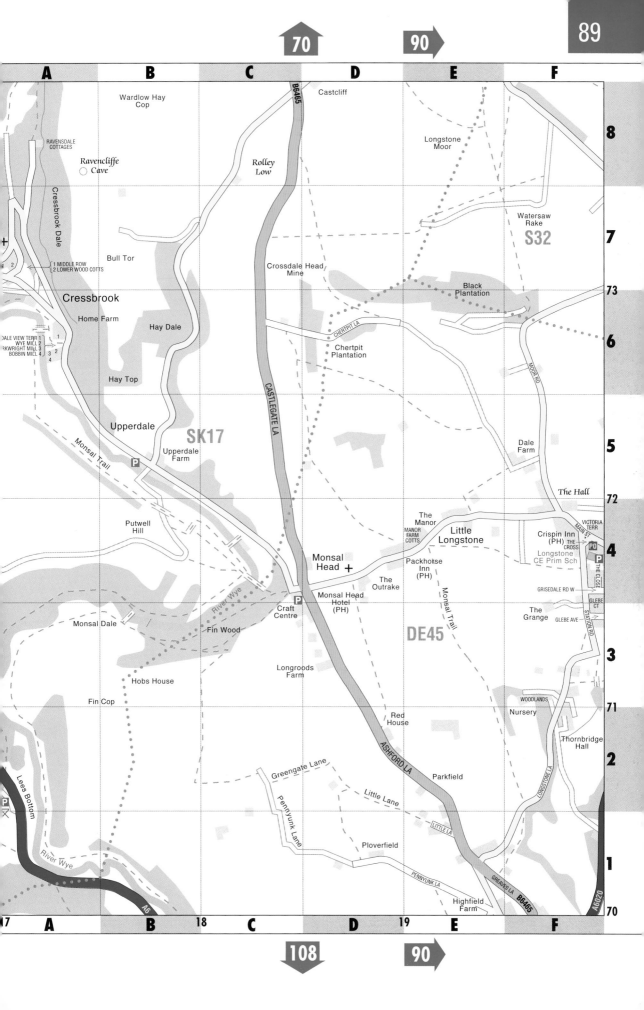

A B C D E F

8

7

73

6

72

5

4

3

71

2

1

70

Wardlow Hay Cop

Castcliff

B6465

Longstone Moor

RAVENSDALE COTTAGES

Ravencliffe Cave

Rolley Low

Watersaw Rake

S32

Cressbrook Dale

Bull Tor

1 MIDDLE ROW
2 LOWER WOOD COTTS

Crossdale Head Mine

Black Plantation

Cressbrook

Home Farm

Hay Dale

CHERTPIT LA

DALE VIEW TERR 1
WYE MILL 2
ARKWRIGHT MILL 3
BOBBIN MILL 4

Chertpit Plantation

MOOR RD

Hay Top

Dale Farm

Upperdale

SK17

The Hall

Monsal Trail

Upperdale Farm

CASTLEGATE LA

VICTORIA TERR

The Manor

The Hall

P

Putwell Hill

MANOR FARM COTTS

Little Longstone

Crispin Inn (PH)

THE CROSS

Longstone CE Prim Sch

PO

P

THE CLOSE

Monsal Head

Packhorse Inn (PH)

GRISEDALE RD W

GLEBE CT

Monsal Trail

River Wye

Craft Centre

P

The Outrake

Monsal Head Hotel (PH)

DE45

The Grange

GLEBE AVE

STATION RD

Monsal Dale

Fin Wood

Longroods Farm

Red House

WOODLANDS

Nursery

Hobs House

Fin Cop

Parkfield

Thornbridge Hall

ASHFORD LA

LONGSTONE LA

Lees Bottom

Greengate Lane

Little Lane

P

Pennyunk Lane

LITTLE LA

Ploverfield

GREAVES LA B6465

River Wye

PENNYUNK LA

A6

Highfield Farm

A6020

7 A 18 B C 19 D E F

A B C D E F

8

Mines
(disused)

Deep Rake

Opencast
Workings

Longstone Moor
Farm

S32

High Rake

Opencast
Workings

Bleaklow

Opencast
Workings

Beacon
Rod

Opencast
Workings

7

Longstone Edge

Opencast
Workings

Opencast
Workings

Hassop
Common

B6001

73

6

Hardrake Lane

Top
Farm

Rowland

Torrs
Farm

Eyre Arms
(PH)

Dog Kennel
Wood

5

Underedge

Hassop Hall
(Hotel)

Home
Farm

Hassop

BEGGARWAY LA

Hermitage
Pond

72

+

Church La

Barn Furlong

Great
Longstone
Bsns Pk

Standhill
Farm

LONGREAVE LA

Long Rake
Plantation

Bowling
Green
Wood

4

The Mires

Great
Longstone

DE45

Hassop
Park

Flatts
Farm

Birchill Bank
Wood

MAIN ST

CROFT RD

1
3 2
4

MIRES LA

GRISEDALE
RD W

GRISEDALE
RD E

EDGE VIEW DR

BURNALL

GLEBE AVE

1 SUNNY BANK
2 SPRING BANK
3 WESTERN VIEW
4 THE MEADOWS

Buskey
Cottage

Oak
Wood

3

Park
Farm

Birchills
Farm

71

Toll Bar
House

Rowdale
House

Monsal Trail

2

A6020

Churchdale
Farm

Cracknowl
Wood

Station
Farm

Nether
Wood

A619

B6048

Hassop Rd

A6020

1

Churchdale
Hall

Flatt
Plantation

A619

Baslow Rd

B6001

Old Hollow
Plantation

Cracknowl
House

70

20 A B 21 C D 22 E F

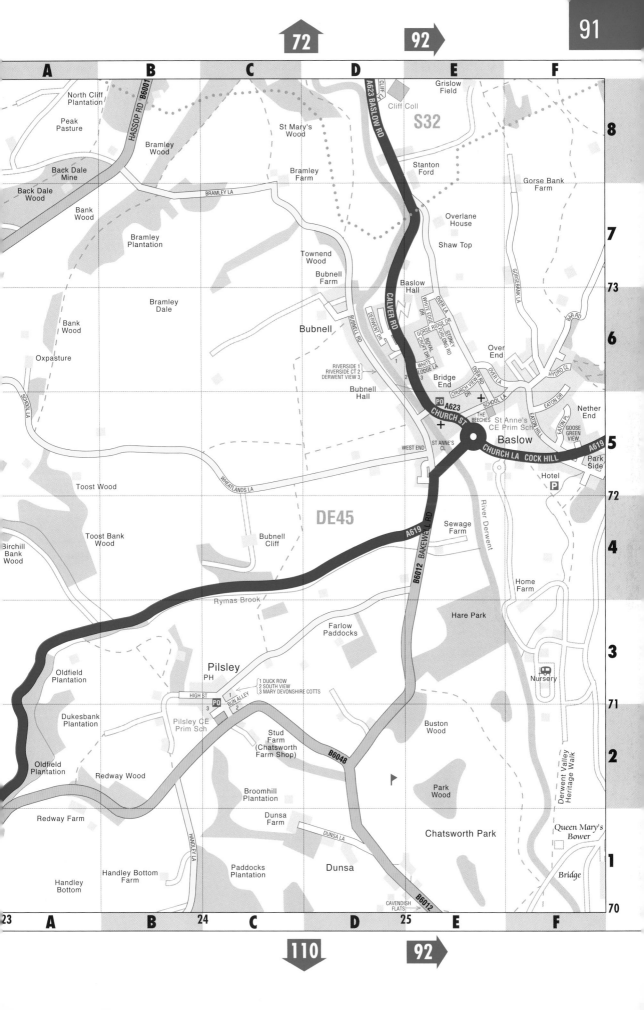

91
73

A   B   C   D   E   F

8

Wellington's
Monument

Jack Flat

Bar Brook

A621

7

SHEFFIELD RD

Gardom's Edge

BAR RD

Baslow Bar

Raddowhole
Plantation

Bar Brook

73

Yeld Wood

Nelson's
Monument

6

Yeldwood
Farm

A621

Far End

Yeld
Farm

Moorside
Farm

Birchen Edge

East Moor

DE45

Robin Hood Inn
(PH)

Newbridge Farm

5

A619

Jumble Coppice

Saw Mill

Robin Hood

P

B6050

Robin Hood
Farm

Park Lodge

Heathy Lea Brook

B6050

72

Chatsworth Park

Robin Hood
Plantations

Stone
Low

4

Dobb Edge

Emperor Stream

S42

A619

Umberley Brook

3

Parkgate

Gibbet
Wood

71

2

The
Hunting
Tower

Bunker's Hill
Wood

Gibbet Moor

1

Emperor
Lake

Stand
Wood

Chatsworth
House

Swiss
Lake

Swiss
Cottage

70

26   A   B   27   C   D   28   E   F

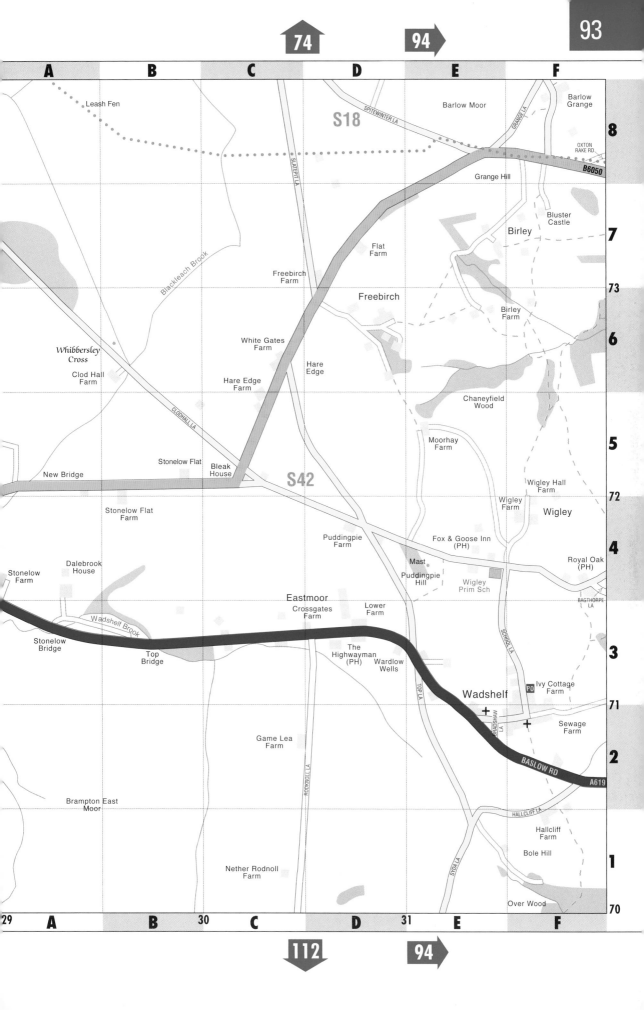

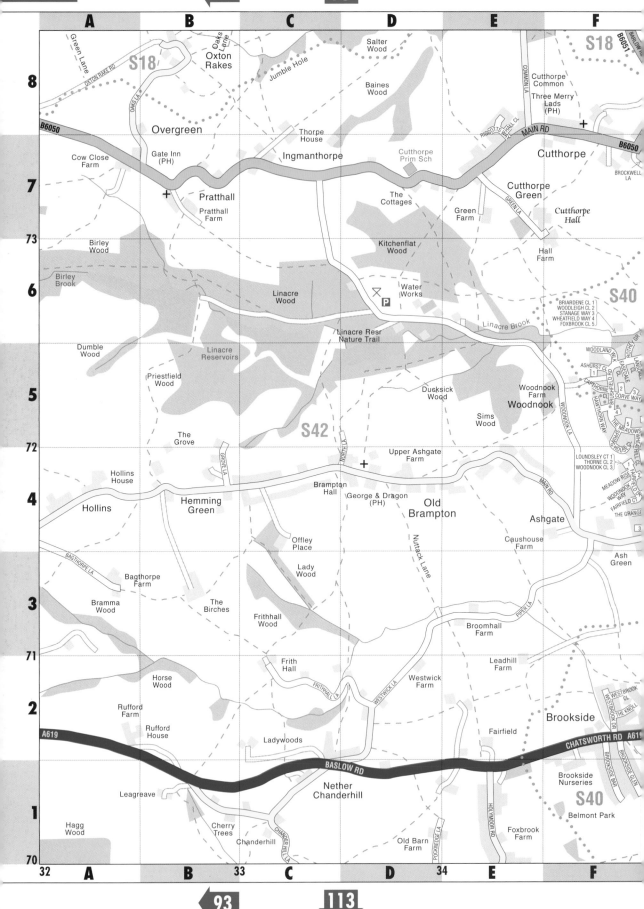
A   B   C   D   E   F

8

S18

Green Lane

OXTON RAKE RD

S18

B6051

BARLOW RD

OAKS LA

Oaks Lane

Oxton
Rakes

Salter
Wood

Jumble Hole

Baines
Wood

COMMON LA

RIGGOTTS WAY

WHALL CL

Cutthorpe
Common

Three Merry
Lads
(PH)

B6050

Overgreen

Thorpe
House

Ingmanthorpe

Cutthorpe
Prim Sch

MAIN RD

Cutthorpe

B6050

BROCKWELL LA

7

Cow Close
Farm

Gate Inn
(PH)

Pratthall

Pratthall
Farm

The Cottages

Cutthorpe

Green
Farm

GREEN LA

Cutthorpe
Green

Cutthorpe
Hall

73

Birley
Wood

Kitchenflat
Wood

Hall
Farm

6

Birley
Brook

Linacre
Wood

Water
Works

P

Linacre Brook

S40

BRIARDENE CL 1
WOODLEIGH CL 2
STANAGE WAY 3
WHEATFIELD WAY 4
FOXBROOK CL 5.

Dumble
Wood

Linacre
Reservoirs

Linacre Resr
Nature Trail

WOODLAND WLK

ROTHER GR

ASHURST CL

CAPTHORNE CL

Priestfield
Wood

Duelsick
Wood

Sims
Wood

Woodnook
Farm

Woodnook

WOODNOOK LA

HAWTHORN WAY

THE MEADOWS

CORVE WAY

5

72

The
Grove

GROVE LA

S42

NORTH LA

Upper Ashgate
Farm

MAIN RD

LOUNDSLEY CT 1
THORNE CL 2
WOODNOOK CL 3

Hollins
House

Hollins

Hemming
Green

Brampton
Hall

George & Dragon
(PH)

Old
Brampton

Ashgate

MEADOW RISE

FAIRFIELD DR

WOODNOOK
WAY

FAIRFIELD CT

THE GRANGE

4

BAGTHORPE LA

Offley
Place

Lady
Wood

Nuttack Lane

Caushouse
Farm

Ash
Green

Bagthorpe
Farm

3

Bramma
Wood

The
Birches

Frithhall
Wood

Broomhall
Farm

PIPER LA

71

Horse
Wood

Frith
Hall

FRITHHALL LA

WESTWICK LA

Westwick
Farm

Leadhill
Farm

WESTBROOK
CL

WESTBROOK DR

THE KNOLL

2

Rufford
Farm

Rufford
House

Ladywoods

Fairfield

Brookside

BROOKSIDE BAR

BROOKSIDE GLEN

A619

BASLOW RD

CHATSWORTH RD

A61

Leagreave

Nether
Chanderhill

HOLYMOOR RD

Brookside
Nurseries

S40

1

Hagg
Wood

Cherry
Trees

Chanderhill

CHANDER HILL LA

Old Barn
Farm

POCKHEDGE LA

Foxbrook
Farm

Belmont Park

70

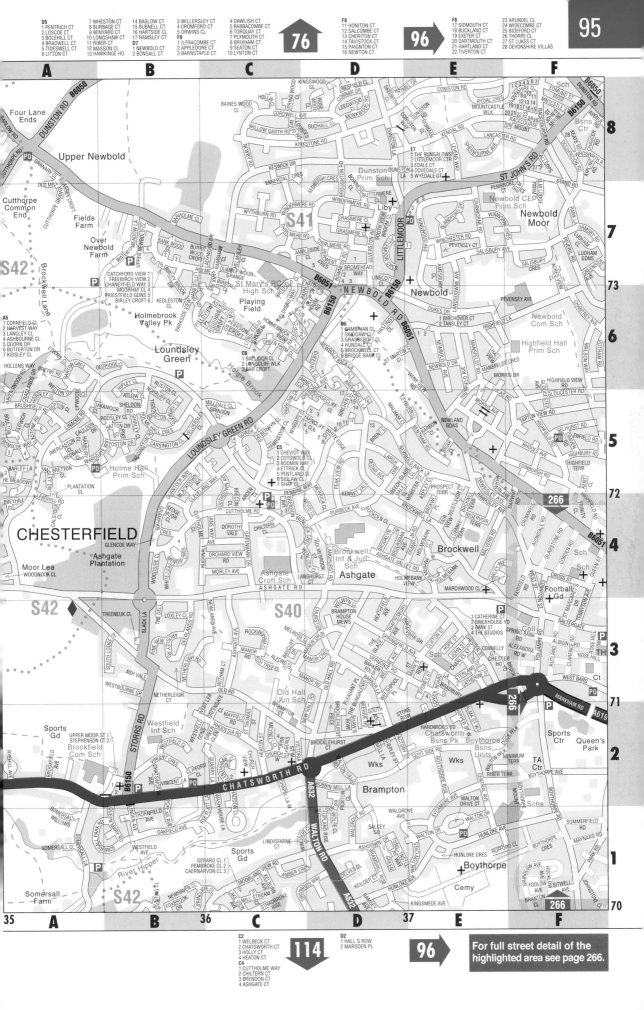

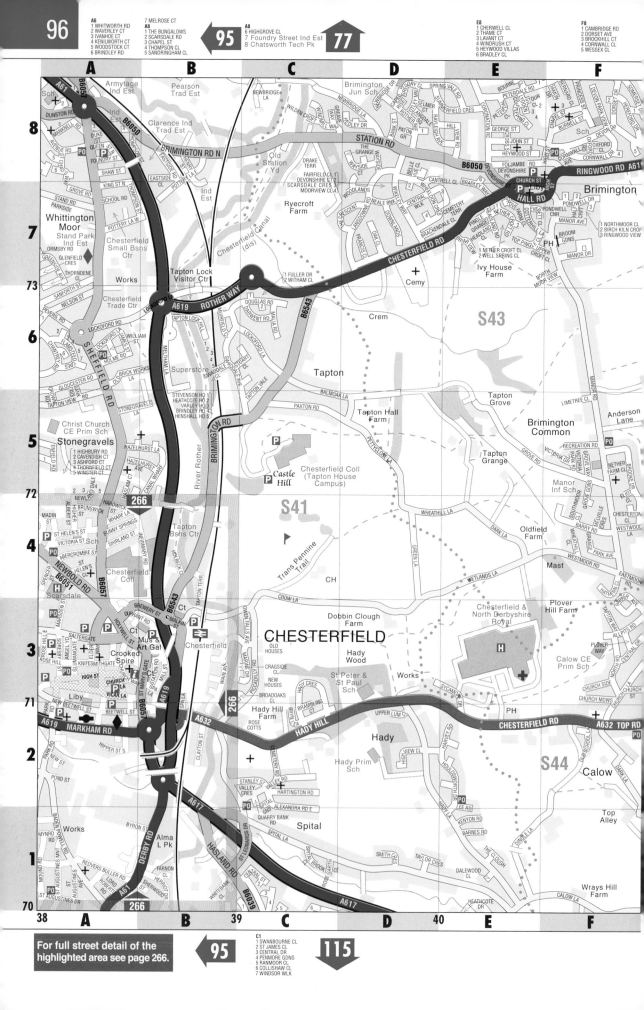

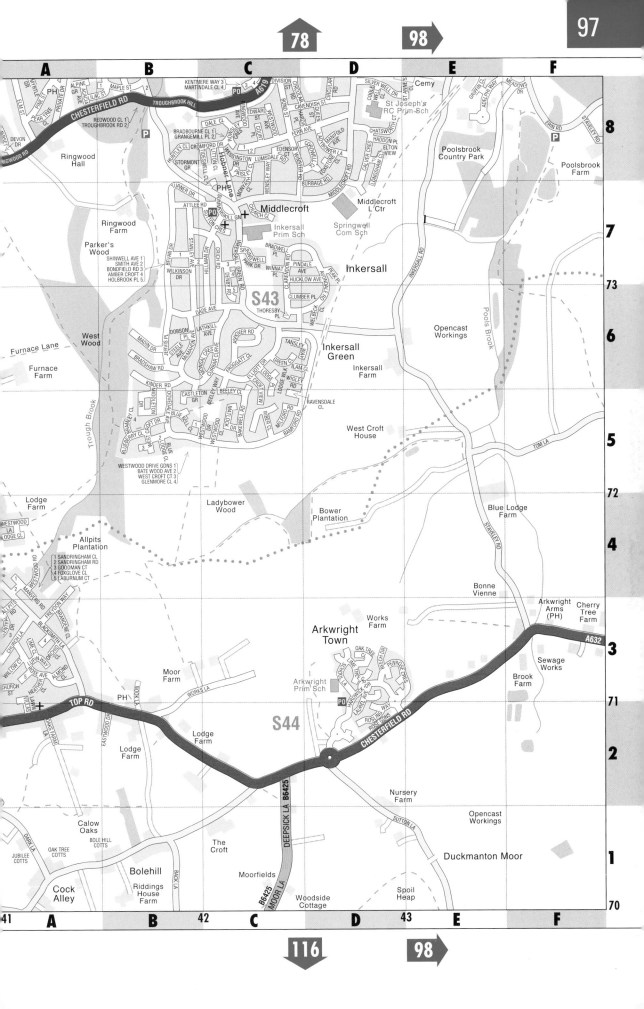

99
81

A B C D E F

DUCHESS ST

A616

Fox
Green

Markland
Farm

Grange
Farm

OXCROFT LA

Elmton

THE
SQUARE

PH

Elm
Tree Farm

Green
Farm

Camp Hill

Oaks
Farm

MARK'S LN

SPRING LA

Archaeological Trail

WOOD LA

CHATSWORTH RD

BULLIVANT AVE

WOOD
AVE

OAKS
AVE

MANSE CT

CENTRAL AVE

RAILWAY

PO

ELMTON RD

BANK
CL

ELMTON CL

WOOD LA

MODEL
VILLAGE

Creswell
Bsns Pk

Crags
Bsns Pk

HAZELEY RD

WELBECK
ST

MORVEN ST

COLLIERY RD

FRITHWOOD LA

S80

FRITHWOOD LA

Frithwood
Farm

The Old
Hag

Frith Wood

OXPASTURE LA

LC

Whaley Moor

Norwood
Farm

MAG LA

Whaley
Hall

WHALEY COMM

Whaley
Common

PH

Whaley

MOORFIELD LA

NG20

Grave
Wood

Whaley
Farm

Mill Pond

Bolsover Moor
Quarry

Mill
Farm

P

Langwith-
Whaley Thorns

PACK VIEW

P

S44

Scarcliffe Park

Owl Sick

Poulter
Country Park

BATHURST
TERR

P

Apsley
Grange

Owl
Spring

Archaeological
Trail

WHALEY RD

River Poulter

P

PO

A632

PH

MAIN RD

POULTER
ST

BOUNDARY
WLK

DEVONSHIRE DR

LANGWITH
MALTINGS

Scarcliffe
Grange

50 A B 51 C D 52 E F

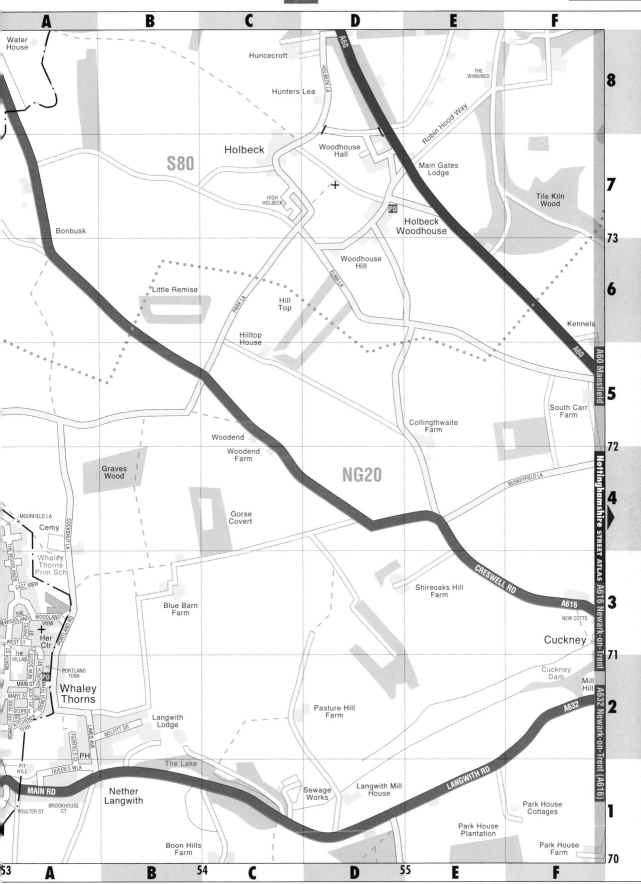

A **B** **C** **D** **E** **F**

Water House

Huncecroft

Hunters Lea

THE WINNINGS

A60

HOLBECK LA

Robin Hood Way

Main Gates Lodge

Tile Kiln Wood

8

S80

Holbeck

Woodhouse Hall

7

HIGH HOLBECK

Bonbusk

PO

Holbeck Woodhouse

73

Little Remise

Woodhouse Hill

ELMA LA

Kennels

6

PARK LA

Hill Top

A60

Hilltop House

5

South Carr Farm

Woodend

Collingthwaite Farm

72

Graves Wood

Woodend Farm

NG20

BUSKEYFIELD LA

4

MOORFIELD LA

Cemy

COCKSHUT LA

Gorse Covert

CRESWELL RD

Shireoaks Hill Farm

A616

3

THE WOODLANDS

Whaley Thorns Prim Sch

NEW COTTS

EAST VIEW

Cuckney

71

THE VILLAS

WOODLAND VIEW

Blue Barn Farm

PORTLAND RD

CHAPEL ST

WEST ST

Her Ctr

Cuckney Dam

THE WOODLANDS

PORTLAND TERR

Mill Hill

NORTH ST

CHURCH ST

A632

MARY ST

NEW SCOTT ST

FRENCH TERR

Whaley Thorns

PO

Langwith Lodge

Pasture Hill Farm

2

JELLICOE ST

GEORGE ST

KITCHENER TERR

Langwith Lodge

LIMES AVE

WELFITT GR

SCARCLIFFE TERR

FAIRFIELD CL

PH

The Lake

LANGWITH RD

Park House Cottages

PIT HILL

QUEEN'S WLK

Sewage Works

Langwith Mill House

1

MAIN RD

Nether Langwith

BROOKHOUSE CT

Park House Plantation

POULTER ST

Boon Hills Farm

Park House Farm

70

A **B** 54 **C** **D** 55 **E** **F**

53

Nottinghamshire STREET ATLAS A616 Newark-on-Trent

A60 Mansfield

A632 Newark-on-Trent (A616)

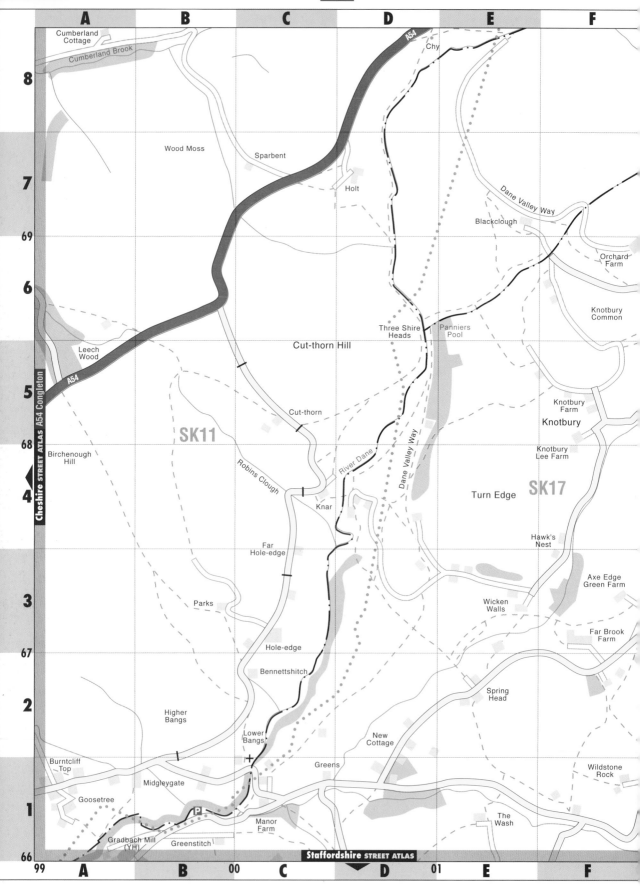

83

Cumberland
Cottage

Cumberland Brook

8

Wood Moss

Sparbent

A54

Chy

7

Holt

Dane Valley Way

69

Blackclough

Orchard
Farm

6

Leech
Wood

Cut-thorn Hill

Three Shire
Heads

Panniers
Pool

Knotbury
Common

Cheshire STREET ATLAS A54 Congleton

A54

5

SK11

Cut-thorn

Knotbury
Farm

Knotbury

68

Birchenough
Hill

Robins Clough

River Dane

Knotbury
Lee Farm

SK17

4

Knar

Dane Valley Way

Turn Edge

Far
Hole-edge

Hawk's
Nest

3

Parks

Axe Edge
Green Farm

67

Hole-edge

Bennettshitch

Wicken
Walls

Far Brook
Farm

2

Higher
Bangs

Lower
Bangs

New
Cottage

Spring
Head

Burntcliff
Top

Midgleygate

P

Greens

Wildstone
Rock

1

Goosetree

Manor
Farm

The
Wash

Gradbach Mill
(YH)

Greenstitch

66

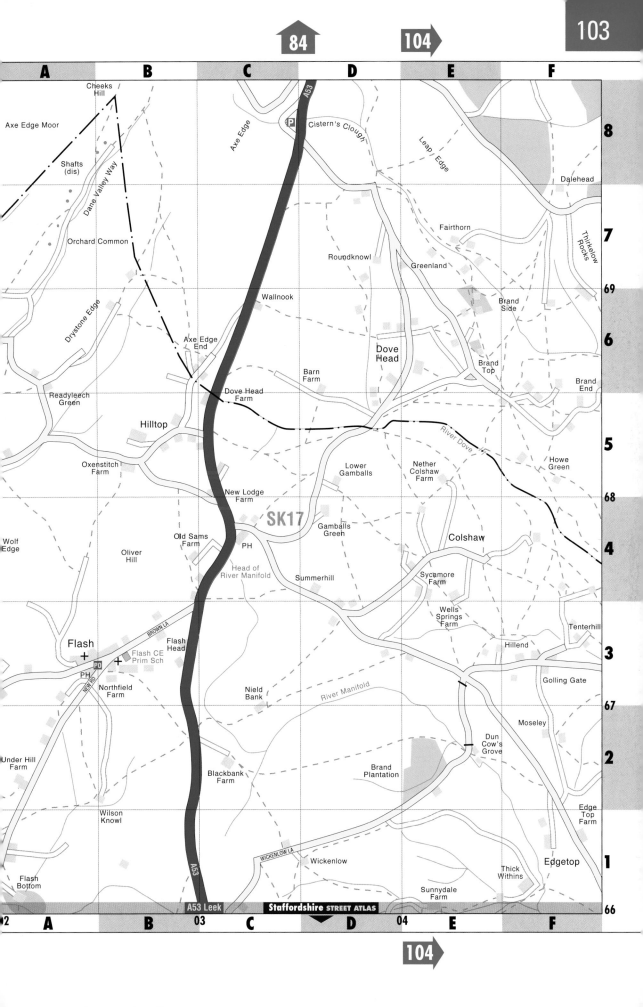

A   B   C   D   E   F

Cheeks
Hill

Axe Edge Moor

8

Shafts
(dis)

Dane Valley Way

Axe Edge

Cistern's Clough

Leap Edge

Dalehead

7

Fairthorn

Thirkelow
Rocks

Orchard Common

Roundknowl

Greenland

69

Drystone Edge

Wallnook

Brand
Side

6

Axe Edge
End

Dove
Head

Brand
Top

Brand
End

Readyleech
Green

Dove Head
Farm

Barn
Farm

Brand
End

Hilltop

River Dove

5

Oxenstitch
Farm

Lower
Gamballs

Nether
Colshaw
Farm

Howe
Green

New Lodge
Farm

68

Wolf
Edge

SK17

Gamballs
Green

Colshaw

4

Old Sams
Farm

PH

Oliver
Hill

Head of
River Manifold

Summerhill

Sycamore
Farm

Wells
Springs
Farm

Tenterhill

Flash

Flash
Head

Hillend

3

Flash CE
Prim Sch

Golling Gate

PH

PO

Northfield
Farm

BROWN LA

NEW RD

Nield
Bank

River Manifold

67

Moseley

Under Hill
Farm

Dun
Cow's
Grove

2

Brand
Plantation

Blackbank
Farm

Wilson
Knowl

Edge
Top
Farm

Flash
Bottom

WICKENLOW LA

Wickenlow

Edgetop

1

Thick
Withins

Sunnydale
Farm

A53

Staffordshire STREET ATLAS

66

A   B   C   D   E   F

02   03   C   04

103
85

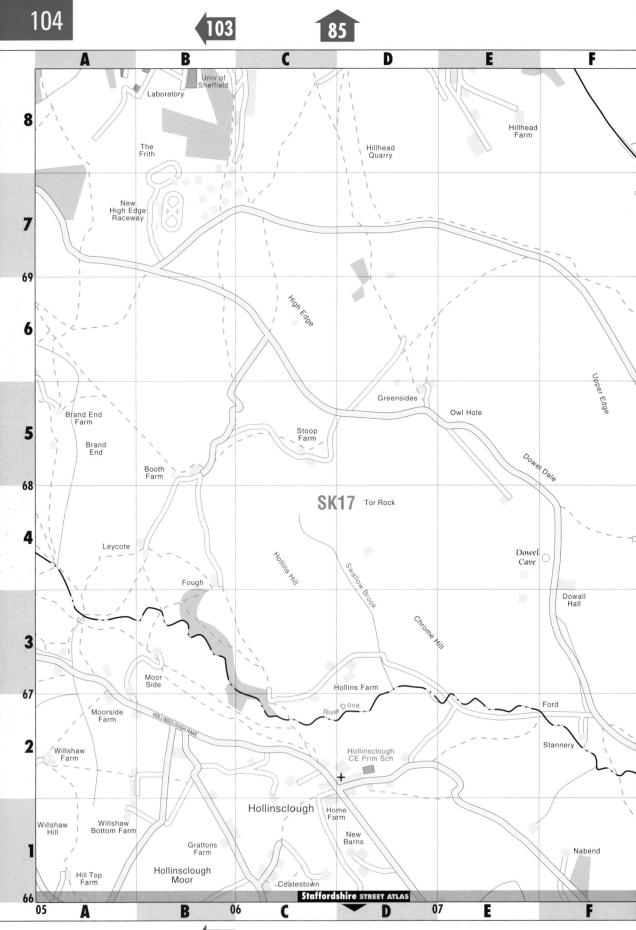

103

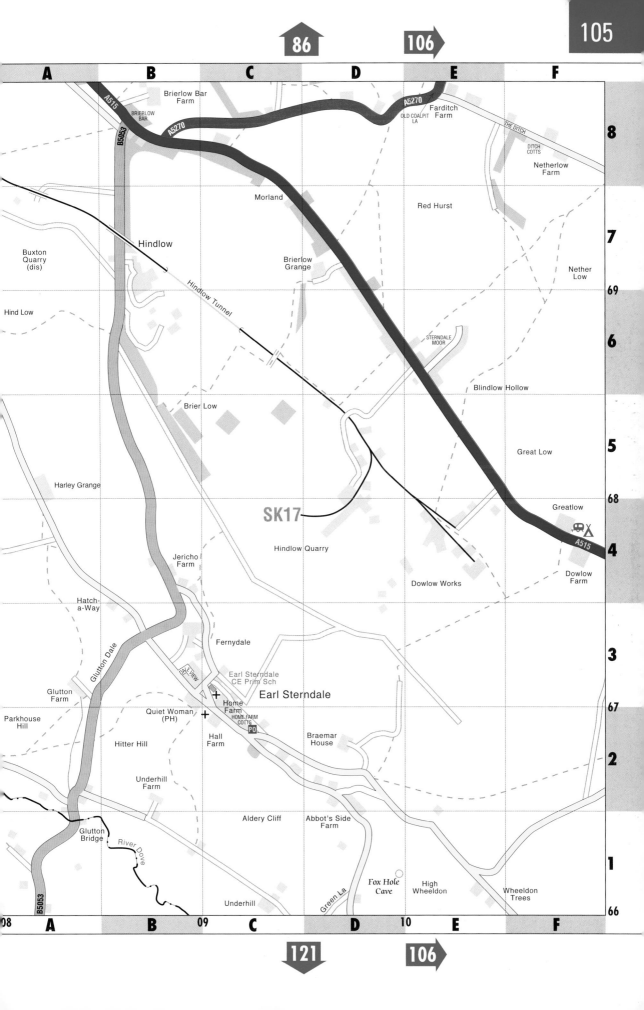

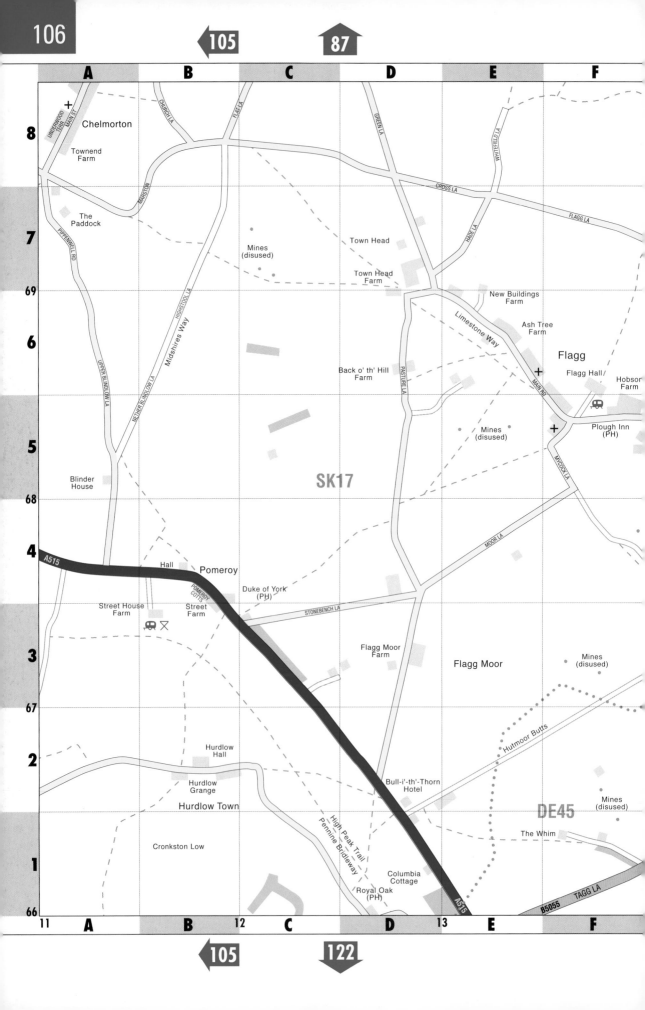

A   B   C   D   E   F

8 Chelmorton
Townend Farm
The Paddock

UNDERWOOD TERR
MAIN ST
CHURCH LA
FLEET LA
GREEN LA
CROSS LA
WHITFIELD LA
FLAGG LA

7 Mines (disused)
Town Head
Town Head Farm
New Buildings Farm

69 Limestone Way
Ash Tree Farm

6 Back o' th' Hill Farm
Flagg
Flagg Hall
Hobson Farm

PIPPENWELL RD
MARSTON
HIGHSTOOL LA
Midshires Way
NETHER BLINDLOW LA
UPPER BLINDLOW LA
PASTURE LA
MAIN RD

Mines (disused)
Plough Inn (PH)

5 Blinder House
MYCOCK LA

68 SK17

MOOR LA

4 A515
Hall   Pomeroy
Duke of York (PH)
Street House Farm
Street Farm
POMEROY COTTS
STONEBENCH LA

Flagg Moor Farm

3 Flagg Moor
Mines (disused)
Hutmoor Butts

67

2 Hurdlow Hall
Hurdlow Grange
Hurdlow Town
Bull-i'-th'-Thorn Hotel
DE45
Mines (disused)

Cronkston Low
High Peak Trail
Pennine Bridleway
Columbia Cottage
The Whim

1 Royal Oak (PH)
A515
TAGG LA
B5055

66
11   A   B   12   C   D   13   E   F

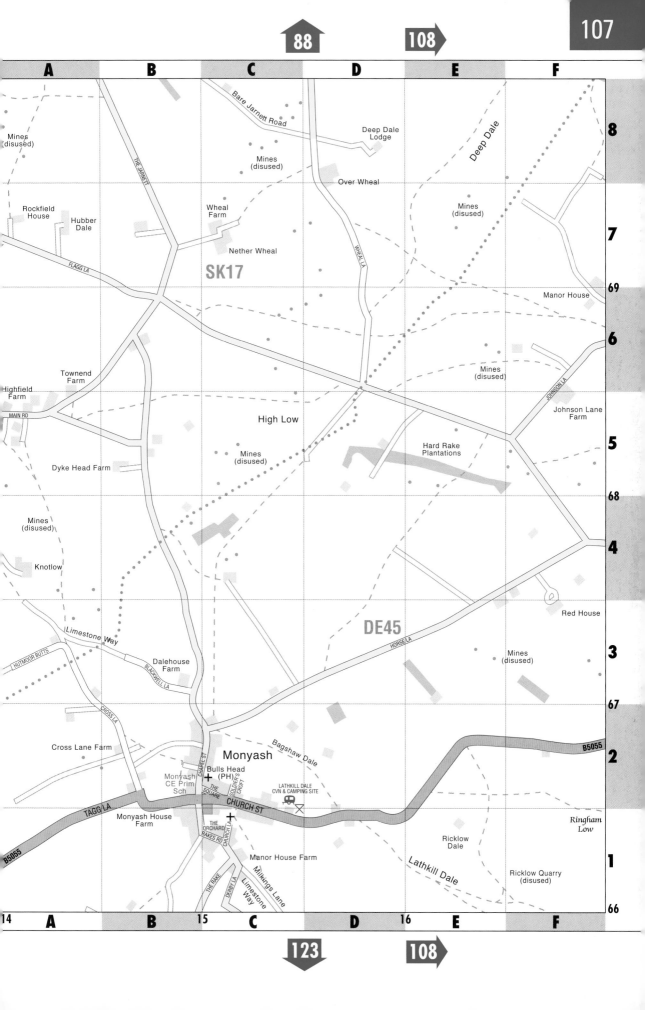

Mines (disused)

Bare Jarnett Road

Deep Dale Lodge

Deep Dale

8

Mines (disused)

Over Wheal

Rockfield House

Hubber Dale

Wheal Farm

7

THE JARNETT

FLAGG LA

Nether Wheal

WHEAL LA

Manor House

69

SK17

6

Highfield Farm

Townend Farm

High Low

Mines (disused)

Johnson Lane Farm

JOHNSON LA

MAIN RD

Hard Rake Plantations

5

Dyke Head Farm

Mines (disused)

68

Mines (disused)

Knotlow

4

Red House

Limestone Way

DE45

Mines (disused)

3

HUTMOOR BUTTS

Dalehouse Farm

BLACKWELL LA

HORSE LA

67

CROSS LA

B5055

Cross Lane Farm

Bagshaw Dale

Monyash

2

Monyash CE Prim Sch

Bulls Head (PH)

CHAPEL ST

SOLDIER'S CROFT

LATHKILL DALE CVN & CAMPING SITE

TAGG LA

THE SQUARE

CHURCH ST

Ringham Low

Monyash House Farm

THE ORCHARD

RAKES RD

CHURCH LA

Manor House Farm

Milkings Lane Limestone Way

Ricklow Dale

1

B5055

THE RAKE

DERBY LA

Lathkill Dale

Ricklow Quarry (disused)

66

14

15

16

A   B   C   D   E   F

8

Great Shacklow Wood

Weir

River Wye

Little Shacklow Wood

I HIGHFIELD
VICARAGE LA
HILL CROSS
GREAVES LA
HALL END LA
A6020
B6465
A6020

TRINITY CL
FENNEL ST
CHURCH ST
GREATS
PH
CHERRY CL
BETTY LA
NEW RD
(BASLOW RD)

THE DUKE S DR
A6020
A6
BUXTON RD

BUXTON RD
MOUNT PLEASANT
CORNBROOK 1
HILLMORTON 2
MILLSTONE LA
JOHN BANK LA

Ashford in the Water

Mill

7

Mast

Arrock Plantation

69

Rose Farm

Opencast Workings

6

Johnson La

Top Farm

PH

Sheldon

Lower Farm

Woodbine Farm

Opencast Workings

Dirtlow Farm

Dirtlow Plantations

Cowden Plantations

Kirk Dale

5

Magpie Mine (disused)

Truebell Lane

68

DE45

Opencast Workings

Green Cowden Farm

4

B5055

Shafts (dis)

Bole Hill

Bole Hill Farm

3

Blores Barn Farm

Green La

Melbourne Farm

67

Haddon Grove Farm

2

B5055

Organ Ground

Opencast Workings

Mandale Rake

Haddon Grove

Mines (dis)

1

Haddon Grove Farms

Twin Dales

HADDON GROVE FARM CAMP SITE

66

Weir

River Lathkill

17 A   B 18 C   D 19 E   F

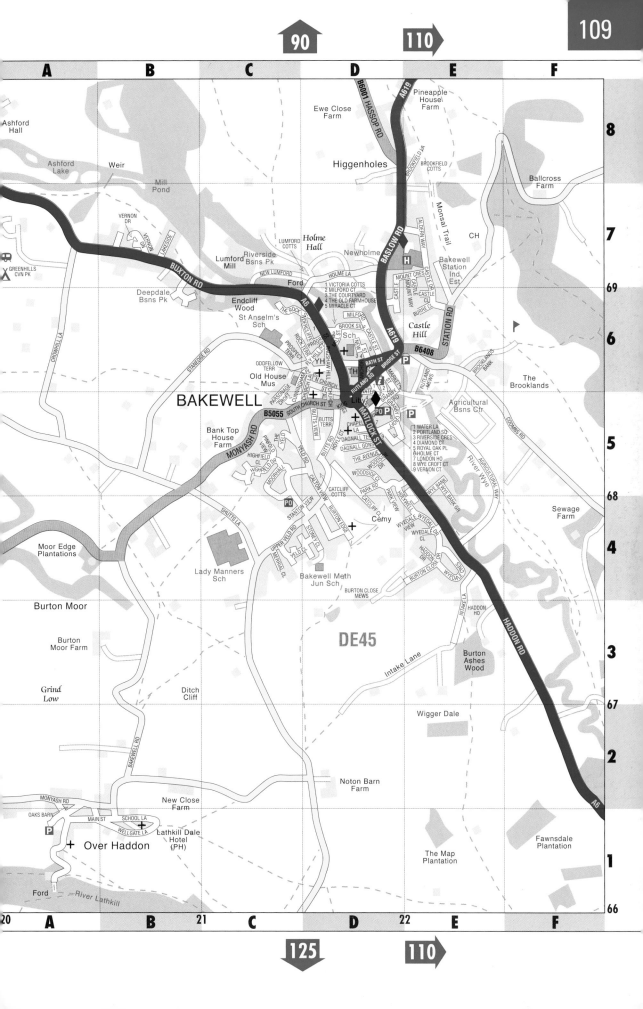

109
91

A   B   C   D   E   F

8

CAVENDISH FLATS

Edensor

B6012

Chatsworth Park

River Derwent

HANDLEY LA

Edensor Forest Nursery

7

Maud's Plantation

Lindup Low

69

Moatless Plantation

New Piece Wood

6

LONG GALLERY

Calton Plantations

Calton Houses

Calton Pastures

P

B6012

5

Lees Wood

DE4

Manners Wood

Calton Lees Farm

Calton Lees

68

DE45

COOMBS RD

4

Coombs Farm

Beech Square Plantation

Lindop Wood

Derwent Valley Heritage Way

Cook Wood

Lees Moor Wood

3

Haddon Park Farm

Rowsleymoor Wood

Bank Wood

Shadyside Plantation

67

PARK RD

Bowling Green Farm

2

Aaron Hole Plantation

Bouns Corner

Shay Knowl

Haddon Park

PARK LA

Sallowbed Plantation

A6

Haddon Hall

River Wye

1

Parkside Wood

CHURCH LA

VICARAGE CROFT
DEVONSHIRE DR 1
SCHOFIELD CT 2
MIDLAND COTTS 3

River Derwent

B6012

RIVERBANK
SUNNY BANK
HINCKLEY CT

CHATSWORTH RD

Haddon Barn

A6

ST KATHERINES

Peak Village
Outlet Sh Ctr

66

23   A   B   24   C   D   25   E   F

109
126

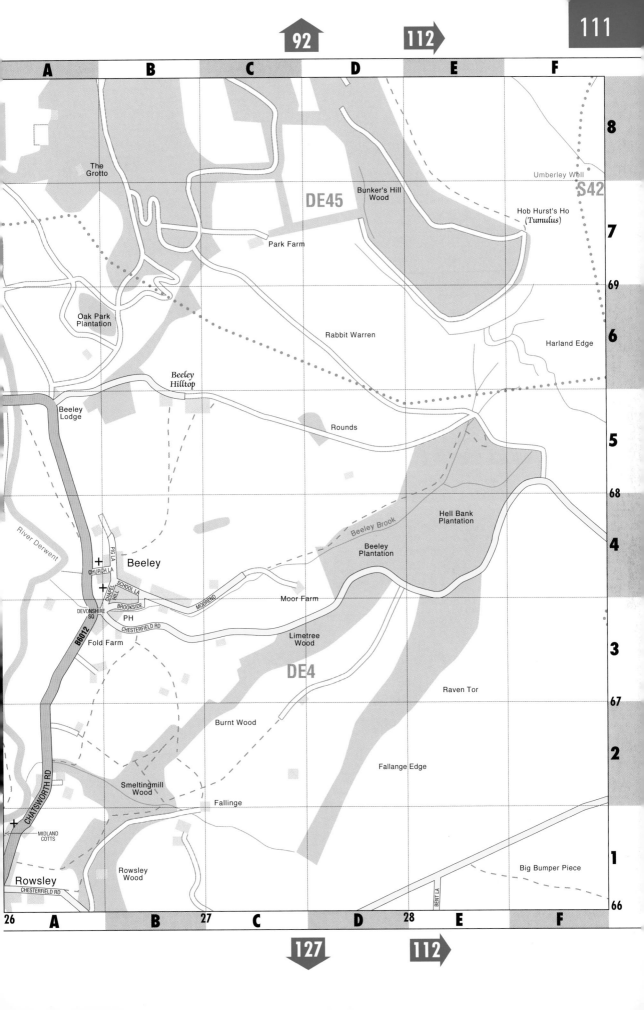

A B C D E F

8

The
Grotto

DE45

Bunker's Hill
Wood

Umberley Well
S42

Hob Hurst's Ho
(Tumulus)

Park Farm

7

69

Oak Park
Plantation

Rabbit Warren

Harland Edge

6

Beeley
Hilltop

Beeley
Lodge

Rounds

5

68

Beeley Brook

Hell Bank
Plantation

4

River Derwent

PIG LA
CHURCH LA
Beeley
SCHOOL LA
CHAPEL HILL
MOOREND
Beeley
Plantation

Moor Farm

BROOKSIDE
DEVONSHIRE
SQ
PH
CHESTERFIELD RD

B6012
Fold Farm
Limetree
Wood

3

DE4

Raven Tor

67

Burnt Wood

2

Fallange Edge

CHATSWORTH RD
Smeltingmill
Wood

Fallinge

MIDLAND
COTTS

1

Big Bumper Piece

Rowsley
Wood

Rowsley

CHESTERFIELD RD

BENT LA

66

26 A B 27 C D 28 E F

← 111
93

A B C D E F

8

Rodknoll Farm

Mast

RODKNOLL LA

LOADSHEAD LA

Loads Head Farm

Loads House Farm

SYDA LA

CLAYPIT LA

Umberley Sick

Upper Loads

7

Well Lane Farm

Syda Farm

WELL LA

LOADS RD

69

S42

LONGSIDE RD

6

DE45

Hipper Sick

Longside Moor

Beeley Moor

Slagmill Plantation

Harland Sick

DE4

5

Arkwright Plantation

Lamb Pasture

Harewood Grange

68

Harewood House Farm

4

Harewood Grange Farm

Millstone Sick

Harewood Moor

3

BEELEY LA

S45

67

2

Moor Hall Farm

B5057

ALICEHEAD RD

Screetham House Farm

Gladwin's Mark

Mast

DE4

Sitchs Plantation

Gladwin's Mark Wood

FLASH LA

SCREETHAM LA

Roach Wood

PEASUNHURST LA

B5057

1

Sitchs

Roach Farm

Peasunhurst

Upper Dogkennel Plantation

66

29   A   B   30   C   D   31   E   F

← 111
128

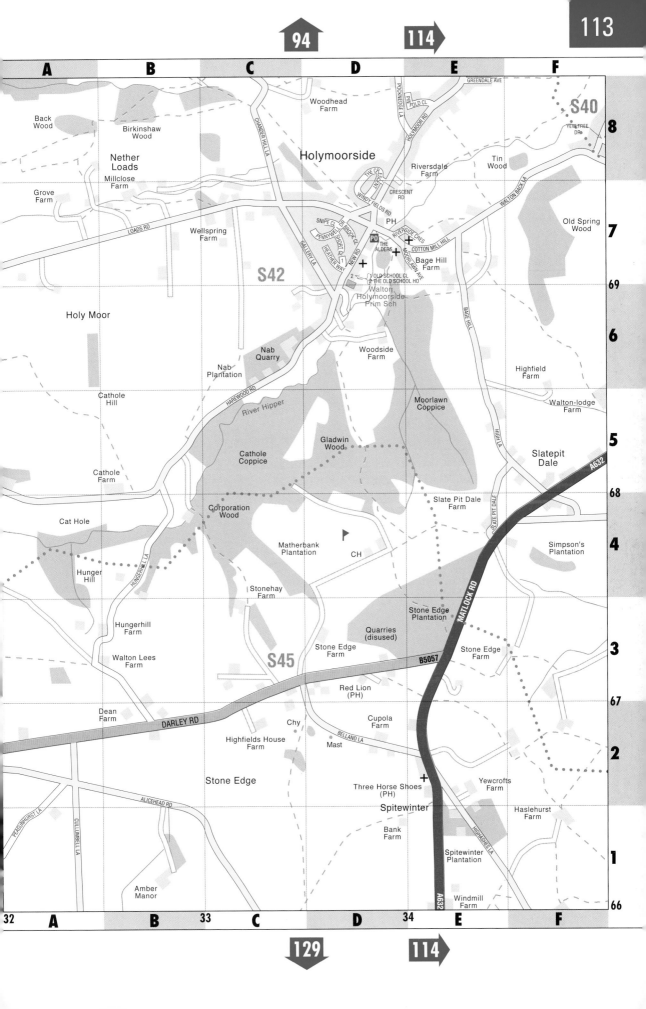

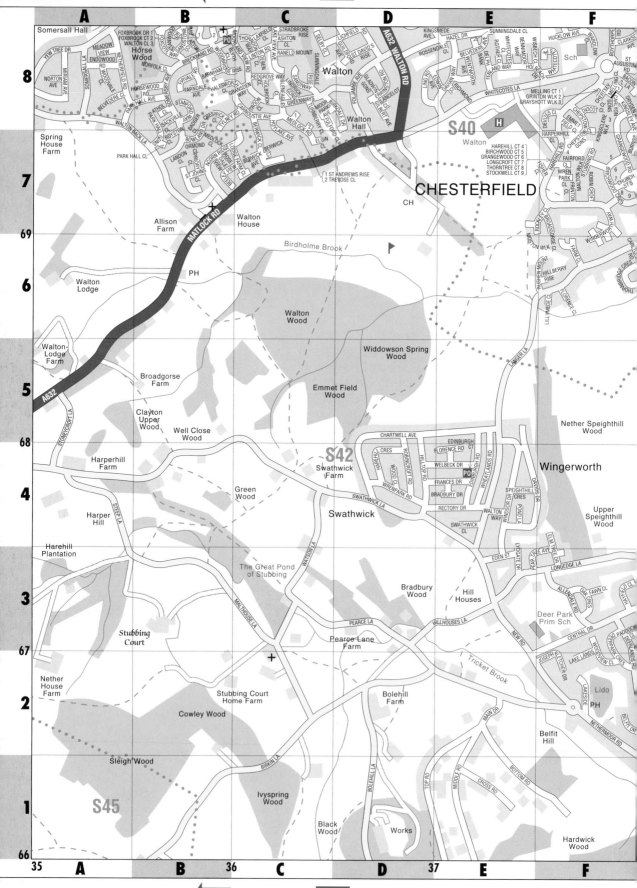

A B C D E F

8
Nether House
Farm
CALOW LA
HALL FLASH LA
Calow
Green
Calowgreen
Farm
BACK LA
MOOR LA
B6425
Spoil Heap
Sutton Lane
Farm

7
Woodnook
Farm
SUTTON LA
Bull
Paddock
Farm

69
HASSOCKY LA
Calow Brook
S44
Rock La
Hall Farm

6
Sutton Springs
Wood
ROCK LA
Yewtree
Farm

A617
S41
Springwood
Farm

5
Muster Brook

RAILWAY
COTTS
Hill
Farm
B6425
SHIRE LA

68
B6039
Bond's
Main
Temple
Normanton Prim
Sch
POSTMANS LA
S42

4
Temple Normanton
Bsns Pk
SPRINGWOOD ST
ELM ST
SUTTON
VIEW
High House
Farm

Grassmoor
Country Park
Cemy
CHURCH LA
Temple
Normanton
A617

3
✠
Philadelphia
BIRKIN LA
CHURCH FARM MEWS
MANSFIELD RD
Musterbrook
Bridge

67

2
High Top
Poultry
Farm
CHESTERFIELD RD
Holmewood
Bsns Pk
Williamthorpe
Ind Pk
Williamthorpe Ponds
(Nature Reserve)
LILAC CL
MOOR DRI CRES
GORSE
BANK
HEATHER CL
SLACK LA
Heath
Prim
Sch
BRAMBLE CL
BRACKEN AVE

Lings
Farm
ENTERPRISE DR WAY
TIPTON WAY
MOORE CL
WOODSOME
PK
Holmewood
Ind Pk
PARK RD
Sewage
Works
FERN CL
HEATH RD
A6175

1
CHESTERFIELD
RD
B6039
SHELLEY ST
FENNYSON ST
SHARL ST
SHAKESPEARE ST
LAWRENCE ST
DICKENS DR
MASEFIELD AVE
WOOD
ST
QUEENS
WLK
Pavilion
Workshops
Works
Holmewood
QUEENSWAY
CAVENDISH CL
DUKES CL
DEVONSHIRE TERR
RAILWAY
COTTS
COMPTON ST
HUNLOKE
RD
HARDWICK
VIEW RD
ASTWITH CL
STANSBY
Holmewood
Est

66
41 A 42 B C 43 D E F
B6038
P

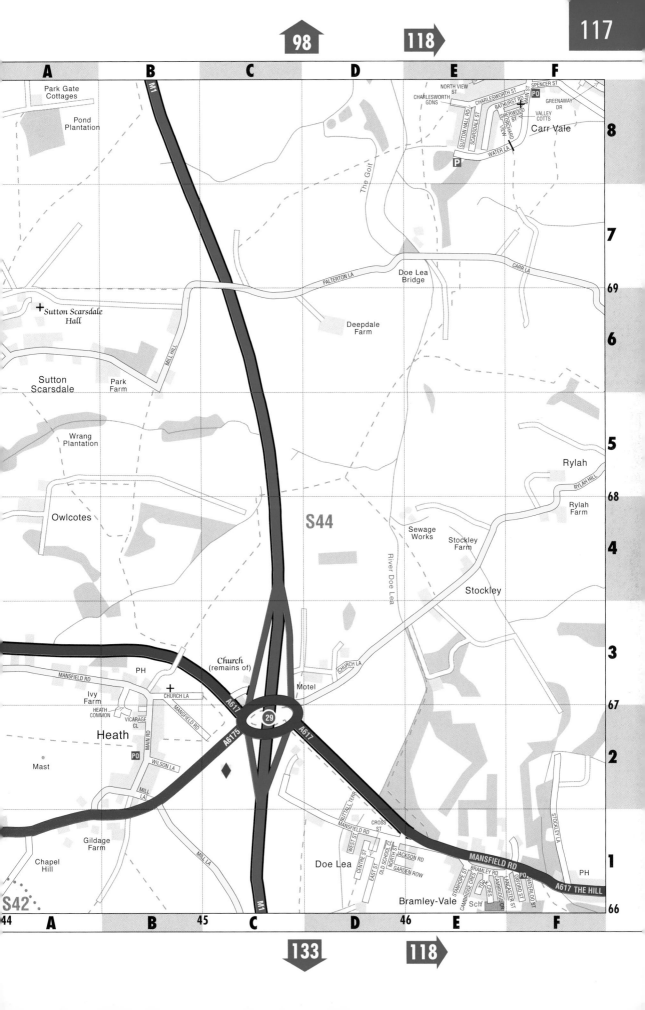

GREENAWAY DR
BROOKFIELD RD
MEADOW VALLEY RD
FAIRFIELD RD
SPITAL CL
VIVADALE DR
RIDGEDALE RD
NEW STATION
EASTERN AVE
HUDSON RD
CAVENDISH RD
CAVENDISH RD
PORTLAND AVE
A632
ST LAWRENCE AVE
LANGWITH RD
B6417

CROMWELL RD 1
POLYFIELDS LA 2
TOWER CRES 3
OWLCOTES VIEW
STOCKLEY VIEW
CRICH VIEW
SUTTON VIEW
VICTORIA ST
MOUNT
NESBIT ST
MIDDLE ST
SELWYN ST
WELLS ST
P
PH
PO
Hillstown

DARWOOD LA
WEST VIEW
CASTLE S
PLEASANT AVE
Hillstown Bsns Ctr

The Meadows

MOOR LA A63

Lidget La
Fox Hill
LANGWITH RD

8

ROTHERHAM RD

7

69

The Elms Farm
CARR LA
CASTLE VIEW
STEEL'S LA
THIRTEEN ROW
PENNINE VIEW
BACK LA

Scarcliffe Prim Sch
DEVONSHIRE COTTS
PH
PO
MAIN ST
WOOD LA
STATION RD

6

S44
PH
EAST ST
GAG LA
MANSFIELD RD
Meadowspot Farm

Scarcliffe

NORTHFIELD LA
MANSFIELD RD

Palterton
Palterton Prim Sch

5

RYLAH HILL
MAIN ST
TRAMWAY TERR

Poulterwell La
Birch Hill Plantation
River Poulter

68

LING LA

4

Fox Covert

Roseland Wood

NG20

ROTHERHAM RD
Archaeological Trail

3

67

Lanes Farm
LOSK LA

NG19

2

Terrace Wood
GLAPWELL LA

LOSK CNR
Water La
WATER LA
Houghton Bassett
Hall Farm
Elm Tree Farm
GREER LA
GREEN LA
Houghton Felley
Stony Houghton

Car Wood

1

BEECH CRES 1
APPLECROFT CL 2
HAWTHORN AVE 3
ROWTHORNE LA 4
THE PINFOLD
BACK LA
CEDAR CL
PARK AVE
PH
BLACKSMITHS CL
Glapwell
B6417

66

A617
THE HILL
HILL ST
1 2 3
A617 MANSFIELD RD

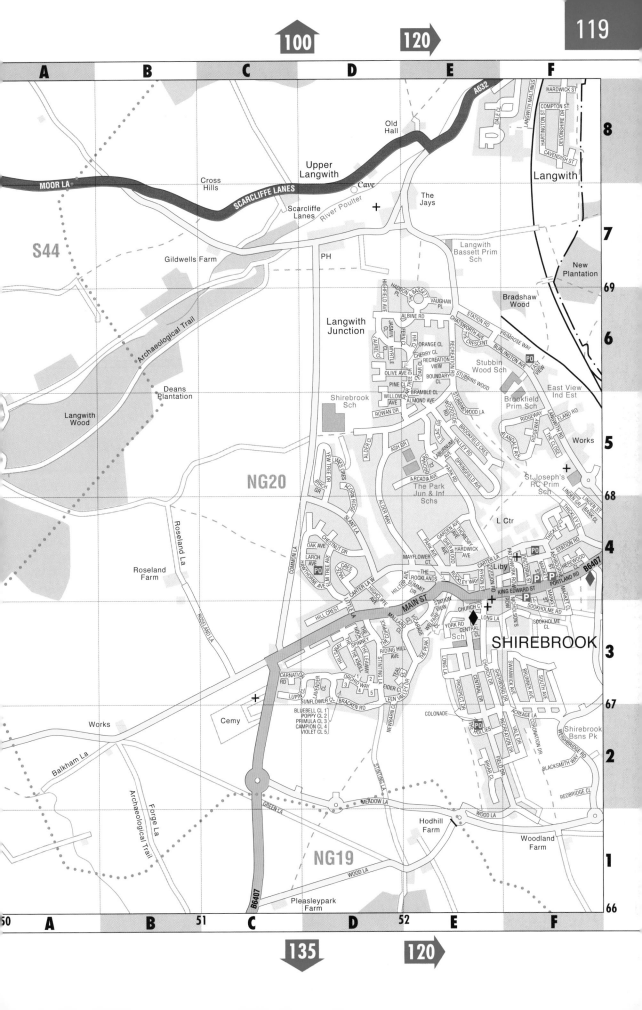

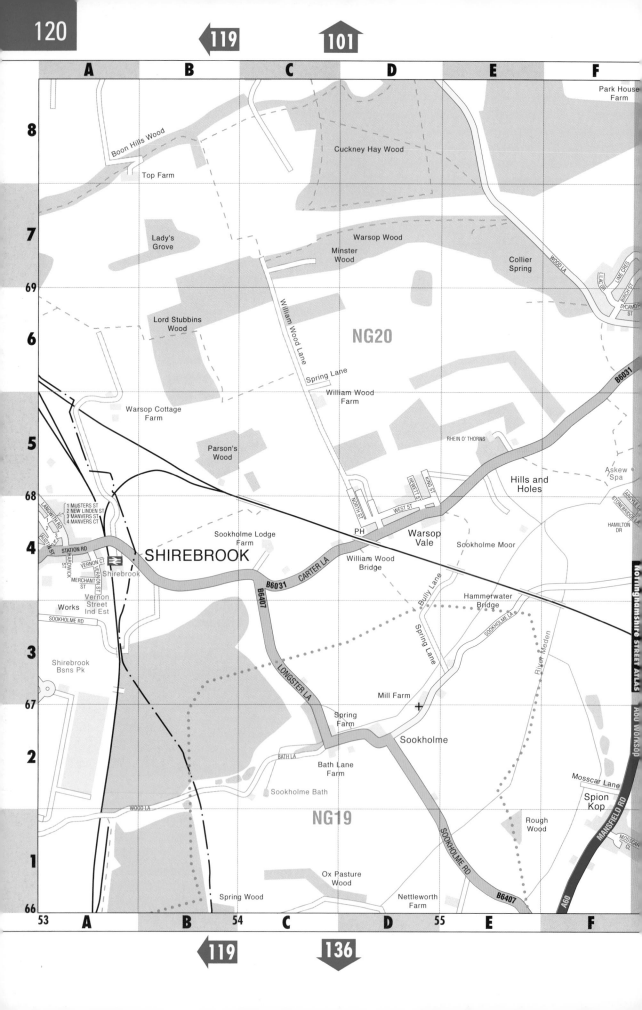

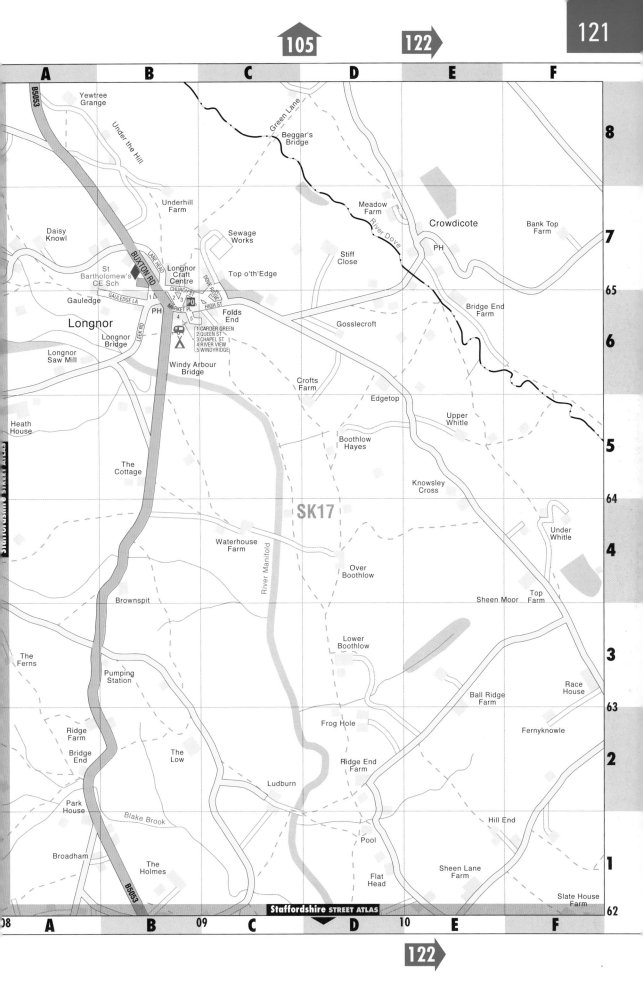

A B C D E F

8
7
65
6
5
64
4
3
63
2
1
62

Yewtree Grange

Under the Hill

Green Lane

Beggar's Bridge

Underhill Farm

Meadow Farm

River Dove

Crowdicote

PH

Bank Top Farm

Daisy Knowl

St Bartholomew's CE Sch

BUXTON RD

LANE HEAD

Longnor Craft Centre

Sewage Works

Top o'th'Edge

Stiff Close

CHURCH ST

DOVE RIDGE

Gauledge

GAULEDGE LA

1

PH

PO

MARKET PL

HIGH ST

Folds End

Bridge End Farm

Longnor

LEEK RD

2 3
4 5

1 CARDER GREEN
2 QUEEN ST
3 CHAPEL ST
4 RIVER VIEW
5 WINDYRIDGE

Gosslecroft

Longnor Bridge

Longnor Saw Mill

Windy Arbour Bridge

Crofts Farm

Edgetop

Upper Whitle

Heath House

Boothlow Hayes

The Cottage

Knowsley Cross

SK17

Under Whitle

Waterhouse Farm

River Manifold

Over Boothlow

Sheen Moor

Top Farm

Brownspit

Lower Boothlow

The Ferns

Pumping Station

Ball Ridge Farm

Race House

Ridge Farm

The Low

Frog Hole

Fernyknowle

Bridge End

Ludburn

Ridge End Farm

Park House

Blake Brook

Hill End

Broadham

The Holmes

Pool

Flat Head

Sheen Lane Farm

Slate House Farm

B5063

A B C D E F

08 09 10

← 121
106

A B C D E F

8

Sparklow

Needham
Grange

Cronkston
Grange

Mines
(dis)

TAGG LA

A515

B5055
Endmoor

High
Needham

7

DE45

Cronkston
Lodge

Clemonseats
Plantation

Middle Street
Farm

65

Waggon Low

6

Mine
(dis)

Midshires Way

A515

Cotesfield

5

Mosey Low

SK17

64

Custard Field
Farm

Pilsbury Castle
Hills

4

Pilsbury
Lodge

Sand
Pit

Broadmeadow
Hall

3

Pilsbury

Vincent
House

River Dove

63

Parks
Barn

Mines
(dis)

2

Sheen
Hill

Carder Low

Long Dale

High Sheen
Farm

HIDE LA

1

Ludwell
Farm

Mines
(dis)

Harris Close

62

11 A B 12 C D 13 E F

← 121
137

107
124

A **B** **C** **D** **E** **F**

Barrowstones Lane

Milkings Lane

Fern Dale

8

Summerhill
Farm

Limestone Way

One Ash
Grange Farm

7

Highlow Farm

DERBY LA.

65

Mines
(dis)

Opencast Workings

DE45

6

Bruntmoor

THE RAKE

Cales Dale

Mines
(dis)

Cales
Farm

Moscar Farm

Benty
Grange

Prospect Mine
(dis)

5

LONG RAKE

64

Crookdale
Plantation

Darley
Farm

4

Parsley
Hay

Upper Oldhams
Farm

Arbor Low
Henge

New Vincent
Farm

Gib Hill

Rookery
Plantation

Pennine Bridleway

Gibhill
Plantation

3

Middleton Common

63

Blake Moor

SK17

2

Midshires Way

Newhaven
Lodge

Tissington Trail

Lean Low

Blakemoor
Plantation

Green Lane

1

Leanlow
Farm

A515

62

14 **A** **B** 15 **C** **D** 16 **E** **F**

138
124

A　　B　　C　　D　　E　　F

8

Palmerston Wood

Lathkill Dale

River Lathkill

Meadow Place
Wood

Low Wood

Lathkill Dale
National Nature
Reserve

Mines
(dis)

Calling Low Dale

Bee Low Wood

7

Cales Dale

65

Calling Low

Limestone Way

6

Bee Low

BACK LA

MOOR LA

Low Moor
Plantation

P

✕

5

Mine

Mines
(dis)

64

Works

LONG RAKE

Lomberdale
Hall

DE45

Crossflat
Plantation

4

River Bradford

Castle
Farm

Greenseats
Plantation

✚

Castle
(remains of)

3

Middleton Common

Bushey
Wood

Flax Dale

Middleton

THE PINFOLD

✚

THE
SQUARE

Thorntree

RAKE LA

Rake
Wood

63

Mere Farm

Middleton
Hall

WEADOW LA

2

Green Lane

WHITFIELD LA

Woodside
Farm

1

Kenslow
Farm

Kenslow
Wood

62

Little Rookery
Plantation

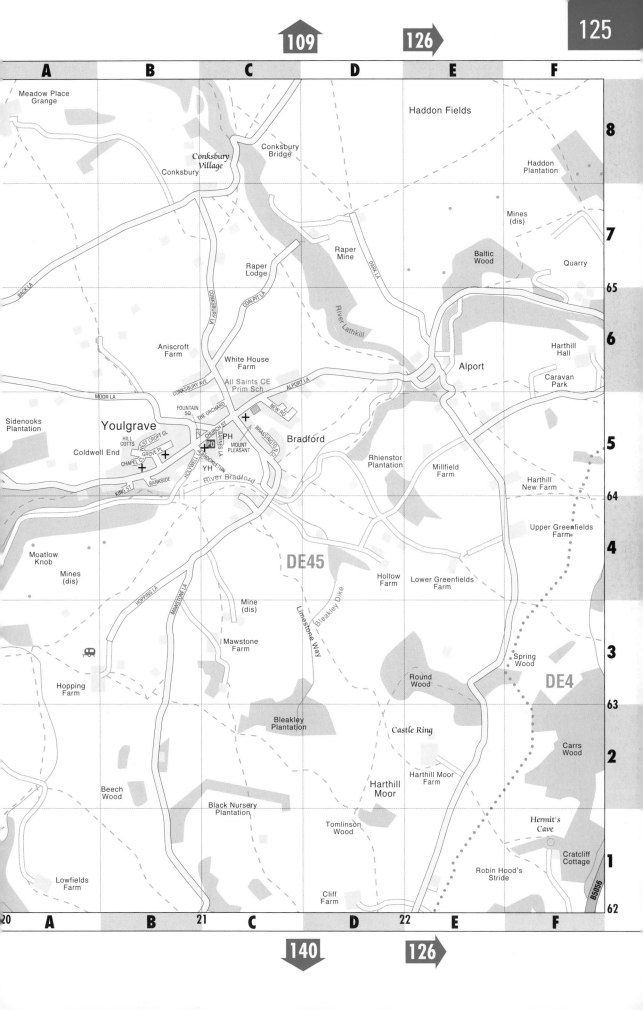

A B C D E F

8

Meadow Place
Grange

Haddon Fields

Conksbury
Village
Conksbury Bridge

Conksbury

Haddon
Plantation

7

Mines
(dis)

BACK LA

Raper
Mine

Raper
Lodge

CONKSBURY LA

COALPIT LA

DARK LA

River Lathkill

Baltic
Wood

Quarry

65

6

Aniscroft
Farm

White House
Farm

All Saints CE
Prim Sch

Alport

Harthill
Hall

Caravan
Park

MOOR LA

CONKSBURY AVE

ALPORT LA

Sidenooks
Plantation

Youlgrave

FOUNTAIN
SQ

THE ORCHARD

NEW RD

Coldwell End

HILL
COTTS

WEST CROFT CL

GROVE PL

CHAPEL CL

CHURCH ST

BARNES LA

PH

PO

MOUNT
PLEASANT

BRASSINGTON LA

Bradford

Rhienstor
Plantation

Millfield
Farm

Harthill
New Farm

5

KING ST

BANKSIDE

HOLYWELL LA

BROOKLETON

YH

River Bradford

64

Moatlow
Knob

Mines
(dis)

DE45

Hollow
Farm

Lower Greenfields
Farm

Upper Greenfields
Farm

4

HOPPING LA

MAWSTONE LA

Mine
(dis)

Limestone Way

Bleakley Dike

Spring
Wood

DE4

3

Hopping
Farm

Mawstone
Farm

Round
Wood

63

Bleakley
Plantation

Castle Ring

Carrs
Wood

2

Beech
Wood

Harthill Moor
Farm

Black Nursery
Plantation

Harthill
Moor

Tomlinson
Wood

Hermit's
Cave

Cratcliff
Cottage

1

Lowfields
Farm

Cliff
Farm

Robin Hood's
Stride

B5056

62

20 A B 21 C D 22 E F

125
110

A   B   C   D   E   F

CHATSWORTH RD

PARK LA

A6

B5056

8

Nutseats Quarry (dis)

Wye Farm

WYE TERR

Cauldwell's Mill & Craft Ctr

PO

CHURCH LA

DALE RD N

OLD STATION CL

SCHOOL LA

Rowsley CE Prim Sch

DALE RD

Shafts (dis)

Pickering Wood

Rowsley

River Wye

River Derwent

STANTONHALL LA

Dove House Farm

PEAKTOR LA

7

Oxclose Wood

River Lathkill

Sewage Farm

Congreave Farm

The Plantation

The Plantation

Peak Tor

WOODHOUSE RD

DE45

Congreave

Pilhough

65

Bowers Hall

Pilhough Farm

6

Tolls Wood

Smithy Wood

PILHOUGH LA

Beighton Houses

Holly Wood

Park Farm

Stanton-in-Peak CE Prim Sch

Sheepwalk Wood

Stanton Woodhouse Farm

PILHOUGH RD

Stanton Woodhouse

5

The Lodge

PH

MIDDLE ST

SCHOOL LA

Stanton in Peak

THE GREEN

THE LANE

PARK LA

Stanton Hall

DE4

64

Stoney Ley Wood

4

Mast

The Scraggs

Hillcarr Wood

Stanton Moor Quarries (dis)

King Stone

Nine Ladies Stone Circle

Tower

Stoney Ley Lodge

BIRCHOVER RD

3

Cow Close Farm

Stanton Moor Plantation

LEES RD

Stanton Lees

63

Black Knowle Plantation

Bee Hill

Eagle Tor

Warrencarr

2

Mires Farm

Stanton Park Quarry

Hill Wood

Hillcarr Farm

Warrencarr Farm

B5056

CLIFF LA

THE HILLS

Dungeon Plantation

Birchover Quarry

1

EAGLE TERR

Barn Farm

Birchover

PH

THE GREEN

WELLCROFT

KEELING LA

UPPER TOWN LA

BARTON HILL

BARN FARM CVN & CAMPING SITE

P

BRADLEY CL

ANNIE'S CL

Brookfield Farm

62

23   A   B   24   C   D   25   E   F

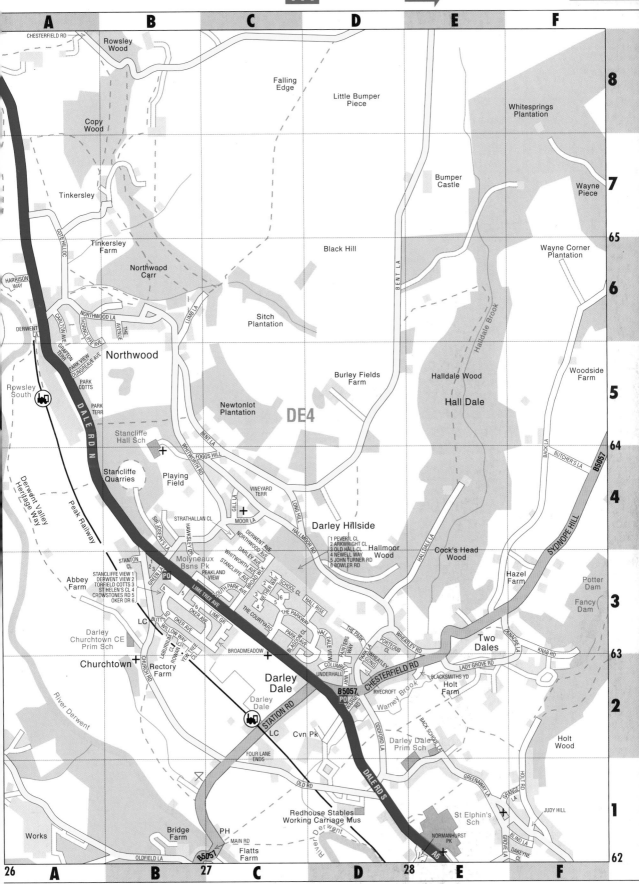

A   B   C   D   E   F

8

Darley Forest
Grange

B5057

Fishpond
Wood

Wilkin
House

7

FLASH LA

BACK LA

Nine Acre
Piece

SCREETHAM LA

Darwin Forest
Holiday
Country
Park

Mast

North
Brittain

S45

HODGE LA

Hodgelane Brook

65

6

Seventy Acre
Plantation

Burnt
Piece

Moor
House

Shooters-Lea
Farm

Nursery
Farm

Flash
Dam

Upper Moor

5

SYDNOPE HILL

Matlock
Farm Park

JAGGERS LA

Rushley
Lodge

Grouse Cottage
Farm

B5057

SYDNOPE
HALL

DE4

64

Black Brook

4

Sydnope Brook

The Warren

Farley
Moor

Middle
Moor

Sydnope
Stand

Clarke's
Plantation

FARLEY LA

3

Tax Farm

63

Matlock
Moor

2

Cuckoostone
Grange

CUCKOOSTONE LA

Cuckoostone
House

SANDY LA

1

Farley
Farm

FARLEY HILL

Farley

Cuckoo
Stone

Bottom
Farm

Cuckoostone
Dale

A632

62

29   A   B   30   C   D   31   E   F

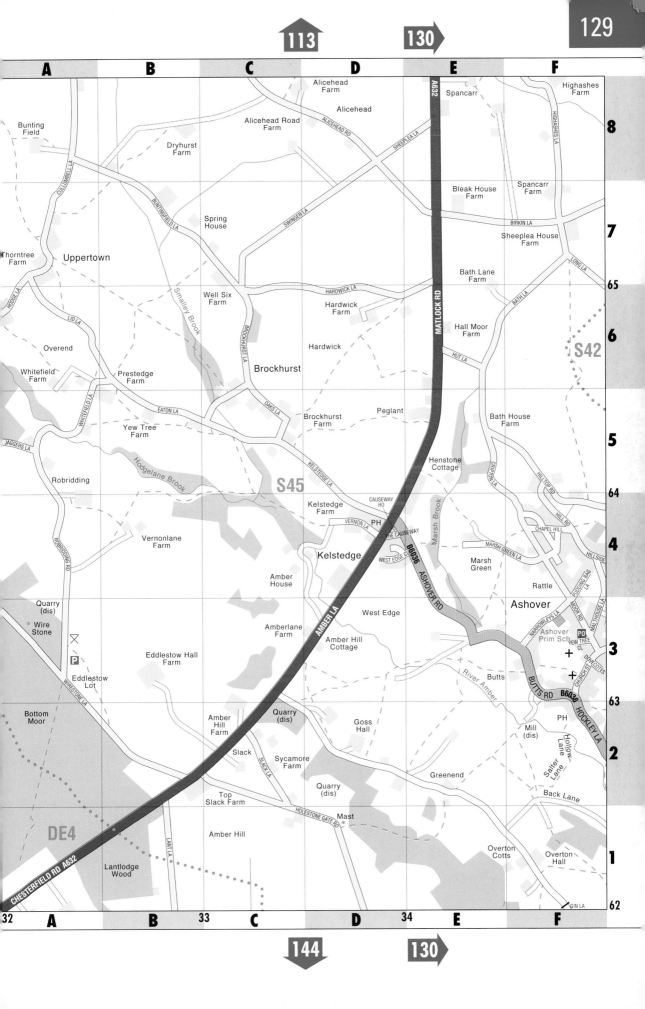

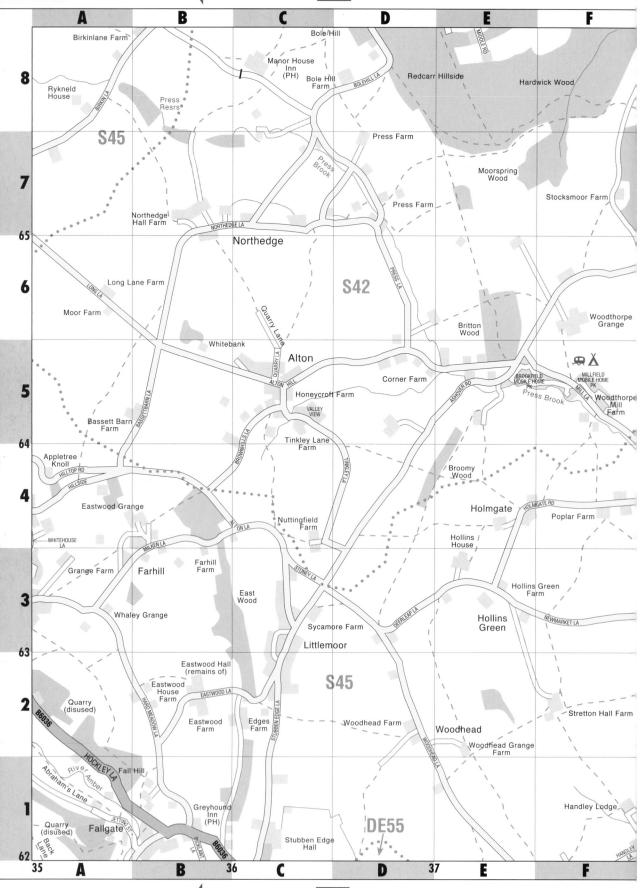

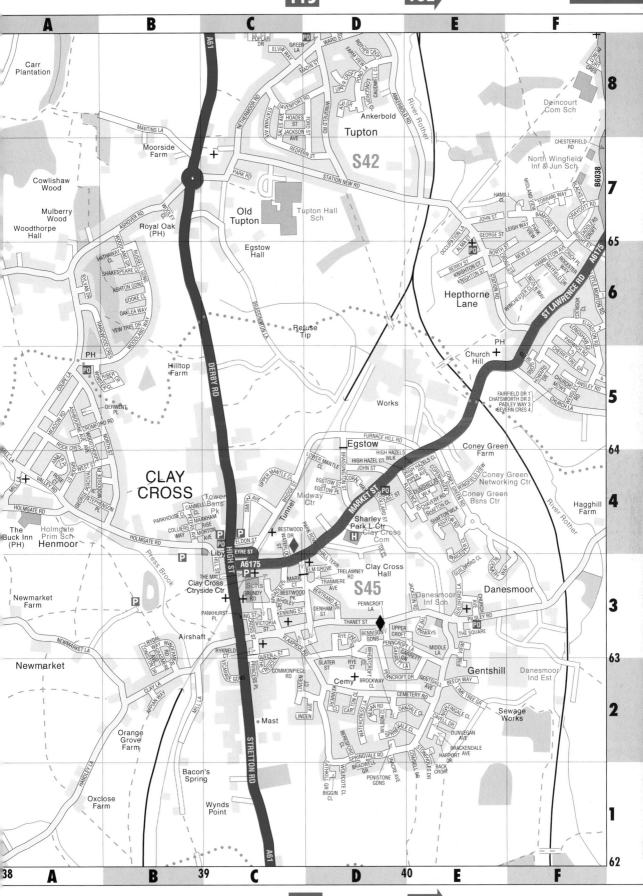

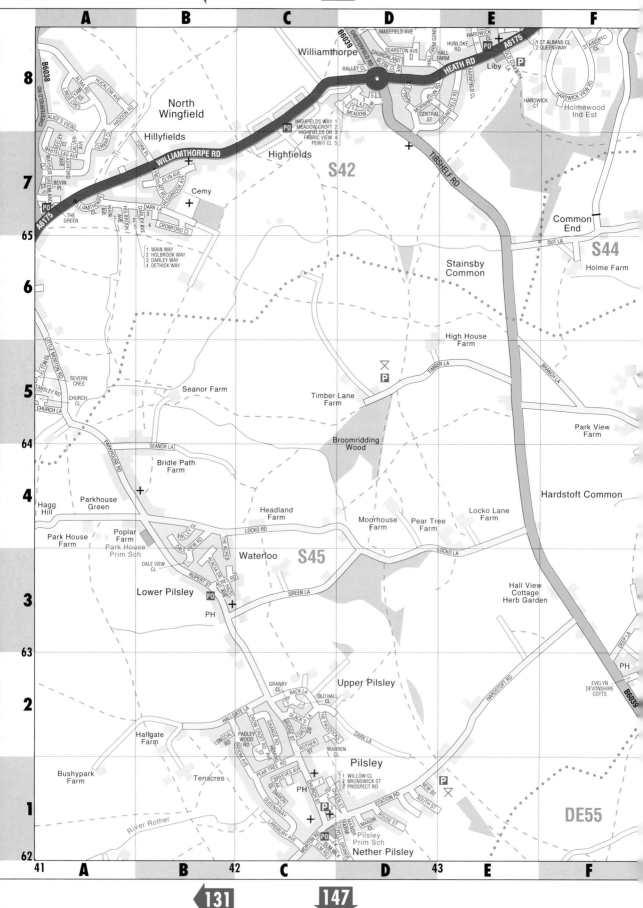

131
116

North Wingfield

Williamthorpe

Hillyfields

Highfields

HIGHFIELDS WAY 1
MEADOW CROFT 2
HIGHFIELDS DR 3
FABRIC VIEW 4
PEWIT CL 5

WILLIAMTHORPE RD

S42

TIBSHELF RD

HEATH RD

Liby

1 ST ALBANS CL
2 QUEENSWAY

Holmewood Ind Est

Hardwick Ct

Cemy

THE GREEN

1 WAIN WAY
2 HOLBROOK WAY
3 DARLEY WAY
4 DETHICK WAY

Common End

S44

Holme Farm

Stainsby Common

High House Farm

Timber Lane Farm

Seanor Farm

Park View Farm

Severn Cres

Church Cl

Church La

Seanor La

Broomridding Wood

Hardstoft Common

Bridle Path Farm

Hagg Hill

Parkhouse Green

Headland Farm

Locko Rd

Moorhouse Farm

Pear Tree Farm

Locko Lane Farm

Park House Farm

Poplar Farm

Park House Prim Sch

Waterloo

S45

Locko La

Lower Pilsley

PH

Hall View Cottage Herb Garden

Upper Pilsley

Evelyn Devonshire Cotts

PH

Hallgate Farm

Pilsley

1 WILLOW CL
2 BRUNSWICK ST
3 PROSPECT RD

Bushypark Farm

Tenacres

PH

Station Rd

Pilsley Prim Sch

DE55

River Rother

Nether Pilsley

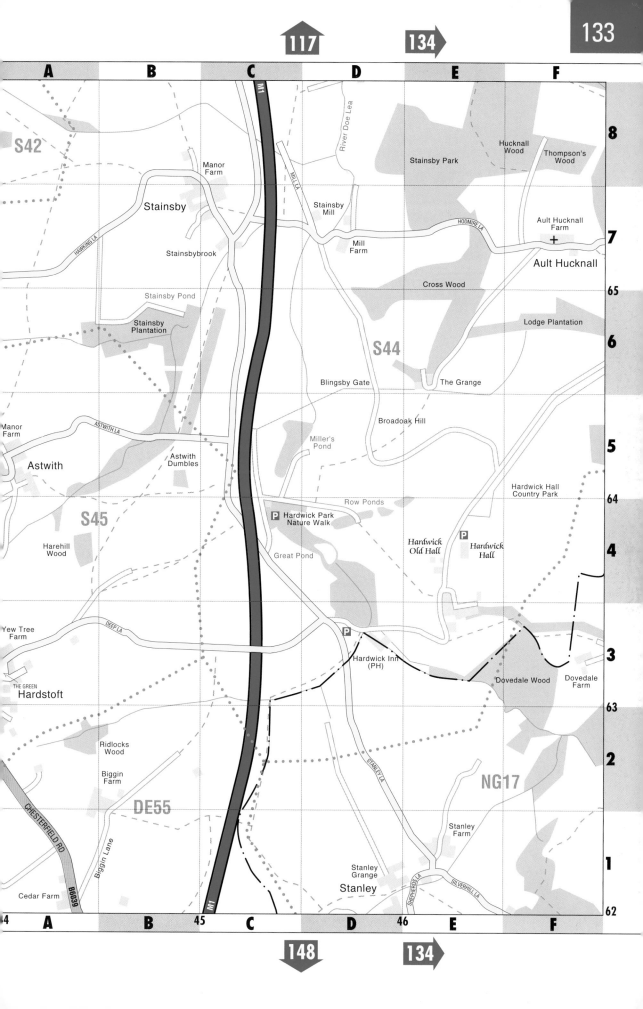

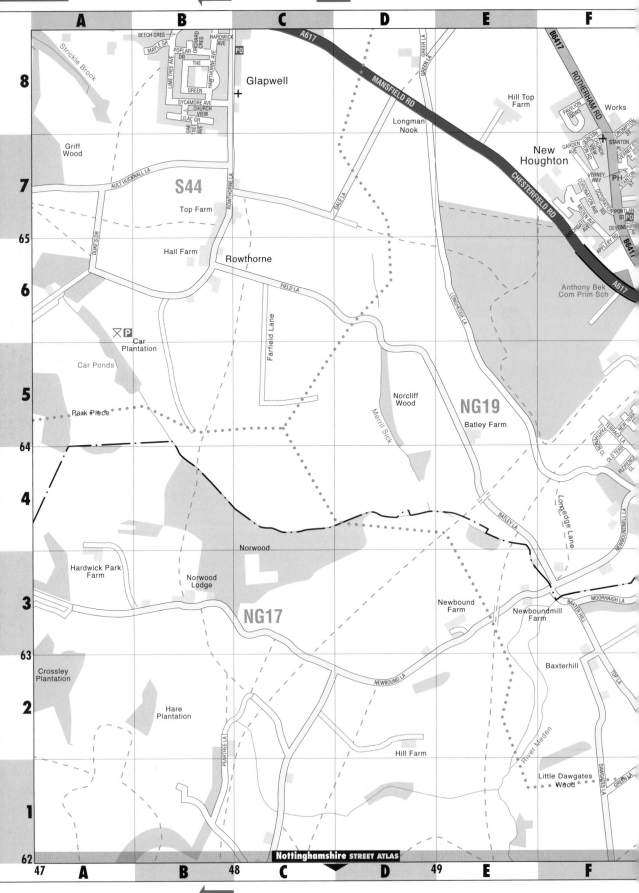

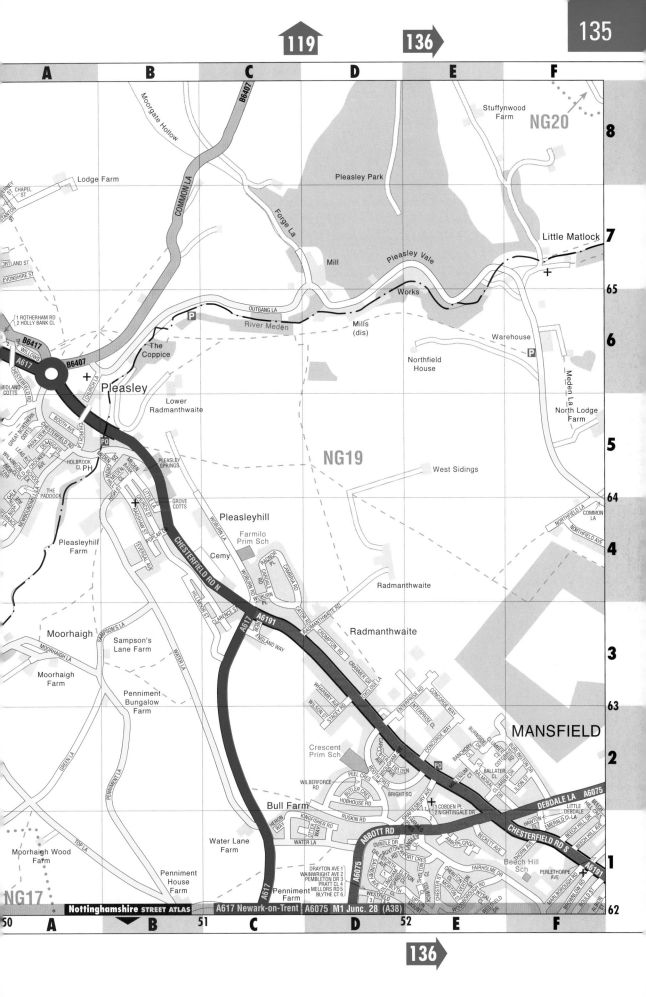

A   B   C   D   E   F

8

NG20

Stuffynwood
Farm

Lodge Farm

CHAPEL
ST

Moorgate Hollow

COMMON LA

B6407

Pleasley Park

Little Matlock

7

Forge La

65

Mill

Pleasley Vale

ORTLAND ST

EVONSHIRE ST

1 ROTHERHAM RD
2 HOLLY BANK CL

P

OUTGANG LA

River Meden

Works

6

Mills
(dis)

Warehouse

P

1 B6417   THE WILLOWS

A617

B6407

The
Coppice

CHURCH LA

Northfield
House

Meden La

CHESTERFIELD RD

MIDLAND
COTTS

Pleasley

Lower
Radmanthwaite

North Lodge
Farm

NORTHFIELD LA

5

GREAT NORTHERN
COTTS
PARK VIEW

BOOTH AVE

LEAS RD

MEDEN SQ

MEDEN BANK

HIGH ST

BEASGATE

BEACON
AVE

PO

Pleasley
Springs

West Sidings

64

WILKINSON ST
OLD SCHOOL

ST CROOKES

HOLBROOK
CL PH

CHURCH ST

LITTLE LA

WOBURN LA

GROVE
COTTS

NORTHFIELD LA

COMMON
LA

DALE BANK
POLISH

THE
PADDOCK

BAGSHAW ST

POPLAR ST

Pleasleyhill

Farmilo
Prim Sch

RADNOR
PL

CAMBRIA RD

4

NEWBOUNDMILL
LA

TENTERSAL AVE

Cemy

WOBURN RD

CROADALE
RD

Radmanthwaite

Pleasleyhill
Farm

HILLMOOR ST

WOBURN
PL

CLARENCE ST

A617

A6191

CATOR RD

RADMANTHWAITE RD

CROMPTON RD

CRANMER GR

Moorhaigh

SAMPSON'S LA

WATER LA

ENGLAND WAY

CRAMMER GR
LA

OXCLOSE LA

Radmanthwaite

MOORHAIGH LA

Sampson's
Lane Farm

3

Moorhaigh
Farm

WHARMBY AVE

WILSON ST

STACEY RD

ENTERPRISE RD

ENTERPRISE CL

CONCORDE WAY

63

Penniment
Bungalow
Farm

BURNSIDE
RD

CUMBER
CL

LIMBER CL

BURLINGTON DR

MANSFIELD

PENNIMENT LA

GREEN LA

Crescent
Prim Sch

CARPENTER AVE

CONCORDE WAY

PO

BANCHORY
CL

COTGRAVE RD

BALLATER
CL

BALMORAL
CL

CUMBER DR

LINTON ST

2

WILBERFORCE
RD

PEEL CRES

BOOTH CRES

FIELDEN

SHAFTESBURY AVE

MILLENNIUM
CT

DEBDALE LA   A6075

BUTLER CRES

HOBHOUSE RD

BRIGHT SQ

1 COBDEN PL
2 NIGHTINGALE DR

HILL SIDE

LITTLE
DEBDALE
CL LA

HAWTON
CL

EMERALD CL LA

BEECH HILL DR

BEECH HILL AVE

Bull Farm

KINGFISHER RD

RUSKIN RD

ABBOTS CROFT

BECKETT AVE

CHESTERFIELD RD S

TOP LA

HERON
WAY

OTTER
WAY

Water Lane
Farm

ABBOTT RD

THORN AVE

BROXTOWE RD

Beech Hill
Sch

A6191

1

Moorhaigh Wood
Farm

Water La

OUNDLE DR

A6075

KINGLAKE
PL

DALESTORTH

AINSWORTH
DR

MORTON ST

CHESTER ST

CHERITON DR

EVERTON ST

FAIRHOLME DR

WYSALL
LA

UPTON

PERLETHORPE
AVE

MARLBOROUGH RD

BOULD ST

NG17

Penniment
House
Farm

A617

Penniment
Farm

DRAYTON AVE 1
WAINWRIGHT AVE 2
PEMBLETON DR 3
PRATT CL 4
MELLORS RD 5
BLYTHE CT 6.

A6075

WESTFIELD

BLYTH

UPTON
MOUNT

SHELTON ST

PORT CRES

ELSTON
CL

BUXTON
CL

GOSWICK

WONBOROUGH RD

WESTFIELD
DR

ALBION ST

62

50   A   B   51   C   D   52   E   F   62

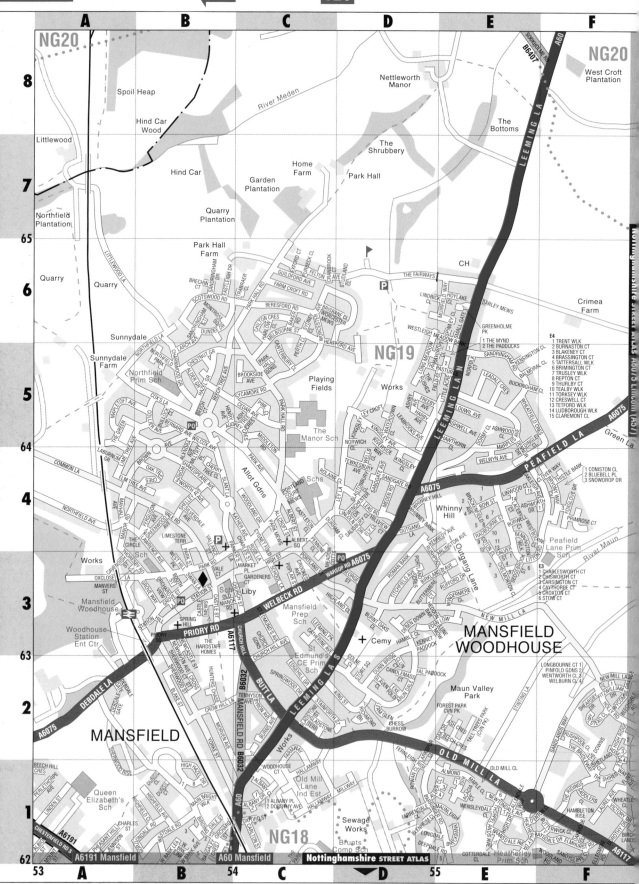

NG20

West Croft
Plantation

NG20

Spoil Heap

Hind Car
Wood

Littlewood

River Meden

Nettleworth
Manor

The Bottoms

The Shrubbery

Hind Car

Home
Farm

Garden
Plantation

Park Hall

Northfield
Plantation

Quarry
Plantation

Park Hall
Farm

CH

Crimea
Farm

Quarry

Quarry

NG19

Sunnydale

Sunnydale
Farm

Northfield
Prim Sch

Playing
Fields

Works

The
Manor Sch

Whinny
Hill

Peafield
Lane Prim
Sch

River Maun

Works

MANSFIELD
WOODHOUSE

Mansfield
Prep Sch

Mansfield
Woodhouse

Woodhouse
Station Ent Ctr

WELBECK RD

PRIORY RD

Cemy

Maun Valley
Park

FOREST PARK
CVN PK

TALL TREES PARK
(CVN PK)

DEBDALE LA

A6075

MANSFIELD

Old Mill
Lane Ind Est

OLD MILL LA

Beech Hill
Cres

Queen
Elizabeth's
Sch

Sewage
Works

Brunts
Comp Sch

Heatherley
Prim Sch

NG18

A6191 Mansfield

A60 Mansfield

Nottinghamshire STREET ATLAS

B1
1 MUSKHAM CT
2 NORWELL CT
3 MISTERTON CT
4 MATTERSEY CT
5 THE WOODLANDS
6 WOODHOUSE RD
7 DUNSIL RD
8 MAIN BRIGHT RD

E1
1 ASPEN CT
2 HOLLY CT
3 BULLACE CT
4 CORNEL CT
5 GLEBE VIEW
6 KINGSTHORPE CL
7 BRACKMILLS CL

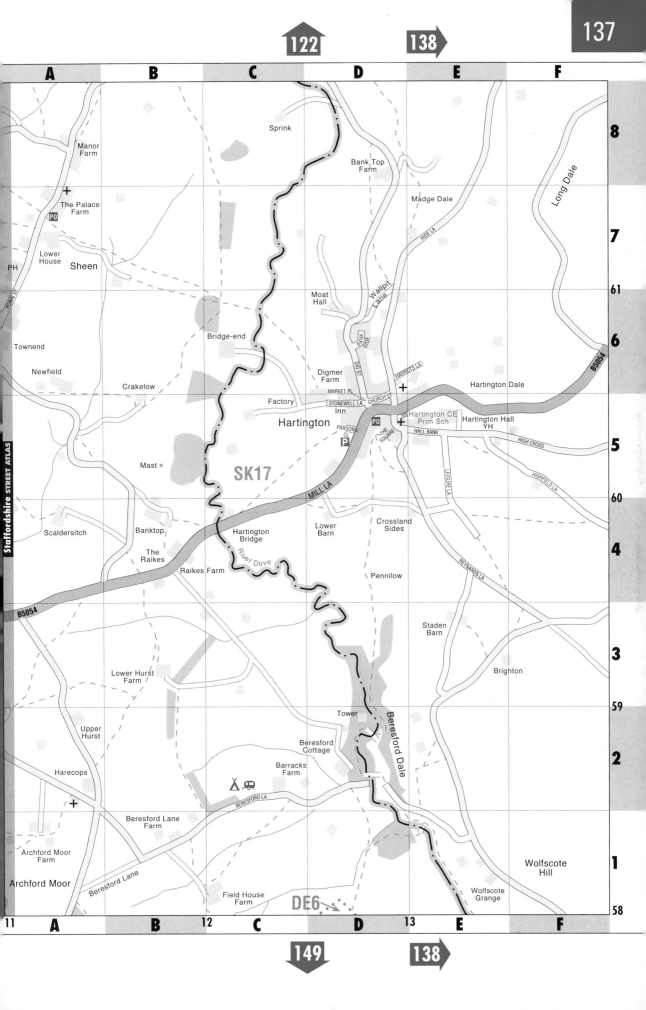

A B C D E F

8
7
61
6
5
60
4
3
59
2
1
58

Staffordshire STREET ATLAS

Manor Farm

The Palace Farm
PO

Lower House

Sheen

PH

Townend

Newfield

Crakelow

Bridge-end

Scaldersitch

Banktop

The Raikes

Raikes Farm

Mast

SK17

Sprink

Bank Top Farm

Madge Dale

HIDE LA

Wallpit Lane

Moat Hall

BANK SIDE

DIG ST

Digmer Farm

MARKET PL

STONEWELL LA

Factory

Inn

Hartington

PARSONS CL

P
PO
THE SQUARE

CHURCH ST

HARROTS LA

Hartington Dale

Hartington CE Prim Sch

Hartington Hall YH

HALL BANK

HIGH CROSS

LEISURE LA

HIGHFIELD LA

Long Dale

B5054

Hartington Bridge

River Dove

Lower Barn

Crossland Sides

Pennilow

MILL LA

REYNARDS LA

Staden Barn

Brighton

Lower Hurst Farm

Upper Hurst

Harecops

Beresford Lane Farm

Archford Moor Farm

Archford Moor

Beresford Lane

BERESFORD LA

Barracks Farm

Beresford Cottage

Tower

Beresford Dale

Wolfscote Hill

Wolfscote Grange

Field House Farm

DE6

A B C D E F

11 12 13

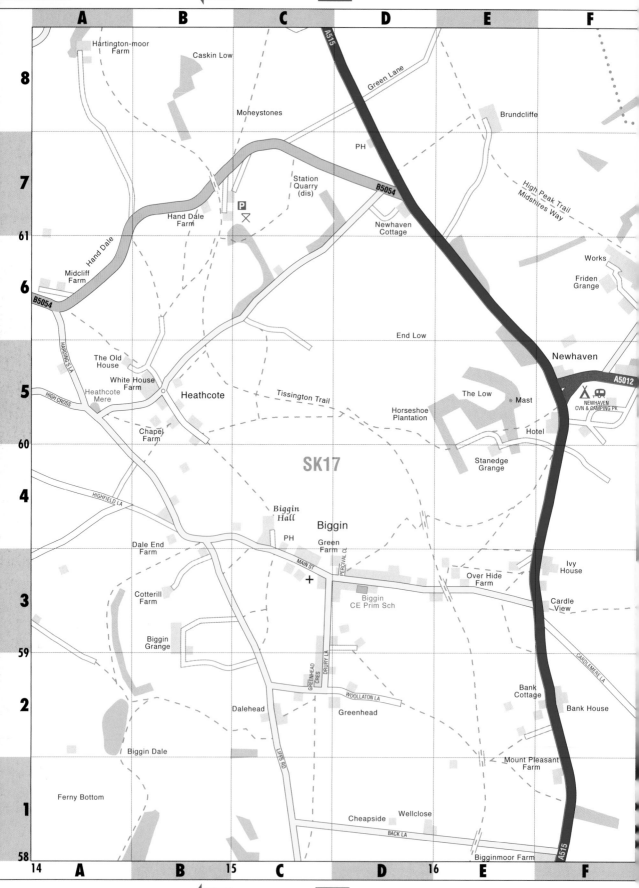

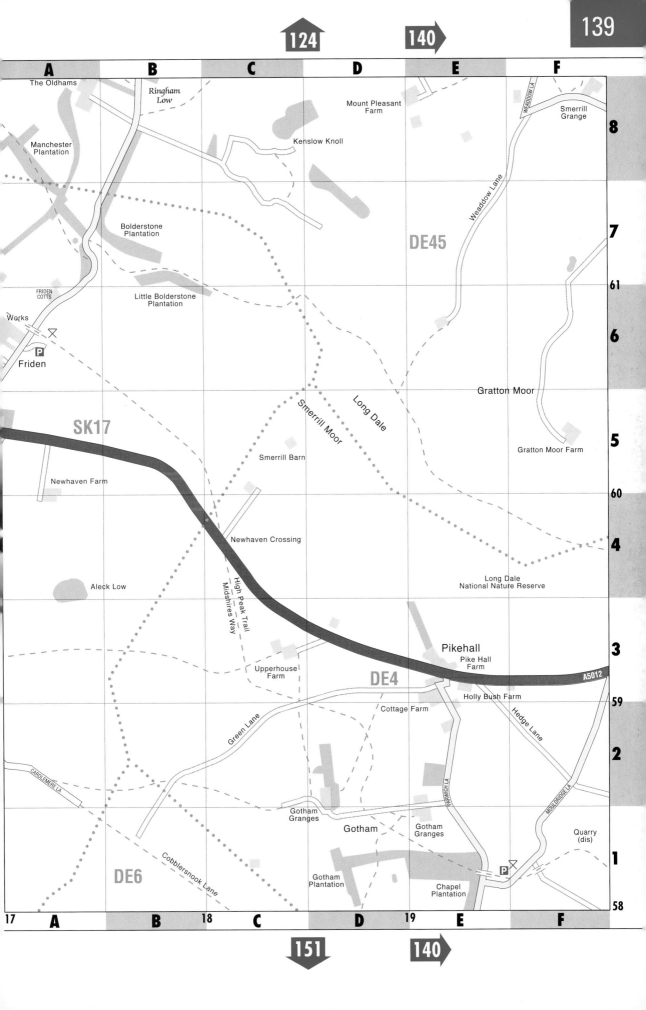

The Oldhams

Ringham Low

Mount Pleasant Farm

Manchester Plantation

Kenslow Knoll

Smerrill Grange

WEADDOW LA

8

Bolderstone Plantation

DE45

Weaddow Lane

7

61

FRIDEN COTTS

Little Bolderstone Plantation

Works

6

P

Friden

Gratton Moor

Long Dale

Smerrill Moor

SK17

5

Newhaven Farm

Smerrill Barn

Gratton Moor Farm

60

Newhaven Crossing

4

Aleck Low

Long Dale National Nature Reserve

High Peak Trail

Midshires Way

Pikehall

3

Pike Hall Farm

Upperhouse Farm

DE4

A5012

Holly Bush Farm

59

Cottage Farm

Hedge Lane

2

Green Lane

PARWICH LA

MOULDRIDGE LA

CARDLEMERE LA

Gotham Granges

Quarry (dis)

Gotham

Gotham Granges

DE6

Cobblersnook Lane

Gotham Plantation

Chapel Plantation

P

1

58

17

18

19

A **B** **C** **D** **E** **F**

8

Fishpond Wood

Gratton Grange Farm

Rock Farm

Dud Wood

Dudwood Farm

B5056

Anthony Hill

Limestone Way

Dale End House

DUDWOOD LA

Dale End

DE45

7

Dale End Farm

GRATTON LA

Bury Cliff Farm

Well Street Farm

Woodbine Farm

61

The Bungalows

WEST END

WELL ST

Elton CE Prim Sch

EAST END

WINSTER LA

Oddo House Farm

PH

PO

MAIN ST

BACK LA

Dark Lane

Elton House Farm

CHAPEL CROFT

YT LA

Elton

6

Gratton Moor

Hungerhill Lane

Gratton Dale

Leadmines Farm

Blake Low

5

Shafts (dis)

MOOR LA

60

Barker Barn

EXLOWMERE LA

4

Elton Common

DE4

Mouldridge Grange

Allsop Barn

Sacheveral Farm

3

A5012

SACHEVERAL LA

Stunstead Lane

MOULDRIDGE LA

Little Wisels Wood

59

Grange Barn

2

Astonhill

A5012

New Barn

1

Pennine Bridleway Midshires Way

Rockhurst Farm

Greenlow Farm

58

20 **A** **B** 21 **C** **D** 22 **E** **F**

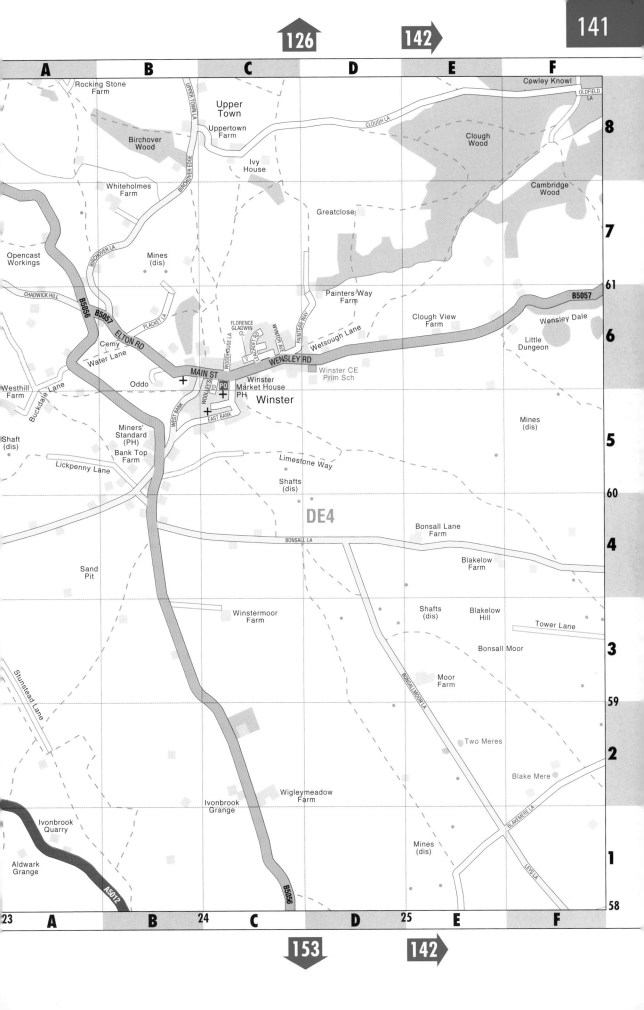

| | A | B | C | D | E | F |

8

Rocking Stone Farm

Cowley Knowl

OLDFIELD LA

Upper Town

CLOUGH LA

Uppertown Farm

Clough Wood

Birchover Wood

Ivy House

Whiteholmes Farm

Cambridge Wood

BIRCHOVER EDGE

7

Greatclose

Opencast Workings

Mines (dis)

BIRCHOVER LA

Painters Way Farm

61

B5057

CHADWICK HILL

B5056

B5057

PLACKET LA

ELTON RD

Clough View Farm

Wensley Dale

Cemy

FLORENCE GLADWIN CL

Wetsough Lane

Little Dungeon

6

WOODHOUSE LA

LEACROFT RD

WYNTOR AV

PAINTERS WAY

Water Lane

MAIN ST

WENSLEY RD

Westhill Farm

Oddo

WOOLLEYS YD

PO

Winster Market House PH

Winster CE Prim Sch

Buckdale Lane

WEST BANK

EAST BANK

Winster

Mines (dis)

5

Shaft (dis)

Miners' Standard (PH)

Bank Top Farm

Limestone Way

Lickpenny Lane

Shafts (dis)

60

DE4

Bonsall Lane Farm

BONSALL LA

4

Sand Pit

Blakelow Farm

Winstermoor Farm

Shafts (dis)

Blakelow Hill

Tower Lane

Stunstead Lane

Bonsall Moor

3

BONSALL MOOR LA

Moor Farm

59

Two Meres

2

Blake Mere

Ivonbrook Grange

Wigleymeadow Farm

BLAKEMERE LA

Ivonbrook Quarry

Mines (dis)

LEYS LA

1

Aldwark Grange

A5012

B5056

58

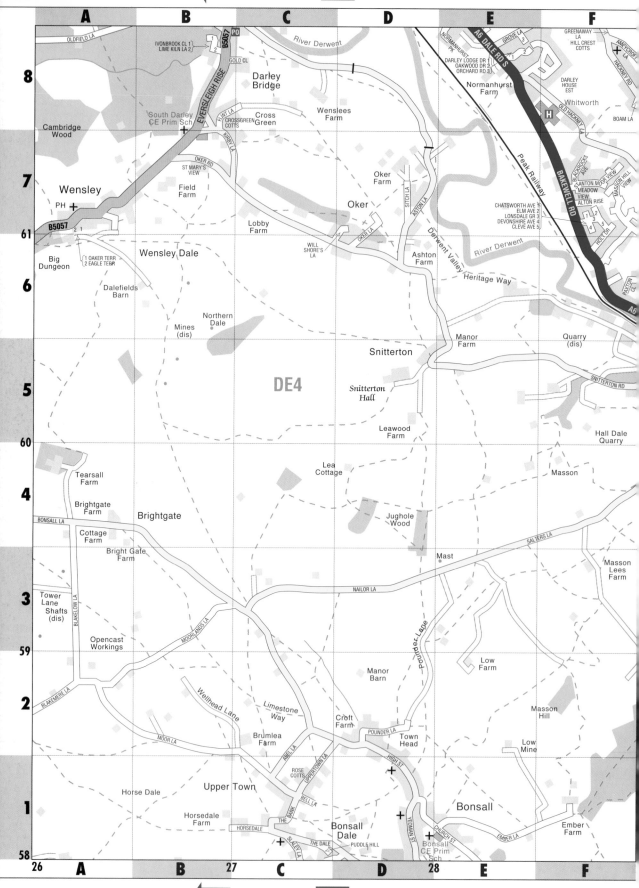

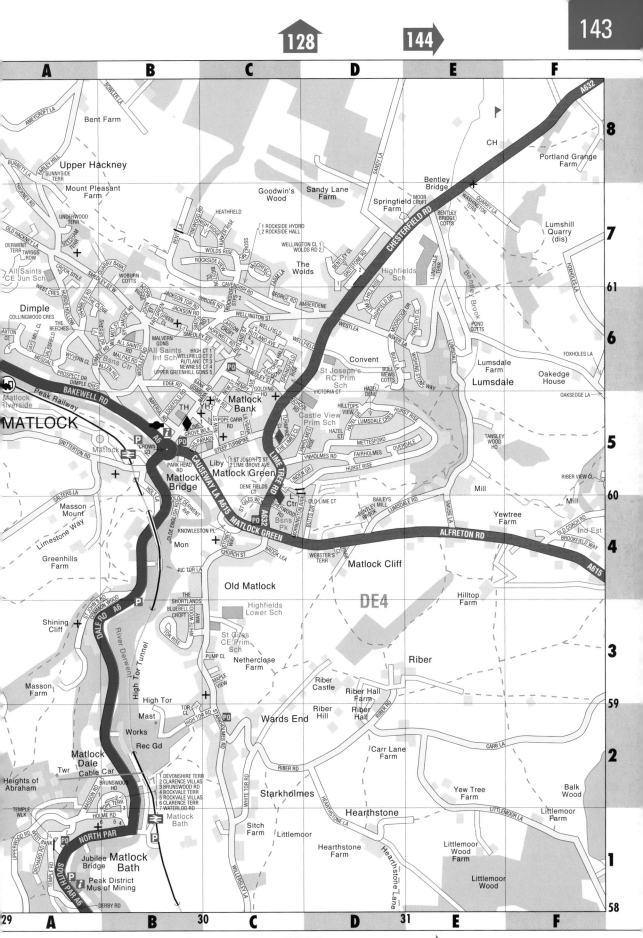

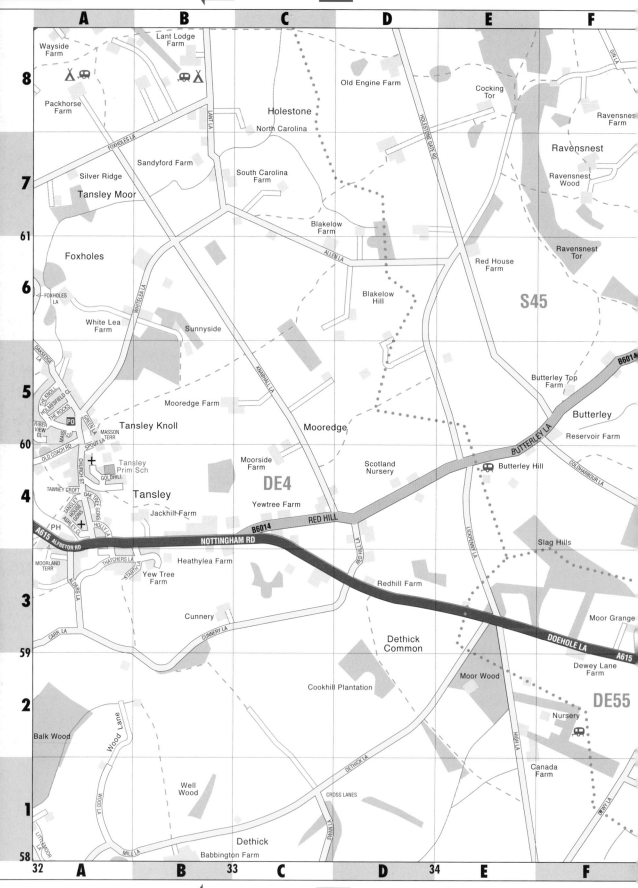

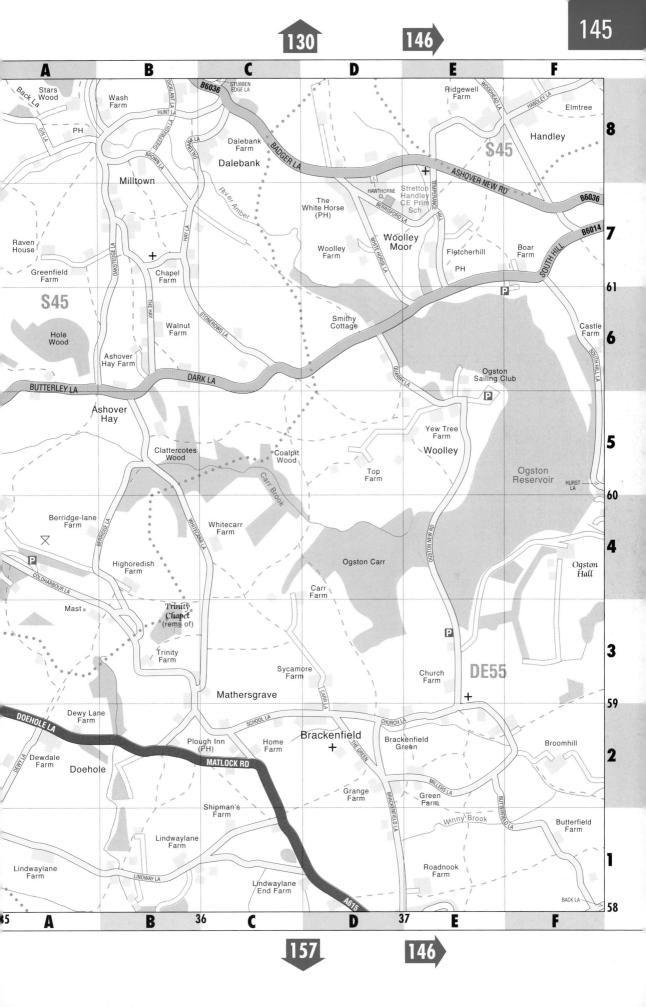

145
131

A B C D E F

8

Menel Farm
S45
Stretton House
Top Farm
STRAW LA
Ain Moor
S45
Opencast Workings
Padley Wood
STRETTON RD
A61
HIGHSTAIRS LA

Cemy
B6036
B6014
ASHOVER RD
Smithy Moor
Stretton Farm
SMITHS LA
Stretton
Averill Farm
EVERSHILL LA

7

Sidness Farm

61

PH
Hillside Farm
MORTON ROAD

6

South Hill
CROW LA
HURST LA
Hilltop Farm
Smithy Brook
PEGGS LA
MAIN RD
Stretton Plantation
STRETTON RD
Haver Hill Farm
EVERSHILL

South Hill Farm
Stretton Hillside
Fold House Farm
BURNSHAW ST
HOLLAND CL
MALTBY AVE
SILWELL VILLAS
Morton
MAIN RD
B6014
BACK LA

5

RESERVOIR HOS
SHERWOOD ST
CEDAR ST
WINTHORPE AVE
BRONTE AVE
PRIESTLEY AVE
TENNYSON ST
MICKLEY LA
Mickley Estate
Northedge Farm
DE55
PH

60

Ogston
SHAKESPEARE AVE
FIR TREE AVE
MILTON AVE
CHURCH RISE
Mickley Inf Sch
Yew Tree Farm
CHURCH
YEW
BLUEBELL HILL
SYCAMORE CL
HIGHAM LA
Stonebroom

4

Ogston Bridge
OGSTON LA
Pingle Farm
Mickley Farm
The Double Six (PH)
JULIA ST
SCHOOL CL
WEST ST
HIGH ST
QUARRY LA
Sch

PH
WELL LA
COMMON LA
CARLYLE RD
SCOTT CRES
WESLEY
QUEENSWAY
KEATS CL
BIRKINSTYLE
ADDISON RD

3

B6013
PO
CHESTERFIELD RD
Goosegreen
BIRKINSTYLE LA
CLEVELAND RD
BRIERLEY RD
BUNYAN WLK
BYRON GR
SHELLEY GR
KINGSLEY CRES

River Amber
Higham
FERN LEA
FERNWOOD CL
THE CROFT
GOOSE GREEN LA
THE BUNGALOWS
KEATS
2

Higham Farm Hotel
STRETTEA LA
NEW ST
SCHOOL LA
TOWN END
PH
Shirland Prim Sch
New Higham
WELLINGTON MEWS
DOG LA

Higham Dairy Farm
BELPER RD
HALLFIELDS RISE
ELM ST
WILLOW
PEE AVE
BURNS ST
ROWAN DR
LILAC WAY
ASPEN RISE
HALLFIELDGATE LA
Shirland
MAIN RD
WELLINGTON PK
CHURCH ST

1

BUMPMILL LA
Hallfield Gate
PIT LA
PO
CLAY ST
GREAVES ST
BEVAN ST
BEVAN CT
St LEONARDS PL
PARK LA
PACK CL
DAM LA

BACK LA
Carr Hill Farm
B6013
Hallfield Hall
A61
CROSS LA

58

38 A 39 B C 40 D E F

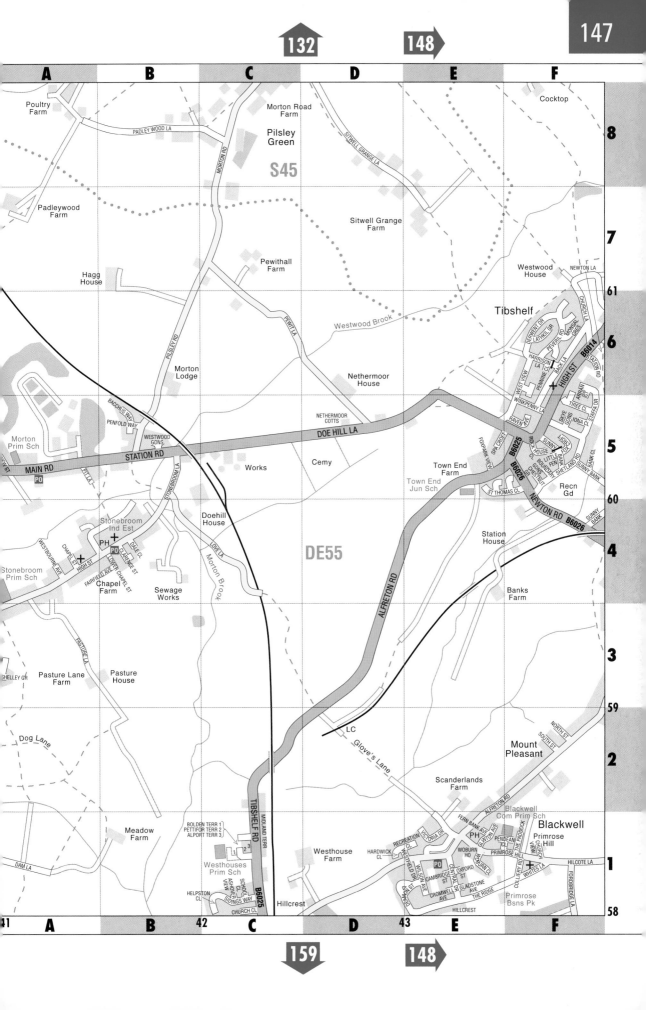

147
133

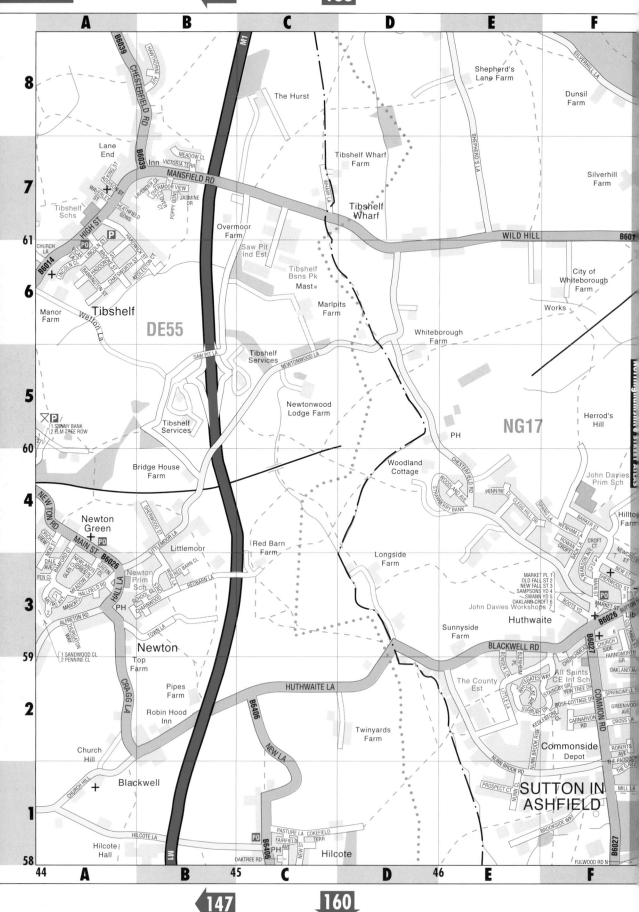

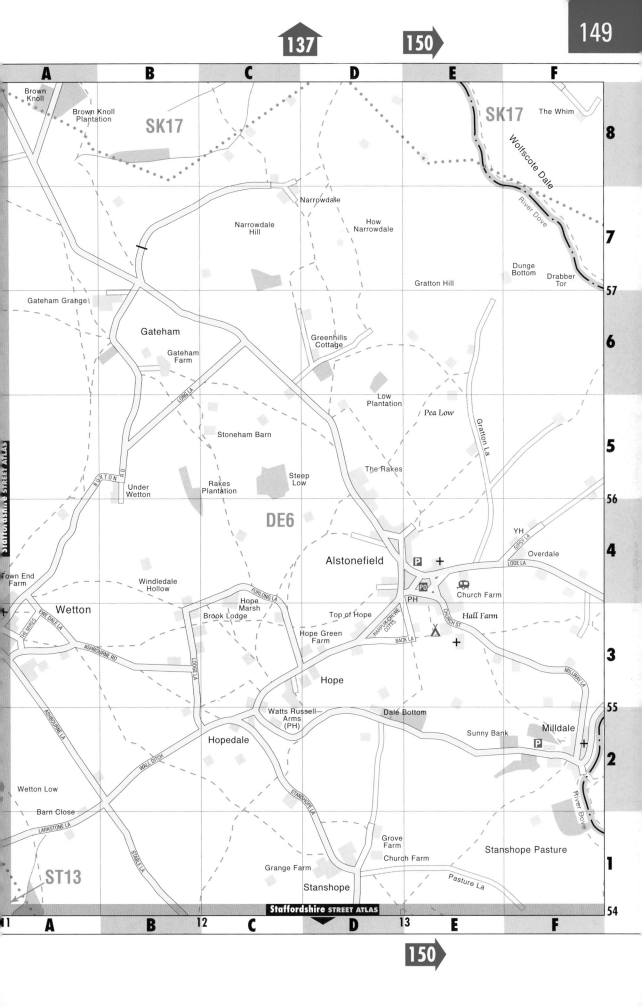

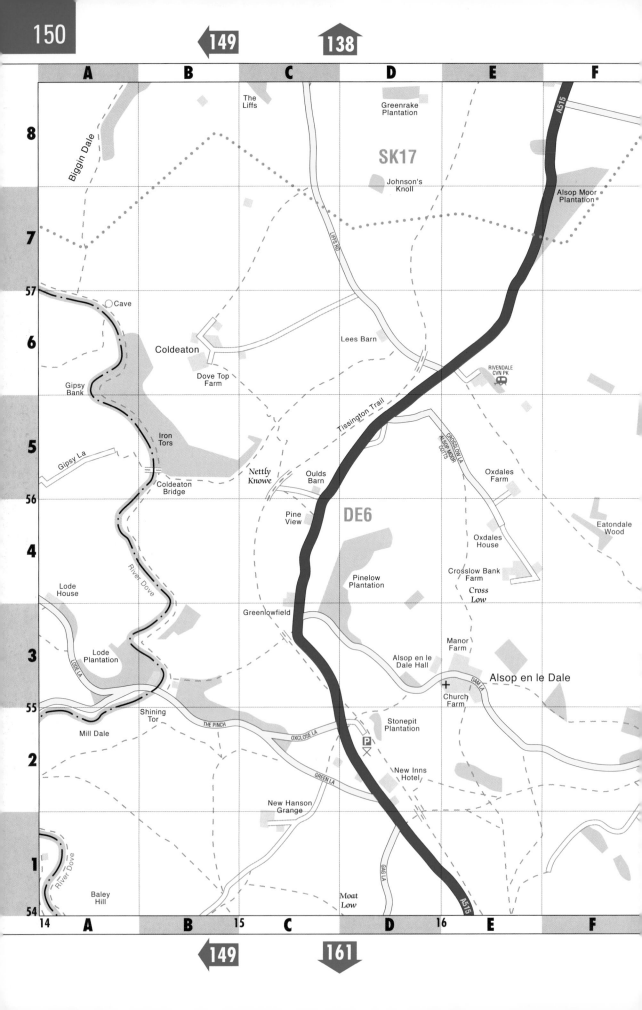

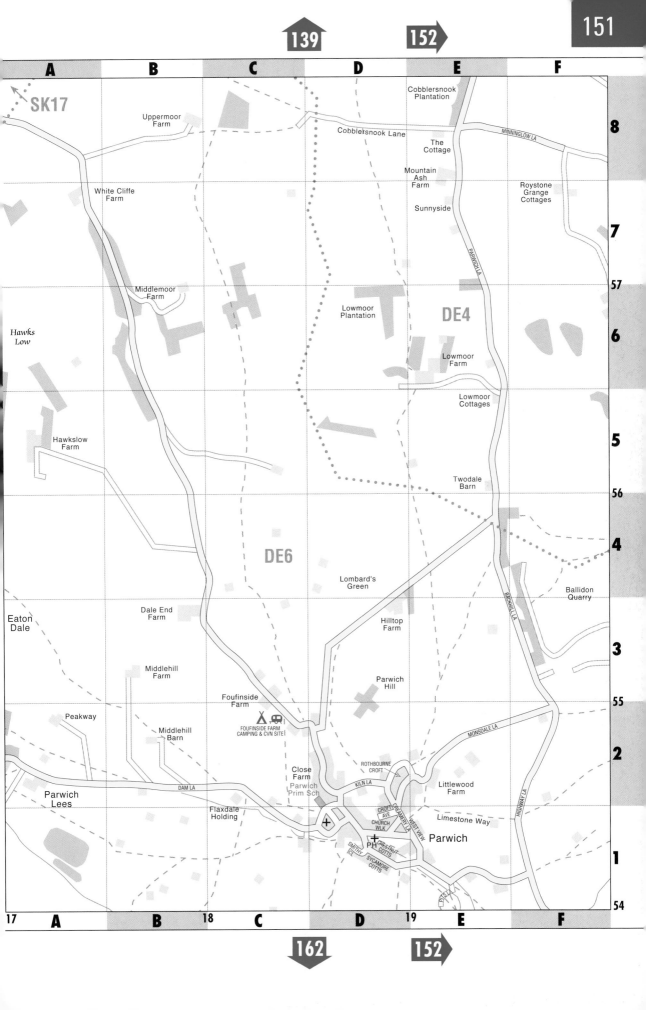

151
140

A **B** **C** **D** **E** **F**

Longedge
Plantation

Rockhurst
Farm

8 Minninglow
Grange

Lidgate
Farm

Works

Minninglow La

Green
Farm

Aldwark

Minning
Low

7 Minninglow
Hill

Tithe
Farm

Hilltop
Farm

Shafts
(dis)

57

Slipper
Low

Slipper Low
Farm

6 Royston
Grange

DE4

Daisy
Bank

Pennine Bridleway

Gallowlow La

Haven Hoe
Farm

5 High Peak Trail
Midshires Way

56 Longcliffe
Farm

B5056

4 Hoe
Grange

Longcliffe

Ballidon
Quarry

Pinder's
Rock

Blackstone's
Low

Ballidonmoor

Beardsley's
Plantation

3 Works

Nut
Wood

55 White
Edge

Black
Rocks

2 DE6

Oldfields
Farm

Black
Plantation

Rainster
Rocks

Ballidonhall
Farm

Lots La

Ballidon

Cow Close
Farm

Limestone Way

PASTURE LA

CHURCH
ST

HILLSIDE

1 Overfields
Barn

Works

Hipley
Farm

Caves

WEST END

WELL ST

Hipley
Hill

Hipley
Barn

Hipley
Works

Middle La

NETHER LA

54 B5056

20 **A** **B** **21** **C** **D** **22** **E** **F**

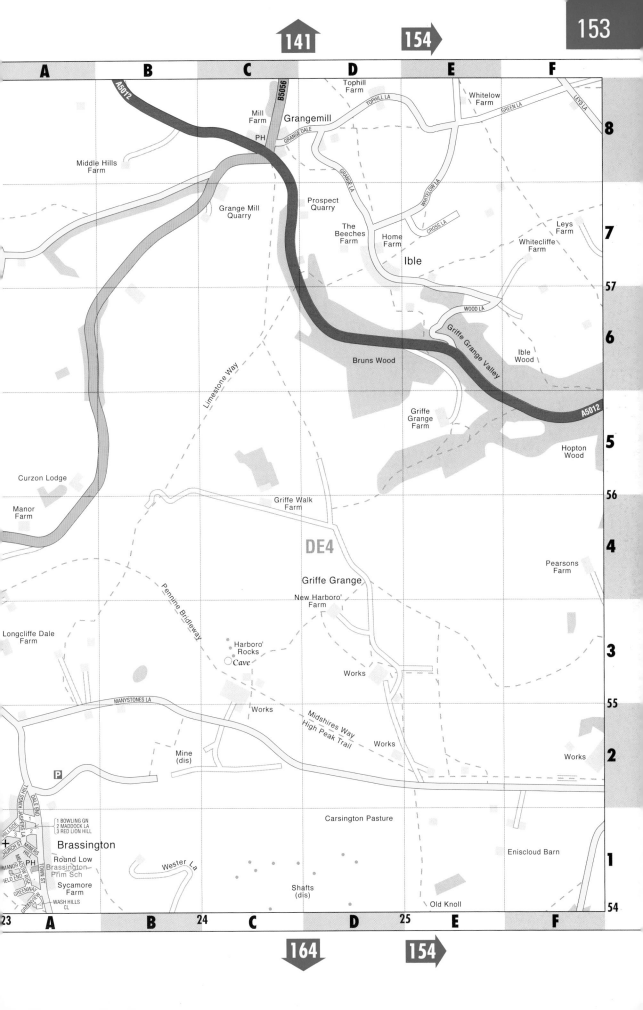

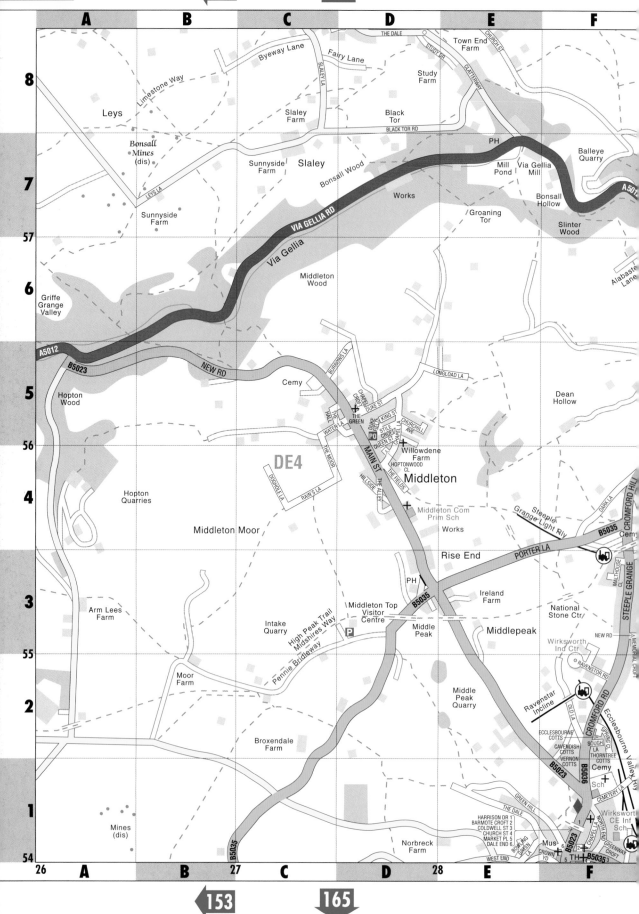

153 142

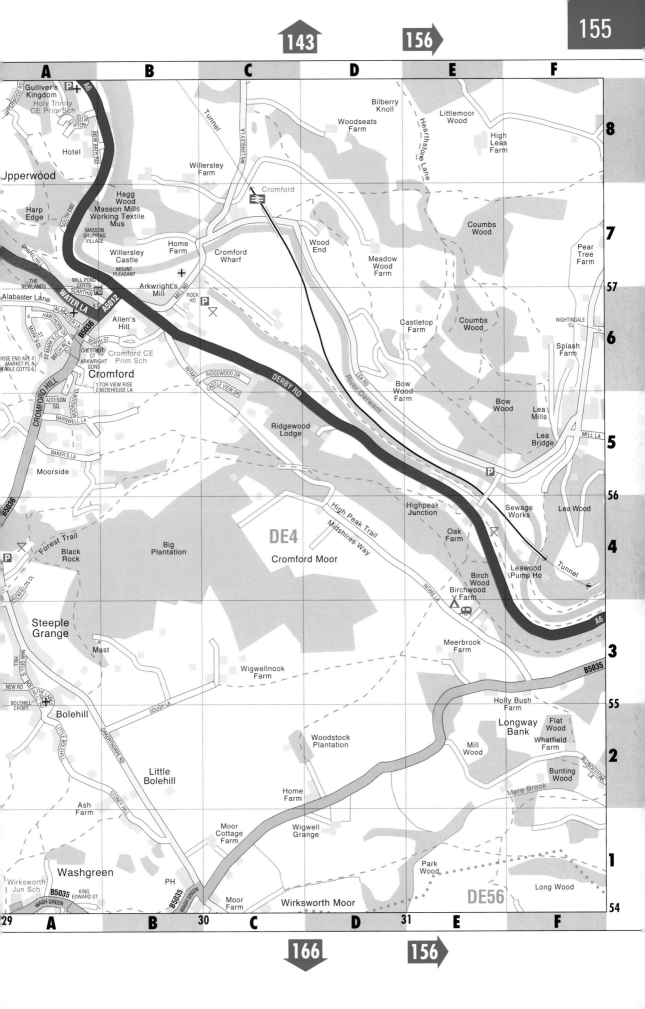

A B C D E F

Gulliver's Kingdom
Holy Trinity CE Prim Sch
Hotel
Upperwood
Harp Edge
Hagg Wood
Masson Mills Working Textile Mus
MASSON SHOPPING VILLAGE
Willersley Castle
MOUNT PLEASANT
Home Farm
THE NEWLANDS
Alabaster Lane
MILL POND COTTS
SCARTHIN
Arkwright's Mill
ROCK HO
Mill Pond Cotts
CROMFORD HILL
CHAPEL HILL
SOUTH END
WATER LA
A5012
Allen's Hill
NORTH ST
CHESTNUT CT
ARKWRIGHT GDNS
Cromford CE Prim Sch
B5036
HAWTHORN DR
ST MARK'S CL
MARK'S CL
BECH NL
Cromford
ADDISON SQ
TOR VIEW RISE
BEDEHOUSE LA
ROSE END AVE
MARKET PL
TABLE COTTS
MOORSIDE CL
BARNWELL LA
BAKER'S LA
Moorside
B5036
Forest Trail
Black Rock
BRICKFIELDS CL
Steeple Grange
MAI GELL'S HILL
BOLEHILL HILL
NEW RD
THE LANES
BOLEHILL CROFT
Bolehill
LITTLE BOLEHILL
OAKERTHORPE RD
STONEY HILL
SOUGH LA
Little Bolehill
Ash Farm
Mast
Wigwellnook Farm
Washgreen
Wirksworth Jun Sch
WASH GREEN
B5035
KING EDWARD ST
PH
B5035
WASH GREEN
Moor Farm
Wirksworth Moor
Moor Cottage Farm
Wigwell Grange
Home Farm
Woodstock Plantation
Willersley Farm
Tunnel
WILLERSLEY LA
Cromford
Cromford Wharf
Wood End
Woodseats Farm
Bilberry Knoll
Littlemoor Wood
High Leas Farm
HEARTHSTONE LANE
Coumbs Wood
Meadow Wood Farm
Pear Tree Farm
RIDGEWOOD DR
CASTLE VIEW DR
INTAKE LA
DERBY RD
Ridgewood Lodge
High Peak Trail
Midshires Way
Cromford Moor
DE4
Castletop Farm
Coumbs Wood
River Derwent
LEA RD
Bow Wood Farm
Bow Wood
Lea Mills
Splash Farm
NIGHTINGALE CL
Lea Bridge
MILL LA
Lea Wood
Highpeak Junction
Sewage Works
Oak Farm
Birch Wood Farm
Birchwood Farm
INTAKE LA
A6
Leawood Pump Ho
Tunnel
Meerbrook Farm
B5035
Holly Bush Farm
Longway Bank
Mill Wood
Flat Wood
Whatfield Farm
BLUNDESTONE LA
Bunting Wood
Mere Brook
Park Wood
Long Wood
DE56

29 30 31

8 7 57 6 5 56 4 3 55 2 1 54

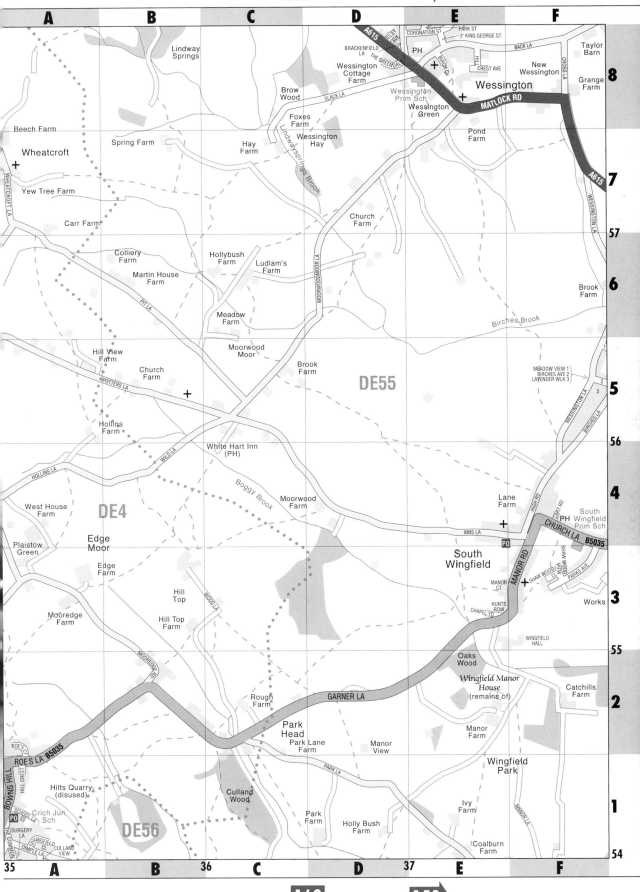

145
158
168
158

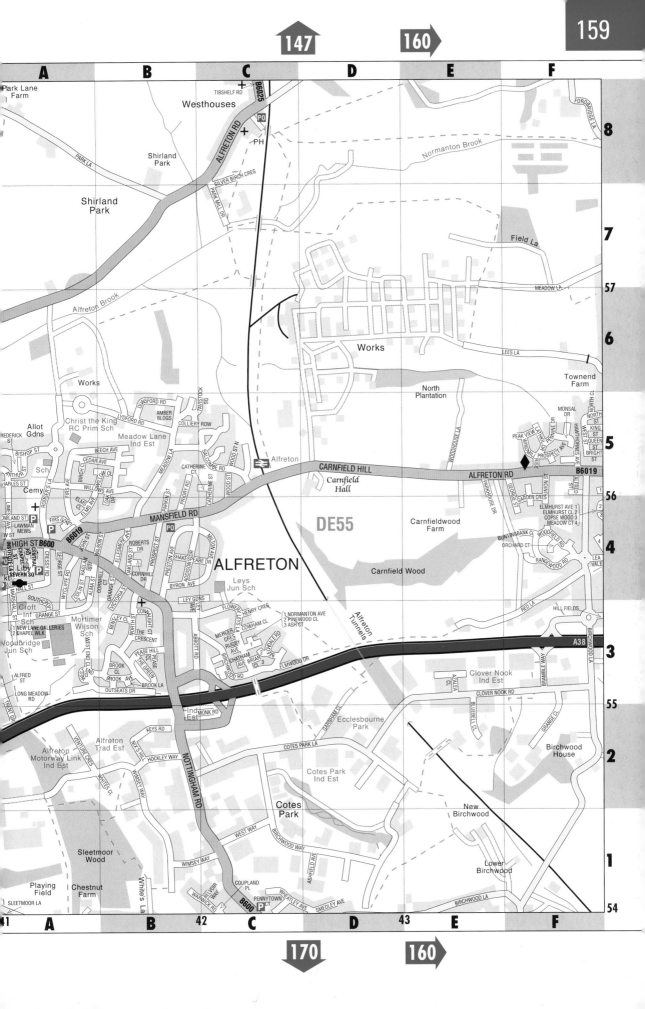

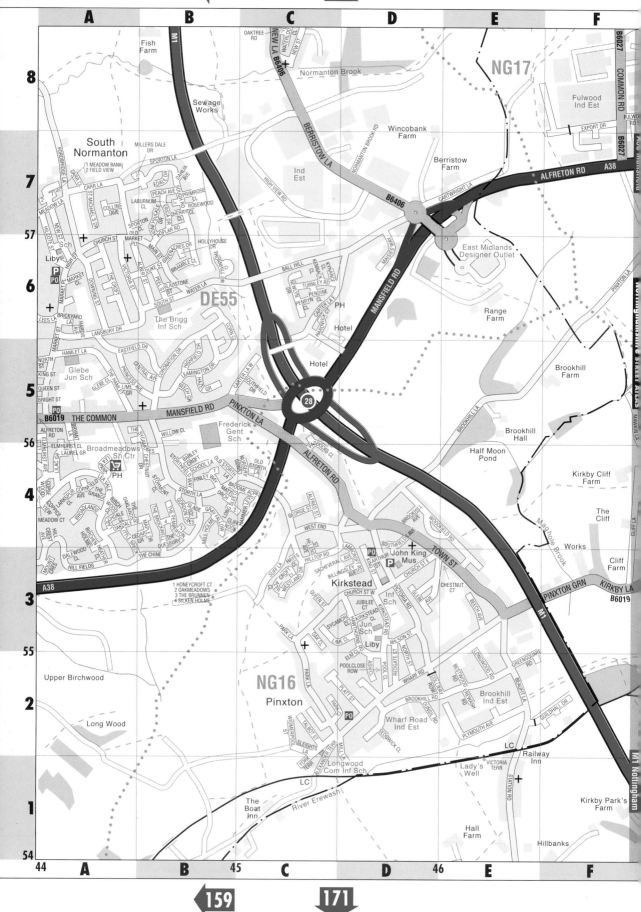

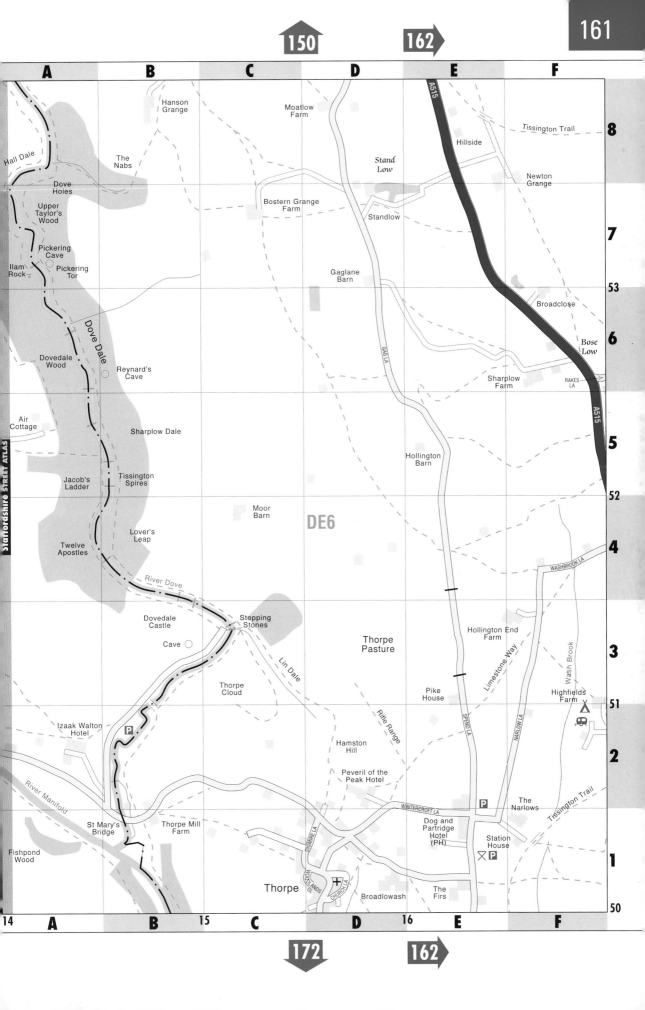

Staffordshire STREET ATLAS

A **B** **C** **D** **E** **F**

8
7
53
6
5
52
4
3
51
2
1
50

14   15   16

Hall Dale
Hanson Grange
Moatlow Farm
Tissington Trail
Hillside
Newton Grange
The Nabs
Stand Low
Standlow
Dove Holes
Bostern Grange Farm
Upper Taylor's Wood
Broadclose
Pickering Cave
Gaglane Barn
Bose Low
Ilam Rock
Pickering Tor
Dove Dale
Sharplow Farm
RAKES LA
Dovedale Wood
Reynard's Cave
Hollington Barn
Air Cottage
Sharplow Dale
A515
Jacob's Ladder
Tissington Spires
Moor Barn
DE6
Lover's Leap
Twelve Apostles
Washbrook La
River Dove
Hollington End Farm
Limestone Way
Wash Brook
Dovedale Castle
Stepping Stones
Thorpe Pasture
Highfields Farm
Cave
Lin Dale
Thorpe Cloud
Pike House
Spend La
Narlow La
Izaak Walton Hotel
Hamston Hill
Rifle Range
River Manifold
Peveril of the Peak Hotel
The Narrows
Tissington Trail
St Mary's Bridge
Thorpe Mill Farm
Wintercroft La
Dog and Partridge Hotel (PH)
Fishpond Wood
Digmire La
Viccars Cl
Woodlands Cl
Church La
Station House
Thorpe
Broadlowash
The Firs

161
151

161
173

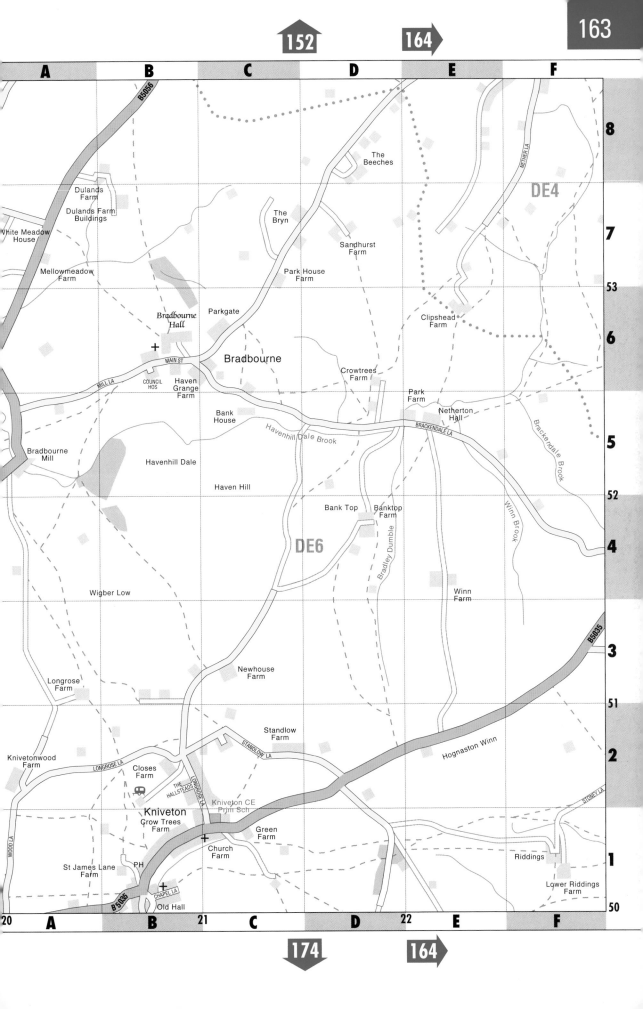

A B C D E F

8

DE4

7

53

6

White Meadow House

Dulands Farm
Dulands Farm Buildings

Mellowmeadow Farm

The Bryn

Sandhurst Farm

The Beeches

Park House Farm

Parkgate

Clipshead Farm

Bradbourne Hall

Bradbourne

MAIN ST

Crowtrees Farm

Park Farm

Netherton Hall

MILL LA

COUNCIL HOS

Haven Grange Farm

Bank House

Havenhill Dale Brook

BRACKENDALE LA

Brackendale Brook

5

Bradbourne Mill

Havenhill Dale

Haven Hill

Winn Brook

52

Bank Top

Banktop Farm

DE6

Bradley Dumble

Winn Farm

4

Wigber Low

B5035

3

Longrose Farm

Newhouse Farm

51

Standlow Farm

Hognaston Winn

Knivetonwood Farm

LONGROSE LA

Closes Farm

STANDLOW LA

STONEY LA

2

WOOD LA

THE HALLSTEADS

LONGROSE LA

Kniveton CE Prim Sch

Kniveton

Crow Trees Farm

Green Farm

Riddings

1

St James Lane Farm

PH

Church Farm

Lower Riddings Farm

CHAPEL LA

B5035

Old Hall

50

20 A B 21 C D 22 E F

◀ **163**
153 ▲

	A	B	C	D	E	F

8

Shafts (dis)

King's Chair

Wester Lane

Mines (dis)

Stone Dene

Carslow

Shafts (dis)

Min (dis

KING'S CL

Carsington

7

WOODSIDE

The Miner's Arms (PH)

Hopton Hall

Hopto

Carsington & Hopton Prim Sch

53

Breach Farm

Brook Knowles

Wash Farm

PINGLE LA

B5035

Wall Lands

DE4

⊠

P

Owslow Farm

6

Wallands Farm

Shiningford Farm

Hall Wood

Kennelmeadow

White House

Big Covert

5

Knockerdown

52

Knockerdown Inn (PH)

BRACKENDALE LA

BIG LA

4

⊠

P

Carsington Water Visitor Ctr

Carsington Water

Sitch Farm

Uppertown Farm

P

Upper Town

B5035

Overtown Farm

3

Lendow Wood

DE6

51

Upperfield Farm

STONEPIT LA

ENSLEY LA

OLDFIELD LA

2

The Green Farm

The Green

BANK HOUSE CT

GREEN LA

Inn

STONEY LA

OLDFIELD LA

BLIND LA

COCKAYNE LA

Church Farm

✚

✚

BENTHEAD LA

Hognaston

MILLS CROFT

OLD BAKERY CL

Brook House Farm

1

HAYS LA

GORSEY LA

The Riddings Farm

BROOM LA

50

	A		B		C		D		E		F
23				24			25				

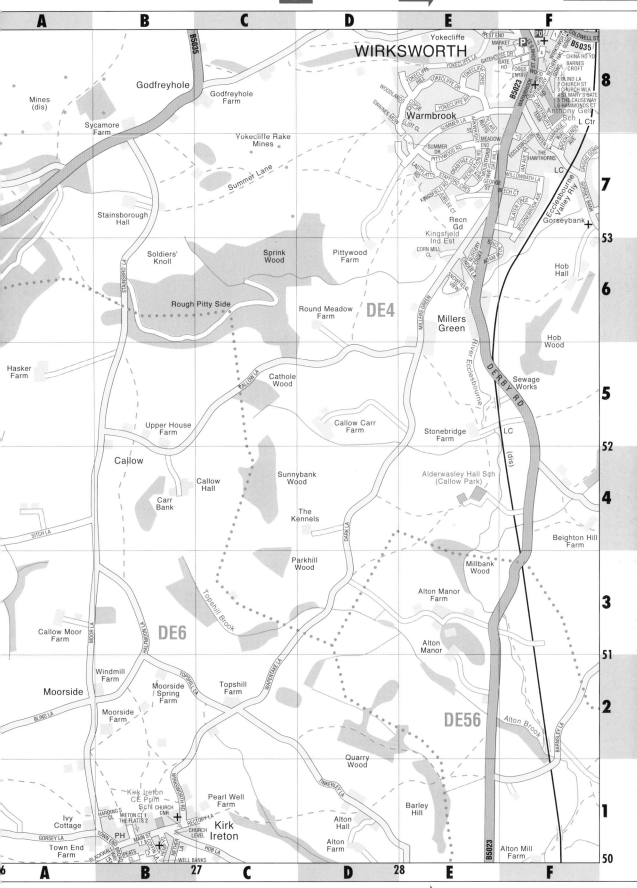

165
155

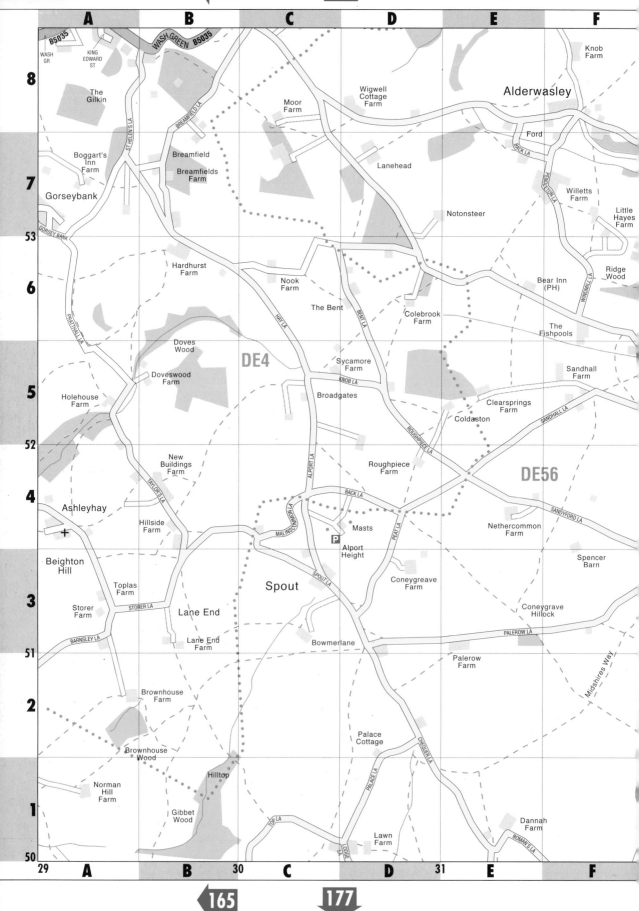

165
177

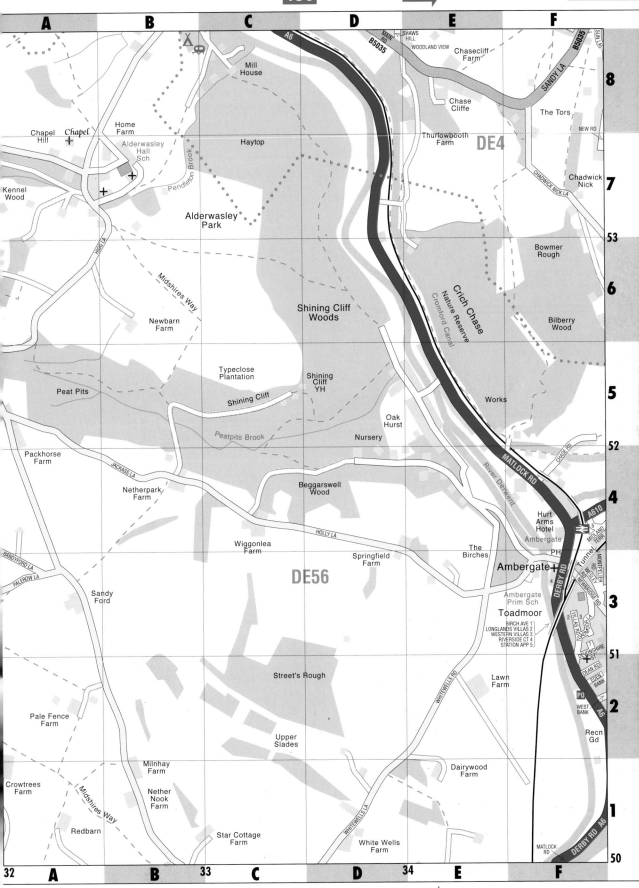

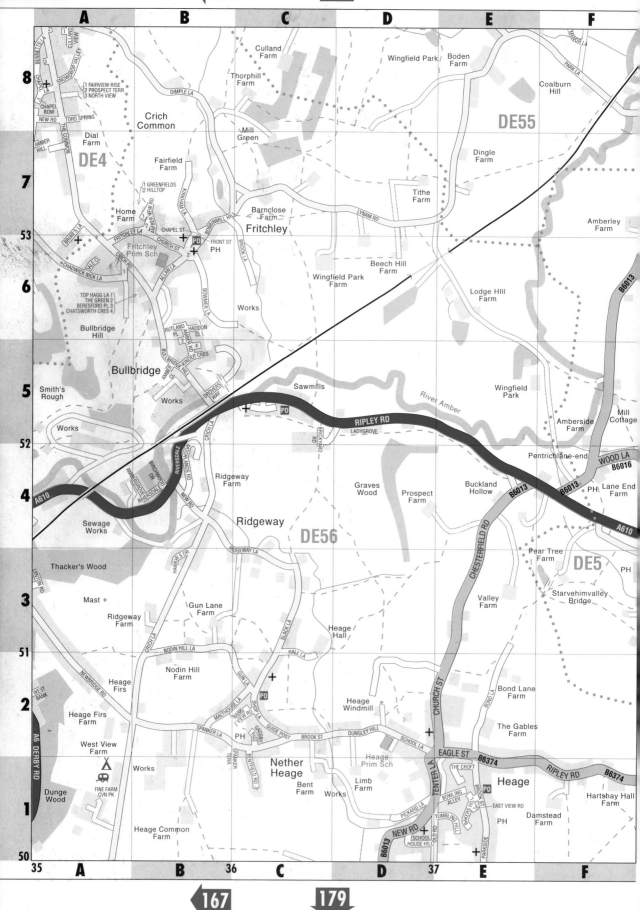

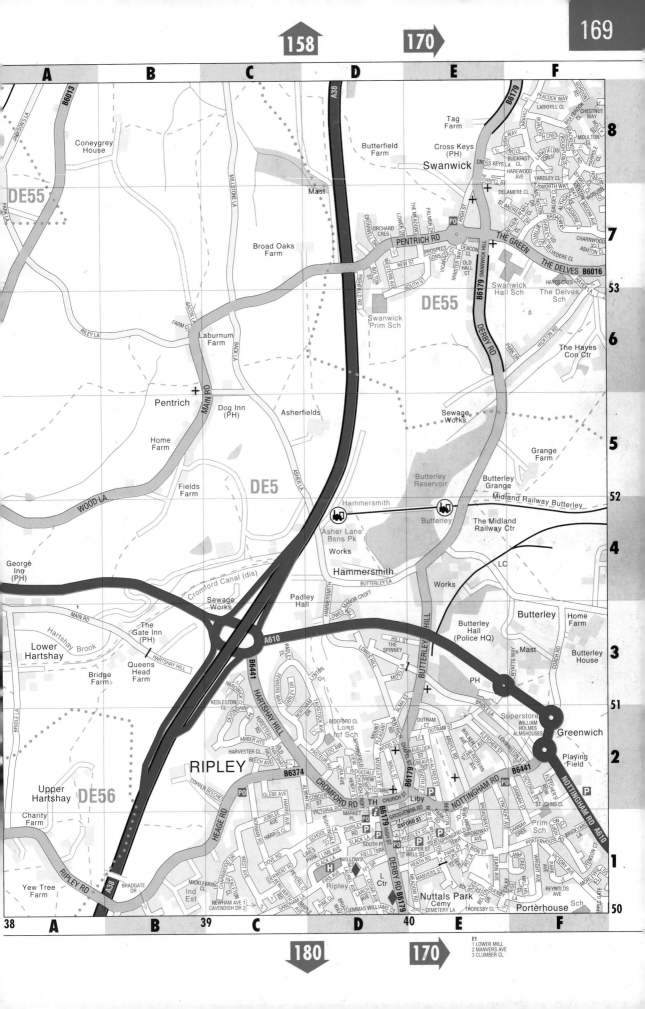

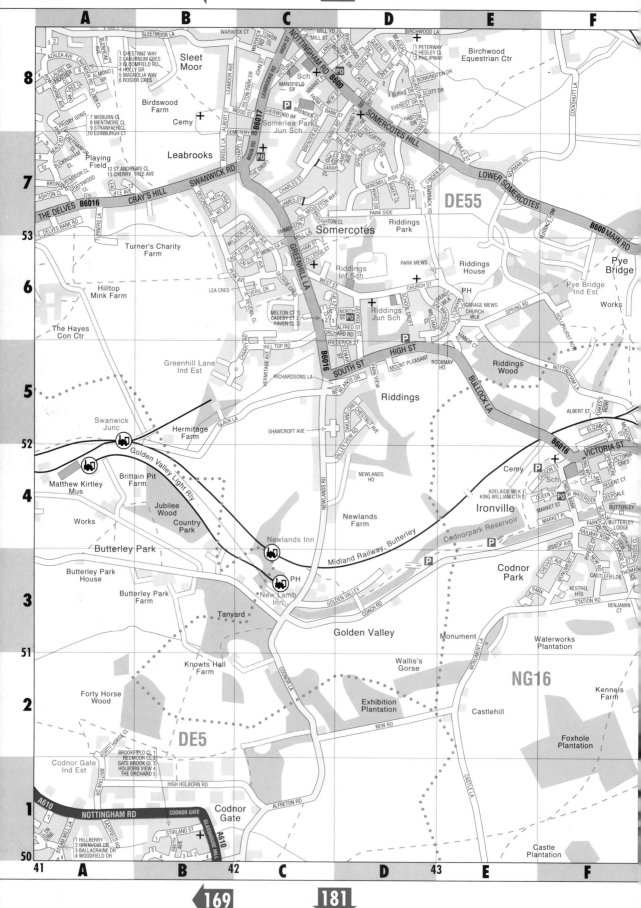

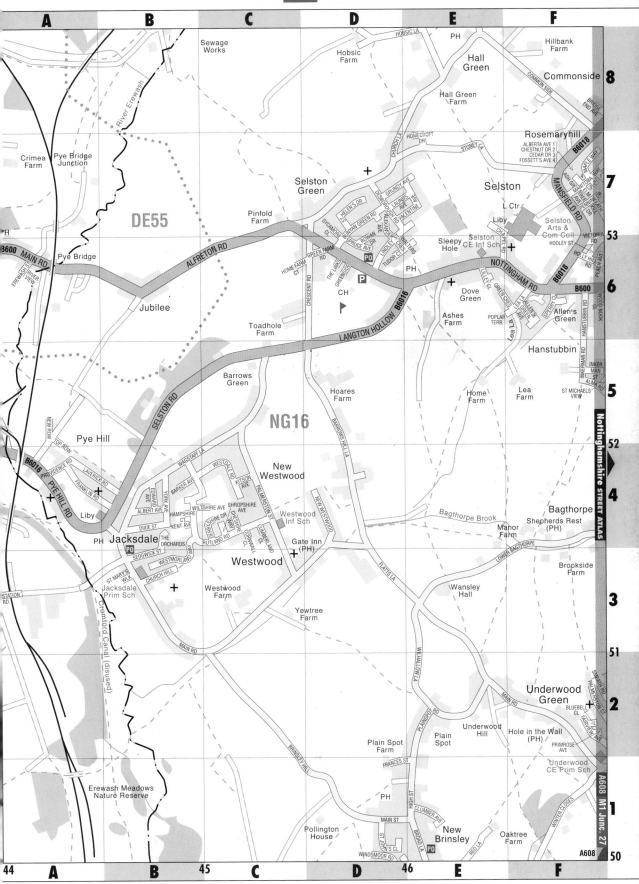

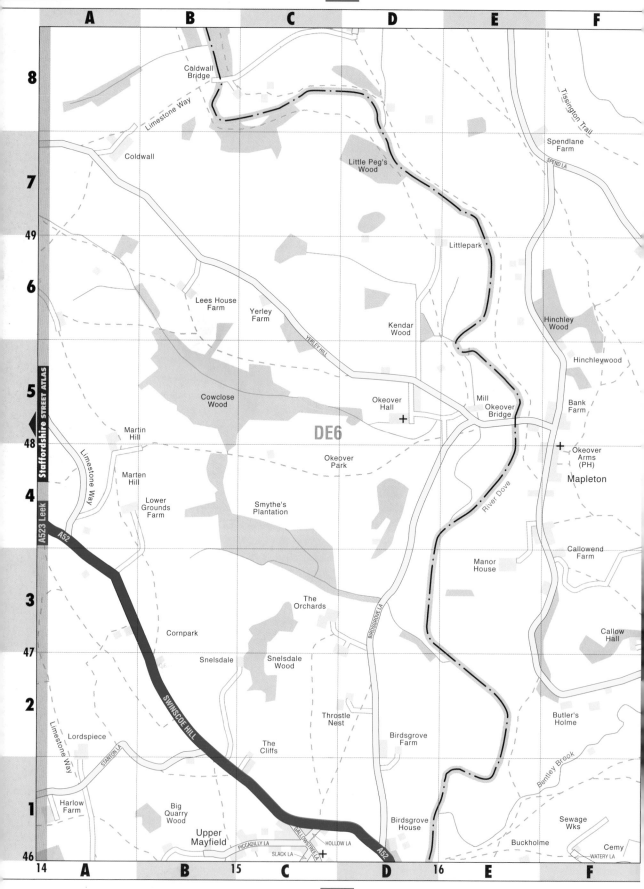

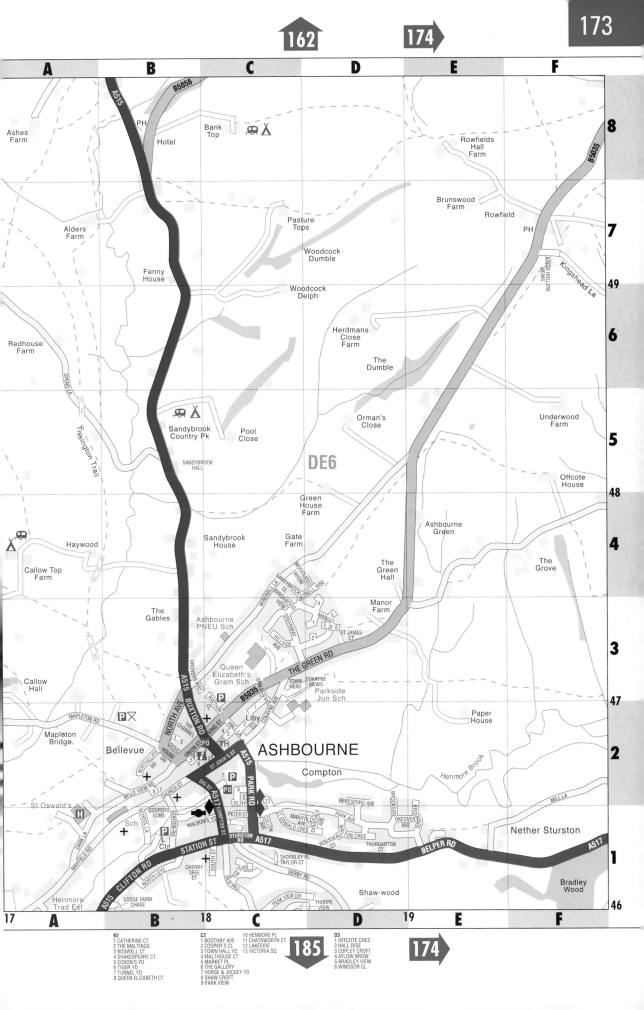

173
163

A B C D E F

8

7

49

6

5

48

4

3

47

2

1

46

20 A B 21 C D 22 E F

WOOD LA
B5035

Brookhouse
Farm

Madge
Hill

Atlow
Winn

Breck
Farm

Shaws

Parkside Brook

WINN LA

Pethills

Kingshead La

Kniveton Brook

Atlowmoat
Farm

Foxhole
Farm

FOXHOLES LA

Woodhead

Green
Farm

Upper
Hallfields

Whitehouse
Farm

Offcote
Grange

DE6

Agnes
Meadow

AGNESMEADOW LA

KNIVETON LA

The
Rough

Ridge La

Annies
Meadow
House

Parkfields
Farm

Ox Close

Agnesmeadow
Bridge

Henmoor Brook

Corley
Farm

Dayfield Brook

Tomlinson
Carr

47

Sturston
Mill

CORLEY LA

A517

Sturston
Hall

MILL LA

Bradley
Pastures

Bradley
Lodge

New House
Farm

A517

Bradley
Wood

Shepherd's
Folly

Bradley
Smithy

YELDERSLEY LA

YEW TREE LA

Airfield
(dis)

Bull
Hill

Bradley
Moor

Bradley
Hall

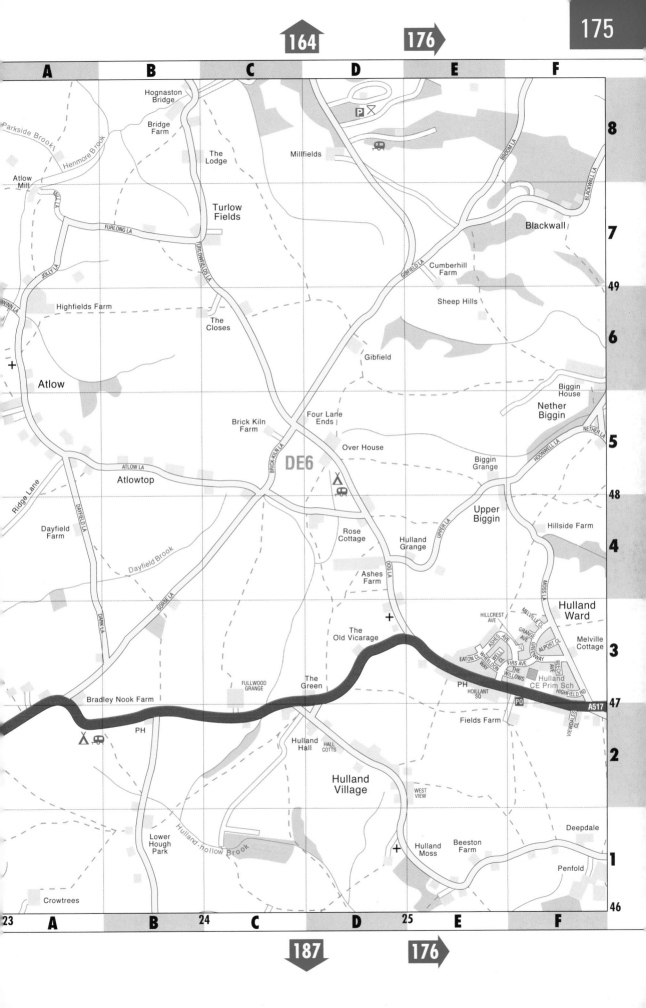

	A	B	C	D	E	F

8

BLACKWALL LA
BROAD WAY
NETHER LA
TOP LONS
BOTTOM LONS
FIELD LA
HOB LA
Addcrofts
TINKERLEY LA
WOOD LA
B5023
JEBB'S LA
(dis)

Field Farm
Winneyhill
Holm Brook

Bennywall Wood

7

The Mountain
Bullhill
Idridgehay Green
JOHNSON LA
CLIFFASH LA

Bennywall Brook

49

Biggin Head Farm
Rakestones Farm
GORSES
CLIFFASH LA
PH LC
ROOD LA

6

Hays Farm
Idridgehay
Southsitch House
WIRKSWORTH RD
B5023
ECCLESBOURNE LA

Biggin
HOONWELL LA
Carr Wood

5

DE6
Cherry Orchard
WINDLEY LA
BIGGINHILL LA
Ford

Nether Biggin
Mill
MAG LA
DE56

48

Millington Green
Hillside Farm
Ireton Wood
NETHER LA

4

Redhouse Farm
NEW RD
White House Farm
Hall
Brook Farm
BULLHILL LA

Lanehead Farm
Iretonwood Farm
Mount Pleasant

Sherbourne Brook

3

BIGGIN LA
Biggin Old Hall
Bull Hill
OLD LA

Stock-a-Sitch
Toad Holes Farm
Lumber Lane Farm
LUMBER LA
HILLCLIFF LA

Springhill Farm

47

A517
Massey's Barn
PH
CROSSWAYS LA
Crossways Farm

2

Cross o' th' hands
A517

Magfield
SMITH-HALL LA

1

Waterlagg Cottage
Beech-hill Farm

Moneyhills
Derbyhill Farm

46

26	A		B	27	C		D	28	E		F

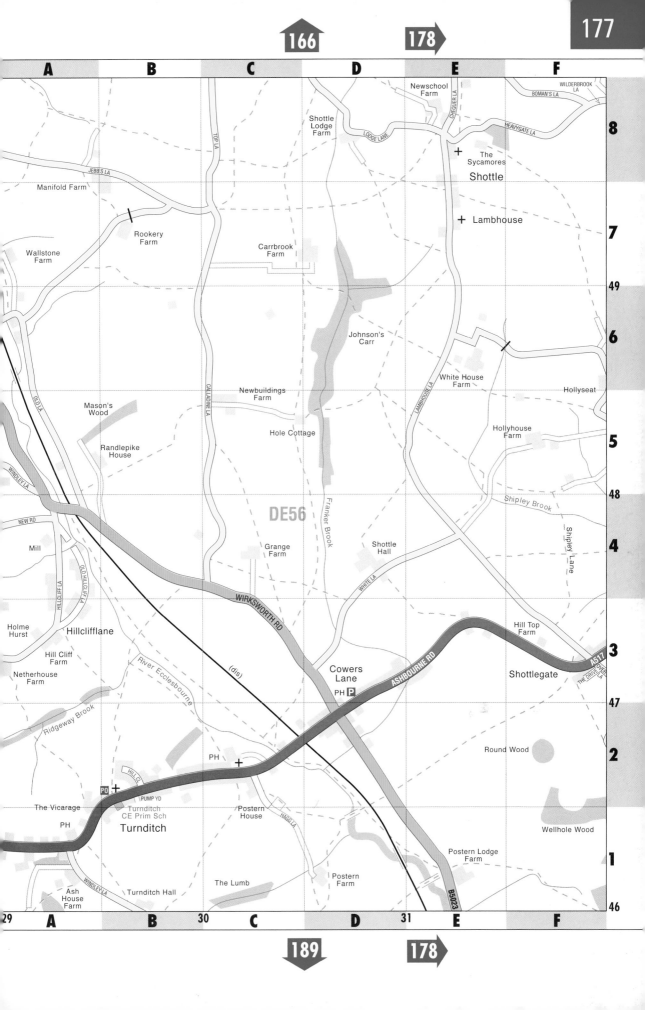

Newschool Farm

WILDERBROOK LA

BOMAN'S LA

Shottle Lodge Farm

LODGE LANE

CHEQUER LA

HEAVYGATE LA

8

The Sycamores

Shottle

Manifold Farm

JEBB'S LA

Lambhouse

7

Rookery Farm

Wallstone Farm

Carrbrook Farm

TOP LA

49

Johnson's Carr

6

White House Farm

Hollyseat

Mason's Wood

Newbuildings Farm

CALLADINE LA

LAMBHOUSE LA

Randlepike House

Hole Cottage

Hollyhouse Farm

5

WINDLEY LA

Shipley Brook

48

OLD LA

DE56

Franker Brook

Grange Farm

Shottle Hall

Shipley Lane

4

Mill

NEW RD

Holme Hurst

Hillclifflane

HILLCLIFF LA

OLD HILLCLIFF LA

WIRKSWORTH RD

WHITE LA

Hill Top Farm

Hill Cliff Farm

(dis)

Cowers Lane

ASHBOURNE RD

Shottlegate

A517

THE DRIVE OVER LA

3

Netherhouse Farm

River Ecclesbourne

PH P

47

Ridgeway Brook

PH

Round Wood

2

HILL CL

The Vicarage

PO

PUMP YD

Turnditch CE Prim Sch

Postern House

HAGG LA

Wellhole Wood

PH

Turnditch

Postern Lodge Farm

1

Ash House Farm

WINDLEY LA

Turnditch Hall

The Lumb

Postern Farm

B5023

46

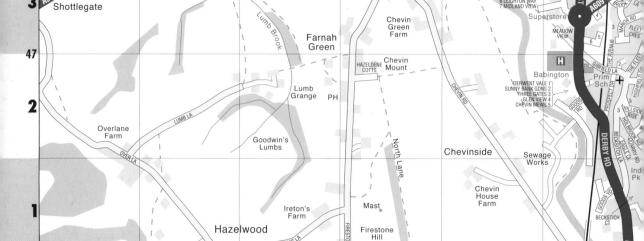

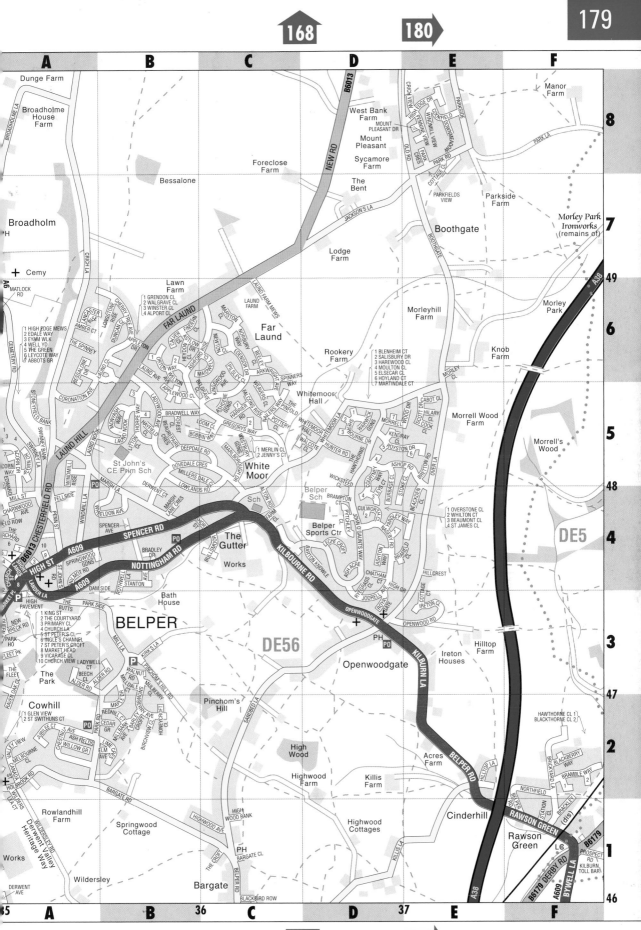

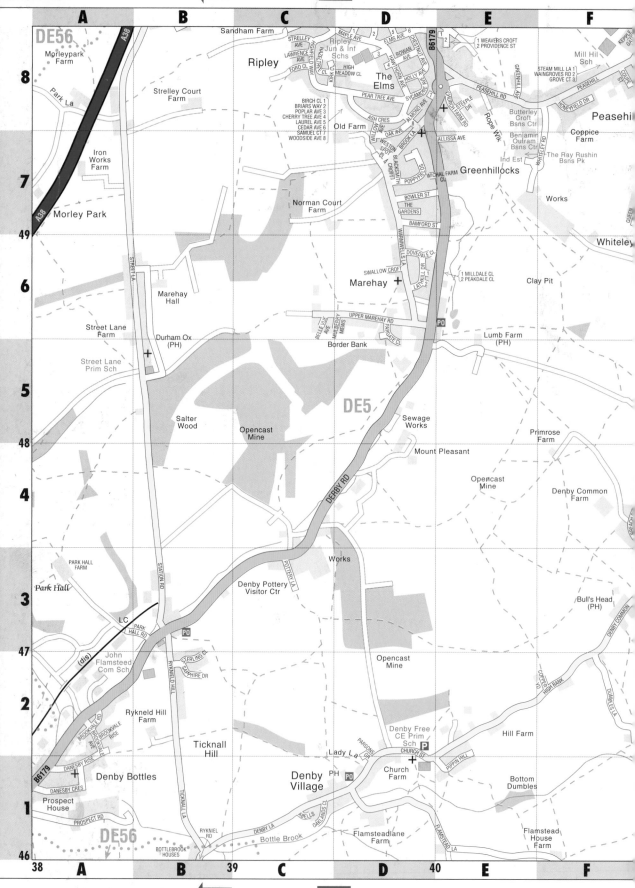

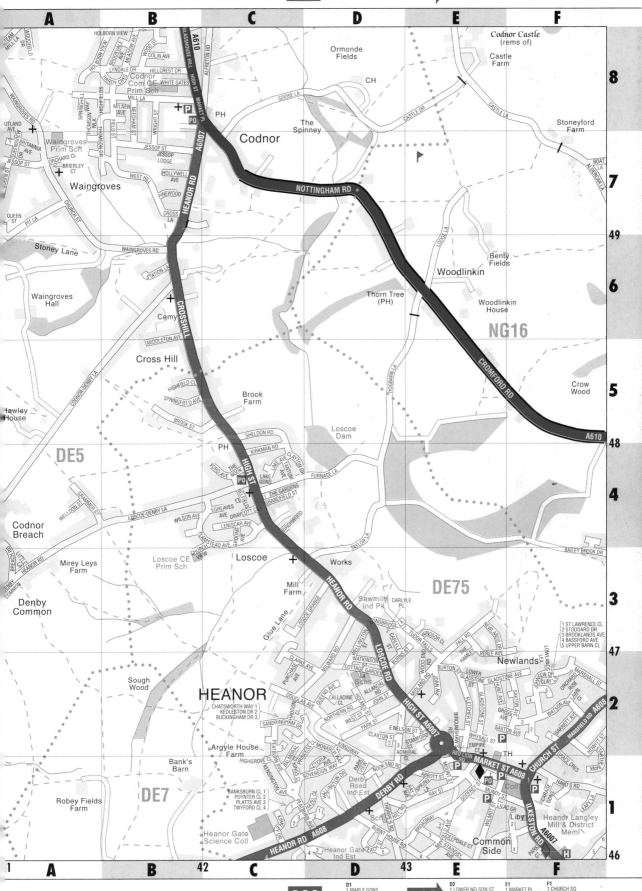

D1
1 MAPLE GDNS
2 CHESTNUT BANK
3 HEANOR GATE
4 HEANOR GATE RD
5 KIRKHAM CL

D2
1 LOWER NELSON ST
2 CLAXTON TERR
3 UPPER NELSON ST
4 HAMPTON CT

E1
1 MARKET PL
2 AMBER CT
3 THE MEADOWS
4 LOCTON AVE

F1
1 CHURCH SQ
2 MERTON CL
3 TRINITY WAY
4 GREYFRIARS CL
5 WESTFIELD AVE
6 ELLA BANK RD

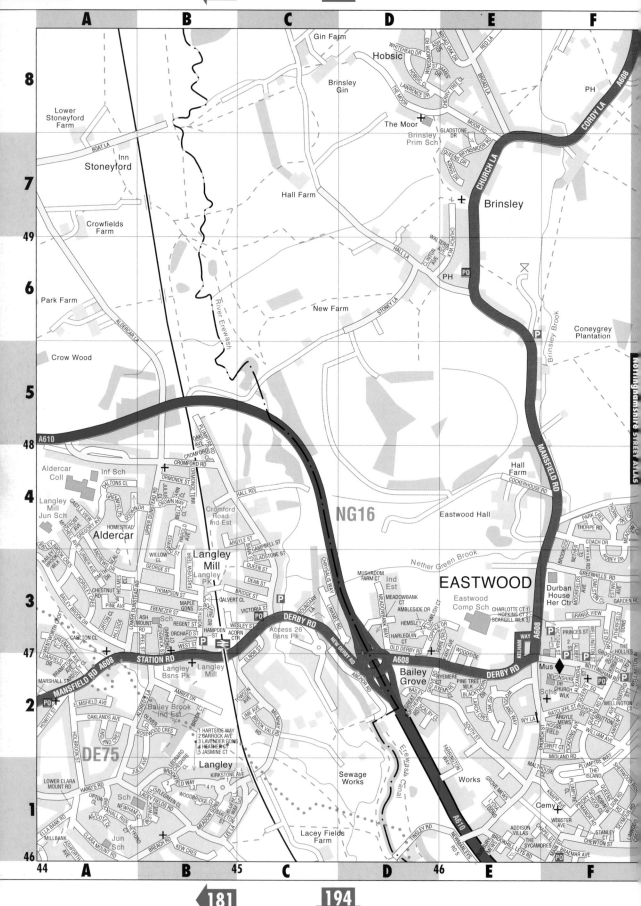

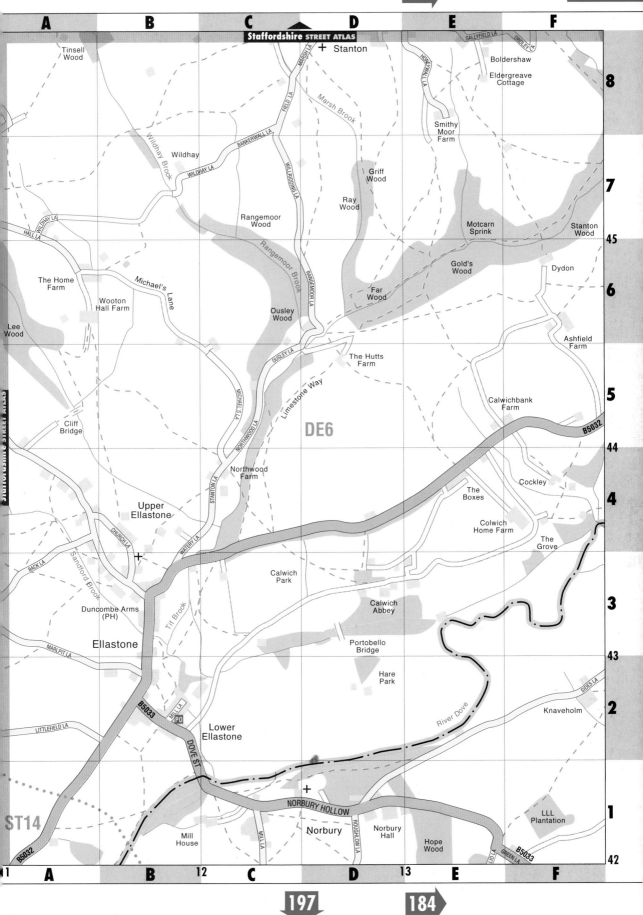

Staffordshire STREET ATLAS

A   B   C   D   E   F

8

7

45

6

5

44

4

3

43

2

1

42

A   12   B   C   13   D   E   F

Tinsell Wood
Stanton
Boldershaw
Eldergreave Cottage
Smithy Moor Farm
Wildhay
Wildhay
Griff Wood
Ray Wood
Rangemoor Wood
Motcarn Sprink
Stanton Wood
The Home Farm
Gold's Wood
Dydon
Wooton Hall Farm
Michael's Lane
Far Wood
Ousley Wood
Ashfield Farm
Lee Wood
The Hutts Farm
Calwichbank Farm
Cliff Bridge
DE6
B5032
Northwood Farm
The Boxes
Cockley
Upper Ellastone
Colwich Home Farm
The Grove
Calwich Park
Duncombe Arms (PH)
Calwich Abbey
Ellastone
Portobello Bridge
Hare Park
River Dove
Knaveholm
B5033
Lower Ellastone
PO
ST14
LLL Plantation
Mill House
Norbury
Norbury Hall
Hope Wood
B5033
B5032
Marsh Brook
Wildhay Brook
Rangemoor Brook
Limestone Way
Sandford Brook
Tit Brook
Dove St
Norbury Hollow
HALL LA
WILDHAY LA
BANKERWALL LA
FIELD LA
WILLRIDDING LA
HONEYWALL LA
SALLYFIELD LA
OROLEY LA
RANGEMOOR LA
OUSLEY LA
MICHAEL'S LA
NORTHWOOD LA
STANTON LA
CHURCH LA
BACK LA
WATERY LA
MARLPIT LA
LITTLEFIELD LA
MILL LA
MILL LA
ROUGHLOW LA
GREEN LA
SIDES LA

183
172

A **B** **C** **D** **E** **F**

8

WATERY LA

A52

Woodside Farm

SLACK LA

OLD BANK

GALLOWSTREE LA

SHINSCOE HILL

Hanging Bridge

MAYFIELD RD

A52

TOLLGATE COTTS

STONE COTTS

Harlow Wood

Limestone Way

Slack Lane

Mayfield

CHURNET CL 1
KINVER CL 2
SUNNY BANK 3
HOLME BANK 4
DOVESIDE 5
OXMEAD 6
SYCAMORE RD 7
EAST VIEW 8

MORRELLS RD

THE PARK

ASHBOURNE RD

MAIN RD

B5032

BRIDGE VIEW

PO

Alrewas Mill

Holme Farm

Hangingbridge

DIAMOND JUBILEE COTTS

7

Wallash

Holme Farm

SLACK LA

HERMITAGE LA

Sch

JUBILEE SQ

DR MAYFIELD AVE

CONYGREE LA

THE CRESCENT

GREEN LA

Doles Farm

Ford

DOLES LA

THE GREENACRE

CLIFTON RD

A515

45

WEIRSIDE

MEADOWSIDE

WATERY LA

CROSS SIDE

THE FAIRWAYS

PO

CLIFTON RD

Clifton CE Prim Sch

6

Middle Mayfield

PH

CHURCH LA

Factory

Clifton Bridge

1 2 3

1 MAYFIELD TERR
2 WEST VIEW
3 SOUTH VIEW

Church Mayfield

River Dove

Hemmore Brook

CHURCH VIEW

COCK HILL

PH

HOLLIES CL

CHAPEL LA

Clifton

CH

5

B5032

Cliff Bank Cottage

SIDES LA

SPRINKSWOODS LA

Cemy

DOBBINHORSE LA

A515

44

Toadhole Foot Bridge

Sides Plantation

DE6

Mountpleasant Farm

4

PARKFIELD LA

Gravelpit Covert

Collycroft

LITTLEFIELD LA

3

OLDFIELD LA

CACKLEHILL LA

Snelston

CHURCH RD

Snelston Hall

BETLINGSPRING LA

Snelston Park

Lower Dumble

Collycroft Farm

Upper Dumble

43

DEEPDALE LA

Old Slade La

Overton Farm

Cackle Hill

Windmill Farm

WINDMILL LA

2

Deepdale

Thornyhill Farm

Brook Farm

Gorse Covert

Ashton Close

Virginsalley

VIRGINSALLEY LA

Lower Brookfarm Dumble

Headlow Fields

1

High Grounds

SNIPES LA

Snelston Firs

Rose Cottage

Anacrehill

A515

42

14 **A** **B** **15** **C** **D** **16** **E** **F**

A B C D E F

8

MAYFIELD RD

Westwood

LODGE FARM CHASE
MARGERY CL
GEORGE ST
LODGE AVE
HIGHFIELD RD
HARBORO

Lodge Farm

CLIFTON • RD
A515

QUIXHILL
NORTHWOOD RISE
CLUMBER CL
PREMIER AVE
BUSCOT DR
HAMILTON
FORSHAW
DUNCOMBE DR

NETHERFIELD CL
Hilltop Inf Sch
Spitalhill

ELIZABETH VILLAS

BOOTH DR
THORNHANGE CL
WRIGHT CRES
SPENCER
WEAVER
MUMFORD DR
SPRINGFIELD AVE
OLD DERBY RD
ROADMEADOW
LAMBOURNE AVE

BRICKYARD COTTS
TREE CL
POPLAR CRES
LIME GR
PINE
CROFT
OAK CRES
WILLOW MEADOW RD
CHESTNUT DR
CEDAR
CL
ROWAN
BEECH DR
WYASTON GDNS
WILLOW

BLOREL PL
CAVENDISH DR
HADDON CT
MILLDALE CT
ILAM RD
SHATTON RD
ASHMEADOW CT

LATHKILL DR

WHITLEY WAY
Dovedale Ct
George Dutton Ind Pk
MOOR FARM RD W
BLENHEIM RD
MOOR FARM RD E

Airfield (dis)

CH

Bank Cottages

1 DERWENT GDNS
2 HAWTHORN CL
3 MAPLE DR
Hilltop
DERBY RD

SNIPE MOOR LA

7

45

GATEWAY CVN PK

Whitemeadow

A52

6

The Hollies

WYASTON RD

Blake House

Centenary Way
Bonnie Prince Charlie Wlk

MOOR LA

Glebe House

5

Briery House

DOBBINHORSE LA

Tinker's Inn

Osmaston Fields Farm

New House Farm

Osmaston CE Prim Sch
CHURCH LA

44

DE6

Osmaston

The Holts

4

New Buildings Farm

A515

Osmaston Pastures

QUILOW LA

Quilow Farm

3

43

Scardale Covert

Copse Hill

Wyaston Brook

THE MEWS
EDLASTON LA

Edlaston Hall

PH

✝ Edlaston

Wyaston

Wyaston Grove

2

Airfield (dis)

Church Farm

Darley Moor Motor Cycle Racing Circuit

ORCHARD LA

1

RODSLEY LA

42

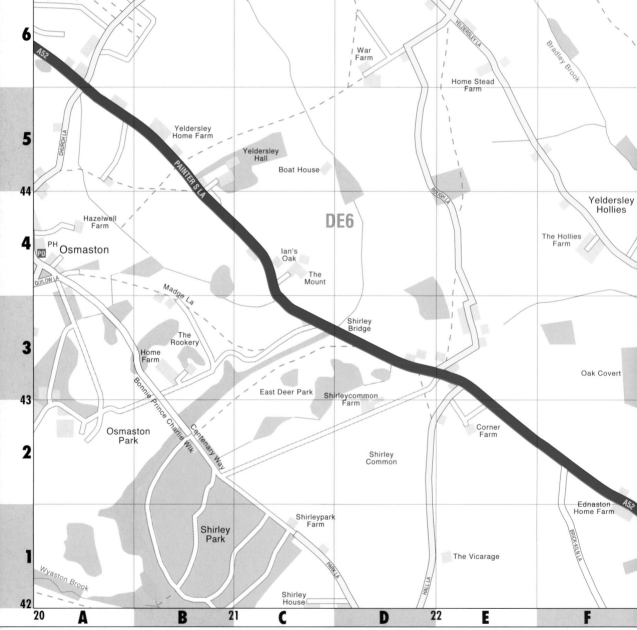

A   B   C   D   E   F

8   Bradley Moor

Park
Farm

Hole
in the
Wall

Lady's
Pond

Bradley

Bradley CE
Prim Sch

Brook
Farm

Moorend

HADLEY LA

PINFOLD LA

Lady Hole
House

Ladyhole
Farm

7

LADY HOLE LA

Firs
Farm

Old Hall
Farm

MILLDAM LA

Knoll
Lodge

45

Airfield
(disused)

DOGKENNEL LA

YELDERSLEY LA

Bradley Brook

6   A52

War
Farm

CHURCH LA

Home Stead
Farm

PAINTER'S LA

Yeldersley
Home Farm

5

Yeldersley
Hall

Boat House

44

ROUGH LA

Yeldersley
Hollies

DE6

Hazelwell
Farm

The Hollies
Farm

4   PH
PO   Osmaston

Ian's
Oak

The
Mount

QUILOW LA

Madge La

Shirley
Bridge

The
Rookery

3

Home
Farm

Oak Covert

East Deer Park

Shirleycommon
Farm

43

Bonnie Prince Charlie Wlk

Corner
Farm

Osmaston
Park

Centenary Way

2

Shirley
Common

Shirleypark
Farm

HALL LA

Ednaston
Home Farm

A52

Shirley
Park

1

BRICK KILN LA

Wyaston Brook

PARK LA

The Vicarage

42   Shirley
House

20   A   B   21   C   D   22   E   F

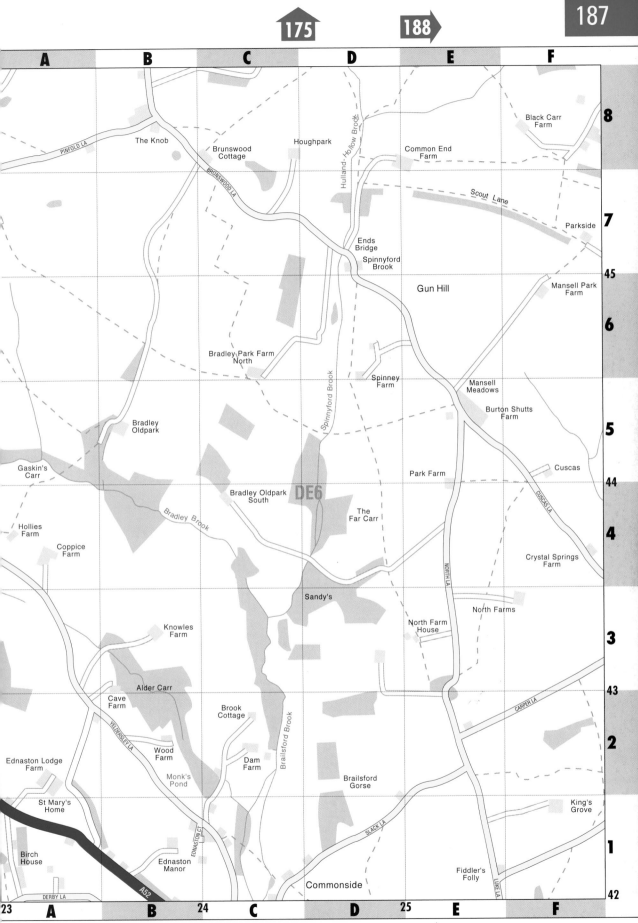

A B C D E F

8

Black Carr
Farm

PINFOLD LA

The Knob

Brunswood
Cottage

Houghpark

Hulland-Hollow Brook

Common End
Farm

Scout Lane

BRUNSWOOD LA

Parkside

7

Ends
Bridge

Spinnyford
Brook

45

Mansell Park
Farm

Gun Hill

6

Bradley Park Farm
North

Spinnyford Brook

Spinney
Farm

Mansell
Meadows

Burton Shutts
Farm

5

Bradley
Oldpark

Cuscas

CUSCAS LA

Gaskin's
Carr

Bradley Oldpark
South

DE6

Park Farm

44

Bradley Brook

The
Far Carr

Hollies
Farm

4

Coppice
Farm

Crystal Springs
Farm

NORTH LA

Sandy's

North Farms

Knowles
Farm

North Farm
House

3

Alder Carr

43

CARPER LA

Cave
Farm

Brook
Cottage

YELDERSLEY LA

Brailsford Brook

2

Ednaston Lodge
Farm

Wood
Farm

Dam
Farm

Monk's
Pond

Brailsford
Gorse

King's
Grove

St Mary's
Home

EDNASTON CT

SLACK LA

1

Birch
House

Ednaston
Manor

Fiddler's
Folly

LUKE LA

A52

DERBY LA

Commonside

42

23 A B 24 C D 25 E F

187 176

A B C D E F

8

Smith Hall Farm

Carr Hall Farm

Waterlagg Brook

Hollinghurst

Works

The Carr

Blackbrook Farm

INTAKES LA

Mast

Common Farm

7

Pit (disused)

Blackbrook Farm

Herbalshaw Meadow Farm

The Clives

SMITH HALL LA

45

DE56

Redmiregap

Parkhill Farm

Muggintonlane End

Mansell Park

Humblebee Hill

6

The Hollies

Black Brook

Park Farm

Old Covert Farm

Highfields Farm

HIGHFIELD LA

5

Sand Pit

Sand Pit

DE6

Old Covert

Cock Inn (PH)

44

Shuckton Manor Farm

MERCASTON LA

Works

BULLHURST LA

Pit (dis)

4

Brook Farm

Ling Hill

CUSPAS LA

Hill Top Farm

Mill House

3

CARPER LA

ALDER LA

Mercaston Green

HUNGER LA

Hunger Hill

Mercaston

Schoolhouse Farm

Hungerhill Brook

Mugginton

43

Brailsford Common

Ford

Mercaston Brook

TAGHOLE LA

Mugginton CE Prim Sch

Malkin Lane

2

The Gables

CHURCH LA

GREEN LA

Greenlane Brook

Hazlehurst

Wood Lane

Top House Farm

Sewage Works

1

ALLEN LA

NEW RD

Centenary Way

Trent Trout Farm

New House Farm

42

26 A B 27 C D 28 E F

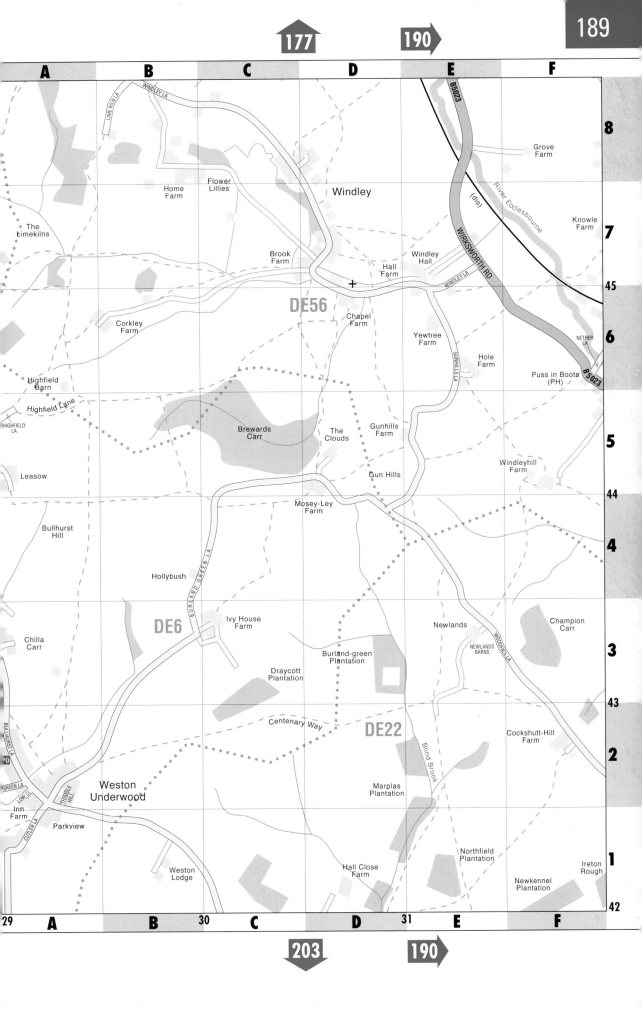

A B C D E F

8

7

45

6

5

44

4

3

43

2

1

42

B5023

Grove Farm

Windley

The Limekilns

Home Farm

Flower Lillies

Knowle Farm

River Ecclesbourne

(dis)

WIRKSWORTH RD

Windley Hall

Brook Farm

Hall Farm

Windley La

DE56

Chapel Farm

Corkley Farm

Yewtree Farm

GUNHILLS LA

Hole Farm

NETHER LA

Puss in Boots (PH)

B 5023

Highfield Barn

Highfield Lane

HIGHFIELD LA

Brewards Carr

The Clouds

Gunhills Farm

Windleyhill Farm

Leasow

Gun Hills

Mosey-Ley Farm

Bullhurst Hill

BURLAND GREEN LA

Hollybush

Champion Carr

DE6

Ivy House Farm

Newlands

NEWLANDS BARNS

WOODFIELD LA

Chilla Carr

Burland-green Plantation

Draycott Plantation

Centenary Way

DE22

Cockshutt-Hill Farm

BULLHURST LA

Blind Brook

Marplas Plantation

GREEN LA

LOW CL

Weston Underwood

THIMBLE HILL

Inn Farm

CUTLER LA

Parkview

Weston Lodge

Hall Close Farm

Northfield Plantation

Newkennel Plantation

Ireton Rough

29 A B 30 C D 31 E F

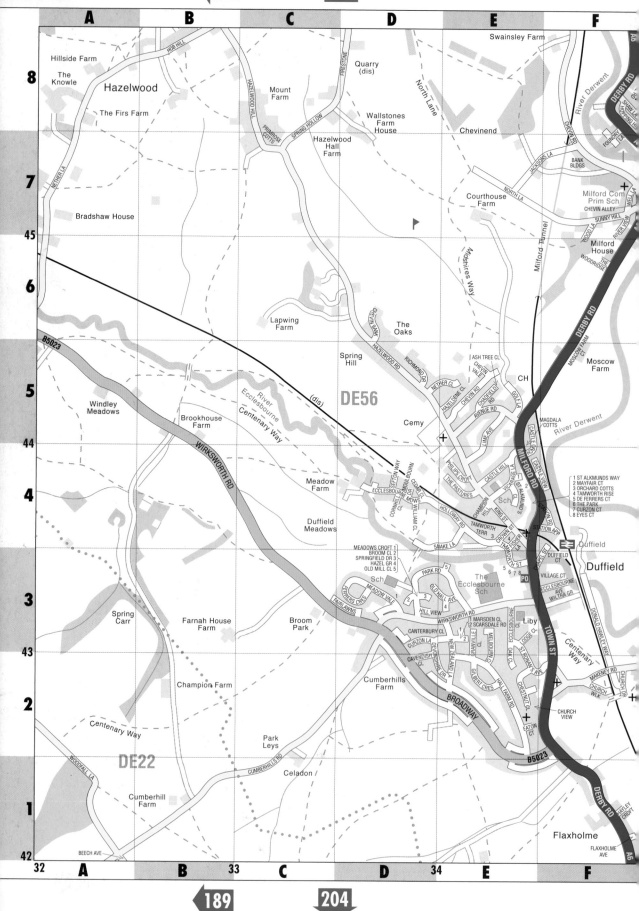

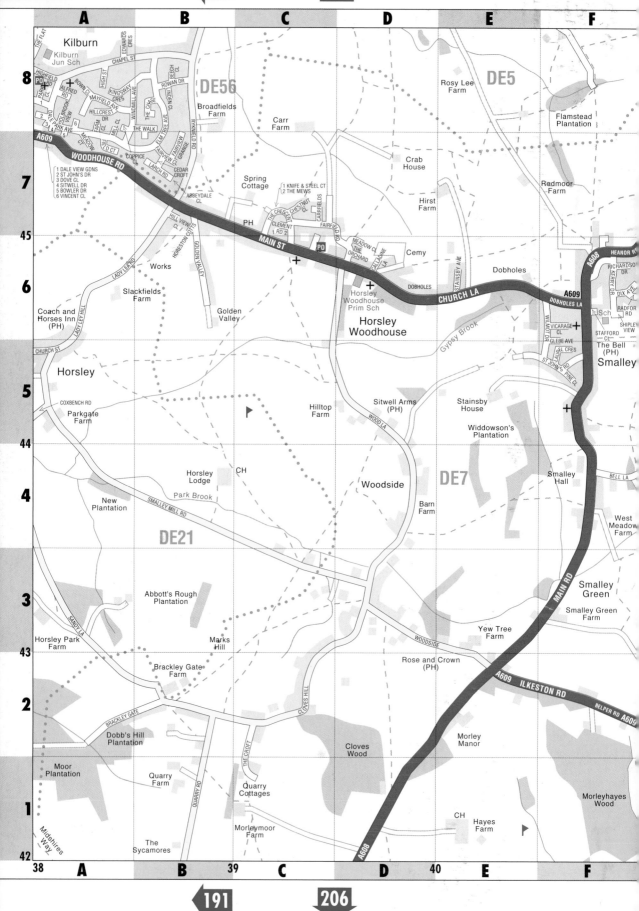

E1
1 BRUSSELLS TERR
2 STAMFORD ST
3 STATION CT
4 FULLWOOD AVE
5 PROVIDENCE PL
6 FULLWOOD ST
7 WHARNCLIFFE RD
8 JACKSON AVE
9 GREGORY ST

F1
1 BURLEIGH ST
2 ESSEX ST
3 DURHAM ST
4 NORTHGATE ST
5 WILTON ST
6 WEST TERR
7 NORTH ST
8 CHAPEL ST
9 UPPER CHAPEL ST

10 RIGLEY AVE

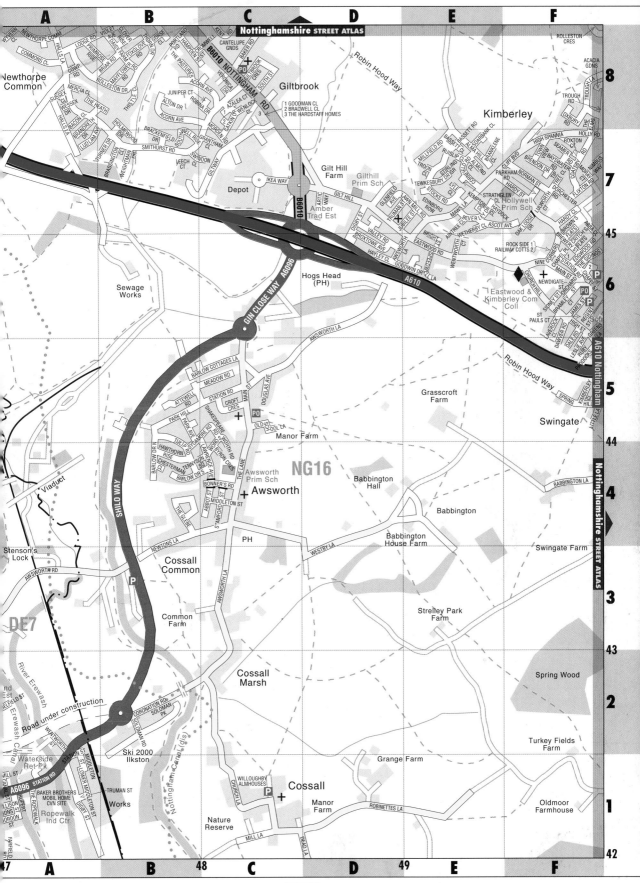

A **B** **C** **D** **E** **F**

Holbrook
Farm

Saltersford Lane

ST10

Folly
Farm

Alverton Hall
Farm

8

B5032

Prestwood La

B5032

Quixhill La

QUIXHILL BANK

7

DENSTONE LA

QUIXHILL LA

Quixhill

41

Windyharbour

Little Park
Farm

Oliver's
Green

THE
WEAVERS

Quixhill
Bridge

Denstone
Hall

Staffordshire Way

Manor
Farm

GREENFIELDS 1
ST CHAD'S CL 2
CROFTSTEAD AVE 3

3 2

MARLPIT LA

ALTON RD

B5031

The Tavern
(PH)

6

Nabb
Farm

HOLLIS LA

COLLEGE RD

COLLEGE RD

THE
WESTLANDS

BIRCH
CL

ELM
VIEW

Denstone

All Saints
CE Fst Sch

HAWTHORN
CL

VERNON GR

LADY MEADOW

Harper
Meadow

Staffordshire STREET ATLAS

5

Denstone
Coll

ST14

STUBWOOD HOLLOW

Stubwood
Farm

Rycroft
CE Mid Sch

B5030

40

Hallriddings

Smalley

TAYLORS LA

B5031

4

Nabb La

Nabb Brook

Riddings

Stubwood

River Churnet

NORTHFIELD AVE 1
ROWAN CT 2

EBBS FARM DR

ASHBOURNE RD

Woodhouse
Farm

Armitage

STUBWOOD LA

JARDINES LA

Works

Churnet
Bridge

CHURNET
ROW

HIGH ST

PO

5

SOUTH
VIEW WLK

RIVERSFIELD DR

WOODLAND DR

DOVEFIELD

ATKINS RD

EATON RD

3

Woodhouse
Fields
Farm

Woodhouse
Fields

HOLLINGTON RD

Banks
Farm

MILL ST 1
WESTGATE CL 2
ABBEY RD 3
CHURCH LA 4
WHITAKER MEWS 5

39

Alders

New
Plantation

2

Woottons
Farm

Alders Brook

Pit Holes
Plantation

Ford

Cornhill
Farm

Woodseat

1

Nothill Brook

Field Head
Farm

B5030

DE6

River Dove

38

A 08 **B** 09 **C** **D** 10 **E** **F**

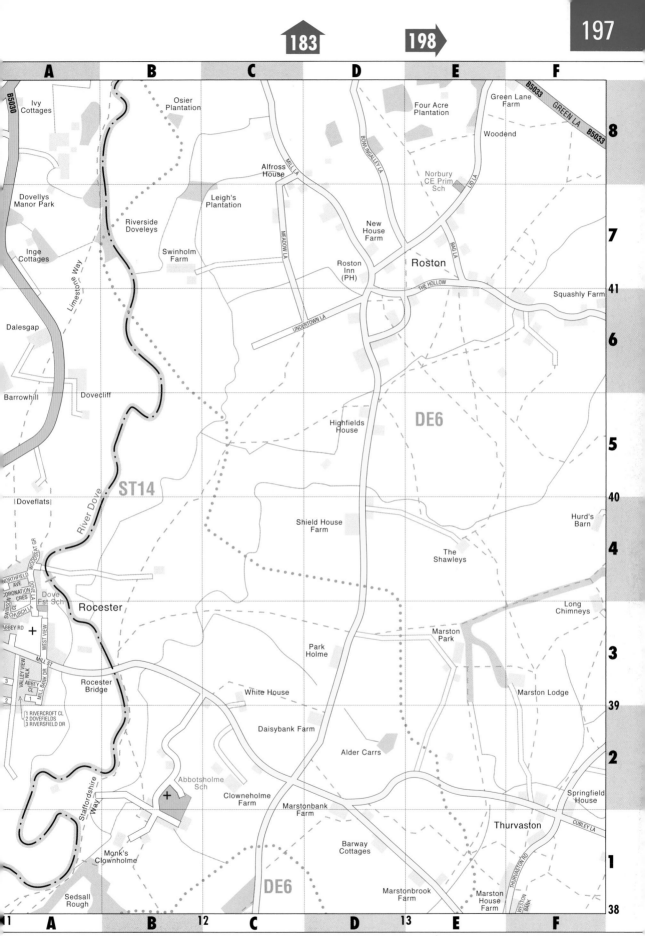

B5030

Ivy Cottages

Osier Plantation

Four Acre Plantation

Green Lane Farm

B5033

GREEN LA

B5033

8

Woodend

Dovellys Manor Park

Riverside Doveleys

Leigh's Plantation

Alfross House

Norbury CE Prim Sch

MILL LA

BOWLING ALLEY LA

LID LA

Inge Cottages

Swinholm Farm

New House Farm

BAG LA

7

Limestone Way

MEADOW LA

Roston Inn (PH)

Roston

Dalesgap

River Dove

Roston

THE HOLLOW

Squashly Farm

41

UNDERTOWN LA

6

Barrowhill

Dovecliff

Highfields House

DE6

ST14

5

40

Doveflats

Shield House Farm

Hurd's Barn

4

WOODSEAT GR

NORTHFIELD AVE

DOVE LA

CORONATION CRES

SWINSON CL

CHURCH LA

Dove Fst Sch

The Shawleys

Long Chimneys

Rocester

ABBEY RD

WEST VIEW

Marston Park

MILL ST

Park Holme

VALLEY VIEW WLK

ABBEY CL

MILL BANK DR

3

3

2

Rocester Bridge

White House

Marston Lodge

39

1 RIVERCROFT CL
2 DOVEFIELDS
3 RIVERSFIELD DR

Daisybank Farm

2

Alder Carrs

Springfield House

Abbotsholme Sch

Clowneholme Farm

Marstonbank Farm

Thurvaston

CUBLEY LA

Staffordshire Way

Monk's Clownholme

Barway Cottages

THURVASTON RD

1

Sedsall Rough

DE6

Marstonbrook Farm

Marston House Farm

WESTON BANK

38

A B C D E F

8

Shepherdswood

Chapel House

Queen Adelaide Arms (PH)

Snelston Common

Old Queen Farm

Flat Covert

Cindershills Wood

Darley Moor

B5033

GREEN LA

SNAPES LA

VIRGINS ALLEY LA

COCKSHEAD LA

B5033

A515

7

Common Farm

Quarry (dis)

John Roe's Covert

Grange Cottage

Top Stydd

41

Grange Farm

Manor House

6

Roston Common

Birchwood Park

Cubley Brook

Birchwoodmoor

5

DE6

Cubley Wood Farm

Marstoncommon Farm

Accession Wood

40

Wood Hay Farm

The Hollies

HOLLIES LA

Side Gate

4

Broad Lane

Whiterley

Sandhills Farm

Cubley Covert

Sammy's Wood

3

Holme Lea

Cubley Common

39

Cubley Cottage Farm

Gorse Covert

Common Farm

2

Mountpleasant Farm

Rough Grounds

THE ROW

1

Birch Field Farm

The Spinney

Brookside Farm

Great Cubley

CUBLEY LA

SHAW LA

A515

DERBY LA

PO

LONG MOW

38

Cubley Fields Farm

Howard Arms (PH)

14 A B 15 C D 16 E F

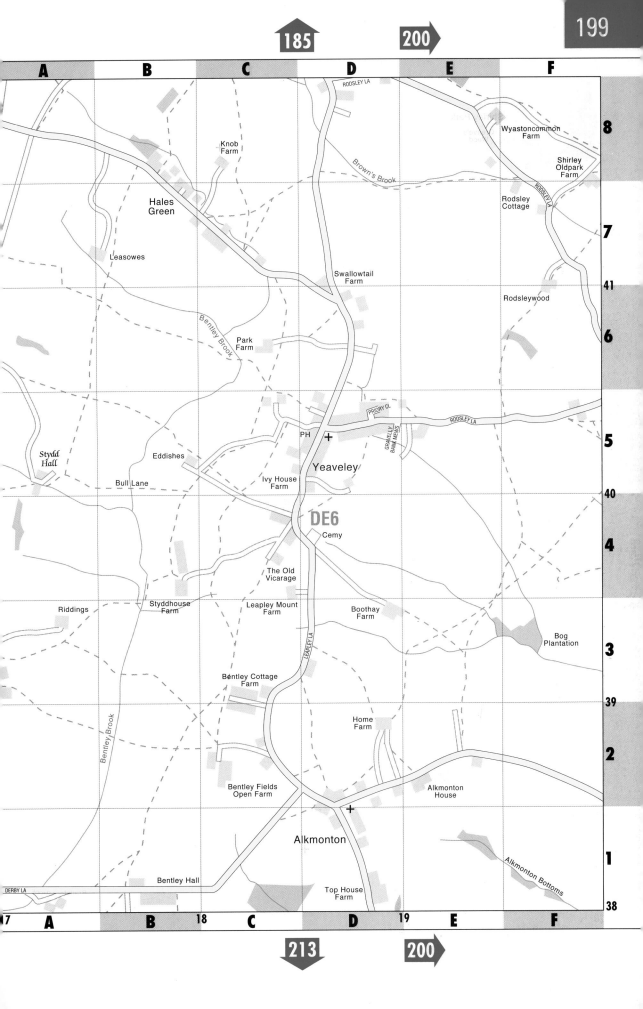

A   B   C   D   E   F

RODSLEY LA

Wyastoncommon
Farm

Shirley
Oldpark
Farm

Brown's Brook

RODSLEY LA

Rodsley
Cottage

8

Hales
Green

Leasowes

Rodsleywood

7

41

Swallowtail
Farm

Bentley Brook

Park
Farm

6

PRIORY CL

RODSLEY LA

GRAVELLY
BANK MEWS

PH

Stydd
Hall

Eddishes

Yeaveley

5

Bull Lane

Ivy House
Farm

40

DE6

Cemy

4

The Old
Vicarage

Riddings

Styddhouse
Farm

Leapley Mount
Farm

Boothay
Farm

Bog
Plantation

3

Bentley Cottage
Farm

39

LEAPLEY LA

Home
Farm

2

Bentley Brook

Bentley Fields
Open Farm

Alkmonton
House

Alkmonton

1

Alkmonton Bottoms

DERBY LA

Bentley Hall

Top House
Farm

38

A   B   C   D   E   F

17   18   19

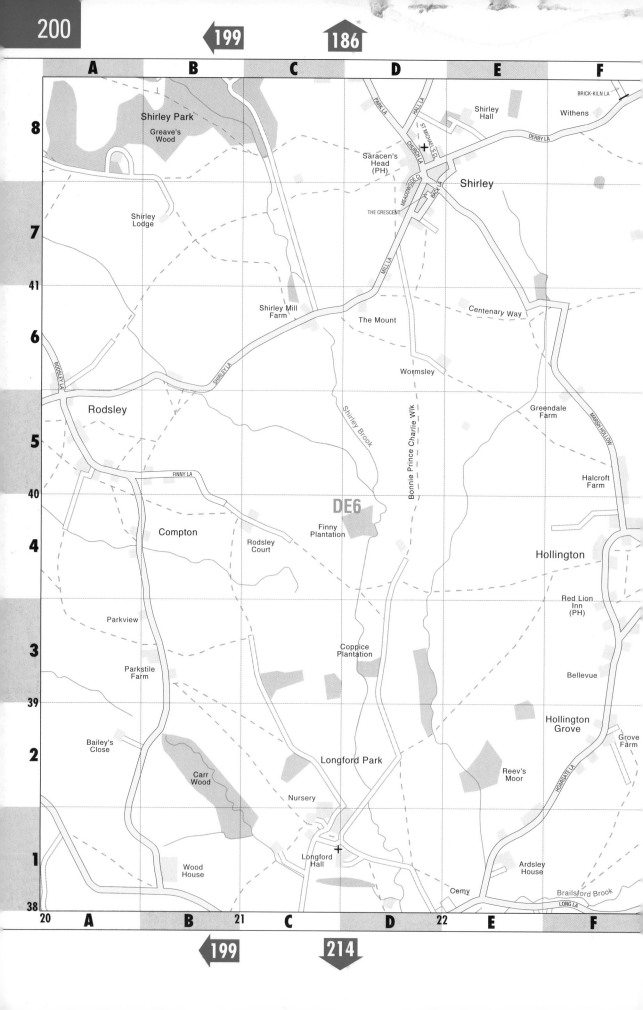

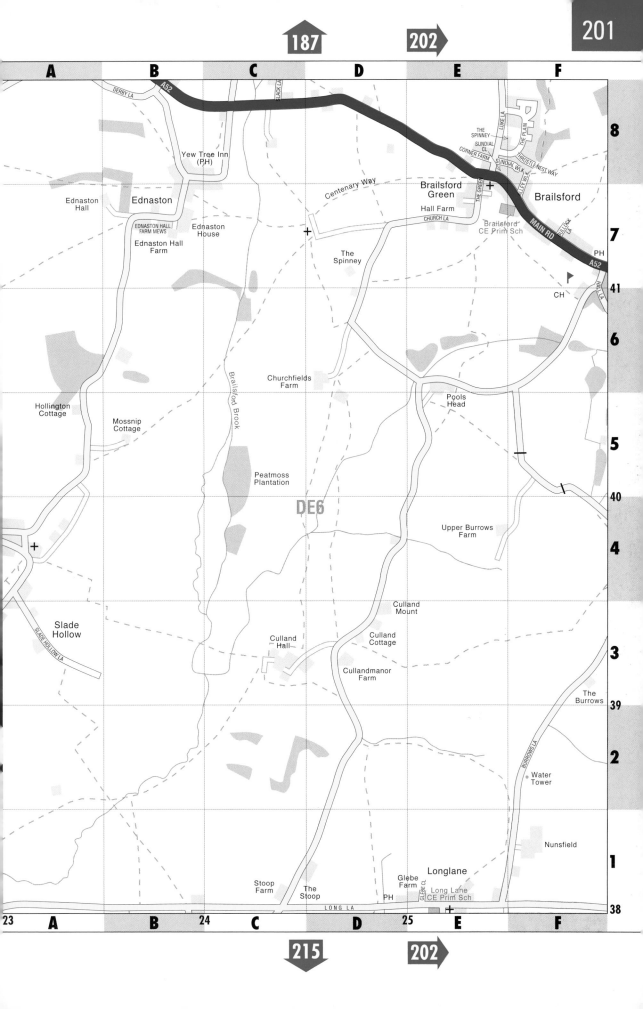

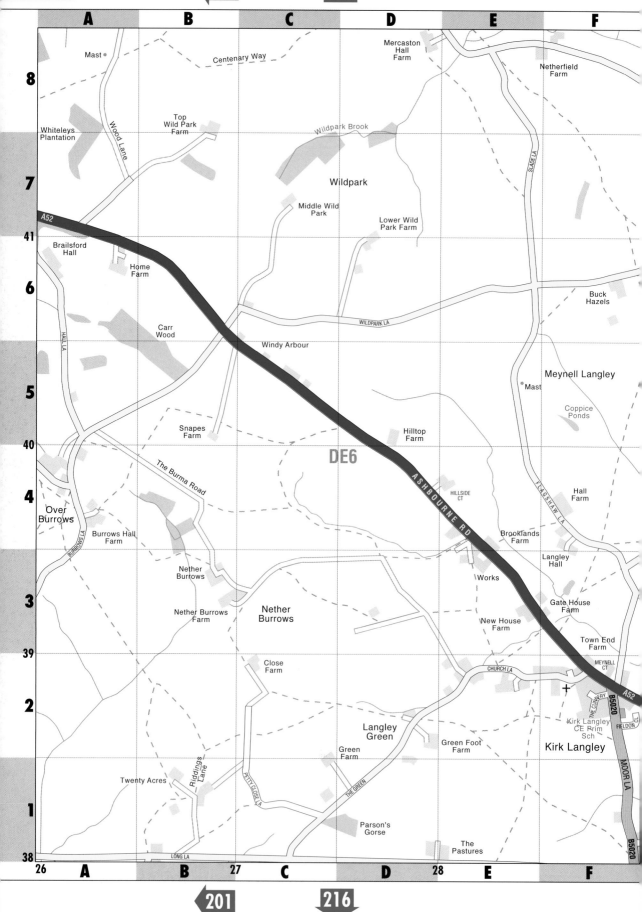

A B C D E F

8

Mast

Centenary Way

Mercaston Hall Farm

Netherfield Farm

Whiteleys Plantation

Wood Lane

Top Wild Park Farm

Wildpark Brook

7

A52

Wildpark

Middle Wild Park

Lower Wild Park Farm

Slade La

41

Brailsford Hall

Home Farm

Wildpark La

Buck Hazels

6

Hall La

Carr Wood

Windy Arbour

Meynell Langley

Mast

Coppice Ponds

5

Snapes Farm

Hilltop Farm

DE6

40

The Burma Road

Hillside Ct

Flagshaw La

Hall Farm

4

Over Burrows

Burrows Hall Farm

Ashbourne Rd

Brooklands Farm

Langley Hall

Burrows La

Nether Burrows

Works

Gate House Farm

3

Nether Burrows Farm

Nether Burrows

New House Farm

Town End Farm

Meynell Ct

39

Close Farm

Church La

A52

2

Kirk Langley CE Prim Sch

B5020

The Cumbery

Fieldon Cl

Langley Green

Green Farm

Green Foot Farm

Kirk Langley

Twenty Acres

Riddings Lane

Petty Close La

Parson's Gorse

Moor La

1

The Green

The Pastures

38

Long La

B5020

26 A B 27 C D 28 E F

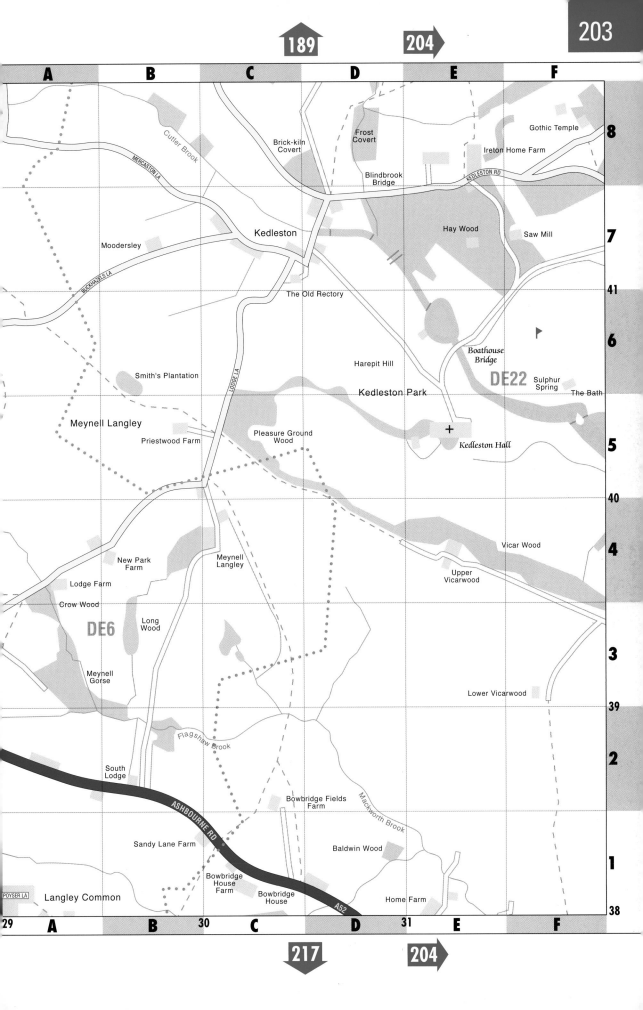

A B C D E F

8
Gothic Temple
Frost Covert
Brick-kiln Covert
Ireton Home Farm
Blindbrook Bridge
KEDLESTON RD
Cutler Brook
MERCASTON LA

7
Kedleston
Hay Wood
Saw Mill
Moodersley
BUCKHAZELS LA

41
The Old Rectory

6
Boathouse Bridge
Harepit Hill
DE22
Sulphur Spring
The Bath
Smith's Plantation
LODGE LA
Kedleston Park

5
Meynell Langley
Pleasure Ground Wood
Kedleston Hall
Priestwood Farm

40

4
Vicar Wood
New Park Farm
Meynell Langley
Upper Vicarwood
Lodge Farm
Crow Wood
Long Wood
DE6

3
Meynell Gorse
Lower Vicarwood

39
Flagshaw Brook

2
South Lodge
Bowbridge Fields Farm
Mackworth Brook
ASHBOURNE RD

1
Sandy Lane Farm
Baldwin Wood
Bowbridge House Farm
Bowbridge House
Home Farm
A52

38
POYSER LA
Langley Common

29 A B 30 C D 31 E F

D2
1 CARSINGTON HO
2 NORBURY CT
3 KEDLESTON CT

F2
1 WICKERSLEY CL
2 MALTBY CL
3 ST HUGH'S CL
4 ST MATTHEW'S WLK

F3
1 BIRCHOVER HO
2 CHURCH LA N
3 TUDOR CT

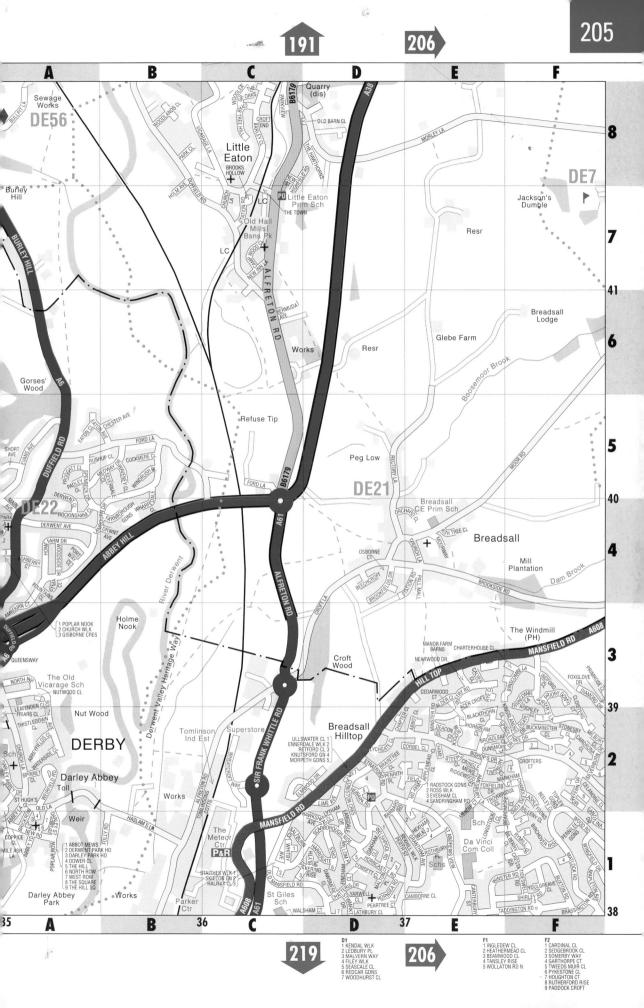

A B C D E F

8

Priory
Cottages
Little
Wood

Breadsall
Priory
Hotel

Morley
Smithy

Smithy
Farm

CH

Almshouses

Morley
Prim Sch

Park
Farm

7

MORLEY LA

MORLEY ALMSHOUSES

Morley
House
Farm

Morley
Hall

Hayes
Park
Farm

Lodge
Farm

Morleymoor

MOOR RD

QUARRY RD

BRICKKILN LA

PRIMROSE DR

PH

MOSES LA

41

The
Mound

Morley

Midshires Way

CHURCH LA

6

DE21

Spring
Oak
Farm

Newtop
Farm

DE7

Jesse
Farm

5

Derby Coll
(Broomfield Campus)

Broomfield
COTTS

40

Broomfield
Farm

Lime
Farm

LIME LA

The
Limes

4

Ferriby Brook

Chaddesden
Common

Kings
Corner

BROOKSIDE
RD

North
Lodge

A608

1 GLENORCHY CT
2 APPLEGATE CL
3 BRAMBLEBERRY CT
4 TISSINGTON DR
5 CRESSBROOK WAY

1 HEDGEROW GDNS
2 HEDGEBANK CT
3 MAYTREE CL

PH

DERBY RD

MANSFIELD
RD

3

PRIMROSE
CL

DERBY

Chaddesden
Wood

CROSSDALE GR

LIME LA

CONSORT
GDNS

SOVEREIGN WAY

ROYAL
GR

CORONET
CT

BARON
CL

HEMLOCK CL

FOXGLOVE DR

1 CELANDINE CL
2 DUNKERY CT
3 SELWORTHY CL
4 PORLOCK CT
5 BONNYRIGG CL
6 HAREBELL CL

DIAMOND
DR

EMERALD
CL

Parkview
Prim Sch

39

Football
Training
Ground

8 ELKSTONE CL
9 CHURCHDOWN CL
10 ARMSCOTE CL
11 BARCHESTON CL
12 CULWORTH CT
13 MOUNTFORD CL
14 LAMPETER CL
15 OXWICH CT
16 BRIDGEND CT
17 SHREWSBURY CL

Birch
Wood

2

Oakwood
L Ctr

DE21

Birchwood
House

Locko
Hall

Locko
Park

1 COLUMBINE CL
2 SWANWICK GDNS
3 ANSTEY CT
4 THURLOW CT
5 DELAMERE CL

Crow
Wood
Farm

1

OAKWOOD DISTRICT CTR

1 THORESBY CL
2 BASSINGHAM CL
3 ROSEBERRY CT
4 FIRTREE GR
5 WHYTELEAFE GR
6 BICKLEY MOSS
7 SAMANTHA CT

Hill
Farm

The Lake

38

Morley Hall
Prep Sch

38 A B 39 C D 40 E F

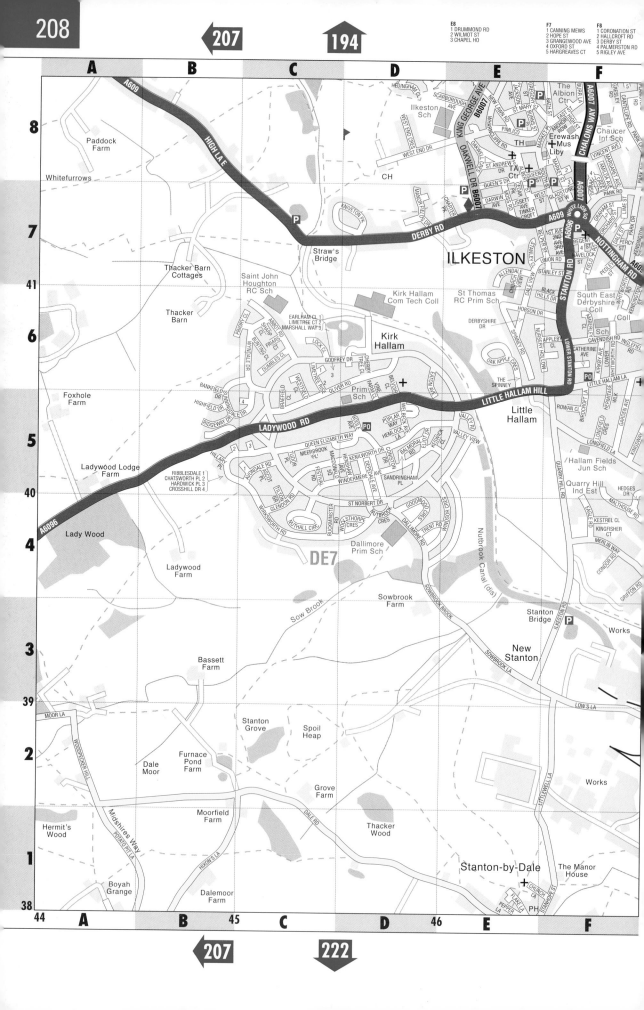

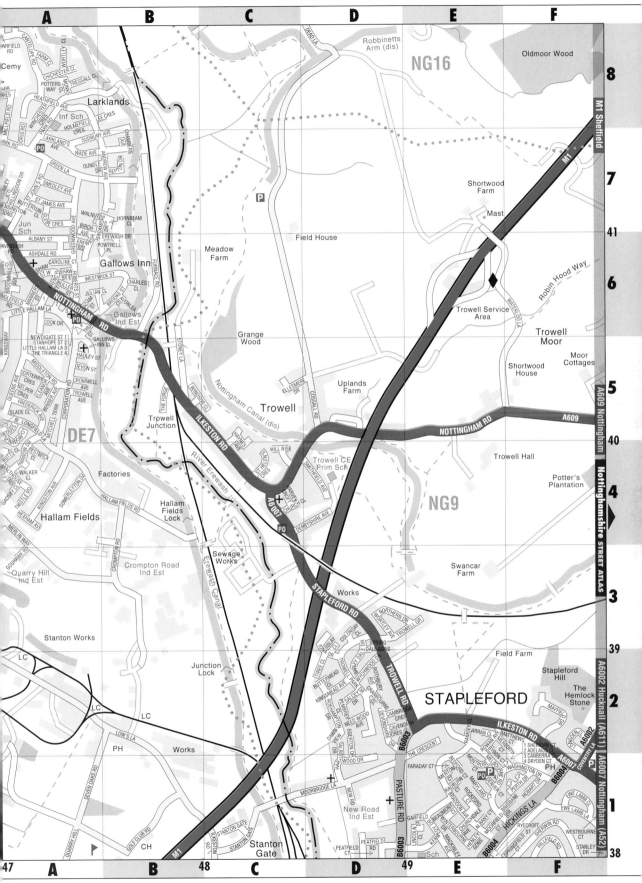

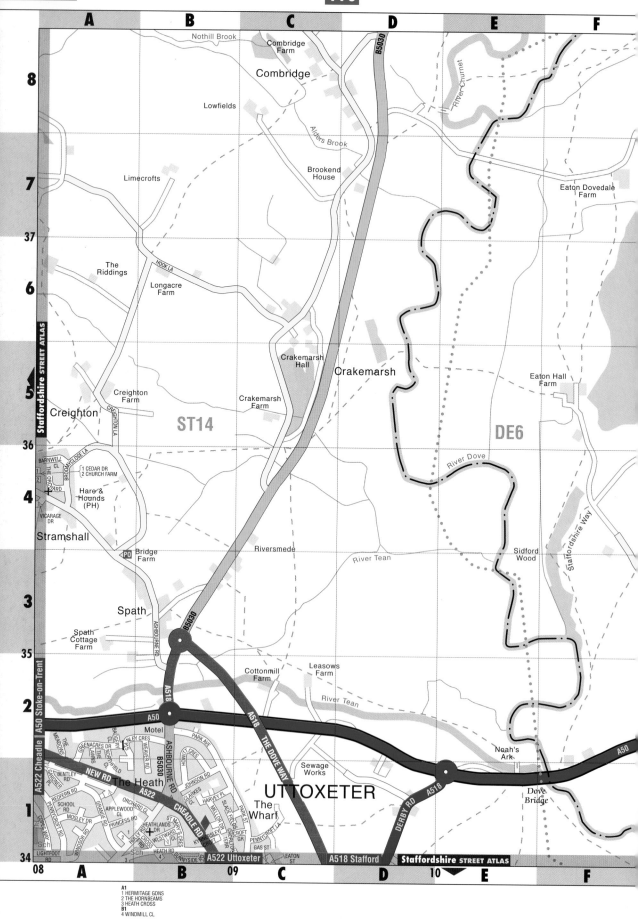

A B C D E F

8

7

37

6

Staffordshire STREET ATLAS

5

36

4

3

35

2

1

34

A50 Stoke-on-Trent

Combridge
Farm

Combridge

Nothill Brook

Lowfields

Limecrofts

The
Riddings

HOOK LA

Longacre
Farm

CREIGHTON LA

Creighton
Farm

Creighton

ST14

BARNWELL
CL

BROOMYCLOSE LA

1 CEDAR DR
2 CHURCH FARM

THE ORCHARD

Hare &
Hounds
(PH)

VICARAGE DR

Stramshall

PO

Bridge
Farm

Spath
Cottage
Farm

Spath

ASHBOURNE RD

B5030

A518

A50

Motel

B5030

THE MEADOWS

GREENACRES DR

BAGGLEY LA

SINLEY CRES

NORFIELD

WEAVER RD

PARK AVE

KINGH

CLADWELL

JOHNSON RD

THE LAWNS

A522 Cheadle

GARDNER PL

BENTLEY RD

REDFERN RD

NEW RD

WINDSOR RD

SCHOOL RD

MOSLEY DR

GRANGE RD

PRINCESS RD

The Heath

ORCHARD CL

APPLEWOOD CL

HEATHLANDS

ST MARY CRES

HOLLY RD

HEATH CROSS

WESTWARD CL

Sch

HEATH RD

SUNNYSIDE

A522

CHEADLE RD

PARK ST

HARVEY PL

WELDON DR

SLADE FIELDS

CHIRCROFT

CHIRCROFT
GR

PARK ST

PENNYCROFT LA

GAS ST

KYNNERSLEY RD

EATON ST

A522 Uttoxeter

The
Wharf

UTTOXETER

Sewage
Works

Cottonmill
Farm

Riversmede

Crakemarsh
Farm

Crakemarsh
Hall

Brookend
House

Alders Brook

B5030

Crakemarsh

Leasows
Farm

River Tean

River Tean

THE DOVE WAY

A518

DERBY RD

A518

A518 Stafford

Staffordshire STREET ATLAS

Noah's
Ark

Dove
Bridge

River Dove

DE6

Eaton Hall
Farm

River Dove

Sidford
Wood

Staffordshire Way

River Churnet

Eaton Dovedale
Farm

A50

08   A   B   09   C   D   10   E   F

197
212

A B C D E F

8
7
37
6
5
36
4
3
35
2
1
34

Morry House Farm

ST14

Manor House

Sch PO 1
PEARL BANK
1 WESTON BANK
2 THURVASTON RD

Marston Montgomery

PH

Eaton Barn

Sedsall Farm

Havenhouse Farm

WALDLEY LA

Beggarsbutts

The Beeches

Banktop

Waldley

Eaton Wood

Waldley Farm

Marston Brook

Marston Woodhouse

Upper Eaton Farm

Old Woodhouse Farm

DE6

Upwoods Farm

Lady Coppice

MARSTON LA

Holmlea Farm

Somersal Farm

Hill Farm

Victory Farm

Woodhouse Farm

Somersal Herbert

Mount Pleasant

The Hall

North Lodge

Brocksford Brook

Grove Cottages

Eaton Lodge

Field Farm

Mill Cottage

Oaklea

UPWOODS RD

DERBY RD

MARSTON LA

PH

MARSTON LA

BABBS LA

GROVE LA

Mill Farm

Doveridge

HALL DR

OAK DR
WEST DR
PARK CRES
EAST DR
LAKE DR
LAKE SIDE
COOK LA
MAPLE CL
HAWTHORN CL
ORCHARD CT
HIGH ST
SAND LA
O DERBY RD
FLORENCE DR
CAVENDISH CT
BAKERS LA

River Dove

MILL LA
CHURCH LA
Sch
PO
PUMP LA
ALMS RD

A50

A B C D E F

1
12
13

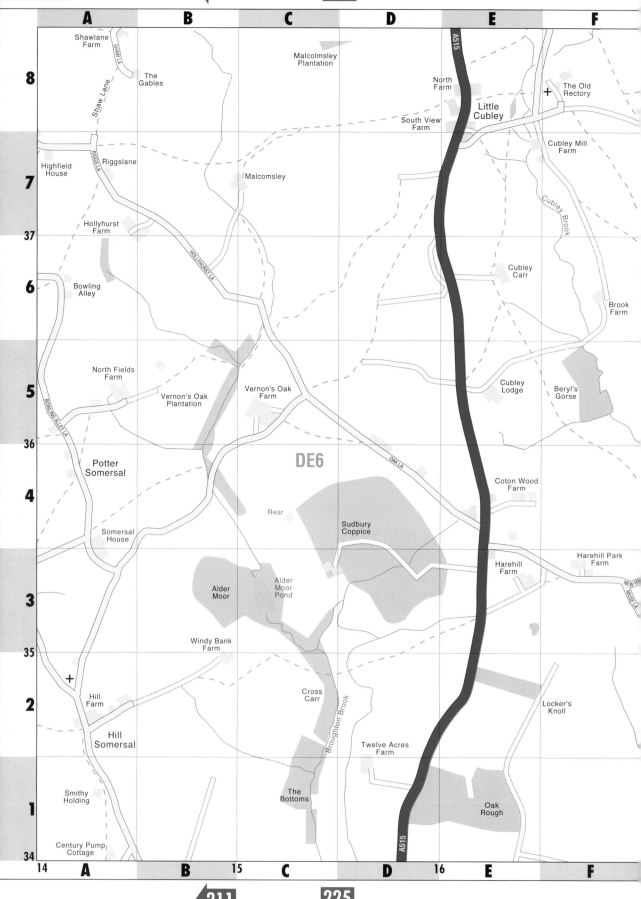

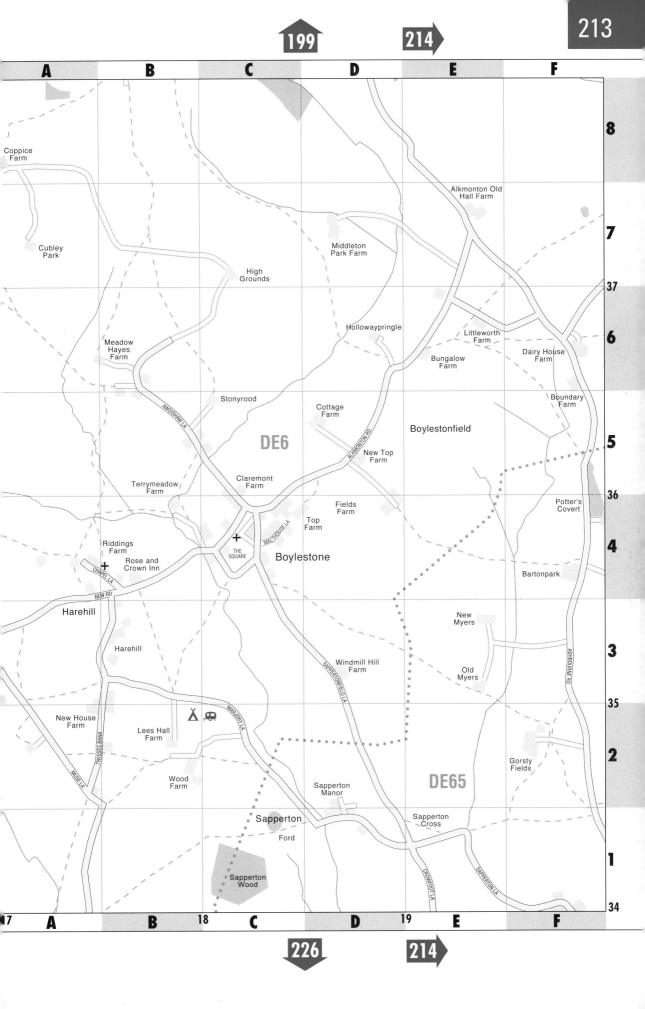

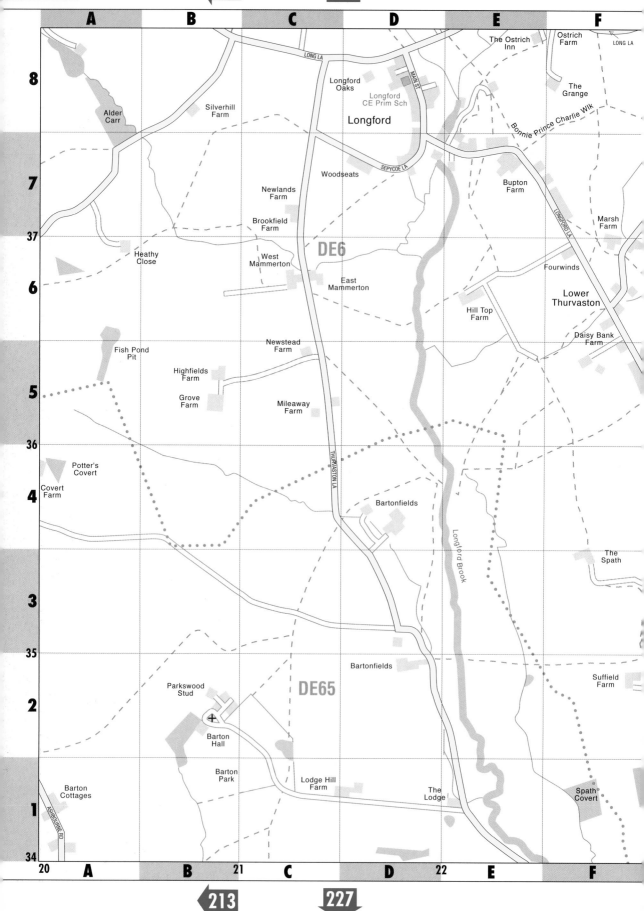

A B C D E F

8

7

37

6

5

36

4

3

35

2

1

34

20 A 21 B C 22 D E F

Alder Carr

Silverhill Farm

LONG LA

Longford Oaks

Longford CE Prim Sch

MAIN ST

Longford

The Ostrich Inn

Ostrich Farm

LONG LA

The Grange

Bonnie Prince Charlie Wlk

Woodseats

SEPYCOE LA

Newlands Farm

Brookfield Farm

DE6

Bupton Farm

LONGFORD LA

Marsh Farm

Heathy Close

West Mammerton

East Mammerton

Fourwinds

Lower Thurvaston

Fish Pond Pit

Newstead Farm

Highfields Farm

Grove Farm

Mileaway Farm

THURVASTON LA

Hill Top Farm

Daisy Bank Farm

Potter's Covert

Covert Farm

Bartonfields

Longford Brook

The Spath

Parkswood Stud

Barton Hall

DE65

Bartonfields

Suffield Farm

Barton Park

Lodge Hill Farm

The Lodge

Spath Covert

Barton Cottages

ASHBOURNE RD

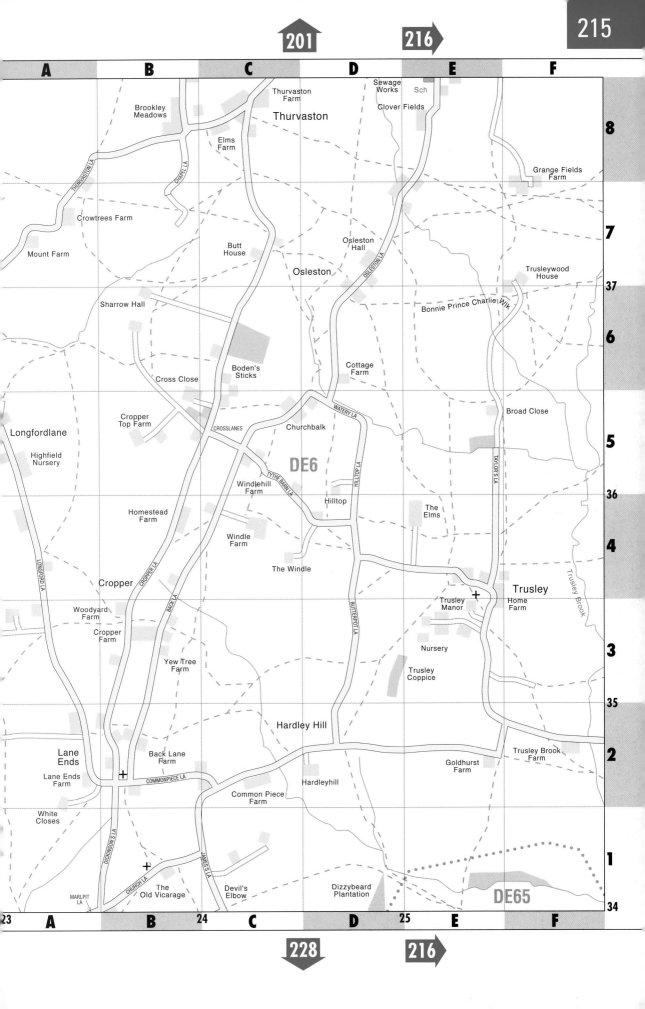

A B C D E F

8

7

37

6

5

36

4

3

35

2

1

34

Thurvaston Farm

Thurvaston

Brookley Meadows

Elms Farm

Sewage Works

Sch

Clover Fields

Grange Fields Farm

Crowtrees Farm

Mount Farm

Butt House

Osleston Hall

Osleston

Trusleywood House

Sharrow Hall

Bonnie Prince Charlie Wlk

Cross Close

Boden's Sticks

Cottage Farm

Broad Close

Longfordlane

Cropper Top Farm

CROSSLANES

Churchbalk

DE6

Highfield Nursery

Windlehill Farm

TYTHE BARN LA

Hilltop

HILLTOP LA

WATERY LA

TAYLOR'S LA

The Elms

Homestead Farm

Windle Farm

Cropper

CROPPER LA

The Windle

Trusley Manor

Trusley

Home Farm

Woodyard Farm

BACK LA

Cropper Farm

Yew Tree Farm

BUTTERPOT LA

Nursery

Trusley Coppice

Hardley Hill

Lane Ends

Back Lane Farm

Goldhurst Farm

Trusley Brook Farm

Lane Ends Farm

COMMONPIECE LA

Hardleyhill

DICKINSON'S LA

White Closes

Common Piece Farm

JAMES'S LA

Devil's Elbow

CHURCH LA

The Old Vicarage

MARLPIT LA

Dizzybeard Plantation

DE65

Longfordlane

LONGFORD LA

Trusley Brook

| | A | B | C | D | E | F |

LONG LA

8

Cherry Tree
Farm

Poplar Grove
Farm

Nunsclough Brook

Lees
Hall

Lees

7

Hillside
Farm

PH

37

Sewage
Works

Black Fir Tree
Farm

Foxfields
Farm

Corner
Farm

6

Rock House
Farm

Hinckley
Farm

Foxfield
Plantation

Bonnie Prince Charlie Wlk

Woodhouse Lane

Thatched
Farm

Radbourne

5

Woodhouse
Farm

DE6

Old Park
Farm

Ravensdale
Lodge

Cunnery
Pond

36

Ravensdale

Daysclose
Plantation

Dog Kennel
Pond

4

Birch
Wood

Radbourne
Hall

Radbourne Brook

The
Rough

3

The
Rookery

Rookhills
Farm

Seedpiece
Plantation

35

White House
Farm

Terrel Hays

2

Dalbury
Hollow

Sandpit
Wood

Smerrills
Farm

Bearwardcote
Hall

HEAGE LA

Manor
Farm

Top
Farm

DE65

1

Dalbury

DE3

The
Cottage

Bannell's
Lane

34

| 26 | A | B | 27 | C | D | 28 | E | F |

A   B   C   D   E   F

8

MOOR LA   PIMM'S RD
B5020   POLE'S RD   ADAMS RD
PH
Brunhouse
Farm
Langley
Common
Bowbridge Wood
A52
Jarvey's La
Wind
Pump
Mackworth
Brook

BRUN LA
Wheathills
Farm
ASHBOURNE RD
GOLD LA   LOWER RD

Squire's
Nursery
Brun
Wood
Works
Mackworth
The Mackworth
Hotel
A52   CHURCH LA

7

Ash House
Farm
DE22
ALDERSGATE 1
SYDENHAM RD 2
REIGATE DR
P 2
Reigate
Prim Sch

37

Radbourne
Common
Brickyard
Wood
EMBANKMENT CL
WESTBOURNE
PROGATE
FINCH
EDGWARE
REIGATE
Pilldock
Wood
ENDSLEIGH GDNS 1
CROYDON WLK 2
Water
Twr   Resr
ACTON CL
OM RD RD
HENLEY
GN

6

Brickyard Wood
Farm
Skitteridge's
Wood
MOORGATE 1
CHELSEA CL 2
FARRINGDON CL 3
HIGHBURY CL 4
MILBANK CL 5
EPPING CL 6.
DILWICH RD
BROMPTON RD
BRIDCAGE
CHISWICK
CL
BAYSWATER
ISLEWORTH DR
DOWNING
Ivy House
Farm
Mackworth
Fields
LOMBARD
ST   BELSIZE
DE6
MAYFAIR   PRINCE CHARLES AVE
MARYLEBONE
CRES

5

LUDGATE
WLK
CHEAM CL   SNOW'S AVE
MUSWELL   THAMES
RD
CL   DOWNING HO
RADBOURNE LA
PUTNEY CL
Silverhill
Farm
Moorcroft
Farm
Derby Coll

36

Silverhill
Wood
RADBOURNE
GATE
STARFLOWER WAY   OOK WA
The Great Northern
(PH)
DERBY
Murray Park
Com Sch

4

CRYSTAL CT
WHISTLESTOP CL
CUTLER WAY 1
LANTERN GR 2
MEWS CT 3
Hackwood
Farm
NAPIER CL   ONSLOW
ADELAIDE CL
RANGEMORE CL
ENGLAND CL   VICTORIA CL
PERTH CL
EARLSWOOD

Slade
Plantation
FARBOURNE DR
INGLEWOOD AVE
ROMSLEY CL
TIVERTON
WETLAND   STAVERTON DR
BELVEDERE CL
MILL LA
MILL
CROFT
CROMFORD   MICKLEROSS DR
BAKEWELL CL
CAIRNS
BRISBANE RD   MURRAY RD
TASMAN CL
Potlocks
Farm
Bonnie Prince Charlie Walk
SAXONDALE   COLTON RD
CAMELLIA
LANGFORD
BONSALL
BUXTON
CLIFTON DR
Ravensdale
Inf & Jun
Schs
NELSON CL
HAMILTON   SYDNEY
MELBOURNE CL

3

Black
Wood
STANSTEAD
BARWELL
MILTON CL
RIGSBY
UPCHURCH RD
LOXLEY   HAILSHAM CL
WESTHALL   EAST AVE
STATION RD
CHESTNUT   THORPE
OPE RD
DEVONSHIRE DR   DARWIN CL
DUNEDIN
AUCKLAND
Derby Univ
(Mickleover
Site)
A516
Bean Hole
Plantation
SANDOWN AVE
BRAMPTON
KINGSMUIR RD   CHELMSFORD CL
STAACROSS CL   CHELSEA CL
BROOMHILL
MARFLEET
MALVERN
ROTHWELL
RD
AVE
RD   LEA DR
PO
NORK
OAK DR
NORTH AVE   CANBERRA
EASTLEIGH
HOBART CL
CHEVIN AVE
A38

35

Osierbed
Wood
NASEBY
CL   WIGMORE
SWAYFIELD   ADWICK
SHELFORD
DAVENTRY
ASHTON
CL   SEATON
Silverhill
Prim Sch
HOYLAKE DR   RISEDALE RD
DENVER
HOYLAKE CT
WINDSOR
CT
MOORLA
APPLETR
WLK
EDALE
AVE   Mickleover
BATH RD   ARUNDEL AVE
B5020

2

BARNWOOD
TAPLOW
CL
WHENBY
CL
FEN CL
STAINES
CL
CHERTSEY
West Dr
FARNWAY
HOPE AVE
Western Rd
DE3
WADE DR
WELLS RD
BRISTOL CL
B5020
UTTOXETER RD

Brown Cross
Plantation
DRESDEN CL
LAMBROOK CL
COOKHAM CL
Recn
Gd
Mickleover
Prim Sch
Liby
PORTLAND CL   THE GROVE
CAVENDISH WAY
HARDWICK
Staff
A38   A516

1

Orchard
Plantation
Bonehill
Farm
GREENSLADE
LIDGATE
FARNHAM CL
GLENGATE
GLENMORE
CROOKHAM
BURNHAM DR
Parkstone
WEAVERS
GREEN
PRESCOT CL
CROMER
CATTERICK DR   CHANTRY CL
PARK RD
VICARAGE RD
HOLLY CL
BURLINGTON WAY
HARRINGTON WAY
ALMA HTS
CARNFORTH   SAW CL   PENDLETON
TELFORD CL
DOWNHAM   BRIERFIELD WAY
WENTWORTH   CARNOUSTIE
LINDRICK CL
BELFRY
BIRKDALE CL
GLENEAGLES
MELLION
CL
CH
DE23

34

HOWDEN CL
MICKLEOVER MANOR
UFFA
MAGNA
PAXTON CL
CUMBRIA
SEDGEFIELD
GREEN
ALVERTON CL
BRUNTON
CL
THE
SQUARE
WARNER
PO
STRETTON
KIPLING DR
WENLOCK
ACACIA AVE
MELBREAK   GARTH CRES
BARF CL   SANDRINGHAM WAY
WANSFELL
BOWLAND   BO   SPRINGHILL
SKIDDAW
A38   A516
1 HOLMESFIELD DR
2 LITTLE LONGSTONE CL
3 ABNEY CL

29   A   B   30   C   D   31   E   F

D1
1 MORLEY HO
2 BRAMBLE MEWS
3 LIMES CT
4 THE PARADE
5 MEADOW CT
6 ALL SAINTS CT

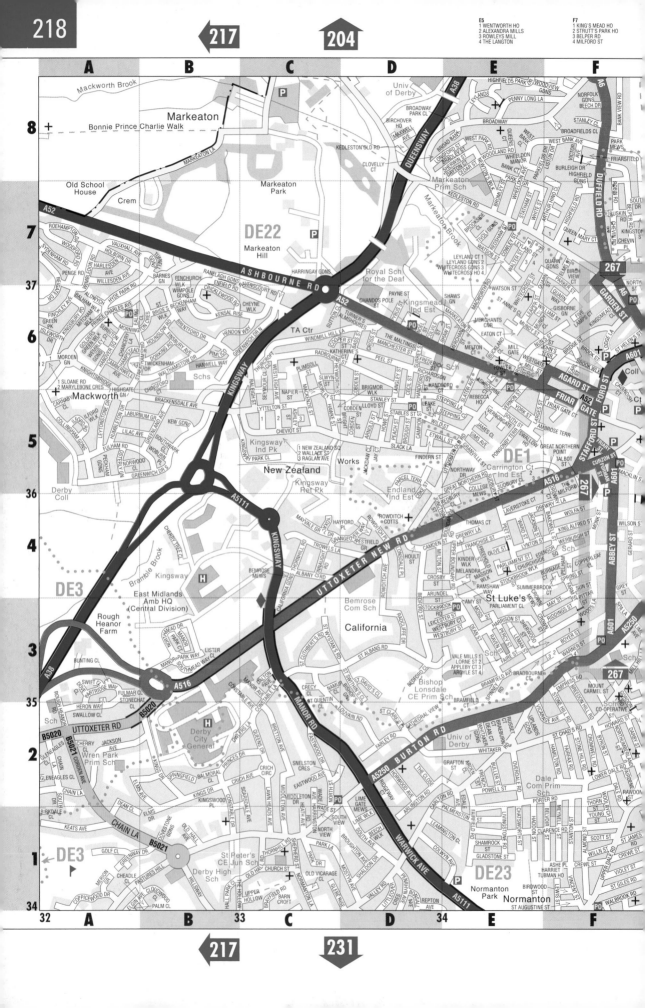

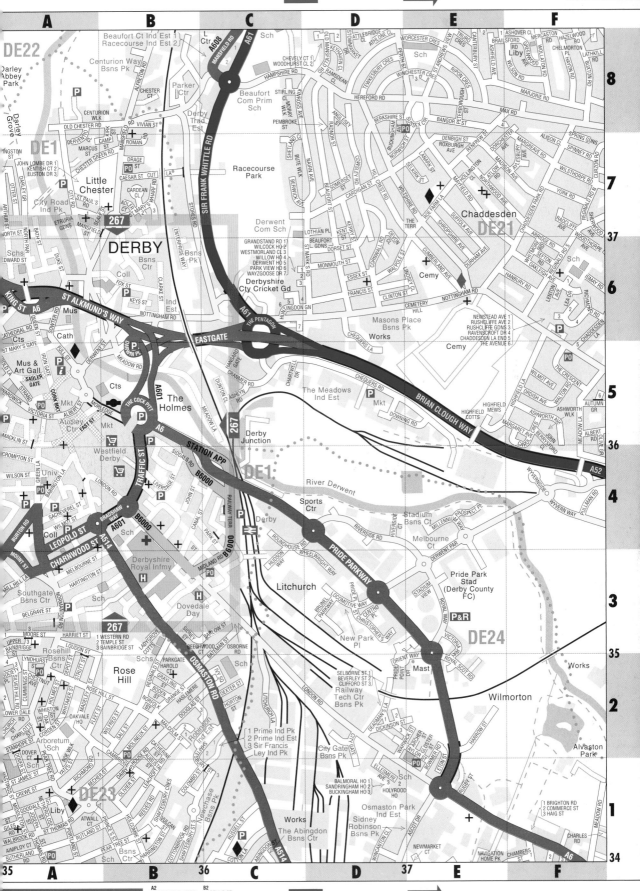

For full street detail of the highlighted area see page 267.

A2
1 PETERHOUSE TERR
2 CO-OPERATIVE ST
3 INDUSTRIAL ST
4 PROVIDENT ST

B2
1 ARTHUR CT
2 TINTAGEL CL
3 ALEXANDRA GDNS

219 206

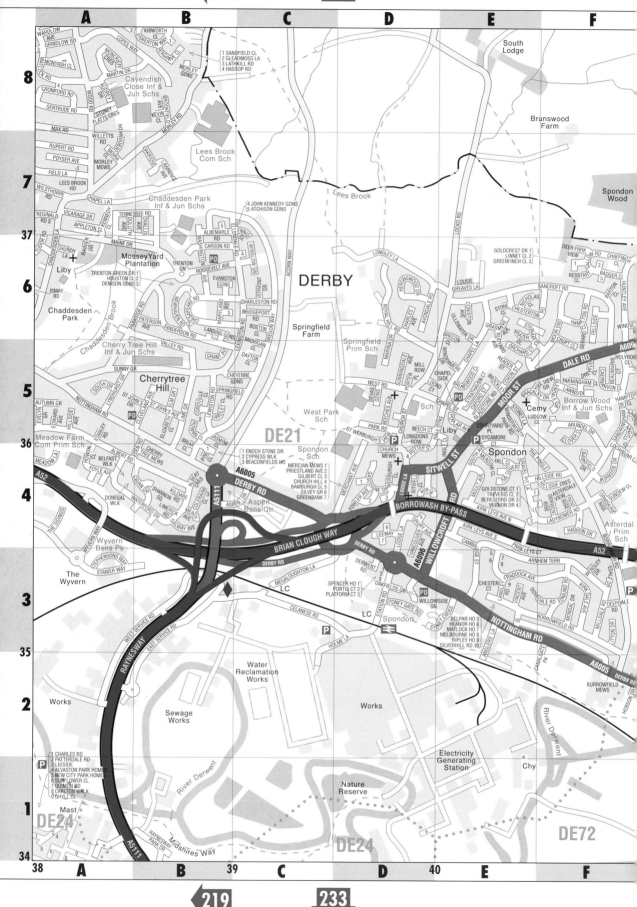

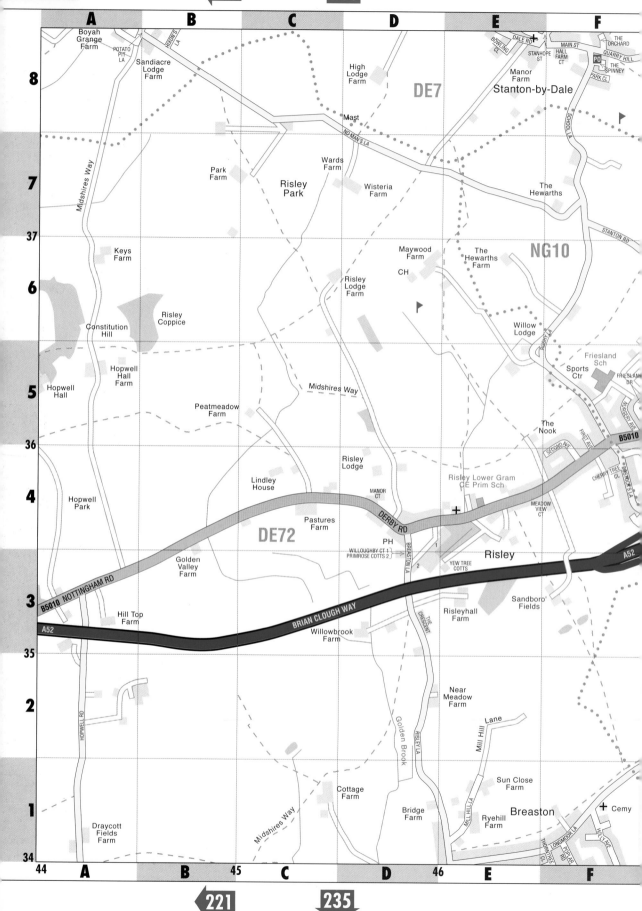

221
208

A **B** **C** **D** **E** **F**

Boyah Grange Farm

POTATO PIT LA

Sandiacre Lodge Farm

HIXON'S LA

Midshires Way

8

High Lodge Farm

Mast

NO MAN'S LA

DE7

BOWLING CL

DALE RD

STANHOPE ST

MAIN ST

THE ORCHARD

QUARRY HILL

PO

PARK CL

HALL FARM CT

THE SPINNEY

Manor Farm

Stanton-by-Dale

Park Farm

Wards Farm

7

Risley Park

Wisteria Farm

The Hewarths

SCHOOL LA

STANTON RD

37

Keys Farm

Maywood Farm

CH

The Hewarths Farm

NG10

6

Risley Lodge Farm

Constitution Hill

Risley Coppice

Willow Lodge

RUSBY LA

Friesland Sch

FRIESLAND DR

Hopwell Hall

Hopwell Hall Farm

Midshires Way

Sports Ctr

5

Peatmeadow Farm

The Nook

FIRST AVE

SECOND AVE

NURSERY AVE

B5010

36

Risley Lodge

Lindley House

Risley Lower Gram CE Prim Sch

MEADOW VIEW CT

CHERRY TREE CL

BOSTOCK LA

4

Hopwell Park

Pastures Farm

MANOR CT

DERBY RD

BREASTON LA

Risley

DE72

PH

WILLOUGHBY CT 1
PRIMROSE COTTS 2

1

2

YEW TREE COTTS

A52

Golden Valley Farm

B5010 NOTTINGHAM RD

3

Hill Top Farm

A52

BRIAN CLOUGH WAY

Willowbrook Farm

THE CRESCENT

Risleyhall Farm

Sandboro' Fields

35

HOPWELL RD

RISLEY LA

Near Meadow Farm

2

Golden Brook

MILL HILL LA

Mill Hill Lane

Sun Close Farm

Cemy

1

Midshires Way

Cottage Farm

Bridge Farm

Ryehill Farm

Breaston

LONGMOOR LA

THORNTREE CL

POPLAR RD

HOLLY LANE

Draycott Fields Farm

34

A **B** **C** **D** **E** **F**

44 45 46

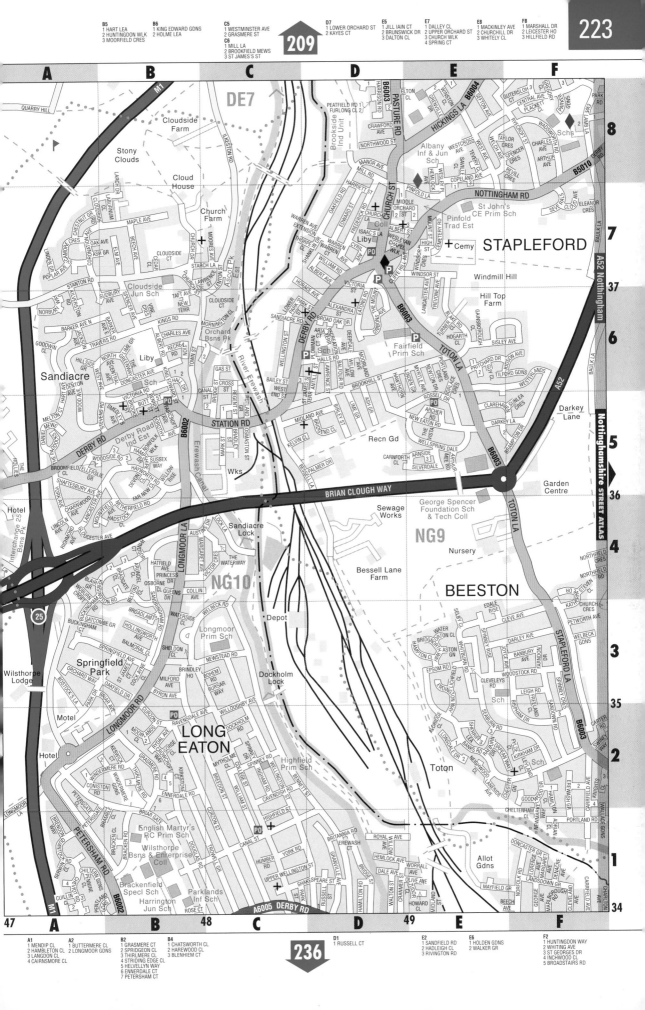

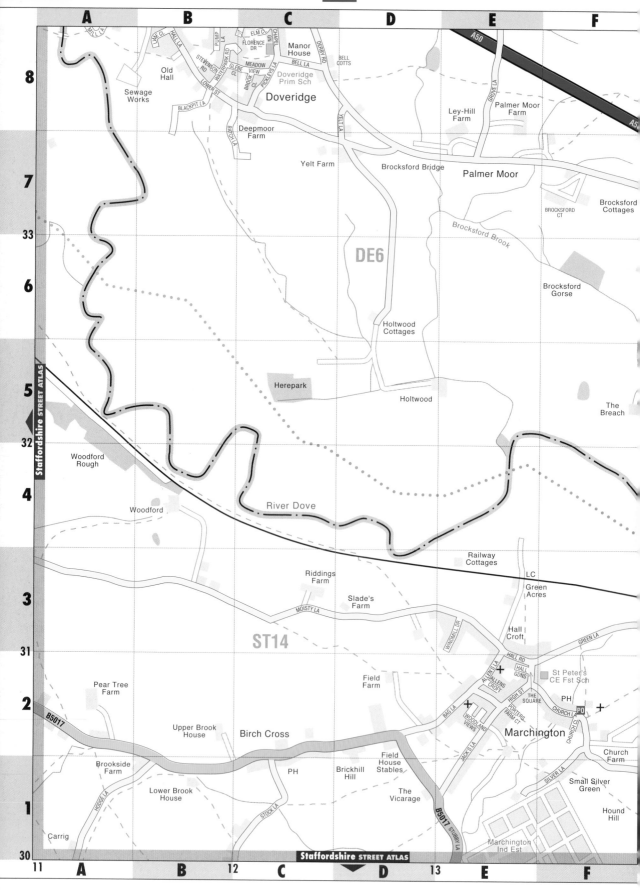

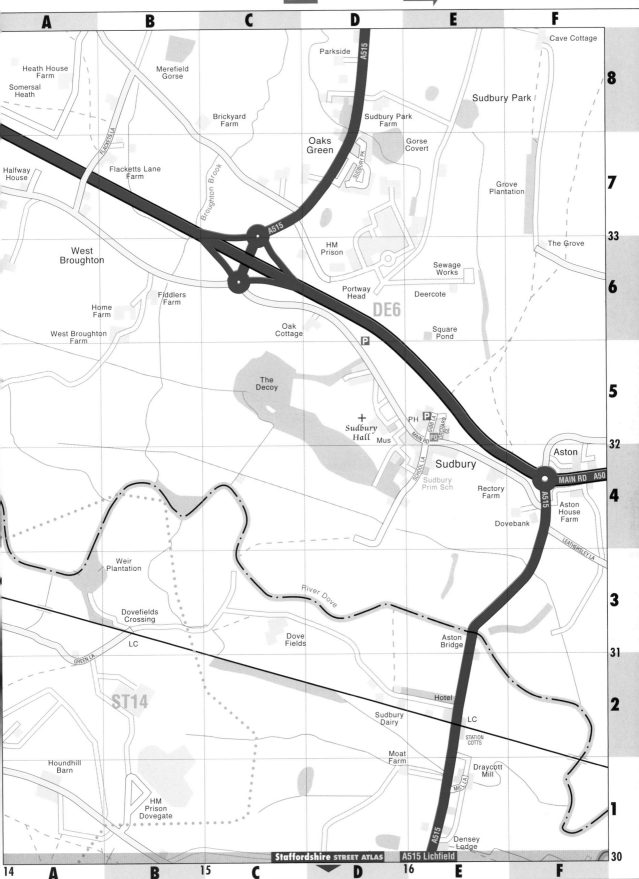

A B C D E F

8

7

33

6

5

32

4

3

31

2

1

30

Cave Cottage

Parkside

Heath House Farm

Somersal Heath

Merefield Gorse

Brickyard Farm

Oaks Green

Sudbury Park Farm

Sudbury Park

Gorse Covert

Grove Plantation

Halfway House

FLACKETS LA

Flacketts Lane Farm

Broughton Brook

A515

SUDBURY PK

A515

The Grove

West Broughton

HM Prison

Sewage Works

Fiddlers Farm

Portway Head

Deercote

DE6

Home Farm

West Broughton Farm

Oak Cottage

Square Pond

The Decoy

Sudbury Hall

PH

Mus

P

P

PO

GIBB LA

ORCHARD CL

MAIN RD

SCHOOL LA

Aston

A50

MAIN RD

Sudbury

Sudbury Prim Sch

Rectory Farm

Dovebank

A515

Aston House Farm

LEATHERSLEY LA

Weir Plantation

River Dove

Dovefields Crossing

LC

GREEN LA

Dove Fields

Aston Bridge

ST14

Hotel

Sudbury Dairy

LC

Moat Farm

STATION COTTS

Houndhill Barn

HM Prison Dovegate

MILL LA

Draycott Mill

A515

Densey Lodge

225
213

A   B   C   D   E   F

8

Mackley House

Fox Hole

Sapperton Brook

The Homestead

SAPPERTON L

Dale Brook

MUSE LA

Foston Mill Farm

CROWFOOT LA

Crowfoot Farm

7

Muselane Farm

MILL LA

Cotefield Farm

WOODHOUSE LA

33

Dalebrook

Ford

Aston Heath

Broomhill Farm

Foston Brook

Conygree Wood

6

Aston Heath Farm

BREACH LA

Haylane Farm

HAY LA

Rough Wood

Breach Gorse

Sailor's Holme

COPLOW LA

DE6

DE65

Lawn House

5

Home Farm

WOODYARD LA

32

MAIN RD

Foston

A50

UTTOXETER RD

UTTOXETER RD

Tomlinson Bsns Pk

4

Maidensley Farm

WOODLAND DR

HM Detention Centre

Lemon's Holme

UTTOXETER RD

A50

Dale Brook

Puddingbag Covert

Roundabout Covert

Fishpond Plantation

Cote House

3

Leathersley Farm

The Churchleys

31

LEATHERSLEY LA

BROOM'S LA

WATERY LA

2

Sweet Holme

Scropton

1

River Dove

River Dove

Brookside Farm

Brookhouse Farm

LC

+ PH

Ivy House Farm

SCROPTON RD

MILL LA

LC

30

17   A   18   B   C   18   D   19   E   F

225
238

A B C D E F

8

The Hall Farm
The Hall
Dizzybeard Plantation
Baldfields Farm

COMMON LA
MARLPIT LA
BROOK LA

Sutton on the Hill
Fields Farm
Gamekeepers Cottage
Ash Gorse

7

DE6
Fieldgate Farm
Arbourfield Covert
Ash Farm
Ash Cottages

33

Acre La
Dishfields Farm
ASH LA

DISH LA

6

Ivy House Farm
Park Farm

5

Hilton Fields
Holly Bush Farm

WILLOWPIT LA

32

Hoon Mount
Roystone House

4

Hoon Ridge
DE65
Burntheath
Blakelow Farm
Badger Farm

Sutton Brook

Hilton Gorse
SUTTON LA
A51f

3

A50
Hallcroft
Hilton Ind Est
DERBY RD
Hilton Lodge

HOON LA

Hoon Villa Farm

31

A5132
A50

2

Moorend
DERBY RD
UTTOXETER RD
The Old School

1 Montgomery Cl
2 Churchill Dr
3 Shaef Cl
4 Sherman Cl

Elm Tree Farm
Hilton Common

MARSTON LA

Hilton Brook

Hilton
PH
Hilton Prim Sch
Hargate Lodge
The Stables

WILLOWBROOK CL
DALE END RD
WEST AV
SHADY GR
PERCY CL
WAKELYN WOOD CL
MAIN ST
PO
FIELD CL
PEACROFT LA
PEACROFT CT
NEW RD
WITHAM CL
EGGINTON RD

1 Marston Brook
2 Dale Brook
3 Sandford Brook

Hargate House Farm

1 HAMBLE WAY
2 WILDHAY BROOK
3 SHERBOURNE DR
4 LYNMOUTH HO
5 RICHMOND HO
6 EDEN CL
7 THE GABLES
8 ORDLEY WLK
9 BUCKINGHAM HO
10 ROTHWELL HO
11 RYTON WAY
12 NENE WAY

Hargate Manor
A5132

30

23 A B 24 C D 25 E F

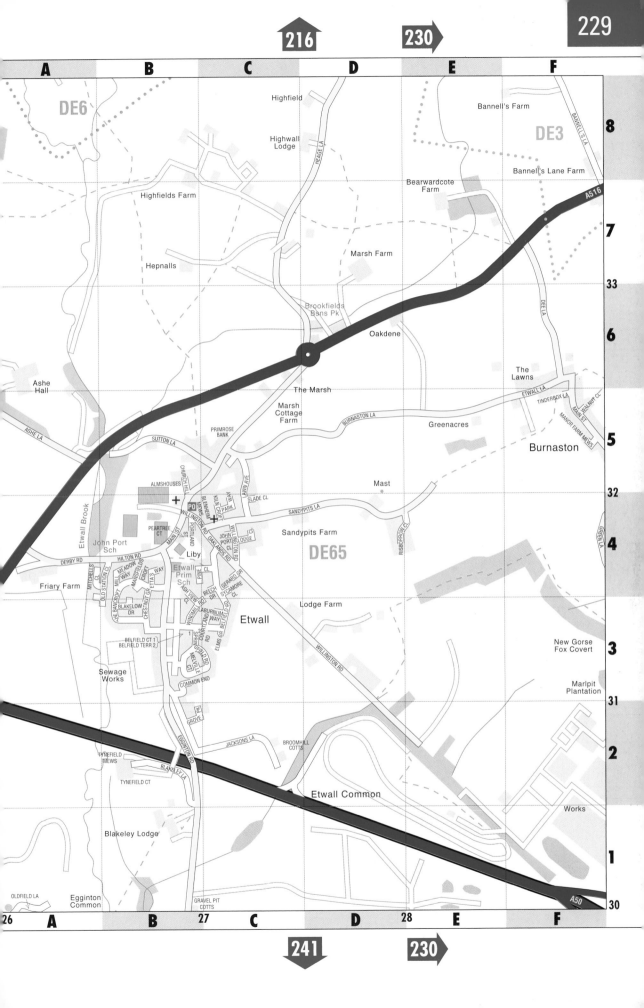

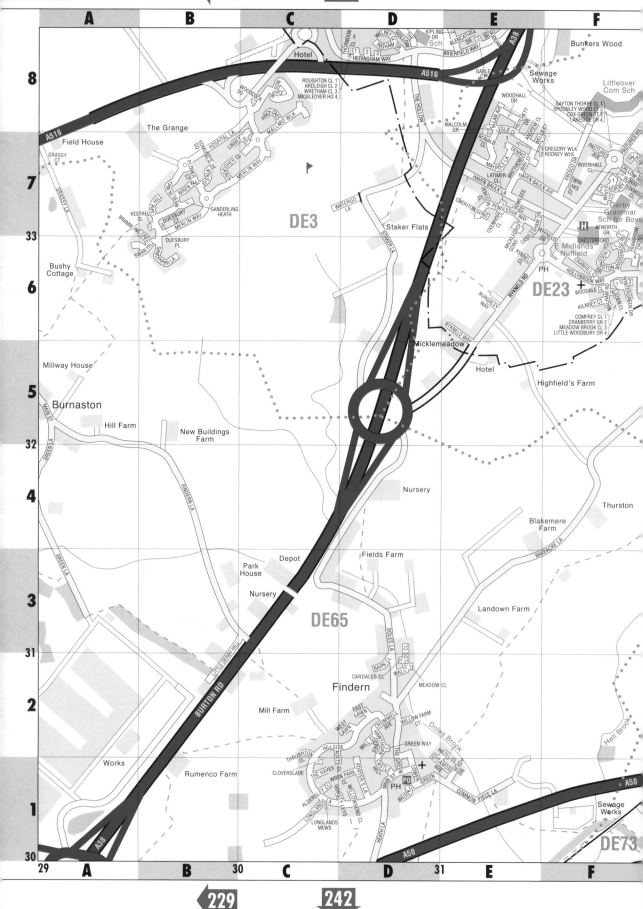

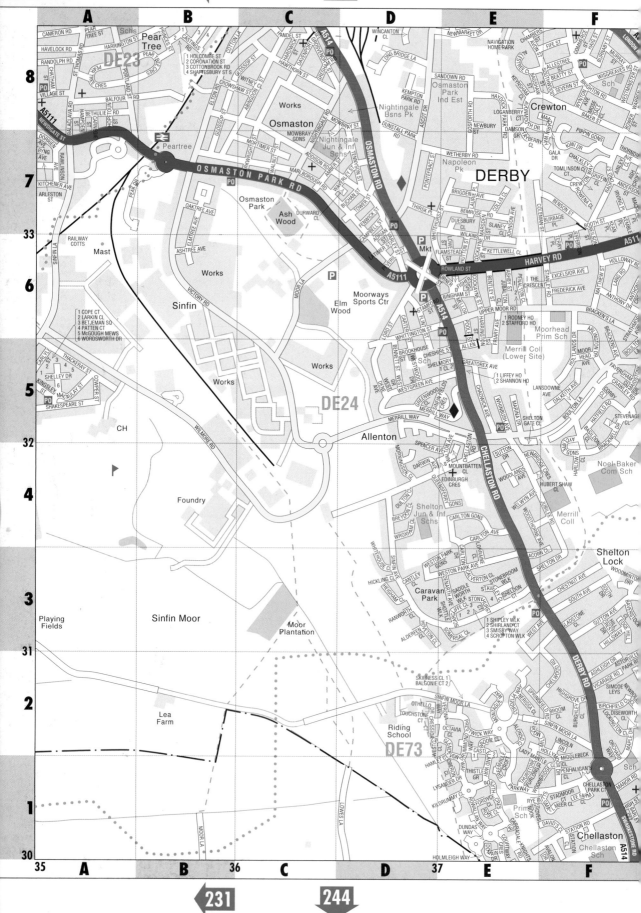

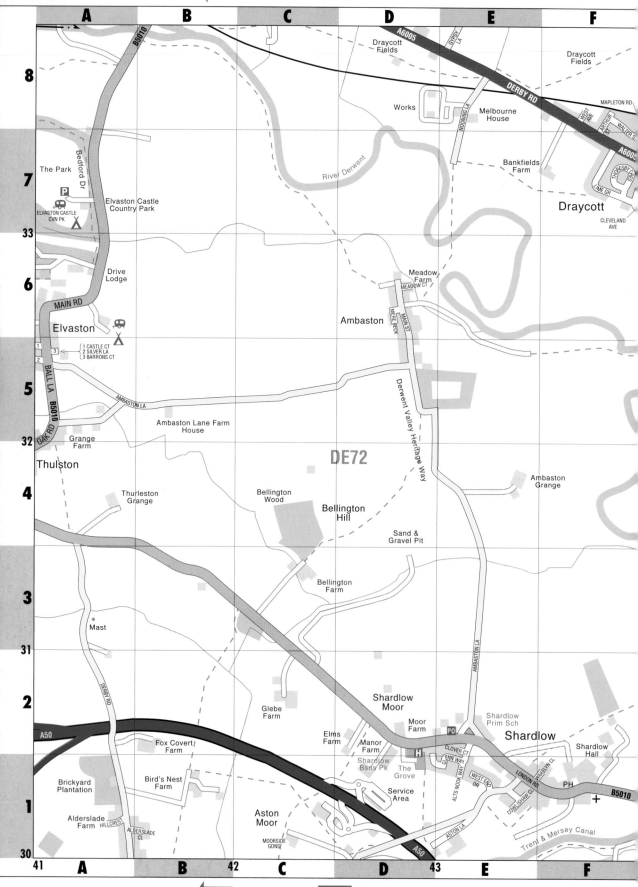

233
221
233
246

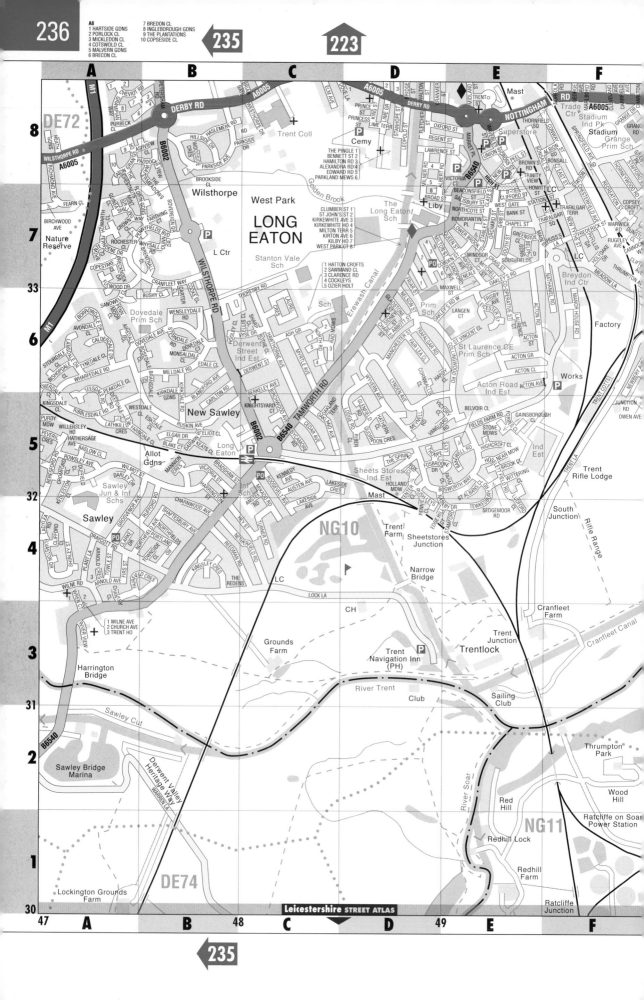

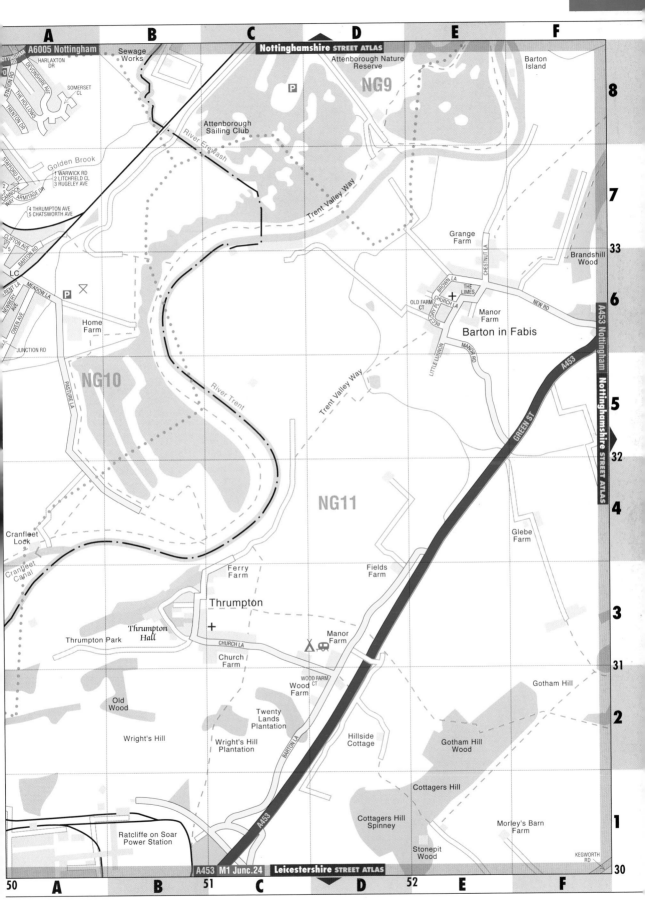

A6005 Nottingham

HARLAXTON DR

SOMERSET CL

Golden Brook
1 WARWICK RD
2 LITCHFIELD CL
3 RUGELEY AVE

4 THRUMPTON AVE
5 CHATSWORTH AVE

Sewage Works

Attenborough Nature Reserve

NG9

Barton Island

Attenborough Sailing Club

River Erewash

Trent Valley Way

Grange Farm

Brandshill Wood

THE LIMES

OLD FARM CT

CHURCH LA

Manor Farm

Barton in Fabis

NEW RD

Home Farm

NG10

River Trent

Trent Valley Way

Barton in Fabis

LITTLE LUNNON

MANOR RD

GREEN ST

A453 Nottingham

NG11

Cranfleet Lock

Cranfleet Canal

Glebe Farm

Ferry Farm

Thrumpton

Fields Farm

Thrumpton Park

Thrumpton Hall

CHURCH LA

Manor Farm

Church Farm

WOOD FARM CT

Wood Farm

Gotham Hill

Old Wood

Twenty Lands Plantation

BARTON LA

Wright's Hill

Wright's Hill Plantation

Hillside Cottage

Gotham Hill Wood

Cottagers Hill

A453

Cottagers Hill Spinney

Morley's Barn Farm

Ratcliffe on Soar Power Station

Stonepit Wood

KEGWORTH RD

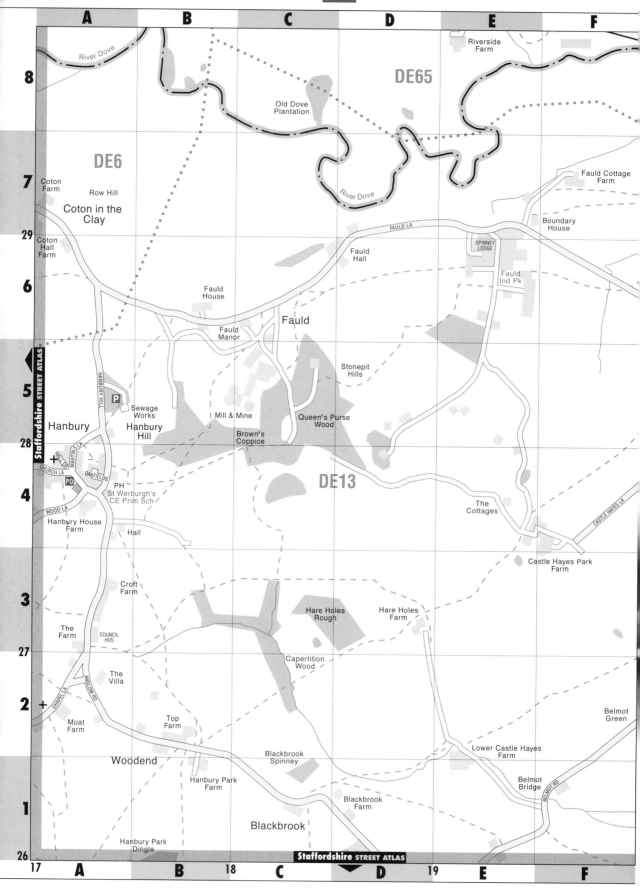

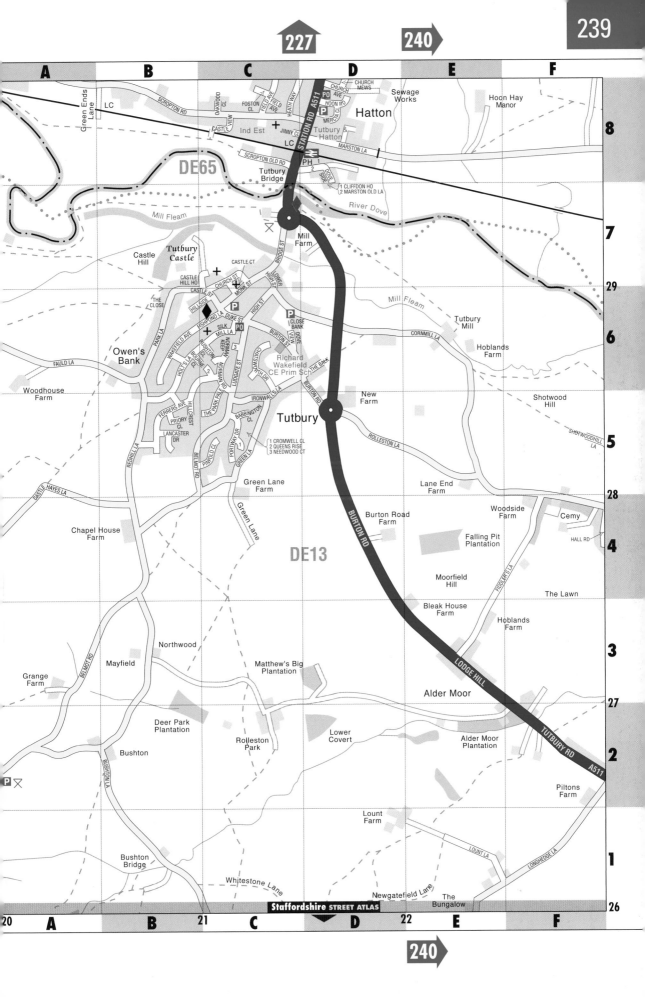

A   B   C   D   E   F

8
29
7
6
5
28
4
3
27
2
1
26

Green Ends Lane
LC
SCROPTON RD
DE65
OAKWOOD CL
FOSTON CL
CASTLE VIEW
FIELD AVE
HEATH WAY
JINNY CL
Ind Est
LC
SCROPTON OLD RD
Tutbury Bridge
CHURCH AVE
CHURCH MEWS
PO
P
MERCIA CL
HOON RD
STATION RD A511
Hatton
Sewage Works
Hoon Hay Manor
Tutbury & Hatton
MARSTON LA
PH
DOVE SIDE
1 CLIFFDON HO
2 MARSTON OLD LA
River Dove

Mill Fleam
Mill Farm
Castle Hill
Tutbury Castle
CASTLE CT
CASTLE HILL HO
THE CLOSE
CHURCH ST
MOWE ST
BRIDGE ST
HIGH ST
OWNER
HILLSIDE
CASTLE ST
FISHPOND LA
DUKE ST
P
PO
SILK MILL LA
CLOSE BANK
P
DOVE VIEW
Mill Fleam
Tutbury Mill
CORNMILL LA
Hoblands Farm

Owen's Bank
PARK LA
WAKEFIELD AVE
HOLT'S LA
BOTHINE
RUSTLOW CL
NORMAN KEEP
LUDGATE ST
CHADSWORTH DR
BURTON ST
Richard Wakefield CE Prim Sch
New Farm
Shotwood Hill
SHOTWOODHILL LA

FAULD LA
Woodhouse Farm
REDHILL LA
HILLCREST
PRIORY CL
FERRERS AVE
LANCASTER DR
THE PARK
PAVE VIEW
IRONWALL LA
BABBINGTON CL
Tutbury
BURTON RD
THE BANK
1 CROMWELL CL
2 QUEENS RISE
3 NEEDWOOD CT

CASTLE HAYES LA
BELMOT RD
PORTWAY DR
PINFOLD CL
GREEN LA
Green Lane Farm
ROLLESTON LA
Lane End Farm
Woodside Farm
Cemy
HALL RD

Chapel House Farm
Green Lane
DE13
Burton Road Farm
Falling Pit Plantation
BURTON RD
RIDDER'S LA
The Lawn

BELMOT RD
Grange Farm
Northwood
Mayfield
Matthew's Big Plantation
Moorfield Hill
Bleak House Farm
Hoblands Farm
LODGE HILL

Deer Park Plantation
Rolleston Park
Lower Covert
Alder Moor
Alder Moor Plantation
TUTBURY RD A511
Piltons Farm

Bushton
BUSHTON LA
Bushton Bridge
Whitestone Lane
Lount Farm
LOUNT LA
Newgatefield Lane
The Bungalow
LONGHEDGE LA

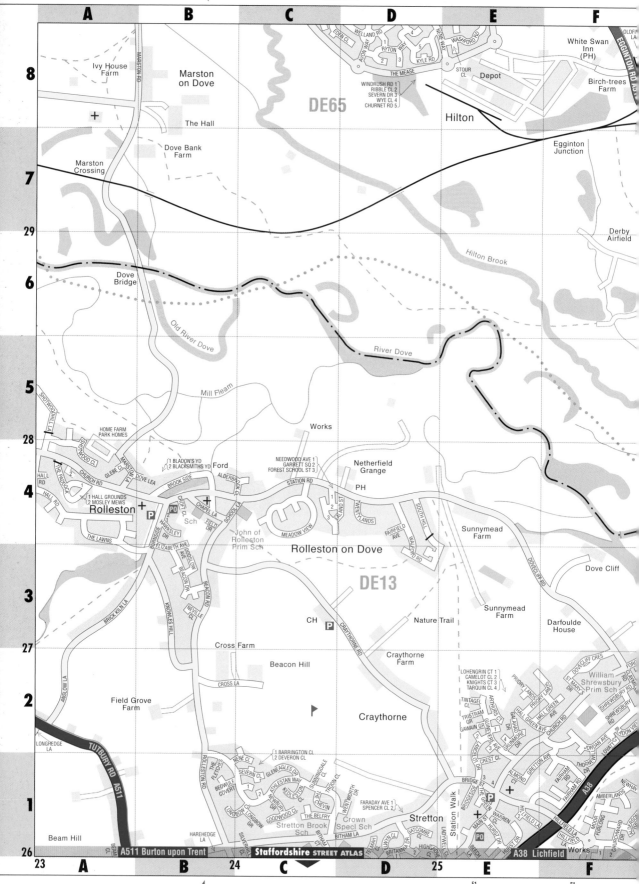

E1
1 PRINCESS WAY
2 CARISBROOKE DR
3 BRIDGE FARM
4 CHILTON CT

F1
1 ALDERHOLME DR
2 MANTON CL

A B C D E F

8

Longlands Plantation

BURTON RD A50

A50

Stenson Junction

A38 B5008

Common Plantation

HEATH LA

PH

Buckford Bridge

Buckford La

Trent and Mersey Canal

Findern Prim Sch

DE73

Hill Farm

ETWALL RD

7

Willington Junction

29

LC

FINDERN LA

LC

LC

Cemy

DERWENT CT

Potlocks House Farm

A5132

6

Willington

CANAL BRIDGE

WILLOW GR

PH

THE GREEN

CHAPEL CL

ORCHARD CL

Willington Prim Sch

THE POTLOCKS

FERN AVE FERN CL

Power Station

WATERSIDE

GREEN LA

A5132

PO

Willington

TWYFORD RD

HAMILTON TERR

OAKS RD

IVY CL

VESEY CL

HILL DR

FORD LA

TWYFORD CL

CALEY CL

ST JAMES CL

WHEATFIELD CT

THE CASTLE WAY

MERCIA DR

HUMPHREY CL

BEECH AVE

TRENT AVE

TRENT CL

SAXON GR

FATLEY DR

REPTON RD

CHURCH CL

HALL LA

BARGATE LA

ST MICHAEL'S CL

FERRY GREEN

COUCH WAY

SPILSBURY CL

5

IVY CL

MESSITER MEWS

THE RIVERBANK

28

Works

SYCAMORE CT

Gravel Pit

Eggington Brook

Willington Bridge

River Trent

DE65

Meadows Farm

Old Trent Water

4

WILLINGTON RD

The Rookery

Brook Farm

Cemy

Askew Hill

3

Repton Sch

MONSOM LA

BURDETT WAY

SAXON CROFT

MILTON RD

27

BROOK END

TANNER'S LA

BROOKSIDE CL

ASKEW GR

FISHER CL

THE CRESCENT

Repton Prim Sch

Parson's Hills

Liby

MITRE DR

BROOK HOUSE MEWS

MARCIE CT

RICHMOND CT

PINFOLD CL

SPRINGFIELD RD

HILL VIEW

1 MEADOW CL
2 LONGLANDS

Repton

2

CHESTNUT WAY

THE PASTURES

THE SPINNEY LODGE

PH

FORGE CL

PINFOLD LA

STRATFORD CL

MOUNT PLEASANT RD

WELL LA

BROOMHILLS LA

SHAKESPEARE MDWS

MAIN ST

Common Farm

BURTON RD

Hill Top Farm

MILL HILL

Mount Pleasant

1

B5008

Cokhay

Cokhay Green

Depot

Ridgeway Farm

26

29 A B 30 C D 31 E F

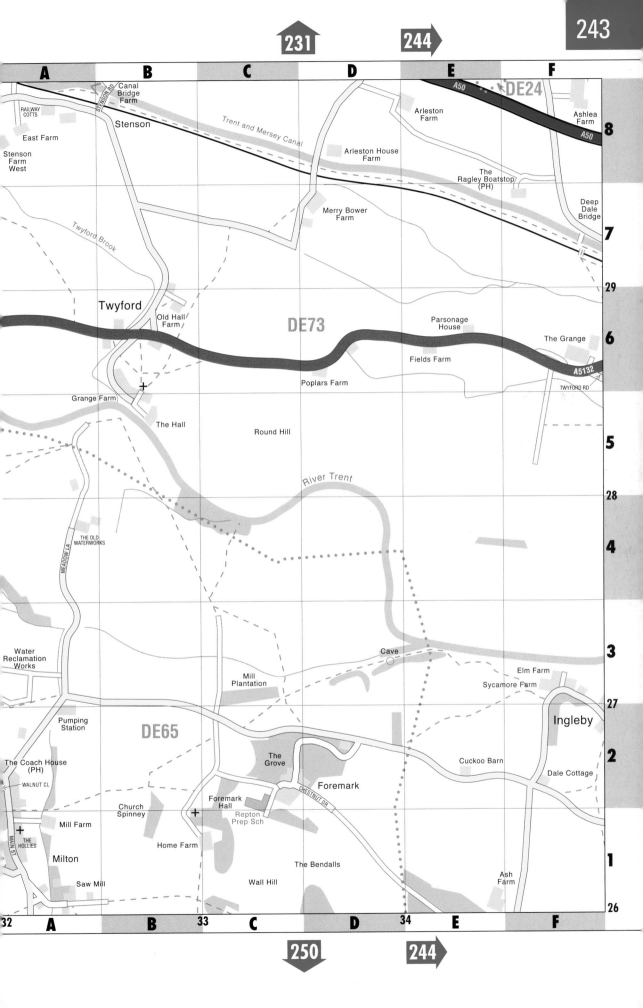

231
244
250
244

A B C D E F

A50
DE24

RAILWAY
COTTS
Canal
Bridge
Farm
Stenson
East Farm
Trent and Mersey Canal
Arleston
Farm
Ashlea
Farm
Stenson
Farm
West
Arleston House
Farm
The
Ragley Boatstop
(PH)
A50
8

Merry Bower
Farm
Deep
Dale
Bridge
7

Twyford Brook
29

Twyford
DE73
Parsonage
House
The Grange
6
Old Hall
Farm
Fields Farm
A5132
Poplars Farm
TWYFORD RD
Grange Farm
The Hall
Round Hill
5

River Trent
28

THE OLD
WATERWORKS
4
MEADOW LA

Cave
Elm Farm
3
Water
Reclamation
Works
Mill
Plantation
Sycamore Farm
27

Ingleby
Pumping
Station
DE65
Cuckoo Barn
Dale Cottage
2
The Coach House
(PH)
The
Grove
Foremark
WALNUT CL
CHESTNUT DR
Church
Spinney
Foremark
Hall
Mill Farm
Repton
Prep Sch
THE
HOLLIES
Home Farm
The Bendalls
Ash
Farm
1
Milton
MAIN ST
Saw Mill
Wall Hill
26

32 A B 33 C D 34 E F

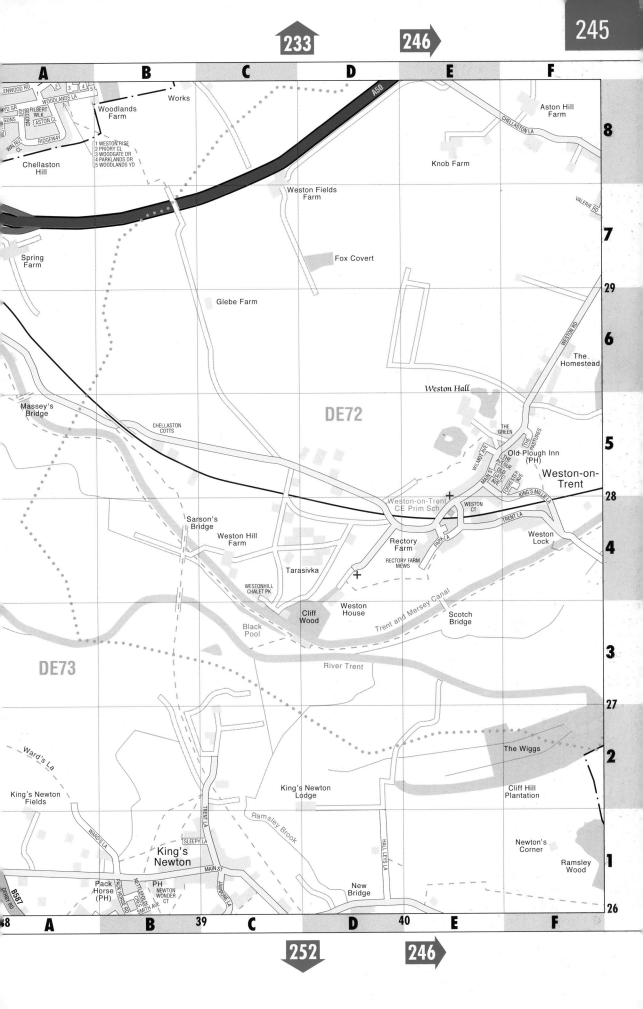

245
234

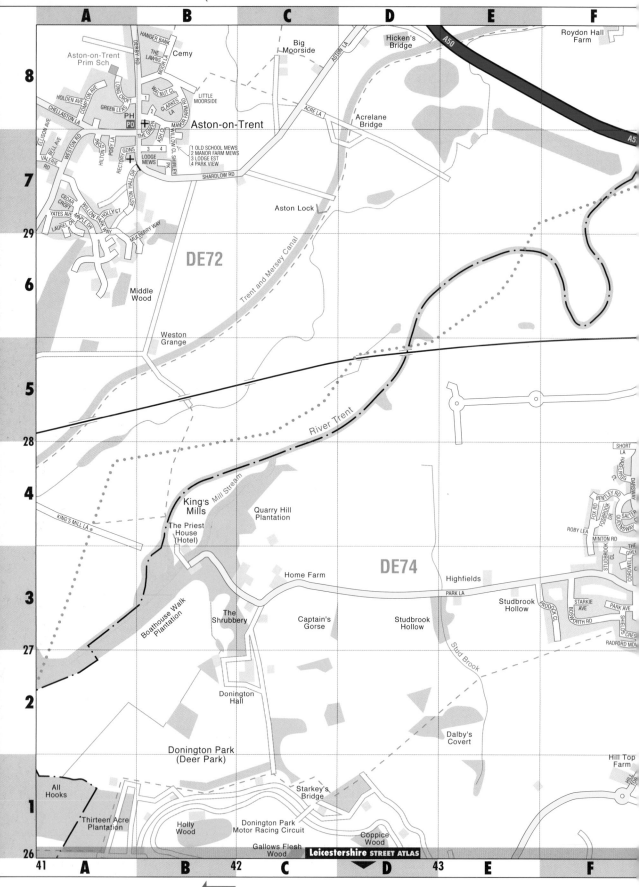

245

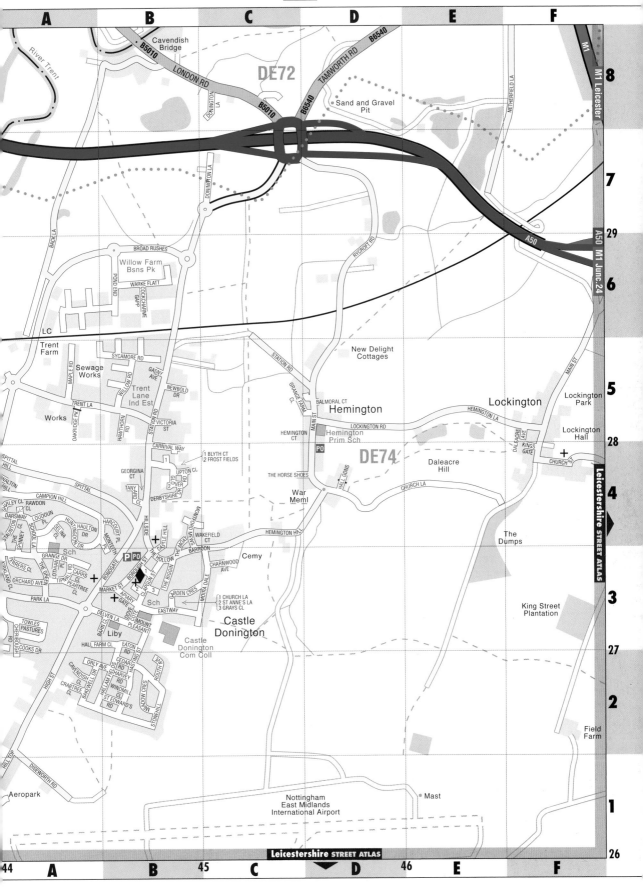

A   B   C   D   E   F

Cavendish
Bridge

B5010

LONDON RD

DONINGTON LA

B5010

TAMWORTH RD

B6540

B6540

DE72

Sand and Gravel
Pit

M1

M1 Leicester

8

DONINGTON LA

7

A50

A50 M1 Junc. 24

RYCROFT RD

29

BROAD RUSHES

Willow Farm
Bsns Pk

POND END

WARKE FLATT

GAPP

COCKCHARME

6

BACK LA

New Delight
Cottages

5

LC

Trent
Farm

Sewage
Works

SYCAMORE RD

MAPLE RD

WILLOW RD

NEWBOLD
DR

GASNY
AVE

STATION RD

GRANGE FARM
CL

Balmoral CT

Lockington

MAIN ST

Lockington
Park

Trent
Lane
Ind Est

TRENT LA

Works

OAKRIDGE PK

HAWTHORN RD

STATION RD

Victoria
ST

Hemington

MAIN ST

HEMINGTON LA

Lockington
Hall

DALEACRE AVE

KINGS
GATE

5

CARNIVAL WAY

HEMINGTON
CT

LOCKINGTON RD

Hemington
Prim Sch

PO

28

CHURCH

SPITTAL
HILL

WALTON
HILL

SPITTAL

Georgina
CT

TANY
ARD CL

UPTON CL

OVER

DERBYSHIRE

1 BLYTH CT
2 FROST FIELDS

1

DE74

The Horse Shoes

Daleacre
Hill

CHURCH

28

SEASLEY CL

DARSWAY

SCHOOL LA

SWING
SPLINE

SELINA

HUNTINGTON
DR

HAULTON
DR

MONTEITH
PL

HARCOURT PL

HILLSIDE

CASTLE HILL

THE MOUNT

MONTROSE CL

CARRS

Rawdon
CL

Campion Hill

LOUDOUN
PL

WAKEFIELD
CT

War
Meml

HALL GDNS

CHURCH LA

4

RAWDON
CL

CASTLE HILL

BARROON

HEMINGTON HIL

The
Dumps

FERRERS CL

ORCHARD AVE

KIRKLAND
CL

THE GREEN

GRANGE DR

ANTHONY
PL

TIPPET
CL

PEARTREE CL

P PO

BONDGATE

BORROW ST

THE HOLLOW

THE BIGGIN

Cemy

CHARNWOOD
AVE

3

PARK LA

MARKET ST

CLAPGUN ST

APARTS
CORE

GARDEN CRES

MOIRA DALE

1 CHURCH LA
2 ST ANNE'S LA
3 GRAYS CL

King Street
Plantation

DELVEN LA

DOVECOTE

Sch

EASTWAY

Castle
Donington

27

Liby

HALL FARM CL

EATON
RD

KINGS RD

MOUNT
PLEASANT

Castle
Donington
Com Coll

27

TOWLES
PASTURES

CHERBOUGH
RD

COOKS DR

CAVENDISH
RD

BAKEWELL
CL

CEDARS
RD

HARVEY
RD

HALLAM
FIELDS RD

WINDMILL
CL

ST EDWARD'S
RD

MOUNT CRES

ROUTH
AVE

STONEHILL

2

HIGH ST

CRABTREE
CL

Field
Farm

HILL TOP

DISEWORTH RD

Aeropark

Nottingham
East Midlands
International Airport

Mast

1

26

44   A   45   B   C   46   D   E   F

Leicestershire STREET ATLAS

Leicestershire STREET ATLAS

242
250

A **B** **C** **D** **E** **F**

8

Repton
Bank House
Farm

New Inn
(PH)

MAIN ST

7

HARTSHORNE RD

Lawn
Bridge

ROBIN'S CROSS LA

DE65

Gravel Pit Hill

Park
Pond

25

Cockey Barn
Farm

6

Dale Farm

Broken
Flatts

The Hayes

RED LA

Loscoe
Farm

Little
Rough

Repton Park
Farm

5

KNIGHT'S LA

Hill Farm
Cottages

Repton Park

Repton
Common

NEWTON LA

Hill
Farm

24

Newton Lane
Farm

4

Shades
Farm

Town Farm

DE15

Repton
Lodge

Cherry Tree
Cottage

Repton
Shrubs

Bretby

THE SQUARE

Mill
(dis)

3

BRETBY LA

MOUNT RD

WATERY LA

The Dower
House

23

Castle
Farm

GEARY LA

HOME FARM
HO

Philosopher's
Wood

Noah's
Ark

White
Hollow

Greysich
Farm

2

BRETBY
MEWS

GREYSICH LA

The
Decoy

CARNARVON
CT

Bretby
Park

REPTON RD

The Gorse

PARK
ROW

Bretby Hall

Hoofies
Wood

1

DE11

Common
Plantation

22

29 **A** **B** 30 **C** **D** 31 **E** **F**

249
243

A B C D E F

8

ROBIN'S CROSS LA

Bendalls
Clump

Heath
Wood

Warsick Lan

Seven Spouts
Farm

7

DE65

Knowle Hill
Farm

Orangehill
Bridge

The Bendalls
Farmhouse

25

Orange Hill

Brookdale Farm

6

Spur's Bottom

Dove Cote
Hill

Repton
Common

Tower

P

P

24

Foremark Reservoir

The Grange

5

BURTON RD
A514

NARROW LA

Sailing
Club

DE73

4

HIGH ST

Fairview Farm

THE GREEN

DE15

SCADDOWS LA

The Scaddows

3

Repton
Shrubs

Repton
Bog

Bondwood
Farm

Foremark Park
Farm

Basfords Hill
Farm

ASHBY RD

Mast

23

The
Scaddows

Pottery
House

Hartshorn
Bog

Carver's
Rocks

2

P

DERBY RD

STAUNTON LA

Top Farm
House

1

DE11

Smith's
Gorse

A514
COAL
LA

Gravelpit Hill

B5006

THE BUILDINGS
FARM

22

32 A 33 B C 34 D E F

244
252

A   B   C   D   E   F

Warsick La

Coppy Hill

Lady Acre Wood

Robin Wood

8

Mount Pleasant

Fox Hole Wood

Melbourne Ride

Ingerholmes Wood

BOURNE CT 1
HOPE ST 2

B587

COCKSHUT LA

Highfields

The Roundlet

7

Gorsey Leys

St BRIDE'S FARM

RIDING BANK

25

Woodside

Melbourne Common

Shaw House

ROBINSON'S HILL

Stanton's Wood

Dovesite Bsns Pk

Bleak House

B587

6

Brickyard Cottage

Hemsley's Barn

SHEPHERD'S LA

Tower

Visitor Ctr

5

STANTON HILL

Derby Hills House Farm

BOG LA

Sailing Club

Dame Catherine Harpur's Sch

GRANGE CL

CHAPEL ST

MELBOURNE LA

Broadstone Lane End

DERBY HILLS HOUSE CT

24

MAIN ST

BROADSTONE LA

BSE LA

DE73

FLETCHING

PO

HARPUR AVE

STONE FRONTS

BANTON'S LA

1 HAYES FARM CT
2 SLADE FARM

Works

Staunton Harold Resr

4

HIGH ST

PH

NARROW LA

Ticknall

B5006

BURTON RD

White Leys

Lodge Plantation

Shaw's Plantation

Derby Hills Farm

Walker's La

Serpentine Wood

3

Middle Lodge

Kennel Cottages

Clay Pit Plantation

23

The Rookery

Mere Pond

Jubilee Plantation

Betty's Pond

Calke Park

Calke Abbey

P

Spring Wood

2

Gorsey Covert

Poker's Leys

Home Farm

LE65

STAUNTON LA

White Hollows Farm

Dark Plantation

Calke

The Gables

Ivanhoe Way

1

22

A   B   C   D   E   F

35   36   37

258
252

251

245

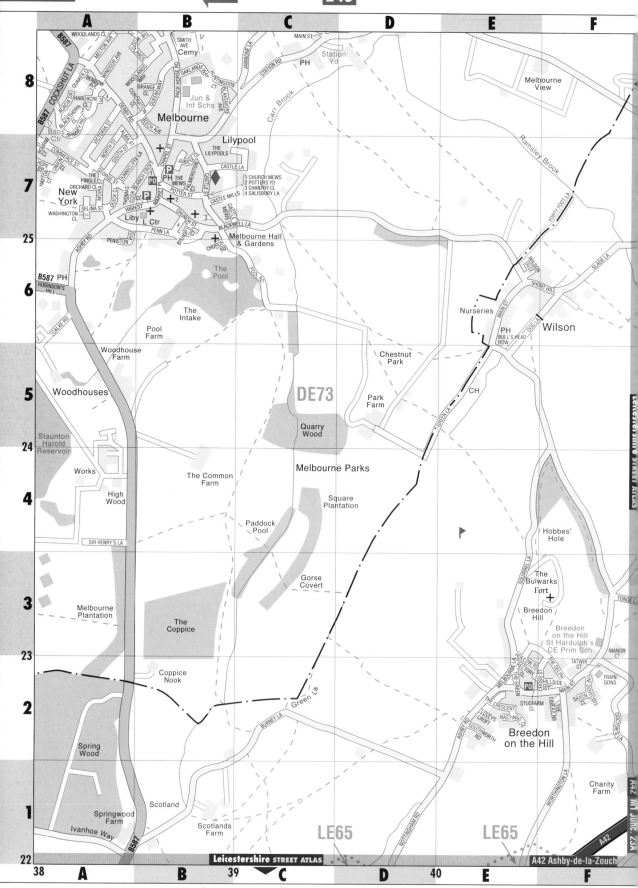

251

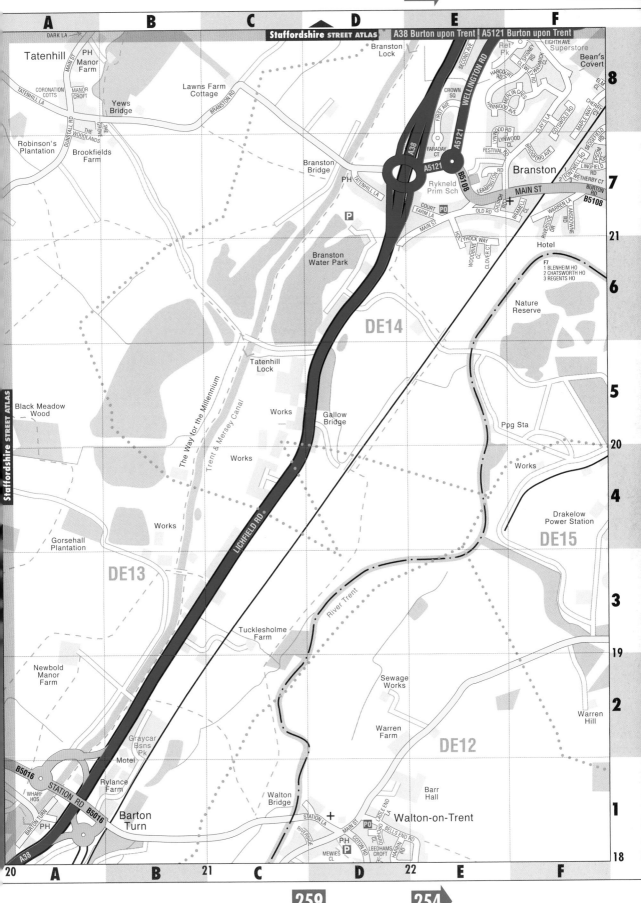

Staffordshire STREET ATLAS | A38 Burton upon Trent | A5121 Burton upon Trent

Tatenhill

Dark La
Manor Farm
PH
Coronation Cotts
Tatenhill La
Manor Croft
Yews Bridge
The Grove
The Woodlands
Dunstall Rd
Robinson's Plantation
Brookfields Farm
Main St

Lawns Farm Cottage
Branston Rd

Branston Lock
Branston Bridge
PH
Tatenhill La
P
Court Farm La
Main St
Rykneld Prim Sch
PO
Old Rd
Holyhock Way
Woodbine Cl
Clover Cl

Branston Water Park

A38
A5121
Faraday Ct
B5108
Crown Sq
First Ave
Second Ave
Wellington Rd
Harcourt Rd
Harwood Ave
Merlin Cres
Festival Rd
Lynwood Rd
Lynwood Cl
Bridford Ave
Leamington Rd
Clays La
Cotswold Rd
Springfield Rd
Clewley Way
Church Rd
Bramley
Barnett
Riverside Dr
Warren La
Lansdowne Rd

Ret Pk
Eighth Ave
Superstore
Bean's Covert
Elm Cl
Cherry Rd
Fonthwell Rd
Efford Rd
Stockfield Rd
Lingfield Rd
Wetherby Ct
Maple Way
Branston
Main St
B5108
Burton Rd
Hotel

8

7

21

6

F7
1 BLENHEIM HO
2 CHATSWORTH HO
3 REGENTS HO

Nature Reserve

DE14

Tatenhill Lock
The Way for the Millennium
Trent & Mersey Canal
Works
Works
Works
Gallow Bridge

Black Meadow Wood

Gorsehall Plantation

DE13

Lichfield Rd

Ppg Sta
Works

Drakelow Power Station

DE15

5

20

4

River Trent
Tucklesholme Farm

3

19

Newbold Manor Farm

Sewage Works
Warren Farm

DE12

Warren Hill

2

Graycar Bsns Pk
Motel
Rylance Farm

Barton Turn

B5016
Station Rd
B5016
Wharf Hos
Barton Turn
PH
A38

Walton Bridge
Station La
Riverside
Mewies Cl
PH
P

Coton Rd
Main St
PO
Cadle End
Bells End Rd
Harbin Rd
Leedhams Croft

Barr Hall
Walton-on-Trent

1

18

Staffordshire STREET ATLAS

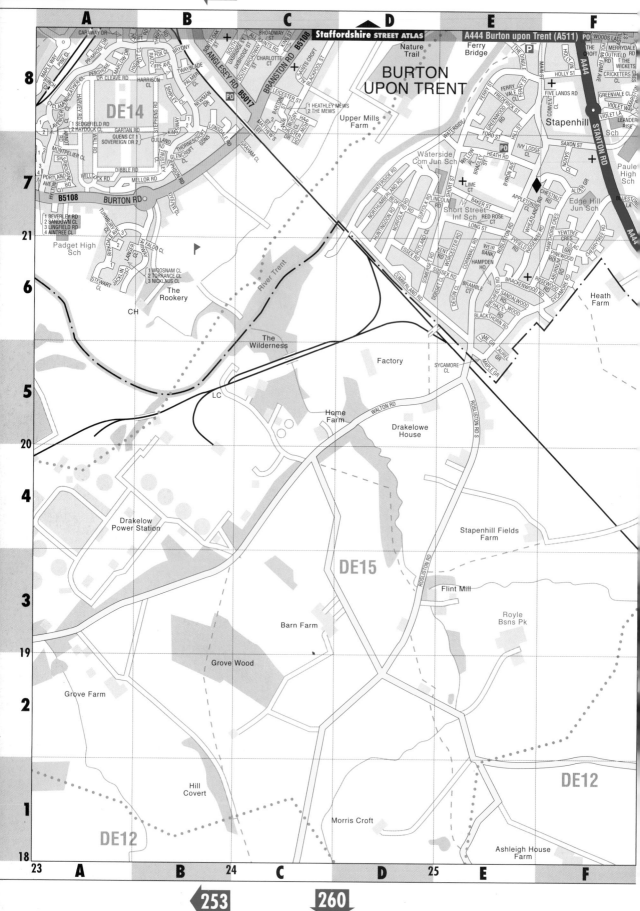

253

Staffordshire STREET ATLAS

A444 Burton upon Trent (A511)

BURTON UPON TRENT

DE14

DE15

DE12

DE12

Drakelow Power Station

The Wilderness

Factory

Home Farm

Drakelowe House

Stapenhill Fields Farm

Flint Mill

Royle Bsns Pk

Barn Farm

Grove Wood

Grove Farm

Hill Covert

Morris Croft

Ashleigh House Farm

Stapenhill

Heath Farm

River Trent

The Rookery

Padget High Sch

Upper Mills Farm

Nature Trail

Ferry Bridge

Paule High Sch

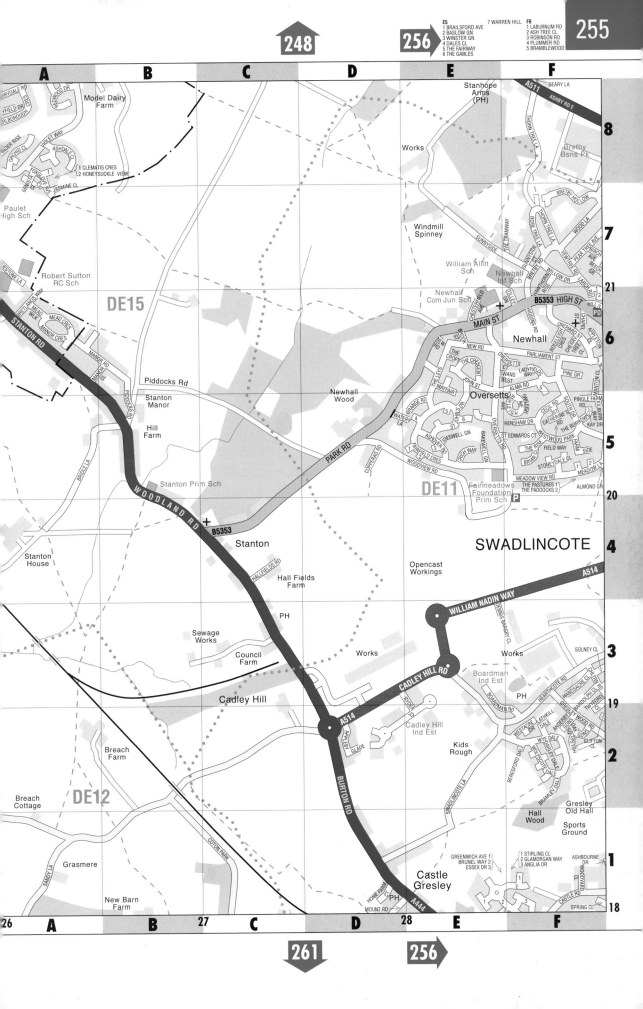

248

256

255

E5
1 BRAILSFORD AVE
2 BASLOW GN
3 WINSTER GN
4 DALES CL
5 THE FAIRWAY
6 THE GABLES

7 WARREN HILL

F6
1 LABURNUM RD
2 ASH TREE CL
3 ROBINSON RD
4 PLUMMER RD
5 BRAMBLEWOOD

A   B   C   D   E   F

8

7

21

6

20

5

4

19

3

2

1

18

Model Dairy Farm

1 CLEMATIS CRES
2 HONEYSUCKLE VIEW

Paulet High Sch

DE15

Robert Sutton RC Sch

STANTON RD

Piddocks Rd

Stanton Manor

Hill Farm

Stanton Prim Sch

WOODLAND RD

B5353

Stanton

Stanton House

Hall Fields Farm

PH

Sewage Works

Council Farm

Cadley Hill

DE12

Breach Farm

Breach Cottage

Grasmere

New Barn Farm

SANDY LA

COTON PARK

BURTON RD

A514

Castle Gresley

A444

HOME FARM

PH

MOUNT RD

Stanhope Arms (PH)

GEARY LA

ASHBY RD E

A511

Works

Windmill Spinney

William Allitt Sch

Newhall Inf Sch

Newhall Com Jun Sch

MAIN ST

B5353 HIGH ST

Newhall

PO

Oversetts

DE11

PARK RD

Newhall Wood

WATERY LA

COPPERAS RD

Fairmeadows Foundation Prim Sch

THE PASTURES
THE PADDOCKS

ALMOND GR

MEADOW VIEW RD

SWADLINCOTE

Opencast Workings

A514

WILLIAM NADIN WAY

CADLEY HILL RD

Boardman Ind Est

PH

Works

SOLNEY CL

Works

Cadley Hill Ind Est

Kids Rough

Hall Wood

Gresley Old Hall

Sports Ground

GREENWICH AVE 1
BRUNEL WAY 2
ESSEX DR 3

1 STIRLING CL
2 GLAMORGAN WAY
3 ANGLIA DR

ASHBOURNE DR

SPRING CL

CASTLE RD

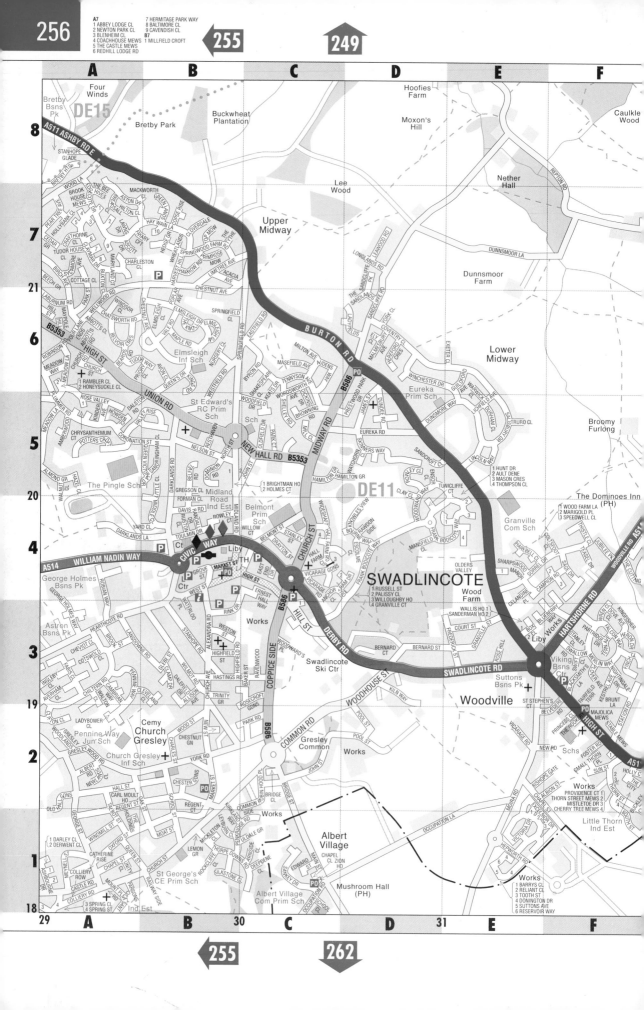

A B C D E F

Henson's Coppice

Wilder House

Coppice House Farm

COAL LA

White Hollows Farm

DE73

Spring Farm

Coppice Farm

Tadsor Farm

Shaw's Alders

SPRINGHILL

BROOK ST

PEAR TREE CL

PO

PH

REPTON RD

MILLPOOL CL

KENDRICKS CL

TICKNALL RD

Pisternhill Plantation

MEROAK LA

DERBY RD

B5006

8

7

21

Manor Farm

Ladyfields Plantation

MAIN ST

Hartshorne CE Prim Sch

Hartshorne

MANOR VIEW

DUNMORE GRANGE

CHURCH ST

P

PH

SLACK LA

Limehouse Dam

Daniel Hayes Farm

Long Alders

The Elms

6

TOWER RD

WOODVILLE RD

Horn Hill

Sharp's Bottom

Pistern Hill

B5006

5

Goseley Dale

DE11

MANCHESTER LA

Several Wood

20

BROOKDALE RD

GOSELEY AVE

HARTSHILL RD

GOSELEY CRES

ELMSDALE RD

BRETBY VIEW

MOUNT RD

BROOKDALE RD

DALE RD

EDWARD ST

1 BELL LA
2 BENTLEY DALE
3 LIMESTONE CL

Short Hazels Farm

Heath Farm

Hartshorne Heath

The Forties

HEATH LA

FORTIES LA

4

Hilltop Farm

PH

BEECH DR

FIELD LA

Stonehouse Farm

Tithe Farm

Smisby

Manor Farm

NELSON PL

CHAPEL ST

MAIN ST

PH

3

MILLFIELD ST

RADLEIGH GR

HIGH ST

ASHBY RD

Boundary

Myrtle Lodge Farm

LE65

19

1 THE SHRUBBERY
2 HOLLY CT
3 CANNER CL
4 THORN ST

THE COTE

SMITHS LA

HEATH LA

Gardens

ANNWELL LA

Tournament Field

2

Blackfordby House

Blackfordby
St Margaret's
CE Prim Sch

Scam-Hazel Farm

Annwell Place

PH

A511

BUTT LA

FENTON AVE

ELSTEAD LA

WELL LA

MAIN ST

ASHBY LA

STRAWBERRY LA 1
CHURCH CL 2
PARKERS CL 3

Hall

Blackfordby

Holywell Farm

1

Works

Leicestershire STREET ATLAS

18

32 33 34

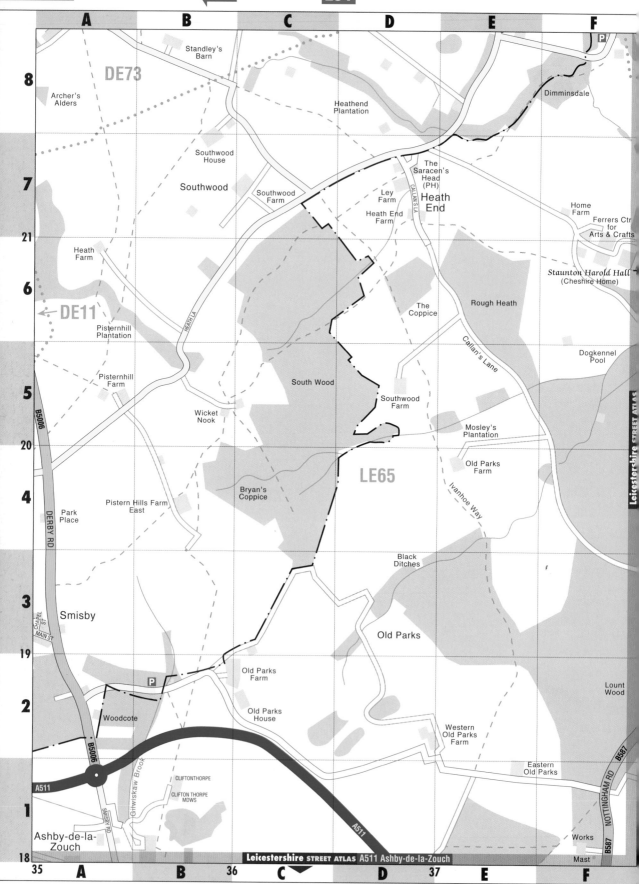

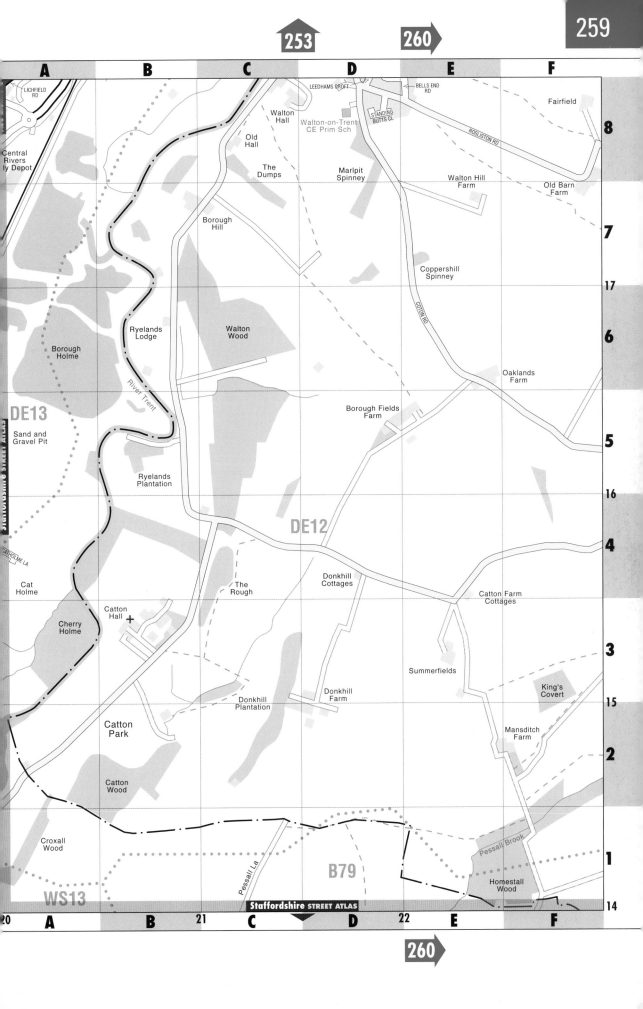

A B C D E F

8
7
17
6
5
16
4
3
15
2
1
14

LICHFIELD
RD

Central
Rivers
ly Depot

Walton
Hall

Old
Hall

The
Dumps

Borough
Hill

LEEDHAMS CROFT

Walton-on-Trent
CE Prim Sch

STANDING
BUTTS CL

BELLS END
RD

Fairfield

ROSLISTON RD

Walton Hill
Farm

Old Barn
Farm

Marlpit
Spinney

Coppershill
Spinney

Ryelands
Lodge

Walton
Wood

COTOM RD

Borough
Holme

River Trent

Oaklands
Farm

DE13

Sand and
Gravel Pit

Ryelands
Plantation

Borough Fields
Farm

DE12

CATHOLME LA

Cat
Holme

The
Rough

Donkhill
Cottages

Catton Farm
Cottages

Catton
Hall

Cherry
Holme

Summerfields

King's
Covert

Donkhill
Plantation

Donkhill
Farm

Mansditch
Farm

Catton
Park

Catton
Wood

Pessall Brook

Croxall
Wood

Pessall La

B79

Homestall
Wood

WS13

20 A 21 B C 22 D E F 14

259
254

A B C D E F

8

ROSLISTON RD

Corner
Farm

Nursery

Rosliston
Forestry
Visitor Ctr

DE15

Priory
Farm

SANDY LA

Walton Lane
Farm

Fox
Covert

The
Royal Oak
(PH)

CHURCH LA

MAIN ST

7

Calves Croft
Farm

Caldwell

17

Moonraker

Pegasus
Sch

Manor
Farm

THE CHASE

BURTON RD

Rosliston CE
Prim Sch

PH

Rosliston

Caldwell
Covert

6

HOLDON CROFT

PO

THE GLEBE

VICARAGE WLK

YEW TREE RD

YEW TREE
GDNS

MAIN ST

NEW ST

CAULDWELL RD

CATTON LA

STRAWBERRY LA

LINTON RD

Blakenhall
Farm

5

COTON RD

Field House
Farm

DE12

COTON LA

Beehive
Farm

P

16

Lads Grave

Longfurlong
Farm

P

4

Coton in the
Elms

BURTON RD

Pessall Brook

Overfields
Farm

Church
Farm

CHURCH CROFT

PO

ELMS RD

CHAPMANS
CROFT

Coton in the
Elms CE Prim
Sch

GREENACRE
PK

GLEBE
CL

ELMS LA

CHAPEL ST

Queen's Head
Inn (PH)

COTON LA

3

CHURCH ST

NEW RD

MILL ST

COALPIT LA

CRAFTY FLATTS LA

15

HILL GREEN CL

Pessall Brook

Malt House
Farm

P

2

Raddle Farm
Wood

LITTLE LIVERPOOL

Pessall Brook

Church Flatts
Farm

1

The Crosses

Grafton
House

14

B79

23 A B 24 C D 25 E F

259
263

261
256

A   B   C   D   E   F

8

Gresley Wood

Littleworth

MOIRA RD

DE11

Boothorpe

7

Gresley Tunnel

P

Spoil Heaps and Clay Pits

RESERVOIR HILL

Gorse La

17

Swainspark

Swainspark Ind Est

Hanging Hill

6

RICKMANS CNR CVN SITE

PARK RD

GORSE LA

P

Hanging Hill Farm

5

A444

Works

SPRING COTTAGE RD

Spring Cottage

OMNI LENIUM AVE

MARQUIS DR

RANTON RD

PH

Conkers Discovery Centre

MARQUIS CT

16

BURTON RD

ALEXANDRA CT

Works

BRITON LODGE CL

4

EDWARD ST

ALEXANDRA RD

ROYAL LA

CORONATION ST

WOODLANDS CRES

ALICE GDNS

STANLEIGH RD

WOODVILLE RD

ROSEDALE VIEW

HARLEY'S

Overseal Prim Sch

P

SLACKEY LA

DE12

Conkers Waterside Centre

Sarah's Wood

Visitors Ctr

FOREST LEA

STATION DR

ASHBY RD

PO

3

Overseal

PH

LULLINGTON MEWS

DAISY LA

HALLCROFT AVE

MOIRA RD

Gorsey Leys

Caravan Pk

Gresley Leys

Blencathra

BATH LA

WHITWORTH CL

VIADE VIANA

PH

Moira

Furnace Lane Ind Est

FURNACE LA

Warren House Farm

ASHBY-DE-LA-ZOUCH

MEASHAM RD

15

LULLINGTON RD

CLIFTON

BRAMBLE WLK

VALLEY RD

AVE

JACKSON CL

ASHLEY CL

ACRESFORD VIEW

PO

SHORTHEATH

Brooklands Farm

SHORT

HEATH RD

Moira Furnace Mus

PARK RD

SCHOOL ST

2

Sewage Works

SQUIRREL WLK

Grange Farm

Rookery Farm

ACRESFORD RD

A444

Short Heath

Shortheath Farm

DONISTHORPE LA

POPLAR AVE

IVANHOE WAY

1

Cadborough Hill

Church Way

Hooborough Brook

Sewage Works

FINNEY CL

JUBILEE TERR

GREENSIDE CL

HILL ST

DAWKIN

DAISY CL

BUTTERCUP AVE

VIOLET CL

COWSLIP CL

BLUEBELL CL

FOXGLOVE AVE

Donisthorpe

Cemy

ASHLAR DR

14

Cadborough Farm

SEALS RD

BARKLAM CL

IVY CL

NEW ST

CHAPEL ST

THE PETERLEAS

PO

CHURCH ST

29   A   B   30   C   D   31   E   F

PRINCESS ST   SPRING ST   BANK ST   STATION ST

ISLAND CL

OCCUPATION RD

COVERT PL

Sch

THE CLOSE

MUSHROOM LA

A B C D E F

8

7

13

6

Edingale
Fields
Farm

Green Lane

Lady
Leys

Hall

COLVILE CL

DAG LA

PH

Home
Farm

Lullington

Woollens
Plantation

DE12

Limes
Farm

New
Plantation

Lullington Park

Westbrook
Farm

West Brook

Fox
Covert

5

12

Bald Hill's
Farm

Seal Brook

4

River Mease

B79

Mill
Farm

LULLINGTON RD

3

PH

11

POTTERS CROFT

TUDOR RISE

MAIN ST

NETHERSEAL RD

Hall

MEASE LA

Newhouse
Farm

CHURCH ST

St Andrew's
CE Prim Sch

ST DAVIDS RD

ST ANDREW'S CL

2

Twizles Lane

Haunton

SMITH LA

CHESTNUT LA

PARSON'S WLK

Clifton
Campville

COPPICE LA

SYERSCOTE LA

1

10

23 A B 24 C D 25 E F

Staffordshire STREET ATLAS

A **B** **C** **D** **E** **F**

8

Woodfields Farm

Grangewood

Broomfields

LODGE RD

GUNBY HILL

GORSEY LA

Seal Brook

West View Farm

The Hawthornes

7

HUNT'S LA

HAWTHORN AVE

CROFT

MAIN ST

Netherseal

PH

THE BROOMHILLS

WOOLSTITCH PK

Hollows Farm

The Grange

13

HOLLY BUSH

PH

PO

STANLEY CL

BLACKSMITHS CL

DOG LA

Grange Fields

CLIFTON RD

MANOR

Hall Farm

CHURCH ST

6

Birchington House

Hillside Cottage

St Peter's CE Prim Sc

Sewage Works

DE12

Yew Tree Farm

5

12

River Mease

Gorse Spinney

4

NETHERSEAL RD

Stones Bridge

Seal Fields Farm

HURST CT

Home Farm

WOODLAND VIEW

Chilcote

3

Clifton Hall

CHURCH LA

Manor Farm

NO MAN'S HEATH RD

11

B79

2

Clifton Lodge Farm

Bandland Farm

Clifton Heath

New Covert

1

Fairview Cottages

QUARRY BERRY LA

10

A **B** **C** **D** **E** **F**

Warwickshire STREET ATLAS

A B C D E F

8

7

13

6

5

12

4

3

11

2

1

10

29 A B 30 C D 31 E F

Donisthorpe

STANLEIGH GDNS 1
IVY CL 2
CHURCH WLK 3
STANLEIGH HO 4

NEW ST

PH
PH

Hall
Farm

Ivanhoe Way

Saltersford Brook

STRETTON VIEW

CORONATION LA

Mine
(dis)

CHAPEL ST

Oak
Villa

Oakthorpe

REPTON RD

A42

M1 Junc. 23A A42 Leicestershire STREET ATLAS

A444

GORSEY LA

Seale
Pastures

COOPERS CL
BROOKFIELD
COTTS

Acresford

PH

Eastfield

ACRESFORD RD

HURCH ST

ACRESFORD RD

Moneyhill
Farm

MEASHAM RD

Saltersford
Cottages

Saltersford
Bridge

Saltersford
Farm

River Mease

Stretton
Bridge

Mill
House

DE12

Hall
Farm

Stretton en le Field

Manor House
Farm

Park
Farm

TAMWORTH RD

MEASHAM RD

Heath
Lodge

Appleby
Magna

Hill
Farm

A444

M42

11

Old
House

B5493

Warwickshire STREET ATLAS M42 Birmingham A444 Nuneaton

Hotel

WHITESTONE RD

RECTORY LA

The Old
Rectory

PARKFIELD CRES

CHURCH ST

ST MICHAEL'S
DR

STONEY LA

OLD END

Index

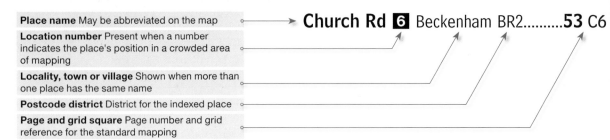

Place name May be abbreviated on the map

Location number Present when a number indicates the place's position in a crowded area of mapping

Locality, town or village Shown when more than one place has the same name

Postcode district District for the indexed place

Page and grid square Page number and grid reference for the standard mapping

Church Rd **6** Beckenham BR2..........**53** C6

Public and commercial buildings are highlighted in magenta **Places of interest** are highlighted in blue with a star★

Abbreviations used in the index

Acad	**Academy**	Comm	**Common**	Gd	**Ground**	L	**Leisure**	Prom	**Promenade**
App	**Approach**	Cott	**Cottage**	Gdn	**Garden**	La	**Lane**	Rd	**Road**
Arc	**Arcade**	Cres	**Crescent**	Gn	**Green**	Liby	**Library**	Recn	**Recreation**
Ave	**Avenue**	Cswy	**Causeway**	Gr	**Grove**	Mdw	**Meadow**	Ret	**Retail**
Bglw	**Bungalow**	Ct	**Court**	H	**Hall**	Meml	**Memorial**	Sh	**Shopping**
Bldg	**Building**	Ctr	**Centre**	Ho	**House**	Mkt	**Market**	Sq	**Square**
Bsns, Bus	**Business**	Ctry	**Country**	Hospl	**Hospital**	Mus	**Museum**	St	**Street**
Bvd	**Boulevard**	Cty	**County**	HQ	**Headquarters**	Orch	**Orchard**	Sta	**Station**
Cath	**Cathedral**	Dr	**Drive**	Hts	**Heights**	Pal	**Palace**	Terr	**Terrace**
Cir	**Circus**	Dro	**Drove**	Ind	**Industrial**	Par	**Parade**	TH	**Town Hall**
Cl	**Close**	Ed	**Education**	Inst	**Institute**	Pas	**Passage**	Univ	**University**
Cnr	**Corner**	Emb	**Embankment**	Int	**International**	Pk	**Park**	Wk, Wlk	**Walk**
Coll	**College**	Est	**Estate**	Intc	**Interchange**	Pl	**Place**	Wr	**Water**
Com	**Community**	Ex	**Exhibition**	Junc	**Junction**	Prec	**Precinct**	Yd	**Yard**

Index of localities, towns and villages

A

Abbeydale Park 55 F6
Abney 51 F4
Acresford 265 C7
Albert Village 256 C1
Aldercar 182 A4
Alders 196 C2
Alderwasley 166 E8
Aldwark 152 F7
Alfreton 159 C4
Alkmonton 199 D1
Allenton 232 D5
Allestree 204 F3
Alsop en le Dale 150 E3
Alstonefield 149 D4
Alton 130 C5
Alvaston 233 B8
Ambaston 234 D6
Ambergate 167 F3
Annwell Place 257 E1
Apperknowle 58 A1
Appleby Magna 265 F1
Arbourthorne 43 E8
Arbourthorne Estate .. 43 E6
Arkwright Town 97 D3
Ashbourne 173 C2
Ashby-de-la-Zouch ... 258 A1
Ashford in the Water .. 108 E7
Ashgate
  Chesterfield 95 D4
  Old Brampton 94 F4
Ashleyhay 166 A4
Ashopton 30 E2
Ashover 129 F3
Ashover Hay 145 B5
Aston
  Hope 39 C4
  Sudbury 225 F4
Aston Heath 226 B6
Aston-on-Trent 246 B8
Astwith 133 A5
Atlow 175 A6
Atlowtop 175 B5
Ault Hucknall 133 F7
Awsworth 195 C4

B

Backmoor 43 C2
Bagshaw 47 F7
Bagthorpe 171 F4
Bailey Grove 182 D2
Bakestone Moor 81 E5
Bakewell 109 C5

Ballidon 152 A2
Bamford 40 B4
Bank Top 53 A8
Bankwood Gate 16 C8
Barber Booth 37 A6
Bargate 179 C1
Barlborough 80 B7
Barlborough Common . 80 B5
Barlow 75 E2
Barrow Hill 78 B4
Barrow upon Trent . 244 B6
Barton in Fabis ... 237 E6
Barton Turn 253 B1
Baslow 91 F5
Bassett 42 E5
Batemoor 57 A5
Batham Gate 66 F4
Beauchief 56 D8
Beeley 111 B4
Beeston 223 E4
Bellevue 173 B2
Belper 179 B3
Belper Lane End ... 178 C7
Belph 82 C4
Bibbington 66 F7
Biggin
  Hartington 138 C4
  Hulland Ward 176 A5
Birch Cross 224 C2
Birchover 126 B1
Birch Vale 25 B2
Birdholme 115 A4
Birley 93 F7
Birleyhay 58 D5
Blackbrook
  Belper 178 B4
  Chapel-en-le-Frith . 47 E6
  Tutbury 238 C1
Blackfordby 257 C1
Blackwall 175 F7
Blackwell
  Sutton in Ashfield . 147 F1
  Taddington 87 D5
Bolehill
  Calow 97 B1
  Common Side 75 C2
  Sheffield 43 A2
  Wirksworth 155 A2
Bolsover 99 B3
Bonsall 142 E1
Bonsall Dale 142 D1
Boothgate 179 E7
Boothorpe 262 F8
Borrowash 221 C2
Boulton 233 B6
Boundary 257 C2
Bowden Head 35 D1

Bowshaw 56 F4
Boylestone 213 C4
Boylestonfield 213 E5
Boythorpe 95 E1
Brackenfield 145 D2
Bradbourne 163 C6
Bradley 186 F8
Bradway 56 C5
Bradway Bank 56 A6
Bradwell 51 B7
Bradwell Hills 51 B6
Brailsford 201 F7
Bramley 58 F3
Bramley-Vale 117 E1
Brampton 95 D2
Branston 253 F7
Brassington 153 A1
Breadsall 205 E4
Breadsall Hilltop . 205 D2
Breaston 235 D7
Breck End 35 C1
Breedon on the Hill . 252 E4
Bretby 249 A3
Bretton 71 A8
Brick Houses 55 D8
Bridgefield 17 B7
Bridgeholm Green . 47 A8
Bridgemont 33 E2
Brierley Green ... 34 B2
Brightgate 142 B4
Brimington 96 F7
Brimington Common . 96 F5
Brindwoodgate 75 D5
Brinsley 182 E7
Broadbottom 16 A8
Broadholm 179 A7
Brockhurst 129 C6
Brockwell 95 E4
Brook Bottom 23 F1
Brookfield 9 E3
Brookside 94 F2
Brough 39 D2
Brushfield 88 D4
Bubnell 91 D6
Bullbridge 168 B5
Bull Farm 135 C2
Burbage 84 E6
Burnaston 229 F5
Burntheath 228 C4
Burrfields 47 C6
Burton upon Trent . 254 D8
Butterley
  Ripley 169 F3
  Tansley 144 F5
Buxton 85 A7
Buxworth 34 A1

C

Caldwell 260 E7
California 218 D3
Calke 251 E1
Callow 165 B4
Calow 96 F1
Calow Green 116 A8
Calton Lees 110 F5
Calver 72 C2
Calver Sough 72 C2
Canholes 84 E5
Carr Vale 117 F8
Carsington 164 E7
Cartledge 75 B7
Castle Donington . 247 C3
Castle Gresley ... 255 E1
Castleton 38 C2
Causeway Head 55 C8
Chaddesden 219 E7
Chapel-en-le-Frith . 47 B6
Chapel Milton 47 B8
Charlestown 17 C6
Charlesworth 16 C6
Chellaston 233 A1
Chelmorton 87 B1
Cherrytree Hill .. 220 B5
Chesterfield 266 B2
Chevinside 178 E2
Chew 16 A5
Chilcote 264 F3
Chinley 34 F1
Chinley Head 34 F5
Chisworth 16 B5
Church Broughton . 227 B8
Church Broughton,
  Heathtop 227 A6
Church Gresley ... 256 B2
Church Mayfield .. 184 D6
Churchtown 127 B2
Church Town 60 E6
Cinderhill 179 E1
Clay Cross 131 B4
Clay Mills 241 A3
Clifton 184 F6
Clifton Campville . 263 F1
Clowne 80 D3
Coal Aston 57 B4
Cock Alley 97 A1
Cockyard 46 E4
Codnor 181 C7
Codnor Breach 181 A4
Codnor Gate 170 B1
Codnor Park 170 E3
Coldeaton 150 B6

Colshaw 103 E4
Combridge 210 C8
Combs 46 E1
Common End 132 F7
Commonside
  Brailsford 187 D1
  Selston 171 F8
  Sutton in Ashfield . 148 F2
Common Side
  Barlow 75 D3
  Heanor 181 E1
Compstall 15 A3
Compton 173 D2
Congreave 126 D7
Coplow Dale 50 E3
Corbriggs 115 F5
Cordwell 74 E6
Cossall 195 C1
Cossall Common ... 195 B3
Cossall Marsh 195 C2
Cote Green 15 C1
Cotes Park 159 C2
Cotmanhay 194 E4
Coton in the Clay . 238 F3
Coton in the Elms . 260 C4
Coton Park 261 D8
Cowers Lane 177 D3
Cowhill 179 A2
Cowley 75 D7
Cowley Bar 75 B8
Coxbench 191 F3
Crakemarsh 210 D5
Craythorne 240 D2
Creighton 210 A3
Cressbrook 89 A6
Creswell 81 F2
Crewton 232 F8
Crich 156 F1
Crich Common 168 B8
Crist 46 B8
Cromford 155 A6
Cropper 215 B4
Cross Hill 181 B5
Crowden 6 E3
Crowdicote 121 E7
Crowhole 75 D4
Cuckney 101 F3
Curbar 72 E2
Cutthorpe 94 F7
Cutthorpe Green .. 94 C3

D

Dalbury 216 B3
Dale Abbey 207 F2
Dalebank 145 C8

Dale End
Bradwell 51 A6
Elton 140 C7
Danebank 32 E5
Danesmoor 131 E3
Darfoulds 63 F1
Darley Abbey 205 A2
Darley Bridge 142 C8
Darley Dale 127 C2
Darley Hillside 127 D4
Deep Pit 43 F8
Denby Bottles 180 A1
Denby Common 181 A3
Denby Village 180 C1
Denstone 196 D6
Derby 267 C4
Derwent 30 C6
Dethick 156 B8
Dimple 143 A6
Disley 32 C5
Doehole 145 A2
Doe Lea 117 D1
Donisthorpe 262 F1
Dore 55 E7
Dove Head 103 D6
Dove Holes 47 E2
Doveridge 211 A1
Draycott 234 F7
Dronfield 56 E2
Duckmanton 98 A5
Duffield 190 F3
Duffieldbank 191 A3
Dunnshill 207 C1

E
Eagle Tor 126 A2
Earl Sterndale 105 C3
Eastmoor 93 D4
Eastwood 182 E3
Eccles Fold 46 C8
Eckington 59 C4
Edale 37 C8
Edale End 29 D2
Edensor 110 E8
Edgetop 103 F1
Edlaston 185 C2
Egginton 241 B6
Egstow 131 D5
Ellastone 183 B3
Elmton 100 A7
Elton 140 E6
Elvaston 234 A6
Emmett Carr 79 C7
Etwall 229 C3
Etwall Common 229 D2
Eyam 71 D6

F
Fairfield 85 D8
Far Laund 179 C6
Farley 128 B1
Farnah Green 178 C3
Fauld 238 C6
Fenny Bentley 162 A1
Fernilee 45 E1
Findern 230 D2
Flagg 106 F6
Flash 103 A3
Flaxholme 190 F1
Foolow 70 E6
Ford 58 E5
Foremark 243 D2
Foston 226 D4
Fourlane Ends 158 C4
Fox Green 100 F8
Freebirch 93 D6
Friden 139 A6
Fritchley 168 C7
Froggatt 72 C5
Furness Vale 33 C3

G
Gallows Inn 209 B6
Gamesley 9 D1
Gentshill 131 E2
Giltbrook 195 C8
Glapwell 134 C8
Glasshouse Common 77 D5
Gleadless Valley 43 E3
Glossop 10 B2
Godfreyhole 165 B8
Golden Valley 170 D3
Goosegreen 146 D3
Gorseybank 166 A7
Gorsey Leys 262 C4
Gosforth Valley 56 E2
Gotham 139 D1
Gowhole 33 E4
Grangemill 153 D8
Grasshill 115 E4
Grassmoor 115 F3
Great Cubley 198 F1
Great Hucklow 70 B8
Great Longstone 90 B4
Great Wilne 235 C2
Green Fairfield 67 C2
Greenhill 56 F7
Greenhillocks 180 E7
Greenside 58 C3
Greenwich 169 F2
Griffe Grange 153 D4
Grindleford 72 C7

Grindlow 70 C8
Grindsbrook Booth 37 C8

H
Hadfield 10 B5
Hady 96 D2
Hague Bar 32 F8
Hales Green 199 B7
Halfway 59 F7
Hallam Fields 209 A4
Hallam Moors 41 E8
Hall Green 171 E8
Hallhill 46 F7
Hallowes 76 C8
Hammersmith 169 D4
Hanbury 238 A5
Handley 145 F8
Hangingbridge 184 F8
Hanstubbin 171 F5
Hardhurst 76 E6
Hardley Hill 215 C2
Hardstoft 133 A3
Harehill 213 A3
Hargatewall 68 B3
Harlesthorpe 80 E5
Harpur Hill 85 C3
Harthill 61 F6
Hartington 137 D5
Hartshorne 257 A6
Hasland 115 D7
Hasland Green 115 C7
Hassop 90 F5
Hathersage 53 B7
Hatton 239 D8
Haunton 263 B2
Hayfield 25 C2
Hazelford 53 A5
Hazelwood 190 A8
Heage 168 E1
Heanor 181 C2
Heanor Gate 193 C8
Hearthstone 143 D1
Heath 117 B2
Heathcote 138 B5
Heath End 258 D7
Heathtop 227 A6
Heeley 43 B6
Hemington 247 D5
Hemming Green 94 B4
Hemsworth 43 D3
Henmoor 131 A4
Hepthorne Lane 131 E6
Herdings 43 F3
Hidebank 33 C8
Higham 146 C3
High Cross Bank 261 E8
Higher Bibbington 67 A6
Higher Buxton 85 C6
Higher Chisworth 16 B4
Higher Crossings 46 F6
Higher Dinting 10 A8
Higher Disley 32 E5
Higher Gamesley 16 D8
Highfield 43 A8
Highfields 132 C1
Highgate 25 D1
High Lane 32 A8
High Low 52 E5
Hilcote 148 C1
Hillclifflane 177 A4
Hillcross 231 C7
Hillfoot 55 D5
Hilltop
Chapel-en-le-Frith 46 B6
Flash 103 B5
Hill Top 76 A7
Hillyfields 132 B7
Hilton 228 C1
Hilton Common 228 F2
Hindlow 105 B7
Hobsic 182 D8
Hockley 115 A2
Hodthorpe 82 C6
Hognaston 164 A1
Holbeck 101 C7
Holbeck Woodhouse 101 E7
Holbrook
Belper 191 D6
Sheffield 60 A8
Holbrook Moor 191 D7
Holehouse 16 C5
Holestone 144 C8
Hollington 200 F4
Hollingworth 9 C6
Hollins 94 A4
Hollinsclough 104 C1
Hollins Green 130 E3
Hollin Wood 34 B1
Holloway 156 B5
Holme 2 F8
Holmesdale 57 C2
Holmesfield 75 A8
Holmesfield Common 74 E8
Holmewood 116 E1
Holmgate 130 E4
Holmley Common 57 A3
Holymoorside 113 D8
Hope
Alstonefield 149 D3
Castleton 38 F4
Hopedale 149 C2
Hopton 164 F7

Horsley 191 F6
Horsleygate 74 E6
Horsley Woodhouse 192 D6
Horwich End 45 D5
Hulland Village 175 D2
Hulland Ward 175 F3
Hundall 77 B7
Hunloke Estate 115 C2
Hurl Field 43 E5
Huthwaite 148 E3

I
Ible 153 E7
Idridgehay 176 F6
Idridgehay Green 176 E7
Ilkeston 208 E7
Ingleby 243 F2
Ingmanthorpe 94 C7
Inkersall 97 D7
Inkersall Green 97 D6
Ireton Wood 176 D4
Ironville 170 E4

J
Jacksdale 171 B4
Jordanthorpe 57 B7
Jubilee 171 B6

K
Kedleston 203 C7
Kelstedge 129 D4
Kilburn 192 A8
Killamarsh 60 E6
Kimberley 195 F8
King's Newton 245 B1
King Sterndale 86 C5
Kirk Hallam 208 D6
Kirk Ireton 165 C1
Kirk Langley 202 F2
Kirkstead 160 D3
Kniveton 163 B1
Knotbury 102 F5

L
Ladmanlow 84 E4
Lambhouse 177 E7
Lane 2 E8
Lane Ends
Disley 32 E4
Marple 15 D1
Sutton on the Hill 215 A2
Lane Head 69 E5
Langley 182 B1
Langley Common 217 B8
Langley Green 202 D2
Langley Mill 182 B3
Larklands 209 B8
Lea 156 B7
Lea Bridge 156 A6
Leabrooks 170 B7
Leadmill 53 B5
Leam 53 A3
Lee Head 16 C6
Lees 216 B7
Leys 154 A8
Lightwood
Eckington 58 F2
Sheffield 57 F8
Lilypool 252 B7
Limekiln Field 99 A3
Linton 261 D6
Litchurch 219 C3
Little Bolehill 155 B2
Little Chester 219 A7
Little Cubley 212 E8
Little Eaton 205 C8
Little Hallam 208 E5
Little Hayfield 25 B1
Little Hucklow 50 E2
Little Longstone 89 E4
Little Matlock 135 F7
Littlemoor 130 C3
Little Norton 57 A8
Littleover 231 B8
Littleworth 262 D6
Litton 69 F3
Litton Mill 88 E7
Lockington 247 F5
Longcliffe 152 F4
Long Duckmanton 98 A3
Long Eaton 236 C7
Longford 214 D8
Longfordlane 215 A5
Longnor 121 A6
Loscoe 181 C3
Loundsley Green 95 B6
Lowedges 57 A6
Lower Bradway 56 C6
Lower Crossings 46 F6
Lower Dinting 10 B1
Lower Ellastone 183 C2
Lower Hartshay 169 A3
Lower Kilburn 191 F7
Lower Midway 256 E6
Lower Pilsley 132 B3
Lower Thurvaston 214 F6
Lowfield 43 B8
Lowgates 78 F3

Low Leighton 33 D8
Lullington 263 E7
Lumsdale 143 E6
Lydgate 74 D8

M
Mackworth 217 E8
Makeney 191 A6
Malcoff 35 E2
Mansfield 135 F2
Mansfield Woodhouse 136 E2
Mapleton 172 F4
Mapperley 193 E3
Marchington 224 E2
Marehay 180 D6
Markeaton 218 B8
Marlpool 193 F8
Marple 23 A5
Marpleridge 23 A2
Marsh Lane 58 F3
Marston Montgomery 211 F8
Marston on Dove 240 B8
Martinside 47 D3
Mastin Moor 79 D4
Mathersgrave 145 C3
Matlock 143 A5
Matlock Bank 143 C5
Matlock Bath 143 C5
Matlock Bridge 143 B5
Matlock Cliff 143 D4
Matlock Dale 143 A2
Matlock Green 143 C5
Mayfield 184 C8
Meersbrook 43 B5
Meersbrook Bank 43 A5
Melbourne 252 B8
Mellor 23 D5
Mercaston 188 B3
Mercaston Green 188 B3
Mickleover 217 E2
Mickley 56 B3
Middlecroft 97 C7
Middle Handley 77 F8
Middle Mayfield 184 B6
Middlepeak 154 E3
Middleton
Wirksworth 154 D4
Youlgrave 124 E3
Milehill 115 F5
Milford 191 A7
Mill Brow 23 E8
Milldale 149 F2
Miller's Dale 88 A2
Millers Green 165 E6
Millington Green 176 A4
Millthorpe 74 F5
Milltown 145 B8
Milton 243 A1
Moira 262 E3
Monsal Head 89 D4
Monyash 107 C2
Mooredge 144 C5
Moorend
Bradley 186 D8
Marple 24 A6
Moorhaigh 135 A3
Moorhall 74 D2
Moorside 165 A2
Morley 206 C4
Morton 146 F5
Mosborough 59 D7
Mottram in Longdendale . . 9 B4
Mount Pleasant
Belper 178 D6
Blackwell 147 F2
Castle Gresley 261 E7
Melbourne 251 F8
Repton 242 E1
Mudd 9 A2
Mugginton 188 F2
Muggintonlane End 188 E6

N
Nether Biggin 175 F5
Nether Booth 29 A1
Nether Burrows 202 C3
Nether Chanderhill 94 C1
Nether Green 60 D7
Nether Handley 77 F7
Nether Heage 168 C1
Nether Langwith 101 B1
Nether Padley 53 E1
Nether Pilsley 132 D1
Netherseal 264 E7
Nether Sturston 173 F1
Netherthorpe 79 A2
New Barlborough 80 D5
Newbold 95 E6
Newbold Moor 95 F7
New Bolsover 98 F2
New Brimington 77 F1
New Brinsley 171 E1
Newfield Green 43 D5
Newgate 75 D1
Newhall 255 F6
Newhaven 138 F5
New Horwich 45 E6
New Houghton 134 F7
Newlands 181 F2
Newmarket 131 A2
New Mills 33 D7
New Sawley 236 B5
New Smithy 35 A1
New Stanton 208 E3

Newthorpe 195 A8
Newthorpe
Common 195 A8
Newton 148 B3
Newton Green 148 A4
Newton Solney 248 E8
New Totley 55 E4
Newtown 33 B6
New Westwood 171 C4
New York 252 A7
New Zealand 218 C5
Ninham End 84 F8
Norbriggs 79 C3
Norbury 183 D1
Normanton 231 F7
Northedge 130 C6
North Wingfield 132 B8
Northwood 127 B5
Norton 57 B8
Norton Lees 43 A4
Norton
Woodseats 43 A2
Norwood 60 F8
Nuttals Park 169 E1

O
Oakerthorpe 158 C3
Oaks Green 225 D7
Oakthorpe 265 F5
Oakwood 206 A2
Ockbrook 221 D5
Offerton 52 D7
Ogston 146 A4
Oker 142 D7
Old Brampton 94 D4
Old Dam 49 B4
Old Glossop 10 E2
Old Matlock 143 C4
Old Tupton 131 C7
Old Whittington 77 B1
Ollerbrook Booth 37 D8
Openwoodgate 179 D3
Osleston 215 D7
Osmaston
Ashbourne 185 F4
Derby 232 C8
Over Burrows 202 A4
Overgreen 94 B8
Over Haddon 109 B1
Over Leigh 45 F6
Overseal 262 A3
Oversetts 255 E5
Over Woodhouse 98 E3
Owen's Bank 239 B6
Owlcotes 117 A4
Owler Bar 55 B1
Owlthorpe 59 B8
Oxton Rakes 94 B8

P
Padfield 10 C5
Palmer Moor 224 E7
Palterton 118 A5
Park Head 157 C2
Parsley Hay 123 B4
Parwich 151 E1
Parwich Lees 151 A2
Peak Dale 67 B5
Peak Forest 49 B3
Peakley Hill 75 C6
Pear Tree 232 B8
Peasehill 180 F8
Pentrich 169 B5
Perryfoot 48 E7
Pikehall 139 E3
Pilhough 126 E7
Pilsley
Baslow 91 C3
Clay Cross 132 D1
Pilsley Green 147 C8
Pinxton 160 C2
Plaistow 156 F6
Plaistow Green 156 F6
Pleasley 135 B6
Pleasleyhill 135 C4
Poolsbrook 98 A7
Porterhouse 169 F1
Potter Somersal 212 A4
Pratthall 94 B7
Priestcliffe 87 F3
Priestcliffe Ditch 87 D4
Pye Bridge 170 F6
Pye Hill 171 A5

Q
Quarndon 204 D6
Quixhill 196 E7
Quoit Green 57 B1

R
Radbourne 216 F5
Radmanthwaite 135 D3
Ravensnest 144 F7
Rawson Green 179 F1
Renishaw 79 B8
Repton 242 E2
Riber 143 E3
Riddings
Denstone 196 B4
Somercotes 170 D5

Ridgeway
Bullbridge 168 C4
Sheffield 58 E8
Ridgeway Moor 58 E7
Ringinglow 42 F4
Ripley 169 C2
Rise End 154 E3
Risley 222 E3
River's Vale 84 F7
Robin Hood 92 D5
Rocester 197 A3
Rodsley 200 A5
Rolleston 240 A4
Rollestone 43 D5
Rolleston on Dove 240 C3
Rose Hill 219 B2
Rosemaryhill 171 F7
Rosliston 260 D6
Roston 197 E7
Rowarth 24 E7
Rowland 90 C5
Rowsley 111 A1
Rowthorne 134 C6
Rylah 117 F5

S

St Augustines 115 B7
St Luke's 218 E3
Sandiacre 223 A6
Sapperton 213 C1
Sawley 236 A4
Scarcliffe 118 E6
Scropton 226 E1
Selston 171 E7
Selston Green 171 D7
Shacklecross 221 D1
Shardlow 234 E2
Shatton 39 F1
Sheen 137 A7
Sheepbridge 76 E2
Sheffield 44 D6
Sheldon 108 A6
Shelton Lock 232 F3
Shipley 194 B6
Shipley Common 194 C4
Shirebrook 119 F3
Shireoaks 63 E6
Shirland 146 D2
Shirley 200 E8
Short Heath 262 D2
Shottle 177 E8
Shottlegate 177 F3
Shuttlewood 98 F7
Simmondley 17 A7
Sinfin 231 F4
Slackhall 47 F8
Slaley 154 C7
Sleat Moor 170 B8
Smalldale
Bradwell 50 F8
Peak Dale 67 D7
Smalley 192 F5
Smalley Common 193 A2

Smalley Green 192 F3
Smisby 257 F3
Smithfield 47 C6
Smithy-Hill 51 A7
Smithy Moor 146 B7
Snape Hill 57 A2
Snelston 184 C3
Snitterton 142 D5
Somercotes 170 C7
Somersal Herbert 211 E3
Sookholme 120 D2
South Normanton ... 160 A7
South Wingfield 157 E3
Southwood 258 B7
Sparrowpit 48 B6
Spath 210 A3
Spinkhill 60 D2
Spion Kop 120 F2
Spital 96 C1
Spitalhill 185 C8
Spitewinter 113 D1
Spondon 220 E4
Spout 166 C3
Spring Cottage 262 D5
Springfield Park 223 A3
Staden 85 E5
Stainsby 133 B7
Stanfree 99 B8
Stanhope Bretby 248 F1
Stanley
Tibshelf 133 D1
West Hallam 207 C5
Stanley Common 193 B1
Stanshope 149 D1
Stanton
Mayfield 183 D8
Swadlincote 255 C4
Stanton by Bridge ... 244 D3
Stanton-by-Dale 222 E8
Stanton Gate 209 C1
Stanton in Peak 126 C5
Stanton Lees 126 F3
Stapenhill 254 F8
Stapleford 223 C4
Starkholmes 143 C2
Staveley 78 D1
Steeple Grange 155 A3
Stenson 243 B8
Stockley 117 E4
Stoke 72 C6
Stonebroom 146 F4
Stonegravels 96 A5
Stoneyford 182 A7
Stoney Middleton 72 A4
Stony Houghton 118 F1
Stramshall 210 A4
Stretton
Clay Cross 146 C7
Rolleston on Dove ... 240 D1
Stretton en le Field .. 265 D4
Stretton Hillside 146 B5
Strines 23 C2
Stubwood 196 D4
Sudbury 225 E4
Summerley 57 E2

Sunny Hill 231 D5
Sutton in Ashfield ... 148 F1
Sutton on the Hill ... 228 B8
Sutton Springs Wood . 116 C6
Swadlincote 256 D4
Swainspark 262 B7
Swanwick 169 E8
Swarkestone 244 D6
Swathwick 114 D4
Swingate 195 F5

T

Taddington 88 B3
Tansley 144 B4
Tansley Knoll 144 A5
Tapton 96 C6
Tatenhill 253 A8
Taxal 45 D4
Temple Normanton ... 116 B3
The Banks 23 E3
The Brushes 76 F3
The Elms 180 D8
The Flourish 207 D2
The Forties 257 F4
The Gutter 179 C4
The Heath 210 A1
The Wharf 210 C1
Thornhill 39 F3
Thornsett 24 F3
Thorpe 161 C1
Thorpe Salvin 62 F6
Thrumpton 237 C3
Thulston 233 F4
Thurvaston
Longford 215 C8
Marston Montgomery . 197 F1
Tibshelf 148 A6
Tibshelf Wharf 148 D7
Ticknall 251 A4
Tintwistle 10 B8
Tissington 162 B6
Toadhole Furnance ... 158 C6
Toadmoor 167 F3
Tomthorn 66 E4
Torr Top 33 C8
Totley 55 E4
Totley Brook 55 E5
Totley Rise 55 F5
Toton 223 E2
Townend 47 C7
Town End
Eyam 71 E6
Tideswell 69 C3
Townhead 55 C7
Town Head
Eyam 71 C6
Tideswell 69 C5
Trentlock 236 E3
Troway 58 B4
Trowell 209 C5
Trusley 215 F4
Tunstead 67 F2

Tunstead Milton 46 C5
Tupton 131 D8
Turlow Fields 175 C7
Turnditch 177 B1
Tutbury 239 C5
Tutbury, Fauld 238 C6
Two Dales 127 E3
Twyford 243 B6

U

Underwood Green 171 F2
Unstone 76 E7
Unstone Green 76 E6
Unthank 74 D5
Upper Biggin 175 E4
Upper Booth 36 E7
Upper Bradway 56 B5
Upperdale 89 B5
Upper Ellastone 183 B4
Upper End 67 B5
Upper Hackney 143 A8
Upper Hartshay 169 A2
Upper Holloway 156 C5
Upper Langwith 119 D8
Upper Mayfield 172 B1
Upper Midway 256 C7
Upper Newbold 95 A8
Upper Padley 53 D2
Upper Pilsley 132 D2
Upperthorpe 60 E5
Uppertown 129 A7
Upper Town
Birchover 141 C8
Bonsall 142 C1
Hognaston 164 B4
Upperwood 155 A8
Uttoxeter 210 C1

W

Wadshelf 93 E3
Waingroves 181 A7
Wakebridge 156 D3
Waldley 211 C7
Wallash 184 C7
Walton 114 D8
Walton-on-Trent 253 D1
Wardlow 70 C2
Wardlow Mires 70 C4
Wards End 143 C2
Warhill 9 A3
Warmbrook 165 E8
Warsop Vale 120 D4
Wash 35 C1
Washgreen 155 A1
Waterloo 132 C3
Water Swallows 67 A3
Waterswallows Green . 66 F3
Wensley 142 A7
Wensley Dale 142 B6
Wessington 157 E8
West Broughton 225 A6

Westfield 59 F8
West Hallam 207 F8
West Hallam Common . 207 D8
West Handley 77 D8
Westhouses 159 C8
Weston-on-Trent 245 F5
Weston Underwood .. 189 A2
Westthorpe 60 D4
Westwood 171 C3
Wetton 149 A3
Whaley 100 D4
Whaley Bridge 45 D7
Whaley Thorns 101 A2
Whatstandwell 156 C1
Wheatcroft 157 A7
Wheston 68 F5
Whitehough 46 D8
Whitehough Head 46 E8
Whiteley 180 F6
White Moor 179 C5
Whitfield 17 D8
Whittington Moor 96 A7
Whitwell 81 E6
Wigley 93 F4
Wilday Green 75 A2
Williamthorpe 132 C8
Willington 242 A6
Wilmorton 219 E2
Wilson 252 F6
Wilsthorpe 236 B7
Windley 189 D7
Windmill 69 F8
Wingerworth 114 F4
Winshill 248 B3
Winsick 115 E6
Winster 141 C5
Wirksworth 165 E8
Woodall 61 C6
Woodend
Disley 32 C8
Hanbury 238 A1
Woodhead
Crowden 7 C4
Littlemoor 130 E2
Woodhouses 252 A5
Woodlinkin 181 E6
Woodnook 94 E5
Woodseats 16 A6
Woodside 192 D4
Woodthorpe 79 C2
Woodville 256 E3
Woolley 145 E5
Woolley Moor 145 D7
Wormhill 68 C1
Wyaston 185 D2

Y

Yeaveley 199 D5
Yeldersley Hollies ... 186 F4
Youlgreave 125 B5

A

1st Ave DE7 . . . . 208 F7
2nd Ave DE7 . . . . 208 F7
3rd Ave DE7 . . . . 208 F7

A

Abba Cl NG16 . . . . 195 F7
Abbey Brook Ct **1** S8 . . . . 56 E8
Abbey Brook Dr S8 . . . . . . 56 E8
Abbey Cl ST14 . . . . 197 A3
Abbey Croft
 Chesterfield S40 . . . . 95 A7
 Renishaw S21 . . . . 79 C8
Abbeydale Cl DE56 . . . . . . 192 B7
Abbeydale Ct S17 . . . . 56 A7
Abbeydale Industrial Mus★
 S7 . . . . 56 B8
Abbeydale Park Cres S17 . . 55 F6
Abbeydale Park Rise S17 . . 55 F6
Abbeydale Rd S7 . . . . 43 A8
Abbeydale Rd S S41 . . . . 56 A7
Abbeyfields Cl DE22 . . . . . . 205 A2
Abbey Gdns SK14 . . . . 9 A3
Abbey Hill DE21, DE22 . . . . 205 B4
Abbeyhill Cl S42 . . . . 95 A4
Abbey Hill Rd DE22 . . . . . . 204 D2
Abbey La DE22 . . . . 205 A1
Abbey Lodge Cl **1** DE11 . 256 A7
Abbey Pl S21 . . . . 79 C8
Abbey St
 Derby DE1, DE22 . . . . 267 A2
 Ilkeston DE7 . . . . 194 F2
Abbey View Dr S8 . . . . 43 A3
Abbey View Hts **3** S8 . . . . 43 A3
Abbey View Rd S8 . . . . 43 A3
Abbey Yd DE22 . . . . 205 A1
Abbot Beyne Sch DE15 . . . 248 A3
Abbot Cl DE21 . . . . 205 E2
Abbot Mews DE22 . . . . 205 A1
Abbot Rd DE7 . . . . 208 C6
Abbots Croft NG19 . . . . 135 E1
Abbotsford Mews DE7 . . . 194 D3
Abbots Gr DE56 . . . . 179 A5
Abbotsholme Sch ST14 . . . 197 B2
Abbot St NG16 . . . . 195 C4
Abbott Rd
 Alfreton DE55 . . . . 159 A5
 Mansfield NG19 . . . . 135 D1
Abbotts Barn Cl DE22 . . . . 267 A2
Abbotts Cl DE11 . . . . 256 A6
Abbotts Rd DE11 . . . . 256 A6
Abbott St
 Heanor DE75 . . . . 181 E1
 Long Eaton NG10 . . . . 236 D6
Abel La DE4 . . . . 142 C2
Abells DE5 . . . . 180 C1
Abels Mill **1** DE1 . . . . 267 A4
Abercrombie Prim Sch
 S41 . . . . 266 B4
Abercrombie St S41 . . . . . . 266 B4
Aberdare Cl DE21 . . . . 206 B2
Abingdon Bsns Ctr The
 DE24 . . . . 219 C1
Abingdon St DE24 . . . . 232 C8
Abney Cl
 Chesterfield S40 . . . . 95 D6
 Derby DE3 . . . . 217 F2
 Sheffield S14 . . . . 43 C6
Abney Dr S14 . . . . 43 C6
Abney Rd S14 . . . . 43 C6
Acacia Ave
 Brimington S43 . . . . 97 A8
 Derby DE3 . . . . 217 E1
 Swadlincote DE11 . . . . 256 B7
Acacia Cres S21 . . . . 60 B5
Acacia Ct NG19 . . . . 136 E1
Acacia Dr
 Melbourne DE73 . . . . 252 A8
 Pilsley S45 . . . . 132 B3
Acacia Gdns NG16 . . . . 195 F8
Access 26 Bsns Pk NG16 182 C3
Acer Cl
 Killamarsh S21 . . . . 60 C5
 Pinxton NG16 . . . . 160 C3
Acer Croft DE21 . . . . 205 E3
Acorn Ave NG16 . . . . 195 C8
Acorn Ct DE24 . . . . 232 E3
Acorn Ctr NG16 . . . . 182 C3
Acorn Dr DE56 . . . . 179 A5
Acorn Ridge
 Chesterfield S40 . . . . 114 B7
 Matlock DE4 . . . . 143 B6
 Shirebrook NG20 . . . . 119 D5
Acorn Terr SK22 . . . . 33 B6
Acorn Way
 Belper DE56 . . . . 179 A5
 Derby DE21 . . . . 220 C6
Acreage La NG20 . . . . 119 F2
Acre Ct **5** SK13 . . . . 17 C7
Acrefield Way DE73 . . . . . . 233 B2
Acre La DE72 . . . . 246 D7
Acresford Rd
 Donisthorpe DE12 . . . . 265 D7
 Netherseal DE12 . . . . 265 B6
 Overseal DE12 . . . . 262 B2
Acresford View DE12 . . . . . 262 B3
Acres Rd S45 . . . . 132 B3
Acre St **4** SK13 . . . . 17 C7
Acre St S45 . . . . 132 B4
Acresview Cl DE22 . . . . 204 D4
Acres View Cl S41 . . . . 95 F7

Acton Ave NG10 . . . . 236 E6
Acton Cl NG10 . . . . 236 E6
Acton Ct **1** S43 . . . . 78 B3
Acton Gr **1** NG10 . . . . 236 E6
Acton Rd
 Derby DE22 . . . . 217 F6
 Long Eaton NG10 . . . . 236 E6
Acton Road Ind Est
 NG10 . . . . 236 E6
Acton St NG10 . . . . 236 E6
Adale Rd DE7 . . . . 193 B8
Adam's Rd DE6 . . . . 217 A8
Adam Bede Cres DE4 . . . . . 165 F6
Adams Cl DE75 . . . . 193 D7
Adams Ct DE7 . . . . 194 E3
Adam St DE7 . . . . 209 A6
Adastral Ave S12 . . . . 44 A2
Adderley Pl SK13 . . . . 9 F1
Adderley Rd SK13 . . . . 9 F1
Addison Dr DE55 . . . . 159 B4
Addison Rd
 Derby DE24 . . . . 232 C7
 Stonebroom DE55 . . . . 146 F3
Addison Sq DE4 . . . . 155 A5
Addison St DE55 . . . . 148 A7
Addison Villas NG16 . . . . . 182 E1
Adelaide Cl
 Derby DE3 . . . . 217 E4
 Stapleford NG9 . . . . 209 F1
Adelaide Cres DE15 . . . . . . 248 C2
Adelaide Wlk NG16 . . . . . . 170 F4
Adelphi Cl DE23 . . . . 231 A6
Adelphi Way S43 . . . . 97 E8
Adin Ave S44 . . . . 98 F6
Adler Ct DE1 . . . . 219 B7
Adlington Ave S42 . . . . 115 C2
Adlington La S32 . . . . 72 C8
Admiral Cl DE75 . . . . 181 D2
Adrian Cl NG9 . . . . 223 F1
Adrian St DE24 . . . . 232 D6
Adwick Cl DE3 . . . . 217 C2
Agard St DE1 . . . . 267 A4
Agnesmeadow La DE6 . . . 174 D4
Agricultural Bsns Ctr
 DE45 . . . . 109 E5
Agricultural Way DE45 . . . 109 E5
Aimploy Ct DE23 . . . . 219 A1
Ainley Cl DE24 . . . . 232 F7
Ainsworth Dr DE23 . . . . . . 231 E7
Aintree Ave S21 . . . . 59 B3
Aintree Cl
 Burton u T DE14 . . . . 254 A7
 Kimberley NG16 . . . . 195 E7
Airedale Cl DE24 . . . . 233 C6
Airedale Wlk **3** DE24 . . . 233 C6
Akley Bank Cl S17 . . . . 55 F5
Alabaster La DE4 . . . . 155 A6
Alandale Ave NG20 . . . . . . 119 F5
Albany Cl NG19 . . . . 136 C1
Albany Ct NG9 . . . . 209 E1
Albany Dr NG19 . . . . 136 C1
Albany Inf & Jun Schs
 NG9 . . . . 223 E8
Albany Jun Sch NG9 . . . . . 209 E1
Albany Pl NG19 . . . . 136 C1
Albany Rd DE22 . . . . 218 C4
Albany St DE7 . . . . 209 A6
Albemarle Rd DE21 . . . . . . 220 B7
Alberta Ave NG16 . . . . 171 F7
Albert Ave
 Chesterfield S43 . . . . 77 D3
 Jacksdale NG16 . . . . 171 B4
 Stapleford NG9 . . . . 223 D7
Albert Cres DE21 . . . . 220 B4
Albert Ct SK17 . . . . 85 C6
Albert Rd
 Breaston DE72 . . . . 235 B7
 Chesterfield S43 . . . . 77 D3
 Derby DE21 . . . . 220 A4
 Long Eaton NG10 . . . . 236 D8
 Ripley DE5 . . . . 169 C2
 Sandiacre NG10 . . . . 223 B6
 Sheffield, Heeley S8 . . . . . . 43 A6
 Swadlincote DE11 . . . . 256 A2
Albert St N S41 . . . . 76 F1
Albert Sq NG19 . . . . 136 C4
Albert St
 Belper DE56 . . . . 178 F4
 Derby DE1 . . . . 267 B3
 Eastwood NG16 . . . . 182 F3
 Eckington S21 . . . . 59 D2
 Glossop SK13 . . . . 10 A5
 Ilkeston DE7 . . . . 208 E8
 Ironville NG16 . . . . 170 F5
 Mansfield Woodhouse
  NG19 . . . . 136 C4
 Ripley DE5 . . . . 169 E1
 Somercotes DE55 . . . . 170 B8
 South Normanton DE55 . . . 160 B6
 Stapleford NG9 . . . . 223 D7
Albert Village Com Prim Sch
 DE11 . . . . 256 C1
Albine Rd NG20 . . . . 119 E6
Albion Ctr The DE7 . . . . . . 208 F8
Albion Mill SK14 . . . . 9 C5
Albion Rd
 Chesterfield S40 . . . . 266 A3
 Long Eaton NG10 . . . . 236 F8
 New Mills SK22 . . . . 33 B8
Albion St
 Derby DE1 . . . . 267 B3
 Ilkeston DE7 . . . . 194 F1

Albion St continued
 Mansfield NG19 . . . . 135 F1
 Ripley DE5 . . . . 169 E1
 Woodville DE11 . . . . 256 F2
Albrighton Ave DE24 . . . . . 231 D2
Aldam Cl S17 . . . . 55 E4
Aldam Croft S17 . . . . 55 E4
Aldam Rd S17 . . . . 55 F4
Aldam Way S17 . . . . 55 E4
Alder Brook DE65 . . . . 34 E2
Alderbrook Cl DE13 . . . . . . 240 B4
Aldercar Com Language Coll
 NG16 . . . . 182 A4
Aldercar Inf Sch NG16 . . . 182 A4
Aldercar La NG16 . . . . 182 A6
Alder Cl
 Derby DE21 . . . . 205 E3
 Glossop SK13 . . . . 9 F4
 Mansfield NG19 . . . . 136 E1
 Shirebrook NG20 . . . . 119 D5
Alder Com High Sch SK14 15 A8
Alder Ct S41 . . . . 266 B4
Alderfen Cl DE24 . . . . 232 D3
Alder Gr
 Burton u T DE15 . . . . 254 F7
 Buxton SK17 . . . . 85 A8
 Chapel-en-le-F SK23 . . . . . . 47 A6
 Mansfield Woodhouse
  NG19 . . . . 136 B5
Alderholme Dr **1** DE13 . 240 F1
Alder La DE6 . . . . 188 A3
Alderley Ct DE21 . . . . 206 A2
Alderney Rd **3** S8 . . . . 43 A7
Aldern Way DE45 . . . . 109 E7
Alder Rd DE56 . . . . 179 A3
Alder Rise SK23 . . . . 45 D8
Alders Ave S23 . . . . 34 E1
Alders Brook DE65 . . . . 228 D1
Aldersgate
 Derby DE21 . . . . 217 F7
 New Mills SK22 . . . . 33 B8
Alders La
 Chinley SK23 . . . . 34 E2
 Tansley DE4 . . . . 144 A3
Alderslade Cl DE72 . . . . . . 234 B1
Aldersley Cl DE65 . . . . 230 C1
Alderson Dr DE13 . . . . 240 F1
Alderson Pl S2 . . . . 43 A8
Alderson Rd S2 . . . . 43 A8
Alderson Rd N S2 . . . . 43 A8
Alders Rd SK12 . . . . 32 A7
Alders The S42 . . . . 113 D7
Alderwasley Hall Sch
 DE56 . . . . 167 B7
Alderwasley Hall Sch (Callow
 Park) DE4 . . . . 165 E4
Alder Way NG20 . . . . 119 D4
Alder Wlk DE23 . . . . 267 B1
Aldred's La DE75, NG16 . . 182 B2
Aldred Cl S21 . . . . 60 E8
Aldridge Cl NG9 . . . . 223 E2
Aldwark Rd SK17 . . . . 85 C6
Aldwych DE22 . . . . 218 A6
Alexander Ave NG16 . . . . . 171 D7
Alexander Rd SK17 . . . . 47 F1
Alexander Terr NG16 . . . . . 160 C1
Alexandra Ave NG19 . . . . . 136 B5
Alexandra Ct
 Burton u T DE15 . . . . 248 A3
 Overseal DE12 . . . . 262 B4
Alexandra Gdns **3** DE23. 219 B2
Alexandra Mills **2** DE1 . . 218 E5
Alexandra Rd
 Burton u T DE15 . . . . 248 A3
 Buxton SK17 . . . . 85 C5
 Dronfield S18 . . . . 57 B2
 Long Eaton NG10 . . . . 236 D8
 Overseal DE12 . . . . 262 B4
 Sheffield S2 . . . . 43 B7
 Swadlincote DE11 . . . . 256 B3
Alexandra Rd E S41 . . . . 96 C1
Alexandra Rd W S40 . . . . . 266 A3
Alexandra St
 Eastwood NG16 . . . . 182 F2
 Stapleford NG9 . . . . 223 D6
Alexandre Cl DE23 . . . . 231 D6
Alford Cl S40 . . . . 95 C3
Alfred Rd DE56 . . . . 192 A8
Alfred St
 Alfreton DE55 . . . . 158 F3
 Pinxton NG16 . . . . 160 C4
 Ripley DE5 . . . . 169 E2
 Somercotes DE55 . . . . 170 D6
 South Normanton DE55 . . . 159 F5
Alfreton & Mansfield
 Parkway Sta DE55 . . . . . . 159 C5
Alfreton Motorway Link Ind
 Est DE55 . . . . 159 A2
Alfreton Park Com Specl Sch
 DE55 . . . . 158 F4
Alfreton Rd
 Blackwell DE55 . . . . 147 E2
 Breadsall DE21 . . . . 205 B2
 Codnor DE5 . . . . 170 C1
 Holbrook DE21 . . . . 191 D2
 Little Eaton DE21 . . . . 205 C6
 Matlock DE4 . . . . 143 E4
 Pinxton NG16 . . . . 160 C4
 Selston DE55, NG16 . . . . . 171 C6
 Somercotes DE55 . . . . 170 C6
 Stapleford NG9 . . . . 223 D7
Alfreton Trad Est DE55 . . . 159 B2
Algar Cl S2 . . . . 43 E7

Algar Cres S2 . . . . 43 F7
Algar Dr S2 . . . . 43 E7
Algar Pl S2 . . . . 43 E7
Algar Rd S2 . . . . 43 E7
Alice's View S42 . . . . 132 A8
Alice Gdns DE12 . . . . 262 B4
Alicehead Rd S45 . . . . 113 B2
Alice St DE1 . . . . 267 C4
Alice Way S18 . . . . 76 E5
Alison Cl DE21 . . . . 219 F7
Alkmonton Rd DE6 . . . . . . 213 D5
Alkmund Cl DE1 . . . . 267 B4
Allan Ave DE23 . . . . 230 E8
Allandale Rd DE75 . . . . 181 D2
Allan La DE56 . . . . 168 B6
Allcroft St NG19 . . . . 136 C2
Allen's Green Ave NG16 . . 171 F6
Allen's La S14 . . . . 224 E2
Allenby Cl S8 . . . . 56 E7
Allenby Dr S8 . . . . 56 E7
Allendale DE7 . . . . 208 E7
Allendale Rd S42 . . . . 114 F3
Allendale Way NG19 . . . . . 136 E1
Allen Hill DE4 . . . . 143 B6
Allen La
 Ashover DE4 . . . . 144 C6
 Weston Underwood DE6 . . 188 C3
Allens Croft ST14 . . . . 224 E2
Allenton Com Prim Sch
 DE24 . . . . 232 D5
Allestree Cl DE24 . . . . 232 E8
Allestree Dr S18 . . . . 56 C1
Allestree La DE22 . . . . 204 D3
Allestree Pk★ DE22 . . . . . . 204 F5
Allestree St DE24 . . . . 232 F8
Alley The DE4 . . . . 154 D4
Alley Wlk DE4 . . . . 154 D4
Allison Ave DE11 . . . . 256 B3
Allison Gdns DE7 . . . . 195 A1
Allissa Ave DE5 . . . . 180 E7
Allpits Rd S44 . . . . 96 F3
Allport Terr S44 . . . . 78 B4
All Saints' Rd DE4 . . . . 143 B6
All Saints CE Fst Sch
 ST14 . . . . 196 E6
All Saints CE Jun Sch
 DE4 . . . . 143 A7
All Saints CE Prim Sch
 Marple SK6 . . . . 23 A5
 Youlgreave DE45 . . . . 125 C5
All Saints Cl DE7 . . . . 193 B1
All Saints Croft DE14 . . . . 254 C8
All Saints Ct **6** DE3 . . . . . 217 D1
All Saints Inf Sch DE4 . . . 143 B6
All Saints RC Prim Sch
 SK13 . . . . 10 D2
All Saints Rd DE14 . . . . . . 254 C8
Allsops Pl S41 . . . . 95 F8
Allstone Lee DE56 . . . . 178 F5
Alma Cl NE7 . . . . 194 E5
Alma Cres S18 . . . . 57 A3
Alma Hill NG16 . . . . 195 E7
Alma Hts DE3 . . . . 217 E1
Alma L Pk★ S40 . . . . 266 C1
Alma Rd
 North Wingfield S42 . . . . . 132 A8
 Selston NG16 . . . . 171 F5
 Swadlincote DE11 . . . . 255 F6
 Tideswell SK17 . . . . 69 C5
Alma St W S40 . . . . 95 E2
Alma Sq SK17 . . . . 85 D8
Alma St
 Alfreton DE55 . . . . 159 A4
 Buxton SK17 . . . . 85 D8
 Derby DE22 . . . . 267 A2
 Melbourne DE73 . . . . 252 A7
 North Wingfield S42 . . . . . 131 E6
 Ripley DE5 . . . . 169 D3
Almond Ave
 Ripley DE5 . . . . 180 D8
 Shirebrook NG20 . . . . 119 E5
Almond Cl
 Calow S44 . . . . 97 A3
 Kimberley NG16 . . . . 195 E7
Almond Cres S43 . . . . 79 C4
Almond Ct DE13 . . . . 240 E1
Almond Dr S21 . . . . 60 C5
Almond Gr
 Swadlincote DE11 . . . . 256 A5
 Swanwick DE55 . . . . 170 A8
Almond Rise NG19 . . . . 136 E1
Almond St DE23 . . . . 218 F1
Almshouses
 Etwall DE65 . . . . 229 B5
 Newton Solney DE15 . . . . . 248 E8
Alms Rd DE6 . . . . 211 C1
Alnwick Dr S12 . . . . 44 C5
Alnwick Rd S12 . . . . 44 B5
Alonso Cl DE73 . . . . 232 E2
Alpha Rd S43 . . . . 34 E2
Alpine Gr S43 . . . . 97 A8
Alport Ave
 Buxton SK17 . . . . 85 D7
 Sheffield S12 . . . . 44 E5
Alport Cl
 Belper DE56 . . . . 179 D5
 Hulland Ward DE6 . . . . 175 F3
Alport Dr S12 . . . . 44 E5
Alport Gr
 3 Gamesley SK13 . . . . 9 E2
 Sheffield S12 . . . . 44 E5

1st–And 271

Alport La
 Spout DE4, DE56 . . . . 166 C4
 Youlgreave DE45 . . . . 125 C6
Alport Lea **2** SK13 . . . . 9 E2
Alport Pl S12 . . . . 44 E4
Alport Rd S12 . . . . 44 E5
Alport Rise S18 . . . . 56 D2
Alport Terr DE55 . . . . 147 C1
Alport Way **1** SK13 . . . . 9 E2
Alsager Cl DE21 . . . . 206 A1
Alsfeld Way S22 . . . . 33 A8
Alsop Moor Cotts DE6 . . . 150 E5
Alsop Pl SK17 . . . . 85 E7
Alsop Way SK17 . . . . 85 E7
Alstonefield YH★ DE6 . . . 149 F4
Alstonfield Dr DE22 . . . . . 204 E1
Alston Rd SK23 . . . . 47 B5
Althorp Cl DE55 . . . . 169 F7
Alton Cl
 Chesterfield S40 . . . . 114 B8
 Derby DE22 . . . . 204 D3
 Dronfield S18 . . . . 75 D8
Alton Dr NG16 . . . . 195 B8
Alton Hill S42 . . . . 130 C5
Alton La S45 . . . . 130 C4
Alton Rd
 Belper DE56 . . . . 179 C4
 Denstone ST14 . . . . 196 D6
Alton Rise DE4 . . . . 142 F7
Alts Nook Way DE72 . . . . . 234 E1
Alum Chine Cl S41 . . . . 115 C8
Alum Cl DE24 . . . . 233 C7
Alvaston Inf Sch DE24 . . . 233 C7
Alvaston Jun Sch DE24 . . . 233 C7
Alvaston Park Homes
 DE24 . . . . 220 A1
Alvaston St DE24 . . . . 233 B8
Alvenor St DE7 . . . . 194 F1
Alverton Cl DE21 . . . . 217 C1
Alvaston Pk Homes
 DE24 . . . . 233 A8
Alward's Cl DE24 . . . . 233 A6
Ambaston La
 Elvaston DE72 . . . . 234 A5
 Shardlow DE72 . . . . 234 E2
Amber Bldgs DE55 . . . . 159 B5
Amber Cl DE56 . . . . 168 B5
Amber Cres S40 . . . . 95 C1
Amber Croft S43 . . . . 97 C7
Amber Ct
 Belper DE56 . . . . 179 A4
 Chesterfield S41 . . . . 266 B4
 2 Heanor DE75 . . . . 181 E1
Amberdene DE4 . . . . 143 D6
Amber Dr NG16 . . . . 182 B2
Ambergate Prim Sch
 DE56 . . . . 167 F3
Ambergate Sta DE56 . . . . . 167 F4
Amber Gr DE55 . . . . 158 F2
Ambergrove DE56 . . . . 168 B4
Amber Hill DE4 . . . . 168 A7
Amber Hts DE5 . . . . 169 C2
Amber La S45 . . . . 129 D3
Amberlands DE13 . . . . 240 F1
Amberley Cl DE7 . . . . 208 F6
Amberley Dr
 Buxton SK17 . . . . 85 C5
 Derby DE22 . . . . 231 F5
Amber Pl S45 . . . . 131 A4
Amber Rd
 Bullbridge DE56 . . . . 168 B6
 Derby DE22 . . . . 204 D1
Amber St DE24 . . . . 232 C7
Amber Terr DE55 . . . . 158 B6
Amber Trad Est NG16 . . . . 195 D7
Ambervale Cl DE23 . . . . . . 231 A6
Amber View Rd DE56 . . . . 168 B7
Amberwood DE11 . . . . 256 A5
Ambleside Cl
 Chesterfield S41 . . . . 95 C7
 Sheffield S20 . . . . 59 E6
Ambleside Dr
 Bolsover S44 . . . . 98 F1
 Eastwood NG16 . . . . 182 D3
Ambrose Terr DE1 . . . . 218 E5
Amen Alley DE1 . . . . 267 B3
American Adventure Theme
 Pk The★ DE75 . . . . 194 B5
Amesbury Cl S41 . . . . 95 C1
Amesbury La DE21 . . . . 205 E2
Ameycroft La DE4 . . . . 143 A8
Amilda Ave DE7 . . . . 208 F8
Amy St DE22 . . . . 218 E4
Anchor Ave SK23 . . . . 47 C6
Anchor Cl DE11 . . . . 256 C4
Anchor Fold SK23 . . . . 47 D6
Anchor Rd NG16 . . . . 182 D2
Anchor Row DE7 . . . . 208 F8
Anchor Sq DE45 . . . . 109 D6
Anderby Gdns DE11 . . . . . 255 F2
Anderson Cl S43 . . . . 77 E3
Anderson St DE24 . . . . 232 F7
Andrew Ave DE7 . . . . 209 B7
Andrew Cl DE23 . . . . 230 E8
Andrews Dr
 Langley Mill NG16 . . . . . . 182 A3
 Stanley Common DE7 . . . . 193 A1
Andrew St SK6 . . . . 15 A2
Andwell La S10 . . . . 42 F6

Angel Yd S40 . . . . **266** B3
Angerford Ave S8 . . . . . . **43** A4
Anglers' La DE21 . . . . **220** E3
Anglesey Rd
　Burton u T DE14 . . . . **254** B8
　Dronfield S18 . . . . **76** A8
Anglesey St DE21 . . . . . . **219** D8
Angleton Ave S2 . . . . **44** C8
Angleton Cl S2 . . . . **44** C8
Angleton Gdns S2 . . . . . . **44** C8
Angleton Gn S2 . . . . **44** C8
Angleton Mews S2 . . . . . . **44** C8
Anglia Dr DE11 . . . . **255** F1
Ankerbold Rd S42 . . . . . . **131** D8
Anncroft Rd SK17 . . . . . . **84** D5
Anne Potter Cl DE72 . . . . **221** D5
Annesley Cl
　Chesterfield S41 . . . . **115** C8
　Sheffield S8 . . . . **56** F7
Annesley Rd S8 . . . . **56** F7
Annie's Cl DE4 . . . . **126** B1
Anns Grove Prim Sch S2 . **43** A7
Anns Rd S2 . . . . **43** A7
Anns Rd N S2 . . . . **43** B7
Ann St S80 . . . . **81** E1
Annwell La LE65 . . . . **257** E2
Anslow La DE13 . . . . **240** A2
Anslow Rd DE13 . . . . **238** B2
Anson Wlk DE7 . . . . **194** F3
Anstee Rd NG10 . . . . **236** C5
Anstey Ct DE21 . . . . **206** A1
Anthony Bek Com Prim Sch
　NG19 . . . . **134** F6
Anthony Cres DE24 . . . . . **232** F6
Anthony Dr DE24 . . . . **232** F6
Anthony Gell Sch DE4 . . . **165** F8
Antill St NG9 . . . . **223** D6
Apiary Gate DE74 . . . . . . **247** B3
Apperknowle Com Prim Sch
　S18 . . . . **58** A1
Appian Cl DE72 . . . . **221** C1
Appian Way
　Clay Cross S45 . . . . **131** B2
　Derby DE24 . . . . **233** D5
Appleby Cl DE7 . . . . **208** F6
Appleby Glade DE11 . . . . **255** F6
Appleby Rd NG19 . . . . . . **134** F6
Applecroft Cl S44 . . . . . . **118** B1
Applecross Ct DE24 . . . . **231** E3
Appledore Cl **2** S41 . . . . **95** F8
Appledore Dr DE21 . . . . . **206** B1
Appledown Way DE23 . . . **231** A6
Applegarth Cl S12 . . . . . . **44** A6
Applegarth Dr S12 . . . . . . **44** A6
Applegate Cl DE21 . . . . . **206** B3
Applemead Cl DE21 . . . . **205** E2
Apple St SK14 . . . . **15** C7
Appleton Cl
　Burton u T DE15 . . . . **254** E7
　Derby DE21 . . . . **220** A7
　Swadlincote DE11 . . . . . . **255** F6
Appleton Dr
　Belper DE56 . . . . **179** B6
　Glossop SK13 . . . . **17** F8
Appletree Cl DE72 . . . . . **221** C1
Appletree Dr S18 . . . . **57** A1
Appletree Rd
　Bolsover S44 . . . . **80** B1
　Hatton DE65 . . . . **227** C1
Apple Tree Rd SK22 . . . . . **24** B1
Appletree Wlk DE3 . . . . . **217** D2
Applewood Cl
　Belper DE56 . . . . **179** B5
　Uttoxeter ST14 . . . . **210** A1
Appleyard Ct S41 . . . . . . **266** A4
Arbor Cl DE22 . . . . **267** A2
Arboretum Prim Sch
　DE23 . . . . **219** A2
Arboretum Sq DE23 . . . . **267** C1
Arboretum St DE23 . . . . . **267** C1
Arbor Gr SK17 . . . . **84** F7
Arbor Low (Henge)★
　DE45 . . . . **123** E4
Arbor Cl S41 . . . . **115** D6
Arbour Hill DE7 . . . . **207** E3
Arbourthorne Com Prim Sch
　S2 . . . . **43** D6
Arbourthorne Cotts S2 . . **43** D8
Arbourthorne Rd S2 . . . . . **43** E6
Arcadia Ave NG20 . . . . . . **119** E5
Archdale Cl S2 . . . . **44** B8
Archdale Rd S2 . . . . **44** A8
Archer Rd NG9 . . . . **223** E5
Archer St
　Derby DE24 . . . . **219** E2
　Ilkeston DE7 . . . . **194** E3
Arden Cl
　Chesterfield S40 . . . . **95** C5
　Derby DE23 . . . . **218** E2
　Glossop SK13 . . . . **17** A8
Arden Est SK22 . . . . **33** D7
Arden St SK22 . . . . **33** C7
Ardleigh Cl DE3 . . . . **230** D8
Ardsley Cl
　Heanor DE75 . . . . **182** A2
　Sheffield S20 . . . . **44** F2
Ardsley Dr S20 . . . . **44** F2
Ardsley Gr S20 . . . . **44** F2
Ardsley Rd S40 . . . . **95** B3
Argyle Cl
　Market Warsop NG20 . . . **120** F4
　Sheffield S8 . . . . **43** B5
Argyle Mews NG16 . . . . . **182** C4
Argyle Rd S8 . . . . **43** B5

Argyle St
　Derby DE22 . . . . **218** F3
　Langley Mill NG16 . . . . . **182** C4
Argyll Cl DE21 . . . . **220** F5
Argyll Rd DE5 . . . . **169** E2
Aria Ct NG9 . . . . **223** D6
Arkendale Wlk **4** DE24 . . **233** C6
Arkle Gn DE24 . . . . **231** E4
Arklow Cl S41 . . . . **115** D8
Arkwright's Mill★ DE4 . . **155** B7
Arkwright Ave DE56 . . . . **179** C6
Arkwright Cl DE4 . . . . **127** C3
Arkwright Dr SK6 . . . . **23** A6
Arkwright Gdns DE4 . . . . **155** A6
Arkwright Mill SK17 . . . . . **89** A6
Arkwright Prim Sch S44 . **97** D3
Arkwright Rd SK6 . . . . **23** A6
Arkwright St
　Derby DE24 . . . . **232** C7
　Wirksworth DE4 . . . . **165** E8
Arleston La DE24 . . . . . . **231** D2
Arleston St DE23 . . . . **231** F7
Arlington Ave NG19 . . . . **136** E4
Arlington Dr
　Derby DE24 . . . . **232** F6
　Swanwick DE55 . . . . **169** F7
Armitage Dr NG10 . . . . . . **237** A7
Armscote Cl DE21 . . . . . . **206** B2
Arms Park Dr S20 . . . . **59** F8
Arnfield La SK13 . . . . **9** F8
Arnhem Terr DE21 . . . . . . **220** F3
Arnold Ave
　Long Eaton NG10 . . . . . . **236** A4
　Sheffield S12 . . . . **44** B1
Arnold Cl DE11 . . . . **261** E7
Arnold Cres NG10 . . . . . . **236** A4
Arnold St DE22 . . . . **218** D5
Arnot Rd DE14 . . . . **254** A7
Arnside NG9 . . . . **223** E5
Arnside Cl
　Chesterfield S41 . . . . **76** D1
　Swadlincote DE11 . . . . . . **256** C1
Arran Cl
　Derby DE24 . . . . **231** E3
　Stapleford NG9 . . . . **209** E2
Arran Ct DE55 . . . . **147** F6
Arreton Ct DE24 . . . . **233** C5
Arridge Rd DE21 . . . . **219** F6
Arrowscroft Ct SK14 . . . . . **9** D5
Arrowscroft Way SK14 . . . **9** D4
Arthington Blgs S2 . . . . . . **43** A6
Arthington St S8 . . . . **43** A6
Arthur Ave NG9 . . . . **223** F8
Arthur Ct **1** DE23 . . . . . . **219** B2
Arthur Hind Cl DE22 . . . . **218** F7
Arthur Mee Rd NG9 . . . . **223** E5
Arthurs Ct DE13 . . . . **240** E4
Arthur Short Cl S80 . . . . . **82** A6
Arthur St
　Alfreton DE55 . . . . **159** A5
　Derby DE1 . . . . **267** B5
　Draycott DE72 . . . . **234** F8
　Linton DE11 . . . . **261** E7
　Pinxton NG16 . . . . **160** D3
Arthurs View NG16 . . . . . **170** F4
Arthurs Way S33 . . . . **38** A2
Artic Way NG16 . . . . **195** D7
Artisan View S8 . . . . **43** A6
Arun Dale NG19 . . . . **136** D2
Arundel Ave DE3 . . . . **217** F2
Arundel Cl
　23 Chesterfield S41 . . . . **95** F8
　Dronfield S18 . . . . **56** D1
　Sandiacre NG10 . . . . **223** B4
Arundel Ct **6** S43 . . . . . . **78** E2
Arundel Dr DE21 . . . . **220** F5
Arundel Grange SK13 . . . **17** A8
Arundel St
　Derby DE22 . . . . **218** D4
　Glossop SK13 . . . . **10** C1
Asbourne Ct DE7 . . . . **194** D1
Ascot Ave NG16 . . . . **195** E7
Ascot Cl
　Burton u T DE15 . . . . **248** A3
　West Hallam DE7 . . . . . . **207** D7
Ascot Dr DE24 . . . . **232** D8
Ascot Park Est NG10 . . . . **223** C7
Ascot Pl DE7 . . . . **208** C5
Ascott Dr DE11 . . . . **256** A7
Ash Acre DE56 . . . . **179** D4
Ashberry Ct DE21 . . . . . . **205** A4
Ashbourne Ave S45 . . . . . **131** A5
Ashbourne Ct **4** S40 . . . . **95** A5
Ashbourne Ct
　3 Glossop SK13 . . . . . . **17** E8
Ashbourne Dr DE11 . . . . **256** A1
Ashbourne La
　Chapel-en-le-F SK23 . . . . **47** D5
　Wetton DE6 . . . . **149** A2
Ashbourne PNEU Sch
　DE6 . . . . **173** C3
Ashbourne Rd
　Alstonefield DE6 . . . . **149** B3
　Belper DE56 . . . . **178** C4
　Buxton SK17 . . . . **85** D4
　Church Broughton DE65 . **213** F3
　Derby DE22 . . . . **218** C7
　Kirk Langley DE6 . . . . . . **202** D4
　Mackworth DE22 . . . . . . **217** E8
　Mayfield DE6 . . . . **184** C7
　Rocester ST14 . . . . **196** F4
　Shottle DE56 . . . . **177** D3
　Uttoxeter ST14 . . . . **210** B1
Ashbourne St NG20 . . . . **119** F4
Ashbrook DE15 . . . . **248** A1

Ashbrook Ave DE72 . . . . **221** C2
Ashbrook Cl DE22 . . . . . . **204** C3
Ashbrook Inf Sch DE72 . . **221** B2
Ashbrook Jun Sch DE72 . **221** B2
Ashbury Dr S8 . . . . **43** C2
Ashbury La S8 . . . . **43** C2
Ashby Ave NG19 . . . . **136** D5
Ashby La DE11 . . . . **257** C1
Ashby Rd
　Blackfordby DE11, LE65 . **257** D2
　Breedon on t H DE73 . . . **252** E2
　Burton u T DE15 . . . . **248** B2
　Melbourne DE73 . . . . . . **252** A6
　Moira DE12 . . . . **262** F4
Ashby Rd E DE15 . . . . . . **248** E1
Ashby St DE24 . . . . **232** E6
Ash Cl
　Aston-on-T DE72 . . . . . . **246** B7
　Barlborough S43 . . . . **80** B6
　Derby DE22 . . . . **204** D4
　Killamarsh S21 . . . . **60** C5
　Mottram in L SK14 . . . . . . **9** A4
　Pinxton NG16 . . . . **160** D2
Ashcombe Gdns DE21 . . **206** B1
Ash Cres
　Eckington S21 . . . . **59** B1
　Mansfield Woodhouse
　NG19 . . . . **136** E2
　Ripley DE5 . . . . **180** D8
Ashcroft Cl DE24 . . . . . . **232** F7
Ashcroft Ct S41 . . . . **77** B3
Ashcroft Dr S41 . . . . **77** B2
Ash Croft Prim Sch
　DE24 . . . . **231** E2
Ash Ct DE55 . . . . **159** C3
Ashdale Cl DE15 . . . . **255** A8
Ashdale Rd DE7 . . . . **209** A6
Ashdene Gdns DE56 . . . . **179** C5
Ashdown Dr S40 . . . . **95** D1
Ashe La DE65 . . . . **229** A5
Ashe Pl DE23 . . . . **218** F1
Asher La DE5 . . . . **169** C5
Ashes Ave DE6 . . . . **175** F3
Ashes La
　Fenny Bentley DE6 . . . . . **162** A1
　Glossop SK13 . . . . **10** B2
Ashes The SK13 . . . . **10** B2
Ashfield Ave
　Derby DE21 . . . . **219** E8
　Somercotes DE55 . . . . . . **159** D1
Ashfield Cl S12 . . . . **43** F4
Ashfield Dr S12 . . . . **43** F4
Ashfield Gr SK6 . . . . **15** B1
Ashfield Rd
　Chapel-en-le-F SK23 . . . . **47** D6
　Chesterfield S41 . . . . **115** D8
　Glossop SK13 . . . . **9** F3
Ash Fields DE56 . . . . **179** C6
Ashford Ave S42 . . . . **132** A4
Ashford Cl S18 . . . . **75** D8
Ashford Ct
　Chesterfield S41 . . . . **96** A5
　West Hallam DE7 . . . . . . **207** D8
Ashford Gn **2** SK13 . . . . **9** E1
Ashford La DE45 . . . . **89** D2
Ashford Mews SK13 . . . . . **9** E1
Ashford Pl DE7 . . . . **194** E5
Ashford Rd S18 . . . . **75** D8
Ashford Rise DE56 . . . . . **179** C6
Ashforth Ave DE75 . . . . . **194** A8
Ashfurlong Cl S17 . . . . . . **55** F7
Ashfurlong Dr S17 . . . . . . **55** F7
Ashfurlong Rd S17 . . . . . . **55** F7
Ashgate Ave S40 . . . . **95** C3
Ashgate Croft Sch S40 . . **95** C4
Ashgate Ct **4** S40 . . . . . . **95** C4
Ashgate Prim Sch DE22 . **218** D6
Ashgate Rd S40 . . . . **95** C4
Ashgate Valley Rd S40 . . **95** D4
Ash Gr
　Brinsley NG16 . . . . **182** D8
　Chinley SK23 . . . . **34** E1
　Long Eaton NG10 . . . . . . **236** C6
　Mastin Moor S43 . . . . **79** B4
　Sandiacre NG10 . . . . **223** B4
　Selston NG16 . . . . **171** F7
　Shirebrook NG20 . . . . . . **119** C5
　Stapleford NG9 . . . . **223** D5
　Tupton S42 . . . . **131** D8
Ash La
　Chesterfield S21 . . . . **77** D8
　Sutton on t H DE6, DE65 . **228** C3
　Unstone S18 . . . . **57** F3
Ashland Rd S21 . . . . **59** E3
Ashlar Dr DE12 . . . . **262** F1
Ashlea Dr DE6 . . . . **184** D7
Ashlea Wlk S43 . . . . **81** A5
Ashleigh Ave
　Glossop SK13 . . . . **10** B2
　Sheffield S12 . . . . **43** F5
　Swadlincote DE11 . . . . . . **255** F5
Ashleigh Dr
　Chellaston DE73 . . . . **232** F2
　Sheffield S12 . . . . **43** F5
Ashleigh Pl S12 . . . . **43** F5
Ashleigh Rd S43 . . . . **80** B7
Ashley Cl
　Killamarsh S21 . . . . **60** D6
　Overseal DE12 . . . . **262** B3
　Tansley DE4 . . . . **144** A4
Ashley Ct DE15 . . . . **248** A3

Ashley La S21 . . . . **60** D6
Ashley St DE22 . . . . **218** C5
Ashlyn Rd DE21 . . . . **219** C5
Ashmeadow DE72 . . . . . . **221** B1
Ashmeadow Ct DE6 . . . . **185** D8
Ashmore Ave S21 . . . . . . **59** B2
Ash Mount Rd NG16 . . . . **182** B3
Ashop Rd DE56 . . . . **179** D5
Ashopton Ave DE23 . . . . **231** F8
Ashopton Dr S33 . . . . **40** B4
Ashopton Rd
　Bamford S33 . . . . **40** A6
　Chesterfield S41 . . . . **95** C6
Ashover Cl DE21 . . . . **219** F8
Ashover New Rd DE55,
　S45 . . . . **145** E8
Ashover Prim Sch S45 . . **129** E3
Ashover Rd
　Alton S45 . . . . **130** E5
　Ashover S45 . . . . **129** E4
　Brackenfield DE55 . . . . . **146** B7
　1 Derby, Chaddesden
　DE21 . . . . **219** E8
　Derby DE22 . . . . **204** D3
　Staveley S43 . . . . **97** C6
　Swadlincote DE11 . . . . . . **255** E5
　Tupton S42 . . . . **131** E5
Ashover View DE55 . . . . **147** C1
Ash St
　Buxton SK17 . . . . **85** B6
　Ilkeston DE7 . . . . **194** E4
　Sheffield, Mosborough S20 . **59** C8
Ash Terr SK17 . . . . **85** C8
Ashton Cl
　Chesterfield S40 . . . . **114** C8
　Derby DE3 . . . . **217** C3
　Killamarsh S21 . . . . **60** C6
　Swanwick DE55 . . . . **170** A7
Ashton Gdns
　Clay Cross S42 . . . . **131** B6
　1 Glossop SK13 . . . . . . **17** C7
Ashton Rd S45 . . . . **131** E4
Ashton St SK13 . . . . **17** C7
Ashton Way DE56 . . . . . . **179** D4
Ashtree Ave DE24 . . . . . . **232** B6
Ash Tree Cl
　Breadsall DE21 . . . . **205** E4
　Chesterfield S40 . . . . **95** C3
　Duffield DE56 . . . . **190** E5
　2 Swadlincote DE11 . . . **255** F6
Ash Tree Cres NG16 . . . . **136** C5
Ash Tree Rd S43 . . . . **80** E2
Ashurst Cl S40 . . . . **94** F5
Ash Vale S40 . . . . **95** B3
Ashview Cl NG10 . . . . **236** A8
Ash View Cl DE65 . . . . . . **229** B3
Ashwater Cl DE24 . . . . . . **231** F2
Ashwell Ave NG19 . . . . . **136** E5
Ashwood SK13 . . . . **16** F8
Ashwood Cl
　Buxton SK17 . . . . **85** C7
　Mansfield Woodhouse
　NG19 . . . . **136** E5
Ashwood Rd
　Buxton SK17 . . . . **66** E1
　Disley SK12 . . . . **32** D6
Ashworth Ave
　Burton u T DE15 . . . . **248** C2
　Derby DE21 . . . . **219** F5
Ashworth Dr NG19 . . . . . **136** E4
Ashworth La SK14 . . . . **9** A3
Ashworth Wlk DE21 . . . . **219** F5
Askerfield Ave DE22 . . . . **204** C4
Asker La DE4 . . . . **143** D6
Askew Gr DE65 . . . . **242** D2
Asline Rd S2 . . . . **43** A8
Aspen Bsns Ctr DE21 . . . **220** B4
Aspen Cl
　Buxton SK17 . . . . **66** E1
　Killamarsh S21 . . . . **60** C6
Aspen Ct **1** NG19 . . . . . . **136** E1
Aspen Dr DE21 . . . . **220** C4
Aspen Rd S21 . . . . **59** B1
Aspen Rise DE55 . . . . . . **146** D1
Aspen Way SK6 . . . . **32** A7
Aspley Cl S40 . . . . **95** E5
Asptcote Cl DE75 . . . . . . **182** A1
Asterdale Prim Sch
　DE21 . . . . **220** F3
Asterdale View DE21 . . . **220** F4
Aster Gdns DE23 . . . . . . **231** B6
Astil St DE15 . . . . **254** F8
Astlow Dr DE56 . . . . **179** B6
Aston Cl
　Chellaston DE73 . . . . **245** A8
　Dronfield S18 . . . . **57** C3
Aston Ct S43 . . . . **78** F2
Aston Dr DE11 . . . . **256** A7
Aston Gn NG9 . . . . **223** E3
Aston Hall Dr DE72 . . . . . **246** A7
Aston Hall Hospl DE72 . . **246** A6
Aston La
　Chellaston DE73 . . . . **233** B1
　Hope S33 . . . . **39** C4
　Shardlow DE72 . . . . **234** E1
　Sudbury DE6 . . . . **226** A5
　Wensley DE4 . . . . **142** D7
Aston-on-Trent Prim Sch
　DE72 . . . . **246** A8
Aston Rd DE23 . . . . **231** C5
Astorville Park Rd DE73 . **232** F2
Astron Bsns Pk DE11 . . . **256** A3
Astwith Cl S44 . . . . **116** F1
Astwith La S44, S45 . . . . **133** B5
Atchison Gdns DE21 . . . . **220** B7
Atherfield Wlk DE24 . . . . **233** C5

Atherstone Rd DE12 . . . . **265** D1
Atherton Ave SK14 . . . . . . **9** A4
Atherton Cl S2 . . . . **43** F6
Atherton Gr SK14 . . . . **9** A4
Atherton Rd
　Ilkeston DE7 . . . . **194** F3
　Sheffield S2 . . . . **43** F6
Athlestan Way DE13 . . . . **240** C1
Athlone Cl DE21 . . . . **219** D8
Athol Cl
　Chesterfield S40 . . . . **114** B8
　Derby DE24 . . . . **231** E4
Atkin Pl S2 . . . . **43** A8
Atkinson Ct S40 . . . . **266** B1
Atkinson Mews S21 . . . . . **59** C3
Atkins Way ST14 . . . . **196** F3
Atlantic Cres **1** S8 . . . . . **56** E6
Atlantic Dr S8 . . . . **56** E6
Atlantic Way S8 . . . . **56** E6
Atlantic Wlk S8 . . . . **56** E6
Atlow Brow **4** DE6 . . . . **173** D3
Atlow Cl S40 . . . . **95** B5
Atlow La DE6 . . . . **175** A5
Atlow Rd DE21 . . . . **219** E7
Attenborough Nature
　Reserve★ NG9 . . . . **237** D8
Attewell Ct DE72 . . . . **235** B7
Attewell Rd NG16 . . . . . . **195** B5
Attlebridge Cl DE21 . . . . **219** D8
Attlee Rd S43 . . . . **97** B7
Atwall Ct DE23 . . . . **219** A1
Atworth Gr DE23 . . . . **230** F7
Auburn Cl DE7 . . . . **207** B8
Auckland's Pl S40 . . . . . . **266** B2
Auckland Cl DE3 . . . . **217** F3
Auckland Dr S20 . . . . **59** E5
Auckland Rise S20 . . . . . . **59** E6
Auckland Way S20 . . . . . . **59** E6
Auction Cl DE6 . . . . **173** C2
Auden Cl DE65 . . . . **227** A8
Audens Way DE11 . . . . . . **256** C6
Audley Cl DE7 . . . . **194** D3
Audley Ctr DE1 . . . . **267** B3
Audrey Cotts S32 . . . . **71** C6
Audrey Cres NG19 . . . . . **136** C5
Audrey Dr DE21 . . . . **220** A8
Audrey Rd S13 . . . . **44** C7
Aughton Cl S13 . . . . **44** D7
Aughton Cres S13 . . . . . . **44** D7
Aughton Dr S13 . . . . **44** C8
Augusta St DE23 . . . . **219** B2
Ault Dene DE11 . . . . **256** E4
Ault Hucknall La S44 . . . **134** A7
Aults DE65 . . . . **230** C1
Austen Ave
　Derby DE23 . . . . **231** B8
　Long Eaton NG10 . . . . . . **236** C5
Austins Dr NG10 . . . . **223** B4
Austin Sq DE23 . . . . **231** F7
Austin St NG20 . . . . **120** A4
Autumn Gr DE21 . . . . **219** F5
Avalon Dr DE73 . . . . **244** B8
Avenue 1 S41 . . . . **115** B8
Avenue 2 S41 . . . . **115** B8
Avenue 3 S41 . . . . **115** B8
Avenue 4 S41 . . . . **115** B8
Avenue 5 S41 . . . . **115** B8
Avenue 6 S41 . . . . **115** B8
Avenue 7 S41 . . . . **115** B8
Avenue 8 S41 . . . . **115** B8
Avenue Cl S32 . . . . **72** C3
Avenue Rd
　Chesterfield S41 . . . . **96** A5
　Duffield DE56 . . . . **190** E5
Avenue The
　Bakewell DE45 . . . . **109** D5
　Belper DE56 . . . . **178** F2
　Chapel-en-le-F SK23 . . . . **46** E2
　Derby, Chaddesden DE21 . **219** F5
　Derby DE1 . . . . **267** B2
　Dronfield S18 . . . . **57** B2
　Glossop SK13 . . . . **10** A4
　Northwood DE4 . . . . **127** C4
　Spinkhill S21 . . . . **60** D2
　Stoney Middleton S32 . . . **72** A3
　Tissington DE6 . . . . **162** A5
　Weston-on-T DE72 . . . . . **245** E5
Averham Cl
　Derby DE21 . . . . **206** A1
　Swadlincote DE11 . . . . . . **256** A3
Aviemore Cl S43 . . . . **77** E4
Aviemore Way DE24 . . . . **231** E4
Avis Ave DE75 . . . . **193** F7
Avocet Ct DE24 . . . . **231** D4
Avon Cl
　Derby DE24 . . . . **231** D2
　Dronfield S18 . . . . **57** B3
　Swadlincote DE11 . . . . . . **256** B6
Avon Ct S41 . . . . **266** C4
Avondale Cl NG10 . . . . . . **236** A6
Avondale Rd
　Bolsover S44 . . . . **118** A8
　Chesterfield S40 . . . . **266** A4
　Derby DE23 . . . . **267** B1
　Derby, Spondon DE21 . . . **220** D6
　Ilkeston DE7 . . . . **208** C5
　Staveley S43 . . . . **97** D7
Avonlea Cl DE7 . . . . **209** B6
Avonmouth Dr DE24 . . . . **232** E8
Avon St DE24 . . . . **232** E8
Avon Way
　Burton u T DE15 . . . . **248** A1
　Hilton DE65 . . . . **228** D1
Awdishaw La DE6 . . . . . . **213** B5
Awsworth La
　Cossall NG16 . . . . **195** C3
　Kimberley NG16 . . . . **195** D6

Awsworth Prim Sch
NG16. . . . . .195 C4
Awsworth Rd DE7 . . . . . .194 F2
Aycliffe Gdns DE24. . . . .232 F4
Aylesbury Ave DE21 . . . .219 F7
Aylward Cl S2 . . . . .43 F7
Aylward Rd S2. . . . . .43 F7
Ayncourt Rd S42. . . . . . .132 B7
Ayr DE21. . . . . .220 D4
Azalea Ave DE55. . . . . . .170 A8
Azalea Cl DE55. . . . . . . .159 E3
Azalea Ct NG16 . . . . .195 C8

B

Babbacombe Cl DE24 . . .233 C7
Babbacombe Ct 5 S41. . .95 F8
Babbington Cl DE13. . . . .239 C5
Babbington La NG16. . . . .195 F4
Babbington St DE55. . . . .148 A6
Babbs La DE6. . . . . .211 C1
Babington Bsns Coll
DE1. . . . . .267 B1
Babington Cl S2 . . . . .43 F7
Babington St S2 . . . . .43 F7
Babington Hospl DE56 . .178 F2
Babington La DE1. . . . . . .267 B2
Bacchus Way DE55 . . . . .147 B5
Back Bridge St SK22 . . . .24 C1
Back Croft S45 . . . . .131 E2
Backhill La DE6. . . . . .151 F3
Back Jodrell St SK22. . . .33 B7
Back La
Alderwasley DE56 . . . . . .166 E7
Alstonefield DE6 . . . . .149 E3
Biggin SK17 . . . . .138 D1
Brackenfield DE55. . . . . . .146 A1
Calow S44. . . . . .116 B8
Castle Donington DE74 . . .247 A5
Chellaston DE73 . . . . .233 A2
Darley Dale DE4 . . . . .127 F4
Eckington S21. . . . . .59 B3
Ellastone DE6. . . . . .183 A3
Elton DE4. . . . . .140 E6
Glapwell S44. . . . . .118 B1
Glossop SK13. . . . . .16 E6
Hathersage S32. . . . . .53 A7
Hilton DE65 . . . . .228 D2
Ilkeston DE7 . . . . .194 E2
Mottram in L SK14. . . . . . .9 A4
Palterton S44. . . . . .118 B5
Pilsley S45. . . . . .132 C2
Ripley DE5 . . . . .169 C6
Shirley DE6 . . . . .200 D7
Spout DE4 . . . . .166 D4
Stonebroom DE55. . . . . . .146 F5
Sutton in A NG17. . . . . . . .148 F4
Thorpe Salvin S80. . . . . . .63 B6
Thurvaston DE6. . . . . .215 B3
Tibshelf DE55 . . . . .147 F6
Unstone S18 . . . . .57 F1
Wessington DE55 . . . . . . .157 F8
Youlgreave DE45. . . . . . . .125 A6
Back Mellor SK22. . . . . . .24 C1
Back Moor SK14. . . . . . . .9 A4
Backmoor Cres S8. . . . . .43 C2
Backmoor Rd S8. . . . . . . .43 D2
Back Rd S18. . . . . .57 F1
Back School La DE7. . . . .127 E2
Back Sitwell St DE1. . . . .267 B2
Back South St S43 . . . . . .77 D3
Back St S33 . . . . .38 C3
Back Union Rd 3 S42. . . .33 C7
Back Wyver La DE56 . . . .178 F5
Bacon Cl NG16. . . . . .195 A8
Bacon La DE5. . . . . .169 B6
Bacons La S40. . . . . .115 A8
Baden Powell Ave S40 . .266 B2
Baden Powell Rd S40 . . .266 B2
Badger Cl
Chesterfield S40 . . . . .114 B7
Derby DE21 . . . . .220 F6
Badgerdale DE23 . . . . . . .231 A4
Badger La S45 . . . . .145 C8
Badgers Way SK13 . . . . . .17 B7
Badgery Cl ST14 . . . . .210 A1
Badway La DE65 . . . . .227 C8
Bage Hill S42. . . . . .113 E6
Baggaley Cres NG19 . . . .136 B1
Bag La
Marchington ST14. . . . . . .224 E2
Roston DE6 . . . . .197 E7
Bagot St DE7. . . . . .207 C8
Bagshaw's Rd S12 . . . . . .44 B6
Bagshawe Ave SK23. . . . .46 F6
Bagshawe Cavern S33. . .51 A6
Bagshaw Hill DE45 . . . . . .109 D6
Bagshaw La SK17. . . . . . .48 B6
Bagshaw St
Derby DE24 . . . . .232 E8
Pleasley NG19. . . . . .135 B4
Bagthorpe La S42. . . . . . .94 A3
Bailey Ave DE12 . . . . .262 A3
Bailey Brook Cres
Aldercar NG16. . . . . .182 A4
Langley Mill NG16. . . . . . .182 A3
Bailey Brook Ind Est
NG16. . . . . .182 B2
Bailey Brook Rd NE7. . . .194 F5
Bailey Brook Wlk NG16. .182 A3
Bailey Dr S21. . . . . .60 E8
Bailey Gr SK17 . . . . .85 E8
Bailey Grove Rd NG16 . . .182 D2
Baileys Mill DE4 . . . . .143 D4
Bailey St
Derby DE23. . . . . .267 A1
Stapleford NG9 . . . . .223 C6
Bainbridge Rd S44. . . . . .98 F1
Bainbridge St DE23. . . . .219 A3
Baines Wood S41 . . . . . . .95 C8
Bains Dr DE72 . . . . .221 D1
Bakeacre La DE65. . . . . . .230 E3
Bakehouse La DE72. . . . .221 C5
Bakehurst Cl SK22 . . . . . .33 C7
Baker's La
Cromford DE4 . . . . .155 A5
Doveridge DE6. . . . . .211 C1
Baker Ave DE75 . . . . .193 F7
*Baker Brothers Mobil Home
Cvn Site* DE7 . . . . .195 A1
Baker Cl DE55 . . . . .170 D7
Baker Dr S21 . . . . .60 C6
Baker Rd
Eastwood NG16 . . . . .195 C8
Mansfield Woodhouse
NG19. . . . . .136 C6
Bakers Hill DE56. . . . . . . .168 E1
Bakers La DE4 . . . . .156 A8
Baker St
Burton u T DE15. . . . . . . .254 E7
Creswell S80 . . . . .81 E2
Ilkeston DE7 . . . . .194 F1
Swadlincote DE11 . . . . . . .256 C3
Bakestone Moor S80. . . . .81 F5
Bakewell Bank 39 SK13. .9 D1
Bakewell CE Inf Sch
DE45. . . . . .109 D6
Bakewell Cl
Derby DE3 . . . . .217 E3
40 Gamesley SK13. . . . . . .9 D1
Bakewell Dr DE74. . . . . . .247 A2
Bakewell Fold 37 SK13. . .9 D1
Bakewell Gdns 41 SK13. .9 D1
Bakewell Gn
38 Gamesley SK13. . . . . . .9 D1
Swadlincote DE11 . . . . . . .255 E5
Bakewell Gr 38 SK13 . . . .9 D1
Bakewell Lea 34 SK13 . . .9 D1
Bakewell Meth Jun Sch
DE45. . . . . .109 D6
Bakewell Mews 38 SK13. .9 D1
Bakewell Rd
Baslow DE45 . . . . .91 E4
Buxton SK17 . . . . .85 C7
Darley Dale DE4 . . . . .142 F7
Long Eaton NG10 . . . . . . .236 E5
Matlock DE4 . . . . .143 A5
Over Haddon DE45 . . . . . .109 B2
Staveley S43 . . . . .97 C5
Bakewell St DE22 . . . . . . .218 F4
Bakewell Station Ind Est
DE45. . . . . .109 E7
Bakewell Wlk 44 SK13 . . .9 D1
Balaclava Rd DE23 . . . . . .232 A8
Balfour Rd
Derby DE23 . . . . .232 A8
Stapleford NG9 . . . . .223 C6
Balgonie DE73 . . . . .232 E2
Balham Wlk DE22 . . . . . . .218 A6
Balk The DE13 . . . . .239 D6
Ballacraine Dr DE5. . . . . .170 A1
Ballards Way DE72 . . . . . .221 D1
Ballater Cl
Derby DE24 . . . . .231 E4
Mansfield NG19 . . . . .135 D2
Balleny Cl DE21. . . . . .205 F2
Ball Hill DE55. . . . . .160 C6
Ballidon Cl 1 S41. . . . . . . .95 C6
Ball La DE7. . . . . .234 A5
Balmoak La S41. . . . . .96 C5
Balmoral Cl
Derby DE23 . . . . .218 B2
Heanor DE75 . . . . .181 C1
Mansfield Woodhouse
NG19. . . . . .136 C6
Sandiacre NG10 . . . . .223 B3
Balmoral Cres
Dronfield S18. . . . . .56 D2
Sheffield S10 . . . . .42 F8
Balmoral Ct DE74 . . . . . . .247 D5
Balmoral Dr NG19. . . . . . .135 D2
Balmoral Rd
Borrowash DE72 . . . . .221 C1
Burton u T DE15. . . . . . . .248 A3
Ilkeston DE7 . . . . .208 D5
Balmoral Way S43 . . . . . . .77 E4
Baltimore Cl 8 DE11. . . . .256 A7
Bamburgh Cl DE21 . . . . . .220 D4
Bamford Ave
Derby DE23 . . . . .231 F8
North Wingfield S42 . . . . .131 F7
Bamford Fold 3 SK13. . . . .9 E1
Bamford Gn 4 SK13. . . . . .9 E1
Bamford Ho S33 . . . . .40 B3
Bamford La SK13. . . . . . . .9 E1
Bamford Mews SK13 . . . . .9 E1
Bamford Mills S33. . . . . . .40 B3
Bamford Prim Sch S33. . .40 B4
Bamford Rd S43 . . . . .97 C5
Bamford St
Chesterfield S43 . . . . .77 D4
Newton DE55 . . . . .148 A3
Ripley DE5. . . . . .180 D7
Bamford Sta S33. . . . . . . .40 B1
Banbury Ave NG9 . . . . . . .223 F3
Banchory Cl NG19. . . . . . .135 C2
Bancroft DE65 . . . . .228 D1
Bancroft Dr DE24 . . . . . . .204 C4
Bancroft The DE65 . . . . . .229 B3
Bangor St DE21 . . . . .219 E8
Bank Bldgs DE56. . . . . . . .190 F7
Bankbottom SK13. . . . . . .10 A5
Bolsover S44. . . . . .99 A3
Creswell S80 . . . . .100 D8
Shirebrook NG20. . . . . .119 F4
Tibshelf DE55 . . . . .147 F5
Bank Ct DE22 . . . . .218 E8
Bankerwall La DE6. . . . . . .183 C7
Bankfield Dr
Derby DE21 . . . . .220 F4
Ilkeston DE7 . . . . .208 B6
Bankgate SK14 . . . . .16 A8
Bank Gdns DE4 . . . . .143 B6
Bankholmes Cl DE24 . . . .231 E2
Bank House DE6 . . . . .164 A2
Bank La SK13 . . . . .10 A7
Bank Rd
Chesterfield S41 . . . . .96 A6
Matlock DE4 . . . . .143 C5
Bank Row SK13 . . . . .10 A7
Banksburn Cl DE75. . . . . .181 C1
Bankside DE45. . . . . .125 B5
Bank Side
Derby DE22. . . . . .204 E2
Hartington SK17 . . . . .137 D6
Bankside Cl SK6. . . . . .15 C1
Banks Rd NG9 . . . . .223 E2
Bank St
Brimington S43 . . . . .96 D8
Broadbottom SK14. . . . . . .16 A8
Chesterfield S40 . . . . .95 E3
Glossop SK13. . . . . .17 D8
Hadfield SK13 . . . . .10 A5
Hayfield SK22 . . . . .25 D3
Langley Mill NG16. . . . . . .182 C3
Long Eaton NG10 . . . . . . .236 E7
Somercotes DE55 . . . . . . .170 C8
Swadlincote DE11 . . . . . . .262 A8
Bankswood Cl SK13 . . . . . .10 A4
Bank Terr SK13 . . . . .10 A5
Bank The
Bonsall DE4. . . . . .142 C1
Glossop SK13. . . . . .17 D8
Hayfield SK22 . . . . .25 B4
Stoney Middleton S32 . . . .71 F4
Bank Top La S30. . . . . .72 C8
Bank Vale Rd SK22. . . . . . .25 C3
Bank View SK17 . . . . .69 B5
Bank View Rd
Derby DE22 . . . . .218 F8
Nether Heage DE56. . . . . .168 C2
Bankwood Cl S14. . . . . . . .43 D5
Bank Wood Cl S40 . . . . . . .95 B7
Bankwood Com Prim Sch
S14. . . . . .43 D5
Bankwood Rd S14. . . . . . . .43 D5
Bannels Ave DE23. . . . . . .231 B7
Banton's La DE73 . . . . . . .251 A4
Banwell Cl DE3 . . . . .217 C3
Barber's La S21. . . . . .60 D7
Barber St DE7 . . . . .194 E3
Barber St SK13 . . . . .10 B5
Barbon Cl S40 . . . . .95 E5
Barchester Dr DE21 . . . . .206 B2
Barclay Ct DE7. . . . . .194 D3
Barclay Grange S41. . . . . .266 C3
Bar Croft 3 S40 . . . . .95 C6
Barden Dr DE22 . . . . .204 F3
Bardolph Cl DE11 . . . . . . .255 F3
Bardsey Ct DE21 . . . . .206 B3
Bare Jarnett Rd SK17 . . . .88 B1
Bare La DE72 . . . . .221 C5
Bargate S33 . . . . .38 C2
Bargate DE56 . . . . .179 C1
Bargate La DE65 . . . . .242 B5
Bargate Rd DE56. . . . . . . .179 B1
Barholme Cl S41. . . . . .95 B7
Barker Ave NG16 . . . . .171 B4
Barker Ave N NG10. . . . . .223 A6
Barker Cl DE7 . . . . .193 B1
Barker Fold S40 . . . . .95 D3
Barker Gate DE7 . . . . .194 F2
Barker La S40 . . . . .95 D3
Barker St NG17. . . . . .148 F4
Barklam Cl DE12. . . . . . . .262 E1
Barlborough Hall Sch S43 61 B1
Barlborough Prim Sch
SK43 . . . . .80 B7
Barlborough Rd S43 . . . . .80 D5
Barley Cft DE73 . . . . .232 F1
Barley Cl DE21 . . . . .205 C8
Barleycorn Cl DE55 . . . . .148 A1
Barley Corn Cl DE21. . . . .206 C2
Barleycroft SK13 . . . . .9 F4
Barley Croft
Belper DE56. . . . . .179 B2
South Normanton DE55. . .160 B4
Barley Dale Dr NG9 . . . . .209 D2
Barley La S42. . . . . .95 A5
Barley Mews
Dronfield S18. . . . . .56 B2
Mansfield Woodhouse
NG19. . . . . .136 E6
Barling Dr DE7. . . . . .194 C2
Barlow CE Prim Sch S18 . 75 E3
Barlow Cottages La
NG16. . . . . .195 C5
Barlow Dr N NG16. . . . . . .195 B4
Barlow Dr S NG16. . . . . . .195 B4
Barlow Lees La S18 . . . . .75 F7
Barlow Rd
Chapel-en-le-F SK23 . . . . .47 C6
Cutthorpe S18, S42. . . . . . .94 F8
Staveley S43 . . . . .78 E1
Barlow St DE1, DE24. . . . .267 D1
Barlow View S18. . . . . .76 B7
Barlow Wood Dr SK6. . . . .23 B3
Barmote Croft DE4. . . . . .154 F1
Barms Way SK17 . . . . .66 D1
Barnard Ave S18. . . . . . . .57 D3
Barnard Rd DE21. . . . . . . .205 D2
Barn Cl
Castle Donington DE74 . . .247 B3
Chesterfield S41 . . . . .95 D6
Findern DE65. . . . . .230 D2
Glossop SK13. . . . . .17 D7
Quarndon DE22 . . . . .204 C6
Barn Croft DE23 . . . . .218 C1
Barnes Ave S18 . . . . .56 E2
Barnes Croft
Heanor DE75 . . . . .193 C8
Wirksworth DE4 . . . . .165 F8
Barnes Gn DE22. . . . . .218 B7
Barnes La
Dronfield S18. . . . . .56 C3
Youlgreave DE45 . . . . .125 C5
Barnes Rd S41. . . . . .96 C1
*Barn Farm Cvn & Camping
Site* DE4. . . . . .126 C1
Barnfield Cl
Holmewood S42. . . . . .132 E8
1 Staveley S43. . . . . .78 E2
Barnfield Dr S32. . . . . .52 F7
Barnfields S32. . . . . .52 F7
Barnfield Wlk S32 . . . . . . .78 E2
Barn Furlong DE45. . . . . . .90 A4
Barnham Cl S40 . . . . .114 B8
Barnhill Gr DE23 . . . . .231 A7
Barnsfold Ct S42. . . . . . . .25 D3
Barnsley La DE4, DE56 . . .165 F2
Barnstaple Cl DE21. . . . . .206 A2
Barnstaple Ct 3 S41. . . . .95 F8
Barns The S42. . . . . .115 B4
Barnwell Cl ST14. . . . . . . .210 A4
Barnwell La DE4 . . . . .155 A5
Barnwood Cl DE3 . . . . . . .217 C2
Baron Cl DE21 . . . . .206 D3
Barrack Rd S18 . . . . .58 A1
Barrack Yd DE55 . . . . .170 D7
Barratt Rd S21. . . . . .59 D2
Bar Rd
Baslow DE45 . . . . .91 F6
Curbar S32 . . . . .72 F2
Barrett St DE24 . . . . .233 A7
Barrie Dr DE24. . . . . .231 F5
Barringer Rd NG19. . . . . . .136 D1
Barrington Cl DE13 . . . . . .240 C1
Barron's Way DE72. . . . . .221 C1
Barrons Ct DE72 . . . . .234 A5
Barroon DE74. . . . . .247 B3
Barrow Hill Prim Sch S43 78 B3
*Barrow Hill Roundhouse Rly
Ctr* S43. . . . . .78 A4
Barrow La DE73. . . . . .244 C6
Barrows Hill La NG16. . . .171 D5
Barrow St S43 . . . . .78 F2
Barry Rd S43 . . . . .96 F4
Barrys Cl DE11. . . . . .256 E1
Barson Gr SK17 . . . . .85 E2
Bartle Ave S12. . . . . .43 A4
Bartle Dr S12. . . . . .43 A4
Bartle Rd S12. . . . . .43 A4
Bartle Way S12. . . . . .43 A4
Barton Cl DE21 . . . . .220 F6
Barton Cres S40 . . . . .95 A6
Barton Hill DE4 . . . . .126 C1
Barton Knowle DE56. . . . .179 D4
Barton La NG11 . . . . .237 C2
Barton Rd
Long Eaton NG10 . . . . . . .237 A6
Sheffield S8 . . . . .43 A6
Barton St
Burton u T DE14. . . . . . . .254 C8
Clowne S43 . . . . .80 C4
Barton Turn DE13. . . . . . . .253 A1
Barway DE7 . . . . .211 E8
Basegreen Ave S12. . . . . .44 B3
Basegreen Cl S12. . . . . . .44 C3
Basegreen Cres S12. . . . .44 B3
Basegreen Dr S12 . . . . . . .44 C3
Basegreen Pl S12. . . . . . .44 B3
Basegreen Rd S12. . . . . . .44 C3
Basegreen Way S12. . . . . .44 C3
Basil Cl S41 . . . . .266 B3
Basildon Cl DE24 . . . . . . .232 F5
Basingwerke Ct SK22 . . . .25 D3
Baslow Cl
22 Gamesley SK13 . . . . . . .9 E1
Long Eaton NG10 . . . . . . .236 A5
Baslow Cl 14 S40 . . . . .95 D5
Baslow Dr DE22. . . . . .204 F3
Baslow Fold 21 SK13. . . . .9 E1
Baslow Gn
23 Gamesley SK13 . . . . . . .9 E1
2 Swadlincote DE11 . . . . .255 E5
Baslow Gr SK17 . . . . .85 E6
Baslow Mews SK13 . . . . . .9 E1
Baslow Rd
Bakewell DE45. . . . . .109 D2
Curbar S32 . . . . .72 D1
Holymoorside S42. . . . . . .94 C1
Sheffield S17 . . . . .55 C4
Baslow Way 24 SK13 . . . . .9 E1
Bass's Cres DE11. . . . . . . .261 E7
Bassettbarn La S42. . . . . .130 B5
Bassett Cl
Ilkeston DE7 . . . . .194 C3
Kimberley NG16. . . . . .195 E7
Bassett La S10. . . . . .42 E6
Bassett Rd NG16 . . . . .195 E7
Bassett The NG20. . . . . . .119 E6
Bassford Ave DE75. . . . . .181 F2
Bassingham Cl DE21 . . . . .206 B1
Bassledene Ct S2. . . . . . . .44 A8
Bassledene Rd S2. . . . . . .44 A8
Bass St DE22 . . . . .218 D6
Batch La DE6 . . . . .224 B7
Bateman Cl S43. . . . . .77 D4
Bateman St DE23 . . . . . . .219 C3
Batemill Rd SK22 . . . . .24 D2
Batemoor Cl S8. . . . . .57 A6
Batemoor Dr S8. . . . . .57 A6
Batemoor Pl S8. . . . . .57 A6
Batemoor Rd S8. . . . . .57 A5
Batemoor Wlk S8. . . . . . . .57 A6
Bate Wood Ave S43. . . . . .97 B5
Batham Gate SK17 . . . . . . .48 F1
Batham Gate Rd SK17 . . . .67 B6
Batham Rd S33 . . . . .51 A8
Bath La
Ashover S45 . . . . .129 F6
Moira DE12 . . . . .262 D4
Shirebrook NG19. . . . . . . .120 C2
Bath Rd
Buxton SK17 . . . . .85 B6
Derby DE3 . . . . .217 E2
Bath St
Bakewell DE45. . . . . .109 D6
Derby DE1. . . . . .267 B5
Ilkeston DE7 . . . . .194 E1
Bathurst Rd S44. . . . . .117 F8
Bathurst Terr NG20 . . . . . .100 F2
Batley La NG19 . . . . .134 E4
Batt St 9 S8. . . . . .43 A8
Baulk La
Beeston NG9 . . . . .223 F7
Hathersage S32. . . . . .53 A6
Baverstock Cl DE73. . . . . .232 F3
Baxter Hill NG19 . . . . .134 F3
Baxter Sq DE23 . . . . .231 F6
Baycliff Dr S40 . . . . .95 C3
Bay Ct S21 . . . . .60 C5
Bayleaf Cres DE21 . . . . . .206 B3
Baysdale Croft S20. . . . . .59 D7
Baysdale Dr NG19 . . . . . . .136 F1
Bayswater Cl DE22 . . . . . .217 F6
Bayswater Rd NG16 . . . . .195 F7
Bazley Rd S2 . . . . .43 F6
Beackden Cl DE56 . . . . . . .179 C4
Beacomfold SK6. . . . . .15 B3
Beacon Dr DE13 . . . . .240 D5
Beaconfields Ho DE21. . . .220 B4
Beacon Rd DE13 . . . . .240 D5
Beaconsfield St NG10 . . .236 E7
Beam Cl DE21 . . . . .240 A1
Beamwood Cl 3 DE21 . . .205 F1
Beard Cres S32. . . . . .33 D8
Beardmore Cl DE21 . . . . .205 F2
Beards Rd DE11. . . . . .256 A6
Bearwood Hill Rd DE15. .248 A3
Beatrix Dr SK13. . . . . .9 E3
Beatty St DE24 . . . . .232 F8
Beatty Wlk DE7 . . . . .194 F3
Beauchief Abbey La S8. . .56 C8
Beauchief Abbey (rems of)
S8. . . . . .56 C8
Beauchief Dr S17 . . . . .56 C7
Beauchief Gdns DE55 . . .170 D8
Beaufit La NG16 . . . . .160 E2
Beaufort Com Prim Sch
DE21. . . . . .219 C8
Beaufort Court Ind Est
DE21. . . . . .219 C8
Beaufort St
Burton u T DE15. . . . . . . .248 B1
Derby DE24 . . . . .231 D2
Beaufort St DE21 . . . . . . .219 D7
Beaulieu Way DE55 . . . . .170 A7
Beaumaris Ct DE21. . . . . .220 F5
Beaumont Cl
Barrow u T DE73 . . . . .244 A5
Belper DE56. . . . . .179 D4
Stapleford NG9 . . . . .209 L1
Beaumont Dr SK17. . . . . . .47 F1
Beaumont Wlk DE23 . . . . .231 E6
Beaurepaire Cres DE56. . .179 B5
Beaureper Ave DE22 . . . .204 E3
Beauvale Dr DE7 . . . . .194 E5
Becher St DE23 . . . . .219 A1
Beck Cl S44 . . . . .99 C2
Beckenham Way DE22. . . .218 B6
Becket Ave S8. . . . . .56 D6
Becket Cres S8. . . . . .56 E6
Becket Prim Sch DE22 . . .218 F4
Becket Rd S8. . . . . .56 E6
Becket St DE1. . . . . .267 A3
Beckett Ave NG19 . . . . . . .135 E1
Becket Well La DE1. . . . . .267 B3
Becket Wlk S8. . . . . .56 E6
Beckingham Way S40 . . .266 B2
Beckitt Cl DE24. . . . . .233 A8
Becksitch Ct DE56. . . . . . .178 F2
Becksitch Ct DE56 . . . . . .178 F2
Bedehouse La DE4 . . . . . .155 A6
Bedford Cl DE22 . . . . .218 D3
Bedford Ct NG9. . . . . .209 E1
Bedford Rd DE15 . . . . .254 D7
Bedford St DE22 . . . . .218 D3
Bedgrave Cl S21 . . . . .60 F8
Beech Ave
Alfreton DE55 . . . . .159 B5
Borrowash DE72 . . . . .221 C3
Breaston DE72. . . . . .235 F8
Creswell S80 . . . . .81 F1
Derby DE23 . . . . .233 B7
Glossop SK13. . . . . .17 A8
Hulland Ward DE6 . . . . . . .175 F3
Long Eaton NG10 . . . . . . .223 L1
Melbourne DE73 . . . . .252 B8
New Mills SK22 . . . . .24 D1

Beech Ave *continued*
Pinxton NG16 .... 160 E3
Quarndon DE22 .... 204 B8
Ripley DE5 .... 169 C2
Sandiacre NG10 .... 223 B7
Willington DE65 .... 242 B5
Beech Cl
Belper DE56 .... 179 A3
Kilburn DE56 .... 192 B8
Beech Cres
Eckington S21 .... 59 B1
Glapwell S44 .... 134 B8
Killamarsh S21 .... 60 D5
Mansfield Woodhouse NG19 .... 136 E2
Beechcroft DE21 .... 205 D4
Beech Ct
Derby DE21 .... 220 D5
Mansfield Woodhouse NG19 .... 136 B5
Wirksworth DE4 .... 165 F7
Beechdale Cl S40 .... 95 D5
Beechdale Rd
Alfreton DE55 .... 159 C3
Mansfield NG19 .... 136 F2
Beech Dr
Arkwright Town S44 .... 97 D3
Ashbourne DE6 .... 185 D8
Derby DE22 .... 218 F8
Etwall DE65 .... 229 C4
Findern DE65 .... 230 E1
Woodville DE11 .... 257 B2
Beeches Ave DE21 .... 220 D5
Beeches Dr S2 .... 43 C8
Beeches The
Baslow DE45 .... 91 E5
Crich DE4 .... 156 F1
Heanor DE75 .... 193 C8
Matlock DE4 .... 143 A6
Beechfield Rd SK13 .... 9 F3
Beech Gdns DE24 .... 233 B7
Beech Gr
Long Duckmanton S44 .... 98 A4
South Normanton DE55 .... 160 B5
Swadlincote DE11 .... 255 F7
Beech Hill Ave NG19 .... 135 F1
Beech Hill Cres NG19 .... 135 F1
Beech Hill Dr NG19 .... 135 F1
Beech Hill Sch NG19 .... 135 F1
Beech La
Burton u T DE13 .... 240 E1
Dove Holes SK17 .... 66 E8
West Hallam DE7 .... 207 D7
Beechley Dr DE21 .... 206 B1
Beech Rd SK23 .... 45 E7
Beech Rise SK23 .... 45 C5
Beech St S43 .... 78 A1
Beech Tree Ave NG19 .... 136 B5
Beech Tree Dr S43 .... 80 F2
Beech Way
Clay Cross S45 .... 131 E2
Dronfield S18 .... 57 A3
Beech Wlk
Cromford DE4 .... 155 A6
Derby DE23 .... 218 D1
Beechwood SK13 .... 16 F7
Beechwood Cl DE56 .... 178 E5
Beechwood Cres DE23 .... 231 C8
Beechwood Ct DE23 .... 219 B3
Beechwood Dr SK6 .... 23 A6
Beechwood Park Dr DE22 .... 204 F1
Beechwood Rd S18 .... 56 F1
Beehive Rd S40 .... 95 D2
Bee Hives The DE11 .... 256 A7
Beeley Cl
Belper DE56 .... 179 C6
Creswell S80 .... 81 D1
Derby DE22 .... 204 D2
Derby, Oakwood DE21 .... 205 F2
North Wingfield S42 .... 132 A7
Staveley S43 .... 97 C6
Beeley La DE4 .... 112 B3
Beeley View S40 .... 114 B7
Beeley Way S43 .... 97 C5
Beelow Cl SK17 .... 47 F2
Beeston Cl S18 .... 56 C2
Beetwell St S40 .... 266 B2
Beggarway La DE45 .... 90 B5
Beighton St DE5 .... 169 E1
Beldon Cl S2 .... 43 D7
Beldon Pl S2 .... 43 D7
Beldon Rd S2 .... 43 D7
Belfast Wlk DE21 .... 220 A4
Belfield Ct
Etwall DE65 .... 229 B3
Heanor DE75 .... 181 C4
Belfield Gdns NG10 .... 236 E7
Belfield Rd
Etwall DE65 .... 229 C3
Swadlincote DE11 .... 256 B5
Belfield St DE7 .... 194 F2
Belfield Terr DE65 .... 229 B3
Belfit Dr S42 .... 114 F2
Belf Moor Cl S80 .... 82 A5
Belfry Cl DE3 .... 217 F1
Belfry The DE13 .... 240 C1
Belgrade Ave SK23 .... 34 E1
Belgrave Cl DE56 .... 179 C5
Belgrave Sq 6 S2 .... 43 A8
Belgrave St DE23 .... 267 B1
Belklane Dr S21 .... 60 E7
Bella Cl NG16 .... 182 B4
Belland La S45 .... 113 D2
Bell Ave DE72 .... 246 A7
Bell Cotts DE6 .... 224 C8
Belle Acre Cl 3 DE56 .... 178 F3
Belle View Rd DE6 .... 173 B2
Belle Vue Ave DE5 .... 180 C6
Belle Vue Cl S43 .... 96 D8
Bellhouse La S43 .... 78 F3
Bell House La S43 .... 78 F3
Bellhouse View S43 .... 78 F3
Bellingham Ct DE22 .... 204 C2
Bell La
Bonsall DE4 .... 142 C1
Doveridge DE6 .... 224 C8
Hartshorne DE11 .... 257 A3
Heanor DE7, DE75 .... 193 C5
Bells End Rd DE12 .... 253 D1
Bellsfield Cl S80 .... 82 A5
Belmont Ave DE72 .... 235 E8
Belmont Dr
Borrowash DE72 .... 221 B1
Marple SK6 .... 15 B1
Staveley S43 .... 78 F2
Belmont Prim Sch DE11 .... 256 C4
Belmont St DE11 .... 256 C4
Belmont Terr 1 SK17 .... 85 B7
Belmot Rd DE13 .... 239 B4
Belpar Ho DE21 .... 220 E3
Belper La DE56 .... 178 E6
Belper Rd
Ashbourne DE6 .... 173 E1
3 Derby DE22 .... 218 F7
Holbrook DE56 .... 191 C8
Kilburn DE56 .... 179 E2
Morley DE7 .... 192 F2
Shirland DE55 .... 146 C2
Stanley Common DE7 .... 193 B1
West Hallam DE7 .... 207 C8
Belper Sch DE56 .... 179 D4
Belper St DE7 .... 208 F7
Belper Sta DE56 .... 178 F4
Belsize Cl DE22 .... 217 F6
Belton Cl
Dronfield S18 .... 56 C1
Sandiacre NG10 .... 223 B4
Belton Dr DE5 .... 169 E1
Belvedere Ave S40 .... 114 E8
Belvedere Cl
Chesterfield S40 .... 114 A8
Derby DE3 .... 217 D3
Swanwick DE55 .... 169 F7
Belvedere Rd DE11 .... 256 F2
Belvedere Terr 1 SK17 .... 85 B6
Belvoir Cl
Breaston DE72 .... 235 D7
Ilkeston DE7 .... 208 D6
Long Eaton NG10 .... 236 E5
Belvoir Cres DE11 .... 256 A6
Belvoir St DE23 .... 218 F1
Belvoir Way DE55 .... 159 C1
Bembridge Dr DE24 .... 233 C5
Bemrose Com Sch DE22 .... 218 D4
Bemrose Gate S33 .... 40 A6
Bemrose Mews DE22 .... 218 C4
Bemrose Rd DE24 .... 232 E7
Benbow Ave DE73 .... 252 A8
Benches La SK6 .... 15 E3
Bench Rd SK17 .... 85 D8
Bendall Gn DE23 .... 231 C5
Bend Oak Dr DE15 .... 248 C4
Bend Oak Jun Sch DE15 .... 248 C3
Benjamin Ct NG16 .... 170 F3
Benjamin Outram Bsns Ctr DE5 .... 180 E7
Benmore Ct DE21 .... 206 B3
Benner Ave DE7 .... 209 A5
Bennerley Ave DE7 .... 194 F4
Bennerley Fields Sch DE7 .... 194 F4
Bennerley Sch DE7 .... 194 F4
Bennetts La DE4 .... 168 A8
Bennett St
Buxton SK17 .... 85 C6
Derby DE24 .... 232 D5
Hollingworth SK14 .... 9 D5
Long Eaton NG10 .... 223 C2
Sandiacre NG10 .... 223 B5
Bennimoor Way S40 .... 114 E8
Bennington Wlk NG19 .... 136 E4
Bennion Gr ST14 .... 196 E5
Bennison Gdns S45 .... 131 D3
Bensley Cl DE73 .... 233 A1
Benson St DE24 .... 232 F7
Bentfield Rd DE56 .... 168 C1
Bentham Rd S40 .... 95 E5
Benthead La DE6 .... 164 F1
Bentinck Dr S43 .... 81 A4
Bentinck Rd S44 .... 98 F7
Bentink Cl S80 .... 81 C1
Bent La
Church Broughton DE65 .... 227 C6
Darley Dale DE4 .... 127 D6
Matlock DE4 .... 143 B7
Spout DE4, DE56 .... 166 C6
Staveley S43 .... 79 A3
Tissington DE6 .... 162 D5
Bentley Bridge Cotts DE4 .... 143 E7
Bentley Brook
Hilton DE65 .... 228 D1
Matlock DE4 .... 143 D4
Bentley Cl
Alfreton DE55 .... 159 B3
Matlock DE4 .... 143 D7
Bentley Dale DE11 .... 257 A3
Bentley Fields Open Farm★ DE6 .... 199 C2
Bentley Rd
Castle Donington DE74 .... 246 F4
Uttoxeter ST14 .... 210 A2
Bentley St DE24 .... 232 E6
Benton Dr SK6 .... 23 C8
Bents Cres S18 .... 57 C3
Bentside Rd SK12 .... 32 D5
Bents La S18 .... 57 C3
Bent The S32 .... 72 E3
Beowulf Covert DE13 .... 240 B1
Beresford Ave
Ashbourne DE6 .... 173 D2
Chapel-en-le-F SK23 .... 47 C6
Beresford Cl S45 .... 131 D2
Beresford Dale DE11 .... 255 F2
Beresford Dr
Derby DE21 .... 220 E4
Ilkeston DE7 .... 194 E5
Beresford La SK17 .... 137 C2
Beresford Pl DE56 .... 168 B6
Beresford Rd
Chapel-en-le-F SK23 .... 47 C6
Long Eaton NG10 .... 236 A5
Mansfield Woodhouse NG19 .... 136 C6
Berkeley Ave NG10 .... 236 C6
Berkeley Cl DE23 .... 231 D7
Berkley Ct SK23 .... 45 D6
Berkshire St DE21 .... 219 D8
Berle Ave DE75 .... 181 E2
Bermuda Ave DE21 .... 205 C6
Bernard Ave NG19 .... 136 B5
Bernard Cl S43 .... 96 F8
Bernard Ct DE11 .... 256 D3
Bernard St
Glossop SK13 .... 10 C1
Swadlincote DE11 .... 256 D3
Bernard Walker Ct SK6 .... 15 B2
Berners Cl S2 .... 43 E6
Berners Dr S2 .... 43 E6
Berners Pl S2 .... 43 E6
Berners Rd S2 .... 43 E6
Berridge La S45 .... 145 B4
Berrisford La DE55 .... 145 D7
Berristow La DE55 .... 160 C7
Berry Ave S21 .... 59 C3
Berry Gdns DE15 .... 248 C4
Berry Hedge La DE15 .... 248 C4
Berry Park Cl DE22 .... 204 E1
Berry St S42 .... 131 E6
Bertrand Ave S45 .... 131 D3
Berwick Ave
Chesterfield S40 .... 114 C7
Derby DE21 .... 219 C7
Berwick Cl DE24 .... 233 B5
Berwick Ct S40 .... 114 C7
Berwick Dr DE24 .... 231 D3
Berwick Rd SK17 .... 85 C4
Berwin Cl NG10 .... 223 A1
Berwyn Cl S40 .... 95 C5
Besom La S32 .... 53 A8
Bessalone Dr DE56 .... 179 A6
Bessell La NG9 .... 223 D5
Bessie La S33 .... 51 B6
Best Ave DE15 .... 248 B1
Besthill Cotts SK14 .... 16 B8
Besthorpe Cl DE21 .... 206 B1
Bestwick Ave DE75 .... 182 B1
Bestwick Cl DE7 .... 209 A4
Bestwood Dr S45 .... 131 D3
Bestwood Pk S45 .... 131 C3
Bestwood Rd NG16 .... 160 E2
Bethel Terr S81 .... 63 E7
Bethulie Rd DE23 .... 232 A8
Betjeman Sq DE24 .... 232 A5
Betlingspring La DE6 .... 184 D3
Betony Cl S21 .... 60 B5
Betony Rd DE15 .... 248 C2
Betty La DE45 .... 108 F8
Bevan Ct DE55 .... 146 E1
Bevan Dr S43 .... 97 B7
Bevan Rd S45 .... 131 D2
Bevan St DE55 .... 146 E1
Beverley Dr NG16 .... 195 E7
Beverley Rd DE14 .... 254 A7
Beverleys Rd S8 .... 43 A4
Beverley St DE24 .... 219 D2
Bevin Pl S42 .... 132 A7
Bewdley Cl DE73 .... 233 A3
Bexhill Wlk DE21 .... 205 E1
Bexley Cl SK13 .... 10 C3
Bicester Ave DE24 .... 231 C2
Bickley Moss DE21 .... 206 B1
Bideford Cl DE5 .... 169 D2
Bideford Ct 25 S41 .... 95 F8
Bideford Dr DE23 .... 231 D6
Bidston Cl DE4 .... 143 C7
Bidworth La SK13 .... 9 D1
Biggin CE Prim Sch SK17 .... 138 D3
Biggin Cl S45 .... 131 D1
Biggin La DE6 .... 176 B3
Biggin mill La DE6 .... 176 C5
Biggin The DE74 .... 247 B3
Big La DE6 .... 164 A4
Bilberry Cl DE21 .... 205 F1
Bilby La S43 .... 77 E1
Billam St S21 .... 59 B3
Billingsley Ave NG16 .... 160 D3
Bingham St DE24 .... 232 E6
Bings Rd SK23 .... 45 F8
Bingswood Ave SK23 .... 45 E8
Bingswood Ind Est SK23 .... 45 E8
Bingswood Rd SK23 .... 45 E7
Binscombe La DE21 .... 205 F3
Birch Ave
Ambergate DE56 .... 167 F3
Ilkeston DE7 .... 209 A7
Swadlincote DE11 .... 256 A7
Birch Cl
Alfreton DE55 .... 159 A5
Birch Cl *continued*
Burton u T DE14 .... 254 A8
Buxton SK17 .... 66 B1
Denstone ST14 .... 196 D6
Derby DE21 .... 221 A6
Grassmoor S42 .... 115 F3
Killamarsh S21 .... 60 C5
Ripley DE5 .... 180 D8
Wessington DE55 .... 157 E8
Birchen Cl
Chesterfield S40 .... 95 D5
Dronfield S18 .... 56 D1
Birchen Holme DE55 .... 160 A4
Birches Ave DE55 .... 157 F5
Birches Fold S18 .... 57 C4
Birches La
Dronfield S18 .... 57 C4
South Wingfield DE55 .... 158 A5
Birches Rd DE22 .... 204 D4
Birches The SK22 .... 25 C2
Birch Farm Ave S8 .... 57 A8
Birchfield Cl DE73 .... 232 F2
Birchfield Pk DE75 .... 193 F7
Birchfield Rd DE15 .... 254 E6
Birch Gn SK13 .... 10 E1
Birch Gr
Hatton DE65 .... 227 D2
Shirebrook NG20 .... 119 D5
Birch Hall Cl SK22 .... 25 B2
Birch Holt Gr S18 .... 76 E5
Birch House Way S18 .... 57 C1
Birchills The S80 .... 81 C1
Birchitt Cl S17 .... 56 C5
Birchitt Ct S17 .... 56 C5
Birchitt Pl S17 .... 56 C5
Birchitt Rd S17 .... 56 C5
Birchitt View S18 .... 57 A3
Birch Kiln Croft S43 .... 96 F7
Birch La S43 .... 78 A1
Birchlands NG19 .... 136 F1
Birchlands Dr S21 .... 60 D5
Birchover Ct S41 .... 95 E6
Birchover Edge DE4 .... 141 B8
Birchover Ho
1 Derby, Allestree DE22 .... 204 F3
Derby, Markeaton DE22 .... 218 D8
Birchover La DE4 .... 141 B7
Birchover Pl DE7 .... 194 E5
Birchover Rd DE4 .... 126 C3
Birchover Rise DE21 .... 205 F1
Birchover Way DE22 .... 204 E2
Birch Rd S80 .... 82 C6
Birchside Ave SK13 .... 10 B2
Birch St NG20 .... 120 F6
Birch Vale DE56 .... 178 F5
Birch Vale Ind Est SK22 .... 25 A2
Birchvale Rd S12 .... 44 D3
Birch Vale Terr SK22 .... 24 F3
Birchview Cl DE56 .... 179 B2
Birch View Ct DE1 .... 218 F7
Birchway Gr DE23 .... 231 A6
Birchwood DE75 .... 181 C4
Birchwood Ave
Derby DE23 .... 231 D6
Long Eaton, Breaston NG10 .... 236 A7
Long Eaton, New Sawley NG10 .... 236 C5
Birchwood Cl
7 Sheffield S20 .... 59 E8
South Normanton DE55 .... 160 A4
Birchwood Cres
Chesterfield S40 .... 114 F7
Somercotes DE55 .... 170 D8
Birchwood Croft S20 .... 59 E8
Birchwood Ct S40 .... 114 F7
Birchwood Dr DE56 .... 168 B4
Birchwood Gdns 6 S20 .... 59 E8
Birchwood Gr S20 .... 59 E8
Birchwood La DE55 .... 159 E3
Birchwood Rd
Alfreton DE55 .... 159 C3
Eckington S21 .... 58 D4
Birchwood Rise 5 S20 .... 59 E8
Birchwood View
Ashbourne DE6 .... 173 C3
Sheffield S20 .... 59 E8
Birchwood Way
16 Sheffield S20 .... 59 E8
Somercotes DE55 .... 159 C1
Bircumshaw's Rd DE75 .... 181 E2
Birdcage Wlk DE22 .... 217 F6
Birdcroft La DE7 .... 208 F5
Birdholme Cres S40 .... 115 A8
Birdholme Inf Sch S40 .... 115 A7
Birding St NG19 .... 136 B1
Birdsgrove La
Ashbourne DE6 .... 172 D3
Mayfield DE6 .... 172 D4
Bird St S43 .... 78 F2
Birdwood St DE23 .... 218 F1
Birkdale Ave DE14 .... 254 A6
Birkdale Cl
Derby DE3 .... 218 A2
Ilkeston DE7 .... 194 D1
Birkdale Dr S40 .... 114 D8
Birk Hill Inf Sch S21 .... 59 B2
Birkin Ave S42 .... 115 C1
Birkin La
Grassmoor S42 .... 115 F2
Holmewood S42 .... 116 A3
Wingerworth S40, S42 .... 114 C1
Birkin La W S42 .... 115 F2
Birkinstyle Ave DE55 .... 146 F3
Birkinstyle La DE55 .... 146 E3
Birkland Ave NG19 .... 136 D3
Birks Cl S80 .... 82 D6
Birley Brook Dr S40 .... 95 B7
Birley Com Coll S12 .... 44 D2
Birley Com Prim Sch S12 .... 44 D3
Birley Croft S41 .... 95 B7
Birley La
Bamford S32 .... 40 F2
Sheffield S12 .... 44 D2
Birley Moor Ave S12 .... 44 E3
Birley Moor Cl S12 .... 44 E3
Birley Moor Cres S12 .... 44 E2
Birley Moor Dr S12 .... 44 E2
Birley Moor Pl S12 .... 44 E2
Birley Moor Rd S12 .... 44 E4
Birley Moor Way S12 .... 44 E2
Birley School Mews S13 .... 44 E5
Birley Spa Com Prim Sch S12 .... 44 F4
Birley Spa La S12 .... 44 F3
Birley St NG9 .... 223 D5
Birley Vale Ave S12 .... 44 C5
Birley Vale Cl S12 .... 44 C4
Birstall Cl S41 .... 95 C7
Biscay Ct DE21 .... 206 C2
Bishop's Ct DE73 .... 252 A7
Bishop's Dr DE21 .... 205 E2
Bishop's Gn DE22 .... 218 D3
Bishop's House Mus★ S8 .... 43 A4
Bishopdale Cl NG10 .... 236 A6
Bishopdale Dr S20 .... 59 A8
Bishopdale Rise S20 .... 59 A8
Bishop Lonsdale CE Prim Sch DE22 .... 218 E3
Bishopscourt Rd S8 .... 43 A5
Bishops Ct
Melbourne DE73 .... 252 B7
Sheffield S8 .... 43 B5
Bishops Gate DE11 .... 256 E2
Bishops La SK17 .... 84 E7
Bishop St
Alfreton DE55 .... 159 A5
Eastwood NG16 .... 182 F2
Bispham Dr NG9 .... 223 F2
Bitham Ct DE13 .... 240 C1
Bitham La DE13 .... 240 D1
Blaby Cl DE23 .... 231 E6
Blacka Moor Cres S17 .... 55 C6
Blacka Moor Rd S17 .... 55 C6
Blacka Moor View S17 .... 55 C6
Blackberry Ct S43 .... 80 D4
Blackberry Flats S20 .... 59 E7
Blackberry Way DE56 .... 179 F2
Blackbird Row DE56 .... 179 C1
Blackbrook La SK23 .... 47 E6
Blackburn Pl DE7 .... 194 E3
Blackcliff Field Cl S80 .... 82 A5
Blackdown Ave S40 .... 95 B5
Blackfordby St Margaret's CE Prim Sch DE11 .... 257 C1
Black Harry La S32 .... 71 B2
Black Hills Dr DE7 .... 208 F6
Blackmore St DE23 .... 231 F7
Blackmount Ct 5 DE24 .... 231 D3
Blackpit La DE6 .... 224 B8
Blackpool St DE14 .... 254 C8
Black Rock★ DE4 .... 155 A4
Blackrocks Ave DE4 .... 142 F7
Blackshaw Clough SK13 .... 10 E3
Blackshaw Rd SK13 .... 10 E2
Blacks La S42 .... 131 F7
Blacksmith's La
Egginton DE65 .... 241 A6
Newton Solney DE15 .... 248 E8
Woodville DE11 .... 256 F3
Blacksmith Croft DE5 .... 180 D7
Blacksmith La S44 .... 97 A3
Blacksmiths Cl
Glapwell S44 .... 118 C1
Netherseal DE12 .... 264 F7
Blacksmiths Yd
Darley Dale DE4 .... 127 E2
Rolleston DE13 .... 240 B4
Blacksmith Way NG20 .... 119 F2
Blackstock Cl S14 .... 43 D2
Blackstock Cres S14 .... 43 D2
Blackstock Dr S14 .... 43 D2
Blackstock Rd S14 .... 43 D4
Blackstone Cl DE55 .... 170 D7
Blackthorn Cl
Chesterfield S41 .... 115 D8
Derby DE21 .... 205 E2
Melbourne DE73 .... 252 A8
Blackthorn Dr NG16 .... 182 E2
Blackthorne Cl DE56 .... 179 F2
Blackthorn Rd DE15 .... 254 E6
Black Tor Rd DE4 .... 154 D8
Blackwall La DE6 .... 176 A8
Blackwell Ave DE7 .... 194 F5
Blackwell Com Prim Sch DE55 .... 147 F1
Blackwell La
Melbourne DE73 .... 252 A7
Monyash DE45 .... 107 B3
Blackwell Mill Cotts SK17 .... 87 A6
Blackwell Rd NG17 .... 148 E3
Bladon House Sch DE15 .... 248 B6
Bladon St DE15 .... 248 C4
Bladon View DE13 .... 241 A2
Blagdon Cl DE4 .... 127 C3
Blagreaves Ave DE23 .... 231 C5
Blagreaves La DE23 .... 231 C6
Blair Gr NG10 .... 223 A4
Blair Ho DE23 .... 231 C5
Blakebrook Dr DE73 .... 233 A3
Blake Ct NG10 .... 236 B5
Blakeley La DE65 .... 229 B2
Blakelow Dr DE65 .... 229 B3
Blakelow La DE4 .... 142 A3
Blakemere La DE4 .... 141 F1

Blakemore Ave DE73 . . . . 252 B8
Blakeney Ct
  Derby DE21 . . . . 206 C1
  3 Mansfield Woodhouse
  NG19. . . . . 136 E4
Blake Rd NG9 . . . . 223 E6
Blake St
  Ilkeston DE7 . . . . . . 194 F1
  Mansfield Woodhouse
  NG19. . . . . 136 B2
Blanch Croft DE73 . . . . 252 B7
Blandford Ave NG10. . . . 236 B6
Blandford Cl DE24 . . . . 233 D6
Blandford Dr S41 . . . . . 95 E7
Blankney Cl DE24 . . . . . 231 D2
Blay Ct S43 . . . . 77 C4
Bleaklow Wlk 29 SK13. . . . 9 E1
Blencathra Dr DE3 . . . . 230 E8
Blenheim Ave DE55 . . . . 170 A8
Blenheim Cl
  Burton u T DE15. . . . . 248 C3
  4 Glossop SK13. . . . . 10 A5
  Mansfield NG19. . . . . 136 D1
  3 Swadlincote DE11 . . . 256 A7
Blenheim Ct DE56 . . . . . 179 D5
Blenheim Dr DE22 . . . . 204 D4
Blenheim Ho 1 DE14 . . . 253 F7
Blenheim Mews DE55 . . . 229 C4
Blenheim Par DE22 . . . . 204 D4
Blenheim Pl NG17. . . . . 148 E3
Blenheim Rd DE6 . . . . . 185 E7
Blenhiem Ct 3 NG10. . . . 223 B4
Blind La
  Bolsover S44 . . . . . . 98 F3
  Breaston DE72. . . . . . 235 D8
  Darley Dale DE4 . . . . . 127 F1
  Kirk Ireton DE6 . . . . . 165 A2
  Wirksworth DE4 . . . . . 165 F8
Blisworth Way DE55 . . . 169 F8
Blithe Cl DE65 . . . . . . 228 E1
Blithfield Gdns DE73 . . . 233 A2
Bloomery Way S45. . . . . 131 E3
Bloomfield Cl
  Derby DE1 . . . . 267 C1
  Hilton DE65 . . . . 228 D1
Bloomfield Rd DE55 . . . . 170 A8
Bloomfield St DE1 . . . . . 267 D1
Bloomsgrove Rd DE7. . . . 194 F2
Bloom St DE1 . . . . 267 B2
Blore Cl DE6. . . . . 185 D8
Blossom Cres S12. . . . . . 44 B3
Blossom Wlk DE65 . . . . 227 C1
Bluebank View S43 . . . . . 77 D3
Bluebell Cl
  Barlborough S43 . . . . . 80 B6
  Derby DE24 . . . . 231 D2
  Donisthorpe DE12 . . . . 262 E1
  Hayfield SK22 . . . . . . 25 C3
  Shirebrook NG20. . . . . 119 D3
  Somercotes DE55 . . . . 159 E2
  Underwood Green NG16 . 171 F2
Blue Bell Cl S43 . . . . . . 97 B5
Bluebell Croft DE4 . . . . 143 B3
Bluebell Hill DE55 . . . . 146 C4
Bluebell Pl NG19. . . . . . 136 F4
Bluebell Way DE75 . . . . 182 B1
Blueberry Cl S43. . . . . . 97 B5
Blueberry Way DE11 . . . 256 F3
Bluebird Ct DE24. . . . . 231 D4
Blue Cedars Dr DE15 . . . 248 B7
Blue Lodge Cl S43 . . . . . 97 B5
Blue Mountains DE56 . . . 191 B1
Bluestone La DE15 . . . . 255 A7
Blundestone La DE4. . . . 156 A2
Blunt Ave S43 . . . . 79 C4
Blunt St DE7. . . . . 193 A2
Blyth Cl
  Chesterfield S40 . . . . . 114 B8
  Mansfield NG19. . . . . 135 D1
Blyth Ct DE74. . . . . . . 247 B4
Blythe Ct NG19 . . . . . . 135 D1
Blyth Pl DE21 . . . . 205 D1
Boam La DE4 . . . . 142 F8
Boardman Ind Est DE11 . . 255 E3
Boardman Rd DE11 . . . . 255 E3
Boarfold La SK13, SK14. . . 15 E5
Boars Head Ind Est DE1 . . 267 C4
Boarslack La SK17 . . . . . 69 F2
Boarstones La SK17 . . . . 85 E8
Boat La NG16. . . . . . . 182 A7
Boatmans Cl DE7 . . . . . 194 F2
Bobbin Mill Cl S17 . . . . . 89 A6
Bobbinmill Hill DE56. . . . 168 B7
Bobbin Mill La S40. . . . . 95 D2
Bobbin Way DE56 . . . . . 179 C5
Bochum Parkway S8. . . . . 57 C8
Bocking La S8. . . . . 56 E8
Bocking Rise S8. . . . . . . 56 E8
Boden St DE23 . . . . . . 219 B2
Bodmin Cl DE24 . . . . . 231 D3
Bodmin Way 3 S40. . . . . 95 C5
Boggard La SK13. . . . . . 16 D6
Bogguard Rd SK6. . . . . . 24 A4
Boggy La
  Bradwell S33. . . . . . . 51 B6
  Church Broughton DE65 . 227 A7
  Church Broughton, Heathtop
  DE65. . . . . 227 A6
Bog La DE73. . . . . 251 E5
Bohem Rd NG10. . . . . . 223 C3
Boiley La S21. . . . . 60 C4
Boland Rd S8. . . . . 56 D5
Bolden Terr DE1 . . . . . 147 C1
Bold La DE1 . . . . 267 B3
Bole Hill S8 . . . . 43 A2
Bole Hill Cotts S44. . . . . 97 A1
Bolehill Croft DE4. . . . . 155 A3

Bolehill Ct 3 S40. . . . . . 95 D5
Bolehill La
  Eckington S21 . . . . . . 58 F2
  Northedge S42. . . . . . 130 C7
  Wingerworth S42 . . . . 114 D1
Bolehill Rd DE4 . . . . . . 155 A3
Bolsover Bsns Pk S44. . . . 98 E2
Bolsover Castle ★ S44. . . . 99 A2
Bolsover CE Jun Sch S44. . 99 A2
Bolsover Cl DE5 . . . . . . 169 E1
Bolsover Hill S44. . . . . . 99 A2
Bolsover Inf Sch S44. . . . 99 A2
Bolsover Local Hospl S44 99 C2
Bolsover Rd
  Mastin Moor S43. . . . . 79 D2
  Shuttlewood S44 . . . . . 98 F6
Bolsover Sch The S44. . . . 99 C1
Bolton St DE55. . . . . . 169 D7
Boman's La DE56. . . . . 177 F8
Bonchurch Cl DE24 . . . . 233 C5
Bondfield Rd S43 . . . . . . 97 C7
Bondgate DE74. . . . . . 247 B3
Bondhay La S80 . . . . . . 62 C2
Bond La DE56. . . . . . . 168 E2
Bond St S43 . . . . 97 C8
Bonington Rise SK6. . . . . 23 B8
Bonner's Rd NG16. . . . . 195 C4
Bonnington Dr DE55 . . . 170 D8
Bonnyrigg Dr DE21. . . . 206 A2
Bonsall Ave DE23 . . . . . 231 D8
Bonsall CE Prim Sch
  DE4. . . . . 142 E1
Bonsall Cl SK13. . . . . . . 9 E2
Bonsall Dr
  2 Chesterfield S41 . . . . 95 D7
  Long Eaton NG10. . . . . 236 F8
Bonsall Fold SK13. . . . . . 9 E2
Bonsall La
  Alfreton DE55 . . . . . . 158 F4
  Winster DE4 . . . . . . 141 C4
Bonsallmoor La DE4 . . . 141 E3
Bonsall St NG10. . . . . . 236 E8
Bonser Cres NG17. . . . . 148 E2
Booth's Ct 1 SK13. . . . . 10 D1
Booth Ave NG19 . . . . . 135 A5
Boothby Ave 1 DE6. . . . 173 C4
Booth Cres NG19. . . . . 135 D2
Booth Dr DE6. . . . . . . 185 C8
Boothgate DE56. . . . . . 179 E7
Boot Hill DE56 . . . . . . 242 C3
Booth St
  Derby DE24 . . . . 232 F7
  Hollingworth SK14. . . . 9 C5
  Mansfield Woodhouse
  NG19. . . . . 136 B3
  Ripley DE5 . . . . 169 E2
Booth Trad Est NE7 . . . . 194 F2
Boots Yd NG17. . . . . . 148 F3
Border Cl S43 . . . . 80 F3
Border Cres DE24 . . . . . 233 B5
Border La S80 . . . . 80 F2
Borlace Cres NG9. . . . . 223 E6
Borough St DE74. . . . . 247 B3
Borrowash By-pass
  DE72. . . . . 221 C3
Borrowash By-pass DE72 . 220 F4
Borrowdale Ave 3 S20. . . 59 E6
Borrowdale Cl 2 S20 . . . 59 E6
Borrowdale Dr
  Long Eaton NG10. . . . . 236 A6
  Sheffield S20. . . . . . . 59 E6
Borrowdale Rd S20. . . . . 59 E6
Borrowfield Rd DE21. . . . 220 F3
Borrowfields DE72. . . . . 221 B1
Borrow Wood Inf Sch
  DE21. . . . . 220 F5
Borrow Wood Jun Sch
  DE21. . . . . 220 F5
Boscastle Rd DE24 . . . . 233 B6
Boscawen Ct NE7. . . . . 194 F4
Boscowan Ct DE7 . . . . . 194 F4
Bosley Mews DE56. . . . . 178 F5
Bostock's La
  Long Eaton NG10. . . . . 223 A3
  Risley DE72. . . . . . . 222 F4
Bostock Rd SK14. . . . . . 16 A8
Boston Cl DE24 . . . . . . 220 C6
Boswell Ct 3 DE6. . . . . 173 B2
Boswell Sq DE23 . . . . . 231 F7
Bosworth Ave DE23 . . . . 231 E6
Bosworth Rd DE74 . . . . 246 F3
Bosworth Way NG10. . . . 236 B5
Bothe Cl NG10. . . . . . . 223 B1
Bottlebrook Houses DE5 180 B1
Bottomhill Rd SK17. . . . . 69 E1
Bottom Lons DE56 . . . . 176 B8
Bottom Rd S42. . . . . . . 114 E1
Boughton Dr DE55 . . . . 169 F8
Boughton La S43 . . . . . 80 D4
Bould St NG19 . . . . . . 135 F1
Boulevard The SK14. . . . . 9 D4
Boulton Cl S40 . . . . . . 95 A5
Boulton Dr DE24 . . . . . 233 A6
Boulton La
  Derby, Allenton DE24. . . 232 F5
  Derby DE24 . . . . 233 A6
Boulton Prim Sch DE24 . 233 A6
Boundary Cl
  Shirebrook NG20 . . . . . 119 E6
  Staveley S43 . . . . 79 A3
Boundary Gdns DE55 . . . 147 F5

Boundary La NG16. . . . . 182 C3
Boundary Rd
  Derby DE22 . . . . 218 E4
  Egginton DE65. . . . . . 241 D8
Boundary Wlk NG20. . . . 100 F1
Bournebrook Ave DE4. . . 165 F7
Bourne Cl
  Brimington S43 . . . . . . 96 E8
  Tutbury DE13. . . . . . . 239 B6
Bourne Dr NG16. . . . . . 182 B3
Bourne Mill Cl S43. . . . . 80 B6
Bourne Sq DE72 . . . . . 235 E7
Bourne St DE1 . . . . . . 267 B2
Bourne Way DE1 . . . . . 256 D4
Bowbank Cl DE23 . . . . . 231 A6
Bowbridge Ave DE23 . . . 231 C5
Bowden Cl SK22 . . . . . . 25 C3
Bowden Cres SK22 . . . . . 33 D8
Bowden Hey Rd SK23. . . . 47 C7
Bowden La
  Chapel-en-le-F SK23. . . . 47 C7
  Hope S33. . . . . 39 A4
Bowden Rd SK13. . . . . . 10 C3
Bowdon Ave S43 . . . . . 80 A6
Bower Dr DE4 . . . . . . 156 F1
Bower Farm Rd S41. . . . . 77 B2
Bower St DE24 . . . . . . 232 F8
Boweswell Rd DE7. . . . . 194 E2
Bowland Cl DE3. . . . . . 217 E1
Bowland Dr S40 . . . . . . 114 B7
Bowland Rd SK13. . . . . . 17 A8
Bowlees Ct DE23 . . . . . 230 E7
Bowler Dr DE56. . . . . . 192 A7
Bowler La
  Darley Dale DE4 . . . . . 143 B8
  Matlock DE4. . . . . . . 143 B8
Bowler Rd DE4 . . . . . . 127 C3
Bowler St DE5 . . . . . . 180 D7
Bowling Alley S43. . . . . 168 E1
Bowlingalley La DE56 . . . 197 D8
Bowling Alley La DE6 . . . 212 A5
Bowling Cl DE7 . . . . . . 222 E8
Bowling Gn DE4 . . . . . 153 A1
Bowling Green La DE4 . . 154 E1
Bowman Cl S12. . . . . . . 43 F2
Bowmer La DE56. . . . . . 168 B6
Bowmer Rd DE24 . . . . . 219 E1
Bown Cl DE56. . . . . . . 192 A8
Bowness Cl
  Chesterfield S41 . . . . . 95 D7
  Dronfield S18. . . . . . . 56 E1
Bowness Rd S41 . . . . . . 95 D7
Bowns Hill S44 . . . . . . 157 A1
Bowns Yd DE55 . . . . . . 170 D8
Bowshaw S18 . . . . 56 F4
Bowshaw Ave S8 . . . . . . 57 A5
Bowshaw Cl S8. . . . . . . 57 A5
Bowshaw S8 . . . . 57 A5
Bowshaw W8 . . . . 57 A5
Bow St NG19 . . . . 136 E4
Box Cl S41 . . . . 256 E3
Boxmoor Cl DE23 . . . . . 230 F7
Boyd Gr DE73. . . . . . . 245 A8
Boyer St DE1 . . . . 267 A1
Boyer Wlk DE22. . . . . . 267 A1
Boylestone Rd DE23 . . . . 231 C5
Boythorpe Ave S40 . . . . 266 A2
Boythorpe Bsns Units S40 95 E2
Boythorpe Cres S40. . . . 266 A1
Boythorpe Mount S40. . . 266 A2
Boythorpe Rd S40 . . . . . 266 A2
Boythorpe Rise S40. . . . . 95 E2
Brabyns Brow SK6 . . . . . 23 A7
Bracken's La DE24 . . . . 232 F6
Bracken Ave S44. . . . . . 116 F1
Bracken Cl
  Hollingworth SK14. . . . . 9 D6
  Long Eaton NG10. . . . . 223 B1
  Marple SK6. . . . . 23 C7
Brackendale Ave S45 . . . 131 E2
Brackendale Cl S43. . . . . 96 D7
Brackendale La DE6. . . . 163 E5
Brackendale Rd DE56 . . . 169 F8
Brackenfield Ave NG19. . . 136 E6
Brackenfield Dr NG16. . . 195 B7
Brackenfield Gr S12 . . . . 44 D3
Brackenfield La
  Brackenfield DE55. . . . . 145 D1
  Wessington DE55 . . . . 157 D8
Brackenfield Specl Sch
  NG10. . . . . 223 B1
Bracken La DE4 . . . . . . 156 B5
Bracken Rd
  Long Eaton NG10. . . . . 223 B1
  Shirebrook NG20. . . . . 119 D3
Brackens Ave DE24 . . . . 232 F5
Brackenwood Rd DE15 . . 254 E6
Brackensdale Ave DE22 . . 218 B5
Brackensdale Inf Sch
  DE22. . . . . 218 B6
Brackensdale Jun Sch
  DE22. . . . . 218 B6
Brackens La S43. . . . . . 80 B6
Brackley DE56 . . . . . . 179 F1
Brackley Dr DE21. . . . . 220 E5
Brackley Gate DE7 . . . . 192 A2
Brackmills Cl 7 NG19. . . 136 E1
Bracknell Dr DE24 . . . . 232 F5
Bradbourne Cl DE22 . . . 218 E3
Bradbury Cl
  Borrowash DE72 . . . . . 221 C1
  Chesterfield S40 . . . . . 95 E3
Bradbury Dr S42. . . . . . 114 E4
Bradbury St S8 . . . . 43 A6
Braddon Ave NG9 . . . . . 209 E1
Bradgate Cl NG10 . . . . . 223 B4
Bradgate Croft S41 . . . . 115 C7

Bradgate Ct DE23 . . . . . 231 E6
Bradgate Dr DE5 . . . . . 169 B1
Brading Cl DE24 . . . . . 233 D5
Bradley CE Prim Sch
  DE6. . . . . 186 F8
Bradley Cl
  Birchover DE4 . . . . . . 126 B1
  6 Brimington S43. . . . . 96 E8
Bradley Dr DE56 . . . . . 179 B4
Bradley La S18 . . . . 75 C4
Bradley St
  Burton u T DE15. . . . . 254 E7
  Derby DE22 . . . . 218 E8
  Sandiacre NG10. . . . . . 223 C5
Bradley View 5 DE6. . . . 173 D3
Bradley Way S41 . . . . . . 96 F1
Bradmoor Gr DE73 . . . . 233 B2
Bradshaw Ave S55. . . . . 170 E6
Bradshaw Cres SK6. . . . . 23 A7
Bradshaw Croft DE56 . . . 178 E6
Bradshaw Dr DE56 . . . . 191 C6
Bradshaw La
  Old Brampton S42 . . . . 93 E2
  Stoney Middleton S32 . . . 70 E8
Bradshaw Mdw DE65 . . . 227 C1
Bradshaw Rd
  Marple SK6. . . . . 23 A7
  Staveley S43 . . . . 97 B6
Bradshaw St NG10. . . . . 236 B5
Bradshaw Way DE1 . . . . 267 C2
Bradway Cl S17. . . . . . . 56 B5
Bradway Dr S17. . . . . . . 56 B5
Bradway Grange Rd S17. . . 56 C5
Bradway Rd
  Sheffield, Bradway S17. . . 56 B5
  Sheffield, Lower Bradway
  S17. . . . . 56 C6
Bradwell CE Inf Sch S33. . 51 B7
Bradwell Cl
  Derby DE3 . . . . 217 E1
  Dronfield S18. . . . . . . 56 C1
  Eastwood NG16 . . . . . 195 C8
Bradwell Cl 4 S40. . . . . 95 D5
Bradwell Fold 10 SK13. . . 9 E1
Bradwell Gr S45 . . . . . . 131 D2
Bradwell Head Rd S33. . . 51 A8
Bradwell Jun Sch S33. . . . 51 A7
Bradwell Lea 12 SK13. . . . 9 E1
Bradwell Pl S43 . . . . . . 97 C7
Bradwell Terr 11 S2. . . . . 43 B6
Bradwell St 1 S2. . . . . . 43 B6
Bradwell Way DE56 . . . . 179 B5
Braeburn Cl S43 . . . . . . 218 E2
Braefield Cl DE7 . . . . . 208 C5
Braemar Ave NG16 . . . . 182 F1
Braemar Cl
  Chesterfield S43 . . . . . 77 D4
  11 Derby DE24 . . . . . 231 D3
Brafield Cl DE56 . . . . . 179 D4
Brailsford Ave
  4 Gamesley SK13. . . . . 9 E2
  1 Swadlincote DE11 . . . 255 E5
Brailsford CE Prim Sch
  DE6. . . . . 201 E7
Brailsford Cl 7 SK13. . . . 9 E2
Brailsford Gdns 8 SK13. . . 9 E1
Brailsford Gn 5 SK13. . . . 9 E1
Brailsford Mews 6 SK13. . . 9 E1
Brailsford Rd DE21 . . . . 219 F8
Braintree Cl DE21 . . . . . 205 D2
Braithwell Cl DE22 . . . . 204 F2
Bramah Edge Ct SK13 . . . 9 F7
Bramall Cl S2 . . . . 43 A8
Bramall La S2 . . . . 43 A8
Bramble Bank SK13 . . . . 17 C6
Brambleberry Ct DE21. . . 206 B3
Bramble Cl
  Holmewood S44. . . . . . 116 F1
  Long Eaton NG10. . . . . 223 B2
  Shirebrook NG20. . . . . 119 E6
  South Normanton DE55. . 160 B6
Bramble Ct DE15 . . . . . 254 E6
Bramble Mews 2 DE3 . . . 217 D1
Bramble St DE1. . . . . . 267 A3
Bramble Way
  Kilburn DE56 . . . . . . 179 E6
  South Normanton DE55. . 159 F3
Bramblewick Dr DE23 . . . 231 A6
Bramble Wlk DE12. . . . . 262 A3
Bramblewood 5 DE11. . . 255 F6
Brambling Cres S41 . . . . 96 C2
Brambling DE14 . . . . . . 253 F7
Bramfield Ave DE22 . . . . 218 E3
Bramfield Ct DE22 . . . . 218 E4
Bramham Rd SK6 . . . . . 23 A4
Bramley Ave S13. . . . . . 44 F8
Bramley Cl
  Derby DE21 . . . . 206 C3
  Sheffield S20. . . . . . . 59 C7
  Staveley S43 . . . . 97 B5
Bramley Ct
  Hatton DE65 . . . . 227 C1
  Kimberley NG16. . . . . 195 F6
Bramley Dale DE11. . . . . 255 F2
Bramley Hall Rd S13 . . . . 44 F8
Bramley La
  Baslow DE45 . . . . 91 C7
  Sheffield S13. . . . . . . 44 F8
Bramley Mews S21. . . . . 59 D3
Bramleymoor La S21. . . . 58 E1
Bramley Park Cl S13 . . . . 44 F8
Bramley Pk S21. . . . . . . 58 F3
Bramley Rd
  Bramley-Vale S44 . . . . . 117 D4
  Eckington S21 . . . . . . 58 E1
Bramley St DE55 . . . . . 170 E7

Bramley Vale Prim Sch
  S44. . . . . 117 E1
Bramlyn Cl S43 . . . . . . 80 D5
Bramlyn Cl S43 . . . . . . 80 D5
Brampton Ave DE75. . . . 182 A2
Brampton Cl DE3 . . . . . 217 C3
Brampton Ct
  Belper DE56. . . . . . . 179 D4
  Chesterfield S40 . . . . . 95 C2
Brampton Dr NG9. . . . . 223 F5
Brampton House Mews
  S40. . . . . 95 D3
Brampton Prim Sch S40. . 95 E3
Bramshill Rise S40. . . . . 95 D1
Branch La S45 . . . . 132 F5
Brancliffe La S81 . . . . . . 63 F8
Brandelhow Ct DE21. . . . 206 C3
Brandene Cl S45. . . . . . 97 A3
Brandreth Dr NG16. . . . 195 A8
Branklene Cl NG16 . . . . 195 E7
Branksome Ave DE24. . . 233 C7
Branksome Chine Ave
  S41. . . . . 115 C8
Bransdale Ave NG19 . . . . 136 E1
Bransdale Cl NG10 . . . . 236 B6
Branston Rd
  Burton u T DE14. . . . . 254 C8
  Tatenhill DE13, DE14. . . 253 C8
Branton Cl S40 . . . . . . 266 A1
Brassington Cl
  Eastwood NG16. . . . . . 195 B7
  West Hallam DE7 . . . . . 207 E8
  Youlgreave DE45 . . . . . 125 C5
Brassington Cres 4 NG19. 136 E1
Brassington La S42, S45. . 131 C6
Brassington Prim Sch
  DE4. . . . . 153 A1
Brassington Rd DE21. . . . 205 F1
Brassington St S45. . . . . 131 D4
Braybrook Ct DE55 . . . . 169 F8
Brayfield Ave DE23 . . . . 231 D8
Brayfield Rd DE23. . . . . 231 C8
Breach La
  Barrow u T DE73 . . . . . 244 E1
  Hatton DE65 . . . . 227 D3
  Scropton DE6. . . . . . . 226 C5
Breach Rd
  Denby DE5. . . . . 181 A4
  Heanor DE7 . . . . 194 A8
Breadsall CE Prim Sch
  DE21. . . . . 205 E4
Breadsall Cl DE11 . . . . . 256 A7
Breadsall Dr DE7. . . . . . 194 F3
Breadsall Hill Top Inf Sch
  DE21. . . . . 205 E1
Breadsall Hill Top Jun Sch
  DE21. . . . . 205 E1
Breamfield La DE4 . . . . 166 B8
Brearley Ave S41 . . . . . . 77 B3
Brearley Ct S41 . . . . . . 77 B3
Brearley Hall S41 . . . . . 77 C4
Brearley St S41 . . . . . . 77 C4
Breaston Ind Est DE72. . . 235 C7
Breaston La DE72. . . . . 222 D3
Brechin Ct NG19 . . . . . 136 B6
Breck La S21, S43. . . . . . 78 C6
Breckland Rd S40, S42. . . 114 B8
Brecknock Dr NG10 . . . . 236 A7
Brecon Cl
  Chesterfield S40 . . . . . 95 C5
  Derby DE21 . . . . 220 E6
  6 Long Eaton NG10. . . . 236 A8
Bredon Cl 7 NG10 . . . . 236 A8
Breedon Ave DE23 . . . . 231 D8
Breedon Hill Rd DE23 . . . 218 F3
Breedon on the Hill St
  Hardulph's CE Prim Sch
  DE73. . . . . 252 F3
Breedon St NG10 . . . . . 223 C2
Brendan Gdns DE22 . . . . 204 E1
Brenden Ave DE55 . . . . 170 C7
Brenden Cl DE55 . . . . . 170 C8
Brendon Ave S44 . . . . . 95 C4
Brendon Cl SK13. . . . . . 17 A8
Brendon Ct 3 S40 . . . . . 95 C4
Brendon Dr NG16 . . . . . 195 F7
Brendon Way NG10 . . . . 223 A1
Brent Cl S41 . . . . 95 D5
Brentford Dr DE22 . . . . 218 B6
Brentnall Cl NG10 . . . . 236 B7
Brentwood Ave S33 . . . . 40 B3
Brentwood Rd S33 . . . . . 40 B3
Bren Way DE65. . . . . . 228 C2
Bretby Bsns Pk DE15 . . . 255 F8
Bretby Fairways DE15 . . . 248 F2
Bretby Hollow DE11. . . . 255 F7
Bretby Hts DE11 . . . . . 256 A8
Bretby La
  Bretby DE15. . . . . . . 248 E3
  Burton u T DE15. . . . . 248 D2
Bretby Rd
  Chesterfield S40 . . . . . 95 A6
  Swadlincote DE11 . . . . 255 F7
Bretby Sq DE23 . . . . . . 231 C5
Bretby View DE11 . . . . . 257 A4
Bretlands Way DE15. . . . 255 A6
Bretton Ave
  Bolsover S44 . . . . 99 C2
  Derby DE23 . . . . 218 C2
Bretton Cl S40. . . . . . . 95 A5
Bretton Gr S12 . . . . 44 D3
Bretton Rd DE56 . . . . . 179 E5

Brewery St
Chesterfield S41 . . . . .266 C3
Kimberley NG16 . . . . .195 F6
Breydon Cl DE24 . . . . .232 D4
Breydon Ind Ctr NG10 . . .236 F7
Brian Clough Way
Derby DE21 . . . . .220 C4
Risley DE72 . . . . .222 C3
Stapleford NG9 . . . . .223 D5
Briar's La DE4 . . . . .168 A7
Briar Ave NG10 . . . . .223 A3
Briar Briggs Rd S44 . . . . . .98 F3
Briar Cl
Alfreton DE55 . . . . .159 C3
Borrowash DE72 . . . . .221 C2
Chesterfield S41 . . . . .95 E5
Derby DE21 . . . . .220 B5
Shirebrook NG20 . . . . .119 E2
Swadlincote DE11 . . . . . . .255 F5
Briardene Cl S40 . . . . .94 F5
Briarfield Ave S12 . . . . .44 A3
Briarfield Cres S12 . . . . . . .44 A2
Briarfield Rd S12 . . . . .44 A3
Briar Gate NG10 . . . . .223 B1
Briargrove Rd SK22 . . . . . . .24 C4
Briar Lea Cl DE24 . . . . .231 F4
Briar Rd NG16 . . . . .195 B8
Briars Cl S21 . . . . .60 D5
Briarsgate DE22 . . . . .204 D2
Briars Way DE5 . . . . .180 D8
Briar View S43 . . . . .96 E7
Briarwood Cl SK6 . . . . .23 A3
Briarwood Way DE23 . . . .231 C6
Brickbridge Rd SK6 . . . . . . .23 A3
Brickfields Cl DE4 . . . . . . .155 A4
Brickfield St SK13 . . . . .10 B5
Brickhouse La S17 . . . . .55 C8
Brickhouse Yd S40 . . . . .95 E3
Brickkiln La DE7 . . . . .206 C8
Brick-kiln La
Brailsford DE6 . . . . .186 F1
Hulland Ward DE6 . . . . . . .175 C5
Brick Kiln La DE13 . . . . . . .240 A3
Brick Row DE22 . . . . .205 A1
Brick St DE1 . . . . .218 E6
Brickyard Cotts DE6 . . . . .185 D8
Brickyard La
Kilburn DE56 . . . . .179 F2
Ripley DE5 . . . . .169 F1
South Normanton DE55 . . .160 A6
Brickyard Rd DE56 . . . . . .168 C5
Brickyard The DE7 . . . . . .193 B1
Bricky Cl S43 . . . . .80 D5
Bridge Bank Cl ⬛ S40. . . . .95 D6
Bridge Cl
Swadlincote DE11 . . . . . . .256 C2
Whitwell S80 . . . . .82 A5
Bridge End Ave NG16 . . . .171 F8
Bridge Farm ⬛ DE13 . . . . .240 E1
Bridgefield ⬛ SK13 . . . . . . .17 B8
Bridge Field DE72 . . . . . . .235 C7
Bridgefield Ct ⬛ DE56 . . . .178 F4
Bridge Foot DE56 . . . . . . .178 F5
Bridge Hill DE56 . . . . .178 E5
Bridgeholm Mill SK23 . . . . .47 A8
Bridgend Cl NG9 . . . . .223 D5
Bridgend Ct DE21 . . . . . . .206 C2
Bridgeness Rd DE23 . . . . .230 F6
Bridgeport Rd DE21 . . . . . .220 C6
Bridgeside DE13 . . . . .240 E1
Bridge St
Bakewell DE45 . . . . .109 D6
Belper DE56 . . . . .178 F4
Bradwell S33 . . . . .51 A7
Burton u T, Stretton DE13 .240 E1
Buxton SK17 . . . . .85 C8
Chesterfield S40 . . . . .266 B1
Clay Cross S45 . . . . .131 C3
Derby DE1 . . . . .267 A4
Ilkeston DE7 . . . . .194 F4
Killamarsh S21 . . . . .60 D6
Langley Mill NG16 . . . . . . .182 C3
Linton DE11 . . . . .261 E8
Long Eaton NG10 . . . . .223 D1
New Mills SK22 . . . . .24 C1
Pilsley S45 . . . . .132 C2
Sandiacre NG10. . . . . .223 C5
Swadlincote DE11 . . . . . . .256 C2
Tupton S42 . . . . .115 D1
Tutbury DE13 . . . . .239 C7
Whaley Bridge SK23 . . . . . .45 E7
Bridge View
Belper DE56 . . . . .191 A7
Mayfield DE6 . . . . .184 D8
Bridgewater St S42 . . . . . .115 C1
Bridgeway SK23 . . . . .47 B4
Bridge Way S41 . . . . .76 D3
Bridgford Ave DE14 . . . . .253 F7
Bridgnorth Way NG9 . . . .223 B3
Bridgwater Cl DE24 . . . . . .233 C7
Bridle Cl DE73 . . . . .233 A1
Bridle La
Ripley, Greenwich DE5. . . .169 E2
Ripley, Lower Hartshay DE5,
DE56. . . . . .169 A2
Somercotes DE55 . . . . .170 B7
Swadlincote DE15 . . . . . . .170 A5
Bridle Rd
Bolsover S44 . . . . .80 B1
Staveley S43 . . . . .79 B2
Bridle Stile S20 . . . . .59 C7
Bridle Stile Cl S20 . . . . .59 C7
Bridle Stile Gdns S20 . . . . .59 B7
Bridleway SK22 . . . . .24 D1
Bridleway The NG19 . . . . .136 F1

Brierfield Way DE3 . . . . . .230 E8
Brierley Cl S43 . . . . .78 E1
Brierley Pk SK23 . . . . .34 B1
Brierley Rd
Stonebroom DE55 . . . . . . .146 F3
Unstone Green S18 . . . . . . .76 E6
Brierlow Bar SK17 . . . . . . .105 B8
Brigden Ave DE24 . . . . . . .232 E1
Brigg Inf Sch The DE55 . . .160 B6
Brighstone Cl DE24 . . . . . .233 C5
Brightman Ho DE11 . . . . . .256 B5
Bright Mdw S20 . . . . .60 A5
Brighton Rd DE24 . . . . . . .232 F8
Bright Sq NG19 . . . . .135 D2
Bright St
Derby DE22 . . . . .218 D5
Ilkeston DE7 . . . . .194 E3
Kimberley NG16 . . . . .195 E6
North Wingfield S42 . . . . . .131 F6
South Normanton DE55. . . .159 F5
Brigmor Wlk DE24 . . . . . . .218 C5
Brimington Cl NE7 . . . . . . .194 F6
Brimington Ct ⬛ NG19 . . . .136 E4
Brimington Jun Sch S43 . . .96 D8
Brimington Rd S41 . . . . . . .96 B5
Brimington Rd N S41 . . . . .96 B8
Brimmesfield Cl S2 . . . . . . .43 F7
Brimmesfield Dr S2 . . . . . . .43 E8
Brimmesfield Rd S2 . . . . . . .43 E7
Brincliffe Cl S40 . . . . .95 B1
Brindle Way DE23 . . . . . . .231 A5
Brindley Cl S8 . . . . .43 A4
Brindley Cres S8 . . . . .43 A4
Brindley Ct S21 . . . . .60 C6
Brindley Ho
Chesterfield S41 . . . . .96 B6
Long Eaton NG10 . . . . .223 B3
Brindley Rd ⬛ S41 . . . . . . .96 A6
Brindley Way S43 . . . . .78 F2
Brindley Wlk DE24 . . . . . . .231 E2
Brinkburn Cl S17 . . . . .55 F6
Brinkburn Cl S17 . . . . .55 F6
Brinkburn Dr S17 . . . . .55 F6
Brinkburn Vale Rd S17 . . . .55 F6
Brinsley Hill NG16 . . . . . . .171 C2
Brinsley Prim Sch NG16 . .182 D8
Brisbane Cl NG19 . . . . . . .136 C6
Brisbane Dr NG9 . . . . .209 F1
Brisbane Rd DE3 . . . . .217 F3
Briset Cl DE24 . . . . .231 E2
Bristol Dr DE3 . . . . .217 E2
Bristol Rd DE7 . . . . .194 E1
Britannia Ave DE5 . . . . . . .181 A7
Britannia Ct DE1 . . . . .267 B4
Britannia Dr DE13 . . . . . . .240 D1
Britannia Rd
Chesterfield S40 . . . . .115 B7
Long Eaton NG10 . . . . .223 D1
Briton Lodge Cl DE12 . . . .262 F4
Brittain Dr DE5 . . . . .170 A1
Brittain Pit Farm* DE5. . . .170 A1
Brixham Ct ⬛ S41 . . . . .95 F8
Brizlincote La DE15 . . . . . .248 D1
Broad Bank DE22 . . . . .218 E8
Broadbottom CE Prim Sch
SK14 . . . . .15 F8
Broadbottom Sta SK14 . . . .16 A8
Broadfield Rd S2 . . . . .43 A7
Broadfields Cl DE22 . . . . . .218 E8
Broadgorse Cl S40 . . . . . . .114 F7
Broadhey View SK22 . . . . . .24 B1
Broadholme La DE56 . . . . .179 A8
Broad La
Brinsley NG16 . . . . .182 E8
Creswell S80 . . . . .82 D6
Elvaston DE72 . . . . .233 F4
Broadlands
Sandiacre NG10. . . . . .223 B3
South Normanton DE55. . . .160 A4
Broadleaf Cl DE21 . . . . . . .205 E2
Broadley Rd S13 . . . . .44 C7
Broadleys S45 . . . . .131 C3
Broadmeadow DE4 . . . . . . .127 C3
Broadmeadows Sh Ctr
DE55. . . . . .160 A4
Broad Oak Dr
Brinsley NG16 . . . . .182 E8
Stapleford NG9 . . . . .223 D6
Broadoaks Cl S41 . . . . .266 C3
Broad Pavement S40. . . . . .266 B3
Broad Pl S80 . . . . .82 C6
Broad Rushes DE74 . . . . . .247 B6
Broad St NG10 . . . . .236 D7
Broadstairs Rd ⬛ NG9 . . . .223 F2
Broadstone Cl DE21 . . . . . .206 A1
Broadstone La DE73 . . . . . .251 D4
Broadway
Derby DE22 . . . . .218 E8
Duffield DE56 . . . . .190 E2
Heanor DE75 . . . . .181 E1
Ilkeston DE7 . . . . .194 E3
Ripley DE5 . . . . .169 E1
Swanwick DE55 . . . . .169 F7
Broad Way DE6 . . . . .176 B8
Broadway Ave DE5 . . . . . . .169 E1
Broadway La SK17 . . . . .88 A5
Broadway Park Cl DE22 . . .218 E8
Broadway St DE14 . . . . . . .254 C4
Broad Wlk
Buxton SK17 . . . . .85 B7
Darley Dale DE4 . . . . .127 C3
Brockhall Rise DE75. . . . . .182 A1
Brockhill Ct ⬛ S43 . . . . . . .96 F8
Brockholes SK13. . . . . .16 F8
Brockhurst La S45 . . . . . . .129 C6
Brocklehurst Ave S8 . . . . . .57 C8
Brocklehurst Ct S40 . . . . . .95 D2

Brocklehurst Piece S40 . .95 D2
Brockley DE21 . . . . .220 E5
Brockley Ave S44 . . . . .98 F6
Brockley La SK17 . . . . .69 C3
Brockley Prim Sch S44. . . .98 F7
Brocksford Ct DE6 . . . . . . .224 F7
Brockway Cl S45 . . . . .131 D2
Brockwell Ct ⬛ S41. . . . . . .95 D6
Brockwell Inf & Jun Sch
S40. . . . . .95 D4
Brockwell La
Chesterfield S40 . . . . .95 E4
Cutthorpe S42 . . . . .94 F7
Brockwell Pl S40 . . . . .95 E4
Brockwell Terr S40 . . . . . . .95 E4
Brockwell The DE55. . . . . .160 B4
Brodie Cl DE73 . . . . .232 E2
Bromehead Way S41. . . . . .95 D7
Bromley Ct DE7 . . . . .209 A7
Bromley St DE22 . . . . .218 E7
Brompton Rd DE22 . . . . . . .217 F6
Bromyard Dr DE73 . . . . . . .233 A3
Bronte Cl NG10 . . . . .236 A7
Bronte Pl DE23 . . . . .231 B8
Bronte St DE55 . . . . .146 C5
Brook Ave DE5 . . . . .159 B3
Brookbank Ave S40 . . . . . . .95 D4
Brookbank Rd S43 . . . . . . .80 F4
Brook Bldgs S33 . . . . .51 A7
Brook Bottom Rd SK22. . . .33 A8
Brookbridge Ct DE1. . . . . .267 A4
Brook Cl
Alfreton DE55 . . . . .159 B3
Doveridge DE6. . . . . .224 C8
Findern DE65 . . . . .230 D1
Hatton DE65 . . . . .227 D2
Holymoorside S42 . . . . . . .113 D7
Long Eaton NG10 . . . . .236 E5
Quarndon DE22 . . . . .204 C4
Brook Cotts DE7 . . . . .194 F3
Brook Ct
Elvaston DE72 . . . . .233 F4
Heanor DE75 . . . . .182 B2
Brookdale Ave SK6. . . . . . . .23 A4
Brookdale Dr DE23 . . . . . .231 A5
Brookdale Rd DE11 . . . . . .257 A4
Brooke Dr S43 . . . . .96 F5
Brook End DE65 . . . . .242 D3
Brooke St
Ilkeston DE7 . . . . .209 B6
Sandiacre NG10. . . . . .223 B5
Tibshelf DE55 . . . . .148 A6
Brookfield DE73 . . . . .244 A6
Brookfield Ave
Chesterfield S40 . . . . .95 A2
Derby, Chaddesden DE21 . .220 B8
Derby, Littleover DE23. . . .231 D6
Brookfield Cl DE5 . . . . .170 B1
Brookfield Com Sch S40 . .95 A2
Brookfield Cotts
Acresford DE12 . . . . .265 C7
Bakewell DE45. . . . . .109 E8
Brookfield Cres NG20 . . . .119 C5
Brookfield Ind Est SK13 . . .9 E3
Brookfield La DE45. . . . . . .109 E8
Brookfield Mews ⬛
NG10 . . . . .223 C6
Brookfield Mobile Home Pk
S42. . . . . .130 F5
Brookfield Park Ind Est
DE4 . . . . .143 F4
Brookfield Prim Sch
Derby DE3 . . . . .230 D8
Shirebrook NG20. . . . . . . .119 F5
Brookfield Rd S44 . . . . . . .118 A8
Brookfields
Calver S32 . . . . .72 C1
Horsley DE56. . . . . .191 E7
Brookfields Bsns Pk
DE65 . . . . .229 D6
Brookfields Dr DE21 . . . . .205 D4
Brookfield Way
Heanor DE75 . . . . .182 B1
Tansley DE4 . . . . .143 F4
Brook Fold SK23 . . . . .47 C7
Brookhill S43 . . . . .80 F4
Brookhill Ave NG16 . . . . . .160 D4
Brookhill Ind Est NG16 . . .160 E2
Brookhill La NG16. . . . . . . .160 E5
Brookhill Leys Rd NG16 . .182 E1
Brookhill Rd NG16 . . . . . . .160 D2
Brookhill St NG9. . . . . .223 D6
Brook Ho ⬛ DE1. . . . . .267 A4
Brookhouse Ct
Hayfield SK22 . . . . .25 D3
Whaley Thorns NG20 . . . . .101 A1
Brook House Mews
Repton DE65 . . . . .242 D2
Swadlincote DE11 . . . . . . .256 A2
Brookhouse St DE24 . . . . . .232 D5
Brook La
Alfreton DE55 . . . . .159 B3
Clowne S43 . . . . .80 F4
Crich DE56. . . . . .168 C6
Hatton DE65 . . . . .227 C3
Ripley DE5 . . . . .180 D7
Sutton on t H DE6 . . . . . . .228 A4
Brooklands SK17. . . . . .85 C8
Brooklands Ave
Chapel-en-le-F SK23 . . . . . .47 D6
Heanor DE75 . . . . .181 F2
Wirksworth DE4 . . . . .165 F7
Brooklands Bank DE45. . . .109 E6
Brooklands Dr
Derby DE23 . . . . .231 C8
Glossop SK13. . . . . .17 B7

Brooklands Prim Sch
NG10. . . . . .236 D6
Brooklands Rd SK23 . . . . . .47 D6
Brook Lea DE4. . . . . .143 C4
Brookleton DE45. . . . . .125 C5
Brooklyn Dr S40 . . . . .95 D4
Brooklyn Pl ⬛ S8. . . . . .43 A5
Brooklyn Rd ⬛ S8 . . . . .43 A5
Brook Mdw SK13. . . . . .10 E1
Brook Rd
Borrowash DE72 . . . . .221 B1
Elvaston DE72 . . . . .233 F4
Sheffield S8 . . . . .43 A5
Brooks Hollow DE21 . . . . .205 C7
Brookside
Ashbourne DE6 . . . . .173 D1
Beeley DE4 . . . . .111 B3
Bradwell S33 . . . . .51 A7
Burton u T DE15. . . . . .248 B5
Derby DE1 . . . . .267 A4
Eastwood NG16 . . . . .182 F4
Glossop SK13. . . . . .17 B8
New Mills SK22 . . . . .24 E7
Whaley Bridge SK23 . . . . . .34 A1
Brook Side
Bakewell DE45. . . . . .109 D6
Belper DE56. . . . . .178 F3
Rolleston DE13 . . . . .240 B4
Brookside Ave NG19 . . . . .136 C5
Brookside Bar S40 . . . . .94 F1
Brookside Cl
Derby DE1 . . . . .218 E7
Glossop SK13. . . . . .9 F4
Long Eaton NG10 . . . . .236 B8
Repton DE65 . . . . .242 D2
Brookside Glen S40 . . . . . . .94 F1
Brookside Gr SK17 . . . . . . .24 E7
Brookside Ind Unit NG9 . .223 D8
Brookside Rd
Breadsall DE21 . . . . .205 E4
Chapel-en-le-F SK23 . . . . . .47 B5
Brookside Way NG17 . . . . .148 F1
Brooks Rd S43 . . . . .78 B4
Brook St
Clay Cross S45 . . . . .131 A4
Derby DE1 . . . . .267 A4
Glossop SK13. . . . . .10 C1
Hartshorne DE11 . . . . .257 A7
Heage DE56. . . . . .168 E1
Heanor DE75 . . . . .181 B5
Nether Heage DE56. . . . . .168 C2
Renishaw S21 . . . . .79 C8
Swadlincote DE11 . . . . . . .256 A3
Swadlincote, Newhall
DE11 . . . . .255 E6
Brookvale Ave
Codnor DE5 . . . . .181 B8
Denby Village DE5 . . . . . . .180 A2
Brook Vale Cl S18. . . . . .75 D3
Brookvale Rd DE5. . . . . . . .180 A2
Brook Vale Rd NG16 . . . . .182 C2
Brookvale Rise DE5 . . . . . .180 A2
Brookview Ct S18. . . . . .57 A3
Brook Walkway DE1. . . . . .267 A4
Brook Yd S40. . . . . .266 A3
Broom's La DE6 . . . . .226 B2
Broom Ave
Pilsley S45 . . . . .132 C2
Swanwick DE55 . . . . .169 F7
Broombank Pk S41 . . . . . . .76 C3
Broombank Rd S41 . . . . . . .76 C3
Broom Bsns Pk S41. . . . . . .76 C3
Broom Cl
Belper DE56. . . . . .178 E6
Chellaston DE73 . . . . .232 F2
Chesterfield S41 . . . . .95 D7
Derby, Sinfin DE73. . . . . . .231 E2
Duffield DE56. . . . . .190 D3
Broom Dr S42 . . . . .115 E2
Broome Acre DE55 . . . . . . .160 C4
Broomfield Ave S41. . . . . . .115 D7
Broomfield Cl NG10 . . . . . .223 A5
Broomfield Cotts DE7 . . . .206 C5
Broom Gdns S43 . . . . .96 F7
Broomhill Ave DE7 . . . . . . .209 A6
Broomhill Cl
Derby DE3 . . . . .217 D3
Eckington S21 . . . . .59 B3
Broomhill Cotts DE65 . . . .229 C2
Broomhill Ct S41 . . . . .76 F2
Broomhill Rd S41. . . . . .76 F2
Broomhills La DE65 . . . . . .242 D1
Broomhills The DE12. . . . . .264 F7
Broom La DE6 . . . . .175 E7
Broomyclose La ST14 . . . . .210 A4
Brosscroft SK13 . . . . .10 A6
Brosscroft Cl
Glossop SK13. . . . . .10 A6
Hadfield SK13. . . . . .10 A6
Brosscroft Village SK13 . . .10 A6
Brosterfield Cvn Site S32. .70 D5
Brougham Ave NG19 . . . . .135 C2
Brough La S33. . . . . .51 C7
Brough Rd DE15 . . . . .248 C3
Brough St DE22 . . . . .218 D5
Broughton Ave DE23 . . . . .218 D1
Broughton Cl
Church Broughton DE65 . . .227 A8
Ilkeston DE7 . . . . .194 D2
Somercotes DE55 . . . . .170 C7
Broughton Rd S41. . . . . . . .95 D7
Brow Cres S20 . . . . .59 F7
Brown Edge Rd SK17. . . . . .66 C2
Brownhill La HD9 . . . . .3 B8

Brownhills La S42 . . . . .130 C4
Brown Hills La S10. . . . . . . .42 E8
Browning Cir DE23 . . . . . . .231 F7
Browning Rd DE11 . . . . . . .256 C5
Browning St DE23. . . . . . . .231 F7
Brown La
Ashover S45 . . . . .145 B8
Barton in F NG11. . . . . . . .237 E6
Dronfield S18. . . . . .57 C3
Flash SK17. . . . . .103 B3
Brownlow Rd NG19 . . . . . .135 F1
Broxtowe Ave NG16 . . . . . .195 D6
Broxtowe Coll Arthur Mee
Ctr (Coll of F Ed) The
NG9. . . . . .223 D7
Brunel Parkway DE24 . . . .219 D3
Brunel Way
Castle Gresley DE11 . . . . .255 F6
Church Gresley DE11. . . . .261 F8
Brun La DE6, DE22. . . . . . .217 B8
Brunnen The DE55 . . . . . . .160 B4
Brunner Ave NG20 . . . . . . .119 F3
Brunswick Dr ⬛ NG9 . . . . .223 E8
Brunswick St
Chesterfield S41 . . . . .266 C4
Derby DE23 . . . . .231 F8
Pilsley S45 . . . . .132 C2
Brunswood Cl DE21 . . . . . .220 E5
Brunswood Ho DE4 . . . . . . .143 B2
Brunswood La DE6. . . . . . . .187 C7
Brunswood Rd DE4 . . . . . . .143 B1
Brunt La DE11 . . . . .256 F3
Brunton Cl DE3 . . . . .217 C1
Brunts Comp Sch NG19 . .136 C4
Brushes S15 . . . . .4 A3
Brushes Rd SK15. . . . . .4 A3
Brushfield Gr S12 . . . . .44 D4
Brushfield Rd S40 . . . . .94 F5
Brussells Terr ⬛ DE7 . . .194 E1
Bryant La DE55 . . . . .160 A5
Bryn Lea S41 . . . . .96 C2
Brynsmoor Rd NG16. . . . . .182 E7
Bryony DE14 . . . . .254 B8
Bryony Cl
Derby DE21 . . . . .206 A1
Killamarsh S21 . . . . .60 C6
Bryony Way NG19 . . . . . . .136 F4
Bubnell Ct ⬛ S40 . . . . .95 D5
Bubnell Rd DE45 . . . . .91 D6
Buchanan St DE1 . . . . .267 B4
Buchan St DE24. . . . . .232 D7
Buckden Cl S40. . . . . .95 D4
Buckfast Cl DE55. . . . . .169 C8
Buckford La DE65, DE73. .242 E8
Buckhazels La DE6, DE22.203 B7
Buckingham Ave DE21 . . . .219 D8
Buckingham Cl
⬛ Dronfield S18. . . . . .56 C1
Mansfield Woodhouse
NG19. . . . . .136 E5
Swanwick DE55 . . . . .170 A7
Buckingham Ct
Burton u T DE15. . . . . .248 C3
Sandiacre NG10. . . . . .223 A3
Buckingham Dr
Church Gresley DE11. . . . .261 D7
Heanor DE75 . . . . .181 C2
Buckingham Ho DE65 . . . .228 D1
Buckingham Rd NG10 . . . .223 A4
Buckland Cl DE1 . . . . .218 E6
Buckland Ct ⬛ S41 . . . . . . .95 F8
Buckland Gr SK14. . . . . . . .15 A8
Buckleather La S18. . . . . . . .74 C1
Buckley Cl DE11 . . . . .256 F2
Buckminster Cl DE21 . . . . .205 F2
Buckminster Rd DE7 . . . . .208 C4
Buck Wood View S14 . . . . . .43 D5
Bull's Head Row DE73. . . . .252 B6
Bullace Ct ⬛ NG19. . . . . . .136 E1
Bullbridge Hill DE56 . . . . .168 B5
Buller St
Derby DE23 . . . . .218 E2
Ilkeston DE7 . . . . .209 A6
Bullhill La DE56 . . . . .176 E3
Bullhurst La DE6 . . . . .188 F4
Bulling La DE4. . . . . .156 F1
Bullivant Ave S80 . . . . .100 C8
Bull La DE4 . . . . .143 D6
Bull Mews Cotts DE4 . . . . .143 C5
Bullock Cl NG19 . . . . .136 C5
Bullock La
Brailsford DE6 . . . . .201 F7
Ironville NG16, DE55. . . . .170 C5
Bullpit La DE56 . . . . .205 A8
Bullsmoor DE56. . . . . .179 C4
Bulltor La SK17 . . . . .88 B5
Bumpmill La DE55 . . . . . . .146 A3
Bun Alley DE45 . . . . .91 C3
Bungalows The
Chesterfield, Brampton
S40 . . . . .95 D4
Chesterfield, Hady S41 . . .266 C4
⬛ Chesterfield, Newbold
S41 . . . . .95 C7
⬛ Chesterfield, Whittington
Moor S41 . . . . .96 A3
Clowne S43 . . . . .81 A4
Elton DE4 . . . . .140 D6
Killamarsh S21 . . . . .60 C6
New Mills SK22 . . . . .24 D1
Stonebroom DE55 . . . . . . .146 C3
Bunker's Hill S80 . . . . .62 D8
Bunkers Hill S21. . . . . .60 E6
Buntingbank Cl DE55. . . . .159 F4
Bunting Cl
Chesterfield S42 . . . . .95 B1
Derby DE3 . . . . .218 A3
Ilkeston DE7 . . . . .208 C6

Bunting Cl continued
Sheffield S8 . . . . **43** B2
Buntingfield La S45 . . . . **129** B7
Bunting Ho S41 . . . . **77** A3
Bunting Nook S8 . . . . . . **43** B1
Bunyan Cres DE55 . . . . **146** F3
Bunyan Green Rd NG16. . **171** D7
Burbage Bank SK13 . . . . . . **9** E2
Burbage Cl
Belper DE56. . . . . **179** D5
Dronfield S18. . . . . **56** D2
Burbage Ct 8 S40 . . . . . **95** D5
Burbage Gr
Gamesley SK13 . . . . **9** E2
Sheffield S12 . . . . **44** D5
Burbage Pl DE24 . . . . . . **232** F7
Burbage Rd S43 . . . . **97** D8
Burbage Way SK13. . . . . . . **9** E2
Burch Pl S32 . . . . **71** E6
Burcot Cl DE7 . . . . **207** E8
Burdekin Cl SK23 . . . . . . **47** C6
Burdett Way DE65 . . . . **242** D3
Burdock Cl DE21 . . . . . . **205** E2
Burgess Cl S41 . . . . **115** D7
Burghley Cl DE73 . . . . . **232** F2
Burghley Way DE23 . . . **230** E6
Burke Dr DE55 . . . . **170** D8
Burkitt Dr S43 . . . . **79** B3
Burland Green La DE6. . . **189** B4
Burleigh Cres DE55 . . . . **169** F8
Burleigh Dr DE22 . . . . . **218** F8
Burleigh St 1 DE7 . . . . **194** F1
Burley Bank La HD9. . . . . . . **2** E7
Burley Cl S40 . . . . **115** A7
Burley Dr DE22 . . . . . . **204** E2
Burley Hill DE22 . . . . . . **205** A7
Burley La DE22 . . . . . . **204** E7
Burlington Ave NG20 . . . **119** F6
Burlington Cl
Breaston DE72. . . . . **235** D8
Sheffield S17 . . . . **55** E7
Burlington Dr NG19 . . . . **135** F2
Burlington Glen S17 . . . . **55** E7
Burlington Gr S17 . . . . . . **55** E7
Burlington Rd
Buxton SK17 . . . . **85** A7
Derby DE22 . . . . **217** F6
Sheffield S17 . . . . **55** E7
Burlington St S40 . . . . . **266** B3
Burlington Way DE3 . . . **217** D1
Burlow Ave SK17 . . . . . . **85** C3
Burlow Rd SK17. . . . . **85** D2
Burnaby St DE24 . . . . . . **232** F8
Burnage Ct DE22 . . . . . . **218** F4
Burnaston Cl S18 . . . . . . **56** C1
Burnaston Ct 2 NG19 . . **136** E4
Burnaston La DE65 . . . . **229** D5
Burnbridge Rd S41 . . . . . **77** C3
Burncroft DE7 . . . . **207** E7
Burnell St S43 . . . . **96** F4
Burnett La DE4 . . . . . . **143** A8
Burney La DE73 . . . . . . **252** C2
Burnham Cl DE7 . . . . . . **207** D8
Burnham Dr DE3 . . . . . . **217** C2
Burns Ave NG19 . . . . . . **136** C2
Burns Cl
Chesterfield S40 . . . . . . **114** F7
Derby DE23 . . . . **231** B8
Burns Dr
Dronfield S18. . . . . **76** C8
Grassmoor S42 . . . . **115** E3
Burnshaw St DE55 . . . . **146** C5
Burnside
Glossop SK13. . . . . **9** F4
Rolleston DE13 . . . . **240** B4
Burnside Ave
Chapel-en-le-F SK23 . . . . **47** C7
Sheffield S8 . . . . **43** A5
Shirland DE55 . . . . **146** D1
Burnside Cl DE24 . . . . . **231** D3
Burnside Dr S24 . . . . . . **233** A8
Burnside Dr
Derby DE21 . . . . **220** F4
Mansfield NG19 . . . . . . **135** E2
Burnside St DE24 . . . . . **233** A8
Burns St
Heanor DE75 . . . . **181** D2
Ilkeston DE7 . . . . **208** E8
Burnt House Rd DE75 . . . **181** D1
Burnt Oaks Cl NG19 . . . . **136** D3
Burre Cl DE45 . . . . **109** E6
Burrfields Rd SK23 . . . . . **47** B6
Burr La DE7 . . . . **194** F1
Burrowfield Mews DE21. **220** F2
Burrows La
Brailsford DE6. . . . . **201** F2
Middleton DE4 . . . . **154** D5
Burrows The DE11 . . . . **255** F5
Burrows Wlk DE1 . . . . . **267** B2
Burrs Wood Croft S41. . . . **95** B7
Bursar Way NG10 . . . . . **223** C3
Bursdon Cl S41 . . . . **77** A1
Burton Close Dr DE45 . . **109** E4
Burton Close Mews
DE45. . . . . **109** D4
Burton Edge DE45 . . . . . **109** D4
Burton Rd
Burton u T DE14. . . . . . **254** B7
Castle Gresley DE11 . . . . **255** D2
Coton in t E DE12 . . . . . **260** D3
Derby DE23 . . . . **218** C1
Findern DE65 . . . . **230** D4
Overseal DE12 . . . . **262** A4
Repton DE15, DE65 . . . . **242** B2
Rosliston DE12 . . . . **260** C6
Swadlincote DE11 . . . . . **256** D6
Ticknall DE73. . . . . **250** F4

Burton Rd continued
Tutbury DE13 . . . . **239** D4
Willington DE65 . . . . . . **241** F7
Burton St
Heanor DE75 . . . . **181** E2
Tutbury DE13 . . . . **239** C6
Burwell Cl SK13. . . . . **17** A8
Burwell Ct NG19 . . . . . . **136** E4
Buscott Dr DE6 . . . . . . **185** B8
Bushey Wood Gr S17. . . . **55** D7
Bushey Wood Rd S17 . . . **55** E6
Bushton La DE13 . . . . . . **239** B2
Bushy Cl NG10 . . . . **236** B6
Buskeyfield La NG20 . . . **101** F4
Butcher's La DE4 . . . . . . **127** F4
Bute St SK13. . . . . **10** E3
Bute Wlk DE21. . . . . **219** C7
Butler Cres NG19 . . . . . **135** D2
Butler Way S21 . . . . **60** C6
Buttercup Ave DE12 . . . . **262** E1
Buttercup Cl S18 . . . . . . **17** E8
Butterfield Cres DE55 . . **169** F7
Butterfield La DE55 . . . . **145** E1
Butterhall Cl S80 . . . . **82** A5
Butterley Cl NE7 . . . . . . **194** F6
Butterley Croft Bsns Ctr
DE5. . . . . **180** E8
Butterley Cl NG16. . . . . . **170** F4
Butterley Hill DE5 . . . . . **169** E3
Butterley La
Ashover DE4, S45 . . . . . **144** E5
Ripley DE5. . . . . **169** D4
Butterley La NG16 . . . . . **170** D4
Butterley Sta DE5 . . . . . **169** E4
Buttermead NG9 . . . . . . **209** D2
Buttermere Cl
Chesterfield S41 . . . . **95** D7
1 Long Eaton NG10 . . . **223** B2
Buttermere Ct NG19 . . . **136** D3
Buttermere Dr
Derby DE22 . . . . **204** E3
Dronfield S18. . . . . **56** E1
Buttermilk La S44. . . . . . . **98** D4
Butterpot La DE6 . . . . . **215** D3
Butterton Cl DE7 . . . . . **209** A7
Butterton Dr 6 S40. . . . **95** A5
Butterwick Cl
Derby DE23 . . . . **231** E5
Forest Town NG19 . . . . . **136** F1
Butt Hill S80. . . . . **81** F6
Butt Hill Cl S80. . . . . **81** F6
Butt La
Blackfordby DE11 . . . . . **257** A1
Mansfield Woodhouse
NG19. . . . . **136** C2
Buttonoak Dr DE73. . . . . **233** A3
Butts Cl DE7 . . . . **209** A4
Butts Dr DE4. . . . . **143** D4
Butts Hill S17. . . . . **55** D4
Butts Rd
Ashover S45 . . . . **129** F3
Bakewell DE45 . . . . **109** D5
Darley Dale DE4 . . . . . . **127** B3
Butt St NG10. . . . . **223** B5
Butts Terr DE45 . . . . . . **109** D5
Butts The DE56 . . . . **179** A3
Butts View DE45 . . . . . . **109** D5
Buxton Ave DE75. . . . . . **193** F7
Buxton Cl
17 Gamesley SK13 . . . . . . **9** E2
Swadlincote DE11 . . . . . **256** A7
Buxton Com Sch SK17. . . **85** A6
Buxton Ct DE7 . . . . **194** D1
Buxton Ctry Pk* SK17 . . . **84** E6
Buxton Dr
Derby DE3 . . . . **217** E3
Little Eaton DE21. . . . . . **191** D2
Buxton Gn DE75 . . . . . . **193** F2
Buxton Hospl SK17. . . . . **85** C5
Buxton Inf Sch SK17 . . . . **85** C7
Buxton Jun Sch SK17 . . . **85** B6
Buxton Mews SK13. . . . . . **9** E2
Buxton Mus & Art Gal*
SK17 . . . . **85** B7
Buxton New Rd SK11. . . . **83** A6
Buxton Old Rd SK12. . . . . **32** E4
Buxton Rd
Alstonefield DE6 . . . . . . **149** B5
Ashbourne DE6 . . . . **173** D2
Ashford in t W DE45 . . . . **108** E8
Bakewell DE45. . . . . **109** B7
Castleton S33 . . . . **38** B2
Chapel-en-le-F SK17, SK23 . **47** E5
Chinley SK23 . . . . **34** F2
Derby DE21 . . . . **219** F8
Dove Holes SK17 . . . . . . **66** F8
High Lane SK12 . . . . **32** A6
Horwich End, New Horwich
SK23. . . . . **45** E6
Longnor SK17 . . . . **121** B7
Mansfield NG19 . . . . . . **135** D1
New Mills SK22, SK23 . . . . **33** C4
Tideswell SK17 . . . . **69** C3
Whaley Bridge SK23. . . . . **33** E1
Buxton Rd W SK12 . . . . . **32** B5
Buxton Sta SK17 . . . . . . **85** B8
Buxton Terr SK14 . . . . **9** D5
Buxton Wlk 9 SK13 . . . . . **9** E1
Buxworth Prim Sch SK23 . **34** A1
Byfield Cl DE21 . . . . **206** B2
Byng Ave DE23 . . . . **231** F7
Byron Ave
Alfreton DE55 . . . . **159** B4
Burton u T DE15. . . . . . **254** E7
Long Eaton NG10 . . . . . **223** B3
Mansfield Woodhouse
NG19. . . . . **136** C2

Byron Cl
Dronfield S18. . . . . **76** C7
Grassmoor S42 . . . . **115** E3
Byron Cres NG16 . . . . . . **195** C4
Byron Ct NG9 . . . . **209** E2
Byron Gr DE55 . . . . **146** F3
Byron Lo SK17 . . . . **85** C6
Byron Rd
Chesterfield S40 . . . . . . **115** A8
Swadlincote DE11 . . . . . **256** C6
Byron St
Buxton SK17 . . . . **85** C6
Chesterfield S40 . . . . . . **266** C1
Derby DE23 . . . . **218** F2
Ilkeston DE7 . . . . **194** F1
Shirebrook NG20 . . . . . . **119** E4
Shirland DE55 . . . . **146** C1
Bywell La DE56 . . . . **179** F1

C

Cabot Cl DE56 . . . . **179** E5
Cacklehill La DE6 . . . . . **184** C2
Cadeby Cl DE55 . . . . . . **170** C6
Cadgwith Dr DE22 . . . . **204** E3
Cadley Hill Ind Est DE11. **255** E2
Cadley Hill Rd DE11 . . . . **255** E3
Cadman Ct S20 . . . . **59** D6
Cadman Rd S12 . . . . **44** C6
Cadman St S20 . . . . **59** D6
Cadwell Cl DE24 . . . . . . **233** D6
Caerhays Ct DE24 . . . . . **231** D3
Caernarvon Cl
Chesterfield S40 . . . . **95** C1
Derby DE21 . . . . **220** F5
Caernarvon Rd S18 . . . . . **76** B8
Caesar St DE1 . . . . **219** B7
Cairn Dr S43. . . . . **77** D4
Cairngorm Cl S43 . . . . . . **77** D4
Cairngorm Dr DE24 . . . . **231** D3
Cairns Cl
Burton u T DE15. . . . . . **248** C3
Derby DE3 . . . . **217** E3
Cairnsmore Cl 4 NG10. . **223** A1
Caldene Terr SK23 . . . . . . **45** E7
Calder Cl
Derby DE22 . . . . **204** E3
Hilton DE65 . . . . **228** D1
Calderdale Dr NG10 . . . . **236** A6
Caldermill Dr DE21 . . . . **206** A2
Caldey Rd S18. . . . . **76** A8
Cale Rd SK22 . . . . **33** D8
Calesdale Cl SK17 . . . . . . **85** B5
Calf Croft S80 . . . . **82** A5
Calgary Cres DE15 . . . . . **248** D3
Calico Cres SK15. . . . . **4** A6
Calico La SK23. . . . . **33** D4
California Gdns DE22. . . . **218** C4
California La S43 . . . . **80** A7
Calke Abbey* LE65 . . . . . **251** D2
Calke Rd NG17. . . . . **148** E2
Calke Rise DE5 . . . . **169** F1
Calladine Cl DE75 . . . . . **181** D2
Calladine La
Horsley Woodhouse DE7 . **192** D6
Shottle DE56 . . . . **177** C5
Callan's La LE65 . . . . . . **258** D7
Calley Ave NE7 . . . . **194** F6
Callow Dr S14 . . . . **43** D5
Callow Hill Way DE23 . . . **231** A7
Callow La DE4, DE6 . . . . **165** C5
Callow Mount S14 . . . . . . **43** D5
Callow Pl S14. . . . . **43** D5
Callow Rd S14 . . . . **43** C5
Callywhite La S18 . . . . . . **57** C1
Calow CE Prim Sch S44 . . **96** F3
Calow Cl S13 . . . . **9** E2
Calow Gn SK13 . . . . **9** E2
Calow La
Calow S41, S44 . . . . **96** F1
Chesterfield S41 . . . . . . **115** E8
Calow Lane Ind Est S41. . **115** E8
Calstock Cl S40 . . . . **95** A4
Calton View DE45 . . . . . **109** D5
Calver Ave S42 . . . . **132** A7
Calver Bank 8 SK13 . . . . . **9** D2
Calver Cl
Belper DE56. . . . . **179** B6
Derby DE21 . . . . **205** E3
10 Gamesley SK13 . . . . . . **9** E2
Calver Cres S43 . . . . **97** D8
Calver Fold 6 SK13 . . . . . **9** D2
Calver Mews SK13 . . . . **9** E2
Calver Mill S32 . . . . **72** D2
Calver Pl 7 SK13 . . . . **9** D2
Calver Rd DE45 . . . . **91** D6
Calver St NG19 . . . . **136** E4
Calvert Cl NG16 . . . . . . **182** B3
Calverton Cl DE24 . . . . . **232** E3
Calvert St DE1 . . . . **267** D2
Calvin Cl DE24 . . . . **233** A5
Camberwell Ave DE22. . . **218** A6
Camberwell Ct 10 S43 . . . **78** B3
Camborne Cl DE21 . . . . . **205** E1
Cambrian Cl 1 S40 . . . . . **95** D6
Cambrian Way DE11 . . . **256** A3
Cambria Rd NG17 . . . . . **135** C4
Cambridge Cres
Bramley-Vale S44 . . . . . **117** E1
Stapleford NG9 . . . . **209** D2
Cambridge Ct 13 S8. . . . . **43** B6
Cambridge Lo S8 . . . . **43** B6
Cambridge Rd
1 Brimington S43 . . . . . . **96** F8

Cambridge Rd continued
Sheffield S8 . . . . **43** B6
Cambridge St
Blackwell DE55 . . . . . . **147** E1
Derby, Rose Hill DE23 . . **219** B2
Derby, Spondon DE21 . . **220** E3
Camdale Rise S12. . . . . . . **44** F1
Camdale View S12. . . . . . **44** F1
Camden St DE22 . . . . . . **218** D4
Camellia Cl DE3 . . . . . . **217** D3
Camelot Cl DE3 . . . . **240** E2
Cameron Cl DE15 . . . . . **248** B1
Cameron Rd DE23. . . . . . **231** F8
Camerory Way S43. . . . . . **77** D5
Cam Height S32 . . . . **41** F2
Camlough Wlk S41. . . . . **266** C2
Camms CE Prim Sch S21. **59** D4
Camms Cl S21 . . . . **59** D4
Campbell Ct S43 . . . . **77** A4
Campbell Dr S43 . . . . **78** B4
Campbell St
Belper DE56. . . . . **178** F3
Derby DE24 . . . . **232** D7
Langley Mill NG16 . . . . . **182** C4
Campion Cl NG20 . . . . . **119** D3
Campion Dr S21 . . . . **60** C6
Campion Hill DE74 . . . . . **247** A4
Campion Rd DE11 . . . . . **256** F4
Campion St DE22 . . . . . . **218** D5
Campsie Ct 8 DE24 . . . . **231** D3
Camp St DE1 . . . . **219** B7
Camp Wood Cl DE21 . . . **205** C7
Canada St DE56 . . . . . . **179** A2
Canal Bank DE72. . . . . . **235** A1
Canal Bridge
Killamarsh S21 . . . . **60** D6
Willington DE65 . . . . . . **242** A6
Canalgate Pk DE21. . . . . **220** F3
Canal Mews S41 . . . . . . **266** B4
Canalside S21 . . . . **60** B1
Canal Side SK23 . . . . **33** F1
Canal St
Derby DE1 . . . . **267** C2
Ilkeston DE7 . . . . **195** A1
Long Eaton NG10 . . . . . **223** C1
Marple SK6 . . . . **23** A6
Sandiacre NG10. . . . . . . **223** C6
Whaley Bridge SK23 . . . . **45** E8
Canal Wharf S41. . . . . . . **96** B5
Canberra Cl
Derby DE3 . . . . **217** E2
Stapleford NG9 . . . . **209** F1
Candlemass Ct NG19 . . . **136** D2
Cannell Cl S45 . . . . **131** B4
Canner Cl DE11 . . . . **257** A2
Canning Mews 1 DE7. . . **208** F7
Cannock Way NG10 . . . . **237** A7
Cannon Fields S32 . . . . . . **52** E8
Cannon St SK14 . . . . **9** C5
Canon's Wlk DE22 . . . . . **204** F2
Cantelupe Gdns NG16 . . **195** C4
Cantelupe Rd DE7 . . . . . **209** A8
Canterbury Cl
Chesterfield S40 . . . . . . **115** A8
Duffield DE56. . . . . **190** E3
Mansfield Woodhouse
NG19. . . . . **136** C5
Canterbury Rd
Burton u T DE15. . . . . . **248** C3
Sheffield S8 . . . . **43** B5
Wirksworth DE4 . . . . . . **165** F8
Canterbury Terr DE4 . . . **165** F8
Cantley Cl DE24 . . . . . . **232** D3
Cantley Rd DE55 . . . . . . **170** C6
Cantrell Cl S43 . . . . **96** D8
Capel Rise S43 . . . . **96** D8
Capthorne Cl S40 . . . . . . **94** F5
Caraway Dr DE4 . . . . . . **254** A8
Cardale Rd NG19 . . . . . . **135** C4
Cardales DE65 . . . . **230** D2
Cardean Cl DE1 . . . . **219** B7
Carder Gn SK17 . . . . **121** B6
Cardigan St DE21 . . . . . . **219** D7
Cardinal Cl 1 DE21 . . . . **205** F2
Cardlemere La SK17 . . . . **138** F2
Cardrona Pl DE21 . . . . . . **205** F2
Cardwell Ave S13 . . . . . . **44** F7
Cardwell Dr S13 . . . . **44** F7
Carfield Ave S8. . . . . **43** B5
Carfield La S8 . . . . **43** C5
Carfield Pl S8 . . . . **43** C5
Carfield Prim Sch S8 . . . . **43** B5
Carisbrooke Dr 2 DE13 . **240** E1
Carisbrooke Gdns DE23 . **231** C6
Carlin Cl DE72 . . . . **235** E8
Carlin St S13 . . . . **44** E6
Carlisle Ave DE23 . . . . . **231** B8
Carlisle Gr SK17 . . . . **85** A8
Carlisle Rd SK17 . . . . **84** F8
Carl Moult Ho DE11 . . . . **256** A2
Carlton Ave
Derby DE24 . . . . **232** E4
Northwood DE4 . . . . . . **127** A6
Carlton Cl
Clay Cross S45 . . . . **131** D2
Heanor DE75 . . . . **182** A3
Sheffield S20 . . . . **59** C6
Carlton Dr S24 . . . . **232** E3
Carlton Gdns DE24 . . . . **232** E4
Carlton Mews S42 . . . . . . **43** E7
Carlton Rd
Chesterfield S40 . . . . . . **115** A6
Derby DE23 . . . . **218** C2
Long Eaton NG10 . . . . . **236** B5
Mansfield NG19 . . . . . . **136** C1

Carlton Wlk
Derby DE24 . . . . **220** A1
Derby DE24 . . . . **233** A8
Carlyle Inf Sch DE23 . . . **231** B8
Carlyle Pl DE75 . . . . **181** D3
Carlyle Rd DE55. . . . . . . **146** F3
Carlyle St
Derby DE24 . . . . **231** F5
Heanor DE75 . . . . **181** D3
Carlyon Gdns S40 . . . . . **114** F8
Carnaby Cl DE22 . . . . . . **218** A5
Carnarvon Ct DE15 . . . . **249** C2
Carnarvon Rd NG17 . . . . **148** F2
Carnation Rd NG20. . . . . **119** C3
Carnegie St DE23 . . . . . . **232** A8
Carnfield Hall* DE55 . . . **159** D5
Carnfield Hill DE55 . . . . **159** D5
Carnforth Cl
Derby DE3 . . . . **217** E1
Stapleford NG9 . . . . **223** D5
Carnival Way DE74 . . . . . **247** B4
Carnoustie Ave S40 . . . . **114** C8
Carnoustie Cl DE13 . . . . **217** F2
Carol Cres DE21 . . . . . . **219** F5
Caroline Cl DE24. . . . . . . **233** D7
Caroline Ct
Hope S33 . . . . **38** F4
Ilkeston DE7 . . . . **209** A6
Carpenter Ave
Mansfield NG19 . . . . . . **135** D2
Mastin Moor S43 . . . . . . **79** B3
Carpenter Cl DE15 . . . . . **248** C2
Carpenter Croft S12 . . . . **44** C6
Carpenter Gdns S12 . . . . **44** C6
Carpenter Mews S12. . . . **44** C6
Carper La DE6 . . . . **187** F2
Carradale Gr DE73 . . . . . **232** E1
Carr Bank SK13 . . . . **17** E6
Carr Brook Cl SK23 . . . . . **45** E5
Carr Brow SK6. . . . . **32** A7
Carr Cl DE55 . . . . **160** A4
Car Rd S18 . . . . **74** B6
Carrfield Ave
Beeston NG9 . . . . **223** F2
Long Eaton NG10 . . . . . **223** F1
Carrfield Ct 8 S8. . . . . . . **43** B6
Carrfield Dr S8 . . . . **43** B6
Carrfield La S8 . . . . **43** B6
Carrfield Rd S8. . . . . **43** B6
Carrfields DE7 . . . . **192** C7
Carrfield St S8. . . . . **43** B6
Carrhouse La SK14. . . . . . . **9** C4
Carriage Dr The SK13 . . . . **9** F5
Carriers Mdw SK23. . . . . . **47** B7
Carriers Rd DE55 . . . . . . **241** D6
Carrington Ct Ind Est
DE1. . . . . **218** E5
Carrington St DE1 . . . . . **267** C2
Carr La
Brackenfield DE55 . . . . . **145** D3
Dronfield S18. . . . . **56** C2
Matlock DE4 . . . . **143** E2
Scarcliffe S44 . . . . **117** F7
South Normanton DE55. . **160** A7
Thornhill S33 . . . . **39** F5
Carr Lane Mews S18 . . . . **56** D2
Carrock Ave DE75 . . . . . **182** B1
Carron Cl DE24 . . . . **231** E4
Carrs Cl DE74 . . . . **247** A3
Carr Vale Rd S44 . . . . **98** F1
Carrwood Rd
Chesterfield S41 . . . . **76** C4
Renishaw S21 . . . . **79** B8
Carsington Cl S40. . . . . . . **95** B5
Carsington Cres DE22. . . **204** D1
Carsington Ct 3 NG19 . . **136** E3
Carsington Ho 1 DE22. . . **204** D2
Carsington & Hopton Prim
Sch DE4. . . . . **164** E7
Carsington Mews DE22. . **204** D2
Carsington Water Visitor
Ctr* DE6. . . . . **164** C4
Carson Croft DE4 . . . . . . **143** C6
Carson Mount S12. . . . . . **44** B3
Carson Rd DE21. . . . . . . **220** B6
Carter Cl NG10. . . . . **236** B6
Carter Grange 11 S8 . . . . **43** B6
Carterhall La S12 . . . . . . **44** C2
Carterhall Rd S12. . . . . . . **44** B2
Carter La
Shirebrook NG20 . . . . . . **119** E4
Shirebrook, Warsop Vale
NG20. . . . . **120** C4
Carter La E DE55 . . . . . . **160** C6
Carter La W
Shirebrook NG20 . . . . . . **119** D4
South Normanton DE55. . **160** C5
Carter Pl S8 . . . . **43** B6
Carter Rd
Beeston NG9 . . . . **223** F2
Sheffield S8 . . . . **43** A6
Carter St DE24 . . . . **232** D6
Cartledge La S18 . . . . . . **75** A7
Cartmel Cl S18 . . . . **56** E1
Cartmel Cres S41 . . . . . . **95** E8
Cart Rd DE55 . . . . **157** F4
Cartworth Moor Rd HD9. . **3** E8
Cartwright La DE55 . . . . **160** E7
Cartwright St S81. . . . . . . **63** F7
Car Vale Dr S13. . . . . **44** C8
Car Vale View S13 . . . . . . **44** C8
Carver Cl S26. . . . . **61** E6
Carver Way S26 . . . . **61** E6
Cary Gr S2 . . . . **43** F8

Cary Rd
Eckington S21 59 B3
Sheffield S2 44 A8
Cascade Gr DE23 231 A7
Casson Ave DE24 233 A6
Casson Dr S26 61 E7
Casson St NG16 170 F4
Castings Rd DE23 232 B8
Castlebeck Ave S2 44 C8
Castlebeck Dr S2 44 C8
Castle Cl
Bakewell DE45 109 E6
Borrowash DE72 221 D2
Castlecraig Ct DE24 231 E2
Castle Croft
Derby DE24 233 D5
Linton DE11 261 E8
Castle Ct
Elvaston DE72 234 A5
Glossop SK13 10 A4
Tutbury DE13 239 C7
Castledale Croft S2 44 B8
Castledale Gr S2 44 C8
Castledale Pl S2 44 B8
Castle Donington Com Coll DE74 247 B3
Castle Dr
Bakewell DE45 109 E7
Codnor NG16 181 E8
Somercotes DE55 170 D8
Castle Edge Rd SK22 24 B2
Castlefields NG16 170 F3
Castlefields Main Ctr DE1 267 C2
Castlegate La SK17, DE45 89 C5
Castle Gn S44 118 B7
Castle Gresley Inf Sch DE11 261 E7
Castle Hayes La DE13 239 A5
Castle Hill
Castle Donington DE74 247 B4
Duffield DE56 190 E4
Eckington S21 59 D4
Findern DE65 230 D1
Glossop SK13 10 E2
Castle Hill Cl S21 59 D4
Castle Hill Ho DE13 239 B7
Castle Ho DE1 267 D2
Castle Ind Est S44 98 E2
Castle La
Bolsover S44 99 A1
Ironville NG16 170 E1
Melbourne DE73 252 A7
Castleland Way DE73 232 E2
Castle Mews
Mansfield Woodhouse NG19 136 B3
Melbourne DE73 252 B7
Castle Mews The 5 DE11 256 A7
Castle Mills DE73 252 B7
Castle Mount Cres DE45 109 D7
Castle Mount Way DE45 109 E7
Castle Orch DE56 190 E4
Castle Rd DE11 255 F1
Castlerigg Way 1 S18 56 E1
Castle Row S17 56 B6
Castlerow Cl S17 56 B6
Castlerow Dr S17 56 B6
Castlerow View S17 56 B6
Castleshaw Dr DE23 230 E7
Castle St
Bakewell DE45 109 D6
Bolsover S44 99 A2
Castleton S33 38 B2
Glossop SK13 10 A4
Mansfield Woodhouse NG19 136 B3
Melbourne DE73 252 B7
Tutbury DE13 239 C6
Castleton Ave
Derby DE23 231 F8
Ilkeston DE7 194 E5
Somercotes DE55 170 C6
Castleton Bank 27 SK13 9 E1
Castleton CE Prim Sch S33 38 C2
Castleton Cl NG19 136 C4
Castleton Cres SK13 9 E1
Castleton Gn 26 SK13 9 E1
Castleton Gr
28 Gamesley SK13 9 E1
Staveley S43 97 B5
Castleton Rd
Hathersage S32 52 E8
Hope S33 38 E3
Castleton Terr 25 SK13 9 E1
Castleton YH★ S33 38 C2
Castle View
Aldercar NG16 182 A4
Duffield DE56 190 E4
Eckington S21 59 D3
Hatton DE65 239 C7
Palterton S44 118 B6
Castle View Dr DE4 155 C6
Castle View Prim Sch DE4 143 D5
Castle Way The DE65 241 F5
Castle Wlk DE1 267 C2
Catchford View S40 95 B7
Catcliff Cl DE45 109 D4
Catcliff Cotts DE45 109 D5
Cat & Fiddle La DE7 207 E5
Cathedral Rd DE1 267 B4
Cathedral View DE22 218 D2
Catherine Ave
Ilkeston DE7 208 F6
Mansfield Woodhouse NG19 136 C3
Catherine Ct
Alfreton DE55 159 C5
1 Ashbourne DE6 173 B2
Chesterfield S40 95 E3
Catherine McAuley Ho DE22 204 E1
Catherine Rise DE11 256 A1
Catherine St
Alfreton DE55 159 C4
Chesterfield S40 95 E3
Derby DE23 219 B2
Cath of All Saints, Derby★ DE1 267 B4
Catholme La DE12 259 A4
Catkin Dr NG16 195 C8
Cat La S2, S8 43 C5
Cator Rd NG19 135 D3
Catterick Dr DE3 217 C1
Catterwood Dr SK6 15 B2
Catton La DE12 260 B5
Caudwell's Mill & Craft Ctr★ DE4 126 F8
Caudwell Cl S42 131 D8
Cauldon Dr S40 95 A5
Cauldwell Rd DE12 261 B6
Causeway DE22 204 E2
Causeway Gdns S17 55 D8
Causeway Glade S17 55 C8
Causeway Head Rd S17 55 D8
Causeway Ho S45 129 D4
Causeway La
Crich DE4 156 F5
Matlock DE4 143 C5
Causeway The
Ashover S45 129 D4
Eyam S32 71 E5
Sheffield S17 55 D7
Wirksworth DE4 165 F8
Cavan Dr DE21 220 B4
Cavell Dr S45 131 E2
Cavendish Ave
Buxton SK17 84 F6
Derby DE22 204 F3
Sheffield, Abbeydale Park S17 55 F7
Cavendish Cir 6 SK17 85 B8
Cavendish Cl
Castle Donington DE74 247 A2
Creswell S80 81 D1
Doveridge DE6 211 C1
Duffield DE56 190 D2
Holmewood S42 116 E1
Shardlow DE72 235 B2
9 Swadlincote DE11 256 A7
Cavendish Close Inf Sch DE21 220 A8
Cavendish Close Jun Sch DE21 220 B8
Cavendish Cotts DE4 154 F2
Cavendish Cres NG9 209 D2
Cavendish Ct
Chesterfield S41 96 A5
Derby DE1 267 A4
Shardlow DE72 235 A1
Cavendish Dr
Ashbourne DE6 185 D8
Clowne S43 81 A4
Ripley DE5 169 C1
Cavendish Flats
Edensor DE45 110 E8
Pilsley DE45 91 E1
Cavendish Hospl The SK17 85 A8
Cavendish Jun Sch S41 95 F8
Cavendish Pl S43 78 B3
Cavendish Rd
Bolsover S44 99 B1
Ilkeston DE7 208 F6
Long Eaton NG10 223 C2
Matlock DE4 143 C7
Cavendish Rise S18 75 F8
Cavendish St N S41 77 A2
Cavendish Sq S21 77 D8
Cavendish St
Chesterfield S40 266 B3
Derby DE1 267 A3
Langwith NG20 119 F8
Mansfield Woodhouse NG19 136 A3
Staveley S43 97 D8
Cavendish Way DE3 217 E2
Cavendish Wlk S44 99 A2
Caversfield Cl DE23 231 A8
Caversham Way DE7 207 D8
Cavill Rd S8 43 A3
Cawdor Rd S2 43 F6
Caxterway La SK17 86 E3
Caxton Cl S43 77 D3
Caxton Ct DE23 231 E6
Caxton St
Derby DE23 231 F6
Derby, Normanton DE23 231 E7
Caythorpe Ct 4 NG19 136 E3
Ceal The SK6 15 B2
Cecil Ave S18 57 A2
Cecil Rd
Dronfield S18 57 A2
Swadlincote DE11 255 F5
Cecil St DE22 218 D6
Cedar Ave
Alfreton DE55 159 A5
Chesterfield S40 95 D5
Long Eaton NG10 236 C5
Cedar Ave *continued*
Mansfield Woodhouse NG19 136 C5
Ripley DE5 169 D1
Cedar Cl
Ashbourne DE6 185 D7
Duffield DE56 190 D4
Eckington S21 59 B2
Glapwell S44 118 B1
Glossop SK13 10 B2
Killamarsh S21 60 C5
Sandiacre NG10 223 B7
Shirebrook NG20 119 E6
Cedar Croft
Aston-on-T DE72 246 A7
Kilburn DE56 192 B7
Cedar Dr
Ockbrook DE72 221 C4
Selston NG16 171 F7
Uttoxeter ST14 210 A4
Cedar Gr
Belper DE56 179 B2
Linton DE12 261 C6
South Normanton DE55 160 B4
Swadlincote DE11 256 A7
Cedar Park Dr S44 99 C2
Cedar Pk DE7 208 E7
Cedar Rd
Castle Donington DE74 247 B2
Linton DE11 261 E7
Cedar St
Brimington S43 78 A1
Derby DE22 218 E8
Shirland DE55 146 C5
Cedarwood Ct DE21 205 E2
Celandine Cl
Burton u T DE15 248 C2
Derby DE21 206 A2
Celandine Ct S17 56 A5
Celandine Gdns S17 56 A5
Celandine Pl DE11 256 E4
Celanese Rd DE21 220 C3
Cemetery Hill DE21 219 E6
Cemetery La
Ripley DE5 169 E1
Staveley S43 78 E1
Wirksworth DE4 154 F1
Cemetery Rd
Belper DE56 179 A5
Chesterfield S41 96 C2
Clay Cross S45 131 E2
Dronfield S18 76 B8
Glossop SK13 10 C4
Somercotes DE55 170 C7
Stapleford NG9 223 E7
Cemetery Terr S43 96 E7
Centenary Ho DE1 267 B1
Central Ave
Borrowash DE72 221 B1
Chesterfield S40 95 E2
Creswell S80 100 D8
Sandiacre NG10 223 B6
South Normanton DE55 160 B5
Stapleford NG9 223 F8
Central Cl
Shirebrook NG20 119 E3
Unstone Green S18 76 E6
Central Dr
Blackwell DE55 147 E1
Buxton SK17 85 D5
Calow S44 96 F3
3 Chesterfield S41 96 C1
Shirebrook NG20 119 E3
Wingerworth S42 114 F3
Central Pavement S40 266 B3
Central Rd DE55 159 A4
Central St
Chesterfield S41 96 C1
Holmewood S42 132 E8
Central Store 6 SK13 10 C1
Central Wlk S43 96 D7
Centre Ct DE1 267 C1
Centre St S44 117 D1
Centro Pl DE24 219 D3
Centrum East Ret Pk DE14 253 F8
Centurion Way Bsns Pk DE21 219 B8
Chaddesden Cl S18 56 C1
Chaddesden La DE21 220 A6
Chaddesden Lane End DE21 219 F6
Chaddesden Park Inf Sch DE21 220 B6
Chaddesden Park Jun Sch DE21 220 B7
Chaddesden Park Rd DE21 219 F7
Chadfield Rd DE56 190 E5
Chadwick Ave DE24 232 E5
Chadwick Ct S43 78 D1
Chadwick Hill DE4 141 A6
Chadwick Nick La
Crich DE4 167 F7
Fritchley DE4 168 A6
Chadwick Rd S13 44 C7
Chadwick St SK13 17 B8
Chaffinch Cl DE21 220 F6
Chain La DE3 218 A2
Chalfont Sq DE21 206 B2
Chalkley Cl DE24 232 F7
Challands Cl S41 115 C8
Challands Way S41 115 C8
Challis Ave DE21 220 B7
Challoner Gn S20 59 E8
Challoner Way S20 59 E8
Chalons Cl DE7 194 F1
Chalons Way DE7 208 F8
Chambers Ave DE7 209 B7
Chambers Ct SK14 9 A3
Chambers St DE24 219 F1
Champion Ave DE7 194 C3
Champion Hill DE56 190 E4
Chancel Pl DE22 267 A1
Chancery La DE22 218 A6
Chancet Wood Cl S8 56 F8
Chancet Wood Dr S8 56 F8
Chancet Wood Rd 1 S8 56 F8
Chancet Wood Rise S8 56 F8
Chancet Wood View S8 56 F8
Chander Hill La S42 113 C8
Chandlers Ford DE21 205 F2
Chandos Cres S21 60 D6
Chandos Pole St DE22 218 D6
Chandres Ct DE22 204 E4
Chaneyfield Way S40 95 B7
Channel The DE6 173 B2
Chantrey Ave S41 96 A6
Chantrey Rd S8 43 A3
Chantry Cl
Derby DE3 217 C1
Disley SK12 32 E5
Long Eaton NG10 236 A4
Melbourne DE73 252 A7
Chantry Ct SK17 69 C4
Chantry Fold SK12 32 E6
Chantry La SK17 69 D4
Chantry Rd SK12 32 E6
Chapel Brow
Broadbottom SK13 16 E6
Glossop SK13 10 A7
Chapel Cl
Clowne S43 80 E4
Moira DE11 256 C1
Willington DE65 242 B6
Youlgreave DE45 125 B5
Chapel Croft
Elton DE4 140 E6
Middleton DE4 154 D5
Chapel Ct DE7 194 F4
Chapel-en-le-Frith CE Prim Sch SK23 47 C6
Chapel-en-le-Frith High Sch SK23 47 A5
Chapel-en-le-Frith Sta SK23 47 B3
Chapel Gn DE6 224 C8
Chapel Hill
Ashover S45 129 F4
Beeley DE4 111 B4
Cromford DE4 155 A7
Chapel Ho 3 DE7 208 E8
Chapel Houses SK6 23 A5
Chapel Inf Sch SK23 47 B6
Chapel La
Apperknowle S18 58 A1
Bakewell DE45 109 D5
Barrow u T DE73 244 A6
Boylestone DE6 213 B4
Chellaston DE73 233 A1
Church Broughton DE65 227 B8
Clifton DE6 184 F6
Crich DE4 168 A8
Derby, Chaddesden DE21 220 A7
Derby, Spondon DE21 220 E5
Glossop SK13 9 F5
Hanbury DE13 238 A2
Holloway DE4 156 B5
Kniveton DE6 163 B1
Middleton DE4 154 D5
Rolleston DE13 240 B4
Sheffield, Hillfoot S17 55 D4
Taddington SK17 88 B3
Thurvaston DE6 215 B8
Tissington DE6 162 B6
Wirksworth DE4 154 F1
Chapel La E S41 115 D7
Chapel La W S40 95 C2
Chapel Lofts SK13 10 B5
Chapel Pl NG16 195 F6
Chapel Rd
Bolsover S44 98 F1
Grassmoor S42 115 F3
Hayfield SK22 25 D2
Horwich End SK23 45 E5
Selston NG16 171 E6
Chapel Row
Borrowash DE72 221 B2
Crich DE4 168 A8
Chapel Side DE21 220 E5
Chapel St
Alfreton DE55 159 A4
Belper DE56 178 F3
Brimington S43 96 F8
Buxton SK17 85 B7
3 Chesterfield S41 96 A8
Coton in t E DE12 260 D3
Derby DE1 267 B4
Derby, Spondon DE21 220 E5
Donisthorpe DE12 265 E8
Donisthorpe, Oakthorpe DE12 265 F6
Duffield DE56 190 F3
Eastwood NG16 182 F1
Fritchley DE56 168 B6
Glossop SK13 10 C1
Hayfield SK22 25 D2
Heanor DE75 194 A8
Holbrook DE56 191 C7
8 Ilkeston DE7 194 F1
Kilburn DE56 192 A8
Kimberley NG16 195 F6
Linton DE11 261 E8
Long Eaton NG10 236 E7
Longnor SK17 121 B6
Melbourne DE73 252 B7
Chapel St *continued*
Monyash DE45 107 B2
New Houghton NG19 135 A7
New Mills, Rowarth SK22 24 E7
New Mills SK22 33 B6
Ripley DE5 169 D2
Sheffield S20 59 C6
Smisby LE65 257 F3
Somercotes DE55 170 C7
Stonebroom DE55 147 A4
Swadlincote, Church Gresley DE11 256 A1
Swadlincote, Newhall DE11 255 F6
Swanwick DE55 169 E8
Ticknall DE73 251 A5
Whaley Bridge SK23 45 E8
Whaley Thorns NG20 101 A3
Woodville DE11 256 F2
Chapel Way S42 115 D1
Chapel Wlk
Alfreton DE55 159 A4
Curbar S32 72 E2
Chapel Yd
Dronfield S18 57 A2
Harthill S26 61 E6
South Wingfield DE55 157 E3
Chapman Ave DE24 233 B6
Chapman La S42 115 F3
Chapmans Croft DE12 260 D3
Chapter Cl DE21 205 D2
Chardin Ave SK6 23 C8
Charing Ct DE1 267 C5
Charingworth Rd DE21 206 B2
Chariot Cl DE24 233 D5
Charity Rd DE55 170 C5
Charlbury Cl DE23 231 A8
Charles Ashmore Rd S8 57 A8
Charles Ave
Derby DE21 220 D6
Sandiacre NG10 223 B6
Stapleford NG9 223 F8
Charles Cl DE7 209 B6
Charles La SK13 10 E3
Charles Rd DE24 220 A1
Charles St
Alfreton DE55 159 A5
4 Buxton SK17 85 C8
Chesterfield S40 95 E3
Glossop SK13 10 C1
Long Eaton NG10 236 D6
Mansfield NG19 136 A1
Somercotes DE55 170 C7
Swadlincote DE11 256 B2
Charleston Cl DE11 256 A7
Charleston Rd DE21 220 C6
Charlestown SK13 17 C6
Charlestown Dr DE22 204 D4
Charlestown Rd SK13 17 C7
Charlesworth Cl SK23 33 D3
Charlesworth Cres SK23 33 D3
Charlesworth Ct 1 NG19 136 E3
Charlesworth Gdns S44 117 E8
Charlesworth Prim Sch SK13 16 C6
Charlesworth Rd SK23 33 D3
Charlesworth St S44 117 E8
Charley La SK23 47 A8
Charlotte Ct
Burton u T DE14 254 C8
Eastwood NG16 182 F3
Sheffield S2 43 B8
Charlotte Inf Sch DE7 194 E2
Charlotte La S33 51 A7
Charlotte Rd S2 43 B8
Charlotte St
Derby DE23 219 A2
Ilkeston DE7 194 E3
Charlton Ave NG10 223 F1
Charlton Cl DE12 261 D5
Charnock Ave S12 44 B2
Charnock Cres S12 44 A3
Charnock Dale Rd S12 44 B2
Charnock Dr S12 44 B3
Charnock Gr S12 44 B2
Charnock Hall Prim Sch S12 44 B2
Charnock Hall Rd S12 44 A2
Charnock View Rd S12 44 B2
Charnock Wood Rd S12 44 B1
Charnwood Ave
Belper DE56 179 A4
Borrowash DE72 221 C2
Castle Donington DE74 247 C3
Derby DE23 231 D5
Long Eaton NG10 236 B4
Sandiacre NG10 223 A4
Charnwood Cl DE55 169 F7
Charnwood Cres DE55 148 B3
Charnwood Dr DE5 169 C1
Charnwood Gr NG19 136 B5
Charnwood St DE1 267 B2
Charterhouse Cl DE21 205 F3
Charter Pk DE7 208 E7
Charterstone La DE22 204 E4
Chartwell Ave S42 114 D5
Chartwell Dr DE21 219 C5
Chase Cl DE73 233 B2
Chasecliff Cl S40 95 D5
Chase Rd DE56 167 F4
Chase The
Derby DE24 231 F4
Kilburn DE56 192 B8
Little Eaton DE21 191 D2
Rosliston DE12 260 C6
Chase View DE4 156 F1
Chatfield Cl DE15 248 C1

Chatham Ave DE55 . . . . .159 C3
Chatham St DE56 . . . . .179 D4
Chatham St DE23 . . . . .232 A8
Chatsworth Ave
　Chesterfield S40 . . . . .95 B2
　Clowne S43 . . . . .80 F4
　Crich DE4 . . . . .156 F1
　Darley Dale DE4 . . . . .142 F7
　Long Eaton NG10 . . . . . . .237 A6
　Shirebrook NG20 . . . . . . .119 E6
Chatsworth Bsns Pk S40 . .95 E2
Chatsworth Cl
　Alfreton DE55 . . . . .158 F3
　Bolsover S44 . . . . .99 C2
　🄵 Sandiacre NG10 . . . . .223 B4
Chatsworth Cres
　Bullbridge DE56 . . . . . . .168 B5
　Derby DE22 . . . . .204 F3
Chatsworth Ct
　🄹 Ashbourne DE6 . . . . . .173 C2
　🄶 Chesterfield S40. . . . . . .95 C2
　Derby DE24 . . . . .231 F4
　Staveley S43 . . . . .97 D8
　West Hallam DE7. . . . . . .207 E8
Chatsworth Dr
　Derby DE3 . . . . .217 E3
　Little Eaton DE21. . . . . . .191 D2
　North Wingfield S42 . . . . .131 F6
　Tutbury DE13 . . . . .239 C6
Chatsworth Farm Shop★
　DE45 . . . . .91 C2
Chatsworth Ho
　Baslow DE45 . . . . .92 A1
　🄶 Branston DE14. . . . . . .253 F7
Chatsworth Lo SK17. . . . . . .85 A8
Chatsworth Park Ave S12. . .44 A5
Chatsworth Park Cl S12. . . .44 A5
Chatsworth Park Gr S12. . . .44 A5
Chatsworth Park Rd S12 . . .44 A5
Chatsworth Park Rise
　S12. . . . . .44 A5
Chatsworth Pl
　Dronfield S18. . . . . .56 D2
　Ilkeston DE7 . . . . .208 B5
Chatsworth Rd
　Buxton SK17 . . . . .85 E7
　Chesterfield S40. . . . . .95 C2
　Creswell S80 . . . . .81 C1
　Rowsley DE4 . . . . .111 A2
　Sheffield S17 . . . . .55 F6
　Swadlincote DE11 . . . . . . .256 A6
Chatsworth St
　Derby DE23 . . . . .218 C1
　Tibshelf DE55 . . . . .148 A6
Chatsworth Tech Pk 🄼
　S41. . . . . .96 A8
Chatsworth View S32 . . . .72 E1
Chatsworth Way DE75 . . .181 C2
Chatteris Dr DE21. . . . . . . .205 D1
Chatterton La
　Marple SK6 . . . . .24 A8
　Mellor SK6. . . . . .24 B8
Chaucer Dr S18. . . . . .76 C7
Chaucer Inf Sch DE7 . . . .208 F8
Chaucer Jun Sch DE7 . . . .194 F1
Chaucer Rd S41 . . . . .95 F8
Chaucer St DE7 . . . . .194 F1
Chaucer Terr DE23 . . . . . . .231 F7
Chavery Rd S45 . . . . .131 E4
Cheadle Cl DE23 . . . . .218 E8
Cheadle Rd ST14. . . . . .210 B1
Cheam Cl DE22 . . . . .217 E6
Cheapside
　🄶 Belper DE56. . . . . .178 F3
　Derby DE1 . . . . .267 B3
Chedworth Dr DE24 . . . . .233 D6
Cheedale SK17. . . . . .85 D7
Cheedale Ave S40. . . . . .95 D6
Cheedale Cl
　Burton u T DE15. . . . . . . .248 B5
　Chesterfield S40 . . . . .95 D6
Cheetham Ave S18. . . . . . . .76 E5
Chellaston Cotts DE72. . . . .45 A6
Chellaston Inf Sch DE73 . .233 A2
Chellaston Jun Sch
　DE73 . . . . .232 F1
Chellaston La
　Aston-on-T DE72, DE73. . .233 D1
　Aston-on-Trent DE72 . . . .245 F8
Chellaston Park Ct DE73. .232 F2
Chellaston Rd DE24 . . . . . .232 E4
Chellaston Sch DE73. . . . . .232 F1
Chelmarsh Cl DE73. . . . . . .233 A3
Chelmorton Cl NG19 . . . . .136 E3
Chelmorton Pl DE7 . . . . . .219 F8
Chelmsford Cl DE3. . . . . . .217 C3
Chelmsford Way 🄶 S43 . . .78 B3
Chelsea Cl DE22 . . . . .217 E6
Cheltenham Cl NG9 . . . . .223 F2
Chelwood Rd DE73. . . . . . .232 F2
Chendre Cl SK22. . . . . .25 C3
Chepstow Cl S40. . . . . .114 F8
Chepstow Gdns S40. . . . . .114 F7
Chequer La DE56 . . . . .166 D2
Chequers La DE21 . . . . . . .219 D6
Chequers Rd DE21 . . . . . . .219 D5
Cheribough Rd DE74 . . . . .247 A3
Cheriton Cl NG19 . . . . . . .135 E1
Cheriton Ct 🄳 S41 . . . . . . .95 F8
Cheriton Dr DE7 . . . . .194 C3
Cheriton Gdns DE23 . . . . .230 E7
Cherry Bank Rd S8. . . . . . . .43 A3
Cherry Cl
　Ashford in t W DE45 . . . .108 F8
　Breaston DE72. . . . . .235 E8
　Derby DE3 . . . . .218 A2
　Shirebrook NG20 . . . . . . .119 E6

Cherry Cl continued
　South Normanton DE55. . .160 B7
Cherry Ct DE14 . . . . .253 E6
Cherrydale Ct DE23 . . . . . .231 A6
Cherry Garth DE65 . . . . . .228 D2
Cherry Leys DE15 . . . . . . .248 C4
Cherry St S2. . . . . .43 A8
Cherry St S S2. . . . . .43 A8
Cherry Tree Ave
　Belper DE56. . . . . .179 B6
　Ripley DE5 . . . . .180 D8
　Shireoaks S81. . . . . .63 F7
　Swanwick DE55. . . . . .170 A7
Cherry Tree Cl
　Bolsover S44 . . . . .99 C1
　Brinsley NG16 . . . . .182 E8
　Clowne S43 . . . . .80 E3
　Derby DE22 . . . . .218 B4
　Hilton DE65 . . . . .228 D2
　Ilkeston DE7 . . . . .208 D6
　Mansfield Woodhouse
　　NG19. . . . . .136 B4
　Risley DE72 . . . . .222 F4
　Swadlincote DE11 . . . . . . .255 F6
Cherry Tree Ct
　Ashbourne DE6 . . . . .173 B1
　Chapel-en-le-F SK23 . . . . .47 A6
Cherry Tree Dr
　Buxton SK17 . . . . .66 D1
　Creswell S80 . . . . .81 D2
　Killamarsh S21 . . . . .60 D2
　Long Duckmanton S44. . . .98 A4
Cherry Tree Gr
　Mastin Moor S43. . . . . . . .79 C3
　North Wingfield S42 . . . . .131 F5
Cherry Tree Hill Inf Sch
　DE21. . . . . .220 B5
Cherry Tree Hill Jun Sch
　DE21. . . . . .220 B5
Cherry Tree Mews
　Derby DE22 . . . . .220 B4
　Woodville DE11 . . . . .256 F2
Cherrytree Rd DE15 . . . . . .254 F6
Cherry Tree Sq SK17. . . . . .69 C3
Chertsey Cl S40. . . . . .114 F8
Chertsey Ct DE7 . . . . .207 D8
Chertsey Rd DE3 . . . . .217 C2
Cherwell Cl 🄵 S43. . . . . . .96 E8
Chesapeake Rd DE21. . . . .220 B6
Chesham Cl
　Glossop SK13. . . . . .10 B5
　Hadfield SK13 . . . . .10 B5
Cheshire St DE24 . . . . .232 E5
Cheshire Way NG16 . . . . .171 C4
Chess Burrow NG19 . . . . .136 D2
Chessel Cl S8. . . . . .43 A4
Chester Ave DE22 . . . . . . .205 B5
Chester Ct
　Derby, Little Chester
　　DE21. . . . . .219 B8
　Derby, Spondon DE21 . . . .220 E3
　Eckington S21 . . . . .59 B2
Chesterfield Art Gall & Mus★
　S41. . . . . .266 C3
Chesterfield Ave
　Chesterfield S43 . . . . .77 E3
　Long Eaton NG10. . . . . . .236 E4
　Swadlincote DE11 . . . . . . .255 E6
Chesterfield Coll S41 . . . .266 B4
Chesterfield Coll Clowne
　Campus
　Clowne S43 . . . . .80 D3
　Clowne S43 . . . . .80 E4
Chesterfield Coll (Tapton
　House Campus) S41. . . . .96 C5
Chesterfield Dr DE12 . . . .261 D4
Chesterfield & North
　Derbyshire Royal Hospl
　S44. . . . . .96 E3
Chesterfield Rd
　Alfreton DE55 . . . . .158 F5
　Barlborough S43 . . . . .80 A5
　Beeley DE4 . . . . .111 B4
　Belper DE56. . . . . .179 A4
　Brimington, Middlecroft S43 97 B8
　Brimington, Tapton S41,
　　S43. . . . . .96 D7
　Calow S41, S44. . . . . .96 E2
　Darley Dale DE4 . . . . .127 D2
　Dronfield S18. . . . . .57 B1
　Eckington S21 . . . . .59 B2
　Grassmoor S42 . . . . .115 F1
　Heage DE56. . . . . .168 D4
　Holmewood S42. . . . . . . .116 C2
　Long Duckmanton S44. . . .98 C3
　Matlock DE4 . . . . .143 C7
　New Houghton NG19 . . . .134 F7
　North Wingfield S42 . . . . .132 A4
　Pilsley DE5, S45. . . . . . . .133 A1
　Pleasley NG19. . . . . .135 A6
　Rowsley DE4 . . . . .111 A1
　🄶 Sheffield S8 . . . . .43 A6
　Shirland DE55 . . . . .146 C3
　Shuttlewood S44 . . . . .98 E5
　Sutton in A NG17. . . . . . .148 E4
Chesterfield Rd N NG19 . .135 D3
Chesterfield Rd S S8. . . . . .57 A6
Chesterfield Small Bsns Ctr
　S41. . . . . .96 A7
Chesterfield Sta S41 . . . . .266 C3
Chesterfield Trade Ctr
　S41. . . . . .96 A4
Chesterfield Trad Est S41. .76 C3
Chester Gdns DE11. . . . . .256 B2
Chester Gn NG9 . . . . .223 F7
Chester Green Rd DE1 . . .219 A7

Chester Ho S40 . . . . .95 E3
Chesterman Cl NG16 . . . . .195 B4
Chester St
　Chesterfield S40 . . . . .95 E3
　Mansfield NG19. . . . . .135 E1
Chesterton Ave DE23. . . . .231 E7
Chesterton Cl S43 . . . . .96 F4
Chesterton Rd DE21. . . . . .220 E6
Chestnut Ave
　Belper DE56. . . . . .179 A2
　Chellaston DE73 . . . . .232 F3
　Derby DE3 . . . . .217 D3
　Derby, Rose Hill DE23 . . . .219 A2
　Eckington S21 . . . . .59 B2
　Holbrook DE56 . . . . .191 C7
　Killamarsh S21 . . . . .60 C5
　Ripley DE5 . . . . .180 D8
　Somercotes DE55 . . . . . . .170 D5
　Swadlincote DE11 . . . . . . .256 B6
Chestnut Bank 🄵 DE75. . . .181 D1
Chestnut Centre
　Conservatory Pk★ SK23. .47 E8
Chestnut Cl
　Buxton SK17 . . . . .66 B1
　Dronfield S18. . . . . .76 C8
　Duffield DE56. . . . . .190 E2
　Horsley Woodhouse DE7. .192 C7
　New Mills SK22 . . . . .24 E1
Chestnut Cotts DE6 . . . . .151 D1
Chestnut Ct
　Cromford DE4 . . . . .155 A6
　Pinxton NG16 . . . . .160 E3
Chestnut Dr
　Ashbourne DE6 . . . . .185 D7
　Clowne S43 . . . . .80 D4
　Creswell S80 . . . . .81 D2
　Repton DE65 . . . . .243 D2
　Selston NG16 . . . . .171 F7
　Shirebrook NG20. . . . . . . .119 D4
　South Normanton DE55. . .160 B4
Chestnut Gn DE11 . . . . . . .256 B2
Chestnut Gr
　Borrowash DE72 . . . . .221 C3
　Etwall DE65 . . . . .229 B3
　Mansfield Woodhouse
　　NG19. . . . . .136 B5
　Sandiacre NG10. . . . . . . .223 A7
　Tibshelf DE55 . . . . .147 F5
Chestnut La
　Barton in F NG11. . . . . . .237 E6
　Clifton Campville B79 . . .263 F2
Chestnut Rd
　Burton u T DE15. . . . . . . .254 F7
　Langley Mill NG16 . . . . . .182 A3
Chestnuts The NG10 . . . . .236 A8
Chestnut Way
　Repton DE65 . . . . .242 C2
　Swanwick DE55. . . . . .170 A8
Chevely Ct DE21 . . . . .219 D8
Cheverton Cl DE24 . . . . . .233 D5
Chevin Alley DE56. . . . . . .190 F7
Chevin Ave
　Borrowash DE72 . . . . .221 C2
　Derby DE3 . . . . .217 F2
Chevin Bank DE56 . . . . . . .190 D6
Chevin Mews DE56. . . . . . .178 F2
Chevin Pl DE1 . . . . .218 F7
Chevin Rd
　Belper, Chevinside DE56 . .178 E2
　Belper, Milford DE56 . . . .190 F8
　Derby DE1 . . . . .218 F7
　Duffield DE56. . . . . .190 E5
Chevin The DE13. . . . . . . .240 C1
Chevin Vale DE56 . . . . . . .190 E5
Chevin View DE56 . . . . . . .178 F4
Cheviot Ave NG16. . . . . . . .170 F3
Cheviot Cl DE11. . . . . .256 A3
Cheviot Rd NG10 . . . . .223 A1
Cheviot St DE22. . . . . .218 C5
Cheviot Way 🄵 S40. . . . . . .95 C5
Chew Rd OL3 . . . . .5 C8
Chewton St NG16 . . . . . . .182 F1
Cheyenne Gdns DE21. . . . .220 C5
Cheyne Wlk DE22 . . . . . . .218 C6
Chichester Cl DE7 . . . . . . .209 A8
Chigwell Way 🄶 S43. . . . . .78 B3
Chilson Dr DE3 . . . . .217 C3
Chiltern Cl
　Chesterfield S40 . . . . .95 C4
　Grassmoor S42 . . . . .115 F3
Chiltern Ct 🄶 S40. . . . . . . .95 C4
Chiltern Dr DE7 . . . . .207 E8
Chiltern Gdns NG10 . . . . .223 A1
Chiltern Rd DE11. . . . . . . .256 A3
Chilton Cres NG19 . . . . . .136 C6
Chilton Ct 🄴 DE13 . . . . . .240 E1
Chime Cl DE21 . . . . .205 E2
China House Yd DE4 . . . . .165 F8
Chine The DE55. . . . . .160 B3
Chingford Ct DE22 . . . . . .218 B6
Chinley Lo SK23 . . . . .34 E2
Chinley Prim Sch SK23 . . .35 A1
Chinley Rd DE21 . . . . .206 A1
Chinley Sta SK23. . . . . .34 E2
Chippinghouse Rd S2. . . . .43 A7
Chisworth Cl DE22 . . . . . .217 F6
Chiswick Ct 🄲 S43. . . . . . .78 B3
Chisworth Ct 🄶 NG19 . . . .136 E3
Chiverton Cl S18. . . . . .57 A2
Chorlton Terr ST14. . . . . . .210 B1
Christ Church CE Prim Sch
　S41. . . . . .96 A5
Christchurch Ct DE1 . . . . .267 B4
Christ the King RC Prim Sch
　DE55 . . . . .159 A5
Chrysalis Way NG16 . . . . .182 D3
Chrysanthemum Ct
　DE11 . . . . .256 A5

Chunal La SK13. . . . . .17 D5
Chunal Lane Flats SK13 . . .17 C6
Church Al DE45 . . . . .109 D5
Church Alley DE45 . . . . . . .109 D5
Church Ave
　Buxton SK17 . . . . .67 B5
　Clay Cross S45 . . . . .131 E3
　Hatton DE65 . . . . .239 D8
　Long Eaton NG10 . . . . . . .236 A4
　Swadlincote DE11 . . . . . . .256 B3
　Tideswell SK17 . . . . .69 C4
Church Bank S32 . . . . .53 A8
Church Bk S43. . . . . .45 D7
Church Broughton CE Prim
　Sch DE65 . . . . .227 B8
Church Broughton Rd
　DE65 . . . . .227 C3
Church Brow
　Chapel-en-le-F SK23 . . . . .47 B6
　Mottram in L SK14. . . . . . .9 A3
Church Cl
　Barrow u T DE73. . . . . . . .244 C3
　Blackfordby DE11 . . . . . . .257 B1
　Blackwell DE55 . . . . .147 C1
　Burton u T DE15. . . . . . . .248 B3
　Chellaston DE73 . . . . .233 A1
　Clowne S43 . . . . .80 F3
　Glossop SK13. . . . . .10 A2
　Marchington ST14 . . . . . .224 F2
　North Wingfield S45 . . . . .132 A5
　Peak Forest SK17 . . . . . . .49 A3
　Renishaw S21 . . . . .79 B8
　Staveley S43 . . . . .97 C7
　Trowell NG9. . . . . .209 C4
　Willington DE65 . . . . .242 B5
　Wingerworth S42 . . . . . . .115 A4
Church Cnr DE6 . . . . .165 B1
Church Cres NG9 . . . . . . .223 F3
Church Croft
　Coton in t E DE12 . . . . . .260 C3
　Ripley DE5 . . . . .169 D2
Church Ct NG20 . . . . .119 E3
Churchdale Ave NG9 . . . . .209 E1
Churchdale Mews S12 . . . .44 D4
Churchdale Rd S12. . . . . . .44 D4
Churchdown Cl DE21. . . . .206 B2
Church Dr
　Duffield DE56. . . . . .190 F2
　Ilkeston DE7 . . . . .194 D4
　Sandiacre NG10. . . . . . . .223 B7
　Shirebrook NG20. . . . . . . .119 E3
Church Farm ST14 . . . . . .210 A4
Church Farm Mews S42 . .116 B3
Church Farm Rd DE5. . . . .180 E8
Churchfields S80 . . . . .81 E1
Church Fold SK13. . . . . . . .16 C7
Church Gdns NG19 . . . . . .136 C3
Church Gresley Inf Sch
　DE11. . . . . .256 B2
Church Hill
　Derby DE21 . . . . .220 D4
　Etwall DE65 . . . . .229 B5
　Jacksdale NG16 . . . . .171 B3
　Kimberley NG16. . . . . . . .195 F6
　Mansfield Woodhouse
　　NG19. . . . . .136 C3
　Newton DE55. . . . . .148 A1
Church Hill Ave NG19 . . . .136 C3
Church Hill St DE15 . . . . .248 B3
Churchill Ave DE4. . . . . . . .154 D5
Churchill Cl DE72 . . . . . . .235 D8
Churchill Dr
　Hilton DE65 . . . . .228 E2
　🄶 Stapleford NG9 . . . . . .223 E8
Church La
　Bakewell DE45 . . . . .109 D6
　Barrow u T DE73. . . . . . . .244 A5
　Barton in F NG11. . . . . . .237 E6
　Baslow DE45 . . . . .91 E5
　Beeley DE4 . . . . .111 A4
　Belper DE56. . . . . .179 A4
　Brackenfield DE55 . . . . . .145 D2
　Brailsford DE6. . . . . .201 E7
　Breadsall DE21 . . . . .205 E4
　Brinsley NG16 . . . . .182 E7
　Buxton SK17 . . . . .86 B7
　Caldwell DE12 . . . . .260 E7
　Calow S44 . . . . .97 A3
　Castle Donington DE74 . . .247 B3
　Chapel-en-le-F SK23 . . . . .47 B6
　Chelmorton SK17. . . . . . .106 B8
　Chesterfield S40 . . . . .266 B3
　Chilcote DE12 . . . . .264 E3
　Clowne S43 . . . . .80 F3
　Cossall NG16. . . . . .195 C1
　Derby, Chaddesden DE21. .220 A6
　Derby, Darley Abbey DE22 .205 A2
　Doveridge DE6 . . . . .211 B1
　Eckington S12 . . . . .58 E7
　Ellastone DE6 . . . . .183 B4
　Great Longstone DE45. . . .90 A4
　Hanbury DE13 . . . . .238 A4
　Heath S44 . . . . .117 B3
　Heath, Stockley S44 . . . . .117 D3
　Hemington DE74 . . . . . . .247 E4
　Holmewood S42. . . . . . . .116 B3
　Horsley Woodhouse DE7. .192 E6
　Killamarsh S21 . . . . .60 E6
　Kirk Langley DE6 . . . . . . .202 E2
　Little Eaton DE21. . . . . . .205 C7
　Mackworth DE22 . . . . . . .217 F7
　Marchington ST14 . . . . . .224 F2
　Marple SK6 . . . . .23 A5
　Mayfield DE6 . . . . .184 C6
　Monyash DE45. . . . . .107 C1
　Morley DE7 . . . . .206 E6
　New Mills SK22 . . . . .33 C8
　Newton Solney DE15 . . . .248 D8

Church La continued
　North Wingfield S42 . . . . .131 F5
　Osmaston DE6. . . . . .186 A5
　Peak Forest SK17 . . . . . . .49 A3
　Pleasley NG19. . . . . .135 A5
　Rocester ST14 . . . . .197 A3
　Rowsley DE4 . . . . .110 E1
　Selston NG16. . . . . .171 E7
　Sheffield, Townhead S17 . . .55 D6
　Shirley DE6 . . . . .200 D8
　South Wingfield DE55 . . . .157 F4
　Stanton-by-D DE7 . . . . . .208 F1
　Stapleford NG9 . . . . .223 D7
　Stonebroom DE55 . . . . . .146 F5
　Sutton on t H DE6 . . . . . .215 B1
　Thorpe DE6 . . . . .161 D1
　Thrumpton NG11. . . . . . .237 C3
　Tibshelf DE55 . . . . .147 F6
　Ticknall DE73. . . . . .251 A4
　Tideswell SK17 . . . . .69 D4
　Weston Underwood DE6. .188 E2
Church La N
　Chesterfield S41 . . . . .77 A3
　🄶 Derby DE22 . . . . .204 F3
Churchland Ave S42 . . . . .132 D8
Church Level DE6 . . . . . . .165 B1
Church Mdws
　Calow S44 . . . . .96 F3
　North Wingfield S42 . . . . .131 F5
Churchmead NG17 . . . . . .148 F3
Church Mews
　Derby DE21 . . . . .220 D4
　Hatton DE65 . . . . .227 D1
　Killamarsh S21 . . . . .60 E7
　Melbourne DE73 . . . . . . .252 B7
　Sheffield S20 . . . . .59 D7
Church Rd
　Branston DE14. . . . . .253 E7
　Burton u T DE13. . . . . . . .240 E7
　Church Broughton DE65 . .227 A8
　Darley Dale DE4 . . . . .127 B2
　Egginton DE65 . . . . .241 B4
　Hollingworth SK14. . . . . . .9 A4
　Marple SK6 . . . . .23 E6
　New Mills SK22 . . . . .33 C7
　Quarndon DE22 . . . . .204 C5
　Rolleston DE13 . . . . .240 A4
　Shuttlewood S44 . . . . .99 A6
　Shuttlewood, Stanfree S44. .99 B8
　Snelston DE6 . . . . .184 C3
　Swadlincote DE11 . . . . . . .256 A6
Church Rise S44 . . . . .146 C4
Church St E NG16 . . . . . . .160 D3
Church St N S41 . . . . .77 A3
Church St S
　Chesterfield S40 . . . . .115 A7
　Glossop SK13. . . . . .10 E2
Church St W
　Chesterfield S40 . . . . .95 C2
　Pinxton NG16. . . . . .160 D3
Churchside
　Grassmoor S41 . . . . .115 D5
　Willington DE65 . . . . .242 A5
Church Side
　Calow S44 . . . . .96 F3
　Sutton in A NG17. . . . . . .148 F3
Churchside La S41. . . . . . . .115 D6
Churchside Wlk DE22. . . . .218 E4
Church Sq
　🄵 Heanor DE75 . . . . .181 F1
　Melbourne DE73 . . . . . . .252 B6
Church St
　Alfreton DE55 . . . . .158 F4
　Alstonefield DE6 . . . . . . .149 D3
　Appleby Magna DE12. . . .265 F1
　Ashbourne DE6 . . . . .173 B2
　Ashford in t W DE45 . . . .108 F8
　Ashover S45 . . . . .129 F3
　Barlborough S43 . . . . .80 B7
　Baslow DE45 . . . . .91 E5
　Belper DE56. . . . . .179 A3
　Bolsover S44 . . . . .99 A1
　Bonsall DE4 . . . . .142 A4
　Bradwell S33 . . . . .51 A7
　Brassington DE4 . . . . .153 A1
　Brimington S43 . . . . .96 E8
　Buxton SK17 . . . . .85 B6
　Calow S44 . . . . .96 F3
　Clifton Campville B79 . . .263 E2
　Clowne S43 . . . . .80 E3
　Coton in t E DE12 . . . . . .260 C3
　Creswell S80 . . . . .81 F1
　Denby Village DE5. . . . . . .180 D1
　Derby, Alvaston DE24 . . . .233 C1
　Derby DE23 . . . . .218 C1
　Derby, Rose Hill DE23 . . . .219 A2
　Derby, Spondon DE21 . . . .220 D5
　Donisthorpe DE12 . . . . . .262 F1
　Dronfield S18. . . . . .57 A1
　Eastwood NG16. . . . . . . .182 F2
　Eckington S21 . . . . .59 E4
　Eyam S32. . . . . .71 D5
　Fritchley DE56 . . . . .168 B5
　Glossop SK13. . . . . .10 D2
　Hadfield SK13 . . . . .10 A4
　Hartington SK17 . . . . . . .137 D5
　Hartshorne DE11 . . . . . . .257 B6
　Hayfield SK22 . . . . .25 D2
　Heage DE56. . . . . .168 E2
　Holbrook DE56. . . . . .191 C6
　Holloway DE4 . . . . .156 A6
　Horsley DE21 . . . . .191 F5
　Ilkeston DE7 . . . . .194 F1
　Kilburn DE56 . . . . .191 F8
　Lockington DE74 . . . . . . .247 F4

Church St *continued*
Longnor SK17 . . . . .121 B6
Mansfield Woodhouse
NG19. . . . . .136 C3
Marple SK6 . . . . .23 A5
Matlock DE4 . . . . .143 C4
Melbourne DE73 . . . . .252 B7
Monyash SK17 . . . . .107 C2
Netherseal DE12 . . . . .264 F6
Ockbrook DE72 . . . . .221 C4
Pilsley S45. . . . . .132 C1
Pleasley NG19 . . . . .135 B4
Ripley DE5 . . . . .169 D2
Ripley, Waingroves DE5 . . . .181 A7
Sandiacre NG10. . . . . .223 B7
Shirland DE55 . . . . .146 D2
Somercotes DE55 . . . . .170 D6
South Normanton DE55. . . .160 A6
Stapleford NG9 . . . . .223 D7
Staveley S43 . . . . .78 E2
Swadlincote DE11 . . . . .256 B6
Swadlincote, Lower Midway
DE11 . . . . .256 C4
Swadlincote, Newhall
DE11 . . . . .256 A6
Tansley DE4 . . . . .144 A4
Tideswell SK17 . . . . .69 C4
Tintwistle SK13 . . . . .10 A7
Tutbury DE13 . . . . .239 C7
Unstone S18 . . . . .76 E2
Whaley Thorns NG20 . . . . . .101 A2
Wirksworth DE4 . . . . .165 F8
Youlgreave DE45 . . . . .125 C5
Church Street Mews S33 . 51 A7
Church Terr SK13 . . . . .10 D2
Church View
Barlborough S43 . . . . .80 A7
Belper DE56. . . . . .179 A4
Blackwell DE55 . . . . .147 F1
Breaston DE72 . . . . .235 D7
Chesterfield S40 . . . . .95 C2
Clifton DE6. . . . . .184 F6
Clowne S43 . . . . .80 F3
Duffield DE56 . . . . .190 E2
Glapwell S44 . . . . .134 B8
Heanor DE75 . . . . .181 B4
Ilkeston DE7 . . . . .208 E7
Killamarsh S21 . . . . .60 E7
Mottram in L SK14. . . . . .9 A3
New Houghton NG19 . . . . .134 F7
New Mills SK22 . . . . .33 C8
Church View Cotts SK17 . .84 E6
Church View Dr DE45 . . . . .91 E6
Churchward Dr DE13 . . . . .240 F1
Church Way S40 . . . . .266 B3
Church Wlk
Brinsley NG16 . . . . .182 E6
Chesterfield, Glasshouse
Common S43. . . . . .77 D4
Chesterfield S40 . . . . .266 B3
Derby DE22 . . . . .204 F4
Donisthorpe DE12 . . . . .265 E8
Duffield DE56. . . . . .190 F2
Eastwood NG16. . . . . .182 F2
Glossop SK13. . . . . .10 E2
Parwich DE6 . . . . .151 D1
Somercotes DE55 . . . . .170 E6
3 Stapleford NG9 . . . . . .223 E7
Wirksworth DE4 . . . . .165 F8
Churnet Cl DE6 . . . . .184 C7
Churnet Rd DE65. . . . . . . .240 D8
Churnet Row ST14 . . . . . .196 F3
Churston Rd S40. . . . . .95 D3
Cinder Bank NG16 . . . . . .170 F4
Cinder Hill S81 . . . . .63 D7
Cinderhill La S8 . . . . .57 C8
Cinder La
Killamarsh S21 . . . . .60 F7
Wirksworth DE4 . . . . .165 E6
Cinder Rd DE55 . . . . .170 D7
Circle Cl S2 . . . . .44 B8
Circle The
Derby DE24 . . . . .231 E5
Mansfield Woodhouse
NG19. . . . . .136 B6
Sheffield S2. . . . . .44 A8
Circular Dr S21 . . . . .79 B8
Circular Rd
Chesterfield S40 . . . . .115 B8
Staveley S43 . . . . .78 D1
City Gate DE24. . . . . .219 D2
City Gate Bsns Pk DE24 . .219 D2
City Rd
Derby DE1. . . . . .219 A7
Sheffield S12, S2. . . . . .43 F8
City Road Ind Pk DE1 . . . .219 A7
City Sch The S13. . . . . .44 F6
City The
Blackfordby DE11 . . . . .257 A4
Woodville DE11 . . . . .256 F2
Civic Ctr S18 . . . . .57 A1
Civic Way DE11 . . . . .256 B4
Clamp Dr DE11 . . . . .256 B3
Clapgun St DE74. . . . . .247 B3
Clara Mount Rd DE75 . . . .182 A1
Clarehaven NG9 . . . . .223 E5
Clare Ho DE1 . . . . .267 B1
Claremont Cl 15 NG19 . . . .136 E4
Clarence Ind Trad Est
S41 . . . . .96 B8
Clarence Rd
Chesterfield S40 . . . . .266 A3
Derby DE23 . . . . .218 F1
Long Eaton NG10. . . . . .236 C6

Clarence St
Chesterfield S40 . . . . .266 A3
Pleasley NG19 . . . . .135 C3
Stonebroom DE55 . . . . .147 B4
Clarence Terr DE4 . . . . . . .143 A1
Clarence Villas DE4 . . . . . .143 B2
Clarendon Rd S43 . . . . .97 C7
Clarke Ave DE75 . . . . .181 C2
Clarke Dr NG10 . . . . .236 A4
Clarkes Cl ST14 . . . . .210 B1
Clarkes La DE72 . . . . .246 B8
Clarke St DE1. . . . . .267 C4
Clarkson Ave S40 . . . . .266 B1
Clatterway DE4 . . . . .154 E8
Claverhouse Rd DE15 . . . . .248 A2
Claxton St DE75 . . . . .181 D2
Claxton Terr 2 DE75 . . . . .181 D2
Clay's La DE14 . . . . .253 F8
Clay Cross Com Hospl
S45 . . . . .131 D4
Clay Cross Countryside Ctr ★
S45 . . . . .131 C3
Clay Cross Inf & Jun Sch
S45 . . . . .131 C3
Claye St NG10 . . . . .236 E7
Clay La
Clay Cross S45 . . . . .131 B2
Heanor DE75 . . . . .181 F2
Claylands SK14 . . . . .9 D4
Claylands Gr S80 . . . . .81 E5
Claylands Pl S80. . . . . .81 E5
Claylands Rd S80 . . . . .81 E5
Claymar Dr DE11 . . . . .256 A7
Claymills Rd DE13 . . . . . . .241 A2
Claypit La S42 . . . . .112 F8
Clay Pit Way S43. . . . . .80 C6
Clay St E DE15 . . . . .248 A1
Clay St
Burton u T DE15 . . . . .248 A1
Draycott DE72 . . . . .235 A7
Shirland DE55 . . . . .146 E1
Cleave Rd DE14 . . . . .254 A8
Clegg Hill Dr NG17 . . . . . . .148 E4
Clematis Cres DE15 . . . . . .255 B3
Clement La SK17 . . . . .50 C6
Clement Rd
Horsley Woodhouse DE7 . .192 C7
Marple SK6 . . . . .23 C7
Cleve Ave
Beeston NG9 . . . . .223 F3
Darley Dale DE4 . . . . .142 F7
Cleveland Ave
Derby DE21 . . . . .220 B5
Draycott DE72 . . . . .235 A7
Long Eaton NG10. . . . . .223 F1
Cleveland Cl DE11 . . . . . . .256 B3
Cleveland Ct DE15 . . . . . . .248 B3
Cleveland Rd DE55 . . . . . . .146 F3
Cleveland Way S40 . . . . . . .95 C5
Cleveleys Rd NG9 . . . . .223 B3
Clewley Rd DE14 . . . . .253 F8
Cliffash La DE56 . . . . .176 E6
Cliff Bottom S32 . . . . .71 F4
Cliff Bvd NG16 . . . . .195 F7
Cliff Coll S32 . . . . .91 D8
Cliffdon Ho DE65 . . . . .239 D8
Cliffefield Rd S8. . . . . .43 A5
Cliffe Field Rd S8. . . . . .43 A4
Cliffe Hill Ave NG9 . . . . . . .223 D7
Cliffe La
Hathersage S32. . . . . .52 F8
Tideswell SK17 . . . . .69 C4
Cliffe Rd SK13 . . . . .17 D8
Cliffe View Rd S8. . . . . .43 A5
Cliff Hill S43. . . . . .80 D3
Cliff La
Curbar S32 . . . . .72 E1
Elton DE4. . . . . .140 D8
Kirby-in-A NG16 . . . . .160 F4
Cliff Nook DE55. . . . . .160 B4
Clifford Cl
Chesterfield S40 . . . . .95 B2
Long Eaton NG10. . . . . .236 A4
Clifford St
Derby DE24 . . . . .219 D2
Long Eaton NG10. . . . . .236 E7
Cliff Rd SK17 . . . . .85 D2
Clifton Ave
Barlborough S43 . . . . .80 A7
Long Eaton NG10. . . . . .237 A7
Clifton CE Prim Sch DE6 .184 F6
Clifton Cl
Overseal DE12. . . . . .262 A3
Swadlincote DE11 . . . . .256 A2
Clifton Dr
Buxton SK17 . . . . .85 C4
Derby DE3 . . . . .217 E3
Clifton Rd
Ashbourne DE6 . . . . .185 A8
Buxton SK17 . . . . .85 C7
Derby DE22 . . . . .204 D3
Matlock Bath DE4 . . . . .155 A8
Netherseal DE12 . . . . .264 D6
Clifton St
Chesterfield S40 . . . . .95 E3
Derby DE1. . . . . .267 D1
Cliftonthorpe LE65 . . . . . . .258 B1
Clifton Thorpe Mdws
LE65. . . . . .258 B1
Clifton Way DE15 . . . . .248 B2
Clinthill La S80 . . . . .81 E7
Clinton Ave NG16 . . . . .182 D6
Clinton St DE21 . . . . .219 D6
Clipstone Gdns DE21 . . . . .206 B2
Clive Ho DE15 . . . . .248 C3

Clock Tower Bsns Ctr The
S43 . . . . .78 B2
Clodhall La
Curbar S32 . . . . .72 F2
Old Brampton S42 . . . . .93 B5
Cloisters Ct DE21 . . . . .205 F2
Cloonmore Croft S8 . . . . . . .43 C1
Cloonmore Dr S8 . . . . .43 C1
Close Bank DE13 . . . . .239 C6
Close The
Derby, Allestree DE22 . . . . .204 F2
Derby, Normanton Park
DE23. . . . . .218 D2
Great Longstone DE45. . . . . .89 F4
Linton DE12 . . . . .261 C5
Marple SK6 . . . . .15 B1
Matlock DE4 . . . . .143 B6
Moira DE11 . . . . .262 D8
Shirebrook NG20. . . . . .119 F5
Tutbury DE13 . . . . .239 B6
Cloud Ave NG9 . . . . .223 F7
Cloudside Ct NG10 . . . . . . .223 B7
Cloudside Jun Sch NG10 .223 B7
Cloudside Rd NG10 . . . . . . .223 B7
Cloudwood Cl DE23 . . . . . .218 B1
Clough Ave SK6. . . . . .23 C6
Clough Bank S2 . . . . .43 B8
Clough Field Cl S23 . . . . . . .45 D8
Clough La
Hayfield SK22 . . . . .25 C5
Sheffield S10. . . . . .42 F5
Wensley DE4 . . . . .141 D8
Clough Mill SK22 . . . . .25 C5
Cloughside SK12. . . . . .32 E6
Clough Side SK6. . . . . .23 C7
Clough St SK17 . . . . .85 B7
Clough The
Bamford S33 . . . . .40 C4
Chesterfield S41 . . . . .96 C1
Clovelly Ct DE22 . . . . .218 D8
Clover Cl DE21 . . . . .220 F5
Clover Ct
Branston DE14. . . . . .253 E6
Shardlow DE72 . . . . .234 E2
Sheffield S8. . . . . .43 C2
Tibshelf DE55 . . . . .148 B7
Cloverdale DE11 . . . . .256 B7
Cloverdale Dr DE24 . . . . . . .231 F2
Clover Fields Touring Cvn Pk
SK17 . . . . .85 C1
Clover Nook Ind Est
DE55. . . . . .159 E3
Clover Nook Rd DE55. . . . . .159 E3
Clover Rise NG16 . . . . .195 B8
Cloverslade DE65 . . . . .230 C1
Clover Way NG19 . . . . .136 F4
Clowne Jun & Inf Schs
S43 . . . . .80 E3
Clowne Rd
Barlborough S43 . . . . .80 C6
Shuttlewood S44 . . . . .99 A8
Club La DE73 . . . . .244 A5
Clubmill Terr S40 . . . . .95 E4
Club Row S32 . . . . .71 E6
Clumber Ave NG16 . . . . . . .171 E1
Clumber Cl
Ashbourne DE6 . . . . .185 B8
Clowne S43 . . . . .80 F4
8 Ripley DE5 . . . . .169 E1
Clumber Ct
Ilkeston DE7 . . . . .194 F5
Mansfield NG19 . . . . .135 E2
Clumber Dr NG19 . . . . .135 E2
Clumber Pl S43 . . . . .97 C6
Clumber St NG10 . . . . .236 D7
Clun Ct NG19 . . . . .136 D2
Clune St S43 . . . . .81 A5
Cluster Rd DE56 . . . . .178 F4
Clusters Ct 3 DE56 . . . . . .178 F4
Clyde St DE65. . . . . .228 D1
Coach Dr
Eastwood NG16. . . . . .182 F4
Quarndon DE22 . . . . .204 D7
Coachhouse Mews 4
DE11 . . . . .256 A7
Coach Rd
Hollingworth SK14. . . . . .9 C5
Ironville DE55 . . . . .170 D3
Ripley DE5 . . . . .169 F3
Shireoaks S81 . . . . .63 F6
Coach Way DE65. . . . . .242 C5
Coachways DE7. . . . . .193 F3
Coal La DE11, DE73 . . . . . . .257 D8
Coalpit La
Coton in t E DE12 . . . . .260 E3
Youlgreave DE45 . . . . .125 C6
Coarses View SK23. . . . . . . .47 C7
Coasthill DE4 . . . . .156 F7
Coatsby Rd NG16 . . . . .195 F7
Cobden Pl NG19 . . . . .135 E2
Cobden Rd
Chesterfield S40 . . . . .266 A4
Matlock DE4 . . . . .143 C6
Cobden St
Derby DE22 . . . . .218 D5
Long Eaton NG10. . . . . .236 E7
Ripley DE5 . . . . .169 D2
Cobham Cl DE24 . . . . .231 D3
Cobnar Ave S8. . . . . .43 A2
Cobnar Dr
Chesterfield S41 . . . . .95 D8
Sheffield S8. . . . . .43 A2
Cobnar Rd S8 . . . . .43 A2
Cobnar Wood Cl S18. . . . . . .76 B3
Cobthorn Dr DE22 . . . . . . .204 C3
Coburn Pl DE1. . . . . .267 A3
Cock Ayne Cl NG10. . . . . . .223 B3

Cockayne La DE6 . . . . .164 B2
Cockayne St N DE24. . . . . .232 E6
Cockayne St S DE24 . . . . . .232 E6
Cock Brow SK14 . . . . .15 C7
Cockcharme Gapp DE74 . .247 B6
Cockerhouse Rd NG16 . . . .182 E4
Cock Hill
Baslow DE45 . . . . .91 F5
Clifton DE6. . . . . .184 F6
Cockleys NG10 . . . . .236 C6
Cock Pitt The DE1 . . . . .267 C3
Cockshead La DE1 . . . . . . .198 D7
Cockshut La
Melbourne DE73 . . . . .251 F7
Whaley Thorns NG20 . . . . . .101 A2
Cockshut Lane Bsns Ctr
DE73. . . . . .252 A7
Cockshutt Ave S8. . . . . .56 D8
Cockshutt Dr S8 . . . . .56 D8
Cockshutt La DE55 . . . . . . .170 F8
Cockshutt Rd S8. . . . . .56 D8
Cod Beck Cl DE24 . . . . .233 D6
Coddington La DE4 . . . . . . .156 E2
Codnor Com CE Prim Sch
DE5 . . . . .181 B8
Codnor-Denby La DE5 . . . .181 A5
Codnor Gate DE5 . . . . .170 B1
Codnor Gate Ind Est
DE5. . . . . .170 A1
Codnor La DE5 . . . . .170 C2
Coffin La DE6. . . . . .165 B1
Coggers La S32. . . . . .52 F8
Coisley Hill S13. . . . . .44 F6
Cokayne Ave DE6 . . . . .173 C2
Cokayne Mews DE6 . . . . . .173 C3
Cokefield Terr DE55. . . . . . .148 C1
Coke St DE22 . . . . .218 D5
Coldharbour La S45. . . . . . .145 A4
Cold Side S33 . . . . .14 F3
Coldstream Wlk DE24 . . . . .231 E4
Coldwell St DE4 . . . . .165 F8
Cole La DE72 . . . . .221 D3
Coleman St DE24 . . . . .232 E7
Coleraine Cl DE21 . . . . .220 B4
Coleridge St
Derby, Littleover DE23. . . . .231 E6
Derby, Normanton DE23 . . .231 F7
Colin Ave DE5 . . . . .181 B8
College Ave S43 . . . . .78 D1
College Mews DE1 . . . . . . .218 E5
College Rd
Buxton SK17 . . . . .85 A6
Denstone ST14 . . . . .196 C6
Spinkhill S21 . . . . .60 D2
College St NG10 . . . . .223 C2
College View S43 . . . . .80 E3
College Way SK17. . . . . .85 D2
Collier Ave NG19 . . . . .136 B5
Collier La DE72 . . . . .221 C4
Collier St SK13. . . . . .17 C8
Colliers Trek S43 . . . . .80 C5
Colliers Way S45. . . . . .131 B4
Colliery Cl S43. . . . . .78 F1
Colliery La DE12 . . . . .261 D4
Colliery Rd
Blackwell DE55 . . . . .147 F1
Creswell S80 . . . . .100 E8
Swadlincote DE11 . . . . .256 A1
Colliery Row
Alfreton DE55 . . . . .159 B5
Pinxton NG16. . . . . .160 D2
Swadlincote DE11 . . . . .256 A1
Collin Ave NG10 . . . . .223 B4
Collingham Gdns DE22 . . . .218 A5
Collingham Rd NG19 . . . . . .135 D1
Collingwood Cres DE4 . . . .143 A6
Collingwood Rd NG10 . . . . .236 E6
Collins Ave DE55 . . . . .160 A7
Collins Yd S18 . . . . .57 B1
Collis Cl DE24 . . . . .232 E7
Collishaw Cl 6 S41 . . . . . . .96 C1
Collumbell Ave DE72. . . . . .221 C5
Colne Cl NG19 . . . . .136 D2
Colombo St DE23 . . . . .219 B1
Colonade NG20 . . . . .119 E2
Colonnade The 3 SK17 . . .85 B8
Colonsay Cl NG9 . . . . .209 D3
Colton Cl S41. . . . . .76 E1
Coltsfoot Cl DE11 . . . . .256 F4
Coltsfoot Dr DE24. . . . . .231 F2
Coltsworth La S43 . . . . .80 E8
Columbell Way DE4 . . . . . .127 D2
Columbia St NG17 . . . . .148 F3
Columbine Cl DE21 . . . . . . .206 A1
Colver Rd S2 . . . . .43 A8
Colvile Cl DE12 . . . . .263 D7
Colvile St DE22 . . . . .218 D6
Colwell Dr DE24 . . . . .233 D5
Colwick Cl NG19 . . . . .135 E1
Colwyn Ave DE23 . . . . .218 D1
Colyear St DE1. . . . . .267 B3
Combs Bank 53 SK13 . . . . . .9 D2
Combs Cl S43. . . . . .33 A8
Combs Fold 51 SK13 . . . . . . .9 D2
Combs Gdns 2 SK13 . . . . . . .9 D1
Combs Gr 49 SK13 . . . . .9 D2
Combs Inf Sch SK23. . . . . . .46 E1
Combs Lea 1 SK13 . . . . .9 D1
Combs Mews 48 SK13 . . . . . .9 D2
Combs Rd S43. . . . . .46 E3
Combs Terr 50 SK13. . . . . . . .9 D2
Combs Way 52 SK13. . . . . . . .9 D2
Comfrey Cl DE23 . . . . .230 F6
Commerce St
Derby DE24 . . . . .232 F8
Melbourne DE73 . . . . .252 A7

Commercial Rd SK17. . . . . . .69 C4
Commercial Row S32 . . . . . .72 C8
Common End DE65. . . . . . . .229 B3
Common La
Chelmorton SK17. . . . . .87 A1
Cutthorpe S42 . . . . .94 E8
Mansfield Woodhouse
NG19. . . . . .136 A4
Shirebrook NG20. . . . . .119 C4
Shirland DE55 . . . . .146 C3
Stanley DE7 . . . . .207 A7
Sutton on t H DE6 . . . . .228 A8
Commonpiece La DE6. . . . . .215 B2
Common Piece La DE65 . . . .230 E1
Commonpiece Rd S45. . . . . .131 C3
Common Rd
Harthill S26 . . . . .62 B5
Sutton in A NG17 . . . . .148 F2
Swadlincote DE11 . . . . .256 C2
Thorpe Salvin S80 . . . . .62 F6
Commons Rd NG16 . . . . . . .195 A8
Common Side
Selston NG16. . . . . .171 E8
Swadlincote DE11 . . . . .256 C2
Commonside Rd S18. . . . . . .75 D2
Common The
Crich DE4. . . . . .168 A7
Quarndon DE22 . . . . .204 C8
South Normanton DE55. . . .160 A5
Common Wood DE4. . . . . . .143 B3
Compass Cres S41 . . . . .77 C3
Compstall Mills Ests SK6 . .15 B2
Compstall Rd
Compstall SK6 . . . . .15 A3
Marple SK6 . . . . .15 A2
Compton Ave DE72. . . . . . . .246 A8
Compton Cl 6 DE24 . . . . . .233 C6
Compton Dr S80 . . . . .81 D1
Compton Gr SK17 . . . . .85 B6
Compton Rd SK17 . . . . .85 B6
Compton St
Ashbourne DE6 . . . . .173 C2
Chesterfield S40 . . . . .266 A4
Holmewood S42 . . . . .116 E1
Langwith NG20 . . . . .119 F8
Conalan Ave S17. . . . . .56 B5
Concert Pl 6 SK17. . . . . . . .85 B7
Concorde Way NG19 . . . . . .135 E3
Condliff Rd SK17. . . . . .69 E5
Condor Rd DE7 . . . . .208 F4
Conduit Rd S44 . . . . .118 B8
Conduit St
Glossop SK13. . . . . .9 F7
Tintwistle SK13 . . . . .9 F7
Coney Green Bsns Ctr
S45 . . . . .131 E4
Coney Green Networking Ctr
S45 . . . . .131 E4
Coney Green Rd S45. . . . . . .131 E4
Coniston Ave DE21 . . . . . . .220 E6
Coniston Cl NG19 . . . . .136 F4
Coniston Cres DE21 . . . . . .205 D2
Coniston Dr
Clay Cross S45 . . . . .131 B2
Ilkeston DE7 . . . . .208 C3
Coniston Rd
Chesterfield S41 . . . . .95 C8
Dronfield S18. . . . . .56 E1
Long Eaton NG10. . . . . .223 A2
Coniston Way S41 . . . . .95 E8
Conjoint La SK17. . . . . .69 E4
Conkers Discovery Ctr ★
DE12. . . . . .262 D5
Conkers Waterside Ctr ★
DE12. . . . . .262 D4
Conksbury Ave DE45 . . . .125 C6
Conksbury La DE45 . . . . . .125 C6
Connaught Ct DE55 . . . . . .159 B3
Connaught Rd DE22 . . . . . .218 C4
Connelly Ct S40. . . . . .95 E3
Consett Cl DE21. . . . . .205 D1
Consort Gdns DE21 . . . . . .206 C3
Constable Ave DE23. . . . . . .218 C2
Constable Cl
3 Dronfield S18. . . . . .56 E1
Sheffield S14 . . . . .43 E2
Constable Dr
Derby DE23 . . . . .218 B1
Marple SK6 . . . . .23 B8
Sheffield S14 . . . . .43 D2
Constable La DE23 . . . . . . .218 C3
Constable Pl S14 . . . . .43 E2
Constable Rd S14. . . . . .43 D2
Constable Way S14 . . . . .43 D2
Convent Cl DE15 . . . . .254 F8
Conway Ave DE72. . . . . .221 D2
Conway Rd NG10. . . . . .236 F8
Conway St NG10 . . . . .236 F8
Conygree La DE6 . . . . .184 D7
Cook Cl DE56. . . . . .179 E5
Cook Dr DE7. . . . . .209 A6
Cooke & Beard Homes S8 .43 B5
Cooke Cl
Clay Cross S42 . . . . .131 B6
Long Eaton NG10. . . . . .236 B7
Cookfield DE56 . . . . .179 C6
Cookham Cl DE3 . . . . .217 C2
Cook La DE6. . . . . .211 B1
Cooks Dr DE74. . . . . .247 A3
Coole Well Cl S43. . . . . .97 D8
Coombes La SK13. . . . . .16 C5
Coombes View SK14 . . . . . .15 F8
Coombs Rd DE45. . . . . .109 F5
Cooper's Cl 2 DE6. . . . . . . .173 C2
Co-operative St
Derby DE23 . . . . .218 F2
Disley SK12. . . . . .32 D6
Long Eaton NG10. . . . . .236 E6

Coopers Cl
Acresford DE12 . . . . **265** B7
Borrowash DE72 . . . . **221** D1
Coopers Croft DE65 . . . . . **227** C1
Coopers Gdns DE6 . . . . . . **173** B1
Cooper St
Derby DE22 . . . . **218** D6
Glossop SK13 . . . . **10** B1
Ripley DE5 . . . . **169** D1
Copecastle Sq DE1 . . . . . . **267** C2
Cope St DE24 . . . . **232** A5
Copeland Ave NG9 . . . . . . **223** E8
Copeland St DE1 . . . . **267** C2
Copenhagen Rd S45 . . . . . **131** E4
Copestake Cl NG10 . . . . . . **236** A7
Copes Way
Derby DE21 . . . . **220** A8
Uttoxeter ST14 . . . . **210** A1
Copley Croft 3 DE6 . . . . . **173** D3
Coplow La DE65 . . . . **226** D5
Copperas Rd DE11 . . . . . . **255** D5
Copper Beech Dr SK13 . . . . **9** E1
Copper Beeches DE5 . . . . . **169** C2
Copperleaf Cl DE22 . . . . . . **267** A4
Copper Yd DE5 . . . . **180** F2
Coppice Ave
High Lane SK12 . . . . **32** A6
Ilkeston DE7 . . . . **194** D5
Coppice Cl
Chesterfield S41 . . . . **115** D6
Derby DE22 . . . . **204** F1
High Lane SK12 . . . . **32** A6
Kilburn DE56 . . . . **192** A7
Coppice Ct
Eastwood NG16 . . . . **182** D3
Heanor DE75 . . . . **193** F7
Coppice Dr
Eastwood NG16 . . . . **182** D3
Heanor DE75 . . . . **193** F7
Coppice End Rd DE22 . . . . **204** C1
Coppice La
Clifton Campville B79 . . . . **263** F1
High Lane SK12 . . . . **32** A5
Coppice Mews DE75 . . . . . **193** F7
Coppice Prim Sch DE75 . . **193** E8
Coppice Side DE11 . . . . . . **256** C3
Coppice The
Horwich End SK23 . . . . **45** F5
Shirebrook NG20 . . . . **119** F5
Coppice View S45 . . . . **160** A4
Coppicewood Dr DE23 . . . . **218** A1
Copse Cl DE4 . . . . **165** E8
Copse Gr DE23 . . . . **231** A4
Copse Rise DE11 . . . . **256** B7
Copseside Cl 10 NG10 . . . **236** A8
Copse The
Ilkeston DE7 . . . . **194** D5
Marple SK6 . . . . **23** C8
Copsewood DE55 . . . . **160** A4
Copsey Croft Ct NG10 . . . **236** F7
Copthorne Com Inf Sch
DE55 . . . . **159** A5
Copthurst Rd HD9 . . . . **3** E7
Coral Way S45 . . . . **131** D4
Corbar Grange SK17 . . . . . **85** A8
Corbar Rd SK17 . . . . **66** B1
Corbar Woods La SK17 . . . **66** A1
Corbel Cl DE21 . . . . **205** E2
Corbridge Gr DE21 . . . . . . **231** A4
Corbriggs Cvn Site S42 . . . **115** F5
Corby Cl DE24 . . . . **232** F5
Cordelia Way DE73 . . . . . . **232** E2
Corden Ave DE3 . . . . **218** A2
Corden St DE23 . . . . **219** A2
Cordville Cl DE21 . . . . **220** B5
Cordwell Ave S41 . . . . **95** C8
Cordwell Cl
Castle Donington DE74 . . . **246** F3
Staveley S43 . . . . **97** D8
Cordwell La S18 . . . . **74** E5
Cordy La
Brinsley NG16 . . . . **182** F8
Selston NG16 . . . . **182** F8
Corfe Cl DE23 . . . . **231** D6
Corfield Ave DE75 . . . . **193** F7
Corfield CE Inf Sch
DE75 . . . . **181** D1
Coriander Gdns DE23 . . . . **231** D4
Corinium Cl DE24 . . . . **233** D5
Corker Rd S12 . . . . **44** A6
Corks La SK12 . . . . **32** E5
Corley La DE6 . . . . **174** D2
Cornbrook DE45 . . . . **108** F7
Corn Cl DE55 . . . . **160** B6
Cornel Ct 4 NG19 . . . . . . **136** E1
Corner Farm DE6 . . . . **201** E8
Cornfield Ave DE55 . . . . . . **160** A4
Cornfield Cl 1 S42 . . . . . . **95** A5
Cornfield Rd NG16 . . . . . . **195** E7
Cornflower Dr DE21 . . . . . **206** B3
Cornhill DE22 . . . . **204** F4
Cornhill Cl DE56 . . . . **190** D4
Cornhill Dr DE55 . . . . **159** B4
Cornmill Cl
Bolsover S44 . . . . **99** B2
Calver S32 . . . . **72** C1
Derby DE72 . . . . **233** D5
Corn Mill Cl DE4 . . . . **165** E6
Cornmill Ho SK13 . . . . **10** D1
Cornmill La DE13 . . . . **239** E6
Corn Mkt DE1 . . . . **267** B3
Corn St SK13 . . . . **10** D1
Cornwall Ave
Brimington S43 . . . . **96** F8
Buxton SK17 . . . . **85** E7
Cornwall Cl
4 Brimington S43 . . . . . . **96** F8
Westwood NG16 . . . . **171** C4
Cornwall Dr
Brimington S43 . . . . **96** F8

Cornwall Dr continued
Grassmoor S42 . . . . **115** F3
Cornwallis Cl NG10 . . . . . . **236** D6
Cornwall Rd
Burton u T DE15 . . . . **254** E6
Derby DE21 . . . . **219** D6
Shireoaks S81 . . . . **63** F7
Coronation Ave
Belper DE56 . . . . **179** A5
Derby DE24 . . . . **233** C5
New Houghton NG19 . . . . **134** F7
Sandiacre NG10 . . . . **223** A7
Coronation Cl DE73 . . . . . **252** B8
Coronation Cotts DE13 . . . **253** A8
Coronation Cres ST14 . . . . **197** A4
Coronation Dr
Shirebrook NG20 . . . . **119** F2
South Normanton DE55 . . . **160** B5
Coronation La DE12 . . . . . . **265** F6
Coronation Rd
Brimington S43 . . . . **96** E8
Cossall DE7, NG16 . . . . . . **195** A2
Mapperley DE7 . . . . **193** F3
Stanley DE7 . . . . **207** C6
Coronation St
Derby DE23 . . . . **232** B8
1 Ilkeston DE7 . . . . **208** F8
Overseal DE12 . . . . **262** A4
Swadlincote DE11 . . . . . . **256** A5
Whitwell S80 . . . . **82** A6
Coronet Ct DE21 . . . . **206** D3
Corporation Rd DE7 . . . . . **209** A5
Corporation St
Chesterfield S41 . . . . **266** C3
Derby DE1 . . . . **267** B3
Corve Way S40 . . . . **94** F5
Cossall Rd NG9 . . . . **209** D5
Cote Bottom La DE65 . . . . **227** A7
Cote Green La SK6 . . . . **15** B1
Cote Green Rd SK6 . . . . **15** C1
Cote Hilloc DE4 . . . . **127** A6
Cote La SK22 . . . . **25** D3
Cotes Park Ind Est DE55 . . **159** D2
Cotes Park La DE55 . . . . . . **159** C2
Cotgrave Rd NG19 . . . . **135** F2
Cotman Dr SK6 . . . . **23** C8
Cotmanhay Inf & Jun Sch
DE7 . . . . **194** E5
Cotmanhay Rd DE7 . . . . . . **194** F3
Coton Cl NG19 . . . . **136** E4
Coton in the Elms CE Prim
Sch DE12 . . . . **260** D3
Coton La
Coton in t E DE12 . . . . **260** F3
Rosliston DE12 . . . . **260** D5
Coton Pk DE12 . . . . **255** C1
Coton Rd DE12 . . . . **259** E6
Cotswold Cl
2 Chesterfield S40 . . . . . . **95** C5
Derby DE23 . . . . **231** C8
Glossop SK13 . . . . **17** A8
4 Long Eaton NG10 . . . . . **236** B8
Swadlincote DE11 . . . . . . **256** A3
Cotswold Dr S42 . . . . **115** E3
Cotswold Rd DE14 . . . . **253** F8
Cottage Cl
Heage DE56 . . . . **179** E8
Ilkeston DE7 . . . . **194** D3
Poolsbrook S43 . . . . **98** A7
Swadlincote DE11 . . . . . . **256** A7
Cottage Dr DE56 . . . . **179** E3
Cottage Garden La DE75 . . **181** D2
Cottage La SK13 . . . . **9** E2
Cottages The SK23 . . . . **47** B6
Cottam Cres SK6 . . . . **23** B7
Cottam Dr S43 . . . . **80** C6
Cotterdale Cl NG19 . . . . . . **136** E1
Cotterhill La S43 . . . . **96** E7
Cottesmore Cl DE15 . . . . . **248** B1
Cottesmore Rd DE15 . . . . . **248** A1
Cottisford Cl DE23 . . . . **231** A8
Cottonbrook Rd DE23 . . . . **232** B8
Cotton La DE24 . . . . **219** C1
Cotton Mill Hill S42 . . . . . . **113** E7
Cotton St S44 . . . . **99** A1
Cotts The SK17 . . . . **86** D5
Council Hos
Bradbourne DE6 . . . . **163** B6
Hanbury DE13 . . . . **238** A3
Countess Gr DE73 . . . . **244** F8
Counting House Rd SK12 . . **32** E5
Countisbury Dr DE21 . . . . . **206** A2
County Est The NG17 . . . . **148** E2
Coupe La S42, S45 . . . . **131** A5
Coupe St DE5 . . . . **180** F8
Coupland Cl S41 . . . . **77** C4
Coupland Pl DE55 . . . . **159** C1
Court Farm La DE14 . . . . . **253** E7
Court La DE45 . . . . **108** E8
Courtland Dr DE24 . . . . . . **233** B6
Courtland Gdns DE24 . . . . **233** B7
Courtland Rd DE55 . . . . . . **229** C3
Courtney Way DE56 . . . . . . **179** D5
Court Pl S43 . . . . **97** C8
Court St DE11 . . . . **256** E1
Court The DE24 . . . . **233** B6
Court View S43 . . . . **80** E3
Courtway Cres DE73 . . . . . **244** F8
Courtyard Mews DE24 . . . **233** A6
Courtyard Pl DE21 . . . . . . **220** E5
Courtyard The
Bakewell DE45 . . . . **109** D6
Belper DE56 . . . . **179** A4
Darley Dale DE4 . . . . **127** C3
Hollingworth SK14 . . . . **9** D5
Coventry Cl DE11 . . . . **256** D6
Coventry La NG9 . . . . **209** F2
Coverdale Wlk DE24 . . . . . **233** C7

Covert Pl DE11 . . . . **262** C8
Covert The DE21 . . . . **220** E4
Cowbrook Ave SK13 . . . . . . **10** F1
Cowbrook Cl SK13 . . . . **10** F1
Cowburn Dr SK22 . . . . **24** C1
Cowdale Cotts SK17 . . . . . . **86** A4
Cowdray Cl DE24 . . . . **231** D2
Cowham Cl DE55 . . . . **159** C3
Cow La S43 . . . . **77** E1
Cowley Bottom S18 . . . . . . **75** E8
Cowley Cl S41 . . . . **266** C3
Cowley Gdns S20 . . . . **59** E8
Cowley La S18 . . . . **75** D7
Cowley St DE22 . . . . **218** E7
Cowlishaw Cl DE72 . . . . . . **234** E1
Cowlow La S17, SK23 . . . . . **47** C2
Cowper Rd NG16 . . . . **195** A8
Cowper St DE24 . . . . **232** A5
Cowpingle La S43 . . . . **77** E1
Cowsell Dr S45 . . . . **131** E2
Cowsley Rd DE21 . . . . **219** D7
Cowslip Cl DE12 . . . . **262** E1
Cowslip Mdw DE72 . . . . . . **235** A7
Cox's La NG19 . . . . **136** B5
Coxbench Rd DE21 . . . . . . **191** F4
Cox Green Ct DE23 . . . . . . **230** F7
Coxon's Yd 5 DE6 . . . . . . **173** B2
Coxon St DE21 . . . . **220** E5
Crabtree Ave SK12 . . . . **32** E5
Crabtree Cl
Castle Donington DE74 . . . **247** A2
Derby DE22 . . . . **204** C4
Wirksworth DE4 . . . . **165** E7
Crabtree Cl SK12 . . . . **32** D6
Crabtree Hill DE22 . . . . . . **204** C4
Crab Tree Hill DE21 . . . . . . **205** C8
Cracken Cl SK23 . . . . **34** C3
Craddock Ave DE21 . . . . . . **220** B3
Cradock Mews S2 . . . . **43** E7
Cradock Rd S2 . . . . **43** F7
Crafty Flats La DE12 . . . . . **260** F3
Cragdale Gr S20 . . . . **59** D7
Cragg La DE55 . . . . **148** A2
Craggon Dr S43 . . . . **77** D4
Craggs Dr S43 . . . . **80** E3
Craggs Rd S44 . . . . **99** A2
Craglands Gr S40 . . . . **95** A5
Crags Bsns Pk S80 . . . . . . **100** E8
Cragside Cl S41 . . . . **96** C3
Crags Rd S80 . . . . **82** A1
Crags View S80 . . . . **81** F1
Craig Dr SK23 . . . . **45** E6
Craiglee Ct 1 DE24 . . . . . . **231** D3
Craig St NG10 . . . . **236** E1
Cranberry Gr DE23 . . . . . . **230** F6
Cranborne Rd S41 . . . . **95** E7
Cranbourne Cl NG9 . . . . . . **209** D2
Cranbrook Ct NG19 . . . . . . **136** C6
Cranfleet Way NG10 . . . . . **236** B7
Cranhill Cl DE23 . . . . **230** F6
Cranleigh Rd S43 . . . . **79** B3
Cranmer Cl NG19 . . . . **135** D3
Cranmer Rd DE21 . . . . **267** D3
Cranmer St
Ilkeston DE7 . . . . **194** F1
Long Eaton NG10 . . . . **223** D1
Cratcliff View DE4 . . . . **126** A1
Craven Rd S41 . . . . **95** F5
Crawford Ave NG9 . . . . **223** D8
Crawford Rd S8 . . . . **43** A4
Crawley Rd DE24 . . . . **232** F5
Crawshaw Ave S8 . . . . **56** D8
Crawshaw Gr S8 . . . . **56** D8
Crawshaw Mews S18 . . . . . **56** C1
Cray's Hill DE55 . . . . **170** B7
Crayford Rd DE24 . . . . **233** A5
Craythorne Cl DE11 . . . . . . **256** A7
Craythorne Rd DE13 . . . . . **240** D3
Creamery La DE6 . . . . **151** D1
Crecy Cl DE22 . . . . **218** C3
Creighton La ST14 . . . . **210** A5
Crescent S26 . . . . **61** E5
Crescent Dr SK22 . . . . **33** C2
Crescent Prim Sch
NG19 . . . . **135** D4
Crescent Rd
Ashover S42 . . . . **113** D7
Selston NG16 . . . . **171** D6
Crescent Row SK22 . . . . . . **25** A2
Crescent The
Alfreton DE55 . . . . **159** B3
Barlborough S43 . . . . **80** C6
Bradwell S33 . . . . **51** A8
Breaston DE72 . . . . **235** C2
Breedon on t H DE73 . . . . **252** E2
Brimington S43 . . . . **96** C7
Buxton SK17 . . . . **85** B8
Chapel-en-le-F SK23 . . . . . **47** C7
Clay Cross S45 . . . . **131** C2
Derby, Boulton DE24 . . . . **232** E6
Derby, Chaddesden DE21 . **219** F5
Holmesfield S18 . . . . **75** A8
Holymoorside S42 . . . . . . **113** D8
Hope S33 . . . . **39** A4
Horsley Woodhouse DE7 . . **192** C2
Mayfield DE6 . . . . **184** D7
New Mills SK22 . . . . **33** B8
Repton DE65 . . . . **242** D2
Risley DE72 . . . . **222** D3
Sheffield S17 . . . . **55** E5
Shirebrook NG20 . . . . **119** E6
Shirley DE6 . . . . **200** D7
Stanley DE7 . . . . **207** B8
Stapleford NG9 . . . . **209** B8
Swadlincote DE11 . . . . . . **255** E6
Cressbrook Ave S42 . . . . . . **132** B7
Cressbrook Way DE21 . . . . **206** B3
Cressida Ct DE73 . . . . **232** D2

Cresswell Ave SK22 . . . . . . **33** C8
Cresswellpart La S33 . . . . . **50** E7
Cresswell St SK22 . . . . **33** C8
Cressy Rd DE55 . . . . **159** A4
Cresta Gr DE21 . . . . **205** F3
Crest Cl DE13 . . . . **240** E1
Crest The
Derby DE22 . . . . **204** E2
Linton DE12 . . . . **261** C6
Creswell Bsns Pk S80 . . . . **100** E8
Creswell CE Inf Sch S80 . . **81** E1
Creswell Crags Visitor Ctr*
S80 . . . . **82** B1
Creswell Ct 12 NG19 . . . . . **136** E4
Creswell Jun Sch S80 . . . . **81** E1
Creswell Rd
Clowne S43 . . . . **80** F4
Cuckney NG20 . . . . **101** E3
Creswell Sta S80 . . . . **81** E1
Creswick Cl S40 . . . . **114** B8
Crewe St DE23 . . . . **218** F1
Crewton Way DE24 . . . . . . **232** F7
Crich Ave DE23 . . . . **218** C2
Crich Carr CE Prim Sch
DE4 . . . . **156** C1
Crich CE Inf Sch DE4 . . . . **156** F1
Crich Cir DE23 . . . . **218** C2
Crich Jun Sch DE4 . . . . . . **157** A1
Crich La
Belper DE56 . . . . **179** A4
Ridgeway DE56 . . . . **168** B3
Crich Pl
Buxton SK17 . . . . **85** E7
North Wingfield S42 . . . . . **131** F6
Crich Rd
Fritchley DE56 . . . . **168** A6
Staveley S43 . . . . **97** C7
Crich Tramway Village*
DE4 . . . . **156** C2
Crich View
Bolsover S44 . . . . **118** B8
Heage DE56 . . . . **179** E8
Newton DE55 . . . . **148** A4
Crich Way DE11 . . . . **255** C5
Cricket Cl DE15 . . . . **248** E8
Cricketers Cl DE15 . . . . . . **254** F8
Cricketers Ct DE23 . . . . . . **231** B8
Cricket View S43 . . . . **80** E2
Cricklewood Ct 7 S43 . . . . **78** B3
Cricklewood Rd DE22 . . . . **218** B6
Cringle Mews DE21 . . . . . **205** E2
Cripton La S45 . . . . **129** E5
Crispin Cl S12 . . . . **44** A4
Crispin Dr S12 . . . . **44** A4
Crispin Gdns S12 . . . . **44** A4
Crispin Rd 3 S12 . . . . **44** A4
Critch's Flats NG16 . . . . . **195** F6
Critchley St DE7 . . . . **194** F1
Croft Ave DE6 . . . . **151** D1
Croft Cl
Dale Abbey DE7 . . . . **207** F2
Derby DE21 . . . . **220** F5
Netherseal DE12 . . . . **264** F7
Ockbrook DE72 . . . . **221** C4
Pinxton NG16 . . . . **160** D3
Rolleston DE13 . . . . **240** B4
Croft Cres NG16 . . . . **195** C5
Croft Ct NG17 . . . . **148** F4
Croft End DE21 . . . . **205** C8
Crofters Cl S21 . . . . **60** C4
Crofters Ct DE21 . . . . **205** E2
Croft Gr ST14 . . . . **210** C1
Croft Inf Sch DE55 . . . . . . **159** A3
Croft La DE21 . . . . **205** D3
Croft Lea S18 . . . . **56** C2
Croft Manor SK13 . . . . **10** C1
Crofton Cl S18 . . . . **56** F1
Crofton Rise S18 . . . . **56** F1
Croft Rd
Great Longstone DE45 . . . . **90** A4
Sheffield, Intake S12 . . . . . **44** B5
Croftstead Ave ST14 . . . . . **196** D6
Crofts The S32 . . . . **53** A8
Croft The
Bamford S33 . . . . **40** B3
Belper DE56 . . . . **179** C5
Burton u T DE15 . . . . **254** F8
Derby DE23 . . . . **231** D8
Draycott DE72 . . . . **235** A6
Glossop SK13 . . . . **10** A6
Heage DE56 . . . . **168** E1
2 Melbourne DE73 . . . . . **252** A8
Morley DE7 . . . . **192** C2
Mottram in L SK14 . . . . **9** A4
Shirland DE55 . . . . **146** D2
Somercotes DE55 . . . . **170** C7
South Normanton DE55 . . . **160** A6
Swadlincote DE11 . . . . . . **255** D6
Taddington SK17 . . . . **88** A3
Croft View
Clowne S43 . . . . **80** F3
Staveley S43 . . . . **97** C6
Croft Wlk S80 . . . . **82** A6
Cromarty Cl DE24 . . . . **231** E4
Cromarty Rise S18 . . . . **56** D2
Cromdale Ave S43 . . . . **77** D4
Cromer Cl DE3 . . . . **217** C1
Cromford Bank 21 SK13 . . . **9** D2
Cromford CE Prim Sch
DE4 . . . . **155** B6
Cromford Cl
Aldercar NG16 . . . . **182** B4
22 Gamesley SK13 . . . . . . **9** D2
Long Eaton NG10 . . . . **236** A5
North Wingfield S42 . . . . . **132** B7
Cromford Ct
4 Chesterfield S41 . . . . . . **95** D7
Horwich End SK23 . . . . **45** E6

Cromford Dr
Derby DE3 . . . . **217** E4
Staveley S43 . . . . **97** C8
Cromford Fold 23 SK13 . . . . **9** D2
Cromford Gn 20 SK13 . . . . . **9** D2
Cromford Gr 18 SK13 . . . . . **9** D2
Cromford Hill DE4 . . . . **155** A5
Cromford La SK17 . . . . **85** E7
Cromford Lea 19 SK13 . . . . . **9** D2
Cromford Mews SK23 . . . . . **45** E5
Cromford Pl
Buxton SK17 . . . . **85** E7
24 Gamesley SK13 . . . . . . **9** D2
Cromford Rd
Aldercar NG16 . . . . **182** B4
Clay Cross S45 . . . . **131** A5
Crich DE4 . . . . **156** F2
Derby DE21 . . . . **220** A8
Heanor NG16 . . . . **181** B5
Ripley DE5 . . . . **169** C2
Wirksworth DE4 . . . . **154** F1
Cromford Road Ind Est
NG16 . . . . **182** B4
Cromford Sta SK13 . . . . . . **155** C7
Cromford Way 17 SK13 . . . . **9** D2
Cromford Wharf* DE4 . . . . **155** C7
Crompton Rd
Ilkeston DE7 . . . . **209** B4
Mansfield NG19 . . . . **135** D3
Staveley S43 . . . . **78** F2
Crompton Road Ind Est
DE7 . . . . **209** B3
Crompton St
Derby DE1 . . . . **267** B2
New Houghton NG19 . . . . **134** F8
Cromwell Ave
Blackwell DE55 . . . . **147** E1
Chapel-en-le-F SK23 . . . . . **47** A5
Findern DE65 . . . . **230** D2
Ilkeston DE7 . . . . **209** A5
Cromwell Cl DE13 . . . . **239** C5
Cromwell Dr DE55 . . . . **169** C4
Cromwell Rd
Bolsover S44 . . . . **118** B8
Chesterfield S40 . . . . **266** A4
Derby DE23 . . . . **218** F2
Cromwell St NG16 . . . . **195** C8
Crooked Spire (St Mary & All
Saints Church)* S40. . . **266** B3
Crookes Ave
Mansfield Woodhouse
NG19. . . . . **136** C3
Pleasley NG19 . . . . **135** A5
Crook Stile DE4 . . . . **143** A7
Cropper La DE6 . . . . **215** B4
Cropston Cl S41 . . . . **115** C2
Cropton Cl DE24 . . . . **233** C6
Crosby St DE22 . . . . **218** D4
Cross Chantrey Rd S8 . . . . **43** A3
Cross Cl DE23 . . . . **231** C8
Cross Gr SK13 . . . . **17** E8
Crossdale Gr DE21 . . . . . . **206** C3
Crossfield Gr SK6 . . . . **15** B1
Crossgate La SK13 . . . . **9** F7
Crossgreen Cotts DE4 . . . . **142** B8
Crosshill DE5 . . . . **181** B6
Crosshill Dr DE7 . . . . **208** C5
Crossings Ave SK23 . . . . . . **47** A6
Crossings Mdw SK23 . . . . . **47** A6
Crossings Rd SK23 . . . . **46** F6
Cross Keys La DE55 . . . . . **169** E7
Cross Keys Row SK23 . . . . . **47** B8
Cross La
Calver S32 . . . . **72** B2
Codnor DE5 . . . . **181** B7
Dronfield, Coal Aston S18 . . **57** C3
Dronfield, Quoit Green S18 . **57** B4
Dronfield S18 . . . . **57** C5
Flagg SK17 . . . . **106** E7
Ible DE4 . . . . **153** E7
Monyash DE45 . . . . **107** B2
Rolleston DE13 . . . . **240** B2
Sheffield S17 . . . . **55** C8
Shirland DE55 . . . . **158** E8
Sutton in A NG17 . . . . **148** F2
Wessington DE55 . . . . **157** F8
Crossland Dr S12 . . . . **44** A3
Crossland Pl S12 . . . . **44** A4
Crossland Rd S32 . . . . **53** A7
Crosslands Cl SK13 . . . . . . **17** D8
Crossland Villas S32 . . . . . **53** A7
Crosslanes DE6 . . . . **215** C5
Cross Lanes DE4 . . . . **144** C1
Cross Lea DE7 . . . . **207** F2
Crossley St DE5 . . . . **169** E2
Cross London St S43 . . . . . **77** D3
Crosslow La DE6 . . . . **150** E5
Cross Myrtle Rd S2 . . . . . . **43** B7
Cross Park Rd 1 S8 . . . . . . **43** A5
Cross Rd ST14 . . . . **210** B1
Cross Rise SK13 . . . . **17** E8
Cross Side DE6 . . . . **184** F7
Cross St
Bolsover S44 . . . . **118** C8
Bramley-Vale S44 . . . . **117** D1
Breedon on t H DE73 . . . . **252** F2
Brimington S43 . . . . **96** B6
8 Broadbottom SK14 . . . . . **16** A8
Buxton SK17 . . . . **85** D8
Castleton S33 . . . . **38** B2
Chapel-en-le-F SK23 . . . . . **47** B6
Chesterfield S40 . . . . **266** A4
Clay Cross S45 . . . . **131** C3
Derby DE22 . . . . **218** D6
Glossop SK13. . . . . **10** C1

Cross St *continued*
Grassmoor S42 . . . . **115** F3
Hadfield SK13 . . . . **10** A5
Hollingworth SK14 . . . . **9** D4
Killamarsh S21 . . . . **60** F7
Linton DE11 . . . . **261** E8
Long Eaton NG10 . . . . **236** E8
Mansfield Woodhouse
NG19 . . . . **136** B2
New Mills SK22 . . . . **33** C8
North Wingfield S42 . . **131** E6
Sandiacre NG10 . . . . . . **223** C6
Cross The
1 Glossop SK13 . . . . **10** A5
Great Longstone DE45 . . . . **89** F4
Crossways La DE6 . . . . . **176** B2
Cross Wellington St S43 . . **77** D3
Crow Croft Rd S45 . . . . . **132** C4
Crowcroft Way NG10 . . . **223** B2
Crowden Dr SK13 . . . . . . **10** B5
Crowden YH★ SK13 . . . . . . **6** E3
Crowestones SK17 . . . . . **85** C6
Crowfoot La DE65 . . . . . **226** E8
Crow Hill NG19 . . . . **135** B5
Crowhill La DE45 . . . . . **109** A6
Crow Hill La NG19 . . . . **136** B2
Crow La
Brackenfield DE55 . . . . . **146** A6
Chesterfield S41 . . . . **96** C3
Unstone S18 . . . . **76** F7
Crown Cl
Chesterfield S43 . . . . **77** D3
Long Eaton NG10 . . . . **236** A7
Crown Hill Way DE7 . . . **207** B8
Crownland Dr DE73 . . . . **233** D6
Crown Mews DE22 . . . . **218** C3
Crown Rd S41 . . . . **96** A5
Crown Specl Sch DE13 . . **240** C1
Crown Sq
Branston DE14 . . . . **253** E8
Matlock DE4 . . . . **143** B5
Crown St
Clowne S43 . . . . **80** E3
Derby DE22 . . . . **218** B4
Duffield DE56 . . . . **190** E4
Crown Terr 2 DE56 . . . . **178** F4
Crown Way
Aldercar NG16 . . . . **182** B4
Chellaston DE73 . . . . . . **244** F8
Crown Wlk DE1 . . . . . . **267** B2
Crown Yd DE4 . . . . **154** F1
Crowshaw St DE24 . . . . **232** B8
Crowstones Rd DE4 . . . **127** B3
Crowther Pl 7 S7 . . . . . **43** A8
Croxton Ct 5 NG19 . . . **136** E3
Croydon Wlk DE22 . . . . **217** F6
Cruck Cl S18 . . . . **56** E2
Crystal Cl DE3 . . . . **217** D4
Cubley La DE6 . . . . **198** B1
Cuckmere Cl DE22 . . . . **205** B5
Cuckoostone La DE4 . . . **128** F2
Cuillin Cl NG10 . . . . . . **223** A1
Cullabine Ct S2 . . . . **44** A7
Cullabine Rd S2 . . . . **44** A7
Culland Rd DE14 . . . . . **254** B7
Culland View DE4 . . . . . **168** A8
Cullen Ave DE6 . . . . . . **173** C1
Cullumbell La S45 . . . . **129** A7
Culworth Cl DE56 . . . . **179** D4
Culworth Ct DE21 . . . . **206** B2
Cumberhills Rd DE22,
DE56 . . . . **190** C1
Cumberland Ave DE21 . . **219** E6
Cumberland Cl
Buxton SK17 . . . . **85** D4
Westwood NG16 . . . . . . **171** C4
Cumberland Cres DE72 . . **221** B2
Cumberland Rd DE15 . . **254** D6
Cumbria Wlk DE3 . . . . . **217** C1
Cummings St DE23 . . . . **219** A2
Cundy Rd S44 . . . . **99** A3
Cunliffe St S18 . . . . **57** C4
Cunnery La DE4 . . . . . . **144** B3
Cunnery The DE6 . . . . . **202** F2
Cunningham Pl DE45 . . . **109** D6
Cupola Park Cvn Pk DE4 **156** B3
Curbar Cl S42 . . . . **132** A7
Curbar Curve S43 . . . . . **97** C6
Curbar Hill S32 . . . . **72** D2
Curborough Dr DE24 . . **233** D6
Curlew Ave S21 . . . . **59** B3
Curlew Cl DE24 . . . . . . **231** D4
Curlew Way SK13 . . . . . **16** F8
Curtis Gr SK13 . . . . **10** A5
Curzon Ave S18 . . . . **75** F8
Curzon CE Prim Sch The
DE22 . . . . **204** D6
Curzon Cl
Derby DE22 . . . . **204** C4
Killamarsh S21 . . . . **60** D6
Curzon Ct DE56 . . . . . . **190** E3
Curzon La
Derby DE24 . . . . **233** A8
Duffield DE56 . . . . **190** D3
Curzon Rd
Buxton SK17 . . . . **85** C7
Derby DE15 . . . . **219** F7
Curzon St
Derby DE1 . . . . **267** A3
Long Eaton NG10 . . . . **223** B8
Curzon Terr SK17 . . . . . . **88** D7
Cuscas La DE6 . . . . **187** F4
Cut La DE1, DE21 . . . . . **219** D2
Cutler Cl S21 . . . . **60** B7

Cutler La DE6 . . . . **189** A1
Cutler Way DE3 . . . . . . **217** D4
Cuttholme Cl S40 . . . . . **95** B4
Cuttholme Rd S40 . . . . . **95** C4
Cuttholme Way 1 S40 . . . **95** C4
Cutthorpe Grange S40 . . **95** A4
Cutthorpe Prim Sch S42 **94** D7
Cutthorpe Rd S40 . . . . . **95** A8
Cutting The DE11 . . . . . **256** F4
Cuttlebrook Cl DE23 . . **231** E6
Cyclamen Cl DE14 . . . . **254** A8
Cygnet Fold NG19 . . . . **136** C4
Cypress Ave S8 . . . . **43** C1
Cypress Cl S21 . . . . **60** C5
Cypress Way SK6 . . . . . . **32** A7
Cypress Wlk DE21 . . . . **220** B5
Cyprus Rd S8 . . . . **43** A5
Cyril Ave NG9 . . . . **223** D7

D

Dade Ave S43 . . . . **97** C6
Dag La DE12 . . . . **263** E7
Dagnall Gdns DE45 . . . **109** D5
Dagnall Terr DE45 . . . . **109** D5
Dagnam Cl S2 . . . . **43** F6
Dagnam Cres S2 . . . . **43** F6
Dagnam Dr S2 . . . . **43** F7
Dagnam Pl S2 . . . . **43** F6
Dagnam Pl S2 . . . . **43** F7
Dahlia Ave DE55 . . . . . **160** B7
Dahlia Dr DE21 . . . . . . **206** C3
Dairy House Rd DE23 . . **219** B1
Daisy Cl DE12 . . . . **262** E1
Daisy Farm Rd NG16 . . **195** B8
Daisy La DE12 . . . . **262** B3
Daisymere La SK17 . . . . **67** A2
Dakeyne Cl DE4 . . . . . . **127** F1
Dakin Ave SK17 . . . . **85** D8
Dakin Ct SK17 . . . . **66** E1
Dalbury Rd S18 . . . . **56** C1
Dalbury Wlk DE23 . . . . **231** C5
Daleacre Ave DE74 . . . . **247** F5
Dale Ave
Long Eaton NG10 . . . . **223** D1
Newton DE55 . . . . **148** A3
Somercotes DE55 . . . . . **170** C6
Dale Bank Cres S43 . . . . **77** D3
Dalebank La S45 . . . . . **145** B8
Dale Brook DE65 . . . . . **228** E1
Dalebrook Rd DE15 . . . **248** B5
Dale Cl
Breaston DE72 . . . . **235** D8
Fritchley DE56 . . . . **168** A6
Langwith NG20 . . . . . . **119** E8
Staveley S43 . . . . **97** C8
Stonebroom DE55 . . . . **147** B4
Whaley Thorns NG20 . . **100** F1
Dale Com Prim Sch
DE23 . . . . **218** F1
Dale Cres
Hathersage S32 . . . . **53** B8
Tupton S42 . . . . **115** C1
Dale Ct DE56 . . . . **191** F8
Dale End
Brassington DE4 . . . . . . **153** A4
Wirksworth DE4 . . . . . . **154** F1
Dale End Rd DE65 . . . . **228** C2
Dalefield Dr DE11 . . . . **256** B3
Dalehead Ct S32 . . . . . . **71** E5
Dale Hill DE55 . . . . **158** B5
Dale La
Buxton SK17 . . . . **85** E8
Glapwell S44 . . . . **134** D7
Dale Park Ave DE56 . . . **192** A8
Dale Rd
Buxton, Higher Buxton
SK17 . . . . **85** C7
Buxton, Peak Dale SK17 . . **67** B7
Derby, Alvaston DE24 . . **233** B7
Derby DE21, DE72 . . . . **221** A6
Derby, Normanton DE23 . **218** F2
Dronfield S18 . . . . **76** B8
Killamarsh S21 . . . . **60** E6
Kimberley NG16 . . . . . **195** F6
Matlock Bath DE4 . . . . **143** B3
New Mills SK22 . . . . **33** C7
Stanley DE7 . . . . **207** C4
Stanton-by-D DE7 . . . . **208** C1
Tupton S42 . . . . **115** C1
Dale Rd N DE4 . . . . **127** A5
Dale Rd S DE4 . . . . **127** D1
Dales Cl 4 DE11 . . . . . **255** E5
Dalesfield DE4 . . . . **143** A6
Dalesgate Cl DE23 . . . . **231** C5
Daleside DE15 . . . . **248** B1
Dale Side SK17 . . . . **85** B7
Dale St
Ilkeston DE7 . . . . **208** F7
Mansfield NG19 . . . . . . **136** B1
Dales The DE7 . . . . **207** E7
Dale Terr SK17 . . . . **85** B6
Dale The
Bonsall DE4 . . . . **142** D1
Hathersage S32 . . . . **53** B8
Stoney Middleton S32 . . **71** E4
Wirksworth DE4 . . . . . . **154** F1
Dale View
Earl Sterndale SK17 . . . **105** B3
Ilkeston DE7 . . . . **208** E7
Litton SK17 . . . . **69** E3
Mottram in L SK14 . . . . . **9** A3
Shirland DE55 . . . . **146** C4
Dale View Cl S45 . . . . . **132** B3
Dale View Gdns DE56 . . **191** F8
Dale View Rd S45 . . . . . **132** B4

Dale View Terr SK17 . . . . **89** A6
Dalewood Cl
Chesterfield S41 . . . . **96** E1
South Normanton DE55 . . **160** A3
Dalkeith Ave DE24 . . . . **232** F5
Dalley Cl 1 NG9 . . . . . **223** E7
Dalley La DE56 . . . . . . **178** C6
Dallimore Prim Sch DE7 **208** D4
Dallimore Rd DE7 . . . . **208** D4
Dalness Ct 7 DE24 . . . . **231** D3
Dalston Rd DE11 . . . . . **256** A5
Dalton Ave
Burton u T DE15 . . . . . **248** B1
Derby DE22 . . . . **218** C3
Dalton Cl 3 NG9 . . . . . **223** E5
Daltons DE6 . . . . **182** A4
Dalvey Way S43 . . . . **77** D5
Dame Catherine Harpur's
Sch DE73 . . . . **251** A5
Dam La
Alsop en le D DE6 . . . . **150** E3
Shirland DE55 . . . . **146** F1
Damon Cl S45 . . . . **132** C1
Damon Dr S43 . . . . **96** F8
Damsbrook Dr S43 . . . . **80** E3
Damsbrook La
Bolsover S80 . . . . **99** D8
Clowne S43 . . . . **80** D1
Dam Side DE56 . . . . . . **179** A4
Damside La SK17 . . . . . . **49** A3
Damson Croft S43 . . . . . **78** A2
Damson Gr DE24 . . . . . **232** E8
Danbury Cl S42 . . . . . . **115** E3
Danby Ave S41 . . . . **77** B2
Dane Bank Dr SK12 . . . . **32** D6
Danebridge Cres DE21 . **206** A1
Dane Gr SK17 . . . . **85** C4
Dane Hill Cl SK12 . . . . . **32** D5
Danesby Cres DE5 . . . . **180** A1
Danesby Rise DE5 . . . . **180** A1
Danesmoor Ind Est S45 **131** F2
Danesmoor Inf Sch S45 **131** E3
Danesway SK23 . . . . **47** B6
Daniel Mews NG10 . . . . **223** A5
Dannah Cres DE5 . . . . **169** F1
Dannah St DE5 . . . . . . **169** F2
Darby St DE23 . . . . **218** F2
Darcy Rd S21 . . . . **59** C3
Daresbury Cl S2 . . . . . . **43** D6
Daresbury Dr S2 . . . . . . **43** D6
Daresbury Pl S2 . . . . . . **43** D6
Daresbury Rd S2 . . . . . **43** D6
Daresbury View S2 . . . . **43** D6
Darfield Ave S20 . . . . . . **44** F2
Darfield Cl S20 . . . . **44** F2
Darfield Dr DE75 . . . . . **182** A2
Darfield La DE6 . . . . . . **162** C4
Darkey La NG9 . . . . **223** E5
Dark La
Ashbourne DE6 . . . . . . **173** A1
Ashover DE55 . . . . **145** C6
Bradley DE6 . . . . **175** B3
Calow S44 . . . . **96** F2
Chesterfield S44 . . . . . . **96** E4
Crich DE4 . . . . **156** F5
Cromford DE4 . . . . **154** F4
Holbrook DE56 . . . . . . **191** B7
North Wingfield S42 . . **132** B7
Pilsley S45 . . . . **132** D2
Tatenhill DE13 . . . . **253** A8
Wirksworth DE4, DE56 **165** D3
Youlgreave DE45 . . . . . **125** D7
Darklands La DE11 . . . **256** A4
Darklands Rd DE11 . . . **256** B5
Darley Abbey Dr DE22 . **204** F2
Darley Abbey Pk★ DE22 **205** A1
Darley Ave
Beeston NG9 . . . . **223** E4
Darley Dale DE4 . . . . . **127** C4
North Wingfield S42 . . **132** B7
Darley Churchtown CE Prim
Sch DE4 . . . . **127** B3
Darley Cl
Burton u T DE15 . . . . . **248** C1
Harthill S26 . . . . **61** E6
Staveley S43 . . . . **78** E1
Swadlincote DE11 . . . . **256** A1
Darley Dale DE11 . . . . **255** F2
Darley Dale Prim Sch
DE4 . . . . **127** E2
Darley Dale Sta★ DE4 . **127** C2
Darley Dr
Long Eaton NG10 . . . . **236** A5
Ripley DE5 . . . . **169** C3
West Hallam DE7 . . . . **207** E8
Darley Gr
Buxton SK17 . . . . **85** D6
Derby DE1 . . . . **219** A7
Darley House Est DE4 . . **142** E8
Darley La DE1 . . . . **267** B4
Darley Lodge Dr DE4 . . **142** E8
Darley Moor Motor Cycle
Racing Circuit DE6 . . **185** A1
Darley Park Dr DE22 . . **204** F1
Darley Park Ho DE22 . . **205** A1
Darley Park Rd DE22 . . **204** F1
Darley Rd S45 . . . . **113** B2
Darley Sq DE7 . . . . **194** E5
Darley St DE22 . . . . . . **205** A1
Darley Way
Buxton SK17 . . . . **85** E7
North Wingfield S42 . . **132** B7
Darnley Dr S2 . . . . **44** A8
Darsway DE74 . . . . **246** F4
Dartford Pl DE24 . . . . . **233** A5
Dartmouth Ct 20 S41 . . . **95** F8
Dartnall S42 . . . . **32** A6
Darwent Rd S41 . . . . . . **96** C6

Darwin Ave
Buxton SK17 . . . . **85** C7
Chesterfield S40 . . . . **95** E5
Derby DE24 . . . . **232** D4
Ilkeston DE7 . . . . **208** E7
Darwin Cl DE15 . . . . . **248** C1
Darwin Pl DE1 . . . . . . **267** C3
Darwin Rd
Chesterfield S40 . . . . . **266** A4
Derby DE3 . . . . **217** C3
Long Eaton NG10 . . . . **236** B5
Darwin Sq DE1 . . . . . . **267** B2
Darwood La S44 . . . . . **118** B8
Dashwood St DE1 . . . . **267** B1
Datchet Cl DE23 . . . . . **231** A8
Daveham Ave SK17 . . . . **85** C6
Davenport Rd
Derby DE24 . . . . **232** C8
Tupton S42 . . . . **131** C8
Daventry Cl DE3 . . . . . **217** C3
Davey Ct S44 . . . . **98** F3
Davian Way S40 . . . . . **114** E8
David's Cl DE73 . . . . . . **232** F1
Davids Dr S42 . . . . **114** E4
Da Vinci Com Coll DE21 **205** E1
Davis Ho 2 DE1 . . . . . **267** B2
Davis Rd DE11 . . . . . . **256** B4
Dawber La S21 . . . . **60** F7
Dawes Cl DE14 . . . . . . **254** B7
Dawgates La NG17, NG19. **134** F2
Dawkins Rd DE12 . . . . **262** E1
Dawlish Ct
4 Chesterfield S41 . . . . **95** F8
Derby DE24 . . . . **233** C7
Eastwood NG16 . . . . . . **182** D3
Dawn View NG9 . . . . . **209** D2
Dawsmere Cl DE21 . . . **205** D1
Dawson Cl DE21 . . . . . **220** C5
Dayton Cl DE21 . . . . . **220** C5
Dayton Ct DE21 . . . . . **218** E8
Deacon Cl
Derby DE21 . . . . **205** E2
Swanwick DE55 . . . . . **169** E7
Dead La NG16 . . . . **195** D1
Deadman's La DE24 . . . **219** D2
Deamon St DE55 . . . . . **147** L1
Dean Cl DE23 . . . . **218** A2
Dean Ct DE23 . . . . **218** A2
Deanhead Dr S20 . . . . . . **44** F2
Dean Rd DE56 . . . . **167** F2
Deans Dr DE72 . . . . . . **221** B2
Deansgate NG19 . . . . . **135** A5
Dean St
Derby DE22 . . . . **218** E3
Langley Mill NG16 . . . . **182** C3
Debdale La NG19 . . . . . **136** A2
Deben Cl S40 . . . . **114** C8
Deben Down NG19 . . . . **136** D3
Deborah Dr DE21 . . . . **220** A7
Dee Cl DE24 . . . . **231** E3
Dee La DE65 . . . . **229** F6
Deepdale NG16 . . . . . . **170** F4
Deepdale Ave
Borrowash DE72 . . . . . **221** C3
Stapleford NG9 . . . . . . **223** D6
Deepdale Bsns Pk DE45 **109** B6
Deepdale Cl
Burton u T DE15 . . . . . **248** B6
Staveley S43 . . . . **78** E3
Deepdale Ct DE55 . . . . **181** E1
Deepdale La DE6 . . . . . **184** A2
Deep Dale La
Barrow u T DE73 . . . . . **244** A7
Derby DE24, DE73 . . . . **231** F1
Deepdale Rd
Belper DE56 . . . . **179** B5
Bolsover S44 . . . . **98** F3
Derby DE21 . . . . **220** F3
Long Eaton NG10 . . . . **236** A5
Mansfield NG19 . . . . . . **136** C1
Deepdene Cl DE11 . . . . **256** C1
Deep La S44, S45 . . . . . **133** B3
Deepsick La S44 . . . . . . **97** C1
Deepwell Ave S20 . . . . . **59** F6
Deepwell Bank S20 . . . . **59** F6
Deepwell Ct S20 . . . . . . **59** F6
Deepwell View S20 . . . . **59** F6
Deerlands Rd
Chesterfield S40 . . . . **95** B3
Wingerworth S42 . . . . . **114** F2
Deerleap La S42 . . . . . . **130** D3
Deerpark Cres S42 . . . . **114** F3
Deer Park Prim Sch S42 **114** F3
Deer Park View DE21 . . **220** F6
De Ferrers Cl DE56 . . . **190** E3
Degge St DE1 . . . . **267** B2
Deincourt Cl DE21 . . . **221** A6
Deincourt Com Sch S42 **131** F8
Deincourt Cres S42 . . . **131** F8
Delamere Cl
Breaston DE72 . . . . **235** D8
Derby DE21 . . . . **206** A1
Swanwick DE55 . . . . . **169** F7
Delf St S2 . . . . **43** B7
Delhi Cl DE15 . . . . **248** C3
Dell The S40 . . . . **95** B3
Delph Bank S40 . . . . . . **114** E8
Delph Cl S32 . . . . **71** D6
Delph The DE73 . . . . . **252** F2
Delven La DE74 . . . . . . **247** B3
Delves Cl S40 . . . . **95** D1
Delves Ct S40 . . . . **193** E8

Delves Rd
Heanor DE75 . . . . **193** D8
Killamarsh S21 . . . . **60** C6
Delves Sch The DE55 . . **169** F7
Delves The DE55 . . . . . **169** F7
Denacre Ave NG10 . . . . **223** A5
Denacre La DE4 . . . . . . **127** C3
Denarth Ave DE24 . . . . **232** E3
Denbigh St DE21 . . . . . **219** E2
Denby Comm DE5 . . . . **180** F3
Denby Free CE Prim Sch
DE5 . . . . **180** D1
Denby Hall Rd NE7 . . . **194** F6
Denby La DE5, DE56 . . . **180** C1
Denby Pottery Visitor Ctr★
DE5 . . . . **180** C3
Denby Rd S43 . . . . **97** C7
Denefield Cl SK6 . . . . . . **15** B1
Dene Fields Ct DE4 . . . **143** C5
Denham St S45 . . . . . . **131** B3
Denison Gdns DE21 . . . **220** B6
Denman Cres S32 . . . . . **72** A3
Denmark Rd S2 . . . . **43** B6
Dennis Barsby Cl DE11 . **255** E3
Dennis Cl DE23 . . . . . . **230** E7
Dennor Dr NG19 . . . . . **136** C5
Denson Cl 4 S2 . . . . . . **43** B6
Denstone Coll ST14 . . . **196** B5
Denstone Dr DE24 . . . . **233** A4
Denstone La ST14 . . . . **196** C7
Dentdale Ct DE24 . . . . **233** C7
Dent La S12 . . . . **44** F2
Denton Ave NG10 . . . . **223** A6
Denton Cl NG19 . . . . . . **136** E1
Denton Way DE55 . . . . **169** F7
Denver Cl NG9 . . . . **209** E1
Denver Rd DE3 . . . . . . **217** D3
Depedale Ave DE7 . . . . **208** D5
Depot St DE23 . . . . **219** A2
Derby Ass Rm★ DE1 . . . **267** B3
Derby City General Hospl
DE23 . . . . **218** A5
Derby Coll DE22 . . . . . **218** A5
Derby Coll (Broomfield
Campus) DE7 . . . . **206** B5
Derby Gram Sch for Boys
DE23 . . . . **230** F7
Derby High Sch DE23 . . **218** B4
Derby Hills House Ct
DE73 . . . . **251** A2
Derby Industrial Mus★
DE1 . . . . **267** B3
Derby Knoll SK23 . . . . . **33** F1
Derby La
Brailsford DE6 . . . . **201** B3
Derby DE23 . . . . **231** F8
Great Cubley DE6 . . . . **198** F1
Monyash DE45 . . . . **123** C7
Shirley DE6 . . . . **200** E8
Derby Moor Com Sports Coll
DE23 . . . . **231** B2
Derby Mus & Art Gallery★
DE1 . . . . **267** B3
Derby Pl S2 . . . . **43** C6
Derby Rd
Alfreton DE55 . . . . **158** F3
Ambergate DE56 . . . . . **167** F3
Ashbourne DE6 . . . . . . **185** E4
Aston-on-T DE72 . . . . . **234** A2
Borrowash DE72, DE21 **221** A2
Burton u T DE13 . . . . . **241** A1
Chellaston DE73 . . . . . **232** F2
Clay Cross S45, S42 . . . **131** C5
Cromford DE4 . . . . **155** C6
Dale Abbey DE7, DE21 **206** E3
Derby, Spondon DE21 . **220** C3
Doveridge DE6 . . . . . . **211** B1
Draycott DE72 . . . . . . **234** E8
Duffield DE56 . . . . **190** F6
Duffield, Flaxholme DE56 **190** F1
Eastwood NG16 . . . . . . **182** E2
Egginton DE65 . . . . . . **241** C4
Etwall DE65 . . . . **229** A4
Hatton DE65 . . . . **227** E2
Heanor DE75 . . . . **181** D1
Hilton DE65 . . . . **228** F3
Horsley DE21, DE56. . . **191** D5
Ilkeston DE7 . . . . **208** D7
Kilburn DE56 . . . . **179** F1
Langley Mill NG16 . . . **182** C3
Long Eaton NG10 . . . . **236** B8
Marston on D DE65 . . . **228** B2
Melbourne DE73 . . . . . **252** A8
New Mills SK22 . . . . . . **24** D1
Ripley DE5 . . . . **180** C3
Sandiacre NG10 . . . . . **223** A5
Smisby LE65 . . . . **258** A4
Stanley DE7 . . . . **207** B4
Stapleford NG9 . . . . . . **223** D6
Swadlincote DE11 . . . . **256** C3
Swanwick DE55, DE5 . . **169** E5
Ticknall DE11, DE73. . . **257** F7
Uttoxeter ST14 . . . . . . **210** D1
Wingerworth S42 . . . . . **115** A6
Wirksworth DE4 . . . . . **165** C6
Derby Road Ind Est
Heanor DE75 . . . . **181** D1
Sandiacre NG10 . . . . . **223** B5
Derbyshire Ave
Trowell NG9 . . . . **209** D4
West Hallam DE7 . . . . **207** E8
Derbyshire Cl DE7 . . . . **207** E8
Derbyshire Cty Cricket Gd
DE21 . . . . **219** C3
Derbyshire Dr
Castle Donington DE74 . **247** B4
Ilkeston DE7 . . . . **208** E6

Derbyshire Dr *continued*
Westwood NG16 . . . . 171 C4
Derbyshire La S8 . . . . 43 A3
Derbyshire Level SK13 . . 17 F6
Derbyshire Royal Infmy
DE1 . . . . 267 C1
Derby Small Bsns Ctr
Derby DE1 . . . . 267 C2
Derby, Pear Tree DE23 . . 219 B1
Derby St
Glossop SK13 . . . . 17 C8
3 Ilkeston DE7 . . . . 208 F8
Sheffield S2 . . . . 43 C6
Derby Sta DE1 . . . . 219 C4
Derby Terr S2 . . . . 43 C6
Derby Trad Est DE21 . . 219 B8
Derventio CI DE1 . . . . . . 219 A7
Derwent Ave
Belper DE56 . . . . 179 A1
Borrowash DE72 . . . . 221 C3
Darley Dale DE4 . . . . 127 C4
Derby DE72 . . . . 205 A4
Grindleford S32 . . . . 72 C8
Ilkeston DE7 . . . . 194 D2
West Hallam DE7 . . . . . . 207 E8
Derwent Bsns Ctr DE1 . 267 C4
Derwent CI
Derby DE22 . . . . 205 A4
Dronfield S18 . . . . 57 B3
Glossop SK13 . . . . 17 F8
Grindleford S32 . . . . 72 C8
Swadlincote DE11 . . . . . . 256 A1
Derwent Com Prim Sch DE21 219 C7
Derwent Cres S41 . . . . . 95 D7
Derwent Ct
5 Belper DE56 . . . . 179 B4
5 Sheffield S8 . . . . 56 A5
Willington DE65 . . . . 242 B6
Derwent Dr
Baslow DE45 . . . . 91 D6
Chinley SK23 . . . . 34 E1
Derby DE24 . . . . 231 D2
Tibshelf DE55 . . . . 147 F6
Derwent Gdns DE6 . . . . 185 D8
Derwent Gr DE55 . . . . . 158 F2
Derwent Ho DE21 . . . . . 219 C6
Derwent La
Derwent S33 . . . . 30 B7
Hathersage S32 . . . . 52 F8
Northwood DE4 . . . . 127 A6
Derwent Par DE21, DE72 219 E3
Derwent Park Ho DE22 . 205 A1
Derwent PI S45 . . . . 131 A5
Derwent Rise
Burton u T DE15 . . . . 248 A2
Buxton SK17 . . . . 85 C6
Derby DE21 . . . . 220 D3
Dronfield S18 . . . . 57 B3
Ripley DE5 . . . . 169 C1
Derwent Rise DE21 . . . . 220 F4
Derwentside Ind Pk
DE56 . . . . 178 F1
Derwent Sq SK23 . . . . . . 34 E1
Derwent St
Belper DE56 . . . . 178 F3
Derby DE1 . . . . 267 C4
Draycott DE72 . . . . 235 A7
Long Eaton NG10 . . . . . . 236 C6
Derwent Street Ind Est
NG10 . . . . 236 C6
Derwent Terr DE4 . . . . . 143 A7
Derwent Vale DE56 . . . . 178 F2
Derwent View
Baslow DE45 . . . . 91 E6
Belper, Milford DE56 . . . 191 A8
Belper, Mount Pleasant
DE56 . . . . 178 F5
Darley Dale DE4 . . . . 127 B3
Mastin Moor S43 . . . . 79 C3
Desborough Rd NG16 . . 171 D7
De Sutton PI S26 . . . . . . 61 E5
Dethick La DE4 . . . . 144 D1
Dethick Way S42 . . . . . . 132 B7
Devas Gdns DE21 . . . . . 220 D5
Deveron CI DE13 . . . . . . 240 C1
Deveron Rd S20 . . . . 59 F7
Devizes CI S40 . . . . 114 F8
Devon CI
Burton u T DE15 . . . . 254 E6
Grassmoor S42 . . . . 115 F2
Sandiacre NG10 . . . . 223 B5
Devon Dr S43 . . . . 96 F8
Devonish Royal Hospl The
SK17 . . . . 85 B8
Devon Park View S43 . . 96 F8
Devonshire Ave
Borrowash DE72 . . . . 221 C2
Darley Dale DE4 . . . . 142 F7
Derby DE22 . . . . 204 F3
Long Eaton NG10 . . . . . . 237 A8
Ripley DE5 . . . . 169 C2
Devonshire Ave E S41 . . 115 C8
Devonshire Ave N S43 . . 77 E3
Devonshire Bsns Ctr S43 78 B2
Devonshire CI
Chesterfield S41 . . . . 95 F8
Dronfield S18 . . . . 75 F8
Ilkeston DE7 . . . . 194 E5
2 Staveley S43 . . . . 78 E2
Devonshire Cotts S44 . . 118 E6
Devonshire Ct S43 . . . . . 96 D7
Devonshire Dr
Chinley SK23 . . . . 34 E2
Creswell S80 . . . . 81 C1

Devonshire Dr *continued*
Derby DE3 . . . . 217 E3
Duffield DE56 . . . . 190 D2
Eastwood NG16 . . . . 182 F2
Langwith NG20 . . . . 119 F8
Rowsley DE4 . . . . 110 F1
Sheffield S17 . . . . 55 F7
Somercotes DE55 . . . . . . 170 B7
Stapleford NG9 . . . . 209 D2
Devonshire Glen S17 . . . 55 F6
Devonshire Gr S17 . . . . . 55 E6
Devonshire Pk S43 . . . . . 96 E8
Devonshire Rd
Buxton SK17 . . . . 85 B8
Sheffield S17 . . . . 55 F6
Devonshire Rd E S41 . . . 115 C8
Devonshire Rd N S43 . . . 77 E3
Devonshire Sq DE4 . . . . 111 A3
Devonshire St
Ambergate DE56 . . . . 167 F3
Brimington S43 . . . . 96 E8
Chesterfield S41 . . . . 266 B3
New Houghton NG19 . . . 135 A7
3 Staveley S43 . . . . 78 E2
Devonshire Terr
Holmewood S42 . . . . 116 E1
Matlock Bath DE4 . . . . . . 143 A2
Devonshire Terrace Rd
S17 . . . . 55 D7
Devonshire Villas **23** S41 . 95 F8
Devonshire Way S43 . . . 81 A4
Devon St DE7 . . . . 209 A5
De Warren PI S26 . . . . . . 61 F5
Dewchurch Dr DE23 . . . 231 E5
Dewint Ave SK6 . . . . 23 B8
Dew Pond La SK17 . . . . . 85 E8
Dewsnap La SK14 . . . . . . 9 A6
Dewy La DE4, DE55 . . . . 144 F1
Dexter St DE23 . . . . 219 C2
D H Lawrence Mus ★
NG16 . . . . 182 F3
Dialstone S33 . . . . 51 A7
Diamond Ct DE45 . . . . . . 109 D5
Diamond Dr DE21 . . . . . . 205 F3
Diamond Jubilee Cotts
DE6 . . . . 184 E8
Dibble Rd DE14 . . . . 254 A7
Dickens Dr
Holmewood S42 . . . . 116 D1
Swadlincote DE11 . . . . . . 256 C5
Dickenson Rd S41 . . . . . . 266 C1
Dickens Sq DE23 . . . . . . 231 F7
Dickinson's La DE6 . . . . 215 B1
Dickinson St DE24 . . . . . 219 D2
Dicklant La S45 . . . . 145 B8
Didcot CI S40 . . . . 114 F8
Didsbury Terr SK22 . . . . 25 E2
Digby St
Cossall DE7 . . . . 195 A1
Kimberley NG16 . . . . 195 D7
Diglands Ave SK22 . . . . . 24 D1
Diglands CI SK22 . . . . . . 24 D1
Diglee Rd SK23 . . . . 33 C3
Digmire La DE6 . . . . 161 D1
Dig St
Ashbourne DE6 . . . . 173 B2
Hartington SK17 . . . . 137 D6
Dimple Cres DE4 . . . . . . 143 B5
Dimple La DE56 . . . . 168 B8
Dimple Rd DE4 . . . . 143 A6
Dimple Road Bsns Ctr
DE4 . . . . 143 B6
Dingle CI SK13 . . . . 17 A8
Dingle La S41, S44 . . . . . 96 E1
Dingle The DE15 . . . . 254 E8
Dingley CI NG19 . . . . 136 E5
Dinmore Grange DE11 . . 257 B6
Dinting CE Prim Sch
SK13 . . . . 10 A1
Dinting La SK13 . . . . 10 A1
Dinting Lane Trad Est
SK13 . . . . 10 A1
Dinting Lodge Ind Est SK13 9 F2
Dinting Rd SK13 . . . . 10 B2
Dinting Sta SK13 . . . . . . 10 A2
Dinting Vale SK13 . . . . . 10 A1
Dinting Vale Bsns Pk SK13 . 9 F2
Discovery Way S41 . . . . . 77 A1
Diseworth CI DE73 . . . . . 232 F2
Diseworth Rd DE74 . . . . 247 A1
Dish La DE6, DE65 . . . . . 228 B6
Dishwell La S26 . . . . 61 E6
Disley Prim Sch SK12 . . 32 D6
Disley Sta SK12 . . . . 32 C6
Disraeli Cres DE7 . . . . . . 208 F8
Ditch Cotts SK17 . . . . . . 105 F8
Ditch The SK17 . . . . 105 F8
Division Rd NG20 . . . . . . 119 E4
Division St S43 . . . . 97 C8
Dix Ave DE7 . . . . 192 F6
Dixie St NG16 . . . . 171 B4
Dixon's Rd S41 . . . . 266 C2
Dixon Croft S43 . . . . 77 D4
Dixon Ct S41 . . . . 77 B3
Dobbinhorse La DE6 . . . 185 B5
Dobbin La S18 . . . . 75 C6
Dobbs CI S21 . . . . 60 C6
Dobholes DE7 . . . . 192 D6
Dobholes La DE7 . . . . . . 192 F6
Dobson PI S43 . . . . 97 B6
Dockholm Rd NG10 . . . . 223 C2
Dock Wlk S40 . . . . 266 A2
Doctor's La DE73 . . . . . . 252 F2
Doctor La S26 . . . . 61 F5
Dodburn Ct DE24 . . . . . . 231 D4
Dodslow Ave DE13 . . . . . 240 B3
Doe Hill La DE55 . . . . . . 147 D5

Doehole La
Ashover DE4, DE55 . . . . . 144 F3
Brackenfield DE55 . . . . . . 145 A2
Doe La S12 . . . . 58 C5
Doghole La DE4 . . . . 154 C4
Dogkennel La DE6 . . . . . 186 E7
Dog La
Hulland Ward DE6 . . . . . . 175 D4
Netherseal DE12 . . . . 264 F6
Stonebroom DE55 . . . . . . 146 E2
Wilson DE73 . . . . 252 E6
Dolby Rd SK17 . . . . 85 D2
Doles La
Clifton DE6 . . . . 184 F7
Findern DE65 . . . . 230 D3
Whitwell S80 . . . . 82 B7
Dolly La
Chinley SK23 . . . . 34 A2
Furness Vale SK23 . . . . . . 33 F3
Dolly Wood CI SK23 . . . . 34 B1
Dolphin CI DE21 . . . . 221 A6
Domain Dr DE73 . . . . 232 E1
Dominion Rd DE11 . . . . . 256 B5
Dominoe Gr S12 . . . . 44 D5
Donald Hawley Way
DE56 . . . . 190 F3
Doncaster Ave NG10 . . . 223 B6
Doncaster Gr NG10 . . . . 223 F1
Donegal Wlk DE21 . . . . . 220 A4
Donington CI DE23 . . . . . 231 E5
Donington Dr
Derby DE23 . . . . 231 E5
Woodville DE11 . . . . 256 E1
Donington La DE72, DE74 247 C7
Donisthorpe La DE12 . . . 262 E2
Donkey La S32 . . . . 72 C2
Donner Cres DE7 . . . . . . 194 E5
Dorchester Ave DE21 . . . 219 F7
Dorchester Rd NG16 . . . 195 F7
Dore CI S17 . . . . 56 A7
Dore Ct S17 . . . . 56 A7
Dore Hall Croft S17 . . . . 55 D7
Dore La S32 . . . . 53 A7
Dore Prim Sch S17 . . . . . 55 D6
Dore Rd S17 . . . . 55 E8
Dore Sta S17 . . . . 56 A7
Doris Rd DE7 . . . . 209 A7
Dorking Rd DE22 . . . . . . 218 B6
Dormy CI NG19 . . . . 136 E5
Dorothy Ave
Mansfield Woodhouse
NG19 . . . . 136 C1
Sandiacre NG10 . . . . 223 B5
Dorothy Dr NG19 . . . . . . 136 F1
Dorothy Vale S40 . . . . . . 95 C4
Dorrien Ave DE23 . . . . . . 232 A7
Dorset Ave **2** S43 . . . . . 96 F8
Dorset CI
Brimington S43 . . . . 77 F1
Burton u T DE15 . . . . 254 E6
Buxton SK17 . . . . 85 D4
Dorset Dr S43 . . . . 96 F8
Dorset St DE21 . . . . 219 D6
Dorterry Cres DE7 . . . . . 209 A5
Douglas Ave
Awsworth NG16 . . . . 195 C5
Heanor DE75 . . . . 181 C2
Douglas Rd
Chesterfield S41 . . . . 96 C6
Long Eaton NG10 . . . . . . 223 B1
Somercotes DE55 . . . . . . 170 D8
Douglas St DE23 . . . . 219 B2
Douse Croft La S10 . . . . . 42 F6
Dove Bk SK6 . . . . 23 F6
Dove CI
Derby DE3 . . . . 218 A3
Kilburn DE56 . . . . 192 A8
Woodville DE11 . . . . 256 F1
Dovecliff Cres DE13 . . . . 240 F2
Dovecliff Rd DE13 . . . . . 240 E3
Dovecote DE74 . . . . 247 B3
Dovecote Dr DE72 . . . . . 221 B2
Dovecotes S45 . . . . 129 F3
Dovecote The
Breedon on t H DE73 . . . 252 F2
Horsley DE21 . . . . 191 F6
Dovedale Ave
Ashbourne DE6 . . . . 173 D1
Derby DE24 . . . . 233 C7
Long Eaton NG10 . . . . . . 236 B6
Staveley S43 . . . . 97 B5
Dovedale Circ DE7 . . . . . 194 E5
Dovedale CI
Burton u T DE15 . . . . 248 B5
Ripley DE5 . . . . 180 D6
Dovedale Cres
Belper DE56 . . . . 179 B5
Buxton SK17 . . . . 84 F6
Dovedale Ct
Ashbourne DE6 . . . . 185 E8
4 Chesterfield S41 . . . . 95 E7
1 Glossop SK13 . . . . . . 10 F1
Long Eaton NG10 . . . . . . 236 B6
Dovedale Day Hospl
DE1 . . . . 267 C1
Dovedale Prim Sch
NG10 . . . . 236 B6
Dovedale Rd DE21 . . . . . 220 T3
Dovedale Rise DE22 . . . . 204 D1
Dovedales The DE3 . . . . 217 D2
Dovefields ST14 . . . . 196 T3
Dove Fst Sch ST14 . . . . . 197 A3
Dove Gr DE65 . . . . 241 A5
Dove Holes CE Prim Sch
SK17 . . . . 47 T1
Dove Holes Sta SK17 . . . 47 E1
Dove House Gn DE6 . . . . 173 B2

Dove La
Long Eaton NG10 . . . . . . 236 C8
Rocester ST14 . . . . 197 A3
Dove Lea DE13 . . . . 240 B4
Dover CI DE21 . . . . 219 A2
Dover Rd DE5 . . . . 169 C5
Dove Ridge SK17 . . . . . . 121 C6
Doveridge CI S41 . . . . . . 77 A2
Doveridge Gr DE7 . . . . . . 85 E6
Doveridge Prim Sch
Doveridge DE6 . . . . 211 A1
Doveridge, Manor House
DE6 . . . . 224 C8
Doveridge Rd DE55 . . . . 248 B1
Doveridge Wlk DE23 . . . 231 C5
Dove Rise DE65 . . . . 228 C2
Dover St
Creswell S80 . . . . 81 C1
Derby DE23 . . . . 219 A1
Doveside DE6 . . . . 184 D7
Dove Side DE65 . . . . 239 D8
Dovesite Bsns Pk DE73 . 251 E6
Dove St DE56 . . . . 183 B2
Dovestone Gdns DE23 . . 218 B1
Dove Valley Pk DE65 . . . 227 A5
Dove View DE13 . . . . 239 C6
Dove Way The ST14 . . . . 210 C2
Dovewood CI DE23 . . . . . 231 A7
Dowcarr La S26 . . . . 61 C5
Dowdeswell St S41 . . . . . 266 B4
Dower CI DE21 . . . . 205 A1
Dowie Way DE4 . . . . 156 F2
Downham CI DE3 . . . . . . 217 E1
Downing CI DE22 . . . . . . 217 F6
Downing Ho DE22 . . . . . . 217 F6
Downing Rd
Derby DE21 . . . . 219 D5
Sheffield S8 . . . . 56 E4
Downing Row S32 . . . . . . 52 F8
Downing St DE55 . . . . . . 160 A6
Downings The S26 . . . . . 61 F5
Downlands S43 . . . . 96 D7
Downlee CI SK23 . . . . 46 F5
Downmeadow DE56 . . . . 179 E8
Downs The NG19 . . . . 136 F1
Drabbles Rd DE4 . . . . . . 143 A6
Drage St DE1 . . . . 219 B7
Drake Terr S43 . . . . 96 C8
Draycott CI DE75 . . . . . . 181 C4
Draycott Com Prim Sch
DE72 . . . . 235 A7
Draycott Ct DE7 . . . . 194 F3
Draycott Dr DE3 . . . . 217 C3
Draycott Mills DE72 . . . . 235 A7
Draycott PI S18 . . . . 75 D8
Draycott Rd
Borrowash DE72 . . . . 221 C1
Breaston DE72 . . . . 235 C7
Long Eaton NG10 . . . . . . 236 A4
North Wingfield S42 . . . . 131 F7
Drayton Ave
Derby DE22 . . . . 217 F6
Mansfield NG19 . . . . 135 D1
Drayton St DE11 . . . . 256 C4
Dresden CI DE3 . . . . 217 C2
Drewry Ct DE1 . . . . 218 F5
Drewry La DE22 . . . . 218 F4
Dreyfus CI DE21 . . . . 220 F5
Drive The DE56 . . . . 177 F3
Dronfield Inf Sch S18 . . . 57 A1
Dronfield Jun Sch S18 . . 57 A1
Dronfield PI DE7 . . . . 194 E5
Dronfield Rd S21 . . . . 59 B2
Dronfield Sta S18 . . . . . . 57 A1
Drovers Way
Ashbourne DE6 . . . . 173 B3
Bullbridge DE56 . . . . 168 B5
Drovers Wlk **3** SK13 . . . 10 D1
Drummond Rd DE7 . . . . . 194 E1
Drummond Way DE73 . . . 232 E1
Drum The DE21 . . . . 204 F3
Drury Ave DE21 . . . . 220 D4
Drury La
Biggin SK17 . . . . 138 C2
Dronfield S18 . . . . 57 C3
Sheffield S17 . . . . 55 D7
Dryden Ave S40 . . . . 115 A8
Dryden St NG9 . . . . 209 E1
Dryden St DE23 . . . . 231 F7
Dryhurst Dr SK12 . . . . . . 32 D6
Dryhurst La SK12 . . . . . . 32 D6
Drysdale Rd DE3 . . . . 217 D3
Duchess St
Creswell S80 . . . . 81 F1
Whitwell S80 . . . . 82 A6
Duchess Way DE73 . . . . 244 E8
Duckmanton Prim Sch
S44 . . . . 98 A5
Duckmanton Rd S44 . . . . 98 A5
Duck Row DE45 . . . . 91 C3
Ducksett La S21 . . . . 59 E2
Duck St DE55 . . . . 241 B5
Dudwood La DE4 . . . . . . 140 F7
Duesbury CI DE24 . . . . . . 232 E7
Duesbury CI DE3 . . . . 230 B7
Duesbury PI DE3 . . . . 230 B7
Duesbury The DE55 . . . . 160 B4
Duewell Ct **9** S43 . . . . . 78 B3
Duffield Bank DE56 . . . . 191 A4
Duffield CI NG10 . . . . 236 A5
Duffield Ct DE56 . . . . 190 F3
Duffield Rd DE22 . . . . . . 205 A5
Duffield Sta DE56 . . . . . . 190 F4
Duke's Bldgs DE11 . . . . . 191 B4
Duke's Dr
Buxton SK17 . . . . 85 C5
Glapwell S44 . . . . 134 C7
Duke's Dr The DE45 . . . . 108 E8

Duke Field DE4 . . . . 154 D5
Duke of Norfolk CE Prim Sch
SK13 . . . . 10 D1
Duke of Norfolk CE Prim Sch
(Annexe) SK13 . . . . 10 E2
Dukeries Ct S43 . . . . 80 F3
Dukeries La DE21 . . . . . . 206 B2
Dukes CI S42 . . . . 116 E1
Dukes Dr
Chesterfield S41 . . . . 95 E6
Curbar S32 . . . . 72 D2
Dukes Fold SK13 . . . . 17 B7
Dukes PI DE7 . . . . 194 E4
Dukes St SK13 . . . . 17 C8
Duke St
Buxton SK17 . . . . 84 E6
Chesterfield S41 . . . . 96 A8
Clowne S43 . . . . 81 A4
Creswell S80 . . . . 81 F1
Derby DE1 . . . . 267 A4
Ilkeston DE7 . . . . 194 F3
Middleton DE4 . . . . 154 D5
Sheffield S20 . . . . 59 D6
South Normanton DE55 . . 160 B6
Staveley S43 . . . . 78 E2
Tutbury DE13 . . . . 239 C6
Whitwell S80 . . . . 82 A6
Duluth Ave DE21 . . . . . . 220 A7
Dulverton Ave DE24 . . . . 231 C2
Dulwich Ct **11** S43 . . . . . 78 B3
Dulwich Rd DE22 . . . . . . 217 C6
Dumb Hall La S80 . . . . . . 63 B4
Dumbles CI DE7 . . . . 208 C6
Dumbles La DE5 . . . . 180 F2
Dumbles Rd S44 . . . . 98 F1
Dumbleton Rd S21 . . . . . 60 E5
Dumble Wood Grange
S41 . . . . 95 C7
Dunbar CI DE24 . . . . 231 E2
Duncan CI DE56 . . . . 179 B6
Duncan Rd DE23 . . . . 231 F8
Duncombe Dr DE6 . . . . . 185 C8
Dundas Way DE73 . . . . . 232 E1
Dundee Dr NG19 . . . . 136 B6
Dundee Rd DE11 . . . . 256 D5
Dundonald Rd S40 . . . . . 266 B1
Dunedin CI DE3 . . . . 217 E3
Dunedin Cres DE15 . . . . 248 C2
Dunedin Glen S20 . . . . . . 59 E6
Dunedin Gr S20 . . . . 59 E6
Dungley Hill DE56 . . . . . 168 D2
Dungreave Ave DE4 . . . . 127 A5
Dunkirk DE22 . . . . 267 A2
Dunlow La S32 . . . . 71 C5
Dunn Brigg NG19 . . . . . . 136 D2
Dunn Dr NG10 . . . . 236 B7
Dunne La SK13 . . . . 10 E2
Dunnicliffe La DE73 . . . . 252 A7
Dunnsmoor La DE11 . . . . 256 E7
Dunoon CI DE24 . . . . 231 E3
Dunsa La DE45 . . . . 91 D1
Dunsford Rd DE55 . . . . . 159 B5
Dunshill Wlk S45 . . . . . . 131 E4
Dunsil CI NG19 . . . . 136 B1
Dunsil Ct NG19 . . . . 136 B1
Dunsil Rd
7 Mansfield NG19 . . . . 136 B1
Pinxton NG16 . . . . 160 D2
Dunsmore Dr DE21 . . . . . 205 F2
Dunsmore Way DE11 . . . 256 D5
Dunstall Brook DE15 . . . 248 A4
Dunstall Park Rd DE24 . . 232 D8
Dunstall Rd DE13 . . . . . . 253 A7
Dunston CI NG10 . . . . . . 236 F7
Dunston Ct S41 . . . . 76 F1
Dunston La S41 . . . . 95 D8
Dunston PI S41 . . . . 76 F1
Dunston Prim Sch S41 . . 95 D8
Dunston Rd S41 . . . . 76 D2
Dunston Tech Pk S41 . . . 76 E1
Dunston Trad Est S41 . . . 76 E2
Dunton CI DE21 . . . . 267 D3
Dunvegan Ave S45 . . . . . 131 E4
Dunvegan CI DE24 . . . . . 231 D2
Duper La S32 . . . . 51 E5
Durban CI DE15 . . . . 248 C3
Durban House Her Ctr ★
NG16 . . . . 182 F3
Durham Ave
Chesterfield S43 . . . . 77 D3
Derby DE21 . . . . 219 E6
Grassmoor S42 . . . . 115 F2
Durham CI
Chesterfield S43 . . . . 77 D3
Mansfield Woodhouse
NG19 . . . . 136 D4
Swadlincote DE11 . . . . . . 256 E5
Durham St **3** DE7 . . . . . 194 F1
Durley Chine Dr S41 . . . . 115 C8
Durley CI DE24 . . . . 233 C7
Durlstone CI S12 . . . . 44 A5
Durlstone Cres S12 . . . . . 44 A5
Durlstone Dr S12 . . . . . . 44 A5
Durlstone Gr S12 . . . . . . 44 A5
Durrant Rd S41 . . . . 266 B3
Durvale Ct S17 . . . . 55 E6
Durward CI DE24 . . . . . . 232 C7
Dyche CI S8 . . . . 57 B6
Dyche Dr S8 . . . . 57 B6
Dyche La S8, S18 . . . . . . 57 B5
Dyche PI S8 . . . . 57 B6
Dyche Rd S8 . . . . 57 B6
Dye House La SK22 . . . . . 33 C8
Dykes CI S44 . . . . 99 A2

Dyke Vale Rd S12 . . . . 44 F5
Dymond Gr S42 . . . . 115 F3
Dystelegh Rd SK12 . . . . . . 32 D6

E

Each Well La DE55 . . . . . . 158 F3
Eagle Cl DE56 . . . . 178 F2
Eagle Ctr DE1 . . . . 267 C2
Eagle Hts DE15 . . . . 248 D3
Eagle Par **9** SK17 . . . . 85 B7
Eagle Rd DE7 . . . . 208 F4
Eagle St
 4 Buxton SK17 . . . . 85 B7
 Heage DE56 . . . . 168 E2
Eagle Terr
 Birchover DE4 . . . . 126 B1
 Wensley DE4 . . . . 142 A7
Ealand St DE13 . . . . 240 D4
Ealing Cl DE22 . . . . 218 B6
Ealing Ct **8** S43 . . . . 78 B3
Eardley Cl DE21 . . . . 220 B5
Earlham Cl DE7 . . . . 208 C6
Earls Cres DE65 . . . . 206 B2
Earl Sterndale CE Prim Sch
 SK17 . . . . 105 C3
Earlsway **5** SK13 . . . . 17 B8
Earlswood Cl DE72 . . . . . . 235 D8
Earlswood Dr DE3 . . . . . . 217 F4
Earnshaw St SK14 . . . . 9 D4
Easedale Cl S40 . . . . 94 F5
East Ave
 Derby DE3 . . . . 217 E3
 Stanfree S44 . . . . 80 B1
East Bank DE4 . . . . 141 C5
East Bank Pl S2 . . . . 43 D6
East Bank Rd S2 . . . . 43 D6
East Bank Way S2 . . . . 43 D6
Eastbrae Rd DE23 . . . . . . 231 D7
Eastbrook Cl SK23 . . . . 47 C6
East Cl DE22 . . . . 204 E2
Eastcliffe Ct S2 . . . . 43 C8
East Cres
 Holbrook DE56 . . . . 191 C8
 Long Duckmanton S44 . . . . 98 A6
East Croft Ave DE23 . . . . . 231 D5
Eastcroft Cl S20 . . . . 59 F8
Eastcroft Dr S20 . . . . 59 F8
Eastcroft Glen S20 . . . . . . 59 F8
Eastcroft View S20 . . . . . . 59 F7
Eastcroft Way **7** S20 . . . . . 59 F8
East Dr DE6 . . . . 211 B1
East End DE4 . . . . 140 F7
East End Dr DE11 . . . . . . 256 C4
Eastern Ave
 Bolsover S44 . . . . 118 B8
 Sheffield S2 . . . . 43 E7
Eastern Cres S2 . . . . 43 D6
Eastern Dr S2 . . . . 43 D7
Eastern Wlk S2 . . . . 43 D7
Eastfield Dr DE55 . . . . . . 160 A5
Eastfield Rd
 Dronfield S18 . . . . 76 C8
 Ripley DE5 . . . . 170 A1
 Swadlincote DE11 . . . . . . 256 C6
Eastgate DE1 . . . . 267 C4
East Glade Ave S12 . . . . . . 44 E3
East Glade Cl S12 . . . . 44 E3
East Glade Cres S12 . . . . . . 44 E4
East Glade Dell S12 . . . . . . 44 E4
East Glade Pl S12 . . . . 44 E3
East Glade Rd S12 . . . . 44 E3
East Glade Sq S12 . . . . 44 E3
East Glade Way S12 . . . . . . 44 E4
East Hill Sec Sch S2 . . . . . . 43 C8
East Lawn DE65 . . . . 230 D2
Eastleigh Ct S41 . . . . 115 D8
Eastleigh Dr
 Derby DE3 . . . . 217 E2
 Mansfield Woodhouse
 NG19 . . . . 136 B6
East Midlands Designer
 Outlet DE55 . . . . 160 E6
East Midlands International
 Airport DE74 . . . . 247 C1
East Midlands Nuffield Hospl
 DE23 . . . . 230 F6
Eastmoor Rd S43 . . . . 96 F4
East Nelson St DE75 . . . . . 181 D2
East Par S80 . . . . 82 A5
East Rd S2 . . . . 43 B7
East Service Rd DE21 . . . . 220 B3
Eastside Cl S41 . . . . 96 B8
Eastside Rd S41 . . . . 96 B8
East St
 Bramley-Vale S44 . . . . . . 117 D1
 Burton u T DE15 . . . . . . 248 C3
 Clay Cross S45 . . . . 131 D4
 Clowne S43 . . . . 81 A5
 Creswell S80 . . . . 81 D1
 Derby DE1 . . . . 267 B3
 Heanor DE75 . . . . 194 A8
 Ilkeston DE7 . . . . 208 F8
 Long Eaton NG10 . . . . . . 236 F8
 Renishaw S21 . . . . 79 B8
 Scarcliffe S44 . . . . 118 E6
East Vale SK6 . . . . 23 A5
East View
 Chesterfield S40 . . . . . . 266 B2
 Mayfield DE6 . . . . 184 D7
 Shirebrook NG20 . . . . . . 119 F6
 Whaley Thorns NG20 . . . . 101 A3
East View Ave S21 . . . . . . 59 C2
East View Ind Est NG20 . . 119 F6

East View Rd DE56 . . . . . 168 E1
Eastview Terr NG16 . . . . . 182 B3
Eastway DE74 . . . . 247 B3
Eastwood Ave DE23 . . . . . 218 C2
Eastwood Cl S41 . . . . 115 D8
Eastwood Comp Sch
 NG16 . . . . 182 E3
Eastwood Cotts S32 . . . . . 53 B8
Eastwood Dr
 Calow S44 . . . . 97 B2
 Derby DE23 . . . . 218 C2
Eastwood Jun & Inf Schs
 NG16 . . . . 182 F2
Eastwood & Kimberley Com
 Coll NG16 . . . . 195 F6
Eastwood La S45 . . . . 130 B2
Eastwood Park Appartments
 S41 . . . . 115 C7
Eastwood Park Dr S41 . . . . 115 D8
Eastwood Rd NG16 . . . . . 195 E6
Eather Ave NG19 . . . . . . 136 C4
Eaton Ave
 Derby DE22 . . . . 205 B5
 Ilkeston DE7 . . . . 208 D6
Eaton Bank DE56 . . . . . . 191 A1
Eaton Cl
 Derby DE22 . . . . 205 A5
 Hatton DE65 . . . . 227 D1
 Hulland Ward DE6 . . . . . 175 E3
Eaton Ct
 Derby DE1 . . . . 218 E6
 Duffield DE56 . . . . 190 E2
Eaton Dr DE45 . . . . 91 F5
Eaton Fold S32 . . . . 71 F3
Eaton Grange Dr NG10 . . . 236 A8
Eaton Hill DE45 . . . . 91 F5
Eaton La S45 . . . . 129 B5
Eaton Pl DE45 . . . . 91 F5
Eaton Rd
 Castle Donington DE74 . . . 247 B3
 Rocester ST14 . . . . 196 F3
Eatons Rd NG9 . . . . 223 D6
Eaton St ST14 . . . . 210 C1
Eaves Ave SK23 . . . . 47 C5
Eaves Knoll Rd SK22 . . . . . 33 B8
Ebenezer St
 Glossop SK13 . . . . 17 D7
 Ilkeston DE7 . . . . 194 F3
 Langley Mill NG16 . . . . . 182 B3
Ecclesbourne Ave DE56 . 190 F3
Ecclesbourne Cl
 Duffield DE56 . . . . 190 E3
 Wirksworth DE4 . . . . . . 165 F1
Ecclesbourne Cotts DE4 . 154 F2
Ecclesbourne Dr SK17 . . . . 85 A6
Ecclesbourne La DE6 . . . . 176 F5
Ecclesbourne Mdws
 DE56 . . . . 190 D4
Ecclesbourne Pk DE55 . 159 D2
Ecclesbourne Sch The
 DE56 . . . . 190 E3
Ecclesbourne Valley Rly ★
 DE4 . . . . 154 F2
Eccles Cl
 Hope S33 . . . . 39 A4
 Whaley Bridge SK23 . . . . 45 D8
Eccles Fold SK23 . . . . 47 A6
Eccles Rd
 Chapel-en-le-F, Higher
 Crossings SK23 . . . . . . 47 A6
 Chapel-en-le-F, Hilltop SK23 46 C7
Eccles Terr SK23 . . . . 46 D8
Eckington Bsns Pk S21 . . 59 F4
Eckington Cl DE7 . . . . . . 207 E8
Eckington Hall S21 . . . . . . 59 D5
Eckington Jun Sch S21 . . . 59 D3
Eckington Mews S20 . . . . . 59 D5
Eckington Rd
 Chesterfield S43 . . . . . . 77 D5
 Dronfield S18 . . . . 57 D4
 Sheffield S20 . . . . 59 F8
 Staveley S43 . . . . 78 F4
Eckington Sch S21 . . . . . . 59 A3
Eckington Way S20 . . . . . . 59 F8
Edale Ave
 Derby, Alvaston DE24 . . . . 233 D4
 Derby DE23 . . . . 218 E2
 Derby, Mickleover DE3 . . . 217 D2
Edale Bank SK13 . . . . 9 E2
Edale CE Prim Sch S33 . 37 C8
Edale Cl
 Derby DE22 . . . . 204 D1
 Gamesley SK13 . . . . 9 E2
 Long Eaton NG10 . . . . . . 236 B6
Edale Cres SK13 . . . . 9 E1
Edale Ct **3** S41 . . . . 95 E7
Edale Dr
 Derby DE21 . . . . 220 F3
 South Normanton DE55 . . 160 B7
Edale Fold SK13 . . . . 9 E2
Edale Gr SK17 . . . . 85 E7
Edale Mews SK17 . . . . 85 E7
Edale Mill S33 . . . . 37 E7
Edale Rd
 Hayfield SK22 . . . . 26 A2
 Hope S33 . . . . 38 F7
 Mastin Moor S43 . . . . . . 79 C4
Edale Rise NG9 . . . . 223 F8
Edale Sq DE7 . . . . 194 E5
Edale Sta S33 . . . . 37 C7
Edale Way DE56 . . . . 179 A5
Edale YH ★ S33 . . . . 29 A2
Eden Bank DE56 . . . . 167 F2
Eden Cl DE65 . . . . 240 C8
Edenhall Rd S2 . . . . 43 F7
Eden Low NG19 . . . . 136 E3
Eden Rd DE21 . . . . 220 B4
Edensor Ave SK17 . . . . . . 85 E7

Edensor Cl S42 . . . . 131 F6
Edensor Ct S43 . . . . 97 C8
Edensor Dr DE56 . . . . . . 179 C6
Edensor Sq DE22 . . . . . . 218 F4
Eden St
 Derby DE24 . . . . 233 A8
 Wingerworth S42 . . . . . . 114 E3
Edes Farm Dr ST14 . . . . . 196 F4
Edgbaston Ct DE23 . . . . . 231 C8
Edgecote Dr DE11 . . . . . . 256 A7
Edgefold Rd DE4 . . . . . . 143 B5
Edgehill DE56 . . . . 191 A2
Edge Hill DE73 . . . . 232 F3
Edge Hill Ct NG10 . . . . . . 236 D4
Edgehill Gr NG10 . . . . . . 236 C2
Edge Hill Jun Sch DE15 . . 254 F7
Edge La S33 . . . . 51 B6
Edgelaw Ct **2** DE24 . . . . . 231 D3
Edge Mount View S32 . . . . 72 E2
Edge Rd
 Eyam S32 . . . . 71 E7
 Matlock DE4 . . . . 143 B6
Edge View S32 . . . . 72 B3
Edge View Cl S32 . . . . . . 72 C7
Edge View Dr DE45 . . . . . 90 A4
Edgware Rd DE22 . . . . . . 217 F6
Edgwood Rd NG16 . . . . . 195 F6
Edinboro Row NG16 . . . . 195 E7
Edinburgh Cres DE24 . . . . 232 E4
Edinburgh Ct
 Chesterfield S42 . . . . . . 114 E1
 Swanwick DE55 . . . . 170 A7
Edinburgh Rd
 Chesterfield S41 . . . . . . 95 F5
 Wingerworth S42 . . . . . . 114 E4
Edith Wood Cl DE24 . . . . 233 B5
Edlaston La DE6 . . . . 185 B2
Edmonton Pl DE15 . . . . . 248 D2
Edmund Ave S17 . . . . 56 D6
Edmund Cl S17 . . . . 56 D6
Edmund Dr S17 . . . . 56 D6
Edmund Rd
 Derby DE21 . . . . 220 F3
 Sheffield S2 . . . . 43 B8
Edmund St S41 . . . . 95 F8
Edmunds Ave DE23 . . . . . 231 D5
Ednaston Hall Farm Mews
 DE6 . . . . 201 B7
Edward Ave
 Derby DE21 . . . . 220 A5
 Jacksdale NG16 . . . . 171 A4
Edward Rd NG10 . . . . . . 236 D8
Edwards Cres DE56 . . . . . 192 A8
Edward St
 Aldercar NG16 . . . . 182 B4
 Belper DE56 . . . . 179 A4
 Derby DE1 . . . . 267 B4
 Eckington S21 . . . . 59 D3
 Glossop SK13 . . . . 10 C1
 Hartshorne DE11 . . . . . . 257 A3
 Marple SK6 . . . . 15 B1
 Moira DE11 . . . . 256 C1
 Overseal DE12 . . . . 262 A4
 Stapleford NG9 . . . . 223 D7
 Staveley S43 . . . . 97 C8
Edward Wlk S42 . . . . 115 D1
Edwin Ave S40 . . . . 114 D8
Edwin Rd S2 . . . . 43 C6
Edwinstowe Rd DE21 . . . . 206 B1
Egerton Dr NG9 . . . . 209 D2
Egerton Rd S18 . . . . 57 B2
Eggesford Rd DE24 . . . . . 231 D2
Eggington Rd DE65 . . . . . 240 F8
Egginton Prim Sch DE65 . 241 B5
Egginton Rd DE65 . . . . . . 229 B2
Egmanton Cl DE21 . . . . . 206 B1
Egreaves Ave DE75 . . . . . 181 C4
Egstow Pl S45 . . . . 131 D4
Egstow St S45 . . . . 131 D4
Ehlinger Ave SK13 . . . . . . 10 A5
Eider Cl NG20 . . . . 119 D3
Eighth Ave DE14 . . . . 253 F8
Eland Cl DE21 . . . . 221 A6
Eland Rd NG20 . . . . 119 F5
Elder Cl DE55 . . . . 170 A8
Elder Ct S21 . . . . 60 C5
Elder Way S40 . . . . 266 B3
Eldon Cl SK23 . . . . 47 C6
Eldon Ho **5** DE1 . . . . 267 B2
Eldon La SK17 . . . . 49 B5
Eldon St
 Burton u T DE15 . . . . . . 248 B3
 Clay Cross S45 . . . . 131 C4
Eleanor Ave DE7 . . . . 209 A5
Eleanor Cres NG9 . . . . . . 223 F7
Elesmere Ct DE7 . . . . 194 D1
Eley Cl DE7 . . . . 194 C2
Eley Wlk DE1 . . . . 267 A1
Elgar Dr NG10 . . . . 236 B5
Elgin Ave DE23 . . . . 218 A1
Elgin Cl S40 . . . . 114 C7
Eliot Cl
 Calow S43 . . . . 96 F5
 Long Eaton NG10 . . . . . . 236 B5
 Wirksworth DE4 . . . . . . 165 E8
Eliot Dr DE7 . . . . 208 D5
Eliot Rd DE23 . . . . 231 B8
Elizabeth Ave
 Buxton SK17 . . . . 85 D7
 Disley SK12 . . . . 32 D5
 Rolleston DE13 . . . . 240 B3
Elizabeth Cl
 Derby DE21 . . . . 220 B5
 West Hallam DE7 . . . . . . 207 D8
Elizabeth Ct
 Burton u T DE15 . . . . . . 248 C3
 Ilkeston DE7 . . . . 194 D1

Elizabeth Pk NG16 . . . . . 170 F5
Elizabeth Villas DE6 . . . . . 185 C8
Elkstone Rd S40 . . . . 95 A5
Ella Bank Rd DE75 . . . . . 182 A1
Ellastone Gdns DE24 . . . . 233 B7
Ellendale Rd DE21 . . . . . 220 B7
Ellerslie Gr NG10 . . . . . . 223 A5
Ellesmere Ave
 Alfreton DE55 . . . . 159 B4
 Derby DE24 . . . . 219 D1
Ellesmere Dr NG9 . . . . . . 209 C5
Ellesmere Rd NG19 . . . . . 136 F1
Elliott Ave S33 . . . . 51 A8
Elliott Dr S43 . . . . 97 C6
Ellis Cl NG10 . . . . 236 C6
Ellison Ave DE72 . . . . . . 246 A7
Ellison Cl SK14 . . . . 9 D5
Ellisons Rd S21 . . . . 60 F8
Ellison St SK13 . . . . 10 D1
Elma La S80 . . . . 101 D6
Elm Ave
 Belper DE56 . . . . 179 B2
 Darley Dale DE4 . . . . . . 142 F7
 Long Eaton NG10 . . . . . . 236 C8
 Sandiacre NG10 . . . . . . 223 B7
Elm Cl
 Bolsover S44 . . . . 99 C1
 Branston DE14 . . . . 253 F8
 Chesterfield S41 . . . . . . 95 F8
 Doveridge DE6 . . . . 224 C8
 Killamarsh S21 . . . . 60 C5
 Pinxton NG16 . . . . 160 D3
Elm Cres S20 . . . . 59 C8
Elm Dr
 Hilton DE65 . . . . 228 D2
 Killamarsh S21 . . . . 60 C5
Elmfield SK23 . . . . 47 A5
Elm Gr
 Clay Cross S45 . . . . 131 D3
 Derby, Cherrytree Hill
 DE21 . . . . 220 B5
 Derby DE22 . . . . 204 D5
 Glossop SK13 . . . . 10 C2
Elmhurst DE65 . . . . 241 A4
Elmhurst Ave DE55 . . . . . 160 A4
Elmhurst Cl DE55 . . . . . . 160 A4
Elmhurst Rd NG19 . . . . . 136 F1
Elm Lodge Farm Cl S41 . 95 F7
Elm Park Ct DE1 . . . . 267 A5
Elm Rd
 Eckington S21 . . . . 59 C2
 Pilsley S45 . . . . 132 C1
Elms Ave
 Alfreton DE55 . . . . 159 A4
 Derby DE23 . . . . 218 B2
 Ripley DE5 . . . . 180 D8
Elms Cl DE55 . . . . 159 A4
Elmsdale Rd DE11 . . . . . 257 A4
Elms Dr DE23 . . . . 218 B1
Elms Farm Way DE23 . . . . 231 A8
Elmsfield Ave DE75 . . . . . 182 A2
Elms Gr DE65 . . . . 229 C3
Elmslea Ave DE12 . . . . . . 260 D3
Elmsleigh Cl DE11 . . . . . 256 B6
Elmsleigh Dr DE11 . . . . . 256 B6
Elmsleigh Gr DE11 . . . . . 256 B6
Elmsleigh Inf Sch DE11 . . 256 B6
Elms Rd
 Burton u T DE15 . . . . . . 248 A1
 Coton in t E DE12 . . . . . 260 D3
Elms St DE1 . . . . 218 F7
Elm St
 Borrowash DE72 . . . . . . 221 B2
 Brimington S43 . . . . 97 A8
 Holmewood S42 . . . . . . 116 B4
Elms The NG16 . . . . 195 F7
Elmton Cl
 Clowne S43 . . . . 80 C3
 Creswell S80 . . . . 100 D8
Elmton La S44 . . . . 99 C3
Elmton Rd S80 . . . . 81 E1
Elmton View S80 . . . . . . 81 D2
Elmtree Ave
 Derby DE24 . . . . 232 B7
 Selston NG16 . . . . 171 F7
Elm Tree Ave
 Kilburn DE56 . . . . 192 B3
 Mansfield Woodhouse
 NG19 . . . . 136 A4
 Shirebrook NG20 . . . . . . 119 D4
 Shirland DE55 . . . . 146 C1
Elmtree Cl S81 . . . . 63 F7
Elm Tree Cres S18 . . . . . . 57 A3
Elm Tree Dr S42 . . . . 114 F4
Elm Tree Ho S12 . . . . 44 A6
Elm Tree Row DE55 . . . . . 148 A5
Elm View ST14 . . . . 196 E6
Elm Wlk S45 . . . . 132 C1
Elmwood Dr
 Alfreton DE55 . . . . 159 C3
 Derby DE21 . . . . 205 D2
 Sheffield S20 . . . . 59 D6
Elnor Ave S45 . . . . 45 E5
Elnor La SK23 . . . . 45 F4
Elnor St NG16 . . . . 182 C1
Elsecar Cl DE56 . . . . 179 D5
Elstead Cl DE11 . . . . 257 B1
Elston Cl NG19 . . . . 135 D1
Elstree Dr S12 . . . . 44 B4
Elstree Rd S12 . . . . 44 B4
Elton Bank **6** SK13 . . . . . 9 D1
Elton CE Prim Sch DE4 . 140 E6
Elton Cl
 8 Gamesley SK13 . . . . . . 9 D1
 North Wingfield S42 . . . . 132 A5
 Stapleford NG9 . . . . 223 D8

Elton Gr SK17 . . . . 85 E6
Elton Lea **7** SK13 . . . . . . 9 D1
Elton Pl **9** SK13 . . . . 9 D1
Elton Rd
 Derby DE24 . . . . 232 B3
 Winster DE4 . . . . 141 B6
Elton St S40 . . . . 266 C4
Elton View S43 . . . . 97 D8
Elvaston Castle ★ DE21 . . 233 F7
Elvaston Castle Ctry Pk ★
 DE21 . . . . 233 F6
Elvaston Castle Cvn Pk
 DE72 . . . . 234 A7
Elvaston Cl S18 . . . . 56 B1
Elvaston Dr NG10 . . . . . . 236 A4
Elvaston Estate Mus ★
 DE72 . . . . 233 F7
Elvaston La DE24 . . . . . . 233 C7
Elvaston Rd S42 . . . . 131 F6
Elvaston St DE72 . . . . . . 235 B7
Elveden Dr DE7 . . . . 194 C3
Elvin Way S42 . . . . 131 C8
Elwood Rd S17 . . . . 56 C6
Elwyn Cl DE13 . . . . 240 D1
Ely Cl
 Mansfield Woodhouse
 NG19 . . . . 136 C6
 Swadlincote DE11 . . . . . 256 D6
Elyn Ave S42 . . . . 132 B7
Elysee Gdns SK17 . . . . . . 85 C3
Embankment Cl DE22 . . . 217 F7
Ember La DE4 . . . . 142 E1
Embridge Cswy SK10 . . . . 64 B5
Emerald Cl
 Derby DE21 . . . . 206 A3
 Mansfield NG19 . . . . . . 135 F1
Emerson Sq DE23 . . . . . . 231 F6
Emery Cl DE12 . . . . 261 D5
Emmas Williams Ct SK6 169 D1
Emmerson Rd DE55 . . . . 170 C7
Emmet Field Cl S40 . . . . . 114 F8
Emmett Carr Cl S21 . . . . . 79 C8
Emmett Carr Dr S21 . . . . . 79 C8
Emmett Carr La S21 . . . . . 79 C8
Empire Cl DE75 . . . . 181 E2
Empire Rd DE15 . . . . 248 B5
Empress Rd DE23 . . . . . . 267 A1
Emsworth Cl DE7 . . . . . . 194 D3
Endland Ind Est DE1 . . . 218 C5
Endowood Rd S40 . . . . . . 114 A8
Endsleigh Gdns DE22 . . . 217 F2
End The DE15 . . . . 248 E8
Enfield Cl DE65 . . . . 228 C2
Enfield Rd
 Chesterfield S41 . . . . . . 96 A5
 Derby DE22 . . . . 218 B6
England Cres DE75 . . . . . 182 A2
English Martyrs RC Prim Sch
 NG10 . . . . 223 B1
Ennerdale Ave **4** S20 . . . . 59 C6
Ennerdale Cl S18 . . . . 56 E1
Ennerdale Cres S41 . . . . . 95 C8
Ennerdale Ct **6** NG10 . . . 223 B2
Ennerdale Dr S20 . . . . 59 C6
Ennerdale Rd NG10 . . . . . 223 B2
Ennerdale Wlk DE21 . . . . 205 D2
Ennis Cl DE21 . . . . 220 C4
Enoch Stone Dr DE21 . . . 220 B4
Enslet La DE6 . . . . 164 B2
Ensor Cl DE11 . . . . 256 D5
Ensor Way SK22 . . . . 33 C7
Enterprise Cl NG19 . . . . . 135 E2
Enterprise Ct
 Creswell S80 . . . . 81 E1
 Ilkeston DE7 . . . . 194 D1
Enterprise Dr S42 . . . . . . 116 C1
Enterprise Rd NG19 . . . . . 135 E3
Enterprise Way DE21 . . . . 267 C4
Epping Cl DE22 . . . . 217 F6
Epsom Cl DE14 . . . . 253 F7
Epsom Rd NG9 . . . . 223 E3
Epworth Dr DE24 . . . . . . 233 A4
Epworth Ho DE15 . . . . . . 248 D3
Erdington Way NG9 . . . . . 223 E3
Erewash Ct
 Ilkeston DE7 . . . . 194 D1
 Long Eaton NG10 . . . . . . 223 D1
Erewash Dr DE7 . . . . 209 B3
Erewash Gr NG9 . . . . 223 F2
Erewash Mus ★ DE7 . . . . 208 F8
Erewash Rd NG16 . . . . . . 160 E2
Erewash Sq DE7 . . . . 209 A6
Erewash St DE55 . . . . . . 171 A4
Erica Dr DE55 . . . . 160 B7
Erin Rd S43, S44 . . . . 98 B7
Ernest Hall Way DE14 . . . 256 C4
Ernocroft La SK6 . . . . 15 C3
Ernocroft Rd SK6 . . . . . . 15 B1
Errington Ave S2 . . . . 43 E6
Errington Cl S2 . . . . 43 E6
Errington Cres S2 . . . . . . 43 E6
Errington Rd
 Chesterfield S40 . . . . . . 114 C8
 Sheffield S2 . . . . 43 E6
Errington Way S2 . . . . . . 43 E7
Errwood Ave SK17 . . . . . . 85 A6
Errwood Forest Walks ★
 SK17 . . . . 64 E2
Erskine Cres S2 . . . . 43 C7
Erskine Rd S2 . . . . 43 C7
Erskine St SK6 . . . . 15 B3
Erskine View S2 . . . . 43 C7
Escolme Cl DE11 . . . . . . 256 D4
Eskdale Cl
 Bolsover S44 . . . . 98 F1
 Dronfield S18 . . . . 56 E1
 Long Eaton NG10 . . . . . . 236 B5
Eskdale Wlk DE24 . . . . . 233 D6

Essendine Cres S8 . . . . . 43 B3
Essex Dr DE11 . . . . 255 E1
Essex Rd DE15 . . . . 254 D6
Essex St
  Derby DE21 . . . . 219 D6
  2 Ilkeston DE7. . . . . . 194 F1
Estwic Ave NG16 . . . . . . 182 F3
Etchells The DE65. . . . . 227 A8
Etherow Brow 6 SK14 . . 16 A8
Etherow Ctry Pk★ SK6 . . 15 C3
Etherow Ctry Pk Visitor Ctr★
  SK6. . . . . 15 B2
Etherow Ind Est SK13. . . . 9 E5
Etherow Way SK13. . . . . . 9 E5
Eton Ct DE7 . . . . 207 D8
Eton St DE24 . . . . 219 E1
Etruria Gdns DE1 . . . . . 267 B5
Etta's Way 4 S40. . . . . . 95 C5
Ettrick Cl 4 S40 . . . . . . 95 C5
Ettrick Dr DE24 . . . . . . 231 E2
Etwall Cl S40 . . . . 95 A6
Etwall La DE65. . . . . . . 229 F5
Etwall Prim Sch DE65 . . 229 B4
Etwall Rd
  Derby DE3 . . . . 217 C1
  Egginton DE65 . . . . . . 241 B7
  Willington DE65 . . . . . 242 A7
Etwall St DE22 . . . . 218 E5
Eureka Prim Sch DE11 . . 256 D5
Eureka Rd DE11. . . . . . . 256 D5
Euston Dr DE1 . . . . 219 B7
Evans Ave DE22 . . . . . . 205 A3
Evans Cl S33. . . . . 51 A7
Evanston Gdns DE21 . . . 220 B6
Evelyn Devonshire Cotts
  S45. . . . . 132 F2
Evelyn Gr DE21 . . . . . . 220 A5
Everard Ave S17 . . . . . . 56 A5
Everard Dr S17 . . . . 56 A5
Everard Glade 3 S17 . . . 56 A5
Everest Dr DE55 . . . . . . 170 D8
Everett Cl S43 . . . . 96 E7
Evergreen Cl DE21 . . . . 206 A3
Evershill Cl DE55 . . . . . 146 F5
Evershill La DE55 . . . . . 146 F6
Eversleigh Rise DE4. . . . 142 B8
Everton St NG19 . . . . . . 135 E1
Evesham Ave SK13 . . . . . 10 A5
Evesham Cl DE21 . . . . . 205 E1
Ewart La DE55 . . . . 158 F3
Ewe Dale La DE6. . . . . . 149 A3
Ewe Lamb Cl NG9. . . . . 209 F1
Ewe Lamb La NG9. . . . . 209 F1
Excalibur Way S41 . . . . 266 C3
Excelsior Ave DE24. . . . 232 F6
Excelsior Dr DE11 . . . . . 256 E2
Exchange St DE1. . . . . . 267 B3
Exe Fold NG19 . . . . 136 D2
Exeter Cl DE11. . . . . . . 256 E6
Exeter Ct 19 S41 . . . . . . 95 F8
Exeter Ho DE1 . . . . 267 C3
Exeter Pl DE1. . . . . 267 C3
Exeter St DE1. . . . . 267 C4
Exford Ct NG19 . . . . . . 136 C6
Exlowmere La DE4. . . . . 140 F5
Export Dr NG17 . . . . . . 160 F8
Eyam Cl
  Burton u T DE15. . . . . 248 B2
  15 Gamesley SK13. . . . . 9 D2
  North Wingfield S42 . . 132 A8
Eyam Fold 29 SK13. . . . . . 9 D2
Eyam Gdns 28 SK13 . . . . . 9 D2
Eyam Gn 16 SK13 . . . . . . 9 D2
Eyam Gr 17 SK13 . . . . . . 9 D2
Eyam Hall★ S32 . . . . . . 71 D5
Eyam La SK13. . . . . 9 E2
Eyam Lea SK13 . . . . 9 E2
Eyam Mews SK13 . . . . . . 9 E2
Eyam Moor Stone Circ★
  S32. . . . . 52 F3
Eyam Mus★ S32 . . . . . . 71 D6
Eyam Wlk DE56 . . . . . . 179 A5
Eyam YH★ S32 . . . . 71 D6
Eyes Ct DE56 . . . . 194 F2
Eyre's Gdns DE7 . . . . . . 194 F2
Eyre Gdns S40. . . . . . . 266 A4
Eyre St E S41 . . . . 115 C8
Eyre St
  Clay Cross S45. . . . . . 131 C3
  Creswell S80 . . . . 81 D1
Eyrie The
  Burton u T DE15. . . . . 248 C3
  Derby DE24 . . . . 231 E3

F

Fabis Cl DE11. . . . . 256 A3
Fabric View S42. . . . . . 132 D8
Factory La DE7 . . . . 194 E2
Factory St S40. . . . . 95 D2
Fairbourne Dr DE21 . . . 217 D4
Fairburn Croft Cres S43. . 80 B6
Faircroft Ave NG10. . . . 223 B5
Fairdene DE23 . . . . 218 F2
Faires Cl DE72. . . . . . . 221 D1
Faire St DE22 . . . . 218 E3
Fairfax Dr S2 . . . . 44 B8
Fairfax Rd
  Derby DE23 . . . . 218 F2
  Sheffield S2 . . . . 44 B8
Fairfax Rise S2 . . . . 44 B8
Fairfield Ave
  Borrowash DE72. . . . . 221 C3
  Hilcote DE55 . . . . 148 C1
  Rolleston DE13 . . . . . 240 D4
  Stonebroom DE55. . . . 147 B4

Fairfield Cl
  Brimington S43 . . . . . . 96 D8
  Whaley Thorns NG20. . 101 A2
Fairfield Cres
  Long Eaton NG10 . . . . 236 B4
  Swadlincote DE11 . . . . 255 E5
Fairfield Cl S42. . . . . . . 94 F4
Fairfield Dr S42. . . . . . . 94 F4
Fairfield Endowed CE Jun
  Sch SK17. . . . . 85 E7
Fairfield Inf Sch SK17. . . 85 E8
Fairfield Prim Sch NG9. . 223 D6
Fairfield Rd
  Bolsover S44. . . . . 118 A3
  Buxton SK17 . . . . 85 C8
  Chesterfield S40 . . . . . 266 A4
  Derby DE23 . . . . 218 E1
  Horsley Woodhouse DE7. . 192 C7
Fairfield Terr DE1 . . . . . 256 F3
Fairfield Villas S40. . . . 266 A4
Fairford Cl S40 . . . . 114 F7
Fairford Gdns DE23 . . . 231 A6
Fairholme Dr NG19 . . . . 135 E1
Fairholmes DE4. . . . . . . 143 D5
Fairisle Cl DE21. . . . . . 206 C3
Fairlawns DE56. . . . . . . 190 E5
Fair Lea Cl NG10. . . . . . 236 D6
Fairleigh S2. . . . . 44 A8
Fairmeadows Foundation
  Prim Sch DE11 . . . . . . 255 E5
Fair View S40. . . . . 95 E4
Fairview Ave NG16 . . . . 171 F2
Fairview Cl
  Derby DE23 . . . . 231 A8
  Kilburn DE56. . . . . . . 192 B7
Fairview Grange DE56. . 192 B7
Fairview Rd S18 . . . . 57 A3
Fairview Rise DE4. . . . . 168 A8
Fairway DE14 . . . . 254 B6
Fairway Cl DE22 . . . . . . 204 E2
Fairway Cres DE22 . . . . 204 D2
Fairways Cl SK13 . . . . . . 10 F1
Fairways The
  Clay Cross S45. . . . . . 131 E3
  Clifton DE6. . . . . 184 F6
  Mansfield Woodhouse
  NG19. . . . . 136 D6
Fairway The 5 DE11 . . . 255 E5
Fairwinds Cl S18. . . . . . . 57 A1
Fairwood Dr DE24 . . . . 233 D6
Fairy Bank Cres SK22 . . . 25 C3
Fairy Bank Rd SK22 . . . . 25 D3
Falaise Way DE65 . . . . . 228 E2
Falcon Cl SK22. . . . . 33 D8
Falcon Ct DE7 . . . . 194 D1
Falcon Rd S18 . . . . 57 C3
Falcon Rise S18 . . . . 57 D3
Falcons Rise DE56 . . . . 179 C5
Falcon Way
  Derby DE21 . . . . 231 E2
  Woodville DE11 . . . . . 256 F3
Falcon Yd S40 . . . . 266 B3
Faldo Cl DE14. . . . . 254 B6
Falkland Rise S18. . . . . . 76 A8
Fallowfield Rd S43. . . . . 77 D3
Fallow Rd DE21 . . . . . . 220 F6
Fall Rd DE7 . . . . 181 E3
Falmouth Rd DE24 . . . . 233 C5
Fal Paddock NG19 . . . . 136 D2
Fanny Ave S21. . . . . 60 E5
Fan Rd S43 . . . . 78 F1
Fan Road Ind Est S43 . . . 78 F2
Fanshaw Ave S21 . . . . . . 59 C2
Fanshaw Bank S18. . . . . 57 A1
Fanshaw Cl S21. . . . . . . 59 C2
Fanshaw Dr S21. . . . . . . 59 C2
Fanshawe Gate La S17,
  S18. . . . . 55 C1
Fanshaw Rd
  Dronfield S18. . . . . . . 57 B2
  Eckington S21 . . . . . . 59 C2
Fanshaw Way S21 . . . . . 59 C2
Faraday Ave DE13. . . . . 240 D1
Faraday Ct
  Branston DE14. . . . . . 253 E7
  Stapleford NG9. . . . . . 209 E1
Far Clay Gr S81. . . . . . . 63 F7
Far Croft DE72. . . . . . . 235 D8
Far Cross DE4 . . . . 143 C7
Farfield Rd DE7 . . . . . . 209 A8
Far Gn DE4 . . . . 143 B6
Far Hill S33. . . . . 51 A7
Farish Pl 5 S2 . . . . 43 B6
Far La
  Barlow S18 . . . . 75 B3
  Ockbrook DE72. . . . . . 221 D6
Far Laund DE56 . . . . . . 179 B6
Farley Hill DE4. . . . . . . 143 A6
Farley La DE4. . . . . 128 B3
Farley Rd DE23 . . . . . . 218 D2
Farm Cl
  Belper DE56. . . . . 179 C4
  Chesterfield S40 . . . . . 114 F6
  Dronfield S18. . . . . . . 57 B4
  Hilton DE65 . . . . 228 B1
  Ilkeston DE7 . . . . 209 A8
  Kilburn DE56. . . . . . . 192 A8
  Long Eaton NG10. . . . 236 E5
  Ripley DE5. . . . . 169 B6
  Sheffield S12 . . . . 44 A4
  Somercotes DE55 . . . . 170 C8
Farm Cres S20 . . . . 59 C6
Farm Croft Rd NG19 . . . 136 C6
Farm Dr DE24. . . . . 233 A5
Farmfields Cl S44. . . . . . 98 E3
Farmhouse Rd DE24. . . . 231 E2
Farmilo Cres NG19 . . . . 135 E1

Farmilo Prim Sch NG19 . 135 C4
Farm La
  High Lane SK12 . . . . . . 32 A6
  Matlock DE4 . . . . 143 C7
  Newton Solney DE15 . . 248 E7
Farmlands La DE23 . . . . 231 B6
Farm Side DE11. . . . . . . 255 F5
Farm St DE22 . . . . 267 A1
Farmstead Cl S14. . . . . . 43 D5
Farm View S41 . . . . 131 D8
Farm Way NG19 . . . . . . 136 C2
Farm Wlk S20 . . . . 59 C7
Farnah Green Rd DE56. . 178 D3
Farnborough Gdns DE22 209 D3
Farncombe La DE21. . . . 205 F3
Farndale Ave S40. . . . . . 114 B8
Farndale Cl NG10 . . . . . 236 A5
Farndale Ct 5 DE24. . . . 233 C6
Farndale Rd S43 . . . . . . 78 E4
Farndon Dr NG9 . . . . . . 223 F3
Far New Cl NG10. . . . . . 223 B5
Farnham Cl DE3. . . . . . 217 C1
Farnham Wlk DE7. . . . . 207 D8
Farningham Cl DE21 . . . 220 F5
Farnon Cl S40 . . . . 266 C1
Farnsley La S32. . . . . . . 71 B4
Farnsworth Gr NG17 . . . 148 F3
Farnsworth St S41 . . . . 115 C8
Farnway DE22 . . . . 204 E1
Farrendale Cl NG19 . . . . 136 D1
Farrier Gdns DE23 . . . . 231 A7
Farriers Croft DE7 . . . . 194 C3
Farringdon Cl DE22 . . . 217 F6
Farrington Way NG16 . . 182 E1
Farthing Ct NG10 . . . . . 236 B7
Farwater Cl S18 . . . . 76 A8
Farwater La S18 . . . . 56 F1
Far Woodseats La SK13 . . 15 F5
Fauld Ind Pk DE13 . . . . 238 C6
Fauld La
  Tutbury DE13. . . . . . . 239 A6
  Tutbury, Fauld DE13. . . 238 D7
Fauvel Pl SK13. . . . . 10 C1
Fauvel Rd SK13. . . . . . . 10 C2
Faversham Cl DE24 . . . . 232 F5
Fawn Cl S42. . . . . 114 F3
Fay Gdns SK13 . . . . 9 E4
Faywood Dr SK6. . . . . . 23 A6
Fearn Ave DE5 . . . . 169 E1
Fearn Cl
  Church Broughton DE65 227 B8
  Long Eaton DE72 . . . . 236 A7
Featherbed La
  Bolsover S44. . . . . 99 A5
  Darfoulds S80 . . . . . . 63 F2
Felkin St S41 . . . . 266 C3
Fellbrigg Rd S2. . . . . . . 43 D7
Fellow Lands Way DE73 . 233 A2
Fellside
  Belper DE56. . . . . 179 A4
  Derby DE21 . . . . 220 F6
Felton Ave NG19 . . . . . 136 C6
Fenchurch Wlk DE22 . . . 218 B7
Fen Cl DE55 . . . . 148 A3
Fenland Way S40. . . . . . 114 E8
Fennel St DE45 . . . . . . 108 E8
Fenton Ave DE11. . . . . . 257 B1
Fenton Rd DE3. . . . . . . 217 C2
Fenton St S21 . . . . 59 B2
Fenwick St DE24 . . . . . . 232 D7
Ferguson Ave NG19 . . . 136 B4
Fern Ave
  Staveley S43 . . . . 97 D8
  Willington DE65 . . . . . 242 C6
Fernbank S33 . . . . 51 A7
Fern Bank Ave DE55. . . . 147 E1
Fernbank Dr S21. . . . . . 59 B3
Fern Cl
  Eckington S21 . . . . . . 59 B3
  Holmewood S44. . . . . 116 F1
  Shirebrook NG20 . . . . 119 E6
  Willington DE65. . . . . 242 C6
Fern Cres NG16. . . . . . . 182 D3
Ferncroft Ave S20 . . . . . 59 C7
Ferndale Ave SK17 . . . . . 67 C4
Ferndale Cl S18. . . . . . . 57 D3
Ferndale Rd
  Buxton SK17 . . . . 67 C4
  Dronfield S18. . . . . . . 57 D3
Ferndale Rise S18 . . . . . 57 D3
Ferndene Dr NG10 . . . . 236 A7
Fernello Cl DE73 . . . . . 244 A6
Ferneydale Ave SK17. . . . 85 C4
Fernhill SK6. . . . . 23 B6
Fernhill Cl SK13 . . . . . . 10 D3
Fernhill Cl DE73 . . . . . . 233 A3
Fernilee Cl
  New Mills SK22 . . . . . . 24 C1
  West Hallam DE7. . . . . 207 E8
Fernilee Cotts SK23. . . . 45 E1
Fernilee Gdns DE21 . . . 205 E1
Fern Lea
  Hollingworth SK14. . . . . 9 D6
  Shirland DE55 . . . . . . 146 D3
Fernlea Cl S43. . . . . 9 E4
Fernleigh Rise NG19 . . . 136 D5
Fern Rd SK17 . . . . 85 B5
Fern Royd S32. . . . . 53 A7
Fern Sq S32. . . . . 71 D6
Fernway SK17 . . . . 85 C4
Fern Way S21. . . . . 59 B3
Fernwood SK6. . . . . 23 C7
Fernwood Cl
  Chesterfield S41 . . . . . 115 C7
  Derby DE23 . . . . 231 D4
  Shirland DE55 . . . . . . 146 D3

Ferrers Ave DE13 . . . . . 239 B5
Ferrers Cl DE74. . . . . . . 247 A3
Ferrers Cres DE56 . . . . . 190 D3
Ferrers Ctr for Arts &
  Crafts★ LE65 . . . . 258 F7
Ferrers Way
  Derby DE22 . . . . 204 E2
  Ripley DE5 . . . . 169 C3
Ferry Gn DE65 . . . . 242 B5
Ferry St DE15. . . . . 254 E8
Ferry Vale Cl DE15 . . . . 254 E8
Festival Ave DE72. . . . . 235 E6
Festival Rd
  Branston DE14. . . . . . 253 E7
  Ilkeston DE7 . . . . 208 C7
Fiddler's Elm DE13 . . . . 239 F4
Fiddle St SK17 . . . . 85 C3
Fidlers Cl S33. . . . . 40 B3
Fidlers Well S33. . . . . . . 40 B4
Field Ave
  Hatton DE65 . . . . 239 C8
  Renishaw S21 . . . . 79 B8
Field Cl
  Borrowash DE72. . . . . 221 B3
  Breaston DE72. . . . . . 235 F7
  Dronfield S18. . . . . . . 56 C2
  Hilton DE65 . . . . 228 D2
  Mansfield Woodhouse
  NG19. . . . . 136 D5
Field Cres DE24 . . . . . . 233 A5
Field Ct
  Chesterfield S43 . . . . . 77 D4
  Kilburn DE56. . . . . . . 192 A8
Field Dr
  Derby DE24 . . . . 233 A5
  Rolleston DE13 . . . . . 240 A3
  Shirebrook NG20 . . . . 119 C2
Fielden Ave NG19 . . . . . 135 D2
Field End DE4 . . . . 153 A1
Fieldfare Ct DE23 . . . . . 231 A6
Fieldfare Ho S41. . . . . . 77 B3
Fieldgate Dr DE21 . . . . 205 F2
Fieldhead Rd S8. . . . . . . 43 A7
Fieldhead Way S41 . . . . 95 C6
Field Head Way DE21 . . 206 D2
Field House Inf Sch DE7 208 F6
Field House La SK6. . . . 23 A6
Fielding's Rd S80 . . . . . 81 F1
Field La
  Belper DE56. . . . . 178 F4
  Blackfordby DE11 . . . . 257 C2
  Derby, Boulton DE24 . . 233 B5
  Derby, Chaddesden DE21 220 A7
  Glapwell NG19, S44. . . 134 C6
  Killamarsh S21 . . . . . . 60 B5
  Kirk Ireton DE6. . . . . 176 B8
  Mayfield DE6 . . . . 183 C8
Field Rd DE7 . . . . 208 F7
Field Rise S23 . . . . 231 C7
Field Row 5 DE56 . . . . 178 F4
Fields Cres SK14 . . . . . . 9 D6
Fields Farm Rd NG10. . . 236 E5
Fields Gr SK14 . . . . 9 D5
Fields La DE11 . . . . 261 F6
Field St DE5 . . . . 181 B8
Fields The DE6 . . . . 154 D4
Fieldsway Dr DE21 . . . . 205 E2
Field Terr DE5 . . . . 169 D1
Field The DE75 . . . . . . 194 A6
Field View
  Chesterfield S40 . . . . . 115 A7
  Clowne S43 . . . . 80 F3
  South Normanton DE55. 160 A7
Field View Cl DE24. . . . 233 B5
Fieldview Pl S41. . . . . . . 95 C6
Field Way DE11 . . . . . . 255 F5
Fife St DE24 . . . . 232 F8
Filbert Wlk DE73. . . . . . 245 A8
Filey Wlk 4 DE21 . . . . . 205 D1
Fincham Cl DE21. . . . . . 205 D1
Finch Cl DE11. . . . . 256 F3
Finch Cres DE3 . . . . . . 230 C8
Finchley Ave DE22. . . . . 217 F6
Findern Cl
  Belper DE56. . . . . 179 B6
  Derby DE22 . . . . 204 D1
Findern La
  Burnaston DE65. . . . . 230 B4
  Willington DE65 . . . . . 242 B6
Findern Prim Sch DE65 . 242 E8
Findern St DE22 . . . . . . 218 D5
Fine Farm Cvn Pk DE56. . 178 B1
Finley Way DE55 . . . . . . 160 B4
Finmere Cl DE23 . . . . . 231 A8
Finney Cl DE12 . . . . 262 E1
Finningley Dr DE22 . . . 204 F2
Finny La DE6 . . . . 200 B5
Finsbury Ave DE22 . . . . 218 B6
Finsley Wlk DE23 . . . . . 231 E6
Firbeck La S80. . . . . 63 A1
Fir Cl NG20 . . . . 119 E6
Firestone DE56 . . . . . . 178 D5
Firfield Ave DE72 . . . . . 235 E8
Firfield Prim Sch DE72. . 235 E7
Fir Pl S21 . . . . 60 C5
Fir Rd S21 . . . . 59 C2
Firs Ave
  Alfreton DE55 . . . . . . 159 A5
  Hulland Ward DE6 . . . 175 F3
  Ripley DE5. . . . . 169 D1
Firs Cres DE22 . . . . 204 E4
Firs Estate Prim Sch
  DE22. . . . . 218 E3
Firs Gdns DE55 . . . . . . 159 A4
Firs Parade DE4. . . . . . 143 C6
Firs St NG10 . . . . 236 A4
Fir St S43 . . . . 78 B1

First Ave
  Branston DE14. . . . . . 253 E7
  Risley NG10. . . . . 222 F5
Firs The SK6. . . . . 173 C1
Firth Ct S43 . . . . 77 D4
Firthwood Ave S18. . . . . 57 D3
Firthwood Cl S18 . . . . . 57 D3
Firthwood Rd S18. . . . . 57 D3
Fir Tree Ave DE55. . . . . 146 C4
Fir Tree Dr DE73. . . . . . 244 A6
Firtree Gr DE21 . . . . . . 206 B2
Firvale S26 . . . . 61 E5
Firvale Rd S40 . . . . 114 B8
Fisher Cl
  Chesterfield S40 . . . . . 114 F7
  Repton DE65 . . . . 242 D2
Fisher Ct DE7 . . . . 194 F4
Fisher St DE56 . . . . 190 E4
Fishers Bridge SK22. . . . 25 D2
Fishers Cl S42. . . . . 115 A3
Fishponds Cl S42 . . . . . 115 A3
Fishponds Rd S13. . . . . 44 C7
Fishponds Rd W S13. . . . 44 C7
Fiskerton Way DE21 . . . 206 B1
Fitzalan St SK13 . . . . . . 10 C1
Fitzherbert CE Prim Sch
  DE6 . . . . 162 A1
Fitzhubert Rd
  Sheffield S2 . . . . 44 A7
  Sheffield S2 . . . . 44 A8
Fitzroy Rd S2. . . . . 43 B6
Fitzwilliam Dr NG19 . . . 136 F2
Five Lamps Ct DE1. . . . 218 F6
Five Lamps Ho DE1 . . . 267 A4
Five Lands Rd DE15 . . . 254 F8
Five Trees Ave S17. . . . . 56 A6
Five Trees Cl S17 . . . . . 56 A6
Five Trees Dr S17. . . . . . 56 A6
Flackets La DE6. . . . . . . 225 B7
Flagg La S17 . . . . 106 F7
Flagshaw La DE6. . . . . . 202 F4
Flake La DE7 . . . . 208 E1
Flamstead Ave DE75 . . . 181 C4
Flamstead La DE5. . . . . 180 E1
Flamstead Rd DE7 . . . . 194 F1
Flamstead St DE24 . . . . 232 E4
Flamsteed Cres S41. . . . 96 A6
Flash CE Prim Sch SK17. 103 B3
Flash La DE4 . . . . 128 A7
Flat La SK17 . . . . 106 B8
Flat The DE56. . . . . 191 F8
Flatts La NG16 . . . . 171 D3
Flatts The DE6 . . . . 165 B1
Flax Croft DE65. . . . . . . 227 C1
Flaxholme Ave DE56 . . . 190 F1
Flaxpiece Rd S45 . . . . . 131 D3
Fleet Cres DE56 . . . . . . 178 F3
Fleet Pk DE56. . . . . 179 A3
Fleet St DE23 . . . . 219 A2
Fleet The DE56 . . . . . . 178 F2
Fletcher's Row DE5 . . . 169 F2
Fletcher Ave S18 . . . . . . 57 A1
Fletcher St
  Heanor DE75 . . . . 181 E2
  Long Eaton NG10 . . . . 236 D8
  Ripley DE5. . . . . 169 E2
Fletches The DE13 . . . . 240 B1
Fleury Cl S14 . . . . 43 E4
Fleury Cres S14 . . . . . . 43 E4
Fleury Pl S14 . . . . 43 E4
Fleury Rd S14 . . . . 43 E4
Fleury Rise S14 . . . . 43 E4
Flint Ave NG19 . . . . 136 F1
Flint La DE4 . . . . 142 B8
Flintson Ave S43 . . . . . . 77 D4
Flint St DE24 . . . . 232 D6
Flixton Rd NG16 . . . . . . 195 F7
Flood St DE72 . . . . 221 C4
Florence Ave NG10. . . . 223 F1
Florence Cl
  Chesterfield S40 . . . . . 114 F6
  Pleasley NG19 . . . . . . 134 F4
Florence Ct
  Derby DE1 . . . . 267 D2
  Ilkeston DE7 . . . . 194 F4
Florence Dr DE6. . . . . . 224 C8
Florence Gladwin Cl
  DE4 . . . . 141 C6
Florence Rd
  Clay Cross S45. . . . . . 131 E4
  Wingerworth S42 . . . . 114 E4
Florence Way SK14 . . . . . 9 D5
Florin Gdns NG10 . . . . . 236 B7
Flowery Leys La DE55. . . 159 C3
Fly Hill DE45. . . . . 109 D6
Foggs Entry DE4 . . . . . . 165 F8
Foggs Hill DE4. . . . . . . 127 C4
Folds La S23 . . . . 45 F3
Folds Yd DE4 . . . . 156 F2
Fold The S32 . . . . 71 F4
Foljambe Ave S40. . . . . 114 C8
Foljambe Rd
  Brimington S43 . . . . . . 96 E8
  Chesterfield S40 . . . . . 266 A3
Folkestone Dr DE24 . . . 233 A5
Folly Rd DE22 . . . . 205 B1
Fontwell Rd DE14 . . . . . 253 F7
Foolow Ave S40 . . . . . . 266 A1
Foolow Ct S40. . . . . 266 A1
Forbes Cl NG10 . . . . . . 236 E5
Ford Ave DE75 . . . . 181 C4
Fordbridge La DE55 . . . 160 A7

Ford Cl
Dronfield S18. . . . . 56 F1
Ripley DE5. . . . . 180 C8
Ford Gr SK14. . . . . 9 A4
Ford La
Breadsall DE21. . . . . 205 C5
Derby DE22. . . . . 205 B5
Eckington S12, S21. . . . . 58 E5
Willington DE65. . . . . . . 242 C5
Ford Rd S21. . . . . 58 E4
Ford St
Belper DE56. . . . . 178 F4
Burton u T DE15. . . . . . . 254 E7
Derby DE1. . . . . 267 A4
Tupton S42. . . . . 131 D8
Ford Way SK14. . . . . 9 A4
Fordwells Cl DE23. . . . . 231 A8
Fordyce Cl DE73. . . . . . 232 E1
Foremark Ave DE23. . . . 231 E8
Forest Ave SK17. . . . . . . 85 C6
Forest Cl DE56. . . . . 179 B5
Forest Ct S43. . . . . 80 B6
Forest Dr S45. . . . . 132 C2
Foresters Rd DE5. . . . . 169 C2
Forester St DE1. . . . . . . 267 B2
Forest La SK17. . . . . 50 C2
Forest Lea DE12. . . . . . . 262 E4
Forest Park Cvn Pk
NG19. . . . . 136 E2
Forest School St DE13. . 240 C4
Forest View DE12. . . . . . 262 B4
Forge Cl DE65. . . . . 242 D2
Forge La
Burton u T DE13. . . . . . . 241 A2
Killamarsh S21. . . . . 60 B7
Forge Mill Pl DE56. . . . . 191 A6
Forge Rd S43. . . . . 45 E7
Forge Stps DE56. . . . . . 191 A6
Forge Terr SK23. . . . . 34 E1
Forge The
Dronfield S18. . . . . 57 A1
Trowell NG9. . . . . 209 B5
Forman Cl DE11. . . . . . . 256 B4
Forman St DE1, DE22. . . 267 A3
Forrester's La S18. . . . . . 57 C4
Forrester Ave DE72. . . . 245 F5
Forshaw Cl DE6. . . . . . . 185 C8
Forth Ave S18. . . . . 56 D2
Forties La LE65. . . . . . . 257 F3
Forty Foot La DE73. . . . 252 F7
Forty Horse Cl DE5. . . . 170 A2
Forum Cl DE24. . . . . 233 D5
Fosbrook Dr DE74. . . . . 246 F4
Fosbrooke Dr NG10. . . . 236 D5
Fosse Cl DE72. . . . . 221 C1
Fossett's Ave NG16. . . . 171 F7
Foster Rd DE11. . . . . 256 F2
Foston Cl DE65. . . . . 239 C8
Foston Dr S40. . . . . 95 B5
Foufinside Farm Camping &
Cvn Site DE6. . . . . 151 D2
Foundry Cl 1 SK22. . . . . 33 C7
Foundry La DE56. . . . . . 190 F8
Foundry St S41. . . . . 96 A8
Foundry Street Ind Est 7
S41. . . . . 96 A8
Foundry The S41. . . . . . 266 C2
Fountains Cl DE22. . . . . 205 A4
Fountain Sq
Disley SK12. . . . . 32 D6
Tideswell SK17. . . . . 69 C4
Youlgreave DE45. . . . . . . 125 B5
Fountain St SK17. . . . . . . 85 B7
Four Lane Ends
Darley Dale DE4. . . . . . . 127 C1
Swadlincote DE11. . . . . . 256 A6
Four Lanes SK14. . . . . 9 A4
Fowler Ave DE21. . . . . . 220 D4
Fowler St
Chesterfield S41. . . . . 76 F2
Derby DE22. . . . . 218 E6
Draycott DE72. . . . . 235 B7
Foxbrook Cl
Chesterfield S42. . . . . 94 F5
Derby DE23. . . . . 231 A8
Foxbrook Ct S40. . . . . . . 114 B8
Foxbrook Dr S40. . . . . . . 114 B8
Fox Cl
Burton u T DE14. . . . . . . 254 B8
Derby DE24. . . . . 231 D2
Long Eaton NG10. . . . . . 236 D5
Foxcote Way S40. . . . . . 114 B8
Fox Croft DE55. . . . . 147 F5
Foxcroft Chase S21. . . . . 60 C6
Foxcroft Dr S21. . . . . 60 C5
Foxcroft Gr S21. . . . . 60 C6
Foxdale Ave S12. . . . . . . 44 B5
Foxdell Way DE73. . . . . 233 A2
Foxes Wlk DE22. . . . . . . 204 E4
Foxes Yd SK17. . . . . 66 D1
Fox Field DE11. . . . . 261 F8
Foxfields Dr DE21. . . . . 205 C2
Foxglove Ave
Burton u T DE15. . . . . . . 255 A8
Donisthorpe DE12. . . . . 262 E1
Foxglove Cl S44. . . . . 97 A3
Foxglove Dr DE21. . . . . 206 A3
Foxglove Gr NG19. . . . . 136 F4
Foxglove Rd NG16. . . . . 195 B8
Foxhall La S10. . . . . 42 F6
Foxholes La
Kniveton DE6. . . . . 174 B6
Tansley DE4. . . . . 144 A7
Fox La
Holmesfield S18. . . . . 74 B5

Fox La continued
Sheffield, Base Green S12. . 44 C3
Sheffield, Lower Bradway
S17. . . . . 56 D6
Foxlands Ave DE22. . . . . 204 F2
Fox Lane Ct S12. . . . . 44 C4
Fox Lane View S12. . . . . . 44 C4
Foxlea SK13. . . . . 16 F8
Foxley Ct DE21. . . . . 206 A2
Foxley Oaks S41. . . . . . . 77 B1
Foxpark View DE55. . . . 147 E5
Fox Rd
Castle Donington DE74. . 246 F4
Whitwell S80. . . . . 82 A6
Fox St DE1. . . . . 267 C4
Foxstone Cl S43. . . . . 97 D8
Foxton Cl DE7. . . . . 194 C3
Foxwood Ave S12. . . . . . 44 B6
Foxwood Cl
Chesterfield S41. . . . . . . 115 D6
Chesterfield, Sheepbridge
S41. . . . . 76 F1
Foxwood Dr S12. . . . . . . 44 B6
Foxwood Gr S12. . . . . . . 44 B5
Foxwood Ind Pk S41. . . . 76 F1
Foxwood Rd
Chesterfield S41. . . . . 76 F2
Sheffield S12. . . . . 44 B6
Foxwood Way S41. . . . . . 76 E2
Foyers Way S41. . . . . . . 266 C3
Foyle Ave DE21. . . . . . . 220 A4
Frain Gdns DE73. . . . . . 252 F2
Framlingham Pl S2. . . . . 43 D7
Framlingham Rd S2. . . . . 43 D7
Frampton Gdns DE23. . . 230 F6
Frances Dr S42. . . . . 114 E4
Frances St NG16. . . . . . . 171 D1
Franchise St DE22. . . . . 218 E4
Francis Cl S43. . . . . 96 D7
Francis St DE21. . . . . . . 219 D6
Frank Bodicote Way
DE11. . . . . 256 D4
Franklin Ave S80. . . . . . . 81 F5
Franklin Cl DE15. . . . . . 248 B1
Franklin Cres S80. . . . . . 81 F5
Franklin Rd NG16. . . . . . 171 A4
Franklyn Dr
Derby DE24. . . . . 233 A6
Staveley S43. . . . . 78 F3
Franklyn Rd S40. . . . . . . 95 E4
Frazer Cl DE21. . . . . 220 E6
Frecheville St S43. . . . . . 78 D1
Frederic Ave DE75. . . . . 193 F7
Frederick Ave
Derby DE24. . . . . 232 F6
Ilkeston DE7. . . . . 209 A5
Frederick Gent Sch
DE55. . . . . 160 B5
Frederick Harrison Inf Sch
NG9. . . . . 223 F8
Frederick Rd NG9. . . . . 223 D7
Frederick St
Alfreton DE55. . . . . 159 A5
Burton u T DE15. . . . . . . 254 E8
Derby DE22. . . . . 218 D6
Grassmoor S42. . . . . 115 E3
Long Eaton NG10. . . . . . 236 F7
Somercotes DE55. . . . . . 170 C5
Woodville DE11. . . . . 256 E3
Freebirch View S40. . . . . 95 B7
Freeby Ave NG19. . . . . . 136 D5
Freehold St DE22. . . . . . 218 E4
Freeland Cl NG9. . . . . . . 223 F3
Freeman Ave DE23. . . . . 231 E6
Freesia Cl DE3. . . . . 217 E1
Freetown SK13. . . . . 17 C8
Fremantle Rd DE22. . . . . 217 E3
French La DE21. . . . . 191 F5
French St
Derby DE23. . . . . 218 E2
Ilkeston DE7. . . . . 209 A6
French Terr NG20. . . . . . 101 A2
Fresco Dr DE23. . . . . 230 F7
Fresh Ct SK13. . . . . 16 F7
Freshfield Cl SK6. . . . . . . 15 B1
Freshfields Farm Donkey
Sanctuary * SK17. . . . . . 48 D2
Freshwater Ho DE24. . . . 233 C7
Freshwaters S42. . . . . . . 116 D1
Fretson Cl S2. . . . . 44 A8
Fretson Gn S2. . . . . 44 A8
Fretson Rd S2. . . . . 44 A8
Fretson Rd S S2. . . . . 44 A8
Freydon Way S44. . . . . . 97 A3
Friar Gate DE1. . . . . 218 F5
Friar Gate Ct DE1. . . . . . 218 F5
Friar Gate House Sch
DE1. . . . . 218 E6
Friar Gr SK17. . . . . 85 C6
Friars Cl DE22. . . . . 205 A2
Friars Ct DE7. . . . . 208 C6
Friarsfield DE22. . . . . . . 218 F8
Friar St NG10. . . . . 236 D7
Friary Ave DE24. . . . . . . 232 E6
Friary Croft DE11. . . . . . 256 A7
Friary St DE1. . . . . 267 A3
Friden Cotts SK17. . . . . 139 A6
Friesland Dr NG10. . . . . 222 F5
Friesland Sch NG10. . . . 222 F5
Frinton Cl S40. . . . . 114 F7
Frisby Ave NG10. . . . . . 236 F6
Fritchley CE Prim Sch
DE56. . . . . 168 B6
Fritchley Cl DE21. . . . . . 206 A1
Fritchley La DE56. . . . . . 168 A7
Frith Cl S12. . . . . 44 B5
Frithhall La S42. . . . . 94 C2

Frith Knoll Rd SK23. . . . . 47 D7
Frith Rd S12. . . . . 44 B5
Frith View SK23. . . . . 47 A5
Frithwood Dr S18. . . . . . 57 C2
Frithwood La
Creswell S80. . . . . 100 F8
Elmton S80. . . . . 100 F8
Frizams La DE73. . . . . . . 242 F7
Froggatt Cl
Derby DE22. . . . . 205 A5
Staveley S43. . . . . 97 C6
Froggett Ct DE55. . . . . . 170 D7
Front St DE56. . . . . 168 B6
Frood Cl S13. . . . . 47 C7
Frost Ave NG16. . . . . . . 182 A4
Frost Fields DE74. . . . . . 247 B4
Fryar Rd NG16. . . . . 182 F4
Fulbrook Rd DE23. . . . . 231 A8
Fulford Cl S40. . . . . 114 C8
Fulham Rd DE22. . . . . . . 218 A5
Fuller Dr S41. . . . . 96 C6
Fulleylove Ct S44. . . . . . . 99 B1
Full St DE1. . . . . 267 B3
Fullwood Ave 4 DE7. . . 194 E1
Fullwood Grange DE6. . 175 C3
Fullwood St 6 DE7. . . . . 194 E1
Fullwood Stile La S33. . . 38 F6
Fulmar Cl DE3. . . . . 218 A3
Fulwood Dr NG10. . . . . . 236 A7
Fulwood Head Rd S10. . . 42 D7
Fulwood Ind Est NG17. . 160 F8
Fulwood La S10, S11. . . . 42 E5
Fulwood Rd N NG17. . . . 148 F1
Fulwood Rd S NG17. . . . 160 F1
Furlong Cl NG9. . . . . 223 D8
Furlong La
Alstonefield DE6. . . . . . . 149 C4
Atlow DE6. . . . . 175 B7
Furnace Cl S42. . . . . 115 E2
Furnace Hillock Way
S41. . . . . 115 E5
Furnace Hill Rd S45. . . . 131 D5
Furnace La
Barlow S18. . . . . 75 F3
Heanor DE75. . . . . 181 D4
Moira DE12. . . . . 262 E3
Furnace Lane Ind Est
DE12. . . . . 262 E3
Furnace Rd DE7. . . . . . . 209 B6
Furnace Row DE55. . . . . 170 F7
Furnall Ave DE45. . . . . . . 90 A3
Furness Cl 2 SK13. . . . . 17 F8
Furness Lodge Cl SK23. . 33 D4
Furness Vale Bsns Ctr
SK23. . . . . 33 D4
Furness Vale Prim Sch
SK23. . . . . 33 D3
Furness Vale Sta SK23. . . 33 D4
Furniss Ave S17. . . . . 55 D6
Furniss Mews S17. . . . . . 55 E6
Furrows DE21. . . . . 206 C3
Fyfield Rd DE15. . . . . . . 254 E6
Fylde Cl NG9. . . . . 223 F2

G

Gable Ct DE3. . . . . 230 E8
Gables Cl S42. . . . . 132 D8
Gables The
Hilton DE65. . . . . 228 D1
6 Swadlincote DE11. . . 255 E5
Gadley Cl SK17. . . . . 84 F8
Gadley La SK17. . . . . 84 F8
Gadsby Cl DE7. . . . . 209 A4
Gadsby Rise DE56. . . . . 168 C2
Gag La DE6. . . . . 161 D6
Gainsborough Ave SK6. . 23 B8
Gainsborough Cl
Derby DE21. . . . . 206 B1
Long Eaton NG10. . . . . . 236 E5
Stapleford NG9. . . . . 223 E6
Gainsborough Rd S18. . . 75 E8
Gainsborough Way DE15 248 B3
Gairloch Cl DE24. . . . . . 231 D2
Gala Dr DE24. . . . . 232 F7
Galahad Dr DE13. . . . . . 240 E2
Gallery La S42. . . . . 113 D7
Gallery The 6 DE6. . . . . 173 C2
Gallows Ind Est DE7. . . 209 B6
Gallows Inn Cl DE7. . . . . 209 A5
Gallowstree La DE6. . . . 184 C8
Galway Ave DE21. . . . . . 220 B4
Gamesley Com Prim Sch
SK13. . . . . 9 E2
Gander La S43. . . . . 80 B5
Gang La S44. . . . . 118 E5
Gannow Ct S21. . . . . 60 F7
Gapsick La S43, S80. . . . 81 B5
Garden Ave
Ilkeston DE7. . . . . 208 F5
New Houghton NG19. . . 134 F7
Renishaw S21. . . . . 79 B7
Shirebrook NG20. . . . . . 119 E4
Garden Cl S43. . . . . 77 D3
Garden Cres
Castle Donington DE74. . 247 B3
South Normanton DE55. . 159 F4
Gardeners Ct
Bolsover S44. . . . . 99 A2
Mansfield Woodhouse
NG19. . . . . 136 C3
Garden Rd NG16. . . . . . 182 F3
Garden Row S44. . . . . . . 117 D1
Garden St
7 Broadbottom SK14. . . 16 A8
Derby DE1. . . . . 267 A4

Gardens The
Heanor DE75. . . . . 181 C4
Ripley DE5. . . . . 180 D7
Gardner Pl ST14. . . . . . . 210 A1
Gardom Cl S18. . . . . 56 D1
Garfield Ave DE72. . . . . 235 A7
Garfield Cl
Derby DE23. . . . . 231 C6
Stapleford NG9. . . . . 209 E1
Garland Cl S20. . . . . 59 E7
Garland Croft S20. . . . . . 59 E7
Garland Mount 15 S20. . 59 E7
Garland Way S20. . . . . . . 59 E7
Garner La DE4, DE55. . . 157 D2
Garnett Ave DE75. . . . . 181 F2
Garnham Cl DE55. . . . . . 159 D2
Garrett Gn S45. . . . . 131 E3
Garrett La S45. . . . . 131 D2
Garrett Sq DE13. . . . . . . 240 C4
Garrick St DE24. . . . . . . 233 A7
Garry Cl DE24. . . . . 231 D2
Garsdale Cl DE24. . . . . . 233 D6
Gartan Rd DE14. . . . . . . 254 A8
Garth Cres DE24. . . . . . 233 B6
Garthorpe Ct 4 DE21. . . 205 F2
Garth Rd SK6. . . . . 23 A6
Garth Way S18. . . . . 56 F1
Garth Way Cl S18. . . . . . . 56 F1
Gartrice Gdns S20. . . . . . 60 A5
Gartrice Gr S20. . . . . 60 A5
Gary Cl DE23. . . . . 231 D5
Gascoigne Dr DE21. . . . 220 D4
Gashouse La S20, S21. . . 59 D5
Gaskell Ave DE23. . . . . . 231 E7
Gasny Ave DE74. . . . . . . 247 B5
Gas St
Hollingworth SK14. . . . . . 9 D5
Sandiacre NG10. . . . . . . 223 C6
Uttoxeter ST14. . . . . 210 C1
Gatcombe Cl
Burton u T DE13. . . . . . . 240 D1
Derby DE21. . . . . 206 B2
Gatcombe Gr NG10. . . . 223 A3
Gate Brook Cl DE5. . . . . 170 B1
Gatefield Cl S41. . . . . 95 C7
Gate Ho DE4. . . . . 165 F4
Gate Ho The S32. . . . . . . 72 D2
Gatehouse Dr DE4. . . . . 165 F8
Gateland La S18. . . . . 75 E5
Gateway Christian Sch
DE7. . . . . 207 F2
Gateway Cvn Pk DE6. . . 185 D7
Gauledge La SK17. . . . . 121 B6
Gaunt Cl
Killamarsh S21. . . . . 60 C6
Sheffield S14. . . . . 43 D3
Gaunt Dr S14. . . . . 43 D3
Gaunt Pl S14. . . . . 43 D4
Gaunt Rd S14. . . . . 43 D3
Gaunt Way S14. . . . . 43 D3
Gawain Gr DE13. . . . . . . 240 E2
Gawsworth Cl SK13. . . . . 10 A5
Gayton Ave DE23. . . . . . 231 D6
Gayton Com Jun Sch
DE23. . . . . 231 D6
Gayton Rd NE7. . . . . 194 D1
Gayton Thorpe Cl DE23. 230 F7
Geary La DE15. . . . . 248 F2
Geer La S12. . . . . 58 D5
Gelderd Pl S18. . . . . 76 A8
Gema Cl DE22. . . . . 205 A4
Genista Cl DE15. . . . . . . 255 A8
Gentshill Ave S45. . . . . . 131 E2
George Ave NG10. . . . . . 223 F1
George Cres DE55. . . . . 170 C6
George Dutton Ind Pk
DE6. . . . . 185 E8
George Holmes Bsns Pk
DE11. . . . . 256 A4
George Holmes Way
DE11. . . . . 256 A3
George Inn Ct S80. . . . . . 81 F6
George Percival Pl S45. . 131 A4
George Rd DE4. . . . . 143 C6
George Spencer Foundation
Sch & Tech Coll NG9. . 223 F5
George St
Alfreton DE55. . . . . 159 A4
Ashbourne DE6. . . . . . . 185 B8
Belper DE56. . . . . 178 F4
Brimington S43. . . . . 96 E8
7 Buxton SK17. . . . . 85 B8
Chesterfield S41. . . . . . . 76 F2
Compstall SK6. . . . . 15 B2
Derby DE1. . . . . 267 A3
Glossop SK13. . . . . 17 C8
Langley Mill NG16. . . . . 182 B3
Mansfield Woodhouse
NG19. . . . . 136 D3
Melbourne DE73. . . . . . 252 A7
North Wingfield S42. . . . 131 E7
Pinxton NG16. . . . . 160 C4
Somercotes DE55. . . . . . 170 D8
Somercotes, Riddings
DE55. . . . . 170 D6
South Normanton DE55. . 159 F5
Swadlincote DE11. . . . . . 256 A1
Whaley Bridge SK23. . . . 45 E7
Whaley Thorns NG20. . . 101 A2
Georgina Ct DE74. . . . . . 247 B4
Gerard Cl
Chesterfield S40. . . . . 95 C1
Derby DE21. . . . . 220 A2
15 Sheffield S8. . . . . 43 B6
Gerard Ct DE1. . . . . 267 A2
Gerard Gr DE65. . . . . . . 229 C2
Gerard St
Derby DE1. . . . . 267 A2

Gerard St continued
Sheffield S8. . . . . 43 B6
Gertrude Rd
Derby DE21. . . . . 220 A1
Draycott DE72. . . . . 235 A7
Gervase Ave S8. . . . . 56 E6
Gervase Dr S8. . . . . 56 E6
Gervase Pl S8. . . . . 56 E6
Gervase Rd S8. . . . . 56 E6
Gervase Wlk 2 S8. . . . . . 56 E6
Ghyll Cl DE24. . . . . 220 A1
Gibb Ct S43. . . . . 77 D4
Gibb La
Marple SK6. . . . . 23 E5
Sudbury DE6. . . . . 225 E5
Gibbons Ave NG9. . . . . . 223 D8
Gibbons Dr S14. . . . . 43 E2
Gibbons Way S14. . . . . . 43 E2
Gibbons Wlk S14. . . . . . . 43 E2
Gibb St NG10. . . . . 236 E7
Gibfield La
Belper DE56. . . . . 178 F2
Kirk Ireton DE6. . . . . 175 F7
Gifford Rd S8. . . . . 43 A7
Gilbert Ave S40. . . . . . . 114 C8
Gilbert Cl DE21. . . . . . . 220 D4
Gilbert Cres DE56. . . . . 190 E2
Gilbert Heathcote Inf Sch
S41. . . . . 96 A3
Gilbert St DE24. . . . . . . 233 B6
Gilderdale Way DE21. . . 206 B3
Gill's La S42. . . . . 115 E2
Gillamoor Ct DE24. . . . . 233 D6
Gilleyfield Ave S17. . . . . 55 E7
Gilliver Gdns DE72. . . . . 235 A7
Gill La DE4. . . . . 127 C4
Gillott St DE75. . . . . 194 A8
Giltbrook Cres NG16. . . 195 C8
Gilt Hill NG16. . . . . 195 D7
Gilthill Prim Sch NG16. . 195 D7
Giltway NG16. . . . . 195 C7
Gimson Cl DE7. . . . . 194 C3
Gin Close Way NG16. . . 195 C6
Gin La S45. . . . . 144 F8
Gipsyhill La S80. . . . . 81 B8
Gipsy La
Alstonefield DE6. . . . . . . 149 F4
Apperknowle S18. . . . . . 58 A1
Chesterfield S41. . . . . 77 B1
Gird La SK6. . . . . 15 E1
Girdon Cl SK17. . . . . 84 F6
Gisborne Cl DE3. . . . . . . 217 E3
Gisborne Cres DE22. . . . 204 F4
Gisborne Gn DE1. . . . . . 218 E6
Gisbourne Cl S43. . . . . . 78 F1
Gisbourne Dr SK23. . . . . 47 B5
Glade Cl S40. . . . . 95 E5
Glade Croft S12. . . . . . . 44 A4
Glade Lea S12. . . . . 44 A4
Glade The
Buxton SK17. . . . . 85 A8
Chesterfield S40. . . . . 95 D3
Gladstone Ave
Blackwell DE55. . . . . 147 E1
Heanor DE75. . . . . 181 F2
Gladstone Cl
Chellaston DE73. . . . . . . 232 F3
Glossop SK13. . . . . 17 D8
Gladstone Dr NG16. . . . 182 E7
Gladstone Rd
Alfreton DE55. . . . . 158 F3
Chesterfield S40. . . . . . . 266 A4
Derby DE21. . . . . 220 E5
Gladstone St W DE7. . . . 208 F7
Gladstone St
Derby DE23. . . . . 218 E1
Glossop SK13. . . . . 17 C8
Hadfield SK13. . . . . 10 A4
Heanor DE75. . . . . 181 E2
Langley Mill NG16. . . . . 182 C3
Long Eaton NG10. . . . . . 236 D6
Mansfield Woodhouse
NG19. . . . . 136 C2
South Normanton DE55. . 160 B6
Gladstone Terr NG19. . . 136 C2
Gladwin Gdns S40. . . . . 114 D8
Gladys Buxton Com Ed Ctr
S18. . . . . 57 C2
Glaisdale Nook DE24. . . 233 D6
Glamis Cl DE21. . . . . 206 B2
Glamorgan Way DE11. . . 255 F1
Glapwell La S44. . . . . . . 118 B2
Glasshouse Hill DE5. . . 181 B8
Glasshouse La S43. . . . . 77 D4
Glastonbury Cl NG19. . . 136 D4
Glastonbury Rd DE24. . 233 C2
Glaven Cl NG19. . . . . . . 136 D2
Gleadless Ave S12. . . . . 44 A4
Gleadless Bank S12. . . . 43 F4
Gleadless Comm S12. . . 44 A5
Gleadless Ct S2. . . . . 43 B6
Gleadless Dr S12. . . . . . 43 F4
Gleadless Mount S12. . . 44 A3
Gleadless Prim Sch S12. . 44 B5
Gleadless Rd S12, S14, S2. 43 D5
Gleadless Rise
1 Sheffield, Gleadless
Townend S12. . . . . 44 A3
Sheffield S12. . . . . 43 F5
Gleadless View
2 Sheffield, Gleadless
Townend S12. . . . . 44 A3
Sheffield S12. . . . . 43 F5
Gleadsmoss La DE21. . . 206 A1
Glebe Ave
Great Longstone DE45. . . 90 A3
Harthill S26. . . . . 61 E7
Pinxton NG16. . . . . 160 D3

Glebe Ave *continued*
Ripley DE5 . . . 169 C2
Smalley DE7 . . . 192 F6
Glebe Cl
Coton in t E DE12 . . . 260 C3
Doveridge DE6 . . . 224 B8
Holmewood S42 . . . 132 D8
Rolleston DE13 . . . 240 A4
South Normanton DE55 . . . 160 A5
Thurvaston DE6 . . . 201 E1
Glebe Cres
Ilkeston DE7 . . . 209 A7
Stanley DE7 . . . 207 B6
Glebe Farm Cl S26 . . . 61 E7
Glebe Field Cl DE4 . . . 156 F1
Glebe Gdns S42 . . . 131 F5
Glebe Jun Sch DE55 . . . 160 A5
Glebe Rd SK17 . . . 85 D8
Glebe Rise DE23 . . . 218 D1
Glebe St DE11 . . . 256 B3
Glebe The
Awsworth NG16 . . . 195 B4
Chesterfield S41 . . . 77 A2
Rosliston DE12 . . . 260 C6
Glebe View
Barlborough S43 . . . 80 B6
5 Forest Town NG19 . . . 136 E1
Glebe Way The S41 . . . 77 A2
Gledhill Cl S18 . . . 57 A1
Glen Ave DE56 . . . 191 C7
Glenavon Cl S43 . . . 77 D5
Glenbrook Hill SK13 . . . 10 C2
Glen Cl DE55 . . . 148 A3
Glencoe Way S40 . . . 95 B4
Glencroft Cl DE14 . . . 254 B7
Glencroft Dr DE24 . . . 231 D3
Glendale Dr DE21 . . . 220 F5
Glendevon Way DE73 . . . 232 E2
Glendon Rd
Derby DE24 . . . 231 D3
Ilkeston DE7 . . . 208 C4
Glendon St DE7 . . . 193 A1
Gleneagles Cl
Chesterfield S40 . . . 114 C8
Derby DE3 . . . 217 F2
Gleneagles Dr DE13 . . . 240 C1
Glenfield Ave NG16 . . . 195 D7
Glenfield Cres
Chesterfield S41 . . . 96 A7
Derby DE3 . . . 217 C2
Glenfield Rd NG10 . . . 236 D5
Glengarry Way DE24 . . . 231 E4
Glenholme Dr S13 . . . 44 E7
Glenholme Pl S13 . . . 44 F7
Glenholme Rd S13 . . . 44 F7
Glenholme Way S13 . . . 44 E7
Glenmoor Rd SK17 . . . 66 D1
Glenmore Cl S43 . . . 97 B5
Glenmore Croft S12 . . . 44 C6
Glenmore Dr DE24 . . . 231 D3
Glenmoy Cl DE23 . . . 231 D7
Glenn Way DE72 . . . 234 E1
Glenorchy Ct DE21 . . . 206 B3
Glen Park Cl DE73 . . . 244 F8
Glen Rd DE4 . . . 156 D1
Glenthorn Cl S81 . . . 63 F7
Glenthorne Cl S40 . . . 95 C2
Glen Vale S18 . . . 56 D1
Glen View DE56 . . . 178 F2
Glen View Rd S8 . . . 56 E8
Glen Vine DE5 . . . 170 A1
Glenwood Rd DE73 . . . 245 A8
Glinton Ave DE55 . . . 147 E1
Glossop's Croft S41 . . . 77 B2
Glossopbrook Bsns Pk SK13 . . . 10 C1
Glossop Brook Rd SK13 . . 10 B1
Glossop Central Sta SK13 10 C1
Glossopdale Com Coll SK13 . . . 10 C2
Glossopdale Comm Coll (Annexe) SK13 . . . 10 A4
Glossop Heritage Ctr★ SK13 . . . 10 C1
Glossop Rd
Broadbottom SK13 . . . 16 D7
Gamesley SK13 . . . 9 E1
Hayfield SK22 . . . 25 C6
Marple SK6 . . . 15 D3
Glossop St DE24 . . . 232 B8
Gloster St DE24 . . . 219 E2
Gloucester Ave
Chesterfield S41 . . . 95 F5
Sandiacre NG10 . . . 223 A4
Gloucester Rd S41 . . . 95 F5
Gloucester Way
Burton u T DE15 . . . 248 B1
4 Glossop SK13 . . . 17 F8
Glover Rd
Castle Donington DE74 . . . 247 B4
Sheffield, Highfield S8 . . . 43 A7
Sheffield, Totley Rise S17 . . 55 F5
Gloves La DE55 . . . 147 D2
Glumangate S40 . . . 266 B3
Goathland Rd DE24 . . . 231 D2
Goatscliffe Cotts S32 . . . 72 C7
Goddard La
Glossop SK13 . . . 10 A6
New Mills SK22 . . . 24 E7
Goddard Rd SK13 . . . 10 A4
Godfrey Dr DE7 . . . 208 D6
Godfrey St DE75 . . . 181 E1
Godkin Dr NG16 . . . 182 A4
Godward Rd SK22 . . . 33 B8
Gold Cl DE4 . . . 142 B8
Goldcrest Dr DE21 . . . 220 F6
Goldcrest Ho S41 . . . 77 B3
Golden Valley
Horsley Woodhouse DE7 . . 192 B6
Somercotes DE55 . . . 170 D3
Golden Valley Light Rly★ DE5 . . . 170 B4
Golders Green Wlk DE22 218 A6
Goldhill DE4 . . . 144 A4
Golding Ho DE4 . . . 143 C6
Gold La DE22 . . . 217 E8
Goldstone Ct DE21 . . . 220 E4
Golf Cl DE23 . . . 218 A1
Golf Club Rd DE7 . . . 209 B1
Golf La DE56 . . . 190 E5
Golf Terr SK17 . . . 66 D1
Gomersal La S18 . . . 57 A1
Goodale St DE23 . . . 219 A1
Goodman Cl NG16 . . . 195 C8
Goodman Ct S44 . . . 97 A3
Goodrington Rd DE21 . . . 206 C3
Goodsmoor Rd DE23, DE24 . . . 231 E5
Goodsmoor Rd Ind Est DE24 . . . 231 E5
Goods Rd DE56 . . . 178 F2
Goods Yd DE56 . . . 178 F1
Goodwin's La DE56 . . . 178 C1
Goodwin Cl NG10 . . . 223 A6
Goodwin Dr NG16 . . . 195 E6
Goodwin Rd 6 S8 . . . 43 A6
Goodwood Cl DE13 . . . 240 C1
Goodwood Cres DE7 . . . 208 D4
Goodwood Dr
Beeston NG9 . . . 223 F2
Derby DE24 . . . 233 C6
Gooker La DE55 . . . 158 F3
Goole Ave DE7 . . . 208 D5
Goose Green La DE55 . . . 146 D3
Goose Green View DE45 . . 91 F5
Goosehill S33 . . . 38 B2
Goose La DE5 . . . 181 C8
Gordon Ave S8 . . . 43 A2
Gordon Cres DE55 . . . 160 B4
Gordondale Rd NG19 . . . 136 B1
Gordon Rd
Borrowash DE72 . . . 221 B1
Derby DE23 . . . 218 F3
Swanwick DE55 . . . 169 F8
Tideswell SK17 . . . 69 C3
Gordon St DE7 . . . 195 A1
Gordon Works 12 S2 . . . 43 A6
Gore La S33 . . . 51 A8
Gorman Cl S41 . . . 95 E8
Gorse Bank S44 . . . 116 F2
Gorsebank La DE45 . . . 91 F7
Gorse Cl
Derby DE23 . . . 231 B6
Eastwood NG16 . . . 195 B8
Long Eaton NG10 . . . 223 B2
Gorse Dr S21 . . . 60 D5
Gorsehill Gr DE23 . . . 231 A7
Gorse La
Bradley DE6 . . . 175 B3
Moira DE12 . . . 262 E6
Sheffield S10 . . . 42 F7
Gorse Ridge Dr DE45 . . . 91 E6
Gorses
Alderwasley DE56 . . . 178 C8
Idridgehay DE6 . . . 176 D5
Gorse Valley Rd S41 . . . 115 E7
Gorse Valley Way S41 . . . 115 E7
Gorse Way SK13 . . . 17 F7
Gorsey Bank DE4 . . . 165 F7
Gorsey Brigg S18 . . . 56 D1
Gorseybrigg Prim Sch S18 . . . 56 D1
Gorsey Brow SK14 . . . 9 A1
Gorsey Cl DE56 . . . 178 E6
Gorsey Intakes SK14 . . . 16 A8
Gorsey La
Kirk Ireton DE6 . . . 165 A1
Netherseal DE12 . . . 265 A7
Gorsty Leys DE65 . . . 230 D1
Gosber Rd S21 . . . 59 E3
Gosber St S21 . . . 59 D3
Goseley Ave DE11 . . . 257 A4
Goseley Cres DE11 . . . 257 A4
Gosforth Ave NE7 . . . 194 E6
Gosforth Cl S18 . . . 56 F1
Gosforth Cres 3 S18 . . . 56 F1
Gosforth Dr S18 . . . 75 D8
Gosforth Gn S18 . . . 56 F1
Gosforth La S18 . . . 56 F1
Gosforth Rd DE24 . . . 232 E8
Goshawk Rd DE7 . . . 209 A3
Gower Cres S40 . . . 95 C5
Gower St DE1 . . . 267 B2
Goyt's La SK17 . . . 65 A3
Goyt Forest Walks★ SK11 83 E7
Goytlands SK17 . . . 84 F6
Goyt Pl SK23 . . . 45 E7
Goyt Rd
Disley SK12 . . . 32 D5
Horwich End SK23 . . . 45 E6
New Mills SK22 . . . 33 D6
Goyt Side Rd S40 . . . 95 E2
Goyt Valley Ind Est SK23 . . 33 D4
Goyt View SK22 . . . 33 B6
Grace Cres DE75 . . . 181 F2
Gradbach Mill (YH)★ SK17 . . . 102 A1
Grafham Cl DE73 . . . 233 A2
Grafton Rd DE15 . . . 248 B1
Grafton St DE23 . . . 218 E2
Grafton Terr DE4 . . . 127 A5
Graham Cl DE14 . . . 254 C7
Graham Dr SK12 . . . 32 C6
Graham St DE7 . . . 208 F7
Grammer St DE5 . . . 181 A4
Grampian Cres S40 . . . 95 B4
Grampian Prim Sch DE24 . . . 231 D4
Grampian Way
Derby DE24 . . . 231 E4
Long Eaton NG10 . . . 236 A8
Granary Cl S40 . . . 95 A8
Granby Ave SK23 . . . 34 E1
Granby Cl S45 . . . 132 C2
Granby Croft DE45 . . . 109 D5
Granby Jun Sch DE7 . . . 194 E3
Granby Rd
Bakewell DE45 . . . 109 D5
Bradwell S33 . . . 50 F7
Buxton SK17 . . . 85 D7
Granby St DE7 . . . 194 E2
Grandfield St DE75 . . . 181 C4
Grandstand Rd DE21 . . . 219 C6
Grange Ave
Breaston DE72 . . . 235 D8
Chapel-en-le-F SK23 . . . 47 B5
Derby DE23 . . . 231 E7
Dronfield S18 . . . 56 E1
Hulland Ward DE6 . . . 175 F3
Grange Cl
Melbourne DE73 . . . 252 B8
Somercotes DE55 . . . 159 F2
Ticknall DE73 . . . 251 A4
Grange Ct DE65 . . . 241 B5
Grange Dale DE4 . . . 153 C8
Grange Dr
Castle Donington DE74 . . . 247 A3
Long Eaton NG10 . . . 236 F8
Grange Farm Cl DE74 . . . 247 D5
Grange Gate DE22 . . . 267 A1
Grange La
Barlow S18 . . . 75 B1
Darley Dale DE4 . . . 127 F1
Ible DE4 . . . 153 D7
Grangemill Pl S43 . . . 97 C8
Grangeover Way DE22 . . . 218 D4
Grange Park Ave
Calow S43 . . . 96 F4
Chapel-en-le-F SK23 . . . 47 B5
Grange Park Rd SK23 . . . 47 B5
Grange Pk NG10 . . . 236 F8
Grange Prim Sch NG10 . . 236 F8
Grange Rd
Buxton SK17 . . . 85 C7
Derby DE24 . . . 233 B6
Long Eaton NG10 . . . 236 F8
Pilsley S45 . . . 132 C2
Swadlincote DE11 . . . 255 E5
Uttoxeter ST14 . . . 210 A1
Grange Rd S SK14 . . . 15 A8
Grange St
Alfreton DE55 . . . 159 A3
Derby DE23 . . . 219 B2
Grange The
Brimington S43 . . . 96 D8
Chesterfield S42 . . . 94 F4
Smalley DE75 . . . 193 C8
South Normanton DE55 . . . 160 A4
Grange View NG16 . . . 182 F3
Grange Wlk S42 . . . 115 E2
Grangewood Ave 3 DE7 208 F7
Grangewood Ct S40 . . . 114 F7
Grangewood Dr DE56 . . . 191 A7
Grangewood Gdns DE12 261 D6
Grangewood Rd S40 . . . 114 F7
Gransden Way S40 . . . 114 C8
Grant Ave DE21 . . . 220 B5
Grantham Ave DE21 . . . 205 E1
Grantham Cl NG16 . . . 195 C7
Granville Ave NG10 . . . 223 D1
Granville Cl
Chesterfield S41 . . . 115 D8
Duffield DE56 . . . 190 E3
Hatton DE65 . . . 227 D1
Granville Com Sch DE11. 256 E4
Granville Ct DE11 . . . 256 C4
Granville St
Derby DE1 . . . 218 E5
Woodville DE11 . . . 256 E3
Graphite Way
Glossop SK13 . . . 9 F6
Hollingworth SK13 . . . 9 F6
Grasmere Ave
Clay Cross S45 . . . 131 B3
Derby DE21 . . . 220 E6
Grasmere Cl
Burton u T DE15 . . . 248 B1
Chesterfield S41 . . . 95 D7
Grasmere Cres DE24 . . . 231 E4
Grasmere Ct 1 NG10 . . . 223 B2
Grasmere Rd
Dronfield S18 . . . 56 D1
Long Eaton NG10 . . . 223 B2
Grasmere St 2 NG10 . . . 223 C5
Grasscroft Cl 3 S40 . . . 95 D6
Grasscroft Mobile Home Pk S43 . . . 77 D5
Grassdale View S12 . . . 44 F3
Grassmoor Cl S12 . . . 43 F5
Grassmoor Cres SK13 . . . 9 D2
Grassmoor Ctry Pk★ S42, S41 . . . 116 A4
Grassmoor Prim Sch S42 . . . 115 F2
Grass St DE7 . . . 194 E3
Grassthorpe Cl DE21 . . . 206 B1
Grassthorpe Rd S12 . . . 44 B4
Grassy Ct DE3 . . . 230 A7
Grassy La DE65 . . . 230 A7
Gratton Ct S43 . . . 78 F3
Gratton La DE45 . . . 140 C7
Gravelly Bank Mews DE6 . . . 199 D5
Gravel Pit Cotts DE65 . . . 229 B1
Gravel Pit Hill DE65 . . . 249 E7
Gravel Pit La DE21 . . . 220 E4
Graves Park Animal Farm★ S8 . . . 43 B1
Graves Tennis & L Ctr S8 . 57 B7
Graves Trust Homes
Sheffield, Common Side S12 . . . 44 A5
Sheffield, Greenhill S8 . . . 56 F8
Sheffield, Little Norton S8 . . 57 A8
Graycar Bsns Pk DE13 . . . 253 B2
Gray Fallow DE55 . . . 160 B4
Grayling St DE23 . . . 219 B2
Grays Cl DE74 . . . 247 B3
Grayshott Wlk S40 . . . 114 F8
Gray St
Clowne S43 . . . 80 F4
Sheffield, Mosborough S20 . 59 C7
Grayston Ct SK6 . . . 23 B7
Grayswood Cl DE55 . . . 170 A7
Great Common Cl S43 . . . 80 B6
Great Croft S18 . . . 56 D2
Great Hucklow Prim Sch SK17 . . . 51 B1
Great Longstone Bsns Pk DE45 . . . 90 A4
Great Northern Cotts NG19 . . . 135 A5
Great Northern Point DE22 . . . 218 F4
Great Northern Rd
Derby DE1 . . . 218 F5
Eastwood NG16 . . . 182 D2
Greatorex Ave DE24 . . . 232 E5
Greaves La DE45 . . . 108 F8
Greaves St
Ripley DE5 . . . 169 E2
Shirland DE55 . . . 146 E1
Greave Way S43 . . . 96 C8
Greenacre Ave DE75 . . . 182 A3
Greenacre Pk DE12 . . . 260 C3
Greenacres DE23 . . . 231 B8
Greenacres Cl S18 . . . 76 C7
Greenacres Dr
South Normanton DE55 . . . 160 B6
Uttoxeter ST14 . . . 210 A2
Greenacre The DE6 . . . 184 F7
Green Ave DE73 . . . 233 A1
Greenaway Dr S44 . . . 118 A8
Greenaway La DE4 . . . 127 E1
Greenbank
Derby DE21 . . . 220 D4
Hollingworth SK13 . . . 9 F5
Green Bank SK13 . . . 16 F7
Greenbank Dr S40 . . . 95 C4
Greenbank Rd SK6 . . . 15 B1
Greenburn Cl DE23 . . . 231 C6
Green Chase S21 . . . 59 C3
Green Cl
Curbar S32 . . . 72 E2
Matlock DE4 . . . 143 B6
Newton DE55 . . . 148 A3
Renishaw S21 . . . 79 B8
Staveley S43 . . . 97 C6
Unstone Green S18 . . . 76 E6
Willington DE65 . . . 242 A6
Green Cres NG16 . . . 171 E6
Green Cross S18 . . . 57 B2
Greendale Ave S42 . . . 113 E8
Greendale Ct S18 . . . 57 B2
Greendale Sh Ctr S18 . . . 57 B2
Greendale The DE55 . . . 157 D8
Green Farm Cl S40 . . . 95 C6
Green Farm Rd NG16 . . . 171 D6
Greenfield Ave S80 . . . 82 C6
Greenfield Cl
New Mills SK22 . . . 33 A8
Sheffield S8 . . . 56 F7
Greenfield Dr
Linton DE12 . . . 261 C6
Sheffield S8 . . . 56 F7
Greenfield Ho SK13 . . . 10 A6
Greenfield Rd S8 . . . 56 F7
Greenfields
Aldercar NG16 . . . 182 A4
Denstone ST14 . . . 196 D6
Eckington S21 . . . 59 C3
Fritchley DE56 . . . 168 B7
Greenfields Ave DE23 . . . 231 B8
Greenfield St SK13 . . . 10 A6
Greenfinch Cl DE21 . . . 220 F6
Greengate Cl S40 . . . 95 C2
Green Glen S40 . . . 95 C2
Greenhall Rd S21 . . . 59 C3
Greenhead S33 . . . 40 B4
Greenhead Cres SK17 . . . 138 C2
Greenhead Pk S33 . . . 40 B4
Green Hill DE4 . . . 154 E1
Greenhill Ave
Ripley DE5 . . . 180 E8
Sheffield S8 . . . 56 F8
Greenhill La DE55 . . . 170 C6
Greenhill Lane Ind Est DE55 . . . 170 B5
Greenhill Main Rd
Sheffield S8 . . . 56 F7
Sheffield S8 . . . 57 A7
Greenhill Parkway S8 . . . 56 D6
Greenhill Prim Sch S8 . . . 56 E7
Greenhills Cvn Pk DE45 . 109 A7
Greenhills Rd NG16 . . . 182 F3
Greenhill Wlk SK12 . . . 32 D6
Greenholme Pk NG19 . . . 136 E6
Greenhouse La S10 . . . 42 F5
Green Inf Sch The DE55 . 160 A6
Green La
Alsop en le D DE6 . . . 150 C2
Green La *continued*
Bakewell DE45 . . . 108 C3
Barrow u T DE73 . . . 244 A5
Belper DE56 . . . 178 F4
Bonsall DE4 . . . 153 F8
Burnaston DE65 . . . 230 A4
Buxton SK17 . . . 85 A6
Buxton, Water Swallows SK17 . . . 67 C2
Chelmorton SK17 . . . 106 D8
Chesterfield S41 . . . 96 D4
Chinley SK23 . . . 34 E2
Clifton DE6 . . . 184 E7
Compstall SK14 . . . 15 B8
Creswell S80 . . . 82 C5
Cutthorpe S42 . . . 94 E7
Darley Dale DE4 . . . 127 B3
Derby, Alvaston DE24 . . . 233 C8
Derby DE1 . . . 267 B2
Disley SK12 . . . 32 D4
Dronfield S18 . . . 57 B2
Glossop, Brookfield SK13 . . . 9 F4
Glossop SK13 . . . 16 F8
Hognaston DE6 . . . 164 B2
Hollingworth SK14 . . . 9 D6
Ilkeston DE7 . . . 209 A7
Killamarsh S21 . . . 60 C3
Mansfield NG19 . . . 135 A2
Marchington ST14 . . . 225 A2
Ockbrook DE72 . . . 221 C5
Overseal DE12 . . . 261 F4
Pilsley S45 . . . 132 C3
Pleasley S44 . . . 134 D8
Roston DE6 . . . 197 F8
Shirebrook NG19, NG20 . . 119 C2
Tansley DE4 . . . 144 A5
Tupton S42 . . . 115 D1
Tutbury DE13 . . . 239 C5
Weston Underwood DE6 . . 188 F2
Wilson DE73 . . . 252 E5
Greenland Ave DE22 . . . 218 B5
Greenland Cl S42 . . . 132 A7
Green Lands DE11 . . . 256 B7
Green Lea S18 . . . 56 C2
Green Leas DE72 . . . 246 A8
Greenmount Cl DE23 . . . 231 A6
Green Oak Ave S17 . . . 55 E4
Green Oak Cres S17 . . . 55 E4
Green Oak Dr S17 . . . 55 E4
Green Oak Gr S17 . . . 55 E4
Green Oak Rd S17 . . . 55 E4
Green Park Ave SK23 . . . 47 C6
Green Pastures S17 . . . 55 E7
Green Pk DE22 . . . 218 A6
Green Rd The DE6 . . . 173 C3
Greens Ct DE7 . . . 194 D1
Greenshall La SK12 . . . 32 F5
Greenside NG16 . . . 171 D6
Greenside Ave S41 . . . 96 A7
Greenside Cl
Barlborough S43 . . . 80 C4
Donisthorpe DE12 . . . 262 E1
Long Eaton NG10 . . . 236 E7
Greenside Ct DE3 . . . 217 C2
Greens La NG16 . . . 195 F6
Greensmith Cl DE15 . . . 248 C3
Greensquare Rd NG16 . . . 160 E2
Green St
Barton in F NG11 . . . 237 F5
Chesterfield S41 . . . 77 A2
Green The
Alfreton DE55 . . . 159 B3
Aston-on-T DE72 . . . 246 B8
Bamford S33 . . . 40 B4
Belper DE56 . . . 179 A5
Birchover DE4 . . . 126 B1
Brackenfield DE55 . . . 145 D2
Bradwell S33 . . . 51 B6
Brailsford DE6 . . . 201 E7
Breedon on t H DE73 . . . 252 E2
Burton u T DE13 . . . 240 E1
Castle Donington DE74 . . . 247 A3
Chesterfield S41 . . . 115 D7
Clowne S43 . . . 80 E4
Crich DE4 . . . 156 D1
Curbar S32 . . . 72 E2
Derby DE22 . . . 204 D1
Derby, Mickleover DE3 . . . 217 D1
Draycott DE72 . . . 235 A7
Findern DE65 . . . 230 D1
Fritchley DE56 . . . 168 B6
Froggatt S32 . . . 72 D5
Glapwell S44 . . . 134 B8
Glossop SK13 . . . 17 A7
Hardstoft S45 . . . 133 A3
Kirk Langley DE6 . . . 202 C1
Mansfield Woodhouse NG19 . . . 136 A5
Marple SK6 . . . 23 A3
Middleton DE4 . . . 154 D5
North Wingfield S42 . . . 132 A7
Sheffield S17 . . . 55 D4
Stanton in Peak DE4 . . . 126 C5
Sutton in A NG17 . . . 148 F1
Swanwick DE55 . . . 169 E7
Ticknall DE73 . . . 250 F3
Tissington DE6 . . . 162 B5
Weston-on-T DE72 . . . 245 F5
Willington DE65 . . . 242 A6
Greenvale Cl DE15 . . . 254 F8
Greenview DE4 . . . 153 A1
Greenville Croft DE73 . . . 232 E1
Green Water Mdw SK14 . . . 9 D5
Greenway
Ashbourne DE6 . . . 173 C3

Greenway continued
Brassington DE4 . . . . 153 A1
Burton u T DE15 . . . . . . 248 A4
Hulland Ward DE6 . . . . . 175 F3
Whitwell S80 . . . . 81 F6
Wingerworth S42 . . . . . . 115 C2
Green Way DE65 . . . . . . 230 D2
Greenway Cl DE72 . . . . . 221 B3
Greenway Croft DE4 . . . . 154 F1
Greenway Dr DE23 . . . . . 218 A1
Greenways S40 . . . . 114 C8
Greenway The
Derby DE72 . . . . 233 D5
Sandiacre NG10 . . . . . . 223 B6
Sheffield S8 . . . . 56 F8
Greenwich Ave DE11 . . . 255 E1
Greenwich Ct 12 S43 . . . 78 B3
Greenwich Dr N DE22 . . 218 C6
Greenwich Dr S DE22 . . 218 B5
Greenwood Ave
Derby DE21 . . . . 219 F8
Ilkeston DE7 . . . . 209 A7
Mansfield Woodhouse
NG19 . . . . 136 B4
Sutton in A NG17 . . . . . 148 F2
Greenwood Cl DE24 . . . . 232 D5
Greenwood Ct DE1 . . . . . 267 B4
Greenwood Rd DE15 . . . 254 E8
Greer La S44 . . . . 118 D1
Gregg Ave DE75 . . . . . . 181 F2
Greggs Ave SK23 . . . . . . 46 F5
Gregory Ave
Aldercar NG16 . . . . 182 A4
Breaston DE72 . . . . 235 C8
Gregory Cl
Brimington S43 . . . . 96 E7
Stapleford NG9 . . . . . . 223 F8
Gregory Ct 10 S8 . . . . . . 43 B6
Gregory La S8 . . . . 77 D1
Gregory Rd S8 . . . . 43 A6
Gregory St DE7 . . . . . . 208 E8
Gregorys Way DE56 . . . . 179 C5
Gregory Wlk DE23 . . . . . 230 E7
Gregson Cl DE11 . . . . . . 256 B5
Grendon Cl DE56 . . . . . . 179 B6
Grenfell Ave DE23 . . . . . 231 E6
Grenville Dr
Ilkeston DE7 . . . . 194 F3
Stapleford NG9 . . . . . . 223 F8
Grenvoir Dr DE5 . . . . . . 170 A1
Gresham Rd DE24 . . . . . 232 C8
Gresley Rd
Ilkeston DE7 . . . . 194 F1
Sheffield S8 . . . . 56 E5
Gresley Wlk S8 . . . . 56 E5
Gresley Woodlands
DE11 . . . . 256 A2
Gresley Wood Rd
Swadlincote DE11 . . . . . 255 F2
Woodville DE11 . . . . . . 256 A2
Gretton Ave DE13 . . . . . 240 E1
Gretton Rd SK17 . . . . . . 85 D8
Greyfriars Cl 4 DE75 . . 181 F1
Greysich La DE65 . . . . . . 249 F2
Grey St DE22 . . . . 267 A2
Greystones Ct S26 . . . . . 61 D6
Griffe Field Prim Sch
DE23 . . . . 231 A6
Griffin Cl
Derby DE24 . . . . 232 F7
New Mills SK22 . . . . . . 33 D6
Staveley S43 . . . . 97 E8
Griffon Rd DE7 . . . . . . 208 F4
Griggs Gdns DE4 . . . . . 165 F7
Grimshaw Ave DE24 . . . 233 B7
Grindleford Gdns 16 SK13 . 9 E2
Grindleford Dyke 13 SK13 . 9 E2
Grindleford Lea 14 SK13 . . 9 E2
Grindleford Prim Sch S32 72 C8
Grindleford Sta S32 . . . . 53 D2
Grindleford Wlk 15 SK13 . 9 E2
Grindlow Ave S40 . . . . . 266 A1
Grindlow Cl S14 . . . . . . 43 C6
Grindlow Dr S14 . . . . . . 43 C6
Grindlow Rd DE21 . . . . . 220 A8
Grindon Cl S40 . . . . 95 C5
Grindslow Ave DE7 . . . . 207 E8
Grinlow Cl SK17 . . . . . . 85 C3
Grinlow Cvn Pk SK17 . . . 84 F5
Grin Low Rd SK17 . . . . . 85 B3
Grinton Wlk S40 . . . . . . 114 F8
Grisedale Rd E DE45 . . . . 90 A4
Grisedale Rd W DE45 . . . 90 A4
Grisedale Wlk S18 . . . . . 56 E1
Gritstone Rd DE4 . . . . . 143 D7
Grizedale Cl DE15 . . . . . 248 B1
Groombridge Cres DE23 . 231 A6
Groome Ave DE75 . . . . . 181 C4
Grosvenor Ave
Breaston DE72 . . . . 235 F8
Long Eaton NG10 . . . . . 236 A4
Grosvenor Dr DE23 . . . . 231 A6
Grosvenor Rd
Eastwood NG16 . . . . . . 182 F2
Marple SK6 . . . . 23 A7
Ripley DE5 . . . . 169 C2
Grosvenor St DE24 . . . . 232 C8
Grove Ave S17 . . . . 55 D5
Grovebury Dr DE23 . . . . 231 C5
Grove Cl DE72 . . . . 233 F4
Grove Cotts NG19 . . . . . 135 B4
Grove Ct
Elvaston DE72 . . . . 233 F4
Ripley DE5 . . . . 180 F8
Grove Farm Cl S43 . . . . . 96 E7

Grove Gdns S43 . . . . 96 F5
Grove Ho DE23 . . . . 267 B1
Grove Hospl The DE72 . . 234 D1
Grove House Ct S17 . . . . 55 E5
Grove La
Buxton SK17 . . . . 85 C6
Darley Dale DE4 . . . . . 127 E1
Old Brampton S42 . . . . . 94 B4
Somersal Herbert DE6 . . 211 F2
Grove Mews DE1 . . . . . . 182 E1
Grove Par 2 SK17 . . . . . 85 B8
Grove Pk DE65 . . . . 229 B2
Grove Pl DE45 . . . . 125 B5
Grove Rd
Calow S43 . . . . 96 E5
Chesterfield S41 . . . . . . 96 A7
Sheffield, Totley Brook S17 . 55 F5
Groves Nook DE73 . . . . . 232 E1
Grove St
Chesterfield S41 . . . . . . 115 C8
Derby DE23 . . . . 267 B1
Mansfield Woodhouse
NG19 . . . . 136 B3
New Mills SK22 . . . . . . 33 B7
Swadlincote DE11 . . . . . 256 B4
Grove The
Breaston DE72 . . . . 235 F8
Derby DE3 . . . . 217 E2
Glossop SK13 . . . . 9 F4
Poolsbrook S43 . . . . 98 A8
Sheffield, Hillfoot S17 . . . 55 D5
Tatenhill DE13 . . . . 253 A4
Grove Way
Calow S43 . . . . 96 F5
Mansfield Woodhouse
NG19 . . . . 136 B3
Grundy Ave NG16 . . . . . 171 D7
Grundy Nook S80 . . . . . . 82 A5
Grundy Rd S45 . . . . 131 C3
Grunmore Dr DE13 . . . . 240 E2
Guernsey Rd S2 . . . . 43 A7
Guide Post DE56 . . . . . . 168 C2
Guildford Ave
Chesterfield S40 . . . . . . 114 D8
Mansfield Woodhouse
NG19 . . . . 136 C6
Sheffield S8 . . . . 43 D8
Swadlincote DE11 . . . . . 256 E6
Guildford Cl S45 . . . . . . 131 E3
Guildford La S45 . . . . . . 131 E3
Guildford Rise S2 . . . . . . 43 E8
Guildford View S2 . . . . . 43 E7
Guildhall Dr NG16 . . . . . 160 F2
Guildhall Theatre★ DE1 . 267 B3
Guinea Cl NG10 . . . . . . 236 A7
Guinevere Ave DE13 . . . 240 E2
Gulliver's Kingdom★
DE4 . . . . 155 A8
Gunby Hill DE12 . . . . . . 261 F2
Gunhills La DE56 . . . . . . 189 E6
Gun La DE56 . . . . 168 C2
Gun Rd SK6 . . . . 16 C2
Gurney Ave DE23 . . . . . 231 D6
Gutersloh Ct NG9 . . . . . 223 F8
Guy Cl NG9 . . . . 223 E6
Gypsy La
Creswell S80 . . . . 81 E1
Draycott DE72 . . . . 221 E1

H

Hackney La S18 . . . . 75 F1
Hackney Rd DE4 . . . . . . 143 A7
Hackthorn Rd 4 S8 . . . . 43 A3
Haddon Ave S43 . . . . . . 81 A4
Haddon Cl
Alfreton DE55 . . . . 158 F3
Bullbridge DE56 . . . . . . 168 B6
Chesterfield S40 . . . . . . 95 C1
Derby DE22 . . . . 204 D3
Dronfield S18 . . . . 57 B2
Heanor DE75 . . . . 181 C2
West Hallam DE7 . . . . . 207 E8
Haddon Ct DE6 . . . . . . 185 D8
Haddon Dr
Bakewell DE45 . . . . 109 E4
Derby DE22 . . . . 204 D3
Derby, Mickleover DE3 . . 217 E3
Derby, Spondon DE21 . . . 220 F4
Little Eaton DE21 . . . . . 191 C2
Haddon Gn 31 SK13 . . . . 9 D2
Haddon Grove Farm Camp
Site DE45 . . . . 108 B1
Haddon Hall★ DE45 . . . 110 B1
Haddon Ho DE45 . . . . . 109 E3
Haddon Lea 32 SK13 . . . . 9 D2
Haddon Mews 30 SK13 . . 9 D2
Haddon Nurseries DE7 . . 194 E3
Haddon Pl
Shirebrook NG20 . . . . . 119 E6
Staveley S43 . . . . 97 D8
Haddon Rd
Bakewell DE45 . . . . 109 F3
Buxton SK17 . . . . 85 D8
North Wingfield S42 . . . 132 A8
Haddon St
Derby DE23 . . . . 218 E1
Ilkeston DE7 . . . . 194 E3
Tibshelf DE55 . . . . 148 A6
Haddon Way NG10 . . . . 235 F4
Hade La SK17 . . . . 106 F2
Hades La SK17 . . . . 88 B3
Hadfield Ind Est SK13 . . . 9 F6
Hadfield Inf Sch SK13 . . . 9 F5
Hadfield Pl SK13 . . . . . . 17 C8
Hadfield Rd
Glossop SK13 . . . . 9 F4

Hadfield Rd continued
Hadfield SK13 . . . . 10 A5
Hadfields Ave SK14 . . . . 9 D5
Hadfield Sq 1 SK13 . . . . 17 C8
Hadfield St SK13 . . . . . . 17 C8
Hadfield Sta SK13 . . . . . 10 A5
Hadleigh Cl 2 NG9 . . . . 223 E2
Hadley La DE6 . . . . 186 E8
Hadley St DE7 . . . . 209 A5
Hadstock Cl NG10 . . . . . 223 B4
Hady Cres S41 . . . . 96 C3
Hady Hill S41 . . . . 96 C2
Hady La S41 . . . . 96 E1
Hady Prim Sch S41 . . . . 96 D2
Hag Bank La SK12 . . . . . 32 D7
Hagg La
Dale Abbey DE7 . . . . . . 207 D4
Turnditch DE56 . . . . . . 177 C1
Hague Ave S21 . . . . 79 B8
Hague Bar Prim Sch SK22 32 E8
Hague Bar Rd SK22 . . . . 32 F8
Hague Fold Rd SK22 . . . . 32 F8
Hague La S21, S43 . . . . . 79 B6
Hague Rd SK14 . . . . 16 A8
Hague St SK13 . . . . 17 D7
Haig Hill Farm Hamlet
S42 . . . . 115 E1
Haigh Meml Homes S8 . . 57 A7
Haigh Moor Rd S13 . . . . 44 F8
Haigh Moor Wlk S13 . . . 44 F8
Haig St DE24 . . . . 232 F8
Hailsham Cl DE3 . . . . . . 217 D3
Haines Cl DE24 . . . . 231 F4
Halcyon App S42 . . . . . . 115 C2
Halcyon Cl S12 . . . . 44 F3
Haldane Cl S80 . . . . 81 E2
Haldane Cres S44 . . . . . 98 F2
Halesworth Cl S40 . . . . 114 B8
Half Acre La S18 . . . . . . 76 D8
Half Croft S45 . . . . 96 F7
Halfmoon La DE6 . . . . . 165 B3
Halfway Ctr S20 . . . . . . 59 E7
Halfway Dr S20 . . . . 59 E7
Halfway Gdns S20 . . . . . 59 E7
Halfway Inf Sch S20 . . . . 59 F7
Halfway Jun Sch S20 . . . 59 E6
Halifax Cl
Derby DE21 . . . . 205 C1
Hilton DE65 . . . . 228 E2
Hall's Ct SK13 . . . . 10 C1
Hall's Row 1 S40 . . . . . 95 D2
Hallam Ct
Dronfield S18 . . . . 76 A8
Ilkeston DE7 . . . . 194 F3
Hallam Fields DE74 . . . . 247 B2
Hallam Fields Jun Sch
DE7 . . . . 208 F5
Hallam Fields Rd DE7 . . 209 B4
Hallamway NG19 . . . . . 136 C1
Hallam Way DE7 . . . . . . 207 D8
Hall Bank
Buxton SK17 . . . . 85 B7
Hartington SK17 . . . . . 137 E5
Hall Cl
Cutthorpe S42 . . . . 94 E8
Dronfield S18 . . . . 56 C2
Mottram in L SK14 . . . . 9 A5
Sandiacre NG10 . . . . . . 223 B6
Hallcliff La S42 . . . . 93 F1
Hall Cotts DE6 . . . . 175 D2
Hallcroft Ave DE12 . . . . 262 B3
Hallcroft Rd 2 DE7 . . . . 208 F8
Hall Ct DE7 . . . . 207 E7
Halldale La DE4 . . . . . . 127 E3
Hall Dale View DE4 . . . . 127 D3
Hall Dr
Doveridge DE6 . . . . 211 A1
Hanbury DE13 . . . . 238 A4
Mottram in L SK14 . . . . 9 A5
Sandiacre NG10 . . . . . . 223 B6
Hall End La DE45 . . . . . 108 F8
Hall Farm S42 . . . . 132 D8
Hall Farm Cl
Castle Donington DE74 . . 247 B3
Chesterfield S41 . . . . . . 115 D7
Swadlincote DE11 . . . . . 256 C4
Whaley Bridge SK23 . . . 45 D8
Hall Farm Ct DE7 . . . . . 222 F8
Hall Farm Gdns S42 . . . 132 D8
Hall Farm Rd
Duffield DE56 . . . . 190 E2
Swadlincote DE11 . . . . . 256 C4
Hallfield Cl S42 . . . . . . 115 A4
Hallfieldgate La DE55 . . 146 D1
Hallfield Rd DE55 . . . . . 148 A3
Hallfields Rd DE15 . . . . 255 C4
Hallfields Rise DE55 . . . 146 C1
Hallflash La SK14 . . . . . 116 A8
Hallgate Cl DE21 . . . . . 206 C3
Hallgate La S45 . . . . . . 132 B2
Hall Gate View S33 . . . . 51 A8
Hall Gdns
Hemington DE74 . . . . . 247 D4
Marchington ST14 . . . . 224 E2
Hall Green Ave DE13 . . . 240 F2
Hall Grounds DE13 . . . . 240 A4
Hallington Dr DE75 . . . . 181 D1
Hall La
Ashbourne DE6 . . . . . . 173 C2
Brailsford DE6 . . . . 202 A6
Brinsley NG16 . . . . 182 D6
Donisthorpe DE12 . . . . 265 E8
Doveridge DE6 . . . . 224 B8
Litton SK17 . . . . 69 E3
Mayfield DE6 . . . . 183 A4
Nether Heage DE56 . . . . 168 C3
Newton DE55 . . . . 148 A3
Shirley DE6 . . . . 200 D8

Hall La continued
Staveley S43 . . . . 78 D3
Willington DE65 . . . . . . 242 B5
Hall Leys La DE73 . . . . . 245 D1
Hall Meadow Croft S20 . 59 F5
Hall Meadow Dr S20 . . . 59 F5
Hall Meadow Gr S20 . . . 59 F5
Hall Meadow Rd SK13 . . 10 D2
Hallmoor Rd DE4 . . . . . 127 C4
Hallowes Ct S18 . . . . . . 57 B1
Hallowes Dr S18 . . . . . . 76 B8
Hallowes La S18 . . . . . . 76 B8
Hallowes Rise S18 . . . . . 76 C8
Hall Park Cl DE23 . . . . . 218 A5
Hall Pk DE73 . . . . 244 A5
Hall Rd
Aldercar NG16 . . . . 182 C4
Brimington S43 . . . . 96 E7
Marchington ST14 . . . . 224 E2
Rolleston DE13 . . . . . . 239 F4
Hall Rise
2 Ashbourne DE6 . . . . 173 D3
Darley Dale DE4 . . . . . 127 D3
Hallside Ct S20 . . . . 59 D6
Halls La NG16 . . . . 195 A8
Halls Rd NG9 . . . . 223 D6
Hall St
Alfreton DE55 . . . . 159 A4
Derby DE24 . . . . 233 A7
New Mills SK22 . . . . . . 33 B8
Swadlincote DE11 . . . . . 256 A2
Hallsteads SK17 . . . . . . 47 F1
Hallsteads Cl SK17 . . . . 47 F1
Hallsteads The DE6 . . . . 163 B2
Hall Terr S45 . . . . 131 D3
Hall The
Glossop SK13 . . . . 17 A7
Middleton DE4 . . . . 154 D5
Hall View S41 . . . . 95 E6
Hall View Cottage Herb
Gdn★ S45 . . . . 132 E3
Hall Wlk S42 . . . . 115 D1
Hallworth Wlk S21 . . . . 58 E2
Hallyburton Cl S2 . . . . . 43 C6
Hallyburton Dr S2 . . . . . 43 C6
Hallyburton Rd S2 . . . . . 43 C6
Halstead Cl NG19 . . . . . 136 F2
Halstock Dr DE24 . . . . . 233 C8
Halton Cl S41 . . . . 76 E1
Hamble Cl NG19 . . . . . . 136 D3
Hambledon Cl S40 . . . . . 95 C5
Hambledon Dr DE24 . . . 231 D2
Hambleton Ave S42 . . . . 131 F6
Hambleton Cl
Ashbourne DE6 . . . . . . 185 C8
2 Long Eaton NG10 . . . 223 A1
Hambleton Rise NG19 . . 136 F1
Hamble Way DE65 . . . . 228 C1
Hamblin Cres DE24 . . . . 231 F4
Hamill Cl S42 . . . . 131 F7
Hamilton Cl
Beeston NG9 . . . . 223 F2
Derby DE3 . . . . 217 F3
Hamilton Dr
Market Warsop NG20 . . 120 F4
Swadlincote DE11 . . . . . 256 C5
Hamilton Fields DE15 . . 248 A3
Hamilton Gr DE11 . . . . . 256 D5
Hamilton Rd
Burton u T DE15 . . . . . 248 A2
Derby DE23 . . . . 218 F2
Long Eaton NG10 . . . . . 223 D1
Hamilton Terr DE65 . . . 242 B6
Hamlet Ct DE73 . . . . . . 232 E1
Hamlet La DE55 . . . . . . 160 A5
Hamlet The
Heanor DE75 . . . . 181 E3
South Normanton DE55 . 160 A5
Hammer Leys DE55 . . . . 160 C4
Hammersmith DE5 . . . . 169 D4
Hammersmith Sta★ DE5 169 D4
Hammonds Ct DE4 . . . . 165 F8
Hampden Ho DE15 . . . . 254 E6
Hampden St
Derby DE23 . . . . 232 A8
Eastwood NG16 . . . . . . 195 B8
Langley Mill NG16 . . . . 182 B3
Hampshire Cl SK13 . . . . 17 F8
Hampshire Ct NG16 . . . 171 B4
Hampshire Dr NG10 . . . 223 B5
Hampshire Rd DE21 . . . 219 C8
Hampstead Dr DE22 . . . 218 A6
Hampton Cl
Beeston NG9 . . . . 223 E3
Derby DE21 . . . . 220 D5
West Hallam DE7 . . . . . 207 D8
Hampton Ct 4 DE75 . . . 181 D2
Hampton St S41 . . . . . . 115 D7
Hanbury Ave DE65 . . . . 227 D1
Hanbury Cl
Chesterfield S40 . . . . . . 95 A5
Dronfield S18 . . . . 56 F1
Hanbury Hill DE13 . . . . 238 A5
Hanbury Rd DE21 . . . . . 219 F6
Hanchurch Cl DE15 . . . . 248 A4
Hand's Rd DE75 . . . . . . 182 A1
Handby St S41 . . . . 115 D7
Handby St S41 . . . . 115 D7
Handel Mews DE6 . . . . . 185 D8
Handel St DE24 . . . . . . 232 C8
Handford St DE22 . . . . . 218 D6
Handford St DE22 . . . . . 218 D6
Handley Ct S43 . . . . 77 D4
Handley La
Ashover S45 . . . . 145 F8
Clay Cross S45 . . . . 131 A1
Pilsley DE45 . . . . 91 B1

Handley Rd S43 . . . . 77 D5
Handsacre Cl DE11 . . . . 255 F5
Handyside St DE1 . . . . . 267 B4
Hangar Hill S80 . . . . 82 A6
Hanger Bank DE72 . . . . 246 B8
Hanley Cl SK12 . . . . 32 D5
Hannage Way DE4 . . . . 165 F7
Hanover Sq DE22 . . . . . 218 A6
Hansard Gate DE21 . . . . 267 D3
Hanslynn DE72 . . . . . . 233 F4
Hanston Ct S43 . . . . 77 D4
Hanstubbin Rd NG16 . . 171 F6
Hanwell Way DE22 . . . . 218 B6
Harbin Rd DE12 . . . . . . 253 D1
Harboro Cl DE6 . . . . . . 185 B8
Harby Ave NG19 . . . . . . 136 D5
Harcourt Cl
Chesterfield S41 . . . . . . 115 C7
Ilkeston DE7 . . . . 194 D1
Harcourt Pl DE74 . . . . . 247 B4
Harcourt Rd DE14 . . . . . 253 F8
Harcourt St DE1 . . . . . . 267 B2
Hardacre Cl DE73 . . . . . 252 A8
Hardcastle Mews SK23 . . 47 B6
Hardhurst Rd
Derby DE24 . . . . 233 B5
Unstone Green S18 . . . . 76 E6
Hardie Ave DE55 . . . . . 160 A6
Hardie Pl S43 . . . . 97 D8
Hardie St S21 . . . . 59 D3
Harding's Cl DE6 . . . . . 165 B1
Harding's La SK17 . . . . . 138 A5
Hard La S26 . . . . 61 E8
Hard Meadow La S45 . . 130 B2
Hardstaff Homes The
Eastwood NG16 . . . . . . 195 C8
Mansfield Woodhouse
NG19 . . . . 136 B3
Hardstoft Rd S45 . . . . . 132 C2
Hardwick's Yd S40 . . . . 95 C2
Hardwick Ave
Chesterfield S43 . . . . . . 77 D3
Derby DE22 . . . . 204 D3
Glapwell S44 . . . . 134 B8
Shirebrook NG20 . . . . . 119 E4
West Hallam DE7 . . . . . 207 E8
Hardwick Cl
Blackwell DE55 . . . . . . 147 D1
Clowne S43 . . . . 81 A4
Dronfield S18 . . . . 57 C2
Holmewood S42 . . . . . . 132 E8
Ripley DE5 . . . . 169 C3
Hardwick Ct
Holmewood S42 . . . . . . 132 E8
Long Eaton NG10 . . . . . 235 F4
South Normanton DE55 . 160 C6
5 Staveley S43 . . . . . . 78 E2
Hardwick Dr
Arkwright Town S44 . . . 97 D3
Derby DE3 . . . . 217 E2
Hardwick Gdns 6 SK17 . 85 B7
Hardwick Hall★ S44 . . . 133 E4
Hardwick Hall Ctry Pk★ S44,
NG17 . . . . 133 F5
Hardwick La S45 . . . . . . 129 D6
Hardwick Mount SK17 . . 85 C7
Hardwick Old Hall★ S44 133 D4
Hardwick Park Nature Wlk★
S44 . . . . 133 C5
Hardwick Pl DE7 . . . . . . 208 C5
Hardwick Prim Sch
DE23 . . . . 219 A1
Hardwick Sq E SK17 . . . 85 C7
Hardwick Sq N SK17 . . . 85 C7
Hardwick Sq S SK17 . . . 85 B7
Hardwick Sq W SK17 . . 85 B7
Hardwick St
Buxton SK17 . . . . 85 B8
Chesterfield S41 . . . . . . 266 B4
Derby DE24 . . . . 232 C8
Langwith NG20 . . . . . . 119 F8
Shirebrook NG20 . . . . . 120 A4
Tibshelf DE55 . . . . 148 A7
Hardwick View Rd S42 . . 132 E8
Hardy Barn DE75 . . . . . 194 A7
Hardybarn La SK17 . . . . 67 B2
Hardy Cl
Kimberley NG16 . . . . . 195 F7
Long Eaton NG10 . . . . . 236 D6
Hardy Cres DE5 . . . . . . 181 B8
Hardy La SK17 . . . . 69 C4
Hardy St
Alfreton DE55 . . . . 158 F5
Kimberley NG16 . . . . . 195 F7
Harebell Cl
Derby DE21 . . . . 206 A3
Swadlincote DE11 . . . . . 256 E4
Harehedge La DE13 . . . . 240 C4
Harehill Cres S42 . . . . . 114 D4
Harehill Ct S40 . . . . 114 F7
Harehill Rd S40 . . . . . . 114 F7
Harepit Cl DE24 . . . . . . 233 A5
Harewood SK14 . . . . 16 A8
Harewood Ave DE55 . . . 169 F6
Harewood Cl
Belper DE56 . . . . 179 C5
2 Sandiacre NG10 . . . . 223 B4
Harewood Cres S42 . . . . 131 B6
Harewood Lo SK14 . . . . 16 A8
Harewood Rd
Derby DE22 . . . . 204 D3
Holymoorside S42 . . . . 113 C5
Hargate Hill La SK13 . . . 16 E2
Hargate Rd
Burton u T DE15 . . . . . 248 C1
Buxton SK17 . . . . 84 F6
Hargrave Ave DE72 . . . 221 C5
Hargreaves Cl DE23 . . . 231 A6

Hargreaves Ct **5** DE7 ... 208 F7
Harlaxton Dr NG10 ...... 237 A8
Harlech Cl
  Derby DE21 .... 221 A5
  Ilkeston DE7 .... 194 C3
Harlequin Ct NG16 ...... 182 D3
Harlesden Ave DE22 .... 218 A7
Harlesthorpe Ave S43 .... 80 F5
Harlesthorpe La S43 .... 80 E5
Harley's Ct DE12 ...... 262 C4
Harlow Cl
  Derby DE24 .... 232 F4
  Mansfield Woodhouse
    NG19 .... 136 C6
Harlow Ct DE7 .... 207 D7
Harold Ave NG16 .... 182 B4
Harold Ct DE23 .... 219 B2
Harperhill Cl S40 ...... 114 F7
Harpole Cl DE55 .... 169 F8
Harport Dr S45 .... 131 E2
Harpswell Cl DE22 ...... 204 E2
Harpur Ave
  Derby DE23 .... 231 B8
  Ticknall DE73 .... 251 A4
Harpur Crewe Cotts DE6 149 D3
Harpur Hill Bsns Pk SK17 . 85 B2
Harpur Hill Prim Sch
    SK17 .... 85 C4
Harpur Hill Rd SK17 .... 85 C4
Harrier Rd DE56 .... 179 C5
Harrier Way DE24 ...... 231 E3
Harriet St DE23 .... 219 A3
Harriet St NG9 .... 223 D7
Harriet Tubman Ho
    DE23 .... 218 F1
Harrimans Dr DE72 ..... 235 F8
Harringay Gdns DE22 ... 218 C6
Harrington Ave DE7 ... 221 C2
Harrington Jun Sch
    NG10 .... 223 B1
Harrington Rd
  Derby DE23 .... 218 C1
  10 Sheffield S2 .... 43 A8
Harrington St
  Derby, Allenton DE24 .. 232 E6
  Derby, Normanton DE23 . 232 A8
  Draycott DE72 .... 235 B7
  Long Eaton NG10 ...... 236 B5
Harris Ave DE5 .... 169 C2
Harris Cl DE5 .... 169 C1
Harrison Cl DE14 ...... 254 B6
Harrison Dr DE4 .... 154 F1
Harrison La
  Sheffield S10 .... 42 F7
  Tibshelf DE55 .... 147 F6
Harrison Rd NG9 .... 223 D8
Harrison St DE22 ...... 218 E3
Harrison Way DE4 ...... 127 A6
Harris Rd SK17 .... 85 C3
Harrogate Cres DE21 ... 205 D1
Harrop La S10 .... 42 F6
Harrots La SK17 .... 137 D6
Harrow Dr
  Burton u T DE14 ...... 254 C8
  Ilkeston DE7 .... 209 A4
Harrow Rd DE11 .... 256 B7
Harrow St DE24 .... 219 E2
Hart Ave NG10 .... 223 A6
Hartford Cl S41 .... 115 B7
Hartford Cl S8 .... 43 A3
Hartford Rd S8 .... 43 A3
Harthill La S43 .... 61 E1
Harthill Field Rd S26 ... 62 A3
Harthill Prim Sch S26 ... 61 E5
Harthill Rd
  Sheffield S13 .... 44 B7
  Thorpe Salvin S80 ..... 62 D7
Hartington CE Prim Sch
    SK17 .... 137 D5
Hartington Ct DE7 .... 207 E8
Hartington Ct
  Clowne S43 .... 81 A4
  Dronfield S18 .... 57 B2
Hartington Dr
  Chinley SK23 .... 34 E1
  Creswell S80 .... 81 C1
Hartington Gdns **11** SK17 . 85 B7
Hartington Hall YH★
    SK17 .... 137 E5
Hartington Ind Est S43 .. 78 E4
Hartington Pl DE7 .... 194 E5
Hartington Rd
  Buxton SK17 .... 85 B7
  Chesterfield S41 .... 96 C2
  Dronfield S18 .... 57 B2
Hartington St
  Derby DE1, DE23 ...... 267 B1
  Langwith NG20 .... 119 F8
Hartington View S43 .... 78 F4
Hartland Ct **21** S41 ... 95 F8
Hartland Dr DE23 ...... 231 E6
Hartland Way S41 ...... 77 A1
Hart Lea **1** NG10 .... 223 B5
Hartley St S2 .... 43 A7
Hartopp Ave S2 .... 43 C6
Hartopp Cl S2 .... 43 C6
Hartopp Dr S2 .... 43 D6
Hartopp Rd S2 .... 43 C6
Hartshay Hill DE5 ..... 169 C2
Hartshill DE11 .... 257 A4
Hartshorne CE Prim Sch
    DE11 .... 257 B6
Hartshorne Rd
  Derby DE23 .... 231 C5
  Repton DE65 .... 249 E7
  Woodville DE11 .... 256 F3
Hartside Cl **16** S40 ... 95 D5

Hartside Gdns **1** NG10 . 236 A8
Hartside Way DE75 .... 182 B1
Hartwood Dr NG9 ...... 209 D1
Harvester Cl DE5 ...... 169 C2
Harvest Hill DE11 ...... 256 B7
Harvest Way
  2 Chesterfield S42 ... 95 A5
Harvey Clough Mews S8 . 43 B3
Harvey Clough Rd S8 ... 43 B3
Harvey Croft NG9 ...... 209 C4
Harvey Ct S44 .... 98 F2
Harvey Pl ST14 .... 210 B1
Harvey Rd
  Burton u T DE14 ...... 254 A8
  Castle Donington DE74 . 247 B2
  Chesterfield S41 ...... 96 C2
  Derby DE24 .... 232 E6
Harwich Rd S2 .... 43 F8
Harwood Ave DE14 ..... 253 F8
Harwood Cl S2 .... 43 A8
Harwood Dr **2** S2 ... 43 A8
Hasgill Cl DE21 .... 206 C3
Haslam Ct DE23 ...... 219 B2
Haslam La DE21, DE23 .. 205 B1
Haslam Cres S8 .... 56 E6
Haslam Ct
  Bolsover S44 .... 98 F2
  Chesterfield S41 ...... 266 B4
Hasland Hall Com Sch
    S41 .... 115 C7
Hasland Inf Sch S41 ... 115 C7
Hasland Jun Sch S41 .. 115 C7
Hasland Rd S41 .... 115 C8
Haslemere Ct DE23 ... 219 B2
Haslemere Rd NG10 ... 236 B8
Haslin Rd SK17 .... 85 D2
Hassall Rd DE65 ...... 227 D1
Hassock La N DE75 .... 194 B7
Hassock La S DE7, DE75 . 194 C6
Hassocky La S44, S42 .. 116 B6
Hassop Cl
  Chesterfield S41 ...... 95 C6
  Dronfield S18 .... 57 C2
Hassop Rd
  Calver S32 .... 72 B1
  Derby DE21 .... 220 A8
  Hassop DE45 .... 90 D1
  Staveley S43 .... 78 F3
Hastilar Cl S2 .... 44 B8
Hastilar Rd S2 .... 44 B8
Hastilar Rd S S13 .... 44 C7
Hastings Cl
  Breedon on t H DE73 ... 252 F2
  Chesterfield S41 ...... 95 D6
Hastings Rd
  Buxton SK17 .... 85 C4
  Swadlincote DE11 ..... 256 B3
Hastings St DE23 ..... 219 A1
Hasting St DE74 ...... 247 B2
Haston Dr DE55 .... 170 D8
Hatchmere Cl DE21 ... 206 A1
Hatfield Ave NG10 .... 223 B4
Hatfield Rd DE24 ..... 232 F5
Hathaway Cl S42 ..... 131 B6
Hathern Cl
  Calow S43 .... 96 F4
  Derby DE23 .... 231 E5
  Long Eaton NG10 ..... 236 D5
Hathersage Ave
  Derby DE23 .... 231 E8
  Long Eaton NG10 ..... 235 F5
Hathersage Cres SK13 .. 9 E2
Hathersage Dr
  Glossop SK13 .... 17 F8
  Somercotes DE55 ..... 170 D7
Hathersage Pk S32 .... 53 A7
Hathersage Rd
  Bamford S32, S33 ..... 40 B1
  Sheffield S11, S17 .... 54 D6
Hathersage Sta S32 ... 53 A7
Hathersage YH★ S32 .. 52 F7
Hatton Cl S18 .... 75 D8
Hatton Crofts NG10 ... 236 C6
Hatton Ct DE73 .... 252 A7
Hatton Dr S40 .... 95 B5
Haulton Dr DE74 ..... 247 A4
Havelock Rd DE23 .... 232 A8
Havelock St
  Ilkeston DE7 .... 208 F7
  Ripley DE5 .... 169 E2
Haven Baulk Ave DE23 . 230 E7
Haven Baulk La DE23 .. 230 E7
Haven Ct DE24 .... 233 D6
Havenwood Gr DE23 .. 231 C5
Havercroft Terr S21 ... 60 B7
Hawfield La DE15 ..... 248 E4
Hawk's Dr DE15 ...... 248 D3
Hawke St DE22 .... 218 C5
Hawk Green Rd SK6 ... 23 A3
Hawkhill Rd S32 ...... 71 D6
Hawkinge Ho **13** S41 . 95 D5
Hawking La S44 ...... 133 A7
Hawkins Ct DE7 ...... 194 F4
Hawkins Dr DE56 ..... 168 B3
Hawk Rd SK22 .... 33 E8
Hawksdale Cl DE73 ... 233 A2
Hawkshead Ave
  Derby DE21 .... 205 D1
  Dronfield S18 .... 56 E1
Hawkshead Fold SK13 .. 10 E3
Hawkshead Rd SK13 ... 10 E3
Hawksley Ave S40 .... 95 E4
Hawksley Dr
  Darley Dale DE4 ...... 127 B4
  Rolleston DE13 .... 240 A4
Hawksway S21 .... 59 B3
Hawley Cl DE4 .... 143 E6

Hawley St S18 .... 58 A1
Hawthorn Ave
  Breaston DE72 .... 235 F8
  Derby DE24 .... 233 A7
  Mastin Moor S43 ...... 79 C4
  Netherseal DE12 ...... 264 F7
  Ripley DE5 .... 180 D8
  Stapleford NG9 ...... 223 D6
Hawthorn Bank
  Glossop SK13 .... 9 F4
  New Mills SK22 .... 33 B6
Hawthorn Cl
  Ashbourne DE6 .... 185 D8
  Chinley SK23 .... 34 E1
  Clowne S43 .... 80 C4
  Denstone ST14 .... 196 E6
  Doveridge DE6 .... 211 B1
  Hilton DE65 .... 228 D1
  Hope S33 .... 39 A4
  Mansfield Woodhouse
    NG19 .... 136 E5
Hawthorn Cres
  Burton u T DE15 ...... 254 F7
  Findern DE65 .... 230 D2
Hawthorn Ct DE1 ..... 267 A5
Hawthorn Dr DE4 ..... 155 A6
Hawthorne Ave
  Borrowash DE72 ...... 221 C2
  Creswell S80 .... 81 E2
  Dronfield S18 .... 57 A3
  Glapwell S44 .... 134 B8
  Long Eaton NG10 ..... 236 C6
  Shirebrook NG20 ..... 119 D4
  Shirland DE55 .... 146 C5
  Tibshelf DE55 .... 148 B8
Hawthorne Cl
  Ashover DE55 .... 145 D8
  Barlborough S43 ..... 80 A6
  Kilburn DE56 .... 179 F2
  Killamarsh S21 ...... 60 D5
Hawthorn Rd NG16 .... 160 D3
Hawthornes Ave DE55 . 159 F5
Hawthorne St S40 .... 266 C1
Hawthorn Gr SK14 ..... 9 D6
Hawthorn Hill S43 .... 78 F6
Hawthorn Rd
  Castle Donington DE74 . 247 B5
  Eckington S21 .... 59 B2
Hawthorn Rise
  Awsworth NG16 ...... 195 B4
  Swadlincote DE11 .... 255 F7
Hawthorn St DE24 .... 232 C8
Hawthorns The
  Belper DE56 .... 179 D5
  Chapel-en-le-F SK23 .. 47 B4
  Little Eaton DE21 .... 205 D8
  Wirksworth DE4 ...... 165 F7
Hawthorn Way S42 .... 94 F5
Hawton Cl NG19 ...... 135 F1
Hawtrey Gdns DE24 ... 233 A7
Haxby Cl S13 .... 44 E6
Haxby Pl S13 .... 44 E6
Haxby St S13 .... 44 E6
Haybrook Ct S17 ..... 55 E5
Haycroft Cl NG19 .... 136 E5
Haycroft Ct DE23 .... 231 A7
Haycroft Gdns S43 ... 79 B4
Hayden Ct **1** SK13 ... 10 C1
Haydn Rd DE21 ...... 219 F3
Haydock Cl
  Burton u T DE14 ..... 254 A7
  Kimberley NG16 ..... 195 E7
Haydock Park Rd DE24 . 232 E8
Hayes Ave
  Breaston DE72 .... 235 B7
  Derby DE23 .... 231 D6
Hayes Cl
  Pinxton NG16 .... 160 C3
  West Hallam DE7 .... 207 E8
Hayes Con Ctr The DE55 170 A6
Hayes Cres DE55 ..... 169 F7
Hayes Ct S20 .... 59 E6
Hayes Dr S20 .... 59 E6
Hayes Farm Ct DE73 .. 251 A4
Hayes La DE55 .... 169 F7
Hayes The DE55 ...... 230 C1
Hayes Wood Rd DE7 .. 193 A1
Hayfield Cl
  Belper DE56 .... 179 B5
  Dronfield S18 .... 56 D1
  Staveley S43 .... 78 F3
  Wingerworth S42 ..... 114 F3
Hayfield Cres S12 ..... 44 D3
Hayfield Dr S12 ...... 44 D3
Hayfield Gdns DE23 ... 231 B6
Hayfield Pl S12 ...... 44 D3
Hayfield Prim Sch SK22 . 25 C3
Hayfield Rd
  Chapel-en-le-F SK23 .. 47 B8
  Chinley SK23 .... 35 A3
  New Mills SK22 ..... 24 E1
Hayfield Rd E SK23 ... 47 C6
Hayfield View S21 .... 59 C3
Hayfield Vistor Ctr★ SK22 25 D4
Hayford Pl DE22 ..... 218 D4
Hayford Way S43 ..... 78 E1
Hay La
  Ashover S45 .... 145 B7
  Scropton DE65 ...... 226 E5
  Spout DE4 .... 166 C5
Hayley Cl NG16 ...... 195 D6
Hayley Croft DE56 ... 190 F1
Hayling Cl DE7 ...... 194 C3
Haynes Ave NG9 ..... 209 C5
Hays Cl DE7 .... 194 D2
Hays La DE6 .... 164 L1
Hays The DE65 ...... 227 C2

Hay The S45 .... 145 B6
Hay Wain La DE11 .... 256 D7
Haywards Cl SK13 .... 10 C3
Haywood Cl DE24 .... 233 A5
Hayworth Rd NG10 ... 223 B5
Hazel Ave
  Derby DE23 .... 231 D6
  Killamarsh S21 ...... 60 C5
  Pilsley S45 .... 132 B3
Hazelbadge Cres S12 .. 44 E3
Hazelby Rd S80 ...... 100 F8
Hazel Cl
  Ashbourne DE6 ...... 185 D8
  Dronfield S18 .... 76 B8
  Findern DE65 .... 230 E2
  Heanor DE75 .... 181 D1
  Swadlincote DE11 ... 256 A5
Hazel Cres NG20 .... 119 D4
Hazel Ct
  Dronfield S18 ...... 76 B8
  Matlock DE4 .... 143 D5
Hazel Dene DE4 .... 143 D5
Hazeldene Cl DE56 .. 190 E5
Hazeldene Cotts DE56 . 178 D2
Hazel Dr
  Chesterfield S40 .... 114 E8
  Derby DE21 .... 221 A6
  Wingerworth S42 .... 115 B3
Hazel Gr
  Calver S32 .... 72 C2
  Duffield DE56 .... 190 E3
  Mansfield Woodhouse
    NG19 .... 136 B5
  Mastin Moor S43 .... 79 C4
  Matlock DE4 .... 143 D5
  South Normanton DE55 160 B5
Hazel Rd S21 .... 59 C2
Hazelrigg Cl DE74 ... 246 F4
Hazeltree Cl DE5 .... 180 C8
Hazelwood Cl **5** S18 .. 56 C1
Hazelwood Hill DE56 . 190 C8
Hazelwood Rd
  Burton u T DE15 ..... 254 E6
  Derby DE21 .... 219 F8
  Duffield DE56 .... 190 D5
Hazlebarrow Cl S8 .... 57 C7
Hazlebarrow Cres S8 .. 57 C7
Hazlebarrow Dr S8 ... 57 B7
Hazlebarrow Gr S8 ... 57 C7
Hazlebarrow Rd S8 ... 57 B7
Hazlehurst Ave S41 .. 96 B5
Hazlehurst La
  Chesterfield S41 ..... 96 B5
  Eckington S8 .... 57 F8
Hazlewood Dr S43 ... 80 C8
Headingley Ct DE23 .. 231 C8
Headland Cl S43 ..... 96 C7
Headland Rd S43 .... 96 C7
Heage La DE65 ...... 229 D8
Heage Prim Sch DE56 . 168 D2
Heage Rd DE5 .... 169 C1
Heage Windmill★ DE56 168 D2
Healaugh Way S40 ... 115 B8
Heale St S43 .... 80 C3
Heanor Gate **3** DE7 .. 181 D1
Heanor Gate Ind Est
    DE75 .... 193 D8
Heanor Gate Rd DE75 . 193 D8
Heanor Gate Science Coll
    DE75 .... 181 C1
Heanor Ho DE21 .... 220 E3
Heanor Langley Mill &
    District Meml Hospl
    DE75 .... 181 F1
Heanor Rd
  Denby DE5 .... 181 A3
  Ilkeston DE7 .... 194 D3
  Smalley DE7, DE75 ... 193 B7
Heanor Rd, DE75 .... 181 D1
Hearthcote Rd DE11 .. 256 A3
Hearthstone La DE4 .. 143 D1
Heath Ave
  Derby DE23 .... 218 C1
  Killamarsh S21 ...... 60 C5
Heath Comm S44 .... 117 B2
Heathcote Cl DE24 ... 233 C5
Heathcote Dr S41 ... 115 E8
Heathcote Ho S41 ... 96 B6
Heath Cross **3** ST14 . 210 A1
Heath Ct
  Chesterfield S40 .... 115 A8
  Derby DE24 .... 231 E3
Heather Ave S44 .... 117 B2
Heather Bank Cl **2** SK13 . 17 A7
Heather Cl
  Burton u T DE14 ..... 254 A8
  Calow S44 .... 97 A3
  Derby DE24 .... 231 D2
  South Normanton DE55 160 A3
  Swanwick DE55 ..... 170 A8
Heather Cres
  Breaston DE72 ...... 235 F7
  Derby DE23 .... 231 C6
Heather Ct DE75 .... 182 B1
Heather Falls SK22 ... 33 B8
Heather Gdns S41 ... 115 C6
Heather Gr SK14 ..... 9 D6
Heather La S32 ...... 53 A6
Heather Lea Ave S17 . 55 C7
Heather Lea Pl S17 .. 55 C7
Heatherley Dr NG19 .. 136 C1
Heatherley Prim Sch
    NG19 .... 136 C1

Heathermead Cl **2** DE21 205 F1
Heathers Edge S32 ... 53 A6
Heather Vale S41 .... 115 E7
Heather Vale Cl S41 .. 115 E7
Heather Vale Rd S41 .. 115 D7
Heather Way S42 .... 113 D7
Heathfield DE4 ...... 143 C7
Heathfield Ave
  Chesterfield S40 .... 95 D3
  Ilkeston DE7 .... 209 A8
Heathfield Cl
  Dronfield S18 .... 75 F8
  Wingerworth S42 .... 115 B4
Heathfield Gdns
  Buxton SK17 .... 85 A8
  Tibshelf DE55 ...... 148 A7
Heathfield Nook Rd SK17 . 85 C6
Heathfield Rd S12 ... 44 D4
Heath Fields Prim Sch
    DE65 .... 227 C1
Heath Gdns DE72 .... 236 A8
Heath Gr SK17 ...... 85 C6
Heath La
  Blackfordby DE11 ... 257 C2
  Findern DE65 .... 242 D8
  Hartshorne DE11 .... 257 E4
  Smisby LE65 .... 258 B6
Heathlands Dr ST14 .. 210 B1
Heathley Mews DE14 . 254 C8
Heath Park Rd S17 ... 85 C6
Heath Prim Sch S44 .. 116 F1
Heath Rd
  Burton u T DE15 ..... 254 E7
  Glossop SK13 .... 10 D2
  Holmewood S44 ..... 116 E1
  Holmewood, Williamthorpe
    S42 .... 132 E8
  Ripley DE5 .... 169 E5
  Uttoxeter ST14 ..... 210 B1
Heath St S17 .... 85 B6
Heath The
  Eastwood NG16 ..... 195 A8
  Glossop SK13 ...... 10 C3
Heath View S17 ..... 85 C1
Heath Way DE65 .... 227 D1
Heaton Cl S18 ...... 56 D1
Heaton Ct **4** S40 .. 95 C2
Heaton Pl SK17 ..... 85 E8
Heaton St S40 ...... 95 C2
Heavygate La DE56 .. 177 F8
Hebden Cl DE23 .... 230 F6
Hebden Dr SK13 .... 17 F8
Hebrides Cl DE24 ... 231 D3
Heddon Bar NG19 ... 136 E3
Hedgebank Ct DE21 .. 206 B7
Hedge Gr DE11 ..... 256 B7
Hedgerow Gdns DE21 . 206 C3
Hedges Dr DE7 ..... 209 A5
Hedgevale Cl DE23 .. 231 A7
Hedingham Cl NE7 .. 194 D1
Hedingham Way DE3 . 230 D8
Hedley Cl DE55 .... 170 D8
Hedley Dr S43 ...... 96 D8
Heeley Arches S2 ... 43 A7
Heeley Bank Rd S2 .. 43 B7
Heeley City Farm★ S2 . 43 B7
Heeley Gn S2 ...... 43 B6
Heigham Cl DE24 ... 232 D3
Heights of Abraham★
    DE4 .... 143 A2
Heights of Abraham Cable
    Car★ DE4 .... 143 A2
Helmsley Ave S20 ... 59 E7
Helmsley Cl S41 ... 95 C7
Helmton Dr S8 ..... 43 A2
Helmton Rd S8 ..... 43 A2
Helpston Cl DE55 ... 147 C1
Helston Cl
  Chesterfield S41 .... 115 B8
  Derby DE24 .... 233 B6
  Linton DE12 .... 261 D5
Helvellyn Way **5** NG10 . 223 B2
Heming Ave S45 .... 132 C2
Hemington Ct DE74 .. 247 C5
Hemington Hill DE74 . 247 C4
Hemington La DE74 .. 247 E5
Hemington Prim Sch
    DE74 .... 247 D5
Hemlock Ave
  Long Eaton NG10 ... 223 D1
  Stapleford NG9 .... 223 D1
Hemlock Cl DE21 ... 206 A3
Hemlock La DE7 .... 208 D5
Hemlock Stone The★
    NG9 .... 209 F2
Hemper Gr S8 ...... 56 D7
Hemper La S8 ...... 56 D7
Hemp Yd DE6 ...... 165 B1
Hemsley Dr NG16 ... 182 D3
Hemsworth Rd S8, S14 . 43 C2
Hendon Way DE22 ... 218 B6
Henley Ave S8 ..... 57 C8
Henley Gdns NG9 ... 209 E1
Henley Gn DE22 .... 217 F6
Henley Way DE7 .... 207 D8
Henmore Pl **10** DE6 . 173 C2
Henmore Trad Est DE6 . 173 A1
Hennymoor Cl S80 .. 82 A5
Hennymoor La S80 .. 82 C2
Henry Ave
  Mansfield Woodhouse
    NG19 .... 136 B5
  Matlock DE4 .... 143 C6
Henry Bradley Inf Sch
    S43 .... 96 F8

Henry Cres DE55........159 C3
Henry Fanshawe Sch S18 57 B2
Henry Prince CE Fst Sch The
DE6....................184 D7
Henry St
 Chesterfield S41.........96 B8
 Derby DE1..............267 A4
 Eckington S21...........59 D3
 Glossop SK13...........10 C1
 Grassmoor S42.........115 E3
 Ripley DE5.............169 D2
Henshall Ho S41..........96 B6
Henshaw Ave DE7.......208 D5
Henshaw Pl DE7.........194 E4
Hepworth Rd DE11.......256 E1
Herald Gr DE73.........244 E8
Herbert St DE15.........248 B3
Herbert Strutt Prim Sch
DE56...................178 F2
Herdings Ct S12..........44 A3
Herdings Rd S12..........44 A3
Herdings View S12........44 A3
Hereford Ave NG19......136 D5
Hereford Cl S17...........85 C4
Hereford Cres DE11......256 D6
Hereford Dr S43..........96 F8
Hereford Rd
 Buxton SK17............85 C4
 Derby DE21............219 D8
Hereward's Rd S14........43 D1
Herewood Cl NG20......119 F4
Heritage Com Sch S43....80 D4
Heritage Ct 4 DE56......178 F3
Heritage Dr S43...........80 D5
Heritage Way DE15......248 A1
Hermitage Ave
 Borrowash DE72.......221 C2
 Somercotes DE55......170 C5
Hermitage Ct DE21......206 B1
Hermitage Gdns 1 S14 210 A1
Hermitage La DE6.......184 B6
Hermitage Park Way 7
DE11...................256 A7
Hermitage Wlk DE7......208 F6
Hernstone La SK17........49 B2
Heron Cl SK13............17 F8
Heron Dr DE11...........256 F3
Heronswood Dr DE21....220 D6
Heron View SK13.........16 F8
Heron Way
 Derby DE3.............218 A2
 Mansfield NG19.......135 C1
Herriot Dr S40...........266 C1
Hessey St S13............44 F6
Hewers Holt S43..........80 B6
Hewett St NG20.........120 D5
Hewitt Pl S26.............61 E5
Hexham Ave DE7........209 A4
Hexham Wlk DE21......205 E1
Heyden Bank 26 SK13.....9 D2
Heyden Fold 27 SK13......9 D2
Heyden Terr 25 SK13......9 D2
Heydon Cl DE56.........179 B6
Heyford Ct DE75.........182 A1
Heysbank Rd SK12........32 D5
Hey St NG10............236 C4
Heywood St S43..........96 E8
Heywood View S43........80 C6
Heywood Villas 5 S43....96 E8
Heyworth Rd SK23........47 C6
Heyworth St DE22.......218 D6
Hibbert St S42............33 B6
Hickings La NG9.........223 E8
Hickingwood La S43......81 A5
Hickinwood Cres S43.....80 F5
Hickleton Cl DE5........169 C1
Hickling Cl DE24........232 D3
Hickton Rd DE55........169 F6
Hide La SK17............137 E7
Hides Gn S44.............99 A2
Higger La S32............52 F8
Higgins Rd DE11........255 F6
Higg La DE56...........167 A6
Higgott Cl DE14........254 B8
Higham La
 Compstall SK14.........15 A7
 Stonebroom DE55.....146 E4
Highashes La S45.........113 E1
Highbank SK13...........9 F7
High Bank DE5..........180 F2
Highbank Rd SK13.......17 F7
High Bank Rd DE15......248 B3
Highbury Cl DE22........217 F6
Highbury Rd S41.........95 F5
Highcliffe Ave NG20.....119 D4
Highcroft Cl NG10......236 E5
High Cross
 Hartington SK17.......137 F5
 Linton DE11...........261 F7
High Ct DE4.............143 C6
High Edge Dr DE56......179 B8
High Edge Mews DE56...179 A5
Higher Albert St S41....266 B4
Higher Barn Rd SK13......9 F4
Higher Dinting SK13......10 A2
Higher Hallsteads SK17...47 F3
Higher La SK12...........32 E1
Higher Noon Sun SK22....24 F2
Higher Sq SK13...........10 A7
Highfield DE45..........108 E8
Highfield Ave
 Chesterfield S41.........95 E6
 Dove Holes SK17........47 L1
 Mansfield NG19.......136 B1
 Shirebrook NG20......119 D6

Highfield Cl
 Bakewell DE45.........109 C5
 Heanor DE75...........181 B5
 Mansfield NG19.......136 B1
Highfield Cotts
 Alfreton DE55.........158 D3
 Derby DE21............219 E5
Highfield Ct SK14.........9 A4
Highfield Dr
 Bakewell DE45.........109 C5
 Ilkeston DE7..........208 B5
 Matlock DE4...........143 D6
 South Normanton DE55.160 B5
Highfield Gdns
 Derby DE21............218 F7
 Hollingworth SK14......9 D5
Highfield Hall Prim Sch
S41.....................95 F6
Highfield La
 Chesterfield S41........95 E6
 Derby DE21............219 F5
 Hartington SK17.......137 F5
 Weston Underwood DE6.188 F5
Highfield Mews DE21....219 E5
Highfield Pl S2...........43 A8
Highfield Prim Sch
NG10...................223 C2
Highfield Rd
 Ashbourne DE6........185 B8
 Belper DE56...........178 F2
 Bolsover S44............99 A1
 Chesterfield S41.......266 A4
 Derby DE22............218 F7
 Derby, Littleover DE23..231 C7
 Glossop SK13...........17 D8
 Hayfield SK22..........25 D3
 Hulland Ward DE6.....175 F3
 Kilburn DE56..........191 F8
 Little Eaton DE21......205 C8
 Marple SK6.............23 B6
 Swadlincote DE11......256 B3
 Swanwick DE55........169 D7
Highfields
 Buxton SK17............67 B5
 Codnor DE5............181 B8
Highfields Cres S18.......76 A8
Highfields Dr
 Holmewood S42........132 D8
 Linton DE12...........261 C6
Highfields Lower Sch
DE4....................143 C3
Highfields Park Dr DE22.204 E1
Highfields Rd S18.........76 A8
Highfields Sch DE4......143 E7
Highfield St
 Long Eaton NG10......223 C2
 Swadlincote DE11......256 B3
Highfields Way S42......132 D8
Highfield Terr
 Chesterfield S41........95 F5
 New Mills SK22.........33 D8
Highfield View Rd S41....95 F5
Highfield Way DE5......180 C8
Highgate Cl S43..........77 D3
Highgate Dr
 Dronfield S18...........76 C7
 Ilkeston DE7..........194 D3
Highgate Gn DE22.......218 A5
Highgate La S18..........76 C7
Highgate Rd SK22........25 E1
Highgates DE1..........267 B2
High Gr
 Belper DE56...........179 D4
 Mansfield NG19.......136 C1
Highgrove Cl
 Burton u T DE13.......240 C1
 6 Chesterfield S41.....96 A8
 Heanor DE75...........181 C1
Highgrove Dr DE73......232 F2
High Hazel Ct S45.......131 D4
High Hazel Dr NG19.....136 B1
High Hazels Cl S45......131 E4
High Hazels Rd S43.......80 B5
High Hazels Wlk S45....131 E4
High Hill Rd SK22.........24 D1
High Holbeck S80.......101 C7
High Holborn DE7.......194 E3
High Holborn Rd DE5....170 B1
High La
 Broadbottom SK13......16 E7
 Eckington S12..........44 E1
 Holloway, Dethick Common
 DE4..................144 E2
 Holloway, Upper Holloway
 DE4..................156 E1
 Holymoorside S42......113 E5
 Sheffield S12...........58 F8
High La Central DE7....193 F1
High La E DE7..........208 B8
Highland Cl
 Buxton SK17............85 C5
 Mansfield Woodhouse
 NG19.................136 D3
Highland Rd S43.........77 D4
Highlands Dr DE15......248 A4
Highlands Pl S41.........76 F1
High La W DE7..........193 E1
High Lea Rd SK22........33 A8
High Leys Rd S43.........80 E2
Highlightley La S18.......75 C5
Highlow Cl S40...........95 C5
High Mdws SK13.........17 B7
High Meadow Cl DE56...180 D8
High Pavement DE56....179 A3
High Rd DE55...........157 F4
High Ridge
 Mansfield NG19.......136 F2
 Matlock DE4...........143 C7

High St E SK13..........10 D1
High St W SK13..........10 B1
High Spannia NG16......195 F7
High St
 Alfreton DE55.........159 A4
 Apperknowle S18........58 A1
 Barlborough S43........80 A7
 Belper DE56...........179 A4
 Bonsall DE4...........142 D1
 Brimington S43..........96 F7
 Brinsley NG16.........171 E1
 Buxton SK17............85 B7
 Calver S32.............72 B2
 Castle Donington DE74..247 A2
 Chapel-en-le-F SK23.....47 B6
 Chellaston DE73........233 A1
 Chesterfield S41, S43....77 D4
 Chesterfield, Stonegravels
 S40..................266 B3
 Clay Cross S45.........131 C3
 Clowne S43.............80 D3
 Codnor DE5............181 B8
 Doveridge DE6.........211 B1
 Dronfield S18...........57 A1
 Eckington S21..........59 D3
 Ilkeston DE7..........208 F8
 Kilburn DE56..........192 A8
 Killamarsh S21..........60 D6
 Kimberley NG16.......195 F6
 Linton DE12...........261 C6
 Long Eaton NG10......236 E8
 Longnor SK17.........121 C6
 Mansfield Woodhouse
 NG19.................136 C3
 Marchington ST14.....224 E2
 Melbourne DE73.......252 A7
 New Mills SK22.........33 C8
 Pilsley DE45............91 C3
 Pleasley NG19.........135 B5
 Repton DE65..........242 D2
 Ripley DE5............169 D1
 Rocester ST14.........196 F3
 Sheffield, Dore S17......55 D7
 Sheffield, Mosborough S20.59 D7
 Somercotes DE55......170 C8
 Somercotes, Riddings
 DE55.................170 D5
 South Normanton DE55.160 A6
 Stapleford NG9........223 E7
 Staveley S43............78 E2
 Stonebroom DE55......147 A4
 Stoney Middleton S32...71 F3
 Swadlincote, Church Gresley
 DE11.................256 C3
 Swadlincote, Newhall
 DE11.................256 A6
 Swanwick DE55........169 F7
 Tibshelf DE55.........148 A7
 Ticknall DE73.........251 A4
 Tideswell SK17.........69 C4
 Tutbury DE13.........239 C6
 Whitwell S80............81 F6
 Woodville DE11........256 F2
Highstairs La DE55......146 C8
Highstones Gdns SK13...10 F2
Highstool La SK17......106 B6
High Street Mews S20....59 C7
High Tor★ DE4.........143 B3
High Tor Rd DE4........143 B2
High Trees S17...........55 D7
Highview SK13...........17 A7
High View Cl S41.........96 D2
High View Rd DE55.....160 C7
Highway La DE6.........151 F2
Highwood Ave DE56....179 C1
High Wood Bank DE56..179 C1
Highwood Cl SK13.......17 B8
High Wood Fold SK6.....23 C8
Highwood La S80.........81 D5
Highwood Pl S21.........59 C3
High Wood Way S43......80 C5
Hilary Cl DE56..........179 E5
Hilcote La DE55.........148 B1
Hilcote St DE55.........160 A6
Hilderstone Cl DE24....233 D6
Hillary Pl DE7..........208 B5
Hillberry DE5...........170 A1
Hillberry Rise S40.......114 F6
Hill Brow DE1..........267 B2
Hill Cl
 Derby DE21............220 E4
 Stanley Common DE7..193 A1
 Turnditch DE56........177 B2
Hillcliff La
 Hulland Ward DE56....176 F2
 Turnditch DE56........177 A3
Hill Cotts DE45.........125 B5
Hillcrest
 Aston-on-T DE72.......234 A1
 Belper DE56...........179 E4
 Blackwell DE55.......147 E1
 Tutbury DE13.........239 B5
Hill Crest
 Crich DE4.............157 A1
 Shirebrook NG20......119 D3
Hillcrest Ave
 Burton u T DE15.......248 A4
 Hulland Ward DE6.....175 F3
 South Normanton DE55.160 A4
Hill Crest Ave DE55.....157 E8
Hill Crest Cotts DE4....142 F8
Hillcrest Dr
 Codnor DE5............181 B8
 Kilburn DE56..........192 A8
Hillcreste Dr DE73......232 F3
Hillcrest Gr S43..........78 F4
Hillcrest Rd S41.........115 D7

Hill Crest Rd DE21......219 D7
Hillcroft Dr DE72.......221 C4
Hill Cross DE45.........108 F8
Hill Cross Ave DE23....231 C7
Hill Cross Dr DE23.....231 B7
Hill Dr SK23.............45 D8
Hillend SK14.............9 A1
Hillend La SK14..........9 A1
Hillfield La DE13........240 F1
Hillfield Rd NG9.........209 F1
Hill Fields DE55.........160 A3
Hillfoot Ct S17...........55 D4
Hillfoot Rd S17..........55 D5
Hill Gr S43..............78 B4
Hill Green Cl DE12......260 D3
Hill Head S33............51 A7
Hillhead La SK17.........85 E1
Hillhouses La S42.......114 E3
Hillingdon Dr DE7......209 A7
Hill La S32..............52 F8
Hillman Dr S43..........97 C7
Hillmoor St NG19.......135 C3
Hillmorton DE45........108 F7
Hill Nook Cl DE73......233 A1
Hillock The S32..........72 E2
Hill Pond Ave SK22......24 D1
Hill Rd
 Ashover S45...........129 F4
 Heanor DE75..........181 D1
Hill Rise NG9...........209 C4
Hill Rise Cl DE12.......231 D8
Hillsdale Rd DE15......248 B5
Hillside
 Ashover S45...........130 A4
 Brassington DE4......152 F1
 Buxton SK17............85 D3
 Castle Donington DE74..247 B4
 Chinley SK23...........47 B8
 Curbar S32.............72 E2
 Findern DE65..........230 C2
 Holloway DE4.........156 A6
 Langley Mill NG16.....182 A3
 Middleton DE4.........154 D4
 Sheffield S20...........59 C7
 Tutbury DE13.........239 C6
 Whitwell S80............81 F5
Hillside Ave
 Ashbourne DE6........173 C3
 Derby DE21............220 A5
 Dronfield S18...........76 A8
Hillside Cl
 Disley SK12............32 E6
 Glossop SK13............9 E3
 Whitwell S80............81 F5
Hillside Cotts S32........53 B7
Hillside Cres DE21......220 F4
Hillside Ct
 Breedon on t H DE73...252 F2
 Kirk Langley DE6......202 E4
Hillside Dr
 Chesterfield S40........95 D1
 Long Eaton NG10......236 B8
 Mastin Moor S43.......79 C3
Hillside Gdns DE11......255 F6
Hillside Gr
 Marple SK6.............15 B1
 Sandiacre NG10.......223 A6
Hillside Pk DE55.........158 B4
Hillside Rd
 Derby DE21............220 F4
 Linton DE12...........261 D7
Hillside Rise DE56......178 F2
Hillside View SK22.......33 A8
Hill Sq The DE22........205 A1
Hills Rd DE72...........235 C7
Hill St
 Burton u T DE15.......254 E8
 Clay Cross S45.........131 C3
 Donisthorpe DE12.....262 E1
 Ripley DE5............169 D3
 Sheffield S2............43 A8
 Swadlincote, Church Gresley
 DE11.................256 C3
 Swadlincote DE11......255 F6
Hills The S33.............44 F1
Hillstown Bsns Ctr S44..118 B7
Hillsway
 Chellaston DE73.......232 F3
 Derby DE23............218 B1
 Shirebrook NG20......119 D3
Hill The
 Derby DE22............205 A1
 Glapwell S44..........118 A1
 Hilltop DE56...........168 B7
Hill Top
 Bolsover S44............99 A2
 Castle Donington DE74..247 A4
 Derby DE21............205 E3
Hilltop Ave NG20........119 E4
Hilltop Cl S44..........118 B1
Hilltop Inf Sch DE6.....185 C8
Hilltop La
 Belper DE56...........179 E2
 Thurvaston DE6.......215 D5
Hilltop Rd
 Ashover S45...........129 F5
 Chesterfield S41........77 B2
 Dronfield S18...........76 B7
 Glossop SK13...........10 B3
 Pinxton NG16.........160 C3
 Wingerworth S42......114 D4
Hill Top Rd DE55.......170 C5
Hill Top Rise SK23.......45 D8
Hilltops View DE4.......143 D5
Hilltop Way S18.........76 A7
Hill View
 Duffield DE56.........190 D3
 Repton DE65..........242 E2

Hill View continued
 Whaley Bridge SK23....45 C8
Hill View Cl DE7........192 B7
Hillview Ct NG19........136 D4
Hill View Gr DE21......220 E5
Hillview Ho 1 DE1......267 B2
Hill View Rd S43.........96 E5
Hillwood Dr SK13........17 F8
Hilton Cl
 Derby DE3............217 D1
 Long Eaton NG10......235 F4
 Swadlincote DE11......256 A7
Hilton Gdns DE72.......246 A7
Hilton Ind Est DE65....228 D3
Hilton Park Dr DE55....170 C8
Hilton Prim Sch DE65..228 D2
Hilton Rd
 Disley SK12............32 B7
 Egginton DE65........241 B7
 Etwall DE65...........229 B4
Hinckley Ct DE4........110 F1
Hind Ave DE72..........235 C8
Hindersitch La DE4.....156 C2
Hindscarth Cres DE3...217 E1
Hinton Gr SK14.........15 A8
Hipley Cl S40............95 B6
Hipper St S S40.........266 B2
Hipper St W S40.........95 E2
Hipper St S40...........266 B2
Hixon's La DE7.........208 B1
Hoades St S42..........131 C8
Hoargate La DE6........200 F2
Hobart Cl
 Burton u T DE15.......248 C8
 Derby DE3............217 F2
Hobart Dr NG9.........209 F1
Hob Hill DE56..........190 B8
Hob Hill Mdws SK13.....17 D7
Hobhouse Rd NG19.....135 D2
Hob Hurst's Ho★ DE45.111 F7
Hobkirk Dr DE24.......231 E2
Hob La DE6.............176 B8
Hobsic Cl NG16........182 D8
Hobsic La NG16........171 E8
Hobson Dr
 Derby DE21............220 F2
 Ilkeston DE7..........208 E6
Hobson Moor Rd SK14....9 A7
Hockerley Ave SK23.....45 D8
Hockerley Cl SK23......45 D8
Hockerley La SK23......45 D8
Hockerley New Rd SK23..45 D8
Hockley La
 Ashover S45...........130 A1
 Wingerworth S42......115 A3
Hockley Way DE55......159 B2
Hodder Cl DE4.........156 F2
Hodge Beck Cl DE24...233 D6
Hodge Fold SK14........15 F8
Hodge La
 Ashover S45...........128 E7
 Broadbottom SK14......15 F8
 Marchington ST14.....224 A1
Hodmire La S44.........133 E7
Hodthorpe Cl DE21.....206 B1
Hodthorpe Prim Sch S80. 82 C5
Hogarth Cl NG9.........223 E6
Hogarth Rd SK6.........23 B8
Hogarth Rise S18........75 F8
Hogbarn La DE75, NG16.181 D5
Hoggs Field NG16......182 F2
Hogshaw Villas Rd 1
SK17...................85 C8
Hoillant Sq DE6.........175 E3
Holbeach Dr S40........114 E8
Holbeck Ave S44.........99 C2
Holbeck Cl S41.........266 C4
Holbeck La S80.........101 D8
Holbeck St S80...........81 D1
Holbein Cl S18...........75 F8
Holborn Dr DE22.......218 A4
Holborn View DE5......170 B1
Holbrook Ave
 North Wingfield S42...132 A7
 Sheffield S20............60 A8
Holbrook Centre For Autism
DE56...................191 D5
Holbrook CE Prim Sch
DE56...................191 C7
Holbrook Cl
 Chesterfield S40.......114 C8
 Pleasley NG19.........135 A5
Holbrook Dr S13.........44 B6
Holbrook Gn S20.........60 A8
Holbrook Pl S43..........97 C6
Holbrook Rd
 Belper DE56...........178 F2
 Derby DE24...........233 B6
 Sheffield S13...........44 B7
Holbrook St DE75.......182 A4
Holbrook View DE56....192 A8
Holbrook Way S42......132 A7
Holburn Ave S18.........57 A2
Holcombe St DE23......219 B3
Holden Ave DE72.......246 A8
Holden Ct DE24.........233 A8
Holden Gdns 1 NG9....223 E6
Holderness Cl DE24....231 D2
Holdings The DE11......256 A1
Holdon Croft DE12......260 C6
Holestone Gate Rd S45..129 D1
Holker Ave SK17.........85 C8
Holker St S17............85 C7
Holkham Cl DE7........194 C3
Holland Cl DE55........146 F5
Holland Mdw NG10.....236 D5
Holland Pl 8 S2.........43 A8

Holland Rd
Chesterfield S41 ....76 F2
Sheffield S2 ....43 A8
Hollbank Cotts DE55 ....158 B3
Hollens Way S40 ....95 A5
Hollies Cl
Clifton DE6 ....184 F6
Dronfield S18 ....76 C8
Newton Solney DE15 ....248 E8
Hollies Dr SK6 ....23 A5
Hollies Farm Cl DE73 ....244 E3
Hollies La DE6 ....198 C4
Hollies Rd DE22 ....204 D3
Hollies The
Eastwood NG16 ....182 F2
Repton DE65 ....243 A1
Sandiacre NG10 ....223 A5
Shirebrook NG20 ....119 E2
Hollin Cl S41 ....95 C8
Hollin Cross La SK13 ....17 C8
Hollindale Dr S12 ....44 C5
Hollin Dr SK23 ....47 B5
Hollington Cl DE21 ....219 E7
Hollington Rd ST14 ....196 D3
Hollingwood Cres S43 ....78 A1
Hollingwood Prim Sch
S43 ....78 A1
Hollingworth Ave NG10 ....223 B3
Hollingworth Prim Sch
SK14 ....9 C5
Hollinhey Terr SK14 ....9 C5
Hollin Hill Rd S43 ....81 A3
Hollins Ave SK17 ....85 B7
Hollins Bank 41 SK13 ....9 D2
Hollins Cl 40 SK13 ....9 D2
Hollinsclough CE Prim Sch
SK17 ....104 D2
Hollinsclough Rake
SK17 ....104 B2
Hollinsend Ave S12 ....44 C5
Hollinsend Pl S12 ....44 C5
Hollinsend Rd S12 ....44 B5
Hollins Fold 43 SK13 ....9 D2
Hollins Gdns 46 SK13 ....9 D2
Hollins Gr 42 SK13 ....9 D2
Hollins Ind Pk SK13 ....10 B5
Hollins La
Crich DE4 ....157 A4
Marple SK6 ....23 C8
Hollins Mews 44 SK13 ....9 D2
Hollinsmoor Rd SK6, SK22 ....24 D7
Hollins Mount SK6 ....23 B8
Hollins Spring Ave S18 ....76 A8
Hollins Spring Rd S18 ....76 A8
Hollins St SK17 ....85 B7
Hollins The DE4 ....156 A6
Hollins Way 45 SK13 ....9 D2
Hollins Wood Cl DE4 ....156 A5
Hollinwood La SK6 ....23 B2
Hollinwood Rd SK12 ....32 D6
Hollis La
Chesterfield S41 ....266 C2
Denstone ST14 ....196 B6
Hollis St DE24 ....233 A8
Holllins Ave 47 SK13 ....9 D2
Holloway Rd
Derby DE24 ....232 F6
Duffield DE56 ....190 E4
Hollow Cres DE15 ....248 C4
Hollowford Rd S33 ....38 B4
Hollowford Training &
Conference Ctr S33 ....38 C4
Hollow Gate S33 ....51 A7
Hollow La
Burton u T DE15 ....248 C4
Mayfield DE6 ....184 C7
Sheffield, Mosborough S20 ....59 D6
Hollow O'the Moor SK17 ....87 E4
Hollowood Ave DE23 ....231 C8
Hollow Rd DE73 ....252 E2
Hollows The NG10 ....237 A8
Hollow The
Bamford S33 ....40 B3
Castle Donington DE74 ....247 B4
Derby, Littleover DE23 ....231 C8
Derby, Mickleover DE3 ....230 D8
Holloway DE4 ....156 B5
Roston DE6 ....197 E7
Holly Ave
Breaston DE72 ....222 F1
Ripley DE5 ....180 D8
Hollybank S12 ....44 B6
Hollybank Ave S12 ....44 C6
Hollybank Cl
Sheffield S12 ....44 D6
Swadlincote DE11 ....256 A7
Holly Bank Cl
New Houghton NG19 ....135 A6
South Wingfield DE55 ....158 B3
Hollybank Cres S12 ....44 C6
Holly Bank Ct DE4 ....156 F1
Hollybank Dr S12 ....44 B6
Hollybank Rd S12 ....44 C6
Hollybank Way S12 ....44 D6
Hollybrook Way DE23 ....230 F6
Holly Brook Way DE23 ....230 F6
Holly Bush Cl DE12 ....264 F7
Holly Bush La DE56 ....191 A6
Holly Cl
Ashbourne DE6 ....185 D8
Chesterfield S41 ....77 A3
Draycott DE72 ....235 A7
Killamarsh S21 ....60 C5
Holly Croft DE15 ....248 C2

Holly Ct
Aston-on-T DE72 ....246 A7
3 Chesterfield S40 ....95 C2
2 Mansfield NG19 ....136 E1
Woodville DE11 ....256 F2
Holly Gdns S12 ....44 C6
Holly Gn DE15 ....254 F8
Holly Gr
Sheffield S12 ....44 C6
Swanwick DE55 ....169 F8
Holly Hill Rd NG16 ....171 F6
Hollyhock Way DE14 ....253 E6
Hollyhouse Dr DE55 ....160 B6
Holly House La DE56 ....178 C4
Holly House Specl Sch
S41 ....77 A3
Hollyhurst La DE6 ....212 B6
Hollyhurst Row DE55 ....170 F6
Holly La
Alderwasley DE56 ....167 D4
Tansley DE4 ....144 A4
Hollymoor Dr DE73 ....232 F2
Holly Mount 2 SK13 ....10 D1
Holly Rd
Kimberley NG16 ....195 F7
Mansfield NG19 ....136 F2
Uttoxeter ST14 ....210 B1
Holly St DE15 ....254 F8
Hollythorpe Cl S41 ....115 D8
Hollythorpe Cres S8 ....43 A4
Hollythorpe Rd S8 ....43 B4
Hollythorpe Rise S8 ....43 B4
Hollywell Ave DE5 ....181 B7
Hollywell Prim Sch
NG16 ....195 F7
Hollywood Rd SK6 ....23 F8
Holm Ave DE21 ....205 B7
Holm Cl S18 ....56 D2
Holme Bank DE6 ....184 D7
Holmebank Cl S40 ....95 E4
Holmebank E S40 ....95 E4
Holmebank View S40 ....95 E4
Holmebank W S40 ....95 E4
Holmebrook Ct S40 ....95 E4
Holmebrook View S41 ....95 C6
Holme Cl
Hatton DE65 ....227 C1
Holloway DE4 ....156 A5
Ilkeston DE7 ....194 D2
Holme Croft DE7 ....207 E7
Holme Ct DE45 ....109 D5
Holme Farm Ave DE15 ....254 F8
Holmefield Cres DE7 ....209 A8
Holmefield Rd S80 ....82 A6
Holme Hall Cres S40 ....95 B5
Holme Hall Prim Sch S40 ....95 B5
Holme La
Bakewell DE45 ....109 D7
Derby DE21 ....220 C3
Holme Lea 2 NG10 ....223 B6
Holme Park Ave S41 ....95 C7
Holme Rd
Chesterfield S41 ....96 A6
Matlock Bath DE4 ....143 B1
Holmes Cl NG16 ....182 A3
Holmes Ct DE11 ....256 B5
Holmesdale Cl S18 ....57 C3
Holmesdale Inf Sch S18 ....57 C2
Holmesdale Rd S18 ....57 C3
Holmesfield Cl DE4 ....144 A5
Holmesfield Dr
Derby DE3 ....217 F2
Shipley DE75 ....194 A8
Holmesfield Rd S18 ....56 F1
Holmes Rd DE72 ....235 D8
Holmes St
Derby DE23 ....219 A2
Heanor DE75 ....181 D4
Holmewood Ave NE7 ....194 F5
Holmewood Bsns Pk
S42 ....116 C2
Holmewood Dr NG16 ....195 B8
Holmewood Ind Est S42 ....132 F8
Holmewood Ind Pk S42 ....116 D1
Holme Woods La HD9 ....2 F6
Holmfield
Buxton SK17 ....84 E6
Derby DE23 ....231 E7
Holmgate Prim Sch S45 ....131 A4
Holmgate Rd S45 ....131 A4
Holm La DE55 ....158 A4
Holmleigh Way DE73 ....244 F8
Holmley Bank S18 ....57 A3
Holmley La S18 ....57 A3
Holmoak Cl DE21 ....206 B3
Holmshaw Dr S13 ....44 E8
Holmshaw Gr S13 ....44 E8
Holmwood Terr 2 SK17 ....85 C8
Holt's La DE13 ....239 B6
Holt Ave DE24 ....233 C6
Holt Dr DE4 ....142 F7
Holt La
Lea DE4 ....156 B7
Matlock DE4 ....143 B5
Holtlands Dr DE24 ....232 F5
Holt Rd DE4 ....127 F1
Holyhead Dr DE21 ....206 B3
Holymoor Rd S42 ....113 E8
Holyoake Ave S13 ....44 E8
Holyoake Dr NG10 ....236 F7
Holyrood Cl DE21 ....221 A5
Holyrood Ho DE24 ....219 D1
Holy Rosary RC Prim Sch
DE15 ....248 A3
Holy Trinity CE Prim Sch
DE4 ....155 A8
Holywell DE45 ....109 D4

Holywell La DE45 ....125 B5
Holywell Rd DE7 ....194 C3
Holywell St S41 ....266 B3
Homecroft Dr NG16 ....171 E7
Home Farm Cl DE72 ....221 C5
Home Farm Cotts SK17 ....105 C3
Home Farm Ct
Castle Gresley DE11 ....255 D1
Selston NG16 ....171 C6
Home Farm Dr DE22 ....205 A4
Home Farm Ho DE15 ....249 A3
Home Farm Park Homes
DE13 ....240 A5
Homefields Prim Sch
DE73 ....232 E1
Homemoss Ho SK17 ....85 A8
Homeport Mews S41 ....266 B4
Homer Dr S6 ....23 B8
Homestead NG16 ....182 A4
Homestead Rd S41 ....32 C6
Homestead Way SK23 ....47 C5
Honeycroft Cl DE6 ....179 B2
Honeycroft Ct DE55 ....160 B4
Honeyfield Dr DE5 ....180 F8
Honeysuckle Cl DE11 ....256 A6
Honeysuckle Dr DE55 ....160 B7
Honeysuckle View DE15 ....255 A8
Honeywall La DE6 ....183 E8
Honingham Rd DE7 ....194 C3
Honiton Ct 11 S41 ....95 F8
Hook La ST14 ....210 B6
Hoole St S41 ....115 D8
Hooley Cl NG10 ....236 B6
Hooley St NG16 ....171 F6
Hoon La DE65 ....228 A3
Hoonwell La DE6 ....175 F5
Hope Ave DE3 ....217 D2
Hopedale Rd S12 ....44 D4
Hopefield Ave S12 ....44 D4
Hope Prim Sch S33 ....39 A4
Hope Rd S33 ....39 D2
Hope St
Chesterfield S40 ....95 E3
Derby DE1 ....267 C2
Glossop SK13 ....10 C2
2 Ilkeston DE7 ....208 F7
Melbourne DE73 ....252 A7
Hope Sta S33 ....39 C3
Hope Terr DE4 ....143 B2
Hopetoun St DE23 ....232 A8
Hope Valley Coll S33 ....38 F3
Hopewell Rd DE4 ....143 C6
Hopewell Wlk DE7 ....194 F5
Hop Inge The S26 ....61 F5
Hopkins Ct NG16 ....182 F3
Hopmeadow Way DE15 ....248 A1
Hopping Hill DE56 ....190 F8
Hopping Hill Terr E
DE56 ....191 A7
Hopping Hill Terr W
DE56 ....191 A7
Hopping La DE45 ....125 B3
Hopton Cl
Derby DE21 ....206 A1
Ripley DE5 ....169 F1
Hoptonwood Cl DE4 ....154 D4
Hopwell Rd DE72 ....222 A2
Horace Ave NG9 ....223 D6
Hordern Cl SK13 ....10 A4
Hordens La SK13 ....47 B5
Hordens Park Rd SK23 ....47 B5
Hordens Rd SK23 ....47 A5
Horeston Cotts DE7 ....192 B7
Hornbeam Cl
Brimington S43 ....78 A2
Derby DE21 ....205 D1
Hornbeams The 2 ST14 ....210 A1
Horncastle Rd DE21 ....205 D1
Horner Rd 1 S7 ....43 A7
Hornscroft Rd S44 ....99 A1
Hornsea Rd DE21 ....205 D1
Hornthorpe Rd S21 ....59 C2
Horridge St DE7 ....194 F4
Horsecroft Cl DE7 ....194 C2
Horsedale DE4 ....142 C1
Horse Fair Ave SK23 ....47 A6
Horsehead La S44 ....99 C2
Horse & Jockey Yd 7
DE6 ....173 C2
Horseshoe Ave SK17 ....47 F1
Horse Shoes The DE74 ....247 D4
Horsewood Rd S40 ....114 B8
Horsley CE Prim Sch
DE21 ....191 F5
Horsley Cl S40 ....95 A5
Horsley Cres
Holbrook DE56 ....191 C7
Langley Mill NG16 ....182 A3
Horsleygate La S18 ....74 E7
Horsleygate Rd S17, S18 ....74 B7
Horsley La DE21 ....191 E4
Horsley Rd DE21, DE56 ....191 F6
Horsley Woodhouse Prim
Sch DE7 ....192 D6
Horton Cl
Sheffield S20 ....59 E7
Swanwick DE55 ....169 E8
Horton Dr S20 ....59 E7
Horton St DE23 ....219 C2
Horwood Ave DE23 ....218 D2
Hoselett Field Rd NG10 ....236 E5
Hospital La DE3 ....230 B7
Houfton Cres S44 ....98 F3
Houfton Rd S44 ....98 F3
Houghton Ave DE7 ....194 C3
Houghton Cl SK22 ....25 C2

Houghton Ct 7 DE21 ....205 F2
Houldsworth Cres S44 ....98 F2
Houldsworth Dr S41 ....96 E2
Hoult St DE22 ....218 D4
Houndkirk Rd S11 ....42 F2
Hounslow Rd DE22 ....218 B6
Houston Cl DE21 ....220 B6
Hoveton Cl DE24 ....232 D3
Howard Cl
Glossop SK13 ....10 B2
11 Long Eaton NG10 ....223 F1
Howard Dr
Chesterfield S41 ....77 A2
North Wingfield S42 ....131 F5
Howards Mdw SK13 ....17 B7
Howard St
Derby DE23 ....218 F2
Glossop SK13 ....10 C1
Howarth Cl NG10 ....236 A7
Howden Cl
Derby DE3 ....217 C1
Staveley S43 ....78 F2
Swadlincote DE11 ....256 A5
Howden Rd SK22 ....24 C1
Howells Pl S43 ....79 B3
Howe St DE22 ....218 D5
Howitt Cres ST14 ....210 B2
Howitt St
Heanor DE75 ....181 F2
Long Eaton NG10 ....236 E7
How La S33 ....38 C3
Howth Cl DE21 ....220 A4
Hoylake Ave S40 ....114 C7
Hoylake Cl NG19 ....136 E6
Hoylake Ct DE3 ....217 C3
Hoylake Dr DE3 ....217 C3
Hoyland Ct DE56 ....179 E5
Hoyle Cl DE45 ....109 D5
Hubert Shaw Cl DE24 ....232 E4
Huckerby Rd DE7 ....194 C2
Hucklow Ave
Chesterfield S40 ....266 A1
North Wingfield S42 ....132 A8
Staveley S43 ....97 D7
Hucklow Bank 36 SK13 ....9 D2
Hucklow Cl 35 SK13 ....9 D2
Hucklow Ct DE21 ....206 B3
Hucklow Fold 34 SK13 ....9 D2
Hucklow Lanes 33 SK13 ....9 D2
Hucknall Ave S40 ....95 C4
Hudson Cl S26 ....61 E7
Hudson Mount S44 ....118 B8
Hudson Way DE24 ....219 C3
Hufton's Ct DE75 ....194 A7
Hufton's Dr DE75 ....194 A7
Hugh La S33 ....51 A7
Hugh St SK13 ....10 B1
Hulland CE Prim Sch
DE6 ....175 F3
Hulland St DE1 ....267 D1
Hulland View DE22 ....204 D1
Humber Cl DE24 ....233 C6
Humber Rd NG10 ....223 C1
Humber St DE65 ....228 C1
Humbleton Dr DE22 ....218 A5
Humphrey Rd S8 ....56 E8
Hundall Ct 4 S40 ....95 D6
Hundall La
Chesterfield S41 ....77 A4
Unstone S18 ....77 A7
Hungerhill La S42, S45 ....113 B4
Hunger La DE6 ....188 E3
Hungry La
Bradwell S33 ....51 A6
Hathersage S32 ....53 B8
Hunloke Ave S40 ....95 E1
Hunloke Cres S40 ....95 E1
Hunloke Park Prim Sch
S42 ....115 A4
Hunloke Rd S42 ....132 E8
Hunloke View S42 ....115 B4
Hunsdon Rd S21 ....59 C3
Hunstone Ave S8 ....57 A7
Hunt Ave DE75 ....181 E2
Hunt Dr DE11 ....256 E4
Hunter's La S13 ....44 C6
Hunter Dr DE56 ....191 F8
Hunter Pk S18 ....57 C1
Hunter Rd DE56 ....179 D5
Hunters Chase NG19 ....136 B2
Hunters Croft DE24 ....231 E2
Hunters Green Cl SK23 ....34 E1
Hunters La SK13 ....16 F8
Huntingdon Ave S40 ....99 B1
Huntingdon Ct DE73 ....252 B8
Huntingdon Dr DE74 ....247 A4
Huntingdon Gn DE21 ....219 C6
Huntingdon Rd DE15 ....254 D7
Huntingdon Way 1 NG9 ....223 F2
Huntingdon Wlk 2
NG10 ....223 B5
Hunt La S45 ....145 B8
Huntley Ave DE21 ....220 F5
Huntley Cl S43 ....97 B8
Hunts La DE12 ....264 E8
Huntsman Rd S43 ....78 F2
Huntspill Rd DE65 ....228 E1
Hunts Row DE55 ....157 E3
Hunt Way DE11 ....256 E4
Hurdlow Gn 10 SK13 ....9 D1
Hurdlow Lea 11 SK13 ....9 D1
Hurdlow Mews SK13 ....9 D1
Hurdlow Way 12 SK13 ....9 D1
Hurds Hollow DE4 ....143 A6
Hurker Rise DE4 ....143 C7
Hurl Dr S12 ....43 F5
Hurley Ct DE7 ....207 E8
Hurlfield Ct S12 ....44 A6

Hurlfield Dr S12 ....43 F6
Hurlfield Rd S12 ....43 F5
Hurstbrook Cl SK13 ....10 E1
Hurst Cl SK13 ....10 E1
Hurstclough La S32, S33 ....40 D2
Hurst Cres SK13 ....17 E8
Hurst Ct DE12 ....264 F4
Hurst Dr
Burton u T DE13 ....240 E1
Stanley DE7 ....207 C6
Hurst La DE55 ....146 A5
Hurst Lea Rd SK22 ....33 C7
Hurst Rd SK13 ....10 F1
Hurst Rise DE4 ....143 D5
Huss's La NG10 ....236 F7
Hutchings Cres S43 ....80 D5
Huthwaite All Saints CE Inf
Sch NG17 ....148 E2
Huthwaite La DE55 ....148 C2
Hut La
Ashover S45 ....129 E6
Killamarsh S21 ....60 F4
Hutmoor Butts SK17 ....107 A3
Hutton St DE24 ....232 E6
Huxley Cl DE23 ....231 F7
Hyde Bank Ct SK22 ....33 C7
Hyde Bank Rd SK22 ....33 C8
Hyde Park Rd DE22 ....218 A6
Hyde Rd SK14 ....9 A4
Hydro Cl DE45 ....91 F6
Hylton Cl DE14 ....254 A7
Hyndley Rd S44 ....98 F3

I

Ian Ave DE4 ....165 F7
Ians Way S45 ....95 C4
Ibbotsons Croft S32 ....53 A8
Ibbotsons Farm Cotts S32 ....53 A8
Ibsley Cl DE24 ....233 C6
Ida's St S21 ....59 D4
Ikea Way NG16 ....195 C7
Ilam Cl S43 ....97 C6
Ilam Ct NG16 ....185 D8
Ilam Dr DE7 ....194 D3
Ilam Sq DE7 ....194 E5
Ilford Cl DE7 ....194 D3
Ilford Rd DE22 ....218 A5
Ilford Wlk DE22 ....218 A5
Ilfracombe Ct 1 S41 ....95 F8
Ilion St NG19 ....135 F2
Ilkeston Com Hospl DE7 ....194 D4
Ilkeston Rd
Heanor DE75 ....193 F3
Sandiacre DE7, NG10 ....223 C8
Smalley DE7 ....192 F2
Stanton-by-D DE7 ....208 F3
Stapleford NG9 ....209 F2
Trowell NG9 ....209 C5
Ilkeston Sch DE7 ....208 D8
Immingham Gr S43 ....78 D1
Imperial Ct DE22 ....204 D5
Imperial Rd DE4 ....143 B5
Inchwood Cl 4 NG9 ....223 F2
Independent Hill DE55 ....158 F3
Industrial St 3 DE23 ....219 A2
Infirmary Rd S41 ....266 C4
Ingham Dr DE3 ....230 D8
Ingham Rd NG10 ....223 C2
Ingleborough Gdns 8
NG10 ....236 A8
Ingleby Ave DE23 ....231 F7
Ingleby Cl
Dronfield S18 ....56 C1
Swadlincote DE11 ....256 A5
Ingleby La DE73 ....251 A5
Ingleby Rd
Barrow u T DE73 ....244 D3
Long Eaton NG10 ....235 F4
Ingle Cl DE21 ....220 E5
Ingledew Cl 1 DE21 ....205 F1
Inglefield Rd DE7 ....209 A6
Ingleton Rd S41 ....115 B7
Inglewood Ave DE3 ....217 D4
Ingliston Cl DE24 ....233 D6
Inkerman Cl NE7 ....194 E5
Inkerman Rd NG16 ....171 F5
Inkerman St NG16 ....171 F5
Inkersall Dr S20 ....59 E8
Inkersall Green Rd S43 ....97 C7
Inkersall Prim Sch S43 ....97 C7
Inkersall Rd S43 ....97 E7
Inn La DE22 ....204 B7
Institute La DE55 ....159 A4
Instow Dr DE23 ....231 D6
Intake La
Bakewell DE45 ....109 E3
Cromford DE4 ....155 B6
Holloway DE4 ....155 E4
Intake Prim Sch S12 ....44 C6
Intake Rd S44 ....98 E3
Intakes La DE56 ....188 C7
Interchange 25 Bsns Pk
NG10 ....223 A4
Inveraray Cl DE24 ....231 D3
Invernia Cl DE23 ....231 E5
Iona Cl
Derby DE24 ....231 E4
Tibshelf DE55 ....147 F5
Iona Dr NG9 ....209 D2
Ireland Cl S43 ....78 F1
Ireland St S43 ....78 F2
Ireland Trad Est S43 ....78 F1

Ireton Cl DE56 . . . . 179 E3
Ireton Ct DE6 . . . . 165 B1
Iron Cliff Rd S44 . . . . 98 F3
Irongate S40 . . . . 266 B3
Iron Gate DE1 . . . . 267 B3
Ironside Cl S14 . . . . 43 D3
Ironside Pl S14 . . . . 43 E3
Ironside Rd S14 . . . . 43 E3
Ironside Wlk S14 . . . . 43 D2
Ironville & Codnor Park Prim Sch NG16 . . . . 170 F4
Ironwalls La DE13 . . . . . . 239 C5
Irvine Cl DE24 . . . . 231 D3
Irving Pl DE24 . . . . 232 F7
Isaac's La NG9 . . . . 223 D7
Island DE11 . . . . 262 C8
Island The NG16 . . . . 182 F1
Islay Cl NG9 . . . . 209 D3
Islay Rd DE24 . . . . 231 E4
Isleworth Dr DE22 . . . . . . 217 F6
Ismay Rd DE21 . . . . 219 F6
Ivan Brook Cl 4 S18 . . . . . 56 C1
Ivanhoe Cl S42 . . . . 115 C1
Ivanhoe Ct 3 S41 . . . . 96 A6
Iveagh Wlk DE55 . . . . 170 C5
Ivonbrook Cl DE4 . . . . . . 142 B8
Ivybridge Cl DE22 . . . . . . 206 C3
Ivy Cl
  Chesterfield S41 . . . . 77 A2
  Donisthorpe DE12 . . . . . 262 E1
  Willington DE65 . . . . 242 A5
Ivycroft SK13 . . . . 9 E4
Ivy Ct
  Derby DE3 . . . . 217 D1
  Egginton DE65 . . . . 241 A5
  Hilton DE65 . . . . 228 D1
  Sheffield S8 . . . . 43 C2
Ivy Farm Cl S43 . . . . 80 E3
Ivy Gr DE5 . . . . 169 D1
Ivy House Sch DE23 . . . . 219 C2
Ivy La
  Eastwood NG16 . . . . 182 E2
  Elton DE4 . . . . 140 E6
Ivyleaf Way DE23 . . . . . . 231 B6
Ivy Lodge Cl DE15 . . . . . 254 E7
Ivy Side Cl S21 . . . . 60 D6
Ivy Side Gdns S21 . . . . 60 D6
Ivy Spring Cl S42 . . . . 115 B4
Ivy Sq DE23 . . . . 219 C2
Ivywood Gdns S44 . . . . . . 98 A5

J

Jack's La ST14 . . . . 224 E2
Jackass La DE56 . . . . 167 B4
Jackdaw Dr DE22 . . . . . . 218 D5
Jacklin Cl DE14 . . . . 254 A6
Jacksdale Cl DE3 . . . . . . 204 D1
Jacksdale Prim Sch NG16 . . . . 171 B3
Jackson's La
  Heage DE56 . . . . 179 D7
  Ripley DE5 . . . . 169 A8
Jackson Ave
  Derby DE3 . . . . 218 A2
  Ilkeston DE7 . . . . 208 E8
  Sandiacre NG10 . . . . 223 A4
  Tupton S42 . . . . 131 C8
Jackson Cl DE12 . . . . 262 B3
Jackson Rd
  Bramley-Vale S44 . . . . . . 117 D1
  Clay Cross S45 . . . . 131 E3
  Matlock DE4 . . . . 143 B6
Jacksons Edge Rd SK12 . . 32 B6
Jacksons La
  Belper DE56 . . . . 190 E7
  Etwall DE65 . . . . 229 C2
Jackson St
  Derby DE22 . . . . 218 E4
  Glossop, Padfield SK13 . . . 10 C5
  Glossop SK13 . . . . 17 C7
  Mottram in L SK14 . . . . . . 9 A3
Jackson Tor Rd DE4 . . . . 143 B6
Jackys La S26 . . . . 61 E6
Jacobean Ct DE15 . . . . . . 248 C4
Jagger's La S32 . . . . 52 E8
Jaggers La DE4 . . . . 128 E5
Jago Ave S43 . . . . 81 A4
James's La DE6 . . . . 215 C1
James Andrew Cl S8 . . . . . 56 F7
James Andrew Cres S8 . . . 56 F7
James Andrew Croft S8 . . . 56 F7
James Ave DE55 . . . . 170 D7
James Brindley Way DE13 . . . . 240 F1
James Cl DE1 . . . . 218 E5
James St
  Chesterfield S41 . . . . 96 A6
  7 Glossop SK13 . . . . 17 C8
  Kimberley NG16 . . . . 195 F6
  Somercotes DE55 . . . . . . 170 C7
  Swadlincote DE11 . . . . . . 256 D5
James Walton Ct S20 . . . . 59 F7
James Walton Dr S20 . . . . 59 F7
James Walton Pl S20 . . . . 59 F7
James Walton View S20 . . 59 F7
Jane La SK23 . . . . 34 B1
Jap La DE45 . . . . 110 E8
Jardine Ct DE72 . . . . 235 B7
Jardines La ST14 . . . . 196 D4
Jarnett The SK17 . . . . 107 B8
Jarvey's La DE22 . . . . 217 E2
Jarvis Ct DE24 . . . . 231 E2
Jarvis Rd DE24 . . . . 231 E2

Jasmin Cl NG20 . . . . 119 D6
Jasmine Cl
  Burton u T DE15 . . . . 255 A8
  Derby DE21 . . . . 220 B5
  Swanwick DE55 . . . . 169 F7
Jasmine Ct DE75 . . . . 182 B1
Jasmine Dr DE55 . . . . . . 148 B7
Jaspers La DE4 . . . . 153 A1
Jaunty Ave S12 . . . . 44 C4
Jaunty Cl S12 . . . . 44 C4
Jaunty Cres S12 . . . . 44 C4
Jaunty Dr S12 . . . . 44 C4
Jaunty La S12 . . . . 44 B4
Jaunty Mount S12 . . . . . . 44 C3
Jaunty Pl S12 . . . . 44 C3
Jaunty Rd S12 . . . . 44 C3
Jaunty View S12 . . . . 44 C3
Jaunty Way S12 . . . . 44 B4
Jawbone La DE73 . . . . . . 252 C8
Jaw Bones Hill S40 . . . . . 115 A8
Jay Ct DE22 . . . . 218 D5
Jebb's La
  Idridgehay DE56 . . . . . . 176 F8
  Shottle DE56 . . . . 177 B8
Jebb Gdns S40 . . . . 95 C2
Jedburgh Cl DE24 . . . . . . 231 E2
Jefferson Pl DE24 . . . . . . 232 F7
Jeffery St 6 S2 . . . . 43 B6
Jeffrey La S33 . . . . 51 A6
Jeffries Ave DE4 . . . . 156 F1
Jeffries La DE4 . . . . 156 F1
Jellicoe St NG20 . . . . 101 A2
Jemison Cl DE23 . . . . 230 E2
Jennison St NG19 . . . . . . 136 A1
Jenny's Ct DE56 . . . . 179 C5
Jephson Rd DE14 . . . . . . 254 B7
Jepson Rd S41 . . . . 115 C7
Jermyn Ave S12 . . . . 44 F4
Jermyn Cl S12 . . . . 44 F3
Jermyn Cres S12 . . . . 44 F4
Jermyn Dr S12 . . . . 44 F3
Jermyn Way S12 . . . . 44 F4
Jersey Rd S2 . . . . 43 A7
Jervis Ct DE7 . . . . 194 F3
Jervis Pl S43 . . . . 97 B6
Jesop Dr DE24 . . . . 231 E2
Jesses La DE56 . . . . 178 C7
Jessop Ave NG16 . . . . . . 170 F4
Jessop Lo DE5 . . . . 181 B7
Jessop St DE5 . . . . 181 B7
Jetting St S45 . . . . 130 A1
Jill Iain Ct 1 NG9 . . . . . . 223 E5
Jinny Cl DE65 . . . . 239 C8
Joan Ave DE75 . . . . 181 E2
Joan La S33 . . . . 40 C3
Jodrell Ave DE56 . . . . . . 179 D3
Jodrell Mdw SK23 . . . . . . 45 E8
Jodrell Rd SK23 . . . . 45 D8
Jodrell St SK22 . . . . 33 B7
John Bank La DE45 . . . . . 108 F7
John Berrysford Cl DE21 219 F5
John Dalton St SK13 . . . . . 9 E1
John Davies Prim Sch NG17 . . . . 148 A4
John Davies Workshops NG17 . . . . 148 A4
John Eaton's Almshouses S8 . . . . 43 B2
John F Kennedy Gdns DE21 . . . . 220 C6
John Flamsteed Com Sch DE5 . . . . 180 B2
John Kennedy Rd SK14 . . . 9 A3
John King Inf Sch NG16 160 D3
John King Workshop Mus★ NG16 . . . . 160 D3
John Lombe Dr DE1 . . . . 219 A7
Johnnygate La S18 . . . . . . 75 A4
John O'Gaunts Way DE56 . . . . 179 D4
John of Rolleston Prim Sch DE13 . . . . 240 C4
John Port Cl DE65 . . . . . 229 C4
John Port Sch DE65 . . . . 229 B4
Johnson Ave DE24 . . . . . 232 E7
Johnson Dr DE75 . . . . . . 181 F2
Johnson La
  Idridgehay DE56 . . . . . . 176 E7
  Monyash DE45 . . . . 107 F6
Johnson Rd ST14 . . . . . . 210 B1
Johnson St SK23 . . . . 45 E8
Johnson Way SK23 . . . . . . 47 D6
John St
  Alfreton DE55 . . . . 159 A4
  Brimington S43 . . . . 96 E8
  Chesterfield S40 . . . . 95 E3
  Clay Cross S45 . . . . 131 D4
  Clowne S43 . . . . 80 D3
  Compstall SK6 . . . . 15 B3
  Creswell S80 . . . . 81 E1
  Derby DE1 . . . . 267 C2
  Eckington S21 . . . . 59 D3
  Glossop SK13 . . . . 17 C8
  Heanor DE75 . . . . 181 D2
  Ilkeston DE7 . . . . 194 F1
  Marple SK6 . . . . 23 A5
  Matlock DE4 . . . . 143 B6
  North Wingfield S42 . . . . 131 E7
  Somercotes DE55 . . . . . . 170 C8
  Swadlincote, Albert Village DE11 . . . . 256 C2
  Swadlincote DE11 . . . . . . 255 E6
  Swadlincote, Lower Medway DE11 . . . . 256 C5
Johnstone Cl S40 . . . . . . 266 A1
John Turner Rd DE4 . . . . 127 C3
Jolly La DE6 . . . . 175 A7
Jones St SK13 . . . . 10 A5

Jordan Ave DE13 . . . . . . 240 F2
Jordan St S13 . . . . 10 E1
Jordanthorpe Ctr S8 . . . . 57 B6
Jordanthorpe Gn S8 . . . . 57 C6
Jordanthorpe Parkway S8 . . . . 57 C6
Jordanthorpe View S8 . . . 57 C7
Joseph Fletcher Dr S42 . 114 F2
Joseph St
  Belper DE56 . . . . 178 F4
  Derby DE23 . . . . 219 A1
  Eckington S21 . . . . 59 D3
  Marple SK6 . . . . 23 A4
Joseph Wright Ctr (Derby Coll) The DE1 . . . . 267 A4
Joseph Wright Terr DE1. 267 B4
Joyce Ave NG9 . . . . 223 B6
Jubalton Cl DE24 . . . . . . 232 E6
Jubilee Ave DE5 . . . . 169 C1
Jubilee Bsns Pk DE21 . . . 267 C4
Jubilee Cl DE23 . . . . 252 B7
Jubilee Cotts S44 . . . . 97 A1
Jubilee Cres
  Clowne S43 . . . . 81 A4
  Killamarsh S21 . . . . 60 E7
  Whitwell S80 . . . . 81 E5
Jubilee Ct
  Belper DE56 . . . . 179 A2
  Pinxton NG16 . . . . 160 D3
  West Hallam DE7 . . . . . . 207 D8
  Wirksworth DE4 . . . . . . 165 E2
Jubilee Gdns
  New Mills SK22 . . . . 33 C7
  Whitwell S80 . . . . 81 F5
Jubilee Parkway DE21 . . . 267 C4
Jubilee Pk DE11 . . . . 256 F4
Jubilee Pl S80 . . . . 81 F5
Jubilee Rd
  Chapel-en-le-F SK23 . . . . 47 B5
  Derby DE24 . . . . 232 F4
  Whitwell S80 . . . . 81 F5
Jubilee Rise DE15 . . . . . . 248 C3
Jubilee Sq DE6 . . . . 184 D7
Jubilee St
  Kimberley NG16 . . . . 195 E7
  New Mills SK22 . . . . 33 C7
Jubilee Terr DE12 . . . . . . 262 E1
Judson Ave NG9 . . . . 223 F6
Judy Hill DE4 . . . . 127 F1
Julia Cres DE55 . . . . 146 F3
Julian Cl DE7 . . . . 209 B6
Julie Ave DE75 . . . . 182 B1
Julius Cl NG16 . . . . 182 B4
Jumble Rd S11 . . . . 42 F1
Junction Rd NG10 . . . . . . 237 A6
Junction St DE1 . . . . 218 E4
Juniper Cl S43 . . . . 78 A2
Juniper Ct NG16 . . . . 195 C8
Juniper Rise S21 . . . . 60 C5
Jura Ave DE5 . . . . 169 D2
Jury St DE1 . . . . 267 A4

K

Kariba Cl S41 . . . . 266 C3
Katherine Dr NG9 . . . . . . 223 F4
Katrine Wlk DE24 . . . . . . 231 E5
Kay Dr DE11 . . . . 255 F5
Kayes Ct 2 NG9 . . . . 223 D7
Kean Pl DE24 . . . . 232 F7
Kearsley Rd S2 . . . . 43 A8
Keats Ave DE23 . . . . 218 A1
Keats Cl NG10 . . . . 236 B5
Keats Dr DE11 . . . . 256 C6
Keats Rd
  Chesterfield S41 . . . . 95 F8
  Stonebroom DE55 . . . . . 146 F3
Keats Way S42 . . . . 115 C4
Keats Wlk DE55 . . . . 146 F3
Keble Cl
  Burton u T DE15 . . . . 248 C2
  Derby DE1 . . . . 267 C1
Kedleston Cl
  Burton u T DE13 . . . . 240 C1
  Chesterfield S41 . . . . 95 C6
  Derby DE22 . . . . 204 D1
  Long Eaton NG10 . . . . . . 236 A5
  Ripley DE5 . . . . 169 C3
Kedleston Ct
  3 Derby DE22 . . . . 204 D2
  4 Staveley S43 . . . . 78 E2
  Tibshelf DE55 . . . . 148 B6
Kedleston Dr
  Heanor DE75 . . . . 181 C2
  Ilkeston DE7 . . . . 194 D3
Kedleston Gdns DE1 . . . . 267 A4
Kedleston Hall★ DE22 . . . 203 E5
Kedleston Old Rd DE22 . . 218 D8
Kedleston Rd
  Buxton SK17 . . . . 85 C7
  Derby DE22 . . . . 218 E7
  Quarndon DE22 . . . . . . 204 B5
  Weston Underwood DE22 203 A8
Kedleston St DE1 . . . . . . 267 A4
Keeling La DE4 . . . . 126 B1
Keeling Terr DE4 . . . . . . 126 B1
Keepers La S18 . . . . 75 E3
Kegworth Ave DE23 . . . . 231 C6
Kegworth Rd NG11 . . . . . 237 F1
Keilder Ct S40 . . . . 95 D1
Kelburn Ave S40 . . . . 95 C1
Keldholme La DE24 . . . . . 232 E6
Kelgate S20 . . . . 59 D6
Kelham Way NG16 . . . . . 182 E3

Kelmoor Rd DE24 . . . . . . 233 B7
Kelsons Ave SK17 . . . . . . 85 D5
Kelso Wlk DE24 . . . . 231 E2
Kelstedge La S45 . . . . . . 129 D5
Kelvedon Dr DE23 . . . . . 231 A6
Kelvin Cl NG9 . . . . 223 C5
Kemble Pl DE24 . . . . 232 F7
Kemp Cl S21 . . . . 60 C6
Kempton Cl NG16 . . . . . . 195 E7
Kempton Park Rd DE24 . . 232 D8
Kempton Rd DE15 . . . . . . 248 A3
Kendal Cl SK17 . . . . 85 C4
Kendal Dr S18 . . . . 56 E1
Kendal Rd S41 . . . . 95 E8
Kendal Wlk 1 DE21 . . . . . 205 D1
Kendon Ave DE23 . . . . . . 231 E6
Kendray Ct DE56 . . . . . . 179 D5
Kendricks Cl DE11 . . . . . 257 A7
Kenilworth Ct 4 S41 . . . . . 96 A4
Kenilworth Dr DE7 . . . . . 208 D5
Kenmare Cl S45 . . . . 131 D2
Kennack Cl S55 . . . . 160 C6
Kennedy Ave
  Long Eaton NG10 . . . . . . 236 C5
  Mansfield Woodhouse NG19 . . . . 136 D4
Kennedy Cl DE21 . . . . . . 220 A7
Kennedy Dr NG9 . . . . . . 209 E1
Kennet Paddock NG19 . . 136 D3
Kennet Gr SK17 . . . . 84 E6
Kennet Vale S40 . . . . 95 D5
Kenninghall Cl S2 . . . . . . 43 D7
Kenninghall Dr S2 . . . . . . 43 D7
Kenninghall Rd S2 . . . . . 43 D7
Kenning St S45 . . . . 131 C3
Kensal Rise DE22 . . . . . . 218 B6
Kensington Ave DE75 . . . 181 C1
Kensington Chase S10 . . . 42 F8
Kensington Cl NG19 . . . . 136 E5
Kensington Dr S10 . . . . . . 42 F8
Kensington Gdns DE7 . . . 208 F7
Kensington Jun Sch DE7 . . . . 209 A7
Kensington Pk S10 . . . . . . 42 F8
Kensington Rd
  Burton u T DE15 . . . . 248 A3
  Sandiacre NG10 . . . . 223 A4
Kensington St
  Derby DE1 . . . . 267 A3
  Ilkeston DE7 . . . . 208 F6
Kent's Bank Rd SK17 . . . . 85 C6
Kent Ave NG16 . . . . 171 B4
Kent Cl S41 . . . . 95 F5
Kent Grange 12 S8 . . . . . . 43 B6
Kent House Cl S12 . . . . . . 58 E8
Kentish Ct DE1 . . . . 219 B7
Kentmere Cl S18 . . . . 56 E1
Kentmere Way S43 . . . . . . 97 C8
Kent Rd
  Burton u T DE15 . . . . 254 E6
  Eastwood NG16 . . . . 195 C8
  Glossop SK13 . . . . 10 D1
  Sheffield S8 . . . . 43 B6
Kent St
  Chesterfield S41 . . . . . . 115 C8
  Derby DE1 . . . . 219 D7
Kenwell Dr S17 . . . . 56 B5
Kenyon Rd S41 . . . . 96 E1
Keppel Ct DE7 . . . . 194 F3
Kepple Gate DE5 . . . . . . 180 F8
Kernel Cl DE3 . . . . 231 A8
Kerry's Yd DE56 . . . . 191 F8
Kerry Dr DE7 . . . . 192 F6
Kerry St DE21 . . . . 219 D7
Kershaw St SK13 . . . . 17 C8
Kershope Dr DE21 . . . . . 206 B3
Kerwin Cl S17 . . . . 55 C8
Kerwin Dr S17 . . . . 55 C8
Kerwin Rd S17 . . . . 55 C8
Kestrel Ave DE11 . . . . . . 256 C7
Kestrel Cl
  Bolsover S44 . . . . 98 F3
  Burnaston DE3 . . . . 230 B7
  Ilkeston DE7 . . . . 208 F4
  Killamarsh S21 . . . . 60 B7
  Marple SK6 . . . . 23 A3
Kestrel Dr S21 . . . . 59 B3
Kestrel Ho DE24 . . . . 231 E2
Kestrel Hts NG16 . . . . . . 170 F3
Kestrels Croft DE24 . . . . 231 E3
Kestrel View SK13 . . . . . . 16 F8
Kestrel Way DE15 . . . . . . 248 D3
Keswick Ave DE23 . . . . . 231 E6
Keswick Cl
  Bolsover S44 . . . . 98 F1
  Ilkeston DE7 . . . . 208 D5
Keswick Ct NG10 . . . . . . 223 B2
Keswick Dr S41 . . . . 95 C8
Keswick Pl S18 . . . . 56 E1
Kettlewell Cl DE24 . . . . . 232 E6
Ketton Ave S8 . . . . 43 B3
Kevin Cl DE21 . . . . 220 B8
Kew Cres
  Heanor DE75 . . . . 182 B1
  Sheffield S12 . . . . 44 A2
Kew Gdns DE22 . . . . 218 B5
Keyhaven Cl DE21 . . . . . 219 D8
Keynsham Cl DE24 . . . . . 232 E8
Keys Rd DE55 . . . . 159 B2
Keys St DE1 . . . . 267 C4
Kibworth Cl
  Chesterfield S41 . . . . . . 115 C7
  Derby DE21 . . . . 220 B8
Kidd Rd SK13 . . . . 17 E6
Kidsley Cl 7 S40 . . . . 95 A5

Kilbourne Rd DE56 . . . . . 179 C4
Kilburn Dr DE7 . . . . 194 D3
Kilburn Inf Sch DE56 . . . 191 F8
Kilburn Jun Sch DE56 . . 192 A8
Kilburn La DE56 . . . . 179 E3
Kilburn Rd S18 . . . . 56 C1
Kilburn Toll Bar DE56 . . 179 F1
Kilburn Way DE11 . . . . . 255 F5
Kilby Ho NG10 . . . . 236 E7
Kildale Gdns S20 . . . . 59 D7
Kildare Rd DE21 . . . . 220 B4
Kildonan Gr S12 . . . . 44 C3
Kildrummy Cl DE73 . . . . 232 E1
Killamarsh Inf Sch S21 . . 60 E7
Killamarsh Jun Sch S21 . . 60 E7
Killamarsh La S21 . . . . . . 61 A6
Killigrew Ave DE24 . . . . . 231 F4
Killis La
  Belper DE56 . . . . 179 D1
  Holbrook DE56 . . . . 191 D8
Kilmorey Fold SK13 . . . . . 10 E3
Kiln Cl DE7 . . . . 193 E1
Kiln Croft DE65 . . . . 229 C4
Kiln Hill S18 . . . . 57 C3
Kiln La
  Glossop SK13 . . . . 10 A5
  Parwich DE6 . . . . 151 D2
Kilnsey Ct DE23 . . . . 230 E6
Kiln Way DE11 . . . . 256 D3
Kilverston Rd NG10 . . . . 223 A4
Kilvington Ave S44 . . . . . 88 B7
Kilvington Cres S13 . . . . . 44 B7
Kilvington Rd S13 . . . . . . 44 B7
Kimberley Cl NG16 . . . . . 195 E7
Kimberley Dr DE15 . . . . . 248 C3
Kimberley Prim Sch NG16 . . . . 195 E7
Kimberley Rd DE72 . . . . . 221 B2
Kinder Ave DE11 . . . . . . 256 A5
Kinder Cl SK13 . . . . 17 A8
Kinder Cres DE56 . . . . . . 168 B5
Kinder Dr SK6 . . . . 23 A6
Kinder Gr SK17 . . . . 85 A6
Kinderlee Way SK13 . . . . . 16 B5
Kinder Rd
  Hayfield SK22 . . . . 25 E2
  Staveley S43 . . . . 97 B6
Kinder Row SK22 . . . . . . 25 F2
Kinder View SK22 . . . . . . 33 C7
Kinder Way SK17 . . . . 85 E7
Kinder Wlk DE22 . . . . . . 218 E4
King's Cl SK17 . . . . 85 D8
King's Mead Wlk DE1 . . . 267 A4
King's Mill La DE72 . . . . . 245 F5
King's Mills La DE72 . . . . 245 F5
King's Rd SK17 . . . . 85 D8
King Alfred St DE22 . . . . 267 A2
King Charles Ct SK13 . . . . 17 C7
King Cup Cl S13 . . . . 17 E8
King Ecgbert Rd S17 . . . . 55 C5
King Ecgbert Sch S17 . . . 55 D6
King Edward Ave SK13 . . . 10 C1
King Edward Gdns 1 NG10 . . . . 223 B7
King Edward St
  Sandiacre NG10 . . . . 223 C6
  Shirebrook NG20 . . . . . . 119 F4
  Wirksworth DE4 . . . . . . 166 A8
Kingfisher Ave DE11 . . . . 256 F3
Kingfisher Cl DE3 . . . . . . 230 B7
Kingfisher Ct
  Bolsover S44 . . . . 98 F3
  Ilkeston DE7 . . . . 208 F4
Kingfisher Ho S41 . . . . . . 77 B3
Kingfisher Mews SK6 . . . 23 A6
Kingfisher Rd NG19 . . . . 135 D1
Kingfisher Way SK13 . . . . 16 F8
Kingfisher Wlk DE24 . . . . 231 E2
King George Ave DE7 . . . 208 E8
King George St
  Wessington DE55 . . . . . . 157 E8
  Wirksworth DE4 . . . . . . 165 E7
King St N S41 . . . . 96 A7
King St S S40 . . . . 115 A7
Kingsbury Cl DE15 . . . . . 248 A4
Kingsbury Rd DE22 . . . . . 218 A4
Kings Cl
  Carsington DE4 . . . . 164 E8
  Clowne S43 . . . . 80 F3
  Creswell S80 . . . . 81 F1
  Heanor DE75 . . . . 181 C1
Kingsclere Ave DE21 . . . . 206 B2
Kingsclere Wlk S40 . . . . . 114 F8
Kings Coppice S17 . . . . . . 55 C6
Kings Croft DE22 . . . . . . 204 C4
Kingscroft Cl S17 . . . . 55 E8
Kings Ct
  Derby DE1 . . . . 267 A4
  5 Glossop SK13 . . . . 17 C8
Kingsdale Cl NG10 . . . . . 236 A5
Kingsdale Gr DE73 . . . . . 244 F8
Kings Dr
  Brinsley NG16 . . . . 182 E7
  Derby DE3, DE23 . . . . . . 218 B2
Kingsfield Ind Est DE4 . . 165 E6
Kingsfield Rd DE4 . . . . . . 165 E7
Kingsgate S32 . . . . 72 C2
Kings Gate DE74 . . . . . . 247 F4
Kings Hill DE4 . . . . 153 A2
Kings Hollow Mews DE6. 173 F7
Kingsland Cl DE21 . . . . . 205 F2
Kingsley Ave
  Chesterfield S40 . . . . . . 114 F8
  Mansfield Woodhouse NG19 . . . . 136 C3
Kingsley Cl NG19 . . . . . . 136 D4

Kingsley Cres
Long Eaton NG10. . . . . . . 236 B4
Stonebroom DE55 . . . . . . 146 F3
Kingsley Ct NG19 . . . . 136 D5
Kingsley Rd DE22 . . . . 204 D4
Kingsley St DE24. . . . . 231 F5
Kingsmead Ave NG9 . . . . . 209 D2
King's Mead Ho 1 DE22. 218 F7
Kingsmead Ind Est DE22 218 D6
Kingsmede Ave S40. . . . . . 95 D1
Kings Mews S21 . . . . 59 E3
Kingsmoor Fields SK13. . . 10 D3
Kingsmoor Rd SK13. . . . . . . 10 D2
Kingsmuir Rd DE3 . . . . 217 C3
Kings Rd
Sandiacre NG10. . . . . . . 223 B6
Swadlincote DE11 . . . . . 256 B6
King St
Alfreton DE55 . . . . 158 F4
Ashbourne DE6 . . . . 173 C2
Bakewell DE45. . . . . 109 D5
Belper DE56 . . . . 178 F3
Brimington S43 . . . . 77 F1
Broadbottom SK14 . . . . . 16 A8
Burton u T DE14. . . . . . . 254 C8
Clay Cross S45 . . . . 131 C3
Clowne S43 . . . . 80 E3
Creswell, Hodthorpe S80. . 82 C6
Creswell S80 . . . . 81 F1
Derby DE1. . . . . 267 B4
Duffield DE56 . . . . 190 E4
Eastwood NG16. . . . . . . 182 F2
Glossop SK13. . . . . 17 C8
Hollingworth SK14. . . . . . 9 D5
Ilkeston DE7 . . . . 194 F1
Long Eaton NG10 . . . . . . 236 D8
Mansfield Woodhouse
NG19. . . . . 136 D2
Middleton DE4. . . . . 154 D5
Pinxton NG16. . . . . 160 D3
Shirebrook NG20. . . . . . 120 D5
South Normanton DE55. . 159 F5
Tibshelf DE55 . . . . 148 A4
Youlgreave DE45 . . . . . . 125 B5
Kingsthorpe Cl 6 NG19 . 136 E1
Kingston Ave DE7 . . . . . . 209 A4
Kingston Ct
3 Barrow Hill S43 . . . . . 78 B3
West Hallam DE7. . . . . . 207 D8
Kingston Rd DE15. . . . . . . 248 C2
Kingston St DE1 . . . . 218 F7
Kingsway
Burton u T DE14. . . . . . . 254 B8
Derby DE22 . . . . 218 B5
Heanor DE75 . . . . 181 D2
Ilkeston DE7 . . . . 209 A5
Kings Way S80. . . . . 82 C6
Kingsway Cres DE56 . . . . 192 A8
Kingsway Hospl DE22 . . . . 218 B4
Kingsway Ind Pk DE22 . . . 218 C5
Kingsway Park Cl DE22 . . . 218 C5
Kingsway Ret Pk DE22 . . . 218 C5
Kingswood Ave DE56. . . . 179 C6
Kingswood Cl S41 . . . . 95 D8
Kingswood Pl DE23 . . . . . 218 B2
King William Ctr NG16 . . 170 F4
King William St NG16 . . . 170 F4
Kinross Ave DE21 . . . . 219 C8
Kintyre Dr DE24. . . . . 231 E2
Kinver Cl DE6. . . . . 184 C8
Kinver Rd DE15 . . . . 248 A4
Kipling Cl S18 . . . . 76 C8
Kipling Dr DE3. . . . . 217 D1
Kipling Rd S41. . . . . 95 F8
Kirby Cl S41 . . . . 115 C7
Kirby La DE4. . . . . 142 B7
Kirk Cl DE5 . . . . 180 C8
Kirkby Ave
Ilkeston DE7 . . . . 208 F6
Sheffield S12. . . . . 44 A4
Kirkby Dr S12. . . . . 44 A4
Kirkby La NG16 . . . . 160 F3
Kirkby Rd S12. . . . . 44 A4
Kirkby View S12. . . . . 44 A4
Kirkby Way S12. . . . . 44 A3
Kirk Cl DE5 . . . . 180 C8
Kirkcroft Ave S21 . . . . 60 D7
Kirkcroft Dr S21 . . . . 60 D6
Kirkcroft La S21 . . . . 60 D6
Kirk Dale Ave DE21 . . . . . 220 F3
Kirkdale Cl S40 . . . . 115 B8
Kirkdale Gdns NG10. . . . . 236 B6
Kirkdale Rd NG10 . . . . . . 236 B6
Kirkewhite Ave NG10. . . . 236 D7
Kirkewhite Ho NG10 . . . . 236 D7
Kirkfield Dr DE72 . . . . 235 A8
Kirk Hallam Com Tech Coll
DE7. . . . . 208 C6
Kirkham Cl 5 DE75 . . . . . 181 D1
Kirkham Dr NG9 . . . . 223 F2
Kirkham La DE56. . . . . . . 168 B7
Kirk Ireton CE Prim Sch
DE6. . . . . 165 B1
Kirkistown Cl DE24. . . . . . 233 C6
Kirkland Cl DE74. . . . . . . 247 A3
Kirkland Way
12 Derby DE24 . . . . 231 D3
Swadlincote DE11 . . . . . 256 B1
Kirk Langley CE Prim Sch
DE6. . . . . 202 F2
Kirkley Dr DE75 . . . . 181 C1
Kirk Leys Ave N DE21 . . . 220 E4
Kirk Leys Ave S DE21. . . . 220 E4
Kirkman Rd DE75 . . . . . . 181 C4
Kirk St DE1 . . . . 219 B8
Kirkstead Cl
Derby DE21 . . . . 206 B1

Kirkstead Cl continued
Pinxton NG16. . . . . 160 D3
Kirkstead Jun Sch NG16 160 D3
Kirkstead Rd NG16 . . . . . 160 D3
Kirkstone Ave DE75. . . . . 182 B1
Kirkstone Ct NG10 . . . . . 223 B2
Kirkstone Rd
Buxton SK17 . . . . 85 D3
Chesterfield S41 . . . . 95 D8
Kirton Ave NG10 . . . . 236 D7
Kishfield La SK23 . . . . 45 A6
Kitchener Ave DE23 . . . . . 231 F7
Kitchener Terr NG20 . . . . 101 A2
Kitson Ave NG16. . . . . . . 171 C4
Kiwi Dr DE24. . . . . 232 F7
Knab Rd DE4 . . . . 127 F3
Knapp Ave NG16 . . . . 182 F1
Knifesmithgate S40. . . . . 266 B3
Knife & Steel Ct DE7 . . . 192 C7
Knight's La DE55 . . . . 249 B5
Knighton Ct S42 . . . . 131 E6
Knighton Rd S42 . . . . 131 E6
Knightsbridge DE22 . . . . 218 A6
Knights Cl
Beeston NG9 . . . . 223 F2
Derby DE24 . . . . 231 E2
Knights Ct DE13 . . . . 240 E2
Knights Rd DE73 . . . . 244 E8
Knightsyard Ct NG10 . . . 236 C5
Knightwake Rd SK22 . . . . 33 A8
Kniveton CE Prim Sch
DE6. . . . . 163 C1
Kniveton La DE6 . . . . 174 C4
Kniveton Pk DE7 . . . . 208 C7
Knob Fields DE11 . . . . . . 261 E8
Knob La DE4. . . . . 166 D5
Knoll Cl DE23 . . . . 231 A8
Knoll St SK22 . . . . 33 B8
Knoll The
Chesterfield S40 . . . . 94 F2
Dronfield S18. . . . . 57 D3
Shirebrook NG20 . . . . . 119 D3
Swadlincote DE11 . . . . . 256 B6
Tansley DE4 . . . . 144 A5
Knowl Ave DE56 . . . . 178 E5
Knowle Ave SK23 . . . . 47 B5
Knowle Gn S17 . . . . 55 C7
Knowle Rd SK6 . . . . 23 C6
Knowles Cl SK17. . . . . 85 E8
Knowles Cres SK17 . . . . . . 85 E8
Knowles Hill DE13 . . . . . 240 B3
Knowles Ind Est SK23 . . . 33 D3
Knowleston Pl DE4. . . . . . 143 C4
Knowles View DE11 . . . . . 256 D4
Knowle Top S20 . . . . 59 E7
Knutsford Gn DE21 . . . . . 205 D2
Kye La S26 . . . . 61 E6
Kyle Cl S21 . . . . 60 B1
Kyle Gr DE21 . . . . 206 B3
Kyle Rd DE65 . . . . 240 D8
Kynance Cl
Derby DE24 . . . . 233 C5
South Normanton DE55. . 160 C6
Kynnersley Croft ST14. . . 210 B1

L

Laburnum Ave NG20 . . . . 119 E5
Laburnum Cl
Bolsover S44. . . . . 99 C1
Creswell S80 . . . . 81 F1
Darley Dale DE4 . . . . . . 127 B3
Sandiacre NG10. . . . . . . 223 B7
South Normanton DE55. . 160 B7
Laburnum Cres
Derby DE22 . . . . 204 D4
Swanwick DE55. . . . . . . 170 A8
Laburnum Ct S44 . . . . 97 A3
Laburnum Gr
Derby DE22 . . . . 218 B5
Killamarsh S21 . . . . 60 C5
Mansfield Woodhouse
NG19. . . . . 136 A4
Laburnum Rd
Burton u T DE15. . . . . . . 254 F6
Swadlincote DE11 . . . . . 256 A6
Laburnum St S43 . . . . 78 B1
Laburnum Way DE65 . . . . 229 C3
Laceby Ct NG19. . . . . 136 E4
Lacey Cl DE7 . . . . 194 C3
Lacey Fields Rd DE75 . . . 182 B1
Ladbroke Gdns DE22 . . . 217 F6
Ladies Spring Ct S17 . . . . 56 A7
Ladies Spring Dr S17 . . . . 56 A7
Ladies Spring Gr S17 . . . . 56 A7
Ladle End La DE12 . . . . . 253 D1
Ladybank Rd
Derby DE3 . . . . 217 C1
Sheffield S20. . . . . 59 D6
Lady Bank View S21 . . . . . 59 D6
Ladybower Cl DE11 . . . . . 256 A2
Ladybower Ct
Glossop SK13. . . . . 10 C1
4 Sheffield S17 . . . . . . 56 A5
Ladybower Dr S32 . . . . . . 53 A7
Ladybower La S43 . . . . 97 D8
Ladybower Rd DE21 . . . . . 220 F4
Ladycroft SK17 . . . . 66 C1
Ladycroft Paddock DE22 204 E4
Ladycross Inf Sch NG10 . 223 B6
Lady Field Rd S80. . . . . . . 62 D8
Ladyfields DE11. . . . . 256 D6
Ladyfields Way DE11 . . . . 255 F6
Ladyflatts Rd DE4. . . . . . 165 E2
Ladygrove DE56 . . . . 168 D5
Ladygrove Cotts DE23 . . 219 B3

Lady Grove Rd DE4. . . . . 127 E2
Lady Hole La DE6 . . . . . . 186 B7
Lady Ida's Dr
Eckington S21 . . . . 59 C4
Sheffield S20, S21 . . . . . . 59 C5
Ladylea Rd NG10. . . . . . . 236 A4
Lady Lea Rd DE21, DE7. . 192 A6
Lady Ley Hill DE21 . . . . . 192 A6
Lady Manners Sch DE45 109 C4
Lady Mantle Cl DE73 . . . 232 E2
Lady Meadow Cl ST14. . . 196 E5
Ladypit Rd SK23 . . . . 33 E4
Ladysmith Rd DE72 . . . . . 221 B2
Ladythorn Ave SK6. . . . . . 23 A5
Ladywell Cl DE13 . . . . . . 240 E1
Ladywell Cl DE56 . . . . . . 179 A3
Ladywood Ave DE56. . . . 179 B5
Ladywood Dr S41 . . . . 95 C7
Ladywood Prim Sch DE7 208 D5
Ladywood Rd DE7 . . . . . . 208 C5
Lake Ave DE75 . . . . 181 C4
Lake Dr
Derby DE23 . . . . 231 F8
Doveridge DE6. . . . . 211 B1
Lake Gdns DE75 . . . . 181 C4
Lake Lands S42 . . . . 114 F2
Lakeside
12 Ashbourne DE6 . . . . 173 C2
Bakewell DE45. . . . . 109 B7
Wingerworth S42 . . . . . . 114 F2
Lake Side
Doveridge DE6. . . . . 211 A1
Glossop SK13. . . . . 10 A6
Lakeside Ave NG10. . . . . 236 C4
Lakeside Bsns Ctr DE75 . 194 A6
Lakeside Com Prim Sch
DE24. . . . . 219 E2
Lakeside Cres NG10. . . . . 236 D5
Lakeside Dr DE23 . . . . . . 231 A7
Lakeside Inf Sch NG10 . . 236 C5
Lakes Rd SK6. . . . . 23 B6
Lake View SK23. . . . . 33 D4
Lake View Ave S40. . . . . . . 95 C1
Lamb Cres DE5 . . . . 169 F1
Lambcroft Rd NG16. . . . . 160 D3
Lambe Ct DE23 . . . . 267 C1
Lambgates SK13 . . . . 10 A5
Lamb Hill Cl S13. . . . . 44 D7
Lambhouse La DE56. . . . . 177 E5
Lambley Dr DE22 . . . . . . 204 C2
Lambourn Ct DE22 . . . . . 205 A3
Lambourn Dr DE22 . . . . . 205 B4
Lambourne Ave DE6 . . . . 185 D8
Lampart La SK17. . . . . 50 D5
Lambrook Cl DE3 . . . . . . 217 C2
Lambton Cl DE7 . . . . 194 E3
Lampad Cl 4 DE73. . . . . 252 A8
Lampeter Cl DE21. . . . . . 206 B2
Lanark St DE21 . . . . 219 E7
Lancaster Ave
Sandiacre NG10. . . . . . . 223 A4
Stapleford NG9 . . . . 223 E7
Lancaster Dr
Hilton DE65 . . . . 228 E2
Tutbury DE13 . . . . 239 B5
Lancaster Rd S41 . . . . 95 E8
Lancaster Rise DE56 . . . . 179 A6
Lancaster Sports Ctr
DE1. . . . . 267 B4
Lancaster St S44. . . . . . . 117 F1
Lancaster Wlk DE21 . . . . 221 A6
Lancelot Cl S40. . . . . 114 D8
Lancelot Cl DE13 . . . . . . 240 E2
Lancing Rd S2. . . . . 43 A8
Landau Forte Coll DE1 . . 267 C4
Lander La DE56 . . . . 179 A4
Landmere DE24 . . . . 231 E3
Landmere Cl DE7 . . . . . . 194 C3
Landon Cl S40 . . . . 114 B7
Landsdowne Ave S41 . . . . 95 A6
Landsdown Gr NG10 . . . . 223 F1
Landseer Cl
4 Dronfield S18. . . . . . . 56 E1
Sheffield S14. . . . . 43 D2
Landseer Dr
Marple SK6. . . . . 23 B7
Sheffield S14. . . . . 43 E2
Landseer Pl S14. . . . . 43 E2
Landseer Wlk S14. . . . . . . 43 E2
Lane Head
Longnor SK17 . . . . 121 B7
Stoney Middleton S32 . . . 71 C3
Tideswell SK17 . . . . 69 D5
Lane Head Gn S33 . . . . . . 37 C7
Lanehead Rd SK23 . . . . . . 45 C5
Lane Head Rd S17 . . . . 55 C4
Lanesend Cotts SK23. . . . 46 A8
Laneside Ave NG9. . . . . . 223 E2
Laneside Cl SK23 . . . . 47 A5
Laneside Rd
New Mills, Rowarth SK22 . 24 E6
New Mills SK22 . . . . 33 E7
Lanes The DE4. . . . . 155 A3
Lane The
Awsworth NG16. . . . . . . 195 C4
Spinkhill S21 . . . . 60 D1
Stanton in Peak DE4. . . . 126 C5
Laneward Cl DE7 . . . . 194 D4
Langdale Cl S40 . . . . 94 F5
Langdale Dr
Derby DE21 . . . . 205 D1
Dronfield S18. . . . . 57 C3
Long Eaton NG10 . . . . . . 236 A6
Langdale Sq S43 . . . . 96 D8
Langdon Cl 3 NG10. . . . . 223 A1
Langen Cl NG16 . . . . 236 E6
Langer Cl DE14 . . . . 254 B6

Langerfield Ave S40 . . . . 115 A7
Langer La S40, S42 . . . . . 114 E3
Langford Rd DE3. . . . . . . 217 D3
Langhurst Ct S40 . . . . 95 D4
Langhurst Rd S40. . . . . . . 95 D4
Langley Ave
Ilkeston DE7 . . . . 194 D5
Somercotes DE55 . . . . . . 170 C8
Langley Bsns Pk NG16 . . 182 B2
Langley Cl
3 Chesterfield S40 . . . . 95 A5
Mansfield NG19. . . . . . . 135 C1
Langley Cls S13 . . . . 10 A5
Langley Dr SK13 . . . . 17 E8
Langley Inf Sch DE75. . . . 182 A1
Langley Mill CE Inf Sch
NG16. . . . . 182 B3
Langley Mill Jun Sch
NG16. . . . . 182 A4
Langley Mill Sta NG16. . . 182 B3
Langley Pk NG16. . . . . . . 182 B3
Langley Rd DE21 . . . . 220 E3
Langley St DE22 . . . . 218 D6
Lang Rd DE24. . . . . 232 F6
Langsett Ave
Sheffield S44. . . . . 99 C1
Langton The 4 DE22. . . . 218 E5
Langsett Cl 13 SK13 . . . . 9 D1
Langsett Dr DE73 . . . . . . 233 A2
Langsett Gn 15 SK13 . . . . 9 D1
Langsett Gr 14 SK13. . . . . 9 D1
Langsett La SK13 . . . . 9 D2
Langsett Lea 25 SK13. . . . 9 D1
Langsett Terr 24 SK13 . . . 9 D1
Langtree Ave S41 . . . . 77 A1
Langwith Bassett Prim Sch
NG20. . . . . 119 E7
Langwith Cl NE7. . . . . 194 F5
Langwith Dr NG20 . . . . . 100 F1
Langwith Maltings NG20 119 F8
Langwith Rd
Bolsover S44. . . . . 118 C8
Cuckney S44 . . . . 101 C1
Scarcliffe S44 . . . . 118 F7
Shirebrook NG20 . . . . . 119 F5
Langwith-Whaley Thorns Sta
NG20. . . . . 100 F2
Lansbury Ave
Mastin Moor S43 . . . . 79 B4
Pilsley S45. . . . . 132 C1
Lansbury Ct S21 . . . . 59 D3
Lansbury Dr DE55 . . . . . . 160 A6
Lansbury Rd S21 . . . . 59 D2
Lanscombe Park Rd
DE22. . . . . 204 E1
Lansdowne Ave DE24. . . . 232 F5
Lansdowne Rd
Branston DE14. . . . . 253 F7
Brimington S43 . . . . 96 D7
Buxton SK17 . . . . 66 B1
Swadlincote DE11 . . . . . 256 A3
Lansing Gdns DE21 . . . . . 220 B6
Lantern Gr DE3 . . . . 217 D4
Lantern Pike View SK22 . . 25 A2
Lantern View SK22 . . . . . . 24 B1
Lant La DE4. . . . . 144 B8
Lapwing Cl DE24. . . . . . . 231 E2
Larch Ave
Killamarsh S21 . . . . 60 C5
Mansfield Woodhouse
NG19. . . . . 136 B5
Ripley DE5 . . . . 169 D1
Shirebrook NG20 . . . . . 119 D4
Larch Cl DE22 . . . . 204 D3
Larch Cres NG16 . . . . 182 C6
Larchdale Cl DE55 . . . . . . 160 A4
Larch Dr NG10 . . . . 223 B7
Larch Rd
Eckington S21 . . . . 59 B2
Kilburn DE56 . . . . 192 B7
Swadlincote DE11 . . . . . 255 F6
Larch Way
Chesterfield S40 . . . . 95 D5
Glossop SK13. . . . . 17 F8
Larges St DE1 . . . . 218 E5
Lark Cl DE23 . . . . 231 C6
Larkfields Cres DE55 . . . . 169 F8
Larkhill DE55 . . . . 169 F8
Lark Hill DE3 . . . . 230 B7
Larkhill Cl DE55 . . . . 169 F8
Larkhill Cres DE24 . . . . . 231 F4
Larkin Cl DE24 . . . . 232 A5
Larkland's Ave DE7 . . . . . 209 A7
Larklands Inf Sch DE7. . . 209 A8
Larkspur Cl
Mansfield NG19. . . . . . . 136 D2
South Normanton DE55. . 160 A4
Larkspur Ct DE21 . . . . . . 206 A3
Larkstone La DE6 . . . . . . 149 A1
Larpit Gn S80. . . . . 82 A5
Lascelles Rd SK17. . . . . . . 85 B8
Lashley Gdns DE21 . . . . . 205 F2
Latham Cl DE15 . . . . 248 C2
Lathbury Cl DE21 . . . . . . 205 D1
Lathkil Dr DE55 . . . . 159 F5
Lathkil Gr
Buxton SK17 . . . . 85 D7
Tibshelf DE55 . . . . 147 F6
Lathkill Ave
Derby DE24 . . . . 233 C7
Ilkeston DE7 . . . . 194 E5
Staveley S43 . . . . 97 C6
Lathkill Cl
Sheffield S13. . . . . 44 C7
West Hallam DE7. . . . . . 207 D8
Lathkill Dale DE11 . . . . . 255 F7
Lathkilldale Cres NG10 . . 236 A5

Kin–Lea 293

Lathkill Dale Cvn & Camping
Site DE45 . . . . 107 C2
Lathkill Dale National Nature
Reserve ★ DE45 . . . . . 124 C8
Lathkill Dr
Ashbourne DE6 . . . . 185 E8
Ripley DE5 . . . . 180 D6
Selston NG16 . . . . 171 F7
Lathkill Gr S45. . . . . 131 D1
Lathkill Rd
Derby DE21 . . . . 219 F8
Sheffield S13. . . . . 44 C7
Latimer Cl DE23 . . . . 230 E7
Latimer St DE24 . . . . 232 D6
Latrigg Cl DE73 . . . . 217 E1
Lauder Cl DE24 . . . . 231 E2
Launceston Rd DE24 . . . . 233 B5
Laund Ave DE56 . . . . 179 B6
Laund Cl DE56 . . . . 179 A6
Laund Farm DE56 . . . . . . 179 C6
Laund Farm Mews DE56. 179 C6
Laund Hill DE56 . . . . 179 A5
Laund Nook DE56 . . . . . . 179 A5
Launds Ave NG16 . . . . . . 171 D7
Laurel Ave
Arkwright Town S44 . . . . 97 D3
Mansfield Woodhouse
NG19. . . . . 136 F1
Ripley DE5 . . . . 169 D1
Laurel Cl
Eckington S21 . . . . 59 C2
Shirebrook NG20 . . . . . 119 D6
Swanwick DE55 . . . . . . 170 A8
Laurel Cres
Brimington S43 . . . . 78 A1
Long Eaton NG10 . . . . . . 236 C6
Smalley DE7. . . . . 192 F5
Laurel Dr
Aston-on-T DE72 . . . . . . 246 A7
Killamarsh S21 . . . . 60 C5
Laurel Garth Cl S41 . . . . . 77 B3
Laurel Gr
Burton u T DE15. . . . . . . 254 E5
South Normanton DE55. . 160 A4
Laurence Cl S41 . . . . 77 A2
Laurie Pl DE24 . . . . 232 E7
Lavant Ct 3 S43 . . . . 96 E8
Lavender Cl
Burton u T DE14. . . . . . . 254 A8
Shirebrook NG20 . . . . . 119 D3
Tibshelf DE55 . . . . 148 B7
Lavender Gdns DE75 . . . . 182 B1
Lavender Gr DE65 . . . . . . 170 A8
Lavender Row DE24 . . . . . 204 F1
Lavender Wlk DE55 . . . . . 157 F5
Laverdene Ave S17. . . . . . 55 F5
Laverdene Cl S17 . . . . 55 F4
Laverdene Dr S17. . . . . . . 55 F4
Laverdene Rd S17 . . . . . . 55 F4
Laverdene Way S17 . . . . . 55 F4
Laverick Rd NG16 . . . . . . 171 A4
Laverock Cl NG16 . . . . . . 195 F6
Laverstoke Ct DE22 . . . . . 218 E4
Lawman Gdns DE55 . . . . 158 F4
Lawman Mews DE55 . . . . 159 A4
Lawn Ave
Derby DE22 . . . . 204 D2
Etwall DE65 . . . . 229 C5
Lawn Cl DE75 . . . . 181 F2
Lawnfold SK13. . . . . 9 E4
Lawn Heads Ave DE23 . . . 218 C2
Lawnlea Cl DE23 . . . . 231 E5
Lawn Mill Rd NG16 . . . . . 195 E7
Lawn Prim Sch DE22 . . . . 204 D1
Lawns Dr DE11 . . . . 256 A4
Lawnside DE21 . . . . 220 F5
Lawns The
Aston-on-T DE72 . . . . . . 246 B8
Rolleston DE13 . . . . 240 A4
Uttoxeter ST14 . . . . 210 A2
Lawn The S18 . . . . 57 B2
Lawn Villas S44. . . . . 97 A2
Lawnswood Cl DE23. . . . . 231 C8
Lawrence Ave
Awsworth NG16. . . . . . . 195 C4
Breaston DE72. . . . . 235 D8
Derby DE21 . . . . 220 B7
Eastwood NG16. . . . . . . 182 F2
Holmewood S42. . . . . . . 116 D1
Mansfield Woodhouse
NG19. . . . . 136 B4
Ripley DE5 . . . . 180 C8
Lawrence Dr NG16 . . . . . 182 D8
Lawrence St
Derby DE23 . . . . 231 F8
Long Eaton NG10. . . . . . 236 D8
Sandiacre NG10. . . . . . . 223 B7
Stapleford NG9 . . . . 223 D6
Lawson Ave NG10 . . . . . . 236 E7
Laxfield Cl S40 . . . . 114 C8
Layton Dr S41 . . . . 77 B1
Lea Bank DE55. . . . . 160 A4
Leabrook Rd S18 . . . . 56 C1
Leabrooks Ave NG19 . . . . 136 D5
Leabrooks Rd DE55 . . . . . 170 C6
Lea Cl DE22. . . . . 204 E3
Lea Cres DE55 . . . . 170 C6
Leacroft Rd
Derby DE23 . . . . 219 B1
Winster DE4 . . . . 141 C6
Lea Ct S41. . . . . 266 B4
Leadale Ave S41 . . . . 170 A7
Leadale Cres NG19 . . . . . 136 E5
Leadbeater Dr S12. . . . . . 44 A5
Leadbeater Rd S12. . . . . . 44 A4

Leaden Knowle SK23 . . . 34 C1
Leadhill Rd S40 . . . . 95 A4
Lea Dr
　Derby, Chaddesden
　　DE21 . . . . 219 F6
　Derby, Mickleover DE3 . . 217 E3
Leafenden Cl DE22 . . . . . 205 A3
Leafgreen La DE23 . . . . . 231 C6
Leafield Rd SK12 . . . . 32 C6
Leafy La DE5 . . . . 181 F1
Lea Gdns★ DE4 . . . . 156 A7
Leaholme Est S44 . . . . . . 98 D2
Leake St DE22 . . . . 218 D5
Lea La NG16 . . . . 171 F6
Lea Main Rd DE4 . . . . 156 B8
Leam Glen NG19 . . . . 136 D2
Leamington Cl DE23 . . . . 218 D1
Leamington Dr DE55 . . . . 160 B5
Leamington Rd DE14 . . . . 253 E7
Leamington St DE5 . . . . . 169 F2
Leamoor Ave DE55 . . . . . 170 B8
Lea Moor Rd DE4 . . . . . . 156 E8
Leander Cl DE23 . . . . 231 D2
Leander Ct **5** S43 . . . . 78 F2
Leander Rise DE15 . . . . . 255 A8
Lean Town SK13 . . . . 17 D6
Leaper St DE1 . . . . 218 E6
Leapley La DE6 . . . . 199 D3
Lea Prim Sch DE4 . . . . . . 156 A7
Lea Rd
　Cromford DE4 . . . . 155 D6
　Dronfield S18 . . . . 57 A1
　Hayfield SK22 . . . . 25 C3
　Lea DE4 . . . . 156 A7
Leas Ave NG19 . . . . 135 A5
Leashaw DE4 . . . . 156 C4
Leashaw Rd DE4 . . . . 156 C3
Leas Park Jun Sch NG19 136 C4
Leas Rd NG19 . . . . 136 D4
Lea St SK22 . . . . 33 B8
Leathersley La DE6, DE65 226 C2
Lea Vale DE55 . . . . 160 A4
Leaway The NG20 . . . . . . 119 D3
Lea Wood Croft DE4 . . . . 156 A5
Leawood Gdns DE21 . . . . 206 B3
Leawood Pump Ho★
　DE4 . . . . 155 F4
Leawood Rd DE11 . . . . . . 256 D7
Leche Croft DE56 . . . . . . 179 D4
Lechlade DE7 . . . . 207 D8
Ledbury Chase DE24 . . . . 231 D2
Ledbury Pl **2** DE21 . . . . . 205 D1
Ledo Ave DE5 . . . . 169 D2
Leebangs Rd SK14 . . . . . . 16 A8
Leech Ct NG16 . . . . 195 B7
Lee Cres DE7 . . . . 209 B8
Lee Dale SK17 . . . . 85 C3
Leedhams Croft DE12 . . . 259 D8
Leeds Pl DE1 . . . . 267 D2
Leeds Rd S81 . . . . 63 F7
Lee Farm Cl DE73 . . . . . . 232 F1
Leefield Rd SK23 . . . . 47 B5
Lee Head SK13 . . . . 16 C5
Leek Rd
　Buxton SK17 . . . . 84 E5
　Longnor SK17 . . . . 121 B6
Lee La DE75 . . . . 182 B1
Leeming La NG19, NG20 . 136 E7
Leeming La N NG19 . . . . 136 E5
Leeming La S NG19 . . . . . 136 C2
Leeming Pk NG19 . . . . . . 136 C3
Lee Mount SK13 . . . . 17 C7
Leen Valley Dr NG20 . . . . 119 D3
Lee Rd S41 . . . . 96 E2
Lees Brook Com Sports Coll
　DE21 . . . . 220 B8
Lees Brook Ho DE21 . . . . 220 A7
Lees Hall Ave S8 . . . . 43 B5
Lees Hall Pl S8 . . . . 43 B5
Lees Hall Rd S8 . . . . 43 B4
Lees House Ct S8 . . . . 43 A4
Leeside DE24 . . . . 220 A1
Lees La DE55 . . . . 159 F6
Lees Mill **4** SK22 . . . . . . 33 C7
Lees Nook S8 . . . . 43 A4
Lees Rd DE4 . . . . 126 E3
Lees Row SK13 . . . . 10 C5
Lees The DE72 . . . . 233 D5
Leeswood Cl S41 . . . . 95 D8
Lee Vale Dr SK13 . . . . 16 D7
Leeway DE21 . . . . 220 D4
Legh Rd SK12 . . . . 32 A6
Leicester Dr SK13 . . . . . . 17 F8
Leicester Ho **2** NG9 . . . 223 F8
Leicester St
　Burton u T DE14 . . . . . . 254 C8
　Derby DE22 . . . . 218 E3
　Long Eaton NG10 . . . . . 236 E6
Leigh Rd NG9 . . . . 223 F3
Leighton Dr
　Marple SK6 . . . . 23 C8
　Sheffield S14 . . . . 43 F3
Leighton Pl S14 . . . . 43 F3
Leighton Rd S14 . . . . 43 E4
Leighton View S14 . . . . . . 43 E5
Leighton Way **6** DE56 . . 178 F3
Leigh Way S42 . . . . 131 F7
Leisure La SK17 . . . . 137 E5
Leman St DE22 . . . . 218 E3
Lemon Gr DE11 . . . . 256 B1
Lemont Rd S17 . . . . 55 E4
Leniscar Ave DE75 . . . . . 181 C4
Lens Rd DE22 . . . . 204 C2
Lenthall Inf Sch S18 . . . . . 57 B3
Lenton Ave DE21 . . . . . . 219 F6

Lenton St NG10 . . . . 223 C7
Leominster St DE21 . . . . . 206 B2
Leonard Cheshire Cl
　DE75 . . . . 182 B1
Leonard Cl
　Derby DE23 . . . . 267 B1
　Sheffield S2 . . . . 44 A7
Leonard St DE1 . . . . 267 C1
Leonard Wlk DE23 . . . . . 267 B1
Leopold St
　Derby DE1 . . . . 267 B2
　Long Eaton NG10 . . . . . 236 D8
Leslie Ave NG16 . . . . 195 F6
Leslie Cl DE23 . . . . 230 E8
Lesser La
　Buxton SK17 . . . . 85 F8
　Chapel-en-le-F SK23 . . . 65 D7
Level La SK17 . . . . 84 D5
Leven Cl DE24 . . . . 231 E2
Levens Way S41 . . . . 95 E8
Leveret Cl DE73 . . . . 233 B2
Lewcote La DE7 . . . . 194 A1
Lewis Rd S13 . . . . 44 C7
Lewis St DE23 . . . . 218 F1
Lewiston Rd DE21 . . . . . . 220 B5
Lexington Rd DE21 . . . . . 220 C6
Ley Ave DE55 . . . . 159 B3
Leyburn Cl
　Chesterfield S40 . . . . . . 95 E5
　Swadlincote DE11 . . . . . 256 B1
Leycote Way DE56 . . . . . 178 F5
Ley Croft
　Hatton DE65 . . . . 227 C1
　Mansfield Woodhouse
　　NG19 . . . . 136 D5
Leyfield Rd S17 . . . . 55 D7
Leygate View SK22 . . . . . 33 B8
Ley Gdns DE55 . . . . 159 B4
Ley La
　Mansfield Woodhouse
　　NG19 . . . . 136 D4
　Marple SK6 . . . . 23 D8
Leyland Cl NG9 . . . . 223 F2
Leyland Ct DE1 . . . . 218 E7
Leyland Gdns DE1 . . . . . . 218 E7
Leylands DE22 . . . . 218 E8
Leylands La SK14 . . . . . . 15 F7
Leyland St DE1 . . . . 218 E7
Leys Ct DE56 . . . . 179 D4
Leys Field Gdns DE73 . . . 233 A2
Leys Jun Sch DE55 . . . . . 159 C4
Leys La DE4 . . . . 154 B7
Leys The
　Little Eaton DE21 . . . . . 191 D2
　Swadlincote DE11 . . . . . 255 E6
Leyton Ct S43 . . . . 77 D4
Leytonstone Dr DE22 . . . 218 A5
Lichfield Ave DE11 . . . . . 256 E5
Lichfield Cl NG9 . . . . 223 E3
Lichfield Dr DE24 . . . . . . 233 A7
Lichfield Rd
　Branston DE13, DE14 . . 253 C4
　Chesterfield S40 . . . . . . 114 D8
Lichford Rd S2 . . . . 43 C6
Lickpenny La DE4 . . . . . . 144 E4
Lidgate Cl DE3 . . . . 217 C1
Lid La
　Ashover S45 . . . . 129 A6
　Roston DE6 . . . . 197 E7
Liffey Ho DE24 . . . . 232 E1
Liffs Rd DE6, SK17 . . . . . 150 C7
Light Alders La SK14 . . . . 32 A6
Lightfoot Rd ST14 . . . . . . 210 A1
Lightwood Ave **3** SK17... 85 C8
Lightwood La
　Chesterfield S21 . . . . . . 77 E8
　Eckington, Middle Handley
　　S21 . . . . 58 E1
　Eckington S8 . . . . 43 F1
Lightwood Rd
　Buxton SK17 . . . . 66 B1
　Eckington S21 . . . . 58 E2
Lilac Ave DE22 . . . . 218 A3
Lilac Cl
　Derby DE24 . . . . 233 A6
　Holmewood S44 . . . . . . 116 F2
Lilac Ct DE24 . . . . 233 A6
Lilac Gr
　Bolsover S44 . . . . 99 C1
　Burton u T DE15 . . . . . . 254 F6
　Glapwell S44 . . . . 134 B8
　Heanor DE75 . . . . 181 E1
　Shirebrook NG20 . . . . . 119 E5
　Shirebrook, Warsop Vale
　　NG20 . . . . 120 F7
　South Normanton DE55... 160 A4
Lilac Mews DE7 . . . . 194 D3
Lilac St
　Brimington S43 . . . . 78 B1
　Staveley S43 . . . . 97 A8
Lilac Way
　Derby DE22 . . . . 204 D2
　Shirland DE55 . . . . 146 D1
Lilian Prime Cl DE24 . . . . 233 B8
Lilley Cl NG16 . . . . 171 E4
Lilley St DE24 . . . . 233 B6
Lillymede Cl S40 . . . . 114 F6
Lilybank Cl DE4 . . . . 143 C5
Lilypools The DE73 . . . . . 252 A7
Limb La S17 . . . . 55 D8
Lime Ave
　Derby, Breadsall Hilltop
　　DE21 . . . . 205 D2
　Derby DE1 . . . . 267 A1
　Duffield DE56 . . . . 190 E5
　Langley Mill NG16 . . . . . 182 C2
　New Mills SK22 . . . . 24 D1

Lime Ave continued
　Ripley DE5 . . . . 169 D1
　Staveley S43 . . . . 78 E1
Lime Cl
　Calow S44 . . . . 97 A3
　Doveridge DE6 . . . . 224 B8
　Pinxton NG16 . . . . 160 D3
Lime Cres
　Belper DE56 . . . . 179 B2
　Shirebrook NG20 . . . . . 120 F7
Lime Croft DE22 . . . . 204 F4
Limecroft View S42 . . . . . 115 B3
Lime Ct DE15 . . . . 254 E7
Limedale Ave DE21 . . . . . 206 B3
Lime Gate Mews DE23... 218 D2
Lime Gr
　Ashbourne DE6 . . . . 185 C8
　Burton u T DE15 . . . . . . 254 E5
　Darley Dale DE4 . . . . . . 127 C3
　Derby DE21 . . . . 220 B5
　Draycott DE72 . . . . 234 F7
　Hatton DE65 . . . . 227 D1
　Long Eaton NG10 . . . . . 236 D8
　Sandiacre NG10 . . . . . . 223 B6
　South Normanton DE55... 160 A5
　Stapleford NG9 . . . . 223 D5
Lime Grove Ave DE4 . . . . 143 C5
Lime Grove Wlk DE4 . . . . 143 B5
Limekiln Fields Rd S44... 99 A3
Lime Kiln La
　Marple SK6 . . . . 23 A5
　Turnditch DE56 . . . . 189 B8
　Wensley DE4 . . . . 142 B8
Lime Kilns The DE73 . . . . 252 E1
Limekiln Way S43 . . . . . . 80 C6
Lime La
　Derby DE21 . . . . 206 C3
　Morley DE7, DE21 . . . . . 206 D5
Lime Rd S21 . . . . 59 B2
Limerick Rd DE21 . . . . . . 220 B4
Limes Ave
　Derby DE3 . . . . 217 D1
　Whaley Thorns NG20 . . . 101 A2
Limes Cl The DE4 . . . . . . 143 C5
Limes Cres NG20 . . . . . . 119 D5
Limes Ct **3** DE3 . . . . . . 217 D1
Limes Pk DE4 . . . . 169 C1
Lime St DE7 . . . . 208 F7
Limes The
　Barton in F NG11 . . . . . 237 E6
　Mapperley DE7 . . . . 193 E3
Limestone Cl DE11 . . . . . 257 A4
Limestone Terr NG19 . . . 136 B4
Lime Terr NG10 . . . . 236 D8
Limetree Ave DE11 . . . . . 256 B7
Lime Tree Ave
　Darley Dale DE4 . . . . . . 127 B3
　Glapwell S44 . . . . 134 B8
　Killamarsh S21 . . . . 60 C5
　Mansfield Woodhouse
　　NG19 . . . . 136 A5
Lime Tree Bsns Pk DE4 . . 143 C4
Limetree Cl S43 . . . . 96 F5
Limetree Ct DE7 . . . . 208 C6
Lime Tree Gr
　Arkwright Town S44 . . . . 97 D3
　Clay Cross S45 . . . . 131 E2
Lime Tree Pk SK17 . . . . . 85 D6
Lime Tree Rd DE4 . . . . . . 143 C5
Limetree Rise DE7 . . . . . 208 C6
Lime Wlk DE23 . . . . 218 D1
Linacre Ave S45 . . . . 131 D2
Linacre Rd S40, S42 . . . . 95 A5
Linacre Reservoir Nature
　Trail★ S42 . . . . 94 D3
Linacres Dr DE73 . . . . . . 233 A2
Linacre Way SK13 . . . . . . 17 F7
Linbery Cl DE55 . . . . 158 B4
Lincoln Ave
　Derby DE24 . . . . 233 A8
　Sandiacre NG10 . . . . . . 223 A4
Lincoln Cl
　Stapleford NG9 . . . . 209 E1
　Tibshelf DE55 . . . . 148 A6
Lincoln Dr NG19 . . . . 136 D4
Lincoln Gn DE73 . . . . 232 F2
Lincoln Rd DE15 . . . . 254 D7
Lincoln St
　Alfreton DE55 . . . . 158 F3
　Chesterfield S40 . . . . . . 115 A8
　Tibshelf DE55 . . . . 148 A6
Lincoln Way
　5 Glossop SK13 . . . . . . 17 F8
　North Wingfield S42 . . . 131 F6
　Swadlincote DE11 . . . . . 256 E5
Lindale Rd S41 . . . . 76 E1
Lindale Way DE73 . . . . . . 233 A2
Linden Ave
　Chesterfield S40 . . . . . . 95 B1
　Clay Cross S45 . . . . 131 D2
　Dronfield S18 . . . . 57 B3
Linden Cl DE56 . . . . 192 B8
Linden Ct S45 . . . . 131 D2
Linden Dr S41 . . . . 115 D6
Linden Gr
　Matlock DE4 . . . . 143 C5
　Sandiacre NG10 . . . . . . 223 A4
　Shirebrook NG20 . . . . . 119 F4
　Stapleford NG9 . . . . 223 E6
Linden Park Gr S40 . . . . . 95 D3
Linden Rd S80 . . . . 81 E2
Linden St
　Mansfield NG19 . . . . . . 136 A1
　Shirebrook NG20 . . . . . 119 F4
Linden Way SK6 . . . . 32 A7
Lindford Cl DE21 . . . . . . 205 F3
Lindisfarne Cl **4** DE24... 231 D3
Lindisfarne Ct S40 . . . . . 95 D1

Lindisfarne Rd S18 . . . . . 76 B8
Lindley St NG16 . . . . 171 D6
Lindon Dr DE24 . . . . 233 C6
Lindrick Cl
　Derby DE3 . . . . 217 F1
　Mansfield Woodhouse
　　NG19 . . . . 136 D6
Lindrick Gdns S40 . . . . . 114 C8
Lindrick Way S43 . . . . . . 80 B5
Lindsey Cl DE21 . . . . 219 E6
Lindway La DE55 . . . . . . 145 B1
Lingfield Rd DE14 . . . . . . 253 F7
Lingfield Rise DE3 . . . . . 217 C3
Lingfoot Ave S8 . . . . 57 B6
Lingfoot Cl S8 . . . . 57 B6
Lingfoot Cres S8 . . . . 57 C6
Lingfoot Dr S8 . . . . 57 B6
Lingfoot Wlk S8 . . . . 57 C6
Ling La S44 . . . . 118 C4
Linglongs Ave SK23 . . . . 45 C5
Linglongs Rd SK23 . . . . . 45 C5
Lings La S40 . . . . 114 D8
Lings Cres S42 . . . . 132 A3
Linkmel Rd NG16 . . . . . . 182 C3
Links Cl DE24 . . . . 231 F4
Links Rd
　Chapel-en-le-F SK23 . . . 46 F5
　Dronfield S18 . . . . 76 B8
Links The NG16 . . . . 171 D6
Links View S17 . . . . 66 D1
Linley La S12, S13 . . . . . . 44 E5
Linnet Cl DE21 . . . . 220 F6
Linnet Hill DE3 . . . . 230 C7
Linscott Cl S41 . . . . 95 D7
Linshaws Rd HD9 . . . . . . 3 E5
Linton Heath DE12 . . . . . 261 E6
Linton Prim Sch DE12 . . . 261 D5
Linton Rd
　Chesterfield S40 . . . . . . 114 C8
　Linton DE11 . . . . 261 E7
　Rosliston DE12 . . . . 260 E5
Linwood Cres NG16 . . . . 182 F1
Linwood Ct NG19 . . . . . . 136 E4
Lipp Ave S21 . . . . 60 C7
Liskeard Dr DE22 . . . . . . 204 D4
Lismore Ct **6** DE24 . . . . 231 D3
Lismore Gr SK17 . . . . 85 A7
Lismore Pk SK17 . . . . 85 A7
Lismore Rd
　Buxton SK17 . . . . 85 A7
　Sheffield S8 . . . . 43 B5
Lissett Ave DE7 . . . . 208 F7
Lister Ave S12 . . . . 44 B3
Lister Cl
　Chesterfield S41 . . . . . . 266 B4
　Derby DE3 . . . . 218 B3
　Sheffield S12 . . . . 44 B3
Lister Cres S12 . . . . 44 B3
Lister Dr S12 . . . . 44 B3
Lister Pl S12 . . . . 44 B3
Lister Way S12 . . . . 44 B3
Liston Dr DE22 . . . . 218 F8
Litchen Cl DE7 . . . . 194 F2
Litchfield Cl NG10 . . . . . 237 A7
Litchurch La DE24 . . . . . 219 C2
Litchurch St DE1 . . . . . . 267 C1
Little Acre NG19 . . . . 136 E5
Little Bolehill DE4 . . . . . . 155 A2
Little Breck DE55 . . . . . . 160 A4
Little Brind Rd S40 . . . . . 95 A5
Littlebrook Cl SK13 . . . . . 10 A4
Little Cl DE11 . . . . 256 B5
Littledale Cl DE21 . . . . . . 206 C3
Little Debdale La NG19... 135 F1
Little Derby Hill DE55 . . . 230 B2
Little Eaton Prim Sch
　DE21 . . . . 205 C2
Little Edge S32 . . . . 71 C6
Little Fen DE55 . . . . 147 F5
Littlefield La
　Ellastone DE6 . . . . 183 A2
　Snelston DE6 . . . . 184 B4
Littlefield Rd DE65 . . . . . 227 C7
Littlefields SK14 . . . . 9 A4
Little Hallam Hill DE7 . . . 208 E6
Little Hallam La DE7 . . . . 209 A6
Little La
　Ashford in t W DE45 . . . 89 E1
　Heanor DE75 . . . . 181 A3
　Kimberley NG16 . . . . . . 195 F5
　Litton SK17 . . . . 69 E3
　Pleasley NG19 . . . . 135 B5
　Sheffield, Woodthorpe Estate
　　S12 . . . . 44 B6
　Shirebrook NG20 . . . . . 119 D3
　Sutton in A NG17 . . . . . 148 E2
　Thorpe Salvin S80 . . . . . 63 B6
Little Liverpool DE12 . . . . 260 C1
Little London DE4 . . . . . . 156 A6
Little Longstone DE3 . . . 217 F2
Little Lunnon NG11 . . . . . 237 E6
Little Meadow Rd DE73... 233 A2
Littlemoor
　Chesterfield S41 . . . . . . 95 D7
　Eckington S21 . . . . 59 E4
Littlemoor Bsns Ctr S21... 59 E4
Littlemoor Cres S41 . . . . 95 D7
Littlemoor Ctr **3** SK13 . . 17 C8
Littlemoor Ctr **2** S41 . . . 95 E7
Littlemoor La
　Matlock Bath DE4 . . . . . 143 F1
　Newton DE55 . . . . 148 B4
Littlemoor Rd SK14 . . . . . 9 A2
Little Moorside DE72 . . . . 246 B8
Little Morton Rd S42,
　S45 . . . . 132 A5

Little Norton Ave S8 . . . . 57 A8
Little Norton Dr S8 . . . . . 57 A8
Little Norton La S8 . . . . . 57 A8
Little Norton Way S8 . . . . 57 A8
Littleover Com Sch DE23 230 F8
Littleover Cres DE23 . . . . 218 D1
Littleover La DE23 . . . . . 231 E8
Little Thorn Ind Est
　DE11 . . . . 256 F2
Littlewell La DE7 . . . . . . 208 F2
Little Woodbury Dr DE23 230 F6
Little Wood Dr S12 . . . . . 44 A3
Littlewood La NG19 . . . . 136 A6
Little Wood La S26, S80... 62 A6
Little Wood Rd S12 . . . . . 44 A3
Litton Bank SK13 . . . . . . 9 E3
Litton CE Prim Sch SK17 . 69 E3
Litton Cl
　Belper DE56 . . . . 179 B5
　Ilkeston DE7 . . . . 194 E4
　Staveley S43 . . . . 97 C8
Litton Ct **6** S40 . . . . 95 D5
Litton Dale SK17 . . . . . . 69 D2
Litton Dr DE21 . . . . 220 F3
Litton Fold **16** SK13 . . . . 9 E3
Litton Gdns **17** SK13 . . . . 9 E3
Litton Mews SK13 . . . . . . 9 E3
Litton Rd NG19 . . . . 136 E4
Littonslack SK17 . . . . . . 88 E7
Liverpool St **4** DE21 . . . . 219 E8
Liversage Almshouses
　DE1 . . . . 267 C2
Liversage Pl DE1 . . . . . . 267 C2
Liversage Rd DE1 . . . . . . 267 C2
Liversage St DE1 . . . . . . 267 C2
Livingstone Rd DE23 . . . . 218 E1
Lloyd St DE22 . . . . 218 D5
Loadshead La S42 . . . . . . 112 C4
Loads Rd S42 . . . . 113 B7
Loake Ct **1** DE21 . . . . . . 252 A8
Lochinvar Cl DE21 . . . . . 220 F4
Lock Cl DE7 . . . . 208 C6
Lockington Cl DE73 . . . . 232 F2
Lockington Rd DE74 . . . . 247 D5
Lock La
　Long Eaton NG10 . . . . . 236 C4
　Sandiacre NG10 . . . . . . 223 C4
Locko Ct DE21 . . . . 220 D5
Lockoford La
　Chesterfield, Stonegravels
　　S41 . . . . 96 A4
　Chesterfield, Tapton S41 . 96 C5
Lockoford Rd S41 . . . . . . 96 A5
Locko Hall DE7 . . . . 206 F2
Locko La S45 . . . . 132 E3
Locko Rd
　Derby DE21 . . . . 220 D7
　Pilsley S45 . . . . 132 C4
Lockside SK6 . . . . 23 A6
Lockton Ave DE75 . . . . . 193 E8
Lock Up Yd DE1 . . . . 267 B3
Lockwood Rd DE22 . . . . . 204 D4
Locomotive Way DE24... 219 D3
Lode La DE6 . . . . 149 F4
Lodes La SK17 . . . . 67 C2
Lodge Ave DE6 . . . . 185 B8
Lodge Bank SK13 . . . . . . 10 A3
Lodge Cl
　Calow S43 . . . . 97 A3
　Duffield DE56 . . . . 190 E3
　Etwall DE65 . . . . 229 C4
Lodge Ct SK14 . . . . 9 A4
Lodge Dr
　Belper DE56 . . . . 178 C5
　Wingerworth S42 . . . . . 115 A4
Lodge Est DE72 . . . . 246 B2
Lodge Farm Chase DE56 . 185 B8
Lodge Farm Cl S40 . . . . . 114 C7
Lodge Hill DE13 . . . . 239 E3
Lodge La
　Alstonefield DE6 . . . . . . 149 B3
　Derby DE1 . . . . 267 A4
　Derby, Spondon DE21... 220 D4
　Heanor NG16 . . . . 181 E6
　Mackworth DE6, DE22... 203 C3
　Shottle DE56 . . . . 177 D8
Lodge Mews DE72 . . . . . 246 B7
Lodge Moor Rd S10 . . . . 42 F8
Lodge Pl S43 . . . . 97 C5
Lodge Rd
　Eastwood NG16 . . . . . . 195 A8
　Long Eaton NG10 . . . . . 236 C4
　Nethers, al DE7 . . . . . . 261 D1
Lodge Row DE7 . . . . 193 E3
Lodge St DE72 . . . . 235 A7
Lodge The
　Glossop SK13 . . . . 10 A3
　Tideswell SK17 . . . . 69 C3
Lodge Wlk S43 . . . . 97 C6
Loganberry Ct DE24 . . . . 232 E8
Lohengrin Ct DE13 . . . . . 240 E2
Lomas Cotts SK17 . . . . . 69 C3
Lombard St DE22 . . . . . . 217 F6
Lomond Ave DE24 . . . . . 231 F2
London Ho DE45 . . . . . . 109 C7
London Rd
　Buxton SK17 . . . . 85 C6
　Castle Donington DE72... 247 B8
　Derby DE23, DE24 . . . . 219 D2
　Shardlow DE72 . . . . 234 E1
　Sheffield, Heeley S2 . . . 43 A6
　Sheffield, Highfield S2 . . 43 A4
London Rd S S2 . . . . 43 A7
London St S43 . . . . 77 D3
Longacre Rd S18 . . . . . . 76 A7
Long Acre View S20 . . . . 60 A8
Long Acre Way S20 . . . . . 60 A8

Longbourne Ct NG19 . . . . 136 F2
Longbow Cl DE13 . . . . 240 C1
Longbow Gr DE13 . . . . 240 C1
Longbridge La
  Buxton SK17 . . . . 67 B4
  Heanor DE75 . . . . 181 D3
Long Bridge La DE24 . . . . . 232 D8
Longcliff Wlk ☑ S41 . . . . 95 C6
Longclough Dr SK13 . . . . . . 17 A8
Longcourse La S44 . . . . 98 A2
Long Croft DE72 . . . . . . 246 A8
Longcroft Ave
  Dronfield S18 . . . . 56 C2
  Ilkeston NE7 . . . . 194 E5
Longcroft Cl S42 . . . . 131 C6
Longcroft Cres S18 . . . . . . 56 C2
Longcroft Rd S40 . . . . 114 F7
Longcroft Rd S18 . . . . 56 C2
Longcroft View S80 . . . . 82 A6
Longdale DE4 . . . . 136 E1
Longdale Dr SK14 . . . . 9 A3
Longdale Gdns SK14 . . . . . . 9 A3
Longden Cl NG9 . . . . 209 F2
Longdendale Com Language
  Coll SK14 . . . . 9 C5
Longdons Row DE21 . . . . 220 D5
Long Eaton Sch The
  NG10 . . . . 236 D7
Long Eaton Sch The (Lower
  Site) NG10 . . . . 236 D5
Long Eaton Sta NG10 . . 236 C5
Long Eaton Trade Ctr
  NG10 . . . . 236 F8
Longedge Gr S42 . . . . 115 B3
Longedge La S42 . . . . 114 F3
Longedge Rise S42 . . . . . . 115 A3
Longfield Cres DE7 . . . . . . 208 F5
Long Field Grange S41 . . . 95 C6
Longfield La DE7 . . . . 208 F5
Longford CE Prim Sch
  DE6 . . . . 214 D8
Longford Cl
  Burton u T DE15 . . . . 248 B2
  Derby DE22 . . . . 204 D1
  Sheffield S17 . . . . 56 A5
Longford Cres S17 . . . . . . 56 A5
Longford Dr S17 . . . . 55 F4
Longford La
  Longford DE6 . . . . 214 F7
  Sutton-On-The-Hill DE6 . . 215 A4
Longford Rd S17 . . . . 56 A4
Longford Spinney S17 . . . 55 F4
Longford St DE22 . . . . 218 E8
Long Gallery DE4 . . . . 110 E6
Longhedge La
  Burton u T DE13 . . . . 239 F1
  Pleasley NG19 . . . . 134 E5
Long Hill
  Darley Dale DE4 . . . . 127 C4
  Whaley Bridge SK17, SK23 . . 65 C5
Longhurst La SK6 . . . . 23 C6
Longhurst View S80 . . . . . . 81 F5
Long La
  Alstonefield DE6 . . . . 149 B5
  Ashover S42 . . . . 130 A6
  Broadbottom SK13 . . . . . . 16 C7
  Chapel-en-le-F, Combs SK23 46 C3
  Chapel-en-le-F SK23 . . . . . 47 B4
  Chesterfield S21 . . . . 77 C7
  Holloway DE4 . . . . 156 B6
  Killamarsh S21 . . . . 60 F6
  Kirk Langley DE6 . . . . . . 202 B1
  Longford DE6 . . . . 214 C8
  Shipley DE75 . . . . 194 E7
  Shirebrook NG20 . . . . . . 119 E3
  Taddington SK17 . . . . 87 E5
  Thurvaston DE6 . . . . 201 B1
Longlands S44 . . . . 99 B2
Longlands Dr SK22 . . . . . . 33 B8
Longlands La DE65 . . . . . 230 C1
Longlands Mews DE65 . . 230 C1
Longlands Rd
  New Mills SK22 . . . . 33 B8
  Swadlincote DE11 . . . . . . 256 D7
Longlands Villas DE55 . . 167 F3
Long Lane CE Prim Sch
  DE6 . . . . 201 E1
Longley La DE21 . . . . 220 D6
Longload La DE4 . . . . 154 E5
Long Mdw
  Great Cubley DE6 . . . . . . 198 F1
  Mansfield Woodhouse
  NG19 . . . . 136 D5
Longmeade Dr DE24 . . . . . 47 B4
Long Meadow La SK17 . . 69 E1
Long Meadow Rd DE55 . . 158 F3
Longmoor Gdns ☑
  NG10 . . . . 223 A2
Longmoor La
  Breaston DE72 . . . . 222 E1
  Sandiacre NG10 . . . . 223 B4
Longmoor Prim Sch
  NG10 . . . . 223 C3
Longmoor Rd
  Glossop SK13 . . . . 17 A7
  Long Eaton NG10 . . . . . . 223 B2
Longnor Craft Ctr★ SK17 121 B7
Longnor Gn ☑ SK13 . . . . . . 9 D2
Longnor Mews ☑ SK13 . . . 9 D2
Longnor Way ☑ SK13 . . . . 9 D2
Long Rake DE4 . . . . 123 D4
Longreave La DE45 . . . . . . 90 C4
Longroad SK17 . . . . 66 F7
Longrose La DE6 . . . . 163 B2
Long Row
  Belper DE56 . . . . 178 F4
  Shardlow DE72 . . . . 235 B2

Long Row Prim Sch
  DE56 . . . . 178 F4
Long Shambles S40 . . . . 266 B3
Longshaw Cl
  North Wingfield S42 . . . . 131 F6
  Staveley S43 . . . . 97 D8
Longshaw Ct ☑ S40 . . . . . 95 D5
Longshaw Estate Trail★
  S11 . . . . 54 A4
Longshaw Estate Visitor Ctr★
  S11 . . . . 54 A4
Longshaw Gdns DE24 . . 233 A6
Longshaw Lo S11 . . . . 54 A4
Longside Rd S42 . . . . 112 E6
Long Sleets DE55 . . . . . . 160 B4
Longs Mill ☑ DE1 . . . . . . 267 A4
Longson Rd SK23 . . . . 47 C6
Long St DE15 . . . . 254 E7
Longster La NG20, NG19 . 120 C3
Longstock Cl DE21 . . . . . 205 E1
Longstone Cres S17 . . . . . . 44 D4
Longstone La DE45 . . . . . . 89 F2
Longstone Rise DE56 . . . 179 B6
Longstone Wlk DE1 . . . . . 267 A4
Longthorpe DE23 . . . . . . 231 A7
Longwalls La DE56 . . . . . 178 C6
Longwood Com Inf Sch
  NG16 . . . . 160 C2
Longwood Rd NG16 . . . . . 160 E2
Lonsdale Dr NG9 . . . . 223 E2
Lonsdale Gr DE4 . . . . 142 F7
Lonsdale Pl DE22 . . . . . . 218 D4
Lonsdale Rd
  Burton u T DE14 . . . . 254 B8
  Pilsley S45 . . . . 132 B2
Lons Inf Sch DE5 . . . . 169 D2
Loom Cl DE56 . . . . 179 C5
Loosemore Dr S12 . . . . 43 F5
Lord Haddon Rd DE7 . . . 194 E1
Lord Roberts Rd S40 . . . 266 B1
Lords Cl S44 . . . . 99 A1
Lordsmill St S41 . . . . 266 C2
Lord St
  Derby DE24 . . . . 232 D6
  Glossop SK13 . . . . 10 D1
  Hollingworth SK14 . . . . 9 D4
Lorne Cl S18 . . . . 56 C2
Lornes Dr DE15 . . . . 248 B3
Lorne St DE22 . . . . 218 F3
Lorraine Cl DE24 . . . . . . 232 E3
Loscoe CE Prim Sch
  DE75 . . . . 181 B3
Loscoe Ct ☑ S40 . . . . 95 D5
Loscoe-Denby La DE5,
  DE75 . . . . 181 B4
Loscoe Grange DE75 . . . 181 D3
Loscoe Rd
  Derby DE21 . . . . 206 A1
  Heanor DE75 . . . . 181 D2
Losehill Hall Study Ctr★
  S33 . . . . 38 C4
Lothian Pl
  Castle Donington DE74 . . 247 A3
  Derby DE21 . . . . 219 D7
Lothlorien Cl DE23 . . . . . 231 B7
Loudon St DE23 . . . . 219 A3
Loudoun Pl DE74 . . . . . . 247 A4
Loundes Rd S18 . . . . 76 E6
Loundes Wood Ave S41 . 95 C8
Loundsley Ct S42 . . . . 94 F4
Loundsley Green Rd S40 . 95 C5
Lount La DE13 . . . . 239 E1
Lousie Greaves La DE21 . 220 E6
Louvain Rd DE22, DE23 . 218 D2
Louwil Ave NG19 . . . . 136 E5
Lovatt Cl DE13 . . . . 240 F2
Loveys Croft DE73 . . . . . . 252 E1
Low's La DE7 . . . . 209 B2
Lowburn Rd S13 . . . . 44 C7
Low Cl DE6 . . . . 189 A2
Low Comm S21 . . . . 79 D7
Lowedges Cres S8 . . . . 56 F6
Lowedges Dr S8 . . . . 56 F6
Lowedges Pl S8 . . . . 57 A6
Lowedges Prim Sch S8 . 56 E6
Lowedges Rd S8 . . . . 56 E6
Lower Bagthorpe NG16 . 171 F3
Lower Bank SK13 . . . . 17 D8
Lower Bank Cl SK13 . . . . . . 9 F3
Lower Barn Rd SK13 . . . . . 9 E4
Lower Bloomsgrove Rd
  DE7 . . . . 194 F2
Lower Brook St NG10 . . 236 E7
Lower Burch Pl S32 . . . . . 71 E5
Lower Chapel St
  ☑ Ilkeston DE7 . . . . 194 F1
  Stonebroom DE55 . . . . . 147 B4
Lower Clara Mount Rd
  DE75 . . . . 182 A1
Lower Dale Rd DE23 . . . . 218 F2
Lower Dr DE55 . . . . 169 D7
Lower Dunstead Rd
  Aldercar NG16 . . . . 182 B3
  Langley Mill NG16 . . . . . 182 A3
Lower Eaves View SK23 . . 47 C5
Lower Eley St DE1 . . . . . . 267 A1
Lower Fold SK6 . . . . 23 B8
Lower Gladstone St
  DE75 . . . . 181 E2
Lower Gn DE65 . . . . 230 D1
Lower Granby St DE7 . . . 194 F2
Lower Greenshall La SK12 32 F6
Lower Grove Rd S40 . . . . 266 A3
Lower Hague SK22 . . . . 32 E8
Lower Hall Cl DE56 . . . . . 191 C6

Lower Hardwick St ☑
  SK17 . . . . 85 B8
Lower Higham Visitor Ctr★
  SK14 . . . . 15 A8
Lower High St DE13 . . . . 239 C7
Lower La SK23 . . . . 34 D1
Lowerlea SK12 . . . . 32 C6
Lower Macclesfield Rd
  SK23 . . . . 45 E6
Lower Mantle Cl S45 . . . 131 D4
Lower Maples DE75 . . . . 194 A8
Lower Market St SK14 . . . 16 B8
Lower Meadow Prim Sch
  S8 . . . . 57 A5
Lower Middleton St DE7. 195 A1
Lower Mill ☑ DE5 . . . . . . 169 C1
Lower Nelson St ☑
  DE7 . . . . 181 D2
Lower Orchard St ☑
  NG9 . . . . 223 D7
Lower Park St NG9 . . . . . 223 C6
Lower Rd DE22 . . . . 217 F8
Lower Rock St ☑ S22 . . . . 33 C7
Lower Smithy La SK17. . . . 88 A3
Lower Somercotes DE55 170 E7
Lower St SK13 . . . . 10 A7
Lower St DE6 . . . . 224 B8
Lower Stanton Rd DE7 . . 208 F6
Lower Strines Rd SK6 . . . 23 A5
Lower Terrace Rd SK17 . . 69 B5
Lower Whitworth Rd
  DE7 . . . . 194 F1
Lower Wood Cotts SK17. . 89 A7
Lowes Hill DE5 . . . . 169 D3
Lowes La DE73 . . . . 244 C7
Lowe St S24 . . . . 232 E6
Lowfield Ave S12 . . . . 58 E8
Lowfield Com Prim Sch
  S2 . . . . 43 A7
Lowfield Ct ☑ S2 . . . . 43 A7
Lowfields S43 . . . . 79 A2
Lowgates S43 . . . . 79 A2
Lowlands Lea DE75 . . . . 181 F2
Lowlands Rd DE56 . . . . . 179 B4
Low Lea Rd SK6 . . . . 23 B6
Low Leighton Rd SK22 . . 33 D8
Low Mdw SK23 . . . . 45 D8
Low Pavement S40 . . . . 266 B3
Lowry Ct SK14 . . . . 9 A4
Lowry Dr
  Dronfield S18 . . . . 56 F1
  Marple SK6 . . . . 23 B8
Lows Ct DE73 . . . . 233 B2
Lowside S32 . . . . 72 B2
Lowside Cl S32 . . . . 72 B2
Loxley
  Chesterfield S40 . . . . 95 B3
  Derby DE21 . . . . 206 B2
Loxley La S80 . . . . 82 A5
Loxton Ct DE3 . . . . 217 D3
Loyne Ct DE24 . . . . 231 F2
Lucas La DE65 . . . . 228 C2
Lucas Rd S41 . . . . 95 E5
Lucas Terr SK22 . . . . 25 C3
Lucas Works S18 . . . . 57 A2
Luccombe Dr DE24. . . . . 233 D5
Lucerne Rd DE21 . . . . . . 206 C3
Ludborough Wlk ☑
  NG19 . . . . 136 E4
Ludford Rd NG10 . . . . . . 236 E4
Ludgate St DE13 . . . . 239 C6
Ludgate Wlk DE22 . . . . . 217 E6
Ludham Cl S41 . . . . 95 F7
Ludham Gdns S41 . . . . . . 95 F7
Ludlam Ave NG16 . . . . . . 195 A8
Ludlam Ho S2 . . . . 43 E6
Ludlow Cl DE21 . . . . 220 F5
Ludworth Prim Sch SK6. . 23 B8
Luke La S6 . . . . 201 E8
Lullington Mews DE12 . . 262 A3
Lullington Rd
  Clifton Campville B79 . . 263 E3
  Overseal DE12 . . . . 262 A3
Lulworth Cl DE23 . . . . . . 231 D6
Lulworth Ct NG16 . . . . . . 195 F7
Lum's Hill Rise DE4 . . . . 143 D6
Lumber La DE6 . . . . 176 D2
Lumb La
  Belper DE56 . . . . 178 C4
  Hazelwood DE56 . . . . . . 178 B2
  Northwood DE4 . . . . 127 B6
Lumford Cotts DE45 . . . 109 D7
Lumsdale DE4 . . . . 143 E6
Lumsdale Cres DE4 . . . . 143 D5
Lumsdale Rd
  Matlock DE4 . . . . 143 D4
  Staveley S43 . . . . 97 C8
Lumsdale Terr DE4 . . . . . 143 E6
Luna Croft S12 . . . . 43 F2
Lunch La SK17 . . . . 88 F8
Lundie Cl DE24 . . . . 231 D2
Lundy Rd S18 . . . . 76 B8
Lune Mdw NG19 . . . . 136 E3
Lupin Cl
  Derby DE21 . . . . 206 C3
  Shirebrook NG20 . . . . . . 119 D3
Lupin Way S44 . . . . 97 A3
Lupton Cres S8 . . . . 56 F6
Lupton Dr S8 . . . . 56 F6
Lupton Rd S8 . . . . 56 F6
Lupton Wlk S8 . . . . 57 A6
Lychgate Cl DE21 . . . . . . 205 D2
Lydden Cl S43 . . . . 96 E8
Lydford Ave S41 . . . . 77 B1
Lydford Rd DE55 . . . . 159 B5
Lydgate S23 . . . . 71 E5
Lydgate Cotts S33 . . . . . . 40 A6
Lydgate Dr S42 . . . . 114 E3

Lydgate La S33 . . . . 40 A6
Lydia Gdns NG16 . . . . . . 182 E1
Lydstep Cl DE21 . . . . 206 C2
Lyle Cl NG16 . . . . 195 E7
Lymefield Terr SK14 . . . . . 16 B7
Lymefield Visitor Ctr★
  SK14 . . . . 16 B8
Lyme Pk
  Chinley SK23 . . . . 34 E2
  Disley SK23 . . . . 32 B1
Lyme Rd SK12 . . . . 32 A6
Lyme Park Ctry Pk★ SK12 32 B2
Lymewood Dr SK12 . . . . . 32 C6
Lynam Rd DE5, DE56 . . . 168 D7
Lyncroft Ave DE5 . . . . . . 169 E1
Lyndale Dr DE5 . . . . 181 B8
Lynden Ave NG10 . . . . . . 236 D5
Lyndhurst Gr DE21 . . . . . 220 A5
Lyndhurst St DE23 . . . . . 219 A2
Lyne Ave SK13 . . . . 17 A8
Lynholmes Rd DE4 . . . . . 143 D5
Lynholmes Rise DE4 . . . 143 D5
Lynmouth Dr DE7 . . . . . . 194 D3
Lynmouth Ho DE65 . . . . 228 C1
Lynne Cl SK13 . . . . 17 F8
Lynton Cl DE5 . . . . 169 D3
Lynton Ct ☑ S41 . . . . 95 F8
Lynton Rd DE5 . . . . 168 A3
Lynton St DE22 . . . . 218 E4
Lynwood Cl
  ☑ Dronfield S18 . . . . 56 D1
Lynwood Rd
  Branston DE14 . . . . 253 E8
  Derby DE24 . . . . 231 F4
Lysander Dr DE73 . . . . . . 232 E1
Lytham Cl DE21 . . . . 205 D1
Lyttelton St DE22 . . . . . . 218 C5

M

M1 Commerce Pk S44 . . . 98 B4
McAdam Cl DE15 . . . . . . 248 B2
MacAulay St DE24 . . . . . 232 A5
McAuley St DE24 . . . . . . 267 B4
Macclesfield Main Rd
  SK17 . . . . 84 D5
Macclesfield Old Rd SK17 84 D6
Macclesfield Rd
  Buxton SK17 . . . . 85 A6
  Horwich End SK23 . . . . . . 45 D6
MacDonald Cl S42 . . . . . 115 F3
MacDonald Sq DE7 . . . . 208 D5
McGough Mews DE24 . . 232 A5
McGregor's Way S40 . . . 115 B7
Machins Ct S18 . . . . 57 A2
Mackenzie St DE22 . . . . 218 C5
Macklin St DE1 . . . . 267 B3
Mackinley Ave NG9 . . . . 209 E1
Macklin St DE1 . . . . 267 B3
Mackworth Cl DE11 . . . . 256 B7
Mackworth Rd DE1, DE22 218 E6
McMahon Ave S43 . . . . . . 97 B6
Macnair Cl SK6 . . . . 23 A5
Macnair Mews SK6 . . . . . . 23 A5
McNeil Gr DE72 . . . . 235 A7
Macready Pl DE24 . . . . . 232 F7
Maddock La DE4 . . . . 153 A1
Madehurst Gdns S2 . . . . . 43 B7
Madehurst Rd S2 . . . . 43 B7
Madehurst Rise S2. . . . . . 43 B7
Madehurst View S2 . . . . . 43 B7
Madeley Cl DE3 . . . . 217 D1
Madeley St DE23 . . . . . . 219 A2
Madin Dr S43 . . . . 97 B6
Madin St
  Chesterfield S41 . . . . . . 266 B4
  Tupton S42 . . . . 131 D8
Madison Ave DE21 . . . . . 219 F7
Madras Rd DE15 . . . . 248 C3
Magdala Cotts DE56 . . . 190 E5
Magee Ct DE21 . . . . 267 C1
Mag La
  Creswell NG20 . . . . 100 D5
  Idridgehay DE56 . . . . . . 176 D5
Magnolia Way DE55 . . . . 170 A8
Maguire Ave SK13 . . . . . . 10 A6
Maidstone Dr DE24 . . . . 232 F5
Maidwell Cl DE56 . . . . . 179 C6
Main Ave
  Derby DE22 . . . . 204 F5
  Sheffield S17 . . . . 55 E4
Main Bright Rd ☑ NG19. 136 B1
Main Bright Wlk NG19. . 136 B1
Main Dr S42 . . . . 114 C2
Maine Dr DE21 . . . . 220 A6
Main Rd
  Bamford S33 . . . . 40 B3
  Bradwell S33 . . . . 51 A8
  Brailsford DE6 . . . . 201 F7
  Chesterfield, Ashgate S42. . 94 E8
  Chesterfield, West Handley
  S21 . . . . 77 D7
  Crich DE4 . . . . 156 D1
  Cutthorpe S42 . . . . 94 E8
  Eckington, Lightwood S21. . 58 F3
  Eckington, Ridgeway S12 . . 58 E8
  Elvaston DE72 . . . . 234 A6
  Flagg SK17 . . . . 106 E6
  Grindleford S32 . . . . 72 C7
  Hathersage S32 . . . . 53 A8
  Heath S44 . . . . 117 B2
  Holmesfield S18 . . . . 75 A8
  Jacksdale NG16 . . . . 171 B3
  Mayfield DE6 . . . . 184 D8
  Renishaw S21 . . . . 79 B8
  Ripley S5 . . . . 169 A3
  Ripley, Pentrich DE5 . . . 169 C5

Main Rd continued
  Shirland DE55 . . . . 146 D1
  Smalley DE7 . . . . 192 F3
  Somercotes, Leabrooks
  DE55 . . . . 170 C7
  Somercotes, Pye Bridge
  DE55 . . . . 170 F6
  Stonebroom DE55 . . . . . 147 A5
  Sudbury, Aston DE6 . . . . 226 A4
  Sudbury DE6 . . . . 225 F4
  Taddington SK17 . . . . 88 A3
  Underwood Green NG16 . 171 F2
  Unstone S18 . . . . 76 E7
  Wensley DE4 . . . . 127 C1
  Whaley Thorns NG20 . . . 101 A1
Main St
  Awsworth NG16 . . . . 195 C5
  Biggin SK17 . . . . 138 C3
  Blackfordby DE11 . . . . . . 257 C1
  Bolsover S44 . . . . 117 F8
  Bradbourne DE6 . . . . 163 B6
  Branston DE14 . . . . 253 F7
  Breaston DE72. . . . . 235 D8
  Breedon on t H DE73 . . . 252 F2
  Brinsley NG16 . . . . 171 D1
  Burnaston DE65 . . . . 229 F5
  Burton u T, Stapenhill
  DE15 . . . . 254 E8
  Burton u T, Stretton DE13 254 E1
  Caldwell DE12 . . . . 260 F7
  Calver S32 . . . . 72 C1
  Chelmorton SK17 . . . . . . 106 A8
  Church Broughton DE65 . 227 B8
  Clifton Campville B79 . . . 263 F2
  Eastwood NG16 . . . . 182 F1
  Egginton DE65 . . . . 241 B5
  Elton DE4 . . . . 140 E6
  Elvaston DE72 . . . . 234 D6
  Etwall DE65 . . . . 229 B4
  Findern DE65 . . . . 230 D1
  Great Longstone DE45. . . 90 A4
  Hartshorne DE11 . . . . . . 257 B6
  Hemington DE74 . . . . . . 247 D5
  Hilton DE65 . . . . 228 C2
  Horsley Woodhouse DE7 . 192 C6
  Kimberley NG16 . . . . 195 F6
  King's Newton DE73 . . . . 245 C1
  Kirk Ireton DE6 . . . . 165 B1
  Linton DE12 . . . . 261 D6
  Lockington DE74 . . . . . . 247 F5
  Long Eaton NG10 . . . . . . 236 E7
  Longford DE6 . . . . 214 D8
  Mapperley DE7 . . . . 193 E3
  Middleton DE4 . . . . 154 D4
  Moira DE11 . . . . 256 C1
  Netherseal DE12 . . . . . . 264 F7
  Newton DE55 . . . . 148 A4
  Newton Solney DE15 . . . 248 E8
  Over Haddon DE45 . . . . . 109 A1
  Overseal DE12 . . . . 262 B3
  Palterton S44 . . . . 118 A5
  Repton DE65 . . . . 242 D1
  Rosliston DE12 . . . . 260 D6
  Scarcliffe S44 . . . . 118 E6
  Shirebrook NG20 . . . . . . 119 E3
  Smisby LE65 . . . . 257 F3
  South Normanton DE55. . 160 B6
  Stanton-by-D DE7 . . . . . 222 F8
  Sutton in a N NG17 . . . . 148 F3
  Swadlincote DE11 . . . . . 255 E6
  Tatenhill DE13 . . . . 253 A8
  Ticknall DE73 . . . . 251 B4
  Ticknall, Milton DE65 . . . 243 A1
  Walton-on-T DE12 . . . . . 253 D1
  Weston-on-T DE72 . . . . . 245 E5
  Whaley Thorns NG20 . . . 101 A2
  Wilson DE73 . . . . 252 E6
  Winster DE4 . . . . 141 C6
Mais Cl DE4 . . . . 144 A5
Maisies Way DE55 . . . . . 160 C6
Maize Cl DE23 . . . . 231 A6
Majolica Mews DE11 . . . 256 F2
Makeney Rd
  Belper DE56 . . . . 191 A6
  Duffield DE56 . . . . 190 F2
  Holbrook DE56 . . . . 191 C6
Makeney Terr DE56 . . . . 191 A6
Malbon's Yd DE6 . . . . . . 173 C1
Malcolm Gr DE23 . . . . . . 230 E8
Malcolm St DE23 . . . . . . 219 B2
Malham Cl S40 . . . . 95 D5
Malham Gdns S20 . . . . . . 59 D7
Malham Gr S20 . . . . 59 E7
Malham Rd DE23 . . . . . . 230 F6
Malia Rd S41 . . . . 96 C6
Malin Cl DE24 . . . . 233 B5
Malinder Cl S21 . . . . 60 D6
Malinscommon La DE56. 166 C4
Malkin St S41 . . . . 266 C3
Mallard Cl NG20 . . . . 119 E3
Mallard Ct ☑ S43 . . . . 78 F2
Mallard Dr S21 . . . . 60 B7
Mallard Wlk DE3 . . . . . . 230 C8
Mallatratt Pl NG19 . . . . . 136 B4
Mallory Cl S41 . . . . 76 E3
Mall The S45 . . . . 131 C3
Malmesbury Ave DE11. . 256 D6
Malpas Rd DE14 . . . . 143 B6
Malson Way S41 . . . . 95 F6
Maltby Ave DE55 . . . . . . 146 E5
Maltby Cl ☑ DE22. . . . . . 204 F2
Malthouse Cl
  Eastwood NG16 . . . . 182 F1
  Wirksworth DE4 . . . . 154 F3

Malthouse Ct
- **4** Ashbourne DE6 . . . . . . .173 C2
- Chesterfield S41 . . . . . . .266 B4

Malthouse La
- Ashover S45 . . . . .129 F3
- Boylestone DE6 . . . . .213 C4
- Froggatt S32 . . . . .72 C5
- Hatton DE65 . . . . .227 D3
- Nether Heage DE56 . . . . . .168 B2
- Wingerworth S42 . . . . . . .114 C3

Malthouse Rd
- Ilkeston DE7 . . . . .208 F4
- Whitwell S80 . . . . .82 A6

Maltings The
- **2** Ashbourne DE6 . . . . . . .173 B2
- Burton u T DE15 . . . . . . .248 A1
- Derby DE1 . . . . .267 B2
- Derby DE22 . . . . .218 D6
- Shardlow DE72 . . . . .235 B1

Malton Pl DE7 . . . . .205 D1
Malton Wlk S40 . . . . .114 F7
Malvern Ave DE15 . . . . . .248 A1
Malvern Cl DE3 . . . . .217 D3

Malvern Gdns
- **5** Long Eaton NG10 . . . . .236 A8
- Matlock DE4 . . . . .143 B6

Malvern Rd S40 . . . . .95 E4
Malvern Rise SK13 . . . . . . .10 A5
Malvern Way **3** DE21 . . .205 D1
Manchester La DE11 . . . . .257 C5

Manchester Rd
- Buxton SK17 . . . . .65 F1
- Chapel-en-le-F SK23 . . . . . .46 E5
- Glossop SK13, SK14 . . . . . . .9 E7
- Tideswell SK17 . . . . .69 B5

Manchester St
- Derby DE22 . . . . .218 D6
- Long Eaton NG10 . . . . . . .236 D6

Mandarin Way DE24 . . . . .232 F8
Manifold Ave
- Ashbourne DE6 . . . . .173 C1
- Staveley S43 . . . . .97 D8
Manifold Dr DE24 . . . . . .233 B8
Manitoba Way NG16 . . . . .171 F7
Manknell Rd S41 . . . . .96 A8
Manners Ave DE7 . . . . . . .194 D1
Manners Cl SK23 . . . . .34 D2
Manners Ind Est DE7 . . . . .194 C1
Manners Rd DE7 . . . . .194 E1
Manners St DE7 . . . . .209 A6
Manning View DE7 . . . . . .194 F2
Mannion Cres NG10 . . . . .236 B5

Manor Ave
- Brimington S43 . . . . .96 F7
- Derby DE23 . . . . .218 C3
- Stapleford NG9 . . . . .223 D8
Manor Bglws **4** S18 . . . . .56 F1

Manor Cl
- Brassington DE4 . . . . .153 A1
- Newton DE55 . . . . .148 A3
- Pilsley S45 . . . . .132 D1
- Swadlincote DE15 . . . . . . .255 A6
Manor Coll F Ed Ctr S40 266 A3
Manor Court Rd S44 . . . . . .98 F3

Manor Cres
- Burton u T DE15 . . . . . . .255 A6
- Chesterfield S40 . . . . .95 D3
- Dronfield S18 . . . . .56 F1

Manor Croft
- Ripley DE5 . . . . .169 D3
- Tatenhill DE13 . . . . .253 A8

Manor Ct
- Barrow u T DE73 . . . . . . .244 B5
- Breaston DE72 . . . . .235 E8
- Breedon on t H DE73 . . . .252 F3
- Clowne S43 . . . . .80 F3
- Risley DE72 . . . . .222 D4
- Somercotes DE55 . . . . . . .170 E5
- South Wingfield DE55 . . . .157 E3

Manor Dr
- Brimington S43 . . . . .96 F7
- Chesterfield S40 . . . . .95 D3
- Netherseal DE12 . . . . .264 F6
Manor Farm S45 . . . . .132 D1
Manor Farm Barns DE21 . .205 E3
Manor Farm Cotts DE45 . . .89 C4

Manor Farm Ct
- Killamarsh S21 . . . . .60 D5
- Whitwell S80 . . . . .81 F6

Manor Farm Mews
- Aston-on-T DE72 . . . . . . .246 B8
- Burnaston DE65 . . . . .229 F5
- Long Duckmanton S44 . . . .98 A3
Manor Farm Rd DE72 . . . . .246 B8
Manor Fields Dr DE7 . . . . .208 D7
Manor Gr S43 . . . . .80 A6
Manor House Rd NG10 . . . .236 F6
Manor Inf Sch S43 . . . . . . .96 F5

Manor La
- Fritchley DE55 . . . . .168 F8
- South Wingfield DE55 . . . .157 F1
Manorleigh DE72 . . . . . . .235 E8
Manor Leigh DE72 . . . . . . .235 E8
Manor Park Ct DE3 . . . . . .218 B3
Manor Park Rd SK13 . . . . . .10 E1
Manor Park View SK13 . . . .10 E2
Manor Park Way DE3 . . . . .218 B3
Manor Pk DE72 . . . . .221 B1

Manor Rd
- Ashbourne DE6 . . . . .173 D3
- Barlborough S43 . . . . .80 A7
- Barton in F NG11 . . . . . . .237 E6
- Belper DE56 . . . . .178 F3
- Borrowash DE72 . . . . . . .221 A1
- Calow S43 . . . . .96 F6

Manor Rd continued
- Chellaston DE73 . . . . . . .232 F1
- Chesterfield S40 . . . . .95 C3
- Derby DE23 . . . . .218 C2
- Eastwood NG16 . . . . .182 F1
- Harthill S26 . . . . .61 F8
- Horwich End SK23 . . . . . . .45 E5
- Ilkeston DE7 . . . . .194 E1
- Killamarsh S21 . . . . .60 E5

Manor Sch The NG19 . . . . .136 C5
Manor St SK13 . . . . .10 D1

Manor View
- Hartshorne DE11 . . . . . . .257 B6
- Sheffield S20 . . . . .59 E7
Manse Ave S80 . . . . .100 D8
Manse Cl S80 . . . . .100 D8
Mansfeldt Cres S41 . . . . . .95 E6
Mansfeldt Rd S41 . . . . . . .95 E6
Mansfield Cl DE11 . . . . . . .256 D4
Mansfield Dr S12 . . . . .44 C6
Mansfield Prep Sch
- NG19 . . . . .136 C3

Mansfield Rd
- Alfreton DE55 . . . . .159 B4
- Bramley-Vale S44 . . . . . . .117 E1
- Brinsley NG16 . . . . .182 F4
- Chesterfield S41 . . . . .115 F6
- Clowne S43 . . . . .80 E2
- Creswell S80 . . . . .81 F1
- Derby DE1, DE21 . . . . . . .267 B4
- Eastwood NG16 . . . . .182 F4
- Glapwell NG19, S44 . . . . . .134 C8
- Heanor DE75 . . . . .182 A2
- Heath S44 . . . . .117 A3
- Holmewood S42 . . . . .116 C3
- Killamarsh S21 . . . . .60 F6
- Mansfield Woodhouse
    NG19 . . . . .136 C2
- Palterton S44 . . . . .118 B6
- Scarcliffe S44 . . . . .118 E5
- Selston NG16 . . . . .171 F7
- Sheffield S12 . . . . .44 B6
- Shirebrook NG20 . . . . . . .120 F1
- South Normanton DE55 . . .160 D6
- Tibshelf DE55 . . . . .148 B7
- Whitwell S80 . . . . .82 F7
Mansfields Croft DE65 . . .229 B4

Mansfield St
- Derby DE1 . . . . .267 B5
- Somercotes DE55 . . . . . . .170 C8
Mansfield View S12 . . . . . .44 B6
Mansfield Woodhouse Sta
- NG19 . . . . .136 A3

Manton Cl
- **2** Burton u T DE13 . . . . . .240 F1
- Swadlincote DE15 . . . . . . .255 F6
Manvers Ave **2** DE5 . . . . .169 E1

Manvers Ct
- Chesterfield S41 . . . . .266 B4
- Shirebrook NG20 . . . . . . .120 A4
Manvers Rd S44 . . . . .97 A4

Manvers St
- Mansfield Woodhouse
    NG19 . . . . .136 A3
- Ripley DE5 . . . . .169 E1
- Shirebrook NG20 . . . . . . .120 A4
Manystones La DE4 . . . . . .153 B3

Maple Ave
- Derby DE23 . . . . .231 D6
- Disley SK12 . . . . .33 A6
- Ripley DE5 . . . . .180 C8
- Sandiacre NG10 . . . . .223 B7
Maplebeck Ct DE1 . . . . . . .267 B5

Maple Cl
- Doveridge DE6 . . . . .211 B1
- Mansfield NG19 . . . . .136 E1

Maple Dr
- Ashbourne DE6 . . . . .185 D7
- Aston-on-T DE72 . . . . . . .246 A7
- Belper DE56 . . . . .179 B2
- Chellaston DE73 . . . . . . .233 A2
- Creswell S80 . . . . .81 E2
- Derby, Boulton DE24 . . . . .233 A6
- Killamarsh S21 . . . . .60 C5
- South Normanton DE55 . . .160 B4

Maple Gdns
- **1** Heanor DE75 . . . . .181 D1
- Langley Mill NG16 . . . . . .182 B3

Maple Gr
- Breaston DE72 . . . . .235 E8
- Burton u T DE15 . . . . . . .254 E5
- Derby DE22 . . . . .204 D5
- Glapwell S44 . . . . .134 C4

Maple Rd
- Castle Donington DE74 . . .247 A5
- Swadlincote DE11 . . . . . . .256 B6
Maple St S43 . . . . .97 B8
Maples The DE75 . . . . . . .194 A7
Mapletoft Ave NG19 . . . . .136 A5
Mapleton Ave DE21 . . . . . .205 F1

Mapleton Rd
- Ashbourne DE6 . . . . .173 B2
- Draycott DE72 . . . . .235 A8
Maple View DE4 . . . . .143 C3

Maple Way
- Branston DE14 . . . . .253 F8
- Burton u T DE14 . . . . . . .254 A8
- Selston NG16 . . . . .171 F7
Mapperley CE Prim Sch
- DE7 . . . . .193 E3
Mapperley La DE7 . . . . . . .193 E2
Mapperley Rd S18 . . . . . . .56 C1
Marchington Cl DE22 . . . .204 E1
Marchwood Cl S40 . . . . . . .95 E4

Marcie Ct DE65 . . . . .242 D2
Marcus St DE1 . . . . .219 A7
Mardale Cl S41 . . . . .76 E1
Marebrook Cvn Pk DE4 . . .156 C2
Maree Cl DE24 . . . . .231 E4
Marfleet Cl DE3 . . . . .217 D3

Margaret Ave
- Derby DE21 . . . . .219 F5
- Ilkeston DE7 . . . . .208 F8
- Long Eaton NG10 . . . . . . .223 F1
- Sandiacre NG10 . . . . .223 B4
Margaret St DE1 . . . . .267 B5
Margery Cl DE6 . . . . .185 D8
Margreave Rd DE21 . . . . . .219 F7
Marigold Cl DE21 . . . . . . .206 B3
Marigold Pl DE11 . . . . . . .256 F4

Marina Dr
- Derby, Allenton DE24 . . . .232 E5
- Derby, Spondon DE21 . . . .220 D5
Marina Rd DE7 . . . . .193 B8
Marine Dr S41 . . . . .96 C3
Marion Ct SK17 . . . . .85 C6
Marjorie Rd DE21 . . . . . . .219 F8
Marjory La DE6, DE65 . . . . .213 C2
Mark's Cl DE23 . . . . .231 D6
Markeaton La DE22 . . . . . .218 B8
Markeaton Prim Sch
- DE22 . . . . .218 E7
Markeaton St DE22 . . . . . .218 E6
Market Arc **2** SK13 . . . . . .10 C1
Market Cl
- Hope S33 . . . . .39 A4
- Shirebrook NG20 . . . . . . .119 F3
- South Normanton DE55 . . .160 A6
Market Head DE56 . . . . . .179 A3

Market Pl
- Alfreton DE55 . . . . .158 F4
- **5** Ashbourne DE6 . . . . . . .173 C2
- Belper DE56 . . . . .179 A3
- Bolsover S44 . . . . .99 A1
- **7** Buxton SK17 . . . . .85 B7
- Castleton S33 . . . . .38 C2
- Chapel-en-le-F SK23 . . . . . .47 B6
- Chesterfield S40 . . . . .266 B3
- Codnor DE5 . . . . .181 B8
- Compstall SK6 . . . . .15 A2
- Crich DE4 . . . . .156 F1
- Cromford DE4 . . . . .155 A6
- Derby DE1 . . . . .267 B3
- Hartington SK17 . . . . .137 D5
- **1** Heanor DE5 . . . . .181 E1
- Ilkeston DE7 . . . . .208 E8
- Ironville NG16 . . . . .170 F4
- Long Eaton NG10 . . . . . . .236 E8
- Longnor SK17 . . . . .121 B6
- Mansfield Woodhouse
    NG19 . . . . .136 C3
- Melbourne DE73 . . . . . . .252 B7
- Mottram in L SK14 . . . . . . .9 A3
- Ripley DE5 . . . . .169 D1
- Somercotes DE55 . . . . . . .170 C8
- Somercotes, Riddings
    DE55 . . . . .170 E6
- South Normanton DE55 . . .160 A6
- Staveley S43 . . . . .78 E2
- Sutton in A NG17 . . . . . . .148 F3
- Tideswell SK17 . . . . .69 C4
- Wirksworth DE4 . . . . .165 F8
Market Sq SK17 . . . . .69 C4

Market St
- Bakewell DE45 . . . . .109 D6
- Broadbottom SK14 . . . . . . .16 A8
- Buxton SK17 . . . . .85 B7
- Castle Donington DE74 . . .247 B3
- Chapel-en-le-F SK23 . . . . . .47 C6
- Clay Cross S45 . . . . .131 D4
- Disley SK12 . . . . .32 D6
- Draycott DE72 . . . . .235 A7
- Eckington S21 . . . . .59 E3
- Glossop SK13 . . . . .10 C1
- Hayfield SK22 . . . . .25 D3
- Heanor DE75 . . . . .181 E1
- Hollingworth SK14 . . . . .9 D5
- Ilkeston DE7 . . . . .208 F8
- Ironville NG16 . . . . .170 F4
- Mottram in L SK14 . . . . . . .9 A4
- New Mills SK22 . . . . .33 B7
- Shirebrook NG20 . . . . . . .119 F4
- South Normanton DE55 . . .160 A5
- Staveley S43 . . . . .78 E2
- Sutton in A NG17 . . . . . . .148 F3
- Swadlincote DE11 . . . . . . .256 A7
- Whaley Bridge SK23 . . . . . .45 E7
Market View **15** SK17 . . . . .85 B7
Markham Cres S43 . . . . . . .78 F2

Markham Ct
- Derby DE21 . . . . .205 F2
- Duckmanton S44 . . . . .98 A5
Markham La S44 . . . . .98 B4
Markham Quay S41 . . . . . .266 C2

Markham Rd
- Chesterfield S40 . . . . .266 B2
- Long Duckmanton S44 . . . .98 B5
Markham Ret Pk S40 . . . . .266 B2
Markham Rise S45 . . . . . . .131 B4
Markland Ave S43 . . . . .81 A4
Markland Cres S43 . . . . . . .81 A4
Markland La S80, S43 . . . . . .81 A2
Markland View S80 . . . . . . .81 B3
Mark St NG10 . . . . .223 C5
Marlborough Cres DE15 . .255 A8
Marlborough Dr DE56 . . . .179 C5

Marlborough Rd
- Breaston DE72 . . . . .235 D7
- Buxton SK17 . . . . .85 B8
- Derby DE24 . . . . .232 C7
- Long Eaton NG10 . . . . . . .223 F1
- Mansfield NG19 . . . . .135 F1

Marlow Brow SK13 . . . . . . .10 A4
Marlow Cres DE7 . . . . .207 D8
Marlow Dr DE14 . . . . .254 A8
Marlowe Ct DE23 . . . . . . .231 F6

Marlow St
- **5** Buxton SK17 . . . . .85 C8
- **5** Glossop SK13 . . . . .10 A5
Marlpit La
- Bolsover S44 . . . . .99 C3
- Denstone ST14 . . . . .196 D6
- Ellastone DE6 . . . . .183 A3
- Sutton on H DE6 . . . . . . .228 A8
Marlpool Inf Sch DE75 . . . .194 A8
Marlpool Jun Sch DE75 . . .182 A1
Marple Rd S18 . . . . .16 B5
Marples Ave NG19 . . . . . . .136 E5
Marple Sta SK6 . . . . .23 A7
Marquis Ct DE12 . . . . .262 E5
Marquis Dr DE12 . . . . .262 E5
Marquis Gdns DE73 . . . . . .244 E8
Marrison Dr S21 . . . . .60 C6
Marsden Cl DE56 . . . . .190 E3
Marsden Pl **2** S40 . . . . . . .95 D2
Marsden Row S33 . . . . .40 B4

Marsden St
- Chesterfield S40 . . . . .266 B3
- Derby DE24 . . . . .232 E7
- Glossop SK13 . . . . .10 A4
Marshall Dr **1** NG9 . . . . . .223 F8

Marshall St
- Alfreton DE55 . . . . .159 A3
- Heanor DE75 . . . . .181 F2
Marshall Way DE7 . . . . . . .208 C6
Marsham Dr SK6 . . . . .23 A5

Marsh Ave
- Dronfield S18 . . . . .57 B3
- Hope S33 . . . . .38 F4
Marshaw Cl DE3 . . . . .217 E1
Marsh Cl S20 . . . . .59 C6
Marshes The S33 . . . . .38 E4
Marshfield Gr S43 . . . . .79 A2
Marshgreen Cl DE24 . . . . .233 D5
Marsh Green La S45 . . . . . .129 F4
Marsh Hall La SK23 . . . . . . .46 F5
Marsh Hollow DE6 . . . . . .200 F5

Marsh La
- Belper DE56 . . . . .179 B5
- New Mills SK22, SK23 . . . . .33 D6
Marsh Lane Cres S18 . . . . . .57 E3
Marsh Lane Prim Sch S21 58 E3
Marsh Lane Trad Est
- SK22 . . . . .33 D7
Marsh View S21 . . . . .59 B2

Marston Cl
- Belper DE56 . . . . .179 C6
- Derby DE23 . . . . .231 D5
- Dronfield S18 . . . . .75 D8
Marstone Cres S17 . . . . . . .55 F5

Marston La
- Doveridge DE6 . . . . .211 B1
- Doveridge DE6 . . . . .211 D4
- Hatton DE65 . . . . .239 D8
- Marston on D DE65 . . . . . .228 B1
- Rolleston DE13 . . . . .240 A4
Marston Montgomery Prim
- Sch DE6 . . . . .211 E8
Marston Old La DE65 . . . . .239 D8
Marston Rd DE65 . . . . .240 A8
Marston Rise DE15 . . . . . .254 F8
Martin's La DE13 . . . . .238 A4
Martin Ct S21 . . . . .59 C3
Martindale Cl S43 . . . . .97 C8
Martindale Ct DE56 . . . . . .179 D5
Martin Dr DE21 . . . . .220 A8
Martin Rise S21 . . . . .59 C3
Martins La S42 . . . . .131 B8
Martlet Ave SK12 . . . . .32 C6
Marx Ct S45 . . . . .131 C3
Mary Ann St S41 . . . . .76 E4
Mary Devonshire Cotts
- DE45 . . . . .91 C2
Mary Howitt Inf Com Sch
- DE75 . . . . .181 D2
Maryland Ct
- Stapleford NG9 . . . . .209 E1
- Swadlincote DE11 . . . . . . .256 A7
Maryland Rd DE21 . . . . . . .220 B6
Marylebone Cres DE22 . . .218 A6
Mary St
- Eckington S21 . . . . .59 D3
- Whaley Thorns NG20 . . . . .101 A2
Mary Swanwick Com Prim
- Sch S41 . . . . .77 A3
Masefield Ave
- Derby DE23 . . . . .231 E7
- Holmewood S42 . . . . .116 D1
- Swadlincote DE11 . . . . . . .256 C6
Masefield Rd S13 . . . . .44 C6
Mason Cres
- Sheffield S13 . . . . .44 D6
- Swadlincote DE11 . . . . . . .256 E4
Mason Gr S13 . . . . .44 D7
Mason Rd DE7 . . . . .194 D2
Masons Cotts S21 . . . . .59 A1
Masons Gr SK13 . . . . .10 A6
Masons Place Bsns Pk
- DE21 . . . . .219 D6
Mason St S80 . . . . .81 F6
Masson Cl **12** S40 . . . . .95 D5
Masson Hill View DE4 . . . .142 F7
Masson Mills Working
Textile Mus DE4 . . . . . .155 A7
Masson Rd DE4 . . . . .143 A7

Masson Shopping Village
- DE4 . . . . .155 A7
Masson Terr DE4 . . . . .144 A5
Masson Wlk DE22 . . . . . . .218 A6
Mastin Ave S43 . . . . .80 D5
Mather's Way S42 . . . . . . .115 D1
Matlock Bank **8** SK13 . . . . . .9 E1
Matlock Bath Sta DE4 . . . .143 B1
Matlock Cl NG10 . . . . .235 F5
Matlock Dr S43 . . . . .97 C5
Matlock Farm Pk ★ DE4 .128 D5
Matlock Gdns **5** SK13 . . . . . .9 E1
Matlock Gn DE4 . . . . .143 C4
Matlock Ho DE21 . . . . .220 E3
Matlock La **7** SK13 . . . . .9 E1
Matlock Pl **6** SK13 . . . . .9 E1

Matlock Rd
- Ambergate DE56 . . . . .167 C5
- Ashover S42, S45 . . . . .113 E3
- Belper DE56 . . . . .178 E8
- Brackenfield DE55 . . . . . . .145 C2
- Derby DE21 . . . . .205 F1
- Holymoorside S42, S40 . . . .114 B7
- Wessington DE55 . . . . . . .157 E8
Matlock Riverside Sta ★
- DE4 . . . . .143 A4
Matlock St DE45 . . . . .109 D5
Matlock Sta DE4 . . . . .143 B5
Mattersey Ct **4** NG19 . . . . .136 B1
Matthew Cl SK13 . . . . .9 E1
Matthew Kirtley Mus ★
- DE5 . . . . .170 A4
Matthews Ct NG9 . . . . .209 E1
Matthews Fold S8 . . . . .43 C1
Matthews La S8 . . . . .43 C1
Matthew St DE24 . . . . .232 F6
Matthew Way DE23 . . . . . .230 E7
Matt Orch DE55 . . . . .160 B4
Maugerhay S8 . . . . .43 C1
Maunleigh NG19 . . . . .136 E1
Mawfa Ave S14 . . . . .43 D2
Mawfa Cres S14 . . . . .43 D2
Mawfa Dr S14 . . . . .43 D2
Mawfa Rd S14 . . . . .43 D2
Mawfa Wlk S14 . . . . .43 D2
Mawkin La NG16 . . . . .160 F5
Maws La NG16 . . . . .195 E2
Mawstone La DE45 . . . . . .125 B3
Maxey Pl S8 . . . . .43 B4
Max Rd DE21 . . . . .219 F8
Maxwell Ave DE22 . . . . . . .218 D8
Maxwell St DE72 . . . . .235 F8
May Ave S41 . . . . .77 C3
Maybank Cl SK23 . . . . .35 A1
Mayfair DE11 . . . . .255 E6
Mayfair Cres DE22 . . . . . . .217 F6
Mayfair Ct DE56 . . . . .190 E4

Mayfield Ave
- Heanor DE75 . . . . .181 E1
- Kilburn DE56 . . . . .192 A8
Mayfield DE6 . . . . .184 C3

Mayfield Dr
- Burton u T DE15 . . . . . . .255 A8
- North Wingfield S42 . . . . .131 F6
- Stapleford NG9 . . . . .209 F2
Mayfield Gr NG10 . . . . . . .223 E1

Mayfield Rd
- Burton u T DE15 . . . . . . .248 A5
- Chesterfield S40 . . . . .95 C2
- Derby DE21 . . . . .219 E2
- Marple SK6 . . . . .15 B1
- Sheffield S10 . . . . .42 F7
Mayfield Terr
- Hathersage S32 . . . . .53 A8
- Mayfield DE6 . . . . .184 D6
Mayflower Ct
- Sheffield S12 . . . . .44 B6
- Shirebrook NG20 . . . . . . .119 E4
Mayflower Rd NG16 . . . . . .195 B8
Mayhall Ave NG19 . . . . . . .136 A4
Maylands DE72 . . . . .221 B1
Maylands Ave DE72 . . . . . .235 E8

Maynard Rd
- Chesterfield S40 . . . . .266 A1
- Grindleford S32 . . . . .53 D1
Maynestone Rd SK23 . . . . . .34 E5
Maypole Hill DE11 . . . . . . .256 A6
Maypole La DE23 . . . . .230 E7
May S DE7 . . . . .194 D3

May St
- Derby DE22 . . . . .218 F3
- Ilkeston DE7 . . . . .194 E4
Maytree Cl DE21 . . . . .206 C3
Mayvale Gr DE22 . . . . .218 C4
Mead Cl DE24 . . . . .231 F4
Mead Cres DE15 . . . . .255 A6

Meadow Ave
- Buxton SK17 . . . . .67 B5
- Codnor DE5 . . . . .181 B8
Meadow Bank
- Glossop SK13 . . . . .16 F7
- Hollingworth SK14 . . . . .9 D6
- Mansfield Woodhouse
    NG19 . . . . .136 C6
- South Normanton DE55 . . .160 A4
Meadowbank Ct NG16 . . . .182 D3
Meadowbank Way NG16 . . .182 D3
Meadow Brook Cl DE23 . . .230 F6
Meadowbrook Ind Est
- S20 . . . . .60 A8

Meadow Cl
- Barlborough S43 . . . . .80 C6
- Bolsover S44 . . . . .118 A8
- Chesterfield S43 . . . . .77 D2
- Derby DE21 . . . . .220 E4
- Dove Holes SK17 . . . . .47 E1
- Draycott DE72 . . . . .235 A7

Meadow Cl continued
Dronfield S18 57 C4
Eastwood NG16 182 F4
Findern DE65 230 D2
Horsley Woodhouse DE7 192 D6
Repton DE65 242 E2
Stoney Middleton S32 72 B3
Tibshelf DE55 148 B7
Whaley Bridge SK23 45 C8
Meadow Cotts NG19 136 C3
Meadow Cres
Castle Donington DE74 247 B2
Sheffield S20 59 B7
Meadowcroft SK14 9 A4
Meadow Croft S42 132 D8
Meadowcroft Gdns S20 59 E8
Meadowcroft Glade S20 59 E8
Meadowcroft Rise 2 S20 59 E8
Meadow Ct
Belper DE56 178 F4
Chesterfield S43 77 D4
5 Derby DE3 217 D1
Elvaston DE72 234 D6
Kilburn DE56 192 A7
South Normanton DE55 159 F4
Meadow End DE4 165 E7
Meadow Farm Com Prim Sch DE21 220 A4
Meadowfield SK23 45 D8
Meadowfield Cl SK13 9 F3
Meadowgate Pk S21 60 D7
Meadow Gdns DE75 182 B1
Meadow Gr
Newton DE55 148 A3
Sheffield S17 55 E4
Meadowgrass Cl DE23 231 B6
Meadow Grove Rd S17 55 D4
Meadowhead S8 56 F8
Meadow Head Ave S8 56 F8
Meadow Head Cl S8 56 E7
Meadow Head Dr S8 56 F8
Meadowhead Sch S8 57 A7
Meadowhill Rd S41 115 D8
Meadow La
Burton u T DE13 248 A8
Derby, Chaddesden DE21 219 F5
Derby DE1, DE21 267 D3
Disley SK12 32 D6
Dove Holes SK17 47 E2
Hilton DE65 228 C1
Long Eaton NG10 236 F7
Newton DE55 159 F7
Repton DE65 243 A4
Roston DE6 197 C7
Shirebrook NG19, NG20 119 D2
Swadlincote DE11 256 A6
Tideswell SK17 69 B2
Meadowlands S44 99 C2
Meadow Lane Ind Est DE55 159 B5
Meadowlark Gr DE21 206 A1
Meadow Nook DE24 233 C5
Meadow Rd
Awsworth NG16 195 C5
Clay Cross S45 131 A5
Derby DE1 267 C3
Derby, Wilmorton DE21, DE24 219 F1
Ripley DE5 169 E1
Meadow Rise
Brassington DE4 153 A1
Chesterfield S42 94 F4
Church Broughton DE65 227 B8
Glossop SK13 16 F7
Meadows Com Sch The S41 77 B3
Meadows Croft DE56 190 D3
Meadows Dr S43 97 F8
Meadowside
Disley SK12 33 A6
Mayfield DE6 184 D6
Whaley Bridge SK23 45 D8
Meadowside Cl
Shirley DE6 200 D8
Wingerworth S42 115 B4
Meadows Ind Est The DE21 219 D5
Meadows Prim Sch DE56 190 D3
Meadows Rd SK22 25 D2
Meadow St
Ilkeston DE7 194 F1
Ironville NG16 170 F5
New Mills SK22 33 C8
Meadows The
Chesterfield S42 95 A5
Dove Holes SK17 47 F1
Great Longstone DE45 90 A4
3 Heanor DE75 181 E1
Killamarsh S21 60 D6
Swanwick DE55 169 F7
Uttoxeter ST14 210 A2
Meadow Vale DE56 190 D3
Meadow View
Belper DE56 178 F3
Bolsover S43 80 F3
Chesterfield S40 114 A8
Darley Dale DE4 142 F7
Doveridge DE6 224 C8
Holmewood S42 132 D8
Rolleston DE13 240 C4
South Wingfield DE55 157 F5
Meadow View Cl DE21 206 B3
Meadow View Ct DE72 222 E4
Meadow View Rd
Sheffield S8 56 F8
Swadlincote DE11 255 F5
Meadow Way
Chellaston DE73 233 A1
Swadlincote DE11 256 A6
Meads The S8 57 B8
Mead The S41 115 C8
Meadway Dr S17 55 D7
Meadway The S17 55 D7
Mead Wlk DE15 255 A6
Meakin St S41 115 D8
Meal Hill Rd HD9 2 F8
Meal St SK22 33 C8
Mear Dr DE72 221 B1
Mear Greaves La DE15 248 B4
Mease La B79 263 B2
Mease The DE65 228 E1
Measham Rd
Appleby Magna DE12 265 F1
Donisthorpe DE12 265 D6
Moira DE12 262 F3
Meath Ave DE21 220 B4
Meden Ave NG19 134 F7
Meden Bank NG19 135 B5
Meden Cl NG19 135 B5
Meden Rd NG19 136 D4
Meden Sq NG19 135 B5
Medina Cl DE24 233 D5
Medlock Cl S40 114 B7
Medlock Rd S40 114 C8
Medway Dr DE22 205 B5
Meerbrook Cl DE21 206 A1
Meerbrook Pl DE7 208 C5
Meersbrook Park Rd S8 43 A5
Meersbrook Rd S8 43 B5
Meersbrook Works 13 S2 43 A6
Meersdale S2 43 C6
Megaloughton La DE21 220 C3
Megdale DE4 143 A6
Melandra Castle Rd SK13 9 D2
Melandra Ct DE22 218 E4
Melandra Rd SK13 9 E3
Melanie Cl SK13 17 A8
Melbourn Cl DE56 190 E3
Melbourne Ave
Burton u T DE15 248 C3
Dronfield S18 56 B1
Melbourne Cl
Belper DE56 179 A2
Derby DE22 204 D2
Derby, Mickleover DE3 217 F3
Melbourne Ct
Derby DE24 219 E4
Long Eaton NG10 235 F4
8 Staveley S43 78 E2
Melbourne Hall & Gdns* DE73 252 C7
Melbourne Ho DE21 220 E3
Melbourne Inf Sch DE73 252 A7
Melbourne Jun Sch DE73 252 A7
Melbourne La
Breedon on t H DE73 252 E1
Ticknall DE73 251 C5
Melbourne Rd NG9 209 E1
Melbourne St
Derby DE1 267 B1
Mansfield Woodhouse NG19 136 C6
Melbreak Cl DE3 217 E1
Melfort Cl DE24 231 F2
Melling Cl S40 114 F8
Melling Ct S40 114 F8
Mellington Cl S8 43 C2
Mellor's La DE56 191 C6
Mellor Dr ST14 210 B1
Mellor La
Barlow S18 75 E1
Chapel-en-le-F SK23 47 A6
Mellor Prim Sch SK6 23 C6
Mellor Rd
Burton u T DE14 254 B7
New Mills SK6, SK22 24 C3
Mellors Rd NG19 135 D1
Mellor St DE24 232 E6
Mellor Way S40 115 A7
Melrose Cl
Chesterfield S40 95 D3
Derby DE24 231 E2
Melrose Ct 7 S41 96 A6
Meltham La S41 96 B6
Melton Ave
Derby DE23 231 C6
Melbourne DE73 252 A8
Melton Ct
Derby DE22 218 E6
Sandiacre NG10 223 A5
Somercotes DE55 170 C6
Melville Cl DE6 175 F3
Melville Cres S43 96 F4
Melville Ct DE65 229 B3
Melville Dr S2 44 A8
Memorial Croft DE4 154 F3
Memorial Pl SK17 67 C5
Memorial Rd DE22 204 C3
Mendip Cl 1 NG10 223 A1
Mendip Cres S40 95 B4
Mendip Ct DE21 205 E2
Menin Rd DE22 204 C2
Mentmore Cl DE55 170 A7
Mercaston Cl S40 95 A5
Mercaston La
Hulland Ward DE6 188 B4
Mackworth DE6, DE22 203 B8
Mercaston Rd DE21 219 F8
Mercer Cres DE55 159 C3
Merchant Ave DE21 220 D4
Merchants Cnr DE22 218 E6
Merchant St
Derby DE22 218 E6
Merchant St continued
Shirebrook NG20 120 A4
Mercia Cl
Eastwood NG16 195 A8
Hatton DE65 239 D8
Mercia Dr
Sheffield S17 55 E6
Willington DE65 242 B5
Mercian Cl DE7 194 E1
Mercian Mews DE21 220 D4
Mercian Pk DE7 194 E1
Mere Beck DE72 234 D6
Meredith Ct NG9 209 E2
Mereoak La DE11, DE73 257 E7
Mereside Gdns SK23 45 D6
Meridian Cl DE7 194 E4
Merion Gr DE23 218 A1
Merlin Ave S44 98 F3
Merlin Cl DE56 179 C5
Merlin Cres DE14 253 F8
Merlin Gn DE24 231 D4
Merlin Way
Burnaston DE3 230 B7
Ilkeston DE7 208 F4
Woodville DE11 256 F3
Merrial Cl DE45 109 C4
Merrick Cl S40 95 D5
Merridale Rd DE23 231 C8
Merrill Coll DE24 232 F4
Merrill Coll (Lower Site) DE24 232 E6
Merrill Way DE24 232 D5
Merrybower Cl DE24 231 D3
Merrydale Rd DE15 255 A8
Mersey Bank Rd SK13 9 F4
Merthyr Ct DE21 206 B2
Merton Cl 2 DE75 181 F1
Merton Ct NG9 209 E1
Mervyn Rd DE15 248 A3
Messiter Mews DE65 242 B5
Metcalfe Ave S21 60 C6
Metcalfe Cl DE24 233 B8
Meteor Ctr The DE21 205 C1
Methley Cl S12 43 F6
Metro Ave DE55 148 A3
Mettesford DE4 143 D5
Meverill Rd SK17 69 D5
Mevril Rd SK23 45 E5
Mevril Springs Way SK23 45 E5
Mewies Cl DE12 253 D1
Mews Ct DE3 217 D4
Mews The
Burton u T DE14 254 C8
Horsley Woodhouse DE7 192 C7
Little Eaton DE56 191 B2
Melbourne DE73 252 A7
New Mills SK22 33 D8
Wyaston DE6 185 B2
Meynell Cl
Burton u T DE15 248 B1
Chesterfield S40 95 C2
Meynell Ct
Derby DE22 204 C2
Kirk Langley DE6 202 F2
Meynell Rd NG10 236 D5
Meynell Rise DE6 173 C4
Meynell St
Derby DE23 218 F1
Swadlincote DE11 256 A1
Meynell Way S21 60 C6
Michael's La DE6 183 C5
Michael Cl S42 115 A5
Michael House Sch DE75 194 A6
Michelle Cl DE24 231 C3
Michigan Cl DE21 220 C5
Michlow Cl S33 51 A8
Michlow Dr S33 51 A8
Michlow La S33 51 A8
Micklebring Cl DE5 169 C1
Micklecroft Gdns DE23 230 E7
Mickledon Cl 1 NG10 236 B8
Mickleover Ho DE3 230 D8
Mickleover Manor DE3 217 C1
Mickleover Prim Sch DE3 217 D2
Mickleross Cl DE3 217 D4
Mickleton Cl DE11 256 B1
Mickley Inf Sch DE55 146 C4
Mickley La
Sheffield S17, S18 55 F4
Shirland DE55 146 C5
Middlebeck Cl DE73 232 F2
Middle Cl DE11 256 B4
Middlecroft L Ctr S43 97 D7
Middlecroft Rd S43 97 D7
Middlefield Cl S17 55 C7
Middlefield Croft S17 55 C7
Middlegate Field Dr S80 82 A5
Middle Hay Cl S14 43 E4
Middle Hay Pl S14 43 E4
Middle Hay Rise S14 43 E4
Middle Hay View S14 43 E4
Middle La
Clay Cross S45 131 E3
Crich DE4 156 D1
Middle Mdw S81 63 E7
Middle Mill 2 DE1 267 A4
Middle Orchard St NG9 223 D7
Middle Ox Cl S20 59 F6
Middle Ox Gdns S20 59 F6
Middle Pavement S40 266 B3
Middle Rd S42 114 E1
Middle Row SK17 89 A7
Middle Shambles S40 266 B3
Middle St
Bolsover, Hillstown S44 118 C8
Bolsover S44 99 A1
Middle St continued
Stanton in Peak DE4 126 C5
Middleton Ave
Codnor DE5 181 B6
Derby DE23 218 C2
Middleton Com Sch DE4 154 D4
Middleton Dr
Derby DE23 218 C2
Staveley S43 97 B5
Middleton La S32 71 D3
Middleton Rd
Ilkeston DE7 209 A5
Mansfield Woodhouse NG19 136 C5
Middleton St
Awsworth NG16 195 C4
Cossall DE7 195 A1
Derby DE23 219 A1
Middleton Top Visitor Ctr* DE4 154 D3
Middleton Way DE55 170 C7
Middletown Mdws S43 80 A6
Midhill Rd S2 43 B7
Midland Ave NG9 223 D5
Midland Cotts
5 Chesterfield S41 115 B7
Grindleford S32 53 D2
Pleasley NG19 135 A6
Rowsley DE4 110 F1
Midland Ct
Barlborough S43 80 A5
6 Chesterfield S41 115 B7
Midland Pl DE1 267 D2
Midland Railway Butterley* DE5 169 F4
Midland Railway Ctr The* DE5 169 E4
Midland Rd
Chapel-en-le-F SK23 47 A6
Derby DE1 267 D1
Eastwood NG16 182 F2
Heanor DE75 181 E2
Swadlincote DE11 256 B4
Midland Road Ind Est DE11 256 B4
Midland St NG10 236 E8
Midland Terr
Ambergate DE56 167 F4
Barrow Hill S43 78 B4
Blackwell DE55 147 C1
4 Chesterfield S41 115 B7
New Mills SK22 33 C7
Midland View
7 Belper DE56 178 F3
North Wingfield S42 131 F7
Midland Way S43 80 A5
Midway DE22 204 E2
Midway Ctr S45 131 D4
Midway Rd DE11 256 C5
Mikado Rd NG10 236 C5
Milbank Cl DE22 217 E6
Milburn Gdns DE21 206 B3
Milbury Cl DE21 205 F2
Mile Ash La DE22 204 F1
Milford DE45 109 D6
Milford Ave NG10 223 B3
Milford Com Prim Sch DE56 190 F7
Milford Ct DE45 109 D6
Milford Dr DE7 194 D3
Milford Rd
Duffield DE56 190 E4
Staveley S43 97 C5
Milford St 4 DE1 218 F7
Milford The DE22 218 F5
Milken La S45 130 B4
Milking La S43 80 B3
Mill DE72 235 A1
Mill Acre Cl DE7 194 D2
Millash La S80 82 B4
Millbank DE75 194 A8
Millbank Ave DE56 179 B2
Millbank Cl DE7 194 D3
Mill Bank Ct S32 53 A8
Mill Bank Dr ST14 197 A3
Millbrook SK14 9 D6
Millbrook Ho SK14 9 E6
Mill Brow
2 Broadbottom SK14 16 A8
Marple SK6 23 D8
Mill Brow Rd SK6 23 E8
Mill Cl
Borrowash DE72 221 C1
Findern DE65 230 D2
Kilburn DE56 192 A7
Newton Solney DE15 248 E8
Swadlincote DE11 256 C5
Swanwick DE55 169 F7
Mill Cliff SK17 85 C7
Mill Cres
Whitwell S80 82 A6
Wingerworth S42 115 C3
Mill Croft DE3 217 D4
Millcross La S18 75 E3
Mill Ct SK13 10 C1
Milldale Ave SK17 84 F6
Milldale Cl
Chesterfield S40 95 C5
Ripley DE5 180 D6
Milldale Ct
Ashbourne DE6 185 D8
Belper DE56 179 B3
Milldale Rd
Derby DE21 220 F3
Long Eaton NG10 236 B6
Sheffield S17 55 F5
Milldam La DE6 186 E7
Millenium Ave DE12 262 E5
Millenium Ct NG19 135 E2
Millennium Cl DE7 194 E3
Millennium Way
Chesterfield S41 76 F1
Derby DE24 219 E4
Miller Ave S43 79 C4
Millers Ct DE1 267 B4
Millersdale Ave DE7 194 E5
Millersdale Cl DE15 248 B5
Millers Dale Cl DE56 179 C5
Millersdale Ct 3 SK13 10 F1
Millers Dale Dr DE55 160 A7
Millersdale Way SK17 85 B6
Millers Gn DE4 165 E6
Millers La DE55 145 E2
Mill Farm Cl S32 72 C1
Millfield DE72 235 B2
Millfield Cl DE7 194 C3
Millfield Croft 1 DE11 256 B7
Millfield Mobile Home Pk S42 130 F5
Millfield Rd
Ilkeston DE7 209 A7
Kimberley NG16 195 E7
Millfield St DE11 257 A2
Mill Fleam DE65 228 E1
Mill Gate DE22 218 E6
Mill Gn
Shardlow DE72 235 A1
Staveley S43 78 E2
Mill Green Way S43 80 E4
Mill Hill
Elvaston DE24 233 C4
Long Duckmanton S44 117 B6
Repton DE65 242 E1
Mill Hill Cl DE5 169 F1
Mill Hill Dr DE15 248 B4
Mill Hill La
Breaston DE72 222 E1
Burton u T DE15 248 B4
Derby DE1, DE23 267 B1
Mill Hill Rd DE23 267 A1
Mill Hil Sch DE5 180 F8
Mill Holme DE55 160 B4
Millhouse Ct DE72 235 B7
Mill La
Ashbourne DE6 173 F1
Atlow DE6 175 A7
Ault Hucknall S44 133 C8
Barlow S18 75 D4
Belper DE56 179 B3
Bolsover S44 99 A3
Bradbourne DE6 163 B6
Castleton S33 38 C3
Chesterfield S40 95 D2
Clay Cross S42, S45 130 F5
Clay Cross S45 131 B2
Codnor DE5 181 B8
Cossall NG16 195 C1
Derby DE3 217 D4
Doveridge DE6 211 A1
Dronfield S18 57 B1
Ellastone DE6 183 B2
Eyam S32 71 E5
Grassmoor S42 115 D3
Hartington SK17 137 D5
Heath S44 117 B1
Hilton DE65 228 C2
Holloway DE4 156 A5
Holmesfield S18 74 F5
Pinxton NG16 160 D1
Renishaw S21 60 A2
Roston DE6 197 D7
1 Sandiacre NG10 223 C6
Scropton DE65 226 F1
Scropton, Foston DE65 226 D7
Sheffield S17 55 F5
Shirley DE6 200 D7
Shuttlewood S44 98 F8
Somercotes DE55 170 C7
Sudbury DE6 225 E1
Sutton in A NG17 148 F1
Whitwell S80 82 A6
Mill Meadow Way DE65 229 B4
Mill Moor Cl DE73 232 F2
Millom Pl DE21 205 D1
Mill Pond Ave SK22 24 D1
Mill Pond Cotts DE4 155 A7
Millpool Cl DE11 257 A7
Mill Rd
Cromford DE4 155 B6
Eckington S21 59 E4
Heanor DE75 194 A8
Stapleford NG9 223 D8
Mill Row DE21 220 D5
Mills Cl DE72 235 A7
Mills Croft DE6 164 B1
Mills Ct DE4 156 F1
Mill St
Bakewell DE45 109 D6
Barlow S18 75 D3
Belper DE56 179 A4
Chesterfield S41 266 C3
Clowne S43 80 E3
Coton in t E DE12 260 D3
Derby DE1 218 E6
Glossop SK13 10 D1
Hayfield SK22 25 D3
Ilkeston DE7 194 F1
Rocester ST14 197 A3
Somercotes DE55 170 C8
Stoney Middleton S32 72 A3
Millstone Cl 1 S18 56 D2
Millstone La
Ashford in t W DE45 108 F7

Millstone La continued
Ripley DE5 . . . . 169 C8
Mill Stream Cl S40 . . . . . . 95 C1
Millthorpe La S18 . . . . 75 A6
Milltown SK13 . . . . 10 D1
Mill View DE56 . . . . 178 F5
Millway NG19 . . . . 136 D1
Millway La DE6 . . . . 149 F3
Mill Wlk
Bolsover S44 . . . . 99 A3
Whitwell S80 . . . . 82 A6
Mill Yd DE55 . . . . 170 C8
Milnbank Ave SK17 . . . . . 85 D8
Milner Ave
Codnor DE5 . . . . 181 B8
Draycott DE72 . . . . 235 A7
Milner Rd NG10 . . . . 236 D8
Milnhay Rd NG16 . . . . . . 182 C2
Milton Ave
Alfreton DE55 . . . . 159 C4
Ilkeston DE7 . . . . 194 E4
Shirland DE55 . . . . 146 C4
Swadlincote DE11 . . . . . . 256 C6
Milton Cl DE3 . . . . 217 C3
Milton Cres S40 . . . . 115 A7
Milton [12] SK17 . . . . 85 B7
Milton La SK23 . . . . 46 B5
Milton Pl S43 . . . . 78 F2
Milton Rd
Ilkeston DE7 . . . . 194 E4
Repton DE65 . . . . 242 D2
Milton St
Derby DE22 . . . . 218 D4
Ilkeston DE7 . . . . 194 E4
Long Eaton NG10 . . . . . . 236 D7
Milton Terr NG10 . . . . . . 236 D7
Milward Rd DE75 . . . . . . 181 D2
Mimosa Cres DE23 . . . . 231 E5
Miners Hill DE4 . . . . 153 A1
Minimum Terr S40 . . . . . 266 A2
Minninglow La DE4 . . . . 151 F8
Minster Rd DE21 . . . . . . 205 E2
Minster Way DE55 . . . . . 169 E7
Mint Gr NG10 . . . . 236 A7
Minton Rd DE74 . . . . 246 F4
Miracle Cl DE45 . . . . 109 D6
Mires La
Great Longstone DE45 . . . 90 B4
Tideswell SK17 . . . . 70 A3
Mires The
Birchover DE4 . . . . 126 A1
Wetton DE6 . . . . 149 A3
Miriam Ave S40 . . . . 114 A8
Miry La DE65 . . . . 227 C4
Misterton Cl DE21 . . . . . 204 E2
Misterton Ct [3] NG19 . . 136 B1
Mistletoe Dr DE11 . . . . . 256 F2
Mitcham Wlk DE22 . . . . 218 A6
Mitchell Ave NG16 . . . . 182 A4
Mitchells Cl DE65 . . . . . 229 A4
Mitchell St
Clowne S43 . . . . 80 F4
Long Eaton NG10 . . . . . . 236 E7
Mitchell Terr DE7 . . . . . 209 A5
Mitchell Villas S43 . . . . 77 E3
Mitchell Way S43 . . . . . . 77 E3
Mitre Dr DE65 . . . . 242 C2
Moat Bank DE15 . . . . . . 248 D2
Moat St DE11 . . . . 256 B1
Moat The DE74 . . . . 247 B4
Model Village S80 . . . . . 100 E8
Model Village Prim Sch
NG20 . . . . 119 E3
Moffatt Rd S2 . . . . 43 B7
Moira Cl DE21 . . . . 220 A7
Moira Dale DE74 . . . . . . 247 C3
Moira Furnace Mus ★
DE12 . . . . 262 E3
Moira Rd
Donisthorpe DE12 . . . . . 262 F1
Moira DE11 . . . . 262 E8
Overseal DE12 . . . . 262 B3
Woodville DE11 . . . . 256 E2
Moira St DE73 . . . . 252 A7
Moisty La
Marchington ST14 . . . . . 224 C3
Stoney Middleton S32 . . . 71 B3
Molineux Ave S43 . . . . . 78 D1
Molineux St DE23 . . . . . 219 B2
Molloy Pl [1] S8 . . . . 43 A6
Molloy St [10] S8 . . . . . . 43 A6
Molyneux Bsns Pk DE4 . 127 B3
Monarch Dr DE21 . . . . . 206 D3
Monarch Way DE75 . . . . 181 D2
Moncreiff Dr DE21 . . . . . 241 A1
Moncrieff Cres DE21 . . . 220 A8
Mondello Dr DE24 . . . . . 233 C6
Monk's Rd SK13 . . . . 17 A4
Monk Rd DE55 . . . . 159 B2
Monks Cl
Derby DE24 . . . . 231 C3
Ilkeston DE7 . . . . 209 A8
Monksdale Cl SK17 . . . . 69 B4
Monksdale La SK17 . . . . 68 F2
Monk's Dale (Nature Reserve) ★ SK17 . . . . . 68 E2
Monk St
Derby DE22 . . . . 267 A2
Tutbury DE13 . . . . 239 C7
Monks Way S81 . . . . 63 F7
Monkton Cl DE7 . . . . 194 D3
Monkwood Rd S41 . . . . . 95 D8
Monmouth St DE21 . . . . 220 A7
Monnies End S43 . . . . . . 80 D5
Monsal Ave SK17 . . . . . . 85 D7

Monsal Cres
Staveley S43 . . . . 97 C6
Tibshelf DE55 . . . . 147 F6
Monsaldale Cl
Burton u T DE15 . . . . 248 B4
Long Eaton NG10 . . . . . . 236 B6
Monsal Dr
Derby DE21 . . . . 220 F3
South Normanton DE55 . . 159 F5
Monsal Gr SK17 . . . . 85 D7
Monsall Ave DE7 . . . . . . 194 E5
Monsom La DE65 . . . . . . 242 D3
Montague Way DE73 . . . 232 E2
Monteith S43 . . . . 247 B4
Montford Mews DE74 . . 247 B4
Montgomery Cl DE65 . . . 228 E2
Montpelier DE21 . . . . 204 D7
Montpelier Cl DE14 . . . . 254 A7
Montpelier [5] SK17 . . . . 85 D8
Montpelier Pl SK17 . . . . 66 D1
Montpelier Rd DE56 . . . . 167 F3
Montrose Cl DE24 . . . . . 231 E4
Montrose Ct NG9 . . . . . . 209 E1
Montrose Pl S18 . . . . 56 D2
Montrose Sq NG19 . . . . . 136 B6
Monument La DE6 . . . . . 170 E3
Monyash CE Prim Sch
DE45 . . . . 107 C1
Monyash Cl
Derby DE21 . . . . 220 A8
Ilkeston DE7 . . . . 194 E3
Staveley S43 . . . . 97 C7
Monyash Ct [32] SK13 . . . 9 D1
Monyash Gr [31] SK13 . . . 9 D1
Monyash Lea [33] SK13 . . 9 D1
Monyash Mews [30] SK13 . 9 D1
Monyash Pl [29] SK13 . . . 9 D1
Monyash Rd
Bakewell DE45 . . . . 109 C5
Over Haddon DE45 . . . . . 109 A2
Monyash Way
Belper DE56 . . . . 179 B5
[1] Gamesley SK13 . . . . . 9 E1
Moonpenny Way S18 . . . 57 A1
Mooracre La S44 . . . . . . 99 D1
Moorbridge La NG9 . . . 209 D1
Moorbrook La S33 . . . . . 50 F7
Moor Cres S20 . . . . 59 C7
Moor Croft DE4 . . . . 143 E7
Moor Dr DE24 . . . . 233 B5
Moore Cl S42 . . . . 116 D1
Mooredge Dr DE4 . . . . . 143 D6
Mooredge Rd DE4 . . . . . 157 B2
Moorend DE4 . . . . 111 C3
Moor End DE21 . . . . 220 F6
Moor End Rd SK6 . . . . . . 24 A5
Moores Ave NG10 . . . . . 223 C7
Moore St DE23 . . . . 219 A3
Moor Farm Ave S20 . . . . 59 B8
Moor Farm Garth S20 . . 59 C8
Moor Farm Rd E DE6 . . . 185 F7
Moor Farm Rd W DE6 . . 185 E8
Moor Farm Rise S20 . . . . 59 B8
Moorfield DE4 . . . . 143 C7
Moorfield Ave S44 . . . . . 99 B1
Moorfield Cres [3] NG10 . 223 B5
Moorfield Ct NG9 . . . . . 209 E1
Moorfield La NG20 . . . . 100 F4
Moorfield Prec SK14 . . . . 9 D5
Moorfield Rd DE56 . . . . 191 C7
Moorfields Ave NG16 . . 182 F3
Moorfield Sq S44 . . . . . . 99 B1
Moorfield St SK14 . . . . . . 9 D5
Moorfield Terr SK14 . . . . 9 D5
Moor Furlong DE13 . . . . 240 F1
Moorgate DE22 . . . . 217 E6
Moorgate Ave NG19 . . . 134 F7
Moorgate Cres S18 . . . . 76 B8
Moorhaigh La NG19 . . . 135 A3
Moorhall DE45 . . . . 109 C5
Moorhay Cl S41 . . . . 95 B7
Moorhead Ave DE24 . . . 232 F5
Moorhead Prim Sch
DE24 . . . . 232 F6
Moorings The SK12 . . . . 32 E6
Moor La
Aston-on-T DE72 . . . . . . 246 B8
Barrow u T DE73 . . . . . . 244 B8
Bolsover S44 . . . . 99 B1
Bonsall DE4 . . . . 142 B2
Calow S44 . . . . 116 C8
Dale Abbey DE7 . . . . 207 F2
Darley Dale DE4 . . . . 127 C4
Derby DE24 . . . . 232 C6
Elton DE4 . . . . 140 E5
Flagg SK17 . . . . 106 E4
Kirk Ireton DE6 . . . . 165 A3
Kirk Langley DE6 . . . . . . 202 F1
Little Eaton DE21 . . . . . . 191 E1
Ockbrook DE72 . . . . 221 C6
Osmaston DE6 . . . . 185 F5
Scarcliffe S44 . . . . 119 A8
Taddington SK17 . . . . . . 87 E1
Youlgreave DE45 . . . . . . 125 B5
Moorland Ave NG9 . . . . 223 D6
Moorland Ctr The ★ S33 . 37 C8
Moorland Dr S44 . . . . . . 116 F2
Moorland Rd
Derby DE3 . . . . 217 D3
Hathersage S32 . . . . 53 A7
Moorlands Cl NG10 . . . . 223 B2
Moorlands Dr DE6 . . . . . 184 C7
Moorlands La
Bonsall DE4 . . . . 142 B3
Froggatt S32 . . . . 72 C5
Moorlands Rd DE56 . . . . 168 B4

Moorland Terr DE4 . . . . 144 A4
Moorland View
Apperknowle S18 . . . . . . 58 A1
Sheffield S12 . . . . 44 A2
Moorland View Rd S40 . . 95 C1
Moorlawn Ave S42 . . . . 113 E7
Moorpark Ave S40 . . . . . 114 C8
Moorpool Cres DE56 . . . 191 C7
Moor Rd
Ashover S45 . . . . 129 F3
Breadsall DE7, DE21 . . . 205 F5
Brinsley NG16 . . . . 182 E8
Great Longstone DE45, S32 89 F6
Moor Rise DE56 . . . . 191 C8
Moorside Cl
Cromford DE4 . . . . 155 A5
Glossop SK13 . . . . 17 B7
Sheffield S20 . . . . 59 C8
Moorside Cres DE24 . . . 231 F4
Moorside Gdns DE72 . . . 234 C1
Moorside La DE56 . . . . . 191 C7
Moor St DE21 . . . . 220 E5
Moor The
Brinsley NG16 . . . . 182 D8
Middleton DE4 . . . . 154 C4
Moorthorpe Gn S20 . . . . 44 F2
Moorthorpe way S20 . . . 44 F2
Moortop Rd S18, S21 . . . 58 B1
Moor Valley S20 . . . . 44 F2
Moorview Cl
Brimington S43 . . . . 96 D7
Wingerworth S42 . . . . . . 115 B3
Moorview Ct [2] S17 . . . . 56 B5
Moor View Rd S43 . . . . . 79 A2
Moorway DE21 . . . . 205 E4
Moorway Croft DE23 . . . 231 B7
Moorway La DE23 . . . . . 231 B6
Moorways Sports Ctr
DE24 . . . . 232 D6
Moorwinstow Croft S17 . 55 E7
Moorwood La S17 . . . . . . 55 C1
Moorwoodmoor La
DE55 . . . . 157 D6
Moray Cl NG16 . . . . 195 F7
Moray Pl S18 . . . . 56 D2
Moray Wlk DE21 . . . . . . 219 C8
Mordaunt Rd S2 . . . . 43 F6
Morden Gn S20 . . . . 218 A6
Morden Rd NG16 . . . . . . 195 C8
Morefern Dr DE21 . . . . . 205 F2
Morland Cl S14 . . . . 43 F3
Morland Dr S14 . . . . 43 F3
Morland Pl S14 . . . . 43 F3
Morland Rd
Hayfield SK22 . . . . 25 B2
Sheffield S14 . . . . 43 F3
Morledge DE1 . . . . 267 C3
Morleston St DE23 . . . . . 267 C1
Morley Almshouses La
DE7 . . . . 206 B7
Morley Ave S40 . . . . 95 C4
Morley Cl
Belper DE56 . . . . 179 E6
Burton u T DE15 . . . . 248 B2
Dronfield S18 . . . . 56 C1
Morley Dr DE7 . . . . 194 D3
Morleyfields Cl DE5 . . . . 169 F1
Morley Gdns DE21 . . . . . 220 B8
Morley Hall Prep Sch
DE7 . . . . 206 C7
Morley Ho
Derby, Alvaston DE24 . . . 233 A7
[1] Derby, Mickleover DE3 217 D1
Morley La
Little Eaton DE7, DE21 . . 205 E8
Stanley DE7 . . . . 207 B6
Morley Mews DE21 . . . . 220 A7
Morley Prim Sch DE7 . . 206 C7
Morley Rd DE21 . . . . 220 B8
Morley St
Derby DE22 . . . . 218 C5
Glossop SK13 . . . . 17 D8
Morlich Dr DE24 . . . . . . 231 E5
Morningside Cl S43 . . . . 77 A3
Mornington Cl NG10 . . . 223 C6
Mornington Cres DE22 . 218 B6
Mornington Rd S42 . . . . 132 D8
Mornington Rise DE4 . . 143 C4
Morpeth Gdns DE21 . . . 205 D2
Morrell Wood Dr DE56 . 179 D5
Morris Ave S41 . . . . 95 E5
Morris Dr S41 . . . . 95 E5
Mortimer Rd S6 . . . . 31 E8
Mortimer St DE24 . . . . . 232 C7
Mortimer Wilson Sch
DE55 . . . . 159 A3
Morton Ave S45 . . . . 131 B4
Morton Gdns S20 . . . . . . 59 F6
Morton La S18, S21 . . . . 58 C1
Morton Mount S20 . . . . . 59 F7
Morton Prim Sch DE55 . 147 A5
Morton Rd
Pilsley S45 . . . . 147 C8
Shirland DE55 . . . . 146 D6
Morton St NG19 . . . . 135 E1
Morven Ave
Bolsover S44 . . . . 99 B1
Mansfield Woodhouse
NG19 . . . . 136 B2
Morven St S80 . . . . 100 F8
Mosborough Hall Dr S20 59 E6
Mosborough Hall Farm
S20 . . . . 59 D6
Mosborough Moor S20 . . 59 B8
Mosborough Prim Sch
S20 . . . . 59 D6
Mosborough Rd S13 . . . . 44 B7
Moscar Cross Rd S6 . . . . 31 F6

Moscow Farm Ct DE56 . 190 F5
Mosedale Cl DE24 . . . . . 232 F8
Moseley St DE5 . . . . 169 D2
Moses La DE7 . . . . 206 E7
Moses View S81 . . . . 63 F7
Mosley Dr ST14 . . . . 210 A1
Mosley Mews DE13 . . . . 240 A4
Mosley Rd SK17 . . . . 85 B6
Mossbank Cl S43 . . . . 9 E4
Moss Beck Ct S21 . . . . . . 59 C2
Mossbrook Ct S21 . . . . . . 59 E4
Mossbrook Sch S8 . . . . . 57 C8
Mosscar Cl NG20 . . . . . . 120 F1
Mossdale Ave S20 . . . . . . 59 D7
Moss Dr S21 . . . . 60 D5
Moss Edge Rd HD9 . . . . . . 3 C8
Moss La
Broadbottom SK14 . . . . . 15 F8
Hulland Ward DE6 . . . . . 175 F4
Ripley DE5 . . . . 169 D3
Moss Rd
Ilkeston DE7 . . . . 208 E7
Sheffield S17 . . . . 55 B4
Moss Rise Pl S21 . . . . . . 59 C3
Moss St
Derby DE22 . . . . 218 E3
Hollingworth SK14 . . . . . . 9 D5
Mossvale Dr DE23 . . . . . 231 A6
Moss View S20 . . . . 59 C6
Moss View Rd SK23 . . . . 47 C5
Moston Wlk S40 . . . . 114 E6
Mostyn Ave DE23 . . . . . 218 D1
Mottistone Cl DE24 . . . . 233 D5
Mottram CE Prim Sch
SK14 . . . . 9 A3
Mottram Fold SK14 . . . . . . 9 A3
Mottram Moor SK14 . . . . 15 B8
Mottram Old Rd SK14 . . . 15 B8
Mottram Rd SK14 . . . . . . 16 A8
Moulbourn Dr DE56 . . . 190 D4
Mouldridge La DE4 . . . . 139 F2
Moult Ave DE21 . . . . 220 E4
Moulton Cl
Belper DE56 . . . . 179 D5
Swanwick DE55 . . . . 169 E8
Mound Rd S40 . . . . 266 B1
Mountbatten Cl DE24 . . 232 E4
Mountbatten Ct DE7 . . . 194 F3
Mount Carmel St DE23 . 267 A1
Mountcastle St S41 . . . . 95 F8
Mountcastle Wlk S41 . . . 95 F8
Mount Cres DE55 . . . . . 160 A3
Mountfield Ave NG10 . . 223 A4
Mountfield Way DE24 . . 233 D4
Mountford Ave DE4 . . . . 165 E7
Mountford Cl DE21 . . . . 206 B2
Mountford Croft S17 . . . 55 E5
Mount Pleasant
Ashford in t W DE45 . . . 108 F8
Castle Donington DE74 . . 247 B3
Cromford DE4 . . . . 155 B7
Ilkeston DE7 . . . . 194 E4
Ripley DE5 . . . . 169 D2
Somercotes DE55 . . . . . 170 D5
Youlgreave DE45 . . . . . . 125 C5
Mount Pleasant Ct S32 . . 72 C8
Mount Pleasant Dr
Belper DE56 . . . . 178 E5
Heage DE56 . . . . 179 E8
Mount Pleasant La DE12 . 265 A8
Mount Pleasant Rd
Grindleford S32 . . . . 72 C8
Linton DE11 . . . . 261 E8
Repton DE65 . . . . 242 E1
Swadlincote DE11 . . . . . 256 A1
Mount Rd
Bretby DE15 . . . . 249 A3
Compstall SK14 . . . . 15 A6
Hartshorne DE11 . . . . . . 257 A4
Linton DE11 . . . . 261 D8
Mount St Mary's RC Coll
S21 . . . . 60 C2
Mount St
Breaston DE72 . . . . 235 F7
Burton u T DE15 . . . . 248 A3
Derby DE1 . . . . 267 B1
Glossop SK13 . . . . 17 C8
Heanor DE75 . . . . 181 E1
Mansfield NG19 . . . . 136 A1
Stapleford NG9 . . . . 223 E7
Mount The
Chesterfield S41 . . . . 77 A3
Stapleford NG9 . . . . 223 D6
Mount View Ave S8 . . . . 43 A3
Mount View Gdns S8 . . . 43 A3
Mount View Lo [2] S8 . . . 43 A3
Mount View Rd S8 . . . . . 43 B3
Mouselow Cl SK13 . . . . . . 9 F3
Mowbray Gdns DE24 . . 232 C7
Mowbray St DE24 . . . . . 232 D8
Moy Ave DE24 . . . . 231 F2
Moyne Gdns DE73 . . . . . 245 A8
Mudhurst La SK12 . . . . . 32 E3
Mugginton CE Prim Sch
DE6 . . . . 188 E2
Muirfield Cl S41 . . . . 96 B6
Muirfield Dr DE3 . . . . . . 217 F2
Muirfield Way NG19 . . . 136 E6
Mulberries Ct DE22 . . . . 204 C5
Mulberry Cl
Belper DE56 . . . . 179 B3
Wingerworth S42 . . . . . . 115 A4
Mulberry Croft
Brimington S43 . . . . 78 A1
Staveley S43 . . . . 78 A1
Mulberry Mews DE5 . . . 180 C6
Mulberry Rd S21 . . . . 59 B2

Mulberry Way
Aston-on-T DE72 . . . . . . 246 A6
Hilton DE65 . . . . 228 E2
Killamarsh S21 . . . . 60 B5
Mull Ct [3] DE24 . . . . . . 231 D3
Mullion Pl DE24 . . . . 233 B5
Mumford Dr DE6 . . . . . . 185 D8
Mundella Pl S8 . . . . 43 A3
Mundella Prim Sch S8 . . 43 A3
Mundy's Dr DE75 . . . . . . 193 F8
Mundy CE Jun Sch DE75 193 F8
Mundy Cl DE1 . . . . 218 E6
Mundy St
Derby DE1 . . . . 218 E6
Heanor DE75 . . . . 181 E1
Ilkeston DE7 . . . . 194 E2
Munro Cl S21 . . . . 60 D6
Munro Ct DE24 . . . . 231 E4
Murrayfield Dr [6] S20 . . 59 E6
Murray Park Com Sch
DE3 . . . . 217 F4
Murray Rd
Derby DE3 . . . . 217 F4
Killamarsh S21 . . . . 60 E7
Murray St DE24 . . . . 232 F8
Musard Pl S43 . . . . 78 D1
Musard Way S21 . . . . 60 C6
Muse La
Boylestone DE6 . . . . 213 A2
Church Broughton DE6 . . 226 B7
Musgrave Ho S33 . . . . . . 40 B3
Mushroom Farm Ct
NG16 . . . . 182 D3
Mushroom La DE11 . . . . 262 D8
Muskham Ave DE7 . . . . 194 F3
Muskham Ct [1] NG19 . . 136 B1
Musters St NG20 . . . . . . 120 A4
Muswell Rd DE22 . . . . . . 217 E5
Mycock La SK17 . . . . 106 F5
Myers Cl DE24 . . . . 231 F4
Mynd The NG19 . . . . 136 E6
Myrtle Ave
Long Eaton NG10 . . . . . . 236 C6
Stapleford NG9 . . . . 223 E6
Myrtle Cl NG20 . . . . 119 D6
Myrtle Gr S43 . . . . 78 A1
Myrtle Rd S2 . . . . 43 B7
Myrtle Springs S12 . . . . . 43 F5
Myrtle Springs Dr S12 . . 43 F5
Myrtle Springs Sch S2 . . 43 F5
Mytham Bridge S33 . . . . 40 B1
Mytholme Cl NG10 . . . . 223 C2

N

Nabb La ST14 . . . . 196 A4
Nailers Way DE56 . . . . . 179 C5
Nailor La DE4 . . . . 142 D3
Nairn Ave DE21 . . . . 219 D7
Nairn Cl DE24 . . . . 231 D3
Nairn Dr S18 . . . . 56 D1
Namur Cl DE22 . . . . 218 C3
Nan Gell's Hill DE4 . . . . 155 A3
Napier Cl DE3 . . . . 217 E4
Napier Cl S43 . . . . 80 B5
Napier St DE22 . . . . 218 C5
Napoleon Pk DE24 . . . . 232 E7
Narlow La DE6 . . . . 161 F2
Narrow La
Denstone ST14 . . . . 196 D6
Donisthorpe DE12 . . . . . 265 E8
Ticknall DE73 . . . . 250 F4
Narrowleys La S45 . . . . . 129 C3
Naseby Cl DE3 . . . . 217 C3
Naseby Dr NG10 . . . . . . 236 E6
Naseby Rd DE56 . . . . . . 179 D4
Nathaniel Rd NG10 . . . . 236 F7
National Stone Ctr ★ DE4 154 F3
National Tramway Mus ★
DE4 . . . . 156 E2
Navan Rd S2 . . . . 44 A7
Navigation Home Pk
Derby DE24 . . . . 219 E1
Derby DE24 . . . . 232 E8
Neal Ct NG16 . . . . 182 A3
Neale Bank S43 . . . . 96 D7
Neale St
Clowne S43 . . . . 80 F4
Long Eaton NG10 . . . . . . 236 E7
Near Mdw NG10 . . . . . . 236 E5
Nearwell Cl SK23 . . . . . . 46 F6
Nearwood Dr DE21 . . . . 205 E3
Needham St DE5 . . . . . . 181 B6
Needham Terr DE4 . . . . 143 A7
Needwood Ave DE13 . . . 240 C4
Needwood Ct DE13 . . . . 239 C6
Neighwood Cl NG9 . . . . 223 E2
Neilson St DE24 . . . . 232 F7
Nelper Cres DE7 . . . . . . 209 A5
Nelson Cl DE3 . . . . 217 F3
Nelson Pl LE65 . . . . 257 F3
Nelson St
Burton u T DE15 . . . . 248 C1
Chesterfield S41 . . . . 96 A1
Derby DE1 . . . . 267 D1
Ilkeston DE7 . . . . 194 F3
Long Eaton NG10 . . . . . . 236 D6
Swadlincote DE11 . . . . . 256 B5
Nene Cl DE13 . . . . 240 C1
Nene Way DE65 . . . . 240 D8
Nerissa Cl DE73 . . . . 232 E2
Nesbit St S44 . . . . 118 B8
Nesfield Cl
Chesterfield S41 . . . . 95 D8
Derby DE24 . . . . 233 C7
Nesfield Ct DE7 . . . . 194 E1

Nesfield Rd DE7 . . . . 194 E1
Ness Wlk DE12 . . . . 204 E3
Nestor Cl DE73 . . . . 232 C2
Nether Ave S21 . . . . 60 C6
Nether Blindlow La
  SK17 . . . . 106 B5
Netherby Manor S17 . . . 56 A7
Nether Cl
  Duffield DE56 . . . . 190 E5
  Eastwood NG16 . . . . 182 H4
  Swanwick DE55 . . . . 169 F7
  Wingerworth S42 . . . . . . 115 A2
Netherclose St DE23 . . . 219 A1
Nether Croft Cl S43 . . . . 96 E7
Nether Croft Rd S43 . . . . 96 E7
Netherdene Rd S18 . . . . 57 A1
Nether Farm Cl S43 . . . . 96 F5
Netherfield Cl
  Ashbourne DE6 . . . . 185 C8
  Staveley S43 . . . . 79 A2
Netherfield La DE72,
  DE74 . . . . 247 F8
Netherfield Rd
  Chapel-en-le-F SK23 . . . 47 D6
  Chesterfield S40 . . . . . . 114 A8
  Long Eaton NG10 . . . . . . 236 C4
  Sandiacre NG10 . . . . 223 B4
Netherfields Cres S18 . . . 76 A8
Nether Gdns DE4 . . . . . . 165 F8
Nethergreen Ave S21 . . . 60 D7
Nethergreen Ct S21 . . . . 60 D7
Nethergreen Gdns S21 . . 60 D7
Nether La
  Brassington DE4 . . . . . . 163 F8
  Hazelwood DE56 . . . . . . 190 A7
  Holbrook DE56 . . . . 191 D6
  Kirk Ireton DE6 . . . . 176 B8
Netherleigh Ct S40 . . . . . 95 B3
Netherleigh Rd S40 . . . . 95 B3
Nethermoor Ave S21 . . . 60 D7
Nethermoor Cl S21 . . . . . 60 D7
Nethermoor Cotts DE55 . 147 D5
Nethermoor Dr S21 . . . . . 60 D7
Nethermoor La S21 . . . . . 60 D7
Nethermoor Rd
  Tupton S42 . . . . 131 C8
  Wingerworth S42 . . . . . . 115 A4
Nether Park Dr DE22 . . . 204 C1
Netherseal Rd
  Chilcote DE12 . . . . 264 F4
  Clifton Campville B79 . . . 263 F2
Netherside S33 . . . . 51 A7
Netherside Dr DE73 . . . . 233 B2
Nether Springs Rd S44 . . 98 F3
Netherthorpe S43 . . . . . . 79 A2
Netherthorpe Airfield
  S80 . . . . 63 B5
Netherthorpe Cl
  Killamarsh S21 . . . . 60 C7
  Staveley S43 . . . . 78 F2
Netherthorpe Flash Nature
  Reserve★ S43 . . . . 79 B2
Netherthorpe La S21 . . . 60 C7
Netherthorpe Rd **3** S43 . 78 F2
Nether Thorpe Rd S80 . . 63 B5
Netherthorpe Sch S43 . . 79 A2
Nether Way DE22 . . . . . . 127 C3
Nether Wheel Row S13 . . 44 F5
Netherwood Ct DE22 . . . 204 C3
Nettlefold Cres DE73 . . . 245 B1
Nettleton Cl DE23 . . . . . 231 A6
Nettleton La S43 . . . . 85 D3
Nettleworth Inf Sch
  NG19 . . . . 136 C4
Networkcentre Barlborough
  Links S43 . . . . 80 A5
Neville Cl DE13 . . . . 240 B3
Nevinson Ave DE23 . . . . 231 D7
Nevinson Dr DE23 . . . . . 231 D7
Nevis Cl
  Chesterfield S40 . . . . . . 95 D4
  Derby DE24 . . . . 231 D2
Newark **8** S20 . . . . 59 E8
Newark Rd DE21 . . . . 205 D2
New Bank St SK13 . . . . . . 10 A5
New Barlborough Cl S43 . 80 D5
Newbarn Cl NG20 . . . . . . 119 D2
New Bath Rd DE4 . . . . . . 155 A8
New Beetwell St S40 . . . 266 B2
Newbery Ave NG10 . . . . . 236 F6
Newbold Ave
  Borrowash DE72 . . . . . . 221 C1
  Chesterfield S41 . . . . . . 95 E6
Newbold Back La S40 . . . 95 E5
Newbold CE Prim Sch
  S41 . . . . 95 E7
Newbold Cl DE73 . . . . . . 232 F2
Newbold Com Sch S41 . . 95 F6
Newbold Ct **1** S41 . . . . . 95 D7
Newbold Dr
  Castle Donington DE74 . . 247 B5
  Chesterfield S41 . . . . . . 95 E6
Newbold Rd S40 . . . . 95 D6
New Bolsover Prim Sch
  S44 . . . . 98 F1
Newborough Rd DE24 . . 233 C6
Newbound La NG17 . . . . 134 C2
Newboundmill La NG19 . 135 A4
New Breck Rd DE56 . . . . 179 A3
Newbridge Cl DE7 . . . . . 207 D8
Newbridge Cres DE24 . . 232 E4
Newbridge Dr S43 . . . . . 96 D8
Newbridge La
  Brimington S43 . . . . 96 D8
  Chesterfield S41 . . . . . . 77 B1
Newbridge Rd DE56 . . . . 168 A2
Newbridge St S41 . . . . . . 77 A1

Newburgh Terr S32 . . . . . 72 C2
Newbury Dr DE13 . . . . . . 240 C1
Newbury St DE24 . . . . . . 232 E8
Newby Cl DE15 . . . . 248 B1
Newby Rd S41 . . . . 95 C8
Newcastle St
  Mansfield Woodhouse
    NG19 . . . . 136 B3
  Sutton in A NG17 . . . . . . 148 F3
Newchase Bsns Pk DE23 219 C1
New Church St S33 . . . . . 51 A7
New City Park Homes
  DE24 . . . . 220 A1
New City Pk Homes
  DE24 . . . . 233 A8
New Cl S32 . . . . 71 C6
New Cotts
  Buxton SK17 . . . . 84 E4
  Whaley Thorns NG20 . . . 101 F3
New Derby Rd NG16 . . . . 182 D3
Newdigate St
  Derby DE23 . . . . 232 A8
  Ilkeston DE7 . . . . 209 A6
  Kimberley NG16 . . . . . . 195 F6
  West Hallam DE7 . . . . . . 207 C8
New Eaton Rd NG9 . . . . . 223 E5
Newell Way DE4 . . . . 127 C3
New England Way NG19 . 136 C3
New Fall St NG17 . . . . . . 148 F3
Newfield Cres S17 . . . . . 55 C7
Newfield Croft S17 . . . . . 55 C8
Newfield Farm Cl S14 . . . 43 E5
Newfield Green Rd S2 . . . 43 D6
Newfield La S17 . . . . 55 C7
Newfield Pl S17 . . . . 55 C7
Newfield Rd DE15 . . . . . . 248 B4
Newfield Sec Sch S8 . . . . 43 C3
Newgate St DE73 . . . . . . 233 B2
Newhall Com Jun Sch
  DE11 . . . . 255 E6
Newhall Inf Sch DE11 . . . 255 F7
New Hall Rd S40 . . . . 95 D2
Newham Ave DE55 . . . . . 169 C1
Newham Cl DE75 . . . . . . 182 A1
Newhaven Ave NG19 . . . 136 B3
Newhaven Cl S40 . . . . . . 95 B1
Newholme Hospl DE45 . . 109 D7
New Horwich Rd SK23 . . 45 E7
New Houses
  Chesterfield S41 . . . . . . 96 C3
  Tideswell SK17 . . . . 88 E8
New Inn La DE21 . . . . 205 C7
New La
  Bradwell S33 . . . . 50 E6
  Hilcote DE55 . . . . 148 C1
New Lamb Inn Sta★
  DE55 . . . . 170 C3
Newland Dale S41 . . . . . 266 B4
Newland Gdns S41 . . . . . 95 E5
Newlands Ave
  Chesterfield S40 . . . . . . 95 C3
  Sheffield S12 . . . . 44 A6
Newlands Barns DE22 . . 189 E3
Newlands Cl
  Ripley DE5 . . . . 169 E2
  Swadlincote DE11 . . . . . 256 A2
Newlands Cres DE55 . . . 148 A3
Newlands Dr
  Glossop SK13 . . . . 9 F4
  Heanor DE75 . . . . 181 E3
  Sheffield S12 . . . . 44 A6
  Somercotes DE55 . . . . . 170 D5
Newlands Gr S12 . . . . . . 44 A6
Newlands Ho DE55 . . . . . 170 D4
Newlands Inn Sta★ DE55 170 C3
Newlands Rd
  Sheffield S12 . . . . 44 A6
  Somercotes DE55 . . . . . 170 C4
Newland St DE1 . . . . 267 A3
Newlands The DE4 . . . . . 155 A7
New Lane Galleries
  DE55 . . . . 159 A4
New Lawn Rd DE21 . . . . . 219 F6
New Linden St NG20 . . . 120 A4
New Lumford DE45 . . . . . 109 C7
Newlyn Dr
  Derby DE23 . . . . 231 F8
  South Normanton DE55 . 160 C6
Newlyn Pl S8 . . . . 43 A3
Newman Dr DE14 . . . . . . 254 B8
Newmanleys Rd NG16 . . 194 E8
Newmanleys Rd S NG16 . 194 E8
Newmanleys Road (South)
  NG16 . . . . 182 E1
Newmarket Dr DE24 . . . 219 E1
Newmarket Dr DE24 . . . 232 E8
Newmarket La S43 . . . . . 130 T3
New Market St SK17 . . . . 85 B6
Newmarket Way NG9 . . . 223 F2
New Mill La NG19 . . . . . . 136 E1
New Mills Central Sta
  SK22 . . . . 33 B7
New Mills Heritage Ctr★
  SK22 . . . . 33 B7
New Mills Newtown Sta
  SK22 . . . . 33 B6
New Mills Prim Sch SK22 . 33 B8
New Mills Rd
  Broadbottom SK13 . . . . . 16 B4
  Hayfield SK22 . . . . 25 B3

New Mills Sch & Sixth Form
  Ctr SK22 . . . . 33 C8
New Mount Cl DE23 . . . . 231 D5
Newness Ct DE4 . . . . 143 C6
New Park Ct SK22 . . . . . . 33 D7
New Park Pl DE24 . . . . . . 219 D3
Newport Cres NG19 . . . . 135 E1
Newport Ct DE24 . . . . . . 233 C5
Newquay Pl DE24 . . . . . . 233 C5
New Queen St S41 . . . . . 266 B4
New Rd
  Apperknowle S18 . . . . . . 58 A1
  Bamford S33 . . . . 40 B5
  Barlborough S43 . . . . . . 80 B7
  Barton in F NG11 . . . . . . 237 F6
  Belper DE56 . . . . 178 F3
  Boylestone DE6 . . . . 213 B4
  Bradwell, Bradwell Hills S33 51 A4
  Bradwell S33 . . . . 51 A4
  Coton in t E DE12 . . . . . . 260 D3
  Crich DE4 . . . . 205 A1
  Eyam S32 . . . . 71 F5
  Flash SK17 . . . . 103 A3
  Glossop SK13 . . . . 9 F7
  Grindleford S32 . . . . 72 B5
  Heage DE56 . . . . 179 D8
  Hilton DE65 . . . . 228 E2
  Holmesfield S18 . . . . . . 75 A5
  Holymoorside S42 . . . . . 113 D7
  Horwich End SK23 . . . . . 45 E6
  Idridgehay DE56 . . . . . . 176 F4
  Ironville NG16 . . . . 170 F3
  Middleton DE4 . . . . 154 B5
  Ridgeway S12 . . . . 168 B4
  Somercotes NG16, DE55 . 170 D2
  Stapleford NG9 . . . . 209 D1
  Swadlincote DE11 . . . . . 255 E6
  Uttoxeter ST14 . . . . 210 A1
  Weston Underwood DE6 . 188 D1
  Whaley Bridge, Bridgemont
    SK23 . . . . 33 F1
  Whaley Bridge SK23 . . . 34 A1
  Wingerworth S42 . . . . . . 114 E3
  Wirksworth DE4 . . . . 155 A3
  Woodville DE11 . . . . 256 E2
  Youlgreave DE45 . . . . . . 125 C5
New Rd (Baslow Rd)
  DE45 . . . . 108 F8
New Road Ind Est NG9 . . 209 D1
New Row NG16 . . . . 171 A5
New School Cl S20 . . . . . 59 C7
New School Ct S20 . . . . . 59 C7
New School Rd S20 . . . . 59 C7
New Scott St NG16 . . . . . 101 A1
Newshaw La SK13 . . . . . . 9 F4
New Sq S40 . . . . 266 B3
New St
  Alfreton DE55 . . . . 159 A4
  Bakewell DE45 . . . . 109 D6
  Bolsover S44 . . . . 99 A3
  3 Broadbottom SK14 . . . 16 A8
  Buxton SK17 . . . . 67 B5
  Chesterfield S40 . . . . . . 266 B2
  Derby DE1 . . . . 267 C2
  Donisthorpe DE12 . . . . . 262 E1
  Draycott DE72 . . . . 235 A7
  Grassmoor S42 . . . . 115 F3
  Hilcote DE55 . . . . 160 C8
  Little Eaton DE21 . . . . . . 205 C8
  Long Eaton NG10 . . . . . . 236 E8
  Matlock DE4 . . . . 143 C5
  New Mills SK22 . . . . 33 D7
  Newton DE55 . . . . 148 A4
  North Wingfield S42 . . . . 131 F6
  Ockbrook DE72 . . . . 221 C4
  Pilsley S45 . . . . 132 D1
  Ripley DE5 . . . . 169 E1
  Rosliston DE12 . . . . 260 D6
  Sheffield, Holbrook S20 . . 60 A8
  Shirland DE55 . . . . 146 C2
  Somercotes DE55 . . . . . 170 C8
  South Normanton DE55 . 160 A6
  Stanley DE7 . . . . 207 C6
  Stonebroom DE55 . . . . . 147 A5
  Sutton in A NG17 . . . . . . 148 F3
  Swadlincote DE11 . . . . . 256 B2
  Swanwick DE55 . . . . 169 E7
  Whitwell S80 . . . . 81 E5
New Station Rd S44 . . . . 99 B1
Newstead Ave
  Derby DE21 . . . . 219 F6
  Sheffield S12 . . . . 44 E3
Newstead Cl
  Dronfield S18 . . . . 56 C1
  Sheffield S12 . . . . 44 E3
Newstead Dr S12 . . . . . . 44 E2
Newstead Gr S12 . . . . . . 44 E3
Newstead Pl S12 . . . . . . 44 E2
Newstead Rd
  Long Eaton NG10 . . . . . . 223 C3
  Sheffield S12 . . . . 44 E3
Newstead Rd N DE7 . . . . 194 D3
Newstead Rd S DE7 . . . . 194 D3
Newstead Rise S12 . . . . 44 F2
Newstead Terr **3** SK17 . . 85 B6
Newstead Way S12 . . . . 44 E2
New Street Bus Link S20 . 60 A8
New Terr
  Pleasley NG19 . . . . 134 F5
  Sandiacre NG10 . . . . 223 B6
Newthorpe Comm NG16 . 195 A8
Newton's Wlk DE22 . . . . 218 E4
Newton Cl
  Belper DE56 . . . . 179 C6
  Newton Solney DE15 . . . 248 E8
Newton Ct **16** S41 . . . . . . 95 F8
Newtondale Ave NG19 . . 136 E1

Newton Dr NG9 . . . . 223 E6
Newton La
  Bretby DE15 . . . . 249 A5
  Newton Solney DE15 . . . 248 F7
  Tibshelf DE55 . . . . 147 F6
Newton Leys DE15 . . . . . 248 C4
Newton Park Cl **2** DE11 . 256 A7
Newton Pk DE15 . . . . 248 D7
Newton Prim Sch DE55 . . 148 A3
Newton Rd
  Burton u T DE15 . . . . 248 A5
  Tibshelf DE55 . . . . 147 F6
Newtons Croft Cres S43 . 80 B6
Newtons La NG16 . . . . . . 195 B4
Newton Solney CE Inf Sch
  DE15 . . . . 248 E8
Newton Wonder Ct DE73 245 B1
Newtonwood La DE55,
  NG17 . . . . 148 C5
Newtown Prim Sch SK22 . 33 B6
New Tythe St NG10 . . . . . 236 F7
New Westwood NG16 . . . 171 D4
New Whittington Com Prim
  Sch
  Chesterfield S43 . . . . . . 77 D3
  Chesterfield S43 . . . . . . 77 D4
New Wye St S17 . . . . 55 B7
New Zealand La DE56 . . . 190 E2
New Zealand Sq DE22 . . 218 C5
Nicholas Cl DE21 . . . . . . 220 E6
Nicholas St S41 . . . . 115 C7
Nicholson's Row NG20 . . 119 F3
Nicholson Ct
  9 Sheffield S8 . . . . 43 B6
  Tideswell SK17 . . . . 69 C4
Nicholson Pl **7** S8 . . . . . 43 B6
Nicholson Rd S8 . . . . 43 A6
Nicklaus Cl DE14 . . . . . . 254 A7
Nicola Gdns DE23 . . . . . 231 D4
Nicolas Cl SK17 . . . . 85 E3
Nidderdale Ct DE24 . . . . 233 D6
Nields Way SK6 . . . . 23 C4
Nightingale Ave NG19 . . 135 A4
Nightingale Bsns Pk
  DE24 . . . . 232 D8
Nightingale Cl
  Chesterfield S41 . . . . . . 266 B4
  Clay Cross S45 . . . . 131 C2
  Holloway DE4 . . . . 155 F6
  Ripley DE5 . . . . 169 D1
Nightingale Dr
  Mansfield NG19 . . . . . . 135 E1
  Woodville DE11 . . . . 256 F3
Nightingale Jun & Inf Schs
  DE24 . . . . 232 C7
Nightingale Mews DE1 . . 267 D2
Nightingale Rd DE24 . . . 232 C8
Nikolas Rd S21 . . . . 60 B1
Nimbus Way NG16 . . . . . 195 F6
Nine Corners NG16 . . . . 195 F6
Nine Ladies Stone Circ★
  DE4 . . . . 126 D3
Ninelands Rd S32 . . . . . . 53 A7
Nix's Hill DE55 . . . . 159 B2
Noble St DE1 . . . . 267 B1
Nodder Rd S13 . . . . 44 C7
Nodin Hill La DE56 . . . . . 168 B3
Noe La S33 . . . . 40 A7
Noel-Baker Com Sch
  DE24 . . . . 232 F4
Noel St DE22 . . . . 218 D6
No Man's Heath Rd DE12 264 F3
No Man's La DE7, DE27 . . 222 D7
Nook End Rd DE75 . . . . . 181 D1
Nook La S44 . . . . 97 B3
Nook The
  Barrow u T DE73 . . . . . . 244 A6
  Heanor DE75 . . . . 181 C4
  Holbrook DE56 . . . . 191 D2
  Shirebrook NG20 . . . . . . 119 D3
  Stoney Middleton S32 . . 72 A2
Nooning La DE72 . . . . . . 234 E8
Norbriggs Prim Sch S43 . 79 B3
Norbriggs Rd S43 . . . . . . 79 C2
Norburn Dr S21 . . . . 60 D6
Norbury CE Prim Sch
  DE6 . . . . 197 E7
Norbury Cl
  Chesterfield S40 . . . . . . 95 B5
  Derby DE22 . . . . 204 D1
  Dronfield S18 . . . . 56 D1
Norbury Cres DE23 . . . . 231 C5
Norbury Ct **2** DE22 . . . . 204 D1
Norbury Hollow DE6 . . . 183 D1
Norbury Way
  Belper DE56 . . . . 179 C6
  Sandiacre NG10 . . . . 223 A6
Norfolk Ave S42 . . . . 115 C4
Norfolk Cl S40 . . . . 114 A8
Norfolk Com Prim Sch
  S2 . . . . 43 D8
Norfolk Cl S19 . . . . 136 E5
Norfolk Gdns DE22 . . . . 218 C4
Norfolk Park Ave S2 . . . . 43 D8
Norfolk Rd
  Burton u T DE15 . . . . 254 D7
  Long Eaton NG10 . . . . . . 223 C3
Norfolk Sq **3** SK13 . . . . . 10 C1
Norfolk St
  Derby DE23 . . . . 219 B2
  Glossop SK13 . . . . 10 D1
Norfolk Wlk NG10 . . . . . . 223 B5
Norgreave Way S20 . . . . 59 E7
Norman Ave DE23 . . . . . 231 D7
Norman Cres DE7 . . . . . . 194 E3
Normandy Rd DE65 . . . . 228 C4
Normanhurst Pk DE4 . . . 127 C4
Norman Keep DE13 . . . . 239 C6

Norman Rd
  Ripley DE5 . . . . 169 C1
  Somercotes DE55 . . . . . 170 C7
  Tutbury DE13 . . . . 239 C6
Norman St
  Ilkeston DE7 . . . . 194 E3
  Kimberley NG16 . . . . . . 195 F7
Normanton Ave S17 . . . . 159 C3
Normanton Brook Rd
  DE55 . . . . 160 C3
Normanton Gr S13 . . . . . 44 F6
Normanton Hill S13 . . . . 44 F6
Normanton Ho **3** SK17 . . 85 A7
Normanton House Prim Sch
  DE23 . . . . 231 F8
Normanton Jun Sch
  DE23 . . . . 231 E7
Normanton La DE23 . . . . 231 C8
Normanton Lo DE23 . . . . 231 E8
Normanton Rd DE1 . . . . 267 B1
Normanton Spring Ct S13 44 F6
Normanton Spring Rd
  S13 . . . . 44 F5
Normanton Village Inf Sch
  DE23 . . . . 231 F8
Northacre Rd DE21 . . . . 206 B2
Northam Dr DE5 . . . . 169 C2
North Ave
  Ashbourne DE6 . . . . 173 B2
  Derby, Darley Abbey DE22 205 A3
  Derby DE3 . . . . 217 E2
  Sandiacre NG10 . . . . 223 A6
North Brook Rd SK13 . . . 9 F4
North Church St DE45 . . . 109 D6
North Cl
  Derby DE3 . . . . 217 E3
  Glossop SK13 . . . . 9 F7
  South Normanton DE55 . 159 F5
  Unstone Green S18 . . . . 76 E6
  Willington DE65 . . . . . . 242 B5
Northcliffe Rd DE6 . . . . . 173 B2
Northcote Ave S2 . . . . . . 43 B6
Northcote Rd S2 . . . . 43 B6
Northcote St NG10 . . . . . 236 E7
North Cres
  Duckmanton S44 . . . . . . 98 A5
  Killamarsh S21 . . . . 60 E8
North Derbyshire Tertiary
  Coll (Markland Campus)
  S80 . . . . 81 E3
Northedge La S42 . . . . . . 130 B7
North End DE4 . . . . 154 F1
Northern Ave S2 . . . . 43 E7
Northern Comm S18 . . . . 56 B2
Northern Dr NG9 . . . . 209 D3
Northern Rd DE75 . . . . . 181 D2
North Farm Cl S26 . . . . . 61 E7
Northfield
  Derby DE24 . . . . 231 D3
  Kilburn DE56 . . . . 179 F2
Northfield Ave
  Ilkeston DE7 . . . . 194 E1
  Long Eaton NG10 . . . . . . 236 B4
  Mansfield Woodhouse
    NG19 . . . . 136 A4
  Rocester ST14 . . . . 197 A4
Northfield Cl ST14 . . . . . 210 A2
Northfield Cres DE22 . . . 223 F4
Northfield Jun Sch S18 . . 57 C3
Northfield La
  Mansfield Woodhouse
    NG19 . . . . 135 F4
  Mansfield Woodhouse
    NG19 . . . . 136 B5
  Palterton S44 . . . . 118 C6
Northfield Pk NG19 . . . . 136 B5
Northfield Prim Sch
  NG19 . . . . 136 B5
Northfield Rd NG9 . . . . . 223 F4
Northfields
  Clowne S43 . . . . 80 F3
  Long Eaton NG10 . . . . . . 236 B4
Northgate DE1 . . . . 267 B4
North Gate S44 . . . . 98 E3
Northgate Ho S21 . . . . . . 59 D3
Northgate St **4** DE7 . . . . 194 F1
North Gr S44 . . . . 98 A6
North La
  Belper, Milford DE56 . . . 190 E4
  Brailsford DE6 . . . . 187 E4
  Old Brampton S42 . . . . . 94 D4
Northlands
  4 Buxton SK17 . . . . 85 D8
  Harthill S26 . . . . 61 E7
North Leys DE6 . . . . 173 B1
Northmead Dr DE3 . . . . . 218 B3
North Mill DE56 . . . . 178 F5
Northmoor Cl S43 . . . . . . 96 F7
North Moor View S43 . . . 96 F7
North Par
  Derby DE1 . . . . 267 B4
  Matlock Bath DE4 . . . . . 143 A1
North Rd
  Buxton SK17 . . . . 66 D1
  Calow S44 . . . . 96 F3
  Clowne S43 . . . . 80 E4
  Glossop SK13 . . . . 10 C3
  Hayfield SK22 . . . . 25 D3
  Long Eaton NG10 . . . . . . 236 C6
North Row DE22 . . . . 205 A1
Northside S42 . . . . 115 C1
North Side S42 . . . . 115 C1
North St
  Alfreton DE55 . . . . 159 B3
  Blackwell DE55 . . . . 147 F2

North St continued
Bramley-Vale S44 . . . .**117** D1
Burton u T DE15. . . . .**248** B3
Clay Cross S45 . . . .**131** B5
Cromford DE4 . . . .**155** A6
Derby DE1 . . . .**267** B5
Derby DE23 . . . .**218** C2
7 Ilkeston DE7. . . . .**194** F1
Langley Mill NG16 . . . . . .**182** B3
Melbourne DE73 . . . .**252** A2
North Wingfield S42 . . . . . .**131** E6
Pinxton NG16. . . . .**160** D3
Shirebrook NG20. . . . . . .**120** D4
Somercotes DE55 . . . .**170** D6
South Normanton DE55. . . . .**159** F5
Swadlincote DE11 . . . .**256** B5
Whaley Thorns NG20. . . . . .**101** A3
North Terr 1 S41. . . . .**115** B7
Northumberland Rd
DE15 . . . .**254** D7
Northumberland St
DE23 . . . .**218** F2
North View
Crich DE4. . . . .**168** A8
Derby DE23 . . . .**218** C1
North View St S44 . . . .**98** F1
Northway DE7 . . . .**218** E4
North Wingfield Inf & Jun
Sch S42 . . . .**131** F7
North Wingfield Rd S42 . .**115** E3
Northwood Ave
Darley Dale DE4 . . . . . .**127** C3
Derby DE21 . . . .**219** E7
Northwood La
Ellastone DE6 . . . .**183** C5
Northwood DE4 . . . .**127** A6
Northwood Rise DE6 . . . . .**185** B8
Northwood St NG9 . . . . . .**223** D8
Norton Ave
Chesterfield S40 . . . .**114** A8
Sheffield S14 . . . .**43** E2
Shuttlewood S44 . . . .**98** C4
Norton Church Glebe S8 . .**43** C1
Norton Church Rd S8 . . . .**43** B1
Norton Free CE Prim Sch
S8 . . . .**43** C1
Norton Green Cl S8 . . . . .**43** C1
Norton Hall S8 . . . .**43** B1
Norton Hall Ct S8 . . . . . .**43** B1
Norton La S8 . . . .**43** C1
Norton Lawns S8 . . . .**43** C1
Norton Lees Cl S8 . . . . . .**43** A3
Norton Lees Cres S8 . . . . .**43** A4
Norton Lees Glade S8. . . .**43** A4
Norton Lees La S8 . . . . . .**43** A4
Norton Lees Rd S8 . . . . . .**43** A4
Norton Lees Sq S8 . . . . . .**43** A3
Norton Mews S8 . . . .**43** C1
Norton Park Ave S8 . . . . .**57** B8
Norton Park Cres S8 . . . . .**57** A8
Norton Park Dr S8 . . . . . .**57** A8
Norton Park Rd S8 . . . . . .**57** B8
Norton Park View S8. . . .**57** B8
Norwell Ct 2 NG19 . . . . . .**136** E1
Norwich Cl NG19. . . . . . .**136** D5
Norwich St DE21 . . . .**219** D7
Norwood Ave S41. . . . . . .**115** E6
Norwood Cl
Chesterfield S41 . . . .**115** E6
Derby DE22 . . . .**218** A5
Norwood Cres S21. . . . . . .**60** F7
Norwood Ind Est S21. . . . .**60** E8
Norwood Pl S21 . . . .**60** F7
Nothills DE73 . . . .**233** A1
Nottingham Canal Nature
Reserve The★ DE7,
NG16. . . . .**195** C1
Nottingham S42. . . . .**115** B3
Nottingham Dr S42 . . . . . .**115** B3
Nottingham East Midlands
Airport Aeropark★
DE74. . . . .**247** A1
Nottingham La NG16 . . . . .**170** F5
Nottingham Rd
Alfreton DE55 . . . .**159** B2
Ashby-de-la-Z LE65 . . . . . .**258** F1
Belper DE56. . . . .**179** B4
Borrowash DE72 . . . .**221** D2
Breedon on t H DE73. . . . . .**252** D1
Codnor DE5, NG16. . . . . .**181** C8
Derby DE1 . . . .**267** C4
Derby, Chaddesden DE21 . . . .**219** E6
Derby DE1, DE21. . . . . . .**267** C4
Derby, Spondon DE21. . . . . .**220** E3
Eastwood, Bailey Grove
NG16. . . . .**182** E2
Eastwood, Giltbrook NG16 .**195** C8
Ilkeston DE7 . . . .**209** A6
Long Eaton NG10. . . . . . .**236** F8
Ripley DE5. . . . .**169** E2
Selston NG16. . . . .**171** F6
Stapleford NG9 . . . .**223** E7
Tansley DE4 . . . .**144** B4
Trowell NG9. . . . .**209** E6
Nowill Ct 2 S8 . . . .**43** A6
Nowill Pl 3 S8 . . . .**43** A6
Nun's St DE1 . . . .**218** E6
Nunbrook Gr SK17 . . . . . .**85** C8
Nunn Brook Rd NG17. . . . .**148** E2
Nunn Brook Rise NG17. . . .**148** E2
Nunn Cl NG17. . . . .**148** E1
Nunsfield Dr DE24 . . . . . .**233** B7
Nunsfield Rd SK17 . . . . . .**66** C1
Nursery Ave
Sandiacre NG10. . . . . . .**222** F5
West Hallam DE7. . . . . . .**207** E7

Nursery Cl
Borrowash DE72 . . . .**221** B2
4 Glossop SK13. . . . . . .**17** C8
Swadlincote DE11 . . . .**256** B6
Nursery Croft DE4 . . . . . .**165** E6
Nursery Dr
Bolsover S44 . . . .**98** F2
Buxton SK17 . . . .**66** C2
Nursery Gdns DE55 . . . . .**160** C4
Nursery Hollow DE7. . . . .**208** E6
Nursery La SK17 . . . .**84** E6
Nutbrook Cres DE7 . . . . . .**208** D4
Nuthall Circ DE7. . . . . . .**208** C4
Nuttall Cl DE55 . . . .**158** F3
Nuttall St DE55 . . . .**158** F3
Nuttall Terr S44 . . . .**117** D1
Nutwood Cl DE22 . . . .**205** A3

O

Oadby Dr S41. . . . .**115** C7
Oadby Rise DE23. . . . . . .**231** E6
Oakamoor Cl S40 . . . .**95** A5
Oak Apple Cres DE7 . . . . .**208** E6
Oak Ave
Aldercar NG16. . . . . . .**182** B5
Disley SK12. . . . .**33** A6
Ripley DE5. . . . .**180** D7
Sandiacre NG10. . . . . . .**223** A4
Shirebrook NG20. . . . . . .**119** D4
Oak Bank SK12 . . . .**33** A6
Oak Bank Ave S41 . . . . . .**77** B2
Oakbank Ct S17. . . . .**55** E5
Oak Cl
Brimington S43 . . . .**96** D7
Chapel-en-le-F SK23 . . . . .**47** C5
Derby DE22 . . . .**204** E4
Duffield DE56. . . . . . .**190** E2
Killamarsh S21 . . . .**60** C5
Linton DE11. . . . .**261** E7
Mottram in L SK14. . . . . .**9** A4
Ockbrook DE72 . . . .**221** C5
Pinxton NG16. . . . .**160** C3
Oak Cres
Ashbourne DE6 . . . .**185** C7
Derby DE23 . . . .**231** C8
Wingerworth S42 . . . .**114** F3
Oakdale Cl S45 . . . .**131** E2
Oakdale Gdns DE21 . . . . .**206** B3
Oakdale Rd DE55 . . . .**160** A4
Oakdell S18 . . . .**57** D3
Oak Dr
Alfreton DE55 . . . .**159** B4
Derby, Boulton DE24 . . . .**233** A6
Derby DE3 . . . .**217** E2
Doveridge DE6. . . . . . .**211** B1
Eastwood NG16. . . . . . .**182** E2
Hilton DE65 . . . .**228** D2
Mansfield Woodhouse
NG19. . . . .**136** E2
Oaker Terr DE4 . . . .**142** A7
Oakerthorpe Rd DE4 . . . . .**155** B2
Oakes's Row NG16 . . . . . .**170** F5
Oakes Cl DE55 . . . .**170** C7
Oakes Park Sch S8 . . . . . .**43** C1
Oakes The S8. . . . .**43** D1
Oakfield Ave S40 . . . .**95** B1
Oakfield Ct DE7 . . . .**193** A2
Oakfield Dr NG10 . . . . . .**223** B3
Oakfield Rd
Glossop SK13. . . . . . .**9** E3
Stapleford NG9 . . . .**223** D7
Oakfields DE13 . . . .**238** A4
Oakfields Gr DE21. . . . . .**220** D3
Oak Grove Gn S17 . . . . . .**55** E4
Oakham Cl DE21 . . . .**205** D1
Oakham Way DE7 . . . .**194** E3
Oakhill Rd S18. . . . .**57** C3
Oakhurst Cl DE56 . . . . . .**178** D6
Oak La DE6 . . . .**212** D4
Oakland Ave
Long Eaton NG10. . . . . . .**236** C5
Sutton in A NG17. . . . . . .**148** F2
Oakland Cres DE55. . . . . .**170** D5
Oakland Croft NG17. . . . .**148** E3
Oaklands SK22. . . . .**25** C3
Oaklands Ave
Derby DE23 . . . .**231** C5
Heanor DE75 . . . .**182** A2
Marple SK6. . . . .**23** C8
Oaklands Cl DE55. . . . . . .**180** D1
Oaklands Rd DE65 . . . . . .**229** C4
Oakland St DE55 . . . .**159** B4
Oaklands The DE55 . . . . .**160** A4
Oaklands Way DE73 . . . . .**252** B8
Oakland Terr NG10. . . . . .**236** C5
Oaklea SK17. . . . .**85** C5
Oaklea Way S44 . . . .**131** B6
Oakleigh Ave
Derby DE21 . . . .**219** F6
Mansfield Woodhouse
NG19. . . . .**136** E4
Swadlincote DE11 . . . . . .**255** F5
Oakley's Rd NG10 . . . . . .**236** E7
Oakley's Rd W NG10 . . . . .**236** D6
Oakley Ave S40 . . . .**95** E4
Oak Lodge Dr NG16 . . . . .**195** F7
Oakmeadows DE55. . . . . .**160** B4
Oakover Dr DE22. . . . . . .**204** D2
Oak Rd
Denstone ST14 . . . .**196** D5
Elvaston DE72 . . . .**233** F4
Grassmoor S42 . . . .**115** F3
Matlock DE4 . . . .**143** C5
Shardlow DE72 . . . .**234** A5

Oak Rd continued
Sheffield, Gleadless Townend
S12. . . . .**44** A2
Oakridge DE21. . . . .**220** B7
Oakridge Cl NG19 . . . . . .**136** F1
Oakridge Pk DE74. . . . . . .**247** A5
Oaks Ave
Creswell S80 . . . .**100** C8
Hayfield SK22. . . . . . .**25** D2
Oaks Barn DE45 . . . .**109** A2
Oaksedge La DE4 . . . .**144** A5
Oaks Farm La S44 . . . .**97** A2
Oakside Way DE21 . . . . . .**206** B3
Oaks La
Ashover S45 . . . .**129** C5
Cutthorpe S18, S42 . . . . . .**94** A8
Oak Sq DE11. . . . .**255** F2
Oak St
Brimington S43 . . . .**78** A1
Derby DE23 . . . .**219** A2
Glossop SK13. . . . . . .**10** C1
Sheffield, Heeley S8 . . . . .**43** A7
Sheffield S20 . . . .**59** C8
Swadlincote DE11 . . . . . .**256** A2
Oakstedge La S45. . . . . . .**145** B7
Oaks The
Glossop SK13. . . . . . .**17** A7
Little Eaton DE21. . . . . .**205** C8
Oaktree Ave DE24. . . . . . .**232** B7
Oak Tree Ave S44 . . . . . .**134** B8
Oak Tree Cl
Arkwright Town S44 . . . . .**97** C3
Swanwick DE55 . . . .**170** A8
Oak Tree Cotts S44 . . . . . .**97** A1
Oak Tree Cres NG19 . . . . .**136** B4
Oak Tree Ct DE72 . . . . . .**221** D1
Oak Tree Gdns DE4 . . . . .**144** A4
Oak Tree Rd S43 . . . .**80** E2
Oakvale Ho DE23. . . . . . .**219** A4
Oakwell Cres DE7. . . . . . .**208** E8
Oakwell Dr
Crich DE4. . . . .**156** F1
Ilkeston DE7. . . . .**208** E8
Oakwood Cl
Derby DE65 . . . .**231** D2
Hatton DE65 . . . .**239** C8
Oakwood District Ctr
DE21. . . . .**206** A1
Oakwood Dr
Darley Dale DE4 . . . . . .**142** E8
Derby DE21 . . . .**206** B2
Oakwood Inf Sch DE24 . .**233** A6
Oakwood Jun Sch DE24 . .**233** A6
Oakwood Rd SK12 . . . . . .**32** D6
Oakwood Way S43 . . . . . .**79** B4
Oakworth Cl 1 S20. . . . . .**59** E6
Oakworth Dr S20 . . . .**59** D6
Oakworth Gr S20 . . . .**59** D6
Oakworth View S20. . . . . .**59** D6
Oat Hill DE4 . . . .**165** F7
Oats Orch S20 . . . .**59** D6
Oberon Cl DE73 . . . .**232** E1
Occupation Cl S43 . . . . . .**80** A6
Occupation La
North Wingfield S42 . . . . .**131** E7
Sheffield, Birley S12. . . . .**44** F3
Woodville DE11 . . . .**256** D1
Occupation Rd
Chesterfield S41 . . . .**95** F8
Moira DE11 . . . .**262** C8
New Houghton NG19. . . . . .**134** F7
Ochbrook Ct DE7 . . . .**194** F3
Octavia Cl DE73. . . . . . .**232** E2
Octavia Ct S40. . . . .**266** E6
Oddfellows Cotts 16 SK17 .**85** B7
Oddfellows Rd S32. . . . . .**53** A7
Oddfellows Row S32. . . . . .**53** A7
Oddfellows Terr S32 . . . . .**53** A7
Oddfellow Terr DE45 . . . . .**109** D6
Oddford La DE4. . . . .**127** D2
Odom Ct S2 . . . .**43** B6
Offcote Cres 1 DE6. . . . . .**173** D3
Offerton Ave DE23 . . . . . .**231** B8
Offridge Cl S43 . . . .**80** F2
Off Spring Bank SK22 . . . .**33** C8
Ogden St SK14. . . . .**16** B8
Ogston La DE55 . . . .**146** B4
Ogston New Rd DE55. . . . .**145** E4
Okeover Ave DE6 . . . .**173** D1
Oker Ave DE4. . . . .**127** B3
Oker Dr DE4. . . . .**127** B3
Oker La DE4 . . . .**142** D6
Oker Rd DE4. . . . .**127** B3
Old Bakery Cl
Chesterfield S41 . . . .**77** A2
Hognaston DE6 . . . .**164** B1
Old Bank DE6. . . . .**184** D8
Old Barn Cl DE21 . . . . . .**205** D8
Old Brick Works La S41 . .**96** A6
Oldbury Cl DE21 . . . .**206** A2
Old Chester Rd DE1 . . . . .**219** A8
Old Church Cl DE22 . . . . .**204** C5
Old Coach Rd DE4. . . . . . .**143** F4
Old Coalpit La SK17 . . . . .**86** F1
Old Colliery La S42 . . . . .**132** E8
Old Coppice Side DE75 . .**193** E7
Old Court House Shops 4
SK17 . . . .**85** B8
Old Cross SK13 . . . .**10** E2
Old Dam La SK17 . . . .**49** C4
Old Derby Rd
Ashbourne DE6 . . . .**185** D8
Eastwood NG16 . . . .**182** D3
Olde Derwent Ave DE4 . .**143** B4

Olde English Rd DE4. . . .**143** B4
Old End DE12 . . . .**265** F1
Olders Valley DE11. . . . . .**256** E4
Old Fall St NG17 . . . .**148** F3
Old Farm Ct NG11. . . . . . .**237** E6
Old Farmhouse The
DE45 . . . .**109** D6
Oldfield Dr DE11 . . . .**256** C5
Oldfield La
Egginton DE65 . . . .**241** A8
Hognaston DE6 . . . .**164** B2
Kirk Ireton DE6 . . . .**164** F2
Snelston DE6 . . . .**184** B3
Wensley DE4 . . . .**142** A8
Old Forge Bsns Pk 5 S2. .**43** A7
Old Forge Cl DE65 . . . . . .**241** A5
Old Gate HD9 . . . .**2** F7
Old Gate Ave DE72 . . . . . .**245** C6
Old Hackney La DE4. . . . . .**142** F8
Old Hall Ave
Derby, Alvaston DE24 . . . .**233** B7
Derby DE23 . . . .**218** B1
Duffield DE56. . . . . . .**190** E3
Old Hall Cl
Darley Dale DE4 . . . . . .**127** C3
Glossop SK13. . . . . . .**10** D2
Pilsley S45 . . . .**132** C2
Old Hall Ct DE55 . . . .**169** E7
Old Hall Dr
Horwich End SK23. . . . . .**45** E4
Willington DE65. . . . . . .**242** B5
Old Hall Gdns
Stoney Middleton S32 . . . . .**72** A4
Swadlincote DE11 . . . . . .**256** A2
Old Hall Jun Sch S40 . . . .**95** C2
Old Hall La
Church Broughton DE65 . . .**227** B8
Marple SK6. . . . .**23** C5
Mottram in L SK14. . . . . .**9** A5
Whitwell S80 . . . .**81** F6
Old Hall Mills Bsns Pk
DE21. . . . .**205** C7
Old Hall Rd
Chesterfield S40 . . . .**95** D3
Derby DE23 . . . .**218** C1
Old Hall Sq 3 SK13 . . . . .**10** A5
Old Hartshay Hill DE5 . .**169** C2
Oldhay Cl S17 . . . .**55** D6
Old Hay Gdns S17. . . . . . .**55** C6
Old Hay La S17. . . . .**55** C6
Old Hill DE6 . . . .**173** C1
Old Hillcliff La DE56. . . . .**177** A3
Old House Mus★ DE45 . . . .**109** C6
Old House Rd S40. . . . . . .**95** D6
Old Houses S41. . . . .**96** C3
Oldicote La DE15 . . . .**248** E3
Oldknow Rd SK6. . . . .**23** A6
Old La
Derby DE22 . . . .**205** A2
Idridgehay DE56 . . . . . .**176** F3
Sheffield S20 . . . .**60** A7
Shottle DE56 . . . .**177** A5
Wirksworth DE4 . . . .**154** F2
Old Lime Ct DE4. . . . .**143** C5
Old Longhill Rd SK17. . . .**65** B4
Old Manor Rd NG19 . . . . .**136** C3
Old Mansfield Rd DE21. . .**205** C1
Old Market Pl DE55 . . . . .**160** A6
Old Mill Cl
Duffield DE56. . . . . . .**190** E3
Mansfield NG19. . . . . . .**136** E1
Old Mill Dr S40 . . . .**95** A8
Old Mill La
Calver S32. . . . .**72** D2
Mansfield NG19. . . . . . .**136** E1
Old Mill Lane Ind Est
NG19. . . . .**136** C1
Old Park Ave S8 . . . .**56** D7
Old Park Rd S8 . . . .**56** D7
Old Peverel Rd S44 . . . . . .**98** A4
Old Pit La DE7 . . . .**193** A6
Old Pond The DE75 . . . . .**194** A8
Old Post Office Row S33 .**40** B4
Old Quarry Cl S43. . . . . . .**80** C6
Old Rd
Branston DE14. . . . . . .**253** E7
Buxton SK17, SK23. . . . . .**65** C5
Chesterfield S40 . . . .**95** C3
Darley Dale DE4 . . . . . .**127** C1
Furness Vale SK23. . . . . .**33** D4
Glossop SK13. . . . . . .**10** A7
Heage DE56. . . . .**179** E8
Horwich End, New Horwich
SK23. . . . .**45** E6
Mottram in L SK14. . . . . .**9** A5
Oldridge Cl S40. . . . .**95** B6
Old School Cl
Bramley-Vale S44 . . . . . .**117** D1
Holymoorside S42 . . . . . .**113** D7
Tideswell SK17 . . . .**69** C4
Old School Ho The S42. .**113** D7
Old School La
Awsworth NG16. . . . . . .**195** C5
Chesterfield S44 . . . .**96** F2
Pleasley NG19 . . . .**135** A5
Old School Mews DE72. .**246** B8
Old School The DE65. . . .**228** C2
Old Ship La S40. . . . .**266** B3
Old Smithy Row SK22. . . . .**33** C7
Old St SK14. . . . .**16** A8
Old Station Cl
Etwall DE65 . . . .**229** C3
Rowsley DE4. . . . .**126** F8
Old Station Yd S43 . . . . . .**79** C2
Old Storth La DE55. . . . . .**160** B4
Old Swanwick Colliery Rd
DE55 . . . .**158** F1

Old Tennis Courts The
SK17 . . . .**85** B8
Old Terr NG19 . . . .**134** F4
Old Vicarage Cl DE23. . . .**218** C3
Old Vicarage La DE22 . . .**204** C5
Old Vicarage Sch The
DE22. . . . .**205** A3
Old Waterworks The
DE73 . . . .**243** A4
Oldwell Cl S17. . . . .**55** D4
Old Whittington La S18 . .**76** E6
Olive Ave
Long Eaton NG10. . . . . . .**223** E1
Shirebrook NG20. . . . . . .**119** D6
Olive Cres S12. . . . .**44** A2
Olive Gr DE21. . . . .**219** F5
Olive Grove Rd S2 . . . . . .**43** B8
Oliver Cl DE75 . . . .**182** B2
Olive Rd S20. . . . .**59** D7
Oliver Ho S41. . . . .**266** C3
Oliver Rd DE7. . . . .**208** C6
Olive St DE22 . . . .**218** E4
Olive Terr 1 SK14. . . . . .**16** A8
Olivet Rd S8 . . . .**43** A3
Olivier St DE23. . . . .**219** B1
Ollersett Ave SK22 . . . . . .**33** D8
Ollersett Dr SK22 . . . .**33** D8
Ollersett Ho SK22 . . . .**33** D8
Ollersett La SK22 . . . .**24** E1
Olton Rd DE3 . . . .**217** C4
Onslow Rd DE3 . . . .**217** E4
Onward Cotts SK17 . . . . . .**85** E8
Opal Cl DE21 . . . .**206** A2
Openacre NG16. . . . .**170** F4
Openwoodgate DE56 . . . . .**179** E3
Openwood Rd DE56 . . . . . .**179** E3
Orange Cl NG20. . . . .**119** E6
Orange St DE55 . . . .**159** B4
Orchard Ave
Castle Donington DE74 . . . .**247** A3
Whaley Bridge SK23 . . . . .**45** D7
Orchard Bsns Pk
Ilkeston DE7. . . . .**194** D1
Sandiacre NG10. . . . . . .**223** C6
Orchard Cl
Barlborough S43 . . . .**80** A7
Belper DE56. . . . .**191** B8
Bolsover S44 . . . .**99** B1
Breadsall DE21 . . . .**205** D4
Breaston DE72. . . . . . .**235** F8
Clowne S43 . . . .**80** E3
Derby DE23 . . . .**231** C7
Elvaston DE24 . . . .**233** D4
Hilton DE65 . . . .**228** D1
Melbourne DE73 . . . .**252** A4
Ockbrook DE72 . . . .**221** C4
Ripley DE5. . . . .**181** A7
Shirebrook NG20. . . . . . .**119** E5
Sudbury DE6 . . . .**225** E5
Uttoxeter ST14 . . . .**210** B1
Walton-on-T DE12 . . . . . .**253** D1
West Hallam DE7. . . . . . .**207** E2
Willington DE65. . . . . . .**242** B4
Orchard Com Prim Sch
DE74. . . . .**247** A3
Orchard Cotts DE56 . . . . .**190** E4
Orchard Cres
Glapwell S44 . . . .**134** B8
Swanwick DE55 . . . .**169** D7
Orchard Ct
Derby DE23 . . . .**220** E5
Doveridge DE6. . . . . . .**211** B1
Langley Mill NG16 . . . . . .**182** B3
South Normanton DE55. . . . .**159** F4
Orchard Dr
Creswell S80 . . . .**81** E2
Gamesley SK13. . . . . . .**9** E1
Orchard La DE6. . . . .**185** D1
Orchard Lee S26. . . . .**61** E6
Orchard Pl S21 . . . .**60** D6
Orchard Rd
Compstall SK6. . . . . . .**15** B2
Darley Dale DE4 . . . . . .**142** E8
Matlock Bath DE4 . . . . . .**143** A1
Somercotes DE55 . . . .**170** C6
Whaley Bridge SK23 . . . . .**45** D7
Orchard Rise DE75 . . . . . .**181** F2
Orchard Sq S18. . . . .**56** D2
Orchard St
Derby DE1 . . . .**267** A4
Derby, Mickleover DE3 . . .**217** D1
Ilkeston DE7. . . . .**208** F7
Kimberley NG16 . . . .**195** F6
Langley Mill NG16 . . . . . .**182** B3
Long Eaton NG10. . . . . . .**236** E7
Mansfield NG19. . . . . . .**136** B1
Swadlincote DE11 . . . . . .**255** F6
Orchards The
Derby DE22 . . . .**204** D3
Jacksdale NG16. . . . . . .**171** B4
Orchards Way S40 . . . . . .**95** D1
Orchard The
Belper DE56. . . . .**179** A4
Codnor DE5 . . . .**170** B1
Disley SK12. . . . .**32** D6
Horsley Woodhouse DE7. . .**192** D6
Stanton-by-D DE7 . . . . . .**222** F8
Uttoxeter ST14 . . . .**210** A4
Youlgreave DE45 . . . .**125** C5
Orchard View
Bolsover S44 . . . .**117** F8
Mansfield Woodhouse
NG19. . . . .**136** B3
Orchard View Rd S40 . . . .**95** C4
Orchard Way
Chellaston DE73 . . . .**232** F2
Sandiacre NG10. . . . . . .**223** A3

Orchid Cl
Burton u T DE15 . . . 255 A8
Calow S44 . . . 97 A3
Orchid Way NG20 . . . 119 D3
Ordish Ave DE21 . . . 219 F5
Ordley La DE6 . . . 183 F8
Ordley Wlk DE65 . . . 228 D1
Oregon Way DE21 . . . 220 C6
Orford Ave SK12 . . . 32 D6
Organ Way SK14 . . . 9 D5
Oriel Ct DE1 . . . 267 C1
Orient Way DE24 . . . 219 E2
Orkney Cl DE24 . . . 231 D3
Orly Ave DE74 . . . 247 A2
Ormesby Cl S18 . . . 56 C1
Ormond Cl
Chesterfield S40 . . . 114 B7
Sheffield S8 . . . 57 B6
Ormond Dr S8 . . . 57 B6
Ormonde St NG16 . . . 182 B4
Ormonde Terr NG16 . . . 182 B4
Ormond Rd S8 . . . 57 B7
Ormond Way S8 . . . 57 B7
Ormsby Rd S41 . . . 95 F7
Ormskirk Rise DE21 . . . 220 F4
Orpean Way NG9 . . . 223 E2
Orpen Dr S14 . . . 43 E2
Orpen Ho S8 . . . 43 D2
Orpen Way S14 . . . 43 E2
Orton Way DE56 . . . 179 B6
Orwins Cl 5 S41 . . . 95 D7
Osborne Cl NG10 . . . 223 B4
Osborne Croft S26 . . . 61 F6
Osborne Ct DE21 . . . 205 D4
Osborne Pl SK13 . . . 10 A5
Osborne Rd DE23 . . . 219 C3
Osborne St
Burton u T DE15 . . . 248 A3
Derby DE23 . . . 267 D1
Osbourne Gdns DE15 . . . 248 A3
Oscar Ct S43 . . . 77 D3
Osiers Cl DE22 . . . 204 C1
Osleston La DE6 . . . 215 D7
Osmaston CE Prim Sch
DE6 . . . 185 F4
Osmaston Cl NG10 . . . 235 F5
Osmaston Park Ind Est
DE24 . . . 232 E8
Osmaston Park Rd DE23,
DE24 . . . 232 C7
Osmaston Rd DE23, DE24 . 219 B2
Osmaston St NG10 . . . 223 C5
Osmaton Park Ind Est
DE24 . . . 219 D1
Osmund Ct S21 . . . 59 C3
Osmund Rd S21 . . . 59 C3
Osprey Cl
Burton u T DE15 . . . 248 D4
Derby DE24 . . . 231 E2
Osterly Gn DE22 . . . 218 A5
Oswestry Cl DE21 . . . 206 B3
Othello Dr DE73 . . . 232 D2
Otterburn Dr DE22 . . . 204 C2
Otter St
Derby DE1 . . . 219 A7
Hilton DE65 . . . 228 D1
Otter Way NG19 . . . 135 D1
Oulton Cl DE24 . . . 232 D4
Oundle Dr
Ilkeston DE7 . . . 209 B7
Mansfield NG19 . . . 135 D1
Ousley La DE6 . . . 183 C5
Outfield Rd DE15 . . . 254 F8
Outgang La
Mansfield Woodhouse
NG19 . . . 136 D4
Pleasley NG19 . . . 135 C6
Out La S42, S44 . . . 132 F6
Outlands Rd S33 . . . 50 F6
Outram Cl DE72 . . . 221 B1
Outram Ct DE5 . . . 169 E2
Outram Dr DE11 . . . 256 D4
Outram Rd S41 . . . 95 F6
Outram St DE5 . . . 169 E2
Outram Way DE24 . . . 231 E2
Outseats Dr DE55 . . . 159 B3
Oval Ct DE23 . . . 231 C8
Oven Hill Rd SK22, SK23 . . . 34 A5
Overcroft Rise S17 . . . 55 D4
Overdale DE4 . . . 143 D5
Overdale Ave SK17 . . . 85 D8
Overdale Cl NG10 . . . 236 A6
Overdale Dr SK13 . . . 17 B8
Overdale Gdns S17 . . . 55 D6
Overdale Rd
Derby DE23 . . . 218 E2
New Mills SK12 . . . 32 F6
Overdale Rise S17 . . . 55 C6
Overend Cl S14 . . . 43 D4
Overend Dr S14 . . . 43 D4
Overend Rd S14 . . . 43 D4
Overend Way S14 . . . 43 D4
Over La
Baslow DE45 . . . 91 E6
Belper DE56 . . . 179 E5
Hazelwood DE56 . . . 178 A2
Overlees S18 . . . 75 D3
Overmoor View DE55 . . . 148 B7
Over Rd DE45 . . . 91 E6
Overseal Prim Sch DE12 . 262 B4
Oversetts Ct DE11 . . . 255 F6
Oversetts Rd DE11 . . . 255 E5
Overstone Cl DE56 . . . 179 D4
Overton Cl S43 . . . 78 F3
Owen Ave NG10 . . . 237 A6
Owen Falls Ave S41 . . . 96 C3
Owers Ave DE75 . . . 193 F7
Owlcotes View S44 . . . 118 A8
Owler Bar Rd S11 . . . 54 B4
Owler Car La S18 . . . 57 F5
Owlers La DE23 . . . 218 C2
Owlers The SK23 . . . 45 E6
Owlston Cl NG16 . . . 182 F3
Owlswick Cl DE23 . . . 231 A8
Owlthorpe Ave S20 . . . 59 B8
Owlthorpe Cl S20 . . . 59 B8
Owlthorpe Dr S20 . . . 59 B8
Owlthorpe Gr S20 . . . 59 B8
Owlthorpe La S20 . . . 59 B8
Owlthorpe Rise S20 . . . 59 B8
Oxbury Rd NG16 . . . 195 F8
Ox Cl S45 . . . 131 D3
Ox Close Ave S17 . . . 56 A5
Oxclose Dr 2 S18 . . . 56 C1
Oxclose La
Alsop en le D DE6 . . . 150 C2
Dronfield S18 . . . 56 C1
Mansfield NG19 . . . 135 D3
Mansfield Woodhouse
NG19 . . . 136 A3
Oxclose Park Gdns S20 . . . 59 F6
Oxclose Park Rd S20 . . . 59 F6
Oxclose Park Rd N S20 . . . 59 F7
Oxclose Park View S20 . . . 59 F6
Oxcroft Est S44 . . . 99 D7
Oxcroft Ind Est S44 . . . 99 A8
Oxcroft La
Bolsover S44 . . . 99 B6
Elmton S44 . . . 99 E8
Oxcroft View S44 . . . 99 B8
Oxcroft Way S43 . . . 80 B5
Oxenhope Cl DE23 . . . 230 E7
Oxford Cl S43 . . . 96 F8
Oxford Rd S43 . . . 96 F8
Oxford St
Blackwell DE55 . . . 147 E1
Bramley-Vale S44 . . . 117 F1
Derby DE1 . . . 267 C1
Derby, Spondon DE21 . . . 220 E5
Eastwood NG16 . . . 182 F2
4 Ilkeston DE7 . . . 208 F7
Long Eaton NG10 . . . 236 D8
Mansfield Woodhouse
NG19 . . . 136 C1
Ripley DE5 . . . 169 D1
Swadlincote DE11 . . . 256 A1
Ox Hill S20 . . . 60 A5
Oxley Rd DE15 . . . 248 A3
Oxmead DE6 . . . 184 D7
Oxpasture La NG20 . . . 100 B5
Oxton Rake Rd S18 . . . 94 A8
Oxwich Ct DE21 . . . 206 B2
Oyster Cl DE14 . . . 254 B7
Ozier Holt NG10 . . . 236 C6

P

Packenham Bvd DE65 . . . 227 A4
Packer's Row S40 . . . 266 B3
Pack Horse Rd DE73 . . . 252 B8
Packman La S26, S80 . . . 62 C6
Paddington Ct S43 . . . 78 B4
Paddock Cl
Castle Donington DE74 . . . 246 F3
Wingerworth S42 . . . 114 F3
Paddock Cres S2 . . . 43 E5
Paddock Croft 9 DE21 . . . 205 F2
Paddock La SK23 . . . 45 F5
Paddocks Cl NG16 . . . 160 C4
Paddocks The
Mansfield Woodhouse
NG19 . . . 136 E5
Pilsley S45 . . . 132 C2
Sandiacre NG10 . . . 223 A5
Staveley S43 . . . 79 C3
Sutton in A NG17 . . . 148 F2
Swadlincote DE11 . . . 255 F5
Paddocks View NG10 . . . 236 B8
Paddock The
Blackwell DE55 . . . 147 F1
Bolsover S44 . . . 99 B1
Burton u T DE15 . . . 248 B4
Buxton SK17 . . . 84 F7
Elvaston DE24 . . . 233 D4
Glossop SK13 . . . 9 E5
Holbrook DE56 . . . 191 C6
Hollingworth SK14 . . . 9 E5
Horwich End SK23 . . . 45 F6
Ockbrook DE72 . . . 221 C4
Pleasley NG19 . . . 135 A5
Rolleston DE13 . . . 240 A3
Paddock Way S18 . . . 57 B3
Padfield Com Prim Sch
SK13 . . . 10 B5
Padfield Gate SK13 . . . 17 D7
Padfield Main Rd SK13 . . . 10 C5
Padget High Sch DE14 . . . 254 A7
Padley Cl
Derby DE22 . . . 205 A5
Ripley DE5 . . . 169 C3
Padley Hill S32 . . . 53 E1
Padley Rd S32 . . . 53 D1
Padley Way S42 . . . 131 F5
Padley Wood La S45 . . . 147 B8
Padley Wood Rd S45 . . . 132 C2
Padstow Cl 13 DE24 . . . 231 D3
Padstow Rd DE24 . . . 233 C5
Paignton Ct 15 S41 . . . 95 F8
Painter's La DE6 . . . 186 B5
Painters Way
Darley Dale DE4 . . . 127 D3
Winster DE4 . . . 141 C6
Paisley Cl S43 . . . 97 C8
Palace La DE56 . . . 166 D1
Palace Rd SK17 . . . 85 B8
Palatine Gr DE23 . . . 230 F7
Palerow La DE56 . . . 166 E3
Palissy Cl DE11 . . . 256 D4
Palladium Dr DE23 . . . 231 A6
Pall Mall DE21 . . . 205 E4
Palm Cl DE23 . . . 218 A1
Palmer Cl DE14 . . . 254 B8
Palmer Cres 3 S18 . . . 57 B1
Palmer Dr
Stapleford NG9 . . . 223 D5
Swanwick DE55 . . . 169 E7
Palmersgate S40 . . . 266 B3
Palmerston Ct DE73 . . . 252 B7
Palmerston Rd 4 DE7 . . 208 F8
Palmerston St
Derby DE23 . . . 218 E1
Underwood Green NG16 . . . 171 F2
Westwood NG16 . . . 171 C4
Palterton La S44 . . . 117 D7
Palterton Prim Sch S44 . 118 B5
Pankhurst Pl S45 . . . 131 C3
Parade The
4 Derby DE3 . . . 217 D1
Sheffield S12 . . . 44 A6
Paradise St SK13 . . . 10 A5
Parcel Terr DE22 . . . 218 D5
Pares Way DE72 . . . 221 C5
Pargate Cl DE5 . . . 180 D6
Park Ave
Ashbourne DE6 . . . 173 D1
Awsworth NG16 . . . 195 B5
Castle Donington DE74 . . . 246 F3
Darley Dale DE4 . . . 127 C3
Dronfield S18 . . . 57 B2
Eastwood NG16 . . . 182 E3
Furness Vale SK23 . . . 33 D3
Glapwell S44 . . . 118 C1
Holmesfield S18 . . . 75 A8
Ilkeston DE7 . . . 208 F8
Mansfield Woodhouse
NG19 . . . 136 C4
Ripley DE5 . . . 169 F1
Scropton DE65 . . . 227 A5
Shirebrook NG20 . . . 119 E4
Stanley DE7 . . . 207 C6
Uttoxeter ST14 . . . 210 B2
Park Cl
Chesterfield S40 . . . 115 A7
Glossop SK13 . . . 10 D2
Kilburn DE56 . . . 192 A8
Linton DE12 . . . 261 C6
Little Eaton DE21 . . . 205 B8
Matlock DE4 . . . 143 D4
Pinxton NG16 . . . 160 C2
Shirland DE55 . . . 146 E1
Stanton-by-D DE7 . . . 222 F8
Park Cotts DE4 . . . 127 A5
Park Cres
Chapel-en-le-F SK23 . . . 47 B5
Doveridge DE6 . . . 211 B1
Eastwood NG16 . . . 182 F4
Furness Vale SK23 . . . 33 D3
Glossop SK13 . . . 10 B3
Heage DE56 . . . 179 E8
Ilkeston DE7 . . . 209 A8
Park Ct
Heanor DE75 . . . 181 F1
Swadlincote DE11 . . . 256 C5
Park Dene Dr SK13 . . . 10 C2
Park Dr
Chesterfield S41 . . . 266 C1
Derby DE23 . . . 218 C1
Ilkeston DE7 . . . 208 F7
Sandiacre NG10 . . . 223 A3
Swanwick DE55 . . . 169 F6
Park Edge S32 . . . 52 F8
Parker's La NG19 . . . 136 C3
Parker Ave S44 . . . 96 F3
Parker Cl DE1 . . . 267 A4
Parker Ctr DE21 . . . 219 B8
Parke Rd SK17 . . . 69 C4
Parker Gdns NG9 . . . 223 F8
Parkers Cl DE11 . . . 257 B1
Parkers La S17 . . . 55 D8
Parker St DE1 . . . 218 F7
Park Farm S18 . . . 56 C2
Park Farm Ctr DE22 . . . 204 D2
Park Farm Dr DE22 . . . 204 D2
Park Farm Mews S21 . . . 60 D1
Parkfield Cres DE12 . . . 265 F1
Parkfield Ct SK17 . . . 85 A7
Parkfield La DE6 . . . 184 D4
Parkfield Pl S2 . . . 43 A8
Parkfields S43 . . . 80 E3
Parkfields Dr DE22 . . . 218 E8
Parkfields View DE56 . . . 179 E8
Parkgate
Derby DE23 . . . 219 B2
Dronfield S18 . . . 57 C2
Parkgate Cl S20 . . . 59 A8
Parkgate Croft S20 . . . 59 A8
Parkgate Dr S20 . . . 59 A8
Parkgate La S21, S43 . . . 77 E5
Park Gr DE22 . . . 218 E7
Park Grange Ct S2 . . . 43 C8
Park Grange Dr S2 . . . 43 C8
Park Grange Mount S2 . . . 43 C8
Park Grange Rd S2 . . . 43 D7
Park Grange Rise S2 . . . 43 C8
Park Grange View S2 . . . 43 D8
Park Hall SK17 . . . 85 B8
Park Hall Ave S40, S42 . . . 114 B8
Park Hall Cl S40 . . . 114 B7
Park Hall Farm DE5 . . . 180 A3
Park Hall Gdns
Chesterfield S40 . . . 114 B7
Mansfield Woodhouse
NG19 . . . 136 C5
Parkhall La S21 . . . 60 D2
Park Hall La
Mapperley DE7 . . . 193 D2
West Hallam DE7 . . . 207 C8
Park Hall Rd
Denby Village DE5 . . . 180 A3
Mansfield Woodhouse
NG19 . . . 136 C5
Parkham Rd NG16 . . . 195 F7
Park Head Rd DE4 . . . 143 B5
Park Hill
Awsworth NG16 . . . 195 B5
Eckington S21 . . . 59 E3
Park Hill Cl SK22 . . . 24 C1
Park Hill Dr DE23 . . . 231 F7
Park Ho DE56 . . . 179 A3
Parkhouse Cl S45 . . . 131 B4
Parkhouse Dr DE55 . . . 159 E5
Park House Prim Sch
S45 . . . 132 B4
Parkhouse Rd S42, S45 . . . 132 A4
Parkin St DE55 . . . 159 B4
Park Jun & Inf Schs The
NG20 . . . 119 E5
Park La
Castle Donington DE74 . . . 246 E3
Chesterfield S41 . . . 95 F7
Darley Dale DE4 . . . 127 D2
Derby, Allestree DE22 . . . 204 F4
Derby, Normanton Park
DE23 . . . 218 C1
Hayfield SK22 . . . 25 D5
Heage DE56 . . . 179 F8
Holbeck NG20, S80 . . . 101 C6
Over Haddon DE45, DE4 . . . 110 C1
Pinxton NG16 . . . 160 C2
Ripley DE5 . . . 169 A7
Shirland DE55 . . . 159 A8
Shirley DE6 . . . 200 D8
South Wingfield DE55 . . . 157 D1
Stanton in Peak DE4 . . . 126 C5
Tutbury DE13 . . . 239 B6
Weston-on-T DE72 . . . 245 E4
Parkland Ave SK22 . . . 24 C1
Parkland Dr S42 . . . 115 A2
Parkland Mews NG10 . . . 236 D8
Parklands Dr DE73 . . . 245 A8
Parklands Inf Sch NG10 . 223 B1
Park Leys Ct DE21 . . . 220 E4
Park Mews
Derby DE22 . . . 218 F8
Mansfield Woodhouse
NG19 . . . 136 C4
Somercotes DE55 . . . 170 D6
Park Mill Dr DE55 . . . 159 C7
Park Pale The DE13 . . . 239 C5
Park Rd
Ashbourne DE6 . . . 173 C2
Bakewell DE45 . . . 109 D5
Belper DE56 . . . 179 A2
Buxton SK17 . . . 85 A8
Chapel-en-le-F SK23 . . . 47 B6
Chesterfield S40 . . . 266 A2
Derby DE3 . . . 217 D2
Derby, Spondon DE21 . . . 220 D5
Donisthorpe DE12 . . . 262 E2
Duffield DE56 . . . 190 D3
Glossop SK13 . . . 10 A4
Heage DE56 . . . 179 E8
High Lane SK12 . . . 32 A6
Holmewood S42 . . . 116 E1
Horwich End SK23 . . . 45 D6
Ilkeston DE7 . . . 208 F7
Mansfield Woodhouse
NG19 . . . 136 B3
New Mills SK22 . . . 33 C7
Over Haddon DE45 . . . 110 B2
Overseal DE12 . . . 262 A6
Ripley DE5 . . . 169 E1
Shirebrook NG20 . . . 119 E5
Stapleford NG9 . . . 223 F8
Swadlincote, Church Gresley
DE11 . . . 256 C2
Swadlincote DE11, DE15 . . 255 D5
Tupton S42 . . . 131 C7
Park Rise S18 . . . 75 A8
Park Row
Bretby DE15 . . . 249 B1
Clay Cross S45 . . . 131 D4
Parks Ave DE55 . . . 157 F3
Parkside
Buxton SK17 . . . 85 A8
Chesterfield S41 . . . 96 A7
Heage DE56 . . . 179 E8
Renishaw S21 . . . 60 B1
Park Side
Belper DE56 . . . 179 A3
Somercotes DE55 . . . 170 D7
Parkside Ave NG10 . . . 236 B8
Parkside Cl NG16 . . . 170 F4
Parkside Com Sch S40 . . . 266 A2
Parkside Dr
Ironville NG16 . . . 170 F4
Long Eaton NG10 . . . 236 B8
Parkside Jun Sch DE6 . . . 173 C2
Parkside La SK6 . . . 23 C6
Parkside Rd DE21 . . . 220 B6
Parkside Sh Ctr S21 . . . 60 D7
Parkside View S40 . . . 95 B6
Park Spring Dr S2 . . . 43 C8
Park Spring Pl S2 . . . 43 C8
Park Spring Way S2 . . . 43 C8
Park St
Alfreton DE55 . . . 158 F3
Barlborough S43 . . . 80 B7
Breaston DE72 . . . 235 F8
Chesterfield S40 . . . 115 A7
Derby DE1 . . . 267 D2
Park St continued
Heanor DE75 . . . 181 D2
Long Eaton NG10 . . . 223 C1
Mansfield Woodhouse
NG19 . . . 136 B3
Ripley DE5 . . . 169 E1
Stapleford NG9 . . . 223 D6
Swadlincote DE11 . . . 256 A6
Uttoxeter ST14 . . . 210 C1
Wessington DE55 . . . 157 E8
Parkstone Ct DE3 . . . 217 C2
Parkstone Delph S12 . . . 44 A2
Park Studios S40 . . . 266 A2
Park Terr DE4 . . . 127 A5
Park The
Darley Dale DE4 . . . 127 D3
Duffield DE56 . . . 190 E3
Ironville NG16 . . . 170 E3
Mansfield Woodhouse
NG19 . . . 136 C1
Mayfield DE6 . . . 184 C8
Parkview DE21 . . . 205 C8
Park View
9 Ashbourne DE6 . . . 173 C2
Aston-on-T DE72 . . . 246 B7
Bakewell DE45 . . . 109 D5
Barlborough S43 . . . 80 B7
Chesterfield S41 . . . 115 D7
Clowne S43 . . . 80 F5
Heanor DE75 . . . 181 D1
Northwood DE4 . . . 127 A5
Pleasley NG19 . . . 135 A5
Somercotes DE55 . . . 170 D5
Whaley Thorns NG20 . . . 100 F2
Park View Ave S20 . . . 59 E7
Park View Cl DE22 . . . 204 F4
Park View Ct S8 . . . 43 A2
Park View Dr SK23 . . . 47 B6
Park View Ho DE21 . . . 219 C6
Parkview Prim Sch DE21 206 A2
Park View Rise SK22 . . . 24 C1
Parkville Cl SK17 . . . 85 D5
Parkway
Chellaston DE73 . . . 232 E1
New Mills SK22 . . . 24 C1
Whitwell S80 . . . 82 B6
Park Way DE65 . . . 229 C4
Parkway Ct S8 . . . 56 F7
Parkway The DE4 . . . 127 C3
Parliament Cl DE22 . . . 218 E4
Parliament St
Derby DE22 . . . 218 E4
Swadlincote DE11 . . . 255 F6
Parson's Wlk B79 . . . 263 F2
Parsonage Cl S20 . . . 59 D6
Parsonage Croft DE45 . . . 109 C5
Parsonage Gdns SK6 . . . 23 A4
Parsons Cl
Hartington SK17 . . . 137 D5
Swadlincote DE11 . . . 256 A1
Parsons Gate S33 . . . 40 A6
Parsons Gr DE5 . . . 180 D2
Parsons La S33 . . . 39 D3
Parthenon Cl NG19 . . . 134 F5
Partington Ct 2 SK13 . . . 10 F1
Partington Pk SK13 . . . 10 C3
Partridge Cl S21 . . . 59 B3
Partridge Dr DE11 . . . 256 F3
Partridge Way DE3 . . . 218 A3
Parwich Cl S40 . . . 95 A5
Parwich La DE4 . . . 151 E7
Parwich Prim Sch DE6 . . 151 D2
Parwich Rd S42 . . . 131 F5
Pasteur Ave DE5 . . . 169 D2
Pasture Gr S21 . . . 59 C3
Pasture La
Brassington DE4 . . . 152 D1
Flagg SK17 . . . 106 D6
Hilcote DE55 . . . 148 C1
Long Eaton NG10 . . . 237 A5
Stonebroom DE55 . . . 147 A3
Pasture Rd NG9 . . . 209 D1
Pastures Ave DE23 . . . 230 F7
Pastures Hill DE23 . . . 218 B1
Pastures The
Duffield DE56 . . . 190 E4
Eastwood NG16 . . . 195 B8
Mansfield Woodhouse
NG19 . . . 136 E5
Repton DE65 . . . 242 C2
Swadlincote DE11 . . . 255 F5
Weston-on-T DE72 . . . 245 F5
Patchwork Row NG20 . . . 119 F4
Paterson Ave DE21 . . . 220 B6
Patmore Sq DE23 . . . 231 F7
Paton Gr S43 . . . 96 D8
Patrick Cl DE12 . . . 261 D5
Patten Ct DE24 . . . 232 A5
Patterdale Cl 2 S18 . . . 56 E1
Patterdale Rd DE24 . . . 220 A1
Pattison St S44 . . . 98 F6
Paulet High Sch DE15 . . . 254 F7
Pavilion Cl S43 . . . 80 E2
Pavilion Ct DE7 . . . 207 D7
Pavilion Gdns
Buxton SK17 . . . 85 B7
New Houghton NG19 . . . 134 F8
Pavilion Mans 3 SK17 . . . 85 B7
Pavilion Rd DE23 . . . 231 C8
Pavilion Workshops S42 116 D1
Paxton Cl
Derby DE3 . . . 217 C1
Matlock DE4 . . . 143 A6
Paxton Ct S14 . . . 43 F4
Paxton Rd S41 . . . 96 C5

Payler Cl S2 . . . . 44 A8
Payne St DE22 . . . . 218 D6
Peach Ave
　Selston NG16 . . . . 171 F6
　South Normanton DE55 . . 160 B7
Peach St
　Derby DE22 . . . . 218 D5
　Heanor DE75 . . . . 181 D1
Peacock Cl
　Glossop SK13 . . . . 9 E4
　Killamarsh S21 . . . . 60 D6
Peacock Gr DE23 . . . . 231 B6
Peacock Pl DE7 . . . . 194 D4
Peacock Way DE55 . . . . 169 F8
Peacroft Ct DE65 . . . . 228 C2
Peacroft La DE65 . . . . 228 D2
Peafield La NG19 . . . . 136 F4
Peafield Lane Prim Sch
　NG19 . . . . 136 F3
Peak Ave DE55 . . . . 170 B6
Peak Cavern★ S33 . . . . 38 E2
Peak Cl S45 . . . . 132 C1
Peakdale Cl
　Long Eaton NG10 . . . . 236 A6
　Ripley DE5 . . . . 180 D6
Peakdale Cres S12 . . . . 44 E5
Peak Dale Prim Sch SK17 . . 67 B5
Peakdale Rd
　Glossop SK13 . . . . 9 E3
　Marple SK6 . . . . 23 A4
Peak District Mus of Mining★
　DE4 . . . . 143 A4
Peak Dr DE23, DE24 . . . . . . 232 A7
Peak Forest CE Prim Sch
　SK17 . . . . 49 A3
Peak Ho SK13 . . . . 10 A5
Peakland View DE4 . . . . . . 127 C3
Peaknaze Cl SK13 . . . . 17 B8
Peak Pl S43 . . . . 97 D7
Peak Rd SK22 . . . . 33 D8
Peak Rly★ DE4 . . . . 143 A5
Peak Sch SK23 . . . . 34 F4
Peaks The S43 . . . . 46 C5
Peak The NG20 . . . . 119 E3
Peaktor La DE4 . . . . 126 E7
Peak View
　Clowne S43 . . . . 80 D5
　Glossop SK13 . . . . 9 F4
　South Normanton DE55 . . 159 F5
Peak View Cl S32 . . . . 72 B2
Peak View Dr DE6 . . . . 173 C1
Peak View Rd S40 . . . . 95 D5
Peak Village Outlet Sh Ctr
　DE4 . . . . 110 F1
Pearce St DE22 . . . . 114 D3
Pearl Bank DE6 . . . . 211 B8
Pearl Cl DE21 . . . . 206 A2
Pearl Way SK14 . . . . 9 A2
Pearson Croft S41 . . . . 95 C6
Pearson Trad Est S41 . . . . . 96 B8
Pear Tree Ave
　Ripley DE5 . . . . 180 D8
　Swadlincote DE11 . . . . . . 255 F7
　Wingerworth S42 . . . . 114 E3
Peartree Cl DE74 . . . . 247 A3
Pear Tree Cl
　Brimington S43 . . . . 97 A8
　Glossop SK13 . . . . 9 E4
　Hartshorne DE11 . . . . 257 A7
　Killamarsh S21 . . . . 60 C5
　Marple SK6 . . . . 23 B8
Pear Tree Com Jun Sch
　DE23 . . . . 219 A1
Pear Tree Cres DE23 . . . . . 232 A8
Peartree Ct
　Derby DE21 . . . . 205 D1
　Etwall DE65 . . . . 229 B4
Pear Tree Dr
　Linton DE12 . . . . 261 C6
　Shirebrook NG20 . . . . 119 E6
Peartree La NG17 . . . . 134 B1
Pear Tree Rd
　Derby DE23 . . . . 219 A1
　Pilsley S45 . . . . 132 C1
Peartree Sta DE23 . . . . 232 B7
Pease Cl DE55 . . . . 159 B3
Peasehill DE5 . . . . 180 F8
Pease Hill DE55 . . . . 159 B3
Peasehill Rd DE5 . . . . 180 E8
Peasunhurst La S45 . . . . . . 113 A1
Peatfield Ct NG9 . . . . 209 D1
Peatfield Rd
　Killamarsh S21 . . . . 60 F7
　Stapleford NG9 . . . . 209 D1
Peat La DE4, DE56 . . . . 166 D4
Peats Cl DE6 . . . . 165 B1
Peckham Gdns DE22 . . . . . 218 A5
Pedley Ave ④ S20 . . . . 59 E8
Pedley Dr S20 . . . . 59 E8
Pedley St DE7 . . . . 208 F7
Peebles Cl DE24 . . . . 231 E2
Peel Cres NG19 . . . . 135 D2
Peel Gdns S18 . . . . 56 F1
Peel St
　Derby DE22 . . . . 218 D6
　Glossop SK13 . . . . 10 C5
　Langley Mill NG16 . . . . . . 182 B3
　Long Eaton NG10 . . . . . . 236 E8
　South Normanton DE55 . . 160 B6
Peers Cl DE21 . . . . 206 B2
Peet St DE22 . . . . 218 E4
Pegasus Cl S44 . . . . 99 B1
Pegasus Sch DE12 . . . . 260 F7
Pegasus Way DE65 . . . . . . 228 E2

Peggars Cl S43 . . . . 80 B6
Peggs Wlk DE23 . . . . 231 E7
Peggy La DE55 . . . . 146 B6
Pegwell Cl DE23 . . . . 231 D7
Pelham Ave DE7 . . . . 194 E1
Pelham St
　Derby DE22 . . . . 218 F4
　Ilkeston DE7 . . . . 194 E1
Pemberton The DE55 . . . . 160 B4
Pembleton Dr NG19 . . . . . 135 D1
Pembrey Cl NG9 . . . . 209 D2
Pembroke Cl S40 . . . . 95 C1
Pembroke Ct S41 . . . . 95 F7
Pembroke Rd
　Dronfield S18 . . . . 76 A8
　Shireoaks S81 . . . . 63 F7
Pembroke St DE21 . . . . . . 219 D8
Penalton Cl DE24 . . . . 232 E6
Pencroft Gr DE23 . . . . 231 C5
Pendean Cl DE55 . . . . 147 E1
Pendennis Cl DE24 . . . . . . 233 B6
Pendine Cl DE55 . . . . 160 C6
Pendlebury Dr DE7 . . . . . . 217 E1
Pendleside Way DE23 . . . . 230 E7
Pendleton La DE56 . . . . . . 166 F7
Penfold Way DE55 . . . . . . 147 B5
Penge Rd DE22 . . . . 218 A7
Penhaligan's Cl DE73 . . . . 232 F1
Penistone Gdns S45 . . . . . 131 D2
Peniston Rise DE73 . . . . . . 252 A7
Penkridge Rd DE11 . . . . . . 256 B1
Penmore Cl S41 . . . . 115 C8
Penmore Gdns ④ S41 . . . . 96 C1
Penmore La S41 . . . . 115 C8
Penmore St S41 . . . . 115 C8
Penncroft Dr S45 . . . . 131 D2
Penncroft La S45 . . . . 131 D3
Pennie Cl NG10 . . . . 236 D4
Penniment La NG19 . . . . . 135 B2
Pennine Cl
　Long Eaton NG10 . . . . . . 223 A1
　Mansfield Woodhouse
　　NG19 . . . . 136 C4
　Newton DE55 . . . . 148 A3
　Sutton in Ashfield NG17 . . 148 E4
　Tibshelf DE55 . . . . 147 F6
Pennine Dr
　Selston NG16 . . . . 171 F7
　South Normanton DE55 . . 159 F5
Pennine Rd SK13 . . . . 17 A8
Pennine View
　Heage DE56 . . . . 179 E8
　Palterton S44 . . . . 118 A5
Pennine Way
　Chesterfield S40 . . . . 95 C5
　Grassmoor S42 . . . . 115 F3
　Swadlincote DE11 . . . . . . 256 A3
Pennine Way Jun Sch
　DE11 . . . . 256 A2
Pennine Wlk S42 . . . . 115 F3
Penn La DE73 . . . . 252 B7
Penn Moor Cl NG10 . . . . . 236 A6
Penns Rd S2 . . . . 43 C6
Penn St DE56 . . . . 179 A4
Penny Acres Prim Sch
　S18 . . . . 74 F8
Pennycress Cl DE23 . . . . . 231 A7
Pennycroft La ST14 . . . . . . 210 C1
Pennycroft Rd ST14 . . . . . . 210 A1
Penny Engine La S21 . . . . . 59 E4
Pennyfields Bvd NG10 . . . 236 B7
Penny Gn S80 . . . . 82 A5
Penny La S17 . . . . 55 C5
Penny Long La DE22 . . . . . 218 E8
Pennytown Ct DE55 . . . . . 159 C1
Pennyunk La DE45 . . . . 89 E1
Pennywell Dr S42 . . . . 113 D7
Penrhyn Ave DE23 . . . . . . 218 D1
Penrith Pl DE21 . . . . 205 D2
Penrose Cres S44 . . . . 97 D3
Penryn Cl DE55 . . . . 160 C6
Pentagon The DE21 . . . . . . 219 C6
Pentewen Cl DE22 . . . . . . 204 E2
Penthorpe Cl S12 . . . . 44 B6
Pentland Cl
　⑤ Chesterfield S40 . . . . . 95 C5
　Derby DE21 . . . . 206 A2
Pentland Gdns NG10 . . . . 223 A1
Pentland Rd S18 . . . . 56 D1
Pentrich Ct ① S40 . . . . 95 D5
Pentrich Rd
　Ripley DE5 . . . . 169 D2
　Swanwick DE55 . . . . 169 D7
Pentridge Dr DE7 . . . . 194 C3
Penzance Rd DE24 . . . . . . 233 B5
Pepper La DE7 . . . . 208 L1
Percival Cl SK17 . . . . 138 D3
Percy St
　Derby DE22 . . . . 218 D3
　Ilkeston DE7 . . . . 208 F7
Percy Wood Cl DE65 . . . . . 228 C2
Peregrine Cl
　Burton u T DE15 . . . . 248 D3
　Derby DE24 . . . . 231 D4
Peregrine Way S26 . . . . 61 E5
Perlethorpe Ave NG19 . . . 136 A1
Pershore Dr DE14 . . . . 254 A8
Perth Cl
　Burton u T DE15 . . . . 248 C2
　Derby DE3 . . . . 217 D1
　Mansfield Woodhouse
　　NG19 . . . . 136 C5
Perth Dr NG9 . . . . 209 F1
Perth St DE21 . . . . 205 D1
Peter Baines Ind Est
　DE22 . . . . 267 A1
Peterborough St DE21 . . . 219 E8

Peterdale Cl S43 . . . . 96 E8
Peterdale Rd S43 . . . . 96 E8
Peterhouse Terr ①
　DE23 . . . . 219 A2
Peterleas The DE12 . . . . . . 262 E1
Peterlee Pl DE24 . . . . 233 A5
Peter More Hill S80 . . . . . . 81 E4
Peters Ave S45 . . . . 131 B4
Peters Ct DE55 . . . . 227 D1
Petersgate NG10 . . . . 223 A1
Petersgate Cl NG10 . . . . . 223 A2
Petersham Ct ⑦ NG10 . . . 223 B2
Petersham Dr DE24 . . . . . . 233 C6
Petersham Rd NG10 . . . . . 223 A1
Peter St
　Ashbourne DE6 . . . . 173 C1
　Glossop SK13 . . . . 10 A6
Peterway DE55 . . . . 170 D8
Pettifor Terr DE55 . . . . . . 147 C1
Pettyclose La S41, S43 . . . . 96 D5
Petty Close La DE6 . . . . . . 202 C1
Petworth Ave NG9 . . . . . . 223 F3
Pevensey Ave S41 . . . . 95 E6
Pevensey Ct S41 . . . . 95 E7
Peveril Ave
　Borrowash DE72 . . . . 221 C2
　New Mills SK22 . . . . 24 C1
Peveril Castle★ S33 . . . . . . 38 C2
Peveril Cres
　Long Eaton NG10 . . . . . . 235 F5
　West Hallam DE7 . . . . . . 207 E8
Peveril Ct
　① Glossop SK13 . . . . 17 F8
　Ripley DE5 . . . . 169 C1
Peveril Dr
　Ilkeston DE7 . . . . 194 D2
　Somercotes DE55 . . . . . . 170 C6
Peveril Gdns SK12 . . . . 33 A6
Peveril Ho SK17 . . . . 85 A6
Peveril Mews SK17 . . . . . . 33 A6
Peveril Rd
　Bolsover S44 . . . . 98 F3
　Buxton SK17 . . . . 85 C7
　Castleton S33 . . . . 38 C2
　Chesterfield S41 . . . . 95 F7
　Eckington S21 . . . . 59 E3
　Tibshelf DE55 . . . . 147 F6
Peveril St DE24 . . . . 232 D6
Pewit Cl S42 . . . . 132 D8
Pewit La DE55 . . . . 147 C4
Pheasant Field Dr DE21 . . 221 A6
Pheasant Hill NG19 . . . . . 136 A1
Philip Howard Rd SK13 . . . 17 C8
Philips Croft DE56 . . . . . . 190 E4
Philipway DE55 . . . . 170 D8
Phoenix Cl S12 . . . . 44 E1
Phoenix Rd S12 . . . . 44 E1
Phoenix St DE1 . . . . 267 B4
Phyllis Gr NG10 . . . . 236 F7
Piccadilly La DE6 . . . . 172 C1
Piccadilly Rd S41 . . . . 96 C3
Pickard Cres S13 . . . . 44 B8
Pickard Dr S13 . . . . 44 B8
Pickard La DE56 . . . . 168 A1
Pickburns Gdns DE56 . . . . 191 F8
Pickering Ave NG16 . . . . . 182 F2
Pickering Rise DE21 . . . . . 205 D1
Pickford Pl SK23 . . . . 47 B6
Pickleys La DE6 . . . . 224 C8
Pickton Cl S40 . . . . 95 D2
Pictor Gr SK17 . . . . 85 D7
Pic Tor La DE4 . . . . 143 B4
Pictor Rd SK17 . . . . 85 D7
Piddocks Rd DE15 . . . . . . 255 B5
Pighills La S18 . . . . 57 B4
Pig La DE4 . . . . 111 B4
Pike's La SK13 . . . . 17 B8
Pike Cl
　Chesterfield S40 . . . . 95 B5
　Hayfield SK22 . . . . 25 C3
Pike View Cl SK23 . . . . 34 E2
Pilgrim Ct S81 . . . . 63 F7
Pilgrims Way DE24 . . . . . . 231 C3
Pilhough La DE4 . . . . 126 D6
Pilhough Rd DE4 . . . . 126 E5
Pillar Butts DE4 . . . . 165 E8
Pilsley CE Prim Sch DE45 . 91 C2
Pilsley Cl DE56 . . . . 179 C6
Pilsley Prim Sch S45 . . . . . 132 C1
Pilsley Rd
　Clay Cross S45 . . . . 131 E3
　Stonebroom DE55 . . . . . . 147 B6
Pimlico
　Derby DE22 . . . . 218 B6
　Ilkeston DE7 . . . . 208 E8
Pimm's Rd DE6 . . . . 217 A8
Pinchom's Hill Rd DE56 . . 179 B3
Pinch The DE6 . . . . 150 B2
Pindale Ave S43 . . . . 97 C7
Pindale Rd S33 . . . . 38 E1
Pine Ave NG16 . . . . 182 A3
Pine Cl
　Burton u T DE14 . . . . 254 A8
　Creswell S80 . . . . 81 F1
　Derby DE21 . . . . 220 B4
　Etwall DE65 . . . . 229 C4
　Killamarsh S21 . . . . 60 C5
　Mansfield Woodhouse
　　NG19 . . . . 136 C5
　Ripley DE5 . . . . 169 D1
　Shirebrook NG20 . . . . 119 E6
　Smalley DE7 . . . . 192 F5
Pine Croft DE6 . . . . 185 D7
Pinecroft Ct DE21 . . . . . . 206 B1

Pine Gr DE11 . . . . 255 F6
Pine St S41 . . . . 97 A8
Pines The DE72 . . . . 235 B7
Pine Tree Wlk NG16 . . . . . 182 E2
Pine View
　Chesterfield S40 . . . . 95 B3
　Clay Cross S45 . . . . 131 E3
Pine Wlk DE11 . . . . 261 E1
Pinewood Cl DE55 . . . . . . 181 B7
Pinewood Cl DE55 . . . . . . 159 C3
Pinewood Rd
　Belper DE56 . . . . 178 E6
　Burton u T DE15 . . . . 254 E6
　Matlock DE4 . . . . 143 B7
Pinfold SK13 . . . . 9 A1
Pinfold Cl
　Holymoorside S42 . . . . . . 113 E8
　Repton DE65 . . . . 242 D2
　Tutbury DE13 . . . . 239 C5
Pinfold Cres SK17 . . . . 69 C3
Pinfold Gdns NG19 . . . . . 136 F2
Pinfold Hill S32 . . . . 72 E2
Pinfold La
　Bradley DE6 . . . . 187 A8
　Repton DE65 . . . . 242 D2
　Stapleford NG9 . . . . 223 E7
Pinfold Rd SK17 . . . . 69 C3
Pinfold St S21 . . . . 59 D3
Pinfold The
　Belper DE56 . . . . 179 C5
　Elvaston DE72 . . . . 233 F4
　Glapwell S44 . . . . 118 B1
　Middleton DE45 . . . . 124 E3
Pinfold Trad Est NG9 . . . . 223 F7
Pinfold View DE45 . . . . . . 109 C5
Pingle DE22 . . . . 204 E4
Pingle Cres DE56 . . . . 178 F5
Pingle Farm Rd DE11 . . . . 255 F5
Pingle Grange S43 . . . . 96 E7
Pinglehill Way DE73 . . . . . 233 B2
Pingle La
　Belper DE56 . . . . 178 F5
　Carsington DE4 . . . . 164 F2
Pingle Rd S21 . . . . 60 E7
Pingle Sch The DE11 . . . . . 256 A5
Pingle The
　Derby DE21 . . . . 220 F4
　Long Eaton NG10 . . . . . . 236 D8
　Melbourne DE73 . . . . 252 A7
Pingot Rd SK22 . . . . 33 D8
Pingott La S10 . . . . 15 A5
Pingreaves Dr DE73 . . . . . 233 A2
Pintail Dr DE24 . . . . 231 D4
Pinxton Gn NG16 . . . . 160 E3
Pinxton La
　Kirby-in-A NG17 . . . . 160 E1
　South Normanton DE55 . . 160 C5
Piper Ave S45 . . . . 131 E4
Piper La S42 . . . . 94 E3
Pipers Ct NG16 . . . . 170 F3
Pipeyard La S21 . . . . 59 C2
Pippin Gdns DE24 . . . . . . 232 F7
Pippin Hill DE5 . . . . 180 E1
Pipworth La S21 . . . . 59 F4
Pitch Cl S43 . . . . 80 E2
Pit Close La DE73 . . . . 233 A1
Pit La
　Codnor DE5 . . . . 181 A7
　Crich DE4, DE55 . . . . 157 B6
　Ripley DE5 . . . . 169 E1
　Sheffield S12 . . . . 44 A6
　Shipley DE75 . . . . 194 B6
　Shirland DE55 . . . . 158 D8
　Stonebroom DE55 . . . . . . 147 A5
Pits La DE6 . . . . 151 E1
Pittar St DE22 . . . . 267 A2
Pitt Hill NG20 . . . . 100 F2
Pittlemere La SK17 . . . . . . 50 A1
Pitt St S21 . . . . 59 C2
Pittywood Rd DE4 . . . . . . 165 E7
Placket La DE4 . . . . 141 B6
Plackett Cl
　Breaston DE72 . . . . 235 D8
　Stapleford NG9 . . . . 223 F8
Plains La DE56 . . . . 178 B4
Plainspot Rd NG16 . . . . . . 171 E2
Plain The DE6 . . . . 201 F8
Plaistow Green Rd DE4 . . . 156 F2
Plantain Gdns DE23 . . . . . 231 C5
Plantation Cl
　Chesterfield S40 . . . . 95 A5
　Whitwell S80 . . . . 81 E5
Plantation Rd ⑦ S8 . . . . . . 43 A6
Plantations The ⑨ NG10 . 236 A8
Plantin Rise S20 . . . . 59 E7
Plantin The S20 . . . . 59 E7
Plant La NG10 . . . . 236 A4
Platform Ct DE21 . . . . 220 D3
Platts Ave DE75 . . . . 181 C1
Platt St
　Glossop SK13 . . . . 10 B5
　Pinxton NG16 . . . . 160 D2
Playhouse Theatre★
　DE1 . . . . 267 C2
Pleasant Ave S44 . . . . 118 B7
Pleasant Cl S12 . . . . 44 B6
Pleasant Pl S40 . . . . 95 D3
Pleasant Rd S12 . . . . 44 B6
Pleasant View SK6 . . . . 15 B3
Pleasley Springs NG19 . . . 135 B5
Plimsoll Ct DE24 . . . . 267 A1
Plimsoll St DE22 . . . . 218 C6
Ploughfield Cl DE23 . . . . . 231 B6
Plough Gate DE22 . . . . . . 204 F2
Plover Ave DE11 . . . . 256 F3
Plover Cl SK13 . . . . 17 F8
Plover Ct DE3 . . . . 230 B7

Plover Way S44 . . . . 96 F3
Plowman Ct NG9 . . . . 223 D6
Plowright Cl S14 . . . . 43 D5
Plowright Dr S14 . . . . 43 D5
Plowright Mount S14 . . . . 43 D5
Plowright Way S14 . . . . . . 43 D5
Plucksbridge Rd SK6 . . . . . 23 B8
Plumbley Hall Mews S20 . . 59 C6
Plumbley Hall Rd S20 . . . . 59 C6
Plumbley La S20 . . . . 59 B6
Plumbleywood La S12,
　S20 . . . . 58 F6
Plummer Rd DE11 . . . . . . 256 A5
Plumptre Cl NG16 . . . . . . 182 F1
Plumptre Rd NG16 . . . . . . 182 B5
Plumptre Way NG16 . . . . 182 F1
Plymouth Ave NG16 . . . . . 160 E2
Plymouth Ct ⑦ S41 . . . . . 95 F8
Pocknedge La S42 . . . . 113 D8
Podnor La SK6 . . . . 24 A6
Pole's Rd DE6 . . . . 217 A8
Pole La S22, SK6 . . . . 24 B4
Pollards Oaks DE72 . . . . . 221 C1
Polly Froggatt La S32 . . . . 72 B2
Polyfields La S44 . . . . 118 B8
Pomegranate Theatre★
　S41 . . . . 266 C3
Pomeroy Cotts SK17 . . . . 106 B4
Pond Cotts DE4 . . . . 143 E6
Pond End DE74 . . . . 247 B6
Pond La
　Tupton S42 . . . . 131 C6
　Wingerworth S42 . . . . . . 114 E4
Pondor La SK6 . . . . 24 A6
Pond Rd DE56 . . . . 191 C7
Pond St S40 . . . . 266 B2
Pondwell Cnr S43 . . . . 96 F7
Pondwell Dr S43 . . . . 96 F7
Ponsonby Terr DE1 . . . . . 218 E5
Pontefract St DE24 . . . . . 232 D7
Pontypool Cl DE21 . . . . . . 206 B2
Pool's La S21 . . . . 77 C7
Pool Cl
　Elvaston DE24 . . . . 233 C4
　Pinxton NG16 . . . . 160 D2
Poolclose Row NG16 . . . . 160 D2
Poole's Cavern★ SK17 . . . 85 A6
Poole St DE24 . . . . 232 E6
Pool Rd DE73 . . . . 252 D6
Poolsbrook Ave S43 . . . . . 98 A8
Poolsbrook Country Pk★
　S43 . . . . 97 C7
Poolsbrook Cres S43 . . . . . 98 A8
Pools Brook Ctry Pk★
　S43 . . . . 79 B1
Poolsbrook Prim Sch S43 . 98 A7
Poolsbrook Rd S44 . . . . . . 98 A5
Poolsbrook Sq S43 . . . . . . 98 A8
Poolsbrook View S43 . . . . 98 A8
Pool St DE11 . . . . 256 B7
Pope Carr Rd DE4 . . . . . . 143 C5
Poplar Ave
　Chesterfield S40 . . . . 95 B2
　Derby DE21 . . . . 220 B5
　Moira DE12 . . . . 262 E2
　New Mills SK22 . . . . 24 D1
　Ripley DE5 . . . . 180 D5
　Sandiacre NG10 . . . . 223 A7
　Swadlincote DE11 . . . . . . 256 B6
Poplar Cl
　Derby DE24 . . . . 233 B7
　Dronfield S18 . . . . 76 C7
　Killamarsh S21 . . . . 60 C5
Poplar Cres DE6 . . . . 185 D8
Poplar Dr
　Chesterfield S42 . . . . 115 C1
　Glapwell S44 . . . . 134 B8
　Pleasley NG19 . . . . 135 B4
Poplar Nook DE22 . . . . . . 204 F4
Poplar Rd
　Breaston DE72 . . . . 235 F8
　Eckington S21 . . . . 59 C2
　South Normanton DE55 . . 160 B7
Poplar Row DE21 . . . . 205 A1
Poplar St NG19 . . . . 136 C3
Poplars The
　Derby DE22 . . . . 204 F4
　Whitwell S80 . . . . 82 A5
Poplar Terr
　Chapel-en-le-F SK23 . . . . 47 B5
　Selston NG16 . . . . 171 L6
Poplar Way
　High Lane SK6 . . . . 32 A7
　Ilkeston DE7 . . . . 208 D5
Poppy Cl NG20 . . . . 119 D3
Poppyfields DE5 . . . . 180 D7
Poppy Gdns DE55 . . . . . . 148 A3
Porlock Cl ② NG10 . . . . . 236 A8
Porlock Ct DE21 . . . . 206 A2
Porteous Cl DE4 . . . . 127 D3
Porter's La
　Derby DE21 . . . . 205 F3
　Findern DE65 . . . . 230 D1
Porter Ho ⑨ S43 . . . . 78 E2
Porterhouse Rd DE5 . . . . . 169 F1
Porter La DE4 . . . . 154 C3
Porter Pl DE21 . . . . 220 D5
Porter Rd DE23 . . . . 218 F2
Porters Farm Ct ST14 . . . . 224 E2
Porters La DE21 . . . . 205 F3
Porter St S43 . . . . 78 E2
Porthcawl Pl DE24 . . . . . . 206 C2
Portico Rd DE23 . . . . 231 A6
Portis St DE21 . . . . 220 D3
Portland Ave
　Bolsover S44 . . . . 99 B1
　Burton u T DE14 . . . . 254 A7
　Creswell S80 . . . . 81 E1

Portland Cl
Chesterfield S41 . . . . **266** B4
Derby DE3 . . . . **217** D2
Portland Court Mews
NG19 . . . . **136** C4
Portland Cres
Bolsover S44 . . . . **99** B1
Mansfield Woodhouse
NG19 . . . . **136** D3
Stapleford NG9 . . . . **223** E6
Portland Gr SK23 . . . . **34** E2
Portland Rd
Beeston NG9 . . . . **223** F1
Eastwood NG16 . . . . **195** B8
Ilkeston DE7 . . . . **194** F3
Long Eaton NG10 . . . . . . **236** B4
New Mills SK22 . . . . **24** D1
Shirebrook NG20 . . . . . . **119** F4
Whaley Thorns NG20 . . . . **101** A3
Portland Sq DE45 . . . . **109** D6
Portland St
Clowne S43 . . . . **81** A4
Derby DE23 . . . . **232** A8
Etwall DE65 . . . . **229** B4
Mansfield Woodhouse
NG19 . . . . **136** C3
New Houghton NG19 . . . . **135** A2
Whitwell S80 . . . . **81** F6
Portland Terr NG20 . . . **101** A2
Portman Chase DE24 . . **231** D2
Portreath Dr DE22 . . . . **204** E3
Port Way DE21, DE56 . . **191** D5
Portway Cl DE22 . . . . . **205** A4
Portway Dr DE13 . . . . . **239** C5
Portway Inf Sch DE22 . . **204** E4
Portway Jun Sch DE22 . . **204** E4
Portwood Ind Est DE11 . **256** A1
Postmans La S42 . . . . . **116** C4
Post Office Row SK17 . . **69** E3
Post St SK13 . . . . **10** B5
Posy La DE72 . . . . **246** A7
Potato Pit La
Dale Abbey DE7 . . . . **208** A1
Stanton-by-D DE7 . . . . . **222** A8
Potlocks The DE65 . . . . **242** C6
Potter Rd SK13 . . . .**9** E3
Potters Cl S41 . . . . **77** C2
Potters Croft
Clifton Campville B79 . . . **263** E2
Swadlincote DE11 . . . . . **256** A5
Potters La DE4, DE55 . . **157** B5
Potters Nook S81 . . . . . **63** F7
Potter St
Derby DE21 . . . . **220** D4
Melbourne DE73 . . . . . . **252** B7
Potters Way DE7 . . . . . **209** A8
Potters Yd DE73 . . . . . **252** B7
Pottery Cl DE56 . . . . . . **179** C5
Pottery La DE5 . . . . . . **180** C3
Pottery La E S41 . . . . . . **96** B8
Pottery La W S41 . . . . . **96** A7
Pottery Prim Sch DE56 . **179** C4
Poulter Cty Pk ★ NG20 . **100** E2
Poulter St NG20 . . . . . **100** F1
Pounder La DE4 . . . . . **142** D2
Powell Dr S21 . . . . **60** C6
Powell St DE23 . . . . . . **218** E2
Pown St SK17 . . . . **137** A6
Powtrell Pl DE7 . . . . . . **209** B6
Poynter Cl DE75 . . . . . . **181** C1
Poynton Wood Cres S17 . **56** A6
Poynton Wood Glade S17 **56** A6
Poyser Ave DE21 . . . . . **220** A7
Poyser La DE6 . . . . **203** A1
Pratt Cl NG19 . . . . **135** D1
Pratthall La DE4 . . . . . . **166** A6
Premier Ave DE6 . . . . . **185** B8
Prescot Cl DE3 . . . . . . **217** C1
Press La S42 . . . . **130** D6
Prestbury Cl DE21 . . . . **206** B1
Preston Ave DE55 . . . . **159** B4
Preston St S8 . . . . **43** A7
Prestwick Way DE73 . . **232** E2
Prestwold Way S41 . . . **115** C7
Prestwood La ST14 . . . . **196** F8
Prestwood Park Dr
DE11 . . . . **256** D5
Pretoria St S44 . . . . **98** F6
Pride Park Stad (Derby
County FC) ★ DE24 . . . **219** E3
Pride Parkway DE24 . . **219** D3
Pride Pl DE24 . . . . **219** D3
Pride Point Dr DE24 . . . **219** D2
Priestcliffe Lees (Nature
Reserve) ★ SK17 . . . . . **88** B7
Priestcliffe Rd SK17 . . . **87** F4
Priestfield Gdns S41 . . . **95** B7
Priestland Ave DE21 . . . **220** D4
Priestley Ave DE55 . . . **146** C5
Primary DE56 . . . . **179** A4
Prime Ind Est DE23 . . . **219** C2
Prime Ind Pk DE23 . . . . **219** C2
Prime Parkway DE1 . . . **267** C4
Primrose Ave NG16 . . . **171** F2
Primrose Bank DE65 . . **229** C5
Primrose Bsns Pk DE55 **147** F1
Primrose Cl
Derby DE21 . . . . **205** F3
Killamarsh S21 . . . . **60** E7
South Normanton DE55 . . **160** B7
Primrose Cotts
Hazelwood DE56 . . . . . **190** C7
Risley DE72 . . . . **222** D3
Primrose Cotts 🟦 SK13 . **17** B8
Primrose Ct
Hayfield SK22 . . . . **25** D3
Mansfield Woodhouse
NG19 . . . . **136** F4

Primrose Dr
Burton u T DE14 . . . . . . **254** A8
Morley DE7 . . . . **206** C8
Primrose Hill
Blackwell DE55 . . . . . . **147** F1
Glossop SK13 . . . . **17** B8
Ilkeston NE7 . . . . **194** E3
Primrose La
Glossop SK13 . . . . **17** B8
Hayfield SK22 . . . . **25** C5
Killamarsh S21 . . . . **60** E7
Marple SK6 . . . . **24** A4
Tideswell SK17 . . . . **69** C3
Primrose Mdw DE11 . . . **256** B7
Primrose Rise NG16 . . . **195** B8
Primrose St DE7 . . . . . **194** E3
Primrose Terr 🟦 SK13 . . **17** B8
Primrose Vale Cotts SK22 **25** C5
Primrose Way NG20 . . . **119** F6
Primula Cl NG20 . . . . . **119** D3
Primula Way DE23 . . . . **231** D4
Prince's St DE23 . . . . . **219** B1
Prince's Rd SK17 . . . . . **85** D8
Prince's St DE7 . . . . . . **219** B1
Prince Charles Ave
DE22 . . . . **218** A6
Prince Edward Prim Sch
S12 . . . . **44** A7
Prince of Wales Rd S2 . . **44** B7
Princes Dr DE23 . . . . . **218** B2
Princes Rd SK23 . . . . . **34** E2
Princess Ave
Linton DE12 . . . . **261** C5
South Normanton DE55 . . **160** A5
Princess Cl
Heanor DE75 . . . . **181** D2
Woodville DE11 . . . . . . **256** F2
Princess Ct S2 . . . . **44** B8
Princess Dr
Borrowash DE72 . . . . . **221** A2
Sandiacre NG10 . . . . . . **223** B4
Princess Pl S45 . . . . . . **131** C2
Princess Rd
Dronfield S18 . . . . **57** B2
Uttoxeter ST14 . . . . . . **210** A1
Princess St
Brimington S43 . . . . **96** F8
Chesterfield S40 . . . . . **266** A4
Glossop SK13 . . . . **17** C8
Long Eaton NG10 . . . . . **236** D8
Swadlincote DE11 . . . . . **261** F8
Princes St NG16 . . . . . **182** F3
Princess Way DE13 . . . **240** E1
Prince St
Ilkeston DE7 . . . . **194** E4
Long Eaton NG10 . . . . . **236** D8
Printers Dr SK15 . . . .**4** A6
Printers Fold SK14 . . . . . .**9** D5
Printers Pk SK14 . . . .**9** E5
Priors Barn Cl DE72 . . . **221** D2
Priorway Ave DE72 . . . **221** D2
Priorway Gdns DE72 . . . **221** C1
Priory Cl
Chellaston DE73 . . . . . . **245** A8
Ilkeston DE7 . . . . **208** C6
Swadlincote DE11 . . . . . **256** A6
Tutbury DE13 . . . . **239** B5
Yeaveley DE6 . . . . **199** D5
Priory Ct S26 . . . . **61** E5
Priory Gdns
Derby DE21 . . . . **205** F3
Swanwick DE55 . . . . . . **170** A8
Priory Lands DE13 . . . . **240** F2
Priory Rd
Alfreton DE55 . . . . **159** B5
Eastwood NG16 . . . . . . **182** F1
Mansfield Woodhouse
NG19 . . . . **136** B3
Priory Sq NG19 . . . . . . **136** B3
Pritchard Dr NG9 . . . . . **223** E6
Pritchett Dr DE23 . . . . . **230** E8
Private DE7 . . . . **78** A1
Progress Ct DE45 . . . . . **109** D6
Prospect Ave DE55 . . . **159** F5
Prospect Cotts S43 . . . . **80** E5
Prospect Ct
🟦 Sheffield S17 . . . . **56** B5
Sutton in A NG17 . . . . . **148** E1
Prospect Dr
Belper DE56 . . . . **178** F2
Matlock DE4 . . . . **143** A6
Sheffield S17 . . . . **55** F5
Shirebrook NG20 . . . . . **119** B3
Prospect Gdns DE55 . . . **169** E7
Prospect Ho S43 . . . . . . **78** F1
Prospect Pl
Derby DE24 . . . . **219** E4
Sheffield S17 . . . . **56** A5
Prospect Rd
Chesterfield S41 . . . . . . **76** F2
Denby Village DE5 . . . . . **180** A1
Dronfield S18 . . . . **57** D3
Heanor DE75 . . . . **194** A8
Pilsley S45 . . . . **132** C1
Sheffield, Bradway Bank
S17 . . . . **56** A5
Sheffield, Lowfield S2 . . . **43** A7
Prospect St DE55 . . . . . **159** B4
Prospect Terr
Bakewell DE45 . . . . . . **109** C6
Chesterfield S40 . . . . . . **95** A4
Crich DE4 . . . . **168** A8
Providence Ct DE11 . . . **256** F2
Providence Pl
Alfreton DE55 . . . . **158** F3
🟦 Ilkeston DE7 . . . . . . **194** E1
Providence Rd NG16 . . . **171** A4
Providence St DE5 . . . . **180** E8
Provident St 🟦 DE23 . . **219** A2

Pryor Mede S26 . . . . . . **61** E5
Pudding Bag La S45 . . . **129** F4
Puddle Hill DE4 . . . . . . **142** C1
Pulborough Gdns DE23 . **231** A6
Pullman Cl S43 . . . . **78** F3
Pullman Rd DE21 . . . . . **219** F4
Pump Cl DE4 . . . . **143** C3
Pump La DE6 . . . . **224** B8
Pump Yd DE56 . . . . **177** B2
Punch Bowl Pk SK17 . . . **85** A8
Purbeck Ave S40 . . . . . . **95** D4
Purbeck Cl
Long Eaton NG10 . . . . . **236** A8
Mansfield Woodhouse
NG19 . . . . **136** C6
Purchase Ave DE75 . . . **181** C2
Purdy Mdw NG10 . . . . . **235** F5
Pursglove Dr S17 . . . . . **69** D4
Pursglove Rd SK17 . . . . **69** C4
Putney Cl DE22 . . . . . . **217** E5
Pybus St DE22 . . . . **218** D6
Pye Bridge Ind Est DE55 . **170** F6
Pyegrove SK13 . . . . **10** F1
Pyegrove Rd SK13 . . . . . **10** E1
Pye Hill Rd NG16 . . . . . **171** A4
Pykestone Cl 🟦 DE21 . . **205** F2
Pym Leys NG10 . . . . . . **235** F5
Pynot Rd S41 . . . . **77** B2
Pytchley Cl DE56 . . . . . **179** D4

Q

Quadrant Mews 🟦 SK17 . . **85** B8
Quadrant The
Buxton SK17 . . . . **85** B8
Sheffield S17 . . . . **55** E5
Quaker Cl DE73 . . . . . . **252** A7
Quantock Cl DE24 . . . . **231** D2
Quantock Rd NG10 . . . . **223** A1
Quantock Way S40 . . . . **95** B5
Quarndon Hts DE22 . . . **204** C3
Quarndon View DE22 . . **204** C3
Quarn Dr DE22 . . . . . . **204** C3
Quarn Gdns DE1 . . . . . **218** F7
Quarn St DE1 . . . . **218** E6
Quarn Way DE1 . . . . . . **218** F6
Quarry Bank DE4 . . . . . **143** B7
Quarry Bank Rd S41 . . . . **96** C2
Quarry Berry La DE12 . . **264** F1
Quarry Cl SK13 . . . . **10** D1
Quarry Hill
Eckington S21 . . . . **58** D2
Sheffield S20 . . . . **59** A8
Stanton-by-D DE7 . . . . . **223** A8
Quarry Hill Ind Est DE7 . . **208** F5
Quarry Hill Rd DE7 . . . . **208** F5
Quarry La
Alton S42 . . . . **130** C5
Brackenfield DE55 . . . . . **145** D6
Chesterfield S40 . . . . . . **95** C2
Matlock DE4 . . . . **143** E7
Stonebroom DE55 . . . . . **146** F3
Quarry Rd
Apperknowle S18 . . . . . **58** A1
Belper DE56 . . . . **178** F2
Bolsover S44 . . . . **99** A3
Hayfield SK22 . . . . **24** F2
Killamarsh S21 . . . . **60** C7
Morley DE7 . . . . **192** B1
New Mills SK22 . . . . . . **33** D7
Sheffield, Totley Brook S17 . **55** E5
Somercotes DE55 . . . . . **170** C4
Quarry Vale Gr S12 . . . . **44** C4
Quarry Vale Rd S12 . . . . **44** C4
Queen's Ave SK17 . . . . . **85** D8
Queen's Ct S41 . . . . . . **266** A4
Queen's Dr
Belper DE56 . . . . **178** E5
Glossop SK13 . . . . **10** F1
Ilkeston DE7 . . . . **208** E8
Swadlincote DE11 . . . . . **256** B6
Queen's Park Sports Ctr
S40 . . . . **266** A2
Queen's Rd SK17 . . . . . . **85** D8
Queen's Sq NG16 . . . . . **182** F2
Queen's Way S42 . . . . . **115** D1
Queen's Wlk
Tupton S42 . . . . **115** D1
Whaley Thorns NG20 . . . **101** A1
Queen Anne Ct S14 . . . . **43** E3
Queen Elizabeth's Gram Sch
DE6 . . . . **173** C3
Queen Elizabeth's Sch
NG19 . . . . **136** A1
Queen Elizabeth Ct
🟦 Ashbourne DE6 . . . . **173** B2
Sheffield S14 . . . . **43** E3
Queen Elizabeth Way
DE7 . . . . **208** C5
Queen Mary Cl S2 . . . . . **44** A7
Queen Mary Cres S2 . . . **44** A8
Queen Mary Ct
Derby DE21 . . . . **218** F7
Sheffield S2 . . . . **44** A8
Queen Mary Gr S2 . . . . . **43** F7
Queen Mary Mews S2 . . **44** A7
Queen Mary Rd
Chesterfield S40 . . . . . . **95** B1
Sheffield S2 . . . . **44** B8
Queen St N S41 . . . . . . **96** A2
Queens Ave
Heanor DE75 . . . . **181** D2
Ilkeston DE7 . . . . **209** A5
Stanley DE7 . . . . **207** C6
Queensbury Chase DE23 . **231** A6
Queensby Cl S80 . . . . . . **82** C5

Queens Ct
Burton u T DE14 . . . . . . **254** B8
Buxton SK17 . . . . **85** D8
Creswell S80 . . . . **81** F2
Derby DE22 . . . . **218** E8
Draycott DE72 . . . . . . **235** A7
Queen's Ct SK6 . . . . **23** A6
Queens Dr
Brinsley NG16 . . . . **182** E7
Derby DE23 . . . . **218** C6
Sandiacre NG10 . . . . . . **223** B4
Queensferry Gdns DE24 . **232** E4
Queensgate Dr DE73 . . . **244** F8
Queens Gdns S2 . . . . . . **43** C8
Queensland Cl DE3 . . . . **217** E4
Queensland Cres DE15 . . **248** C2
Queens Mews S2 . . . . . . **43** C8
Queens Rd
Creswell S80 . . . . **82** C6
Sheffield, Lowfield S2 . . . **43** B8
Queens Rd N NG16 . . . . **182** F2
Queens Rd S NG16 . . . . **182** F1
Queens Ret Pk S2 . . . . . **43** B8
Queens Rise DE13 . . . . **239** C6
Queens Stables S2 . . . . **43** C8
Queen St
Belper DE56 . . . . **179** A3
Brimington S43 . . . . **77** F1
Chesterfield S40 . . . . . **266** A4
Clay Cross S45 . . . . **131** C3
Creswell S80 . . . . **81** F1
Derby DE1 . . . . **267** B4
Eckington S21 . . . . **59** E3
Glossop SK13 . . . . **17** B8
Hadfield SK13 . . . . **10** A4
Ilkeston DE7 . . . . **208** E8
Ironville NG16 . . . . **170** F4
Langley Mill NG16 . . . . . **182** C3
Long Eaton NG10 . . . . . **236** E7
Longnor SK17 . . . . **121** B6
Marple SK6 . . . . **23** A6
Middleton DE4 . . . . . . **154** D5
Pilsley S45 . . . . **132** D1
Pinxton NG16 . . . . **160** C3
Ripley DE5 . . . . **181** A7
Sheffield, Mosborough S20 . **59** C7
Somercotes DE55 . . . . . **170** D8
South Normanton DE55 . . **159** F5
Staveley S43 . . . . **97** D8
Swadlincote DE11 . . . . . **256** A1
Tideswell SK17 . . . . **69** C4
Queens View S2 . . . . . . **43** C8
Queensview Dr DE5 . . . . **181** A7
Queensway
Castle Donington DE74 . . **246** F4
Derby DE22 . . . . **204** F2
Holmewood S42 . . . . . . **116** E1
Melbourne DE73 . . . . . **252** B8
Pilsley S45 . . . . **132** C1
Stonebroom DE55 . . . . . **146** F3
Queens Wlk S42 . . . . . . **116** E1
Queen Victoria Dr DE11 . **256** B5
Queen Victoria Rd
Sheffield S17 . . . . **55** F5
Tupton S42 . . . . **115** C1
Quenby La DE5 . . . . . . **169** E1
Quentin Rd SK23 . . . . . **47** C6
Quick Cl DE73 . . . . **252** A7
Quick Hill Rd DE24 . . . . **231** D2
Quillings Way DE72 . . . **221** D1
Quilow La DE6 . . . . **185** E3
Quintin Rd DE24 . . . . . **233** A8
Quixhill Bank ST14 . . . . **196** F8
Quixhill Cl DE65 . . . . . . **185** B8
Quixhill La ST14 . . . . . . **196** F8
Quoit Gn S18 . . . . **57** B1
Quorn Cl DE73 . . . . **252** A7
Quorndon Cres NG10 . . **236** D5
Quorn Dr 🟦 S40 . . . . . . **95** A5
Quorn Rise DE23 . . . . . **231** E6

R

Rabown Ave DE23 . . . . **231** D8
Racecourse Ind Est
DE21 . . . . **219** C8
Racecourse Mount S41 . . **95** F8
Racecourse Rd
Chesterfield S41 . . . . . . **76** F1
Chesterfield S41 . . . . . . **95** F8
Radbourne Comm 🟦 S18 . **56** D1
Radbourne Gate DE3 . . . **217** D5
Radbourne La DE22 . . . . **217** E6
Radbourne St
Derby DE22 . . . . **218** C6
Mansfield Woodhouse
NG19 . . . . **136** E4
Radburn Ct NG9 . . . . . . **209** E1
Radcliffe Ave DE21 . . . . **219** F7
Radcliffe Dr DE22 . . . . . **218** C3
Radford Mdw DE74 . . . . **246** F3
Radford Rd DE7 . . . . . . **192** F6
Radford St DE24 . . . . . **232** F7
Radleigh Gr DE11 . . . . . **257** A2
Radleigh Grange DE11 . . **257** A2
Radmanthwaite Rd
NG19 . . . . **135** D3
Rad Mdws NG10 . . . . . **236** C6
Radnor Pl NG19 . . . . . . **135** C4
Radnor St DE21 . . . . . . **219** D7
Radstock Gdns DE21 . . . **205** C1
Radstone Cl DE21 . . . . . **206** A2
Raeburn Cl S14 . . . . **43** E2
Raeburn Dr
Beeston NG9 . . . . **223** E2
Marple SK6 . . . . **23** B8
Raeburn Pl S14 . . . . **43** E3

Raeburn Rd S14 . . . . . . **43** E3
Raeburn Way S14 . . . . . **43** E2
Raglan Ave DE22 . . . . . **218** C5
Raglan St DE55 . . . . . . **159** A4
Railway Ave S80 . . . . . **100** D8
Railway Cotts
Bolsover S44 . . . . **98** C2
Derby DE24 . . . . **232** A6
Egginton DE65 . . . . **241** B7
Holmewood S42 . . . . . . **116** F1
Kimberley NG16 . . . . . . **195** F6
Temple Normanton S41 . . **116** A5
Railway Row NG16 . . . . **170** F4
Railway Side DE11 . . . . **256** B1
Railway St
Glossop SK13 . . . . **10** C1
Hadfield SK13 . . . . **10** A5
Railway Technical Centre Bsns
Pk DE24 . . . . **219** D2
Railway Terr
Buxton SK17 . . . . **85** C8
🟦 Chesterfield S41 . . . **115** B7
Derby DE1 . . . . **267** D2
Derby SK12 . . . . **32** D6
Rain's La DE4 . . . . **154** C4
Rainham Gdns DE24 . . . **233** A5
Rainier Dr DE21 . . . . . . **220** A6
Rake Head Rd HD9 . . . . . .**2** E7
Rake La DE45 . . . . **124** D3
Rakes La DE4 . . . . **162** A6
Rakes Rd DE45 . . . . . . **107** C5
Rake The DE45 . . . . . . **123** B6
Raleigh Cl DE7 . . . . . . **194** F3
Raleigh Rd S2 . . . . **43** B6
Raleigh St DE22 . . . . . . **218** C6
Ralley Cl S42 . . . . **132** D8
Ralph Dr DE55 . . . . . . **170** C7
Ralph Rd S43 . . . . **79** A2
Ralston Croft S20 . . . . . **59** E6
Ralston Ct S20 . . . . **59** D6
Ralston Gr S20 . . . . **59** D6
Ralston Pl S20 . . . . **59** D6
Rambler Cl DE11 . . . . . **256** A5
Ramblers Dr DE21 . . . . **206** C3
Ramper Ave S43 . . . . . . **80** E2
Ramscliff Ave DE12 . . . **265** F8
Ramsdean Cl DE21 . . . . **219** D8
Ramsden Cl SK13 . . . . . **10** D2
Ramsden La HD9 . . . .**3** B7
Ramsden Rd HD9 . . . .**3** C7
Ramsey Ave S40 . . . . . . **95** D1
Ramsey Cl NG9 . . . . . . **209** E2
Ramshaw Cl S41 . . . . . . **95** C7
Ramshaw Rd S18 . . . . . . **76** E6
Ramshaw Way DE22 . . . **218** E4
Ramsley Ct 🟦 S17 . . . . . **95** D5
Randal Cres SK23 . . . . . **45** E5
Randall Dr DE11 . . . . . **256** B4
Randall Pl 🟦 S2 . . . . . . **43** A8
Randall St S21 . . . . **59** B2
Randolph Rd DE23 . . . . **231** F8
Ranelagh Gdns DE22 . . . **218** B7
Raneld Mount S40 . . . . **114** C8
Rangemoor La DE6 . . . . **183** D6
Rangemore Cl DE3 . . . . **217** E4
Rangewood Rd DE55 . . . **159** F4
Ranmoor Cl S41 . . . . . . **115** C8
Ranmoor Hill S32 . . . . . **52** E8
Ranmoor La S32 . . . . . . **52** F8
Rannoch Cl
Derby DE24 . . . . **204** E3
Derby, Spondon DE21 . . . **220** F5
Ranworth Cl DE24 . . . . **232** D3
Ratcliffe Ave DE14 . . . . **254** B8
Ratcliffe Cl S41 . . . . . . **115** C7
Ratcliffe La S80 . . . . . . **82** D6
Ratcliffe St NG16 . . . . . **182** F2
Rauche Ct DE23 . . . . . . **267** C1
Raven Ave DE55 . . . . . . **147** F5
Ravencar Rd S21 . . . . . . **59** B3
Raven Cl DE55 . . . . . . **170** C6
Raven Oak Cl DE56 . . . . **179** A3
Ravens Cl SK13 . . . . **16** F8
Ravenscourt Rd DE22 . . **218** C6
Ravenscroft Ave S13 . . . **44** E8
Ravenscroft Cl S13 . . . . **44** E8
Ravenscroft Cres S13 . . . **44** E8
Ravenscroft Ct S13 . . . . **44** E8
Ravenscroft Dr
Derby DE21 . . . . **219** F6
Sheffield S13 . . . . **44** E7
Ravenscroft Oval S13 . . . **44** E8
Ravenscroft Pl S13 . . . . **44** E8
Ravenscroft Rd S13 . . . . **44** E7
Ravenscroft Way S13 . . . **44** E8
Ravensdale Ave NG10 . . **223** E2
Ravensdale Cl S43 . . . . . **97** C5
Ravensdale Cotts SK17 . . **89** A8
Ravensdale Inf & Jun Schs
DE3 . . . . **217** E3
Ravensdale Rd
Derby DE22 . . . . **204** C3
Dronfield S18 . . . . **56** D1
Ravenside Ret Pk S40 . . **266** B2
Raven St DE22 . . . . **218** C3
Ravenstor Rd DE4 . . . . . **154** F2
Ravenstor YH ★ SK17 . . . **88** C7
Ravensworth Rd S40 . . . **95** A5
Ravenwood DE11 . . . . . **256** C3
Rawdon Cl DE74 . . . . . **247** A4
Rawdon Rd DE12 . . . . . **262** C6
Rawdon Side DE11 . . . . **256** D4
Rawdon St DE23 . . . . . **218** F2
Rawlins Ct S18 . . . . **57** C4

Rawlinson Ave DE23 . . . . . . 232 A7
Rawson Gn DE56 . . . . 179 F1
Ray's Ave DE75 . . . . 181 E1
Rayleigh Ave S43 . . . . 96 C8
Raynald Rd S2 . . . . 44 A8
Rayneham Rd DE7 . . . . . . 194 C4
Raynesway
  Derby, Alvaston DE21 . . . . 233 B8
  Derby DE21 . . . . 220 A2
Raynesway Park Dr
  DE21 . . . . 220 B1
Ray Rushin Bsns Pk The
  DE5 . . . . 180 E7
Ray St DE75 . . . . 181 E1
Reader St DE21 . . . . 220 E5
Realm Cl DE73 . . . . 244 E8
Rebecca Ho DE1 . . . . 218 E5
Recreation Cl
  Blackwell DE55 . . . . 147 E1
  Clowne S43 . . . . 80 E4
Recreation Dr NG20 . . . . . 119 F2
Recreation Gd The
  (Chesterfield FC) S40 . . 266 A4
Recreation Rd
  Calow S43 . . . . 96 F5
  New Houghton NG19 . . . . 134 F7
  Sandiacre NG10 . . . . . . 223 B6
  Shirebrook NG20 . . . . . . 119 E6
  Tideswell SK17 . . . . 69 C4
  Wirksworth DE4 . . . . . . 165 E7
Recreation St NG10 . . . . . 236 F7
Recreation Terr NG9 . . . . . 223 D6
Recreation View NG20 . . . 119 E6
Rectory Cl
  Breedon on t H DE73 . . . . 252 E2
  Eckington S21 . . . . 59 E4
  Long Duckmanton S44 . . . 98 A3
Rectory Dr S42 . . . . 114 E4
Rectory Farm Mews
  DE72 . . . . 245 E4
Rectory Gdns
  Aston-on-T DE72 . . . . . . 246 A7
  Harthill S26 . . . . 61 E6
  Killamarsh S21 . . . . 60 D6
  Long Duckmanton S44 . . . 98 A3
Rectory La
  Appleby Magna DE12 . . . . 265 E1
  Breadsall DE21 . . . . 205 D5
  Kirk Ireton DE6 . . . . 165 B1
Rectory Mews DE65 . . . . . 241 B4
Rectory Pl NG11 . . . . 237 E6
Rectory Rd
  Breaston DE72 . . . . 235 E8
  Clowne S43 . . . . 80 E4
  Killamarsh S21 . . . . 60 D5
  Long Duckmanton S44 . . . 98 A4
  Staveley S43 . . . . 78 E2
Reculver Cl DE23 . . . . 231 D7
Redacre Cl S44 . . . . 99 C2
Red Barn Cl DE55 . . . . . . 148 B3
Redbarn La DE55 . . . . 148 B3
Redbridge Cl NG20 . . . . . 119 F2
Redbrook Ave S41 . . . . . . 115 B8
Redbrow Hollow SK6 . . . . . 15 A2
Redbury Cl DE1 . . . . 218 E4
Redcar Gdns 6 DE21 . . . . 205 D1
Reddish Ave S43 . . . . 45 D6
Reddish La SK23 . . . . 45 D6
Reddish Rd S43 . . . . 45 D6
Redens The NG10 . . . . . . 236 B4
Redfern Ave DE55 . . . . . . 169 E2
Redfern Cl SK13 . . . . 10 A6
Redfern Rd ST14 . . . . 210 A1
Redfern St S42 . . . . 131 C7
Redgap La SK17 . . . . 86 A8
Redgate SK13 . . . . 10 C4
Redgate St NG16 . . . . 160 D2
Redgrove Way S40 . . . . . . 114 C8
Red Hill DE4 . . . . 144 C4
Redhill Ct DE56 . . . . 179 B2
Redhill Foundation Prim Sch
  DE72 . . . . 221 C5
Redhill La DE13 . . . . 239 B5
Red Hill La DE4 . . . . 144 D3
Redhill Lodge Rd 6
  DE11 . . . . 256 A7
Redhouse Cl S43 . . . . 77 D4
Redhouse La SK12 . . . . . . 32 E7
Redhouse Stables Working
  Carriage Mus* DE4. . .127 D1
Red La
  Belper DE56 . . . . 191 B6
  Brinsley NG16 . . . . 171 E1
  Chesterfield S41 . . . . . . 77 C1
  Disley SK12 . . . . 32 C5
  Repton DE65 . . . . 249 F6
  South Normanton DE55 . . 159 F3
Redland Cl
  Derby DE24 . . . . 231 F4
  Ilkeston DE7 . . . . 194 F3
Red Lion Hill DE4 . . . . 153 A1
Red Lion Row S32 . . . . . . 72 C8
Red Lion Sq DE75 . . . . . . 181 E1
Red Lo SK12 . . . . 32 A6
Redmires Dr DE73 . . . . . . 233 A2
Redmires Rd S10 . . . . 42 B8
Redmoor Cl
  Burton u T DE15 . . . . . . 248 A3
  Codnor DE5 . . . . 170 B1
Redmoor La
  Disley SK12 . . . . 33 B6
  New Mills SK22 . . . . 33 B6
Rednall Cl S40 . . . . 95 C6
Red Rose Ct DE15 . . . . . . 254 E7
Redruth Pl DE24 . . . . 233 C5

Redshaw St DE1 . . . . 218 E7
Redstart Cl DE21 . . . . 220 F6
Redthorn Rd S13 . . . . 44 F8
Redvers Buller Rd S40 . . . 266 B1
Redway Croft 3 DE73 . . . 252 A8
Redwing Croft DE23 . . . . . 231 D7
Redwood Ave S21 . . . . . . 60 C5
Redwood Cl S43 . . . . 97 B8
Redwood Dr DE15 . . . . . . 255 A8
Redwood Inf Sch DE24 . . 231 F3
Redwood Jun Sch DE24 . . 231 F3
Redwood Rd DE24 . . . . . . 231 E3
Reedman Rd NG10 . . . . . . 236 B4
Reeves Ave S45 . . . . 132 C1
Reeves Rd DE23 . . . . 219 B1
Regal Gate DE73 . . . . 244 F8
Regency Cl
  Derby DE23 . . . . 231 D7
  4 Glossop SK13 . . . . . . 10 D1
Regent Ct
  Ironville NG16 . . . . 170 F4
  Swadlincote DE11 . . . . . 256 B2
Regent Gdns S41 . . . . 266 B4
Regents Ho 3 DE14 . . . . . 253 F7
Regent St
  Clowne S43 . . . . 80 D4
  Derby DE1 . . . . 267 C1
  Glossop, Padfield SK13 . . 10 B5
  Glossop SK13 . . . . 10 D1
  Ilkeston DE7 . . . . 208 F7
  Kimberley NG16 . . . . . . 195 F6
  Langley Mill NG16 . . . . . 182 B3
  Long Eaton NG10 . . . . . . 236 D8
  Stapleford NG10 . . . . . . 223 C5
  Swadlincote DE11 . . . . . 256 B2
Reginald Rd N DE21 . . . . . 219 F7
Reginald Rd S DE21 . . . . . 219 F6
Reginald St DE23 . . . . 219 B3
Regis Cl DE21 . . . . 206 B2
Reigate Dr DE22 . . . . 218 A7
Reigate Prim Sch DE22. . 217 F7
Reliant Cl DE11 . . . . 256 E1
Rembrandt Dr S18 . . . . . . 56 E1
Rempstone Dr S41 . . . . . . 115 C7
Renals St DE23 . . . . 267 B1
Reney Ave S8 . . . . 56 D6
Reney Cres S8 . . . . 56 D6
Reney Dr S8 . . . . 56 D6
Reney Rd S8 . . . . 56 E7
Reney Wlk S8 . . . . 56 D6
Renfrew St DE21 . . . . 219 E7
Renishaw Hall Gdns* S21 59 F1
Renishaw Hall (Mus & Craft
  Ctr)* S21 . . . . 59 F2
Renishaw Rd S43 . . . . 79 C4
Renshaw Dr DE11 . . . . . . 255 F5
Repton Ave DE23 . . . . 218 D1
Repton Cl S40 . . . . 95 A5
Repton Ct 8 NG19 . . . . . 136 E4
Repton Dr DE7 . . . . 209 B7
Repton Pl S18 . . . . 56 C1
Repton Prep Sch DE65 . . 243 C2
Repton Prim Sch DE65 . . 242 E2
Repton Rd
  Appleby Magna DE12 . . . . 265 F5
  Hartshorne DE11 . . . . . . 256 F8
  Long Eaton NG10 . . . . . . 235 F4
  Newton Solney DE15 . . . . 248 F8
  Willington DE65 . . . . 242 A5
Repton Sch DE65 . . . . . . 242 C3
Reservoir Hill DE12 . . . . . 262 D6
Reservoir Hos DE55 . . . . . 146 A5
Reservoir Rd SK23 . . . . . . 45 D7
Reservoir Terr S40 . . . . . . 95 E4
Reservoir Way DE11 . . . . . 256 E1
Resthaven DE11 . . . . 256 B5
Retford Cl DE21 . . . . 205 D2
Revill Cl DE7 . . . . 194 C2
Revill Cres NG9 . . . . 223 F8
Revolution House Mus The*
  S41 . . . . 77 A2
Reynard Cres S21 . . . . . . 79 B8
Reynards La SK17 . . . . . . 137 E4
Reynolds Ave DE5 . . . . . . 169 F1
Reynolds Cl S18 . . . . 75 E8
Reynolds Dr SK6 . . . . 23 B8
Rhein O' Thorns NG20 . . . 120 E5
Rhodes Ave S41 . . . . 95 F5
Rhodes Cotts S43 . . . . . . 80 F4
Rhodes Ho DE15 . . . . 248 C3
Rhodesia Rd S40 . . . . 95 C2
Rhodes St S13 . . . . 10 B5
Rhodeswood Dr SK13 . . . . 10 A6
Rhuddlan Pl SK23 . . . . . . 34 D1
Ribble Cl DE65 . . . . 240 D8
Ribblesdale DE7 . . . . 208 C5
Ribblesdale Cl DE22 . . . . 204 C2
Ribblesdale Dr S12 . . . . . 44 F1
Ribblesdale Rd NG10 . . . . 236 A5
Riber Ave DE55 . . . . 170 D8
Riber Bank 14 SK13 . . . . . 9 E1
Riber Cl
  20 Gamesley SK13 . . . . . 9 E1
  Long Eaton NG10 . . . . . . 236 D5
  Staveley S43 . . . . 97 C5
  West Hallam S43 . . . . . . 207 E8
Riber Cres S42 . . . . 131 B5
Riber Ct 11 S40 . . . . 95 D5
Riber Fold 18 SK13 . . . . . . 9 E1
Riber Gn 19 SK13 . . . . 9 E1
Riber Rd
  Lea DE4 . . . . 156 A8
  Matlock DE4 . . . . 143 C2
Riber Terr S40 . . . . 266 A2
Riber View Cl DE4 . . . . . . 144 A5
Richard La SK17 . . . . 69 C3
Richards Ct 2 S2 . . . . 43 B6

Richardson Dr DE7 . . . . . . 192 F6
Richardson Endowed Prim
  Sch DE7 . . . . 192 F6
Richardsons La DE55 . . . . 170 C5
Richardson St DE22 . . . . . 218 D6
Richards Rd S2 . . . . 43 B6
Richard Wakefield CE Prim
  Sch DE13 . . . . 239 C6
Richmond Ave
  Derby DE23 . . . . 231 C8
  Ilkeston DE7 . . . . 194 F4
  Long Eaton DE72 . . . . . . 236 A8
  Sandiacre NG10 . . . . . . 223 A4
  Sheffield S13 . . . . 44 F8
Richmond Cl
  Chesterfield S40 . . . . . . 114 E8
  Derby DE23 . . . . 231 A7
  Glossop SK13 . . . . 10 A5
  West Hallam DE7 . . . . . . 207 D8
Richmond Ct
  5 Barrow Hill S43 . . . . . 78 B3
  Repton DE65 . . . . 242 D2
  Sheffield S13 . . . . 44 D7
Richmond Dr
  Duffield DE56 . . . . 190 D5
  Mansfield Woodhouse
  NG19 . . . . 136 D2
Richmond Farm Mews
  S13 . . . . 44 D7
Richmond Gdns S41 . . . . . 266 B4
Richmond Gr S13 . . . . 44 E8
Richmond Hall Ave S13 . . 44 D8
Richmond Hall Cres S13 . . 44 D7
Richmond Hall Dr S13 . . . 44 D8
Richmond Hall Rd S13 . . . 44 D8
Richmond Hall Way S13 . . 44 D7
Richmond Hill Ho S13 . . . 44 D7
Richmond Hill Rd S13 . . . 44 D7
Richmond Ho DE65 . . . . . 228 C1
Richmond Pl S13 . . . . 44 D7
Richmond Rd
  Derby, Chaddesden
  DE21 . . . . 219 F6
  Derby, Rose Hill DE23 . . . 219 A1
  Sheffield S13 . . . . 44 D7
Richmond Terr SK6 . . . . . 23 B1
Richworth Rd S13 . . . . . . 44 F8
Rickmans Cnr Cvn Site
  DE12 . . . . 262 A6
Ricroft Rd SK6 . . . . 15 B3
Riddings DE22 . . . . 204 E4
Riddings Cl S2 . . . . 44 A7
Riddings Croft S41 . . . . . . 95 C6
Riddings Inf Sch DE55 . . 170 D6
Riddings Jun Sch DE55 . . 170 D6
Riddings La S32 . . . . 72 D4
Riddings St DE22 . . . . 218 F3
Ridd Way S42 . . . . 115 A3
Ridge Ave SK6 . . . . 23 A4
Ridge Cl SK13 . . . . 9 E3
Ridge Cres S43 . . . . 23 A3
Ridgedale Rd S44 . . . . . . 118 A8
Ridgedale View DE5 . . . . . 169 D2
Ridge End Fold SK6 . . . . . 23 A2
Ridgehill Ave S12 . . . . . . 44 B5
Ridgehill Gr S12 . . . . 44 B5
Ridge La SK23 . . . . 46 E1
Ridge Rd
  Eckington S21 . . . . 58 E2
  Marple SK6 . . . . 23 A3
Ridge The
  Blackwell DE55 . . . . 147 E1
  Marple SK6 . . . . 23 A3
Ridge Top La SK22 . . . . . 25 C2
Ridgeway
  Chellaston DE73 . . . . . . 245 A8
  Clowne S43 . . . . 80 F2
  Dronfield S18 . . . . 57 D3
  Heanor DE75 . . . . 193 F8
  Shirebrook NG20 . . . . . . 119 F5
Ridgeway Ave
  Bolsover S44 . . . . 99 C2
  Derby DE23 . . . . 231 D6
Ridgeway Craft* S12. 58 E8
Ridgeway Cres S12 . . . . . 44 A6
Ridgeway Ct DE23 . . . . . . 218 D2
Ridgeway Dr
  Ilkeston DE7 . . . . 208 B5
  Sheffield S12 . . . . 44 A6
Ridgeway Inf Sch DE23 . . 231 D6
Ridgeway La DE56 . . . . . . 168 C4
Ridgeway Moor S12 . . . . . 58 E6
Ridgeway Prim Sch S12 . . 58 E8
Ridgeway Rd
  Burton u T DE15 . . . . . . 254 E7
  Sheffield S12 . . . . 44 A5
Ridgeways The SK22 . . . . 25 D2
Ridgeway W S43 . . . . 80 E2
Ridgewood Ct DE21 . . . . . 205 E2
Ridgewood Dr DE4 . . . . . 155 C6
Ridgway The SK12 . . . . . . 32 C6
Riding Bank DE73 . . . . . . 251 F6
Riding Hill Ave NG20 . . . . 119 D3
Ridings Rd SK13 . . . . 9 F5
Ridings The
  Mansfield NG19 . . . . 136 F1
  Ockbrook DE72 . . . . 221 D5
Rigga La DE56 . . . . 191 B1
Riggotts Way S42 . . . . . . 94 E8
Riggs La DE6 . . . . 212 A7
Rigley Ave 10 DE7 . . . . . . 194 F1
Rigsby Ct DE3 . . . . 217 C3
Riley Ave DE55 . . . . 157 D2
Riley Back La S32 . . . . . . 71 E6
Riley La DE5 . . . . 169 A6
Rimsdale Cl DE24 . . . . . . 231 E3
Ringer La S43 . . . . 80 E3
Ringer Way S43 . . . . 80 E3

Ringinglow Rd S10, S11. . 42 E4
Ring-o-Bells La SK12 . . . . 32 D6
Ringstone Way SK23 . . . . 45 D8
Ringwood Ave
  Chesterfield S41 . . . . . . 95 E7
  Compstall SK14 . . . . 15 A8
  Staveley S43 . . . . 97 C8
Ringwood Cl 3 DE21 . . . . 219 E8
Ringwood Rd S43 . . . . 96 F8
Ringwood View S43 . . . . . 96 F7
Rink Dr DE11 . . . . 256 B3
Ripley Ho DE21 . . . . 220 E3
Ripley Hospl DE5 . . . . . . 169 D1
Ripley Inf Sch DE5 . . . . . 180 D8
Ripley Jun Sch DE5 . . . . 180 D8
Ripley Rd
  Bullbridge DE56 . . . . . . 168 D5
  Heage DE56 . . . . 169 A1
Ripon Cres DE21 . . . . 219 E8
Ripon Gdns SK17 . . . . . . 85 D5
Risborrow Cl DE65 . . . . . . 229 D4
Rises The SK13 . . . . 9 F5
Rise The
  Derby DE22 . . . . 204 E2
  Horwich End SK23 . . . . . 45 C4
  Swadlincote DE11 . . . . . 255 F5
Risings The SK22 . . . . . . 24 B1
Risley Ct DE7 . . . . 194 F3
Risley La DE72 . . . . 222 D2
Risley Lower Gram CE Prim
  Sch DE72 . . . . 222 E4
Rivendale Cvn Pk DE6 . . . 150 E6
Rivenhall Cl DE23 . . . . . . 230 F7
Riverbank DE4 . . . . 110 F1
Riverbank The DE56 . . . . . 242 B5
Riverbank Way SK13 . . . . 17 F7
Rivercroft Cl ST14 . . . . . . 197 A3
River Ct S17 . . . . 56 A7
River St DE1 . . . . 267 B4
Riverdale S32 . . . . 72 C2
Riverdale Cl DE15 . . . . . . 248 E5
Rivermead Ho DE1 . . . . . 267 B5
Riversdale DE56 . . . . 168 B4
Riversfield Dr ST14 . . . . . 196 F3
Riverside
  Baslow DE45 . . . . 91 D6
  Walton-on-T DE12 . . . . . 253 C1
Riverside Bsns Pk DE45. 109 C7
Riverside Cres
  Bakewell DE45 . . . . 109 D6
  Holymoorside S42 . . . . . 113 E7
Riverside Ct
  Baslow DE45 . . . . 91 E6
  Calver S32 . . . . 72 D1
Riverside Dr
  Branston DE14 . . . . 253 F7
  Calver S32 . . . . 72 D1
Riverside Rd DE21 . . . . . . 219 D4
Riverside Studios S18. . 57 B1
Riverside Way
  Bolsover S44 . . . . 98 E2
  Mansfield Woodhouse
  NG19 . . . . 136 D5
River View
  Aldercar DE55 . . . . 171 A6
  Belper DE56 . . . . 190 F7
  Chesterfield S40 . . . . . . 115 A8
  Long Eaton NG10 . . . . . . 236 A3
  Longnor SK17 . . . . 121 B6
  Tideswell SK17 . . . . 88 D7
Riverview Cotts 2 SK13. . 17 C7
Rivington Rd 3 NG9 . . . . 223 E2
Roadmeadow Cl DE6 . . . . 185 D8
Robert Cl S18 . . . . 76 E5
Robert Rd S8 . . . . 57 A7
Roberts Ave NG17 . . . . . . 148 F2
Roberts Dr DE55 . . . . 159 B4
Robertson's Ave S44 . . . . 98 A4
Robertson Rd SK17 . . . . . 85 B6
Roberts St DE7 . . . . 209 A6
Robey Dr NG16 . . . . 182 F3
Robian Way DE11 . . . . . . 256 A4
Robin's Cross La DE65 . . . 227 C6
Robina Dr NG16 . . . . 195 C8
Robin Croft S40 . . . . 114 F7
Robincroft Rd S42 . . . . . . 114 D4
Robin Croft Rd DE22 . . . . 204 E4
Robinettes La NG16 . . . . . 195 D1
Robin Hood Cl NG16 . . . . 182 F1
Robin Hood Rd DE4 . . . . . 256 C1
Robin Hood Prim Sch
  NG19 . . . . 136 B3
Robin Hood Rd DE4 . . . . . 156 C2
Robinia Cl DE21 . . . . 206 C3
Robinlands La S33 . . . . . . 38 B4
Robin Rd DE1 . . . . 218 F7
Robins Cl DE72 . . . . 233 D5
Robinscross DE72 . . . . . . 221 B1
Robinson's Ind Est DE23 . 219 B2
Robinson Rd DE11 . . . . . . 256 A6
Robinson Way S21 . . . . . . 60 C6
Robinwood Lo 30 SK13 . . 9 E1
Robridding Rd S45 . . . . . . 129 A4
Robson Dr DE24 . . . . 233 A7
Roby Lea DE74 . . . . 246 F4
Rocester Way S42 . . . . . . 131 F6
Roche 9 S20 . . . . 59 E8
Rochester Cl
  Derby DE23 . . . . 233 A5

Rochester Cl continued
  Long Eaton NG10. . . . . . 236 A7
Rochley Cl DE21 . . . . 205 F2
Rock Bank
  Buxton SK17 . . . . 85 C3
  Horwich End SK23 . . . . . 45 E6
Rockbourne Cl DE24 . . . . 233 D6
Rockcliffe Cl DE11 . . . . . . 256 B1
Rockcrete The S21 . . . . . . 191 E4
Rock Cres S45 . . . . 131 A5
Rockfield Rd SK17 . . . . . . 85 D8
Rockhall Terr S22 . . . . . . 25 E2
Rock Ho DE4 . . . . 155 B6
Rock House Cl DE55 . . . . 147 F5
Rockhouse Rd DE24 . . . . 233 A6
Rockingham 11 S20 . . . . . 59 E8
Rockingham Cl
  Chesterfield S40 . . . . . . 95 C3
  Derby DE22 . . . . 205 A4
  3 Dronfield S18 . . . . . . 56 C1
Rock La S44 . . . . 116 E6
Rockley Cl S40 . . . . 114 F7
Rockley Way NG20 . . . . . 119 E4
Rockmay Ho DE55 . . . . . . 147 F5
Rock Mill Bsns Pk S32. . 71 E4
Rock Mill La SK22 . . . . . . 33 B7
Rock Side SK16 . . . . 195 F6
Rockside Cotts S43 . . . . . 80 E4
Rockside Hall DE4 . . . . . . 143 C6
Rockside Hydro DE4 . . . . 143 C6
Rockside Stps DE4 . . . . . 143 C6
Rockside View DE4 . . . . . 143 C7
Rock Sq S32 . . . . 71 D6
Rock St S22 . . . . 33 C7
Rocks The DE4 . . . . 144 A5
Rock Terr
  Bakewell DE45 . . . . 109 D6
  Buxton SK17 . . . . 85 B6
Rock The S45 . . . . 109 C6
Rockvale Terr DE4 . . . . . . 143 B1
Rockvale Villas DE4 . . . . . 143 B1
Rock View SK17 . . . . 88 A7
Rodge Croft S41 . . . . 77 A3
Rodger's La DE55 . . . . . . 159 A5
Rodknoll La S42 . . . . 93 D2
Rod Moor Rd S17, S18. . . 56 B4
Rodney Cl DE65 . . . . 228 C2
Rodney Ho DE24 . . . . 232 E6
Rodney Way DE7 . . . . 194 F3
Rodney Wlk DE23 . . . . . . 230 E7
Rodsley Cl S40 . . . . 95 B5
Rodsley Cres DE23 . . . . . 231 D5
Rodsley La
  Rodsley DE6 . . . . 199 F7
  Yeaveley DE6 . . . . 199 E5
Rodwood Ave S43 . . . . . . 80 A4
Roe's La DE4 . . . . 157 A1
Roebuck Pl SK23 . . . . 47 B6
Roecar Cl S41 . . . . 77 C4
Roe Cross Ind Est SK14. . 9 A5
Roe Cross Rd SK14. . . . . . 9 A5
Roe Farm La DE21 . . . . . . 219 E7
Roe Farm Prim Sch
  DE21 . . . . 219 E8
Roehampton Dr
  Derby DE23 . . . . 218 A7
  Stapleford NG9 . . . . 209 E2
Roe's Ct DE4 . . . . 157 A2
Roe Wlk DE23 . . . . 219 A1
Rogers Ave S80 . . . . 81 D1
Rogers Cl DE55 . . . . 227 D1
Rolaine Cl NG19 . . . . 136 C4
Rolleston Cres NG16 . . . . 195 F8
Rolleston Dr NG16 . . . . . . 195 B8
Rolleston La DE13 . . . . . . 239 D5
Rolleston Rd DE13 . . . . . 240 B1
Rollins La SK6 . . . . 15 A1
Roman Bank NG19 . . . . . 136 D3
Roman Rd DE1 . . . . 219 B7
Roman Way DE72 . . . . . . 221 C1
Romeley La S43 . . . . 80 D3
Romeley La S43 . . . . 80 B2
Romford Way 4 S43 . . . . 78 B3
Romney Dr S18 . . . . 56 E1
Romney Gdns S2 . . . . 43 B6
Romorantin Pl NG10 . . . . 236 F2
Romsley Cl DE3 . . . . 217 D4
Rona Cl DE24 . . . . 231 E4
Ronald Cl DE23 . . . . 230 E7
Rood La
  Clowne S43 . . . . 80 E3
  Idridgehay DE56 . . . . . . 176 F6
Rookery The DE11 . . . . . . 256 F2
Roosevelt Ave
  Derby DE21 . . . . 220 E5
  Long Eaton NG10 . . . . . . 236 C5
Roost The S32 . . . . 53 A6
Roper Ave DE75 . . . . 193 F7
Roper Hill S10 . . . . 42 D7
Ropewalk Ind Ctr DE7. . 195 A1
Ropewalk The
  Heanor DE75 . . . . 193 F8
  Ilkeston DE7 . . . . 195 A1
  Stanley Common DE7 . . . 193 B1
Rosamond's Ride DE23 . . 231 D8
Rosamond Ave S17 . . . . . 56 A6
Rosamond Cl S17 . . . . . . 56 A6
Rosamond Ct S17 . . . . . . 56 A5
Rosamond Dr S17. . . . . . . 56 A6
Rosamond Glade S17 . . . . 56 A6
Rosamond Pl S17 . . . . . . 56 A6
Rose Ave
  Borrowash DE72 . . . . . . 221 C1
  Burton u T DE13. . . . . . . 241 A2
  Calow S44 . . . . 97 A3
  Clowne S43 . . . . 81 A5

Rose Ave *continued*
Ilkeston DE7 . . . . **194** E2
Rose Bank Cl SK14 . . . . **9** D5
Roseberry Ct DE21 . . . . . **206** B1
Rose Cl DE73 . . . . **232** E1
Rose Cottage Dr NG17 . . **148** F2
Rose Cotts
Bonsall DE4 . . . . **142** C1
Chesterfield S41 . . . . **96** C2
Rose Cres S43 . . . . **79** C4
Rosecroft Gdns DE11 . . **256** C3
Rose Ct
Clay Cross S45 . . . . **131** A4
Long Eaton NG10 . . . . . . **223** B1
Rosedale Ave
Chesterfield S40 . . . . **115** B8
Derby DE24 . . . . **233** A6
Rosedale Cl DE21 . . . . . **236** B6
Rosedale View S18 . . . . **114** B7
Rosedale Way NG19 . . . . **136** F2
Rosedene View DE12 . . . **262** C4
Rose End Ave DE4 . . . . . **155** A6
Rose Garth S41 . . . . **96** C1
Rose Gdns S44 . . . . **97** D2
Roseheath Cl DE23 . . . . **231** E5
Rose Hill
Chesterfield S40 . . . . **266** B3
Sheffield S20 . . . . **59** B8
Woodville DE11 . . . . **256** C3
Rose Hill Ave S20 . . . . . . **59** B8
Rosehill Bsns Ctr DE23 . **219** A2
Rose Hill Cl S20 . . . . **59** B8
Rosehill Ct S44 . . . . **99** A1
Rose Hill Dr S20 . . . . **59** B8
Rose Hill E S40 . . . . **266** B3
Rosehill Inf Sch DE23 . . **219** B3
Rose Hill Mews S20 . . . . **59** B8
Rose Hill St DE23 . . . . . **219** A2
Rose Hill View S20 . . . . . **59** B8
Rose Hill W S40 . . . . . . **266** A3
Rose La
Mansfield Woodhouse
NG19 . . . . **136** C3
Ticknall DE73 . . . . **251** A4
Roseland La NG20 . . . . . **119** C3
Roseleigh Cres DE11 . . . **255** F6
Rosemary Ct 1 S8 . . . . . . **43** A3
Rosemary Dr DE24 . . . . . **233** A5
Rosemoor La DE21 . . . . . **206** B1
Rosemount Ct DE22 . . . . **204** C3
Rosengrave St DE1 . . . . . **267** B2
Rose Tree La DE11 . . . . . **255** F7
Rosette Ct DE21 . . . . **206** C3
Rose Valley DE11 . . . . . . **256** A5
Rose Way S21 . . . . **60** D5
Rosewood Cl
Derby DE24 . . . . **233** B7
South Normanton DE55 . . **160** B7
Rose Wood Cl S41 . . . . . . **95** D8
Rosewood Cres DE75 . . . **182** B2
Rosewood Rd DE15 . . . . **254** F6
Roseybank SK23 . . . . **34** B1
Rosier Cres DE55 . . . . . . **170** A8
Rosling Way S44 . . . . **97** D2
Rosliston CE Prim Sch
DE12 . . . . **260** C6
Rosliston Forestry Visitor
Ctr ★ DE12 . . . . **260** C8
Rosliston Rd
Burton u T DE15 . . . . . . **254** D3
Burton u T DE15 . . . . . . **254** E6
Walton-on-T DE12 . . . . . **259** E8
Rosliston Rd S DE15 . . . **254** E5
Roslyn Cres S32 . . . . **53** A7
Roslyn Rd S32 . . . . **53** A7
Rosell Dr NG9 . . . . **223** E5
Rossendale DE7 . . . . **194** E4
Rossendale Cl S40 . . . . . **114** E8
Rosser Ave S43 . . . . **43** F2
Rossington Dr DE23 . . . . **230** F6
Rosslyn Gdns DE24 . . . . **233** A6
Ross Wlk DE21 . . . . **205** E1
Roston Cl 3 S18 . . . . **56** D1
Rosyth Cres DE73 . . . . . **232** E1
Rothay Cl S18 . . . . **75** E8
Rothbourne Croft DE6 . . **151** D2
Rothbury Ave NG9 . . . . . **209** D2
Rothbury Pl DE21 . . . . . . **205** E1
Rother Ave S43 . . . . **96** D8
Rother Cl S40 . . . . **114** E8
Rother Croft S42 . . . . . . **131** D8
Rotherham Cl S21 . . . . . . **60** F8
Rotherham Rd
Bolsover S44 . . . . **99** E2
Eckington S20, S21 . . . . . **59** F6
Killamarsh S21 . . . . **60** F8
New Houghton NG19 . . . . **134** F7
Scarcliffe S44 . . . . **118** C7
Shirebrook S44, NG19 . . . **118** D3
Spinkhill S43 . . . . **61** D2
Rotherham Rd N S20 . . . **59** F8
Rother Jun Sch S40 . . . . . **115** A8
Rotherside Rd S21 . . . . . **59** F4
Rother St S45 . . . . **132** C2
Rothervale Rd S40 . . . . . **115** A8
Rother Valley Ctry Pk ★
S21 . . . . **60** C8
Rother Valley Way S20 . . **60** B8
Rother Way S41 . . . . **96** B6
Rotherwood Rd S21 . . . . . **60** E7
Rothesay Cl DE24 . . . . . **231** E4
Rothey Gr S40 . . . . **94** F5
Rothwell Ho DE65 . . . . . **228** D1
Rothwell Ho DE56 . . . . . **179** B4
Rothwell Rd DE3 . . . . . . **217** D3
Rough Heanor Rd DE3 . . **218** A2
Rough La DE6 . . . . **186** E4
Roughlow La DE6 . . . . . . **183** D1

Roughpiece La DE4 . . . . . **166** D5
Roughton Cl DE3 . . . . . . **230** D8
Round Hill Cl SK13 . . . . **9** F3
Roundhouse Rd DE24 . . . **219** C4
Round Way SK22 . . . . **33** D8
Rouse St S45 . . . . **132** D1
Rousseau Ct DE6 . . . . . . **173** D1
Routh Ave DE74 . . . . **247** B2
Rowan Ave
Ripley DE5 . . . . **180** D8
Stapleford NG9 . . . . **209** E2
Rowan Cl
Creswell S80 . . . . **81** E2
Darley Dale DE4 . . . . **127** B3
Derby, Cherrytree Hill
DE21 . . . . **220** B5
Derby, Sinfin DE24 . . . . . **231** D3
Ilkeston DE7 . . . . **208** F5
Mansfield NG19 . . . . **136** D1
Rowan Croft NG17 . . . . . **148** F4
Rowan Ct ST14 . . . . **196** F4
Rowan Dr
Kilburn DE56 . . . . **192** B8
Selston NG16 . . . . **171** D6
Shirebrook NG20 . . . . . . **119** D5
Shirland DE55 . . . . **146** D1
Rowan Park Cl DE23 . . . . **231** D7
Rowan Rd
Eckington S21 . . . . **59** C1
Mastin Moor S43 . . . . **79** C3
Rowan Sch The S17 . . . . . **55** E6
Rowan Tree Cl
Ashbourne DE6 . . . . **185** D8
Killamarsh S21 . . . . **60** C5
Rowan Tree Dell S17 . . . . **55** E3
Rowan Tree Rd S21 . . . . . **60** C5
Rowan Wlk SK13 . . . . **9** E4
Rowarth Ave S43 . . . . **9** D2
Rowarth Bank 9 SK13 . . . . **9** D2
Rowarth Cl 10 SK13 . . . . . **9** D2
Rowarth Fold 12 SK13 . . . . **9** D2
Rowarth Way 11 SK13 . . . . **9** D2
Rowbury Dr DE15 . . . . . . **248** B2
Rowdale Cres S12 . . . . . . **44** D5
Rowditch Ave DE22 . . . . **218** D4
Rowditch Cotts DE1 . . . . **218** D4
Rowditch Pl DE22 . . . . . . **218** D4
Rowena Cl DE24 . . . . **232** F7
Rowland Ct DE55 . . . . . . **158** F4
Rowland Rd 8 S2 . . . . **43** A8
Rowland St
Alfreton DE55 . . . . **159** A4
Derby DE24 . . . . **232** E4
Rowley Cl DE11 . . . . **256** D5
Rowley Cl DE11 . . . . **256** D5
Rowley Gdns DE23 . . . . . **231** C7
Rowley La DE23 . . . . **231** C2
Rowleys Mill 3 DE1 . . . . **218** E5
Rowsley Ave
Derby DE23 . . . . **231** D8
Long Eaton NG10 . . . . . . **236** A5
Rowsley CE Prim Sch
DE4 . . . . **126** F8
Rowsley Cl SK13 . . . . **9** E2
Rowsley Cres S43 . . . . . . **97** C8
Rowsley Gn SK13 . . . . **9** E2
Rowsley Gr SK13 . . . . **9** E2
Rowsley Mews SK13 . . . . . . **9** E2
Rowsley South Sta ★
DE4 . . . . **127** A5
Rowsley Wlk SK13 . . . . **9** E2
Row The
Great Cubley DE6 . . . . . . **198** E1
Lea DE4 . . . . **156** B8
Rowthorne Ave DE55 . . . **170** A8
Rowthorne La S44 . . . . . **134** B7
Rowton Grange Rd SK23 . **47** B5
Roxburgh Ave DE21 . . . . **219** E7
Roxton Ave 2 S8 . . . . **56** F8
Roxton Ct NG16 . . . . **195** F7
Royal App DE73 . . . . **244** F8
Royal Ave NG10 . . . . **223** D1
Royal Cl DE72 . . . . **221** B1
Royal Croft Dr DE45 . . . . **91** E6
Royal Crown Derby Visitor
Ctr ★ DE1 . . . . **267** C1
Royale Cl S21 . . . . **59** E3
Royal Gate DE56 . . . . . . **179** D3
Royal Gr DE21 . . . . **206** D3
Royal Hill Rd DE21 . . . . . **220** D6
Royal La DE12 . . . . **262** B4
Royal Oak Ct S43 . . . . **79** D4
Royal Oak Pl DE45 . . . . . **109** D5
Royal Oak Rd S42 . . . . . . **32** D5
Royal Sch for the Deaf
DE22 . . . . **218** D6
Royal Scot Rd DE24 . . . . **219** E2
Royal Way DE24 . . . . **219** E3
Roydon Cl DE3 . . . . **217** C3
Royle Ave SK13 . . . . **10** D1
Royston Cl
Ashbourne DE6 . . . . **185** C8
Chesterfield S40 . . . . **114** B7
Royston Dr DE56 . . . . . . **179** D5
Rubens Cl
Dronfield S18 . . . . **56** F1
Marple SK6 . . . . **23** C8
Ruby Ho S8 . . . . **43** B5
Ruby Paddocks NG16 . . . **195** F5
Rudyard Ave DE21 . . . . . **220** E4
Rufford Cl S40 . . . . **95** E8
Rufford Dr NG19 . . . . . . **136** E3
Rufford Rd NG10 . . . . . . **236** B4
Ruffstone Cl DE56 . . . . . **191** C7
Rugby Cl DE14 . . . . **254** C8

Rugby St DE24 . . . . **219** E1
Rugeley Ave NG10 . . . . . **237** A7
Ruislip Cl NG16 . . . . **195** E7
Rupert Rd DE21 . . . . **220** A7
Rupert St
Ilkeston DE7 . . . . **195** A1
Pilsley DE55 . . . . **132** B3
Rushcliffe Ave DE21 . . . **219** F6
Rushcliffe Gdns DE21 . . **219** F6
Rushdale Ave
Derby DE23 . . . . **231** D6
Sheffield S8 . . . . **43** B5
Rushdale Mount 4 S8 . . . **43** A5
Rushdale Rd S8 . . . . **43** B5
Rushdale Terr 3 S8 . . . . **43** A5
Rushen Mount S40 . . . . **114** F6
Rushes The
Glossop SK13 . . . . **9** F4
Mansfield Woodhouse
NG19 . . . . **136** D5
Rushleigh Ct S17 . . . . **55** D7
Rushley Ave S17 . . . . **55** D8
Rushley Cl S17 . . . . **55** D8
Rushley Dr S17 . . . . **55** D7
Rushley Rd S17 . . . . **55** D7
Rush Leys NG10 . . . . **236** D5
Rushmere SK13 . . . . **17** E8
Rushpool Ave NG19 . . . . **136** D3
Rushpool Cl NG19 . . . . . **136** F2
Rushton Cl DE13 . . . . . . **239** C6
Rushton Dr SK6 . . . . **23** A5
Rushup Cl DE22 . . . . **205** A5
Rushup La SK17, SK23 . . . **48** D8
Rushycroft SK13 . . . . **9** A4
Rushy La NG10, DE72 . . . **222** E6
Ruskin Ave NG10 . . . . . . **236** B5
Ruskin Rd
Derby DE1 . . . . **218** F7
Mansfield NG19 . . . . **135** D1
Ruskin Sq S8 . . . . **43** A6
Ruskin Way DE23 . . . . . . **231** B8
Rusk The S43 . . . . **80** B6
Russell Ct 1 NG10 . . . . . **223** D1
Russell Gdns S42 . . . . . . **131** B6
Russell St
Compstall SK6 . . . . **15** B3
Derby DE24 . . . . **219** C1
Long Eaton NG10 . . . . . . **223** D1
Swadlincote DE11 . . . . . . **256** C3
Russet Cl
Derby DE21 . . . . **206** B1
Hatton DE65 . . . . **227** C1
Russet Ct DE23 . . . . **218** E3
Ruston Cl
Chesterfield S40 . . . . **95** B6
Swadlincote DE11 . . . . . . **256** B4
Rutherford Rise 8 DE21 **205** F2
Ruthyn Ave S43 . . . . **80** A7
Rutland Ave
Bolsover S44 . . . . **99** A1
Borrowash DE72 . . . . . . **221** C2
Matlock DE4 . . . . **143** C6
Ripley DE5 . . . . **181** A7
Rutland Cl DE15 . . . . . . **254** D6
Rutland Ct
Ilkeston DE7 . . . . **194** D1
Matlock DE4 . . . . **143** C6
Rutland Dr DE3 . . . . **217** E3
Rutland Gr NG10 . . . . . . **223** C5
Rutland Mews DE45 . . . . **109** E6
Rutland Pl DE56 . . . . **168** B6
Rutland Rd
Chesterfield S40 . . . . **266** A3
Westwood NG16 . . . . **171** C4
Rutland Sq DE45 . . . . . . **109** D6
Rutland St
Chesterfield S41 . . . . **77** A2
Derby DE23 . . . . **219** A1
Ilkeston DE7 . . . . **194** F2
Matlock DE4 . . . . **143** C6
Rutland Terr
Barlow S18 . . . . **75** E3
Ilkeston DE7 . . . . **194** F2
Rutland Way SK23 . . . . . . **34** D2
Ryal Cl DE72 . . . . **221** C5
Ryan Cl DE24 . . . . **231** E3
Rycroft CE Mid Sch
ST14 . . . . **196** E4
Rycroft Rd DE74 . . . . . . **247** D6
Rydal Ave NG10 . . . . **223** B2
Rydal Cl
Derby DE22 . . . . **204** E4
Dronfield S18 . . . . **56** D1
Rydal Cres S41 . . . . **95** E8
Rydal Way S45 . . . . **131** B3
Ryde Ho DE24 . . . . **233** C7
Ryder Cl DE11 . . . . **255** E2
Rye Butts DE73 . . . . **232** F1
Rye Cl DE21 . . . . **205** E3
Rye Cres S45 . . . . **131** D3
Ryecroft DE4 . . . . **127** D2
Ryecroft Glen Rd S17 . . . **56** A8
Ryecroft St NG9 . . . . **223** B8
Ryecroft View S17 . . . . . . **55** D8
Rye Ct S45 . . . . **131** D3
Ryedale Gdns DE23 . . . . **231** C5
Rye Flatt La S40 . . . . **95** C2
Rye Flatts La DE65 . . . . . **227** D1
Ryegrass Cl DE56 . . . . . . **179** D4
Ryegrass Rd DE21 . . . . . **206** C2
Ryehill Ave S40 . . . . **95** A2
Ryemere Cl NG16 . . . . . . **182** E2
Ryemere Ct NG16 . . . . . . **182** E2
Ryknield Cl DE23 . . . . . . **230** E6
Ryknield Ct S45 . . . . **131** C3
Ryknield Dr DE23 . . . . . **230** D7
Ryknield Prim Sch DE14 . **253** F2
Ryknield Rd DE23 . . . . . **230** E6

Rykneld Rise S42 . . . . . . **115** A3
Rykneld Sq S40 . . . . **266** B3
Rykneld Way DE23 . . . . . **230** E6
Ryknield Hill DE5 . . . . . . **180** B2
Ryknield Rd DE56, DE7 . . **192** B8
Rylah Hill S44 . . . . **118** A5
Rymill Dr DE21 . . . . **205** F1
Ryton Way DE65 . . . . . . **228** D1

S

Sacheveral La DE4 . . . . . **140** F4
Sacheverall Ave NG16 . . **160** D3
Sacheverel St DE1 . . . . . **267** B2
Sackerville Terr S21 . . . . . **60** B7
Sackville Cl S40 . . . . **114** B8
Sackville St DE23 . . . . . . **231** F8
Saddlers Cl NG19 . . . . . . **136** F1
Saddlers Croft S42 . . . . . **131** F7
Saddletree View S43 . . . . **79** B4
Saddleworth Wlk DE24 . . **232** E3
Sadler Gate DE1 . . . . **267** B3
Saffron Dr DE21 . . . . **206** A1
Sage Dr DE11 . . . . **256** F4
Sage Mews SK23 . . . . **47** B8
St Agnes Ave DE22 . . . . . **204** D4
St Aidan's Ave S2 . . . . . . **43** E8
St Aidan's Dr S2 . . . . **43** E8
St Aidan's Pl S2 . . . . **43** E8
St Aidan's Rd S2 . . . . **43** E8
St Aidan's Way S2 . . . . . . **43** E8
St Alban's RC Prim Sch
DE21 . . . . **219** F6
St Albans Cl
Holmewood S42 . . . . **132** E8
Long Eaton NG10 . . . . . . **236** E5
St Albans Rd DE22 . . . . . **218** D3
St Albans St SK22 . . . . . . **33** C8
St Alkmund's Cl DE56 . . . **190** E4
St Alkmund's Way DE1 . . **267** B4
St Alkmunds Way DE56 . . **190** E4
St Andrew's CE Jun Sch
SK13 . . . . **9** F4
St Andrew's CE Methodist
Prim Sch S18 . . . . **56** D1
St Andrew's CE Prim Sch
Clifton Campville B79 . . . **263** E2
Stanley DE7 . . . . **207** B5
St Andrew's Cl B79 . . . . . **263** F2
St Andrew's Cl DE7 . . . . . **194** D1
St Andrew's Dr
Ilkeston DE7 . . . . **208** E8
Swanwick DE55 . . . . **169** F7
St Andrews Ct SK13 . . . . . **10** A4
St Andrews Rise S40 . . . **114** C8
St Andrews Sch DE21 . . . **205** E1
St Andrews View DE21 . . **205** E1
St Andrews Wlk SK22 . . . . **33** D8
St Ann's Cl SK23 . . . . **46** F6
St Anne's CE Prim Sch
DE45 . . . . **91** E5
St Anne's Cl
Baslow DE45 . . . . **91** E5
Derby DE1 . . . . **218** E6
Staveley S43 . . . . **97** E8
St Anne's La DE74 . . . . . **247** B3
St Anne's RC Prim Sch
SK17 . . . . **66** B1
St Anne's Well (Micrarium) ★
SK17 . . . . **85** B8
St Annes St 4 SK14 . . . . . **16** A8
St Anselm's Sch DE45 . . . **109** C6
St Augustines Ave S40 . . **115** A8
St Augustines Cres S40 . . **115** A8
St Augustines Dr S40 . . . **266** B1
St Augustines Mount
S40 . . . . **266** B1
St Augustines Rd S40 . . . **115** A8
St Augustines Rise 1
S40 . . . . **115** A8
St Augustine St S40 . . . . **218** F1
St Barnabas Ho 12 S2 . . . **43** A8
St Barnabas La 4 S2 . . . . **43** A8
St Barnabas Rd 5 S2 . . . . **43** A8
St Bartholomew's CE Sch
SK17 . . . . **121** B7
St Benedict RC Sch &
Performing Arts Coll
DE22 . . . . **204** E4
St Benedicts Cl S2 . . . . . . **43** D8
St Bride's Farm DE73 . . . **251** D7
St Bride's Wlk DE22 . . . . **218** B6
St Catherine's Rd DE11 . . **255** F5
St Catherines Prep Sch
SK6 . . . . **23** B7
St Chad's CE Inf Sch
DE23 . . . . **218** F2
St Chad's Cl
Denstone ST14 . . . . **196** D6
Draycott DE72 . . . . **235** A7
St Chad's Rd DE23 . . . . . **218** F2
St Chad's Way S41 . . . . . . **96** A8
St Charles's RC Prim Sch
SK13 . . . . **9** E5
St Charles Cl SK13 . . . . **9** F5
St Christopher's Way
DE24 . . . . **219** D3
St Clare's Cl DE22 . . . . . **218** D3
St Clare's Sch DE3 . . . . . **218** A2
St Cuthbert's Rd DE22 . . **218** D3
St David's Cl DE22 . . . . . **218** D3
St David's Rise S40 . . . . . **114** D8
St Davids Cl NG16 . . . . . **170** F3
St Davids Rd B79 . . . . . . **263** F2
St Edmund's Ave NG19 . . **136** C3

Ros–St J 305

St Edmund's CE Prim Sch
NG19 . . . . **136** C3
St Edmund's Cl DE22 . . . **204** F4
St Edward's CE Prim Sch
DE74 . . . . **247** B3
St Edward's RC Prim Sch
DE11 . . . . **256** B5
St Edward's Rd DE74 . . . **247** B2
St Edwards Ct DE11 . . . . **255** E5
St Elizabeth's RC Prim Sch
DE56 . . . . **178** F5
St Elizabeth Cl S2 . . . . . . **43** B8
St Elphin's CE Sch DE4 . . **127** C1
St George's CE Prim Sch
New Mills SK22 . . . . **33** C8
Swadlincote DE11 . . . . . . **256** B1
St George's Cl DE22 . . . . **204** F3
St George's Pl 1 DE56 . . **178** F4
St George's RC Prim Sch
DE23 . . . . **231** C7
St Georges Dr 3 NG9 . . . **223** F2
St George's Ho DE21 . . . **204** F3
St Georges Rd SK22 . . . . . **33** C8
St Giles CE Prim Sch
Killamarsh S21 . . . . **60** C6
Matlock DE4 . . . . **143** C3
St Giles Cl S40 . . . . **115** B8
St Giles Rd DE23 . . . . . . **218** F1
St Giles Sch DE21 . . . . . **205** C1
St Giles Wlk DE4 . . . . . . **143** C4
St Helen's Cl
Chesterfield S41 . . . . **266** B4
Darley Dale DE4 . . . . **127** B3
Grindleford S32 . . . . **72** D8
St Helen's Cres NG9 . . . **209** C4
St Helen's Croft S32 . . . . **72** D8
St Helen's Dr NG16 . . . . **171** D7
St Helen's La DE4 . . . . . . **166** A7
St Helen's St
Chesterfield S41 . . . . **266** B4
Derby DE1 . . . . **267** A4
St Helens Ave NG16 . . . . **160** C4
St Hugh's Cl DE22 . . . . . **205** A2
St Jame's CE Jun Sch
DE23 . . . . **219** B3
St James' CE Inf Sch
DE23 . . . . **267** C1
St James' Dr NG16 . . . . . **182** D8
St James' Rd DE23 . . . . . **218** F1
St James's Ct SK13 . . . . . **85** C3
St James's Sq 3 NG9 . . . **223** C6
St James' St
14 Buxton SK17 . . . . **85** B7
Derby DE1 . . . . **267** B3
Derby, Rose Hill DE23 . . . **219** A1
St James' Terr SK17 . . . . . **85** B7
St James Ave DE7 . . . . . **209** A7
St James CE Prim Sch
SK13 . . . . **17** B8
St James Cl
Belper DE56 . . . . **179** D4
2 Chesterfield S41 . . . . . **96** C1
Glossop SK13 . . . . **17** C7
Willington DE65 . . . . **242** C5
St James Ct
Ashbourne DE6 . . . . **173** D3
Sandiacre NG10 . . . . **223** B3
St James Sq
Chesterfield S40 . . . . **266** B3
Chesterfield S40 . . . . **266** B3
St James's Terr NG9 . . . **223** D6
St John's 4 SK17 . . . . **85** A7
St John's Ave DE21 . . . . **220** B5
St John's CE Prim Sch
Belper DE56 . . . . **179** B5
Ripley DE5 . . . . **169** F1
Stapleford NG9 . . . . **223** E7
St John's Cl
Brinsley NG16 . . . . **171** D1
Derby DE22 . . . . **204** D3
St John's Cres S43 . . . . . . **80** F3
St John's Dr
Derby DE21 . . . . **220** B5
Kilburn DE56 . . . . **192** A8
Swadlincote DE11 . . . . . . **255** E5
St John's Mount S41 . . . . **95** F8
St John's Rd
Belper DE56 . . . . **179** A4
Buxton SK17 . . . . **85** A7
Chesterfield S41 . . . . **95** F8
Dronfield S18 . . . . **76** E7
Ilkeston DE7 . . . . **209** A7
Matlock Bath DE4 . . . . . . **143** B3
Smalley DE7 . . . . **192** F5
Tideswell SK17 . . . . **69** C4
St John's St
Long Eaton NG10 . . . . . . **236** D7
Wirksworth DE4 . . . . **165** F8
St John's Terr DE1 . . . . . **218** F6
St John Fisher RC Prim Sch
DE24 . . . . **233** C8
Saint John Houghton RC Sch
DE7 . . . . **208** D4
St Johns Cl
Bamford S33 . . . . **40** B3
Chesterfield S40 . . . . **114** B7
Ripley DE5 . . . . **169** F2
St Johns Pl S43 . . . . **78** D1
St Johns Rd S43 . . . . **78** D1
St Johns Road Bsns Ctr
S41 . . . . **95** F8
St John St SK22 . . . . **25** D2
St Joseph's Convent Sch
S41 . . . . **266** A4

St Joseph's RC Prim Sch
Derby DE23 . . . . .267 A1
Matlock DE4 . . . . .143 D6
Shirebrook NG20 . . . . . . .119 F5
Staveley S43 . . . . .97 D8
St Joseph's St DE4. . . . . .143 C5
St Katherines Cl DE4 . . . .110 E1
St Katherine's Ct DE22 . .218 D6
St Laurence CE Prim Sch
NG10. . . . . .236 E6
St Laurence Ct NG10 . . . .236 E6
St Laurence Gdns **10**
DE56 . . . . .178 F4
St Lawrence Ave S44. . . . .118 C8
St Lawrence Cl DE75 . . . .181 F2
St Lawrence Rd S42. . . . .131 F6
St Lawrence View S80 . . . .81 F5
St Leonards Dr S41 . . . . . .96 C1
St Leonards Pl DE55 . . . .146 E1
St Luke's CE Prim Sch
Glossop SK13. . . . . .10 C1
Shireoaks S81 . . . . .63 F7
St Lukes Ct **27** S41 . . . . . .95 F8
St Lukes View S81 . . . . . . .63 F7
St Margaret's Dr S40. . . .266 A3
St Margaret's RC Prim Sch
SK13. . . . . .16 D8
St Mark's Rd
Chesterfield S40 . . . . . . .95 E3
Derby DE21 . . . . .219 D6
St Marks Cl DE4 . . . . . . .155 A6
St Martin's Cl S41. . . . . . .95 D6
St Martin's Rd SK6. . . . . .23 A6
St Martin's Sch DE24. . . .232 F8
St Martin's Wlk S80 . . . . .82 C6
St Martins Ct DE55 . . . . .158 F4
St Mary's Ave DE72 . . . . .235 A7
St Mary's CE Fst Sch
ST14 . . . . .210 B1
St Mary's Cl
Chinley SK23 . . . . .34 E2
Derby DE24 . . . . .233 A6
Newton Solney DE15 . . .248 E8
St Mary's Cres ST14 . . . .210 B1
St Mary's Ct DE1 . . . . . . .267 B4
St Mary's Dr DE13 . . . . .240 F2
St Mary's Gate
Chesterfield S41 . . . . . .266 C3
Derby DE1 . . . . .267 B3
Wirksworth DE4 . . . . . .165 F8
St Mary's Pl S41 . . . . . . .266 C3
St Mary's RC High Sch
S41 . . . . .95 C7
St Mary's RC Prim Sch
Chesterfield S40 . . . . . .266 A4
Derby DE1 . . . . .267 B4
Glossop SK13. . . . . .17 D8
Marple SK6 . . . . .23 B7
New Mills SK22 . . . . .33 B8
St Mary's Rd
Disley SK12 . . . . .32 D5
Glossop SK13. . . . . .17 C8
New Mills SK22 . . . . .33 B8
St Mary's View DE4 . . . .142 B7
St Mary's Wlk NG16. . . . .171 B3
St Mary & All Saints Church
(Crooked Spire)* S40. . .266 B3
St Mary's Ct SK14. . . . . . . .9 C5
St Mary's RC Prim Sch
DE22. . . . . .204 F1
St Mary St DE7 . . . . .208 E8
St Marys Wharf Rd DE1 . .219 B7
St Matthew's Cl S21. . . . . .60 B1
St Matthew's St DE14 . . .254 C8
St Matthew's Wlk **4**
DE22 . . . . .204 F2
St Mawes Cl DE22. . . . . .204 D4
St Mellion Cl DE3 . . . . . .217 F1
St Michael's CE Prim Sch
S32. . . . . .53 A8
St Michael's Cl
Holbrook DE56. . . . . . . .191 C6
Shirley DE6 . . . . .200 D8
Willington DE65. . . . . . .242 B5
St Michael's Dr
Appleby Magna DE12. . . .265 F1
South Normanton DE55. .160 A7
St Michael's La DE1. . . . .267 B4
St Michaels Cl
Crich DE4. . . . . .156 F2
Derby DE24 . . . . .233 C7
St Michaels View
Derby DE24 . . . . .233 C7
Selston NG16. . . . . .171 F5
St Nicholas Cl DE24. . . . .204 D2
St Nicholas Pl DE1 . . . . .267 A5
St Norbert Dr DE7 . . . . .208 D4
St Oswald's CE Inf Sch
DE6. . . . . .173 B1
St Oswald's Hospl DE6 . .173 A1
St Oswald Cres DE6 . . . .173 C1
St Pancras Way DE1 . . . .267 C5
St Paul's Rd DE1 . . . . . . .219 A7
St Pauls Ave S41. . . . . . .115 D6
St Pauls Ct NG16. . . . . . .195 F6
St Peter's CE Fst Sch
ST14 . . . . .224 F2
St Peter's CE Jun Sch
DE23. . . . . .218 C1
St Peter's CE Prim Sch
DE12. . . . . .264 D6
St Peter's Churchyard
DE1 . . . . .267 B3
St Peter's Cl DE56 . . . . . .179 A4

St Peter's Rd
Buxton SK17 . . . . .66 D1
Chellaston DE73 . . . . . .233 A1
Thorpe Salvin S80 . . . . .62 E7
St Peter's St DE1 . . . . . . .267 B3
St Peter & St Paul Sch
S41 . . . . .96 D3
St Peters Cl S44 . . . . .98 A4
St Peters Croft DE56 . . . .179 A4
St Peters Ct DE24 . . . . . .233 A8
St Peter's Way DE1 . . . . .267 B2
St Philip's Dr S41. . . . . . .115 B8
Saint Philip Howard Comp
Sch SK13 . . . . .10 B1
St Philip Howard RC Comp
Sch SK13 . . . . .17 B8
St Quentin Cl
Derby DE22 . . . . .218 C3
Sheffield S17 . . . . .56 B5
St Quentin Dr S17. . . . . . .56 B5
St Quentin Mount S17. . . .56 B5
St Quentin Rise S17. . . . . .56 B5
St Quentin View S17 . . . . .56 B5
St Ronan's Ave DE56 . . . .190 E2
St Stephen's Cl DE23 . . . .231 D6
St Stephen's Ct S41. . . . .256 E3
St Stephens Dr DE72 . . . .221 B1
St Swithin's Cl DE7 . . . . .218 D3
St Swithuns Ct DE56 . . . .179 A2
St Theresa's RC Prim Sch
S2. . . . . .44 B7
St Thomas' St S40 . . . . . .95 C2
St Thomas Cl DE55. . . . .147 E5
St Thomas More RC Sch
SK17 . . . . .85 B8
St Thomas of Canterbury RC
Prim Sch S8. . . . . .56 F8
St Thomas RC Prim Sch
DE7 . . . . .208 E6
St Thomas Rd DE23 . . . . .219 A1
St Vincent Cl NG10. . . . . .236 E6
St Werburgh's CE Prim Sch
Derby DE21 . . . . .220 D1
Hanbury DE13 . . . . .238 A4
St Werburgh's View
DE21 . . . . .220 D5
St Wilfrid's Rd
11 Sheffield S2 . . . . .43 A8
West Hallam DE7 . . . . . .207 E8
St Wystan's Rd DE22 . . . .218 C3
St Wystans Sch DE65. . . .242 C2
Salcey Cl DE55. . . . . .169 F7
Salcey Dr NG9 . . . . .209 D2
Salcey Sq S40 . . . . .95 D1
Salcombe Ct **12** S41. . . . . .95 F8
Salcombe Rd DE55. . . . . .159 C5
Sale & Davys CE Sch
DE73. . . . . .244 A6
Sales Ave S42 . . . . .131 C8
Sales La DE15 . . . . .248 C4
Sale St DE23 . . . . .219 B2
Salisbury Ave
Burton u T DE15. . . . . . .248 D3
Chesterfield S41 . . . . . . .95 E7
Dronfield S18. . . . . .76 A7
Salisbury Cl NG19 . . . . . .136 D4
Salisbury Cres S41. . . . . . .95 F7
Salisbury Dr
Belper DE56. . . . . .179 D5
Swadlincote DE11 . . . . . .256 E5
Salisbury Ho **1** SK17. . . . .85 C7
Salisbury La DE73 . . . . . .252 B7
Salisbury Rd S18. . . . . . . .76 B8
Salisbury St
Derby DE1 . . . . .267 B1
Glossop SK13. . . . . .10 A5
Long Eaton NG10. . . . . . .236 E7
Sallyfield La DE6. . . . . . . .183 E8
Sallywood Cl DE24 . . . . . .231 D2
Saltburn Cl DE21. . . . . . .205 C1
Salter Cl DE74 . . . . .246 F4
Saltergate S40. . . . . .266 B3
Saltergate La S33 . . . . . . .40 B2
Salters La DE4 . . . . .142 F4
Salvin Cres S43 . . . . .80 E4
Samantha Ct DE21 . . . . . .206 B1
Sampson's La NG19 . . . . .135 B3
Sampsons Yd NG17 . . . . .148 F3
Samuel Cl S2. . . . . .43 D7
Samuel Ct DE5. . . . . .180 D8
Samuel Dr S2 . . . . .43 D7
Samuel Pl S2. . . . . .43 D7
Samuel Rd S2 . . . . .43 D8
Samuel St SK14 . . . . .9 C4
Sancroft Ave DE21 . . . . . .220 E6
Sancroft Rd DE21 . . . . . . .220 F6
Sandalwood Cl DE24 . . . .233 C7
Sandalwood Rd DE15 . . . .254 E6
Sandbach Cl DE21 . . . . . .206 A1
Sandbed La DE56 . . . . . . .179 C2
Sandby Croft S14 . . . . . . .43 E2
Sandby Ct S14. . . . . .43 E2
Sandby Dr
Marple SK6 . . . . .23 B8
Sheffield S14 . . . . .43 E2
Sandcliffe Pk DE11. . . . . .256 D7
Sandcliffe Rd DE11. . . . . .256 D6
Sandcroft Cl DE11 . . . . . .256 D5
Sanderling Heath DE3. . . .230 B7
Sanderman Ho DE1 . . . . .256 E1
Sanders Cl DE7 . . . . .194 C2
Sanderson Rd DE21 . . . . .220 B6
Sandfield Cl DE21. . . . . . .220 B8
Sandfield Rd **1** NG9 . . . . .223 E8
Sandford Ave NG10 . . . . .236 E7
Sandford Brook DE65. . . .228 C1
Sandgate Ave NG19 . . . . .136 D4
Sandgate Cl DE24 . . . . . .233 A6

Sandgate Rd NG19 . . . . . .136 D4
Sandhall La DE56 . . . . . . .166 F5
Sandham La DE55 . . . . . .169 C1
Sandhill La
Broadbottom SK6 . . . . . .16 A2
Marple SK6 . . . . .15 E1
Sandhills Rd S44. . . . . . . .99 C1
Sandiacre Rd NG9 . . . . . .223 C6
Sandiway
Chesterfield S40 . . . . . .114 C8
Glossop SK13. . . . . .17 F7
Sand La DE6. . . . . .211 B1
Sandlands The DE11. . . . .256 D6
Sandlands Way NG19. . . .136 F2
Sandown Ave DE3 . . . . . .217 C3
Sandown Cl
Burton u T DE14. . . . . . .254 A7
Eckington S21 . . . . .59 B2
Sandown Rd
Beeston NG9. . . . . .223 F2
Derby DE24 . . . . .232 E8
Sandpiper La DE3. . . . . . .230 B6
Sandringham Ave DE15 . .248 A1
Sandringham Cl
5 Chesterfield S41. . . . . .96 A8
Swadlincote DE11 . . . . . .256 B5
Sandringham Ct
13 Buxton SK17 . . . . . . .85 B7
Mansfield Woodhouse
NG19. . . . . .136 B6
Sandringham Dr
Derby DE21 . . . . .220 F5
Heanor DE75 . . . . .181 C2
Mansfield Woodhouse
NG19. . . . . .136 B6
Sandringham Ho DE24 . .219 D1
Sandringham Pl DE7 . . . .208 D5
Sandringham Rd
Calow S44 . . . . .97 A4
Derby DE21 . . . . .205 E1
Mansfield Woodhouse
NG19. . . . . .136 E5
Sandiacre NG10. . . . . . . .223 B4
Sands Cl S14 . . . . .43 E4
Sandstone Ave S40 . . . . .114 B8
Sandwell Cl NG10. . . . . . .236 A6
Sandwood Cl DE55 . . . . .148 A3
Sandybank Cl SK13 . . . . . . .9 E4
Sandybrook Cl DE6 . . . . .173 C4
Sandybrook Country Pk
DE6. . . . . .173 B5
Sandybrook Hall DE6. . . .173 B5
Sandy Cl S80 . . . . .81 F5
Sandycliffe Cl NG19. . . . .136 F1
Sandyford La DE56. . . . . .166 F4
Sandyhill Cl DE73. . . . . . .233 A2
Sandy La
Broadbottom SK13 . . . . .16 A4
Caldwell DE12 . . . . .261 A8
Chinley SK23 . . . . .35 B3
Crich DE4. . . . . .167 F8
Farley DE4 . . . . .128 D1
Horsley DE21, DE7 . . . . .192 A3
Matlock DE4 . . . . .143 D8
Whitwell S80 . . . . .81 F5
Sandypits La DE65 . . . . . .229 D4
Sanforth St S41. . . . . .96 A6
Sankey Dr DE11. . . . . . . .256 C1
Santolina Dr DE21 . . . . . .205 F1
Sapperton Cl DE23 . . . . .231 D5
Sappertonfield La DE6,
DE65 . . . . .213 D3
Sapperton La DE65. . . . . .213 E1
Sapphire Dr DE5 . . . . . . .180 B2
Sarah Cl DE55 . . . . .170 C7
Sark Rd S2 . . . . .43 A7
Saundby Ave NG19 . . . . .135 D1
Saundersfoot Way DE21. .206 C2
Savage La S17. . . . . .55 D7
Save Penny La DE56. . . . .191 A5
Saville Cl NG9 . . . . .223 E8
Saville House Sch NG19. .136 B3
Savoy The **2** SK17 . . . . . .85 B7
Sawley Inf Sch NG10 . . . .236 A5
Sawley Jun Sch NG10 . . .236 A5
Sawley Rd
Breaston DE72. . . . . . . .235 E6
Draycott DE72 . . . . .235 B7
Sawmand Cl NG10 . . . . . .236 C6
Sawmills Ind Pk DE5. . . . .181 D3
Saw Pit Ind Est DE5. . . . .148 C6
Sawpit La DE65. . . . . .227 C2
Saw Pit La DE55 . . . . . . .148 B5
Saxon Ave DE75. . . . . . . .181 F2
Saxon Cl
Breedon on t H DE73. . . .252 F7
Burton u T DE15. . . . . . .254 F7
Saxon Croft DE65 . . . . . .242 D3
Saxondale Ave DE3 . . . . .217 C4
Saxon Gr DE65. . . . . .242 A5
Saxon Rd S2. . . . . .43 A6
Saxon St DE15 . . . . .254 F7
Saxton Ave DE75. . . . . . .181 F2
Saxton Cl S41 . . . . .115 C8
Scaddows La DE73 . . . . . .250 E3
Scalby Cl NG16 . . . . .182 D2
Scaliot Cl SK22 . . . . .33 B8
Scalpcliffe Rd DE15 . . . . .248 A2
Scarborough Ave DE7. . . .208 E8
Scarborough Rise DE21 . .205 F1
Scarcliffe Cl DE24. . . . . . .232 E3
Scarcliffe Lanes DE55. . . .119 C7
Scarcliffe Prim Sch S44. . .118 F6
Scarcliffe Terr NG20 . . . .101 A2
Scargill CE Prim Sch
DE7. . . . . .207 D7
Scargill Rd DE7 . . . . .207 E8
Scargill Wlk NG16. . . . . . .182 F3

Scarsdale Ave
Derby, Allestree DE22 . . .204 D3
Derby, Littleover DE23. . .218 C2
Scarsdale Cl S18. . . . . .76 B8
Scarsdale Cres S43 . . . . . .96 D7
Scarsdale Cross **1** S18 . . .57 B1
Scarsdale Hospl S40. . . . .266 B4
Scarsdale Pl **8** SK17. . . . . .85 B7
Scarsdale Rd
2 Chesterfield S41 . . . . .96 A8
2 Dronfield S18. . . . . . .57 B1
Duffield DE56. . . . . .190 E3
Scarsdale St S44. . . . . . . .117 E8
Scarthin DE4 . . . . .155 A6
Schofield Ct DE4. . . . . . . .110 F1
Sch of Nursing (Univ of
Nottingham) DE1 . . . . .267 C2
School Ave S20. . . . . .59 F7
School Board La S40. . . . .95 E3
School Cl
Blackwell DE55 . . . . . . .147 C1
Darley Dale DE55. . . . . .127 C3
Fenny Bentley DE6. . . . .162 A1
Moira DE11 . . . . .256 C1
Newton DE55. . . . . .148 B3
Sheffield S20 . . . . .59 F7
Shirland DE55. . . . . .146 D2
Stonebroom DE55. . . . . .146 F4
School Croft DE55 . . . . . .170 D6
Schoolfield Cl S44. . . . . . .99 C1
School House Hill DE56 . .168 D1
School La
Arkwright Town S44 . . . .97 D3
Ashbourne DE6 . . . . . . .173 B1
Baslow DE45 . . . . .91 E5
Beeley DE4 . . . . .111 B4
Brackenfield DE55. . . . . .145 C2
Castle Donington DE74. . .247 A4
Chellaston DE73 . . . . . .233 A2
Compstall SK6. . . . . . . .15 B4
Crich DE4. . . . . .157 A1
Dronfield S18. . . . . .57 A1
Eckington S21 . . . . .58 E3
Hassop DE45 . . . . .91 A5
Hathersage S32. . . . . . . .53 A8
Heage DE56. . . . . .168 D2
Mansfield Woodhouse
NG19. . . . . .136 C3
Old Brampton S42. . . . . .93 F3
Over Haddon DE45 . . . . .109 B1
Ripley DE5 . . . . .169 D1
Rolleston DE13 . . . . . . .240 A3
Rowsley DE4 . . . . .126 F8
Sheffield, Greenhill S8. . .56 F7
Sheffield S8 . . . . .43 C1
South Normanton DE55. .160 B4
Stanton-by-D DE7, NG10.222 F8
Stanton in Peak DE4 . . . .126 C5
Sudbury DE6. . . . . .225 E4
Taddington SK17. . . . . . .87 F3
School Lane Cl S8 . . . . . . .43 C1
Schoolpiece La DE65. . . . .227 F7
School Rd
Buxton SK17 . . . . .67 B5
Chesterfield S41 . . . . . . .96 A7
Matlock DE4 . . . . .143 D5
Uttoxeter ST14 . . . . . . .210 A1
School Sq DE7 . . . . .207 E7
School St
Eckington S21 . . . . .59 D3
Moira DE12 . . . . .262 F2
Sheffield, Mosborough S20 .59 D7
Swadlincote DE11 . . . . . .256 B2
School Woods Cl DE75 . . .194 A6
School Yd The DE1. . . . . .267 B4
Scotches The DE56 . . . . .178 F5
Scotia Cl S2 . . . . .43 F8
Scotia Dr S2. . . . . .43 F8
Scotland St S80 . . . . .81 F6
Scotswood Rd NG19. . . . .136 B6
Scott Cl S42 . . . . .115 E3
Scott Cres DE55 . . . . .146 F3
Scott Dr
Belper DE56. . . . . .179 E5
Marple SK6 . . . . .23 B8
Somercotes DE55 . . . . . .170 D8
Scott St DE23 . . . . .218 F1
Scotts The DE11 . . . . .261 D8
Scotty Brook Cres SK13 . .17 E8
Scowerdons Cl S12. . . . . . .44 F5
Scowerdons Dr S12. . . . . . .44 F5
Scratta La S80 . . . . .63 C2
Screetham La DE4 . . . . . .112 C1
Scropton Old Rd DE65. . .239 C8
Scropton Rd DE65. . . . . . .239 B8
Scropton Wlk DE24 . . . . .232 E3
Sea Breeze Terr S13 . . . . .44 D8
Seaburn Rd NG9 . . . . . . .223 E2
Seaford Way DE7 . . . . . . .194 F5
Seagrave Cl DE21 . . . . . . .220 B8
Seagrave Cres S12. . . . . . .44 B4
Seagrave Dr
Chesterfield S41 . . . . . .115 C7
Sheffield S12 . . . . .44 B4
Seagrave Rd S12. . . . . . . .44 B4
Seale St DE1. . . . . .267 B5
Sealey Cl DE65. . . . . .242 C5
Seals Rd DE12 . . . . .262 F1
Seal View DE12 . . . . .261 C6
Sealwood La
Linton DE12 . . . . .261 E4
Overseal DE12. . . . . .261 F5
Seamer Rd NG16 . . . . . . .195 F7
Seanor La S45 . . . . .132 B4
Searl St DE1 . . . . .218 F6
Searson Ave S44. . . . . . . .99 A1
Searston Ave DE23 . . . . . .132 D8

Seascale Cl **5** DE21 . . . . .205 D1
Seaton Cl DE3 . . . . .217 C3
Seaton Ct **9** S41. . . . . . . .95 F8
Sebastian Cl SK6. . . . . . . .23 B7
Second Ave
Branston DE14. . . . . . . .253 E8
Chellaston DE73 . . . . . .245 A8
Risley DE72 . . . . .222 F5
Sedbergh Cres S41 . . . . . .95 D8
Sedgebrook Cl **2** DE21. . .205 D8
Sedgebrook St NG19 . . . .136 E3
Sedgefield Gn DE3 . . . . . .217 C1
Sedgefield Rd
Branston DE14. . . . . . . .253 F7
Burton u T DE14. . . . . . .254 A8
Sedgemoor Cl S40 . . . . . .95 B4
Sedgemoor Rd NG10 . . . .236 E5
Sedgemoor Way DE23. . . .231 A5
Sedgwick Cl NG16 . . . . . .160 D2
Sedgwick St
Jacksdale NG16. . . . . . . .171 B3
Langley Mill NG16 . . . . .182 B3
Sefton Ave NG9. . . . . . . .223 E8
Sefton Cl DE15. . . . . .248 B1
Sefton Rd DE21 . . . . .219 F6
Sefton St SK13. . . . . .17 C8
Sefton Way DE56 . . . . . . .190 D4
Selborne St DE24 . . . . . . .219 D2
Selby Cl
Beeston NG9. . . . . .223 E3
Chesterfield S40 . . . . . .114 C8
Selhurst Rd S41 . . . . .95 F5
Selig Par S12. . . . . .44 C2
Selina Cl DE74 . . . . .247 A4
Selina St DE73 . . . . .252 A7
Selkirk St DE21 . . . . .219 E7
Selly Oak Gr S8 . . . . .57 C6
Selly Oak Rd S8. . . . . .57 C6
Selmer Ct S43 . . . . .96 C3
Selston Arts & Com Coll
NG16. . . . . .171 F7
Selston CE Inf Sch NG16 .171 E6
Selston Rd NG16. . . . . . . .171 B5
Selworthy Cl DE21 . . . . . .206 A2
Selwyn St
Bolsover S44. . . . . .118 C8
Derby DE21 . . . . .218 C6
Senners La SK17. . . . . . . .87 A2
Sepycoe La DE6 . . . . .214 D7
Serina Ave DE23 . . . . . . .231 D8
Serlby Dr S26. . . . . .61 F5
Serlby La S26. . . . . .61 F6
Serpentine Wlk S8. . . . . . .57 B8
Setcup La S21 . . . . .59 D2
Sett Cl SK22 . . . . .33 B8
Settlement The DE72. . . .221 D4
Setts Way S42 . . . . .115 B4
Sevenlands Dr DE24. . . . .233 C4
Sevenoaks Ave DE22 . . . .217 F6
Seven Oaks Rd DE7 . . . . .209 A1
Severals S40 . . . . .95 B4
Severn Ave NG9 . . . . .223 F7
Severale Cl DE22 . . . . . . .205 B5
Severn Cl DE13 . . . . .240 C1
Severn Cres S42 . . . . .132 A5
Severn Dr DE65 . . . . .240 C8
Severn Sq DE15 . . . . .159 A4
Severn St DE24 . . . . .232 F8
Sewell Rd S20 . . . . .59 F6
Sexton St SK13. . . . . .9 F7
Seymour Cl DE22 . . . . . . .218 C5
Seymour La S43 . . . . .79 C1
Seymour Rd NG16 . . . . . .182 F1
Shacklecross DE72 . . . . . .221 C1
Shady Gr DE65. . . . . .228 C2
Shaef Cl DE65 . . . . .228 E2
Shaftesbury Ave
Chesterfield S40 . . . . . . .95 D3
Long Eaton NG10. . . . . . .236 A4
Mansfield NG19. . . . . . . .135 C4
Sandiacre NG10. . . . . . . .223 A5
Shaftesbury Cres DE23 . . .219 B1
Shaftesbury St S DE23 . . .219 B1
Shaftesbury St DE23 . . . . .219 B2
Shafton Cl S45. . . . . .131 E4
Shafton Wlk S45. . . . . . . .131 E4
Shakespeare Ave
Creswell S80 . . . . .81 C1
Mansfield Woodhouse
NG19. . . . . .136 B4
Shirland DE55 . . . . .146 C4
Shakespeare Cl
Clay Cross S42. . . . . . . .131 B6
Repton DE65 . . . . .242 D1
Swadlincote DE11 . . . . . .256 C6
Shakespeare Cres S18 . . . .76 C7
Shakespeare Ct **4** DE6. . .173 B2
Shakespeare Dr DE55 . . . .159 B4
Shakespeare Mdws
DE65 . . . . .242 D1
Shakespeare Rd NG16. . . .195 C5
Shakespeare St
Derby DE24 . . . . .232 A5
Grassmoor S42 . . . . .115 E3
Holmewood S42. . . . . . . .116 D1
Long Eaton NG10. . . . . . .223 D1
Shaldon Dr DE23. . . . . . .218 D1
Shalfleet Dr DE24 . . . . . .233 C5
Shallcross Ave SK23 . . . . .45 F4
Shallcross Cres SK23. . . . .45 E4
Shallcross Hall Barns
SK23. . . . . .45 E4
Shallcross Mill Rd SK23 . .45 E5
Shallcross Rd SK23. . . . . .45 E4
Shambles The S40 . . . . . .266 B3
Shamrock Cl S45 . . . . .79 C4
Shamrock St DE23 . . . . . .218 C1
Shandwick Ct **10** DE24. . .231 D3
Shanklin Dr NG9 . . . . . . .223 D7

Shanklin Ho DE24 . . . . 233 C7
Shannon Cl DE23 . . . . 231 D6
Shannon Ho DE24 . . . . 232 E5
Shannon Sq DE21 . . . . 220 B4
Shap Cl **7** S40 . . . . 95 C5
Shardlow Bsns Pk DE72 234 D1
Shardlow Prim Sch
DE72 . . . . 234 E2
Shardlow Rd
Aston-on-T DE72 . . . . . . 246 B7
Derby DE24, DE74 . . . . . 233 C6
Sharman Cl S18 . . . . 58 A1
Sharman Wlk S18 . . . . 58 A1
Sharp Cl
Ilkeston DE7 . . . . 208 C6
Long Eaton NG10 . . . . . . 236 C6
Sharpe Ave S8 . . . . 56 E8
Sharpswood Manor
DE11 . . . . 256 E4
Sharrard Cl S12 . . . . 44 B5
Sharrard Dr S12 . . . . 44 B5
Sharrard Gr S12 . . . . 44 B6
Sharrard Rd S12 . . . . 44 B5
Shatton La
Bamford S33 . . . . 40 A1
Thornhill S32, S33 . . . . . . 51 E7
Shaw's Row S40 . . . . 95 D2
Shaw's Yd DE56 . . . . 191 E8
Shawcroft **8** DE6 . . . . 173 C2
Shawcroft Ave DE55 . . . . 170 C5
Shawfield Rd SK13 . . . . 9 E3
Shaw La
Belper DE56 . . . . 191 B7
Glossop SK13 . . . . 9 F3
Holloway DE4 . . . . 156 C8
Marston Montgomery DE6 198 A1
Shaw St E DE7 . . . . 209 A6
Shaw St W DE7 . . . . 209 A6
Shaws Gn DE22 . . . . 218 D6
Shaws Hill DE4 . . . . 156 D1
Shaw St
Chesterfield S41 . . . . 96 A8
Derby DE22 . . . . 218 E6
Dronfield S18 . . . . 57 C4
Glossop SK13 . . . . 17 C8
Holmewood S42 . . . . 116 D1
Mottram in L SK14 . . . . 9 A4
Somercotes DE55 . . . . . . 170 C6
Shaw The SK13 . . . . 10 A3
Shaw Wood Cl DE55 . . . . 157 F3
Shaw Wood View DE55 . . 157 F3
Sheaf Bank S2 . . . . 43 A7
Sheaf Bank Bsns Pk S2 . 43 A7
Sheardhall Ave SK12 . . . . . 32 E5
Sheards Cl S18 . . . . 56 F1
Sheards Dr S18 . . . . 56 F1
Sheards Way S18 . . . . 56 F1
Shearsby Dr NG16 . . . . . . 136 F2
Shearwater Cl DE23 . . . . . 231 D7
Sheepbridge Bsns Ctr
S41 . . . . 76 E2
Sheepbridge La S41 . . . . . 76 E2
Sheepcote Hill S21 . . . . . . 60 D6
Sheepcote Rd S21 . . . . 60 C6
Sheephill Rd S11, S17 . . . . 42 F1
Sheep La DE55 . . . . 158 C8
Sheeplea La S45 . . . . 129 E8
Sheepwash La S45 . . . . . . 145 B8
Sheets Stores Ind Est
NG10 . . . . 236 D5
Sheffield Coll (Norton Coll)
The S8 . . . . 57 B7
Sheffield Coll The
(Frecheville Ctr) S12 . . . 44 C4
Sheffield Pl DE7 . . . . 267 D2
Sheffield Rd
Baslow DE45 . . . . 92 B7
Chapel-en-le-F SK23 . . . . . 47 E7
Chesterfield S41 . . . . 96 A6
Creswell S80, S43 . . . . 81 D3
Dronfield S18 . . . . 56 F3
Eckington S20, S21 . . . . . . 59 E5
Glossop SK13 . . . . 10 F1
Hathersage S32 . . . . 53 A7
Killamarsh S21 . . . . 60 D7
Renishaw S21, S43 . . . . . . 79 D8
Sheffield S20 . . . . 44 F2
Unstone S18, S41 . . . . 76 E3
Shelden Cl **4** SK13 . . . . . . 9 D1
Shelden Fold **3** SK13 . . . . 9 D1
Shelden Mews SK13 . . . . . . 9 D1
Shelden Pl **5** SK13 . . . . . . 9 D1
Shelden Cl NG10 . . . . 223 B3
Shelden Ct DE24 . . . . 232 E3
Shelden Gdns DE4 . . . . . 156 F1
Shelden Rd
Chesterfield S40 . . . . 95 B5
Heanor DE75 . . . . 181 C5
Shelford Cl DE3 . . . . 217 C3
Shelford La DE4 . . . . 156 B7
Shelley Ave NG19 . . . . . . 136 B4
Shelley Dr
Derby DE24 . . . . 232 A5
Dronfield S18 . . . . 76 C7
Shelley Gr DE55 . . . . 146 F3
Shelley Rd DE11 . . . . 256 C5
Shelley St S42 . . . . 116 D1
Shelmory Cl DE24 . . . . . . 232 E5
Shelton Cl NG19 . . . . 135 E1
Shelton Dr DE24 . . . . 232 F3
Shelton Gate Cl DE24 . . 232 E5
Shelton Jun & Inf Schs
DE24 . . . . 232 D4
Shenington Way DE21 . . 206 B2
Shepherd's La DE73 . . . . 251 D6
Shepherd St DE23 . . . . . . 218 C1
Shepley's Yd S40 . . . . . . 266 B3

Shepley St
Chesterfield S40 . . . . 95 D2
Glossop SK13 . . . . 10 F2
Hadfield SK13 . . . . 9 E3
Shepton Cl DE7 . . . . 194 D3
Sheraton Way SK17 . . . . . . 66 B1
Sherbourne Ave S41 . . . . . 95 E8
Sherbourne Dr
Belper DE56 . . . . 179 D5
Burton u T DE14 . . . . 254 A7
Hilton DE65 . . . . 228 C1
Sherbrooke Rd SK12 . . . . . 32 D6
Sherbrook Gr SK17 . . . . . . 85 C5
Sheridan Ct NG17 . . . . . . 209 F1
Sheridan St DE24 . . . . . . 231 F5
Sheriff Dr DE4 . . . . 143 B6
Sherman Cl DE65 . . . . . . 228 C1
Sherriff's Lea NG9 . . . . . 223 E2
Sherroside Cl DE22 . . . . . 204 D4
Sherston Cl DE21 . . . . . . 206 B2
Sherwin Rd NG9 . . . . 209 F1
Sherwin St DE22 . . . . 218 E8
Sherwood Ave
Borrowash DE72 . . . . 221 D2
Creswell S80 . . . . 81 D1
Derby, Chaddesden DE21 . 219 F7
Derby, Littleover DE23 . . 231 D5
Hope S33 . . . . 39 A3
Pinxton NG16 . . . . 160 D3
Shirebrook NG20 . . . . . . 119 E4
Sherwood Chase S17 . . . . . 55 E5
Sherwood Copse SK17 . . . 69 C4
Sherwood Ct NG19 . . . . . 136 B2
Sherwood Dr NG20 . . . . . 119 E3
Sherwood Fold SK13 . . . . . 16 D7
Sherwood Foresters
Regiment Meml ★ DE4 . 156 E3
Sherwood Pl **2** S18 . . . . . 56 D1
Sherwood Rd
Buxton SK17 . . . . 85 C5
Dronfield S18 . . . . 56 D1
Killamarsh S21 . . . . 60 E7
Matlock DE4 . . . . 143 C4
Tideswell SK17 . . . . 69 C3
Sherwood Rise
Eastwood NG16 . . . . 182 F1
Mansfield Woodhouse
NG19 . . . . 136 A1
Sherwood St
Bolsover S44 . . . . 117 F8
Chesterfield S40 . . . . 266 C1
Derby DE22 . . . . 218 E3
Mansfield Woodhouse
NG19 . . . . 136 B2
Newton DE55 . . . . 148 B4
Shirland DE55 . . . . 146 C5
Somercotes DE55 . . . . . . 170 C5
Sutton in A NG17 . . . . . . 148 F3
Shetland Cl
Derby DE21 . . . . 219 C7
Mansfield NG19 . . . . 136 F1
Shetland Rd
Dronfield S18 . . . . 76 B8
Tibshelf DE55 . . . . 147 F5
Shields Cres DE74 . . . . . 247 A4
Shieling The DE65 . . . . . 227 C2
Shilling Way NG10 . . . . . 236 A7
Shiloh Rd SK22, SK6 . . . . . 24 B6
Shilo Way NG16 . . . . 195 A5
Shining Cliff YH ★ DE56 . 167 D5
Shinwell Ave S43 . . . . 97 B7
Shipley Cl DE14 . . . . 254 A7
Shipley Common La DE7 194 D4
Shipley Country Park Visitor
Ctr ★ DE75 . . . . 193 E7
Shipley Ct DE7 . . . . 194 C3
Shipley Ctry Pk ★ DE7 . 194 A4
Shipley View DE7 . . . . . . 192 F6
Shipley Wlk DE24 . . . . . . 232 E3
Shipman Ct S20 . . . . 59 D7
Shippen Rural Bsns Ctr The
S18 . . . . 75 E2
Shippon La S32 . . . . 72 B2
Shirebrook Bsns Pk
NG20 . . . . 120 A3
Shirebrook Cl NE7 . . . . . 194 F6
Shirebrook Ct S2 . . . . 43 A6
Shirebrook Dr
Glossop SK13 . . . . 17 E8
Glossop SK13 . . . . 17 F8
Shirebrook Rd S8 . . . . 43 A6
Shirebrook Sch NG20 . . . 119 D5
Shirebrook Sta NG20 . . . 120 A4
Shiregate Gdns DE23 . . . 231 A5
Shire Hill Hospl SK13 . . . . 10 E3
Shire La S44 . . . . 116 F4
Shireoaks DE56 . . . . 178 D5
Shireoaks Cl DE23 . . . . . 231 D1
Shireoaks Comm S81 . . . . 63 F7
Shireoaks Rd
Dronfield S18 . . . . 57 C2
Shireoaks S81 . . . . 63 F6
Shireoaks Row S81 . . . . . 63 E7
Shireoaks Sta S81 . . . . . . 63 E7
Shires The NG19 . . . . 136 F1
Shire Way SK13 . . . . 10 E3
Shirland Ct DE24 . . . . . . 232 E3
Shirland Prim Sch DE55 146 D2
Shirland St S41 . . . . 266 B4
Shirley Cl
Castle Donington DE74 . . 247 A4
Chesterfield S40 . . . . 95 B5
Hope S33 . . . . 39 A4
Shirley Cres DE72 . . . . . . 235 D8
Shirley La DE6 . . . . 200 B6
Shirley Pk DE72 . . . . 246 B7

Shirley Rd
Derby DE21 . . . . 205 F1
Ripley DE5 . . . . 169 D1
Swanwick DE55 . . . . 169 F7
Shirley St NG10 . . . . 236 A4
Shop La DE56 . . . . 168 C2
Shop Stones DE72 . . . . . 221 C5
Shoreham St S2 . . . . 43 A8
Short Cl S42 . . . . 113 D7
Shortbrook Bank 10 S20 . . 59 E8
Shortbrook Cl S20 . . . . . . 59 F8
Shortbrook Com Prim Sch
S20 . . . . 59 E8
Shortbrook Croft **6** S20 . 59 E8
Shortbrook Dr S20 . . . . . . 59 F8
Shortbrook Rd S20 . . . . . 59 E8
Shortbrook Way **13** S20 . . 59 F8
Shortbrook Wlk **12** S20 . . 59 E8
Short Cl S42 . . . . 113 D7
Shortheath DE12 . . . . . . 262 C3
Shortheath Rd DE12 . . . 262 E3
Short Hill DE73 . . . . 252 E6
Short La DE74 . . . . 246 F4
Short Lands DE56 . . . . . . 179 A4
Shortlands The DE4 . . . . 143 B3
Short Row **4** DE56 . . . . . 178 F4
Shorts La S17 . . . . 55 B6
Short St
Belper DE56 . . . . 179 B4
Burton u T DE14 . . . . 254 E7
Short Street Inf Sch
DE15 . . . . 254 E7
Shorwell Gdns DE24 . . . . 233 C5
Shottle Wlk DE24 . . . . . . 232 E3
Shotwood Cl DE13 . . . . . 240 A4
Shotwoodhill La DE13 . . 240 A5
Shrewsbury Ct DE21 . . . 206 C2
Shrewsbury Rd DE13 . . . 240 F2
Shrewsbury St SK13 . . . . . 10 C1
Shrewsbury Terr S17 . . . . 55 D4
Shropshire Ave
Derby DE21 . . . . 219 E7
Westwood NG16 . . . . . . 171 C4
Shropshire Dr S18 . . . . . . 17 F8
Shrubbery The DE11 . . . 257 A2
Shuckstone La DE4 . . . . 156 F6
Shudehill Cl SK22 . . . . 25 D3
Shunters Drift S43 . . . . . . 80 B6
Shuttlewood Rd S44 . . . . . 99 A4
Shutts La DE45 . . . . 109 C4
Sickleback La S18 . . . . 57 F4
Sickleholme S33 . . . . 40 B1
Sidcup Ct S43 . . . . 78 B4
Siddals St DE15 . . . . 248 B3
Siddals La DE22 . . . . 204 F4
Siddals Rd DE1 . . . . 267 C2
Siddons St DE24 . . . . 233 A7
Side End La SK23 . . . . 45 A2
Sides La DE6 . . . . 184 B5
Sidings The
Chinley SK23 . . . . 34 E2
Derby DE21 . . . . 220 A4
Kimberley NG16 . . . . . . 195 F6
Whaley Bridge SK23 . . . . 45 E8
Sidings Way DE55 . . . . . 147 C1
Sidlaw Cl **6** S40 . . . . 95 C5
Sidmouth Cl DE24 . . . . . 233 C7
Sidmouth Ct **17** S41 . . . . 95 F8
Sidney Robinson Bsns Pk
DE24 . . . . 219 D1
Sidney St
Derby DE1 . . . . 219 B3
Kimberley NG16 . . . . . . 195 F6
Long Eaton NG10 . . . . . . 236 D6
Siggate S33 . . . . 38 D1
Silken Holme DE55 . . . . 160 B4
Silk Hill S33 . . . . 45 F8
Silk Mill La DE13 . . . . . . 239 C6
Silk St S13 . . . . 10 C1
Silkstone Cl
Sheffield S12 . . . . 44 E4
Swadlincote DE11 . . . . . 256 B1
Silkstone Cres S12 . . . . . . 44 D4
Silkstone Dr S12 . . . . 44 D4
Silkstone Pl S12 . . . . 44 E4
Silkstone Rd S12 . . . . 44 E4
Silver Birch Cres DE55 . . 159 C8
Silverburn Dr DE21 . . . . 206 A2
Silverdale NG9 . . . . 223 E5
Silverdale Ave NG19 . . . 136 B4
Silverdale Cl
Chellaston DE73 . . . . 233 A2
Chesterfield S41 . . . . 76 E1
Silverhill Cl DE13 . . . . . . 240 C1
Silverhill La NG17 . . . . . 148 E5
Silverhill Prim Sch DE3 217 C3
Silverhill Rd DE21 . . . . . 220 E3
Silver Hill Rd DE23 . . . . . 219 A2
Silver La
Elvaston DE72 . . . . 234 A5
Marchington ST14 . . . . . 224 F1
Silverlands SK17 . . . . 85 C7
Silverlands Cl SK17 . . . . . 85 C7
Silverlands Pk SK17 . . . . . 85 C7
Silver Mill Rd S2 . . . . 43 A8
Silverton Dr DE24 . . . . . 231 C2
Silver Well Dr S43 . . . . . . 97 D8
Silvey Gr DE21 . . . . 220 D4
Simcoe Leys DE73 . . . . . 233 A2
Simcrest Ave S21 . . . . 60 D5
Simmondley Gr SK13 . . . . 17 A8
Simmondley La SK13 . . . . 17 A8
Simmondley New Rd
SK13 . . . . 17 A7
Simmondley Prim Sch
SK13 . . . . 17 A7
Simon Fields Cl DE7 . . . 193 A2
Simons Cl SK13 . . . . 17 A7

Simons Wlk SK13 . . . . . . 17 A8
Sims Ave S41 . . . . 218 E5
Sims Croft S41 . . . . 77 C3
Sinclair Cl
Derby DE24 . . . . 231 E4
Heanor DE75 . . . . 193 D8
Sinfin Ave DE24 . . . . 232 D3
Sinfin Central Bsns Pk DE23,
DE24 . . . . 231 F5
Sinfin Com Sch DE24 . . . 231 E3
Sinfin District Ctr DE24 . 231 E3
Sinfin Fields Cres DE24 . 232 D5
Sinfin La
Barrow u T DE73 . . . . . . 244 A6
Derby DE23, DE24 . . . . . 231 F4
Sinfin Moor La DE73 . . . 232 E2
Sinfin Prim Sch DE24 . . . 231 F5
Sir Francis Ley Ind Pk
DE23 . . . . 219 C1
Sir Frank Whittle Rd
DE21 . . . . 219 C7
Sir Harold Jackson Prim Sch
S17 . . . . 56 B5
Sir Henry's La DE73 . . . . 252 A4
Sir Joseph's La DE4 . . . . 127 B4
Sir William Hill Rd
Eyam S32 . . . . 71 C8
Grindleford S32 . . . . 53 B1
Sir William Terr S32 . . . . . 72 C8
Siskin Cl DE3 . . . . 230 B7
Siskin Dr DE24 . . . . 231 D4
Sisley Ave S43 . . . . 223 E6
Sister's La DE72 . . . . 221 C5
Sitch La
Hayfield SK22 . . . . 24 F3
Kirk Ireton DE4 . . . . 165 A4
Wensley DE4 . . . . 142 D7
Sitwell **14** S20 . . . . 59 E8
Sitwell Ave S40 . . . . 266 A1
Sitwell Cl DE21 . . . . 220 D4
Sitwell Dr DE56 . . . . 192 A8
Sitwell Grange La S45 . . 147 D8
Sitwell St
Derby DE1 . . . . 267 B2
Derby, Spondon DE21 . . 220 E4
Eckington S21 . . . . 59 C3
Sitwell Villas DE55 . . . . . 146 E5
Skeavington's La DE7 . . . 194 E5
Skeldale Dr S40 . . . . 115 B8
Skelton Rd S8 . . . . 43 A5
Skelwith Cl S41 . . . . 95 D8
Ski 2000 Ilkeston NG16 . 195 B1
Skiddaw Cl **2** S40 . . . . . . 95 C6
Skiddaw Dr DE3 . . . . 217 E1
Skinner St S80 . . . . 81 D2
Skinners Way DE11 . . . . 256 D5
Skipness Cl DE73 . . . . . . 232 E2
Skipton Cl DE7 . . . . 194 D3
Skipton Gn DE21 . . . . . . 205 C1
Skye Gdns DE55 . . . . 147 F5
Skylark Way DE24 . . . . . 231 D4
Slack's La S45 . . . . 132 C2
Slackey La DE12 . . . . 262 C4
Slack La
Ashover S45 . . . . 129 C2
Brailsford DE6 . . . . 187 D1
Chesterfield S40 . . . . 95 B3
Derby, Allestree DE22 . . 204 F2
Derby, New Zealand DE22 218 D5
Hartshorne DE11 . . . . . . 257 B6
Heath S44 . . . . 116 F2
Mayfield DE6 . . . . 184 C8
Nether Heage DE56 . . . . 168 C3
Ripley DE5 . . . . 169 D1
Shipley DE75 . . . . 193 E8
Somercotes DE55 . . . . . . 170 B5
Wessington DE55 . . . . . 157 D8
Slack Rd DE7 . . . . 193 F3
Slacks Cotts SK17 . . . . . . 84 E4
Slacks La SK22 . . . . 25 C5
Slade Cl
Etwall DE65 . . . . 229 C4
Ilkeston DE7 . . . . 209 A5
South Normanton DE55 . 160 B4
Slade Farm DE73 . . . . . . 251 A4
Slade Fields S17 . . . . 210 B1
Slade Hollow La DE6 . . . 201 A3
Slade La
Weston Underwood DE6 . 202 E7
Wilson DE73 . . . . 252 F6
Slade Lands Dr DE73 . . . 233 A2
Slag La S43 . . . . 77 D6
Slaidburn Cl DE3 . . . . . . 217 C1
Slaley La DE4 . . . . 154 C8
Slaney Cl DE24 . . . . 232 E2
Slant Cl SK13 . . . . 17 E8
Slant La
Mansfield Woodhouse
NG19 . . . . 136 B4
Shirebrook NG20 . . . . . . 119 D4
Slatelands Ave SK13 . . . . 17 B8
Slatelands Rd SK13 . . . . . 17 B8
Slate Pit Dale S42 . . . . . 113 E4
Slatepit La S18, S42 . . . . . 93 C8
Slater Ave DE22 . . . . 218 E6
Slater Cres DE4 . . . . 165 F7
Slater St S45 . . . . 131 D3
Slate St S2 . . . . 43 B8
Slayley Hill S43 . . . . 80 C4
Slayley View S43 . . . . 80 C5
Slayley View Rd S43 . . . . 80 B6
Slaypit La S80 . . . . 62 D6
Sledgegate La DE4 . . . . . 156 B7
Sledmere Cl DE24 . . . . . 233 C7
Sleepy La DE73 . . . . 245 C1
Sleetmoor La DE55 . . . . 170 B8
Sleights La NG16 . . . . . . 160 C4
Slindon Croft DE24 . . . . 233 D6

Slipperlow La SK17 . . . . . 87 F2
Sloade La S12 . . . . 58 D7
Sloane Rd DE22 . . . . 218 A6
Smalldale Cotts SK17 . . . . 67 D7
Smalldale Head Rd S33 . 50 F7
Smalldale Rd
Buxton SK17 . . . . 67 C7
Sheffield S12 . . . . 44 D4
Smalley Dr DE21 . . . . . . 206 B3
Smalley Mill Rd DE21,
DE7 . . . . 192 B4
Small Gate NG19 . . . . . . 136 E6
Small Knowle End SK17 . . 67 C6
Small Meer Cl DE73 . . . . 232 F1
Small Thorn Pl DE11 . . . 256 E1
Smeath Rd NG16 . . . . . . 171 F2
Smeckley Wood Cl S41 . . 76 C3
Smedley's Ave NG10 . . . 223 B5
Smedley Ave
Ilkeston DE7 . . . . 209 A4
Somercotes DE55 . . . . . . 159 D1
Smedley Ct DE65 . . . . . . 241 B5
Smedley Pl SK13 . . . . 10 E2
Smedley St E DE4 . . . . . 143 C5
Smedley St W DE4 . . . . . 143 B7
Smedley St S 143 B6
Smeeton St DE75 . . . . . . 182 B1
Smelter Wood Ave S13 . . 44 E7
Smelter Wood Cl S13 . . . 44 E7
Smelter Wood Cres S13 . 44 F7
Smelter Wood Ct S13 . . . 44 E7
Smelter Wood Dr S13 . . . 44 E7
Smelter Wood La S13 . . . 44 E7
Smelter Wood Pl S13 . . . 44 F7
Smelter Wood Rd S13 . . . 44 E7
Smelter Wood Rise S13 . 44 F7
Smelter Wood Way S13 . 44 E7
Smeltinghouse La S18 . . 75 E3
Smisby Rd LE65 . . . . 258 A1
Smisby Way DE24 . . . . . 232 E3
Smith Ave
Codnor DE5 . . . . 170 B1
King's Newton DE73 . . . . 245 B1
Staveley S43 . . . . 97 C7
Smithbrook Cl SK23 . . . . . 47 C6
Smith Cres S41 . . . . 96 D1
Smith Dr NG16 . . . . 182 A3
Smithfield Ave
Chesterfield S41 . . . . 115 C7
Trowell NG9 . . . . 209 D4
Smithfield Rd S12 . . . . . . 44 A3
Smith-Hall La DE6 . . . . . 176 A1
Smith Hall La DE6 . . . . . 188 A7
Smith Rd DE4 . . . . 143 B6
Smiths La DE55 . . . . 146 C7
Smithson Ave S44 . . . . . . 99 B1
Smithurst Rd NG16 . . . . 195 B7
Smithy Ave S45 . . . . 131 C4
Smithy Brook Rd S21 . . . 79 C8
Smithy Cl
Glossop SK13 . . . . 10 D1
Parwich DE6 . . . . 151 D1
Smithy Croft S18 . . . . 56 D2
Smithy Fold SK13 . . . . . . 10 D1
Smithy Hill S33 . . . . 51 A7
Smithy Knoll Rd S32 . . . . 72 C2
Smithy La
Clifton Campville B79 . . . 263 E2
Marple SK6 . . . . 15 F1
Taddington SK17 . . . . 88 A3
Smithy Mdws S32 . . . . . . 53 A8
Smithy Pl S42 . . . . 115 F2
Smuse La DE4 . . . . 143 E4
Snake La DE56 . . . . 190 E4
Snake Pass SK13 . . . . 11 B1
Snake Rd
Bamford S33 . . . . 29 D6
Derwent S33 . . . . 30 B2
High Peak S33 . . . . 28 D8
Snake Woodland Forest
Wlk ★ S33 . . . . 19 F3
Snape Hill S18 . . . . 57 A2
Snapehill Cl S18 . . . . 57 A3
Snape Hill Cres S18 . . . . . 57 A3
Snape Hill Dr S18 . . . . . . 57 B3
Snape Hill La S18 . . . . . . 57 A2
Snapes La DE6 . . . . 184 B1
Snelsmoor La DE73 . . . . 233 B2
Snelston Cl S18 . . . . 56 D1
Snelston Cres DE23 . . . . 218 D2
Snipe S42 . . . . 113 D7
Snipesmoor La DE6 . . . . 185 F7
Snitterton Rd DE4 . . . . . 143 A5
Snowberry Ave DE56 . . . 179 B3
Snowdon La S21 . . . . 58 B2
Snowdrop Dr NG19 . . . . 136 F4
Snowdrop Valley DE4 . . . 168 A8
Snowfield View DE4 . . . . 165 E6
Soaper La S18 . . . . 57 A2
Soarbank Cl NG16 . . . . . 195 E7
Soar Way DE65 . . . . 228 D1
Society Pl DE23 . . . . 219 A2
Soft Water La S33 . . . . . . 51 A7
Soldier's Croft DE45 . . . 107 C2
Solney Cl DE11 . . . . 255 F3
Soloman Pk NG16 . . . . . 195 B2
Soloman Rd DE7 . . . . . . 195 B2
Solomons View SK17 . . . . 85 C7
Solway Cl DE21 . . . . 206 A2
Solway Rise S18 . . . . 56 D2
Somerby Way **8** DE24 . . 205 F2
Somercotes Hill DE55 . . 170 D8
Somercotes Inf Sch
DE55 . . . . 170 C8
Somercotes Rd S12 . . . . . 44 D5

Somerlea Park Jun Sch
DE55 . . . . **170** C8
Somerleyton Dr DE7 . . **209** A4
Somersal Cl DE24 . . . . . . **232** E3
Somersall La S40 . . . . **95** A1
Somersall Cl S40 . . . . **95** A1
Somersall Park Rd S40 . . **95** A1
Somersall Willows S40 . . **95** A1
Somersby Ave S40 . . . . . **114** B8
Somerset Cl
Buxton SK17 . . . . **85** C4
Long Eaton NG10 . . . . . . **237** A8
Somerset Dr S43 . . . . **97** A8
Somerset Rd DE15 . . . . . . **254** D6
Somerset St DE21 . . . . . . **219** D7
Somme Rd DE22 . . . . **204** B3
Sookholme Cl NG20 . . . . **119** F3
Sookholme La NG20 . . . . **120** E3
Sookholme Rd NG20 . . . . **119** F3
Soresby St S40 . . . . **266** B3
Sorrel Dr DE11 . . . . **256** E4
Sough La
Calver S32 . . . . **72** B2
Taddington SK17 . . . . **87** D2
Wirksworth DE4 . . . . **154** F2
Wirksworth, Steeple Grange
DE4 . . . . **155** B2
Soughley La S10 . . . . **42** C8
Sough Rd DE55 . . . . **160** B7
Southall St 9 S8 . . . . **43** A6
Southard's La S80 . . . . . . **62** E5
South Ave
Buxton SK17 . . . . **85** B7
Chellaston DE73 . . . . **232** F3
Derby, Darley Abbey DE22 **205** A2
Derby DE21 . . . . **218** D1
Derby, Spondon DE21 . . . **220** E4
Shirebrook NG20 . . . . . . **119** F3
Southbourne Ct S17 . . . . . **55** D6
South Brae Cl DE23 . . . . . **231** D7
South Broadway St
DE14 . . . . **254** C8
Southcroft Cl SK13 . . . . . . **9** E4
South Church St DE45 . . **109** D5
South Cl
Glossop SK13 . . . . **9** F7
Unstone Green S18 . . . . . **76** E6
Southcote Dr S18 . . . . **56** D1
South Cres
Bolsover S44 . . . . **99** B1
Duckmanton S44 . . . . **98** A5
Killamarsh S21 . . . . **60** E7
Southcroft
Alfreton DE55 . . . . **159** A3
1 Buxton SK17 . . . . **85** A7
Derby DE23 . . . . **231** D4
South Ct S17 . . . . **55** E7
South Darley CE Prim Sch
DE4 . . . . **142** B7
Southdown Ave S40 . . . . . **95** C5
Southdown Cl DE24 . . . . **231** C2
South Dr
Chellaston DE73 . . . . **232** F3
Derby, Cherrytree Hill
DE21 . . . . **220** A5
Derby, Littleover DE3 . . . **218** F7
Swadlincote DE11 . . . . . **255** F5
South East Derbyshire Coll
Heanor DE75 . . . . **181** F1
Ilkeston DE7 . . . . **208** F2
Southend S42 . . . . **115** F2
South End DE4 . . . . **155** A7
Southfield Ave S41 . . . . . **115** D6
Southfield Cl S80 . . . . **81** F5
Southfield Dr
Dronfield S18 . . . . **76** C8
South Normanton DE55 . . **160** C5
Southfield Ind Site S80 . . **82** A4
Southfield La S80 . . . . **82** A4
Southfield Mount S18 . . . . **76** C8
Southfields
Clowne S43 . . . . **80** F3
Long Eaton NG10 . . . . . . **236** E7
Southfields Ave NG16 . . . **160** D4
Southgate S21 . . . . **59** E3
Southgate Bglws S80 . . . . **81** C7
Southgate Bsns Ctr
DE23 . . . . **267** B1
Southgate Cl DE3 . . . . . . **217** C3
Southgate Cres S43 . . . . . **80** F5
Southgate Ct S21 . . . . **59** E3
Southgate Way S43 . . . . . **78** B4
South Head Dr SK23 . . . . . **47** C7
South Hill
Ashover DE55 . . . . **145** F7
Rolleston DE13 . . . . **240** D4
South Hill La DE55 . . . . . **145** F6
South Lodge Ct S40 . . . . . **95** B3
South Marlow St SK13 . . . . **10** A4
Southmead Way DE3 . . . . **218** B3
South Mews 10 SK17 . . . . . **85** B7
South Oak St DE14 . . . . . **254** B8
South Par DE4 . . . . **143** A1
South Park Ave DE4 . . . . **127** C3
South Pl
Chesterfield, Brampton
S40 . . . . **95** D2
Chesterfield, Stonegravels
S40 . . . . **266** B2
Ripley DE5 . . . . **169** D1
South St N S43 . . . . **77** D3
South St
Ashbourne DE6 . . . . **173** C1

South St continued
Blackwell DE55 . . . . **147** F2
Buxton SK17 . . . . **85** B7
Chesterfield S40 . . . . . . **266** B2
Derby DE1 . . . . **218** E5
Draycott DE72 . . . . **235** A7
Eastwood, Bailey Grove
NG16 . . . . **182** E2
Eastwood, Giltbrook NG16 **195** C8
Ilkeston DE7 . . . . **208** F8
Long Eaton NG10 . . . . . . **236** E7
Melbourne DE73 . . . . . . **252** A7
Pilsley S45 . . . . **132** D1
Sheffield S20 . . . . **59** D6
Somercotes DE55 . . . . . . **170** D5
South Normanton DE55 . . **160** B6
Swanwick DE55 . . . . **169** E7
Woodville DE11 . . . . **257** A1
South Uxbridge St DE14 . **254** B8
South View
Bamford S33 . . . . **40** B4
Chesterfield S41 . . . . **95** D7
Derby DE23 . . . . **218** C1
Mayfield DE6 . . . . **184** D6
New Mills SK22 . . . . **33** B8
Pilsley DE45 . . . . **91** C2
Sheffield S20 . . . . **60** A7
Whitwell S80 . . . . **81** F5
South View Rd SK13 . . . . . **17** F7
South View Wlk ST14 . . . **196** F3
Southwell Rise NG16 . . . **195** B7
South Wingfield Prim Sch
DE55 . . . . **157** F4
Southwood 2 SK17 . . . . . **85** A7
Southwood Ave S18 . . . . . **76** B7
Southwood Dr S43 . . . . . . **80** F3
Southwood St DE24 . . . . **232** F8
Southworth Rd DE73 . . . . **252** E2
Sovereign Dr DE14 . . . . . **254** B8
Sovereign Gr NG10 . . . . . **236** B7
Sovereign Way
Derby DE21 . . . . **206** D3
Heanor DE75 . . . . **181** D1
Sowbrook Brook DE7 . . . **208** D4
Sowbrook La DE7 . . . . . . **208** E3
Sowter Rd DE1 . . . . **267** B4
Sowters Row S40 . . . . . . **266** B3
Spa Brook Cl S12 . . . . **44** F4
Spa Brook Dr S12 . . . . **44** F5
Spa Croft DE55 . . . . **147** E5
Spa Ct DE1 . . . . **267** A1
Spa La
Chesterfield, Hady S41 . . **266** C2
Chesterfield, Hady S41 . . **266** C3
Derby DE1 . . . . **267** A1
Spalden Ave DE6 . . . . . . **173** C3
Spang La NG17 . . . . **148** E4
Spanker La DE56 . . . . . . **168** B2
Spanker Terr DE56 . . . . . **168** C2
Sparrowbusk Cl S43 . . . . . **80** B6
Sparrow Cl
Derby DE24 . . . . **231** D4
Ilkeston DE7 . . . . **209** A5
Spa View Ave S12 . . . . **44** F3
Spa View Dr S12 . . . . **44** F3
Spa View Pl S12 . . . . **44** F3
Spa View Rd S12 . . . . **44** F3
Spa View Terr S12 . . . . **44** F3
Spa View Way S12 . . . . **44** F3
Speedwell SK13 . . . . **9** F7
Speedwell Cavern★ S33 . . **37** F2
Speedwell
Derby DE21 . . . . **206** D3
Glossop SK13 . . . . **9** F7
Woodville DE11 . . . . **256** F4
Speedwell Ind Est S43 . . . **78** F2
Speedwell Inf Sch S43 . . . **78** E1
Speedwell La NG16 . . . . . **195** E6
Speetley View S43 . . . . . . **80** E3
Speighthill Cres S42 . . . . **114** E4
Spenbeck Dr DE22 . . . . . **205** A5
Spencer Ave
Belper DE56 . . . . **179** B4
Derby DE24 . . . . **232** D4
Sandiacre NG10 . . . . **223** B6
Staveley S43 . . . . **79** B2
Spencer Cl
Ashbourne DE6 . . . . **185** C8
Burton u T DE13 . . . . . . **240** D1
Spencer Cres NG9 . . . . . **223** F8
Spencer Dr DE55 . . . . . . **170** D7
Spencer Gr SK17 . . . . **85** B6
Spencer Ho
Derby, Crewton DE24 . . . **233** A8
Derby, Spondon DE21 . . . **220** D3
Spencer Rd
Belper DE56 . . . . **179** B4
Buxton SK17 . . . . **85** B6
Chapel-en-le-F SK23 . . . . **46** F6
Sheffield S2 . . . . **43** A7
Spencer St
Bolsover S44 . . . . **117** F8
Chesterfield S40 . . . . . . **266** B4
Derby DE24 . . . . **233** A8
Stanley Common DE7 . . . **193** A1
Spend La DE6 . . . . **161** E2
Sperry Cl NG16 . . . . **171** F6
Spilsbury Cl DE65 . . . . . . **242** C5
Spindletree Dr DE21 . . . . **205** F2
Spinkhill Ave S13 . . . . **44** C8
Spinkhill Dr S13 . . . . **44** D8
Spinkhill Immaculate
Conception Prim Sch
S21 . . . . **60** C2
Spinkhill La S21 . . . . **60** C1
Spinkhill Rd
Killamarsh S21 . . . . **60** E4

Spinkhill Rd continued
Sheffield S13 . . . . **44** D8
Spinkhill View S21 . . . . . . **60** B1
Spinnerbottom SK22 . . . . . **24** F2
Spinners Way DE56 . . . . **179** C5
Spinneybrook Way DE3 . . **217** D4
Spinney Cl
Derby DE22 . . . . **205** A2
Glossop SK13 . . . . **10** C2
Mansfield Woodhouse
NG19 . . . . **136** E6
Spinney Cres NG9 . . . . . . **223** F3
Spinney Dr NG10 . . . . . . **223** C2
Spinney Hill DE73 . . . . . . **252** A7
Spinney Lo
Repton DE65 . . . . **242** C2
Tutbury DE13 . . . . **238** E6
Spinney Rd
Branston DE14 . . . . **253** F8
Derby, Chaddesden DE21 . **219** F7
Derby DE22 . . . . **218** E3
Ilkeston DE7 . . . . **208** E6
Long Eaton NG10 . . . . . . **223** C2
Spinney Rise NG9 . . . . . . **223** F3
Spinney The
Belper DE56 . . . . **179** A6
Borrowash DE72 . . . . . . **221** C1
Brailsford DE6 . . . . **201** E8
Castle Donington DE74 . . **247** A4
Ilkeston DE7 . . . . **208** E6
Ripley DE5 . . . . **169** D3
Shirebrook NG20 . . . . . . **119** D3
Stanton-by-D NG10 . . . . **222** F8
Spire Hollin SK13 . . . . **10** C2
Spire Hollin Ho SK13 . . . . **10** C2
Spital Brook Cl S41 . . . . . . **96** C1
Spital Gdns S41 . . . . **96** C2
Spital La S41 . . . . **96** C1
Spitewinter La S18, S42 . . . **93** D8
Spittal DE7 . . . . **247** A4
Spittal Gn S44 . . . . **118** A8
Spittal Hill DE74 . . . . **247** A4
Spondon Rd DE7 . . . . **207** D2
Spondon Sch DE21 . . . . . **220** C4
Spondon Sta DE21 . . . . . **220** D3
Spooner Dr S21 . . . . **60** C6
Spooner La S32 . . . . **72** C5
Spoonley Wood Ct DE23 . **230** F7
Sporton Cl DE55 . . . . **160** A7
Sporton La DE55 . . . . **160** B6
Spotswood Cl S14 . . . . **43** E4
Spotswood Dr S14 . . . . . . **43** E5
Spotswood Mount S14 . . . **43** E4
Spotswood Pl S14 . . . . **43** D4
Spotswood Rd S14 . . . . . . **43** D5
Spout La
Spout DE56 . . . . **166** C3
Tansley DE4 . . . . **144** A4
Spridgeon Cl 2 NG10 . . . **223** B2
Springbank SK13 . . . . **9** F5
Spring Bank
Buxton SK17 . . . . **67** C4
Great Longstone DE45 . . . **90** A4
Springbank Gdns SK22 . . . **33** B8
Spring Bank Rd
Chesterfield S40 . . . . . . **266** A3
New Mills SK22 . . . . **33** C8
Spring Cl
Belper DE56 . . . . **178** E6
Breaston DE72 . . . . **235** C8
Renishaw S21 . . . . **79** C7
Swadlincote DE11 . . . . . **256** A1
Wirksworth DE4 . . . . **154** F1
Spring Close Dell S14 . . . . **43** F4
Spring Close Mount S14 . . **43** F4
Spring Close View S14 . . . **43** F4
Spring Cottage Rd DE12 . **262** D5
Spring Ct 4 NG9 . . . . **223** E7
Spring Ct Mews SK14 . . . . . . **9** D5
Springdale Ct DE3 . . . . . . **217** E1
Spring Dale Gdns NG9 . . . **209** D3
Springfarm Rd DE15 . . . . **248** A1
Springfield
Broadbottom SK13 . . . . . . **16** C6
Derby DE23 . . . . **218** B2
Springfield Ave
Ashbourne DE6 . . . . **185** D8
Chesterfield S40 . . . . **95** D3
Heanor DE75 . . . . **181** B5
Long Eaton NG10 . . . . . . **236** F8
Sandiacre NG10 . . . . **223** B3
Shirebrook NG20 . . . . . . **119** E5
Springfield Cl
Bradwell S33 . . . . **51** A7
Clowne S43 . . . . **80** E3
Crich DE4 . . . . **157** A1
Eckington S21 . . . . **59** C3
Glossop SK13 . . . . **9** F7
Swadlincote DE11 . . . . . **256** B6
Springfield Cres
Bolsover S44 . . . . **98** F3
Somercotes DE55 . . . . . . **170** D7
Springfield Ct NG9 . . . . . **209** E1
Springfield Dr DE56 . . . . **190** D3
Springfield Gdns DE7 . . . **194** F2
Springfield Jun Sch
DE11 . . . . **256** C5
Springfield Prim Sch
DE21 . . . . **220** D5
Springfield Rd
Barlow S18 . . . . **75** D3
Bradwell S33 . . . . **51** A8
Chellaston DE73 . . . . . . **232** F2
Derby, Cherrytree Hill
DE21 . . . . **220** B5
Etwall DE65 . . . . **229** B3
Holmewood S42 . . . . **132** E8
Repton DE65 . . . . **242** D2

Springfield Rd continued
Swadlincote DE11 . . . . . **256** B6
Springfield Rise DE4 . . . . **143** C6
Springfield Terr
Burton u T DE15 . . . . . . **248** A1
Hayfield SK22 . . . . **25** D2
Ripley DE5 . . . . **169** E1
Springfield View DE5 . . . **169** D2
Spring Gardens Ctr The
SK17 . . . . **85** B8
Spring Garden Terr DE7 . **194** F2
Spring Gdns
Buxton SK17 . . . . **85** C8
Derby DE21 . . . . **219** F7
Glossop SK13 . . . . **10** A5
Springhill DE11 . . . . **257** A8
Spring Hill
Kimberley NG16 . . . . . . **195** F5
Mansfield Woodhouse
NG19 . . . . **136** B3
Whitwell S80 . . . . **82** A6
Springhill Way DE5 . . . . **181** A8
Spring Hollow DE56 . . . . **190** C8
Spring House Ct S42 . . . . . **94** F5
Spring La
Elmton S80 . . . . **99** F6
Heanor DE75 . . . . **181** A1
Sheffield S2 . . . . **43** E8
Shireoaks S80, S81 . . . . . **63** F5
Springmeadow SK13 . . . . . **16** D7
Spring Mount SK22 . . . . . . **33** C8
Spring Pl S40 . . . . **266** B3
Spring Rd DE55 . . . . **170** E6
Spring Rise SK13 . . . . **16** F7
Spring St
Broadbottom SK14 . . . . . . **16** A8
Glossop SK13 . . . . **10** B1
Hollingworth SK14 . . . . **9** C5
Swadlincote DE11 . . . . . **262** A8
Whitwell S80 . . . . **82** A6
Spring The NG10 . . . . . . **236** D5
Springvale Cl S45 . . . . . . **131** D2
Springvale Rd S45 . . . . . . **131** D2
Spring Vale Rd
Brimington S43 . . . . **96** E8
Hayfield SK22 . . . . **25** E2
Spring Water Ave S12 . . . . **44** F3
Spring Water Dr S12 . . . . . **44** F3
Springwell Com Sch S43 . . **97** D7
Springwell Hill S21 . . . . . . **77** F6
Springwell Park Dr S43 . . . **97** C7
Springwell St NG17 . . . . . **148** F2
Springwood SK13 . . . . **16** F8
Springwood Ct S43 . . . . . . **77** D4
Springwood Dr
Derby DE21 . . . . **206** B2
Mansfield Woodhouse
NG19 . . . . **136** C2
Springwood Farm Rd
DE11 . . . . **256** B7
Springwood Gdns DE56 . **179** A4
Springwood Rd S8 . . . . . . **43** A6
Springwood St S42 . . . . . **116** B4
Sprinkswoods La DE6 . . . **184** E5
Spruce Ave NG16 . . . . . . **171** D6
Spruce Rise S21 . . . . **60** C5
Spurr St S2 . . . . **43** B8
Square The
Boylestone DE6 . . . . **213** C4
Bretby DE15 . . . . **249** B3
8 Buxton SK17 . . . . **85** B8
Clay Cross S45 . . . . **131** E3
Derby, Darley Abbey DE22 **205** A4
Derby DE3 . . . . **217** D1
Elmton S80 . . . . **100** A4
Eyam S32 . . . . **71** E5
Hartington SK17 . . . . . . **137** D5
Marchington ST14 . . . . . **224** E2
Middleton DE45 . . . . **124** F3
Monyash DE45 . . . . **107** C2
Whitwell S80 . . . . **81** F6
Squires La S33 . . . . **38** C3
Squires Way DE23 . . . . . . **231** A6
Squirrel La DE73 . . . . **252** E4
Squirrel Wlk DE12 . . . . . . **262** B3
Stable Cl DE4 . . . . **156** B5
Stable Cotts DE4 . . . . **155** A6
Stable La DE6 . . . . **149** B1
Stable Mews DE11 . . . . . . **256** F2
Stables Ct S44 . . . . **99** C1
Stables Dr S43 . . . . **218** D5
Stables The DE65 . . . . . . **228** F1
Stacey Rd NG19 . . . . **135** D2
Staden Bsns Pk SK17 . . . . . **85** E5
Staden La SK17 . . . . **85** E4
Stadium Bsns Ct DE24 . . **219** E4
Stadium Ind Pk NG10 . . . **236** F8
Stadium View DE24 . . . . **219** E3
Stadmoor Ct DE73 . . . . . **232** F1
Staffa Dr DE55 . . . . **147** F5
Stafford Cl
Dronfield S18 . . . . **56** C2
6 Glossop SK13 . . . . **17** F8
Smalley DE7 . . . . **192** F6
Stafford Cres DE4 . . . . . . **165** E7
Stafford Ho DE24 . . . . . . **232** E6
Stafford St
Derby DE1 . . . . **267** A3
Long Eaton NG10 . . . . . . **236** F8
New Mills SK22 . . . . **24** C1
Staines Cl DE3 . . . . **217** C2
Stainforth St NG19 . . . . **136** C2
Stainsbro' La DE4, DE6 . . **165** B6
Stainsby Ave
Heanor DE75 . . . . **193** E8
Horsley Woodhouse DE7 . **192** E6

Stainsby Cl S42 . . . . **132** F8
Stainsby Gr NG17 . . . . . . **148** F2
Stainsby★ S44 . . . . **133** D7
Staithes Wlk DE21 . . . . . **205** C1
Staker La DE3 . . . . **230** D6
Stalybridge Ctry Pk★ SK15 **4** A2
Stalybridge Rd
Mottram in L SK14 . . . . **9** A4
Mottram in L SK14 . . . . **9** A4
Stamford Cl NG10 . . . . . . **236** E4
Stamford St
Awsworth NG16 . . . . **195** C4
Derby DE24 . . . . **232** D6
Heanor DE75 . . . . **181** E2
2 Ilkeston DE7 . . . . **194** E1
Stamps Cl DE15 . . . . **248** C3
Stanage Dr DE3 . . . . **217** F1
Stanage Rise S12 . . . . **44** E5
Stanage Way S40 . . . . **94** F5
Stancliffe Ave DE4 . . . . . **127** C3
Stancliffe Hall Sch DE4 . **127** B5
Stancliffe View DE4 . . . . **127** B3
Standing Butts Cl DE12 . . **259** D3
Standlow La DE6 . . . . **162** A8
Stand Park Ind Est S41 . . . **96** A7
Stand Rd S41 . . . . **95** F7
Stanedge Rd DE45 . . . . . **109** B6
Stanford Rd S18 . . . . **56** C1
Stanford Way S40 . . . . . . **114** B8
Stanhope Glade DE15 . . . **256** A8
Stanhope Gn DE15 . . . . . **248** F1
Stanhope Rd
Derby DE7 . . . . **217** E3
Sheffield S12 . . . . **44** C5
Swadlincote DE11 . . . . . **256** B6
Stanhope St
Bramley-Vale S44 . . . . . **117** C3
Burton u T DE15 . . . . . . **248** B3
Derby DE23 . . . . **219** A2
Ilkeston DE7 . . . . **209** A6
Long Eaton NG10 . . . . . . **236** D8
Stanton-by-D NG10 . . . . **222** E8
Stanier Way
Derby DE21 . . . . **220** B3
Renishaw S21 . . . . **60** B1
Staniforth Ave S21 . . . . . . **59** B3
Stanleigh Gdns DE12 . . . **265** E8
Stanleigh Ho DE12 . . . . . **265** E8
Stanleigh Rd DE12 . . . . . **262** B4
Stanley Ave
Ripley DE5 . . . . **169** E2
Staveley S43 . . . . **97** B7
Stanley Cl
Derby DE22 . . . . **218** E8
Ilkeston DE7 . . . . **208** E2
Netherseal DE12 . . . . . . **264** F7
Woodville DE11 . . . . **256** F3
Stanley Common CE Prim
Sch DE7 . . . . **193** B1
Stanley Cres ST14 . . . . . . **210** A2
Stanley Ct NG16 . . . . **182** F1
Stanley Dr NG9 . . . . **209** F1
Stanley Hall La SK12 . . . . . **32** C6
Stanley La S44, NG17 . . . **133** C2
Stanley Rd
Derby, Allenton DE24 . . . **232** F4
Derby, Cherrytree Hill
DE21 . . . . **220** A5
Sheffield S8 . . . . **43** B5
Stanley St
Chesterfield S41 . . . . **96** C5
Derby DE22 . . . . **218** E5
Ilkeston DE7 . . . . **208** F7
Killamarsh S21 . . . . **60** D7
Long Eaton NG10 . . . . . . **236** F7
Somercotes DE55 . . . . . . **170** D8
Swadlincote DE11 . . . . . **256** C4
Stanshope La DE6 . . . . . . **149** C2
Stanstead Rd DE56 . . . . . **179** B4
Stanton Ave DE56 . . . . . . **179** B4
Stanton Cl DE4 . . . . **127** B3
Stanton Cres S12 . . . . **44** D4
Stanton Gate DE7 . . . . . . **209** C1
Stantonhall La DE4 . . . . . **126** D7
Stanton Hill DE73 . . . . . . **251** C9
Stanton in Peak CE Prim Sch
DE4 . . . . **126** C6
Stanton La
Ellastone DE6 . . . . **183** C4
Mayfield DE6 . . . . **172** A3
Stanton Moor View DE4 . **142** F7
Stanton Pl NG19 . . . . **134** F7
Stanton Prim Sch DE15 . **255** B5
Stanton Rd
Ashbourne DE6 . . . . **185** D8
Burton u T DE15 . . . . . . **254** F7
Ilkeston DE7 . . . . **208** F2
Sandiacre NG10 . . . . **223** A7
Stanton St
Derby DE23 . . . . **218** F1
New Houghton NG19 . . . **134** F7
Stanton Vale Sch NG10 . . **236** C6
Stanton View DE45 . . . . . **109** C4
Stanwood Dr S40 . . . . . . **114** B8
Stanyforth St S13 . . . . **10** A4
Stapleford La NG9 . . . . . **223** F3
Stapleford Rd NG9 . . . . . **209** D3
Stapleton Rd DE7 . . . . . . **194** E4
Starch La NG10 . . . . **223** C7
Starcross Ct DE3 . . . . **217** C3
Starflower Way DE3 . . . . **217** D5
Starkholmes Rd DE4 . . . . **143** C2
Starkie Ave DE74 . . . . . . **246** F3
Starthe Bank DE75 . . . . . **181** F1
Starth La DE4 . . . . **144** A3
Start La SK23 . . . . **45** B7
Statham Ave S42 . . . . **131** C8
Statham St DE22 . . . . **218** E7

Station App
Ambergate DE56 . . . . . . 167 F4
Buxton SK17 . . . . 85 B8
Derby DE1 . . . . 267 B4
Duffield DE56 . . . . 190 F4
Hathersage S32 . . . . 53 A7
Station Back La S41 . . 266 C3
Station Cl
Chellaston DE73 . . . . 232 F1
Kilburn DE56 . . . . 179 F1
Station Cotts DE6 . . . . . 225 E2
Station Ct 3 DE7 . . . . . 194 E1
Station Dr DE12 . . . . 262 F4
Station Hill NG19 . . . . . 136 B3
Station La
Chesterfield S41, S43 . . . . 77 C2
Codnor DE5 . . . . 181 B6
Walton-on-T DE12 . . . . . 253 D1
Station La Ind Est S41 . . 77 B2
Station New Rd S42 . . . 131 D7
Station Rd
Ashbourne DE6 . . . . 173 B1
Awsworth NG16 . . . . 195 C5
Bakewell DE45 . . . . 109 E6
Bamford S33 . . . . 40 B2
Barrow Hill S43 . . . . 78 B3
Bolsover S44 . . . . 98 F2
Borrowash DE72 . . . . 221 B1
Breadsall DE21 . . . . 205 E4
Brimington, Hollingwood
S43 . . . . 78 A2
Brimington S43 . . . . 96 D8
Burton u T DE13 . . . . 253 A1
Buxton SK17 . . . . 85 B7
Castle Donington DE74 . . 247 C5
Chapel-en-le-F SK23 . . . . 47 B6
Chellaston DE73 . . . . 232 F1
Chesterfield, Old Whittington
S41 . . . . 77 A1
Chesterfield S41 . . . . 266 C3
Chinley SK23 . . . . 34 C2
Clowne S43 . . . . 80 E4
Darley Dale DE4 . . . . 127 C2
Denby Village DE5 . . . . . 180 B3
Derby DE3 . . . . 217 D3
Derby, Spondon DE21 . . 220 D3
Dove Holes SK17 . . . . 47 F1
Draycott DE72 . . . . 235 B7
Duffield DE56 . . . . 190 F4
Furness Vale SK23 . . . . . . 33 D4
Glossop SK13 . . . . 10 A5
Great Longstone DE45 . . . 89 F3
Hathersage S32 . . . . 53 A7
Hatton DE65 . . . . 239 D8
Hayfield, Birch Vale SK22 . 25 A2
Hayfield SK22 . . . . 25 D2
Hope S33 . . . . 39 B3
Ilkeston DE7 . . . . 194 F1
Ironville NG16 . . . . 170 F3
Killamarsh S21 . . . . 60 B6
Kimberley NG16 . . . . 195 F6
Langley Mill NG16 . . . . . . 182 B2
Little Eaton DE21 . . . . . . 205 C7
Long Eaton NG10 . . . . . . 236 F8
Marple SK6 . . . . 23 A7
Marple, Strines SK6, SK22 . 23 D1
Melbourne DE73 . . . . 252 C8
New Mills SK22 . . . . 33 B7
North Wingfield S42 . . . . 131 E6
Pilsley S45 . . . . 132 D1
Renishaw S21 . . . . 60 A2
Rolleston DE13 . . . . 240 C4
Sandiacre NG10 . . . . 223 C5
Scarcliffe S44 . . . . 118 F6
Selston NG16 . . . . 160 E1
Sheffield S20 . . . . 59 E7
Shirebrook NG20 . . . . . . 119 E6
Spinkhill S21 . . . . 60 D2
Stanley DE7 . . . . 207 C6
Stonebroom DE55 . . . . . 147 B5
Tibshelf DE55 . . . . 147 F6
West Hallam DE7 . . . . . . 207 C8
Whaley Bridge SK23 . . . . 34 A1
Whitwell S80 . . . . 82 A5
Woodville DE11 . . . . 256 F2
Station St
Ashbourne DE6 . . . . 173 B1
Cossall DE7 . . . . 195 A1
Glossop SK13 . . . . 10 D1
Long Eaton NG10 . . . . . . 236 E7
Mansfield Woodhouse
NG19 . . . . 136 B3
Swadlincote DE11 . . . . . . 261 F8
Station View NG20 . . . . 119 E4
Station Wlk 1 SK17 . . . 85 D8
Station Yd DE73 . . . . 252 C8
Staton La S18 . . . . 58 A1
Staunton Ave DE23 . . . 231 E6
Staunton Cl
Castle Donington DE74 . . 247 A4
Chesterfield S40 . . . . 115 A6
Staunton Harold Resr Visitor
Ctr* DE73 . . . . 251 F5
Staunton La DE73 . . . . 251 A1
Staveley Cl DE24 . . . . . 232 E3
Staveley Jun Sch S43 . . . 78 E1
Staveley La
Barrow Hill S21, S43 . . . . 78 A5
Eckington S21 . . . . 59 E2
Staveley S43 . . . . 78 E7
Staveley Rd
Chesterfield S43 . . . . 77 E3
Long Duckmanton S44 . . . 97 E4
Poolsbrook S43 . . . . 98 A8
Sheffield S8 . . . . 43 A7
Staverton Dr DE3 . . . . . 217 D4
Stead Mews S21 . . . . . . 59 D3
Stead St S21 . . . . 59 D3

Steam Mill La DE5 . . . . 170 A1
Steel's La S44 . . . . 118 B6
Steele Ave S43 . . . . 97 B6
Steele Ct SK17 . . . . 85 A8
Steel La S44 . . . . 99 B2
Steeping Cl S43 . . . . 96 E8
Steep La S42 . . . . 114 A4
Steeple Cl DE21 . . . . . . 205 E2
Steeple Dr DE5 . . . . 180 E8
Steeple End Fold SK22 . . 25 D2
Steeplegate S40 . . . . 266 B3
Steeple Grange S45 . . . 154 F3
Steeple Grange Light Rly*
DE4 . . . . 154 F4
Steep Turnpike DE4 . . . 143 C5
Steetley La S80 . . . . 63 E3
Stenson Ave DE23 . . . . 231 E6
Stenson Ct DE5 . . . . 169 F1
Stenson Fields Prim Com
Sch DE24 . . . . 231 D2
Stenson Rd DE23, DE24 . 231 D4
Stenton Rd S8 . . . . 56 F7
Stephenson Ct S40 . . . . 95 B2
Stephenson Pl
Chesterfield S40 . . . . 266 B3
Clay Cross S45 . . . . 131 B4
Stephenson Rd S43 . . . . 78 E1
Stephensons Way DE21 . 220 A3
Stephens Rd DE14 . . . . . 254 B8
Stepping Cl DE22 . . . . . 218 E5
Stepping La DE22 . . . . . 218 E5
Sterland St S40 . . . . 95 E3
Sterling Cl DE5 . . . . 180 B2
Sterndale Cl SK17 . . . . . 69 E3
Sterndale Ho 4 DE1 . . 267 B2
Sterndale La S41 . . . . . . 69 E3
Sterndale Moor SK17 . . 105 C6
Sterndale Rd NG10 . . . . 236 B6
Sterry Cl S43 . . . . 80 E2
Stevenage Cl DE24 . . . . 232 F5
Steven Cl NG9 . . . . 223 F4
Stevens La DE72 . . . . . . 235 D8
Stevenson Ave DE72 . . . 235 B8
Stevenson Ho S41 . . . . . 96 B6
Stevenson Jun Sch NG9 . 223 F4
Stevenson Pl DE23 . . . . 231 B8
Stevenson Rd DE6 . . . . 224 B8
Stevens Rd NG10 . . . . . . 223 A5
Steward Gate S33 . . . . . . 40 A6
Stewart Cl
Burton u T DE14 . . . . 254 A6
Derby DE21 . . . . 220 E6
Stewart St DE55 . . . . . . 170 D5
Stile Croft DE4 . . . . 154 D5
Stiles Cl SK13 . . . . 9 E5
Stiles Rd DE24 . . . . 233 B8
Stillman Cl S41 . . . . 115 C8
Stinting La
Mansfield NG19 . . . . 136 E2
Shirebrook NG20 . . . . . . 119 D3
Stirland St DE5 . . . . 170 B1
Stirling Cl
Castle Gresley DE11 . . . . 255 F1
Derby DE21 . . . . 219 C8
Stirling Ct S41 . . . . 266 B4
Stirling Gr NG16 . . . . . . 195 E7
Stirling Way S2 . . . . 44 A8
Stockbrook Rd DE22 . . . 218 D3
Stockbrook St DE22 . . . 218 E4
Stockdove Cl DE24 . . . . 231 D4
Stocker Ave DE24 . . . . . 233 D7
Stock La S14 . . . . 224 C1
Stockley La S44 . . . . 117 F1
Stockley View S44 . . . . . 118 B8
Stockport Rd
Broadbottom SK14 . . . . . . 15 D8
Marple SK6 . . . . 23 A6
Stocks Brow SK13 . . . . . . 10 A7
Stocks Green S17 . . . . . . 55 D4
Stocks Green Dr S17 . . . 55 D4
Stocks Rd NG16 . . . . . . 195 E7
Stocks The S13 . . . . 10 A7
Stockton Dr SK23 . . . . . . 34 E1
Stockwell Ct S40 . . . . . . 114 F7
Stoddard Dr DE75 . . . . . 181 F2
Stodhart Flats SK23 . . . . 47 C8
Stoke Cl DE56 . . . . 179 E5
Stollard St S45 . . . . 131 D4
Stone Bank S18 . . . . 57 B1
Stone Bench La SK17 . . 106 C3
Stone Bench Way SK17 . . 85 E8
Stonebridge La NG20 . . 120 F4
Stonebroom Ind Est
DE55 . . . . 147 B4
Stonebroom La DE55 . . 147 B5
Stonebroom Prim Sch
DE55 . . . . 147 A4
Stonebroom Wlk DE24 . . 232 E3
Stonechat Cl DE3 . . . . . 218 A3
Stone Cl
Derby DE21 . . . . 220 E6
Dronfield S18 . . . . 57 C3
Stonecliff Terr SK17 . . . . 85 D8
Stonecroft Rd S17 . . . . . 55 F5
Stonedale Cl S20 . . . . . . 59 D7
Stone Fronts DE73 . . . . 251 A4
Stonegravels Croft 7
S20 . . . . 59 E6
Stonegravels La S41 . . . 96 A5
Stonegravels Way S20 . . 59 F6
Stoneheads SK23 . . . . . . 45 C8
Stoneheads Rise SK23 . . 45 D8
Stonehill DE4 . . . . 247 B2
Stone Hill Rd DE23 . . . . 218 F2
Stoneholes Dr S45 . . . . 131 E2
Stone La
Chesterfield S43 . . . . 77 D4

Stone La continued
Sheffield S12 . . . . 44 F5
Stoneleigh Way DE55 . . 169 F8
Stoneley Cl S12 . . . . 44 B1
Stoneley Cres S12 . . . . . 44 B1
Stoneley Dell S12 . . . . . 44 B1
Stoneley Dr S12 . . . . 44 B1
Stonelow Cres S18 . . . . . 57 C7
Stonelow Gn S18 . . . . . . 57 B2
Stonelow Jun Sch S18 . . . 57 C2
Stonelow Rd S18 . . . . . . 57 C2
Stone Mdws NG10 . . . . 236 E5
Stonepit La DE6 . . . . . . 164 A3
Stone Rd S18 . . . . 57 C3
Stoneridge SK13 . . . . 9 F5
Stone Row
Chesterfield S40 . . . . 95 D2
Marple SK6 . . . . 23 A6
Stonerows La S45 . . . . . 145 C6
Stonesby Cl DE21 . . . . . 205 F2
Stonesdale Ct 1 DE24 . 233 C6
Stones La DE4 . . . . 156 F1
Stone St S20 . . . . 59 D7
Stonewell La SK17 . . . . 137 D5
Stoney Cl DE45 . . . . 109 D4
Stoneycroft La S42 . . . . 114 A5
Stoney Cross S18 . . . . . 220 E3
Stoneydale Cl DE11 . . . 255 F5
Stoneyfield Bank S18 . . 179 A5
Stoney Flatts Cres DE21 . 220 A8
Stoney Furlong Rd DE45 . 91 E6
Stoney Gate Rd DE21 . . 220 D3
Stoney Hill DE4 . . . . 155 B2
Stoney La
Appleby Magna DE12 . . . 265 F1
Ashover S45 . . . . 130 C3
Brinsley NG16 . . . . 182 D6
Derby DE21 . . . . 220 E5
Hognaston DE6 . . . . 164 A2
Selston NG16 . . . . 171 E7
Trowell NG9 . . . . 209 B5
Stoneyland Dr SK22 . . . . 33 B8
Stoney Middleton CE Prim
Sch S32 . . . . 71 F3
Stoney Way S42 . . . . 143 C4
Stoney Wood Dr DE4 . . 156 C1
Stonyhurst Ct DE24 . . . 232 E3
Stony La DE56 . . . . 191 D6
Stony Ridge Rd S11 . . . . 54 C5
Stoodley Pike Gdns
DE22 . . . . 204 C2
Stoops Cl S40 . . . . 95 D6
Stoppard Cl DE7 . . . . . . 194 D2
Storer La DE4 . . . . 166 A2
Stores Rd DE21 . . . . 267 D4
Storforth La S41 . . . . . . 115 B7
Storforth Lane Terr S41 . 115 C8
Storforth Lane Trad Est
S40 . . . . 115 B8
Stormont Cl DE55 . . . . . 160 B4
Stormont Gr S43 . . . . . . 97 C7
Stornoway Rd 9 DE24 . 231 D3
Storrs Rd S40 . . . . 95 B2
Storth Bank S13 . . . . 16 F7
Storthfield Way DE55 . . 160 B4
Storth La DE55 . . . . 160 B4
Storth Meadow Rd SK13 . 16 F7
Stort Sq NG19 . . . . 136 D2
Stour Cl
Brimington S43 . . . . 96 E8
Hilton DE65 . . . . 240 E8
Stourdale Cl NG10 . . . . 236 A6
Stourport Dr DE73 . . . . 233 A3
Stow Ct 6 NG19 . . . . . . 136 E3
Stowmarket Dr DE21 . . 219 D8
Stradbroke Ave S13 . . . . 44 D7
Stradbroke Cl S13 . . . . . 44 E7
Stradbroke Cres S13 . . . 44 E7
Stradbroke Dr S13 . . . . . 44 E7
Stradbroke Pl S13 . . . . . 44 E7
Stradbroke Prim Sch S13 . 44 D7
Stradbroke Rd S13 . . . . . 44 D7
Stradbroke Rise S40 . . . 114 C8
Stradbroke Way S13 . . . . 44 E7
Stradbroke Wlk S13 . . . . 44 D7
Strand DE1 . . . . 267 B3
Strand Arc DE1 . . . . 267 B3
Stranfaer Cl DE55 . . . . . 170 A7
Stranraer Cl NG19 . . . . 136 C6
Stratford Cl DE65 . . . . . 242 D1
Stratford Rd DE21 . . . . . 205 D2
Stratford St DE7 . . . . . . 194 F4
Strathallan Cl DE4 . . . . 127 C4
Strathaven Ct DE21 . . . . 220 E5
Strathglen Cl NG16 . . . . 195 E7
Strathmore Ave DE24 . . 233 A6
Stratton Rd S42 . . . . 99 A2
Strawberry Bank NG17 . 148 E4
Strawberry La
Blackfordby DE11 . . . . . . 257 B1
Rosliston DE12 . . . . 260 D5
Strawberry Lee La S17 . . 55 B5
Straw La
Clay Cross DE55 . . . . 146 D8
Shirland DE55 . . . . 146 D8
Streatham Rd DE22 . . . . 218 B6
Street Farm Cl S26 . . . . . 61 E6
Streetfield Cres S20 . . . . 59 D6
Streetfields S20 . . . . 59 E6
Street Forest Walks The*
SK17 . . . . 64 E4
Street La DE5 . . . . 180 B6
Street Lane Prim Sch
DE5 . . . . 180 B5
Street The S10, SK17 . . . 64 C5
Strelley Ave DE5 . . . . . . 180 C8
Stretfield Rd S33 . . . . . . 39 B1

Strettea La DE55 . . . . . . 146 C2
Stretton Brook Sch
DE13 . . . . 240 C1
Stretton Cl DE13 . . . . . . 217 D1
Stretton Handley CE Prim
Sch DE55 . . . . 145 D7
Stretton Rd
Clay Cross S45 . . . . 131 C1
Shirland DE55 . . . . 146 C8
Stonebroom DE55 . . . . . 146 E5
Stretton View DE12 . . . . 265 F6
Striding Edge Cl 4
NG10 . . . . 223 B2
Strines Rd
Marple SK6 . . . . 23 B3
New Mills SK6 . . . . 32 D8
Strines Sta SK6 . . . . 23 D1
Stroma Cl DE24 . . . . 233 D4
Strutt's Park Ho 2 DE22 218 F7
Strutt St
Belper DE56 . . . . 178 F3
Derby DE23 . . . . 219 A2
Stuart Cl S41 . . . . 96 C6
Stuart St DE1 . . . . 267 B4
Stubben Edge La S45 . . 130 C2
Stubbing Rd S40 . . . . . . 114 F7
Stubbins La SK23 . . . . . . 34 D2
Stubbins Wood NG20 . . 119 E5
Stubbins Wood La NG20 119 E5
Stubbin Wood Sch NG20 119 E4
Stubby La S14 . . . . 224 E1
Stubley Cl S18 . . . . 56 E2
Stubley Croft S18 . . . . . . 56 D2
Stubley Dr S18 . . . . 56 E2
Stubley Hollow S18 . . . . 56 F2
Stubley La S18 . . . . 56 D2
Stubley Pl S18 . . . . 56 E2
Stubwood Hollow ST14 . 196 D5
Stubwood La ST14 . . . . 196 D4
Studbrook Cl DE74 . . . . 246 F3
Studfarm Cl DE73 . . . . . 252 E2
Studios The S40 . . . . 95 E3
Studland Cl NG19 . . . . . 136 D6
Sturge Croft 3 S2 . . . . . 43 B6
Sturges La DE72 . . . . . . 233 F4
Sturston Rd DE6 . . . . . . 173 C1
Sudbury Ave
Ilkeston DE7 . . . . 209 B7
Sandiacre NG10 . . . . 223 A6
Sudbury Cl
Chesterfield S40 . . . . 95 B5
Derby DE1 . . . . 218 C5
Sudbury Cl NG10 . . . . . . 235 F4
Sudbury Dr NG17 . . . . . 148 E2
Sudbury Hall & Mus of
Childhood* DE6 . . . . . 225 D5
Sudbury Mews NG16 . . 182 E1
Sudbury Pk DE6 . . . . . . 225 D7
Sudbury Prim Sch DE6 . . 225 E4
Sudbury St DE1 . . . . 218 E5
Sudhall Cl S41 . . . . 95 D8
Suff La NG16 . . . . 160 C3
Suffolk Ave DE21 . . . . . . 219 E7
Suffolk Rd DE15 . . . . . . 254 D7
Sugworth Rd S6 . . . . 31 F6
Sulleys Field DE22 . . . . . 204 D7
Summer Cross SK17 . . . 69 B4
Summer Dr DE4 . . . . . . 165 E7
Summerfield Cres S43 . . 96 E8
Summerfield Rd
Chesterfield S40 . . . . 266 A1
Dronfield S18 . . . . 57 B3
Summerfields Way DE7 . 194 D3
Summerfields Way S
DE7 . . . . 194 D2
Summer La
Sheffield S17 . . . . 55 D4
Wirksworth DE4 . . . . 165 D4
Summerley Lower Rd S18 57 F2
Summerley Rd S18 . . . . . 57 F2
Summerskill Gn S43 . . . 97 C7
Summerville DE21 . . . . . 231 B6
Summer Wood Ct DE23 . 231 D7
Summerwood La S18 . . . 56 F3
Summerwood Pl S18 . . . 56 F2
Summit Dr NG20 . . . . . . 119 E4
Sumners Pl SK13 . . . . . . 10 B1
Sumner St SK13 . . . . 17 C8
Sunart Cl DE24 . . . . 231 F2
Sundew Cl DE21 . . . . . . 220 F4
Sundial Cl DE21 . . . . . . 201 E8
Sundial Wlk DE6 . . . . . . 201 E8
Sundown Ave DE23 . . . . 231 D6
Sundown Cl SK22 . . . . . . 33 A8
Sundown Pl S13 . . . . 44 F8
Sundown Rd S13 . . . . . . 44 F8
Sunflower Cl
Derby DE24 . . . . 220 A1
Shirebrook NG20 . . . . . . 119 D3
Sun La DE4 . . . . 156 F1
Sunlaws Ct SK13 . . . . . . 17 B8
Sunlaws St SK13 . . . . . . 17 B8
Sunlea Cres NG9 . . . . . . 223 F5
Sunningdale Ave
Derby DE21 . . . . 220 D5
Heanor DE75 . . . . 193 F8
Sunningdale Cl
Burton u T DE13 . . . . 240 C1
Chesterfield S40 . . . . 114 E8
Sunningdale Dr
Glossop SK13 . . . . 10 E1
Ilkeston DE7 . . . . 208 B5
Sunningdale Pk S42 . . . 115 C1
Sunningdale Rise S40 . . 114 C8
Sunninghill Cl DE7 . . . . 207 D8
Sunnybank DE4 . . . . 110 F1

Sunny Bank
Great Longstone DE45 . . . 90 A4
Mayfield DE6 . . . . 184 C7
Tibshelf DE55 . . . . 147 F5
Sunny Bank Gdns DE56 . 178 F2
Sunny Bank La SK17 . . . 69 C4
Sunny Banks 3 SK13 . . . 17 B8
Sunny Brook Cl S43 . . . . 80 E3
Sunnyfield SK17 . . . . 85 F1
Sunny Gr DE21 . . . . 220 A5
Sunny Hill DE56 . . . . . . 190 F7
Sunnyhill Ave DE23 . . . . 231 E6
Sunnyhill Inf Sch DE23 . . 231 E7
Sunnyside
Swadlincote DE11 . . . . . . 255 E7
Whitwell S80 . . . . 82 A6
Sunnyside Ct DE11 . . . . 255 F7
Sunnyside Rd ST14 . . . . 210 B1
Sunnyside Terr DE4 . . . . 143 A8
Sunny Springs S41 . . . . 266 B4
Sunnyvale Ave S17 . . . . . 55 E4
Sunnyvale Rd S17 . . . . . . 55 D4
Sun St
Derby DE22 . . . . 267 A2
Woodville DE11 . . . . 256 F2
Surbiton Cl DE22 . . . . . 218 A6
Surbiton Ct DE7 . . . . . . 207 D8
Surgery La DE4 . . . . 157 A1
Surprise Villas S32 . . . . . 53 A7
Surrey St
Derby DE22 . . . . 218 C6
Glossop SK13 . . . . 10 C1
Sussex Cir DE21 . . . . . . 219 E8
Sussex Cl NG16 . . . . 195 A8
Sussex Rd DE15 . . . . . . 254 E6
Sussex Way NG10 . . . . . 223 B5
Sutherland Rd DE23 . . . 219 A1
Sutton Ave DE73 . . . . . . 232 F3
Sutton Cl DE22 . . . . 218 D6
Sutton Cres S43 . . . . 97 C7
Sutton Ct NG16 . . . . 182 F2
Sutton Dr DE24 . . . . 232 E4
Sutton Hall Rd S44 . . . . 117 E8
Sutton Ho DE24 . . . . . . 233 C5
Sutton La
Etwall DE65 . . . . 229 B5
Hatton DE65 . . . . 227 E4
Hilton DE65 . . . . 228 D3
Long Duckmanton S44 . . 116 F7
Sutton Rd
Church Broughton DE65 . . 227 D7
Sutton in A NG17 . . . . . . 148 F3
Suttons Ave DE11 . . . . . 256 E1
Suttons Bsns Pk DE11 . . . 256 E3
Sutton Scarsdale Hall*
S44 . . . . 117 A6
Suttons La SK6 . . . . 23 A5
Sutton View
Bolsover S44 . . . . 118 B8
Temple Normanton S42 . . 116 B4
Sutton Way SK13 . . . . . . 10 A5
Swaddale Ave S41 . . . . . 96 B6
Swaddale Cl S41 . . . . . . 96 B6
Swadlincote La DE11 . . 255 E2
Swadlincote Rd DE11 . . 256 E3
Swadlincote Ski Ctr
DE11 . . . . 256 C3
Swaines Mdw DE4 . . . . 165 D8
Swainspark Ind Est DE12 256 B6
Swalebank Cl S40 . . . . . 115 B8
Swaledale Ct 2 DE24 . . 233 C6
Swallow Cl S40 . . . . 218 A3
Swallow Croft DE5 . . . . 180 D6
Swallow Ct DE5 . . . . 180 D6
Swallowdale Rd DE24 . . 231 D4
Swallow Fold SK13 . . . . . 16 F8
Swallow Ho DE1 . . . . . . 218 E5
Swallow House Cres
SK22 . . . . 25 C3
Swallow House La SK22 . 25 C3
Swallow Rd DE11 . . . . . . 256 F3
Swanbourne Cl 1 S41 . . 96 C1
Swan Hill DE3 . . . . 230 B6
Swan La NG19 . . . . 136 B3
Swanmore Rd DE23 . . . 231 A8
Swann Yd NG17 . . . . . . 148 F3
Swanson Ave NG17 . . . . 148 F3
Swans Rest DE11 . . . . . . 255 F6
Swanwick Ave NG20 . . . 119 F3
Swanwick Gdns DE21 . . 206 A1
Swanwick Hall Sch DE55 169 F7
Swanwick Junc Sta*
DE55 . . . . 170 A5
Swanwick Prim Sch
DE55 . . . . 169 D6
Swanwick Rd DE55 . . . . 170 B7
Swanwick St S41 . . . . . . 77 A2
Swarkestone Dr DE23 . . 231 C5
Swarkestone Rd
Barrow u T DE73 . . . . . . 244 B6
Chellaston DE73 . . . . 244 F8
Swathwick Cl S42 . . . . . 114 E4
Swathwick La S42 . . . . . 114 D4
Swayfield Cl DE3 . . . . . . 217 C3
Sweetbriar Cl DE24 . . . . 233 A5
Swift Bank SK13 . . . . 16 F8
Swift Cl
Derby DE22 . . . . 218 A3
Woodville DE11 . . . . 256 F3
Swift Ct NG16 . . . . 182 F2
Swinburne St DE1 . . . . . 267 B1
Swinderby Dr DE21 . . . . 206 B1
Swindon Cl NG16 . . . . . 195 C7
Swiney Way NG9 . . . . . . 223 F2

Swinger La S45 . . . . 129 C7
Swinney Bank DE56 . . . 179 A5
Swinney La DE56 . . . . . . 179 A5
Swinscoe Hill DE6 . . . . 172 B2
Swinscoe Way S40 . . . . . 95 A5
Swinson Cl ST14 . . . . . . 197 A3
Swithland Cl S41 . . . . . . 115 C7
Sycamore Ave
  Chesterfield S40 . . . . 95 E2
  Creswell S80 . . . . 81 E2
  Derby DE22 . . . . 204 D3
  Dronfield S18. . . . . 57 A3
  Findern DE65 . . . . 230 E1
  Glapwell S44 . . . . 134 B8
  Ripley DE5 . . . . 180 D8
  Swadlincote DE11 . . . . . 256 A7
Sycamore Cl
  Bolsover S44 . . . . 99 C2
  Burton u T DE15. . . . . . 254 E5
  Buxton SK17 . . . . 66 B1
  Etwall DE65 . . . . 229 C4
  Linton DE12 . . . . 261 D5
  Mapperley DE7 . . . . 193 F3
  New Mills SK22 . . . . 24 E1
  Pinxton NG16. . . . . 160 D3
  Selston NG16. . . . . 171 D7
  Shirland DE55 . . . . 146 C4
Sycamore Cotts DE6 . . 151 D1
Sycamore Cres NG10 . . 223 A7
Sycamore Ct
  Derby DE21 . . . . 220 E5
  Willington DE65 . . . . . . 242 B5
Sycamore Dr
  Calow S44 . . . . 96 E3
  Ilkeston DE7 . . . . 209 B7
  Killamarsh S21 . . . . 60 C5
Sycamore La
  Barlborough S43 . . . . 80 B6
  Brimington S43 . . . . 78 A1
Sycamore Rd
  Awsworth NG16. . . . . . . 195 C5
  Brimington S43 . . . . 78 A1
  Burton u T DE15. . . . . . 254 F6
  Castle Donington DE74. . 247 B5
  Chapel-en-le-F SK23 . . . . 47 B4
  Hayfield SK22 . . . . 24 F2
  Long Eaton NG10. . . . . . 236 C5
  Mansfield Woodhouse
    NG19. . . . . 136 C5
  Matlock DE4 . . . . 143 B6
  Mayfield DE6 . . . . 184 C7
Sycamore St
  Sheffield S20 . . . . 59 C8
  Shirebrook NG20. . . . . 120 F6
Sycamores The
  Eastwood NG16. . . . . . . 182 E1
  Glossop SK13. . . . . .9 F3
  Sheffield S13 . . . . 44 C6
  South Normanton DE55. . 160 B5
Sycamore Terr SK22 . . . 25 D3
Syda La S42 . . . . 93 E1
Syday La S21 . . . . 60 D1
Sydenham Rd DE22 . . . 218 A7
Sydney Cl
  Derby DE3 . . . . 217 F3
  Mansfield Woodhouse
    NG19. . . . . 136 C6
Sydney Rd DE72 . . . . . . 235 A7
Sydney St S40 . . . . 95 E3
Sydnope Hall DE4 . . . . 128 A5
Sydnope Hill DE4 . . . . 128 A5
Syerscote La B79 . . . . . 263 B2
Sylvan Cl S41 . . . . 266 C1
Sylvan Cliff SK17. . . . . . 85 C7
Sylvan Dr S42 . . . . 131 A6
Sylvan Pk SK17 . . . . 85 C8
Sylvia Rd S18. . . . . 76 D5
Sywell Cl DE55. . . . . . . 169 F8

T

Tabley Gdns SK6. . . . . . . 23 A4
Taddington Cl 2 DE21 . . 219 E8
Taddington Pl 31 SK13 . . .9 E1
Taddington & Priestcliffe
  Sch SK17. . . . . 87 F3
Taddington Rd
  Chesterfield S40 . . . . 95 B5
  Derby DE21 . . . . 205 F1
Taft Ave NG10 . . . . 223 B6
Tagg La DE45 . . . . 107 A1
Taggs Knoll S33 . . . . 40 B4
Taghole La DE6 . . . . . . 188 E2
Tailby Dr DE65 . . . . 242 A5
Talbot Cres S41 . . . . . . 115 D7
Talbot Dr NG9 . . . . 209 D2
Talbot Pl DE12 . . . . 265 E8
Talbot Rd SK13 . . . . 10 C2
Talbot St S8 . . . . 43 C2
Talbot St
  Chesterfield S41 . . . . . . 115 D7
  Derby DE1 . . . . 267 A3
  Glossop SK13. . . . . 10 C1
  Pinxton NG16. . . . . 160 C2
  Swadlincote DE11 . . . . . 256 A1
Talgarth Cl DE21 . . . . . 206 C2
Tall Trees Park (Cvn Pk)
  NG19 . . . . 136 E2
Tallys End S43 . . . . 80 A6
Tamar Ave DE22 . . . . . . 204 D4
Tamworth Rd
  Appleby Magna DE12. . . 265 E2

Tamworth Rd continued
  Castle Donington DE72,
    NG10. . . . . 235 E1
  Long Eaton NG10. . . . . . 236 C5
Tamworth Rise DE56. . . 190 E4
Tamworth St DE56 . . . . 190 E3
Tamworth Terr DE56 . . . 190 E4
Tanner's La DE65 . . . . . 242 C3
Tansley Ave DE7 . . . . . . 193 A1
Tanyard Ct DE74 . . . . . . 247 B4
Tap La S40 . . . . 266 A3
Taplow Cl DE3 . . . . 217 C2
Tapton Bsns Ctr S41 . . . 266 C4
Tapton La S41 . . . . 266 C3
Tapton Lock Hill S41. . . . 96 B6
Tapton Lock Visitor Ctr★
  S41 . . . . 96 B6
Tapton Terr S41 . . . . . . 266 C4
Tapton Vale S41 . . . . 96 C5
Tapton View Rd S41 . . . . 95 F5
Tapton Way S44 . . . . 96 F3
Tarina Cl DE73. . . . . . . 233 A1
Tarn Cl NG16. . . . . 182 B4
Tarnside Fold 1 SK13. . . 17 A7
Tarquin Cl DE13 . . . . . . 240 E2
Tasman Cl DE3 . . . . 217 F3
Tatenhill La
  Branston DE14. . . . . . . 253 D7
  Tatenhill DE13 . . . . 253 A8
Tatham's La DE7. . . . . . 194 E2
Tattersall Wlk 5 NG19. . 136 E4
Tattle Hill DE7 . . . . 207 F2
Tatwin Ct DE73 . . . . . . 252 F2
Taunton Cl DE24 . . . . . 233 C8
Taverners Cres DE23 . . 231 C8
Tavern Rd SK13. . . . . .9 E3
Tavistock Ave DE5 . . . . 169 D2
Tavistock Cl 14 DE24 . . 231 D3
Tavistock Ct 14 S41 . . . . 95 F8
Tavistock Sq DE55 . . . . 159 B5
Tawney Croft DE4. . . . . 144 A4
Tawny Way DE23. . . . . . 231 A7
Taxal & Fernilee CE Prim Sch
  SK23 . . . . 45 D6
Taxal Moor Rd SK23. . . . 45 C3
Tayberry Ct DE24 . . . . . 232 E7
Tay Cl
  Derby DE24 . . . . 231 D2
  Dronfield S18. . . . . 56 D2
Taylor's La
  Spout DE4 . . . . 166 B4
  Trusley DE6 . . . . 215 E6
Taylor Cres
  Chesterfield S41 . . . . 96 C1
  Stapleford NG9 . . . . 223 F8
Taylor Ct DE6 . . . . 173 C1
Taylor La DE75. . . . . . . 181 D4
Taylors La ST14. . . . . . . 196 C4
Taylor St
  Derby DE24 . . . . 219 E2
  Hollingworth SK14. . . . . . .9 D4
  Ilkeston DE7 . . . . 194 F1
Tayside Cl DE24. . . . . . 231 D3
Tay Wlk 10 NG19 . . . . . 136 E4
Teal Cl DE24. . . . . 219 D3
Tean Cl DE15 . . . . 248 A1
Teasel Dr DE11 . . . . 256 F4
Tedder Ave SK17. . . . . . . 85 D3
Tedgness Rd S32 . . . . . . 53 E1
Tedworth Ave DE24 . . . 231 D2
Teesdale Rd
  Long Eaton NG10. . . . . . 236 A6
  Sheffield S12. . . . . 58 F8
Telford Cl DE3 . . . . 217 E1
Telford Cres S43. . . . . . . 78 F2
Telford Rd SK6 . . . . 23 A4
Telmah Cl DE13 . . . . . . 240 D1
Temperance Hill DE55 . 145 E7
Temperance Sq SK14 . . . .9 A4
Temperance St 5 SK14 . 16 A8
Templar Cl DE24 . . . . . . 231 C3
Temple Ave SK13 . . . . . . 10 C5
Templebell Cl DE23 . . . 231 A6
Temple Cl SK17 . . . . 85 A6
Temple Normanton Bsns Pk
  S41 . . . . 116 A4
Temple Normanton Prim Sch
  S42 . . . . 116 C4
Temple Rd
  Buxton SK17 . . . . 85 A6
  Matlock Bath DE4 . . . . . 143 A1
Temple St
  Derby DE23 . . . . 219 A3
  Glossop SK13. . . . . 10 C5
Temple View SK17 . . . . . 85 C7
Temple Wlk DE4 . . . . . . 143 A1
Tenant St DE1. . . . . 267 B3
Tenby Dr DE21 . . . . 206 C2
Ten Foot Cl SK13 . . . . . . 10 B2
Tennessee Rd DE21 . . . 220 B7
Tennyson Ave
  Chesterfield S40 . . . . . . 266 A4
  Mansfield Woodhouse
    NG19. . . . . 136 C2
  Swadlincote DE11 . . . . . 256 C6
Tennyson Rd S80. . . . . . 81 D1

Tennyson Sq NG16 . . . . 195 C4
Tennyson St
  Derby DE24 . . . . 232 D7
  Holmewood S42. . . . . . . 116 D1
  Ilkeston DE7 . . . . 194 E3
  Shirland DE55 . . . . 146 C5
Tennyson Way S42. . . . . 115 E3
Tenter Cl NG10 . . . . . . 236 D5
Tenter La DE55 . . . . . . 168 D1
Tern Ave DE11 . . . . 256 F3
Terrace La NG19 . . . . . . 134 F5
Terrace Rd
  Buxton SK17 . . . . 85 B7
  Chapel-en-le-F SK23 . . . . 47 B6
  Tideswell SK17 . . . . 69 C4
Terret Gr SK17. . . . . 84 D5
Terrey Rd S17 . . . . 55 E5
Terr The DE21 . . . . 219 E7
Terry Pl DE24. . . . . 232 F6
Tetford Wlk 13 NG19 . . 136 E4
Teversal Ave NG19 . . . . 135 B4
Tevery Cl NG9 . . . . 223 E8
Teviot Pl DE21 . . . . 206 A2
Tewkesbury Ave NG19. . 136 D4
Tewkesbury Cres DE21 . 219 D8
Tewkesbury Pl NG16. . . 195 E7
Tewkesbury Rd NG10 . . 236 E4
Thackeray Rd DE55 . . . 146 F3
Thackeray St DE24 . . . . 232 A5
Thame Ct 2 S43. . . . . . . 96 E8
Thames Cl DE22 . . . . . . 217 F5
Thames Way DE65 . . . . 228 D1
Thanet Dr DE24 . . . . . . 233 A6
Thanet St S45 . . . . 131 D3
Thatch Cl DE22 . . . . . . 204 F2
Thatchers La DE4. . . . . 144 A3
Thatchmarsh Cl NE7 . . 194 F6
Theatre La S41 . . . . 266 C3
Theatre Wlk DE1 . . . . . 267 C3
Theatre Yd S40 . . . . . . 266 B3
Thickley Cl NG20. . . . . 119 F4
Thimble Hill DE6. . . . . 189 A2
Thirlmere Ave DE22. . . 204 E3
Thirlmere Cl 3 NG10 . . 223 B2
Thirlmere Dr S18 . . . . . . 57 A2
Thirlmere Rd
  Chesterfield S41 . . . . 95 C7
  Long Eaton NG10. . . . . . 223 B2
Thirlwell Rd S8. . . . . 43 A6
Thirsk Pl DE24. . . . . . . 232 D7
Thirteen Row S44. . . . . 118 A6
Thistle Bank NG19 . . . . 136 F4
Thistle Cl
  Eastwood NG16. . . . . . . 195 B8
  Woodville DE11 . . . . . . 256 F4
Thistledown Cl DE22 . . 205 A2
Thistle Gr DE73 . . . . . . 232 E1
Thistlegreen Cl DE75. . 182 B1
Thistle Rd DE7 . . . . 209 A4
Thomas Chambers 3
  SK13 . . . . 17 C7
Thomas Cl NG16. . . . . . 170 F3
Thomas Cook Cl DE73 . 252 A7
Thomas Ct DE1 . . . . . . 218 E4
Thomas St
  Compstall SK6. . . . . 15 B2
  Glossop SK13. . . . . 10 E1
Thompson Cl
  Chesterfield S41 . . . . 96 A8
  Swadlincote DE11 . . . . . 256 E4
Thompson St
  Chesterfield S41 . . . . 96 A7
  Langley Mill NG16. . . . . 182 B3
Thomson Dr DE5. . . . . . 181 B7
Thomson Wlk DE5 . . . . 181 A8
Thoresby Ave
  Clowne S43. . . . . 81 A4
  Shirebrook NG20. . . . . 119 C4
Thoresby Cl
  Derby DE21 . . . . 206 B1
  Ripley DE5 . . . . 169 E1
Thoresby Cres DE72. . . 234 F7
Thoresby Pl S43 . . . . 97 C6
Thoresby Rd
  Long Eaton NG10. . . . . . 236 C6
  Mansfield Woodhouse
    NG19. . . . . 136 A3
Thorn Ave NG19 . . . . . . 135 F1
Thornborough Cl S2. . . . 43 C7
Thornborough Pl S2. . . . 43 C7
Thornborough Rd S2. . . . 43 C7
Thornbridge Ave S12 . . . 44 D3
Thornbridge Cl S12. . . . 44 D3
Thornbridge Cres
  Chesterfield S40 . . . . . . 115 A6
  Sheffield S12. . . . . 44 D3
Thornbridge Dr S12. . . . 44 D3
Thornbridge Gr S12. . . . 44 D3
Thornbridge La S12. . . . 44 E3
Thornbridge Pl S12. . . . 44 D3
Thornbridge Rise S12 . . 44 E3
Thornbridge Way S12 . . 44 E3
Thornbrook Cl SK23 . . . 47 C5
Thornbrook Rd SK23 . . . 47 C6
Thorn Cl
  Buxton SK17 . . . . 85 E8
  Derby DE21 . . . . 204 D4
Thorncliffe Ave DE4. . . 127 A6
Thorncliffe Rd SK13 . . . . .9 F4
Thorncliffe Terr SK17 . . . 69 C3
Thorndene Cl S41. . . . . . 96 A6
Thorndon Cl DE3 . . . . . 230 D8
Thorndon Way S40. . . . 114 C8
Thorn Dr NG16. . . . . . . 195 B8
Thorne Cl S42 . . . . 94 F4
Thorncliffewood SK14 . . .9 D5

Thornell Cl SK23 . . . . . . 47 C5
Thornescroft Gdns DE14 254 B8
Thorness Cl DE24 . . . . . 233 C5
Thornewill Dr DE13 . . . 240 F1
Thorneywood Rd NG10. . 236 F8
Thornfield Ave S40 . . . . . 95 B1
Thornfield Cl S41. . . . . . . 96 A5
Thornfield Sq DE24 . . . 236 E8
Thornhill Dr DE55. . . . . 160 B6
Thornhill La S33 . . . . 39 F4
Thornhill Rd DE23 . . . . 218 C1
Thornley Pl DE6 . . . . . . 173 C1
Thornsett S22. . . . . 24 E2
Thornsett Ave SK17 . . . . 85 E8
Thornsett Cl SK17. . . . . . 85 E8
Thornsett Gdns S17. . . . 55 F8
Thornsett Prim Sch S22. 24 E3
Thornsett Trad Est S22. . 24 E2
Thorn St
  Derby DE23 . . . . 218 F2
  Woodville DE11 . . . . . . 256 F2
Thorn Street Mews DE11 256 F2
Thornton Pl 1 S18. . . . . 56 C1
Thorntree Cl DE72 . . . . 222 F1
Thorntree Cotts DE4. . . 154 F2
Thorntree Ct S40 . . . . . 114 F7
Thorntree La DE7 . . . . . 267 B3
Thorn Tree Gdns NG16. 182 F4
Thorntree La DE11,
  DE15 . . . . 255 F7
Thornway SK6. . . . . 32 A7
Thornwood Ct SK17. . . . 85 A8
Thorpe Ave
  Dronfield S18. . . . . 57 C4
  Whitwell S80 . . . . 81 F5
Thorpe Cl
  Burton u T DE15. . . . . . 248 C2
  26 Chesterfield S41. . . . . 95 F8
  Stapleford NG9 . . . . 223 D7
Thorpe Croft DE4. . . . . 156 B5
Thorpe Downs Rd DE11 . 256 B1
Thorpe Dr DE3. . . . . . . 217 E3
Thorpe Hill Dr DE5 . . . . 193 E8
Thorpe House Ave S8. . . 43 B4
Thorpe House Rd S8. . . . 43 B4
Thorpe House Rise S8. . . 43 B4
Thorpelands Ave NG19 . 136 E1
Thorpelands Dr DE22 . . 204 E1
Thorpe Leys NG10 . . . . 236 D5
Thorpe Rd
  Eastwood NG16. . . . . . . 182 F4
  Harthill S26 . . . . 62 A7
Thorpe St
  Glossop SK13. . . . . 10 E2
  Ilkeston DE7 . . . . 194 E3
Thorpe View DE6 . . . . . 185 C8
Thorpe Way DE56 . . . . . 179 B5
Thorpleigh Rd S43 . . . . . 79 B2
Three Gates DE56. . . . . 178 F2
Thrift Rd DE14 . . . . 254 B8
Throstle Nest Way S40 . 201 F8
Thrumpton Ave NG10 . . 237 A7
Thrumpton Hall★ NG11 . 237 B3
Thrushton Cl DE55 . . . . 230 C2
Thruxton Cl DE24 . . . . . 233 C6
Thunderpit La S32. . . . . . 71 A3
Thurgarton Ct DE6. . . . 173 D1
Thurgaton Way DE55. . . 148 A3
Thurlby Ct 9 NG19 . . . . 136 E4
Thurlow Ct DE21 . . . . . 206 A1
Thurman St DE7 . . . . . . 209 A6
Thurrows Way DE73. . . . 233 B2
Thurstan Ave S8. . . . . . . 56 E8
Thurston Ave DE55. . . . 170 D8
Thurstone Furlong DE73 232 E1
Thurvaston La
  Longford DE6, DE65 . . . 214 C4
  Thurvaston DE6 . . . . . . 215 A8
Thurvaston Rd DE6 . . . 197 F1
Thyme Cl DE23 . . . . 231 D4
Tiber Cl DE24 . . . . 233 D5
Tibshelf Bsns Pk DE55 . 148 C6
Tibshelf Inf Sch DE55 . . 148 A7
Tibshelf Rd
  Blackwell DE55 . . . . . . 147 C1
  Holmewood S42. . . . . . . 132 E7
Tibshelf Sch DE55 . . . . 148 A7
Tickham Ave DE24 . . . . 231 C2
Ticknall Cl DE11. . . . . . 257 B7
Ticknall Rd DE11 . . . . . 257 B7
Ticknall Wlk DE23. . . . . 231 E6
Tideswell Bank 15 SK13. . .9 E1
Tideswell Cl S43 . . . . 97 C8
Tideswell Ct 5 S40 . . . . . 95 D5
Tideswell Gn DE11 . . . . 255 E5
Tideswell La S32. . . . . . . 71 B6
Tideswell Rd DE21 . . . . 205 F1
Tideswell Wlk 13 SK13 . . .9 E1
Tiger Yd 6 DE6 . . . . 173 B2
Tilbury Pl DE24 . . . . . . 233 A5
Tilford Gdns NG9 . . . . . 223 F6
Tiller Cl DE23 . . . . 231 B6
Tilley Gn DE11 . . . . 255 F6
Tillotson Cl 1 S8. . . . . . 43 A6
Tillotson Rise S8 . . . . . . 43 A6
Tilton Gr DE7. . . . . 208 C5
Timber La S45 . . . . 132 D5
Timbersbrook Cl DE21 . 206 A1
Timsbury Ct DE21 . . . . 205 E2
Tinderbox La DE65 . . . . 229 F5
Tinker Croft DE7 . . . . . 208 E7
Tinkerley La DE6. . . . . . 165 D1
Tinkley La S42. . . . . 130 D4

Tinsell Brook DE65 . . . . 228 E
Tinsley Rd DE756, NG16 . 182 C
Tintagel Cl
  Burton u T DE13. . . . . . 240 C
  2 Derby DE23 . . . . 219 B
Tintwistle CE Prim Sch
  Glossop SK13. . . . . .9 F
  Glossop SK13. . . . . 10 A
Tipnall Rd DE74. . . . . . 247 A
Tipper's La DE65 . . . . . 227 A
Tip Tree Cl NG16. . . . . . 195 F
Tiree Cl
  Derby DE24 . . . . 231 F
  Stapleford NG9 . . . . 209 D
  Tibshelf DE55 . . . . 147 F
Tissington Bank 27 SK13. . 9 D
Tissington Cl S40 . . . . . . 95 B
Tissington Dr DE21. . . . 206 B
Tissington Gn 28 SK13. . . .9 D
Tissington Terr 28 SK13 . . 9 D
Titchfield Ave NG19 . . . 136 D
Titchfield St
  Creswell S80 . . . . 81 F
  Whitwell S80 . . . . 81 F
Tithe Barn Cl SK17 . . . . 69 C
Tithebarn La DE6 . . . . . 215 C
Tiverton Cl DE3 . . . . . . 217 D
Tiverton Ct 22 S41 . . . . . 95 F
Tivoli Gdns DE1. . . . . . . 218 C
Toadmoor La DE56. . . . 167 F
Tobermory Way DE24 . . 231 D
Todbrook Cl SK23. . . . . . 45 D
Todd St S13 . . . . 17 D
Toll Bar Ave S12. . . . . . . 43 E
Toll Bar Cl S12 . . . . 43 E
Toll Bar Dr S12. . . . . 43 F
Toll Bar Rd S12. . . . . 43 E
Tollbridge Rd S43 . . . . . 79 B
Tollemache Cl SK14. . . . .9 A
Tollemache Rd SK14 . . . .9 A
Tollgate Cotts DE6. . . . 184 E
Toll House Mead S20 . . . 59 C
Tom Brads Croft SK23. . . 45 E
Tom La
  Chapel-en-le-F SK23 . . . . 46 D
  Staveley S44 . . . . 97 F
Tomlinson Bsns Pk DE65 226 F
Tomlinson Ct DE24. . . . 232 F
Tomlinson Ind Est DE21 . 205 C
Tomlinsons Cotts DE21. . 205 C
Tomwood Rise SK13. . . . 16 C
Tonbridge Dr DE22 . . . 233 A
Tonge La DE73. . . . . . . 252 F
Tongue La SK17 . . . . 85 E
Tongue Lane Ind Est SK17 85 E
Tooth St DE11 . . . . 256 E
Top Cotts SK17 . . . . 88 F
Top Farm Ct DE56. . . . . 191 F
Top Hagg La DE56 . . . . 168 A
Tophole Rd S33. . . . . 50 F
Top La
  Crich DE4. . . . . 156 D
  Mansfield NG19. . . . . . . 135 A
  Old Brampton S42. . . . . . 93 E
  Shottle DE56. . . . . 166 C
Topley Gdns DE21. . . . . 205 F
Top Lons DE6 . . . . 176 B
Top Manor Cl DE72. . . . 221 C
Top Mdw DE11. . . . . . . 256 B
Toppham Dr S8. . . . . 56 F
Toppham Rd S8 . . . . 56 F
Toppham Way S8. . . . . . 56 F
Top Pingle Cl S43. . . . . . 96 C
Top Rd
  Calow S44. . . . . 97 A
  Wingerworth S42 . . . . . 114 D
Top Row NG16. . . . . . . 171 A
Topshill La DE6 . . . . . . 165 B
Tor Ave DE55. . . . . 170 C
Tor Cl DE4. . . . . 143 B
Torfield Cotts DE4 . . . . 127 B
Torksey Wlk 11 NG19 . . 136 E
Torquay Ct 6 S41 . . . . . 95 F
Torrance Cl DE14 . . . . . 254 A
Torrani Way S42 . . . . . . 131 F
Torridon Cl DE24 . . . . . 231 E
Tor Rise DE4 . . . . 143 B
Torr St SK17. . . . . 85 B
Torrs Valley S22. . . . . . . 33 C
Torr Top St S22. . . . . . . 33 C
Torrvale Rd S22 . . . . 33 B
Torside Mews SK13 . . . . 10 A
Torside Way SK13. . . . . . 10 A
Tors Spring DE4 . . . . . . 168 A
Tors The DE4 . . . . 156 F
Tor View Rise DE4 . . . . 155 A
Torwood Dr S8 . . . . 56 E
Totley All Saints CE Prim Sch
  S17 . . . . 55 D
Totley Ave 42 SK13. . . . . 9 D
Totley Brook Cl S17. . . . 55 D
Totley Brook Croft S17. . 55 D
Totley Brook Glen S17 . . 55 D
Totley Brook Gr S17 . . . . 55 D
Totley Brook Rd S17. . . . 55 E
Totley Brook Way S17. . . 55 D
Totley Cl 47 SK13 . . . . . . 9 D
Totley Gdns 46 SK13 . . . 9 D
Totley Gn 49 SK13 . . . . . 9 D
Totley Grange Cl S17. . . 55 D
Totley Grange Rd S17. . . 55 D
Totley Hall Croft S17. . . 55 D
Totley Hall Dr S17 . . . . . 55 D
Totley Hall La S17 . . . . . 55 D
Totley Hall Mead S17 . . 55 D
Totley La S17. . . . . 56 A

otley Lanes 43 SK13 . . . . . 9 D1
otley Mews 45 SK13 . . . . . 9 D1
otley Mount S43 . . . . . 96 D8
otley Pl 45 SK13 . . . . . 9 D1
otley Prim Sch S17 . . . 55 D4
oton Banks Road Inf Sch NG9. . . . . 223 F2
oton Bispham Drive Jun Sch NG9 . . . . . 223 F3
oton La NG9 . . . . . 223 E6
ouchstone Ct DE73 . . . . . 232 D2
oulmin Dr DE11 . . . . . 256 B4
ower Cl
  Sheffield S2 . . . . . 43 C8
  Somercotes DE55 . . . . . 170 C8
ower Cres S44 . . . . . 118 B8
ower Dr S2 . . . . . 43 C8
ower Ho S2 . . . . . 43 C8
ower Rd
  Burton u T DE15 . . . . . 248 B2
  Hartshorne DE11 . . . . . 257 A6
owers La S32 . . . . . 40 E1
ower St DE24 . . . . . 232 D7
ower View Prim Sch DE15. . . . . 248 C3
owle Cl DE72 . . . . . 221 C1
owles Pastures DE74. . 247 A3
owle St NG10 . . . . . 236 A4
own End
  Apperknowle S18. . . . . 58 A1
  Bolsover S44 . . . . . 99 A1
  Buxton SK17 . . . . . 66 E1
  Kirk Ireton DE6 . . . . . 165 B1
  Shirland DE55 . . . . . 146 D2
own End Jun Sch DE55. 147 E5
own End Rd DE7 . . . . . 235 B7
own Fold SK6 . . . . . 23 B7
own Gate S33 . . . . . 51 A7
own Hall Yd 3 DE6 . . 173 C2
Townhead S32. . . . . 71 C6
Town Head DE6. . . . . 173 C3
Townhead La S33. . . . . 39 F4
Townhead Rd S17 . . . . . 55 C7
Town La
  Bradwell S33 . . . . . 51 A7
  Broadbottom SK13 . . . . . 16 D6
  Newton DE55. . . . . 148 A3
Towncliffe La SK6. . . . . 23 C6
Townsend Gr DE73. . . . . 233 A2
Townside Cl NG10 . . . . . 236 B4
Town St
  Brassington DE4 . . . . . 153 A1
  Duffield DE56. . . . . 190 F3
  Holbrook DE56. . . . . 191 C6
  Marple SK6 . . . . . 23 B7
  Pinxton NG16. . . . . 160 E3
  Sandiacre NG10. . . . . 223 B5
Town The DE21 . . . . . 205 C7
Town View NG16. . . . . 195 F7
Towson Ave NG16. . . . . 182 C2
Trafalgar Rd NG10 . . . . . 236 D6
Trafalgar Sq NG10 . . . . . 236 F7
Trafalgar Terr NG10. . . . . 236 F7
Traffic St DE1 . . . . . 267 C2
Traffic Terr
  2 Chesterfield S41. . . . . 115 B7
Trafford Way DE23. . . . . 231 C8
Trail View SK13 . . . . . 10 B5
Tramway The DE11 . . . . . 255 F7
Tranmere Ave S43. . . . . 131 D3
Transvaal Terr S44. . . . . 118 B5
Traso Bsns Pk S18. . . . . 57 D1
Travers Rd NG10. . . . . 223 B6
Travey Rd S2 . . . . . 44 A7
Treak Cliff Cavern ★ S33. . 37 E3
Tredcroft St SK13 . . . . . 17 B8
Tredegar Dr DE21. . . . . 206 B2
Treeneuk Cl S40. . . . . 95 B3
Trefoil Ct DE23 . . . . . 231 A7
Tregaron Cl DE21 . . . . . 206 C2
Tregony Way DE24. . . . . 231 D3
Trelawney Rd S45 . . . . . 131 D3
Trenchard Dr SK17. . . . . 85 D3
Trent Ave
  Buxton SK17 . . . . . 85 C4
  Willington DE65. . . . . 242 C5
Trent Bridge Ct DE23. . . . . 231 C8
Trent Cl
  Derby DE24 . . . . . 231 D2
  Willington DE65. . . . . 242 C5
Trent Coll NG10 . . . . . 236 C8
Trent Cotts NG10 . . . . . 236 F6
Trent Dr DE23 . . . . . 231 D6
Trent Gr
  Alfreton DE55 . . . . . 159 A2
  Dronfield S18. . . . . 57 B3
Trent Ho NG10 . . . . . 236 M4
Trent La
  Castle Donington DE74. 247 A5
  King's Newton DE73. . . 245 C1
  Long Eaton NG10. . . . . 236 F5
  Newton Solney DE15. . . 248 E8
  Weston-on-T DE72. . . . 245 F4
Trent Lane Ind Est DE74. 247 B5
Trenton Dr NG10. . . . . 237 A8
Trenton Gn DE21. . . . . 220 B6
Trenton Green Dr DE21. 220 B6
Trent Rd DE7 . . . . . 208 D4
Trent Rise DE21. . . . . 220 F4
Trent St
  Derby DE24 . . . . . 233 A7
  Long Eaton NG10 . . . . . 236 E8
Trent Wlk 1 NG19 . . . . . 136 E4
Tresillian Cl DE22 . . . . . 204 E2

Tressall Cl DE7 . . . . . 209 A8
Trevelyn Cl DE15. . . . . 248 C2
Treveris Cl DE21 . . . . . 220 E4
Trevone Ave NG9 . . . . . 223 E6
Trevone Ct DE24 . . . . . 233 C5
Trevose Cl S40 . . . . . 114 C7
Triangle The
  Belper DE56. . . . . 178 F4
  Ilkeston DE7 . . . . . 209 A6
Trickett Cl S33 . . . . . 38 C3
Trinity Cl
  Ashford in t W DE45 . . . 108 F8
  Chesterfield S40 . . . . . 266 A4
  Ilkeston DE7 . . . . . 194 E3
Trinity Ct S41. . . . . 266 A4
Trinity Gr DE11 . . . . . 256 B3
Trinity Mews S41. . . . . 266 A4
Trinity St DE1. . . . . 267 C2
Trinity View NG10 . . . . . 236 E8
Trinity Way 3 DE75. . . . . 181 F1
Trinkey La S32. . . . . 72 A3
Tristram Gr DE13 . . . . . 240 E2
Trocadero Ct DE23 . . . . . 267 B1
Troon Cl
  Burton u T DE13. . . . . 240 C1
  Chesterfield S40 . . . . . 114 C8
  Derby DE23 . . . . . 231 A8
  Kimberley NG16. . . . . 195 E7
Trot La SK17. . . . . 70 A5
Troughbrook Hill S43 . . . 97 B8
Troughbrook Rd S43. . . . . 78 B1
Trough La NG16 . . . . . 195 F8
Trough Rd NG16 . . . . . 195 F8
Troutbeck Gr DE23 . . . . . 231 A7
Trowbridge Cl DE21. . . . . 205 E2
Trowels La DE22 . . . . . 218 C4
Trueman St DE7 . . . . . 194 F4
Truman St
  Cossall DE7 . . . . . 195 A1
  Kimberley NG16. . . . . 195 D7
Truro Cl DE11. . . . . 256 E5
Truro Cres DE21 . . . . . 219 E8
Trusley Brook DE65 . . . . . 228 D1
Trusley Gdns DE23 . . . . . 231 D5
Trusley Wlk 7 NG19 . . . . . 136 E4
Trustley Cl DE14 . . . . . 254 B7
Tudor Cl NG10 . . . . . 223 E1
Tudor Ct
  3 Derby DE22 . . . . . 204 F3
  Selston NG16. . . . . 171 D6
Tudor Falls DE75. . . . . 181 E3
Tudor Field Cl DE11. . . . . 233 A1
Tudor House Cl DE11. . . . . 256 A7
Tudor Pl DE7 . . . . . 208 C5
Tudor Rd DE21. . . . . 220 A6
Tudor Rise B79 . . . . . 263 E2
Tudor St 2 S43. . . . . 78 F2
Tudor Way DE11 . . . . . 256 A6
Tuffolds Cl S2 . . . . . 44 A7
Tufnell Gdns DE22 . . . . . 218 B7
Tulip Rd NG16 . . . . . 195 B5
Tulla Cl DE24 . . . . . 231 E2
Tumbling Hill DE56 . . . . . 168 E1
Tunicliffe Cl DE11. . . . . 256 D4
Tunnel Yd 7 DE6 . . . . . 173 B2
Tunstall Gn S40. . . . . 95 D1
Tunstall Way S40 . . . . . 95 D1
Tuphall Cl DE73. . . . . 233 B2
Tupton Hall Sch S42 . . . . . 131 C2
Tupton Moor Cl S42. . . . . 115 D1
Tupton Prim Sch S42 . . . 115 D1
Tupton Way S42 . . . . . 116 D1
Turf Lea Rd SK6 . . . . . 23 B1
Turlowfields La DE6. . . . . 175 C7
Turnberry Cl
  Chesterfield S40 . . . . . 114 C8
  Ilkeston DE7 . . . . . 194 C2
Turnbull Cl S40 . . . . . 266 A1
Turnbury Cl DE14 . . . . . 254 A7
Turncliffe Cl SK17 . . . . . 84 F6
Turnditch CE Prim Sch DE56. . . . . 177 B2
Turner Ave NG16. . . . . 182 A3
Turner Cl
  Dronfield S18. . . . . 56 F1
  Stapleford NG9 . . . . . 223 E6
Turner Dr
  Eastwood NG16. . . . . 195 B7
  Staveley S43 . . . . . 97 B7
Turner Rd NG10. . . . . 236 C4
Turner's Almshouses DE22. . . . . 218 D6
Turners La DE55 . . . . . 170 A7
Turner St DE24 . . . . . 232 E6
Turnlee Cl SK13. . . . . 17 C7
Turnlee Dr SK13 . . . . . 17 C7
Turnlee Rd SK13 . . . . . 17 C7
Turnlea Rd DE55 . . . . . 160 C6
Turnoak Ave NE7 . . . . . 194 F5
Turnoaks La S40. . . . . 115 A7
Turnpike Bsns Pk DE55. 158 F2
Turnpike Cl
  Alfreton DE55 . . . . . 158 F2
  Matlock DE4 . . . . . 143 C5
Turton Cl NG16 . . . . . 182 A3
Tutbury Castle ★ DE13. . 239 B7
Tutbury & Hatton Sta DE65. . . . . 239 D8
Tutbury Rd DE13. . . . . 240 A1

Tuxford Cl DE21 . . . . . 206 B1
T V DE6 . . . . . 172 B1
Twayblade DE14 . . . . . 254 B8
Tweeds Muir Cl 5 DE21. 205 F2
Twentylands DE14 . . . . . 240 D4
Twentywell Ct S17 . . . . . 56 A7
Twentywell Dr S17 . . . . . 56 B6
Twentywell La S17. . . . . 56 B6
Twentywell Rd S17 . . . . . 56 B5
Twentywell Rise S17. . . . . 56 B6
Twentywell View S17. . . . . 56 B6
Twickenham Cl 11 S20. . 59 E6
Twickenham Cres S20. . . 59 F6
Twickenham Ct 8 S20. . 59 E6
Twickenham Dr DE22 . . . 218 A6
Twickenham Glade 10 S20. . . . . 59 E6
Twickenham Glen S20. . . 59 F5
Twickenham Gr 9 S20. . 59 E6
Twiggs Row DE4 . . . . . 143 A7
Twin Oaks 12 S43 . . . . . 230 F7
Twisses Bank DE6 . . . . . 213 A2
Twyford Cl
  Heanor DE75 . . . . . 193 C8
  Swadlincote DE11 . . . . . 255 F2
  West Hallam DE7. . . . . 207 D8
  Willington DE65. . . . . 242 C5
Twyford Rd
  Barrow u T DE73. . . . . 244 A6
  Long Eaton NG10. . . . . 235 F4
  Willington DE65. . . . . 242 B6
Twyford St DE23 . . . . . 267 B1
Tylney Rd S40 . . . . . 114 B8
Tyndale Chase DE24. . . . . 231 C2
Tynedale Cl NG10. . . . . 236 A6
Tynefield Ct DE65. . . . . 229 B2
Tynefield Mews DE65 . . . 229 B2
Tynsel Parkes CE Fst Sch ST14. . . . . 210 A1
Tythe Barn La DE6 . . . . . 215 C5
Tythe The DE11 . . . . . 256 B7

U

Uffa Magna DE3 . . . . . 217 C1
Uldale Gr DE11 . . . . . 256 C1
Ulley Cres S13 . . . . . 44 B7
Ulley Rd S13 . . . . . 44 B7
Ullswater Ave S20 . . . . . 59 E6
Ullswater Cl
  Derby DE21 . . . . . 205 D2
  Dronfield S18. . . . . 56 E2
  Sheffield S20 . . . . . 59 E6
Ullswater Dr
  Derby DE21 . . . . . 220 E5
  Dronfield S18. . . . . 56 E2
Ullswater Pk S18 . . . . . 56 E2
Ullswater Pl S18 . . . . . 56 E2
Ulverston Rd S41 . . . . . 95 D7
Undercliffe DE45. . . . . 109 C6
Underhall DE4 . . . . . 127 D2
Underhill Ave DE23 . . . . . 231 F7
Underhill Cl DE23 . . . . . 231 E6
Underhill Rd S43 . . . . . 80 B6
Underpass The DE1 . . . . . 267 C4
Undertown La DE6 . . . . . 197 D6
Underwood CE Prim Sch NG16. . . . . 171 F1
Underwood Terr
  Chelmorton SK17. . . . . 106 A8
  Darley Dale DE4 . . . . . 143 A7
Union Rd
  Ilkeston DE7 . . . . . 208 F7
  New Mills SK22. . . . . 33 C7
  Swadlincote DE11 . . . . . 256 B5
Union St
  Ashbourne DE6 . . . . . 173 B2
  Glossop SK13. . . . . 17 C8
  Harthill S26 . . . . . 61 C6
  Long Eaton NG10. . . . . 236 E8
  Melbourne DE73. . . . . 252 A7
  South Normanton DE55. 159 F5
Unity Cl DE11 . . . . . 256 A1
Unity Wlk SK13 . . . . . 17 C7
Univ of Derby DE22 . . . . . 204 D1
Univ of Derby (Buxton Campus) SK17. . . . . 85 D3
Univ of Derby (Green Lane Campus) DE1. . . . . 267 B2
Univ of Derby (Sch of Health & Com Studies) DE23 . . 218 D2
Univ of Sheffield SK17 . . 104 B8
Univ of Sheffield (Research Labs) S3. . . . . 85 E3
Unstone Dronfield By-Pass S18. . . . . 56 F3
Unstone Hill S18. . . . . 76 D7
Unstone Jun Sch S18 . . . 76 E7
Unstone Rd S41 . . . . . 76 F4
Unstone St Mary's Inf Sch S18. . . . . 76 F7
Unthank La S18. . . . . 74 C4
Upchurch Cl DE3. . . . . 217 C3
Upland Rise S40 . . . . . 95 D1
Uplands Ave DE23. . . . . 231 C6
Uplands Gdns DE23 . . . . . 218 C2
Uplands Rd
  Compstall SK14. . . . . 15 A6
  Glossop SK13. . . . . 17 D8
Upper Albert Rd S8 . . . . . 43 B5
Upper Bainbrigge St DE23. . . . . 219 A3
Upper Barn Cl DE75. . . . . 181 F2
Upper Blindlow La SK17. 106 A6
Upper Boundary Rd DE22. . . . . 218 E4

Upper Croft
  Clay Cross S45 . . . . . 131 E3
  Tupton S42. . . . . 131 D8
Upper Croft Cl S43 . . . . . 96 E7
Upper Dale Rd DE23 . . . . . 218 F1
Upper Dunstead Rd NG16. . . . . 182 B4
Upper End Rd SK17 . . . . . 67 C4
Upper Greenhill Gdns DE4 . . . . . 143 C6
Upper Hall Cl DE56. . . . . 191 C6
Upper Hollow DE23 . . . . . 218 C1
Upper King St S43 . . . . . 77 F1
Upper La DE6. . . . . 175 E4
Upper Lum Cl S41 . . . . . 96 D2
Upper Mantle Cl S45 . . . . . 131 C4
Upper Marehay Rd DE5. 180 D6
Upper Moor Rd DE24. . . . . 232 E6
Upper Moor St S40 . . . . . 95 B2
Upper Nelson St 3 DE75. . . . . 181 D2
Upper Newbold Cl S40. . . 95 B7
Upper Orchard St 2 NG9. . . . . 223 E7
Upper School La S18. . . . 76 B8
Upperthorpe Rd S21 . . . . . 60 D4
Upperthorpe Villas S21 . . 60 D5
Uppertown La DE4 . . . . . 142 C1
Upper Town La DE4 . . . . . 126 B1
Upper Valley Rd S8 . . . . . 43 B5
Upper Wellington St NG10. . . . . 223 C1
Upperwood Rd DE4 . . . . . 143 A1
Upper Yeld Rd DE45. . . . . 109 C4
Upton Cl
  Castle Donington DE74. 247 B4
  Heanor DE75. . . . . 182 A1
Upton Mount NG19. . . . . 135 E1
Upwood Cl S40 . . . . . 95 A5
Upwoods Rd DE6 . . . . . 211 A1
Utah Cl DE65 . . . . . 228 E2
Uttoxeter New Rd DE22. 218 C3
Uttoxeter Old Rd DE22 . . 218 E5
Uttoxeter Rd
  Derby DE3 . . . . . 217 E1
  Hatton DE65 . . . . . 227 B2
  Hilton DE65 . . . . . 228 C2
  Scropton DE65. . . . . 226 C4
  Scropton, Foston DE65. . 226 F3
Uxbridge St DE14 . . . . . 254 C8

V

Vale Cl
  Bolsover S44. . . . . 99 A1
  Dronfield S18. . . . . 57 B1
Vale Ct S19 . . . . . 136 B3
Vale Dr NG20 . . . . . 119 F2
Vale House Dr SK13. . . . . 10 A5
Vale Mills DE22 . . . . . 218 F3
Valemount S13 . . . . . 10 A5
Valentine Ave NG16. . . . . 171 E7
Vale Rd
  Hartshorne DE11. . . . . 257 A3
  Mansfield Woodhouse NG19. . . . . 136 B4
  Swadlincote DE11 . . . . . 256 B6
Valerian Cl SK17 . . . . . 85 C7
Valerie Rd DE72 . . . . . 246 A7
Vale The DE7 . . . . . 194 E3
Vallance St NG19 . . . . . 136 B4
Valley Cl S45 . . . . . 132 B4
Valley Cotts S44 . . . . . 117 F8
Valley Cres S41 . . . . . 96 C2
Valley Dr
  Chapel-en-le-F SK23 . . . 47 C6
  Killamarsh S21 . . . . . 60 D7
Valley Gdns S14 . . . . . 15 E8
Valley Park Com Sch S14. 43 F2
Valley Rd
  Barlow S18. . . . . 75 D3
  Bolsover S44. . . . . 118 A8
  Broadbottom SK14 . . . . . 15 E8
  Chesterfield S41 . . . . . 96 C2
  Clay Cross S45 . . . . . 131 A4
  Derby, Cherrytree Hill DE21. . . . . 220 B5
  Derby DE23 . . . . . 218 D1
  Glossop SK13. . . . . 16 F8
  Hayfield SK22. . . . . 25 E2
  Ilkeston DE7 . . . . . 208 E5
  Killamarsh S21 . . . . . 60 D7
  Kimberley NG16. . . . . 195 D7
  Mastin Moor S43. . . . . 79 C4
  Overseal DE12. . . . . 262 A3
  Sheffield, Heeley S8 . . . . 43 A6
  Shirebrook NG20. . . . . 119 E6
Valley Rise
  Barlow S18. . . . . 75 D3
  Swadlincote DE11 . . . . . 256 B5
Valley View
  Alton S42. . . . . 130 C5
  Belper DE56. . . . . 179 A2
  Ilkeston DE7 . . . . . 208 E5
Valley View Cl
  Chesterfield S41 . . . . . 115 E7
  Eckington S21 . . . . . 59 C2
Valley View Dr DE7 . . . . . 193 B1
Valley View Rd DE55 . . . . . 170 D4
Valley View Wlk ST14 . . . 197 A3
Vancouver Ave DE21 . . . . . 220 D4
Vancouver Dr S20 . . . . . 248 C3
Vanguard Rd NG10. . . . . 236 D5
Vanguard Trad Est S40 . . 115 B7
Varley Ho S43 . . . . . 96 B6
Varley St DE24. . . . . 232 D6
Vaughan Pl NG20 . . . . . 119 E6

Vaughan Rd SK23 . . . . . 45 E5
Vauxhall Ave DE22 . . . . . 218 A7
Velvet Mill SK17 . . . . . 69 B4
Ventnor Ho DE24 . . . . . 233 C7
Ventura Ct SK22 . . . . . 24 D1
Venture Cres DE55 . . . . . 159 A2
Venture Ho S41. . . . . 76 F1
Venture Way S41 . . . . . 76 F1
Verbena Dr DE23 . . . . . 231 D4
Vere Cl DE65 . . . . . 242 B5
Vermont Dr DE21 . . . . . 220 C6
Verney St NG19 . . . . . 134 F7
Verney Way NG19 . . . . . 134 F7
Vernon Cotts DE4 . . . . . 154 C1
Vernon Dr
  Bakewell DE45. . . . . 109 D5
  Shirebrook NG20. . . . . 120 A4
Vernon Dr
  Bakewell DE45. . . . . 109 B7
  Derby DE21 . . . . . 220 F4
Vernongate DE1 . . . . . 218 E5
Vernon Gn DE45 . . . . . 109 B7
Vernon La S45 . . . . . 129 D4
Vernon Rd
  Chesterfield S40 . . . . . 95 D3
  Sheffield S17 . . . . . 55 F6
Vernon Rise S42 . . . . . 115 F2
Vernon St
  Derby DE1. . . . . 218 E5
  Ilkeston DE7 . . . . . 194 F4
  Shirebrook NG20. . . . . 120 A4
Vernon Street Ind Est NG20. . . . . 120 A4
Verona Way DE73 . . . . . 232 E2
Veronica Dr NG16. . . . . 195 C8
Vestry Rd DE21 . . . . . 205 E3
Vetchfield Cl DE24 . . . . . 231 F2
Viadevana DE12 . . . . . 262 E3
Via Gellia Rd DE4. . . . . 154 C7
Vicarage Ave
  Derby DE23 . . . . . 218 E2
  Ilkeston DE7 . . . . . 194 D4
Vicarage Cl
  Belper DE56. . . . . 179 A4
  Burton u T DE15. . . . . 248 B4
  Heath S44 . . . . . 117 B2
  Holmesfield S18. . . . . 75 A8
  Shirebrook NG20. . . . . 119 E3
  Smalley DE7. . . . . 192 F6
  Swanwick DE55. . . . . 169 E7
Vicarage Croft DE4 . . . . . 110 E1
Vicarage Ct DE3 . . . . . 217 D1
Vicarage Dr
  Derby DE21 . . . . . 220 A7
  Uttoxeter ST14 . . . . . 210 A4
Vicarage Gdns
  Clay Cross S45 . . . . . 131 C2
  Heanor DE75 . . . . . 181 F1
  Swadlincote DE11 . . . . . 256 C4
Vicarage La
  Ashford in t W DE45 . . . 108 E8
  Duffield DE56. . . . . 190 E4
  Hayfield SK22. . . . . 25 D2
  Ironville NG16. . . . . 170 F4
  Little Eaton DE21. . . . . 205 C8
  Sheffield S17 . . . . . 55 D7
Vicarage Mews DE55 . . . . . 170 E4
Vicarage Rd
  Belper DE56. . . . . 190 F8
  Chellaston DE73. . . . . 232 F2
  Derby DE1. . . . . 217 C2
  Swadlincote DE11 . . . . . 256 C4
  Woodville DE11 . . . . . 256 E2
Vicarage St DE7 . . . . . 194 D4
Vicarage Wlk DE12. . . . . 260 C6
Vicar La
  Chesterfield S40 . . . . . 266 B3
  Tibshelf DE55 . . . . . 148 A4
Vicarwood Ave
  Derby DE22 . . . . . 204 F1
  Holbrook DE56. . . . . 191 C7
Victor Ave DE22. . . . . 218 F8
Victor Cres NG10 . . . . . 223 C4
Victoria Ave
  Borrowash DE72 . . . . . 221 B2
  2 Buxton SK17. . . . . 85 D8
  Draycott DE72 . . . . . 235 A7
  Glossop SK13. . . . . 10 A5
  Heanor DE75 . . . . . 181 D1
  Staveley S43 . . . . . 79 A3
Victoria Cl DE3 . . . . . 217 E4
Victoria Cotts DE45 . . . . . 109 D6
Victoria Cres NG16. . . . . 170 F4
Victoria Ct
  6 Glossop SK13. . . . . 17 C8
  Long Eaton NG10. . . . . 236 D6
  Matlock DE4 . . . . . 143 C6
Victoria Dr
  Blackwell DE55 . . . . . 147 E1
  Woodville DE11 . . . . . 256 E1
Victoria Gr S43 . . . . . 96 F5
Victoria Hall Gdns DE4 . . 143 C6
Victoria Ho S80. . . . . 81 F1
Victoria Mews 2 SK13 . . 17 C8
Victoria Park Rd
  Buxton SK17 . . . . . 85 D7
  Calow S43 . . . . . 96 F5
Victoria Rd
  Bamford S33 . . . . . 40 B3
  Draycott DE72 . . . . . 235 A7
  Pinxton NG16. . . . . 160 D3
  Ripley DE5 . . . . . 169 D2
  Sandiacre NG10. . . . . 223 B6
  Selston NG16. . . . . 171 F6
Victoria St N S41 . . . . . 76 F2

Victoria St W S40 . . . . **95** C2
Victoria Sq 13 DE6 . . . **173** C2
Victoria St
  Alfreton DE55 . . . . **159** B4
  Bolsover S44 . . . . **118** B8
  Brimington S43 . . . . **77** F1
  Castle Donington DE74 . . **247** B5
  Chesterfield S41 . . . . **266** B4
  Clay Cross S45 . . . . **131** C3
  Creswell S80 . . . . **81** F1
  Derby DE1 . . . . **267** B3
  Dronfield S18 . . . . **56** F2
  Glossop SK13 . . . . **17** C8
  Ilkeston DE7 . . . . **194** B3
  Ironville NG16 . . . . **170** F4
  Langley Mill NG16 . . . . **182** C3
  Long Eaton NG10 . . . . **236** B5
  Melbourne DE73 . . . . **252** A7
  New Mills SK22 . . . . **33** B6
  Ripley DE5 . . . . **169** F2
  Shirebrook NG20 . . . . **119** F4
  Somercotes DE55 . . . . **170** C8
  South Normanton DE55 . . . **160** A6
  Stapleford NG9 . . . . **223** D7
Victoria Terr
  Great Longstone DE45 . . . . **89** F4
  Selston NG16 . . . . **160** E1
  Tibshelf DE55 . . . . **148** B7
Victoria Way DE24 . . . . . **219** E3
Victoria Wlk S42 . . . . **115** D1
Victor Rd S17 . . . . **55** F7
Victory Ave DE5 . . . . **169** F1
Victory Cl NG10 . . . . **236** E5
Victory Dr NG19 . . . . **136** F1
Victory Rd DE24 . . . . **232** B6
Viewdales Cl DE6 . . . . **175** F2
View Rd S2 . . . . **43** A7
Viking Bsns Ctr DE11 . . . . . **256** F3
Vikinglea Cl S2 . . . . **44** B8
Vikinglea Dr S2 . . . . **44** B8
Village Cl DE56 . . . . **190** F3
Village St DE23 . . . . **231** F8
Village The
  Dale Abbey DE7 . . . . **207** F2
  West Hallam DE7 . . . . **207** E7
Villas Rd
  Ambergate DE56 . . . . **167** F3
  Bolsover S44 . . . . **98** E2
Villa St DE72 . . . . **235** B7
Villas The
  Bolsover S44 . . . . **99** B2
  Whaley Thorns NG20 . . . . . **101** A2
Villa The SK14 . . . . **9** A5
Villiers Cl S2 . . . . **43** E6
Villiers Dr S2 . . . . **43** E6
Vincent Ave
  Derby DE21 . . . . **220** E3
  Ilkeston DE7 . . . . **208** F8
Vincent Cl DE56 . . . . **192** A8
Vincent Cres S40 . . . . **95** B2
Vincent La S40 . . . . **95** B2
Vincent St DE23 . . . . **218** F1
Vine Cl DE23 . . . . **231** B7
Vine Cres NG10 . . . . **223** B6
Vine Farm Cl DE7 . . . . **208** D5
Vineyard Terr DE4 . . . . . . **127** C4
Viola Cl DE21 . . . . **206** C3
Violet Ave NG16 . . . . **195** B8
Violet Cl
  Donisthorpe DE12 . . . . **262** E1
  Shirebrook NG20 . . . . **119** D3
Violet La DE15 . . . . **254** F8
Violet Lane Inf Sch DE15 **254** F8
Violet St DE23 . . . . **218** F1
Violet Way DE15 . . . . **255** A8
Virginsalley La DE6 . . . . . **184** D2
Vista The NG9 . . . . **223** E5
Vivian St
  Derby DE1 . . . . **219** B8
  Shuttlewood S44 . . . . **98** F6
Vulcan St DE23 . . . . **219** B1
Vyse Dr NG10 . . . . **236** C6

W

Wade Ave
  Derby DE23 . . . . **218** C2
  Ilkeston DE7 . . . . **209** B7
Wadebridge Gr DE24 . . . . **233** C5
Wade Dr DE3 . . . . **217** E2
Wade St DE23 . . . . **218** C1
Wadsworth Ave S12 . . . . . . **44** D5
Wadsworth Cl S12 . . . . **44** D5
Wadsworth Dr S12 . . . . **44** D5
Wadsworth Rd
  Sheffield S12 . . . . **44** C5
  Stapleford NG9 . . . . **223** B4
Wagstaff La NG16 . . . . . . **171** B4
Wagtail Cl DE24 . . . . **231** D4
Wain Ave
  Chesterfield S41 . . . . **266** C4
  North Wingfield S42 . . . . . **132** A7
Wainfleet Cl DE7 . . . . **194** C3
Waingroves Prim Sch
  DE5 . . . . **181** A7
Waingroves Rd
  Codnor DE5 . . . . **181** B6
  Ripley DE5 . . . . **181** A8
Wainhouse Brow SK22 . . . **25** D3
Wains Cl SK17 . . . . **47** F1
Wain Way S42 . . . . **132** A7
Wainwright Ave
  Mansfield NG19 . . . . **135** D1
  Sheffield S13 . . . . **44** D8

Wainwright Cres S13 . . . . **44** D8
Wakami Cres DE73 . . . . . . **233** A3
Wakefield Ave DE13 . . . . **239** B6
Wakefield Croft DE7 . . . . **194** C3
Wakefield Cl DE74 . . . . . . **247** C4
Wakelyn Cl
  Hilton DE65 . . . . **228** C2
  Shardlow DE72 . . . . **234** F1
Walbrook Rd DE23 . . . . . . **218** F1
Walcote Cl DE56 . . . . **179** D5
Waldene Dr DE24 . . . . **233** A6
Walden Rd S2 . . . . **43** B7
Waldley La DE6 . . . . **211** D7
Waldorf Ave DE24 . . . . . . **233** A7
Waldorf Cl DE24 . . . . **233** A7
Walford Rd
  Killamarsh S21 . . . . **60** C6
  Rolleston DE13 . . . . **240** D3
Walgrave Cl DE56 . . . . . . **179** B6
Walgrove Ave S40 . . . . **95** E1
Walgrove Rd S40 . . . . **95** D1
Walk Cl DE72 . . . . **235** A7
Walkdale Brow SK13 . . . . . **17** B7
Walker Ave DE5 . . . . **169** E2
Walker Brow SK17 . . . . **47** F1
Walker Gr 2 NG9 . . . . . . **223** E6
Walker La DE1 . . . . **267** A4
Walkers La S21 . . . . **60** D6
Walk La SK13 . . . . **10** A4
Walk Mill Rd SK22 . . . . **25** D2
Wallace Gdns NG9 . . . . . . **223** F1
Wall Ditch DE6 . . . . **149** B2
Wallfields Cl DE65 . . . . . . **230** D2
Wallis Cl DE72 . . . . **235** A7
Wallis Ho DE11 . . . . **256** E3
Wall Rd DE14 . . . . **254** A7
Walls La S80 . . . . **81** C1
Wall St
  Buxton SK17 . . . . **85** D8
  Ripley DE5 . . . . **169** D2
Walnut Ave
  Derby DE24 . . . . **233** B7
  Shireoaks S81 . . . . **63** F7
Walnut Cl
  Aston-on-T DE72 . . . . **246** B8
  Barrow u T DE73 . . . . **244** A6
  Burnaston DE65 . . . . **229** F5
  Chellaston DE73 . . . . **245** A8
  Ilkeston DE7 . . . . **209** A7
  Repton DE65 . . . . **243** A2
  Swadlincote DE11 . . . . **256** A5
Walnut Dr S21 . . . . **60** C5
Walnut Rd DE56 . . . . **179** B3
Walnut St DE24 . . . . **232** C7
Walpole St DE21 . . . . **219** D6
Walseker La S26 . . . . **61** C7
Walsham Ct DE21 . . . . **205** D1
Walter Evans CE Prim Sch
  DE22 . . . . **204** F2
Walters Ave NG16 . . . . . . **182** E6
Walters Cres NG16 . . . . . . **171** D6
Walter St
  Derby DE1 . . . . **218** E7
  Draycott DE72 . . . . **234** F8
Walters Wood SK23 . . . . . . **45** F5
Waltham Ave DE24 . . . . . . **231** F4
Waltham Croft S41 . . . . . . **115** C7
Walthamstow Dr DE22 . . . **218** B6
Waltheof Rd S2 . . . . **44** A8
Walton Ave DE24 . . . . **232** E4
Walton Back La
  Chesterfield S40 . . . . **114** B7
  Holymoorside S42 . . . . **113** F7
Walton Cl
  Chesterfield S40 . . . . **114** B8
  Dronfield S18 . . . . **56** C2
  Swadlincote DE11 . . . . **256** A3
Walton Cres
  Ashbourne DE6 . . . . **173** D1
  Chesterfield S40 . . . . **95** E1
Walton Ct
  Sheffield S8 . . . . **56** E8
  West Hallam DE7 . . . . **207** E8
Walton Dr
  Chesterfield S40 . . . . **95** E1
  Derby DE23 . . . . **231** E7
Walton Drive Ct S40 . . . . . **95** E1
Walton Fields Rd S40 . . . . **95** D2
Walton Hill DE74 . . . . **247** A4
Walton Holymoorside Prim
  Sch S42 . . . . **113** D7
Walton Hospl S40 . . . . **114** E8
Walton-on-Trent CE Prim
  Sch DE12 . . . . **259** D8
Walton Rd
  Burton u T DE15 . . . . **254** D5
  Chesterfield S40 . . . . **95** D1
  Derby DE21 . . . . **219** F5
Walton St NG10 . . . . **223** D1
Walton Way S42 . . . . **114** E4
Walton Wlk S40 . . . . **266** A2
Wansfell Cl DE3 . . . . **217** E1
Wapentake La DE6 . . . . . **165** C2
Warburton Cl S2 . . . . **43** C7
Warburton Gdns S2 . . . . . **43** C7
Warburton Rd S2 . . . . **43** C7
Ward's La
  Barrow u T DE73 . . . . **244** F3
  Breaston DE72 . . . . **235** D8
  King's Newton DE73 . . . . . **245** A2
Ward Dr DE5 . . . . **170** D7
Wardgate Way S40 . . . . . . **95** A5
Ward La
  Barlborough S43 . . . . **80** B8
  Disley SK12 . . . . **32** F4

Wardlow Ave
  Derby DE21 . . . . **220** A8
  17 Gamesley SK13 . . . . **9** D1
Wardlow Cl S40 . . . . **114** F8
Wardlow Fold 21 SK13 . . . . **9** D1
Wardlow Gdns 19 SK13 . . . **9** D1
Wardlow Gr 22 SK13 . . . . . **9** D1
Wardlow Mews
  16 Gamesley SK13 . . . . **9** D1
  23 Gamesley SK13 . . . . **9** D1
Wardlow Rd
  Ilkeston DE7 . . . . **194** E3
  Sheffield S12 . . . . **44** D5
Wardlow Wlk
  18 Gamesley SK13 . . . . **9** D1
  20 Gamesley SK13 . . . . **9** D1
Ward St
  Derby DE22 . . . . **218** E4
  Tupton S42 . . . . **131** D8
Wards Yd S18 . . . . **57** A1
Wardwick DE1 . . . . **267** B3
Warehouse La S33 . . . . **38** D4
Warhurst Fold 2 SK13 . . . **10** A5
Warke Flatt DE74 . . . . **247** B6
Warmbrook DE4 . . . . **165** F8
Warmbrook Rd SK23 . . . . . **47** C6
Warminster Cl S8 . . . . **43** A4
Warminster Cres S8 . . . . . . **43** B4
Warminster Dr S8 . . . . **43** B3
Warminster Gdns S8 . . . . . **43** A3
Warminster Pl S8 . . . . **43** B2
Warminster Rd S8 . . . . **43** A3
Warmwells La DE5 . . . . . . **180** D6
Warner St
  Chesterfield S41 . . . . **266** C1
  Derby DE22 . . . . **267** A1
  Derby, Mickleover DE3 . . . **217** D1
Warney Rd DE4 . . . . **127** D2
Warren Ave NG9 . . . . **223** D7
Warren Ave Extension
  NG9 . . . . **223** D7
Warren Cl
  Burton u T DE13 . . . . **240** E1
  Pilsley S45 . . . . **132** C2
Warren Cres S21 . . . . **58** E2
Warren Ct NG9 . . . . **223** D7
Warrendale Ct DE73 . . . . . **233** A2
Warren Dr DE12 . . . . **261** C6
Warren Hill 7 DE11 . . . . . **255** E5
Warren La
  Branston DE14 . . . . **253** F7
  Castle Donington DE74,
    NG10 . . . . **236** B2
Warren Lea S6 . . . . **15** B2
Warren Rise S18 . . . . **57** C3
Warren St DE24 . . . . **232** F8
Warren Wlk S21 . . . . **58** E2
Warsop Rd NG19 . . . . **136** D3
Warwick Ave DE23 . . . . . . **218** D1
Warwick Cl
  Branston DE14 . . . . **253** F8
  Glossop SK13 . . . . **17** F8
  Swadlincote DE11 . . . . **256** E5
Warwick Ct DE55 . . . . **170** A6
Warwick Dr DE7 . . . . **194** C3
Warwick Gdns DE56 . . . . . **179** D5
Warwick Rd
  Long Eaton NG10 . . . . **237** A2
  Somercotes DE55 . . . . **159** C1
Warwick St
  Chesterfield S40 . . . . **115** B7
  Derby DE24 . . . . **219** D2
Wasdale Ave 5 S20 . . . . . . **59** E6
Wasdale Cl S20 . . . . **59** E6
Washbrook La DE6 . . . . . . **161** F4
Washford Rd DE65 . . . . . . **240** E8
Wash Gn DE4 . . . . **166** B8
Wash Hills Cl DE4 . . . . . . **153** A1
Washhouse Bottom SK17 . **69** E8
Wash House La S40 . . . . . . **95** C2
Washington Ave DE21 . . . **220** B8
Washington Ave DE3 . . . . **252** A7
Washington Cotts DE72 . . **221** D1
Washington Dr NG9 . . . . . **209** F1
Washington Terr DE4 . . . . **143** E7
Watburn Rd SK22 . . . . **24** D1
Watchorn Cl DE11 . . . . . . **256** D5
Watchorn Cotts DE55 . . . . **158** F3
Watchorn La DE55 . . . . . . **158** F3
Watercress La S45 . . . . . . **131** D2
Waterdown Cl NG19 . . . . . **136** D5
Waterfoot Cotts SK14 . . . . . **9** A4
Waterfoot La SK23 . . . . **45** D6
Waterford Dr DE21 . . . . . . **220** B4
Watergo La DE23 . . . . **230** D7
Wateringbury Gr 1 S43 . . **78** F2
Watering La DE56 . . . . **191** D6
Water La
  Bakewell DE45 . . . . **109** D6
  Bamford S33 . . . . **40** A3
  Bolsover S44 . . . . **117** E8
  Cromford DE4 . . . . **155** A6
  Eyam S32 . . . . **71** E6
  Hollingworth SK14 . . . . **9** D5
  Middleton DE4 . . . . **154** C5
  Pleasley NG19 . . . . **135** B3
  Sheffield S17 . . . . **55** F7
  Shirebrook NG19 . . . . **118** E1
  South Normanton DE55 . . . **160** B6
  Tideswell SK17 . . . . **68** F6
  Wirksworth DE4 . . . . **165** F7
Waterloo Cl DE55 . . . . . . **160** C8
Waterloo Ct DE1 . . . . **267** C5
Waterloo La DE4 . . . . **143** A1
Waterloo Pl DE11 . . . . **256** B4
Waterloo Rd DE4 . . . . **143** A1
Waterloo St
  Clay Cross S45 . . . . **131** C4

Waterloo St *continued*
  Doe Lea S44 . . . . **117** F1
Water Mdws DE73 . . . . . . **244** D6
Watermeade S21 . . . . **59** B2
Water Meadow La S40 . . . . **95** B7
Watermeadow Rd DE24 . . **233** A5
Watermeadows The
  NG10 . . . . **236** A8
Watermint Cl DE23 . . . . . . **231** D6
Water Orton Cl NG9 . . . . . **223** E3
Waterpark Rd DE6 . . . . . . **224** B8
Waters Edge SK6 . . . . **23** B8
Waters Edge La SK23 . . . . . **47** C5
Waterside
  Burton u T DE15 . . . . **254** E7
  Disley SK12 . . . . **32** E7
  Furness Vale SK23 . . . . **33** E3
  Glossop SK13 . . . . **10** A6
  Ironville NG16 . . . . **170** F4
  Marple SK6 . . . . **23** A5
  Willington DE65 . . . . **242** A6
Waterside Bsns Pk SK13 . . . **9** F6
Waterside Cl
  Derby DE22 . . . . **205** A2
  Sandiacre NG10 . . . . **223** B3
Waterside Com Jun Sch
  DE15 . . . . **254** E7
Waterside Ho DE1 . . . . **267** B4
Waterside Rd
  Burton u T DE15 . . . . **254** D7
  Disley SK12, SK22 . . . . **32** E7
Waterside Ret Pk DE7 . . . . . **195** A1
Water St
  Bakewell DE45 . . . . **109** D5
  Buxton SK17 . . . . **85** B8
  Glossop SK13 . . . . **10** E2
Waterswallows La SK17 . . **66** F4
Waterswallows Mews
  SK17 . . . . **66** E1
Waterswallows Rd SK17 . . **66** E1
Waterthorpe Cl 4 S20 . . . . **59** F8
Waterthorpe Cres S20 . . . . **59** F8
Waterthorpe Gdns 3 S20 **59** F8
Waterthorpe Glade 5
  S20 . . . . **59** F8
Waterthorpe Glen 2 S20 . . **59** F8
Waterthorpe Rise 1 S20 . . **59** F8
Waterton Cl DE13 . . . . **241** A1
Waterway The NG10 . . . . . **223** C4
Watery La
  Bretby DE15 . . . . **249** C3
  Clifton DE6 . . . . **184** E7
  Ellastone DE6 . . . . **183** B4
  Holme HD9 . . . . **2** F8
  Scropton DE65 . . . . **226** E2
  Swadlincote DE11 . . . . **255** D5
  Thurvaston DE6 . . . . **215** D5
Watford Bridge Ind Est
  SK22 . . . . **24** D1
Watford Bridge Rd SK22 . **24** D1
Watford La SK22 . . . . **24** C2
Watford Lo SK22 . . . . **24** C1
Watford Rd
  Buxton SK17 . . . . **84** F8
  New Mills SK22 . . . . **24** C2
Watkin Ave SK13 . . . . **9** A4
Watkinson St DE75 . . . . . . **181** D2
Watson Ave DE75 . . . . **181** F2
Watson La S42 . . . . **114** C3
Watson Rd DE7 . . . . **194** C2
Watson St DE1 . . . . **218** E6
Watten Cl DE24 . . . . **231** F2
Watts Gn DE45 . . . . **108** F8
Waveney Cl DE22 . . . . **205** B5
Waverley Ct 2 S41 . . . . **96** A6
Waverley St
  Derby DE24 . . . . **232** D7
  Long Eaton NG10 . . . . **236** D8
  Tibshelf DE55 . . . . **148** A7
Wayfaring Rd DE21 . . . . . . **206** A1
Wayford Ave S41 . . . . **266** C1
Wayside S43 . . . . **96** D8
Wayside Cl S42 . . . . **132** A7
Wayside Ct S43 . . . . **96** D8
Wayzgoose Dr DE21 . . . . . **219** C6
Weaddow La DE45 . . . . . . **124** F2
Weakland Cl S12 . . . . **44** F3
Weakland Cres S12 . . . . . . **44** F3
Weakland Dr S12 . . . . **44** F3
Weakland Way S12 . . . . **44** F3
Weather Hill La HD9 . . . . . . **3** A8
Weathern Field DE12 . . . . **261** D5
Weaver Cl
  Ashbourne DE6 . . . . **185** C8
  Crich DE4 . . . . **156** F1
Weavers Cl
  Belper DE56 . . . . **179** C5
  Borrowash DE72 . . . . **221** D1
Weavers Croft DE5 . . . . . . **180** E8
Weavers Ct SK14 . . . . **9** A4
Weavers Gn DE3 . . . . **217** C1
Weavers The ST14 . . . . . . **196** D6
Weaving Ave S33 . . . . **38** C2
Webbs Orch SK23 . . . . **45** D8
Webster Ave NG16 . . . . . . **182** F1
Webster Croft S41 . . . . **77** B2
Webster Ct S40 . . . . **95** E5
Webster St DE1 . . . . **267** A2
Wedgewood Cl DE15 . . . . **248** B1
Wednesnough S41 . . . . **9** C5
Weighbridge Rd NG20 . . . **119** F2
Weightman Dr NG16 . . . . . **195** B7
Weir Bank DE15 . . . . **254** E6
Weirfield Rd DE22 . . . . **205** A2
Weirside DE6 . . . . **184** D7

Welbeck Ave
  Buxton SK17 . . . . **85** C
  Ilkeston DE7 . . . . **208** C
Welbeck Cl
  Dronfield S18 . . . . **56** C
  Staveley S43 . . . . **97** D
Welbeck Ct
  1 Chesterfield S40 . . . . . . **95** C
  Clowne S43 . . . . **80** F
  7 Staveley S43 . . . . **78** E
Welbeck Dr S42 . . . . **114** E
Welbeck Gdns
  Beeston NG9 . . . . **223** F
  Bolsover S44 . . . . **99** C
Welbeck Gr DE22 . . . . **204** D
Welbeck Rd
  Bolsover S44 . . . . **99** B
  Long Eaton NG10 . . . . **223** C
  Mansfield Woodhouse
    NG19 . . . . **136** C
Welbeck St
  Creswell S80 . . . . **81** E
  Whitwell S80 . . . . **82** B
Welburn Cl NG19 . . . . **136** F
Welbury Gdns S20 . . . . **59** E
Welch Ave NG9 . . . . **223** E
Welfare Ave S40 . . . . **95** D
Welfare Cl NG20 . . . . **119** E
Welfitt Gr NG20 . . . . **101** B
Welland Cl
  Burton u T DE15 . . . . **248** A
  Derby DE3 . . . . **217** D
Welland Rd DE65 . . . . **228** D
Well Banks DE6 . . . . **165** B
Wellcarr Rd S8 . . . . **43** A
Well Cl DE6 . . . . **175** E
Wellcroft DE4 . . . . **126** B
Welldon St DE5 . . . . **181** A
Wellesley Ave DE23 . . . . . **231** D
Wellfield DE4 . . . . **143** C
Wellfield Cl S12 . . . . **44** E
Wellfield Ct DE4 . . . . **143** C
Well Gate SK13 . . . . **10** E
Wellgate La DE45 . . . . **109** B
Wellhead Rd 4 S8 . . . . **43** A
Wellington Cl DE4 . . . . . . **143** D
Wellington Cres DE1 . . . . **267** D
Wellington Ct
  1 Belper DE56 . . . . **178** F
  Eastwood NG16 . . . . **182** F
Wellington Mews DE55 . . **146** D
Wellington Pk DE55 . . . . . **146** D
Wellington Pl NG16 . . . . . **182** F
Wellington Rd DE14 . . . . . **253** E
Wellington St
  Chesterfield S43 . . . . **77** D
  Derby DE1 . . . . **267** D
  Eastwood NG16 . . . . **182** F
  Heanor DE75 . . . . **181** D
  Long Eaton NG10 . . . . **223** C
  Matlock DE4 . . . . **143** C
  Ripley DE5 . . . . **169** C
  Stapleford NG9 . . . . **223** C
Well La
  Belper DE56 . . . . **190** F
  Blackfordby DE11 . . . . **257** B
  Holymoorside S42 . . . . **112** F
  Repton DE65 . . . . **242** C
  Shirland DE55 . . . . **146** C
Well Rd S8 . . . . **43** A
Well Row SK14 . . . . **16** A
Wells Cl NG19 . . . . **136** D
Wells Ct DE23 . . . . **230** E
Wellspring Cl
  Barlborough S43 . . . . **80** B
  Wingerworth S42 . . . . **115** B
Well Spring Cl S43 . . . . **96** F
Wellspring Dale NG9 . . . . **223** E
Wells Rd DE3 . . . . **217** E
Wells St S44 . . . . **118** C
Well St
  Brassington DE4 . . . . **152** F
  Derby DE1 . . . . **267** B
  Elton DE4 . . . . **140** E
  New Mills SK22 . . . . **33** B
  Ripley DE5 . . . . **169** C
Wellwood Rd DE11 . . . . . **256** A
Well Yd
  Belper DE56 . . . . **179** A
  Holbrook DE56 . . . . **191** C
Welney Cl DE3 . . . . **230** D
Welshpool Pl S40 . . . . **95** D
Welshpool Rd DE21 . . . . . **205** D
Welton Ave DE56 . . . . **179** B
Welwyn Ave
  Derby, Alleton DE24 . . . . . **232** E
  Derby DE21 . . . . **204** D
  Mansfield Woodhouse
    NG19 . . . . **136** E
Welwyn Cl
  Chesterfield S40 . . . . **95** D
  Sheffield S12 . . . . **44** B
Welwyn Ct S12 . . . . **44** B
Welwyn Rd S12 . . . . **44** B
Wembley Gdns DE22 . . . . **218** A
Wendover Cl DE3 . . . . **217** C
Wenham La NG17 . . . . **148** F
Wenlock Cl
  Chesterfield S40 . . . . **95** D
  Derby DE1 . . . . **217** E
  Eastwood NG16 . . . . **195** C
Wenlock Cres S40 . . . . **95** D
Wenlock Dr S42 . . . . **115** F
Wenlock Wlk S42 . . . . **115** F
Wensleydale Cl NG19 . . . **136** E
Wensleydale Rd NG10 . . . **236** B
Wensleydale Wlk DE24 . . **233** C
Wensley Dr DE21 . . . . **220** F

Wensley Rd
North Wingfield S42 .... 131 F5
Winster DE4 .... 141 D6
Wensley Way S43 .... 97 C8
Wentworth Ave S40 .... 114 E8
Wentworth Cl
Derby DE3 .... 217 F2
Mansfield NG19 .... 136 F2
Wentworth Croft DE75 .... 182 A3
Wentworth Ct NG16 .... 195 E6
Wentworth Dr DE13 .... 240 D1
Wentworth Ho 1 DE1 .... 218 E5
Wentworth Rd S18 .... 56 C1
Wentworth St DE7 .... 195 A2
Werburgh Cl DE21 .... 220 D4
Werburgh St DE22 .... 267 A2
Werneth Low Ctry Pk★ SK14 .... 15 A7
Werneth Low Rd SK14 .... 15 B6
Werneth Rd SK13 .... 17 A7
Wesleyan Chapel La SK17 88 A3
Wesleyan Chapel Wlk NG9 .... 223 D7
Wesley Ct SK23 .... 47 C6
Wesley Ho 3 SK17 .... 85 D8
Wesley La DE72 .... 221 C5
Wesley Pl NG9 .... 223 E7
Wesley Rd
Ambergate DE56 .... 167 F3
Derby DE24 .... 233 B5
Stonebroom DE55 .... 146 F3
Wesley St
Glossop SK13 .... 10 E2
Hadfield SK13 .... 10 A5
Ilkeston DE7 .... 194 E4
Langley Mill NG16 .... 182 C3
Wessex Cl 5 S43 .... 96 F8
Wessex Dr NG16 .... 195 A8
Wessex Gdns S17 .... 55 D5
Wessington Bank 9 SK13 .... 9 E2
Wessington Dr S43 .... 97 C8
Wessington Fold 12 SK13 .... 9 E2
Wessington Gn 11 SK13 .... 9 E2
Wessington La DE55 .... 158 A6
Wessington Mews
Derby DE22 .... 204 E1
Gamesley SK13 .... 9 E2
Wessington Prim Sch DE55 .... 157 E8
Westacre Dr DE11 .... 255 F2
West Ave
Chellaston DE73 .... 232 E3
Derby DE1 .... 267 A4
Draycott DE72 .... 234 F8
Hilton DE65 .... 228 C2
Ripley DE5 .... 169 C1
Sandiacre NG10 .... 223 A6
Stapleford NG9 .... 223 E8
West Bank
Matlock Bath DE4 .... 143 A1
Toadmoor DE56 .... 168 A2
Winster DE4 .... 141 B5
West Bank Ave
Crich DE4 .... 156 F1
Derby DE22 .... 218 F8
Mansfield NG19 .... 136 B1
Westbank Cl S18 .... 57 B4
West Bank Cl DE22 .... 218 E8
Westbank Ct S18 .... 57 C4
West Bank Lea NG19 .... 136 B1
West Bank Link NG19 .... 136 B1
West Bank Rd DE22 .... 204 E5
West Bars S40 .... 266 A3
Westbourne Ave DE55 .... 147 A4
Westbourne Cl NG19 .... 136 E4
Westbourne Ct NG9 .... 209 F1
Westbourne Gr S40 .... 95 B3
Westbourne Pk DE22 .... 217 F7
Westbridge Rd S43 .... 80 A7
Westbrook Cl
Chapel-en-le-F SK23 .... 47 C5
Chesterfield S40 .... 94 F2
Westbrook Dr S40 .... 94 F2
Westbury Ct DE22 .... 218 E3
Westbury Gdns DE56 .... 179 C5
Westbury St DE22 .... 218 E3
Westby La NG16 .... 195 D3
West Cl DE22 .... 204 E2
West Cres
Duckmanton S44 .... 98 A5
Matlock DE4 .... 143 A6
West Croft Ave DE23 .... 231 D5
West Croft Cl DE45 .... 125 B5
Westcroft Cres S20 .... 59 E8
West Croft Ct S43 .... 97 B5
Westcroft Dr S20 .... 59 E7
West Croft Dr S43 .... 97 B5
Westcroft Gdns S20 .... 59 E8
Westcroft Glen S20 .... 59 E7
Westcroft Gr S20 .... 59 E7
Westcross Ave NG9 .... 223 E8
Westdale Cl NG10 .... 236 A5
Westdale Rd
Mansfield NG19 .... 136 B1
Westwood NG16 .... 171 C4
Westdene Ave DE24 .... 232 D5
West Dr
Derby DE3 .... 217 D2
Doveridge DE6 .... 211 B1
Glossop SK13 .... 9 E7
West Edge Cl S45 .... 129 D4
West End
Alfreton DE55 .... 159 A3
Barlborough S43 .... 80 A7
Baslow DE45 .... 91 E5
Brassington DE4 .... 152 F1
Broadbottom SK14 .... 15 F8
Elton DE4 .... 140 E6

West End *continued*
Pinxton NG16 .... 160 C4
Wirksworth DE4 .... 165 E8
West End Cl DE55 .... 159 A3
West End Cres DE7 .... 208 D8
West End Dr
Ilkeston DE7 .... 208 D8
Shardlow DE72 .... 234 E1
West End St NG9 .... 223 C5
West End View S21 .... 59 C2
Westerlands NG9 .... 223 F6
Western Ave DE55 .... 169 D7
Western Dr DE75 .... 193 F8
Western La SK23 .... 46 A8
Western Rd
Derby DE3 .... 217 E2
Derby, Rose Hill DE23 .... 219 A3
Western View DE45 .... 90 A4
Western Villas DE56 .... 167 F3
Westfield Ave
Chesterfield S40 .... 95 B1
5 Heanor DE75 .... 181 F1
West Field Bank S43 .... 80 A7
Westfield Cl
Chesterfield S40 .... 95 B2
Ilkeston DE7 .... 208 C6
Westfield Cres S20 .... 59 C8
Westfield Ctr S20 .... 59 E8
Westfield Dr
Blackwell DE55 .... 147 E1
Ilkeston DE7 .... 194 D2
Westfield Gdns S40 .... 95 B2
Westfield Gr DE22 .... 218 D4
Westfield Inf Sch S40 .... 95 B2
Westfield La
Barlborough S43 .... 79 F7
Chesterfield S21 .... 77 E8
Westfield Northway S20 .. 59 E8
Westfield Rd
Dronfield S18 .... 76 C8
Killamarsh S21 .... 60 C5
Swadlincote DE11 .... 256 B6
Westfield Sch S20 .... 59 D8
Westfield Southway S20 . 59 E8
Westgate DE1 .... 218 E6
West Gate
Holme HD9 .... 3 F8
Long Eaton NG10 .... 236 E7
Westgate Cl ST14 .... 196 F3
West Gr DE24 .... 232 D5
Westgreen Ave DE24 .... 232 D5
Westhall Rd DE3 .... 217 D3
West Hill DE5 .... 181 B7
Westhill La S42 .... 115 E3
West Hill Pk NG19 .... 136 B3
West Ho S8 .... 43 A4
West Horderns SK23 .... 47 B5
Westhorpe Dr NG10 .... 236 C8
Westhouses Prim Sch DE55 .... 147 C1
Westland Dr NG16 .... 160 C3
Westland Gdns S20 .... 59 D8
Westland Gr 3 S20 .... 59 E8
Westland Rd 1 S20 .... 59 E8
Westlands The ST14 .... 196 D6
West Lawn DE65 .... 230 D2
Westlea DE4 .... 143 D6
West Lea
Chesterfield S40 .... 95 B2
Clowne S43 .... 80 D4
West Lea Cotts S43 .... 80 D4
Westlea View S43 .... 80 D4
West Lees Rd S33 .... 40 B4
Westleigh NG19 .... 136 D6
Westleigh Ave DE22 .... 218 C6
Westleigh Ct S40 .... 95 E5
Westley Cres DE21 .... 191 D2
Westminster Ave 1 NG10 .... 223 C5
Westminster St DE24 .... 232 F8
Westmoor Rd S43 .... 96 F4
Westmorland Cl DE21 .... 219 C6
Westmorland Way NG16. 171 B3
Weston Bank DE6 .... 197 F1
Weston Cl S40 .... 95 A5
Weston Cres NG10 .... 235 F4
Weston Ct DE72 .... 245 E4
Westonhill Chalet Pk DE72 .... 245 C4
Weston-on-Trent CE Prim Sch DE72 .... 245 E4
Weston Park Ave DE24 .. 232 E3
Weston Park Gdns DE24 232 D3
Weston Rd
Aston-on-T DE72 .... 246 A7
Weston-on-T DE72 .... 245 F6
Weston Rise DE73 .... 245 A8
Weston Spot Cl DE5 .... 180 D7
Weston St
Heanor DE75 .... 194 A8
Swadlincote DE11 .... 256 B3
West Park Ct NG10 .... 236 D7
West Park Rd DE22 .... 218 E8
West Park Sch DE21 .... 220 D5
West Rd
Buxton SK17 .... 85 B6
Derby DE21 .... 220 D5
West Road Ho 2 SK17 .... 85 B6
West Row DE22 .... 205 A1
West Service Rd DE21 .... 220 B3
West St
Bramley-Vale S44 .... 117 D1
Burton u T DE15 .... 248 B3
Chesterfield S40 .... 266 A4
Clay Cross S45 .... 131 A4
Clowne S43 .... 81 A5
Creswell S80 .... 81 D1
Dronfield S18 .... 56 F2

West St *continued*
Eckington S21 .... 59 C2
Glossop SK13 .... 9 F7
Heanor DE75 .... 181 D2
Ilkeston DE7 .... 208 E7
Langley Mill NG16 .... 182 B3
Shirebrook NG20 .... 120 D4
Somercotes DE55 .... 170 C6
South Normanton DE55 .... 159 F5
Stonebroom DE55 .... 146 F3
Swadlincote DE11 .... 256 B4
Whaley Thorns NG20 .... 101 A3
West Terr 6 DE7 .... 194 F1
Westthorpe Fields Rd S21 .... 60 C4
Westthorpe Rd S21 .... 60 D5
West Towers Mews SK6 .. 23 A4
West View
Barlborough S43 .... 80 A6
Bolsover S44 .... 118 B8
Hulland Village DE6 .... 175 E2
Mayfield DE6 .... 184 D6
Parwich DE6 .... 151 E1
Rocester ST14 .... 197 A3
Staveley S43 .... 78 D1
Tibshelf DE55 .... 147 F6
West View Ave DE23 .... 231 B7
West View Cl S17 .... 55 F6
West View La S17 .... 55 F6
West View Rd S41 .... 95 E6
Westward Cl ST14 .... 210 B1
West Way DE55 .... 159 C1
Westwell Pl S20 .... 59 D6
Westwick Cres S8 .... 56 D7
Westwick Gr S8 .... 56 E7
Westwick La S42 .... 94 D2
Westwick Pk S41 .... 76 D3
Westwick Rd S8 .... 56 E7
Westwick St DE7 .... 209 B6
Westwood Ave S43 .... 97 C8
Westwood Cl S43 .... 97 C5
Westwood Dr
Derby DE24 .... 232 D5
Staveley S43 .... 97 C5
Westwood Drive Gdns S43 .... 97 B5
Westwood Gdns DE55 .... 147 B5
Westwood Inf Sch NG16 171 C4
Westwood La S43 .... 96 F4
Westwood Pk DE11 .... 255 F5
Westwood Rd S44 .... 97 A4
Wetherby Cl NG16 .... 195 E7
Wetherby Ct DE14 .... 253 F7
Wetherby Rd DE24 .... 232 E7
Wetherel Rd DE15 .... 248 C2
Wetlands La S43, S44 .... 96 E4
Weyacres DE72 .... 221 C1
Weybridge Cl DE7 .... 207 D8
Whaley Bridge Prim Sch SK23 .... 45 E7
Whaley Bridge Sta SK23 .. 45 E8
Whaley La SK23 .... 45 C8
Whaley Rd NG20 .... 100 E2
Whaley Thorns Heritage Ctr★ NG20 .... 101 A3
Whaley Thorns Prim Sch NG20 .... 101 A3
Wharf Ct SK23 .... 45 E7
Wharfedale Cl DE22 .... 205 B4
Wharfedale Rd NG10 .... 236 A6
Wharf Hos DE13 .... 253 A1
Wharf La
Chesterfield S41 .... 266 B4
Staveley S43 .... 78 F3
Tibshelf DE55 .... 148 C7
Wharf Rd
Pinxton NG16 .... 160 D2
Whaley Bridge SK23 .... 45 E7
Wharf Road Ind Est NG16 .... 160 D2
Wharf The DE72 .... 235 A2
Wharmby Ave NG19 .... 135 D3
Wharncliffe Cl SK13 .... 9 E4
Wharncliffe Rd DE7 .... 208 E8
Wharton Dr DE24 .... 266 C3
Whatstandwell Sta DE4 . 156 C1
Wheal La SK17 .... 107 D7
Wheatbridge Rd S40 .... 266 A3
Wheatbridge Ret Pk S40 266 A2
Wheatcroft SK13 .... 9 E4
Wheatcroft Cl
Clay Cross S45 .... 131 D2
Wingerworth S42 .... 115 A4
Wheatcroft La DE4 .... 157 A7
Wheatcroft Way DE21 .... 205 C2
Wheatfield Cres NG19 .... 136 E5
Wheatfield Ct DE65 .... 242 D5
Wheatfields SK23 .... 47 C7
Wheatfield Way S42 .... 94 F5
Wheathill Cl
Calow S43 .... 96 F4
Chesterfield S42 .... 94 F5
Wheathill Gr DE23 .... 231 A6
Wheathill La S41 .... 96 D4
Wheatland Cl DE24 .... 231 C2
Wheatlands DE11 .... 256 B7
Wheatlands La DE45 .... 91 C5
Wheatlands Rd
Burton u T DE15 .... 254 E7
Wingerworth S42 .... 114 E4
Wheatley Ave DE55 .... 159 C1
Wheatley Cl NG19 .... 136 F1
Wheatley Gdns DE4 .... 127 D2
Wheatley La DE15 .... 248 C4
Wheatley Rd DE4 .... 127 D3
Wheatsheaf Cl
Derby DE21 .... 206 C2
Horwich End SK23 .... 45 E6

Wheatsheaf La DE4 .... 156 F1
Wheatsheaf Rd SK23 .... 45 E6
Wheeldon Ave
Belper DE56 .... 179 B4
Derby DE22 .... 218 E7
Wheeldon Cl NE7 .... 194 F6
Wheeldon Cres S43 .... 96 D7
Wheeldon Manor DE22 .. 218 E8
Wheeldon Way DE6 .... 175 E3
Wheelwright Way DE24 . 219 D3
Whenby Cl DE3 .... 217 C2
Whernside Cl DE24 .... 233 D6
Wheston Bank SK17 .... 69 B4
Wheston Ct 7 S40 .... 95 D5
Whetmorhurst La SK6 .... 23 E4
Whilton Cres DE7 .... 207 D8
Whilton Ct DE56 .... 179 D4
Whinacre Cl S8 .... 57 B6
Whinacre Pl S8 .... 57 A6
Whinacre Wlk S8 .... 57 A6
Whinbush Ave DE24 .... 232 E5
Whinney Bank NG19 .... 136 D4
Whinney Hill NG19 .... 136 D4
Whisperwood Cl S44 .... 98 A5
Whistlestop Cl DE3 .... 217 D4
Whiston St DE23 .... 219 A2
Whitaker Gdns DE23 .... 218 E2
Whitaker Mews ST14 .... 196 F3
Whitaker Rd DE23 .... 218 E2
Whitaker St DE23 .... 219 A2
Whitburn Rd NG9 .... 223 E3
Whitby Ave DE21 .... 205 C1
Whitcombe Pl DE5 .... 169 D2
Whitebank Cl S41 .... 266 C1
Whitecarr La DE55, S45 .. 145 B4
Whitecotes Cl S40 .... 114 E8
Whitecotes La S40 .... 114 E8
Whitecotes Pk S40 .... 114 F8
Whitecotes Prim Sch S40 .... 114 F8
Whitecroft Rd SK6 .... 23 C1
Whitecross Ave SK17 .... 69 C4
Whitecross Gdns DE1 .... 218 E7
Whitecross Ho DE1 .... 218 E7
Whitecross Rd SK17 .... 69 D5
Whitecross St DE1 .... 218 E6
White Edge Cl S40 .... 95 D5
White Edge Dr DE45 .... 91 E6
Whitefield La
Ashover S45 .... 129 A5
Chelmorton SK17 .... 106 E8
White Gate Rd HD9 .... 3 D7
Whitegates SK14 .... 9 A1
White Gates DE5 .... 181 B8
Whitegates Way NG17 .. 148 F2
Whitehall Terr SK23 .... 34 D1
White Hart Cnr S21 .... 59 E4
White Hart Yd DE56 .... 191 F8
Whitehaven Gr DE73 .... 233 A3
Whitehead Cl DE7 .... 194 D2
Whitehead Dr NG16 .... 182 D8
Whitehead St 4 S43 .... 78 F2
White Horse La DE55 .... 145 D7
Whitehough Head La SK23 .... 46 E8
Whitehouse Cl DE24 .... 232 D3
Whitehouse Rise DE56 .. 178 E6
Whitehouses S41 .... 266 C1
Whitehurst St DE24 .... 232 D7
White Knowle Cl SK17 .... 85 C5
White Knowle Pk SK17 .... 85 C5
White Knowle Rd SK17 .... 85 C5
White La
Eckington S12 .... 44 C2
Shottle DE56 .... 177 D4
Whitelea La DE4 .... 144 B6
White Leas S40 .... 95 B4
Whiteleas Ave S42 .... 132 A7
Whiteleas Rd SK23 .... 45 D3
Whiteley Rd DE5 .... 180 F7
White Lion Sq DE7 .... 208 F7
White Lodge La DE45 .... 91 E6
Whitelow La
Ible DE4 .... 153 E7
Sheffield S17 .... 55 B7
Whitely Cl 3 NG9 .... 223 E8
Whitemoor Hall DE56 .... 179 D5
Whitemoor La DE56 .... 179 D5
White Rd
New Mills SK22 .... 24 C2
Staveley S43 .... 79 A3
Whites Cl DE55 .... 159 A2
Whites Croft View S43 .... 80 B6
Whites La DE55 .... 147 F1
Whitesmead Cl SK12 .... 32 D5
White St DE22 .... 218 E7
White Thorns Cl S8 .... 57 B5
White Thorns Dr S8 .... 57 B5
White Thorns View S8 .... 57 B6
White Tor Rd DE4 .... 143 C2
Whiteway DE22 .... 204 E2
Whitewell Gdns DE24 .... 233 C5
Whitewells La DE56 .... 178 C8
Whitewells Rd DE56 .... 167 E2
White Woods Way DE4 .. 143 B3
Whitfield Ave SK13 .... 17 C7
Whitfield Cross SK13 .... 17 D7
Whitfield La DE45 .... 124 E2
Whitfield Pk SK13 .... 17 C7
Whitfield Wells SK13 .... 17 D7
Whiting Ave 2 NG9 .... 223 F2
Whiting St 8 S8 .... 43 A6
Whitle Bank Rd SK22 .... 24 B2
Whitle Rd SK22 .... 24 C1
Whitley Way DE6 .... 185 E8
Whitley Wlk SK13 .... 16 F8
Whitmore Ave S42 .... 115 E2
Whitmore Rd DE21 .... 219 F6

Whitstable Cl DE23 .... 231 D7
Whittaker La DE21 .... 191 D2
Whitt Cl DE72 .... 221 C1
Whitting Mews S41 .... 76 F2
Whittington Hill S41 .... 77 A2
Whittington La S18 .... 76 F5
Whittington Rd S43 .... 77 F4
Whittington St DE24 .... 232 D6
Whittington Way S41 .... 77 A1
Whitting Valley Rd S41 .... 77 B1
Whittlebury Dr DE23 .... 230 F7
Whitwell Bank 5 SK13 .... 9 D2
Whitwell Cl
4 Gamesley SK13 .... 9 D2
Ilkeston NE7 .... 194 E6
Whitwell Fold 1 SK13 .... 9 D2
Whitwell Gn 2 SK13 .... 9 D2
Whitwell Lea 3 SK13 .... 9 D2
Whitwell Prim Sch S80 .... 82 A5
Whitwell Rd S80 .... 63 A4
Whitwell Sta S80 .... 82 A5
Whitworth Ave DE4 .... 127 C3
Whitworth Cl DE12 .... 262 E4
Whitworth Hospl DE4 .... 142 F8
Whitworth Rd
1 Chesterfield S41 .... 96 A6
Darley Dale DE4 .... 127 B4
Ilkeston DE7 .... 208 F7
Wholey Pl S45 .... 131 C3
Whysall Rd NG10 .... 236 B7
Whysall St DE75 .... 181 E2
Whyteleafe Gr DE21 .... 206 B1
Wichal Farm Cl DE5 .... 180 D7
Wickenlow La SK17 .... 103 D1
Wickersley Cl 1 DE22 .... 204 F2
Wickets The DE15 .... 254 F8
Wickfield Cl S12 .... 44 F5
Wickfield Dr S12 .... 44 F5
Wickfield Gr S12 .... 44 E4
Wickfield Pl S12 .... 44 F5
Wickfield Rd S12 .... 44 F5
Wickins Pl S43 .... 79 B3
Wicksteed Cl DE56 .... 179 D5
Widdop Cl S13 .... 44 D8
Widdop Croft S13 .... 44 D8
Widdybank Cl DE22 .... 204 C2
Widecombe Ct 24 S41 .... 95 F8
Wideshaft DE11 .... 256 C4
Widmerpool St NG16 .... 160 C2
Wigley Prim Sch S42 .... 93 E4
Wigley Rd S43 .... 97 C6
Wigmore Cl DE3 .... 217 C3
Wikeley Way S43 .... 96 D7
Wilberforce Rd NG19 .... 135 D2
Wilcock Ho DE21 .... 219 C6
Wilcox Ave NG19 .... 136 B5
Wildaygreen La S18 .... 75 B2
Wilden Croft S43 .... 96 C8
Wilderbrook La DE56 .... 178 A8
Wilders Lea Ct DE56 .... 179 A2
Wildersley Rd DE56 .... 179 A1
Wildhay Brook DE65 .... 228 C1
Wildhay La DE6 .... 183 C7
Wild Hill NG17 .... 148 E7
Wild La DE4, DE55 .... 157 B4
Wildpark La DE6 .... 202 D6
Wildsmith St DE24 .... 233 A8
Wild St DE22 .... 218 D5
Wilfred St DE23 .... 219 B2
Wilhallow La NG16 .... 171 E2
Wilkin Hill S18 .... 75 E2
Wilkins Dr DE24 .... 232 E7
Wilkinson Cl
Chesterfield S40 .... 115 A6
Pleasley NG19 .... 135 A5
Wilkinson Dr S43 .... 97 B7
Willbury Dr S12 .... 44 A6
Willcock Rd DE14 .... 254 A7
Willersley Ct 3 S41 .... 95 D7
Willersley Ho NG10 .... 236 A5
Willersley La
Matlock Bath DE4 .... 155 C8
Matlock DE4 .... 143 C1
Willesden Ave DE22 .... 218 A7
Willetts Rd DE21 .... 220 A7
William Allitt Sch DE11 .. 255 E7
William Ave NG16 .... 182 F2
William Cl
Duffield DE56 .... 190 D4
Sheffield S20 .... 59 D6
William Cres S20 .... 59 D6
William Gilbert Endowed Prim Sch DE56 .... 190 E4
William Holmes Almshouses DE5 .... 169 F2
William Howitt Jun Com Sch DE75 .... 181 D2
William Levick Prim Sch S18 .... 56 C2
William Lilley Inf Sch NG9 .... 223 D6
William Nadin Way DE11 255 F4
William Newton Cl DE65. 241 B5
William Rd NG9 .... 223 D7
William Rhodes Prim Sch S40 .... 266 A1
William St N S41 .... 76 F2
Williams Cl DE55 .... 170 D6
William Shrewsbury Prim Sch DE13 .... 240 E1
Williamson Ave SK17 .... 66 C1
Williamson Cres SK23 .... 45 D8
Williamson Rd SK23 .... 45 D8
William St
Belper DE56 .... 178 F4

William St continued
Chesterfield S41 . . . . **96** A6
Derby DE1 . . . . **218** E6
Eckington S21 . . . . **59** D3
Long Eaton NG10 . . . . **223** C2
Williamthorpe Cl S42 . . **132** A7
Williamthorpe Ind Pk
S42 . . . . **116** D2
Williamthorpe Ponds (Nature Reserve) ★ S42 . . . . . . **116** E2
Williamthorpe Rd S42 . . **132** B7
Willington Prim Sch
DE65 . . . . **242** B5
Willington Rd
Etwall DE65 . . . . **229** D3
Findern DE65 . . . . **242** B5
Repton DE65 . . . . **242** B4
Willington Sta DE65 . . . . **242** A6
Wiln St DE23 . . . . **218** F1
Willoughby Almshouses
NG16 . . . . **195** C1
Willoughby Ave NG10 . . **223** C3
Willoughby Cl DE72 . . . . **235** E8
Willoughby Ct DE72 . . . . **222** D4
Willoughby Ho DE11 . . . . **256** C4
Willow Ave
Long Eaton NG10 . . . . **223** D1
Ripley DE5 . . . . **180** C1
Shirebrook NG20 . . . . **119** D5
Stapleford NG9 . . . . **223** D6
Willowbath La DE4 . . . . . **165** F7
Willowbrook Cl DE55 . . . **228** C2
Willowbrook Grange
DE73 . . . . **233** A1
Willow Cl
Aldercar NG16 . . . . **182** B4
Alfreton DE55 . . . . **159** B5
Aston-on-T DE72 . . . . **246** B7
Creswell S80 . . . . **81** F1
Derby DE72 . . . . **204** F2
Pilsley S45 . . . . **132** C1
South Normanton DE55 . . . **160** B5
Stanley Common DE7 . . . . . **193** A2
Willow Croft DE24 . . . . . **233** C4
Willowcroft Rd DE21 . . . **220** E4
Willow Ct
Ashbourne DE6 . . . . **185** D7
Calow S44 . . . . **97** A3
Swadlincote DE11 . . . . **256** C4
Willow Dr
Chapel-en-le-F SK23 . . . . . . **47** B5
Mastin Moor S43 . . . . **79** C4
Swadlincote DE11 . . . . **255** F7
Willow Farm Bsns Pk
DE74 . . . . **247** B6
Willow Farm Ct DE65 . . . **230** D2
Willowfields DE65 . . . . . **228** D2
Willow Garth Rd S41 . . . **95** C8
Willow Gr
Belper DE56 . . . . **179** A2
Willington DE65 . . . . **242** A6
Willowherb Cl DE24 . . . . **231** F2
Willow Ho DE21 . . . . **219** C6
Willow Meadow Rd DE6 . **185** D7
Willow Park Way DE72 . . **246** A7
Willowpit La DE65 . . . . . **228** E5
Willow Pl DE15 . . . . **254** E7
Willow Rd
Castle Donington DE74 . . . **247** B5
Killamarsh S21 . . . . **60** C5
Willow Rise NG10 . . . . . . **223** B5
Willow Row DE1 . . . . **267** A4
Willows Ave DE55 . . . . . . **159** B5
Willows Cl DE5 . . . . **169** C1
Willowsend Cl DE65 . . . . **230** D1
Willowside Gn DE21 . . . . **220** D3
Willow St DE55 . . . . **146** C1
Willows The
Hulland Ward DE6 . . . . **175** F3
Pleasley NG19 . . . . **135** A6
Willow Tree Dr S43 . . . . . **80** F2
Willow Way DE4 . . . . **127** B3
Willridding La DE6 . . . . . **183** C7
Will Shore's La DE4 . . . . **142** D6
Willson Ave DE23 . . . . . . **231** D8
Willson Dr DE55 . . . . **170** C7
Willson Rd DE23 . . . . **231** C8
Wilmans Wlk SK13 . . . . . **10** A6
Wilmington Ave DE24 . . **233** B5
Wilmore Rd DE24 . . . . . . **232** B5
Wilmot Ave
Derby DE21 . . . . **219** F5
Weston-on-T DE72 . . . . **245** E5
Wilmot Dr DE7 . . . . **192** F6
Wilmot Rd
Belper DE56 . . . . **179** A4
Swadlincote DE11 . . . . **256** B3
Wilmot St
Derby DE1 . . . . **267** B2
Heanor DE75 . . . . **181** E1
Ilkeston DE7 . . . . **194** E1
Long Eaton NG10 . . . . **236** A5
Matlock DE4 . . . . **143** B6
Wilmslow Dr DE21 . . . . . **206** B1
Wilne Ave NG10 . . . . **236** A4
Wilne Cl NG10 . . . . **235** F4
Wilne La
Breaston DE72 . . . . **235** D4
Shardlow DE72 . . . . **235** B2
Wilne Rd
Draycott DE72 . . . . **235** B5
Long Eaton NG10 . . . . **235** F4
Wilshaw Cl SK22 . . . . **47** C5
Wilson's Terr SK13 . . . . . **17** B8

Wilson Ave
Blackwell DE55 . . . . **147** E1
Clowne S43 . . . . **80** F5
Heanor DE75 . . . . **181** B4
Wilson Cl
Burnaston DE3 . . . . **230** C8
Clay Cross S45 . . . . **131** D2
Wilson La S44 . . . . **117** B2
Wilson Pl ⑥ S8 . . . . **43** A7
Wilson Rd
Derby DE21 . . . . **219** F8
Dronfield S18 . . . . **57** C4
Eastwood NG16 . . . . **182** F1
Wilson Rise DE73 . . . . . . **252** E6
Wilson St
Alfreton DE55 . . . . **159** B4
Derby DE1 . . . . **267** B2
Dronfield S18 . . . . **76** B8
Mansfield NG19 . . . . **135** D2
Pinxton NG16 . . . . **160** D3
Wilsthorpe Bsns & Enterprise Coll NG10 . . . . . . **223** B1
Wilsthorpe Rd
Breaston DE72 . . . . **235** F8
Derby DE21 . . . . **220** A7
Long Eaton NG10 . . . . **236** B7
Wilton Cl DE24 . . . . **231** C2
Wilton Pl DE7 . . . . **194** F1
Wilton St ⑤ DE7 . . . . **194** F1
Wiltra Gr DE56 . . . . **190** F3
Wiltshire Ave NG16 . . . . **171** B4
Wiltshire Dr SK13 . . . . . **17** F8
Wiltshire Rd DE21 . . . . . **219** E7
Wimbledon Rd DE22 . . . . **218** A7
Wimborne Cres S41 . . . . **95** F7
Wimbourne Cl DE73 . . . . **233** A2
Wimpole Gdns DE22 . . . . **218** B6
Wimsey Way DE55 . . . . . **159** B2
Wincanton Cl DE24 . . . . **219** D1
Winchcombe Dr DE15 . . . **248** B1
Winchcombe Way DE21 . . **206** B2
Winchester Cl S42 . . . . . **131** F6
Winchester Cres DE7 . . . **209** A8
Winchester Dr
Burton u T DE14 . . . . **254** C8
Linton DE12 . . . . **261** D5
Mansfield Woodhouse
NG19 . . . . **136** D4
Swadlincote DE11 . . . . **256** D6
Winchester Rd S41 . . . . . **95** E7
Windermere Ave
Dronfield S18 . . . . **56** E1
Ilkeston DE7 . . . . **208** D5
Windermere Cl NG19 . . . **136** E3
Windermere Cres DE22 . . **204** E3
Windermere Dr DE21 . . . **220** E5
Windermere Gdns NG10 . . **223** B2
Windermere Rd
Chesterfield S41 . . . . **95** D7
Clay Cross S45 . . . . **131** B3
Long Eaton NG10 . . . . **223** B2
Winders Cnr S43 . . . . **80** B5
Winding Wheel The ★
S41 . . . . **266** C3
Windlea Rd DE55 . . . . **170** C6
Windley Cres DE22 . . . . . **204** F1
Windley Dr DE7 . . . . **194** D3
Windley La
Idridgehay DE56 . . . . **176** E5
Turnditch DE56 . . . . **177** A1
Windley DE56 . . . . **189** E7
Windmill Lane Ind Est DE56 . . **192** A8
Windmill Cl
Bolsover S44 . . . . **99** A3
Castle Donington DE74 . . . **247** B2
Elvaston DE24 . . . . **233** D4
Ockbrook DE72 . . . . **221** C5
④ Uttoxeter ST14 . . . . **210** B1
Windmill Dr ST14 . . . . . . **224** E3
Windmill Greenway S20 . . **59** E5
Windmill Hill La DE22 . . **218** C6
Windmill La
Alderwasley DE56 . . . . . . **166** F6
Ashbourne DE6 . . . . **173** C4
Belper DE56 . . . . **179** A4
Eyam S32 . . . . **71** C6
Snelston DE6 . . . . **184** E2
Unstone S18 . . . . **77** A6
Windmill Rd DE65 . . . . . . **229** B3
Windmill Rise
Belper DE56 . . . . **179** A4
Somercotes DE55 . . . . **170** D7
South Normanton DE55 . . . **159** F5
Windmill St DE11 . . . . . . **256** A1
Windmill View DE56 . . . . **179** E8
Windmill Way S43 . . . . . . **96** C8
Windrush Cl DE22 . . . . . . **205** B5
Windrush Ct ④ S43 . . . . . **96** E8
Windrush Rd DE65 . . . . . **240** D8
Windses Est S32 . . . . **53** D2
Windsmoor Rd NG16 . . . . **182** D8
Windsor Ave
Derby DE23 . . . . **231** B8
Melbourne DE73 . . . . **252** A8
Windsor Cl
⑥ Ashbourne DE6 . . . . . . **173** D3
Borrowash DE72 . . . . **221** C1
Chesterfield S40 . . . . **95** C1
Heanor DE75 . . . . **181** E3
Swadlincote DE11 . . . . **256** A6
Swanwick DE55 . . . . **170** A7
Trowell NG9 . . . . **209** B5
Windsor Cres
Ilkeston DE7 . . . . **208** E4
Stapleford NG9 . . . . **223** E2
Windsor Ct
Derby DE3 . . . . **217** D3
Long Eaton NG10 . . . . **236** E7

Windsor Ct continued
Sandiacre NG10 . . . . **223** B4
West Hallam DE7 . . . . **207** D8
Windsor Dr
Derby DE21 . . . . **221** A6
Dronfield S18 . . . . **56** C1
Wingerworth S42 . . . . **114** E4
Windsor Park Rd SK17 . . . **85** D8
Windsor Rd
Buxton SK17 . . . . **85** C8
Linton DE12 . . . . **261** D5
Uttoxeter ST14 . . . . **210** A1
Windsor St NG9 . . . . **223** E7
Windsor Wlk ⑦ S41 . . . . . **96** C1
Windy Fields Rd S42 . . . . **113** D7
Windy House La S2 . . . . . **44** A8
Windy Knowle SK22 . . . . **25** A3
Windy La DE21 . . . . **191** C1
Windyridge SK17 . . . . **121** B6
Winfield Gr SK6 . . . . **15** B1
Wingerworth Ave S8 . . . . **56** D8
Wingerworth Cotts S42 . . **115** E3
Wingerworth Park Rd
DE21 . . . . **220** E5
Wingerworth St S42 . . . . **115** E3
Wingerworth Way S40 . . . **114** F7
Wingfield Cl ⑥ S18 . . . . . **56** C1
Wingfield Cres S12 . . . . . **44** C5
Wingfield Dr
Derby DE21 . . . . **205** F1
Ilkeston DE7 . . . . **194** D3
Wingfield Gr SK13 . . . . . . **17** F7
Wingfield Hall DE55 . . . . **157** F3
Wingfield Manor Ho ★
DE55 . . . . **157** E2
Wingfield Rd
Alfreton DE55 . . . . **158** E3
Tupton S42 . . . . **131** D8
Wingfield View S45 . . . . . **131** E4
Winhill Rd S42 . . . . **24** C1
Winkpenny La DE55 . . . . . **147** F5
Winnat Pl S43 . . . . **97** C7
Winnats S33 . . . . **37** E2
Winnats Cl
Chesterfield S40 . . . . **95** D5
Glossop SK13 . . . . **17** F8
Winney Hill S26 . . . . **61** E5
Winney La S26 . . . . **61** E3
Winnings The S80 . . . . . . **101** E8
Winnington Rd SK6 . . . . . **23** A7
Winn La DE6 . . . . **174** F7
Winshill Inf Sch DE15 . . . **248** B3
Winslow Ave SK14 . . . . . . **9** A2
Winslow Gn DE21 . . . . **220** C6
Winster CE Prim Sch
DE4 . . . . **141** D6
Winster Cl
Belper DE56 . . . . **179** B5
Clay Cross S42 . . . . **131** A5
Winster Ct S41 . . . . **96** A5
Winster Gn ⑧ DE11 . . . . . **255** E5
Winster Gr SK17 . . . . **85** E7
Winster La DE4 . . . . **140** F7
Winster Market Ho ★
DE4 . . . . **141** D6
Winster Mews SK13 . . . . . **9** E2
Winster Rd
Derby DE21 . . . . **205** E1
Staveley S43 . . . . **97** C3
Winster Sq SK17 . . . . **85** E7
Winster Way NG10 . . . . . **235** F5
Winston Cl NG9 . . . . **223** E8
Winterbourne Dr NG9 . . . **209** E1
Winter Closes NG16 . . . . **171** F1
Wintercroft La DE6 . . . . . **161** E1
Wintergreen Dr DE23 . . . **230** F6
Winyard Ct ⑨ S40 . . . . . . **95** D5
Wire La DE55 . . . . **148** B3
Wirestone La S45 . . . . . . **129** A3
Wirksmoor Rd SK22 . . . . **33** B7
Wirksworth Hall Gdns
DE4 . . . . **165** F8
Wirksworth Heritage Ctr Mus ★ DE4 . . . . **154** F1
Wirksworth Ind Ctr DE4 . **154** F3
Wirksworth Inf Sch DE4 . **154** F1
Wirksworth Jun Sch
DE4 . . . . **155** A1
Wirksworth Rd
Duffield DE56 . . . . **190** B4
Holloway DE4 . . . . **156** B2
Idridgehay DE56 . . . . **176** F6
Ilkeston DE7 . . . . **208** C4
Kirk Ireton DE6 . . . . **165** B2
Shottle DE56 . . . . **177** C3
Wisbech Cl S40 . . . . **114** E8
Wisgreaves Rd DE24 . . . . **232** F8
Wishing Stone Way DE4 . **143** E6
Wiston Way S41 . . . . **115** C7
Witham Cl
Chesterfield S41 . . . . **96** C6
Hilton DE65 . . . . **228** E2
Witham St S40 . . . . **95** C3
Witham Dr DE23 . . . . **231** D6
Witney Cl DE24 . . . . **232** C8
Witney St S8 . . . . **43** A8
Wittering Cl NG10 . . . . . . **236** E5
Witton Ct DE24 . . . . **231** D4
Woburn Cl
Blackwell DE55 . . . . **147** E1
Swanwick DE55 . . . . **169** F7
Woburn Cotts DE4 . . . . . . **143** B7
Woburn Croft NG10 . . . . **223** A4
Woburn Ho DE55 . . . . **147** E1
Woburn La NG19 . . . . **135** C4
Woburn Pl
Derby DE22 . . . . **218** B5
Pleasley NG19 . . . . **135** C4

Woburn Rd NG19 . . . . . . **135** C4
Wolds Rd DE4 . . . . **143** D7
Wolds Rise DE4 . . . . **143** C7
Wolfa St DE22 . . . . **267** A2
Wolfcote Cl S45 . . . . **131** D1
Wolfe Cl S40 . . . . **95** D1
Wolfscote Dale DE11 . . . . **255** F2
Wollaton Ave S17 . . . . . . **56** A5
Wollaton Dr S17 . . . . **56** A5
Wollaton Rd
Derby DE21 . . . . **219** F8
Sheffield S17 . . . . **56** A5
Wollaton Rd N ⑤ DE21 . . **205** F1
Wollen Cl S80 . . . . **81** F1
Wolseley Rd ② S8 . . . . . . **43** A7
Wolverley Grange DE24 . **233** D6
Wood's Hospl SK13 . . . . . **10** C3
Woodale Cl DE23 . . . . **230** F6
Woodall La S26 . . . . **61** D6
Woodall Rd S21 . . . . **60** F5
Wood Ave
Creswell S80 . . . . **81** D1
Sandiacre NG10 . . . . **223** A6
Woodbank Ct S17 . . . . . . **56** A7
Woodbeck Ct DE21 . . . . . **206** B2
Woodbine Cl DE14 . . . . . . **253** E6
Woodbine Terr SK23 . . . . **47** A6
Woodborough Rd NG15 . . **135** E1
Woodbourne Rd SK22 . . . **33** A5
Woodbridge Cl
Chellaston DE73 . . . . **232** F1
Heanor DE75 . . . . **182** B1
Woodbridge Jun Sch
DE55 . . . . **159** A3
Woodbridge Rise S40 . . . **114** B8
Woodbrook SK23 . . . . **45** E8
Woodbrook Ct SK23 . . . . . **45** E7
Woodchester Dr DE24 . . . **233** D6
Wood Cl S42 . . . . **114** D4
Woodcock Gr SK13 . . . . . **10** E1
Woodcock Rd SK13 . . . . . **11** A1
Woodcock Sq DE24 . . . . . **230** C8
Woodcote Way DE23 . . . . **231** A7
Wood Croft DE23 . . . . **231** D8
Wood End Rd **156** B6
Wood End La DE73 . . . . . . **244** D1
Wood End Rd DE75 . . . . . **181** E2
Woodfall La
Duffield DE56 . . . . **190** A1
Windley DE22 . . . . **189** D3
Wood Farm Ct NG11 . . . . **237** D2
Wood Farm La DE11 . . . . **256** E4
Woodfield Cl SK13 . . . . . . **9** F5
Woodfield Dr
Ripley DE5 . . . . **170** A1
Swadlincote DE11 . . . . **256** C5
Woodfield Rd
Pinxton NG16 . . . . **160** D4
South Normanton DE55 . . . **159** F4
Woodford Rd DE22 . . . . . . **218** A7
Woodford Way S43 . . . . . **78** B4
Woodgate Dr DE73 . . . . . **233** A1
Wood Gdns SK22 . . . . **25** C3
Woodhall Dr DE23 . . . . . . **230** E8
Woodhall House Farm
S26 . . . . **61** C6
Woodhead La S45 . . . . . . **130** D1
Woodhead Rd
Glossop SK13 . . . . **10** D5
Holme HD9 . . . . **3** A5
Sheffield, Highfield S2 . . . **43** A8
Tintwistle SK13 . . . . **10** B8
Woodhouse La
Barlborough S43 . . . . **79** E5
Bolsover S44 . . . . **98** E3
Mastin Moor S43 . . . . **79** C5
Scropton DE65 . . . . **226** F7
South Normanton DE55 . . . **159** E5
Winster DE4 . . . . **141** C6
Woodhouse Rd
Kilburn DE56, DE7 . . . . **192** A7
⑥ Mansfield NG19 . . . . . . **136** B1
Rowsley DE4 . . . . **126** F7
Sheffield S12 . . . . **44** B6
Woodhouse St DE11 . . . . **256** D3
Woodhouse Station Ent Ctr
NG19 . . . . **136** B3
Woodhurst Cl DE21 . . . . . **219** D8
Wood La
Belper DE56 . . . . **190** F7
Creswell S80 . . . . **100** C8
Crich DE4 . . . . **157** C3
Hanbury DE13 . . . . **238** A4
Hayfield SK22 . . . . **25** C3
Holloway DE4 . . . . **144** A1
Horsley Woodhouse DE7 . . **192** D5
Ible DE4 . . . . **153** E6
Idridgehay DE6, DE56 . . . . **176** E8
Kniveton DE6 . . . . **163** A1
Pleasley NG20 . . . . **119** D1
Ripley DE5 . . . . **169** A4
Scarcliffe S44 . . . . **118** F6
Shirebrook NG20 . . . . **120** F7
Swadlincote DE11 . . . . **256** A7
Woodland Ave
Borrowash DE72 . . . . **221** C2
Breaston DE72 . . . . **235** F8
Ilkeston DE7 . . . . **194** D4
Sutton in A NG17 . . . . **148** E4
Woodland Dr
Rocester ST14 . . . . **196** F3
Scropton DE65 . . . . **226** D4
Sheffield S12 . . . . **44** B2
Woodland Gr
Barlborough S43 . . . . **80** A6
Clay Cross S42 . . . . **131** B6
Clowne S43 . . . . **81** A4

Woodland Gr continued
Mansfield Woodhouse
NG19 . . . . **136** C
Woodland Pl S17 . . . . **55** F
Woodland Rd
Derby DE22 . . . . **218** G
Mansfield NG19 . . . . **136** F
Sheffield S8 . . . . **43** B
Swadlincote DE15 . . . . **255** B
Woodlands
Brimington S43 . . . . **96** D
Great Longstone DE45 . . . **89** F
Wirksworth DE4 . . . . **165** E
Woodlands Ave
Breaston DE72 . . . . **235** F
Derby DE24 . . . . **232** E
Woodlands Brow DE6 . . . **173** D
Woodlands Cl
Glossop SK13 . . . . **9** F
Little Eaton DE21 . . . . **205** B
Melbourne DE73 . . . . **252** A
Thorpe DE6 . . . . **161** D
Woodlands Com Sch
DE21 . . . . **204** D
Woodlands Cres DE12 . . . **262** B
Woodlands La
Chellaston DE73 . . . . **245** A
Quarndon DE22 . . . . **204** C
Woodlands Rd
Chapel-en-le-F SK23 . . . . . **47** B
Derby DE22 . . . . **204** E
High Lane SK12 . . . . **32** A
New Mills SK22 . . . . **33** A
Overseal DE12 . . . . **262** B
Woodlands The
⑤ Mansfield NG19 . . . . . . **136** B
Melbourne DE73 . . . . **252** A
Tatenhill DE13 . . . . **253** A
Whaley Thorns NG20 . . . . . **101** A
Woodlands View DE7 . . . . **193** A
Woodlands Way DE73 . . . **252** B
Woodlands Yd DE73 . . . . **245** A
Woodland View
Buxton SK17 . . . . **85** D
Chilcote DE12 . . . . **264** F
Crich DE4 . . . . **167** E
Hathersage S32 . . . . **53** A
Horwich End SK23 . . . . **45** F
Sheffield, Abbeydale Park
S17 . . . . **56** A
Sheffield, Charnock Hill S12 **44** B
Whaley Thorns NG20 . . . . . **101** A
Woodland Views ST14 . . . **224** E
Woodland Way
Clay Cross S42 . . . . **131** B
Eastwood NG16 . . . . **182** E
Woodland Wlk S40 . . . . . . **94** F
Woodlea Gr DE21 . . . . . . **205** C
Woodlea Rd SK13 . . . . . . **17** B
Woodleigh Cl S40 . . . . . . **94** F
Woodmans Croft DE65 . . . **227** C
Woodmeadow Dr DE73 . . **232** F
Woodminton Dr DE73 . . . **232** F
Woodnook Cl S42 . . . . . . **95** A
Wood Nook Cl NG16 . . . . **171** F
Woodnook Gr S21 . . . . . . **58** E
Woodnook La S42 . . . . . . **94** F
Woodnook Way S42 . . . . . **94** F
Woodpecker Hill DE7 . . . **208** A
Wood Rd
Derby, Chaddesden
DE21 . . . . **220** D
Derby, Oakwood DE21 . . . . **205** F
Derby, Spondon DE21 . . . . **221** A
Woodridge The DE56 . . . **190** F
Woodrising Cl DE21 . . . . **206** B
Woodroffe Wlk DE23 . . . . **231** E
Woodrove Ave S13 . . . . . **44** B
Woodrove Cl S13 . . . . **44** B
Wood St N DE55 . . . . **159** C
Woodseat Gr ST14 . . . . . **197** A
Woodseats La SK13 . . . . . **16** B
Woodshop La DE73 . . . . . **244** D
Woodside
Buxton SK17 . . . . **85** C
Carsington DE4 . . . . **164** E
Eastwood NG16 . . . . **182** E
Horsley DE7 . . . . **192** D
Woodside Ave
Holmesfield S18 . . . . **75** A
Killamarsh S21 . . . . **60** F
Ripley DE5 . . . . **180** D
Woodside Cl
Bakewell DE45 . . . . **109** D
Chesterfield S40 . . . . **95** B
Woodside Cres
Ilkeston DE7 . . . . **194** D
Long Eaton NG10 . . . . **236** B
Woodside Dr
Bakewell DE45 . . . . **109** D
Derby DE22 . . . . **205** A
Woodside Pl S45 . . . . **131** B
Woodside Rd
Sandiacre NG10 . . . . **223** B
Shirebrook NG20 . . . . **119** E
Shireoaks S81 . . . . **63** F
Woodside St SK22 . . . . . . **33** B
Woodside View S18 . . . . . **75** A
Woods La
Burton u T, Stapenhill
DE15 . . . . **254** F
Derby DE22 . . . . **267** A
Woods Mdw DE72 . . . . . . **233** D
Woodsome Pk S42 . . . . . . **116** D
Woodsorrel Dr DE21 . . . . **206** B
Wood St
Alfreton DE55 . . . . **159** C
Codnor DE5 . . . . **181** B

Wood St continued
Derby DE1 . . . . .267 C4
Eastwood NG16 . . . . .182 F3
Glossop SK13 . . . . 17 C8
Hollingworth SK14 . . . . 9 D5
Holmewood S42 . . . . .116 E1
Ilkeston DE7 . . . . .194 F1
New Mills SK22 . . . . 33 B7
Ripley DE5 . . . . .169 D2
Somercotes DE55 . . . . .170 C8
Swadlincote DE11 . . . . .256 B2
Wirksworth DE4 . . . . .165 F8
Woodstock Cl DE22 . . . . .204 D4
Woodstock Ct 5 S41 . . . 96 A6
Woodstock Dr S41 . . . . . .115 C8
Woodstock Rd NG9 . . . . .223 F3
Woodstock Rise S41 . . . .115 C8
Woodthorne Ave DE24 . .232 E4
Woodthorpe Ave
Clay Cross S45 . . . . .131 A4
Derby, Chaddesden DE21 . .219 F6
Woodthorpe CE Prim Sch
S43 . . . . 79 C1
Woodthorpe Cl S44 . . . . 98 F7
Woodthorpe Cres S13 . . . . 44 C8
Woodthorpe Prim Sch
S13 . . . . 44 C7
Woodthorpe Rd
Sheffield S13 . . . . 44 C7
Shuttlewood S44 . . . . 98 F8
Staveley S43 . . . . 79 C2
Woodvale Cl S40 . . . . . . .114 A8
Wood View S21 . . . . 79 A8
Woodview Cl S42 . . . . . .114 F2
Woodview Gdns DE22 . . .218 F8
Wood View Ho S21 . . . . . 59 C3
Woodview Rd DE11 . . . . .255 E5
Woodville CE Jun Sch
DE11 . . . . .256 F2
Woodville Inf Sch DE11 . 256 F2
Woodville Rd
Hartshorne DE11 . . . . .257 A5
Overseal DE12 . . . . .262 B4
Woodward's Pl DE11 . . . .256 C3
Woodwards Cl DE72 . . . .221 D1
Woodward Way DE11 . . . 256 D4
Woodyard Cl DE11 . . . . .255 F1
Woodyard La DE65 . . . . .226 F5
Wooley Cl S42 . . . . .131 B7
Wooliscroft Cl DE7 . . . . .194 C2
Woollaton La SK17 . . . . .138 D2
Woolley's Yd DE4 . . . . . .141 C6
Woolley Bridge Rd
Glossop SK13 . . . . .9 F5
Hadfield SK13 . . . . .9 F5
Woolley Cl SK14 . . . . 9 D4
Woolley La
Hollingworth SK14 . . . . 9 D4
Hollingworth SK14 . . . . 9 D6

Woolley Mill La SK13 . . . . . . .9 E7
Woolley Rd DE4 . . . . . . .143 B6
Woolrych St DE23 . . . . . .218 F2
Woolsthorpe Cres DE7 . .208 D4
Woolstitch Pk DE12 . . . .264 E7
Woosnam Cl DE14 . . . . .254 A6
Worcester Ave NG19 . . . .136 C6
Worcester Cl S45 . . . . . .131 E4
Worcester Cres DE21 . . .219 E8
Worcester Gr SK13 . . . . . 17 F8
Worcester Mews NG19 . .136 C6
Worcester Rd DE15 . . . . .254 E6
Wordsworth Ave
Derby DE24 . . . . .231 F5
Mansfield Woodhouse
NG19 . . . . .136 B4
Swadlincote DE11 . . . . . . .256 C6
Wordsworth Dr DE24 . . . .232 A5
Wordsworth Pl S18 . . . . . 76 C7
Wordsworth Rd
Awsworth NG16 . . . . .195 C5
Chesterfield S41 . . . . 95 F8
Works La S44 . . . . 97 B3
Worksop Rd
Mastin Moor S43 . . . . 79 D4
Thorpe Salvin S80 . . . . 62 E7
Whitwell S80 . . . . 81 F6
Works Rd S43 . . . . 78 B2
Worrall Ave NG10 . . . . . .223 E1
Worthington La DE73 . . . .252 F1
Wortley Ave NG9 . . . . . .209 D3
Wortley Cl DE7 . . . . .209 A8
Wortley Ct S33 . . . . 51 B7
Wragley Way DE24 . . . . .231 D2
Wreakes La S18 . . . . 56 F2
Wren Cl DE11 . . . . .256 F3
Wren Ct NG10 . . . . .236 A3
Wren Nest Cl SK13 . . . . . 17 B8
Wren Nest Rd SK13 . . . . . 10 B1
Wren Nest Terr SK13 . . . . 10 C1
Wren Park Cl
Belper DE56 . . . . .178 E5
Chesterfield S40 . . . . .114 F7
Eckington S12 . . . . 58 E8
Findern DE65 . . . . .230 D1
Wren Park Prim Sch
DE3 . . . . .218 A2
Wrenpark Rd S42 . . . . . .114 D4
Wren Way DE3 . . . . .230 B7
Wretham Cl DE3 . . . . . . .230 D8
Wright Ave DE5 . . . . .169 F1
Wright Cres DE6 . . . . . . .185 D8
Wright St DE5 . . . . .181 B8
Wroxham Cl DE24 . . . . . .232 D4
Wulfric Cl S2 . . . . 43 F8
Wulfric Pl S2 . . . . 43 F8
Wulfric Rd
Eckington S21 . . . . 59 C3
Sheffield S2 . . . . 44 A8

Wyaston Cl DE22 . . . . . . .204 E1
Wyaston Gdns DE6 . . . . .185 D7
Wyaston Rd DE6 . . . . . . .185 C6
Wyatts Way DE5 . . . . . . .169 F3
Wybersley Rd SK6 . . . . . . 32 A8
Wychwood Dr NG9 . . . . .209 D2
Wycliffe Rd DE55 . . . . . .159 A4
Wycombe Grange NG19 . .136 F2
Wye Bank DE45 . . . . .109 E5
Wye Bank Gr DE45 . . . . .109 E4
Wye Cl DE65 . . . . .240 D8
Wye Croft Ct DE45 . . . . .109 D5
Wye Dale DE11 . . . . .255 F2
Wyedale Cl
Bakewell DE45 . . . . .109 E4
Buxton SK17 . . . . 85 B6
Wyedale Cres DE45 . . . . .109 E4
Wyedale Ct 5 S41 . . . . . 95 E7
Wyedale Dr DE45 . . . . . .109 E4
Wyedale View DE45 . . . . .109 E4
Wye Gr SK17 . . . . 85 A7
Wye Head Cl SK17 . . . . . . 84 F7
Wye Ho SK17 . . . . 66 B1
Wyelands Cl SK17 . . . . . . 84 F7
Wye Mill SK17 . . . . 89 A6
Wye St
Buxton SK17 . . . . 85 C8
Derby DE24 . . . . .233 A8
Wye Terr DE4 . . . . .126 F3
Wyming Brook Dr S10 . . . . 42 B8
Wyndale Dr DE7 . . . . . . .208 C6
Wyndham Cres DE15 . . . .248 C3
Wyndham St DE24 . . . . . .233 A7
Wynd The S21 . . . . 79 C7
Wynton Ave DE24 . . . . . .232 F8
Wyntor Ave DE4 . . . . . . .141 C6
Wynyard Cl DE7 . . . . .194 C3
Wysall Cl NG19 . . . . .135 E1
Wystan Ct DE65 . . . . . . .242 D2
Wyston Brook DE65 . . . . .228 D1
Wythburn Rd S41 . . . . 95 C7
Wyver La DE56 . . . . .178 F6
Wyvern Ave NG10 . . . . . .236 D5
Wyvern Bsns Pk DE21 . . .220 A4
Wyvern Cl
Eastwood NG16 . . . . .195 A8
Matlock DE4 . . . . .143 A6
Wyvern Gdns S17 . . . . . . 55 E6
Wyvernside DE21 . . . . . . .219 F4
Wyvern Way DE21 . . . . . .220 A4

Y

Yard Cl DE11 . . . . .256 B4
Yardley Cl DE55 . . . . .169 F8
Yardley Way DE56 . . . . . .179 D4
Yard The 4 SK13 . . . . . . 10 C1
Yarmouth Ho DE24 . . . . . .233 C7

Yarncliff Cl S40 . . . . 95 D5
Yarrow Cl
Burton u T DE15 . . . . .248 B2
Derby DE24 . . . . .231 E2
Yarwell Cl DE21 . . . . .205 D1
Yates Ave DE72 . . . . .246 A3
Yates Rd SK22 . . . . 33 C7
Yates St DE23 . . . . .219 A1
Yeardsley Ave SK23 . . . . . 33 D3
Yeardsley Gn SK23 . . . . . 45 D8
Yeardsley La SK23 . . . . . . 33 D3
Yeld Cl DE45 . . . . .109 C4
Yeldersley Cl S40 . . . . . . 95 B5
Yeldersley La
Brailsford DE6 . . . . .187 B2
Osmaston DE6 . . . . .186 E6
Yeld Rd DE45 . . . . .109 D5
Yeld The DE45 . . . . .109 C5
Yelt La DE6 . . . . .224 D8
Yeoman Park Sch NG19 . .136 C4
Yeoman St DE4 . . . . .142 D1
Yeovil Cl DE24 . . . . .233 C7
Yerley Hill DE6 . . . . .172 C6
Yewdale Gr DE21 . . . . . . .206 C3
Yews Cl DE73 . . . . .233 A1
Yew Tree Ave DE72 . . . . .221 D5
Yew Tree Cl
Ashover S45 . . . . .129 F3
Darley Dale DE4 . . . . .127 B3
Derby DE24 . . . . .233 C7
Yew Tree Cotts DE72 . . . .222 E3
Yewtree Cres DE15 . . . . .254 F7
Yew Tree Ct DE65 . . . . . .227 C2
Yew Tree Dr
Chesterfield S40 . . . . .114 A8
Clay Cross S42 . . . . .131 B6
Shirebrook NG20 . . . . .119 D5
Sutton in A NG17 . . . . .148 F2
Yew Tree Gdns DE12 . . . .260 C6
Yew Tree Hill DE4 . . . . . .156 B5
Yew Tree La
Bradley DE6 . . . . .186 E8
Elvaston DE72 . . . . .233 F4
Yewtree Rd DE11 . . . . . . .255 F7
Yew Tree Rd
Hatton DE65 . . . . .227 D1
Rosliston DE12 . . . . .260 C6
Yokecliffe Ave DE4 . . . . .165 E8
Yokecliffe Cres DE4 . . . . .165 E8
Yokecliffe Dr DE4 . . . . . .165 E8
Yokecliffe Hill DE4 . . . . . .165 E8
Yokecliffe La DE4 . . . . . .165 E8
York Ave
Jacksdale NG16 . . . . .171 B4
Sandiacre NG10 . . . . .223 A5
York Cl DE11 . . . . .256 D6
York Cres S44 . . . . .117 E1
Yorke St NG19 . . . . .136 B2

York Pl
North Wingfield S42 . . . . . .132 B7
Shireoaks S81 . . . . 63 F7
York Rd
Derby DE21 . . . . .219 F7
Long Eaton NG10 . . . . .223 C1
Shirebrook NG20 . . . . .119 E3
Swadlincote DE11 . . . . . . .256 B2
Yorkshire Way SK13 . . . . . 17 F8
York St
Chesterfield S41 . . . . .115 C7
Derby DE1 . . . . .218 E5
Glossop SK13 . . . . 10 E1
York Terr
Glossop SK13 . . . . 17 C8
Pinxton NG16 . . . . .160 C1
Youlgreave Cl DE21 . . . . .205 F1
Youlgreave Cres SK13 . . . . .9 D1
Youlgreave Dr S12 . . . . . . 44 D5
Youlgreave YH* DE45 . . .125 C5
Young St DE23 . . . . .218 F1
Yoxall Dr DE22 . . . . .218 C4
Ypres Rd DE22 . . . . .204 C2

Z

Zetland Cres DE24 . . . . . .231 C2
Zion Ho DE11 . . . . .256 C1

Name and Address	Telephone	Page	Grid reference

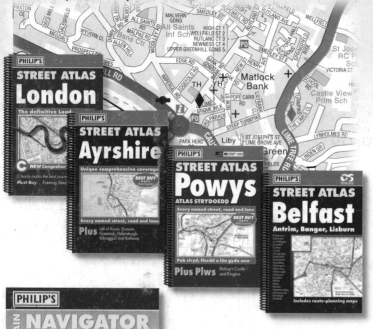